An Introduction to Management Science

Quantitative Approaches to Decision Making

Fifteenth Edition

David R. Anderson
University of Cincinnati

Dennis J. Sweeney
University of Cincinnati

Thomas A. Williams
Rochester Institute
of Technology

Jeffrey D. Camm
Wake Forest University

James J. Cochran
University of Alabama

Michael J. Fry
University of Cincinnati

Jeffrey W. Ohlmann
University of Iowa

CENGAGE

Australia • Brazil • Mexico • Singapore • United Kingdom • United States

Make a better grade with CengageNOWv2
Here's how to make every study moment count

Multi-media study-tools such as videos, games, flashcards, crossword puzzles, and more allow you to review and check your understanding of key concepts to help you prepare for quizzes and exams.

The MindTap eReader is fully optimized for the iPad, provides note-taking and highlighting capabilities, and features an online text-to-speech application that vocalizes the content - providing a fun reading experience.

Flashcards — use the MindTap eReader's pre-made flashcards or make your own. Then print the cards and get to work.

CengageNOW Users Achieve Higher Grades
(Student Grades, Scale = 0-100; N=246)

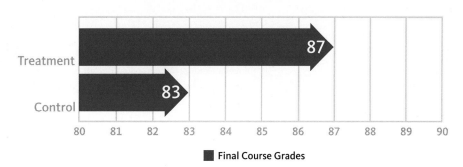

Final Course Grades

"I love the check your work option. Really, when you're having a hard time figuring out an answer, sometimes working backwards is the best way to understand conceptually what you're doing wrong."
Brad Duncan
University of Utah

"[I liked]...the read-a-loud option with the ebook... This helped when first starting a chapter and then when studying for tests."
Jennifer Loughren
Student, Northeast Iowa Community College

Ask your instructor about CengageNOWv2 for this course.

M16016278

ENGAGED WITH YOU | cengage.com

***An Introduction to Management Science: Quantitative Approaches to Decision Making**, Fifteenth Edition*

David R. Anderson, Dennis J. Sweeney, Thomas A. Williams, Jeffrey D. Camm, James J. Cochran, Michael J. Fry, Jeffrey W. Ohlmann

Senior Vice President, Higher Ed Product, Content, and Market Development: Erin Joyner

Vice President, B&E, 4-LTR, and Support Programs: Mike Schenk

Senior Product Team Manager: Joe Sabatino

Senior Product Manager: Aaron Arnsparger

Content Developer: Anne Merrill

Product Assistant: Renee Schnee

Senior Digital Content Designer: Brandon Foltz

Senior Marketing Manager: Nathan Anderson

Content Project Manager: D. Jean Buttrom

Production Service: MPS Limited

Senior Art Director: Michelle Kunkler

Cover and Text Designer: Beckmeyer Design

Cover Image: iStockPhoto.com/tawanlubfah

Intellectual Property

    Analyst: Reba Frederics

    Project Manager: Nick Barrows

For product information and technology assistance, contact us at **Cengage Customer & Sales Support, 1-800-354-9706.**

For permission to use material from this text or product, submit all requests online at **www.cengage.com/permissions.** Further permissions questions can be emailed to **permissionrequest@cengage.com.**

Library of Congress Control Number: 2017953024

ISBN: 978-1-337-40652-9

Cengage
20 Channel Center Street
Boston, MA 02210
USA

Cengage is a leading provider of customized learning solutions with employees residing in nearly 40 different countries and sales in more than 125 countries around the world. Find your local representative at **www.cengage.com.**

Cengage products are represented in Canada by Nelson Education, Ltd.

To learn more about Cengage platforms and services, visit **www.cengage.com.**

To register or access your online learning solution or purchase materials for your course, visit **www.cengagebrain.com.**

Printed in the United States of America
Print Number: 01   Print Year: 2017

Dedication

To My Parents
Ray and Ilene Anderson
DRA

To My Parents
James and Gladys Sweeney
DJS

To My Parents
Phil and Ann Williams
TAW

To My Parents
Randall and Jeannine Camm
JDC

To My Wife
Teresa
JJC

To My Parents
Mike and Cynthia Fry
MJF

To My Parents
Willis and Phyllis Ohlmann
JWO

Brief Contents

Contents

Chapter 11 Waiting Line Models 461

Preface

We are very excited to publish the fifteenth edition of a text that has been a leader in the field for over 25 years. The purpose of this fifteenth edition, as with previous editions, is to provide undergraduate and graduate students with a sound conceptual understanding of the role that management science plays in the decision-making process. The text describes many of the applications where management science is used successfully. Former users of this text have told us that the applications we describe have led them to find new ways to use management science in their organizations.

An Introduction to Management Science: Quantiative Approaches to Decision Making, 15e is applications oriented and continues to use the problem-scenario approach that is a hallmark of every edition of the text. Using the problem scenario approach, we describe a problem in conjunction with the management science model being introduced. The model is then solved to generate a solution and recommendation to management. We have found that this approach helps to motivate the student by demonstrating not only how the procedure works, but also how it contributes to the decision-making process.

From the first edition we have been committed to the challenge of writing a textbook that would help make the mathematical and technical concepts of management science understandable and useful to students of business and economics. Judging from the responses from our teaching colleagues and thousands of students, we have successfully met the challenge. Indeed, it is the helpful comments and suggestions of many loyal users that have been a major reason why the text is so successful.

Throughout the text we have utilized generally accepted notation for the topic being covered so those students who pursue study beyond the level of this text should be comfortable reading more advanced material. To assist in further study, a references and bibliography section is included at the back of the book.

CHANGES IN THE FIFTEENTH EDITION

We are very excited about the changes in the fifteenth edition of Management Science and want to explain them and why they were made. Many changes have been made throughout the text in response to suggestions from instructors and students. While we cannot list all these changes, we highlight the more significant revisions.

Updated Chapter 12: Simulation

The most substantial content change in this latest edition involves the coverage of simulation. We maintain an intuitive introduction by continuing to use the concepts of best-, worst-, and base-case scenarios, but we have added a more elaborate treatment of uncertainty by using Microsoft Excel to develop spreadsheet simulation models. Within the chapter, we explain how to construct a spreadsheet simulation model using only native Excel functionality. The chapter also includes two new appendices. The first appendix describes several probability distributions commonly used in simulation and how to generate values from these distributions using native Excel commands. In the second appendix, we introduce an Excel add-in, Analytic Solver, which facilitates the construction and analysis of spreadsheet simulation models. Nine new problems are introduced, and several others have been updated to reflect the new simulation coverage.

Other Content Changes

A variety of other changes have been made throughout the text. Appendices 4.1 and 7.1 have been updated to reflect changes to Solver in Microsoft Excel 2016. An appendix has been added to Chapter 15 that discusses the Forecast Tool in Microsoft Excel 2016. In addition to updating Appendix A for Microsoft Excel 2016, we have added a section on conducting a what-if analysis using Data Tables and Goal Seek.

Management Science in Action

The Management Science in Action vignettes describe how the material covered in a chapter is used in practice. Some of these are provided by practitioners. Others are based on articles from publications such as *Interfaces* and *OR/MS Today*. We updated the text with nine new Management Science in Action vignettes in this edition.

Cases and Problems

The quality of the problems and case problems is an important feature of the text. In this edition we have updated over 15 problems and added 3 new case problems.

COMPUTER SOFTWARE INTEGRATION

To make it easy for new users of Excel Solver or LINGO, we provide both Excel and LINGO files with the model formulation for every optimization problem that appears in the body of the text. The model files are well-documented and should make it easy for the user to understand the model formulation. The text is updated for Microsoft Excel 2016, but Excel 2010 and later versions allow all problems to be solved using the standard version of Excel Solver. For LINGO users, the text has been updated for LINGO 16.0.

FEATURES AND PEDAGOGY

We have continued many of the features that appeared in previous editions. Some of the important ones are noted here.

Annotations

Annotations that highlight key points and provide additional insights for the student are a continuing feature of this edition. These annotations, which appear in the margins, are designed to provide emphasis and enhance understanding of the terms and concepts being presented in the text.

Notes and Comments

At the end of many sections, we provide Notes and Comments designed to give the student additional insights about the methodology and its application. Notes and Comments include warnings about or limitations of the methodology, recommendations for application, brief descriptions of additional technical considerations, and other matters.

Self-Test Exercises

Certain exercises are identified as self-test exercises. Completely worked-out solutions for those exercises are provided in an appendix at the end of the text. Students can attempt the self-test exercises and immediately check the solution to evaluate their understanding of the concepts presented in the chapter.

ANCILLARY TEACHING AND LEARNING MATERIALS

For Students

Print and online resources are available to help the student work more efficiently.

- **LINGO.** A link to download an educational version of the LINGO software is available on the student website at www.cengagebrain.com.
- **Analytic Solver.** If using Analytic Solver with this text, you can receive the latest Analytic Solver license at Frontline Systems—academic@solver.com or 775-831-0300.

For Instructors

Instructor support materials are available to adopters from the Cengage Learning customer service line at 800-423-0563 or through www.cengage.com. Instructor resources are available on the Instructor Companion Site, which can be found and accessed at login.cengage.com, including:

- **Solutions Manual.** The Solutions Manual, prepared by the authors, includes solutions for all problems in the text.
- **Solutions to Case Problems.** These are also prepared by the authors and contain solutions to all case problems presented in the text.
- **PowerPoint Presentation Slides.** The presentation slides contain a teaching outline that incorporates figures to complement instructor lectures.
- **Test Bank.** Cengage Learning Testing Powered by Cognero is a flexible, online system that allows you to:
  - author, edit, and manage test bank content from multiple Cengage Learning solutions,
  - create multiple test versions in an instant,
  - deliver tests from your LMS, your classroom or wherever you want. The Test Bank is also available in Microsoft Word.

CengageNOWv2

CengageNOWv2 is a powerful course management and online homework tool that provides robust instructor control and customization to optimize the learning experience and meet desired outcomes. CengageNOWv2 features author-written homework from the textbook, integrated eBook, assessment options, and course management tools, including gradebook.

For more information about instructor resources, please contact your Cengage Learning Consultant.

ACKNOWLEDGMENTS

We owe a debt to many of our colleagues and friends whose names appear below for their helpful comments and suggestions during the development of this and previous editions. Our associates from organizations who supplied several of the Management Science in Action vignettes make a major contribution to the text. These individuals are cited in a credit line associated with each vignette.

Art Adelberg
CUNY Queens College

Joseph Bailey
University of Maryland

Ike C. Ehie
Kansas State University

John K. Fielding
University of Northwestern Ohio

Subodha Kumar
Mays Business School
Texas A&M University

Dan Matthews
Trine University

Aravind Narasipur
Chennai Business School

Nicholas W. Twigg
Coastal Carolina University

Julie Ann Stuart Williams
University of West Florida

We are also indebted to our Senior Product Team Manager, Joe Sabatino; our Senior Product Manager, Aaron Arnsparger; our Senior Marketing Manager, Nate Anderson; our Content Developer, Anne Merrill; our Senior Digital Content Designer, Brandon Foltz; our Content Project Manager, Jean Buttrom; and others at Cengage for their counsel and support during the preparation of this text.

David R. Anderson
Dennis J. Sweeney
Thomas A. Williams
Jeffrey D. Camm
James J. Cochran
Michael J. Fry
Jeffrey W. Ohlmann

About the Authors

David R. Anderson. David R. Anderson is Professor of Quantitative Analysis in the College of Business Administration at the University of Cincinnati. Born in Grand Forks, North Dakota, he earned his B.S., M.S., and Ph.D. degrees from Purdue University. Professor Anderson has served as Head of the Department of Quantitative Analysis and Operations Management and as Associate Dean of the College of Business Administration. In addition, he was the coordinator of the College's first Executive Program.

At the University of Cincinnati, Professor Anderson has taught introductory statistics for business students as well as graduate-level courses in regression analysis, multivariate analysis, and management science. He has also taught statistical courses at the Department of Labor in Washington, D.C. He has been honored with nominations and awards for excellence in teaching and excellence in service to student organizations.

Professor Anderson has coauthored 10 textbooks in the areas of statistics, management science, linear programming, and production and operations management. He is an active consultant in the field of sampling and statistical methods.

Dennis J. Sweeney. Dennis J. Sweeney is Professor of Quantitative Analysis and Founder of the Center for Productivity Improvement at the University of Cincinnati. Born in Des Moines, Iowa, he earned a B.S.B.A. degree from Drake University and his M.B.A. and D.B.A. degrees from Indiana University, where he was an NDEA Fellow. During 1978–79, Professor Sweeney worked in the management science group at Procter & Gamble; during 1981–82, he was a visiting professor at Duke University. Professor Sweeney served as Head of the Department of Quantitative Analysis and as Associate Dean of the College of Business Administration at the University of Cincinnati.

Professor Sweeney has published more than 30 articles and monographs in the area of management science and statistics. The National Science Foundation, IBM, Procter & Gamble, Federated Department Stores, Kroger, and Cincinnati Gas & Electric have funded his research, which has been published in *Management Science, Operations Research, Mathematical Programming, Decision Sciences,* and other journals.

Professor Sweeney has coauthored 10 textbooks in the areas of statistics, management science, linear programming, and production and operations management.

Thomas A. Williams. Thomas A. Williams is Professor of Management Science in the College of Business at Rochester Institute of Technology. Born in Elmira, New York, he earned his B.S. degree at Clarkson University. He did his graduate work at Rensselaer Polytechnic Institute, where he received his M.S. and Ph.D. degrees.

Before joining the College of Business at RIT, Professor Williams served for seven years as a faculty member in the College of Business Administration at the University of Cincinnati, where he developed the undergraduate program in Information Systems and then served as its coordinator. At RIT he was the first chairman of the Decision Sciences Department. He teaches courses in management science and statistics, as well as graduate courses in regression and decision analysis.

Professor Williams is the coauthor of 11 textbooks in the areas of management science, statistics, production and operations management, and mathematics. He has been a consultant for numerous *Fortune* 500 companies and has worked on projects ranging from the use of data analysis to the development of large-scale regression models.

Jeffrey D. Camm. Jeffrey D. Camm is the Inmar Presidential Chair and Associate Dean of Analytics in the School of Business at Wake Forest University. Born in Cincinnati, Ohio, he holds a B.S. from Xavier University (Ohio) and a Ph.D. from Clemson University. Prior to joining the faculty at Wake Forest, he was on the faculty of the University of Cincinnati. He has also been a visiting scholar at Stanford University and a visiting professor of business administration at the Tuck School of Business at Dartmouth College.

Dr. Camm has published over 30 papers in the general area of optimization applied to problems in operations management and marketing. He has published his research in *Science*, *Management Science*, *Operations Research*, *Interfaces*, and other professional journals. Dr. Camm was named the Dornoff Fellow of Teaching Excellence at the University of Cincinnati and he was the 2006 recipient of the INFORMS Prize for the Teaching of Operations Research Practice. A firm believer in practicing what he preaches, he has served as an operations research consultant to numerous companies and government agencies. From 2005 to 2010 he served as editor-in-chief of *Interfaces*.

James J. Cochran. James J. Cochran is Professor of Applied Statistics and the Rogers-Spivey Faculty Fellow in the Department of Information Systems, Statistics, and Management Science at The University of Alabama. Born in Dayton, Ohio, he holds a B.S., an M.S., and an M.B.A. from Wright State University and a Ph.D. from the University of Cincinnati. He has been a visiting scholar at Stanford University, Universidad de Talca, the University of South Africa, and Pole Universitaire Leonard de Vinci.

Professor Cochran has published over 30 papers in the development and application of operations research and statistical methods. He has published his research in *Management Science*, *The American Statistician*, *Communications in Statistics - Theory and Methods*, *European Journal of Operational Research*, *Journal of Combinatorial Optimization*, and other professional journals. He was the 2008 recipient of the INFORMS Prize for the Teaching of Operations Research Practice and the 2010 recipient of the Mu Sigma Rho Statistical Education Award. Professor Cochran was elected to the International Statistics Institute in 2005 and named a Fellow of the American Statistical Association in 2011. He received the Founders Award from the American Statistical Association in 2014 and he received the Karl E. Peace Award for Outstanding Statistical Contributions for the Betterment of Society from the American Statistical Association in 2015. A strong advocate for effective operations research and statistics education as a means of improving the quality of applications to real problems, Professor Cochran has organized and chaired teaching effectiveness workshops in Montevideo, Uruguay; Cape Town, South Africa; Cartagena, Colombia; Jaipur, India; Buenos Aires, Argentina; Nairobi, Kenya; Buea, Cameroon; Osijek, Croatia; Kathmandu, Nepal; Havana, Cuba; and Ulaanbaatar, Mongolia. He has served as an operations research or statistical consultant to numerous companies and not-for-profit organizations. From 2007 to 2012 Professor Cochran served as editor-in-chief of *INFORMS Transactions on Education*, and he is on the editorial board of several journals including *Interfaces*, *Significance*, and *ORiON*.

Michael J. Fry. Michael J. Fry is Professor and Head of the Department of Operations, Business Analytics, and Information Systems in the Carl H. Lindner College of Business at the University of Cincinnati. Born in Killeen, Texas, he earned a B.S. from Texas A&M University, and M.S.E. and Ph.D. degrees from the University of Michigan. He has been at the University of Cincinnati since 2002, where he has been named a Lindner Research Fellow and has served as Assistant Director and Interim Director of the Center for Business Analytics. He has also been a visiting professor at the Samuel Curtis Johnson Graduate School of Management at Cornell University and the Sauder School of Business at the University of British Columbia.

Professor Fry has published over 20 research papers in journals such as *Operations Research*, *M&SOM*, *Transportation Science*, *Naval Research Logistics*, *IIE Transactions*, and *Interfaces*. His research interests are in applying quantitative management methods to the areas of supply chain analytics, sports analytics, and public-policy operations. He has worked with many different organizations for his research, including Dell, Inc., Copeland Corporation, Starbucks Coffee Company, Great American Insurance Group, the Cincinnati Fire Department, the State of Ohio Election Commission, the Cincinnati Bengals, and the Cincinnati Zoo. In 2008, he was named a finalist for the Daniel H. Wagner Prize for Excellence in Operations Research Practice, and he has been recognized for both his research and teaching excellence at the University of Cincinnati.

Jeffrey W. Ohlmann. Jeffrey W. Ohlmann is Associate Professor of Management Sciences and Huneke Research Fellow in the Tippie College of Business at the University of Iowa. Born in Valentine, Nebraska, he earned a B.S. from the University of Nebraska, and M.S. and Ph.D. degrees from the University of Michigan. He has been at the University of Iowa since 2003.

Professor Ohlmann's research on the modeling and solution of decision-making problems has produced over twenty research papers in journals such as *Operations Research, Mathematics of Operations Research, INFORMS Journal on Computing, Transportation Science,* the *European Journal of Operational Research,* and *Interfaces.* He has collaborated with companies such as Transfreight, LeanCor, Cargill, the Hamilton County Board of Elections, and three National Football League franchises. Due to the relevance of his work to industry, he was bestowed the George B. Dantzig Dissertation Award and was recognized as a finalist for the Daniel H. Wagner Prize for Excellence in Operations Research Practice.

An Introduction to Management Science

Quantitative Approaches to Decision Making

Fifteenth Edition

CHAPTER 1

Introduction

CONTENTS

Management science, an approach to decision making based on the scientific method, makes extensive use of quantitative analysis. A variety of names exist for the body of knowledge involving quantitative approaches to decision making; in addition to management science, two other widely known and accepted names are operations research and decision science. Today, many use the terms *management science, operations research,* and *decision science* interchangeably.

The scientific management revolution of the early 1900s, initiated by Frederic W. Taylor, provided the foundation for the use of quantitative methods in management. But modern management science research is generally considered to have originated during the World War II period, when teams were formed to deal with strategic and tactical problems faced by the military. These teams, which often consisted of people with diverse specialties (e.g., mathematicians, engineers, and behavioral scientists), were joined together to solve a common problem by utilizing the scientific method. After the war, many of these team members continued their research in the field of management science.

Two developments that occurred during the post–World War II period led to the growth and use of management science in nonmilitary applications. First, continued research resulted in numerous methodological developments. Probably the most significant development was the discovery by George Dantzig, in 1947, of the simplex method for solving linear programming problems. At the same time these methodological developments were taking place, digital computers prompted a virtual explosion in computing power. Computers enabled practitioners to use the methodological advances to solve a large variety of problems. The computer technology explosion continues; smart phones, tablets, and other mobile-computing devices can now be used to solve problems larger than those solved on mainframe computers in the 1990s.

More recently, the explosive growth of data from sources such as smart phones and other personal-electronic devices provide access to much more data today than ever before. Additionally, the Internet allows for easy sharing and storage of data, providing extensive access to a variety of users to the necessary inputs to management-science models.

As stated in the Preface, the purpose of the text is to provide students with a sound conceptual understanding of the role that management science plays in the decision-making process. We also said that the text is application oriented. To reinforce the applications nature of the text and provide a better understanding of the variety of applications in which management science has been used successfully, Management Science in Action articles are presented throughout the text. Each Management Science in Action article summarizes an application of management science in practice. The first Management Science in Action in this chapter, Revenue Management at AT&T Park, describes one of the most important applications of management science in the sports and entertainment industry.

MANAGEMENT SCIENCE IN ACTION

REVENUE MANAGEMENT AT AT&T PARK*

Imagine the difficult position Russ Stanley, Vice President of Ticket Services for the San Francisco Giants, found himself facing late in the 2010 baseball season. Prior to the season, his organization adopted a dynamic approach to pricing its tickets similar to the model successfully pioneered by Thomas M. Cook and his operations research group at American Airlines. Stanley desparately wanted the Giants to clinch a playoff birth, but he didn't want the team to do so *too quickly*.

When dynamically pricing a good or service, an organization regularly reviews supply and demand of the product and uses operations research to determine if the price should be changed to reflect these conditions. As the scheduled takeoff date for a flight nears, the cost of a ticket increases if seats for the flight are relatively scarce. On the other hand, the airline discounts tickets for an approaching flight with relatively few ticketed passengers. Through the use of optimization to dynamically set ticket prices, American Airlines generates nearly $1 billion annually in incremental revenue.

The management team of the San Francisco Giants recognized similarities between their primary product (tickets to home games) and the primary product sold by airlines (tickets for flights) and adopted a similar revenue management system. If a particular Giants' game is appealing to fans, tickets sell quickly and demand far exceeds supply as the date of the game approaches; under these conditions fans will be willing to pay more and the Giants charge a premium for the ticket. Similarly, tickets for less attractive games are discounted to reflect relatively low demand by fans. This is why Stanley found himself in a quandary at the end of the 2010 baseball season. The Giants were in the middle of a tight pennant race with the San Diego Padres that effectively increased demand for tickets to Giants' games, and the team was actually scheduled to play the Padres in San Francisco for the last three games of the season. While Stanley certainly wanted his club to win its division and reach the Major League Baseball playoffs, he also recognized that his team's revenues would be greatly enhanced if it didn't qualify for the playoffs until the last day of the season. "I guess financially it is better to go all the way down to the last game," Stanley said in a late season interview.

"Our hearts are in our stomachs; we're pacing watching these games."

Does revenue management and operations research work? Today, virtually every airline uses some sort of revenue-management system, and the cruise, hotel, and car rental industries also now apply revenue-management methods. As for the Giants, Stanley said dynamic pricing provided a 7% to 8% increase in revenue per seat for Giants' home games during the 2010 season. Coincidentally, the Giants did win the National League West division on the last day of the season and ultimately won the World Series. Several professional sports franchises are now looking to the Giants' example and considering implementation of similar dynamic ticket-pricing systems.

*Based on Peter Horner, "The Sabre Story," *OR/MS Today* (June 2000); Ken Belson, "Baseball Tickets Too Much? Check Back Tomorrow," *NewYork Times.com* (May 18, 2009); and Rob Gloster, "Giants Quadruple Price of Cheap Seats as Playoffs Drive Demand," *Bloomberg Business-week* (September 30, 2010).

1.1 PROBLEM SOLVING AND DECISION MAKING

Problem solving can be defined as the process of identifying a difference between the actual and the desired state of affairs and then taking action to resolve the difference. For problems important enough to justify the time and effort of careful analysis, the problem-solving process involves the following seven steps:

1. Identify and define the problem.
2. Determine the set of alternative solutions.
3. Determine the criterion or criteria that will be used to evaluate the alternatives.
4. Evaluate the alternatives.
5. Choose an alternative.
6. Implement the selected alternative.
7. Evaluate the results to determine whether a satisfactory solution has been obtained.

Decision making is the term generally associated with the first five steps of the problem-solving process. Thus, the first step of decision making is to identify and define the problem. Decision making ends with the choosing of an alternative, which is the act of making the decision.

Let us consider the following example of the decision-making process. For the moment assume that you are currently unemployed and that you would like a position that will lead to a satisfying career. Suppose that your job search has resulted in offers from companies in Rochester, New York; Dallas, Texas; Greensboro, North Carolina; and Pittsburgh, Pennsylvania. Thus, the alternatives for your decision problem can be stated as follows:

1. Accept the position in Rochester.
2. Accept the position in Dallas.
3. Accept the position in Greensboro.
4. Accept the position in Pittsburgh.

The next step of the problem-solving process involves determining the criteria that will be used to evaluate the four alternatives. Obviously, the starting salary is a factor of some

TABLE 1.1   DATA FOR THE JOB EVALUATION DECISION-MAKING PROBLEM

Alternative	Starting Salary	Potential for Advancement	Job Location
1. Rochester	$48,500	Average	Average
2. Dallas	$46,000	Excellent	Good
3. Greensboro	$46,000	Good	Excellent
4. Pittsburgh	$47,000	Average	Good

importance. If salary were the only criterion of importance to you, the alternative selected as "best" would be the one with the highest starting salary. Problems in which the objective is to find the best solution with respect to one criterion are referred to as **single-criterion decision problems.**

Suppose that you also conclude that the potential for advancement and the location of the job are two other criteria of major importance. Thus, the three criteria in your decision problem are starting salary, potential for advancement, and location. Problems that involve more than one criterion are referred to as **multicriteria decision problems.**

The next step of the decision-making process is to evaluate each of the alternatives with respect to each criterion. For example, evaluating each alternative relative to the starting salary criterion is done simply by recording the starting salary for each job alternative. Evaluating each alternative with respect to the potential for advancement and the location of the job is more difficult to do, however, because these evaluations are based primarily on subjective factors that are often difficult to quantify. Suppose for now that you decide to measure potential for advancement and job location by rating each of these criteria as poor, fair, average, good, or excellent. The data that you compile are shown in Table 1.1.

You are now ready to make a choice from the available alternatives. What makes this choice phase so difficult is that the criteria are probably not all equally important, and no one alternative is "best" with regard to all criteria. Although we will present a method for dealing with situations like this one later in the text, for now let us suppose that after a careful evaluation of the data in Table 1.1, you decide to select alternative 3; alternative 3 is thus referred to as the **decision.**

At this point in time, the decision-making process is complete. In summary, we see that this process involves five steps:

1. Define the problem.
2. Identify the alternatives.
3. Determine the criteria.
4. Evaluate the alternatives.
5. Choose an alternative.

Note that missing from this list are the last two steps in the problem-solving process: implementing the selected alternative and evaluating the results to determine whether a satisfactory solution has been obtained. This omission is not meant to diminish the importance of each of these activities, but to emphasize the more limited scope of the term *decision making* as compared to the term *problem solving*. Figure 1.1 summarizes the relationship between these two concepts.

1.2   QUANTITATIVE ANALYSIS AND DECISION MAKING

Consider the flowchart presented in Figure 1.2. Note that it combines the first three steps of the decision-making process under the heading "Structuring the Problem" and the latter two steps under the heading "Analyzing the Problem." Let us now consider in greater detail how to carry out the set of activities that make up the decision-making process.

FIGURE 1.1 THE RELATIONSHIP BETWEEN PROBLEM SOLVING
AND DECISION MAKING

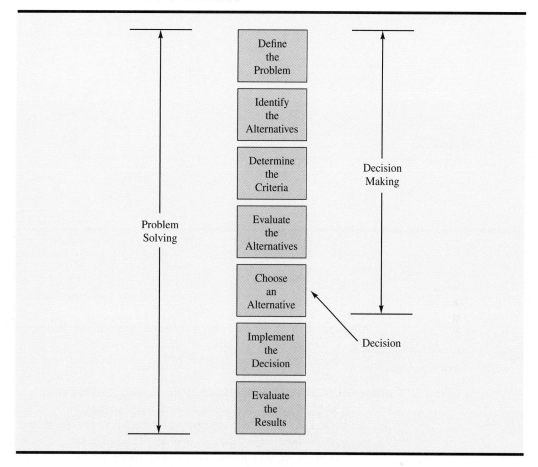

FIGURE 1.2 AN ALTERNATE CLASSIFICATION OF THE DECISION-MAKING PROCESS

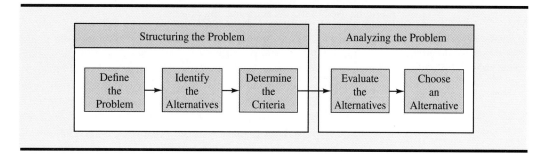

Figure 1.3 shows that the analysis phase of the decision-making process may take two basic forms: qualitative and quantitative. Qualitative analysis is based primarily on the manager's judgment and experience; it includes the manager's intuitive "feel" for the problem and is more an art than a science. If the manager has had experience with similar problems or if the problem is relatively simple, heavy emphasis may be placed upon a qualitative analysis. However, if the manager has had little experience with similar problems, or if the problem is sufficiently complex, then a quantitative analysis of the problem can be an especially important consideration in the manager's final decision.

When using the quantitative approach, an analyst will concentrate on the quantitative facts or data associated with the problem and develop mathematical expressions that

FIGURE 1.3   THE ROLE OF QUALITATIVE AND QUANTITATIVE ANALYSIS

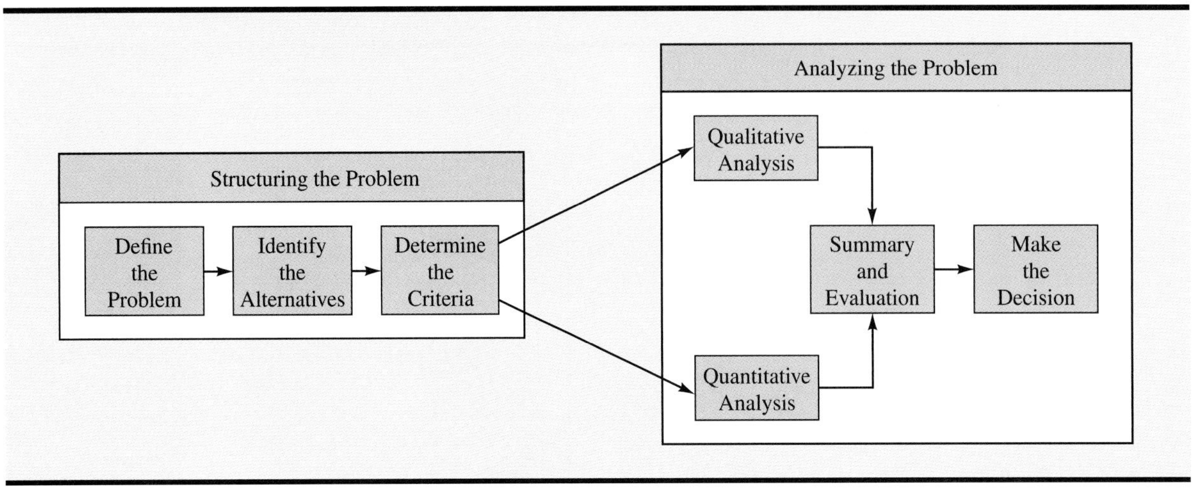

describe the objectives, constraints, and other relationships that exist in the problem. Then, by using one or more quantitative methods, the analyst will make a recommendation based on the quantitative aspects of the problem.

Although skills in the qualitative approach are inherent in the manager and usually increase with experience, the skills of the quantitative approach can be learned only by studying the assumptions and methods of management science. A manager can increase decision-making effectiveness by learning more about quantitative methodology and by better understanding its contribution to the decision-making process. A manager who is knowledgeable in quantitative decision-making procedures is in a much better position to compare and evaluate the qualitative and quantitative sources of recommendations and ultimately to combine the two sources in order to make the best possible decision.

The box in Figure 1.3 entitled "Quantitative Analysis" encompasses most of the subject matter of this text. We will consider a managerial problem, introduce the appropriate quantitative methodology, and then develop the recommended decision.

In closing this section, let us briefly state some of the reasons why a quantitative approach might be used in the decision-making process:

Try Problem 4 to test your understanding of why quantitative approaches might be needed in a particular problem.

1. The problem is complex, and the manager cannot develop a good solution without the aid of quantitative analysis.
2. The problem is especially important (e.g., a great deal of money is involved), and the manager desires a thorough analysis before attempting to make a decision.
3. The problem is new, and the manager has no previous experience from which to draw.
4. The problem is repetitive, and the manager saves time and effort by relying on quantitative procedures to make routine decision recommendations.

1.3   QUANTITATIVE ANALYSIS

From Figure 1.3, we see that quantitative analysis begins once the problem has been structured. It usually takes imagination, teamwork, and considerable effort to transform a rather general problem description into a well-defined problem that can be approached via quantitative analysis. The more the analyst is involved in the process of structuring the problem, the more likely the ensuing quantitative analysis will make an important contribution to the decision-making process.

To successfully apply quantitative analysis to decision making, the management scientist must work closely with the manager or user of the results. When both the management scientist and the manager agree that the problem has been adequately structured, work can begin on developing a model to represent the problem mathematically. Solution procedures can then be employed to find the best solution for the model. This best solution for the model then becomes a recommendation to the decision maker. The process of developing and solving models is the essence of the quantitative analysis process.

Model Development

Models are representations of real objects or situations and can be presented in various forms. For example, a scale model of an airplane is a representation of a real airplane. Similarly, a child's toy truck is a model of a real truck. The model airplane and toy truck are examples of models that are physical replicas of real objects. In modeling terminology, physical replicas are referred to as **iconic models.**

A second classification includes models that are physical in form but do not have the same physical appearance as the object being modeled. Such models are referred to as **analog models**. The speedometer of an automobile is an analog model; the position of the needle on the dial represents the speed of the automobile. A thermometer is another analog model representing temperature.

A third classification of models—the type we will primarily be studying—includes representations of a problem by a system of symbols and mathematical relationships or expressions. Such models are referred to as **mathematical models** and are a critical part of any quantitative approach to decision making. For example, the total profit from the sale of a product can be determined by multiplying the profit per unit by the quantity sold. If we let x represent the number of units sold and P the total profit, then, with a profit of $10 per unit, the following mathematical model defines the total profit earned by selling x units:

$$P = 10x \tag{1.1}$$

The purpose, or value, of any model is that it enables us to make inferences about the real situation by studying and analyzing the model. For example, an airplane designer might test an iconic model of a new airplane in a wind tunnel to learn about the potential flying characteristics of the full-size airplane. Similarly, a mathematical model may be used to make inferences about how much profit will be earned if a specified quantity of a particular product is sold. According to the mathematical model of equation (1.1), we would expect selling three units of the product ($x = 3$) would provide a profit of $P = 10(3) = \$30$.

In general, experimenting with models requires less time and is less expensive than experimenting with the real object or situation. A model airplane is certainly quicker and less expensive to build and study than the full-size airplane. Similarly, the mathematical model in equation (1.1) allows a quick identification of profit expectations without actually requiring the manager to produce and sell x units. Models also have the advantage of reducing the risk associated with experimenting with the real situation. In particular, bad designs or bad decisions that cause the model airplane to crash or a mathematical model to project a $10,000 loss can be avoided in the real situation.

Herbert A. Simon, a Nobel Prize winner in economics and an expert in decision making, said that a mathematical model does not have to be exact; it just has to be close enough to provide better results than can be obtained by common sense.

The value of model-based conclusions and decisions is dependent on how well the model represents the real situation. The more closely the model airplane represents the real airplane, the more accurate the conclusions and predictions will be. Similarly, the more closely the mathematical model represents the company's true profit–volume relationship, the more accurate the profit projections will be.

Because this text deals with quantitative analysis based on mathematical models, let us look more closely at the mathematical modeling process. When initially considering a managerial problem, we usually find that the problem definition phase leads to a specific objective, such as maximization of profit or minimization of cost, and possibly a set of restrictions or **constraints**, such as production capacities. The success of the mathematical model and quantitative approach will depend heavily on how accurately the objective and constraints can be expressed in terms of mathematical equations or relationships.

A mathematical expression that describes the problem's objective is referred to as the **objective function**. For example, the profit equation $P = 10x$ would be an objective function for a firm attempting to maximize profit. A production capacity constraint would be necessary if, for instance, 5 hours are required to produce each unit and only 40 hours of production time are available per week. Let x indicate the number of units produced each week. The production time constraint is given by

$$5x \leq 40 \qquad\qquad (1.2)$$

The value of $5x$ is the total time required to produce x units; the symbol $\leq$ indicates that the production time required must be less than or equal to the 40 hours available.

The decision problem or question is the following: How many units of the product should be scheduled each week to maximize profit? A complete mathematical model for this simple production problem is

$$\text{Maximize} \qquad P = 10x \quad \text{objective function}$$
$$\text{subject to (s.t.)}$$
$$\left.\begin{array}{c} 5x \leq 40 \\ x \geq 0 \end{array}\right\} \text{constraints}$$

The $x \geq 0$ constraint requires the production quantity x to be greater than or equal to zero, which simply recognizes the fact that it is not possible to manufacture a negative number of units. The optimal solution to this model can be easily calculated and is given by $x = 8$, with an associated profit of \$80. This model is an example of a linear programming model. In subsequent chapters we will discuss more complicated mathematical models and learn how to solve them in situations where the answers are not nearly so obvious.

In the preceding mathematical model, the profit per unit (\$10), the production time per unit (5 hours), and the production capacity (40 hours) are environmental factors that are not under the control of the manager or decision maker. Such environmental factors, which can affect both the objective function and the constraints, are referred to as **uncontrollable inputs** to the model. Inputs that are completely controlled or determined by the decision maker are referred to as **controllable inputs** to the model. In the example given, the production quantity x is the controllable input to the model. Controllable inputs are the decision alternatives specified by the manager and thus are also referred to as the **decision variables** of the model.

Once all controllable and uncontrollable inputs are specified, the objective function and constraints can be evaluated and the output of the model determined. In this sense, the output of the model is simply the projection of what would happen if those particular environmental factors and decisions occurred in the real situation. A flowchart of how controllable and uncontrollable inputs are transformed by the mathematical model into output is shown in Figure 1.4. A similar flowchart showing the specific details of the production model is shown in Figure 1.5.

FIGURE 1.4   FLOWCHART OF THE PROCESS OF TRANSFORMING MODEL INPUTS
INTO OUTPUT

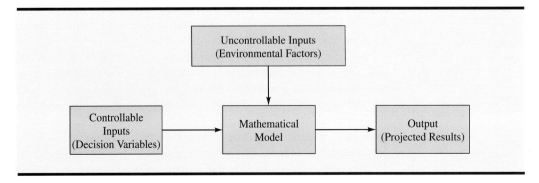

FIGURE 1.5   FLOWCHART FOR THE PRODUCTION MODEL

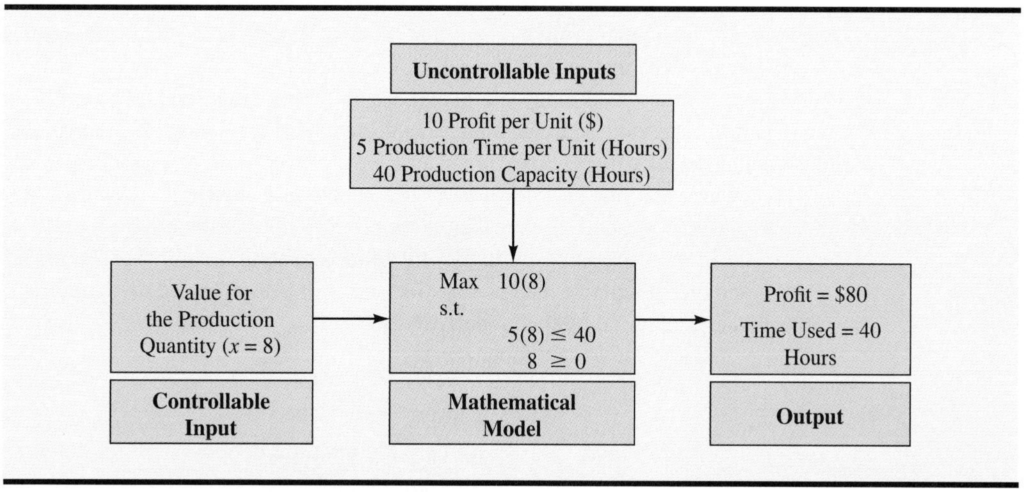

As stated earlier, the uncontrollable inputs are those the decision maker cannot influence. The specific controllable and uncontrollable inputs of a model depend on the particular problem or decision-making situation. In the production problem, the production time available (40) is an uncontrollable input. However, if it were possible to hire more employees or use overtime, the number of hours of production time would become a controllable input and therefore a decision variable in the model.

Uncontrollable inputs can either be known exactly or be uncertain and subject to variation. If all uncontrollable inputs to a model are known and cannot vary, the model is referred to as a **deterministic model**. Corporate income tax rates are not under the influence of the manager and thus constitute an uncontrollable input in many decision models. Because these rates are known and fixed (at least in the short run), a mathematical model with corporate income tax rates as the only uncontrollable input would be a deterministic model. The distinguishing feature of a deterministic model is that the uncontrollable input values are known in advance.

If any of the uncontrollable inputs are uncertain to the decision maker, the model is referred to as a **stochastic** or **probabilistic model**. An uncontrollable input to many production planning models is demand for the product. A mathematical model that treats future demand—which may be any of a range of values—with uncertainty would be called a stochastic model. In the production model, the number of hours of production time required per unit, the total hours available, and the unit profit were all uncontrollable inputs. Because the uncontrollable inputs were all known to take on fixed values, the model was deterministic. If, however, the number of hours of production time per unit could vary from 3 to 6 hours depending on the quality of the raw material, the model would be stochastic. The distinguishing feature of a stochastic model is that the value of the output cannot be determined even if the value of the controllable input is known because the specific values of the uncontrollable inputs are unknown. In this respect, stochastic models are often more difficult to analyze.

Data Preparation

Another step in the quantitative analysis of a problem is the preparation of the data required by the model. Data in this sense refer to the values of the uncontrollable inputs to the model. All uncontrollable inputs or data must be specified before we can analyze the model and recommend a decision or solution for the problem.

In the production model, the values of the uncontrollable inputs or data were $10 per unit for profit, 5 hours per unit for production time, and 40 hours for production capacity. In the development of the model, these data values were known and incorporated into the model as it was being developed. If the model is relatively small and the uncontrollable input values or data required are few, the quantitative analyst will probably combine model development and data preparation into one step. In these situations the data values are inserted as the equations of the mathematical model are developed.

However, in many mathematical modeling situations, the data or uncontrollable input values are not readily available. In these situations the management scientist may know that the model will need profit per unit, production time, and production capacity data, but the values will not be known until the accounting, production, and engineering departments can be consulted. Rather than attempting to collect the required data as the model is being developed, the analyst will usually adopt a general notation for the model development step, and then a separate data preparation step will be performed to obtain the uncontrollable input values required by the model.

Using the general notation

$$c = \text{profit per unit}$$
$$a = \text{production time in hours per unit}$$
$$b = \text{production capacity in hours}$$

the model development step of the production problem would result in the following general model:

$$\text{Max} \quad cx$$
$$\text{s.t.}$$
$$ax \le b$$
$$x \ge 0$$

A separate data preparation step to identify the values for c, a, and b would then be necessary to complete the model.

Many inexperienced quantitative analysts assume that once the problem has been defined and a general model has been developed, the problem is essentially solved. These individuals tend to believe that data preparation is a trivial step in the process and can be easily handled by clerical staff. Actually, this assumption could not be further from the truth, especially with large-scale models that have numerous data input values. For example, a small linear programming model with 50 decision variables and 25 constraints could have more than 1300 data elements that must be identified in the data preparation step. The time required to prepare these data and the possibility of data collection errors will make the data preparation step a critical part of the quantitative analysis process. Often, a fairly large database is needed to support a mathematical model, and information systems specialists may become involved in the data preparation step.

Model Solution

Once the model development and data preparation steps are completed, we can proceed to the model solution step. In this step, the analyst will attempt to identify the values of the decision variables that provide the "best" output for the model. The specific decision-variable value or values providing the "best" output will be referred to as the **optimal solution** for the model. For the production problem, the model solution step involves finding the value of the production quantity decision variable x that maximizes profit while not causing a violation of the production capacity constraint.

One procedure that might be used in the model solution step involves a trial-and-error approach in which the model is used to test and evaluate various decision alternatives. In the production model, this procedure would mean testing and evaluating the model under various production quantities or values of x. Note, in Figure 1.5, that we could input trial values for x and check the corresponding output for projected profit and satisfaction of the production capacity constraint. If a particular decision alternative does not satisfy one or more of

TABLE 1.2   TRIAL-AND-ERROR SOLUTION FOR THE PRODUCTION MODEL
OF FIGURE 1.5

Decision Alternative (Production Quantity) x	Projected Profit	Total Hours of Production	Feasible Solution? (Hours Used $\leq$ 40)
0	0	0	Yes
2	20	10	Yes
4	40	20	Yes
6	60	30	Yes
8	80	40	Yes
10	100	50	No
12	120	60	No

the model constraints, the decision alternative is rejected as being **infeasible**, regardless of the objective function value. If all constraints are satisfied, the decision alternative is **feasible** and a candidate for the "best" solution or recommended decision. Through this trial-and-error process of evaluating selected decision alternatives, a decision maker can identify a good—and possibly the best—feasible solution to the problem. This solution would then be the recommended decision for the problem.

Table 1.2 shows the results of a trial-and-error approach to solving the production model of Figure 1.5. The recommended decision is a production quantity of 8 because the feasible solution with the highest projected profit occurs at $x = 8$.

Although the trial-and-error solution process is often acceptable and can provide valuable information for the manager, it has the drawbacks of not necessarily providing the best solution and of being inefficient in terms of requiring numerous calculations if many decision alternatives are tried. Thus, quantitative analysts have developed special solution procedures for many models that are much more efficient than the trial-and-error approach. Throughout this text, you will be introduced to solution procedures that are applicable to the specific mathematical models that will be formulated. Some relatively small models or problems can be solved by hand computations, but most practical applications require the use of a computer.

Model development and model solution steps are not completely separable. An analyst will want both to develop an accurate model or representation of the actual problem situation and to be able to find a solution to the model. If we approach the model development step by attempting to find the most accurate and realistic mathematical model, we may find the model so large and complex that it is impossible to obtain a solution. In this case, a simpler and perhaps more easily understood model with a readily available solution procedure is preferred even if the recommended solution is only a rough approximation of the best decision. As you learn more about quantitative solution procedures, you will have a better idea of the types of mathematical models that can be developed and solved.

Try Problem 8 to test your understanding of the concept of a mathematical model and what is referred to as the optimal solution to the model.

After a model solution is obtained, both the management scientist and the manager will be interested in determining how good the solution really is. Even though the analyst has undoubtedly taken many precautions to develop a realistic model, often the goodness or accuracy of the model cannot be assessed until model solutions are generated. Model testing and validation are frequently conducted with relatively small "test" problems that have known or at least expected solutions. If the model generates the expected solutions, and if other output information appears correct, the go-ahead may be given to use the model on the full-scale problem. However, if the model test and validation identify potential problems or inaccuracies inherent in the model, corrective action, such as model modification and/or collection of more accurate input data, may be taken. Whatever the corrective action, the model solution will not be used in practice until the model has satisfactorily passed testing and validation.

Report Generation

An important part of the quantitative analysis process is the preparation of managerial reports based on the model's solution. In Figure 1.3, we see that the solution based on the quantitative analysis of a problem is one of the inputs the manager considers before making a final decision. Thus, the results of the model must appear in a managerial report that can be easily understood by the decision maker. The report includes the recommended decision and other pertinent information about the results that may be helpful to the decision maker.

A Note Regarding Implementation

As discussed in Section 1.2, the manager is responsible for integrating the quantitative solution with qualitative considerations in order to make the best possible decision. After completing the decision-making process, the manager must oversee the implementation and follow-up evaluation of the decision. The manager should continue to monitor the contribution of the model during the implementation and follow-up. At times this process may lead to requests for model expansion or refinement that will cause the management scientist to return to an earlier step of the quantitative analysis process.

Successful implementation of results is of critical importance to the management scientist as well as the manager. If the results of the quantitative analysis process are not correctly implemented, the entire effort may be of no value. It doesn't take too many unsuccessful implementations before the management scientist is out of work. Because implementation often requires people to do things differently, it often meets with resistance. People want to know, "What's wrong with the way we've been doing it?" and so on. One of the most effective ways to ensure successful implementation is to include users throughout the modeling process. A user who feels a part of identifying the problem and developing the solution is much more likely to enthusiastically implement the results. The success rate for implementing the results of a management science project is much greater for those projects characterized by extensive user involvement. The Management Science in Action, Quantitative Analysis and Supply Chain Management at the Heracles General Cement Company, discusses the use of management science techniques to optimize the operations of a supply chain.

MANAGEMENT SCIENCE IN ACTION

QUANTITATIVE ANALYSIS AND SUPPLY CHAIN MANAGEMENT AT THE HERACLES GENERAL CEMENT COMPANY*

Founded in 1911, the Heracles General Cement Company is the largest producer of cement in Greece. The company operates three cement plants in the prefecture of Evoia; one each in Volos, Halkis, and Milaki. Heracles' annual cement production capacity is 9.6 million tons, and the company manages 10 quarries that supply limestone, clay, and schist. Seven of these quarries are in the vicinity of the cement plants, and three are managed by Heracles' affiliate LAVA. The company also operates and maintains six distribution centers that are located across Greece; these distribution centers handle 2.5 million tons of domestic cement sales annually, which is over 40% of domestic sales in Greece.

Heracles faces a wide range of logistical challenges in transporting its products to customers. As a result, in 2005 the corporation decided to improve the efficiency of its supply chain by developing a platform for supply chain optimization and planning (SCOP) using mathematical programming. Heracles' objectives in creating SCOP were to (1) improve the efficiency of decision-making processes throughout its supply chain operations by synchronizing production plans, inventory control, and transportation policies; (2) integrate the core business processes of planning and budgeting with supply chain operations; and (3) achieve system-wide cost reductions through global optimization.

SCOP has been extremely successful. In addition to achieving its three initial goals through the development and implementation of SCOP, the platform provides Heracles with guidance for optimal revision of policies and responses to demand and cost fluctuations. The impact and success of SCOP translates into improved internal coordination, lower costs, greater operational efficiency, and increased customer satisfaction.

*Based on G. Dikos and S. Spyropoulou, "SCOP in Heracles General Cement Company," *Interfaces* 43, no. 4 (July/August 2013): 297–312.

NOTES AND COMMENTS

1. Developments in computer technology have increased the availability of management science techniques to decision makers. Many software packages are now available for personal computers. Microsoft Excel and LINGO are widely used in management science courses and in industry.

2. Various chapter appendices provide step-by-step instructions for using Excel and LINGO to solve problems in the text. Microsoft Excel has become the most used analytical modeling software in business and industry. We recommend that you read Appendix A, Building Spreadsheet Models, located in the back of this text.

1.4 MODELS OF COST, REVENUE, AND PROFIT

Some of the most basic quantitative models arising in business and economic applications are those involving the relationship between a volume variable—such as production volume or sales volume—and cost, revenue, and profit. Through the use of these models, a manager can determine the projected cost, revenue, and/or profit associated with an established production quantity or a forecasted sales volume. Financial planning, production planning, sales quotas, and other areas of decision making can benefit from such cost, revenue, and profit models.

Cost and Volume Models

The cost of manufacturing or producing a product is a function of the volume produced. This cost can usually be defined as a sum of two costs: fixed cost and variable cost. **Fixed cost** is the portion of the total cost that does not depend on the production volume; this cost remains the same no matter how much is produced. **Variable cost**, on the other hand, is the portion of the total cost that is dependent on and varies with the production volume. To illustrate how cost and volume models can be developed, we will consider a manufacturing problem faced by Nowlin Plastics.

Nowlin Plastics produces a line of cell phone covers. Nowlin's best-selling cover is its Viper model, a slim but very durable black and gray plastic cover. Several products are produced on the same manufacturing line, and a setup cost is incurred each time a changeover is made for a new product. Suppose that the setup cost for the Viper is $3000. This setup cost is a fixed cost that is incurred regardless of the number of units eventually produced. In addition, suppose that variable labor and material costs are $2 for each unit produced. The cost–volume model for producing x units of the Viper can be written as

$$C(x) = 3000 + 2x \tag{1.3}$$

where

$$x = \text{production volume in units}$$
$$C(x) = \text{total cost of producing } x \text{ units}$$

Once a production volume is established, the model in equation (1.3) can be used to compute the total production cost. For example, the decision to produce $x = 1200$ units would result in a total cost of $C(1200) = 3000 + 2(1200) = \$5400$.

Marginal cost is defined as the rate of change of the total cost with respect to production volume. That is, it is the cost increase associated with a one-unit increase in the production volume. In the cost model of equation (1.3), we see that the total cost $C(x)$ will increase by \$2 for each unit increase in the production volume. Thus, the marginal cost is \$2. With more complex total cost models, marginal cost may depend on the production volume. In such cases, we could have marginal cost increasing or decreasing with the production volume x.

Revenue and Volume Models

Management of Nowlin Plastics will also want information on the projected revenue associated with selling a specified number of units. Thus, a model of the relationship between revenue and volume is also needed. Suppose that each Viper cover sells for \$5. The model for total revenue can be written as

$$R(x) = 5x \qquad (1.4)$$

where

$$x = \text{sales volume in units}$$
$$R(x) = \text{total revenue associated with selling } x \text{ units}$$

Marginal revenue is defined as the rate of change of total revenue with respect to sales volume. That is, it is the increase in total revenue resulting from a one-unit increase in sales volume. In the model of equation (1.4), we see that the marginal revenue is \$5. In this case, marginal revenue is constant and does not vary with the sales volume. With more complex models, we may find that marginal revenue increases or decreases as the sales volume x increases.

Profit and Volume Models

One of the most important criteria for management decision making is profit. Managers need to be able to know the profit implications of their decisions. If we assume that we will only produce what can be sold, the production volume and sales volume will be equal. We can combine equations (1.3) and (1.4) to develop a profit–volume model that will determine the total profit associated with a specified production–sales volume. Total profit, denoted $P(x)$, is total revenue minus total cost; therefore, the following model provides the total profit associated with producing and selling x units:

$$P(x) = R(x) - C(x)$$
$$= 5x - (3000 + 2x) = -3000 + 3x \qquad (1.5)$$

Thus, the profit–volume model can be derived from the revenue–volume and cost–volume models.

Breakeven Analysis

Using equation (1.5), we can now determine the total profit associated with any production volume x. For example, suppose that a demand forecast indicates that 500 units of the product can be sold. The decision to produce and sell the 500 units results in a projected profit of

$$P(500) = -3000 + 3(500) = -1500$$

FIGURE 1.6 GRAPH OF THE BREAKEVEN ANALYSIS FOR NOWLIN PLASTICS

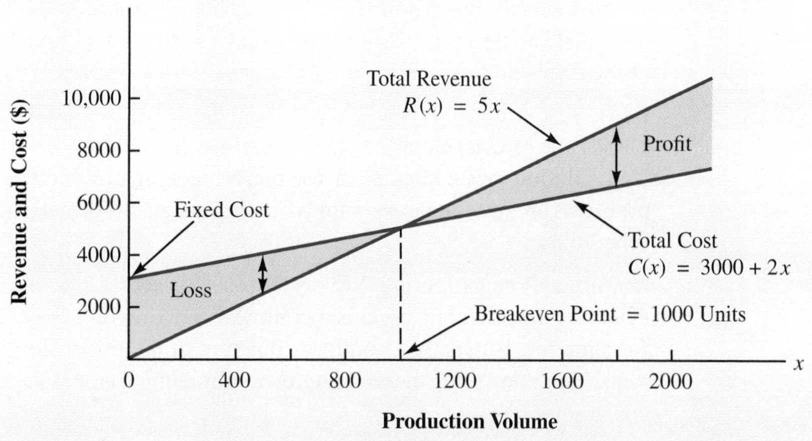

In other words, a loss of $1500 is predicted. If sales are expected to be 500 units, the manager may decide against producing the product. However, a demand forecast of 1800 units would show a projected profit of

$$P(1800) = -3000 + 3(1800) = 2400$$

This profit may be enough to justify proceeding with the production and sale of the product.

We see that a volume of 500 units will yield a loss, whereas a volume of 1800 provides a profit. The volume that results in total revenue equaling total cost (providing $0 profit) is called the **breakeven point**. If the breakeven point is known, a manager can quickly infer that a volume above the breakeven point will result in a profit, whereas a volume below the breakeven point will result in a loss. Thus, the breakeven point for a product provides valuable information for a manager who must make a yes/no decision concerning production of the product.

Let us now return to the Nowlin Plastics example and show how the total profit model in equation (1.5) can be used to compute the breakeven point. The breakeven point can be found by setting the total profit expression equal to zero and solving for the production volume. Using equation (1.5), we have

$$P(x) = -3000 + 3x = 0$$
$$3x = 3000$$
$$x = 1000$$

Try Problem 12 to test your ability to determine the breakeven point for a quantitative model.

With this information, we know that production and sales of the product must be greater than 1000 units before a profit can be expected. The graphs of the total cost model, the total revenue model, and the location of the breakeven point are shown in Figure 1.6. In Appendix 1.1 we also show how Excel can be used to perform a breakeven analysis for the Nowlin Plastics production example.

1.5 MANAGEMENT SCIENCE TECHNIQUES

In this section we present a brief overview of the management science techniques covered in this text. Over the years, practitioners have found numerous applications for the following techniques:

Linear Programming Linear programming is a problem-solving approach developed for situations involving maximizing or minimizing a linear function subject to linear constraints that limit the degree to which the objective can be pursued. The production model developed in Section 1.3 (see Figure 1.5) is an example of a simple linear programming model.

Integer Linear Programming   Integer linear programming is an approach used for problems that can be set up as linear programs, with the additional requirement that some or all of the decision variables be integer values.

Distribution and Network Models   A network is a graphical description of a problem consisting of circles called nodes that are interconnected by lines called arcs. Specialized solution procedures exist for these types of problems, enabling us to quickly solve problems in such areas as supply chain design, information system design, and project scheduling.

Nonlinear Programming   Many business processes behave in a nonlinear manner. For example, the price of a bond is a nonlinear function of interest rates; the quantity demanded for a product is usually a nonlinear function of the price. Nonlinear programming is a technique that allows for maximizing or minimizing a nonlinear function subject to nonlinear constraints.

Project Scheduling: PERT/CPM   In many situations, managers are responsible for planning, scheduling, and controlling projects that consist of numerous separate jobs or tasks performed by a variety of departments, individuals, and so forth. The PERT (Program Evaluation and Review Technique) and CPM (Critical Path Method) techniques help managers carry out their project scheduling responsibilities.

Inventory Models   Inventory models are used by managers faced with the dual problems of maintaining sufficient inventories to meet demand for goods and, at the same time, incurring the lowest possible inventory holding costs.

Waiting-Line or Queuing Models   Waiting-line or queuing models have been developed to help managers understand and make better decisions concerning the operation of systems involving waiting lines.

Simulation   Simulation is a technique used to model the operation of a system. This technique employs a computer program to model the operation and perform simulation computations.

Decision Analysis   Decision analysis can be used to determine optimal strategies in situations involving several decision alternatives and an uncertain or risk-filled pattern of events.

Goal Programming   Goal programming is a technique for solving multicriteria decision problems, usually within the framework of linear programming.

Analytic Hierarchy Process   This multicriteria decision-making technique permits the inclusion of subjective factors in arriving at a recommended decision.

Forecasting   Forecasting methods are techniques that can be used to predict future aspects of a business operation.

Markov Process Models   Markov process models are useful in studying the evolution of certain systems over repeated trials. For example, Markov processes have been used to describe the probability that a machine, functioning in one period, will function or break down in another period.

Methods Used Most Frequently

Our experience as both practitioners and educators has been that the most frequently used management science techniques are linear programming, integer programming, network models (including supply chain models), and simulation. Depending upon the industry, the other methods in the preceding list are used more or less frequently.

Helping to bridge the gap between the manager and the management scientist is a major focus of the text. We believe that the barriers to the use of management science can best be removed by increasing the manager's understanding of how management science can be applied.

The text will help you develop an understanding of which management science techniques are most useful, how they are used, and, most importantly, how they can assist managers in making better decisions.

The Management Science in Action, Impact of Operations Research on Everyday Living, describes some of the many ways quantitative analysis affects our everyday lives.

MANAGEMENT SCIENCE IN ACTION

IMPACT OF OPERATIONS RESEARCH ON EVERYDAY LIVING*

In an interview with Virginia Postrel of the *Boston Globe*, Mark Eisner, associate director of the School of Operations Research and Industrial Engineering at Cornell University, once said that operations research "...is probably the most important field nobody's ever heard of." He further defines Operations Research as "...the effective use of scarce resources under dynamic and uncertain conditions." As Professor Eisner's definition implies, the impact of operations research on everyday living is substantial.

Suppose you schedule a vacation to Florida and use Orbitz to book your flights. An algorithm developed by operations researchers will search among millions of options to find the cheapest fare. Another algorithm will schedule the flight crews and aircraft used by the airline, and yet another algorithm will determine the price you are charged for your ticket. If you rent a car in Florida, the price you pay for the car is determined by a mathematical model that seeks to maximize revenue for the car rental firm. If you do some shopping on your trip and decide to ship your purchases home using UPS, another algorithm tells UPS which truck to put the packages on, the route the truck should follow to avoid congested roads, and where the packages should be placed on the truck to minimize loading and unloading time. Do you subscribe to NetFlix? The organization uses operations research, ratings you provide for movies, and your history of movie selections to recommend other movies that will likely appeal to you. Political campaigns even use operations research to decide where to campaign, where to advertise, and how to spend campaign funds in a manner that will maximize the candidate's chance of getting elected.

Operations Research is commonly used in the healthcare industry. Researchers from the Johns Hopkins Bloomberg School of Public Health, Pittsburgh Supercomputing Center (PSC), University of Pittsburgh, and University of California, Irvine use operations research algorithms in the Regional Healthcare Ecosystem Analyst (RHEA). RHEA is used to assess how increases or decreases in vancomycin-resistant enterococci (VRE) at one hospital ultimately change the incidence of VRE in neighboring hospitals. Because VRE is one of the most common bacteria that cause infections in healthcare facilities, RHEA could dramatically reduce the length of hospital stays and the cost of treatment by reducing the incidence of VRE.

"Our study demonstrates how extensive patient sharing among different hospitals in a single region substantially influences VRE burden in those hospitals," states Bruce Y. Lee, MD, MBA, lead author and associate professor of International Health and Director of Operations Research, International Vaccine Access Center, at the Johns Hopkins Bloomberg School of Public Health. "Lowering barriers to cooperation and collaboration among hospitals, for example, developing regional control programs, coordinating VRE control campaigns, and performing regional research studies could favorably influence regional VRE prevalence."

*Based on Virginia Postrel, "Operations Everything," *The Boston Globe*, June 27, 2004; "How Superbug Spreads Among Regional Hospitals: A Domino Effect," *Science News*, July 30, 2013; and Bruce Y. Lee, S. Levent Yilmaz, Kim F. Wong, Sarah M. Bartsch, Stephen Eubank, Yeohan Song, et al., "Modeling the Regional Spread and Control of Vancomycin-Resistant Enterococci," *American Journal of Infection Control*, 41, no. 8 (2013):668–673.

NOTES AND COMMENTS

The Institute for Operations Research and the Management Sciences (INFORMS) and the Decision Sciences Institute (DSI) are two professional societies that publish journals and newsletters dealing with current research and applications of operations research and management science techniques.

SUMMARY

This text is about how management science may be used to help managers make better decisions. The focus of this text is on the decision-making process and on the role of management science in that process. We discussed the problem orientation of this process and in an overview showed how mathematical models can be used in this type of analysis.

The difference between the model and the situation or managerial problem it represents is an important point. Mathematical models are abstractions of real-world situations and, as such, cannot capture all the aspects of the real situation. However, if a model can capture the major relevant aspects of the problem and can then provide a solution recommendation, it can be a valuable aid to decision making.

One of the characteristics of management science that will become increasingly apparent as we proceed through the text is the search for a best solution to the problem. In carrying out the quantitative analysis, we shall be attempting to develop procedures for finding the "best" or optimal solution.

GLOSSARY

Analog model   Although physical in form, an analog model does not have a physical appearance similar to the real object or situation it represents.

Breakeven point   The volume at which total revenue equals total cost.

Constraints   Restrictions or limitations imposed on a problem.

Controllable inputs   The inputs that are controlled or determined by the decision maker.

Decision   The alternative selected.

Decision making   The process of defining the problem, identifying the alternatives, determining the criteria, evaluating the alternatives, and choosing an alternative.

Decision variable   Another term for controllable input.

Deterministic model   A model in which all uncontrollable inputs are known and cannot vary.

Feasible solution   A decision alternative or solution that satisfies all constraints.

Fixed cost   The portion of the total cost that does not depend on the volume; this cost remains the same no matter how much is produced.

Iconic model   A physical replica, or representation, of a real object.

Infeasible solution   A decision alternative or solution that does not satisfy one or more constraints.

Marginal cost   The rate of change of the total cost with respect to volume.

Marginal revenue   The rate of change of total revenue with respect to volume.

Mathematical model   Mathematical symbols and expressions used to represent a real situation.

Model   A representation of a real object or situation.

Multicriteria decision problem   A problem that involves more than one criterion; the objective is to find the "best" solution, taking into account all the criteria.

Objective function   A mathematical expression that describes the problem's objective.

Optimal solution   The specific decision-variable value or values that provide the "best" output for the model.

Problem solving   The process of identifying a difference between the actual and the desired state of affairs and then taking action to resolve the difference.

Single-criterion decision problem   A problem in which the objective is to find the "best" solution with respect to just one criterion.

Stochastic (probabilistic) model   A model in which at least one uncontrollable input is uncertain and subject to variation; stochastic models are also referred to as probabilistic models.

Uncontrollable inputs   The environmental factors or inputs that cannot be controlled by the decision maker.

Variable cost   The portion of the total cost that is dependent on and varies with the volume.

PROBLEMS

1. Define the terms *management science* and *operations research.*

2. List and discuss the steps of the decision-making process.

3. Discuss the different roles played by the qualitative and quantitative approaches to managerial decision making. Why is it important for a manager or decision maker to have a good understanding of both of these approaches to decision making?

4. A firm just completed a new plant that will produce more than 500 different products, using more than 50 different production lines and machines. The production scheduling decisions are critical in that sales will be lost if customer demands are not met on time. If no individual in the firm has experience with this production operation and if new production schedules must be generated each week, why should the firm consider a quantitative approach to the production scheduling problem?

5. What are the advantages of analyzing and experimenting with a model as opposed to a real object or situation?

6. Suppose that a manager has a choice between the following two mathematical models of a given situation: (a) a relatively simple model that is a reasonable approximation of the real situation, and (b) a thorough and complex model that is the most accurate mathematical representation of the real situation possible. Why might the model described in part (a) be preferred by the manager?

7. Suppose you are going on a weekend trip to a city that is d miles away. Develop a model that determines your round-trip gasoline costs. What assumptions or approximations are necessary to treat this model as a deterministic model? Are these assumptions or approximations acceptable to you?

8. Recall the production model from Section 1.3:

$$\text{Max} \quad 10x$$
$$\text{s.t.}$$
$$5x \leq 40$$
$$x \geq 0$$

Suppose the firm in this example considers a second product that has a unit profit of $5 and requires 2 hours of production time for each unit produced. Use y as the number of units of product 2 produced.
   a. Show the mathematical model when both products are considered simultaneously.
   b. Identify the controllable and uncontrollable inputs for this model.
   c. Draw the flowchart of the input–output process for this model (see Figure 1.5).
   d. What are the optimal solution values of x and y?
   e. Is the model developed in part (a) a deterministic or a stochastic model? Explain.

9. Suppose we modify the production model in Section 1.3 to obtain the following mathematical model:

$$\text{Max} \quad 10x$$
$$\text{s.t.}$$
$$ax \leq 40$$
$$x \geq 0$$

SELF*test*

SELF*test*

where a is the number of hours of production time required for each unit produced. With $a = 5$, the optimal solution is $x = 8$. If we have a stochastic model with $a = 3$, $a = 4$, $a = 5$, or $a = 6$ as the possible values for the number of hours required per unit, what is the optimal value for x? What problems does this stochastic model cause?

10. A retail store in Des Moines, Iowa, receives shipments of a particular product from Kansas City and Minneapolis. Let

$$x = \text{number of units of the product received from Kansas City}$$
$$y = \text{number of units of the product received from Minneapolis}$$

   a. Write an expression for the total number of units of the product received by the retail store in Des Moines.
   b. Shipments from Kansas City cost \$0.20 per unit, and shipments from Minneapolis cost \$0.25 per unit. Develop an objective function representing the total cost of shipments to Des Moines.
   c. Assuming the monthly demand at the retail store is 5000 units, develop a constraint that requires 5000 units to be shipped to Des Moines.
   d. No more than 4000 units can be shipped from Kansas City, and no more than 3000 units can be shipped from Minneapolis in a month. Develop constraints to model this situation.
   e. Of course, negative amounts cannot be shipped. Combine the objective function and constraints developed to state a mathematical model for satisfying the demand at the Des Moines retail store at minimum cost.

11. For most products, higher prices result in a decreased demand, whereas lower prices result in an increased demand. Let

$$d = \text{annual demand for a product in units}$$
$$p = \text{price per unit}$$

Assume that a firm accepts the following price–demand relationship as being realistic:

$$d = 800 - 10p$$

where p must be between \$20 and \$70.
   a. How many units can the firm sell at the \$20 per-unit price? At the \$70 per-unit price?
   b. What happens to annual units demanded for the product if the firm increases the per-unit price from \$26 to \$27? From \$42 to \$43? From \$68 to \$69? What is the suggested relationship between the per-unit price and annual demand for the product in units?
   c. Show the mathematical model for the total revenue (TR), which is the annual demand multiplied by the unit price.
   d. Based on other considerations, the firm's management will only consider price alternatives of \$30, \$40, and \$50. Use your model from part (b) to determine the price alternative that will maximize the total revenue.
   e. What are the expected annual demand and the total revenue corresponding to your recommended price?

SELFtest

12. The O'Neill Shoe Manufacturing Company will produce a special-style shoe if the order size is large enough to provide a reasonable profit. For each special-style order, the company incurs a fixed cost of \$2000 for the production setup. The variable cost is \$60 per pair, and each pair sells for \$80.
   a. Let x indicate the number of pairs of shoes produced. Develop a mathematical model for the total cost of producing x pairs of shoes.
   b. Let P indicate the total profit. Develop a mathematical model for the total profit realized from an order for x pairs of shoes.
   c. How large must the shoe order be before O'Neill will break even?

13. Micromedia offers computer training seminars on a variety of topics. In the seminars each student works at a personal computer, practicing the particular activity that the instructor is presenting. Micromedia is currently planning a two-day seminar on the use of Microsoft Excel in statistical analysis. The projected fee for the seminar is $600 per student. The cost for the conference room, instructor compensation, lab assistants, and promotion is $9600. Micromedia rents computers for its seminars at a cost of $120 per computer per day.

    a. Develop a model for the total cost to put on the seminar. Let x represent the number of students who enroll in the seminar.

    b. Develop a model for the total profit if x students enroll in the seminar.

    c. Micromedia has forecasted an enrollment of 30 students for the seminar. How much profit will be earned if their forecast is accurate?

    d. Compute the breakeven point.

14. Eastman Publishing Company is considering publishing a paperback textbook on spreadsheet applications for business. The fixed cost of manuscript preparation, textbook design, and production setup is estimated to be $160,000. Variable production and material costs are estimated to be $6 per book. The publisher plans to sell the text to college and university bookstores for $46 each.

    a. What is the breakeven point?

    b. What profit or loss can be anticipated with a demand of 3800 copies?

    c. With a demand of 3800 copies, what is the minimum price per copy that the publisher must charge to break even?

    d. If the publisher believes that the price per copy could be increased to $50.95 and not affect the anticipated demand of 3800 copies, what action would you recommend? What profit or loss can be anticipated?

15. Preliminary plans are under way for the construction of a new stadium for a major league baseball team. City officials have questioned the number and profitability of the luxury corporate boxes planned for the upper deck of the stadium. Corporations and selected individuals may buy the boxes for $300,000 each. The fixed construction cost for the upper-deck area is estimated to be $4,500,000, with a variable cost of $150,000 for each box constructed.

    a. What is the breakeven point for the number of luxury boxes in the new stadium?

    b. Preliminary drawings for the stadium show that space is available for the construction of up to 50 luxury boxes. Promoters indicate that buyers are available and that all 50 could be sold if constructed. What is your recommendation concerning the construction of luxury boxes? What profit is anticipated?

16. Financial Analysts, Inc., is an investment firm that manages stock portfolios for a number of clients. A new client is requesting that the firm handle an $800,000 portfolio. As an initial investment strategy, the client would like to restrict the portfolio to a mix of the following two stocks:

Stock	Price/ Share	Maximum Estimated Annual Return/Share	Possible Investment
Oil Alaska	$50	$6	$500,000
Southwest Petroleum	$30	$4	$450,000

Let

x = number of shares of Oil Alaska

y = number of shares of Southwest Petroleum

    a. Develop the objective function, assuming that the client desires to maximize the total annual return.

   b. Show the mathematical expression for each of the following three constraints:
   (1) Total investment funds available are $800,000.
   (2) Maximum Oil Alaska investment is $500,000.
   (3) Maximum Southwest Petroleum investment is $450,000.

   Note: Adding the $x \geq 0$ and $y \geq 0$ constraints provides a linear programming model for the investment problem. A solution procedure for this model will be discussed in Chapter 2.

17. Models of inventory systems frequently consider the relationships among a beginning inventory, a production quantity, a demand or sales, and an ending inventory. For a given production period j, let

s_{j-1} = ending inventory from the previous period (beginning inventory for period j)
x_j = production quantity in period j
d_j = demand in period j
s_j = ending inventory for period j

   a. Write the mathematical relationship or model that describes how these four variables are related.
   b. What constraint should be added if production capacity for period j is given by C_j?
   c. What constraint should be added if inventory requirements for period j mandate an ending inventory of at least I_j?

18. Esiason Oil makes two blends of fuel by mixing oil from three wells, one each in Texas, Oklahoma, and California. The costs and daily availability of the oils are provided in the following table.

Source of Oil	Cost per Gallon	Daily Gallons Available
Texas well	0.30	12,000
Oklahoma well	0.40	20,000
California well	0.48	24,000

   Because these three wells yield oils with different chemical compositions, Esiason's two blends of fuel are composed of different proportions of oil from its three wells. Blend A must be composed of at least 35% of oil from the Texas well, no more than 50% of oil from the Oklahoma well, and at least 15% of oil from the California well. Blend B must be composed of at least 20% of oil from the Texas well, at least 30% of oil from the Oklahoma well, and no more than 40% of oil from the California well.
   Each gallon of Blend A can be sold for $3.10 and each gallon of Blend B can be sold for $3.20. Long-term contracts require at least 20,000 gallons of each blend to be produced.
   Let
   x_i = number of gallons of oil from well i used in production of Blend A
   y_i = number of gallons of oil from well i used in production of Blend B
   i = 1 for the Texas well, 2 for the Oklahoma well, 3 for the California well

   a. Develop the objective function, assuming that the client desires to maximize the total daily profit.
   b. Show the mathematical expression for each of the following three constraints:
   (1) Total daily gallons of oil available from the Texas well is 12,000.
   (2) Total daily gallons of oil available from the Oklahoma well is 20,000.
   (3) Total daily gallons of oil available from the California well is 24,000.
   c. Should this problem include any other constraints? If so, express them mathematically in terms of the decision variables.

19. Brooklyn Cabinets is a manufacturer of kitchen cabinets. The two cabinetry styles manufactured by Brooklyn are contemporary and farmhouse. Contemporary style cabinets sell for $90 and farmhouse style cabinets sell for $85. Each cabinet produced must go through

carpentry, painting, and finishing processes. The following table summarizes how much time in each process must be devoted to each style of cabinet.

	Hours per Process		
Style	**Carpentry**	**Painting**	**Finishing**
Contemporary	2.0	1.5	1.3
Farmhouse	2.5	1.0	1.2

Carpentry costs $15 per hour, painting costs $12 per hour, and finishing costs $18 per hour; and the weekly number of hours available in the processes is 3000 in carpentry, 1500 in painting, and 1500 in finishing. Brooklyn also has a contract that requires the company to supply one of its customers with 500 contemporary cabinets and 650 farmhouse style cabinets each week.
Let

x = the number of contemporary style cabinets produced each week

y = the number of farmhouse style cabinets produced each week

a. Develop the objective function, assuming that Brooklyn Cabinets wants to maximize the total weekly profit.
b. Show the mathematical expression for each of the constraints on the three processes.
c. Show the mathematical expression for each of Brooklyn Cabinets' contractual agreements.

20. PromoTime, a local advertising agency, has been hired to promote the new adventure film *Tomb Raiders* starring Angie Harrison and Joe Lee Ford. The agency has been given a $100,000 budget to spend on advertising for the movie in the week prior to its release, and the movie's producers have dictated that only local television ads and locally targeted Internet ads will be used. Each television ad costs $500 and reaches an estimated 7000 people, and each Internet ad costs $250 and reaches an estimated 4000 people. The movie's producers have also dictated that, in order to avoid saturation, no more than 20 television ads will be placed. The producers have also stipulated that, in order to reach a critical mass, at least 50 Internet ads will be placed. Finally, the producers want at least one-third of all ads to be placed on television.
Let

x = the number of television ads purchased

y = the number of Internet ads purchased

a. Develop the objective function, assuming that the movie's producers want to reach the maximum number of people possible.
b. Show the mathematical expression for the budget constraint.
c. Show the mathematical expression for the maximum number of 20 television ads to be used.
d. Show the mathematical expression for the minimum number of Internet ads to be used.
e. Show the mathematical expression for the stipulated ratio of television ads to Internet ads.
f. Carefully review the constraints you created in part (b), part (c), and part (d). Does any aspect of these constraints concern you? If so, why?

Case Problem   SCHEDULING A GOLF LEAGUE

Chris Lane, the head professional at Royal Oak Country Club, must develop a schedule of matches for the couples' golf league that begins its season at 4:00 P.M. tomorrow. Eighteen couples signed up for the league, and each couple must play every other couple over the course of the 17-week season. Chris thought it would be fairly easy to develop a schedule, but after working on it for a couple of hours, he has been unable to come up with a schedule. Because Chris must have a schedule ready by tomorrow afternoon, he asked you to help him. A possible complication is that one of the couples told Chris that they may have to cancel for the season. They told Chris they will let him know by 1:00 P.M. tomorrow whether they will be able to play this season.

Managerial Report

Prepare a report for Chris Lane. Your report should include, at a minimum, the following items:

1. A schedule that will enable each of the 18 couples to play every other couple over the 17-week season.
2. A contingency schedule that can be used if the couple that contacted Chris decides to cancel for the season.

Appendix 1.1   USING EXCEL FOR BREAKEVEN ANALYSIS

In Section 1.4 we introduced the Nowlin Plastics production example to illustrate how quantitative models can be used to help a manager determine the projected cost, revenue, and/or profit associated with an established production quantity or a forecasted sales volume. In this appendix we introduce spreadsheet applications by showing how to use Microsoft Excel to perform a quantitative analysis of the Nowlin Plastics example.

Refer to the worksheet shown in Figure 1.7. We begin by entering the problem data into the top portion of the worksheet. The value of 3000 in cell B3 is the fixed cost, the value of 2 in cell B5 is the variable labor and material costs per unit, and the value of 5 in cell B7 is the selling price per unit. As discussed in Appendix A, whenever we perform a quantitative analysis using Excel, we will enter the problem data in the top portion of the worksheet and reserve the bottom portion for model development. The label "Model" in cell A10 helps to provide a visual reminder of this convention.

Cell B12 in the Model portion of the worksheet contains the proposed production volume in units. Because the values for total cost, total revenue, and total profit depend upon the value of this decision variable, we have placed a border around cell B12 and screened the cell for emphasis. Based upon the value in cell B12, the cell formulas in cells

FIGURE 1.7   FORMULA WORKSHEET FOR THE NOWLIN PLASTICS PRODUCTION EXAMPLE

	A	B
1	**Nowlin Plastics**	
2		
3	**Fixed Cost**	3000
4		
5	**Variable Cost Per Unit**	2
6		
7	**Selling Price Per Unit**	5
8		
9		
10	**Model**	
11		
12	**Production Volume**	800
13		
14	**Total Cost**	=B3+B5*B12
15		
16	**Total Revenue**	=B7*B12
17		
18	**Total Profit (Loss)**	=B16-B14

FIGURE 1.8 SOLUTION USING A PRODUCTION VOLUME OF 800 UNITS FOR THE NOWLIN PLASTICS PRODUCTION EXAMPLE

MODEL *file*

Nowlin

	A	B
1	Nowlin Plastics	
2		
3	Fixed Cost	$3,000
4		
5	Variable Cost Per Unit	$2
6		
7	Selling Price Per Unit	$5
8		
9		
10	Model	
11		
12	Production Volume	800
13		
14	Total Cost	$4,600
15		
16	Total Revenue	$4,000
17		
18	Total Profit (Loss)	−$600

B14, B16, and B18 are used to compute values for total cost, total revenue, and total profit (loss), respectively. First, recall that the value of total cost is the sum of the fixed cost (cell B3) and the total variable cost. The total variable cost—the product of the variable cost per unit (cell B5) and the production volume (cell B12)—is given by B5*B12. Thus, to compute the value of total cost we entered the formula =B3+B5*B12 in cell B14. Next, total revenue is the product of the selling price per unit (cell B7) and the number of units produced (cell B12), which is entered in cell B16 as the formula =B7*B12. Finally, the total profit (or loss) is the difference between the total revenue (cell B16) and the total cost (cell B14). Thus, in cell B18 we have entered the formula =B16-B14. The worksheet shown in Figure 1.7 shows the formulas used to make these computations; we refer to it as a formula worksheet.

To examine the effect of selecting a particular value for the production volume, we entered a value of 800 in cell B12. The worksheet shown in Figure 1.8 shows the values obtained by the formulas; a production volume of 800 units results in a total cost of $4600, a total revenue of $4000, and a loss of $600. To examine the effect of other production volumes, we only need to enter a different value into cell B12. To examine the effect of different costs and selling prices, we simply enter the appropriate values in the data portion of the worksheet; the results will be displayed in the model section of the worksheet.

In Section 1.4 we illustrated breakeven analysis. Let us now see how Excel's Goal Seek tool can be used to compute the breakeven point for the Nowlin Plastics production example.

Determining the Breakeven Point Using Excel's Goal Seek Tool

The breakeven point is the production volume that results in total revenue equal to total cost and hence a profit of $0. One way to determine the breakeven point is to use a trial-and-error approach. For example, in Figure 1.8 we saw that a trial production volume of 800 units resulted in a loss of $600. Because this trial solution resulted in a loss, a production volume of 800 units cannot be the breakeven point. We could continue to experiment with other production volumes by simply entering different values into cell B12 and observing the resulting profit or loss in cell B18. A better approach is to use Excel's Goal Seek tool to determine the breakeven point.

Excel's Goal Seek tool allows the user to determine the value for an input cell that will cause the value of a related output cell to equal some specified value (called the *goal*). In the

FIGURE 1.9   GOAL SEEK DIALOG BOX FOR THE NOWLIN PLASTICS
PRODUCTION EXAMPLE

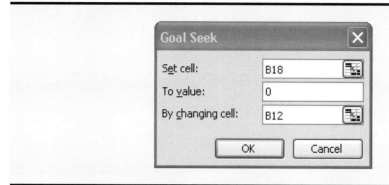

case of breakeven analysis, the "goal" is to set Total Profit to zero by "seeking" an appropriate value for Production Volume. Goal Seek will allow us to find the value of production volume that will set Nowlin Plastics' total profit to zero. The following steps describe how to use Goal Seek to find the breakeven point for Nowlin Plastics:

Step 1. Select the **Data** tab at the top of the Ribbon
Step 2. Select **What-If Analysis** in the **Data Tools** group
Step 3. Select **Goal Seek** in What-If Analysis
Step 4. When the **Goal Seek** dialog box appears:
　　　　Enter *B18* in the **Set cell** box
　　　　Enter *0* in the **To value** box
　　　　Enter *B12* in the **By changing cell** box
　　　　Click **OK**

The completed Goal Seek dialog box is shown in Figure 1.9, and the worksheet obtained after selecting **OK** is shown in Figure 1.10. The Total Profit in cell B18 is zero, and the Production Volume in cell B12 has been set to the breakeven point of 1000.

FIGURE 1.10   BREAKEVEN POINT FOUND USING EXCEL'S GOAL SEEK TOOL
FOR THE NOWLIN PLASTICS PRODUCTION EXAMPLE

	A	B
1	**Nowlin Plastics**	
2		
3	**Fixed Cost**	$3,000
4		
5	**Variable Cost Per Unit**	$2
6		
7	**Selling Price Per Unit**	$5
8		
9		
10	**Model**	
11		
12	**Production Volume**	1000
13		
14	**Total Cost**	$5,000
15		
16	**Total Revenue**	$5,000
17		
18	**Total Profit (Loss)**	$0

CHAPTER 2

An Introduction to Linear Programming

CONTENTS

Linear programming is a problem-solving approach developed to help managers make decisions. Numerous applications of linear programming can be found in today's competitive business environment. For instance, IBM uses linear programming to perform capacity planning and to make capacity investment decisions for its semiconductor manufacturing operations. GE Capital uses linear programming to help determine optimal lease structuring. Marathon Oil Company uses linear programming for gasoline blending and to evaluate the economics of a new terminal or pipeline. The Management Science in Action, Timber Harvesting Model at MeadWestvaco Corporation, provides another example of the use of linear programming. Later in the chapter another Management Science in Action illustrates how IBM uses linear programming and other management science tools to plan and operate its semiconductor supply chain.

To illustrate some of the properties that all linear programming problems have in common, consider the following typical applications:

1. A manufacturer wants to develop a production schedule and an inventory policy that will satisfy sales demand in future periods. Ideally, the schedule and policy will enable the company to satisfy demand and at the same time *minimize* the total production and inventory costs.
2. A financial analyst must select an investment portfolio from a variety of stock and bond investment alternatives. The analyst would like to establish the portfolio that *maximizes* the return on investment.
3. A marketing manager wants to determine how best to allocate a fixed advertising budget among alternative advertising media such as radio, television, newspaper, and magazine. The manager would like to determine the media mix that *maximizes* advertising effectiveness.
4. A company has warehouses in a number of locations throughout the United States. For a set of customer demands, the company would like to determine how much each warehouse should ship to each customer so that total transportation costs are *minimized.*

These examples are only a few of the situations in which linear programming has been used successfully, but they illustrate the diversity of linear programming applications.

MANAGEMENT SCIENCE IN ACTION

TIMBER HARVESTING MODEL AT MEADWESTVACO CORPORATION*

MeadWestvaco Corporation is a major producer of premium papers for periodicals, books, commercial printing, and business forms. The company also produces pulp and lumber, designs and manufactures packaging systems for beverage and other consumables markets, and is a world leader in the production of coated board and shipping containers. Quantitative analyses at MeadWestvaco are developed and implemented by the company's Decision Analysis Department. The department assists decision makers by providing them with analytical tools of quantitative methods as well as personal analysis and recommendations.

MeadWestvaco uses quantitative models to assist with the long-range management of the company's timberland. Through the use of large-scale linear programs, timber harvesting plans are developed to cover a substantial time horizon. These models consider wood market conditions, mill pulpwood requirements, harvesting capacities, and general forest management principles. Within these constraints, the model arrives at an optimal harvesting and purchasing schedule based on discounted cash flow. Alternative schedules reflect changes in the various assumptions concerning forest growth, wood availability, and general economic conditions.

Quantitative methods are also used in the development of the inputs for the linear programming models. Timber prices and supplies as well as mill requirements must be forecast over the time horizon, and advanced sampling techniques are used to evaluate land holdings and to project forest growth. The harvest schedule is then developed using quantitative methods.

*Based on information provided by Dr Edward P. Winkofsky.

A close scrutiny reveals one basic property they all have in common. In each example, we were concerned with *maximizing* or *minimizing* some quantity. In example 1, the manufacturer wanted to minimize costs; in example 2, the financial analyst wanted to maximize return on investment; in example 3, the marketing manager wanted to maximize advertising effectiveness; and in example 4, the company wanted to minimize total transportation costs. *In all linear programming problems, the maximization or minimization of some quantity is the objective.*

All linear programming problems also have a second property: restrictions, or **constraints,** that limit the degree to which the objective can be pursued. In example 1, the manufacturer is restricted by constraints requiring product demand to be satisfied and by the constraints limiting production capacity. The financial analyst's portfolio problem is constrained by the total amount of investment funds available and the maximum amounts that can be invested in each stock or bond. The marketing manager's media selection decision is constrained by a fixed advertising budget and the availability of the various media. In the transportation problem, the minimum-cost shipping schedule is constrained by the supply of product available at each warehouse. *Thus, constraints are another general feature of every linear programming problem.*

2.1   A SIMPLE MAXIMIZATION PROBLEM

Par, Inc., is a small manufacturer of golf equipment and supplies whose management has decided to move into the market for medium- and high-priced golf bags. Par, Inc.'s distributor is enthusiastic about the new product line and has agreed to buy all the golf bags Par, Inc., produces over the next three months.

After a thorough investigation of the steps involved in manufacturing a golf bag, management determined that each golf bag produced will require the following operations:

1. Cutting and dyeing the material
2. Sewing
3. Finishing (inserting umbrella holder, club separators, etc.)
4. Inspection and packaging

The director of manufacturing analyzed each of the operations and concluded that if the company produces a medium-priced standard model, each bag will require $7\!/\!10$ hour in the cutting and dyeing department, $\frac{1}{2}$ hour in the sewing department, 1 hour in the finishing department, and $\frac{1}{10}$ hour in the inspection and packaging department. The more expensive deluxe model will require 1 hour for cutting and dyeing, $\frac{5}{6}$ hour for sewing, $\frac{2}{3}$ hour for finishing, and $\frac{1}{4}$ hour for inspection and packaging. This production information is summarized in Table 2.1.

Par, Inc.'s production is constrained by a limited number of hours available in each department. After studying departmental workload projections, the director of manufacturing estimates that 630 hours for cutting and dyeing, 600 hours for sewing, 708 hours for finishing, and 135 hours for inspection and packaging will be available for the production of golf bags during the next three months.

The accounting department analyzed the production data, assigned all relevant variable costs, and arrived at prices for both bags that will result in a profit contribution[1] of $10 for every standard bag and $9 for every deluxe bag produced. Let us now develop a mathematical model of the Par, Inc., problem that can be used to determine the number of standard bags and the number of deluxe bags to produce in order to maximize total profit contribution.

Problem Formulation

Problem formulation, or **modeling,** is the process of translating the verbal statement of a problem into a mathematical statement. Formulating models is an art that can only be

It is important to understand that we are maximizing profit contribution, not profit. Overhead and other shared costs must be deducted before arriving at a profit figure.

---

[1]From an accounting perspective, profit contribution is more correctly described as the contribution margin per bag; for example, overhead and other shared costs have not been allocated.

TABLE 2.1   PRODUCTION REQUIREMENTS PER GOLF BAG

Department	Production Time (hours)	
	Standard Bag	**Deluxe Bag**
Cutting and Dyeing	7/10	1
Sewing	1/2	5/6
Finishing	1	2/3
Inspection and Packaging	1/10	1/4

mastered with practice and experience. Even though every problem has some unique features, most problems also have common features. As a result, *some* general guidelines for model formulation can be helpful, especially for beginners. We will illustrate these general guidelines by developing a mathematical model for the Par, Inc., problem.

Understand the Problem Thoroughly   We selected the Par, Inc., problem to introduce linear programming because it is easy to understand. However, more complex problems will require much more thinking in order to identify the items that need to be included in the model. In such cases, read the problem description quickly to get a feel for what is involved. Taking notes will help you focus on the key issues and facts.

Describe the Objective   The objective is to maximize the total contribution to profit.

Describe Each Constraint   Four constraints relate to the number of hours of manufacturing time available; they restrict the number of standard bags and the number of deluxe bags that can be produced.

Constraint 1:   Number of hours of cutting and dyeing time used must be less than or equal to the number of hours of cutting and dyeing time available.

Constraint 2:   Number of hours of sewing time used must be less than or equal to the number of hours of sewing time available.

Constraint 3:   Number of hours of finishing time used must be less than or equal to the number of hours of finishing time available.

Constraint 4:   Number of hours of inspection and packaging time used must be less than or equal to the number of hours of inspection and packaging time available.

Define the Decision Variables   The controllable inputs for Par, Inc., are (1) the number of standard bags produced and (2) the number of deluxe bags produced. Let

$$S = \text{number of standard bags}$$
$$D = \text{number of deluxe bags}$$

In linear programming terminology, S and D are referred to as the **decision variables.**

Write the Objective in Terms of the Decision Variables   Par, Inc.'s profit contribution comes from two sources: (1) the profit contribution made by producing S standard bags and (2) the profit contribution made by producing D deluxe bags. If Par, Inc., makes $10 for every standard bag, the company will make $10S$ if S standard bags are produced. Also, if Par, Inc., makes $9 for every deluxe bag, the company will make $9D$ if D deluxe bags are produced. Thus, we have

Total Profit Contribution $= 10S + 9D$

Because the objective—maximize total profit contribution—is a function of the decision variables S and D, we refer to $10S + 9D$ as the *objective function*. Using "Max" as an abbreviation for maximize, we write Par, Inc.'s objective as follows:

$$\text{Max } 10S + 9D$$

Write the Constraints in Terms of the Decision Variables
Constraint 1:

$$\begin{pmatrix} \text{Hours of cutting and} \\ \text{dyeing time used} \end{pmatrix} \leq \begin{pmatrix} \text{Hours of cutting and} \\ \text{dyeing time available} \end{pmatrix}$$

Every standard bag Par, Inc., produces will use $7/10$ hour cutting and dyeing time; therefore, the total number of hours of cutting and dyeing time used in the manufacture of S standard bags is $7/10 S$. In addition, because every deluxe bag produced uses 1 hour of cutting and dyeing time, the production of D deluxe bags will use $1D$ hours of cutting and dyeing time. Thus, the total cutting and dyeing time required for the production of S standard bags and D deluxe bags is given by

$$\text{Total hours of cutting and dyeing time used} = 7/10 S + 1D$$

The units of measurement on the left-hand side of the constraint must match the units of measurement on the right-hand side.

The director of manufacturing stated that Par, Inc., has at most 630 hours of cutting and dyeing time available. Therefore, the production combination we select must satisfy the requirement

$$7/10 S + 1D \leq 630 \tag{2.1}$$

Constraint 2:

$$\begin{pmatrix} \text{Hours of sewing} \\ \text{time used} \end{pmatrix} \leq \begin{pmatrix} \text{Hours of sewing} \\ \text{time available} \end{pmatrix}$$

From Table 2.1, we see that every standard bag manufactured will require $1/2$ hour for sewing, and every deluxe bag will require $5/6$ hour for sewing. Because 600 hours of sewing time are available, it follows that

$$1/2 S + 5/6 D \leq 600 \tag{2.2}$$

Constraint 3:

$$\begin{pmatrix} \text{Hours of finishing} \\ \text{time used} \end{pmatrix} \leq \begin{pmatrix} \text{Hours of finishing} \\ \text{time available} \end{pmatrix}$$

Every standard bag manufactured will require 1 hour for finishing, and every deluxe bag will require $2/3$ hour for finishing. With 708 hours of finishing time available, it follows that

$$1S + 2/3 D \leq 708 \tag{2.3}$$

Constraint 4:

$$\begin{pmatrix} \text{Hours of inspection and} \\ \text{packaging time used} \end{pmatrix} \leq \begin{pmatrix} \text{Hours of inspection and} \\ \text{packaging time available} \end{pmatrix}$$

Every standard bag manufactured will require $1/10$ hour for inspection and packaging, and every deluxe bag will require $1/4$ hour for inspection and packaging. Because 135 hours of inspection and packaging time are available, it follows that

$$1/10 S + 1/4 D \leq 135 \tag{2.4}$$

We have now specified the mathematical relationships for the constraints associated with the four departments. Have we forgotten any other constraints? Can Par, Inc., produce a negative number of standard or deluxe bags? Clearly, the answer is no. Thus, to prevent the decision variables S and D from having negative values, two constraints

$$S \geq 0 \quad \text{and} \quad D \geq 0 \tag{2.5}$$

must be added. These constraints ensure that the solution to the problem will contain nonnegative values for the decision variables and are thus referred to as the **nonnegativity constraints.** Nonnegativity constraints are a general feature of all linear programming problems and may be written in the abbreviated form:

$$S, D \geq 0$$

Try Problem 24(a) to test your ability to formulate a mathematical model for a maximization linear programming problem with less-than-or-equal-to constraints.

Mathematical Statement of the Par, Inc., Problem

The mathematical statement or mathematical formulation of the Par, Inc., problem is now complete. We succeeded in translating the objective and constraints of the problem into a set of mathematical relationships referred to as a **mathematical model.** The complete mathematical model for the Par, Inc., problem is as follows:

$$\begin{aligned}
\text{Max} \quad & 10S + 9D \\
\text{subject to (s.t.)} \quad & \\
& \tfrac{7}{10}S + 1D \leq 630 \quad \text{Cutting and Dyeing} \\
& \tfrac{1}{2}S + \tfrac{5}{6}D \leq 600 \quad \text{Sewing} \\
& 1S + \tfrac{2}{3}D \leq 708 \quad \text{Finishing} \\
& \tfrac{1}{10}S + \tfrac{1}{4}D \leq 135 \quad \text{Inspection and Packaging} \\
& S, D \geq 0
\end{aligned} \tag{2.6}$$

Our job now is to find the product mix (i.e., the combination of S and D) that satisfies all the constraints and, at the same time, yields a value for the objective function that is greater than or equal to the value given by any other feasible solution. Once these values are calculated, we will find the optimal solution to the problem.

This mathematical model of the Par, Inc., problem is **a linear programming model,** or **linear program.** The problem has the objective and constraints that, as we said earlier, are common properties of all *linear* programs. But what is the special feature of this mathematical model that makes it a linear program? The special feature that makes it a linear program is that the objective function and all constraint functions are linear functions of the decision variables.

Mathematical functions in which each variable appears in a separate term and is raised to the first power are called **linear functions.** The objective function $(10S + 9D)$ is linear because each decision variable appears in a separate term and has an exponent of 1. The amount of production time required in the cutting and dyeing department $(\tfrac{7}{10}S + 1D)$ is also a linear function of the decision variables for the same reason. Similarly, the functions on the left-hand side of all the constraint inequalities (the constraint functions) are linear functions. Thus, the mathematical formulation of this problem is referred to as a linear program.

Try Problem 1 to test your ability to recognize the types of mathematical relationships that can be found in a linear program.

Linear *programming* has nothing to do with computer programming. The use of the word *programming* here means "choosing a course of action." Linear programming involves choosing a course of action when the mathematical model of the problem contains only linear functions.

NOTES AND COMMENTS

1. The three assumptions necessary for a linear programming model to be appropriate are proportionality, additivity, and divisibility. *Proportionality* means that the contribution to the objective function and the amount of resources used in each constraint are proportional to the value of each decision variable. *Additivity* means that the value of the objective function and the total resources used can be found by summing the objective function contribution and the resources used for all decision variables. *Divisibility* means that the decision variables are continuous. The divisibility assumption plus the nonnegativity constraints mean that decision variables can take on any value greater than or equal to zero.

2. Management scientists formulate and solve a variety of mathematical models that contain an objective function and a set of constraints. Models of this type are referred to as *mathematical programming models*. Linear programming models are a special type of mathematical programming model in that the objective function and all constraint functions are linear.

2.2   GRAPHICAL SOLUTION PROCEDURE

A linear programming problem involving only two decision variables can be solved using a graphical solution procedure. Let us begin the graphical solution procedure by developing a graph that displays the possible solutions (S and D values) for the Par, Inc., problem. The graph (Figure 2.1) will have values of S on the horizontal axis and values of D on the vertical axis. Any point on the graph can be identified by the S and D values, which indicate the position of the point along the horizontal and vertical axes, respectively. Because every point (S, D) corresponds to a possible solution, every point on the graph is called a *solution point*. The solution point where $S = 0$ and $D = 0$ is referred to as the origin. Because S and D must be nonnegative, the graph in Figure 2.1 only displays solutions where $S \geq 0$ and $D \geq 0$.

FIGURE 2.1   SOLUTION POINTS FOR THE TWO-VARIABLE PAR, INC., PROBLEM

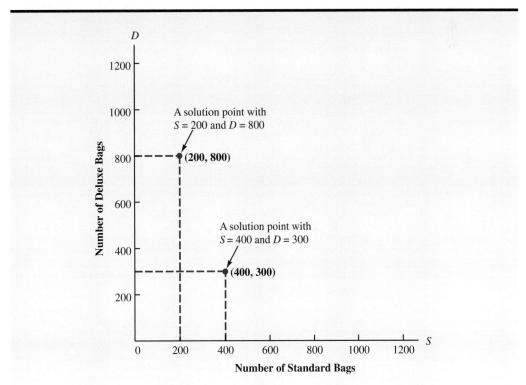

Earlier, we saw that the inequality representing the cutting and dyeing constraint is

$$\tfrac{7}{10}S + 1D \leq 630$$

To show all solution points that satisfy this relationship, we start by graphing the solution points satisfying the constraint as an equality. That is, the points where $\tfrac{7}{10}S + 1D = 630$. Because the graph of this equation is a line, it can be obtained by identifying two points that satisfy the equation and then drawing a line through the points. Setting $S = 0$ and solving for D, we see that the point ($S = 0$, $D = 630$) satisfies the equation. To find a second point satisfying this equation, we set $D = 0$ and solve for S. By doing so, we obtain $\tfrac{7}{10}S + 1(0) = 630$, or $S = 900$. Thus, a second point satisfying the equation is ($S = 900$, $D = 0$). Given these two points, we can now graph the line corresponding to the equation

$$\tfrac{7}{10}S + 1D = 630$$

This line, which will be called the cutting and dyeing *constraint line,* is shown in Figure 2.2. We label this line "C & D" to indicate that it represents the cutting and dyeing constraint line. Recall that the inequality representing the cutting and dyeing constraint is

$$\tfrac{7}{10}S + 1D \leq 630$$

Can you identify all of the solution points that satisfy this constraint? Because all points on the line satisfy $\tfrac{7}{10}S + 1D = 630$, we know any point on this line must satisfy the constraint. But where are the solution points satisfying $\tfrac{7}{10}S + 1D < 630$? Consider two solution points: ($S = 200$, $D = 200$) and ($S = 600$, $D = 500$). You can see from Figure 2.2 that the first solution point is below the constraint line and the second is above the constraint line. Which of these solutions will satisfy the cutting and dyeing constraint? For the point ($S = 200$, $D = 200$), we see that

$$\tfrac{7}{10}S + 1D = \tfrac{7}{10}(200) + 1(200) = 340$$

FIGURE 2.2   THE CUTTING AND DYEING CONSTRAINT LINE

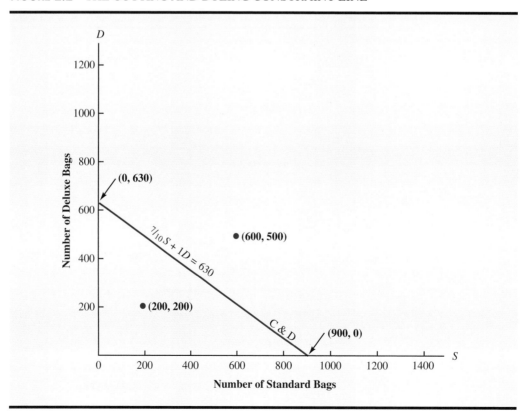

Because the 340 hours is less than the 630 hours available, the ($S = 200$, $D = 200$) production combination, or solution point, satisfies the constraint. For the point ($S = 600$, $D = 500$), we have

$$\tfrac{7}{10}S + 1D = \tfrac{7}{10}(600) + 1(500) = 920$$

The 920 hours is greater than the 630 hours available, so the ($S = 600$, $D = 500$) solution point does not satisfy the constraint and is thus not feasible.

Can you graph a constraint line and find the solution points that are feasible? Try Problem 2.

If a solution point is not feasible for a particular constraint, then all other solution points on the same side of that constraint line are not feasible. If a solution point is feasible for a particular constraint, then all other solution points on the same side of the constraint line are feasible for that constraint. Thus, one has to evaluate the constraint function for only one solution point to determine which side of a constraint line is feasible. In Figure 2.3 we indicate all points satisfying the cutting and dyeing constraint by the shaded region.

We continue by identifying the solution points satisfying each of the other three constraints. The solutions that are feasible for each of these constraints are shown in Figure 2.4.

Four separate graphs now show the feasible solution points for each of the four constraints. In a linear programming problem, we need to identify the solution points that satisfy *all* the constraints *simultaneously*. To find these solution points, we can draw all four constraints on one graph and observe the region containing the points that do in fact satisfy all the constraints simultaneously.

Try Problem 7 to test your ability to find the feasible region given several constraints.

The graphs in Figures 2.3 and 2.4 can be superimposed to obtain one graph with all four constraints. This combined-constraint graph is shown in Figure 2.5. The shaded region in this figure includes every solution point that satisfies all the constraints simultaneously. Solutions that satisfy all the constraints are termed **feasible solutions,** and the shaded region is called the feasible solution region, or simply the **feasible region.** Any solution point on the boundary of the feasible region or within the feasible region is a *feasible solution point.*

FIGURE 2.3 FEASIBLE SOLUTIONS FOR THE CUTTING AND DYEING CONSTRAINT, REPRESENTED BY THE SHADED REGION

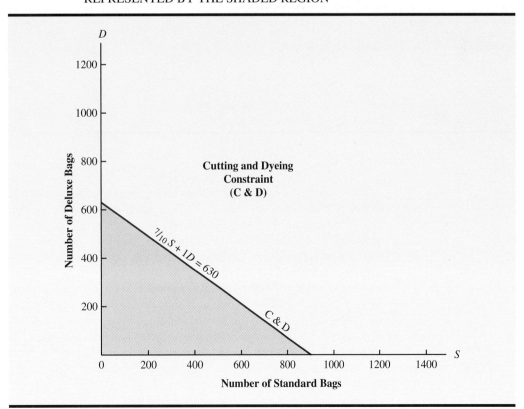

FIGURE 2.4   FEASIBLE SOLUTIONS FOR THE SEWING, FINISHING, AND INSPECTION
AND PACKAGING CONSTRAINTS, REPRESENTED BY THE SHADED REGIONS

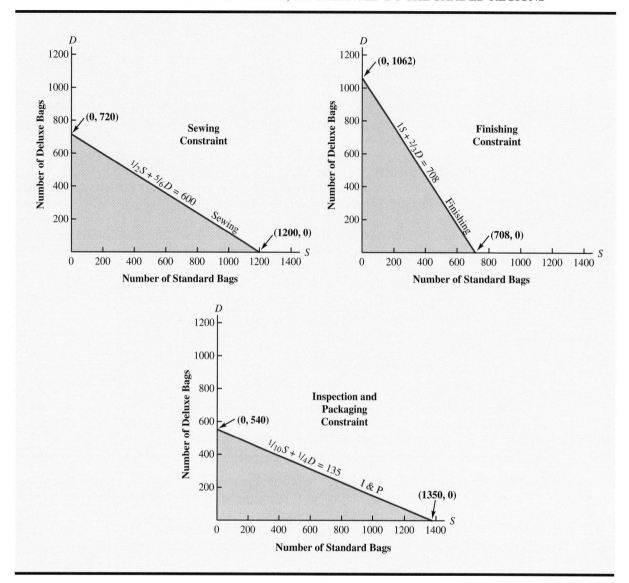

Now that we have identified the feasible region, we are ready to proceed with the graphical solution procedure and find the optimal solution to the Par, Inc., problem. Recall that the optimal solution for a linear programming problem is the feasible solution that provides the best possible value of the objective function. Let us start the optimizing step of the graphical solution procedure by redrawing the feasible region on a separate graph. The graph is shown in Figure 2.6.

One approach to finding the optimal solution would be to evaluate the objective function for each feasible solution; the optimal solution would then be the one yielding the largest value. The difficulty with this approach is the infinite number of feasible solutions; thus, because one cannot possibly evaluate an infinite number of feasible solutions, this trial-and-error procedure cannot be used to identify the optimal solution.

Rather than trying to compute the profit contribution for each feasible solution, we select an arbitrary value for profit contribution and identify all the feasible solutions (S, D) that yield the selected value. For example, which feasible solutions provide a profit contribution

FIGURE 2.5   COMBINED-CONSTRAINT GRAPH SHOWING THE FEASIBLE REGION
FOR THE PAR, INC., PROBLEM

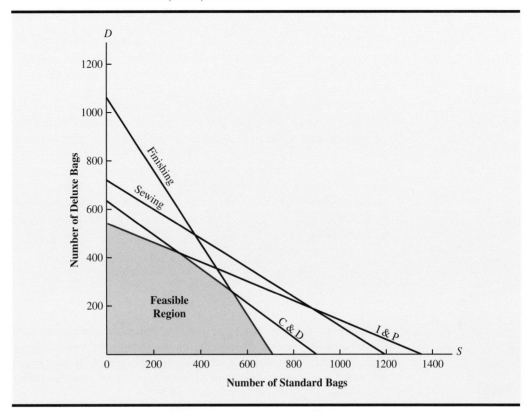

FIGURE 2.6   FEASIBLE REGION FOR THE PAR, INC., PROBLEM

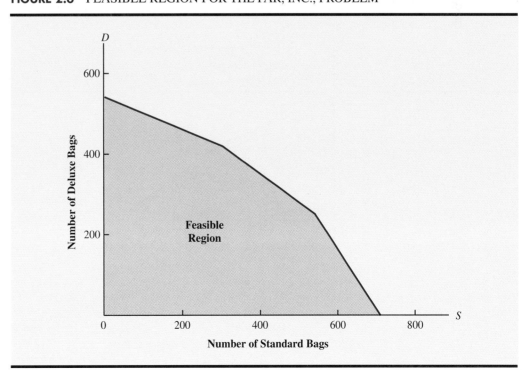

of $1800? These solutions are given by the values of S and D in the feasible region that will make the objective function

$$10S + 9D = 1800$$

This expression is simply the equation of a line. Thus, all feasible solution points (S, D) yielding a profit contribution of $1800 must be on the line. We learned earlier in this section how to graph a constraint line. The procedure for graphing the profit or objective function line is the same. Letting $S = 0$, we see that D must be 200; thus, the solution point ($S = 0$, $D = 200$) is on the line. Similarly, by letting $D = 0$, we see that the solution point ($S = 180, D = 0$) is also on the line. Drawing the line through these two points identifies all the solutions that have a profit contribution of $1800. A graph of this profit line is presented in Figure 2.7.

Because the objective is to find the feasible solution yielding the largest profit contribution, let us proceed by selecting higher profit contributions and finding the solutions yielding the selected values. For instance, let us find all solutions yielding profit contributions of $3600 and $5400. To do so, we must find the S and D values that are on the following lines:

$$10S + 9D = 3600$$

and

$$10S + 9D = 5400$$

Using the previous procedure for graphing profit and constraint lines, we draw the $3600 and $5400 profit lines as shown on the graph in Figure 2.8. Although not all solution points on the $5400 profit line are in the feasible region, at least some points on the line are, and it is therefore possible to obtain a feasible solution that provides a $5400 profit contribution.

Can we find a feasible solution yielding an even higher profit contribution? Look at Figure 2.8, and see what general observations you can make about the profit lines already

FIGURE 2.7 $1800 PROFIT LINE FOR THE PAR, INC., PROBLEM

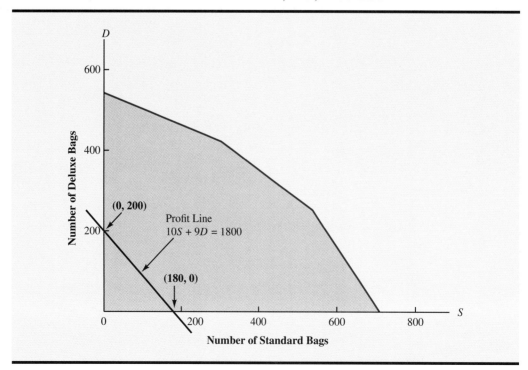

drawn. Note the following: (1) the profit lines are *parallel* to each other, and (2) higher profit lines are obtained as we move farther from the origin. These observations can also be expressed algebraically. Let P represent total profit contribution. The objective function is

$$P = 10S + 9D$$

Solving for D in terms of S and P, we obtain

$$9D = -10S + P$$
$$D = -\tfrac{10}{9}S + \tfrac{1}{9}P \tag{2.7}$$

Equation (2.7) is the *slope–intercept form* of the linear equation relating S and D. The coefficient of S, $-\tfrac{10}{9}$, is the slope of the line, and the term $\tfrac{1}{9}P$ is the D intercept (i.e., the value of D where the graph of equation (2.7) crosses the D axis). Substituting the profit contributions of $P = 1800$, $P = 3600$, and $P = 5400$ into equation (2.7) yields the following slope–intercept equations for the profit lines shown in Figure 2.8:

For $P = 1800$,

$$D = -\tfrac{10}{9}S + 200$$

For $P = 3600$,

$$D = -\tfrac{10}{9}S + 400$$

For $P = 5400$,

$$D = -\tfrac{10}{9}S + 600$$

FIGURE 2.8   SELECTED PROFIT LINES FOR THE PAR, INC., PROBLEM

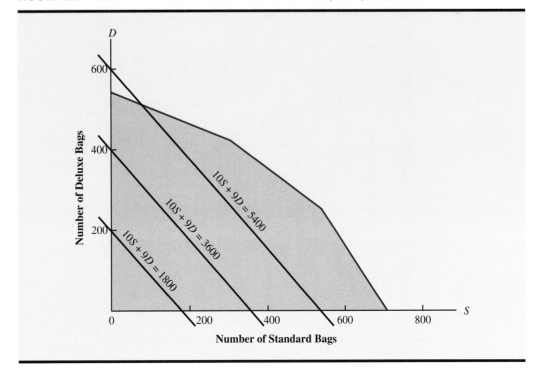

Can you graph the profit line for a linear program? Try Problem 6.

The slope $(-\tfrac{10}{9})$ is the same for each profit line because the profit lines are parallel. Further, we see that the D intercept increases with larger profit contributions. Thus, higher profit lines are farther from the origin.

Because the profit lines are parallel and higher profit lines are farther from the origin, we can obtain solutions that yield increasingly larger values for the objective function by continuing to move the profit line farther from the origin in such a fashion that it remains parallel to the other profit lines. However, at some point we will find that any further outward movement will place the profit line completely outside the feasible region. Because solutions outside the feasible region are unacceptable, the point in the feasible region that lies on the highest profit line is the optimal solution to the linear program.

You should now be able to identify the optimal solution point for this problem. Use a ruler or the edge of a piece of paper, and move the profit line as far from the origin as you can. What is the last point in the feasible region that you reach? This point, which is the optimal solution, is shown graphically in Figure 2.9.

The optimal values of the decision variables are the S and D values at the optimal solution. Depending on the accuracy of the graph, you may or may not be able to determine the *exact* S and D values. Based on the graph in Figure 2.9, the best we can do is conclude that the optimal production combination consists of approximately 550 standard bags (S) and approximately 250 deluxe bags (D).

A closer inspection of Figures 2.5 and 2.9 shows that the optimal solution point is at the intersection of the cutting and dyeing and the finishing constraint lines. That is, the optimal solution point is on both the cutting and dyeing constraint line

$$\tfrac{7}{10}S + 1D = 630 \tag{2.8}$$

FIGURE 2.9 OPTIMAL SOLUTION FOR THE PAR, INC., PROBLEM

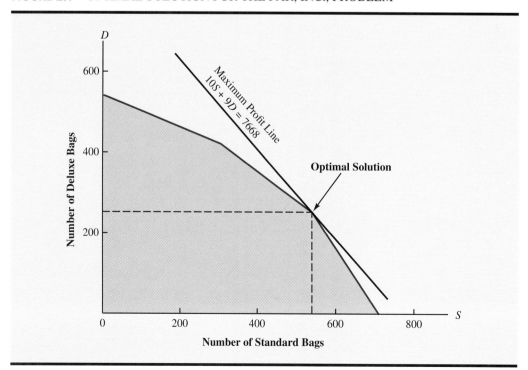

and the finishing constraint line

$$1S + \tfrac{2}{3}D = 708 \tag{2.9}$$

Thus, the optimal values of the decision variables S and D must satisfy both equations (2.8) and (2.9) simultaneously. Using equation (2.8) and solving for S gives

$$\tfrac{7}{10}S = 630 - 1D$$

or

$$S = 900 - \tfrac{10}{7}D \tag{2.10}$$

Substituting this expression for S into equation (2.9) and solving for D provides the following:

$$1(900 - \tfrac{10}{7}D) + \tfrac{2}{3}D = 708$$
$$900 - \tfrac{10}{7}D + \tfrac{2}{3}D = 708$$
$$900 - \tfrac{30}{21}D + \tfrac{14}{21}D = 708$$
$$-\tfrac{16}{21}D = -192$$
$$D = \frac{192}{\tfrac{16}{21}} = 252$$

Using $D = 252$ in equation (2.10) and solving for S, we obtain

$$S = 900 - \tfrac{10}{7}(252)$$
$$= 900 - 360 = 540$$

Although the optimal solution to the Par, Inc., problem consists of integer values for the decision variables, this result will not always be the case.

The exact location of the optimal solution point is $S = 540$ and $D = 252$. Hence, the optimal production quantities for Par, Inc., are 540 standard bags and 252 deluxe bags, with a resulting profit contribution of $10(540) + 9(252) = \$7668$.

For a linear programming problem with two decision variables, the exact values of the decision variables can be determined by first using the graphical solution procedure to identify the optimal solution point and then solving the two simultaneous constraint equations associated with it.

A Note on Graphing Lines

Try Problem 10 to test your ability to use the graphical solution procedure to identify the optimal solution and find the exact values of the decision variables at the optimal solution.

An important aspect of the graphical method is the ability to graph lines showing the constraints and the objective function of the linear program. The procedure we used for graphing the equation of a line is to find any two points satisfying the equation and then draw the line through the two points. For the Par, Inc., constraints, the two points were easily found by first setting $S = 0$ and solving the constraint equation for D. Then we set $D = 0$ and solved for S. For the cutting and dyeing constraint line

$$\tfrac{7}{10}S + 1D = 630$$

this procedure identified the two points $(S = 0, D = 630)$ and $(S = 900, D = 0)$. The cutting and dyeing constraint line was then graphed by drawing a line through these two points.

All constraints and objective function lines in two-variable linear programs can be graphed if two points on the line can be identified. However, finding the two points on the line is not always as easy as shown in the Par, Inc., problem. For example, suppose a company manufactures two models of a small tablet computer: the Assistant (A) and the Professional (P). Management needs 50 units of the Professional model for its own salesforce, and expects sales of the Professional to be at most one-half of the sales of the Assistant. A constraint enforcing this requirement is

$$P - 50 \leq \tfrac{1}{2}A$$

or

$$2P - 100 \leq A$$

or

$$2P - A \leq 100$$

Using the equality form and setting $P = 0$, we find the point ($P = 0$, $A = -100$) is on the constraint line. Setting $A = 0$, we find a second point ($P = 50$, $A = 0$) on the constraint line. If we have drawn only the nonnegative ($P \geq 0$, $A \geq 0$) portion of the graph, the first point ($P = 0$, $A = -100$) cannot be plotted because $A = -100$ is not on the graph. Whenever we have two points on the line but one or both of the points cannot be plotted in the nonnegative portion of the graph, the simplest approach is to enlarge the graph. In this example, the point ($P = 0$, $A = -100$) can be plotted by extending the graph to include the negative A axis. Once both points satisfying the constraint equation have been located, the line can be drawn. The constraint line and the feasible solutions for the constraint $2P - A \leq 100$ are shown in Figure 2.10.

FIGURE 2.10   FEASIBLE SOLUTIONS FOR THE CONSTRAINT $2P - A \leq 100$

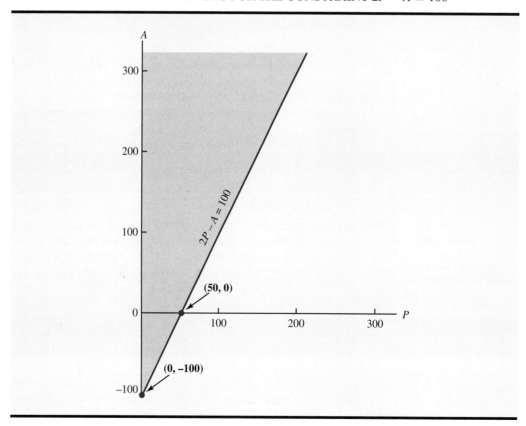

As another example, consider a problem involving two decision variables, R and T. Suppose that the number of units of R produced had to be at least equal to the number of units of T produced. A constraint enforcing this requirement is

$$R \geq T$$

or

$$R - T \geq 0$$

Can you graph a constraint line when the origin is on the constraint line? Try Problem 5.

To find all solutions satisfying the constraint as an equality, we first set $R = 0$ and solve for T. This result shows that the origin ($T = 0$, $R = 0$) is on the constraint line. Setting $T = 0$ and solving for R provides the same point. However, we can obtain a second point on the line by setting T equal to any value other than zero and then solving for R. For instance, setting $T = 100$ and solving for R, we find that the point ($T = 100$, $R = 100$) is on the line. With the two points ($R = 0$, $T = 0$) and ($R = 100$, $T = 100$), the constraint line $R - T = 0$ and the feasible solutions for $R - T \geq 0$ can be plotted as shown in Figure 2.11.

Summary of the Graphical Solution Procedure for Maximization Problems

For additional practice in using the graphical solution procedure, try Problems 24(b), 24(c), and 24(d).

As we have seen, the graphical solution procedure is a method for solving two-variable linear programming problems such as the Par, Inc., problem. The steps of the graphical solution procedure for a maximization problem are summarized here:

1. Prepare a graph of the feasible solutions for each of the constraints.
2. Determine the feasible region by identifying the solutions that satisfy all the constraints simultaneously.
3. Draw an objective function line showing the values of the decision variables that yield a specified value of the objective function.
4. Move parallel objective function lines toward larger objective function values until further movement would take the line completely outside the feasible region.
5. Any feasible solution on the objective function line with the largest value is an optimal solution.

FIGURE 2.11 FEASIBLE SOLUTIONS FOR THE CONSTRAINT $R - T \geq 0$

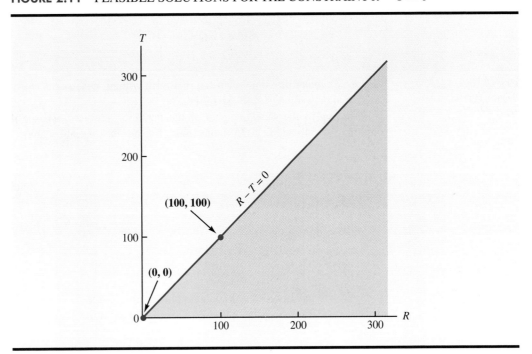

Slack Variables

In addition to the optimal solution and its associated profit contribution, Par, Inc.'s management will probably want information about the production time requirements for each production operation. We can determine this information by substituting the optimal solution values ($S = 540$, $D = 252$) into the constraints of the linear program.

Constraint	Hours Required for $S = 540$ and $D = 252$	Hours Available	Unused Hours
Cutting and Dyeing	$\frac{7}{10}(540) + 1(252) = 630$	630	0
Sewing	$\frac{1}{2}(540) + \frac{5}{6}(252) = 480$	600	120
Finishing	$1(540) + \frac{2}{3}(252) = 708$	708	0
Inspection and Packaging	$\frac{1}{10}(540) + \frac{1}{4}(252) = 117$	135	18

Thus, the complete solution tells management that the production of 540 standard bags and 252 deluxe bags will require all available cutting and dyeing time (630 hours) and all available finishing time (708 hours), while $600 - 480 = 120$ hours of sewing time and $135 - 117 = 18$ hours of inspection and packaging time will remain unused. The 120 hours of unused sewing time and 18 hours of unused inspection and packaging time are referred to as *slack* for the two departments. In linear programming terminology, any unused capacity for a $\leq$ constraint is referred to as the *slack* associated with the constraint.

Can you identify the slack associated with a constraint? Try Problem 24(e).

Often variables, called **slack variables,** are added to the formulation of a linear programming problem to represent the slack, or idle capacity. Unused capacity makes no contribution to profit; thus, slack variables have coefficients of zero in the objective function. After the addition of four slack variables, denoted as S_1, S_2, S_3, and S_4, the mathematical model of the Par, Inc., problem becomes

$$\text{Max} \quad 10S + 9D + 0S_1 + 0S_2 + 0S_3 + 0S_4$$

$$\text{s.t.}$$

$$\frac{7}{10}S + 1D + 1S_1 \qquad\qquad\qquad = 630$$
$$\frac{1}{2}S + \frac{5}{6}D \qquad + 1S_2 \qquad\qquad = 600$$
$$1S + \frac{2}{3}D \qquad\qquad + 1S_3 \qquad = 708$$
$$\frac{1}{10}S + \frac{1}{4}D \qquad\qquad\qquad + 1S_4 = 135$$

$$S, D, S_1, S_2, S_3, S_4 \geq 0$$

Can you write a linear program in standard form? Try Problem 18.

Whenever a linear program is written in a form with all constraints expressed as equalities, it is said to be written in **standard form.**

Referring to the standard form of the Par, Inc., problem, we see that at the optimal solution ($S = 540$ and $D = 252$), the values for the slack variables are

Constraint	Value of Slack Variable
Cutting and Dyeing	$S_1 = 0$
Sewing	$S_2 = 120$
Finishing	$S_3 = 0$
Inspection and Packaging	$S_4 = 18$

Could we have used the graphical solution to provide some of this information? The answer is yes. By finding the optimal solution point in Figure 2.5, we can see that the cutting and dyeing and the finishing constraints restrict, or *bind,* the feasible region at this point. Thus, this solution requires the use of all available time for these two operations. In other words, the graph shows us that the cutting and dyeing and the finishing departments will have zero slack. On the other hand, the sewing and the inspection and packaging constraints are not binding the feasible region at the optimal solution, which means we can expect some unused time or slack for these two operations.

As a final comment on the graphical analysis of this problem, we call your attention to the sewing capacity constraint as shown in Figure 2.5. Note, in particular, that this constraint did not affect the feasible region. That is, the feasible region would be the same whether the sewing capacity constraint were included or not, which tells us that enough sewing time is available to accommodate any production level that can be achieved by the other three departments. The sewing constraint does not affect the feasible region and thus cannot affect the optimal solution; it is called a **redundant constraint.**

NOTES AND COMMENTS

1. In the standard-form representation of a linear programming model, the objective function coefficients for slack variables are zero. This zero coefficient implies that slack variables, which represent unused resources, do not affect the value of the objective function. However, in some applications, unused resources can be sold and contribute to profit. In such cases, the corresponding slack variables become decision variables representing the amount of unused resources to be sold. For each of these variables, a nonzero coefficient in the objective function would reflect the profit associated with selling a unit of the corresponding resource.

2. Redundant constraints do not affect the feasible region; as a result, they can be removed from a linear programming model without affecting the optimal solution. However, if the linear programming model is to be re-solved later, changes in some of the data might make a previously redundant constraint a binding constraint. Thus, we recommend keeping all constraints in the linear programming model even though at some point in time one or more of the constraints may be redundant.

2.3 EXTREME POINTS AND THE OPTIMAL SOLUTION

Suppose that the profit contribution for Par, Inc.'s standard golf bag is reduced from $10 to $5 per bag, while the profit contribution for the deluxe golf bag and all the constraints remain unchanged. The complete linear programming model of this new problem is identical to the mathematical model in Section 2.1, except for the revised objective function:

$$\text{Max } 5S + 9D$$

How does this change in the objective function affect the optimal solution to the Par, Inc., problem? Figure 2.12 shows the graphical solution of this new problem with the revised objective function. Note that without any change in the constraints, the feasible region does not change. However, the profit lines have been altered to reflect the new objective function.

By moving the profit line in a parallel manner toward higher profit values, we find the optimal solution as shown in Figure 2.12. The values of the decision variables at this point are $S = 300$ and $D = 420$. The reduced profit contribution for the standard bag caused a change in the optimal solution. In fact, as you may have suspected, we are cutting back the production of the lower-profit standard bags and increasing the production of the higher-profit deluxe bags.

What observations can you make about the location of the optimal solutions in the two linear programming problems solved thus far? Look closely at the graphical solutions in Figures 2.9 and 2.12. Notice that the optimal solutions occur at one of the vertices, or "corners," of the feasible region. In linear programming terminology, these vertices are referred to as the **extreme points** of the feasible region. The Par, Inc., feasible region

FIGURE 2.12   OPTIMAL SOLUTION FOR THE PAR, INC., PROBLEM WITH AN
OBJECTIVE FUNCTION OF $5S + 9D$

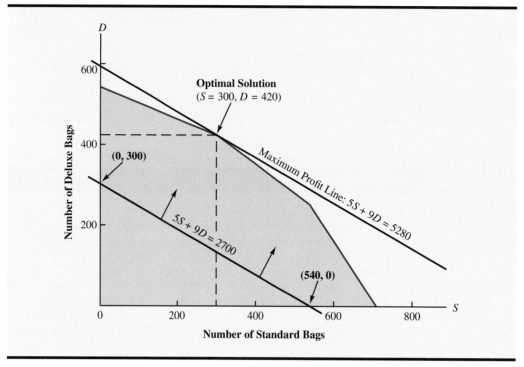

has five vertices, or five extreme points (see Figure 2.13). We can now formally state our observation about the location of optimal solutions as follows:

For additional practice in identifying the extreme points of the feasible region and determining the optimal solution by computing and comparing the objective function value at each extreme point, try Problem 13.

> The optimal solution to a linear program can be found at an extreme point of the feasible region.[2]

This property means that if you are looking for the optimal solution to a linear program, you do not have to evaluate all feasible solution points. In fact, you have to consider *only* the feasible solutions that occur at the extreme points of the feasible region. Thus, for the Par, Inc., problem, instead of computing and comparing the profit contributions for all feasible solutions, we can find the optimal solution by evaluating the five extreme-point solutions and selecting the one that provides the largest profit contribution. Actually, the graphical solution procedure is nothing more than a convenient way of identifying an optimal extreme point for two-variable problems.

2.4   COMPUTER SOLUTION OF THE PAR, INC., PROBLEM

Computer programs designed to solve linear programming problems are now widely available. After a short period of familiarization with the specific features of the package, users are able to solve linear programming problems with few difficulties. Problems involving thousands of variables and thousands of constraints are now routinely solved with computer packages. Some of the leading commercial packages include CPLEX, Gurobi, LINGO, MOSEK, Excel Solver, and Analytic Solver for Excel. Packages are also available for free download. A good example is Clp (COIN-OR linear programming).

---

[2]We will discuss in Section 2.6 the two special cases (infeasibility and unboundedness) in linear programming that have no optimal solution, and for which this statement does not apply.

FIGURE 2.13 THE FIVE EXTREME POINTS OF THE FEASIBLE REGION
FOR THE PAR, INC., PROBLEM

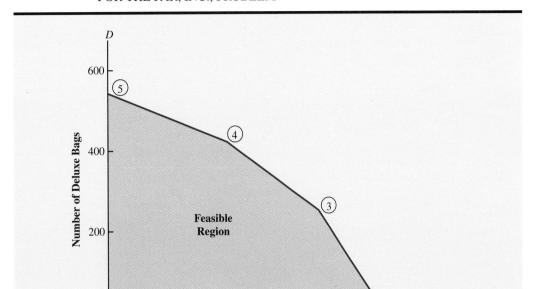

The solution to Par, Inc. is shown in Figure 2.14. The authors have chosen to make this book flexible and not rely on a specific linear programming package. Hence, the output in Figure 2.14 is generic and is not an actual printout from a particular software package. The output provided in Figure 2.14 is typical of most linear programming packages. We use this output format throughout the text. Two common software packages for solving linear programs are Excel Solver and LINGO; descriptions of these two packages are provided in the appendices. In Appendix 2.1 we show how to formulate a spreadsheet model for the Par, Inc., problem and use Excel Solver to solve the problem. In Appendix 2.2 we show how to solve the Par, Inc., problem using LINGO.

Interpretation of Computer Output

Let us look more closely at the output in Figure 2.14 and interpret the computer solution provided for the Par, Inc., problem. The optimal solution to this problem will provide a profit of $7668. Directly below the objective function value, we find the values of the decision variables at the optimal solution. We have $S = 540$ standard bags and $D = 252$ deluxe bags as the optimal production quantities.

Recall that the Par, Inc., problem had four less-than-or-equal-to constraints corresponding to the hours available in each of four production departments. The information shown in the Slack/Surplus column provides the value of the slack variable for each of the departments. This information is summarized here:

Constraint Number	Constraint Name	Slack
1	Cutting and Dyeing	0
2	Sewing	120
3	Finishing	0
4	Inspection and Packaging	18

FIGURE 2.14   THE SOLUTION FOR THE PAR, INC., PROBLEM

Optimal Objective Value =   7668.00000

Variable	Value	Reduced Cost
S	540.00000	0.00000
D	252.00000	0.00000

Constraint	Slack/Surplus	Dual Value
1	0.00000	4.37500
2	120.00000	0.00000
3	0.00000	6.93750
4	18.00000	0.00000

Variable	Objective Coefficient	Allowable Increase	Allowable Decrease
S	10.00000	3.50000	3.70000
D	9.00000	5.28571	2.33333

Constraint	RHS Value	Allowable Increase	Allowable Decrease
1	630.00000	52.36364	134.40000
2	600.00000	Infinite	120.00000
3	708.00000	192.00000	128.00000
4	135.00000	Infinite	18.00000

MODEL file

Par

From this information, we see that the binding constraints (the cutting and dyeing and the finishing constraints) have zero slack at the optimal solution. The sewing department has 120 hours of slack or unused capacity, and the inspection and packaging department has 18 hours of slack or unused capacity.

The rest of the output in Figure 2.14 can be used to determine how changes in the input data impact the optimal solution. We shall defer discussion of reduced costs, dual values, allowable increases and decreases of objective function coefficients, and right-hand-side values until Chapter 3, where we study the topic of sensitivity analysis.

2.5   A SIMPLE MINIMIZATION PROBLEM

M&D Chemicals produces two products that are sold as raw materials to companies manufacturing bath soaps and laundry detergents. Based on an analysis of current inventory levels and potential demand for the coming month, M&D's management specified that the combined production for products A and B must total at least 350 gallons. Separately, a major customer's order for 125 gallons of product A must also be satisfied. Product A requires 2 hours of processing time per gallon and product B requires 1 hour of processing time per gallon. For the coming month, 600 hours of processing time are available. M&D's objective is to satisfy these requirements at a minimum total production cost. Production costs are $2 per gallon for product A and $3 per gallon for product B.

To find the minimum-cost production schedule, we will formulate the M&D Chemicals problem as a linear program. Following a procedure similar to the one used for the

Par, Inc., problem, we first define the decision variables and the objective function for the problem. Let

$$A = \text{number of gallons of product A}$$
$$B = \text{number of gallons of product B}$$

With production costs at \$2 per gallon for product A and \$3 per gallon for product B, the objective function that corresponds to the minimization of the total production cost can be written as

$$\text{Min } 2A + 3B$$

Next, consider the constraints placed on the M&D Chemicals problem. To satisfy the major customer's demand for 125 gallons of product A, we know A must be at least 125. Thus, we write the constraint

$$1A \geq 125$$

For the combined production for both products, which must total at least 350 gallons, we can write the constraint

$$1A + 1B \geq 350$$

Finally, for the limitation of 600 hours on available processing time, we add the constraint

$$2A + 1B \leq 600$$

After adding the nonnegativity constraints ($A, B \geq 0$), we arrive at the following linear program for the M&D Chemicals problem:

$$\text{Min} \quad 2A + 3B$$
$$\text{s.t.}$$
$$
\begin{aligned}
1A \quad\quad\; &\geq 125 \quad \text{Demand for product A} \\
1A + 1B &\geq 350 \quad \text{Total production} \\
2A + 1B &\leq 600 \quad \text{Processing time} \\
A, B &\geq 0
\end{aligned}
$$

Because the linear programming model has only two decision variables, the graphical solution procedure can be used to find the optimal production quantities. The graphical solution procedure for this problem, just as in the Par, Inc., problem, requires us to first graph the constraint lines to find the feasible region. By graphing each constraint line separately and then checking points on either side of the constraint line, the feasible solutions for each constraint can be identified. By combining the feasible solutions for each constraint on the same graph, we obtain the feasible region shown in Figure 2.15.

To find the minimum-cost solution, we now draw the objective function line corresponding to a particular total cost value. For example, we might start by drawing the line $2A + 3B = 1200$. This line is shown in Figure 2.16. Clearly, some points in the feasible region would provide a total cost of \$1200. To find the values of A and B that provide smaller total cost values, we move the objective function line in a lower left direction until, if we moved it any farther, it would be entirely outside the feasible region. Note that the objective function line $2A + 3B = 800$ intersects the feasible region at the extreme point $A = 250$ and $B = 100$. This extreme point provides the minimum-cost solution with an objective function value of 800. From Figures 2.15 and 2.16, we can see that

FIGURE 2.15   THE FEASIBLE REGION FOR THE M&D CHEMICALS PROBLEM

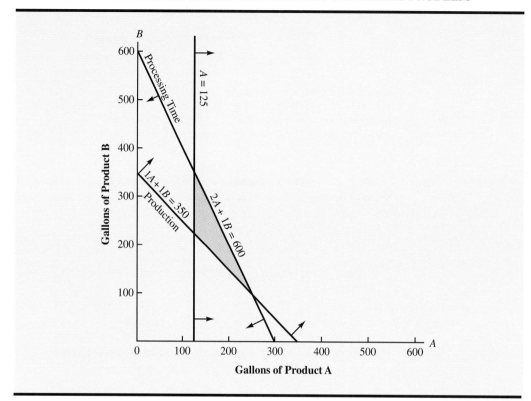

the total production constraint and the processing time constraint are binding. Just as in every linear programming problem, the optimal solution occurs at an extreme point of the feasible region.

Summary of the Graphical Solution Procedure for Minimization Problems

Can you use the graphical solution procedure to determine the optimal solution for a minimization problem? Try Problem 31.

The steps of the graphical solution procedure for a minimization problem are summarized here:

1. Prepare a graph of the feasible solutions for each of the constraints.
2. Determine the feasible region by identifying the solutions that satisfy all the constraints simultaneously.
3. Draw an objective function line showing the values of the decision variables that yield a specified value of the objective function.
4. Move parallel objective function lines toward smaller objective function values until further movement would take the line completely outside the feasible region.
5. Any feasible solution on the objective function line with the smallest value is an optimal solution.

Surplus Variables

The optimal solution to the M&D Chemicals problem shows that the desired total production of $A + B = 350$ gallons has been achieved by using all available processing time of $2A + 1B = 2(250) + 1(100) = 600$ hours. In addition, note that the constraint requiring that product A demand be met has been satisfied with $A = 250$ gallons. In fact, the production of product A exceeds its minimum level by $250 - 125 = 125$ gallons. This excess production

FIGURE 2.16   GRAPHICAL SOLUTION FOR THE M&D CHEMICALS PROBLEM

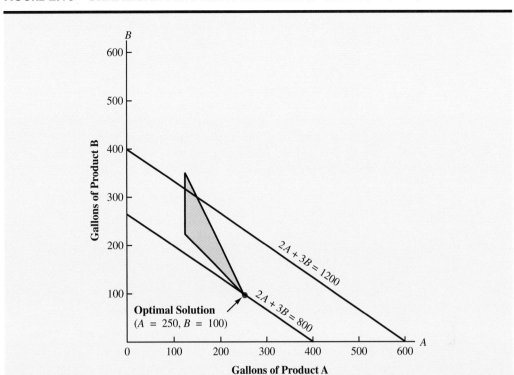

for product A is referred to as *surplus*. In linear programming terminology, any excess quantity corresponding to a $\geq$ constraint is referred to as surplus.

Recall that with a $\leq$ constraint, a slack variable can be added to the left-hand side of the inequality to convert the constraint to equality form. With a $\geq$ constraint, a **surplus variable** can be subtracted from the left-hand side of the inequality to convert the constraint to equality form. Just as with slack variables, surplus variables are given a coefficient of zero in the objective function because they have no effect on its value. After including two surplus variables, S_1 and S_2, for the $\geq$ constraints and one slack variable, S_3, for the $\leq$ constraint, the linear programming model of the M&D Chemicals problem becomes

$$\text{Min} \quad 2A + 3B + 0S_1 + 0S_2 + 0S_3$$

s.t.

$$1A \quad\quad\ -\ 1S_1 \quad\quad\quad\quad = 125$$
$$1A + 1B \quad\quad -\ 1S_2 \quad\quad = 350$$
$$2A + 1B \quad\quad\quad\quad\ +\ 1S_3 = 600$$
$$A, B, S_1, S_2, S_3 \geq 0$$

Try Problem 35 to test your ability to use slack and surplus variables to write a linear program in standard form.

All the constraints are now equalities. Hence, the preceding formulation is the standard-form representation of the M&D Chemicals problem. At the optimal solution of $A = 250$ and $B = 100$, the values of the surplus and slack variables are as follows:

Constraint	Value of Surplus or Slack Variables
Demand for product A	$S_1 = 125$
Total production	$S_2 = 0$
Processing time	$S_3 = 0$

Refer to Figures 2.15 and 2.16. Note that the zero surplus and slack variables are associated with the constraints that are binding at the optimal solution—that is, the total production and processing time constraints. The surplus of 125 units is associated with the nonbinding constraint on the demand for product A.

In the Par, Inc., problem all the constraints were of the ≤ type, and in the M&D Chemicals problem the constraints were a mixture of ≥ and ≤ types. The number and types of constraints encountered in a particular linear programming problem depend on the specific conditions existing in the problem. Linear programming problems may have some ≤ constraints, some = constraints, and some ≥ constraints. For an equality constraint, feasible solutions must lie directly on the constraint line.

Try Problem 34 to practice solving a linear program with all three constraint forms.

An example of a linear program with two decision variables, G and H, and all three constraint forms is given here:

$$\text{Min} \quad 2G + 2H$$
$$\text{s.t.}$$
$$1G + 3H \leq 12$$
$$3G + 1H \geq 13$$
$$1G - 1H = 3$$
$$G, H \geq 0$$

The standard-form representation of this problem is

$$\text{Min} \quad 2G + 2H + 0S_1 + 0S_2$$
$$\text{s.t.}$$
$$1G + 3H + 1S_1 \qquad\qquad = 12$$
$$3G + 1H \qquad -1S_2 = 13$$
$$1G - 1H \qquad\qquad = 3$$
$$G, H, S_1, S_2 \geq 0$$

The standard form requires a slack variable for the ≤ constraint and a surplus variable for the ≥ constraint. However, neither a slack nor a surplus variable is required for the third constraint because it is already in equality form.

When solving linear programs graphically, it is not necessary to write the problem in its standard form. Nevertheless, you should be able to compute the values of the slack and surplus variables and understand what they mean, because the values of slack and surplus variables are included in the computer solution of linear programs.

A final point: The standard form of the linear programming problem is equivalent to the original formulation of the problem. That is, the optimal solution to any linear programming problem is the same as the optimal solution to the standard form of the problem. The standard form has not changed the basic problem; it has only changed how we write the constraints for the problem.

Computer Solution of the M&D Chemicals Problem

The optimal solution to M&D is given in Figure 2.17. The computer output shows that the minimum-cost solution yields an objective function value of $800. The values of the decision variables show that 250 gallons of product A and 100 gallons of product B provide the minimum-cost solution.

The Slack/Surplus column shows that the ≥ constraint corresponding to the demand for product A (see constraint 1) has a surplus of 125 units. This column tells us that production of product A in the optimal solution exceeds demand by 125 gallons. The Slack/Surplus values are zero for the total production requirement (constraint 2) and the processing time limitation (constraint 3), which indicates that these constraints are binding at the optimal solution. We will discuss the rest of the computer output that appears in Figure 2.17 in Chapter 3 when we study the topic of sensitivity analysis.

FIGURE 2.17   THE SOLUTION FOR THE M&D CHEMICALS PROBLEM

```
Optimal Objective Value =              800.00000

        Variable              Value            Reduced Cost
        --------            --------           ------------
           A               250.00000               0.00000
           B               100.00000               0.00000

        Constraint         Slack/Surplus         Dual Value
        ----------         -------------         ----------
            1              125.00000               0.00000
            2                0.00000               4.00000
            3                0.00000              -1.00000

                        Objective         Allowable         Allowable
        Variable        Coefficient        Increase          Decrease
        --------        -----------       ----------        ----------
           A             2.00000           1.00000           Infinite
           B             3.00000           Infinite          1.00000

                           RHS             Allowable         Allowable
        Constraint        Value            Increase          Decrease
        ----------       --------         ----------        ----------
            1            125.00000         125.00000          Infinite
            2            350.00000         125.00000          50.00000
            3            600.00000         100.00000         125.00000
```

MODEL *file*

M&D

2.6   SPECIAL CASES

In this section we discuss three special situations that can arise when we attempt to solve linear programming problems.

Alternative Optimal Solutions

From the discussion of the graphical solution procedure, we know that optimal solutions can be found at the extreme points of the feasible region. Now let us consider the special case in which the optimal objective function line coincides with one of the binding constraint lines on the boundary of the feasible region. We will see that this situation can lead to the case of **alternative optimal solutions;** in such cases, more than one solution provides the optimal value for the objective function.

To illustrate the case of alternative optimal solutions, we return to the Par, Inc., problem. However, let us assume that the profit for the standard golf bag (S) has been decreased to $6.30. The revised objective function becomes $6.3S + 9D$. The graphical solution of this problem is shown in Figure 2.18. Note that the optimal solution still occurs at an extreme point. In fact, it occurs at two extreme points: extreme point ④ ($S = 300$, $D = 420$) and extreme point ③ ($S = 540$, $D = 252$).

The objective function values at these two extreme points are identical, that is

$$6.3S + 9D = 6.3(300) + 9(420) = 5670$$

and

$$6.3S + 9D = 6.3(540) + 9(252) = 5670$$

FIGURE 2.18   PAR, INC., PROBLEM WITH AN OBJECTIVE FUNCTION OF $6.3S + 9D$
(ALTERNATIVE OPTIMAL SOLUTIONS)

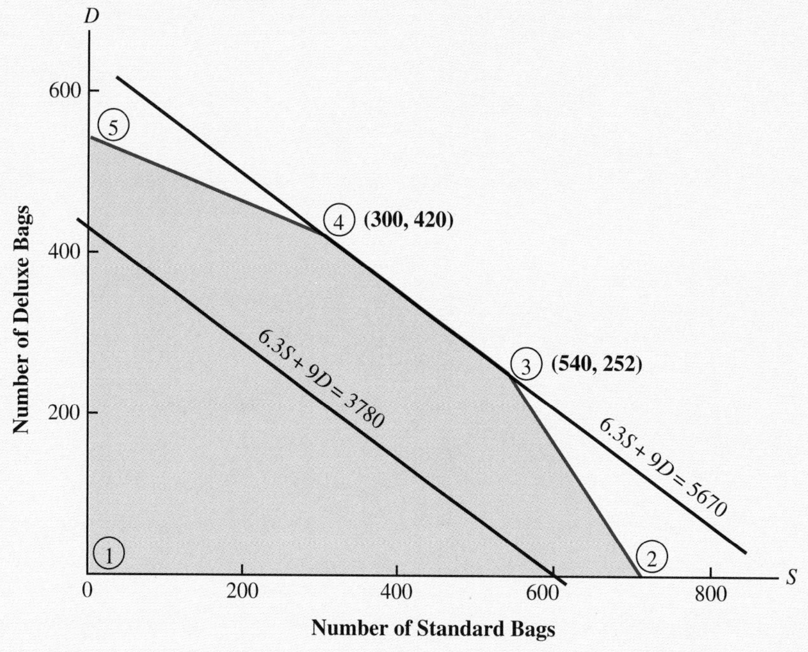

Furthermore, any point on the line connecting the two optimal extreme points also provides an optimal solution. For example, the solution point ($S = 420$, $D = 336$), which is halfway between the two extreme points, also provides the optimal objective function value of

$$6.3S + 9D = 6.3(420) + 9(336) = 5670$$

A linear programming problem with alternative optimal solutions is generally a good situation for the manager or decision maker. It means that several combinations of the decision variables are optimal and that the manager can select the most desirable optimal solution. Unfortunately, determining whether a problem has alternative optimal solutions is not a simple matter.

Infeasibility

Problems with no feasible solution do arise in practice, most often because management's expectations are too high or because too many restrictions have been placed on the problem.

Infeasibility means that no solution to the linear programming problem satisfies all the constraints, including the nonnegativity conditions. Graphically, infeasibility means that a feasible region does not exist; that is, no points satisfy all the constraints and the nonnegativity conditions simultaneously. To illustrate this situation, let us look again at the problem faced by Par, Inc.

Suppose that management specified that at least 500 of the standard bags and at least 360 of the deluxe bags must be manufactured. The graph of the solution region may now be constructed to reflect these new requirements (see Figure 2.19). The shaded area in the lower left-hand portion of the graph depicts those points satisfying the departmental constraints on the availability of time. The shaded area in the upper right-hand portion depicts those points satisfying the minimum production requirements of 500 standard and 360 deluxe bags. But no points satisfy both sets of constraints. Thus, we see that if management imposes these minimum production requirements, no feasible region exists for the problem.

How should we interpret infeasibility in terms of this current problem? First, we should tell management that given the resources available (i.e., production time for cutting and dyeing, sewing, finishing, and inspection and packaging), it is not possible to make 500 standard bags

FIGURE 2.19   NO FEASIBLE REGION FOR THE PAR, INC., PROBLEM WITH
MINIMUM PRODUCTION REQUIREMENTS OF 500 STANDARD
AND 360 DELUXE BAGS

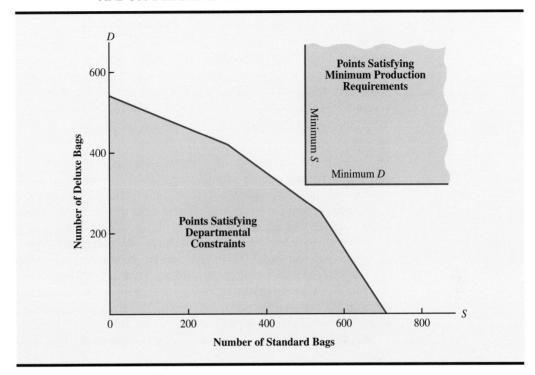

and 360 deluxe bags. Moreover, we can tell management exactly how much of each resource must be expended to make it possible to manufacture 500 standard and 360 deluxe bags. Table 2.2 shows the minimum amounts of resources that must be available, the amounts currently available, and additional amounts that would be required to accomplish this level of production. Thus, we need 80 more hours for cutting and dyeing, 32 more hours for finishing, and 5 more hours for inspection and packaging to meet management's minimum production requirements.

If, after reviewing this information, management still wants to manufacture 500 standard and 360 deluxe bags, additional resources must be provided. Perhaps by hiring another person to work in the cutting and dyeing department, transferring a person from elsewhere in the plant to work part time in the finishing department, or having the sewing people help out periodically with the inspection and packaging, the resource requirements can be met. As you can see, many possibilities are available for corrective management action, once we discover the lack of a feasible solution. The important thing to realize is that linear programming analysis can help determine whether management's plans are feasible. By analyzing the

TABLE 2.2   RESOURCES NEEDED TO MANUFACTURE 500 STANDARD BAGS
AND 360 DELUXE BAGS

Operation	Minimum Required Resources (hours)	Available Resources (hours)	Additional Resources Needed (hours)
Cutting and Dyeing	$\frac{7}{10}(500) + 1(360) = 710$	630	80
Sewing	$\frac{1}{2}(500) + \frac{5}{6}(360) = 550$	600	None
Finishing	$1(500) + \frac{2}{3}(360) = 740$	708	32
Inspection and Packaging	$\frac{1}{10}(500) + \frac{1}{4}(360) = 140$	135	5

problem using linear programming, we are often able to point out infeasible conditions and initiate corrective action.

Whenever you attempt to solve a problem that is infeasible using either LINGO or Excel Solver, you will get an error message indicating that the problem is infeasible. In this case you know that no solution to the linear programming problem will satisfy all constraints, including the nonnegativity conditions. Careful inspection of your formulation is necessary to try to identify why the problem is infeasible. In some situations, the only reasonable approach is to drop one or more constraints and re-solve the problem. If you are able to find an optimal solution for this revised problem, you will know that the constraint(s) that was omitted, in conjunction with the others, is causing the problem to be infeasible.

Unbounded

The solution to a maximization linear programming problem is **unbounded** if the value of the solution may be made infinitely large without violating any of the constraints; for a minimization problem, the solution is unbounded if the value may be made infinitely small. This condition might be termed *managerial utopia;* for example, if this condition were to occur in a profit maximization problem, the manager could achieve an unlimited profit.

However, in linear programming models of real problems, the occurrence of an unbounded solution means that the problem has been improperly formulated. We know it is not possible to increase profits indefinitely. Therefore, we must conclude that if a profit maximization problem results in an unbounded solution, the mathematical model doesn't represent the real-world problem sufficiently. Usually, what happens is that a constraint is inadvertently omitted during problem formulation.

As an illustration, consider the following linear program with two decision variables, X and Y:

$$\text{Max}\quad 20X + 10Y$$
$$\text{s.t.}$$
$$1X \qquad \geq 2$$
$$1Y \leq 5$$
$$X, Y \geq 0$$

In Figure 2.20 we graphed the feasible region associated with this problem. Note that we can only indicate part of the feasible region because the feasible region extends indefinitely in the direction of the X axis. Looking at the objective function lines in Figure 2.20, we see that the solution to this problem may be made as large as we desire. That is, no matter what solution we pick, we will always be able to reach some feasible solution with a larger value. Thus, we say that the solution to this linear program is *unbounded.*

Can you recognize whether a linear program involves alternative optimal solutions or infeasibility, or is unbounded? Try Problems 42 and 43.

Whenever you attempt to solve a problem that is unbounded using either LINGO or Excel Solver you will get a message telling you that the problem is unbounded. Because unbounded solutions cannot occur in real problems, the first thing you should do is to review your model to determine whether you incorrectly formulated the problem. In many cases, this error is the result of inadvertently omitting a constraint during problem formulation.

NOTES AND COMMENTS

1. Infeasibility is independent of the objective function. It exists because the constraints are so restrictive that no feasible region for the linear programming model is possible. Thus, when you encounter infeasibility, making changes in the coefficients of the objective function will not help; the problem will remain infeasible.
2. The occurrence of an unbounded solution is often the result of a missing constraint. However, a change in the objective function may cause a previously unbounded problem to become bounded with an optimal solution. For example, the graph in Figure 2.20 shows an unbounded solution for the objective function Max $20X + 10Y$. However, changing the objective function to Max $-20X - 10Y$ will provide the optimal solution $X = 2$ and $Y = 0$ even though no changes have been made in the constraints.

FIGURE 2.20   EXAMPLE OF AN UNBOUNDED PROBLEM

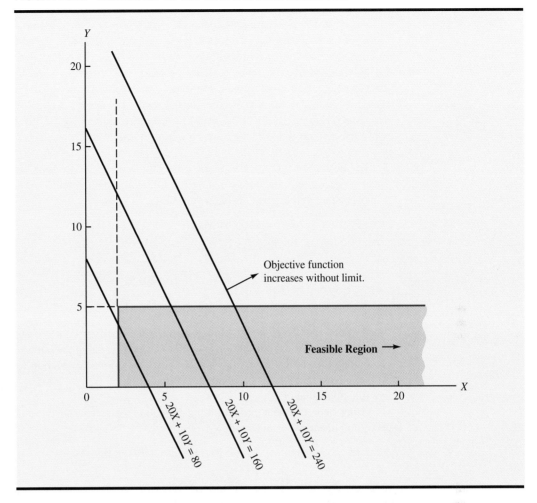

2.7   GENERAL LINEAR PROGRAMMING NOTATION

In this chapter we showed how to formulate linear programming models for the Par, Inc., and M&D Chemicals problems. To formulate a linear programming model of the Par, Inc., problem we began by defining two decision variables: S = number of standard bags and D = number of deluxe bags. In the M&D Chemicals problem, the two decision variables were defined as A = number of gallons of product A and B = number of gallons of product B. We selected decision-variable names of S and D in the Par, Inc., problem and A and B in the M&D Chemicals problem to make it easier to recall what these decision variables represented in the problem. Although this approach works well for linear programs involving a small number of decision variables, it can become difficult when dealing with problems involving a large number of decision variables.

A more general notation that is often used for linear programs uses the letter x with a subscript. For instance, in the Par, Inc., problem, we could have defined the decision variables as follows:

$$x_1 = \text{number of standard bags}$$
$$x_2 = \text{number of deluxe bags}$$

In the M&D Chemicals problem, the same variable names would be used, but their definitions would change:

$$x_1 = \text{number of gallons of product A}$$
$$x_2 = \text{number of gallons of product B}$$

A disadvantage of using general notation for decision variables is that we are no longer able to easily identify what the decision variables actually represent in the mathematical model. However, the advantage of general notation is that formulating a mathematical model for a problem that involves a large number of decision variables is much easier. For instance, for a linear programming model with three decision variables, we would use variable names of x_1, x_2, and x_3; for a problem with four decision variables, we would use variable names of x_1, x_2, x_3, and x_4 (this convention for naming decision variables can be extended to any number of decision variables). Clearly, if a problem involved 1000 decision variables, trying to identify 1000 unique names would be difficult. However, using the general linear programming notation, the decision variables would be defined as $x_1, x_2, x_3, \ldots, x_{1000}$.

To illustrate the graphical solution procedure for a linear program written using general linear programming notation, consider the following mathematical model for a maximization problem involving two decision variables:

$$\text{Max} \quad 3x_1 + 2x_2$$
$$\text{s.t.}$$
$$2x_1 + 2x_2 \leq 8$$
$$1x_1 + 0.5x_2 \leq 3$$
$$x_1, x_2 \geq 0$$

We must first develop a graph that displays the possible solutions (x_1 and x_2 values) for the problem. The usual convention is to plot values of x_1 along the horizontal axis and values of x_2 along the vertical axis. Figure 2.21 shows the graphical solution for this two-variable problem. Note that for this problem the optimal solution is $x_1 = 2$ and $x_2 = 2$, with an objective function value of 10.

Using general linear programming notation, we can write the standard form of the preceding linear program as follows:

$$\text{Max} \quad 3x_1 + 2x_2 + 0s_1 + 0s_2$$
$$\text{s.t.}$$
$$2x_1 + 2x_2 + 1s_1 \qquad = 8$$
$$1x_1 + 0.5x_2 + \qquad 1s_2 = 3$$
$$x_1, x_2, s_1, s_2 \geq 0$$

Thus, at the optimal solution $x_1 = 2$ and $x_2 = 2$; the values of the slack variables are $s_1 = s_2 = 0$.

SUMMARY

We formulated linear programming models for two problems: the Par, Inc., maximization problem and the M&D Chemicals minimization problem. For both problems we showed a graphical solution procedure and provided a computer solution to the problem in a generic solution table. In formulating a mathematical model of these problems, we developed a general definition of a linear programming model.

A linear programming model is a mathematical model with the following characteristics:

1. A linear objective function that is to be maximized or minimized
2. A set of linear constraints
3. Variables that are all restricted to nonnegative values

Slack variables may be used to write less-than-or-equal-to constraints in equality form, and surplus variables may be used to write greater-than-or-equal-to constraints in equality form. The value of a slack variable can usually be interpreted as the amount of unused

FIGURE 2.21   GRAPHICAL SOLUTION OF A TWO-VARIABLE LINEAR PROGRAM
WITH GENERAL NOTATION

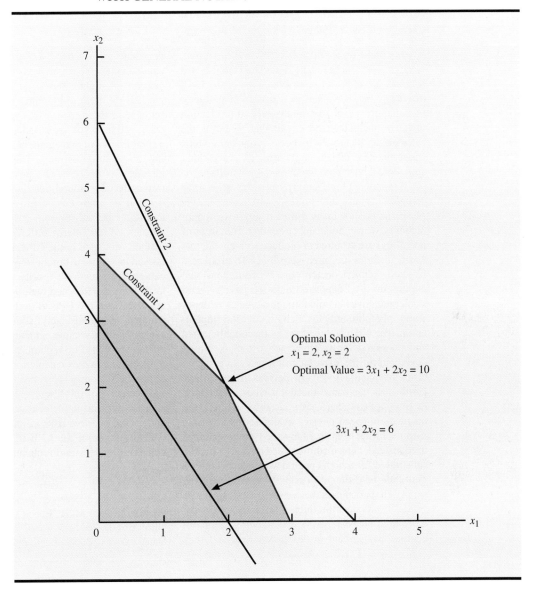

resource, whereas the value of a surplus variable indicates the amount over and above some stated minimum requirement. When all constraints have been written as equalities, the linear program has been written in its standard form.

If the solution to a linear program is infeasible or unbounded, no optimal solution to the problem can be found. In the case of infeasibility, no feasible solutions are possible, whereas, in the case of an unbounded solution, the objective function can be made infinitely large for a maximization problem and infinitely small for a minimization problem. In the case of alternative optimal solutions, two or more optimal extreme points exist, and all the points on the line segment connecting them are also optimal.

This chapter concludes with a section showing how to write a linear program using general linear programming notation. The Management Science in Action, IBM Uses Linear Programming to Help Plan and Execute its Supply Chain Operations, provides another example of the widespread use of linear programming by organizations. In the next two chapters we will see many more applications of linear programming.

MANAGEMENT SCIENCE IN ACTION

IBM USES LINEAR PROGRAMMING TO HELP PLAN AND EXECUTE ITS SUPPLY CHAIN OPERATIONS*

A semiconductor technically refers to the material, usually silicon, used to build integrated circuits that become the main building components for electronic devices. But in casual usage, semiconductor manufacturing refers to the design and production of the actual integrated circuit that performs the calculations necessary to power your computers, smart phones, tablets, and virtually every other electronic device with which you are familiar.

Semiconductor supply chains are very complex because they typically stretch across the globe and include many different suppliers, manufacturers, distributors, and customers. Hundreds of operations are required to produce semiconductors and lead times are often very long. To produce a finished semiconductor, the three-dimensional circuits must be deposited onto the base layer of semiconductive material through a process of deposition, photolithography, etching, and ion implantation. The circuits must then be thoroughly tested and packaged for shipment to customers. Small deviations in the manufacturing process result in different quality (speed) of devices. These different devices can sometimes be used as a substitute in times of shortages. For instance, if there are no medium-speed devices available for a certain manufacturing step, a high-speed device can be used instead, but a medium-speed device cannot be substituted for a high-speed device. This creates a multitude of different possible flows through the supply chain that must be constantly managed.

IBM has been producing semiconductors for more than 50 years. IBM manufactures semiconductors in Asia and in North America, and they distribute them around the world. IBM has been using management science techniques for many years to plan and execute its supply chain strategies. IBM's Central Planning Engine (CPE) is the set of tools the company uses to manage its supply chain activities for semiconductors. The CPE uses a combination of management science tools including linear programming. The model constraints include limitations on production capacities, raw material availabilities, lead time delays, and demand requirements. There are also constraints to enforce the substitution possibilities for certain devices. While many different problem-solving methods are used in the CPE, linear programming is used in several different steps including the allocation of production capacity to devices based on available capacities and materials.

IBM uses the CPE to perform both long-term strategic planning and short-term operational execution for its semiconductor supply chain. Due to the clever use of specific management science tools, these complex calculations can be completed in just a few hours. These fast solution times allow IBM to run several different possible scenarios in a single day and implement sensitivity analysis to understand possible risks in its supply chain. IBM credits the use of the CPE to increasing on-time deliveries by 15% and reducing inventory by 25% to 30%.

*Based on Alfred Degbotse, Brian T. Denton, Kenneth Fordyce, R. John Milne, Robert Orzell, Chi-Tai Wang, "IBM Blends Heuristics and Optimization to Plan Its Semiconductor Supply Chain," *Interfaces* (2012): 1–12.

GLOSSARY

Alternative optimal solutions   The case in which more than one solution provide the optimal value for the objective function.

Constraint   An equation or inequality that rules out certain combinations of decision variables as feasible solutions.

Decision variable   A controllable input for a linear programming model.

Extreme point   Graphically speaking, extreme points are the feasible solution points occurring at the vertices or "corners" of the feasible region. With two-variable problems, extreme points are determined by the intersection of the constraint lines.

Feasible region   The set of all feasible solutions.

Feasible solution   A solution that satisfies all the constraints.

Infeasibility   The situation in which no solution to the linear programming problem satisfies all the constraints.

Linear functions Mathematical expressions in which the variables appear in separate terms and are raised to the first power.

Linear program Another term for linear programming model.

Linear programming model A mathematical model with a linear objective function, a set of linear constraints, and nonnegative variables.

Mathematical model A representation of a problem where the objective and all constraint conditions are described by mathematical expressions.

Nonnegativity constraints A set of constraints that requires all variables to be nonnegative.

Problem formulation The process of translating the verbal statement of a problem into a mathematical statement called the *mathematical model.*

Redundant constraint A constraint that does not affect the feasible region. If a constraint is redundant, it can be removed from the problem without affecting the feasible region.

Slack variable A variable added to the left-hand side of a less-than-or-equal-to constraint to convert the constraint into an equality. The value of this variable can usually be interpreted as the amount of unused resource.

Standard form A linear program in which all the constraints are written as equalities. The optimal solution of the standard form of a linear program is the same as the optimal solution of the original formulation of the linear program.

Surplus variable A variable subtracted from the left-hand side of a greater-than-or-equal-to constraint to convert the constraint into an equality. The value of this variable can usually be interpreted as the amount over and above some required minimum level.

Unbounded If the value of the solution may be made infinitely large in a maximization linear programming problem or infinitely small in a minimization problem without violating any of the constraints, the problem is said to be unbounded.

PROBLEMS

1. Which of the following mathematical relationships could be found in a linear programming model, and which could not? For the relationships that are unacceptable for linear programs, state why.
   a. $-1A + 2B \leq 70$
   b. $2A - 2B = 50$
   c. $1A - 2B^2 \leq 10$
   d. $3\sqrt{A} + 2B \geq 15$
   e. $1A + 1B = 6$
   f. $2A + 5B + 1AB \leq 25$

2. Find the solutions that satisfy the following constraints:
   a. $4A + 2B \leq 16$
   b. $4A + 2B \geq 16$
   c. $4A + 2B = 16$

3. Show a separate graph of the constraint lines and the solutions that satisfy each of the following constraints:
   a. $3A + 2B \leq 18$
   b. $12A + 8B \geq 480$
   c. $5A + 10B = 200$

4. Show a separate graph of the constraint lines and the solutions that satisfy each of the following constraints:
   a. $3A - 4B \geq 60$
   b. $-6A + 5B \leq 60$
   c. $5A - 2B \leq 0$

5. Show a separate graph of the constraint lines and the solutions that satisfy each of the following constraints:
    a. $A \geq 0.25 (A + B)$
    b. $B \leq 0.10 (A + B)$
    c. $A \leq 0.50 (A + B)$

6. Three objective functions for linear programming problems are $7A + 10B$, $6A + 4B$, and $-4A + 7B$. Show the graph of each for objective function values equal to 420.

7. Identify the feasible region for the following set of constraints:

$$0.5A + 0.25B \geq 30$$
$$1A + 5B \geq 250$$
$$0.25A + 0.5B \leq 50$$
$$A, B \geq 0$$

8. Identify the feasible region for the following set of constraints:

$$2A - 1B \leq 0$$
$$-1A + 1.5B \leq 200$$
$$A, B \geq 0$$

9. Identify the feasible region for the following set of constraints:

$$3A - 2B \geq 0$$
$$2A - 1B \leq 200$$
$$1A \leq 150$$
$$A, B \geq 0$$

10. For the linear program

$$\text{Max} \quad 2A + 3B$$
$$\text{s.t.}$$
$$1A + 2B \leq 6$$
$$5A + 3B \leq 15$$
$$A, B \geq 0$$

find the optimal solution using the graphical solution procedure. What is the value of the objective function at the optimal solution?

11. Solve the following linear program using the graphical solution procedure:

$$\text{Max} \quad 5A + 5B$$
$$\text{s.t.}$$
$$1A \leq 100$$
$$1B \leq 80$$
$$2A + 4B \leq 400$$
$$A, B \geq 0$$

12. Consider the following linear programming problem:

$$\text{Max} \quad 3A + 3B$$
$$\text{s.t.}$$
$$2A + 4B \leq 12$$
$$6A + 4B \leq 24$$
$$A, B \geq 0$$

a. Find the optimal solution using the graphical solution procedure.
b. If the objective function is changed to $2A + 6B$, what will the optimal solution be?
c. How many extreme points are there? What are the values of A and B at each extreme point?

SELF_test_

13. Consider the following linear program:

$$\text{Max} \quad 1A + 2B$$

s.t.

$$1A \quad\;\; \le 5$$
$$1B \le 4$$
$$2A + 2B = 12$$
$$A, B \ge 0$$

a. Show the feasible region.
b. What are the extreme points of the feasible region?
c. Find the optimal solution using the graphical procedure.

14. RMC, Inc., is a small firm that produces a variety of chemical products. In a particular production process, three raw materials are blended (mixed together) to produce two products: a fuel additive and a solvent base. Each ton of fuel additive is a mixture of $\frac{2}{5}$ ton of material 1 and $\frac{3}{5}$ of material 3. A ton of solvent base is a mixture of $\frac{1}{2}$ ton of material 1, $\frac{1}{5}$ ton of material 2, and $\frac{3}{10}$ ton of material 3. After deducting relevant costs, the profit contribution is $40 for every ton of fuel additive produced and $30 for every ton of solvent base produced.

RMC's production is constrained by a limited availability of the three raw materials. For the current production period, RMC has available the following quantities of each raw material:

Raw Material	Amount Available for Production
Material 1	20 tons
Material 2	5 tons
Material 3	21 tons

Assuming that RMC is interested in maximizing the total profit contribution, answer the following:
a. What is the linear programming model for this problem?
b. Find the optimal solution using the graphical solution procedure. How many tons of each product should be produced, and what is the projected total profit contribution?
c. Is there any unused material? If so, how much?
d. Are any of the constraints redundant? If so, which ones?

15. Refer to the Par, Inc., problem described in Section 2.1. Suppose that Par, Inc., management encounters the following situations:
a. The accounting department revises its estimate of the profit contribution for the deluxe bag to $18 per bag.
b. A new low-cost material is available for the standard bag, and the profit contribution per standard bag can be increased to $20 per bag. (Assume that the profit contribution of the deluxe bag is the original $9 value.)
c. New sewing equipment is available that would increase the sewing operation capacity to 750 hours. (Assume that $10A + 9B$ is the appropriate objective function.)

If each of these situations is encountered separately, what is the optimal solution and the total profit contribution?

16. Refer to the feasible region for Par, Inc., problem in Figure 2.13.
a. Develop an objective function that will make extreme point ⑤ the optimal extreme point.
b. What is the optimal solution for the objective function you selected in part (a)?
c. What are the values of the slack variables associated with this solution?

SELF_test_

17. Write the following linear program in standard form:

$$\text{Max} \quad 5A + 2B$$

s.t.

$$1A - 2B \le 420$$
$$2A + 3B \le 610$$
$$6A - 1B \le 125$$
$$A, B \ge 0$$

18. For the linear program

$$\text{Max}\quad 4A + 1B$$

s.t.

$$10A + 2B \leq 30$$
$$3A + 2B \leq 12$$
$$2A + 2B \leq 10$$
$$A, B \geq 0$$

    a. Write this problem in standard form.
    b. Solve the problem using the graphical solution procedure.
    c. What are the values of the three slack variables at the optimal solution?

19. Given the linear program

$$\text{Max}\quad 3A + 4B$$

s.t.

$$-1A + 2B \leq 8$$
$$1A + 2B \leq 12$$
$$2A + 1B \leq 16$$
$$A, B \geq 0$$

    a. Write the problem in standard form.
    b. Solve the problem using the graphical solution procedure.
    c. What are the values of the three slack variables at the optimal solution?

20. For the linear program

$$\text{Max}\quad 3A + 2B$$

s.t.

$$A + B \geq 4$$
$$3A + 4B \leq 24$$
$$A \geq 2$$
$$A - B \leq 0$$
$$A, B \geq 0$$

    a. Write the problem in standard form.
    b. Solve the problem.
    c. What are the values of the slack and surplus variables at the optimal solution?

21. Consider the following linear program:

$$\text{Max}\quad 2A + 3B$$

s.t.

$$5A + 5B \leq 400 \quad \text{Constraint 1}$$
$$-1A + 1B \leq 10 \quad \text{Constraint 2}$$
$$1A + 3B \geq 90 \quad \text{Constraint 3}$$
$$A, B \geq 0$$

Figure 2.22 shows a graph of the constraint lines.
    a. Place a number (1, 2, or 3) next to each constraint line to identify which constraint it represents.
    b. Shade in the feasible region on the graph.
    c. Identify the optimal extreme point. What is the optimal solution?
    d. Which constraints are binding? Explain.
    e. How much slack or surplus is associated with the nonbinding constraint?

FIGURE 2.22 GRAPH OF THE CONSTRAINT LINES FOR EXERCISE 21

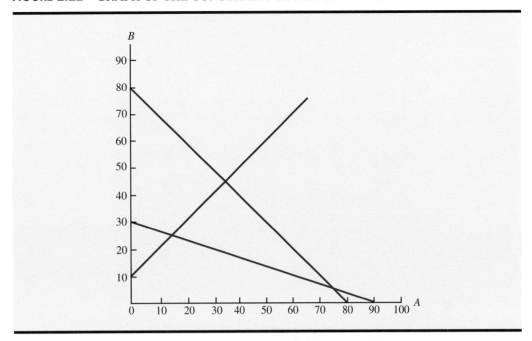

22. Reiser Sports Products wants to determine the number of All-Pro (*A*) and College (*C*) footballs to produce in order to maximize profit over the next four-week planning horizon. Constraints affecting the production quantities are the production capacities in three departments: cutting and dyeing; sewing; and inspection and packaging. For the four-week planning period, 340 hours of cutting and dyeing time, 420 hours of sewing time, and 200 hours of inspection and packaging time are available. All-Pro footballs provide a profit of $5 per unit, and College footballs provide a profit of $4 per unit. The linear programming model with production times expressed in minutes is as follows:

$$\text{Max } 5A + 4C$$

s.t.

$$
\begin{array}{ll}
12A + 6C \leq 20{,}400 & \text{Cutting and Dyeing} \\
9A + 15C \leq 25{,}200 & \text{Sewing} \\
6A + 6C \leq 12{,}000 & \text{Inspection and Packaging} \\
A, C \geq 0 &
\end{array}
$$

A portion of the graphical solution to the Reiser problem is shown in Figure 2.23.
   a. Shade the feasible region for this problem.
   b. Determine the coordinates of each extreme point and the corresponding profit. Which extreme point generates the highest profit?
   c. Draw the profit line corresponding to a profit of $4000. Move the profit line as far from the origin as you can in order to determine which extreme point will provide the optimal solution. Compare your answer with the approach you used in part (b).
   d. Which constraints are binding? Explain.
   e. Suppose that the values of the objective function coefficients are $4 for each All-Pro model produced and $5 for each College model. Use the graphical solution procedure to determine the new optimal solution and the corresponding value of profit.

23. Embassy Motorcycles (EM) manufactures two lightweight motorcycles designed for easy handling and safety. The EZ-Rider model has a new engine and a low profile that make it easy to balance. The Lady-Sport model is slightly larger, uses a more traditional engine, and is specifically designed to appeal to women riders. Embassy produces the engines for both models at its Des Moines, Iowa, plant. Each EZ-Rider engine requires 6 hours of

FIGURE 2.23 PORTION OF THE GRAPHICAL SOLUTION FOR EXERCISE 22

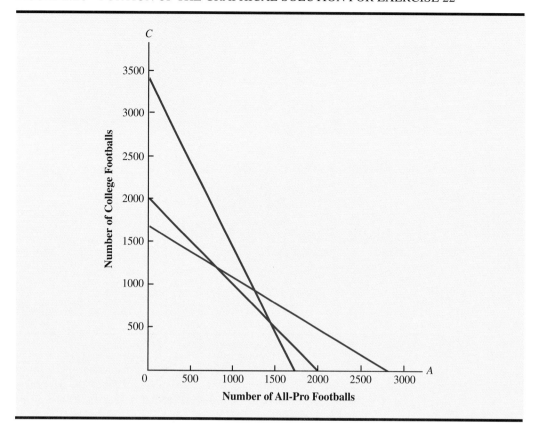

manufacturing time, and each Lady-Sport engine requires 3 hours of manufacturing time. The Des Moines plant has 2100 hours of engine manufacturing time available for the next production period. Embassy's motorcycle frame supplier can supply as many EZ-Rider frames as needed. However, the Lady-Sport frame is more complex and the supplier can only provide up to 280 Lady-Sport frames for the next production period. Final assembly and testing requires 2 hours for each EZ-Rider model and 2.5 hours for each Lady-Sport model. A maximum of 1000 hours of assembly and testing time are available for the next production period. The company's accounting department projects a profit contribution of $2400 for each EZ-Rider produced and $1800 for each Lady-Sport produced.

a. Formulate a linear programming model that can be used to determine the number of units of each model that should be produced in order to maximize the total contribution to profit.
b. Solve the problem graphically. What is the optimal solution?
c. Which constraints are binding?

24. Kelson Sporting Equipment, Inc., makes two different types of baseball gloves: a regular model and a catcher's model. The firm has 900 hours of production time available in its cutting and sewing department, 300 hours available in its finishing department, and 100 hours available in its packaging and shipping department. The production time requirements and the profit contribution per glove are given in the following table:

| Model | Production Time (hours) | | | |
	Cutting and Sewing	Finishing	Packaging and Shipping	Profit/Glove
Regular model	1	½	⅛	$5
Catcher's model	³⁄₂	⅓	¼	$8

Assuming that the company is interested in maximizing the total profit contribution, answer the following:

   a. What is the linear programming model for this problem?

   b. Find the optimal solution using the graphical solution procedure. How many gloves of each model should Kelson manufacture?

   c. What is the total profit contribution Kelson can earn with the given production quantities?

   d. How many hours of production time will be scheduled in each department?

   e. What is the slack time in each department?

25. George Johnson recently inherited a large sum of money; he wants to use a portion of this money to set up a trust fund for his two children. The trust fund has two investment options: (1) a bond fund and (2) a stock fund. The projected returns over the life of the investments are 6% for the bond fund and 10% for the stock fund. Whatever portion of the inheritance he finally decides to commit to the trust fund, he wants to invest at least 30% of that amount in the bond fund. In addition, he wants to select a mix that will enable him to obtain a total return of at least 7.5%.

   a. Formulate a linear programming model that can be used to determine the percentage that should be allocated to each of the possible investment alternatives.

   b. Solve the problem using the graphical solution procedure.

26. The Sea Wharf Restaurant would like to determine the best way to allocate a monthly advertising budget of $1000 between digital advertising and radio advertising. Management decided that at least 25% of the budget must be spent on each type of media, and that the amount of money spent on digital advertising must be at least twice the amount spent on radio advertising. A marketing consultant developed an index that measures audience exposure per dollar of advertising on a scale from 0 to 100, with higher values implying greater audience exposure. If the value of the index for digital advertising is 50 and the value of the index for spot radio advertising is 80, how should the restaurant allocate its advertising budget in order to maximize the value of total audience exposure?

   a. Formulate a linear programming model that can be used to determine how the restaurant should allocate its advertising budget in order to maximize the value of total audience exposure.

   b. Solve the problem using the graphical solution procedure.

27. Blair & Rosen, Inc. (B&R), is a brokerage firm that specializes in investment portfolios designed to meet the specific risk tolerances of its clients. A client who contacted B&R this past week has a maximum of $50,000 to invest. B&R's investment advisor decides to recommend a portfolio consisting of two investment funds: an Internet fund and a Blue Chip fund. The Internet fund has a projected annual return of 12%, whereas the Blue Chip fund has a projected annual return of 9%. The investment advisor requires that at most $35,000 of the client's funds should be invested in the Internet fund. B&R services include a risk rating for each investment alternative. The Internet fund, which is the more risky of the two investment alternatives, has a risk rating of 6 per thousand dollars invested. The Blue Chip fund has a risk rating of 4 per thousand dollars invested. For example, if $10,000 is invested in each of the two investment funds, B&R's risk rating for the portfolio would be $6(10) + 4(10) = 100$. Finally, B&R developed a questionnaire to measure each client's risk tolerance. Based on the responses, each client is classified as a conservative, moderate, or aggressive investor. Suppose that the questionnaire results classified the current client as a moderate investor. B&R recommends that a client who is a moderate investor limit his or her portfolio to a maximum risk rating of 240.

   a. What is the recommended investment portfolio for this client? What is the annual return for the portfolio?

   b. Suppose that a second client with $50,000 to invest has been classified as an aggressive investor. B&R recommends that the maximum portfolio risk rating for an aggressive investor is 320. What is the recommended investment portfolio for this aggressive investor? Discuss what happens to the portfolio under the aggressive investor strategy.

   c. Suppose that a third client with $50,000 to invest has been classified as a conservative investor. B&R recommends that the maximum portfolio risk rating for a conservative investor is 160. Develop the recommended investment portfolio for the conservative investor. Discuss the interpretation of the slack variable for the total investment fund constraint.

28. Tom's, Inc., produces various Mexican food products and sells them to Western Foods, a chain of grocery stores located in Texas and New Mexico. Tom's, Inc., makes two salsa products: Western Foods Salsa and Mexico City Salsa. Essentially, the two products have different blends of whole tomatoes, tomato sauce, and tomato paste. The Western Foods Salsa is a blend of 50% whole tomatoes, 30% tomato sauce, and 20% tomato paste. The Mexico City Salsa, which has a thicker and chunkier consistency, consists of 70% whole tomatoes, 10% tomato sauce, and 20% tomato paste. Each jar of salsa produced weighs 10 ounces. For the current production period, Tom's, Inc., can purchase up to 280 pounds of whole tomatoes, 130 pounds of tomato sauce, and 100 pounds of tomato paste; the price per pound for these ingredients is $0.96, $0.64, and $0.56, respectively. The cost of the spices and the other ingredients is approximately $0.10 per jar. Tom's, Inc., buys empty glass jars for $0.02 each, and labeling and filling costs are estimated to be $0.03 for each jar of salsa produced. Tom's contract with Western Foods results in sales revenue of $1.64 for each jar of Western Foods Salsa and $1.93 for each jar of Mexico City Salsa.
   a. Develop a linear programming model that will enable Tom's to determine the mix of salsa products that will maximize the total profit contribution.
   b. Find the optimal solution.

29. AutoIgnite produces electronic ignition systems for automobiles at a plant in Cleveland, Ohio. Each ignition system is assembled from two components produced at AutoIgnite's plants in Buffalo, New York, and Dayton, Ohio. The Buffalo plant can produce 2000 units of component 1, 1000 units of component 2, or any combination of the two components each day. For instance, 60% of Buffalo's production time could be used to produce component 1 and 40% of Buffalo's production time could be used to produce component 2; in this case, the Buffalo plant would be able to produce 0.6(2000) = 1200 units of component 1 each day and 0.4(1000) = 400 units of component 2 each day. The Dayton plant can produce 600 units of component 1, 1400 units of component 2, or any combination of the two components each day. At the end of each day, the component production at Buffalo and Dayton is sent to Cleveland for assembly of the ignition systems on the following workday.
   a. Formulate a linear programming model that can be used to develop a daily production schedule for the Buffalo and Dayton plants that will maximize daily production of ignition systems at Cleveland.
   b. Find the optimal solution.

30. A financial advisor at Diehl Investments identified two companies that are likely candidates for a takeover in the near future. Eastern Cable is a leading manufacturer of flexible cable systems used in the construction industry, and ComSwitch is a new firm specializing in digital switching systems. Eastern Cable is currently trading for $40 per share, and ComSwitch is currently trading for $25 per share. If the takeovers occur, the financial advisor estimates that the price of Eastern Cable will go to $55 per share and ComSwitch will go to $43 per share. At this point in time, the financial advisor has identified ComSwitch as the higher risk alternative. Assume that a client indicated a willingness to invest a maximum of $50,000 in the two companies. The client wants to invest at least $15,000 in Eastern Cable and at least $10,000 in ComSwitch. Because of the higher risk associated with ComSwitch, the financial advisor has recommended that at most $25,000 should be invested in ComSwitch.
   a. Formulate a linear programming model that can be used to determine the number of shares of Eastern Cable and the number of shares of ComSwitch that will meet the investment constraints and maximize the total return for the investment.
   b. Graph the feasible region.
   c. Determine the coordinates of each extreme point.
   d. Find the optimal solution.

31. Consider the following linear program:

$$\text{Min} \quad 3A + 4B$$
$$\text{s.t.}$$
$$1A + 3B \geq 6$$
$$1A + 1B \geq 4$$
$$A, B \geq 0$$

Identify the feasible region and find the optimal solution using the graphical solution procedure. What is the value of the objective function?

32. Identify the three extreme-point solutions for the M&D Chemicals problem (see Section 2.5). Identify the value of the objective function and the values of the slack and surplus variables at each extreme point.

33. Consider the following linear programming problem:

$$\text{Min} \quad A + 2B$$

s.t.

$$
\begin{aligned}
A + 4B &\leq 21 \\
2A + B &\geq 7 \\
3A + 1.5B &\leq 21 \\
-2A + 6B &\geq 0 \\
A, B &\geq 0
\end{aligned}
$$

a. Find the optimal solution using the graphical solution procedure and the value of the objective function.
b. Determine the amount of slack or surplus for each constraint.
c. Suppose the objective function is changed to max $5A + 2B$. Find the optimal solution and the value of the objective function.

 SELFtest

34. Consider the following linear program:

$$\text{Min} \quad 2A + 2B$$

s.t.

$$
\begin{aligned}
1A + 3B &\leq 12 \\
3A + 1B &\geq 13 \\
1A - 1B &= 3 \\
A, B &\geq 0
\end{aligned}
$$

a. Show the feasible region.
b. What are the extreme points of the feasible region?
c. Find the optimal solution using the graphical solution procedure.

SELFtest

35. For the linear program

$$\text{Min} \quad 6A + 4B$$

s.t.

$$
\begin{aligned}
2A + 1B &\geq 12 \\
1A + 1B &\geq 10 \\
1B &\leq 4 \\
A, B &\geq 0
\end{aligned}
$$

a. Write the problem in standard form.
b. Solve the problem using the graphical solution procedure.
c. What are the values of the slack and surplus variables?

36. As part of a quality improvement initiative, Consolidated Electronics employees complete a three-day training program on teaming and a two-day training program on problem solving. The manager of quality improvement has requested that at least 8 training programs on teaming and at least 10 training programs on problem solving be offered during the next six months. In addition, senior-level management has specified that at least 25 training programs must be offered during this period. Consolidated Electronics uses a consultant to teach the training programs. During the next quarter, the consultant has 84 days of training time available. Each training program on teaming costs $10,000 and each training program on problem solving costs $8000.

a. Formulate a linear programming model that can be used to determine the number of training programs on teaming and the number of training programs on problem solving that should be offered in order to minimize total cost.

    b. Graph the feasible region.

    c. Determine the coordinates of each extreme point.

    d. Solve for the minimum cost solution.

37. The New England Cheese Company produces two cheese spreads by blending mild cheddar cheese with extra sharp cheddar cheese. The cheese spreads are packaged in 12-ounce containers, which are then sold to distributors throughout the Northeast. The Regular blend contains 80% mild cheddar and 20% extra sharp, and the Zesty blend contains 60% mild cheddar and 40% extra sharp. This year, a local dairy cooperative offered to provide up to 8100 pounds of mild cheddar cheese for $1.20 per pound and up to 3000 pounds of extra sharp cheddar cheese for $1.40 per pound. The cost to blend and package the cheese spreads, excluding the cost of the cheese, is $0.20 per container. If each container of Regular is sold for $1.95 and each container of Zesty is sold for $2.20, how many containers of Regular and Zesty should New England Cheese produce?

38. Applied Technology, Inc. (ATI), produces bicycle frames using two fiberglass materials that improve the strength-to-weight ratio of the frames. The cost of the standard grade material is $7.50 per yard, and the cost of the professional grade material is $9.00 per yard. The standard and professional grade materials contain different amounts of fiberglass, carbon fiber, and Kevlar as shown in the following table:

	Standard Grade	Professional Grade
Fiberglass	84%	58%
Carbon fiber	10%	30%
Kevlar	6%	12%

ATI signed a contract with a bicycle manufacturer to produce a new frame with a carbon fiber content of at least 20% and a Kevlar content of not greater than 10%. To meet the required weight specification, a total of 30 yards of material must be used for each frame.

    a. Formulate a linear program to determine the number of yards of each grade of fiberglass material that ATI should use in each frame in order to minimize total cost. Define the decision variables and indicate the purpose of each constraint.

    b. Use the graphical solution procedure to determine the feasible region. What are the coordinates of the extreme points?

    c. Compute the total cost at each extreme point. What is the optimal solution?

    d. The distributor of the fiberglass material is currently overstocked with the professional grade material. To reduce inventory, the distributor offered ATI the opportunity to purchase the professional grade for $8 per yard. Will the optimal solution change?

    e. Suppose that the distributor further lowers the price of the professional grade material to $7.40 per yard. Will the optimal solution change? What effect would an even lower price for the professional grade material have on the optimal solution? Explain.

39. Innis Investments manages funds for a number of companies and wealthy clients. The investment strategy is tailored to each client's needs. For a new client, Innis has been authorized to invest up to $1.2 million in two investment funds: a stock fund and a money market fund. Each unit of the stock fund costs $50 and provides an annual rate of return of 10%; each unit of the money market fund costs $100 and provides an annual rate of return of 4%.

    The client wants to minimize risk subject to the requirement that the annual income from the investment be at least $60,000. According to Innis' risk measurement system, each unit invested in the stock fund has a risk index of 8, and each unit invested in the money market fund has a risk index of 3; the higher risk index associated with the stock fund simply indicates that it is the riskier investment. Innis's client also specified that at least $300,000 be invested in the money market fund.

    a. Determine how many units of each fund Innis should purchase for the client to minimize the total risk index for the portfolio.

    b. How much annual income will this investment strategy generate?

    c. Suppose the client desires to maximize annual return. How should the funds be invested?

40. Eastern Chemicals produces two types of lubricating fluids used in industrial manufacturing. Both products cost Eastern Chemicals $1 per gallon to produce. Based on an analysis of current inventory levels and outstanding orders for the next month, Eastern Chemicals' management specified that at least 30 gallons of product 1 and at least 20 gallons of product 2 must be produced during the next two weeks. Management also stated that an existing inventory of highly perishable raw material required in the production of both fluids must be used within the next two weeks. The current inventory of the perishable raw material is 80 pounds. Although more of this raw material can be ordered if necessary, any of the current inventory that is not used within the next two weeks will spoil—hence, the management requirement that at least 80 pounds be used in the next two weeks. Furthermore, it is known that product 1 requires 1 pound of this perishable raw material per gallon and product 2 requires 2 pounds of the raw material per gallon. Because Eastern Chemicals' objective is to keep its production costs at the minimum possible level, the firm's management is looking for a minimum cost production plan that uses all the 80 pounds of perishable raw material and provides at least 30 gallons of product 1 and at least 20 gallons of product 2. What is the minimum cost solution?

41. Southern Oil Company produces two grades of gasoline: regular and premium. The profit contributions are $0.30 per gallon for regular gasoline and $0.50 per gallon for premium gasoline. Each gallon of regular gasoline contains 0.3 gallons of grade A crude oil, and each gallon of premium gasoline contains 0.6 gallons of grade A crude oil. For the next production period, Southern has 18,000 gallons of grade A crude oil available. The refinery used to produce the gasolines has a production capacity of 50,000 gallons for the next production period. Southern Oil's distributors have indicated that demand for the premium gasoline for the next production period will be at most 20,000 gallons.
   a. Formulate a linear programming model that can be used to determine the number of gallons of regular gasoline and the number of gallons of premium gasoline that should be produced in order to maximize total profit contribution.
   b. What is the optimal solution?
   c. What are the values and interpretations of the slack variables?
   d. What are the binding constraints?

SELF*test*

42. Does the following linear program involve infeasibility, unbounded, and/or alternative optimal solutions? Explain.

$$\begin{aligned} \text{Max} \quad & 4A + 8B \\ \text{s.t.} \quad & \\ & 2A + 2B \le 10 \\ & -1A + 1B \ge 8 \\ & A, B \ge 0 \end{aligned}$$

SELF*test*

43. Does the following linear program involve infeasibility, unbounded, and/or alternative optimal solutions? Explain.

$$\begin{aligned} \text{Max} \quad & 1A + 1B \\ \text{s.t.} \quad & \\ & 8A + 6B \ge 24 \\ & 2B \ge 4 \\ & A, B \ge 0 \end{aligned}$$

44. Consider the following linear program:

$$\begin{aligned} \text{Max} \quad & 1A + 1B \\ \text{s.t.} \quad & \\ & 5A + 3B \le 15 \\ & 3A + 5B \le 15 \\ & A, B \ge 0 \end{aligned}$$

   a. What is the optimal solution for this problem?
   b. Suppose that the objective function is changed to $1A + 2B$. Find the new optimal solution.

45. Consider the following linear program:

$$\text{Max} \quad 1A - 2B$$

s.t.

$$-4A + 3B \le 3$$
$$1A - 1B \le 3$$
$$A, B \ge 0$$

  a. Graph the feasible region for the problem.
  b. Is the feasible region unbounded? Explain.
  c. Find the optimal solution.
  d. Does an unbounded feasible region imply that the optimal solution to the linear program will be unbounded?

46. The manager of a small independent grocery store is trying to determine the best use of her shelf space for soft drinks. The store carries national and generic brands and currently has 200 square feet of shelf space available. The manager wants to allocate at least 60% of the space to the national brands and, regardless of the profitability, allocate at least 10% of the space to the generic brands. How many square feet of space should the manager allocate to the national brands and the generic brands under the following circumstances?
  a. The national brands are more profitable than the generic brands.
  b. Both brands are equally profitable.
  c. The generic brand is more profitable than the national brand.

47. Discuss what happens to the M&D Chemicals problem (see Section 2.5) if the cost per gallon for product A is increased to $3.00 per gallon. What would you recommend? Explain.

48. For the M&D Chemicals problem in Section 2.5, discuss the effect of management's requiring total production of 500 gallons for the two products. List two or three actions M&D should consider to correct the situation you encounter.

49. PharmaPlus operates a chain of 30 pharmacies. The pharmacies are staffed by licensed pharmacists and pharmacy technicians. The company currently employs 85 full-time equivalent pharmacists (combination of full time and part time) and 175 full-time equivalent technicians. Each spring management reviews current staffing levels and makes hiring plans for the year. A recent forecast of the prescription load for the next year shows that at least 250 full-time equivalent employees (pharmacists and technicians) will be required to staff the pharmacies. The personnel department expects 10 pharmacists and 30 technicians to leave over the next year. To accommodate the expected attrition and prepare for future growth, management stated that at least 15 new pharmacists must be hired. In addition, PharmaPlus's new service quality guidelines specify no more than two technicians per licensed pharmacist. The average salary for licensed pharmacists is $40 per hour and the average salary for technicians is $10 per hour.
  a. Determine a minimum-cost staffing plan for PharmaPlus. How many pharmacists and technicians are needed?
  b. Given current staffing levels and expected attrition, how many new hires (if any) must be made to reach the level recommended in part (a)? What will be the impact on the payroll?

50. Expedition Outfitters manufactures a variety of specialty clothing for hiking, skiing, and mountain climbing. Its management decided to begin production on two new parkas designed for use in extremely cold weather: the Mount Everest Parka and the Rocky Mountain Parka. The manufacturing plant has 120 hours of cutting time and 120 hours of sewing time available for producing these two parkas. Each Mount Everest Parka requires 30 minutes of cutting time and 45 minutes of sewing time, and each Rocky Mountain Parka requires 20 minutes of cutting time and 15 minutes of sewing time. The labor and material cost is $150 for each Mount Everest Parka and $50 for each Rocky Mountain Parka, and the retail prices through the firm's mail order catalog are $250 for the Mount Everest Parka and $200 for the Rocky Mountain Parka. Because management believes that the Mount Everest Parka is a unique coat that will enhance the image of the firm, they specified that at least 20% of the total production must consist of this model. Assuming that Expedition Outfitters can sell as many coats of each type as it can produce, how many units of each model should it manufacture to maximize the total profit contribution?

51. English Motors, Ltd. (EML) developed a new all-wheel-drive sports utility vehicle. As part of the marketing campaign, EML produced a video tape sales presentation to send to both owners of current EML four-wheel-drive vehicles as well as to owners of four-wheel-drive sports utility vehicles offered by competitors; EML refers to these two target markets as the current customer market and the new customer market. Individuals who receive the new promotion video will also receive a coupon for a test drive of the new EML model for one weekend. A key factor in the success of the new promotion is the response rate, the percentage of individuals who receive the new promotion and test drive the new model. EML estimates that the response rate for the current customer market is 25%, and the response rate for the new customer market is 20%. For the customers who test drive the new model, the sales rate is the percentage of individuals that make a purchase. Marketing research studies indicate that the sales rate is 12% for the current customer market and 20% for the new customer market. The cost for each promotion, excluding the test drive costs, is $4 for each promotion sent to the current customer market and $6 for each promotion sent to the new customer market. Management also specified that a minimum of 30,000 current customers should test drive the new model and a minimum of 10,000 new customers should test drive the new model. In addition, the number of current customers who test drive the new vehicle must be at least twice the number of new customers who test drive the new vehicle. If the marketing budget, excluding test drive costs, is $1.2 million, how many promotions should be sent to each group of customers in order to maximize total sales?

52. Creative Sports Design (CSD) manufactures a standard-size tennis racquet and an oversize tennis racquet. The firm's racquets are extremely light due to the use of a magnesium–graphite alloy that was invented by the firm's founder. Each standard-size racquet uses 0.125 kilograms of the alloy and each oversize racquet uses 0.4 kilograms; over the next two-week production period only 80 kilograms of the alloy are available. Each standard-size racquet uses 10 minutes of manufacturing time, and each oversize racquet uses 12 minutes. The profit contributions are $10 for each standard-size racquet and $15 for each oversize racquet, and 40 hours of manufacturing time are available each week. Management specified that at least 20% of the total production must be the standard-size racquet. How many racquets of each type should CSD manufacture over the next two weeks to maximize the total profit contribution? Assume that because of the unique nature of their products, CSD can sell as many racquets as they can produce.

53. Management of High Tech Services (HTS) would like to develop a model that will help allocate their technicians' time between service calls to regular contract customers and new customers. A maximum of 80 hours of technician time is available over the two-week planning period. To satisfy cash flow requirements, at least $800 in revenue (per technician) must be generated during the two-week period. Technician time for regular customers generates $25 per hour. However, technician time for new customers only generates an average of $8 per hour because in many cases a new customer contact does not provide billable services. To ensure that new customer contacts are being maintained, the technician time spent on new customer contacts must be at least 60% of the time spent on regular customer contacts. Given these revenue and policy requirements, HTS would like to determine how to allocate technician time between regular customers and new customers so that the total number of customers contacted during the two-week period will be maximized. Technicians require an average of 50 minutes for each regular customer contact and 1 hour for each new customer contact.
   a. Develop a linear programming model that will enable HTS to allocate technician time between regular customers and new customers.
   b. Find the optimal solution.

54. Jackson Hole Manufacturing is a small manufacturer of plastic products used in the automotive and computer industries. One of its major contracts is with a large computer company and involves the production of plastic printer cases for the computer company's portable printers. The printer cases are produced on two injection molding machines. The M-100 machine has a production capacity of 25 printer cases per hour, and the M-200 machine has a production capacity of 40 cases per hour. Both machines use the same chemical material to produce the

printer cases; the M-100 uses 40 pounds of the raw material per hour and the M-200 uses 50 pounds per hour. The computer company asked Jackson Hole to produce as many of the cases during the upcoming week as possible; it will pay $18 for each case Jackson Hole can deliver. However, next week is a regularly scheduled vacation period for most of Jackson Hole's production employees; during this time, annual maintenance is performed for all equipment in the plant. Because of the downtime for maintenance, the M-100 will be available for no more than 15 hours, and the M-200 will be available for no more than 10 hours. However, because of the high setup cost involved with both machines, management requires that each machine must be operated for at least 5 hours. The supplier of the chemical material used in the production process informed Jackson Hole that a maximum of 1000 pounds of the chemical material will be available for next week's production; the cost for this raw material is $6 per pound. In addition to the raw material cost, Jackson Hole estimates that the hourly cost of operating the M-100 and the M-200 are $50 and $75, respectively.

a. Formulate a linear programming model that can be used to maximize the contribution to profit.

b. Find the optimal solution.

55. The Kartick Company is trying to determine how much of each of two products to produce over the coming planning period. There are three departments, A, B, and C, with limited labor hours available in each department. Each product must be processed by each department and the per-unit requirements for each product, labor hours available, and per-unit profit are as shown below.

Labor required in each department

Department	Product (hours/unit) Product 1	Product 2	Labor Hours Available
A	1.00	0.30	100
B	0.30	0.12	36
C	0.15	0.56	50
Profit Contribution	$33.00	$24.00	

A linear program for this situation is as follows:

Let $\quad x_1 =$ the amount of product 1 to produce
$\quad x_2 =$ the amount of product 2 to produce

Maximize $\quad 33 x_1 + 24 x_2$

s.t.

$$1.0 x_1 + 0.30 x_2 \leq 100 \quad \text{Department A}$$
$$0.30 x_1 + 0.12 x_2 \leq 36 \quad \text{Department B}$$
$$0.15 x_1 + 0.56 x_2 \leq 50 \quad \text{Department C}$$
$$x_1, x_2 \geq 0$$

Mr. Kartick (the owner) used trial and error with a spreadsheet model to arrive at a solution. His proposed solution is $x_1 = 75$ and $x_2 = 60$, as shown in Figure 2.24. He said he felt his proposed solution is optimal.

Is his solution optimal? Without solving the problem, explain why you believe this solution is optimal or not optimal.

56. Assume you are given a minimization linear program that has an optimal solution. The problem is then modified by changing an equality constraint in the problem to a less-than-or-equal-to constraint. Is it possible that the modified problem is infeasible? Answer yes or no and justify.

57. Assume you are given a minimization linear program that has an optimal solution. The problem is then modified by changing a greater-than-or-equal-to constraint in the problem to a less-than-or-equal-to constraint. Is it possible that the modified problem is infeasible? Answer yes or no and justify.

FIGURE 2.24 MR. KARTICK'S TRIAL-AND-ERROR MODEL

	A	B	C	D	E
1	**Kartick**				
2	**Data**				
3				Hours	
4	Department	Prod 1	Prod 2	Available	
5	A	1.00	0.30	100	
6	B	0.30	0.12	36	
7	C	0.15	0.56	50	
8	Per unit				
9	Contribution	$33.00	$24.00		
10					
11	**Decisions**				
12					
13		Prod 1	Prod 2		
14	Quantity	75	60		
15					
16					
17	**Model**				
18		Hours	Unused		
19	Department	Used	Hours		
20	A	93	7		
21	B	29.7	6.3		
22	C	44.85	5.15		
23					
24	Contribution	$3,915.00			

58. A consultant was hired to build an optimization model for a large marketing research company. The model is based on a consumer survey that was taken in which each person was asked to rank 30 new products in descending order based on their likelihood of purchasing the product. The consultant was assigned the task of building a model that selects the minimum number of products (which would then be introduced into the marketplace) such that the first, second, and third choice of every subject in the survey is included in the list of selected products. While building a model to figure out which products to introduce, the consultant's boss walked up to her and said: "Look, if the model tells us we need to introduce more than 15 products, then add a constraint which limits the number of new products to 15 or less. It's too expensive to introduce more than 15 new products." Evaluate this statement in terms of what you have learned so far about constrained optimization models.

Case Problem 1   WORKLOAD BALANCING

Digital Imaging (DI) produces color printers for both the professional and consumer markets. The DI consumer division recently introduced two new color printers. The DI-910 model can produce a 4" × 6" borderless color print in approximately 37 seconds. The more sophisticated and faster DI-950 can even produce a 13" × 19" borderless color print. Financial projections show profit contributions of $42 for each DI-910 and $87 for each DI-950.

The printers are assembled, tested, and packaged at DI's plant located in New Bern, North Carolina. This plant is highly automated and uses two manufacturing lines to produce the printers. Line 1 performs the assembly operation with times of 3 minutes per DI-910 printer and 6 minutes per DI-950 printer. Line 2 performs both the testing and packaging operations with times of 4 minutes per DI-910 printer and 2 minutes per DI-950 printer. The shorter time for the DI-950 printer is a result of its faster print speed. Both manufacturing lines are in operation one 8-hour shift per day.

Managerial Report

Perform an analysis for Digital Imaging in order to determine how many units of each printer to produce. Prepare a report to DI's president presenting your findings and recommendations. Include (but do not limit your discussion to) a consideration of the following:

1. The recommended number of units of each printer to produce to maximize the total contribution to profit for an 8-hour shift. What reasons might management have for not implementing your recommendation?
2. Suppose that management also states that the number of DI-910 printers produced must be at least as great as the number of DI-950 units produced. Assuming that the objective is to maximize the total contribution to profit for an 8-hour shift, how many units of each printer should be produced?
3. Does the solution you developed in part (2) balance the total time spent on line 1 and the total time spent on line 2? Why might this balance or lack of it be a concern to management?
4. Management requested an expansion of the model in part (2) that would provide a better balance between the total time on line 1 and the total time on line 2. Management wants to limit the difference between the total time on line 1 and the total time on line 2 to 30 minutes or less. If the objective is still to maximize the total contribution to profit, how many units of each printer should be produced? What effect does this workload balancing have on total profit in part (2)?
5. Suppose that in part (1) management specified the objective of maximizing the total number of printers produced each shift rather than total profit contribution. With this objective, how many units of each printer should be produced per shift? What effect does this objective have on total profit and workload balancing?

For each solution that you develop, include a copy of your linear programming model and graphical solution in the appendix to your report.

Case Problem 2   PRODUCTION STRATEGY

Better Fitness, Inc. (BFI), manufactures exercise equipment at its plant in Freeport, Long Island. It recently designed two universal weight machines for the home exercise market. Both machines use BFI-patented technology that provides the user with an extremely wide range of motion capability for each type of exercise performed. Until now, such capabilities have been available only on expensive weight machines used primarily by physical therapists.

At a recent trade show, demonstrations of the machines resulted in significant dealer interest. In fact, the number of orders that BFI received at the trade show far exceeded its manufacturing capabilities for the current production period. As a result, management decided to begin production of the two machines. The two machines, which BFI named the BodyPlus 100 and the BodyPlus 200, require different amounts of resources to produce.

The BodyPlus 100 consists of a frame unit, a press station, and a pec-dec station. Each frame produced uses 4 hours of machining and welding time and 2 hours of painting and finishing time. Each press station requires 2 hours of machining and welding time and 1 hour of painting and finishing time, and each pec-dec station uses 2 hours of machining and welding time and 2 hours of painting and finishing time. In addition, 2 hours are spent assembling, testing, and packaging each BodyPlus 100. The raw material costs are $450 for each frame, $300 for each press station, and $250 for each pec-dec station; packaging costs are estimated to be $50 per unit.

The BodyPlus 200 consists of a frame unit, a press station, a pec-dec station, and a leg-press station. Each frame produced uses 5 hours of machining and welding time and 4 hours of painting and finishing time. Each press station requires 3 hours of machining and welding time and 2 hours of painting and finishing time, each pec-dec station uses 2 hours of machining and welding time and 2 hours of painting and finishing time, and each leg-press station requires 2 hours of machining and welding time and 2 hours of painting and finishing time. In addition, 2 hours are spent assembling, testing, and packaging each BodyPlus 200. The raw material costs are $650 for each frame, $400 for each press station, $250 for each pec-dec station, and $200 for each leg-press station; packaging costs are estimated to be $75 per unit.

For the next production period, management estimates that 600 hours of machining and welding time, 450 hours of painting and finishing time, and 140 hours of assembly, testing, and packaging time will be available. Current labor costs are $20 per hour for machining and welding time, $15 per hour for painting and finishing time, and $12 per hour for assembly, testing, and packaging time. The market in which the two machines must compete suggests a retail price of $2400 for the BodyPlus 100 and $3500 for the BodyPlus 200, although some flexibility may be available to BFI because of the unique capabilities of the new machines. Authorized BFI dealers can purchase machines for 70% of the suggested retail price.

BFI's president believes that the unique capabilities of the BodyPlus 200 can help position BFI as one of the leaders in high-end exercise equipment. Consequently, he has stated that the number of units of the BodyPlus 200 produced must be at least 25% of the total production.

Managerial Report

Analyze the production problem at Better Fitness, Inc., and prepare a report for BFI's president presenting your findings and recommendations. Include (but do not limit your discussion to) a consideration of the following items:

1. What is the recommended number of BodyPlus 100 and BodyPlus 200 machines to produce?
2. How does the requirement that the number of units of the BodyPlus 200 produced be at least 25% of the total production affect profits?
3. Where should efforts be expended in order to increase profits?

Include a copy of your linear programming model and graphical solution in an appendix to your report.

Case Problem 3   HART VENTURE CAPITAL

Hart Venture Capital (HVC) specializes in providing venture capital for software development and Internet applications. Currently HVC has two investment opportunities: (1) Security Systems, a firm that needs additional capital to develop an Internet security software package, and (2) Market Analysis, a market research company that needs additional capital to develop a software package for conducting customer satisfaction surveys. In exchange for Security Systems stock, the firm has asked HVC to provide $600,000 in year 1, $600,000 in year 2, and $250,000 in year 3 over the coming three-year period. In exchange for their stock, Market Analysis has asked HVC to provide $500,000 in year 1, $350,000 in year 2, and $400,000 in year 3 over the same three-year period. HVC believes that both investment opportunities are worth pursuing. However, because of other investments, they are willing to commit at most $800,000 for both projects in the first year, at most $700,000 in the second year, and $500,000 in the third year.

HVC's financial analysis team reviewed both projects and recommended that the company's objective should be to maximize the net present value of the total investment in Security Systems and Market Analysis. The net present value takes into account the estimated value of the stock at the end of the three-year period as well as the capital outflows that are necessary during each of the three years. Using an 8% rate of return, HVC's financial analysis team estimates that 100% funding of the Security Systems project has a net present value of $1,800,000, and 100% funding of the Market Analysis project has a net present value of $1,600,000.

HVC has the option to fund any percentage of the Security Systems and Market Analysis projects. For example, if HVC decides to fund 40% of the Security Systems project, investments of 0.40($600,000) = $240,000 would be required in year 1, 0.40($600,000) = $240,000 would be required in year 2, and 0.40($250,000) = $100,000 would be required in year 3. In this case, the net present value of the Security Systems project would be 0.40($1,800,000) = $720,000. The investment amounts and the net present value for partial funding of the Market Analysis project would be computed in the same manner.

Managerial Report

Perform an analysis of HVC's investment problem and prepare a report that presents your findings and recommendations. Include (but do not limit your discussion to) a consideration of the following items:

1. What is the recommended percentage of each project that HVC should fund and the net present value of the total investment?
2. What capital allocation plan for Security Systems and Market Analysis for the coming three-year period and the total HVC investment each year would you recommend?
3. What effect, if any, would HVC's willingness to commit an additional $100,000 during the first year have on the recommended percentage of each project that HVC should fund?
4. What would the capital allocation plan look like if an additional $100,000 is made available?
5. What is your recommendation as to whether HVC should commit the additional $100,000 in the first year?

Provide model details and relevant computer output in a report appendix.

Appendix 2.1   SOLVING LINEAR PROGRAMS WITH EXCEL SOLVER

The Excel add-in Analytic Solver, which is used in Chapter 12 of this textbook for simulation problems, can also be used to solve linear programs. Analytic Solver uses more sophisticated algorithms for solving optimization problems and can solve larger problems than Excel Solver. However, since all optimization problems in this textbook can be solved using Excel Solver, we do not specifically discuss the use of Analytic Solver for optimization problems.

In this appendix we will use Excel Solver to solve the Par, Inc., linear programming problem. We will enter the problem data for the Par, Inc., problem in the top part of the worksheet and develop the linear programming model in the bottom part of the worksheet.

Formulation

Whenever we formulate a worksheet model of a linear program, we perform the following steps:

Step 1. Enter the problem data in the top part of the worksheet.
Step 2. Specify cell locations for the decision variables.
Step 3. Select a cell and enter a formula for computing the value of the objective function.
Step 4. Select a cell and enter a formula for computing the left-hand side of each constraint.
Step 5. Select a cell and enter a formula for computing the right-hand side of each constraint.

The formula worksheet that we developed for the Par, Inc., problem using these five steps is shown in Figure 2.25. Note that the worksheet consists of two sections: a data section and a model section. The four components of the model are highlighted, and the cells reserved for the decision variables are B16 and C16. Figure 2.25 is called a formula worksheet because it displays the formulas that we have entered and not the values computed from those formulas. In a moment we will see how Excel Solver is used to find the optimal solution to the Par, Inc., problem. But first, let's review each of the preceding steps as they apply to the Par, Inc., problem.

Step 1. Enter the problem data in the top part of the worksheet.
    Cells B5:C8 show the production requirements per unit for each product. Note that in cells C6 and C7, we have entered the exact fractions. That is, in cell C6 we have entered $=5/6$ and in cell C7 we have entered $=2/3$.

FIGURE 2.25   FORMULA WORKSHEET FOR THE PAR, INC., PROBLEM

	A	B	C	D
1	Par, Inc.			
2				
3		Production Time		
4	Operation	Standard	Deluxe	Time Available
5	Cutting and Dyeing	0.7	1	630
6	Sewing	0.5	0.83333	600
7	Finishing	1	0.66667	708
8	Inspection and Packaging	0.1	0.25	135
9	Profit Per Bag	10	9	
10				
11				
12	Model			
13				
14		Decision Variables		
15		Standard	Deluxe	
16	Bags Produced			
17				
18	Maximize Total Profit	=B9*B16+C9*C16		
19				
20	Constraints	Hours Used (LHS)		Hours Available (RHS)
21	Cutting and Dyeing	=B5*B16+C5*C16	<=	=D5
22	Sewing	=B6*B16+C6*C16	<=	=D6
23	Finishing	=B7*B16+C7*C16	<=	=D7
24	Inspection and Packaging	=B8*B16+C8*C16	<=	=D8

Cells B9:C9 show the profit contribution per unit for the two products.

Cells D5:D8 show the number of hours available in each department.

Step 2.   Specify cell locations for the decision variables.

Cell B16 will contain the number of standard bags produced, and cell C16 will contain the number of deluxe bags produced.

Step 3.   Select a cell and enter a formula for computing the value of the objective function.

Cell B18: $=B9*B16+C9*C16$

Step 4.   Select a cell and enter a formula for computing the left-hand side of each constraint. With four constraints, we have

Cell B21: $=B5*B16+C5*C16$

Cell B22: $=B6*B16+C6*C16$

Cell B23: $=B7*B16+C7*C16$

Cell B24: $=B8*B16+C8*C16$

Step 5.   Select a cell and enter a formula for computing the right-hand side of each constraint. With four constraints, we have

Cell D21: $=D5$

Cell D22: $=D6$

Cell D23: $=D7$

Cell D24: $=D8$

Note that descriptive labels make the model section of the worksheet easier to read and understand. For example, we added "Standard," "Deluxe," and "Bags Produced" in rows 15 and 16 so that the values of the decision variables appearing in cells B16 and C16 can be easily interpreted. In addition, we entered "Maximize Total Profit" in cell A18 to indicate that the value of the objective function appearing in cell B18 is the maximum profit

Appendix A provides a discussion of how to properly build and structure a good spreadsheet model.

contribution. In the constraint section of the worksheet we added the constraint names as well as the "$<=$" symbols to show the relationship that exists between the left-hand side and the right-hand side of each constraint. Although these descriptive labels are not necessary to use Excel Solver to find a solution to the Par, Inc., problem, the labels make it easier for the user to understand and interpret the optimal solution.

Excel Solution

The standard Excel Solver developed by Frontline Systems can be used to solve all of the linear programming problems presented in this text.

The following steps describe how Excel Solver can be used to obtain the optimal solution to the Par, Inc., problem:

Step 1. Select the **Data** tab on the **Ribbon**
Step 2. Select **Solver** from the **Analyze** Group
Step 3. When the **Solver Parameters** dialog box appears (see Figure 2.26):
      Enter *B18* into the **Set Objective** box
      Select the **To: Max** option

FIGURE 2.26   SOLVER PARAMETERS DIALOG BOX FOR THE PAR, INC., PROBLEM

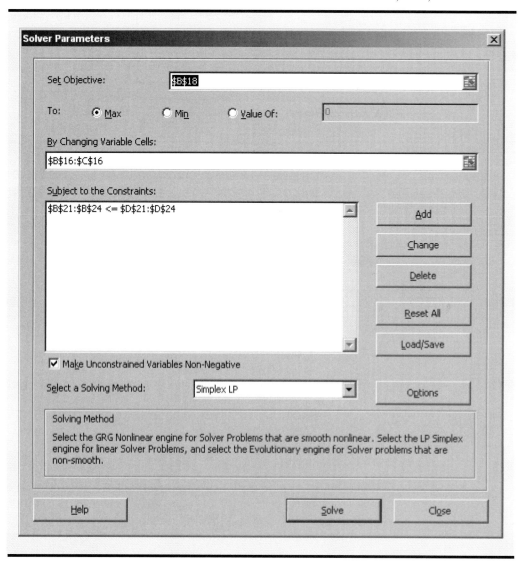

Enter *B16:C16* into the **By Changing Variable Cells** box
Select **Add**

Step 4. When the **Add Constraint** dialog box appears:
Enter *B21:B24* in the left-hand box of the **Cell Reference** area
Select **<=** from the middle drop-down button
Enter *D21:D24* in the **Constraint** area
Click **OK**

Step 5. When the **Solver Parameters** dialog box reappears:
Select the checkbox for **Make Unconstrained Variables Non-Negative**

Step 6. In the **Select a Solving Method** dropdown menu
Select **Simplex LP**

Step 7. Click **Solve**

Step 8. When the **Solver Results** dialog box appears:
Select **Keep Solver Solution**
Click **OK**

Figure 2.26 shows the completed **Solver Parameters** dialog box, and Figure 2.27 shows the optimal solution in the worksheet. The optimal solution of 540 standard bags and 252 deluxe bags is the same as we obtained using the graphical solution procedure. In addition to the output information shown in Figure 2.27, Solver has an option to provide sensitivity analysis information. We discuss sensitivity analysis in Chapter 3.

In Step 5 we selected the **Make Unconstrained Variables Non-Negative** checkbox to avoid having to enter nonnegativity constraints for the decision variables. In general, whenever we want to solve a linear programming model in which the decision variables are all restricted to be nonnegative, we will select this option. In addition, in Step 4 we entered all four less-than-or-equal-to constraints simultaneously by entering *B21:B24* in the left-hand box of the **Cell Reference** area, selecting **<=**, and entering *D21:D24* in the right-hand box. Alternatively, we could have entered the four constraints one at a time.

FIGURE 2.27   EXCEL SOLUTION FOR THE PAR, INC., PROBLEM

	A	B	C	D
4	Operation	Standard	Deluxe	Time Available
5	Cutting and Dyeing	0.7	1	630
6	Sewing	0.5	0.833333333	600
7	Finishing	1	0.666666667	708
8	Inspection and Packaging	0.1	0.25	135
9	**Profit Per Bag**	10	9	
10				
11				
12	**Model**			
13				
14		Decision Variables		
15		Standard	Deluxe	
16	**Bags Produced**	540.00000	252.00000	
17				
18	**Maximize Total Profit**	7668		
19				
20	**Constraints**	Hours Used (LHS)		Hours Available (RHS)
21	Cutting and Dyeing	630	<=	630
22	Sewing	480.00000	<=	600
23	Finishing	708	<=	708
24	Inspection and Packaging	117.00000	<=	135

As a reminder, when entering a fraction into Excel, it is not necessary to convert the fraction into an equivalent or rounded decimal number. For example, simply enter the fraction ⅔ into Excel as =⅔ and do not worry about converting to a decimal or how many decimal places to use. Enter ⁷⁄₁₀ either as =⁷⁄₁₀ or =0.7. When entering a fraction, the "=" sign is necessary; otherwise, Excel will treat the fraction as text rather than a number.

Appendix 2.2   SOLVING LINEAR PROGRAMS WITH LINGO

LINGO is a product of LINDO Systems. It was developed by Linus E. Schrage and Kevin Cunningham at the University of Chicago.

In this appendix we describe how to use LINGO to solve the Par, Inc., problem. When you start LINGO, two windows are immediately displayed. The outer or main frame window contains all the command menus and the command toolbar. The smaller window is the model window; this window is used to enter and edit the linear programming model you want to solve. The first item we enter into the model window is the objective function. Recall that the objective function for the Par, Inc., problem is Max $10S + 9D$. Thus, in the first line of the LINGO model window, we enter the following expression:

$$\text{MAX} = 10*S + 9*D;$$

Note that in LINGO the symbol * is used to denote multiplication and that the objective function line ends with a semicolon. In general, each mathematical expression (objective function and constraints) in LINGO is terminated with a semicolon.

MODEL *file*

Par

Next, we press the Enter key to move to a new line. The first constraint in the Par, Inc., problem is $0.7S + 1D \le 630$. Thus, in the second line of the LINGO model window we enter the following expression:

$$0.7*S + 1*D <= 630;$$

Note that LINGO interprets the $<=$ symbol as $\le$. As was the case when entering the objective function, a semicolon is required at the end of the first constraint. Pressing the Enter key moves us to a new line as we continue the process by entering the remaining constraints as shown here:

$$0.5*S + ⅚*D <= 600;$$
$$1*S + ⅔*D <= 708;$$
$$0.1*S + 0.25*D <= 135;$$

The model window will now appear as follows:

$$\text{MAX} = 10*S + 9*D;$$
$$0.7*S + 1*D <= 630;$$
$$0.5*S + ⅚ *D <= 600;$$
$$1*S + ⅔*D <= 708;$$
$$0.1*S + 0.25*D <= 135;$$

When entering a fraction into LINGO it is not necessary to convert the fraction into an equivalent or rounded decimal number. For example, simply enter the fraction ⅔ into LINGO as ⅔ and do not worry about converting to a decimal or how many decimal places to use. Enter ⁷⁄₁₀ either as ⁷⁄₁₀ or 0.7. Let LINGO act as a calculator for you.

LINGO is very flexible about the format of an equation and it is not necessary to have the variables on the left-hand side of an equation and the constant term on the right. For example

$$0.7*S + 1*D <= 630;$$

could also be entered as

$$0.7*S <= 630 - 1*D;$$

This feature will be very useful later when writing models in a clear and understandable form. Finally, note that although we have expressly included a coefficient of 1 on the variable D above, this is not necessary. In LINGO, $1*D$ and D are equivalent.

If you make an error in entering the model, you can correct it at any time by simply positioning the cursor where you made the error and entering the necessary correction.

To solve the model, select the **Solve** command from the **SOLVER** menu or press the **Solve** button on the toolbar at the top of the main frame window. LINGO will begin the solution process by determining whether the model conforms to all syntax requirements. If the LINGO model doesn't pass these tests, you will be informed by an error message. If LINGO does not find any errors in the model input, it will begin to solve the model. As part of the solution process, LINGO displays a **Solver Status** window that allows you to monitor the progress of the solver. LINGO displays the solution in a new window titled **Solution Report**. The output that appears in the Solution Report window for the Par, Inc., problem is shown in Figure 2.28.

The first part of the output shown in Figure 2.28 indicates that an optimal solution has been found and that the value of the objective function is 7668. We see that the optimal solution is $S = 540$ and $D = 252$, and that the slack variables for the four constraints (rows 2–5) are 0, 120, 0, and 18. We will discuss the use of the information in the Reduced Cost column and the Dual Price column in Chapter 3 when we study the topic of sensitivity analysis.

FIGURE 2.28 PAR, INC., SOLUTION REPORT USING LINGO

```
Global optimal solution found.
Objective value:                              7668.000
Infeasibilities:                              0.000000
Total solver iterations:                             2
Elapsed runtime seconds:                          0.09


Model Class:                                        LP


Total variables:                2
Nonlinear variables:            0
Integer variables:              0


Total constraints:              5
Nonlinear constraints:          0


Total nonzeros:                10
Nonlinear nonzeros:             0


            Variable            Value          Reduced Cost
                   S         540.0000              0.000000
                   D         252.0000              0.000000


                 Row    Slack or Surplus            Dual Price
                   1            7668.000              1.000000
                   2            0.000000              4.375000
                   3            120.0000              0.000000
                   4            0.000000              6.937500
                   5            18.00000              0.000000
```

CHAPTER 3

Linear Programming: Sensitivity Analysis and Interpretation of Solution

CONTENTS

Sensitivity analysis is the study of how the changes in the coefficients of an optimization model affect the optimal solution. Using sensitivity analysis, we can answer questions such as the following:

1. How will a change *in a coefficient of the objective function* affect the optimal solution?
2. How will a change in the *right-hand-side value for a constraint* affect the optimal solution?

Because sensitivity analysis is concerned with how these changes affect the optimal solution, the analysis does not begin until the optimal solution to the original linear programming problem has been obtained. For that reason, sensitivity analysis is sometimes referred to as *postoptimality analysis.*

Our approach to sensitivity analysis parallels the approach used to introduce linear programming in Chapter 2. We begin by showing how a graphical method can be used to perform sensitivity analysis for linear programming problems with two decision variables. Then, we show how optimization software provides sensitivity analysis information.

Finally, we extend the discussion of problem formulation started in Chapter 2 by formulating and solving three larger linear programming problems. In discussing the solution for each of these problems, we focus on managerial interpretation of the optimal solution and sensitivity analysis information.

Sensitivity analysis and the interpretation of the optimal solution are important aspects of applying linear programming. The Management Science in Action, Kimpton Hotels Uses Optimization for Setting Prices on Priceline, provides an example of how Kimpton Hotels uses linear programming and sensitivity analysis to set prices of rooms sold through Priceline. Later in the chapter, other Management Science in Action articles illustrate how Performance Analysis Corporation uses sensitivity analysis as part of an evaluation model for a chain of fast-food outlets, how GE Plastics (now part of the Saudi Basic Industries Corporation) uses a linear programming model involving thousands of variables and constraints

MANAGEMENT SCIENCE IN ACTION

KIMPTON HOTELS USES OPTIMIZATION FOR SETTING PRICES ON PRICELINE*

How to price rooms to maximize revenue is a problem faced by all hotels. If prices are set too low, demand will be higher, but total revenue may be lower than what would have been generated if the customer's willingness to pay was known. If the price is too high, demand may drop, resulting in empty rooms and lost revenue. Revenue management, sometimes called yield management, attempts to determine prices to charge and how many rooms to offer at each price so as to maximize revenue.

Kimpton Hotels owns over 50 boutique four-star hotels in the United States and Canada. Most of Kimpton's customers are business travelers who generally book later and are often willing to pay more than leisure travelers. The shorter lead time of business travelers presents a challenge for Kimpton, since it has less time to react by adjusting its prices when demand does not materialize.

Priceline.com is an Internet site that allows the user to specify the area he or she would like to visit, the dates of the visit, and the level of the hotel (three-star, four-star, etc.) and to make a bid price for a room. Priceline searches a list of participating hotels for a hotel that matches the criteria specified by the user. This is known as opaque marketing because the hotel name is revealed to the user only when a match is found, at which point the user is committed. This opaqueness is important for the hotel, because it allows the hotel to segment the market and offer different prices without diluting its regularly posted prices.

Kimpton participates in the Priceline bidding process and has to submit prices and how many rooms are available at each price level over a specified set of dates. Using historical data, Kimpton predicts future demand and uses a technique known as dynamic programming to set prices. A linear program is then used to determine the number of rooms to offer at each price level. In particular, the dual value on a room availability constraint is utilized to assess whether or not to offer another room at a given price in a given period. Since implementing this new optimization-based approach, rooms sold via Priceline have increased 11% and the average price for the rooms has increased by nearly 4%.

*Based on C. Anderson, "Setting Prices on Priceline," *Interfaces* 39, no. 4 (July/August 2009): 307–315.

to determine optimal production quantities and how Duncan Industries Limited's linear programming model for tea distribution convinced management of the benefits of using quantitative analysis techniques to support the decision-making process.

3.1   INTRODUCTION TO SENSITIVITY ANALYSIS

Sensitivity analysis is important to decision makers because real-world problems exist in a changing environment. Prices of raw materials change, product demand changes, companies purchase new machinery, stock prices fluctuate, employee turnover occurs, and so on. If a linear programming model has been used in such an environment, we can expect some of the coefficients to change over time. We will then want to determine how these changes affect the optimal solution to the original linear programming problem. Sensitivity analysis provides us with the information needed to respond to such changes without requiring the complete solution of a revised linear program.

Recall the Par, Inc., problem from Chapter 2:

$$\text{Max} \quad 10S + 9D$$

s.t.

$$\frac{7}{10}S + 1D \leq 630 \quad \text{Cutting and Dyeing}$$

$$\frac{1}{2}S + \frac{5}{6}D \leq 600 \quad \text{Sewing}$$

$$1S + \frac{2}{3}D \leq 708 \quad \text{Finishing}$$

$$\frac{1}{10}S + \frac{1}{4}D \leq 135 \quad \text{Inspection and Packaging}$$

$$S, D \geq 0$$

The optimal solution, $S = 540$ standard bags and $D = 252$ deluxe bags, was based on profit contribution figures of \$10 per standard bag and \$9 per deluxe bag. Suppose we later learn that a price reduction causes the profit contribution for the standard bag to fall from \$10 to \$8.50. Sensitivity analysis can be used to determine whether the production schedule calling for 540 standard bags and 252 deluxe bags is still best. If it is, solving a modified linear programming problem with $8.50S + 9D$ as the new objective function will not be necessary.

Sensitivity analysis can also be used to determine which coefficients in a linear programming model are crucial. For example, suppose that management believes the \$9 profit contribution for the deluxe bag is only a rough estimate of the profit contribution that will actually be obtained. If sensitivity analysis shows that 540 standard bags and 252 deluxe bags will be the optimal solution as long as the profit contribution for the deluxe bag is between \$6.67 and \$14.29, management should feel comfortable with the \$9-per-bag estimate and the recommended production quantities. However, if sensitivity analysis shows that 540 standard bags and 252 deluxe bags will be the optimal solution only if the profit contribution for the deluxe bags is between \$8.90 and \$9.25, management may want to review the accuracy of the \$9-per-bag estimate. Management would especially want to consider how the optimal production quantities should be revised if the profit contribution per deluxe bag were to drop.

Another aspect of sensitivity analysis concerns changes in the right-hand-side values of the constraints. Recall that in the Par, Inc., problem the optimal solution used all available time in the cutting and dyeing department and the finishing department. What would happen to the optimal solution and total profit contribution if Par, Inc., could obtain additional quantities of either of these resources? Sensitivity analysis can help determine how much each additional hour of production time is worth and how many hours can be added before diminishing returns set in.

3.2   GRAPHICAL SENSITIVITY ANALYSIS

For linear programming problems with two decision variables, graphical solution methods can be used to perform sensitivity analysis on the objective function coefficients and the right-hand-side values for the constraints.

Objective Function Coefficients

Let us consider how changes in the objective function coefficients might affect the optimal solution to the Par, Inc., problem. The current contribution to profit is $10 per unit for the standard bag and $9 per unit for the deluxe bag. It seems obvious that an increase in the profit contribution for one of the bags might lead management to increase production of that bag, and a decrease in the profit contribution for one of the bags might lead management to decrease production of that bag. It is not as obvious, however, how much the profit contribution would have to change before management would want to change the production quantities.

The current optimal solution to this problem calls for producing 540 standard golf bags and 252 deluxe golf bags. The **range of optimality** for each objective function coefficient provides the range of values over which the current solution will remain optimal. Managerial attention should be focused on those objective function coefficients that have a narrow range of optimality and coefficients near the end points of the range. With these coefficients, a small change can necessitate modifying the optimal solution. Let us now compute the ranges of optimality for this problem.

Figure 3.1 shows the graphical solution. A careful inspection of this graph shows that as long as the slope of the objective function line is between the slope of line A (which coincides with the cutting and dyeing constraint line) and the slope of line B (which coincides with the finishing constraint line), extreme point ③ with $S = 540$ and $D = 252$ will be optimal. Changing an objective function coefficient for S or D will cause the slope of the objective function line to change. In Figure 3.1 we see that such changes cause the objective

FIGURE 3.1   GRAPHICAL SOLUTION OF PAR, INC., PROBLEM WITH SLOPE OF
                OBJECTIVE FUNCTION LINE BETWEEN SLOPES OF LINES A AND B;
                EXTREME POINT ③ IS OPTIMAL

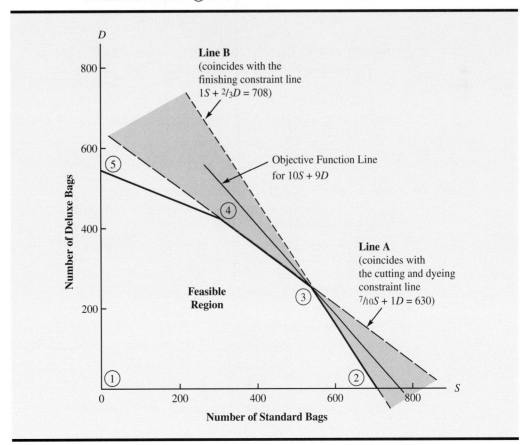

function line to rotate around extreme point ③. However, as long as the objective function line stays within the shaded region, extreme point ③ will remain optimal.

Rotating the objective function line *counterclockwise* causes the slope to become less negative, and the slope increases. When the objective function line rotates counterclockwise (slope increased) enough to coincide with line A, we obtain alternative optimal solutions between extreme points ③ and ④. Any further counterclockwise rotation of the objective function line will cause extreme point ③ to be nonoptimal. Hence, the slope of line A provides an upper limit for the slope of the objective function line.

Rotating the objective function line *clockwise* causes the slope to become more negative, and the slope decreases. When the objective function line rotates clockwise (slope decreases) enough to coincide with line B, we obtain alternative optimal solutions between extreme points ③ and ②. Any further clockwise rotation of the objective function line will cause extreme point ③ to be nonoptimal. Hence, the slope of line B provides a lower limit for the slope of the objective function line.

The slope of the objective function line usually is negative; hence, rotating the objective function line clockwise makes the line steeper even though the slope is getting smaller (more negative).

Thus, extreme point ③ will be the optimal solution as long as

Slope of line B $\leq$ slope of the objective function line $\leq$ slope of line A

In Figure 3.1 we see that the equation for line A, the cutting and dyeing constraint line, is as follows:

$$\tfrac{7}{10}S + 1D = 630$$

By solving this equation for D, we can write the equation for line A in its slope-intercept form, which yields

$$D = -\tfrac{7}{10}S + 630$$

↑   ↑

Slope of   Intercept of
line A   line A on
          D axis

Thus, the slope for line A is $-\tfrac{7}{10}$, and its intercept on the D axis is 630.

The equation for line B in Figure 3.1 is

$$1S + \tfrac{2}{3}D = 708$$

Solving for D provides the slope-intercept form for line B. Doing so yields

$$\tfrac{2}{3}D = -1S + 708$$
$$D = -\tfrac{3}{2}S + 1062$$

Thus, the slope of line B is $-\tfrac{3}{2}$, and its intercept on the D axis is 1062.

Now that the slopes of lines A and B have been computed, we see that for extreme point ③ to remain optimal we must have

$$-\tfrac{3}{2} \leq \text{slope of objective function} \leq -\tfrac{7}{10} \qquad (3.1)$$

Let us now consider the general form of the slope of the objective function line. Let C_S denote the profit of a standard bag, C_D denote the profit of a deluxe bag, and P denote the value of the objective function. Using this notation, the objective function line can be written as

$$P = C_S S + C_D D$$

Writing this equation in slope-intercept form, we obtain

$$C_D D = -C_S S + P$$

and

$$D = -\frac{C_S}{C_D}S + \frac{P}{C_D}$$

Thus, we see that the slope of the objective function line is given by $-C_S/C_D$. Substituting $-C_S/C_D$ into expression (3.1), we see that extreme point ③ will be optimal as long as the following expression is satisfied:

$$-\tfrac{3}{2} \leq -\frac{C_S}{C_D} \leq -\tfrac{7}{10} \qquad\qquad (3.2)$$

To compute the range of optimality for the standard-bag profit contribution, we hold the profit contribution for the deluxe bag fixed at its initial value $C_D = 9$. Doing so in expression (3.2), we obtain

$$-\tfrac{3}{2} \leq -\frac{C_S}{9} \leq -\tfrac{7}{10}$$

From the left-hand inequality, we have

$$-\tfrac{3}{2} \leq -\frac{C_S}{9} \qquad \text{or} \qquad \tfrac{3}{2} \geq \frac{C_S}{9}$$

Thus,

$$\tfrac{27}{2} \geq C_S \qquad \text{or} \qquad C_S \leq \tfrac{27}{2} = 13.5$$

From the right-hand inequality, we have

$$-\frac{C_S}{9} \leq -\tfrac{7}{10} \qquad \text{or} \qquad \frac{C_S}{9} \geq \tfrac{7}{10}$$

Thus,

$$C_S \geq \tfrac{63}{10} \qquad \text{or} \qquad C_S \geq 6.3$$

Combining the calculated limits for C_S provides the following range of optimality for the standard-bag profit contribution:

$$6.3 \leq C_S \leq 13.5$$

In the original problem for Par, Inc., the standard bag had a profit contribution of $10. The resulting optimal solution was 540 standard bags and 252 deluxe bags. The range of optimality for C_S tells Par, Inc.'s management that, with other coefficients unchanged, the profit contribution for the standard bag can be anywhere between $6.30 and $13.50 and the production quantities of 540 standard bags and 252 deluxe bags will remain optimal. Note, however, that even though the production quantities will not change, the total profit contribution (value of objective function) will change due to the change in profit contribution per standard bag.

These computations can be repeated, holding the profit contribution for standard bags constant at $C_S = 10$. In this case, the range of optimality for the deluxe-bag profit contribution can be determined. Check to see that this range is $6.67 \leq C_D \leq 14.29$.

In cases where the rotation of the objective function line about an optimal extreme point causes the objective function line to become *vertical,* there will be either no upper limit or no lower limit for the slope as it appears in the form of expression (3.2). To show how this special situation can occur, suppose that the objective function for the Par, Inc., problem is $18C_S + 9C_D$; in this case, extreme point ② in Figure 3.2 provides the optimal solution. Rotating the objective function line counterclockwise around extreme point ② provides an upper limit for the slope when the objective function line coincides with line B. We showed previously that the slope of line B is $-\tfrac{3}{2}$, so the upper limit for the slope of the objective function line must be $-\tfrac{3}{2}$. However, rotating the objective function line clockwise results in the slope becoming more and more negative, approaching a value of minus infinity as the objective function line becomes vertical; in this case, the slope of the objective function has no lower limit. Using the upper limit of $-\frac{3}{2}$, we can write

$$-\frac{C_S}{C_D} \leq -\frac{3}{2}$$

Slope of the
objective function line

Following the previous procedure of holding C_D constant at its original value, $C_D = 9$, we have

$$-\frac{C_S}{9} \leq -\frac{3}{2} \qquad \text{or} \qquad \frac{C_S}{9} \geq \frac{3}{2}$$

Solving for C_S provides the following result:

$$C_S \geq \frac{27}{2} = 13.5$$

In reviewing Figure 3.2 we note that extreme point ② remains optimal for all values of C_S above 13.5. Thus, we obtain the following range of optimality for C_S at extreme point ②:

$$13.5 \leq C_S < \infty$$

Simultaneous Changes   The range of optimality for objective function coefficients is only applicable for changes made to one coefficient at a time. All other coefficients are assumed to be fixed at their initial values. If two or more objective function coefficients are changed simultaneously, further analysis is necessary to determine whether the optimal solution will change. However, when solving two-variable problems graphically,

FIGURE 3.2   GRAPHICAL SOLUTION OF PAR, INC., PROBLEM WITH AN OBJECTIVE
FUNCTION OF $18S + 9D$; OPTIMAL SOLUTION AT EXTREME POINT ②

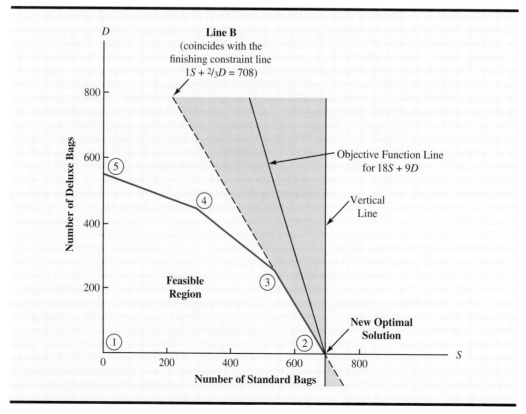

expression (3.2) suggests an easy way to determine whether simultaneous changes in both objective function coefficients will cause a change in the optimal solution. Simply compute the slope of the objective function $(-C_S/C_D)$ for the new coefficient values. If this ratio is greater than or equal to the lower limit on the slope of the objective function and less than or equal to the upper limit, then the changes made will not cause a change in the optimal solution.

Consider changes in both of the objective function coefficients for the Par, Inc., problem. Suppose the profit contribution per standard bag is increased to $13 and the profit contribution per deluxe bag is simultaneously reduced to $8. Recall that the ranges of optimality for C_S and C_D (both computed in a one-at-a-time manner) are

$$6.3 \leq C_S \leq 13.5 \tag{3.3}$$
$$6.67 \leq C_D \leq 14.29 \tag{3.4}$$

For these ranges of optimality, we can conclude that changing either C_S to $13 or C_D to $8 (but not both) would not cause a change in the optimal solution of $S = 540$ and $D = 252$. But we cannot conclude from the ranges of optimality that changing both coefficients simultaneously would not result in a change in the optimal solution.

In expression (3.2) we showed that extreme point ③ remains optimal as long as

$$-\tfrac{3}{2} \leq -\frac{C_S}{C_D} \leq -\tfrac{7}{10}$$

If C_S is changed to 13 and simultaneously C_D is changed to 8, the new objective function slope will be given by

$$-\frac{C_S}{C_D} = -\frac{13}{8} = -1.625$$

Because this value is less than the lower limit of $-\tfrac{3}{2}$, the current solution of $S = 540$ and $D = 252$ will no longer be optimal. By re-solving the problem with $C_S = 13$ and $C_D = 8$, we will find that extreme point ② is the new optimal solution.

Looking at the ranges of optimality, we concluded that changing either C_S to $13 or C_D to $8 (but not both) would not cause a change in the optimal solution. But in recomputing the slope of the objective function with simultaneous changes for both C_S and C_D, we saw that the optimal solution did change. This result emphasizes the fact that a range of optimality, by itself, can only be used to draw a conclusion about changes made to *one objective function coefficient at a time*.

Right-Hand Sides

Let us now consider how a change in the right-hand side for a constraint may affect the feasible region and perhaps cause a change in the optimal solution to the problem. To illustrate this aspect of sensitivity analysis, let us consider what happens if an additional 10 hours of production time become available in the cutting and dyeing department of Par, Inc. The right-hand side of the cutting and dyeing constraint is changed from 630 to 640, and the constraint is rewritten as

$$\tfrac{7}{10}S + 1D \leq 640$$

By obtaining an additional 10 hours of cutting and dyeing time, we expand the feasible region for the problem, as shown in Figure 3.3. With an enlarged feasible region, we now want to determine whether one of the new feasible solutions provides an improvement in the value of the objective function. Application of the graphical solution procedure to the problem with the enlarged feasible region shows that the extreme point with $S = 527.5$ and $D = 270.75$ now provides the optimal solution. The new value for the objective function is

FIGURE 3.3   EFFECT OF A 10-UNIT CHANGE IN THE RIGHT-HAND SIDE
OF THE CUTTING AND DYEING CONSTRAINT

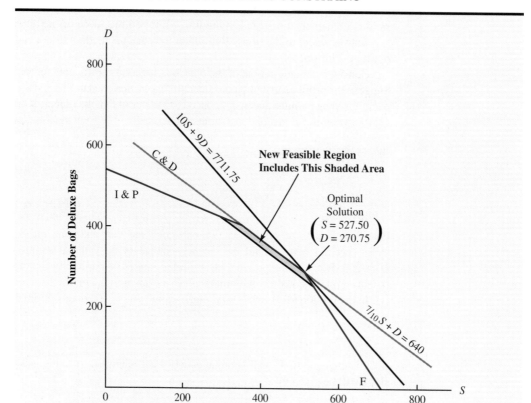

$10(527.5) + 9(270.75) = \$7711.75$, with an increase in profit of $\$7711.75 - \$7668.00 = \$43.75$. Thus, the increased profit occurs at a rate of $\$43.75/10$ hours $= \$4.375$ per hour added.

The *change* in the value of the optimal solution per unit increase in the right-hand side of the constraint is called the **dual value.** Here, the dual value for the cutting and dyeing constraint is $\$4.375$; in other words, if we increase the right-hand side of the cutting and dyeing constraint by 1 hour, the value of the objective function will increase by $\$4.375$. Conversely, if the right-hand side of the cutting and dyeing constraint were to decrease by 1 hour, the objective function would go down by $\$4.375$. The dual value can generally be used to determine what will happen to the value of the objective function when we make a one-unit change in the right-hand side of a constraint.

We caution here that the value of the dual value may be applicable only for small changes in the right-hand side. As more and more resources are obtained and the right-hand-side value continues to increase, other constraints will become binding and limit the change in the value of the objective function. For example, in the problem for Par, Inc., we would eventually reach a point where more cutting and dyeing time would be of no value; it would occur at the point where the cutting and dyeing constraint becomes nonbinding. At this point, the dual value would equal zero. In the next section we will show how to determine the range of values for a right-hand side over which the dual value will accurately predict the improvement in the objective function. Finally, we note that the dual value for any nonbinding constraint will be zero because an increase in the right-hand side of such a constraint will affect only the value of the slack or surplus variable for that constraint.

The dual value is the change in the objective function value per unit increase in a constraint right-hand side. Suppose that we now solve a problem involving the minimization of total cost and that the value of the optimal solution is $100. Furthermore, suppose that the first constraint is a less-than-or-equal-to constraint and that this constraint is binding for the optimal solution. Increasing the right-hand side of this constraint makes the problem easier to solve. Thus, if the right-hand side of this binding constraint is increased by one unit, we expect the optimal objective function value to get better. In the case of a minimization problem, this means that the optimal objective function value gets smaller. If an increase in the right-hand side makes the optimal objective function value smaller, the dual value is negative.

The Management Science in Action, Evaluating Efficiency at Performance Analysis Corporation, illustrates the use of dual values as part of an evaluation model for a chain of fast-food outlets. This type of model will be studied in more detail in Chapter 5 when we discuss an application referred to as data envelopment analysis.

MANAGEMENT SCIENCE IN ACTION

EVALUATING EFFICIENCY AT PERFORMANCE ANALYSIS CORPORATION*

Performance Analysis Corporation specializes in the use of management science to design more efficient and effective operations for a wide variety of chain stores. One such application uses linear programming methodology to provide an evaluation model for a chain of fast-food outlets.

According to the concept of Pareto optimality, a restaurant in a given chain is relatively inefficient if other restaurants in the same chain exhibit the following characteristics:

1. Operate in the same or worse environment
2. Produce at least the same level of *all* outputs
3. Utilize no more of *any* resource and *less* of at least one of the resources

To determine which of the restaurants are Pareto inefficient, Performance Analysis Corporation developed and solved a linear programming model. Model constraints involve requirements concerning the minimum acceptable levels of output and conditions imposed by uncontrollable elements in the environment, and the objective function calls for the minimization of the resources necessary to produce the output. Solving the model produces the following output for each restaurant:

1. A score that assesses the level of so-called relative technical efficiency achieved by the particular restaurant over the time period in question

2. The reduction in controllable resources or the increase of outputs over the time period in question needed for an inefficient restaurant to be rated as efficient

3. A peer group of other restaurants with which each restaurant can be compared in the future

Sensitivity analysis provides important managerial information. For example, for each constraint concerning a minimum acceptable output level, the dual value tells the manager how much one more unit of output would change the efficiency measure.

The analysis typically identifies 40% to 50% of the restaurants as underperforming, given the previously stated conditions concerning the inputs available and outputs produced. Performance Analysis Corporation finds that if all the relative inefficiencies identified are eliminated simultaneously, corporate profits typically increase approximately from 5% to 10%. This increase is truly substantial given the large scale of operations involved.

*Based on information provided by Richard C. Morey of Performance Analysis Corporation.

NOTES AND COMMENTS

1. If two objective function coefficients change simultaneously, both may move outside their respective ranges of optimality and not affect the optimal solution. For instance, in a two-variable linear program, the slope of the objective function will not change at all if both coefficients are changed by the same percentage.

2. Some textbooks and optimization solvers, for example Excel Solver, use the term *shadow price* rather than dual value.

3.3 SENSITIVITY ANALYSIS: COMPUTER SOLUTION

In Section 2.4 we showed how to interpret the output of a linear programming solver. In this section we continue that discussion and show how to interpret the sensitivity analysis output. We use the Par, Inc., problem restated below.

$$\text{Max} \quad 10S + 9D$$

s.t.

$$\frac{7}{10}S + 1D \leq 630 \quad \text{Cutting and dyeing}$$
$$\frac{1}{2}S + \frac{5}{6}D \leq 600 \quad \text{Sewing}$$
$$1S + \frac{2}{3}D \leq 708 \quad \text{Finishing}$$
$$\frac{1}{10}S + \frac{1}{4}D \leq 135 \quad \text{Inspection and packaging}$$
$$S, D \geq 0$$

Let us demonstrate interpreting the sensitivity analysis by considering the solution to the Par, Inc., linear program shown in Figure 3.4.

Interpretation of Computer Output

In Section 2.4 we discussed the output in the top portion of Figure 3.4. We see that the optimal solution is $S = 540$ standard bags and $D = 252$ deluxe bags; the value of the optimal solution is \$7668. Associated with each decision variable is reduced cost. We will interpret the reduced cost after our discussion on dual values.

FIGURE 3.4 THE SOLUTION FOR THE PAR, INC., PROBLEM

MODEL file
Par

Optimal Objective Value =	7668.00000	
Variable	**Value**	**Reduced Cost**
S	540.00000	0.00000
D	252.00000	0.00000

Constraint	**Slack/Surplus**	**Dual Value**
1	0.00000	4.37500
2	120.00000	0.00000
3	0.00000	6.93750
4	18.00000	0.00000

Variable	**Objective Coefficient**	**Allowable Increase**	**Allowable Decrease**
S	10.00000	3.50000	3.70000
D	9.00000	5.28571	2.33333

Constraint	**RHS Value**	**Allowable Increase**	**Allowable Decrease**
1	630.00000	52.36364	134.40000
2	600.00000	Infinite	120.00000
3	708.00000	192.00000	128.00000
4	135.00000	Infinite	18.00000

Immediately following the optimal S and D values and the reduced cost information, the computer output provides information about the constraints. Recall that the Par, Inc., problem had four less-than-or-equal-to constraints corresponding to the hours available in each of four production departments. The information shown in the Slack/Surplus column provides the value of the slack variable for each of the departments. This information is summarized here:

Constraint Number	Constraint Name	Slack
1	Cutting and Dyeing	0
2	Sewing	120
3	Finishing	0
4	Inspection and Packaging	18

From this information, we see that the binding constraints (the cutting and dyeing and the finishing constraints) have zero slack at the optimal solution. The sewing department has 120 hours of slack, or unused capacity, and the inspection and packaging department has 18 hours of slack, or unused capacity.

The Dual Value column contains information about the marginal value of each of the four resources at the optimal solution. In Section 3.2 we defined the *dual value* as follows:

> The dual value associated with a constraint is the *change* in the optimal value of the solution per unit increase in the right-hand side of the constraint.

Try Problem 5 to test your ability to use computer output to determine the optimal solution and to interpret the dual values.

Thus, the nonzero dual values of 4.37500 for constraint 1 (cutting and dyeing constraint) and 6.93750 for constraint 3 (finishing constraint) tell us that an additional hour of cutting and dyeing time increases the value of the optimal solution by \$4.37, and an additional hour of finishing time increases the value of the optimal solution by \$6.94. Thus, if the cutting and dyeing time were increased from 630 to 631 hours, with all other coefficients in the problem remaining the same, Par, Inc.'s profit would be increased by \$4.37, from \$7668 to \$7668 + \$4.37 = \$7672.37. A similar interpretation for the finishing constraint implies that an increase from 708 to 709 hours of available finishing time, with all other coefficients in the problem remaining the same, would increase Par, Inc.'s profit to \$7668 + \$6.94 = \$7674.94. Because the sewing and the inspection and packaging constraints both have slack, or unused capacity, available, the dual values of zero show that additional hours of these two resources will not improve the value of the objective function.

Now that the concept of a dual value has been explained, we define the reduced cost associated with each variable. The **reduced cost** associated with a variable is equal to the dual value for the nonnegativity constraint associated with the variable. From Figure 3.4, we see that the reduced cost on variable S is zero and on variable D is zero. This makes sense. Consider variable S. The nonnegativity constraint is $S \geq 0$. The current value of S is 540, so changing the nonnegativity constraint to $S \geq 1$ has no effect on the optimal solution value. Because increasing the right-hand side by one unit has no effect on the optimal objective function value, the dual value (i.e., reduced cost) of this nonnegativity constraint is zero. A similar argument applies to variable D. In general, if a variable has a nonzero value in the optimal solution, then it will have a reduced cost equal to zero. Later in this section we give an example where the reduced cost of a variable is nonzero, and this example provides more insight on why the term *reduced cost* is used for the nonnegativity constraint dual value.

Referring again to the computer output in Figure 3.4, we see that after providing the constraint information on slack/surplus variables and dual values, the solution output provides ranges for the objective function coefficients and the right-hand sides of the constraints.

Considering the objective function coefficient range analysis, we see that variable S, which has a current profit coefficient of 10, has an *allowable increase* of 3.5 and an *allowable decrease* of 3.7. Therefore, as long as the profit contribution associated with the standard bag is between $10 − $3.7 = $6.30 and $10 + $3.5 = $13.50, the production of $S = 540$ standard bags and $D = 252$ deluxe bags will remain the optimal solution. Therefore, the range of optimality for the objective function coefficient on variable S is from 6.3 to 13.5. Note that the range of optimality is the same as obtained by performing graphical sensitivity analysis for C_S in Section 3.2.

Using the objective function coefficient range information for deluxe bags, we see the following range of optimality (after rounding to two decimal places):

$$9 − 2.33 = 6.67 \leq C_p \leq 9 + 5.29 = 14.29$$

This result tells us that as long as the profit contribution associated with the deluxe bag is between $6.67 and $14.29, the production of $S = 540$ standard bags and $D = 252$ deluxe bags will remain the optimal solution.

The final section of the computer output provides the allowable increase and allowable decrease in the right-hand sides of the constraints relative to the dual values holding. As long as the constraint right-hand side is not increased (decreased) by more than the allowable increase (decrease), the associated dual value gives the exact change in the value of the optimal solution per unit increase in the right-hand side. For example, let us consider the cutting and dyeing constraint with a current right-hand-side value of 630. Because the dual value for this constraint is $4.37, we can conclude that additional hours will increase the objective function by $4.37 per hour. It is also true that a reduction in the hours available will reduce the value of the objective function by $4.37 per hour. From the range information given, we see that the dual value of $4.37 has an allowable increase of 52.36364 and is therefore valid for right-hand-side values up to 630 + 52.36364 = 682.363364. The allowable decrease is 134.4, so the dual value of $4.37 is valid for right-hand-side values down to 630 − 134.4 = 495.6. A similar interpretation for the finishing constraint's right-hand side (constraint 3) shows that the dual value of $6.94 is applicable for increases up to 900 hours and decreases down to 580 hours.

As mentioned, the right-hand-side ranges provide limits within which the dual values give the exact change in the optimal objective function value. For changes outside the range, the problem must be re-solved to find the new optimal solution and the new dual value. We shall call the range over which the dual value is applicable the **range of feasibility.** The ranges of feasibility for the Par, Inc., problem are summarized here:

Try Problem 6 to test your ability to use computer output to determine the ranges of optimality and the ranges of feasibility.

Constraint	Min RHS	Max RHS
Cutting and Dyeing	495.6	682.4
Sewing	480.0	No upper limit
Finishing	580.0	900.0
Inspection and Packaging	117.0	No upper limit

As long as the values of the right-hand sides are within these ranges, the dual values shown on the computer output will not change. Right-hand-side values outside these limits will result in changes in the dual value information.

Cautionary Note on the Interpretation of Dual Values

As stated previously, the dual value is the change in the value of the optimal solution per unit increase in the right-hand side of a constraint. When the right-hand side of the constraint represents the amount of a resource available, the associated dual value is often interpreted as the maximum amount one should be willing to pay for one additional unit of the resource.

However, such an interpretation is not always correct. To see why, we need to understand the difference between sunk and relevant costs. A **sunk cost** is one that is not affected by the decision made. It will be incurred no matter what values the decision variables assume. A **relevant cost** is one that depends on the decision made. The amount of a relevant cost will vary depending on the values of the decision variables.

Let us reconsider the Par, Inc., problem. The amount of cutting and dyeing time available is 630 hours. The cost of the time available is a sunk cost if it must be paid regardless of the number of standard and deluxe golf bags produced. It would be a relevant cost if Par, Inc., only had to pay for the number of hours of cutting and dyeing time actually used to produce golf bags. All relevant costs should be reflected in the objective function of a linear program. Sunk costs should not be reflected in the objective function. For Par, Inc., we have been assuming that the company must pay its employees' wages regardless of whether their time on the job is completely utilized. Therefore, the cost of the labor-hours resource for Par, Inc., is a sunk cost and has not been reflected in the objective function.

Only relevant costs should be included in the objective function.

When the cost of a resource is *sunk,* the dual value can be interpreted as the maximum amount the company should be willing to pay for one additional unit of the resource. When the cost of a resource used is relevant, the dual value can be interpreted as the amount by which the value of the resource exceeds its cost. Thus, when the resource cost is relevant, the dual value can be interpreted as the maximum premium over the normal cost that the company should be willing to pay for one unit of the resource.

The Modified Par, Inc., Problem

The graphical solution procedure is useful only for linear programs involving two decision variables. In practice, the problems solved using linear programming usually involve a large number of variables and constraints. For instance, the Management Science in Action, Determining Optimal Production Quantities at GE Plastics, describes how a linear programming model with 3100 variables and 1100 constraints was solved in less than 10 seconds to determine the optimal production quantities at GE Plastics. In this section we discuss the formulation and computer solution for two linear programs with three decision variables. In doing so, we will show how to interpret the reduced-cost portion of the computer output.

The original Par, Inc., problem is restated as follows:

$$\text{Max} \quad 10S + 9D$$

s.t.

$$\tfrac{7}{10}S + 1D \leq 630 \quad \text{Cutting and dyeing}$$
$$\tfrac{1}{2}S + \tfrac{5}{6}D \leq 600 \quad \text{Sewing}$$
$$1S + \tfrac{2}{3}D \leq 708 \quad \text{Finishing}$$
$$\tfrac{1}{10}S + \tfrac{1}{4}D \leq 135 \quad \text{Inspection and packaging}$$
$$S, D \geq 0$$

Recall that S is the number of standard golf bags produced and D is the number of deluxe golf bags produced. Suppose that management is also considering producing a lightweight model designed specifically for golfers who prefer to carry their bags. The design department estimates that each new lightweight model will require 0.8 hours for cutting and dyeing, 1 hour for sewing, 1 hour for finishing, and 0.25 hours for inspection and packaging. Because of the unique capabilities designed into the new model, Par, Inc.'s management feels they will realize a profit contribution of $12.85 for each lightweight model produced during the current production period.

Let us consider the modifications in the original linear programming model that are needed to incorporate the effect of this additional decision variable. We will let L denote the number of lightweight bags produced. After adding L to the objective function and to each of the four constraints, we obtain the following linear program for the modified problem:

$$\text{Max} \quad 10S + 9D + 12.85L$$

s.t.

$$\begin{aligned}
\tfrac{7}{10}S + 1D + 0.8L &\leq 630 \quad \text{Cutting and dyeing} \\
\tfrac{1}{2}S + \tfrac{5}{6}D + 1L &\leq 600 \quad \text{Sewing} \\
1S + \tfrac{2}{3}D + 1L &\leq 708 \quad \text{Finishing} \\
\tfrac{1}{10}S + \tfrac{1}{4}D + \tfrac{1}{4}L &\leq 135 \quad \text{Inspection and packaging} \\
S, D, L &\geq 0
\end{aligned}$$

Figure 3.5 shows the solution to the modified problem. We see that the optimal solution calls for the production of 280 standard bags, 0 deluxe bags, and 428 of the new lightweight bags; the value of the optimal solution is $8299.80.

Let us now look at the information contained in the Reduced Cost column. Recall that the reduced costs are the dual values of the corresponding nonnegativity constraints. As the computer output shows, the reduced costs for S and L are zero because these decision variables already have positive values in the optimal solution. However, the reduced cost for decision variable D is -1.15. The interpretation of this number is that if the production of deluxe bags is increased from the current level of 0 to 1, then the optimal objective function value will decrease by 1.15. Another interpretation is that if we "reduce the cost" of deluxe bags by 1.15 (i.e., increase the contribution margin by 1.15), then there is an optimal solution where we produce a nonzero number of deluxe bags.

FIGURE 3.5   SOLUTION FOR THE MODIFIED PAR, INC., PROBLEM

MODEL *file*

ParMod

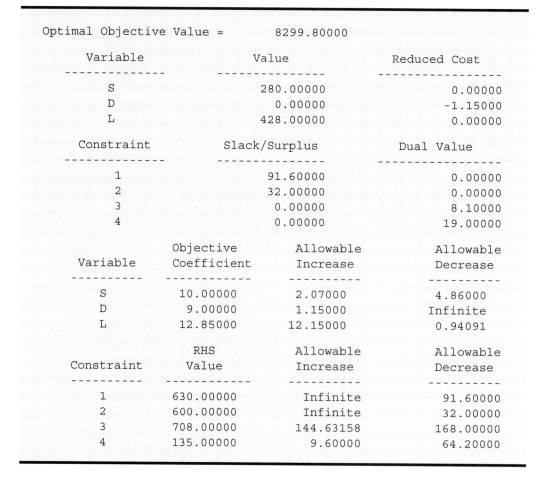

```
Optimal Objective Value =          8299.80000

      Variable              Value              Reduced Cost
    --------------      --------------      ------------------
         S                280.00000               0.00000
         D                  0.00000              -1.15000
         L                428.00000               0.00000

     Constraint          Slack/Surplus            Dual Value
    --------------      --------------      ------------------
         1                 91.60000               0.00000
         2                 32.00000               0.00000
         3                  0.00000               8.10000
         4                  0.00000              19.00000

                        Objective           Allowable           Allowable
      Variable          Coefficient         Increase            Decrease
    ----------        ------------        ----------          ----------
         S               10.00000            2.07000             4.86000
         D                9.00000            1.15000            Infinite
         L               12.85000           12.15000             0.94091

                          RHS               Allowable           Allowable
     Constraint          Value              Increase            Decrease
    ----------        ------------        ----------          ----------
         1              630.00000            Infinite            91.60000
         2              600.00000            Infinite            32.00000
         3              708.00000           144.63158           168.00000
         4              135.00000             9.60000            64.20000
```

Suppose we increase the coefficient of D by exactly $1.15 so that the new value is $9 + $1.15 = $10.15 and then re-solve. Figure 3.6 shows the new solution. Note that although D assumes a positive value in the new solution, the value of the optimal solution has not changed. In other words, increasing the profit contribution of D by *exactly* the amount of the reduced cost has resulted in alternative optimal solutions. Depending on the computer software package used to optimize this model, you may or may not see D assume a positive value if you re-solve the problem with an objective function coefficient of exactly 10.15 for D—that is, the software package may show a different alternative optimal solution. However, if the profit contribution of D is increased by *more than* $1.15, then D will not remain at zero in the optimal solution.

We also note from Figure 3.6 that the dual values for constraints 3 and 4 are 8.1 and 19, respectively, indicating that these two constraints are binding in the optimal solution. Thus, each additional hour in the finishing department would increase the value of the optimal solution by $8.10, and each additional hour in the inspection and packaging department would increase the value of the optimal solution by $19.00. Because of a slack of 91.6 hours in the cutting and dyeing department and 32 hours in the sewing department (see Figure 3.6), management might want to consider the possibility of utilizing these unused labor-hours in the finishing or inspection and packaging departments. For example, some of the employees in the cutting and dyeing department could be used to perform certain operations in either the finishing department or the inspection and packaging department. In the future, Par, Inc.'s management may want to explore the possibility of cross-training employees so that unused capacity in one department could be shifted to other departments. In the next chapter we will consider similar modeling situations.

FIGURE 3.6   SOLUTION FOR THE MODIFIED PAR, INC., PROBLEM WITH THE COEFFICIENT OF D INCREASED BY $1.15

Optimal Objective Value =   8299.80000

Variable	Value	Reduced Cost
S	403.78378	0.00000
D	222.81081	0.00000
L	155.67568	0.00000

Constraint	Slack/Surplus	Dual Value
1	0.00000	0.00000
2	56.75676	0.00000
3	0.00000	8.10000
4	0.00000	19.00000

Variable	Objective Coefficient	Allowable Increase	Allowable Decrease
S	10.00000	2.51071	0.00000
D	10.15000	5.25790	0.00000
L	12.85000	0.00000	2.19688

Constraint	RHS Value	Allowable Increase	Allowable Decrease
1	630.00000	52.36364	91.60000
2	600.00000	Infinite	56.75676
3	708.00000	144.63158	128.00000
4	135.00000	16.15385	18.00000

NOTES AND COMMENTS

1. Computer software packages for solving linear programs are readily available. Most of these provide the optimal solution, dual value or shadow price information, the range of optimality for the objective function coefficients, and the range of feasibility for the right-hand sides. The labels used for the ranges of optimality and feasibility may vary, but the meaning is the same as what we have described here.

2. Whenever one of the right-hand sides is at an end point of its range of feasibility, the dual values and shadow prices only provide one-sided information. In this case, they only predict the change in the optimal value of the objective function for changes toward the interior of the range.

3. A condition called *degeneracy* can cause a subtle difference in how we interpret changes in the objective function coefficients beyond the end points of the range of optimality. Degeneracy occurs when the dual value equals zero for one of the binding constraints. Degeneracy does not affect the interpretation of changes toward the interior of the range of optimality. However, when degeneracy is present, changes beyond the end points of the range do not necessarily mean a different solution will be optimal. From a practical point of view, changes beyond the end points of the range of optimality necessitate re-solving the problem.

4. Managers are frequently called on to provide an economic justification for new technology. Often the new technology is developed, or purchased, in order to conserve resources. The dual value can be helpful in such cases because it can be used to determine the savings attributable to the new technology by showing the savings per unit of resource conserved.

MANAGEMENT SCIENCE IN ACTION

DETERMINING OPTIMAL PRODUCTION QUANTITIES AT GE PLASTICS*

In 2007 GEP was acquired by the Saudi Basic Industries Corporation (SABIC) and relaunched as the subsidiary company SABIC Innovative Plasitcs. SABIC is the largest company in the Middle East, and one of the largest companies in the world. Here we continue to refer to GEP instead of SABIC because the company was known as GE Plastics at the time of this example.

GE Plastics (GEP) is a $5 billion global materials supplier of plastics and raw materials to many industries (e.g., automotive, computer, and medical equipment). GEP has plants all over the globe. In the past, GEP followed a pole-centric manufacturing approach wherein each product was manufactured in the geographic area (Americas, Europe, or Pacific) where it was to be delivered. When many of GEP's customers started shifting their manufacturing operations to the Pacific, a geographic imbalance was created between GEP's capacity and demand in the form of overcapacity in the Americas and undercapacity in the Pacific.

Recognizing that a pole-centric approach was no longer effective, GEP adopted a global approach to its manufacturing operations. Initial work focused on the high-performance polymers (HPP) division. Using a linear programming model, GEP was able to determine the optimal production quantities at each HPP plant to maximize the total contribution margin for the division. The model included demand constraints, manufacturing capacity constraints, and constraints that modeled the flow of materials produced at resin plants to the finishing plants and on to warehouses in three geographical regions (Americas, Europe, and Pacific). The mathematical model for a one-year problem has 3100 variables and 1100 constraints, and can be solved in less than 10 seconds. The new system proved successful at the HPP division, and other GE Plastics divisions are adapting it for their supply chain planning.

*Based on R. Tyagi, P. Kalish, and K. Akbay, "GE Plastics Optimizes the Two-Echelon Global Fulfillment Network at Its High-Performance Polymers Division," *Interfaces* (September/October 2004): 359–366.

3.4   LIMITATIONS OF CLASSICAL SENSITIVITY ANALYSIS

As we have seen, classical sensitivity analysis obtained from computer output can provide useful information on the sensitivity of the solution to changes in the model input data. However, classical sensitivity analysis provided by most computer packages does have its limitations. In this section we discuss three such limitations: simultaneous changes in input data, changes in constraint coefficients, and nonintuitive dual values. We give examples of these three cases and discuss how to effectively deal with these through re-solving the model with changes. In fact, in our experience, it is rarely the case that one solves a model once and makes a recommendaiton. More often than not, a series of models are solved using a variety of input data sets before a final plan is adopted. With improved algorithms and more powerful computers, solving multiple runs of a model is extremely cost and time effective.

Simultaneous Changes

The sensitivity analysis information in computer output is based on the assumption that only one coefficient changes; it is assumed that all other coefficients will remain as stated in the original problem. Thus, the range analysis for the objective function coefficients and the constraint right-hand sides is only applicable for changes in a single coefficient. In many cases, however, we are interested in what would happen if two or more coefficients are changed simultaneously.

Let us consider again the modified Par, Inc., problem, whose solution appears in Figure 3.5. Suppose that after we have solved the problem, we find a new supplier from whom we can purchase the leather required for these bags at a lower cost. Leather is an important component of each of the three types of bags, but is used in different amounts in each type. After factoring in the new cost of leather, the profit margin per bag is found to be $10.30 for a standard bag, $11.40 for a deluxe bag, and $12.97 for a lightweight bag. Does the current plan from Figure 3.5 remain optimal? We can easily answer this question by simply re-solving the model using the new profit margins as the objective function coefficients. That is, we use as our objective function: Maximize $10.3S + 11.4D + 12.97L$ with the same set of constraints as in the original model. The solution to this problem appears in Figure 3.7. The new optimal profit is $8718.13. All three types of bags should be produced.

FIGURE 3.7   THE SOLUTION FOR THE MODIFIED PAR, INC., PROBLEM WITH
REVISED OBJECTIVE FUNCTION COEFFICIENTS

Optimal Objective Value =	8718.12973	
Variable	Value	Reduced Cost
S	403.78378	0.00000
D	222.81081	0.00000
L	155.67568	0.00000

Constraint	Slack/Surplus	Dual Value
1	0.00000	3.08919
2	56.75676	0.00000
3	0.00000	6.56351
4	0.00000	15.74054

Variable	Objective Coefficient	Allowable Increase	Allowable Decrease
S	10.30000	2.08000	2.28600
D	11.40000	4.26053	1.27000
L	12.97000	1.03909	1.82000

Constraint	RHS Value	Allowable Increase	Allowable Decrease
1	630.00000	52.36364	91.60000
2	600.00000	Infinite	56.75676
3	708.00000	144.63158	128.00000
4	135.00000	16.15385	18.00000

Suppose we had not re-solved the model with the new objective function coefficients. We would have used the solution from the original model, the solution found in Figure 3.5. Our profit would have therefore been $10.3(280) + $11.40(0) + $12.97(428) = $8435.16. By re-solving the model with the new information and using the revised plan in Figure 3.7, we have increased total profit by $8718.13 − $8435.16 = $282.97.

Changes in Constraint Coefficients

Classical sensitivity analysis provides no information about changes resulting from a change in the coefficient of a variable in a constraint. To illustrate such a case and how we may deal with it, let us again consider the Modified Par, Inc., problem discussed in Section 3.3.

Suppose we are considering the adoption of a new technology that will allow us to more efficiently finish standard bags. This technology is dedicated to standard bags and would decrease the finishing time on a standard bag from its current value of 1 to ½ of an hour. The technology would not impact the finishing time of deluxe or lightweight bags. The finishing constraint under the new sceanario is

$$\tfrac{1}{2}S + \tfrac{2}{3}D + 1L \leq 708 \quad \text{Finishing with new technology}$$

Even though this is a single change in a coefficient in the model, there is no way to tell from classical sensitivity analysis what impact the change in the coefficient of S will have on the solution. Instead, we must simply change the coefficient and rerun the model. The solution appears in Figure 3.8. Note that the optimal number of standard bags has increased from

FIGURE 3.8   THE SOLUTION FOR THE MODIFIED PAR, INC., PROBLEM WITH NEW STANDARD BAG FINISHING TECHNOLOGY

```
Optimal Objective Value =          9471.31579

        Variable                  Value              Reduced Cost
     --------------          ---------------        -----------------
          S                     521.05263                0.00000
          D                       0.00000               -6.40789
          L                     331.57895                0.00000

      Constraint             Slack/Surplus             Dual Value
     --------------          ---------------        -----------------
          1                       0.00000               12.78947
          2                       7.89474                0.00000
          3                     115.89474                0.00000
          4                       0.00000               10.47368

                         Objective          Allowable           Allowable
        Variable        Coefficient          Increase            Decrease
     ------------      -------------       ------------        ------------
          S              10.00000            1.24375             4.86000
          D               9.00000            6.40789            Infinite
          L              12.85000           12.15000             1.42143

                            RHS             Allowable           Allowable
       Constraint          Value            Increase            Decrease
     ------------      -------------       ------------        ------------
          1             630.00000           30.00000           198.00000
          2             600.00000           Infinite             7.89474
          3             708.00000           Infinite           115.89474
          4             135.00000            2.50000            45.00000
```

280 to 521.1, and the optimal number of lightweight bags decreased from 428 to 331.6. It remains optimal to produce no deluxe bags. Most importantly, with the new technology, the optimal profit increased from $8299.80 to $9471.32, an increase of $1171.52. Using this information with the cost of the new technology will provide an estimate for mangement as to how long it will take to pay off the new technology based on the increase in profits.

Nonintuitive Dual Values

Constraints with variables naturally on both the left-hand and right-hand sides often lead to dual values that have a nonintuitve explantion. To illustrate such a case and how we may deal with it, let us reconsider the Modified Par, Inc., problem discussed in Section 3.3.

Suppose that after reviewing the solution shown in Figure 3.5, management states that they will not consider any solution that does not include the production of some deluxe bags. Management then decides to add the requirement that the number of deluxe bags produced must be at least 30% of the number of standard bags produced. Writing this requirement using the decision variables S and D, we obtain

$$D \geq 0.3S$$

This new constraint is constraint 5 in the modified Par, Inc., linear program. Re-solving the problem with the new constraint 5 yields the optimal solution shown in Figure 3.9.

FIGURE 3.9   THE SOLUTION FOR THE MODIFIED PAR, INC., PROBLEM WITH THE DELUXE BAG REQUIREMENT

Optimal Objective Value =   8183.88000

Variable	Value	Reduced Cost
S	336.00000	0.00000
D	100.80000	0.00000
L	304.80000	0.00000

Constraint	Slack/Surplus	Dual Value
1	50.16000	0.00000
2	43.20000	0.00000
3	0.00000	7.41000
4	0.00000	21.76000
5	0.00000	-1.38000

Variable	Objective Coefficient	Allowable Increase	Allowable Decrease
S	10.00000	2.07000	3.70500
D	9.00000	1.15000	12.35000
L	12.85000	5.29286	0.94091

Constraint	RHS Value	Allowable Increase	Allowable Decrease
1	630.00000	Infinite	50.16000
2	600.00000	Infinite	43.20000
3	708.00000	57.00000	168.00000
4	135.00000	12.00000	31.75000
5	0.00000	101.67568	84.00000

Let us consider the interpretation of the dual value for constraint 5, the requirement that the number of deluxe bags produced must be at least 30% of the number of standard bags produced. The dual value of -1.38 indicates that a one-unit increase in the right-hand side of the constraint will lower profits by $1.38. Thus, what the dual value of -1.38 is really telling us is what will happen to the value of the optimal solution if the constraint is changed to

$$D \geq 0.3S + 1$$

The interpretation of the dual value of -1.38 is correctly stated as follows: If we are forced to produce one deluxe bag over and above the minimum 30% requirement, total profits will decrease by $1.38. Conversely, if we relax the minimum 30% requirement by one bag ($D \geq 0.3S - 1$), total profits will increase by $1.38.

We might instead be more interested in what happens when the requirement of 30% is increased to 31%. Note that dual value does *not* tell us what will happen in this case. Also, because 0.30 is the coefficient of a variable in a constraint rather than an objective function coefficient or right-hand side, no range analysis is given. Note that this is the case just discussed in the previous section. Because there is no way to get this information directly from classical sensitivity analysis, to answer such a question, we need to re-solve the problem using the constraint $D \geq 0.31S$. To test the sensitivity of the solution to changes in the percentage required, we can re-solve the model replacing 0.30 with any percentage of interest.

To get a feel for how the required percentage impacts total profit, we solved versions of the Par, Inc., model with the required percentage varying from 5% to 100% in increments of 5%. This resulted in 20 different versions of the model to be solved. The impact of changing this percentage on the total profit is shown in Figure 3.10, and results are shown in Table 3.1.

What have we learned from this analysis? Notice from Figure 3.10 that the slope of the graph becomes steeper for values greater than 55%. This indicates that there is a shift

FIGURE 3.10   PROFIT FOR VARIOUS VALUES OF REQUIRED PERCENTAGE FOR DELUXE BAGS AS A PERECENTAGE OF STANDARD BAGS

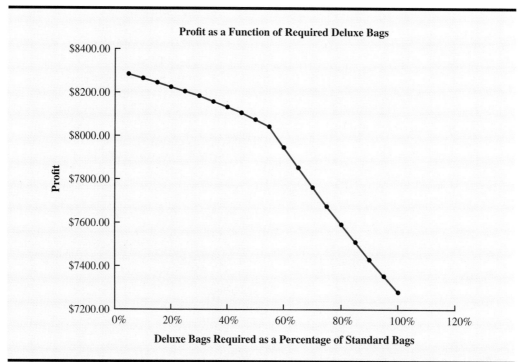

TABLE 3.1 SOLUTIONS FOR VARIOUS VALUES OF REQUIRED PERCENTAGE
FOR DELUXE BAGS AS A PERCENTAGE OF STANDARD BAGS

Percent	Profit	Standard	Deluxe	Lightweight
5%	$8283.24	287.9999	14.4000	410.4000
10%	$8265.71	296.4704	29.6470	391.7648
15%	$8247.11	305.4543	45.8181	372.0002
20%	$8227.35	314.9996	62.9999	351.0002
25%	$8206.31	325.1608	81.2902	328.6455
30%	$8183.88	335.9993	100.7998	304.8005
35%	$8159.89	347.5854	121.6549	279.3110
40%	$8134.20	359.9990	143.9996	252.0008
45%	$8106.60	373.3321	167.9994	222.6677
50%	$8076.87	387.6908	193.8454	191.0783
55%	$8044.77	403.1982	221.7590	156.9617
60%	$7948.80	396.0000	237.6000	144.0000
65%	$7854.27	388.2353	252.3529	132.3529
70%	$7763.37	380.7692	266.5385	121.1538
75%	$7675.90	373.5849	280.1887	110.3774
80%	$7591.67	366.6667	293.3333	100.0000
85%	$7510.50	360.0000	306.0000	90.0000
90%	$7432.23	353.5714	318.2143	80.3571
95%	$7356.71	347.3684	330.0000	71.0526
100%	$7283.79	341.3793	341.3793	62.0690

in the rate of deterioration in profit starting at 55%. Hence, we see that percentages less than or equal to 55% result in modest loss of profit. More pronounced loss of profit results from percentages greater than 55%. So, management now knows that 30% is a reasonable requirement from a profit point of view and that extending the requirement beyond 55% will lead to a more significant loss of profit. From Table 3.1, as we increase the percentage required, fewer lightweight bags are produced.

3.5 THE ELECTRONIC COMMUNICATIONS PROBLEM

The Electronic Communications problem is a maximization problem involving four decision variables, two less-than-or-equal-to constraints, one equality constraint, and one greater-than-or-equal-to constraint. Our objective is to provide a summary of the process of formulating a mathematical model, using software to obtain an optimal solution, and interpreting the solution and sensitivity report information. In the next chapter we will continue to illustrate how linear programming can be applied by showing additional examples from the areas of marketing, finance, and production management. Your ability to formulate, solve, and interpret the solution to problems like the Electronic Communications problem is critical to understanding how more complex problems can be modeled using linear programming.

Electronic Communications manufactures portable radio systems that can be used for two-way communications. The company's new product, which has a range of up to 25 miles, is particularly suitable for use in a variety of business and personal applications. The distribution channels for the new radio are as follows:

1. Marine equipment distributors
2. Business equipment distributors
3. National chain of retail stores
4. Direct mail

TABLE 3.2   PROFIT, ADVERTISING COST, AND PERSONAL SALES TIME DATA
FOR THE ELECTRONIC COMMUNICATIONS PROBLEM

Distribution Channel	Profit per Unit Sold ($)	Advertising Cost per Unit Sold ($)	Personal Sales Effort per Unit Sold (hours)
Marine distributors	90	10	2
Business distributors	84	8	3
National retail stores	70	9	3
Direct mail	60	15	None

Because of differing distribution and promotional costs, the profitability of the product will vary with the distribution channel. In addition, the advertising cost and the personal sales effort required will vary with the distribution channels. Table 3.2 summarizes the contribution to profit, advertising cost, and personal sales effort data pertaining to the Electronic Communications problem. The firm set the advertising budget at $5000, and a maximum of 1800 hours of salesforce time is available for allocation to the sales effort. Management also decided to produce exactly 600 units for the current production period. Finally, an ongoing contract with the national chain of retail stores requires that at least 150 units be distributed through this distribution channel.

Electronic Communications is now faced with the problem of establishing a strategy that will provide for the distribution of the radios in such a way that overall profitability of the new radio production will be maximized. Decisions must be made as to how many units should be allocated to each of the four distribution channels, as well as how to allocate the advertising budget and salesforce effort to each of the four distribution channels.

Problem Formulation

We will now write the objective function and the constraints for the Electronic Communications problem. For the objective function, we can write

Objective function: Maximize profit

Four constraints are necessary for this problem. They are necessary because of (1) a limited advertising budget, (2) limited salesforce availability, (3) a production requirement, and (4) a retail stores distribution requirement.

Constraint 1: Advertising expenditures ≤ Budget

Constraint 2: Sales time used ≤ Time available

Constraint 3: Radios produced = Management requirement

Constraint 4: Retail distribution ≥ Contract requirement

These expressions provide descriptions of the objective function and the constraints. We are now ready to define the decision variables that will represent the decisions the manager must make.

For the Electronic Communications problem, we introduce the following four decision variables:

M = the number of units produced for the marine equipment distribution channel

B = the number of units produced for the business equipment distribution channel

R = the number of units produced for the national retail chain distribution channel

D = the number of units produced for the direct mail distribution channel

Using the data in Table 3.2, the objective function for maximizing the total contribution to profit associated with the radios can be written as follows:

$$\text{Max } 90M + 84B + 70R + 60D$$

Let us now develop a mathematical statement of the constraints for the problem. Because the advertising budget is set at \$5000, the constraint that limits the amount of advertising expenditure can be written as follows:

$$10M + 8B + 9R + 15D \leq 5000$$

Similarly, because the sales time is limited to 1800 hours, we obtain the constraint

$$2M + 3B + 3R \leq 1800$$

Management's decision to produce exactly 600 units during the current production period is expressed as

$$M + B + R + D = 600$$

Finally, to account for the fact that the number of units distributed by the national chain of retail stores must be at least 150, we add the constraint

$$R \geq 150$$

Combining all of the constraints with the nonnegativity requirements enables us to write the complete linear programming model for the Electronic Communications problem as follows:

$$
\begin{array}{lll}
\text{Max} & 90M + 84B + 70R + 60D & \\
\text{s.t.} & & \\
& 10M + 8B + 9R + 15D \leq 5000 & \text{Advertising budget} \\
& 2M + 3B + 3R \leq 1800 & \text{Salesforce availability} \\
& M + B + R + D = 600 & \text{Production level} \\
& R \geq 150 & \text{Retail stores requirement} \\
& M, B, R, D \geq 0 &
\end{array}
$$

Computer Solution and Interpretation

This problem can be solved using either Excel Solver or LINGO. A portion of the standard solution output for the Electronic Communications problem is shown in Figure 3.11. The Objective Function Value section shows that the optimal solution to the problem will provide a maximum profit of \$48,450. The optimal values of the decision variables are given by $M = 25$, $B = 425$, $R = 150$, and $D = 0$.

Thus, the optimal strategy for Electronic Communications is to concentrate on the business equipment distribution channel with $B = 425$ units. In addition, the firm should allocate 25 units to the marine distribution channel ($M = 25$) and meet its 150-unit commitment to the national retail chain store distribution channel ($R = 150$). With $D = 0$, the optimal solution indicates that the firm should not use the direct mail distribution channel.

Now consider the information contained in the Reduced Cost column. Recall that the reduced cost of a variable is the dual value of the corresponding nonnegativity constraint. As the computer output shows, the first three reduced costs are zero because the corresponding decision variables already have positive values in the optimal solution. However, the reduced cost of –45 for decision variable D tells us that profit will decrease by \$45 for every unit produced for the direct mail channel. Stated another way, the profit for the new radios distributed via the direct mail channel would have to increase from its current value of \$60 per unit, by \$45 per unit, to at least \$60 + \$45 = \$105 per unit before it would be profitable to use the direct mail distribution channel.

The computer output information for the slack/surplus variables and the dual values is restated in Figure 3.12.

FIGURE 3.11   A PORTION OF THE COMPUTER OUTPUT FOR THE ELECTRONIC
COMMUNICATIONS PROBLEM

Electronic

```
Optimal Objective Value =          48450.00000

          Variable                 Value              Reduced Cost
        --------------          ---------------      -----------------

             M                     25.00000              0.00000
             B                    425.00000              0.00000
             R                    150.00000              0.00000
             D                      0.00000            -45.00000

          Constraint            Slack/Surplus           Dual Value
        --------------          ---------------      -----------------

             1                      0.00000              3.00000
             2                     25.00000              0.00000
             3                      0.00000             60.00000
             4                      0.00000            -17.00000
```

FIGURE 3.12   OBJECTIVE COEFFICIENT AND RIGHT-HAND-SIDE RANGES FOR THE
ELECTRONIC COMMUNICATIONS PROBLEM

Electronic

```
Optimal Objective Value =          48450.00000

          Variable                 Value              Reduced Cost
        --------------          ---------------      -----------------

             M                     25.00000              0.00000
             B                    425.00000              0.00000
             R                    150.00000              0.00000
             D                      0.00000            -45.00000

          Constraint            Slack/Surplus           Dual Value
        --------------          ---------------      -----------------

             1                      0.00000              3.00000
             2                     25.00000              0.00000
             3                      0.00000             60.00000
             4                      0.00000            -17.00000
```

Variable	Objective Coefficient	Allowable Increase	Allowable Decrease
M	90.00000	Infinite	6.00000
B	84.00000	6.00000	34.00000
R	70.00000	17.00000	Infinite
D	60.00000	45.00000	Infinite

Constraint	RHS Value	Allowable Increase	Allowable Decrease
1	5000.00000	850.00000	50.00000
2	1800.00000	Infinite	25.00000
3	600.00000	3.57143	85.00000
4	150.00000	50.00000	150.00000

The advertising budget constraint has a slack of zero, indicating that the entire budget of $5000 has been used. The corresponding dual value of 3 tells us that an additional dollar added to the advertising budget will increase the objective function (increase the profit) by $3. Thus, the possibility of increasing the advertising budget should be seriously considered by the firm. The slack of 25 hours for the salesforce availability constraint shows that the allocated 1800 hours of sales time are adequate to distribute the radios produced and that 25 hours of sales time will remain unused. Because the production level constraint is an equality constraint, the zero slack/surplus shown on the output is expected. However, the dual value of 60 associated with this constraint shows that if the firm were to consider increasing the production level for the radios, the value of the objective function, or profit, would improve at the rate of $60 per radio produced. Finally, the surplus of zero associated with the retail store distribution channel commitment is a result of this constraint being binding. The negative dual value indicates that increasing the commitment from 150 to 151 units will actually decrease the profit by $17. Thus, Electronic Communications may want to consider reducing its commitment to the retail store distribution channel. A *decrease* in the commitment will actually improve profit at the rate of $17 per unit.

We now consider the additional sensitivity analysis information provided by the computer output shown in Figure 3.12. The allowable increases and decreases for the objective function coefficients are as follows:

Objective Coefficient	Allowable Increase	Allowable Decrease
90.00000	Infinite	6.00000
84.00000	6.00000	34.00000
70.00000	17.00000	Infinite
60.00000	45.00000	Infinite

The current solution or strategy remains optimal, provided that the objective function coefficients do not increase or decrease by more than the allowed amount. Consider the allowable increase and decrease of the direct mail distribution channel coefficient. This information is consistent with the earlier observation for the Reduced Costs portion of the output. In both instances, we see that the per-unit profit would have to increase by $45 to $105 before the direct mail distribution channel could be in the optimal solution with a positive value.

Finally, the sensitivity analysis information on right-hand-side ranges, as shown in Figure 3.12, provides the allowable increase and decrease for the right-hand-side values.

RHS Value	Allowable Increase	Allowable Decrease
5000.00000	850.00000	50.00000
1800.00000	Infinite	25.00000
600.00000	3.57143	85.00000
150.00000	50.00000	150.00000

Try Problems 12 and 13 to test your ability at interpreting the computer output for problems involving more than two decision variables.

Several interpretations of these ranges are possible. In particular, recall that the dual value for the advertising budget enabled us to conclude that each $1 increase in the budget would increase the profit by $3. The current advertising budget is $5000. The allowable increase in the advertising budget is $850 and this implies that there is value in increasing the budget up to an advertising budget of $5850. Increases above this level would not necessarily be beneficial. Also note that the dual value of −17 for the retail stores requirement suggested the desirability of reducing this commitment. The allowable decrease for this constraint is 150,

TABLE 3.3 PROFIT-MAXIMIZING STRATEGY FOR THE ELECTRONIC COMMUNICATIONS PROBLEM

Distribution Channel	Volume	Advertising Allocation	Salesforce Allocation (hours)
Marine distributors	25	$ 250	50
Business distributors	425	3400	1275
National retail stores	150	1350	450
Direct mail	0	0	0
Totals	600	$5000	1775

Projected total profit = $48,450

and this implies that the commitment could be reduced to zero and the value of the reduction would be at the rate of $17 per unit.

Again, the *sensitivity analysis* provided by computer software packages for linear programming problems considers only *one change at a time,* with all other coefficients of the problem remaining as originally specified. As mentioned earlier, simultaneous changes are best handled by re-solving the problem.

Finally, recall that the complete solution to the Electronic Communications problem requested information not only on the number of units to be distributed over each channel, but also on the allocation of the advertising budget and the salesforce effort to each distribution channel. For the optimal solution of $M = 25$, $B = 425$, $R = 150$, and $D = 0$, we can simply evaluate each term in a given constraint to determine how much of the constraint resource is allocated to each distribution channel. For example, the advertising budget constraint of

$$10M + 8B + 9R + 15D \leq 5000$$

shows that $10M = 10(25) = \$250$, $8B = 8(425) = \$3400$, $9R = 9(150) = \$1350$, and $15D = 15(0) = \$0$. Thus, the advertising budget allocations are, respectively, $250, $3400, $1350, and $0 for each of the four distribution channels. Making similar calculations for the salesforce constraint results in the managerial summary of the Electronic Communications optimal solution as shown in Table 3.3.

SUMMARY

We began the chapter with a discussion of sensitivity analysis: the study of how changes in the coefficients of a linear program affect the optimal solution. First, we showed how a graphical method can be used to determine how a change in one of the objective function coefficients or a change in the right-hand-side value for a constraint will affect the optimal solution to the problem. Because graphical sensitivity analysis is limited to linear programs with two decision variables, we showed how to use software to produce a sensitivity report containing the same information.

We continued our discussion of problem formulation, sensitivity analysis and its limitations, and the interpretation of the solution by introducing several modifications of the Par, Inc., problem. They involved an additional decision variable and several types of percentage, or ratio, constraints. Then, in order to provide additional practice in formulating and interpreting the solution for linear programs involving more than two decision variables, we introduced the Electronic Communications problem, a maximization problem with four decision variables, two less-than-or-equal-to constraints, one equality constraint, and one greater-than-or-equal-to constraint.

The Management Science in Action, Tea Production and Distribution in India, illustrates the diversity of problems in which linear programming can be applied and the importance of sensitivity analysis. In the next chapter we will see many more applications of linear programming.

MANAGEMENT SCIENCE IN ACTION

TEA PRODUCTION AND DISTRIBUTION IN INDIA*

In India, one of the largest tea producers in the world, approximately $1 billion of tea packets and loose tea are sold. Duncan Industries Limited (DIL), the third largest producer of tea in the Indian tea market, sells about $37.5 million of tea, almost all of which is sold in packets.

DIL has 16 tea gardens, three blending units, six packing units, and 22 depots. Tea from the gardens is sent to blending units, which then mix various grades of tea to produce blends such as Sargam, Double Diamond, and Runglee Rungliot. The blended tea is transported to packing units, where it is placed in packets of different sizes and shapes to produce about 120 different product lines. For example, one line is Sargam tea packed in 500-gram cartons, another line is Double Diamond packed in 100-gram pouches, and so on. The tea is then shipped to the depots that supply 11,500 distributors through whom the needs of approximately 325,000 retailers are satisfied.

For the coming month, sales managers provide estimates of the demand for each line of tea at each depot. Using these estimates, a team of senior managers would determine the amounts of loose tea of each blend to ship to each packing unit, the quantity of each line of tea to be packed at each packing unit, and the amounts of packed tea of each line to be transported from each packing unit to the various depots. This process requires two to three days each month and often results in stockouts of lines in demand at specific depots.

Consequently, a linear programming model involving approximately 7000 decision variables and 1500 constraints was developed to minimize the company's freight cost while satisfying demand, supply, and all operational constraints. The model was tested on past data and showed that stockouts could be prevented at little or no additional cost. Moreover, the model was able to provide management with the ability to perform various what-if types of exercises, convincing them of the potential benefits of using management science techniques to support the decision-making process.

*Based on Nilotpal Chakravarti, "Tea Company Steeped in OR," *OR/MS Today* (April 2000).

GLOSSARY

Dual value   The change in the value of the objective function per unit increase in the right-hand side of a constraint.

Objective function allowable increase (decrease)   The allowable increase/decrease of an objective function coefficient is the amount the coefficient may increase (decrease) without causing any change in the values of the decision variables in the optimal solution. The allowable increase/decrease for the objective function coefficients can be used to calculate the range of optimality.

Range of feasibility   The range of values over which the dual value is applicable.

Range of optimality   The range of values over which an objective function coefficient may vary without causing any change in the values of the decision variables in the optimal solution.

Reduced cost   The reduced cost of a variable is equal to the dual value on the nonnegativity constraint for that variable.

Relevant cost   A cost that depends upon the decision made. The amount of a relevant cost will vary depending on the values of the decision variables.

Right-hand-side allowable increase (decrease)   The allowable increase (decrease) of the right-hand side of a constraint is the amount the right-hand side may increase (decrease) without causing any change in the dual value for that constraint. The allowable increase (decrease) for the right-hand side can be used to calculate the range of feasibility for that constraint.

Sensitivity analysis   The study of how changes in the coefficients of a linear programming problem affect the optimal solution.

Sunk cost   A cost that is not affected by the decision made. It will be incurred no matter what values the decision variables assume.

PROBLEMS

1. Consider the following linear program:

$$\text{Max} \quad 3A + 2B$$

s.t.

$$1A + 1B \leq 10$$
$$3A + 1B \leq 24$$
$$1A + 2B \leq 16$$
$$A, B \geq 0$$

a. Use the graphical solution procedure to find the optimal solution.
b. Assume that the objective function coefficient for A changes from 3 to 5. Does the optimal solution change? Use the graphical solution procedure to find the new optimal solution.
c. Assume that the objective function coefficient for A remains 3, but the objective function coefficient for B changes from 2 to 4. Does the optimal solution change? Use the graphical solution procedure to find the new optimal solution.
d. The computer solution for the linear program in part (a) provides the following objective coefficient range information:

Variable	Objective Coefficient	Allowable Increase	Allowable Decrease
A	3.00000	3.00000	1.00000
B	2.00000	1.00000	1.00000

Use this objective coefficient range information to answer parts (b) and (c).

2. Consider the linear program in Problem 1. The value of the optimal solution is 27. Suppose that the right-hand side for constraint 1 is increased from 10 to 11.
a. Use the graphical solution procedure to find the new optimal solution.
b. Use the solution to part (a) to determine the dual value for constraint 1.
c. The computer solution for the linear program in Problem 1 provides the following right-hand-side range information:

Constraint	RHS Value	Allowable Increase	Allowable Decrease
1	10.00000	1.20000	2.00000
2	24.00000	6.00000	6.00000
3	16.00000	Infinite	3.00000

What does the right-hand-side range information for constraint 1 tell you about the dual value for constraint 1?
d. The dual value for constraint 2 is 0.5. Using this dual value and the right-hand-side range information in part (c), what conclusion can be drawn about the effect of changes to the right-hand side of constraint 2?

3. Consider the following linear program:

$$\text{Min} \quad 8X + 12Y$$

s.t.

$$1X + 3Y \geq 9$$
$$2X + 2Y \geq 10$$
$$6X + 2Y \geq 18$$
$$A, B \geq 0$$

a. Use the graphical solution procedure to find the optimal solution.
b. Assume that the objective function coefficient for X changes from 8 to 6. Does the optimal solution change? Use the graphical solution procedure to find the new optimal solution.
c. Assume that the objective function coefficient for X remains 8, but the objective function coefficient for Y changes from 12 to 6. Does the optimal solution change? Use the graphical solution procedure to find the new optimal solution.
d. The computer solution for the linear program in part (a) provides the following objective coefficient range information:

Variable	Objective Coefficient	Allowable Increase	Allowable Decrease
X	8.00000	4.00000	4.00000
Y	12.00000	12.00000	4.00000

How would this objective coefficient range information help you answer parts (b) and (c) prior to re-solving the problem?

4. Consider the linear program in Problem 3. The value of the optimal solution is 48. Suppose that the right-hand side for constraint 1 is increased from 9 to 10.
a. Use the graphical solution procedure to find the new optimal solution.
b. Use the solution to part (a) to determine the dual value for constraint 1.
c. The computer solution for the linear program in Problem 3 provides the following right-hand-side range information:

Constraint	RHS Value	Allowable Increase	Allowable Decrease
1	9.00000	2.00000	4.00000
2	10.00000	8.00000	1.00000
3	18.00000	4.00000	Infinite

What does the right-hand-side range information for constraint 1 tell you about the dual value for constraint 1?
d. The dual value for constraint 2 is 3. Using this dual value and the right-hand-side range information in part (c), what conclusion can be drawn about the effect of changes to the right-hand side of constraint 2?

 SELF*test*

5. Refer to the Kelson Sporting Equipment problem (Chapter 2, Problem 24). Letting

$$R = \text{number of regular gloves}$$
$$C = \text{number of catcher's mitts}$$

leads to the following formulation:

$$\text{Max} \quad 5R + 8C$$

s.t.

$$R + \tfrac{3}{2}C \leq 900 \quad \text{Cutting and sewing}$$
$$\tfrac{1}{2}R + \tfrac{1}{3}C \leq 300 \quad \text{Finishing}$$
$$\tfrac{1}{8}R + \tfrac{1}{4}C \leq 100 \quad \text{Packaging and shipping}$$
$$R, C \geq 0$$

The computer solution is shown in Figure 3.13.
a. What is the optimal solution, and what is the value of the total profit contribution?
b. Which constraints are binding?

FIGURE 3.13   THE SOLUTION FOR THE KELSON SPORTING EQUIPMENT PROBLEM

```
Optimal Objective Value =              3700.00000

        Variable              Value              Reduced Cost
     --------------     ---------------     ------------------
           R                500.00000                 0.00000
           C                150.00000                 0.00000

       Constraint         Slack/Surplus            Dual Value
     --------------     ---------------     ------------------
           1                175.00000                 0.00000
           2                  0.00000                 3.00000
           3                  0.00000                28.00000

                       Objective         Allowable          Allowable
        Variable       Coefficient       Increase           Decrease
     -----------     ------------     -----------        -----------
           R            5.00000          7.00000            1.00000
           C            8.00000          2.00000            4.66667

                          RHS            Allowable          Allowable
       Constraint        Value           Increase           Decrease
     -----------     ------------     -----------        -----------
           1           900.00000        Infinite          175.00000
           2           300.00000       100.00000          166.66667
           3           100.00000        35.00000           25.00000
```

c. What are the dual values for the resources? Interpret each.

d. If overtime can be scheduled in one of the departments, where would you recommend doing so?

 SELF*test*

6. Refer to the computer solution of the Kelson Sporting Equipment problem in Figure 3.13 (see Problem 5).

   a. Determine the objective coefficient ranges.

   b. Interpret the ranges in part (a).

   c. Interpret the right-hand-side ranges.

   d. How much will the value of the optimal solution improve if 20 extra hours of packaging and shipping time are made available?

7. Investment Advisors, Inc., is a brokerage firm that manages stock portfolios for a number of clients. A particular portfolio consists of U shares of U.S. Oil and H shares of Huber Steel. The annual return for U.S. Oil is $3 per share and the annual return for Huber Steel is $5 per share. U.S. Oil sells for $25 per share and Huber Steel sells for $50 per share. The portfolio has $80,000 to be invested. The portfolio risk index (0.50 per share of U.S. Oil and 0.25 per share for Huber Steel) has a maximum of 700. In addition, the portfolio is limited to a maximum of 1000 shares of U.S. Oil. The linear programming formulation that will maximize the total annual return of the portfolio is as follows:

$$\text{Max} \quad 3U + 5H \qquad \text{Maximize total annual return}$$

s.t.

$$25U + 50H \leq 80{,}000 \qquad \text{Funds available}$$
$$0.50U + 0.25D \leq \quad 700 \qquad \text{Risk maximum}$$
$$1U \qquad\quad \leq \ 1000 \qquad \text{U.S. Oil maximum}$$
$$U, H \geq 0$$

Problems

FIGURE 3.14 THE SOLUTION FOR THE INVESTMENT ADVISORS PROBLEM

```
Optimal Objective Value =            8400.00000

        Variable              Value          Reduced Cost
    ---------------      ---------------     ---------------
           U                800.00000            0.00000
           H               1200.00000            0.00000

       Constraint         Slack/Surplus        Dual Value
    ---------------      ---------------     ---------------
           1                  0.00000            0.09333
           2                  0.00000            1.33333
           3                200.00000            0.00000

                      Objective       Allowable         Allowable
        Variable      Coefficient     Increase          Decrease
    ----------      ------------    ----------      ----------
           U           3.00000        7.00000          0.50000
           H           5.00000        1.00000          3.50000

                         RHS         Allowable         Allowable
     Constraint         Value        Increase          Decrease
    ----------      ------------    ----------      ----------
           1        80000.00000     60000.00000     15000.00000
           2          700.00000        75.00000       300.00000
           3         1000.00000        Infinite       200.00000
```

The computer solution of this problem is shown in Figure 3.14.
   a. What is the optimal solution, and what is the value of the total annual return?
   b. Which constraints are binding? What is your interpretation of these constraints in terms of the problem?
   c. What are the dual values for the constraints? Interpret each.
   d. Would it be beneficial to increase the maximum amount invested in U.S. Oil? Why or why not?

8. Refer to Figure 3.14, which shows the computer solution of Problem 7.
   a. How much would the return for U.S. Oil have to increase before it would be beneficial to increase the investment in this stock?
   b. How much would the return for Huber Steel have to decrease before it would be beneficial to reduce the investment in this stock?
   c. How much would the total annual return be reduced if the U.S. Oil maximum were reduced to 900 shares?

9. Recall the TJ Inc.'s problem (Chapter 2, Problem 28). Letting

$$W = \text{jars of Western Foods Salsa}$$
$$M = \text{jars of Mexico City Salsa}$$

leads to the formulation:

Max $1W + 1.25M$
s.t.
$$5W + 7M \leq 4480 \quad \text{Whole tomatoes}$$
$$3W + 1M \leq 2080 \quad \text{Tomato sauce}$$
$$2W + 2M \leq 1600 \quad \text{Tomato paste}$$
$$W, M \geq 0$$

FIGURE 3.15   THE SOLUTION FOR THE TJ INC.'S PROBLEM

```
Optimal Objective Value =          860.00000

        Variable              Value              Reduced Cost
      ------------        ------------          ------------
          W                560.00000               0.00000
          M                240.00000               0.00000

      Constraint          Slack/Surplus            Dual Value
      ------------        ------------          ------------
          1                  0.00000               0.12500
          2                160.00000               0.00000
          3                  0.00000               0.18750
```

Variable	Objective Coefficient	Allowable Increase	Allowable Decrease
W	1.00000	0.25000	0.10714
M	1.25000	0.15000	0.25000

Constraint	RHS Value	Allowable Increase	Allowable Decrease
1	4480.00000	1120.00000	160.00000
2	2080.00000	Infinite	160.00000
3	1600.00000	40.00000	320.00000

The computer solution is shown in Figure 3.15.
   a.   What is the optimal solution, and what are the optimal production quantities?
   b.   Specify the objective function ranges.
   c.   What are the dual values for each constraint? Interpret each.
   d.   Identify each of the right-hand-side ranges.

10.   Recall the Innis Investments problem (Chapter 2, Problem 39). Letting

$$S = \text{units purchased in the stock fund}$$
$$M = \text{units purchased in the money market fund}$$

leads to the following formulation:

$$
\begin{array}{llll}
\text{Min} & 8S + & 3M & \\
\text{s.t.} & & & \\
& 50S + 100M \le & 1{,}200{,}000 & \text{Funds available} \\
& 5S + \ \ 4M \ge & 60{,}000 & \text{Annual income} \\
& M \ge & 3{,}000 & \text{Units in money market} \\
& S, M \ge 0 & &
\end{array}
$$

The computer solution is shown in Figure 3.16.
   a.   What is the optimal solution, and what is the minimum total risk?
   b.   Specify the objective coefficient ranges.
   c.   How much annual income will be earned by the portfolio?
   d.   What is the rate of return for the portfolio?
   e.   What is the dual value for the funds available constraint?
   f.   What is the marginal rate of return on extra funds added to the portfolio?

FIGURE 3.16 THE SOLUTION FOR THE INNIS INVESTMENTS PROBLEM

```
Optimal Objective Value =            62000.00000

        Variable              Value              Reduced Cost
      -----------         -------------         --------------
          S                4000.00000              0.00000
          M               10000.00000              0.00000


       Constraint         Slack/Surplus           Dual Value
      -----------         -------------         --------------
          1                   0.00000              -0.05667
          2                   0.00000               2.16667
          3                7000.00000               0.00000


                         Objective        Allowable          Allowable
        Variable        Coefficient        Increase           Decrease
      -----------       -----------       ----------         ----------
          S                8.00000         Infinite           4.25000
          M                3.00000          3.40000           Infinite


                            RHS           Allowable          Allowable
       Constraint          Value          Increase           Decrease
      -----------       -----------       ----------         ----------
          1            1200000.00000     300000.00000       420000.00000
          2              60000.00000      42000.00000        12000.00000
          3               3000.00000       7000.00000         Infinite
```

11. Refer to Problem 10 and the computer solution shown in Figure 3.16.
   a. Suppose the risk index for the stock fund (the value of C_S) increases from its current value of 8 to 12. How does the optimal solution change, if at all?
   b. Suppose the risk index for the money market fund (the value of C_M) increases from its current value of 3 to 3.5. How does the optimal solution change, if at all?
   c. Suppose C_S increases to 12 and C_M increases to 3.5. How does the optimal solution change, if at all?

 SELF*test*

12. Quality Air Conditioning manufactures three home air conditioners: an economy model, a standard model, and a deluxe model. The profits per unit are $63, $95, and $135, respectively. The production requirements per unit are as follows:

	Number of Fans	Number of Cooling Coils	Manufacturing Time (hours)
Economy	1	1	8
Standard	1	2	12
Deluxe	1	4	14

For the coming production period, the company has 200 fan motors, 320 cooling coils, and 2400 hours of manufacturing time available. How many economy models (E), standard models (S), and deluxe models (D) should the company produce in order to maximize profit? The linear programming model for the problem is as follows:

Max $63E + 95S + 135D$

s.t.

$$1E + 1S + 1D \le 200 \quad \text{Fan motors}$$
$$1E + 2S + 4D \le 320 \quad \text{Cooling coils}$$
$$8E + 12S + 14D \le 2400 \quad \text{Manufacturing time}$$
$$E, S, D \ge 0$$

FIGURE 3.17   THE SOLUTION FOR THE QUALITY AIR CONDITIONING PROBLEM

Optimal Objective Value =   16440.00000

Variable	Value	Reduced Cost
E	80.00000	0.00000
S	120.00000	0.00000
D	0.00000	-24.00000

Constraint	Slack/Surplus	Dual Value
1	0.00000	31.00000
2	0.00000	32.00000
3	320.00000	0.00000

Variable	Objective Coefficient	Allowable Increase	Allowable Decrease
E	63.00000	12.00000	15.50000
S	95.00000	31.00000	8.00000
D	135.00000	24.00000	Infinite

Constraint	RHS Value	Allowable Increase	Allowable Decrease
1	200.00000	80.00000	40.00000
2	320.00000	80.00000	120.00000
3	2400.00000	Infinite	320.00000

The computer solution is shown in Figure 3.17.

a. What is the optimal solution, and what is the value of the objective function?
b. Which constraints are binding?
c. Which constraint shows extra capacity? How much?
d. If the profit for the deluxe model were increased to $150 per unit, would the optimal solution change? Use the information in Figure 3.17 to answer this question.

13. Refer to the computer solution of Problem 12 in Figure 3.17.
   a. Identify the range of optimality for each objective function coefficient.
   b. Suppose the profit for the economy model is increased by $6 per unit, the profit for the standard model is decreased by $2 per unit, and the profit for the deluxe model is increased by $4 per unit. What will the new optimal solution be?
   c. Identify the range of feasibility for the right-hand-side values.
   d. If the number of fan motors available for production is increased by 100, will the dual value for that constraint change? Explain.

14. Digital Controls, Inc. (DCI), manufactures two models of a radar gun used by police to monitor the speed of automobiles. Model A has an accuracy of plus or minus 1 mile per hour, whereas the smaller model B has an accuracy of plus or minus 3 miles per hour. For the next week, the company has orders for 100 units of model A and 150 units of model B. Although DCI purchases all the electronic components used in both models, the plastic cases for both models are manufactured at a DCI plant in Newark, New Jersey. Each model A case requires 4 minutes of injection-molding time and 6 minutes of assembly time. Each model B case requires 3 minutes of injection-molding time and 8 minutes of assembly time. For next week, the Newark plant has 600 minutes of injection-molding time available and 1080 minutes of assembly time available. The manufacturing cost is

$10 per case for model A and $6 per case for model B. Depending upon demand and the time available at the Newark plant, DCI occasionally purchases cases for one or both models from an outside supplier in order to fill customer orders that could not be filled otherwise. The purchase cost is $14 for each model A case and $9 for each model B case. Management wants to develop a minimum cost plan that will determine how many cases of each model should be produced at the Newark plant and how many cases of each model should be purchased. The following decision variables were used to formulate a linear programming model for this problem:

$$AM = \text{number of cases of model A manufactured}$$
$$BM = \text{number of cases of model B manufactured}$$
$$AP = \text{number of cases of model A purchased}$$
$$BP = \text{number of cases of model B purchased}$$

The linear programming model that can be used to solve this problem is as follows:

$$\text{Min} \quad 10AM + 6BM + 14AP + 9BP$$

s.t.

$1AM +$		$+ 1AP +$	$=$	100	Demand for model A
	$1BM +$	$1BP =$		150	Demand for model B
$4AM + 3BM$			$\leq$	600	Injection molding time
$6AM + 8BM$			$\leq$	1080	Assembly time
$AM, BM, AP, BP \geq 0$					

The computer solution is shown in Figure 3.18.
a. What is the optimal solution and what is the optimal value of the objective function?
b. Which constraints are binding?
c. What are the dual values? Interpret each.
d. If you could change the right-hand side of one constraint by one unit, which one would you choose? Why?

15. Refer to the computer solution to Problem 14 in Figure 3.18.
a. Interpret the ranges of optimality for the objective function coefficients.
b. Suppose that the manufacturing cost increases to $11.20 per case for model A. What is the new optimal solution?
c. Suppose that the manufacturing cost increases to $11.20 per case for model A and the manufacturing cost for model B decreases to $5 per unit. Would the optimal solution change?

16. Tucker, Inc., produces high-quality suits and sport coats for men. Each suit requires 1.2 hours of cutting time and 0.7 hours of sewing time, uses 6 yards of material, and provides a profit contribution of $190. Each sport coat requires 0.8 hours of cutting time and 0.6 hours of sewing time, uses 4 yards of material, and provides a profit contribution of $150. For the coming week, 200 hours of cutting time, 180 hours of sewing time, and 1200 yards of fabric are available. Additional cutting and sewing time can be obtained by scheduling overtime for these operations. Each hour of overtime for the cutting operation increases the hourly cost by $15, and each hour of overtime for the sewing operation increases the hourly cost by $10. A maximum of 100 hours of overtime can be scheduled. Marketing requirements specify a minimum production of 100 suits and 75 sport coats. Let

$$S = \text{number of suits produced}$$
$$SC = \text{number of sport coats produced}$$
$$D1 = \text{hours of overtime for the cutting operation}$$
$$D2 = \text{hours of overtime for the sewing operation}$$

The computer solution is shown in Figure 3.19.
a. What is the optimal solution, and what is the total profit? What is the plan for the use of overtime?

FIGURE 3.18 THE SOLUTION FOR THE DIGITAL CONTROLS, INC., PROBLEM

```
Optimal Objective Value =          2170.00000
```

Variable	Value	Reduced Cost
AB	100.00000	0.00000
BM	60.00000	0.00000
AP	0.00000	1.75000
BP	90.00000	0.00000

Constraint	Slack/Surplus	Dual Value
1	0.00000	12.25000
2	0.00000	9.00000
3	20.00000	0.00000
4	0.00000	-0.37500

Variable	Objective Coefficient	Allowable Increase	Allowable Decrease
AB	10.00000	1.75000	Infinite
BM	6.00000	3.00000	2.33333
AP	14.00000	Infinite	1.75000
BP	9.00000	2.33333	3.00000

Constraint	RHS Value	Allowable Increase	Allowable Decrease
1	100.00000	11.42857	100.00000
2	150.00000	Infinite	90.00000
3	600.00000	Infinite	20.00000
4	1080.00000	53.33333	480.00000

b. A price increase for suits is being considered that would result in a profit contribution of $210 per suit. If this price increase is undertaken, how will the optimal solution change?

c. Discuss the need for additional material during the coming week. If a rush order for material can be placed at the usual price plus an extra $8 per yard for handling, would you recommend the company consider placing a rush order for material? What is the maximum price Tucker would be willing to pay for an additional yard of material? How many additional yards of material should Tucker consider ordering?

d. Suppose the minimum production requirement for suits is lowered to 75. Would this change help or hurt profit? Explain.

17. The Porsche Club of America sponsors driver education events that provide high-performance driving instruction on actual race tracks. Because safety is a primary consideration at such events, many owners elect to install roll bars in their cars. Deegan Industries manufactures two types of roll bars for Porsches. Model DRB is bolted to the car using existing holes in the car's frame. Model DRW is a heavier roll bar that must be welded to the car's frame. Model DRB requires 20 pounds of a special high alloy steel, 40 minutes of manufacturing time, and 60 minutes of assembly time. Model DRW requires 25 pounds of the special high alloy steel, 100 minutes of manufacturing time, and 40 minutes of assembly time. Deegan's steel supplier indicated that at most 40,000 pounds of the high-alloy steel will be available next quarter. In addition, Deegan estimates that 2000 hours of manufacturing time and 1600 hours of assembly time will be available next quarter. The profit contributions are

FIGURE 3.19 THE SOLUTION FOR THE TUCKER, INC., PROBLEM

```
Optimal Objective Value =        40900.00000
```

Variable	Value	Reduced Cost
S	100.00000	0.00000
SC	150.00000	0.00000
D1	40.00000	0.00000
D2	0.00000	-10.00000

Constraint	Slack/Surplus	Dual Value
1	0.00000	15.00000
2	20.00000	0.00000
3	0.00000	34.50000
4	60.00000	0.00000
5	0.00000	-35.00000
6	75.00000	0.00000

Variable	Objective Coefficient	Allowable Increase	Allowable Decrease
S	190.00000	35.00000	Infinite
SC	150.00000	Infinite	23.33333
D1	-15.00000	15.00000	172.50000
D2	-10.00000	10.00000	Infinite

Constraint	RHS Value	Allowable Increase	Allowable Decrease
1	200.00000	40.00000	60.00000
2	180.00000	Infinite	20.00000
3	1200.00000	133.33333	200.00000
4	100.00000	Infinite	60.00000
5	100.00000	50.00000	100.00000
6	75.00000	75.00000	Infinite

$200 per unit for model DRB and $280 per unit for model DRW. The linear programming model for this problem is as follows:

$$\text{Max} \quad 200DRB + 280DRW$$

s.t.

$$20DRB + 25DRW \le 40{,}000 \quad \text{Steel available}$$
$$40DRB + 100DRW \le 120{,}000 \quad \text{Manufacturing minutes}$$
$$60DRB + 40DRW \le 96{,}000 \quad \text{Assembly minutes}$$
$$DRB, DRW \ge 0$$

The computer solution is shown in Figure 3.20.

a. What are the optimal solution and the total profit contribution?
b. Another supplier offered to provide Deegan Industries with an additional 500 pounds of the steel alloy at $2 per pound. Should Deegan purchase the additional pounds of the steel alloy? Explain.

FIGURE 3.20   THE SOLUTION FOR THE DEEGAN INDUSTRIES PROBLEM

```
Optimal Objective Value =         424000.00000

        Variable              Value              Reduced Cost
     --------------      ---------------      ------------------

          DRB               1000.00000              0.00000
          DRW                800.00000              0.00000


       Constraint         Slack/Surplus           Dual Value
     --------------      ---------------      ------------------

           1                  0.00000              8.80000
           2                  0.00000              0.60000
           3               4000.00000              0.00000


                        Objective          Allowable           Allowable
        Variable        Coefficient        Increase            Decrease
     ----------      ------------       ----------        ----------

          DRB            200.00000         24.00000           88.00000
          DRW            280.00000        220.00000           30.00000


                          RHS            Allowable           Allowable
       Constraint        Value           Increase            Decrease
     ----------      ------------       ----------        ----------

           1          40000.00000        909.09091        10000.00000
           2         120000.00000      40000.00000         5714.28571
           3          96000.00000         Infinite         4000.00000
```

c. Deegan is considering using overtime to increase the available assembly time. What would you advise Deegan to do regarding this option? Explain.

d. Because of increased competition, Deegan is considering reducing the price of model DRB such that the new contribution to profit is $175 per unit. How would this change in price affect the optimal solution? Explain.

e. If the available manufacturing time is increased by 500 hours, will the dual value for the manufacturing time constraint change? Explain.

18. Davison Electronics manufactures two models of LCD televisions, identified as model A and model B. Each model has its lowest possible production cost when produced on Davison's new production line. However, the new production line does not have the capacity to handle the total production of both models. As a result, at least some of the production must be routed to a higher-cost, old production line. The following table shows the minimum production requirements for next month, the production line capacities in units per month, and the production cost per unit for each production line:

Model	Production Cost per Unit		Minimum Production Requirements
	New Line	**Old Line**	
A	$30	$50	50,000
B	$25	$40	70,000
Production Line Capacity	80,000	60,000	

Let

AN = Units of model A produced on the new production line

AO = Units of model A produced on the old production line

BN = Units of model B produced on the new production line

BO = Units of model B produced on the old production line

Davison's objective is to determine the minimum cost production plan. The computer solution is shown in Figure 3.21.

a. Formulate the linear programming model for this problem using the following four constraints:

Constraint 1: Minimum production for model A
Constraint 2: Minimum production for model B
Constraint 3: Capacity of the new production line
Constraint 4: Capacity of the old production line

b. Using computer solution in Figure 3.21, what is the optimal solution, and what is the total production cost associated with this solution?

c. Which constraints are binding? Explain.

FIGURE 3.21   THE SOLUTION FOR THE DAVISON INDUSTRIES PROBLEM

```
Optimal Objective Value =            3850000.00000

        Variable                 Value              Reduced Cost
     --------------        ---------------        -----------------

          AN                 50000.00000               0.00000
          AO                     0.00000               5.00000
          BN                 30000.00000               0.00000
          BO                 40000.00000               0.00000


       Constraint          Slack/Surplus             Dual Value
     --------------        ---------------        -----------------

           1                     0.00000              45.00000
           2                     0.00000              40.00000
           3                     0.00000             -15.00000
           4                 20000.00000               0.00000


                          Objective           Allowable           Allowable
        Variable          Coefficient         Increase            Decrease
     ----------        ------------        ----------        ----------

          AN                30.00000            5.00000            Infinite
          AO                50.00000            Infinite           5.00000
          BN                25.00000           15.00000            5.00000
          BO                40.00000            5.00000           15.00000


                             RHS              Allowable           Allowable
       Constraint           Value             Increase            Decrease
     ----------        ------------        ----------        ----------

           1             50000.00000        20000.00000        40000.00000
           2             70000.00000        20000.00000        40000.00000
           3             80000.00000        40000.00000        20000.00000
           4             60000.00000            Infinite       20000.00000
```

   d. The production manager noted that the only constraint with a positive dual value is the constraint on the capacity of the new production line. The manager's interpretation of the dual value was that a one-unit increase in the right-hand side of this constraint would actually increase the total production cost by $15 per unit. Do you agree with this interpretation? Would an increase in capacity for the new production line be desirable? Explain.

   e. Would you recommend increasing the capacity of the old production line? Explain.

   f. The production cost for model A on the old production line is $50 per unit. How much would this cost have to change to make it worthwhile to produce model A on the old production line? Explain.

   g. Suppose that the minimum production requirement for model B is reduced from 70,000 units to 60,000 units. What effect would this change have on the total production cost? Explain.

Problems 19–32 require formulation and computer solution.

19. Better Products, Inc., manufactures three products on two machines. In a typical week, 40 hours are available on each machine. The profit contribution and production time in hours per unit are as follows:

Category	Product 1	Product 2	Product 3
Profit/unit	$30	$50	$20
Machine 1 time/unit	0.5	2.0	0.75
Machine 2 time/unit	1.0	1.0	0.5

Two operators are required for machine 1; thus, 2 hours of labor must be scheduled for each hour of machine 1 time. Only one operator is required for machine 2. A maximum of 100 labor-hours is available for assignment to the machines during the coming week. Other production requirements are that product 1 cannot account for more than 50% of the units produced and that product 3 must account for at least 20% of the units produced.

   a. How many units of each product should be produced to maximize the total profit contribution? What is the projected weekly profit associated with your solution?

   b. How many hours of production time will be scheduled on each machine?

   c. What is the value of an additional hour of labor?

   d. Assume that labor capacity can be increased to 120 hours. Would you be interested in using the additional 20 hours available for this resource? Develop the optimal product mix assuming the extra hours are made available.

20. Adirondack Savings Bank (ASB) has $1 million in new funds that must be allocated to home loans, personal loans, and automobile loans. The annual rates of return for the three types of loans are 7% for home loans, 12% for personal loans, and 9% for automobile loans. The bank's planning committee has decided that at least 40% of the new funds must be allocated to home loans. In addition, the planning committee has specified that the amount allocated to personal loans cannot exceed 60% of the amount allocated to automobile loans.

   a. Formulate a linear programming model that can be used to determine the amount of funds ASB should allocate to each type of loan in order to maximize the total annual return for the new funds.

   b. How much should be allocated to each type of loan? What is the total annual return? What is the annual percentage return?

   c. If the interest rate on home loans increased to 9%, would the amount allocated to each type of loan change? Explain.

   d. Suppose the total amount of new funds available was increased by $10,000. What effect would this have on the total annual return? Explain.

e. Assume that ASB has the original $1 million in new funds available and that the planning committee has agreed to relax the requirement that at least 40% of the new funds must be allocated to home loans by 1%. How much would the annual return change? How much would the annual percentage return change?

21. Round Tree Manor is a hotel that provides two types of rooms with three rental classes: Super Saver, Deluxe, and Business. The profit per night for each type of room and rental class is as follows:

| | | Rental Class | | |
		Super Saver	Deluxe	Business
Room	Type I	$30	$35	—
	Type II	$20	$30	$40

Type I rooms do not have high-speed Internet access and are not available for the Business rental class.

Round Tree's management makes a forecast of the demand by rental class for each night in the future. A linear programming model developed to maximize profit is used to determine how many reservations to accept for each rental class. The demand forecast for a particular night is 130 rentals in the Super Saver class, 60 rentals in the Deluxe class, and 50 rentals in the Business class. Round Tree has 100 Type I rooms and 120 Type II rooms.

a. Use linear programming to determine how many reservations to accept in each rental class and how the reservations should be allocated to room types. Is the demand by any rental class not satisfied? Explain.

b. How many reservations can be accommodated in each rental class?

c. Management is considering offering a free breakfast to anyone upgrading from a Super Saver reservation to Deluxe class. If the cost of the breakfast to Round Tree is $5, should this incentive be offered?

d. With a little work, an unused office area could be converted to a rental room. If the conversion cost is the same for both types of rooms, would you recommend converting the office to a Type I or a Type II room? Why?

e. Could the linear programming model be modified to plan for the allocation of rental demand for the next night? What information would be needed and how would the model change?

22. Industrial Designs has been awarded a contract to design a label for a new wine produced by Lake View Winery. The company estimates that 150 hours will be required to complete the project. The firm's three graphic designers available for assignment to this project are Lisa, a senior designer and team leader; David, a senior designer; and Sarah, a junior designer. Because Lisa has worked on several projects for Lake View Winery, management specified that Lisa must be assigned at least 40% of the total number of hours assigned to the two senior designers. To provide label-designing experience for Sarah, she must be assigned at least 15% of the total project time. However, the number of hours assigned to Sarah must not exceed 25% of the total number of hours assigned to the two senior designers. Due to other project commitments, Lisa has a maximum of 50 hours available to work on this project. Hourly wage rates are $30 for Lisa, $25 for David, and $18 for Sarah.

a. Formulate a linear program that can be used to determine the number of hours each graphic designer should be assigned to the project in order to minimize total cost.

b. How many hours should each graphic designer be assigned to the project? What is the total cost?

c. Suppose Lisa could be assigned more than 50 hours. What effect would this have on the optimal solution? Explain.

d. If Sarah were not required to work a minimum number of hours on this project, would the optimal solution change? Explain.

23. Vollmer Manufacturing makes three components for sale to refrigeration companies. The components are processed on two machines: a shaper and a grinder. The times (in minutes) required on each machine are as follows:

	Machine	
Component	Shaper	Grinder
1	6	4
2	4	5
3	4	2

The shaper is available for 120 hours, and the grinder is available for 110 hours. No more than 200 units of component 3 can be sold, but up to 1000 units of each of the other components can be sold. In fact, the company already has orders for 600 units of component 1 that must be satisfied. The profit contributions for components 1, 2, and 3 are $8, $6, and $9, respectively.

a. Formulate and solve for the recommended production quantities.
b. What are the objective coefficient ranges for the three components? Interpret these ranges for company management.
c. What are the right-hand-side ranges? Interpret these ranges for company management.
d. If more time could be made available on the grinder, how much would it be worth?
e. If more units of component 3 can be sold by reducing the sales price by $4, should the company reduce the price?

24. National Insurance Associates carries an investment portfolio of stocks, bonds, and other investment alternatives. Currently $200,000 of funds are available and must be considered for new investment opportunities. The four stock options National is considering and the relevant financial data are as follows:

	Stock			
	A	B	C	D
Price per share	$100	$50	$80	$40
Annual rate of return	0.12	0.08	0.06	0.10
Risk measure per dollar invested	0.10	0.07	0.05	0.08

The risk measure indicates the relative uncertainty associated with the stock in terms of its realizing the projected annual return; higher values indicate greater risk. The risk measures are provided by the firm's top financial advisor.

National's top management has stipulated the following investment guidelines: The annual rate of return for the portfolio must be at least 9% and no one stock can account for more than 50% of the total dollar investment.

a. Use linear programming to develop an investment portfolio that minimizes risk.
b. What are the objective coefficient ranges for the four variables? Interpret these ranges.
c. Suppose that the firm decides that the annual rate of return must be at least 10%. What does the dual value associated with this constraint indicate about the change in risk that would occur from this increased rate of return?

25. Georgia Cabinets manufactures kitchen cabinets that are sold to local dealers throughout the Southeast. Because of a large backlog of orders for oak and cherry cabinets, the company decided to contract with three smaller cabinetmakers to do the final finishing operation. For the three cabinetmakers, the number of hours required to complete all the oak cabinets, the number of hours required to complete all the cherry cabinets, the number of hours available for the final finishing operation, and the cost per hour to perform the work are shown here.

	Cabinetmaker 1	Cabinetmaker 2	Cabinetmaker 3
Hours required to complete all the oak cabinets	50	42	30
Hours required to complete all the cherry cabinets	60	48	35
Hours available	40	30	35
Cost per hour	$36	$42	$55

For example, Cabinetmaker 1 estimates it will take 50 hours to complete all the oak cabinets and 60 hours to complete all the cherry cabinets. However, Cabinetmaker 1 only has 40 hours available for the final finishing operation. Thus, Cabinetmaker 1 can only complete $40/50 = 0.80$, or 80%, of the oak cabinets if it worked only on oak cabinets. Similarly, Cabinetmaker 1 can only complete $40/60 = 0.67$, or 67%, of the cherry cabinets if it worked only on cherry cabinets.

a. Formulate a linear programming model that can be used to determine the percentage of the oak cabinets and the percentage of the cherry cabinets that should be given to each of the three cabinetmakers in order to minimize the total cost of completing both projects.

b. Solve the model formulated in part (a). What percentage of the oak cabinets and what percentage of the cherry cabinets should be assigned to each cabinetmaker? What is the total cost of completing both projects?

c. If Cabinetmaker 1 has additional hours available, would the optimal solution change? Explain.

d. If Cabinetmaker 2 has additional hours available, would the optimal solution change? Explain.

e. Suppose Cabinetmaker 2 reduced its cost to $38 per hour. What effect would this change have on the optimal solution? Explain.

26. Benson Electronics manufactures three components used to produce cell telephones and other communication devices. In a given production period, demand for the three components may exceed Benson's manufacturing capacity. In this case, the company meets demand by purchasing the components from another manufacturer at an increased cost per unit. Benson's manufacturing cost per unit and purchasing cost per unit for the three components are as follows:

Source	Component 1	Component 2	Component 3
Manufacture	$4.50	$5.00	$2.75
Purchase	$6.50	$8.80	$7.00

Manufacturing times in minutes per unit for Benson's three departments are as follows:

Department	Component 1	Component 2	Component 3
Production	2	3	4
Assembly	1	1.5	3
Testing & Packaging	1.5	2	5

For instance, each unit of component 1 that Benson manufactures requires 2 minutes of production time, 1 minute of assembly time, and 1.5 minutes of testing and packaging time. For the next production period, Benson has capacities of 360 hours in the production department, 250 hours in the assembly department, and 300 hours in the testing and packaging department.

a. Formulate a linear programming model that can be used to determine how many units of each component to manufacture and how many units of each component to purchase. Assume that component demands that must be satisfied are 6000 units for component 1, 4000 units for component 2, and 3500 units for component 3. The objective is to minimize the total manufacturing and purchasing costs.

b. What is the optimal solution? How many units of each component should be manufactured and how many units of each component should be purchased?

c. Which departments are limiting Benson's manufacturing quantities? Use the dual value to determine the value of an *extra hour* in each of these departments.

d. Suppose that Benson had to obtain one additional unit of component 2. Discuss what the dual value for the component 2 constraint tells us about the cost to obtain the additional unit.

27. Cranberries can be harvested using either a "wet" method or a "dry" method. Dry-harvested cranberries can be sold at a premium, while wet-harvested cranberries are used mainly for cranberry juice and bring in less revenue. Fresh Made Cranberry Cooperative must decide how much of its cranberry crop should be harvested wet and how much should be dry harvested. Fresh Made has 5000 barrels of cranberries that can be harvested using either the wet or dry method. Dry cranberries are sold for $32.50 per barrel and wet cranberries are sold for $17.50 per barrel. Once harvested, cranberries must be processed through several operations before they can be sold. Both wet and dry cranberries must go through dechaffing and cleaning operations. The dechaffing and the cleaning operations can each be run 24 hours per day for the 6-week season (for a total of 1008 hours). Each barrel of dry cranberries requires 0.18 hours in the dechaffing operation and 0.32 hours in the cleaning operation. Wet cranberries require 0.04 hours in the dechaffing operation and 0.10 hours in the cleaning operation. Wet cranberries must also go through a drying process. The drying process can also be operated 24 hours per day for the 6-week season, and each barrel of wet cranberries must be dried for 0.22 hours.

a. Develop a linear program that Fresh Made can use to determine the optimal amount of cranberries to dry harvest and wet harvest.

b. Solve the linear program in part (a). How many barrels should be dry harvested? How many barrels should be wet harvested?

c. Suppose that Fresh Made can increase its dechaffing capacity by using an outside firm for this operation. Fresh Made will still use its own dechaffing operation as much as possible, but it can purchase additional capacity from this outside firm for $500 per hour. Should Fresh Made purchase additional dechaffing capacity? Why or why not?

d. Interpret the dual value for the constraint corresponding to the cleaning operation. How would you explain the meaning of this dual value to management?

28. The Pfeiffer Company manages approximately $15 million for clients. For each client, Pfeiffer chooses a mix of three investment vehicles: a growth stock fund, an income fund, and a money market fund. Each client has different investment objectives and different tolerances for risk. To accommodate these differences, Pfeiffer places limits on the percentage of each portfolio that may be invested in the three funds and assigns a portfolio risk index to each client.

Here's how the system works for Dennis Hartmann, one of Pfeiffer's clients. Based on an evaluation of Hartmann's risk tolerance, Pfeiffer has assigned Hartmann's portfolio a risk index of 0.05. Furthermore, to maintain diversity, the fraction of Hartmann's portfolio invested in the growth and income funds must be at least 10% for each, and at least 20% must be in the money market fund.

The risk ratings for the growth, income, and money market funds are 0.10, 0.05, and 0.01, respectively. A portfolio risk index is computed as a weighted average of the risk ratings for the three funds where the weights are the fraction of the portfolio invested in each of the funds. Hartmann has given Pfeiffer $300,000 to manage. Pfeiffer is currently forecasting a yield of 20% on the growth fund, 10% on the income fund, and 6% on the money market fund.

a. Develop a linear programming model to select the best mix of investments for Hartmann's portfolio.

b. Solve the model you developed in part (a).

    c. How much may the yields on the three funds vary before it will be necessary for Pfeiffer to modify Hartmann's portfolio?

    d. If Hartmann were more risk tolerant, how much of a yield increase could he expect? For instance, what if his portfolio risk index is increased to 0.06?

    e. If Pfeiffer revised the yield estimate for the growth fund downward to 0.10, how would you recommend modifying Hartmann's portfolio?

    f. What information must Pfeiffer maintain on each client in order to use this system to manage client portfolios?

    g. On a weekly basis Pfeiffer revises the yield estimates for the three funds. Suppose Pfeiffer has 50 clients. Describe how you would envision Pfeiffer making weekly modifications in each client's portfolio and allocating the total funds managed among the three investment funds.

29. La Jolla Beverage Products is considering producing a wine cooler that would be a blend of a white wine, a rosé wine, and fruit juice. To meet taste specifications, the wine cooler must consist of at least 50% white wine, at least 20% and no more than 30% rosé, and exactly 20% fruit juice. La Jolla purchases the wine from local wineries and the fruit juice from a processing plant in San Francisco. For the current production period, 10,000 gallons of white wine and 8000 gallons of rosé wine can be purchased; an unlimited amount of fruit juice can be ordered. The costs for the wine are $1.00 per gallon for the white and $1.50 per gallon for the rosé; the fruit juice can be purchased for $0.50 per gallon. La Jolla Beverage Products can sell all of the wine cooler they can produce for $2.50 per gallon.

    a. Is the cost of the wine and fruit juice a sunk cost or a relevant cost in this situation? Explain.

    b. Formulate a linear program to determine the blend of the three ingredients that will maximize the total profit contribution. Solve the linear program to determine the number of gallons of each ingredient La Jolla should purchase and the total profit contribution they will realize from this blend.

    c. If La Jolla could obtain additional amounts of the white wine, should they do so? If so, how much should they be willing to pay for each additional gallon, and how many additional gallons would they want to purchase?

    d. If La Jolla Beverage Products could obtain additional amounts of the rosé wine, should they do so? If so, how much should they be willing to pay for each additional gallon, and how many additional gallons would they want to purchase?

    e. Interpret the dual value for the constraint corresponding to the requirement that the wine cooler must contain at least 50% white wine. What is your advice to management given this dual value?

    f. Interpret the dual value for the constraint corresponding to the requirement that the wine cooler must contain exactly 20% fruit juice. What is your advice to management given this dual value?

30. The program manager for Channel 10 would like to determine the best way to allocate the time for the 11:00–11:30 evening news broadcast. Specifically, she would like to determine the number of minutes of broadcast time to devote to local news, national news, weather, and sports. Over the 30-minute broadcast, 10 minutes are set aside for advertising. The station's broadcast policy states that at least 15% of the time available should be devoted to local news coverage; the time devoted to the combination of local news and national news must be at least 50% of the total broadcast time; the time devoted to the weather segment must be less than or equal to the time devoted to the sports segment; the time devoted to the sports segment should be no longer than the total time spent on the local and national news; and at least 20% of the time should be devoted to the weather segment. The production costs per minute are $300 for local news, $200 for national news, $100 for weather, and $100 for sports.

    a. Formulate and solve a linear program that can determine how the 20 available minutes should be used to minimize the total cost of producing the program.

    b. Interpret the dual value for the constraint corresponding to the available time. What advice would you give the station manager given this dual value?

    c. Interpret the dual value for the constraint corresponding to the requirement that at least 15% of the available time should be devoted to local coverage. What advice would you give the station manager given this dual value?

d. Interpret the dual value for the constraint corresponding to the requirement that the time devoted to the local and the national news must be at least 50% of the total broadcast time. What advice would you give the station manager given this dual value?

e. Interpret the dual value for the constraint corresponding to the requirement that the time devoted to the weather segment must be less than or equal to the time devoted to the sports segment. What advice would you give the station manager given this dual value?

31. Gulf Coast Electronics is ready to award contracts to suppliers for providing reservoir capacitors for use in its electronic devices. For the past several years, Gulf Coast Electronics has relied on two suppliers for its reservoir capacitors: Able Controls and Lyshenko Industries. A new firm, Boston Components, has inquired into the possibility of providing a portion of the reservoir capacitors needed by Gulf Coast. The quality of products provided by Lysehnko Industries has been extremely high; in fact, only 0.5% of the capacitors provided by Lyshenko had to be discarded because of quality problems. Able Controls has also had a high quality level historically, producing an average of only 1% unacceptable capacitors. Because Gulf Coast Electronics has had no experience with Boston Components, it estimated Boston Components' defective rate to be 10%. Gulf Coast would like to determine how many reservoir capacitors should be ordered from each firm to obtain 75,000 acceptable-quality capacitors to use in its electronic devices. To ensure that Boston Components will receive some of the contract, management specified that the volume of reservoir capacitors awarded to Boston Components must be at least 10% of the volume given to Able Controls. In addition, the total volume assigned to Boston Components, Able Controls, and Lyshenko Industries should not exceed 30,000, 50,000, and 50,000 capacitors, respectively. Because of Gulf Coast's long-term relationship with Lyshenko Industries, management also specified that at least 30,000 capacitors should be ordered from Lyshenko. The cost per capacitor is $2.45 for Boston Components, $2.50 for Able Controls, and $2.75 for Lyshenko Industries.

a. Formulate and solve a linear program for determining how many reservoir capacitors should be ordered from each supplier to minimize the total cost of obtaining 75,000 acceptable-quality reservoir capacitors.

b. Suppose that the quality level for reservoir capacitors supplied by Boston Components is much better than estimated. What effect, if any, would this quality level have?

c. Suppose that management is willing to reconsider their requirement that at least 30,000 capacitors must be ordered from Lyshenko Industries. What effect, if any, would this consideration have?

32. PartsTech, Inc., a manufacturer of rechargeable batteries for phones, cameras, and other personal electronic devices, signed a contract with an electronics company to produce three different lithium-ion battery packs for a new line of smartphones. The contract calls for the following:

Battery Pack	Production Quantity
PT-100	200,000
PT-200	100,000
PT-300	150,000

PartsTech can manufacture the battery packs at manufacturing plants located in the Philippines and Mexico. The unit cost of the battery packs differs at the two plants because of differences in production equipment and wage rates. The unit costs for each battery pack at each manufacturing plant are as follows:

	Plant	
Product	Philippines	Mexico
PT-100	$0.95	$0.98
PT-200	$0.98	$1.06
PT-300	$1.34	$1.15

The PT-100 and PT-200 battery packs are produced using similar production equipment available at both plants. However, each plant has a limited capacity for the total number of PT-100 and PT-200 battery packs produced. The combined PT-100 and PT-200 production capacities are 175,000 units at the Philippines plant and 160,000 units at the Mexico plant. The PT-300 production capacities are 75,000 units at the Philippines plant and 100,000 units at the Mexico plant. The cost of shipping from the Philippines plant is $0.18 per unit, and the cost of shipping from the Mexico plant is $0.10 per unit.

a. Develop a linear program that PartsTech can use to determine how many units of each battery pack to produce at each plant in order to minimize the total production and shipping cost associated with the new contract.

b. Solve the linear program developed in part (a) to determine the optimal production plan.

c. Use sensitivity analysis to determine how much the production and/or shipping cost per unit would have to change in order to produce additional units of the PT-100 in the Philippines plant.

d. Use sensitivity analysis to determine how much the production and/or shipping cost per unit would have to change in order to produce additional units of the PT-200 in the Mexico plant.

Case Problem 1   PRODUCT MIX

TJ, Inc.'s makes three nut mixes for sale to grocery chains located in the Southeast. The three mixes, referred to as the Regular Mix, the Deluxe Mix, and the Holiday Mix, are made by mixing different percentages of five types of nuts.

In preparation for the fall season, TJ, Inc.'s just purchased the following shipments of nuts at the prices shown:

Type of Nut	Shipment Amount (pounds)	Cost per Shipment ($)
Almond	6000	7500
Brazil	7500	7125
Filbert	7500	6750
Pecan	6000	7200
Walnut	7500	7875

The Regular Mix consists of 15% almonds, 25% Brazil nuts, 25% filberts, 10% pecans, and 25% walnuts. The Deluxe Mix consists of 20% of each type of nut, and the Holiday Mix consists of 25% almonds, 15% Brazil nuts, 15% filberts, 25% pecans, and 20% walnuts.

An accountant at TJ, Inc. analyzed the cost of packaging materials, sales price per pound, and so forth, and determined that the profit contribution per pound is $1.65 for the Regular Mix, $2.00 for the Deluxe Mix, and $2.25 for the Holiday Mix. These figures do not include the cost of specific types of nuts in the different mixes because that cost can vary greatly in the commodity markets.

Customer orders already received are summarized here:

Type of Mix	Orders (pounds)
Regular	10,000
Deluxe	3,000
Holiday	5,000

Because demand is running high, it is expected that TJ, Inc. will receive many more orders than can be satisfied.

TJ, Inc. is committed to using the available nuts to maximize profit over the fall season; nuts not used will be given to a local charity. Even if it is not profitable to do so, TJ, Inc.'s president indicated that the orders already received must be satisfied.

Managerial Report

Perform an analysis of the TJ, Inc.'s product-mix problem, and prepare a report for the president of TJ, Inc. that summarizes your findings. Be sure to include information and analysis on the following:

1. The cost per pound of the nuts included in the Regular, Deluxe, and Holiday mixes
2. The optimal product mix and the total profit contribution
3. Recommendations regarding how the total profit contribution can be increased if additional quantities of nuts can be purchased
4. A recommendation as to whether TJ, Inc. should purchase an additional 1000 pounds of almonds for $1000 from a supplier who overbought
5. Recommendations on how profit contribution could be increased (if at all) if TJ, Inc. does not satisfy all existing orders

Case Problem 2   INVESTMENT STRATEGY

J. D. Williams, Inc., is an investment advisory firm that manages more than $120 million in funds for its numerous clients. The company uses an asset allocation model that recommends the portion of each client's portfolio to be invested in a growth stock fund, an income fund, and a money market fund. To maintain diversity in each client's portfolio, the firm places limits on the percentage of each portfolio that may be invested in each of the three funds. General guidelines indicate that the amount invested in the growth fund must be between 20% and 40% of the total portfolio value. Similar percentages for the other two funds stipulate that between 20% and 50% of the total portfolio value must be in the income fund, and at least 30% of the total portfolio value must be in the money market fund.

In addition, the company attempts to assess the risk tolerance of each client and adjust the portfolio to meet the needs of the individual investor. For example, Williams just contracted with a new client who has $800,000 to invest. Based on an evaluation of the client's risk tolerance, Williams assigned a maximum risk index of 0.05 for the client. The firm's risk indicators show the risk of the growth fund at 0.10, the income fund at 0.07, and the money market fund at 0.01. An overall portfolio risk index is computed as a weighted average of the risk rating for the three funds where the weights are the fraction of the client's portfolio invested in each of the funds.

Additionally, Williams is currently forecasting annual yields of 18% for the growth fund, 12.5% for the income fund, and 7.5% for the money market fund. Based on the information provided, how should the new client be advised to allocate the $800,000 among the growth, income, and money market funds? Develop a linear programming model that will provide the maximum yield for the portfolio. Use your model to develop a managerial report.

Managerial Report

1. Recommend how much of the $800,000 should be invested in each of the three funds. What is the annual yield you anticipate for the investment recommendation?
2. Assume that the client's risk index could be increased to 0.055. How much would the yield increase and how would the investment recommendation change?
3. Refer again to the original situation where the client's risk index was assessed to be 0.05. How would your investment recommendation change if the annual yield for the growth fund were revised downward to 16% or even to 14%?
4. Assume that the client expressed some concern about having too much money in the growth fund. How would the original recommendation change if the amount invested in the growth fund is not allowed to exceed the amount invested in the income fund?
5. The asset allocation model you developed may be useful in modifying the portfolios for all of the firm's clients whenever the anticipated yields for the three funds are periodically revised. What is your recommendation as to whether use of this model is possible?

Case Problem 3   TRUCK LEASING STRATEGY

Reep Construction recently won a contract for the excavation and site preparation of a new rest area on the Pennsylvania Turnpike. In preparing his bid for the job, Bob Reep, founder and president of Reep Construction, estimated that it would take four months to perform the work and that 10, 12, 14, and 8 trucks would be needed in months 1 through 4, respectively.

The firm currently has 20 trucks of the type needed to perform the work on the new project. These trucks were obtained last year when Bob signed a long-term lease with PennState Leasing. Although most of these trucks are currently being used on existing jobs, Bob estimates that one truck will be available for use on the new project in month 1, two trucks will be available in month 2, three trucks will be available in month 3, and one truck will be available in month 4. Thus, to complete the project, Bob will have to lease additional trucks.

The long-term leasing contract with PennState has a monthly cost of $600 per truck. Reep Construction pays its truck drivers $20 an hour, and daily fuel costs are approximately $100 per truck. All maintenance costs are paid by PennState Leasing. For planning purposes, Bob estimates that each truck used on the new project will be operating eight hours a day, five days a week for approximately four weeks each month.

Bob does not believe that current business conditions justify committing the firm to additional long-term leases. In discussing the short-term leasing possibilities with PennState Leasing, Bob learned that he can obtain short-term leases of 1–4 months. Short-term leases differ from long-term leases in that the short-term leasing plans include the cost of both a truck and a driver. Maintenance costs for short-term leases also are paid by PennState Leasing. The following costs for each of the four months cover the lease of a truck and driver:

Length of Lease	Cost per Month ($)
1	4000
2	3700
3	3225
4	3040

Bob Reep would like to acquire a lease that would minimize the cost of meeting the monthly trucking requirements for his new project, but he also takes great pride in the fact that his company has never laid off employees. Bob is committed to maintaining his no-layoff policy; that is, he will use his own drivers even if costs are higher.

Managerial Report

Perform an analysis of Reep Construction's leasing problem and prepare a report for Bob Reep that summarizes your findings. Be sure to include information on and analysis of the following items:

1. The optimal leasing plan
2. The costs associated with the optimal leasing plan
3. The cost for Reep Construction to maintain its current policy of no layoffs

Appendix 3.1   SENSITIVITY ANALYSIS WITH EXCEL SOLVER

In Appendix 2.1 we showed how Excel Solver can be used to solve a linear program by using it to solve the Par, Inc., problem. Let us now see how it can be used to provide sensitivity analysis.

When Solver finds the optimal solution to a linear program, the **Solver Results** dialog box (see Figure 3.22) will appear on the screen. If only the solution is desired, you simply click **OK**. To obtain the optimal solution and the sensitivity analysis output, you must

FIGURE 3.22   EXCEL SOLVER RESULTS DIALOG BOX

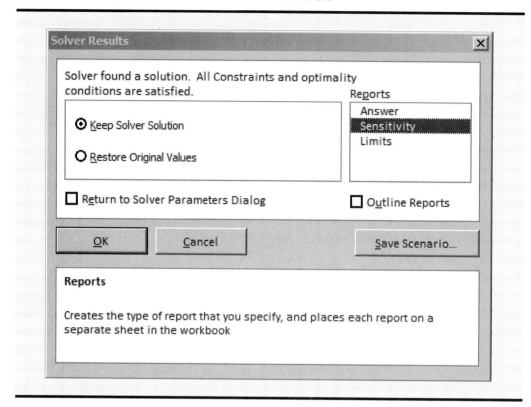

select **Sensitivity** in the **Reports** box before clicking **OK**; the sensitivity report is created on another worksheet in the same Excel workbook. Using this procedure for the Par, Inc., problem, we obtained the optimal solution shown in Figure 3.23 and the sensitivity report shown in Figure 3.24.

Interpretation of Excel Solver Sensitivity Report

In the Adjustable Cells section of the Sensitivity Report, the column labeled Final Value contains the optimal values of the decision variables. For the Par, Inc., problem, the optimal solution is 540 standard bags and 252 deluxe bags. Next, let us consider the values in the Reduced Cost column.[1] For the Par, Inc., problem, the reduced costs for both decision variables are zero; they are at their optimal values.

To the right of the Reduced Cost column in Figure 3.24, we find three columns labeled Objective Coefficient, Allowable Increase, and Allowable Decrease. Note that for the standard bag decision variable, the objective function coefficient value is 10, the allowable increase is 3.5, and the allowable decrease is 3.7. Adding 3.5 to and subtracting 3.7 from the current coefficient of 10 provides the range of optimality for C_S.

$$6.3 \leq C_S \leq 13.5$$

Similarly, the range of optimality for C_D is

$$6.67 \leq C_D \leq 14.29$$

Next, consider the information in the Constraints section of the report. The entries in the Final Value column are the number of hours needed in each department to produce

---

[1]In Excel, if the value of a variable in an optimal solution is equal to the upper bound of the variable, then reduced cost will be the dual value of this upper bound constraint.

FIGURE 3.23 EXCEL SOLUTION FOR THE PAR, INC., PROBLEM

MODEL *file*

Par

	A	B	C	D
1	Par, Inc.			
2				
3		**Production Time**		
4	**Operation**	**Standard**	**Deluxe**	**Time Available**
5	Cutting and Dyeing	0.7	1	630
6	Sewing	0.5	0.83333	600
7	Finishing	1	0.66667	708
8	Inspection and Packaging	0.1	0.25	135
9	**Profit Per Bag**	10	9	
10				
11				
12	**Model**			
13				
14		**Decision Variables**		
15		**Standard**	**Deluxe**	
16	**Bags Produced**	539.99842	252.00110	
17				
18	**Maximize Total Profit**	7668		
19				
20	**Constraints**	**Hours Used** **(LHS)**		**Hours Available** **(RHS)**
21	Cutting and Dyeing	630	<=	630
22	Sewing	479.99929	<=	600
23	Finishing	708	<=	708
24	Inspection and Packaging	117.00012	<=	135

FIGURE 3.24 EXCEL SENSITIVITY REPORT FOR THE PAR, INC., PROBLEM

Adjustable Cells

Cell	Name	Final Value	Reduced Cost	Objective Coefficient	Allowable Increase	Allowable Decrease
$B$16	Bags Produced Standard	540	0	10	3.5	3.7
$C$16	Bags Produced Deluxe	252	0	9	5.285714286	2.3333

Constraints

Cell	Name	Final Value	Shadow Price	Constraint R.H. Side	Allowable Increase	Allowable Decrease
$B$21	Cutting and Dyeing Hours Used (LHS)	630	4.375	630	52.36363636	134.4
$B$22	Sewing Hours Used (LHS)	480	0	600	1E+30	120
$B$23	Finishing Hours Used (LHS)	708	6.9375	708	192	128
$B$24	Inspection and Packaging Hours Used (LHS)	117	0.00000	135	1E+30	18

the optimal production quantities of 540 standard bags and 252 deluxe bags. Thus, at the optimal solution, 630 hours of cutting and dyeing time, 480 hours of sewing time, 708 hours of finishing time, and 117 hours of inspection and packaging time are required. The values in the Constraint R.H. Side column are just the original right-hand-side values: 630 hours of cutting and dyeing time, 600 hours of sewing time, 708 hours of finishing time, and 135 hours of inspection and packaging time. Note that for the Par, Inc., problem, the values of the slack variables for each constraint are simply the differences between the

The sensitivity analysis interpretations provided in this appendix are based on the assumption that only one objective function coefficient or only one right-hand-side change occurs at a time.

entries in the Constraint R.H. Side column and the corresponding entries in the Final Value column.

The entries in the Shadow Price column provide the *shadow price* for each constraint. The shadow price is another, often-used term for the dual value. The last two columns of the Sensitivity Report contain the range of feasibility information for the constraint right-hand sides. For example, consider the cutting and dyeing constraint with an allowable increase value of 52.4 and an allowable decrease value of 134.4. The values in the Allowable Increase and Allowable Decrease columns indicate that the shadow price of $4.375 is valid for increases up to 52.4 hours and decreases to 134.4 hours. Thus, the shadow price of $4.375 is applicable for increases up to 630 + 52.4 = 682.4 and decreases down to 630 − 134.4 = 495.6 hours.

In summary, the range of feasibility information provides the limits where the shadow prices are applicable. For changes outside the range, the problem must be re-solved to find the new optimal solution and the new shadow price.

Appendix 3.2   SENSITIVITY ANALYSIS WITH LINGO

In Appendix 2.2 we showed how LINGO can be used to solve a linear program by using it to solve the Par, Inc., problem. A copy of the Solution Report is shown in Figure 3.25. As we discussed previously, the value of the objective function is 7668, the optimal solution is $S = 540$ and $D = 252$, and the values of the slack variables corresponding to the four constraints (rows 2–5) are 0, 120, 0, and 18. Now let us consider the information in the Reduced Cost column and the Dual Price column.

FIGURE 3.25   PAR, INC., SOLUTION REPORT USING LINGO

```
Global optimal solution found.
Objective value:                          7668.000
Infeasibilities:                          0.000000
Total solver iterations:                         2
Elapsed runtime seconds:                      0.09

Model Class:                                    LP

Total variables:              2
Nonlinear variables:          0
Integer variables:            0

Total constraints:            5
Nonlinear constraints:        0

Total nonzeros:              10
Nonlinear nonzeros:           0


        Variable              Value           Reduced Cost
               S           540.0000               0.000000
               D           252.0000               0.000000

           Row    Slack or Surplus             Dual Price
             1           7668.000               1.000000
             2           0.000000               4.375000
             3           120.0000               0.000000
             4           0.000000               6.937500
             5           18.00000               0.000000
```

LINGO always takes the absolute value of the reduced cost.

For the Par, Inc., problem, the reduced costs for both decision variables are zero because both variables are at a positive value. LINGO reports a **dual price** rather than a dual value. For a maximization problem, the dual value and dual price are identical. For a minimization problem, the dual price is equal to the negative of the dual value. There are historical reasons for this oddity that are beyond the scope of the book. When interpreting the LINGO output for a minimization problem, multiply the dual prices by –1, treat the resulting number as the dual value, and interpret the number as described in Section 3.2. The nonzero dual prices of 4.374957 for constraint 1 (cutting and dyeing constraint in row 2) and 6.937530 for constraint 3 (finishing constraint in row 4) tell us that an additional hour of cutting and dyeing time improves (increases) the value of the optimal solution by $4.37 and an additional hour of finishing time improves (increases) the value of the optimal solution by $6.94.

Next, let us consider how LINGO can be used to compute the range of optimality for each objective function coefficient and the range of feasibility for each of the dual prices. By default, range computations are not enabled in LINGO. To enable range computations, perform the following steps:

Step 1. Choose the **Solver** menu
Step 2. Select **Options...**
Step 3. When the **LINGO Options** dialog box appears:
  Select the **General Solver** tab
  Choose **Prices and Ranges** in the **Dual Computations** box
  Click **Apply**
  Click **OK**

You will now have to re-solve the Par, Inc., problem in order for LINGO to perform the range computations. After re-solving the problem, close or minimize the **Solution Report** window. To display the range information, select the **Range** command from the **Solver** menu. LINGO displays the range information in a new window titled **Range Report**. The output that appears in the **Range Report** window for the Par, Inc., problem is shown in Figure 3.26.

We will use the information in the Objective Coefficient Ranges section of the range report to compute the range of optimality for the objective function coefficients. For example, the current objective function coefficient for S is 10. Note that the corresponding allowable increase is 3.5 and the corresponding allowable decrease is 3.700000. Thus, the range of optimality for C_S, the objective function coefficient for S, is $10 - 3.700000 = 6.300000$ to $10 + 3.5 = 13.5$. After rounding, the range of optimality for C_S is $6.30 \leq C_S \leq 13.50$. Similarly,

FIGURE 3.26 PAR, INC., SENSITIVITY REPORT USING LINGO

```
Ranges in which the basis is unchanged:

                    OBJECTIVE COEFFICIENT RANGES:

                    Current          Allowable         Allowable
    Variable      Coefficient         Increase          Decrease
        S          10.00000          3.500000          3.700000
        D          9.000000          5.285714          2.333333


                    RIGHTHAND SIDE RANGES:

                    Current          Allowable         Allowable
    Row               RHS             Increase          Decrease
     2             630.0000          52.36364          134.4000
     3             600.0000          INFINITY          120.0000
     4             708.0000          192.0000          128.0000
     5             135.0000          INFINITY          18.00000
```

with an allowable increase of 5.285714 and an allowable decrease of 2.333300, the range of optimality for C_D is $6.67 \leq C_S \leq 14.29$.

To compute the range of feasibility for each dual price, we will use the information in the Right-Hand-Side Ranges section of the range report. For example, the current right-hand-side value for the cutting and dyeing constraint (row 2) is 630, the allowable increase is 52.36316, and the allowable decrease is 134.40000. Because the dual price for this constraint is 4.375 (shown in the LINGO solution report), we can conclude that additional hours will increase the objective function by \$4.37 per hour. From the range information given, we see that after rounding the dual price of \$4.37 is valid for increases up to $630 + 52.36 = 682.4$ and decreases to $630 - 134.4 = 495.6$. Thus, the range of feasibility for the cutting and dyeing constraint is 495.6 to 682.4. The ranges of feasibility for the other constraints can be determined in a similar manner.

CHAPTER 4

Linear Programming Applications in Marketing, Finance, and Operations Management

CONTENTS

Linear programming has proven to be one of the most successful quantitative approaches to decision making. Applications have been reported in almost every industry. These applications include production scheduling, media selection, financial planning, capital budgeting, transportation, distribution system design, product mix, staffing, and blending.

The wide variety of Management Science in Actions presented in Chapters 2 and 3 illustrated the use of linear programming as a flexible problem-solving tool. The Management Science in Action, A Marketing Planning Model at Marathon Oil Company, provides another example of the use of linear programming by showing how Marathon uses a large-scale linear programming model to solve a wide variety of planning problems. Later in the chapter other Management Science in Action vignettes illustrate how General Electric uses linear programming for making solar energy investment decisions; how Vestel Electric uses linear programming for production planning; and how the Kellogg Company uses a large-scale linear programming model to integrate production, distribution, and inventory planning.

In this chapter we present a variety of applications from the traditional business areas of marketing, finance, and operations management. We emphasize modeling, computer solution, and interpretation of output. A mathematical model is developed for each problem studied, and solutions are presented for most of the applications. In the chapter appendix we illustrate the use of Excel Solver by solving a financial planning problem.

MANAGEMENT SCIENCE IN ACTION

A MARKETING PLANNING MODEL AT MARATHON OIL COMPANY*

Marathon Oil Company has seven refineries within the United States, operates 61 light product terminals, owns over 170 transport trucks, and owns or leases over 2200 railcars. The Supply and Transportation Division faces the problem of determining which refinery should supply which terminal and, at the same time, determining which products should be transported via pipeline, barge, or tanker to minimize cost. Product demand must be satisfied, and the supply capability of each refinery must not be exceeded. To help solve this difficult problem, Marathon Oil developed a marketing planning model.

The marketing planning model is a large-scale linear programming model that takes into account sales not only at Marathon product terminals but also at all exchange locations. An exchange contract is an agreement with other oil product marketers that involves exchanging or trading Marathon's products for theirs at different locations. All pipelines, barges, and tankers within Marathon's marketing area are also represented in the linear programming

model. The objective of the model is to minimize the cost of meeting a given demand structure, taking into account sales price, pipeline tariffs, exchange contract costs, product demand, terminal operating costs, refining costs, and product purchases.

The marketing planning model is used to solve a wide variety of planning problems that vary from evaluating gasoline blending economics to analyzing the economics of a new terminal or pipeline. With daily sales of over 10 million gallons of refined light product, a savings of even one-thousandth of a cent per gallon can result in significant long-term savings. At the same time, what may appear to be a savings in one area, such as refining or transportation, may actually add to overall costs when the effects are fully realized throughout the system. The marketing planning model allows a simultaneous examination of this total effect.

*Based on information provided by Robert W. Wernert at Marathon Oil Company, Findlay, Ohio.

4.1   MARKETING APPLICATIONS

Applications of linear programming in marketing are numerous. In this section we discuss applications in media selection and marketing research.

Media Selection

Media selection applications of linear programming are designed to help marketing managers allocate a fixed advertising budget to various advertising media. Potential media include

In Section 2.1 we provided some general guidelines for modeling linear programming problems. You may want to review Section 2.1 before proceeding with the linear programming applications in this chapter.

newspapers, magazines, radio, television, and direct mail. In these applications, the objective is to maximize reach, frequency, and quality of exposure. Restrictions on the allowable allocation usually arise during consideration of company policy, contract requirements, and media availability. In the application that follows, we illustrate how a media selection problem might be formulated and solved using a linear programming model.

Relax-and-Enjoy Lake Development Corporation is developing a lakeside community at a privately owned lake. The primary market for the lakeside lots and homes includes all middle- and upper-income families within approximately 100 miles of the development. Relax-and-Enjoy employed the advertising firm of Boone, Phillips, and Jackson (BP&J) to design the promotional campaign.

After considering possible advertising media and the market to be covered, BP&J recommended that the first month's advertising be restricted to five media. At the end of the month, BP&J will then reevaluate its strategy based on the month's results. BP&J collected data on the number of potential customers reached, the cost per advertisement, the maximum number of times each medium is available, and the exposure quality rating for each of the five media. The quality rating is measured in terms of an exposure quality unit, a measure of the relative value of one advertisement in each of the media. This measure, based on BP&J's experience in the advertising business, takes into account factors such as audience demographics (age, income, and education of the audience reached), image presented, and quality of the advertisement. The information collected is presented in Table 4.1.

Relax-and-Enjoy provided BP&J with an advertising budget of \$30,000 for the first month's campaign. In addition, Relax-and-Enjoy imposed the following restrictions on how BP&J may allocate these funds: At least 10 television commercials must be used, at least 50,000 potential customers must be reached, and no more than \$18,000 may be spent on television advertisements. What advertising media selection plan should be recommended?

The decision to be made is how many times to use each medium. We begin by defining the decision variables:

$$DTV = \text{number of times daytime TV is used}$$
$$ETV = \text{number of times evening TV is used}$$
$$DN = \text{number of times daily newspaper is used}$$
$$SN = \text{number of times Sunday newspaper is used}$$
$$R = \text{number of times radio is used}$$

TABLE 4.1   ADVERTISING MEDIA ALTERNATIVES FOR THE RELAX-AND-ENJOY LAKE DEVELOPMENT CORPORATION

Advertising Media	Number of Potential Customers Reached	Cost (\$) per Advertisement	Maximum Times Available per Month*	Exposure Quality Units
1. Daytime TV (1 min), station WKLA	1000	1500	15	65
2. Evening TV (30 sec), station WKLA	2000	3000	10	90
3. Daily newspaper (full page), *The Morning Journal*	1500	400	25	40
4. Sunday newspaper magazine (½ page color), *The Sunday Press*	2500	1000	4	60
5. Radio, 8:00 A.M. or 5:00 P.M. news (30 sec), station KNOP	300	100	30	20

*The maximum number of times the medium is available is either the maximum number of times the advertising medium occurs (e.g., four Sundays per month) or the maximum number of times BP&J recommends that the medium be used.

The data on quality of exposure in Table 4.1 show that each daytime TV (*DTV*) advertisement is rated at 65 exposure quality units. Thus, an advertising plan with *DTV* advertisements will provide a total of 65*DTV* exposure quality units. Continuing with the data in Table 4.1, we find evening TV (*ETV*) rated at 90 exposure quality units, daily newspaper (*DN*) rated at 40 exposure quality units, Sunday newspaper (*SN*) rated at 60 exposure quality units, and radio (*R*) rated at 20 exposure quality units. With the objective of maximizing the total exposure quality units for the overall media selection plan, the objective function becomes

Care must be taken to ensure the linear programming model accurately reflects the real problem. Always review your formulation thoroughly before attempting to solve the model.

$$\text{Max} \quad 65DTV + 90ETV + 40DN + 60SN + 20R \qquad \text{Exposure quality}$$

We now formulate the constraints for the model from the information given:

$$
\begin{array}{rcl}
DTV & \le & 15 \\
ETV & \le & 10 \\
DN & \le & 25 \\
SN & \le & 4 \\
R & \le & 30
\end{array}\left.\right\} \begin{array}{l}\text{Availability}\\ \text{of media}\end{array}
$$

$$1500DTV + 3000ETV + 400DN + 1000SN + 100R \le 30{,}000 \quad \text{Budget}$$

$$
\begin{array}{rcl}
DTV + ETV & \ge & 10 \\
1500DTV + 3000ETV & \le & 18{,}000
\end{array}\left.\right\}\begin{array}{l}\text{Television}\\ \text{restrictions}\end{array}
$$

Problem 1 provides practice at formulating a similar media selection model.

$$1000DTV + 2000ETV + 1500DN + 2500SN + 300R \ge 50{,}000 \quad \text{Customers reached}$$
$$DTV, ETV, DN, SN, R \ge 0$$

The optimal solution to this five-variable, nine-constraint linear programming model is shown in Figure 4.1; a summary is presented in Table 4.2.

FIGURE 4.1   THE SOLUTION FOR THE RELAX-AND-ENJOY LAKE DEVELOPMENT CORPORATION PROBLEM

MODEL *file*
Relax

```
Optimal Objective Value =       2370.00000

     Variable          Value           Reduced Cost
     --------          -----           ------------
       DTV           10.00000             0.00000
       ETV            0.00000           -65.00000
       DN            25.00000             0.00000
       SN             2.00000             0.00000
       R             30.00000             0.00000

    Constraint     Slack/Surplus         Dual Value
    ----------     -------------         ----------
        1             5.00000             0.00000
        2            10.00000             0.00000
        3             0.00000            16.00000
        4             2.00000             0.00000
        5             0.00000            14.00000
        6             0.00000             0.06000
        7             0.00000           -25.00000
        8          3000.00000             0.00000
        9         11500.00000             0.00000
```

Media Availability; Budget; Television Restrictions; Audience Coverage

TABLE 4.2 ADVERTISING PLAN FOR THE RELAX-AND-ENJOY LAKE
DEVELOPMENT CORPORATION

Media	Frequency	Budget
Daytime TV	10	$15,000
Daily newspaper	25	10,000
Sunday newspaper	2	2,000
Radio	30	3,000
		$30,000

Exposure quality units = 2370
Total customers reached = 61,500

The optimal solution calls for advertisements to be distributed among daytime TV, daily newspaper, Sunday newspaper, and radio. The maximum number of exposure quality units is 2370, and the total number of customers reached is 61,500. The Reduced Costs column in Figure 4.1 indicates that the number of exposure quality units for evening TV would have to increase by at least 65 before this media alternative could appear in the optimal solution. Note that the budget constraint (constraint 6) has a dual value of 0.06. Therefore, a $1.00 increase in the advertising budget will lead to an increase of 0.06 exposure quality units. The dual value of −25.000 for constraint 7 indicates that increasing the required number of television commercials by 1 will decrease the exposure quality of the advertising plan by 25 units. Alternatively, decreasing the required number of television commercials by 1 will increase the exposure quality of the advertising plan by 25 units. Thus, Relax-and-Enjoy should consider reducing the requirement of having at least 10 television commercials.

A possible shortcoming of this model is that, even if the exposure quality measure were not subject to error, it offers no guarantee that maximization of total exposure quality will lead to maximization of profit or of sales (a common surrogate for profit). However, this issue is not a shortcoming of linear programming; rather, it is a shortcoming of the use of exposure quality as a criterion. If we could directly measure the effect of an advertisement on profit, we could use total profit as the objective to be maximized.

NOTES AND COMMENTS

1. The media selection model required subjective evaluations of the exposure quality for the media alternatives. Marketing managers may have substantial data concerning exposure quality, but the final coefficients used in the objective function may also include considerations based primarily on managerial judgment. Judgment is an acceptable way of obtaining input for a linear programming model.

2. The media selection model presented in this section uses exposure quality as the objective function and places a constraint on the number of customers reached. An alternative formulation of this problem would be to use the number of customers reached as the objective function and add a constraint indicating the minimum total exposure quality required for the media plan.

Marketing Research

An organization conducts marketing research to learn about consumer characteristics, attitudes, and preferences. Marketing research firms that specialize in providing such information often do the actual research for client organizations. Typical services offered by a marketing research firm include designing the study, conducting market surveys, analyzing the data collected, and providing summary reports and recommendations for the client. In the research design phase, targets or quotas may be established for the number and types of respondents to be surveyed. The marketing research firm's objective is to conduct the survey so as to meet the client's needs at a minimum cost.

Market Survey, Inc. (MSI), specializes in evaluating consumer reaction to new products, services, and advertising campaigns. A client firm requested MSI's assistance in ascertaining consumer reaction to a recently marketed household product. During meetings with the client, MSI agreed to conduct door-to-door personal interviews to obtain responses from households with children and households without children. In addition, MSI agreed to conduct both day and evening interviews. Specifically, the client's contract called for MSI to conduct 1000 interviews under the following quota guidelines:

1. Interview at least 400 households with children.
2. Interview at least 400 households without children.
3. The total number of households interviewed during the evening must be at least as great as the number of households interviewed during the day.
4. At least 40% of the interviews for households with children must be conducted during the evening.
5. At least 60% of the interviews for households without children must be conducted during the evening.

Because the interviews for households with children take additional interviewer time and because evening interviewers are paid more than daytime interviewers, the cost varies with the type of interview. Based on previous research studies, estimates of the interview costs are as follows:

Household	Interview Cost	
	Day	Evening
Children	$20	$25
No children	$18	$20

What is the household, time-of-day interview plan that will satisfy the contract requirements at a minimum total interviewing cost?

In formulating the linear programming model for the MSI problem, we utilize the following decision-variable notation:

DC = the number of daytime interviews of households with children

EC = the number of evening interviews of households with children

DNC = the number of daytime interviews of households without children

ENC = the number of evening interviews of households without children

We begin the linear programming model formulation by using the cost-per-interview data to develop the objective function:

$$\text{Min}\quad 20DC + 25EC + 18DNC + 20ENC$$

The constraint requiring a total of 1000 interviews is

$$DC + EC + DNC + ENC = 1000$$

The five specifications concerning the types of interviews are as follows:

- Households with children:

$$DC + EC \geq 400$$

- Households without children:

$$DNC + ENC \geq 400$$

- At least as many evening interviews as day interviews:

$$EC + ENC \geq DC + DNC$$

- At least 40% of interviews of households with children during the evening:

$$EC \geq 0.4(DC + EC)$$

- At least 60% of interviews of households without children during the evening:

$$ENC \geq 0.6(DNC + ENC)$$

When we add the nonnegativity requirements, the four-variable and six-constraint linear programming model becomes

Min $20DC + 25EC + 18DNC + 20ENC$

s.t.

$DC +$	$EC +$	$DNC +$	ENC	$=$	1000	Total interviews
$DC +$	EC			$\geq$	400	Households with children
		$DNC +$	ENC	$\geq$	400	Households without children
	$EC + ENC \geq DC + DNC$					Evening interviews
	$EC \geq 0.4(DC + EC)$					Evening interviews in households with children
	$ENC \geq 0.6(DNC + ENC)$					Evening interviews in households without children

$$DC, EC, DNC, ENC \geq 0$$

The optimal solution to this linear program is shown in Figure 4.2. The solution reveals that the minimum cost of $20,320 occurs with the following interview schedule:

	Number of Interviews		
Household	Day	Evening	Totals
Children	240	160	400
No children	240	360	600
Totals	480	520	1000

Hence, 480 interviews will be scheduled during the day and 520 during the evening. Households with children will be covered by 400 interviews, and households without children will be covered by 600 interviews.

Selected sensitivity analysis information from Figure 4.2 shows a dual value of 19.200 for constraint 1. In other words, the value of the optimal solution will increase by $19.20 if the number of interviews is increased from 1000 to 1001. Thus, $19.20 is the incremental cost of obtaining additional interviews. It also is the savings that could be realized by reducing the number of interviews from 1000 to 999.

The surplus variable, with a value of 200.000, for constraint 3 shows that 200 more households without children will be interviewed than required. Similarly, the surplus variable, with a value of 40.000, for constraint 4 shows that the number of evening interviews exceeds the number of daytime interviews by 40. The zero values for the surplus variables in constraints 5 and 6 indicate that the more expensive evening interviews are being held at a minimum. Indeed, the dual value of 5.000 for constraint 5 indicates that if one more household (with children) than the minimum requirement must be interviewed during the

FIGURE 4.2   THE SOLUTION FOR THE MARKET SURVEY PROBLEM

MODEL *file*

Market

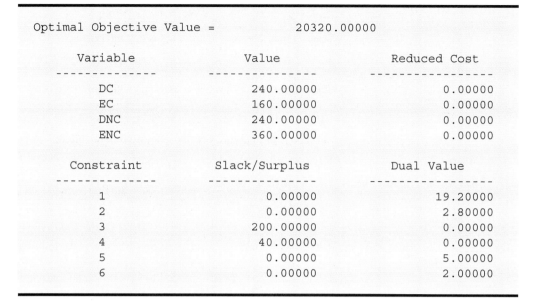

Optimal Objective Value =	20320.00000	
Variable	**Value**	**Reduced Cost**
DC	240.00000	0.00000
EC	160.00000	0.00000
DNC	240.00000	0.00000
ENC	360.00000	0.00000
Constraint	**Slack/Surplus**	**Dual Value**
1	0.00000	19.20000
2	0.00000	2.80000
3	200.00000	0.00000
4	40.00000	0.00000
5	0.00000	5.00000
6	0.00000	2.00000

evening, the total interviewing cost will go up by $5.00. Similarly, constraint 6 shows that requiring one more household (without children) to be interviewed during the evening will increase costs by $2.00.

4.2   FINANCIAL APPLICATIONS

In finance, linear programming can be applied in problem situations involving capital budgeting, asset allocation, portfolio selection, financial planning, and many others. In this section, we describe a portfolio selection problem and a problem involving funding of an early retirement program.

Portfolio Selection

Portfolio selection problems involve situations in which a financial manager must select specific investments—for example, stocks and bonds—from a variety of investment alternatives. Managers of mutual funds, credit unions, insurance companies, and banks frequently encounter this type of problem. The objective function for portfolio selection problems usually is maximization of expected return or minimization of risk. The constraints usually take the form of restrictions on the type of permissible investments, state laws, company policy, maximum permissible risk, and so on. Problems of this type have been formulated and solved using a variety of mathematical programming techniques. In this section we formulate and solve a portfolio selection problem as a linear program.

Consider the case of Welte Mutual Funds, Inc., located in New York City. Welte just obtained $100,000 by converting industrial bonds to cash and is now looking for other investment opportunities for these funds. Based on Welte's current investments, the firm's top financial analyst recommends that all new investments be made in the oil industry, steel industry, or in government bonds. Specifically, the analyst identified five investment opportunities and projected their annual rates of return. The investments and rates of return are shown in Table 4.3.

Management of Welte imposed the following investment guidelines:

1. Neither industry (oil or steel) should receive more than $50,000.
2. Government bonds should be at least 25% of the steel industry investments.
3. The investment in Pacific Oil, the high-return but high-risk investment, cannot be more than 60% of the total oil industry investment.

TABLE 4.3   INVESTMENT OPPORTUNITIES FOR WELTE MUTUAL FUNDS

Investment	Projected Rate of Return (%)
Atlantic Oil	7.3
Pacific Oil	10.3
Midwest Steel	6.4
Huber Steel	7.5
Government bonds	4.5

What portfolio recommendations—investments and amounts—should be made for the available $100,000? Given the objective of maximizing projected return subject to the budgetary and managerially imposed constraints, we can answer this question by formulating and solving a linear programming model of the problem. The solution will provide investment recommendations for the management of Welte Mutual Funds.

Let

$$A = \text{dollars invested in Atlantic Oil}$$
$$P = \text{dollars invested in Pacific Oil}$$
$$M = \text{dollars invested in Midwest Steel}$$
$$H = \text{dollars invested in Huber Steel}$$
$$G = \text{dollars invested in government bonds}$$

Using the projected rates of return shown in Table 4.3, we write the objective function for maximizing the total return for the portfolio as

$$\text{Max} \quad 0.073A + 0.103P + 0.064M + 0.075H + 0.045G$$

The constraint specifying investment of the available $100,000 is

$$A + P + M + H + G = 100{,}000$$

The requirements that neither the oil nor the steel industry should receive more than $50,000 are

$$A + P \leq 50{,}000$$
$$M + H \leq 50{,}000$$

The requirement that government bonds be at least 25% of the steel industry investment is expressed as

$$G \geq 0.25(M + H)$$

Finally, the constraint that Pacific Oil cannot be more than 60% of the total oil industry investment is

$$P \leq 0.60(A + P)$$

By adding the nonnegativity restrictions, we obtain the complete linear programming model for the Welte Mutual Funds investment problem:

Max $0.073A + 0.103P + 0.064M + 0.075H + 0.045G$

s.t.

$A +$	$P +$	$M +$	$H +$	$G = 100{,}000$	Available funds
$A +$	P			$\leq \ 50{,}000$	Oil industry maximum

$$M + \quad H \quad \le 50{,}000 \quad \text{Steel industry maximum}$$

$$G \ge 0.25\,(M + H) \quad \text{Government bonds minimum}$$

$$P \le 0.60\,(A + P) \quad \text{Pacific Oil restriction}$$

$$A, P, M, H, G \ge 0$$

The optimal solution to this linear program is shown in Figure 4.3. Table 4.4 shows how the funds are divided among the securities. Note that the optimal solution indicates that the portfolio should be diversified among all the investment opportunities except Midwest Steel. The projected annual return for this portfolio is $8000, which is an overall return of 8%.

The optimal solution shows the dual value for constraint 3 is zero. The reason is that the steel industry maximum isn't a binding constraint; increases in the steel industry limit of $50,000 will not improve the value of the optimal solution. Indeed, the slack variable for this constraint shows that the current steel industry investment is $10,000 below its limit of $50,000. The dual values for the other constraints are nonzero, indicating that these constraints are binding.

The dual value of 0.069 for constraint 1 shows that the value of the optimal solution can be increased by 0.069 if one more dollar can be made available for the portfolio investment. If more funds can be obtained at a cost of less than 6.9%, management should consider

FIGURE 4.3   THE SOLUTION FOR THE WELTE MUTUAL FUNDS PROBLEM

MODEL *file*

Welte

```
Optimal Objective Value =              8000.00000

        Variable              Value              Reduced Costs
        --------              -----              -------------
           A              20000.00000                0.00000
           P              30000.00000                0.00000
           M                  0.00000               -0.01100
           H              40000.00000                0.00000
           G              10000.00000                0.00000


        Constraint          Slack/Surplus            Dual Value
        ----------          -------------            ----------
            1                  0.00000                0.06900
            2                  0.00000                0.02200
            3              10000.00000                0.00000
            4                  0.00000               -0.02400
            5                  0.00000                0.03000
```

TABLE 4.4   OPTIMAL PORTFOLIO SELECTION FOR WELTE MUTUAL FUNDS

Investment	Amount	Expected Annual Return
Atlantic Oil	$ 20,000	$1460
Pacific Oil	30,000	3090
Huber Steel	40,000	3000
Government bonds	10,000	450
Totals	$100,000	$8000

Expected annual return of $8000
Overall rate of return = 8%

The dual value for the available funds constraint provides information on the rate of return from additional investment funds.

obtaining them. However, if a return in excess of 6.9% can be obtained by investing funds elsewhere (other than in these five securities), management should question the wisdom of investing the entire $100,000 in this portfolio.

Similar interpretations can be given to the other dual values. Note that the dual value for constraint 4 is negative at –0.024. This result indicates that increasing the value on the right-hand side of the constraint by one unit can be expected to decrease the objective function value of the optimal solution by 0.024. In terms of the optimal portfolio, then, if Welte invests one more dollar in government bonds (beyond the minimum requirement), the total return will decrease by $0.024. To see why this decrease occurs, note again from the dual value for constraint 1 that the marginal return on the funds invested in the portfolio is 6.9% (the average return is 8%). The rate of return on government bonds is 4.5%. Thus, the cost of investing one more dollar in government bonds is the difference between the marginal return on the portfolio and the marginal return on government bonds: 6.9% – 4.5% = 2.4%.

Note that the optimal solution shows that Midwest Steel should not be included in the portfolio ($M = 0$). The associated reduced cost for M of –0.011 tells us that the objective function coefficient for Midwest Steel would have to increase by 0.011 before considering the Midwest Steel investment alternative would be advisable. With such an increase the Midwest Steel return would be $0.064 + 0.011 = 0.075$, making this investment just as desirable as the currently used Huber Steel investment alternative.

Finally, a simple modification of the Welte linear programming model permits determining the fraction of available funds invested in each security. That is, we divide each of the right-hand-side values by 100,000. Then the optimal values for the variables will give the fraction of funds that should be invested in each security for a portfolio of any size.

NOTES AND COMMENTS

1. The optimal solution to the Welte Mutual Funds problem indicates that $20,000 is to be spent on the Atlantic Oil stock. If Atlantic Oil sells for $75 per share, we would have to purchase exactly 266⅔ shares in order to spend exactly $20,000. The difficulty of purchasing fractional shares can be handled by purchasing the largest possible integer number of shares with the allotted funds (e.g., 266 shares of Atlantic Oil). This approach guarantees that the budget constraint will not be violated. This approach, of course, introduces the possibility that the solution will no longer be optimal, but the danger is slight

if a large number of securities are involved. In cases where the analyst believes that the decision variables *must* have integer values, the problem must be formulated as an integer linear programming model. Integer linear programming is the topic of Chapter 7.

2. Financial portfolio theory stresses obtaining a proper balance between risk and return. In the Welte problem, we explicitly considered return in the objective function. Risk is controlled by choosing constraints that ensure diversity among oil and steel stocks and a balance between government bonds and the steel industry investment.

Financial Planning

Linear programming has been used for a variety of financial planning applications. The Management Science in Action, General Electric Uses Linear Programming for Solar Energy Investment Decisions, describes how linear programming is used to evaluate various scenarios to guide capital investment strategy over a long-term horizon.

MANAGEMENT SCIENCE IN ACTION

GENERAL ELECTRIC USES LINEAR PROGRAMMING FOR SOLAR ENERGY INVESTMENT DECISIONS*

With growing concerns about the environment and our ability to continue to utilize limited non-renewable sources for energy, companies have begun to place much more emphasis on renewable

forms of energy. Water, wind, and solar energy are renewable forms of energy that have become the focus of considerable investment by companies.

(*continued*)

General Electric (GE) has products in a variety of areas within the energy sector. One such area of interest to GE is solar energy. Solar energy is a relatively new concept with rapidly changing technologies; for example, solar cells and solar power systems. Solar cells can convert sunlight directly into electricity. Concentrating solar power systems focus a larger area of sunlight into a small beam that can be used as a heat source for conventional power generation. Solar cells can be placed on rooftops and hence can be used by both commercial and residential customers, whereas solar power systems are mostly used in commercial settings. In recent years, GE has invested in several solar cell technologies.

Determining the appropriate amount of production capacity in which to invest is a difficult problem due to the uncertainties in technology development, costs, and solar energy demand. GE uses a set of decision support tools to solve this problem. A detailed descriptive analytical model is used to estimate the cost of newly developed or proposed solar cells. Statistical models developed for new product introductions are used to estimate annual solar demand 10 to 15 years into the future. Finally, the cost and demand estimates are used in a multiperiod linear program to determine the best production capacity investment plan.

The linear program finds an optimal expansion plan by taking into account inventory, capacity, production, and budget constraints. Because of the high level of uncertainty, the linear program is solved over multiple future scenarios. A solution to each individual scenario is found and evaluated in the other scenarios to assess the risk associated with that plan. GE planning analysts have used these tools to support management's strategic investment decisions in the solar energy sector.

*Based on B. G. Thomas and S. Bollapragada, "General Electric Uses an Integrated Framework for Product Costing, Demand Forecasting and Capacity Planning for New Photovoltaic Technology Products," *Interfaces* 40, no. 5 (September/October 2010): 353–367.

In the rest of this section, we describe an application of linear programming to minimize the cost of satisfying a company's obligations to its early retirement program. Hewlitt Corporation established an early retirement program as part of its corporate restructuring. At the close of the voluntary sign-up period, 68 employees had elected early retirement. As a result of these early retirements, the company incurs the following obligations over the next eight years:

Year	1	2	3	4	5	6	7	8
Cash Requirement	430	210	222	231	240	195	225	255

The cash requirements (in thousands of dollars) are due at the beginning of each year.

The corporate treasurer must determine how much money must be set aside today to meet the eight yearly financial obligations as they come due. The financing plan for the retirement program includes investments in government bonds as well as savings. The investments in government bonds are limited to three choices:

Bond	Price	Rate (%)	Years to Maturity
1	$1150	8.875	5
2	1000	5.500	6
3	1350	11.750	7

The government bonds have a par value of $1000, which means that even with different prices, each bond pays $1000 at maturity. The rates shown are based on the par value. For purposes of planning, the treasurer assumed that any funds not invested in bonds will be placed in savings and earn interest at an annual rate of 4%.

We define the decision variables as follows:

F = total dollars required to meet the retirement plan's eight-year obligation

B_1 = units of bond 1 purchased at the beginning of year 1

B_2 = units of bond 2 purchased at the beginning of year 1

B_3 = units of bond 3 purchased at the beginning of year 1

S_i = amount placed in savings at the beginning of year i for $i = 1, \ldots, 8$

The objective function is to minimize the total dollars needed to meet the retirement plan's eight-year obligation, or

$$\text{Min} \quad F$$

A key feature of this type of financial planning problem is that a constraint must be formulated for each year of the planning horizon. In general, each constraint takes the form:

$$\begin{pmatrix} \text{Funds available at} \\ \text{the beginning of the year} \end{pmatrix} - \begin{pmatrix} \text{Funds invested in bonds} \\ \text{and placed in savings} \end{pmatrix} = \begin{pmatrix} \text{Cash obligation for} \\ \text{the current year} \end{pmatrix}$$

The funds available at the beginning of year 1 are given by F. With a current price of $1150 for bond 1 and investments expressed in thousands of dollars, the total investment for B_1 units of bond 1 would be $1.15B_1$. Similarly, the total investment in bonds 2 and 3 would be $1B_2$ and $1.35B_3$, respectively. The investment in savings for year 1 is S_1. Using these results and the first-year obligation of 430, we obtain the constraint for year 1:

$$F - 1.15B_1 - 1B_2 - 1.35B_3 - S_1 = 430 \quad \text{year 1}$$

We do not consider future investments in bonds because the future price of bonds depends on interest rates and cannot be known in advance.

Investments in bonds can take place only in this first year, and the bonds will be held until maturity.

The funds available at the beginning of year 2 include the investment returns of 8.875% on the par value of bond 1, 5.5% on the par value of bond 2, 11.75% on the par value of bond 3, and 4% on savings. The new amount to be invested in savings for year 2 is S_2. With an obligation of 210, the constraint for year 2 is

$$0.08875B_1 + 0.055B_2 + 0.1175B_3 + 1.04S_1 - S_2 = 210 \quad \text{year 2}$$

Similarly, the constraints for years 3 to 8 are

$$0.08875B_1 + 0.055B_2 + 0.1175B_3 + 1.04S_2 - S_3 = 222 \quad \text{year 3}$$
$$0.08875B_1 + 0.055B_2 + 0.1175B_3 + 1.04S_3 - S_4 = 231 \quad \text{year 4}$$
$$0.08875B_1 + 0.055B_2 + 0.1175B_3 + 1.04S_4 - S_5 = 240 \quad \text{year 5}$$
$$1.08875B_1 + 0.055B_2 + 0.1175B_3 + 1.04S_5 - S_6 = 195 \quad \text{year 6}$$
$$1.055B_2 + 0.1175B_3 + 1.04S_6 - S_7 = 225 \quad \text{year 7}$$
$$1.1175B_3 + 1.04S_7 - S_8 = 255 \quad \text{year 8}$$

Note that the constraint for year 6 shows that funds available from bond 1 are $1.08875B_1$. The coefficient of 1.08875 reflects the fact that bond 1 matures at the end of year 5. As a result, the par value plus the interest from bond 1 during year 5 is available at the beginning of year 6. Also, because bond 1 matures in year 5 and becomes available for use at the beginning of year 6, the variable B_1 does not appear in the constraints for years 7 and 8. Note the similar interpretation for bond 2, which matures at the end of year 6 and has the par value plus interest available at the beginning of year 7. In addition, bond 3 matures at the end of year 7 and has the par value plus interest available at the beginning of year 8.

Finally, note that a variable S_8 appears in the constraint for year 8. The retirement fund obligation will be completed at the beginning of year 8, so we anticipate that S_8 will be zero and no funds will be put into savings. However, the formulation includes S_8 in the event that the bond income plus interest from the savings in year 7 exceed the 255 cash requirement for year 8. Thus, S_8 is a surplus variable that shows any funds remaining after the eight-year cash requirements have been satisfied.

The optimal solution to this 12-variable, 8-constraint linear program is shown in Figure 4.4. With an objective function value of 1728.79385, the total investment required to meet the retirement plan's eight-year obligation is $1,728,794. Using the current prices of

$1150, $1000, and $1350 for each of the bonds, respectively, we can summarize the initial investments in the three bonds as follows:

Bond	Units Purchased	Investment Amount
1	$B_1 = 144.988$	$1150(144.988) = $166,736
2	$B_2 = 187.856$	$1000(187.856) = $187,856
3	$B_3 = 228.188$	$1350(228.188) = $308,054

The solution also shows that $636,148 (see S_1) will be placed in savings at the beginning of the first year. By starting with $1,728,794, the company can make the specified bond and savings investments and have enough leftover to meet the retirement program's first-year cash requirement of $430,000.

The optimal solution in Figure 4.4 shows that the decision variables S_1, S_2, S_3, and S_4 all are greater than zero, indicating investments in savings are required in each of the first four years. However, interest from the bonds plus the bond maturity incomes will be sufficient to cover the retirement program's cash requirements in years 5 through 8.

In this application, the dual value can be thought of as the present value of each dollar in the cash requirement. For example, each dollar that must be paid in year 8 has a present value of $0.67084.

The dual values have an interesting interpretation in this application. Each right-hand-side value corresponds to the payment that must be made in that year. Note that the dual values are positive, indicating that increasing the required payment in any year by $1000 would *increase* the total funds required for the retirement program's obligation by $1000 times the dual value. Also note that the dual values show that increases in required payments in the early years have

FIGURE 4.4   THE SOLUTION FOR THE HEWLITT CORPORATION CASH
REQUIREMENTS PROBLEM

MODEL *file*

Hewlitt

```
Optimal Objective Value =              1728.79385

        Variable              Value            Reduced Cost
     --------------      ---------------      ---------------

           F             1728.79385              0.00000
           B1             144.98815              0.00000
           B2             187.85585              0.00000
           B3             228.18792              0.00000
           S1             636.14794              0.00000
           S2             501.60571              0.00000
           S3             349.68179              0.00000
           S4             182.68091              0.00000
           S5               0.00000              0.06403
           S6               0.00000              0.01261
           S7               0.00000              0.02132
           S8               0.00000              0.67084


      Constraint        Slack/Surplus           Dual Value
     --------------      ---------------      ---------------

           1                0.00000              1.00000
           2                0.00000              0.96154
           3                0.00000              0.92456
           4                0.00000              0.88900
           5                0.00000              0.85480
           6                0.00000              0.76036
           7                0.00000              0.71899
           8                0.00000              0.67084
```

the largest impact. This makes sense in that there is little time to build up investment income in the early years versus the subsequent years. This suggests that if Hewlitt faces increases in required payments it would benefit by deferring those increases to later years if possible.

NOTES AND COMMENTS

1. The optimal solution for the Hewlitt Corporation problem shows fractional numbers of government bonds at 144.988, 187.856, and 228.188 units, respectively. However, fractional bond units usually are not available. If we were conservative and rounded up to 145, 188, and 229 units, respectively, the total funds required for the eight-year retirement program obligation would be approximately $1254 more than the total funds indicated by the objective function. Because of the magnitude of the funds involved, rounding up probably would provide a workable solution. If an optimal integer solution were required, the methods of integer linear programming covered in Chapter 7 would have to be used.

2. We implicitly assumed that interest from the government bonds is paid annually. Investments such as treasury notes actually provide interest payments every six months. In such cases, the model can be reformulated with six-month periods, with interest and/or cash payments occurring every six months.

4.3   OPERATIONS MANAGEMENT APPLICATIONS

Linear programming applications developed for production and operations management include scheduling, staffing, inventory control, and capacity planning. In this section we describe examples with make-or-buy decisions, production scheduling, and workforce assignments.

A Make-or-Buy Decision

We illustrate the use of a linear programming model to determine how much of each of several component parts a company should manufacture and how much it should purchase from an outside supplier. Such a decision is referred to as a make-or-buy decision.

The Janders Company markets various business and engineering products. Currently, Janders is preparing to introduce two new calculators: one for the business market called the Financial Manager and one for the engineering market called the Technician. Each calculator has three components: a base, an electronic cartridge, and a faceplate or top. The same base is used for both calculators, but the cartridges and tops are different. All components can be manufactured by the company or purchased from outside suppliers. The manufacturing costs and purchase prices for the components are summarized in Table 4.5.

Company forecasters indicate that 3000 Financial Manager calculators and 2000 Technician calculators will be needed. However, manufacturing capacity is limited. The company has 200 hours of regular manufacturing time and 50 hours of overtime that can be scheduled for the calculators. Overtime involves a premium at the additional cost of $9 per hour. Table 4.6 shows manufacturing times (in minutes) for the components.

TABLE 4.5   MANUFACTURING COSTS AND PURCHASE PRICES FOR JANDERS CALCULATOR COMPONENTS

	Cost per Unit	
Component	Manufacture (regular time)	Purchase
Base	$0.50	$0.60
Financial cartridge	$3.75	$4.00
Technician cartridge	$3.30	$3.90
Financial top	$0.60	$0.65
Technician top	$0.75	$0.78

TABLE 4.6   MANUFACTURING TIMES IN MINUTES PER UNIT FOR JANDERS
CALCULATOR COMPONENTS

Component	Manufacturing Time
Base	1.0
Financial cartridge	3.0
Technician cartridge	2.5
Financial top	1.0
Technician top	1.5

The problem for Janders is to determine how many units of each component to manufacture and how many units of each component to purchase. We define the decision variables as follows:

$$BM = \text{number of bases manufactured}$$
$$BP = \text{number of bases purchased}$$
$$FCM = \text{number of Financial cartridges manufactured}$$
$$FCP = \text{number of Financial cartridges purchased}$$
$$TCM = \text{number of Technician cartridges manufactured}$$
$$TCP = \text{number of Technician cartridges purchased}$$
$$FTM = \text{number of Financial tops manufactured}$$
$$FTP = \text{number of Financial tops purchased}$$
$$TTM = \text{number of Technician tops manufactured}$$
$$TTP = \text{number of Technician tops purchased}$$

One additional decision variable is needed to determine the hours of overtime that must be scheduled:

$$OT = \text{number of hours of overtime to be scheduled}$$

The objective function is to minimize the total cost, including manufacturing costs, purchase costs, and overtime costs. Using the cost-per-unit data in Table 4.5 and the overtime premium cost rate of $9 per hour, we write the objective function as

$$\text{Min} \quad 0.5BM + 0.6BP + 3.75FCM + 4FCP + 3.3TCM + 3.9TCP + 0.6FTM$$
$$+ 0.65FTP + 0.75TTM + 0.78TTP + 9OT$$

The first five constraints specify the number of each component needed to satisfy the demand for 3000 Financial Manager calculators and 2000 Technician calculators. A total of 5000 base components are needed, with the number of other components depending on the demand for the particular calculator. The five demand constraints are

$$BM + BP = 5000 \quad \text{Bases}$$
$$FCM + FCP = 3000 \quad \text{Financial cartridges}$$
$$TCM + TCP = 2000 \quad \text{Technician cartridges}$$
$$FTM + FTP = 3000 \quad \text{Financial tops}$$
$$TTM + TTP = 2000 \quad \text{Technician tops}$$

Two constraints are needed to guarantee that manufacturing capacities for regular time and overtime cannot be exceeded. The first constraint limits overtime capacity to 50 hours, or

$$OT \leq 50$$

The second constraint states that the total manufacturing time required for all components must be less than or equal to the total manufacturing capacity, including regular time plus

The same units of measure must be used for both the left-hand side and right-hand side of the constraint. In this case, minutes are used.

overtime. The manufacturing times for the components are expressed in minutes, so we state the total manufacturing capacity constraint in minutes, with the 200 hours of regular time capacity becoming $60(200) = 12{,}000$ minutes. The actual overtime required is unknown at this point, so we write the overtime as $60OT$ minutes. Using the manufacturing times from Table 4.6, we have

$$BM + 3FCM + 2.5TCM + FTM + 1.5TTM \leq 12{,}000 + 60OT$$

The complete formulation of the Janders make-or-buy problem with all decision variables greater than or equal to zero is

Min $0.5BM + 0.6BP + 3.75FCM + 4FCP + 3.3TCM + 3.9TCP$
       $+ 0.6FTM + 0.65FTP + 0.75TTM + 0.78TTP + 9OT$

s.t.

BM				$+$	$BP =$	5000	Bases
	FCM			$+$	$FCP =$	3000	Financial cartridges
		TCM		$+$	$TCP =$	2000	Technician cartridges
			FTM	$+$	$FTP =$	3000	Financial tops
			$TTM +$		$TTP =$	2000	Technician tops
					$OT \leq$	50	Overtime hours
$BM + 3FCM + 2.5TCM + FTM + 1.5TTM \leq 12{,}000 + 60OT$							Manufacturing capacity

The optimal solution to this 11-variable, 7-constraint linear program is shown in Figure 4.5. The optimal solution indicates that all 5000 bases (*BM*), 667 Financial Manager cartridges (*FCM*), and 2000 Technician cartridges (*TCM*) should be manufactured. The remaining 2333 Financial Manager cartridges (*FCP*), all the Financial Manager tops (*FTP*), and all Technician tops (*TTP*) should be purchased. No overtime manufacturing is necessary, and the total cost associated with the optimal make-or-buy plan is $24,443.33.

Sensitivity analysis provides some additional information about the unused overtime capacity. The Reduced Costs column shows that the overtime (*OT*) premium would have to decrease by $4 per hour before overtime production should be considered. That is, if the overtime premium is $9 − $4 = $5 or less, Janders may want to replace some of the purchased components with components manufactured on overtime.

The dual value for the manufacturing capacity constraint 7 is −0.083. This value indicates that an additional hour of manufacturing capacity is worth $0.083 per minute or ($0.083)(60) = $5 per hour. The right-hand-side range for constraint 7 shows that this conclusion is valid until the amount of regular time increases to 19,000 minutes, or 316.7 hours.

Sensitivity analysis also indicates that a change in prices charged by the outside suppliers can affect the optimal solution. For instance, the objective coefficient range for *BP* is $0.600 − 0.017 = 0.583$ to no upper limit. If the purchase price for bases remains at $0.583 or more, the number of bases purchased (*BP*) will remain at zero. However, if the purchase price drops below $0.583, Janders should begin to purchase rather than manufacture the base component. Similar sensitivity analysis conclusions about the purchase price ranges can be drawn for the other components.

NOTES AND COMMENTS

The proper interpretation of the dual value for manufacturing capacity (constraint 7) in the Janders problem is that an additional hour of manufacturing capacity is worth ($0.083)(60) = $5 per hour. Thus, the company should be willing to pay a premium of $5 per hour over and above the current regular time cost per hour, which is already included in the manufacturing cost of the product. Thus, if the regular time cost is $18 per hour, Janders should be willing to pay up to $18 + $5 = $23 per hour to obtain additional labor capacity.

FIGURE 4.5   THE SOLUTION FOR THE JANDERS MAKE-OR-BUY PROBLEM

Optimal Objective Value =   24443.33333

Variable	Value	Reduced Cost
BM	5000.00000	0.00000
BP	0.00000	0.01667
FCM	666.66667	0.00000
FCP	2333.33333	0.00000
TCM	2000.00000	0.00000
TCP	0.00000	0.39167
FTM	0.00000	0.03333
FTP	3000.00000	0.00000
TTM	0.00000	0.09500
TTP	2000.00000	0.00000
OT	0.00000	4.00000

Janders

Constraint	Slack/Surplus	Dual Value
1	0.00000	0.58333
2	0.00000	4.00000
3	0.00000	3.50833
4	0.00000	0.65000
5	0.00000	0.78000
6	50.00000	0.00000
7	0.00000	-0.08333

Variable	Objective Coefficient	Allowable Increase	Allowable Decrease
BM	0.50000	0.01667	Infinite
BP	0.60000	Infinite	0.01667
FCM	3.75000	0.10000	0.05000
FCP	4.00000	0.05000	0.10000
TCM	3.30000	0.39167	Infinite
TCP	3.90000	Infinite	0.39167
FTM	0.60000	Infinite	0.03333
FTP	0.65000	0.03333	Infinite
TTM	0.75000	Infinite	0.09500
TTP	0.78000	0.09500	Infinite
OT	9.00000	Infinite	4.00000

Constraint	RHS Value	Allowable Increase	Allowable Decrease
1	5000.00000	2000.00000	5000.00000
2	3000.00000	Infinite	2333.33333
3	2000.00000	800.00000	2000.00000
4	3000.00000	Infinite	3000.00000
5	2000.00000	Infinite	2000.00000
6	50.00000	Infinite	50.00000
7	12000.00000	7000.00000	2000.00000

Production Scheduling

One of the most important applications of linear programming deals with multiperiod planning such as production scheduling. The solution to a production scheduling problem enables the manager to establish an efficient low-cost production schedule for one or more products over several time periods (weeks or months). Essentially, a production scheduling problem can be viewed as a product-mix problem for each of several periods in the future. The manager must determine the production levels that will allow the company to meet product demand requirements, given limitations on production capacity, labor capacity, and storage space, while minimizing total production costs.

One advantage of using linear programming for production scheduling problems is that they recur. A production schedule must be established for the current month, then again for the next month, for the month after that, and so on. When looking at the problem each month, the production manager will find that, although demand for the products has changed, production times, production capacities, storage space limitations, and so on are roughly the same. Thus, the production manager is basically re-solving the same problem handled in previous months, and a general linear programming model of the production scheduling procedure may be applied frequently. Once the model has been formulated, the manager can simply supply the data—demand, capacities, and so on—for the given production period and use the linear programming model repeatedly to develop the production schedule. The Management Science in Action, Vestel Electronics Uses Linear Programming for Sales and Operations Planning, describes how linear programming is used to plan production to meet sales targets while minimizing total production and procurement costs.

MANAGEMENT SCIENCE IN ACTION

VESTEL ELECTRONICS USES LINEAR PROGRAMMING FOR SALES AND OPERATIONS PLANNING*

Vestel Electronics manufactures a variety of products, including LCD and LED televisions. With a single large manufacturing facility in Manisa, Turkey, it has annual capacity of 15 million units. Vestel's primary market is in Europe, with nearly 90 percent of its products sold to European customers. Vestel is very customer-centric and so it allows mass customization of its products. Since a television is a highly customizable product, the number of possible combinations of attributes such as screen size, speaker type, remote control type etc. opens the possibility of ten thousand different versions of the product. Furthermore, Vestel allows low order quantities and order changes until the time of production. This flexibility, while fantastic for customer relations, leads to incredibly challenging production planning problems.

Vestel uses a multiperiod linear programming model to plan its production. The decision variables

of the linear programming model are how much of each product to produce/procure and how much to hold in inventory at the end of each period during the planning horizon. The objective function is to minimize the total production and procurement cost. Constraints ensure that demand is satisfied (all sales targets are met), resource capacities are not violated, and inventory balance equations calculate how much inventory to hold per period. In addition to more efficient and cost-effective production plans, the optimization has generated other benefits such as decreased planning time, improved planning accuracy, decreased inventory levels, better data visibility, and improved data standardization, and accuracy.

*Based on Z. Taskin et al., "Mathematical Programming-Based Sales and Operations Planning at Vestel Electronics," *Interfaces* 45, no. 4 (July/August, 2015): 325–340.

Let us consider the case of the Bollinger Electronics Company, which produces two different electronic components for a major airplane engine manufacturer. The airplane engine manufacturer notifies the Bollinger sales office each quarter of its monthly requirements for components for each of the next three months. The monthly requirements for the components may vary considerably, depending on the type of engine the airplane engine manufacturer is producing. The order shown in Table 4.7 has just been received for the next three-month period.

TABLE 4.7   THREE-MONTH DEMAND SCHEDULE FOR BOLLINGER
                 ELECTRONICS COMPANY

Component	April	May	June
322A	1000	3000	5000
802B	1000	500	3000

After the order is processed, a demand statement is sent to the production control department. The production control department must then develop a three-month production plan for the components. In arriving at the desired schedule, the production manager will want to identify the following:

1. Total production cost
2. Inventory holding cost
3. Change-in-production-level costs

In the remainder of this section, we show how to formulate a linear programming model of the production and inventory process for Bollinger Electronics to minimize the total cost.

To develop the model, we let x_{im} denote the production volume in units for product i in month m. Here $i = 1, 2$, and $m = 1, 2, 3$; $i = 1$ refers to component 322A, $i = 2$ refers to component 802B, $m = 1$ refers to April, $m = 2$ refers to May, and $m = 3$ refers to June. The purpose of the double subscript is to provide a more descriptive notation. We could simply use x_6 to represent the number of units of product 2 produced in month 3, but x_{23} is more descriptive, identifying directly the product and month represented by the variable.

If component 322A costs \$20 per unit produced and component 802B costs \$10 per unit produced, the total production cost part of the objective function is

$$\text{Total production cost} = 20x_{11} + 20x_{12} + 20x_{13} + 10x_{21} + 10x_{22} + 10x_{23}$$

Because the production cost per unit is the same each month, we don't need to include the production costs in the objective function; that is, regardless of the production schedule selected, the total production cost will remain the same. In other words, production costs are not relevant costs for the production scheduling decision under consideration. In cases in which the production cost per unit is expected to change each month, the variable production costs per unit per month must be included in the objective function. The solution for the Bollinger Electronics problem will be the same regardless of whether these costs are included; therefore, we included them so that the value of the linear programming objective function will include all the costs associated with the problem.

To incorporate the relevant inventory holding costs into the model, we let s_{im} denote the inventory level for product i at the end of month m. Bollinger determined that on a monthly basis inventory holding costs are 1.5% of the cost of the product; that is, $(0.015)(\$20) = \$0.30$ per unit for component 322A and $(0.015)(\$10) = \$0.15$ per unit for component 802B. A common assumption made in using the linear programming approach to production scheduling is that monthly ending inventories are an acceptable approximation to the average inventory levels throughout the month. Making this assumption, we write the inventory holding cost portion of the objective function as

$$\text{Inventory holding cost} = 0.30s_{11} + 0.30s_{12} + 0.30s_{13} + 0.15s_{21} + 0.15s_{22} + 0.15s_{23}$$

To incorporate the costs of fluctuations in production levels from month to month, we need to define two additional variables:

$$I_m = \text{increase in the total production level necessary during month } m$$
$$D_m = \text{decrease in the total production level necessary during month } m$$

After estimating the effects of employee layoffs, turnovers, reassignment training costs, and other costs associated with fluctuating production levels, Bollinger estimates that the cost associated with increasing the production level for any month is $0.50 per unit increase. A similar cost associated with decreasing the production level for any month is $0.20 per unit. Thus, we write the third portion of the objective function as

$$\text{Change-in-production-level costs} = 0.50I_1 + 0.50I_2 + 0.50I_3$$
$$+ 0.20D_1 + 0.20D_2 + 0.20D_3$$

Note that the cost associated with changes in production level is a function of the change in the total number of units produced in month m compared to the total number of units produced in month $m - 1$. In other production scheduling applications, fluctuations in production level might be measured in terms of machine hours or labor-hours required rather than in terms of the total number of units produced.

Combining all three costs, the complete objective function becomes

$$\text{Min } 20x_{11} + 20x_{12} + 20x_{13} + 10x_{21} + 10x_{22} + 10x_{23} + 0.30s_{11}$$
$$+ 0.30s_{12} + 0.30s_{13} + 0.15s_{21} + 0.15s_{22} + 0.15s_{23} + 0.50I_1$$
$$+ 0.50I_2 + 0.50I_3 + 0.20D_1 + 0.20D_2 + 0.20D_3$$

We now consider the constraints. First, we must guarantee that the schedule meets customer demand. Because the units shipped can come from the current month's production or from inventory carried over from previous months, the demand requirement takes the form

$$\begin{pmatrix} \text{Ending} \\ \text{inventory} \\ \text{from previous} \\ \text{month} \end{pmatrix} + \begin{pmatrix} \text{Current} \\ \text{production} \end{pmatrix} - \begin{pmatrix} \text{Ending} \\ \text{inventory} \\ \text{for this} \\ \text{month} \end{pmatrix} = \begin{pmatrix} \text{This month's} \\ \text{demand} \end{pmatrix}$$

Suppose that the inventories at the beginning of the three-month scheduling period were 500 units for component 322A and 200 units for component 802B. The demand for both products in the first month (April) was 1000 units, so the constraints for meeting demand in the first month become

$$500 + x_{11} - s_{11} = 1000$$
$$200 + x_{21} - s_{21} = 1000$$

Moving the constants to the right-hand side, we have

Month 1

$$x_{11} - s_{11} = 500$$
$$x_{21} - s_{21} = 800$$

Similarly, we need demand constraints for both products in the second and third months. We write them as follows:

Month 2

$$s_{11} + x_{12} - s_{12} = 3000$$
$$s_{21} + x_{22} - s_{22} = 500$$

Month 3

$$s_{12} + x_{13} - s_{13} = 5000$$
$$s_{22} + x_{23} - s_{23} = 3000$$

If the company specifies a minimum inventory level at the end of the three-month period of at least 400 units of component 322A and at least 200 units of component 802B, we can add the constraints

$$s_{13} \geq 400$$
$$s_{23} \geq 200$$

Suppose that we have the additional information on machine, labor, and storage capacity shown in Table 4.8. Machine, labor, and storage space requirements are given in Table 4.9. To reflect these limitations, the following constraints are necessary:

Machine Capacity

$$0.10x_{11} + 0.08x_{21} \leq 400 \quad \text{month 1}$$
$$0.10x_{12} + 0.08x_{22} \leq 500 \quad \text{month 2}$$
$$0.10x_{13} + 0.08x_{23} \leq 600 \quad \text{month 3}$$

Labor Capacity

$$0.05x_{11} + 0.07x_{21} \leq 300 \quad \text{month 1}$$
$$0.05x_{12} + 0.07x_{22} \leq 300 \quad \text{month 2}$$
$$0.05x_{13} + 0.07x_{23} \leq 300 \quad \text{month 3}$$

Storage Capacity

$$2s_{11} + 3s_{21} \leq 10,000 \quad \text{month 1}$$
$$2s_{12} + 3s_{22} \leq 10,000 \quad \text{month 2}$$
$$2s_{13} + 3s_{23} \leq 10,000 \quad \text{month 3}$$

One final set of constraints must be added to guarantee that I_m and D_m will reflect the increase or decrease in the total production level for month m. Suppose that the production levels for March, the month before the start of the current production scheduling period, had been 1500 units of component 322A and 1000 units of component 802B for a

TABLE 4.8   MACHINE, LABOR, AND STORAGE CAPACITIES
FOR BOLLINGER ELECTRONICS

Month	Machine Capacity (hours)	Labor Capacity (hours)	Storage Capacity (square feet)
April	400	300	10,000
May	500	300	10,000
June	600	300	10,000

TABLE 4.9   MACHINE, LABOR, AND STORAGE REQUIREMENTS FOR COMPONENTS
322A AND 802B

Component	Machine (hours/unit)	Labor (hours/unit)	Storage (square feet/unit)
322A	0.10	0.05	2
802B	0.08	0.07	3

total production level of 1500 + 1000 = 2500 units. We can find the amount of the change in production for April from the relationship

$$\text{April production} - \text{March production} = \text{Change}$$

Using the April production variables, x_{11} and x_{21}, and the March production of 2500 units, we have

$$(x_{11} + x_{21}) - 2500 = \text{Change}$$

Note that the change can be positive or negative. A positive change reflects an increase in the total production level, and a negative change reflects a decrease in the total production level. We can use the increase in production for April, I_1, and the decrease in production for April, D_1, to specify the constraint for the change in total production for the month of April:

$$(x_{11} + x_{21}) - 2500 = I_1 - D_1$$

Of course, we cannot have an increase in production and a decrease in production during the same one-month period; thus, either I_1 or D_1 will be zero. If April requires 3000 units of production, $I_1 = 500$ and $D_1 = 0$. If April requires 2200 units of production, $I_1 = 0$ and $D_1 = 300$. This approach of denoting the change in production level as the difference between two nonnegative variables, I_1 and D_1, permits both positive and negative changes in the total production level. If a single variable (say, c_m) had been used to represent the change in production level, only positive changes would be possible because of the nonnegativity requirement.

Using the same approach in May and June (always subtracting the previous month's total production from the current month's total production), we obtain the constraints for the second and third months of the production scheduling period:

$$(x_{12} + x_{22}) - (x_{11} + x_{21}) = I_2 - D_2$$
$$(x_{13} + x_{23}) - (x_{12} + x_{22}) = I_3 - D_3$$

Linear programming models for production scheduling are often very large. Thousands of decision variables and constraints are necessary when the problem involves numerous products, machines, and time periods.

The initially rather small, two-product, three-month scheduling problem has now developed into an 18-variable, 20-constraint linear programming problem. Note that in this problem we were concerned only with one type of machine process, one type of labor, and one type of storage area. Actual production scheduling problems usually involve several machine types, several labor grades, and/or several storage areas, requiring large-scale linear programs. For instance, a problem involving 100 products over a 12-month period could have more than 1000 variables and constraints.

Figure 4.6 shows the optimal solution to the Bollinger Electronics production scheduling problem. Table 4.10 contains a portion of the managerial report based on the optimal solution.

Consider the monthly variation in the production and inventory schedule shown in Table 4.10. Recall that the inventory cost for component 802B is one-half the inventory cost for component 322A. Therefore, as might be expected, component 802B is produced heavily in the first month (April) and then held in inventory for the demand that will occur in future months. Component 322A tends to be produced when needed, and only small amounts are carried in inventory.

The costs of increasing and decreasing the total production volume tend to smooth the monthly variations. In fact, the minimum-cost schedule calls for a 500-unit increase in total production in April and a 2200-unit increase in total production in May. The May production level of 5200 units is then maintained during June.

The machine usage section of the report shows ample machine capacity in all three months. However, labor capacity is at full utilization (slack = 0 for constraint 13 in Figure 4.6) in the month of May. The dual value shows that an additional hour of labor capacity in May will decrease total cost by approximately $1.11.

A linear programming model of a two-product, three-month production system can provide valuable information in terms of identifying a minimum-cost production

FIGURE 4.6   THE SOLUTION FOR THE BOLLINGER ELECTRONICS PROBLEM

MODEL *file*

Bollinger

```
Optimal Objective Value =        225295.00000

        Variable              Value            Reduced Cost
        --------            --------            ------------
           X11            500.00000                 0.00000
           X12           3200.00000                 0.00000
           X13           5200.00000                 0.00000
           S11              0.00000                 0.17222
           S12            200.00000                 0.00000
           S12            400.00000                 0.00000
           X21           2500.00000                 0.00000
           X22           2000.00000                 0.00000
           X23              0.00000                 0.12778
           S21           1700.00000                 0.00000
           S22           3200.00000                 0.00000
           S23            200.00000                 0.00000
           I1             500.00000                 0.00000
           I2            2200.00000                 0.00000
           I3               0.00000                 0.07222
           D1               0.00000                 0.70000
           D2               0.00000                 0.70000
           D3               0.00000                 0.62778

       Constraint         Slack/Surplus           Dual Value
       ----------         -------------           ----------
            1                0.00000               20.00000
            2                0.00000               10.00000
            3                0.00000               20.12778
            4                0.00000               10.15000
            5                0.00000               20.42778
            6                0.00000               10.30000
            7                0.00000               20.72778
            8                0.00000               10.45000
            9              150.00000                0.00000
           10               20.00000                0.00000
           11               80.00000                0.00000
           12              100.00000                0.00000
           13                0.00000               -1.11111
           14               40.00000                0.00000
           15             4900.00000                0.00000
           16                0.00000                0.00000
           17             8600.00000                0.00000
           18                0.00000               -0.50000
           19                0.00000               -0.50000
           20                0.00000               -0.42778
```

schedule. In larger production systems, where the number of variables and constraints is too large to track manually, linear programming models can provide a significant advantage in developing cost-saving production schedules. The Management Science in Action, Optimizing Production, Inventory, and Distribution at the Kellogg Company, illustrates the use of a large-scale multiperiod linear program for production planning and distribution.

TABLE 4.10   MINIMUM COST PRODUCTION SCHEDULE INFORMATION
FOR THE BOLLINGER ELECTRONICS PROBLEM

Activity	April	May	June
Production			
Component 322A	500	3,200	5,200
Component 802B	2,500	2,000	0
Totals	3,000	5,200	5,200
Ending inventory			
Component 322A	0	200	400
Component 802B	1,700	3,200	200
Machine usage			
Scheduled hours	250	480	520
Slack capacity hours	150	20	80
Labor usage			
Scheduled hours	200	300	260
Slack capacity hours	100	0	40
Storage usage			
Scheduled storage	5,100	10,000	1,400
Slack capacity	4,900	0	8,600

Total production, inventory, and production-smoothing cost = $225,295

MANAGEMENT SCIENCE IN ACTION

**OPTIMIZING PRODUCTION, INVENTORY, AND DISTRIBUTION
AT THE KELLOGG COMPANY***

The Kellogg Company is the largest cereal producer in the world and a leading producer of convenience foods, such as Kellogg's Pop-Tarts and Nutri-Grain cereal bars. Kellogg produces more than 40 different cereals at plants in 19 countries, on six continents. The company markets its products in more than 160 countries and employs more than 15,600 people in its worldwide organization. In the cereal business alone, Kellogg coordinates the production of about 80 products using a total of approximately 90 production lines and 180 packaging lines.

Kellogg has a long history of using linear programming for production planning and distribution. The Kellogg Planning System (KPS) is a large-scale, multiperiod linear program. The operational version of KPS makes production, packaging, inventory, and distribution decisions on a weekly basis. The primary objective of the system is to minimize the total cost of meeting estimated demand; constraints involve processing line capacities, packaging line capacities, and satisfying safety stock requirements.

A tactical version of KPS helps to establish plant budgets and make capacity-expansion and consolidation decisions on a monthly basis. The tactical version was recently used to guide a consolidation of production capacity that resulted in projected savings of $35 to $40 million per year. Because of the success Kellogg has had using KPS in their North American operations, the company is now introducing KPS into Latin America, and is studying the development of a global KPS model.

*Based on G. Brown, J. Keegan, B. Vigus, and K. Wood, "The Kellogg Company Optimizes Production, Inventory, and Distribution," *Interfaces* (November/December 2001): 1–15.

Workforce Assignment

Workforce assignment problems frequently occur when production managers must make decisions involving staffing requirements for a given planning period. Workforce assignments often have some flexibility, and at least some personnel can be assigned to more than one department or work center. Such is the case when employees have been cross-trained

TABLE 4.11   DEPARTMENTAL LABOR-HOURS PER UNIT AND TOTAL HOURS
AVAILABLE FOR THE McCORMICK MANUFACTURING COMPANY

| Department | Labor-Hours per Unit | | Total Hours Available |
	Product 1	Product 2	
1	0.65	0.95	6500
2	0.45	0.85	6000
3	1.00	0.70	7000
4	0.15	0.30	1400

on two or more jobs or, for instance, when sales personnel can be transferred between stores. In the following application, we show how linear programming can be used to determine not only an optimal product mix, but also an optimal workforce assignment.

McCormick Manufacturing Company produces two products with contributions to profit per unit of \$10 and \$9, respectively. The labor requirements per unit produced and the total hours of labor available from personnel assigned to each of four departments are shown in Table 4.11. Assuming that the number of hours available in each department is fixed, we can formulate McCormick's problem as a standard product-mix linear program with the following decision variables:

$$P_1 = \text{units of product 1}$$
$$P_2 = \text{units of product 2}$$

The linear program is

$$\text{Max} \quad 10P_1 + 9P_2$$
s.t.
$$0.65P_1 + 0.95P_2 \leq 6500$$
$$0.45P_1 + 0.85P_2 \leq 6000$$
$$1.00P_1 + 0.70P_2 \leq 7000$$
$$0.15P_1 + 0.30P_2 \leq 1400$$
$$P_1, P_2 \geq 0$$

The optimal solution to the linear programming model is shown in Figure 4.7. After rounding, it calls for 5744 units of product 1, 1795 units of product 2, and a total profit

FIGURE 4.7   THE SOLUTION FOR THE McCORMICK MANUFACTURING COMPANY
PROBLEM WITH NO WORKFORCE TRANSFERS PERMITTED

```
Optimal Objective Value =            73589.74359

        Variable              Value              Reduced Cost
     -------------        -------------        ----------------
           1                5743.58974              0.00000
           2                1794.87179              0.00000

        Constraint         Slack/Surplus           Dual Value
     -------------        -------------        ----------------
           1                1061.53846              0.00000
           2                1889.74359              0.00000
           3                   0.00000              8.46154
           4                   0.00000             10.25641
```

MODEL _file_

McCormick

of $73,590. With this optimal solution, departments 3 and 4 are operating at capacity, and departments 1 and 2 have a slack of approximately 1062 and 1890 hours, respectively. We would anticipate that the product mix would change and that the total profit would increase if the workforce assignment could be revised so that the slack, or unused hours, in departments 1 and 2 could be transferred to the departments currently working at capacity. However, the production manager may be uncertain as to how the workforce should be reallocated among the four departments. Let us expand the linear programming model to include decision variables that will help determine the optimal workforce assignment in addition to the profit-maximizing product mix.

Suppose that McCormick has a cross-training program that enables some employees to be transferred between departments. By taking advantage of the cross-training skills, a limited number of employees and labor-hours may be transferred from one department to another. For example, suppose that the cross-training permits transfers as shown in Table 4.12. Row 1 of this table shows that some employees assigned to department 1 have cross-training skills that permit them to be transferred to department 2 or 3. The right-hand column shows that, for the current production planning period, a maximum of 400 hours can be transferred from department 1. Similar cross-training transfer capabilities and capacities are shown for departments 2, 3, and 4.

When workforce assignments are flexible, we do not automatically know how many hours of labor should be assigned to or be transferred from each department. We need to add decision variables to the linear programming model to account for such changes.

b_i = the labor-hours allocated to department i for i = 1, 2, 3, and 4

t_{ij} = the labor-hours transferred from department i to department j

The right-hand sides are now treated as decision variables.

With the addition of decision variables b_1, b_2, b_3, and b_4, we write the capacity restrictions for the four departments as follows:

$$0.65P_1 + 0.95P_2 \leq b_1$$
$$0.45P_1 + 0.85P_2 \leq b_2$$
$$1.00P_1 + 0.70P_2 \leq b_3$$
$$0.15P_1 + 0.30P_2 \leq b_4$$

The labor-hours ultimately allocated to each department must be determined by a series of labor balance equations, or constraints, that include the number of hours initially assigned to each department plus the number of hours transferred into the department minus the number of hours transferred out of the department. Using department 1 as an example, we determine the workforce allocation as follows:

$$b_1 = \begin{pmatrix} \text{Hours} \\ \text{initially in} \\ \text{department 1} \end{pmatrix} + \begin{pmatrix} \text{Hours} \\ \text{transferred into} \\ \text{department 1} \end{pmatrix} - \begin{pmatrix} \text{Hours} \\ \text{transferred out of} \\ \text{department 1} \end{pmatrix}$$

Table 4.11 shows 6500 hours initially assigned to department 1. We use the transfer decision variables t_{i1} to denote transfers into department 1 and t_{1j} to denote transfers from department 1. Table 4.12 shows that the cross-training capabilities involving department 1

TABLE 4.12 CROSS-TRAINING ABILITY AND CAPACITY INFORMATION

From Department	Cross-Training Transfers Permitted to Department				Maximum Hours Transferable
	1	2	3	4	
1	—	yes	yes	—	400
2	—	—	yes	yes	800
3	—	—	—	yes	100
4	yes	yes	—	—	200

are restricted to transfers from department 4 (variable t_{41}) and transfers to either department 2 or department 3 (variables t_{12} and t_{13}). Thus, we can express the total workforce allocation for department 1 as

$$b_1 = 6500 + t_{41} - t_{12} - t_{13}$$

Moving the decision variables for the workforce transfers to the left-hand side, we have the labor balance equation or constraint

$$b_1 - t_{41} + t_{12} + t_{13} = 6500$$

This form of constraint will be needed for each of the four departments. Thus, the following labor balance constraints for departments 2, 3, and 4 would be added to the model:

$$b_2 - t_{12} - t_{42} + t_{23} + t_{24} = 6000$$
$$b_3 - t_{13} - t_{23} + t_{34} = 7000$$
$$b_4 - t_{24} - t_{34} + t_{41} + t_{42} = 1400$$

Finally, Table 4.12 shows the number of hours that may be transferred from each department is limited, indicating that a transfer capacity constraint must be added for each of the four departments. The additional constraints are

$$t_{12} + t_{13} \leq 400$$
$$t_{23} + t_{24} \leq 800$$
$$t_{34} \leq 100$$
$$t_{41} + t_{42} \leq 200$$

The complete linear programming model has two product decision variables (P_1 and P_2), four department workforce assignment variables (b_1, b_2, b_3, and b_4), seven transfer variables (t_{12}, t_{13}, t_{23}, t_{24}, t_{34}, t_{41}, and t_{42}), and 12 constraints. Figure 4.8 shows the optimal solution to this linear program.

Variations in the workforce assignment model could be used in situations such as allocating raw material resources to products, allocating machine time to products, and allocating salesforce time to stores or sales territories.

McCormick's profit can be increased by $84,011 - $73,590 = $10,421 by taking advantage of cross-training and workforce transfers. The optimal product mix of 6825 units of product 1 and 1751 units of product 2 can be achieved if $t_{13} = 400$ hours are transferred from department 1 to department 3; $t_{23} = 651$ hours are transferred from department 2 to department 3; and $t_{24} = 149$ hours are transferred from department 2 to department 4. The resulting workforce assignments for departments 1 through 4 would provide 6100, 5200, 8051, and 1549 hours, respectively.

If a manager has the flexibility to assign personnel to different departments, reduced workforce idle time, improved workforce utilization, and improved profit should result. The linear programming model in this section automatically assigns employees and labor-hours to the departments in the most profitable manner.

Blending Problems

Blending problems arise whenever a manager must decide how to blend two or more resources to produce one or more products. In these situations, the resources contain one or more essential ingredients that must be blended into final products that will contain specific percentages of each. In most of these applications, then, management must decide how much of each resource to purchase to satisfy product specifications and product demands at minimum cost.

Blending problems occur frequently in the petroleum industry (e.g., blending crude oil to produce different octane gasolines), chemical industry (e.g., blending chemicals to produce fertilizers and weed killers), and food industry (e.g., blending ingredients to produce soft drinks and soups). In this section we illustrate how to apply linear programming to a blending problem in the petroleum industry.

FIGURE 4.8   THE SOLUTION FOR THE McCORMICK MANUFACTURING
COMPANY PROBLEM WITH WORKFORCE TRANSFERS PERMITTED

Optimal Objective Value =   84011.29945

Variable	Value	Reduced Cost
P1	6824.85900	0.00000
P2	1751.41200	0.00000
B1	6100.00000	0.00000
B2	5200.00000	0.00000
B3	8050.84700	0.00000
B4	1549.15300	0.00000
T41	0.00000	7.45763
T12	0.00000	8.24859
T13	400.00000	0.00000
T42	0.00000	8.24859
T23	650.84750	0.00000
T24	149.15250	0.00000
T34	0.00000	0.00000

Constraint	Slack/Surplus	Dual Value
1	0.00000	0.79096
2	640.11300	0.00000
3	0.00000	8.24859
4	0.00000	8.24859
5	0.00000	0.79096
6	0.00000	0.00000
7	0.00000	8.24859
8	0.00000	8.24859
9	0.00000	7.45763
10	0.00000	8.24859
11	100.00000	0.00000
12	200.00000	0.00000

MODEL *file*

McCormickMod

The Grand Strand Oil Company produces regular and premium gasoline for independent service stations in the southeastern United States. The Grand Strand refinery manufactures the gasoline products by blending three petroleum components. The gasolines are sold at different prices, and the petroleum components have different costs. The firm wants to determine how to mix or blend the three components into the two gasoline products and maximize profits.

Data available show that regular gasoline can be sold for $2.90 per gallon and premium gasoline for $3.00 per gallon. For the current production planning period, Grand Strand can obtain the three petroleum components at the cost per gallon and in the quantities shown in Table 4.13.

Product specifications for the regular and premium gasolines restrict the amounts of each component that can be used in each gasoline product. Table 4.14 lists the product specifications. Current commitments to distributors require Grand Strand to produce at least 10,000 gallons of regular gasoline.

The Grand Strand blending problem is to determine how many gallons of each component should be used in the regular gasoline blend and how many should be used in the premium gasoline blend. The optimal blending solution should maximize the firm's profit,

TABLE 4.13 PETROLEUM COST AND SUPPLY FOR THE GRAND STRAND BLENDING PROBLEM

Petroleum Component	Cost per Gallon	Maximum Available
1	$2.50	5,000 gallons
2	$2.60	10,000 gallons
3	$2.84	10,000 gallons

TABLE 4.14 PRODUCT SPECIFICATIONS FOR THE GRAND STRAND BLENDING PROBLEM

Product	Specifications
Regular gasoline	At most 30% component 1
	At least 40% component 2
	At most 20% component 3
Premium gasoline	At least 25% component 1
	At most 45% component 2
	At least 30% component 3

subject to the constraints on the available petroleum supplies shown in Table 4.13, the product specifications shown in Table 4.14, and the required 10,000 gallons of regular gasoline. We define the decision variables as

$$x_{ij} = \text{gallons of component } i \text{ used in gasoline } j,$$
$$\text{where } i = 1, 2, \text{ or } 3 \text{ for components } 1, 2, \text{ or } 3,$$
$$\text{and } j = r \text{ if regular or } j = p \text{ if premium}$$

The six decision variables are

$$x_{1r} = \text{gallons of component 1 in regular gasoline}$$
$$x_{2r} = \text{gallons of component 2 in regular gasoline}$$
$$x_{3r} = \text{gallons of component 3 in regular gasoline}$$
$$x_{1p} = \text{gallons of component 1 in premium gasoline}$$
$$x_{2p} = \text{gallons of component 2 in premium gasoline}$$
$$x_{3p} = \text{gallons of component 3 in premium gasoline}$$

The total number of gallons of each type of gasoline produced is the sum of the number of gallons produced using each of the three petroleum components.

Total Gallons Produced

$$\text{Regular gasoline} = x_{1r} + x_{2r} + x_{3r}$$
$$\text{Premium gasoline} = x_{1p} + x_{2p} + x_{3p}$$

The total gallons of each petroleum component are computed in a similar fashion.

Total Petroleum Component Used

$$\text{component 1} = x_{1r} + x_{1p}$$
$$\text{component 2} = x_{2r} + x_{2p}$$
$$\text{component 3} = x_{3r} + x_{3p}$$

We develop the objective function of maximizing the profit contribution by identifying the difference between the total revenue from both gasolines and the total cost of the three petroleum components. By multiplying the $2.90 per gallon price by the total gallons of regular gasoline, the $3.00 per gallon price by the total gallons of premium gasoline, and the component cost per gallon figures in Table 4.13 by the total gallons of each component used, we obtain the objective function:

$$\text{Max } 2.90(x_{1r} + x_{2r} + x_{3r}) + 3.00(x_{1p} + x_{2p} + x_{3p})$$
$$- 2.50(x_{1r} + x_{1p}) - 2.60(x_{2r} + x_{2p}) - 2.84(x_{3r} + x_{3p})$$

When we combine terms, the objective function becomes

$$\text{Max } 0.40x_{1r} + 0.30x_{2r} + 0.06x_{3r} + 0.50x_{1p} + 0.40x_{2p} + 0.16x_{3p}$$

The limitations on the availability of the three petroleum components are

$$x_{1r} + x_{1p} \leq 5{,}000 \text{ component 1}$$
$$x_{2r} + x_{2p} \leq 10{,}000 \text{ component 2}$$
$$x_{3r} + x_{3p} \leq 10{,}000 \text{ component 3}$$

Six constraints are now required to meet the product specifications stated in Table 4.14. The first specification states that component 1 can account for no more than 30% of the total gallons of regular gasoline produced. That is,

$$x_{1r} \leq 0.30(x_{1r} + x_{2r} + x_{3r})$$

The second product specification listed in Table 4.14 becomes

$$x_{2r} \geq 0.40(x_{1r} + x_{2r} + x_{3r})$$

Similarly, we write the four remaining blending specifications listed in Table 4.14 as

$$x_{3r} \leq 0.20(x_{1r} + x_{2r} + x_{3r})$$
$$x_{1p} \geq 0.25(x_{1p} + x_{2p} + x_{3p})$$
$$x_{2p} \leq 0.45(x_{1p} + x_{2p} + x_{3p})$$
$$x_{3p} \geq 0.30(x_{1p} + x_{2p} + x_{3p})$$

The constraint for at least 10,000 gallons of regular gasoline is

$$x_{1r} + x_{2r} + x_{3r} \geq 10{,}000$$

The complete linear programming model with six decision variables and 10 constraints is

$$\text{Max } 0.40x_{1r} + 0.30x_{2r} + 0.06x_{3r} + 0.50x_{1p} + 0.40x_{2p} + 0.16x_{3p}$$

s.t.

$$
\begin{aligned}
x_{1r} \quad\quad\quad\quad + x_{1p} \quad\quad\quad\quad &\leq 5{,}000 \\
x_{2r} \quad\quad\quad\quad + x_{2p} \quad\quad &\leq 10{,}000 \\
x_{3r} \quad\quad\quad\quad + x_{3p} &\leq 10{,}000 \\
x_{1r} \quad\quad &\leq 0.30(x_{1r} + x_{2r} + x_{3r}) \\
x_{2r} \quad\quad &\geq 0.40(x_{1r} + x_{2r} + x_{3r}) \\
x_{3r} \quad\quad &\leq 0.20(x_{1r} + x_{2r} + x_{3r}) \\
x_{1p} \quad &\geq 0.25(x_{1p} + x_{2p} + x_{3p}) \\
x_{2p} \quad &\leq 0.45(x_{1p} + x_{2p} + x_{3p}) \\
x_{3p} &\geq 0.30(x_{1p} + x_{2p} + x_{3p}) \\
x_{1r} + x_{2r} + x_{2r} \quad\quad &\geq 10{,}000 \\
x_{1r}, x_{2r}, x_{3r}, x_{1p}, x_{2p}, x_{3p} &\geq 0
\end{aligned}
$$

Try Problem 15 as another example of a blending model.

The optimal solution to the Grand Strand blending problem is shown in Figure 4.9. The optimal solution, which provides a profit of $7100, is summarized in Table 4.15. The

FIGURE 4.9   THE SOLUTION FOR THE GRAND STRAND BLENDING PROBLEM

MODEL *file*

Grand

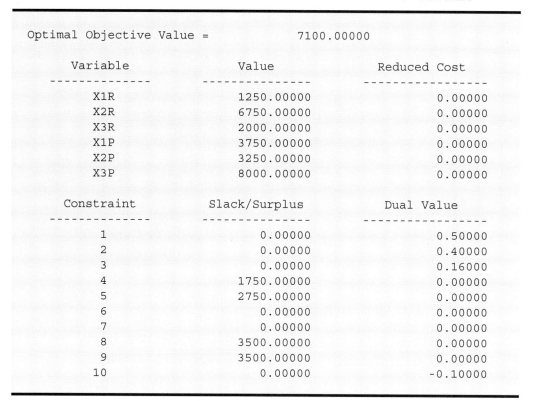

```
Optimal Objective Value =               7100.00000

           Variable              Value            Reduced Cost
        ---------------      ---------------    ------------------

            X1R               1250.00000              0.00000
            X2R               6750.00000              0.00000
            X3R               2000.00000              0.00000
            X1P               3750.00000              0.00000
            X2P               3250.00000              0.00000
            X3P               8000.00000              0.00000


          Constraint         Slack/Surplus          Dual Value
        ---------------      ---------------    ------------------

             1                   0.00000              0.50000
             2                   0.00000              0.40000
             3                   0.00000              0.16000
             4                1750.00000              0.00000
             5                2750.00000              0.00000
             6                   0.00000              0.00000
             7                   0.00000              0.00000
             8                3500.00000              0.00000
             9                3500.00000              0.00000
            10                   0.00000             -0.10000
```

TABLE 4.15   GRAND STRAND GASOLINE BLENDING SOLUTION

| Gasoline | Gallons of Component (percentage) | | | Total |
	Component 1	Component 2	Component 3	
Regular	1,250 (12.5%)	6,750 (67.5%)	2,000 (20%)	10,000
Premium	3,750 (25%)	3,250 (21⅔%)	8,000 (53⅓%)	15,000

optimal blending strategy shows that 10,000 gallons of regular gasoline should be produced. The regular gasoline will be manufactured as a blend of 1250 gallons of component 1, 6750 gallons of component 2, and 2000 gallons of component 3. The 15,000 gallons of premium gasoline will be manufactured as a blend of 3750 gallons of component 1, 3250 gallons of component 2, and 8000 gallons of component 3.

The interpretation of the slack and surplus variables associated with the product specification constraints (constraints 4–9) in Figure 4.9 needs some clarification. If the constraint is a ≤ constraint, the value of the slack variable can be interpreted as the gallons of component use below the maximum amount of the component use specified by the constraint. For example, the slack of 1750.000 for constraint 4 shows that component 1 use is 1750 gallons below the maximum amount of component 1 that could have been used in the production of 10,000 gallons of regular gasoline. If the product specification constraint is a ≥ constraint, a surplus variable shows the gallons of component use above the minimum amount of component use specified by the blending constraint. For example, the surplus of 2750.000 for constraint 5 shows that component 2 use is 2750 gallons above the minimum amount of component 2 that must be used in the production of 10,000 gallons of regular gasoline.

A convenient way to define the decision variables in a blending problem is to use a matrix in which the rows correspond to the raw materials and the columns correspond to the final products. For example, in the Grand Strand blending problem, we define the decision variables as follows:

This approach has two advantages: (1) it provides a systematic way to define the decision variables for any blending problem; and (2) it provides a visual image of the decision variables in terms of how they are related to the raw materials, products, and each other.

		Final Products	
		Regular Gasoline	**Premium Gasoline**
Raw Materials	**Component 1**	x_{1r}	x_{1p}
	Component 2	x_{2r}	x_{2p}
	Component 3	x_{3r}	x_{3p}

SUMMARY

In this chapter we presented a broad range of applications that demonstrate how to use linear programming to assist in the decision-making process. We formulated and solved problems from marketing, finance, and operations management, and interpreted the computer output.

Many of the illustrations presented in this chapter are scaled-down versions of actual situations in which linear programming has been applied. In real-world applications, the problem may not be so concisely stated, the data for the problem may not be as readily available, and the problem most likely will involve numerous decision variables and/or constraints. However, a thorough study of the applications in this chapter is a good place to begin in applying linear programming to real problems.

PROBLEMS

Note: The following problems have been designed to give you an understanding and appreciation of the broad range of problems that can be formulated as linear programs. You should be able to formulate a linear programming model for each of the problems. However, you will need access to a linear programming computer package (e.g., Excel Solver or LINGO) to develop the solutions and make the requested interpretations.

 SELF*test*

1. The Westchester Chamber of Commerce periodically sponsors public service seminars and programs. Currently, promotional plans are under way for this year's program. Advertising alternatives include television, radio, and online. Audience estimates, costs, and maximum media usage limitations are as shown.

Constraint	Television	Radio	Online
Audience per advertisement	100,000	18,000	40,000
Cost per advertisement	$2000	$300	$600
Maximum media usage	10	20	10

To ensure a balanced use of advertising media, radio advertisements must not exceed 50% of the total number of advertisements authorized. In addition, television should account for at least 10% of the total number of advertisements authorized.

a. If the promotional budget is limited to $18,200, how many commercial messages should be run on each medium to maximize total audience contact? What is the allocation of the budget among the three media, and what is the total audience reached?

    b. By how much would audience contact increase if an extra $100 were allocated to the promotional budget?

2. The management of Hartman Company is trying to determine the amount of each of two products to produce over the coming planning period. The following information concerns labor availability, labor utilization, and product profitability:

Department	Product (hours/unit)		Labor-Hours Available
	1	2	
A	1.00	0.35	100
B	0.30	0.20	36
C	0.20	0.50	50
Profit contribution/unit	$30.00	$15.00	

    a. Develop a linear programming model of the Hartman Company problem. Solve the model to determine the optimal production quantities of products 1 and 2.

    b. In computing the profit contribution per unit, management doesn't deduct labor costs because they are considered fixed for the upcoming planning period. However, suppose that overtime can be scheduled in some of the departments. Which departments would you recommend scheduling for overtime? How much would you be willing to pay per hour of overtime in each department?

    c. Suppose that 10, 6, and 8 hours of overtime may be scheduled in departments A, B, and C, respectively. The cost per hour of overtime is $18 in department A, $22.50 in department B, and $12 in department C. Formulate a linear programming model that can be used to determine the optimal production quantities if overtime is made available. What are the optimal production quantities, and what is the revised total contribution to profit? How much overtime do you recommend using in each department? What is the increase in the total contribution to profit if overtime is used?

3. The employee credit union at State University is planning the allocation of funds for the coming year. The credit union makes four types of loans to its members. In addition, the credit union invests in risk-free securities to stabilize income. The various revenue-producing investments together with annual rates of return are as follows:

Type of Loan/Investment	Annual Rate of Return (%)
Automobile loans	8
Furniture loans	10
Other secured loans	11
Signature loans	12
Risk-free securities	9

The credit union will have $2 million available for investment during the coming year. State laws and credit union policies impose the following restrictions on the composition of the loans and investments:

- Risk-free securities may not exceed 30% of the total funds available for investment.
- Signature loans may not exceed 10% of the funds invested in all loans (automobile, furniture, other secured, and signature loans).
- Furniture loans plus other secured loans may not exceed the automobile loans.
- Other secured loans plus signature loans may not exceed the funds invested in risk-free securities.

How should the $2 million be allocated to each of the loan/investment alternatives to maximize total annual return? What is the projected total annual return?

4. Hilltop Coffee manufactures a coffee product by blending three types of coffee beans. The cost per pound and the available pounds of each bean are as follows:

Bean	Cost per Pound	Available Pounds
1	$0.50	500
2	$0.70	600
3	$0.45	400

Consumer tests with coffee products were used to provide ratings on a scale of 0–100, with higher ratings indicating higher quality. Product quality standards for the blended coffee require a consumer rating for aroma to be at least 75 and a consumer rating for taste to be at least 80. The individual ratings of the aroma and taste for coffee made from 100% of each bean are as follows:

Bean	Aroma Rating	Taste Rating
1	75	86
2	85	88
3	60	75

Assume that the aroma and taste attributes of the coffee blend will be a weighted average of the attributes of the beans used in the blend.

a. What is the minimum-cost blend that will meet the quality standards and provide 1000 pounds of the blended coffee product?
b. What is the cost per pound for the coffee blend?
c. Determine the aroma and taste ratings for the coffee blend.
d. If additional coffee were to be produced, what would be the expected cost per pound?

5. Kilgore's Deli is a small delicatessen located near a major university. Kilgore does a large walk-in carry-out lunch business. The deli offers two luncheon chili specials, Wimpy and Dial 911. At the beginning of the day, Kilgore needs to decide how much of each special to make (he always sells out of whatever he makes). The profit on one serving of Wimpy is $0.45, on one serving of Dial 911, $0.58. Each serving of Wimpy requires 0.25 pound of beef, 0.25 cup of onions, and 5 ounces of Kilgore's special sauce. Each serving of Dial 911 requires 0.25 pound of beef, 0.4 cup of onions, 2 ounces of Kilgore's special sauce, and 5 ounces of hot sauce. Today, Kilgore has 20 pounds of beef, 15 cups of onions, 88 ounces of Kilgore's special sauce, and 60 ounces of hot sauce on hand.

a. Develop an LP model that will tell Kilgore how many servings of Wimpy and Dial 911 to make in order to maximize his profit today.
b. Find an optimal solution.
c. What is the dual value for special sauce? Interpret the dual value.
d. Increase the amount of special sauce available by 1 ounce and re-solve. Does the solution confirm the answer to part (c)? Give the new solution.

6. G. Kunz and Sons, Inc., manufactures two products used in the heavy equipment industry. Both products require manufacturing operations in two departments. The following are the production time (in hours) and profit contribution figures for the two products:

Product	Profit per Unit	Labor-Hours	
		Dept. A	Dept. B
1	$25	6	12
2	$20	8	10

For the coming production period, Kunz has available a total of 900 hours of labor that can be allocated to either of the two departments. Find the production plan and labor allocation (hours assigned in each department) that will maximize the total contribution to profit.

7. As part of the settlement for a class action lawsuit, Hoxworth Corporation must provide sufficient cash to make the following annual payments (in thousands of dollars):

Year	1	2	3	4	5	6
Payment	190	215	240	285	315	460

The annual payments must be made at the beginning of each year. The judge will approve an amount that, along with earnings on its investment, will cover the annual payments. Investment of the funds will be limited to savings (at 4% annually) and government securities, at prices and rates currently quoted in *The Wall Street Journal*.

Hoxworth wants to develop a plan for making the annual payments by investing in the following securities (par value = $1000). Funds not invested in these securities will be placed in savings.

Security	Current Price	Rate (%)	Years to Maturity
1	$1055	6.750	3
2	$1000	5.125	4

Assume that interest is paid annually. The plan will be submitted to the judge and, if approved, Hoxworth will be required to pay a trustee the amount that will be required to fund the plan.
a. Use linear programming to find the minimum cash settlement necessary to fund the annual payments.
b. Use the dual value to determine how much more Hoxworth should be willing to pay now to reduce the payment at the beginning of year 6 to $400,000.
c. Use the dual value to determine how much more Hoxworth should be willing to pay to reduce the year 1 payment to $150,000.
d. Suppose that the annual payments are to be made at the end of each year. Reformulate the model to accommodate this change. How much would Hoxworth save if this change could be negotiated?

8. The Clark County Sheriff's Department schedules police officers for 8-hour shifts. The beginning times for the shifts are 8:00 A.M., noon, 4:00 P.M., 8:00 P.M., midnight, and 4:00 A.M. An officer beginning a shift at one of these times works for the next 8 hours. During normal weekday operations, the number of officers needed varies depending on the time of day. The department staffing guidelines require the following minimum number of officers on duty:

Time of Day	Minimum Officers on Duty
8:00 A.M.–Noon	5
Noon–4:00 P.M.	6
4:00 P.M.–8:00 P.M.	10
8:00 P.M.–Midnight	7
Midnight–4:00 A.M.	4
4:00 A.M.–8:00 A.M.	6

Determine the number of police officers that should be scheduled to begin the 8-hour shifts at each of the six times (8:00 A.M., noon, 4:00 P.M., 8:00 P.M., midnight, and 4:00 A.M.) to minimize the total number of officers required. (*Hint:* Let x_1 = the number of officers beginning work at 8:00 A.M., x_2 = the number of officers beginning work at noon, and so on.)

SELF*test*

9. Epsilon Airlines services predominately the eastern and southeastern United States. A vast majority of Epsilon's customers make reservations through Epsilon's website, but a small percentage of customers make reservations via phone. Epsilon employs call-center personnel to handle these reservations along with any problems with the website reservation system and for the rebooking of flights for customers if their plans change or their travel is disrupted. Staffing the call center appropriately is a challenge for Epsilon's management team. Having too many employees on hand is a waste of money, but having too few results in very poor customer service and the potential loss of customers.

   Epsilon analysts have estimated the minimum number of call-center employees needed by day of week for the upcoming vacation season (June, July, and the first two weeks of August). These estimates are as follows:

Day	Minimum Number of Employees Needed
Monday	75
Tuesday	50
Wednesday	45
Thursday	60
Friday	90
Saturday	75
Sunday	45

   The call-center employees work five consecutive days and then have two consecutive days off. An employee may start work any day of the week. Each call-center employee receives the same salary. Assume that the schedule cycles and ignore start-up and stopping of the schedule. Develop a model that will minimize the total number of call-center employees needed to meet the minimum requirements. Find the optimal solution. Give the number of call-center employees that exceed the minimum required.

10. An investment advisor at Shore Financial Services wants to develop a model that can be used to allocate investment funds among four alternatives: stocks, bonds, mutual funds, and cash. For the coming investment period, the company developed estimates of the annual rate of return and the associated risk for each alternative. Risk is measured using an index between 0 and 1, with higher risk values denoting more volatility and thus more uncertainty.

Investment	Annual Rate of Return (%)	Risk
Stocks	10	0.8
Bonds	3	0.2
Mutual funds	4	0.3
Cash	1	0.0

   Because cash is held in a money market fund, the annual return is lower, but it carries essentially no risk. The objective is to determine the portion of funds allocated to each investment alternative in order to maximize the total annual return for the portfolio subject to the risk level the client is willing to tolerate.

   Total risk is the sum of the risk for all investment alternatives. For instance, if 40% of a client's funds are invested in stocks, 30% in bonds, 20% in mutual funds, and 10% in cash, the total risk for the portfolio would be $0.40(0.8) + 0.30(0.2) + 0.20(0.3) + 0.10(0.0) = 0.44$. An investment advisor will meet with each client to discuss the client's investment objectives and to determine a maximum total risk value for the client. A maximum total risk value of less than 0.3 would be assigned to a conservative investor; a maximum total risk value of between 0.3 and 0.5 would be assigned to a moderate tolerance to risk; and a maximum total risk value greater than 0.5 would be assigned to a more aggressive investor.

Shore Financial Services specified additional guidelines that must be applied to all clients. The guidelines are as follows:

- No more than 75% of the total investment may be in stocks.
- The amount invested in mutual funds must be at least as much as invested in bonds.
- The amount of cash must be at least 10%, but no more than 30% of the total investment funds.

a. Suppose the maximum risk value for a particular client is 0.4. What is the optimal allocation of investment funds among stocks, bonds, mutual funds, and cash? What is the annual rate of return and the total risk for the optimal portfolio?

b. Suppose the maximum risk value for a more conservative client is 0.18. What is the optimal allocation of investment funds for this client? What is the annual rate of return and the total risk for the optimal portfolio?

c. Another more aggressive client has a maximum risk value of 0.7. What is the optimal allocation of investment funds for this client? What is the annual rate of return and the total risk for the optimal portfolio?

d. Refer to the solution for the more aggressive client in part (c). Would this client be interested in having the investment advisor increase the maximum percentage allowed in stocks or decrease the requirement that the amount of cash must be at least 10% of the funds invested? Explain.

e. What is the advantage of defining the decision variables as is done in this model rather than stating the amount to be invested and expressing the decision variables directly in dollar amounts?

11. Edwards Manufacturing Company purchases two component parts from three different suppliers. The suppliers have limited capacity, and no one supplier can meet all the company's needs. In addition, the suppliers charge different prices for the components. Component price data (in price per unit) are as follows:

		Supplier	
Component	1	2	3
1	$12	$13	$14
2	$10	$11	$10

Each supplier has a limited capacity in terms of the total number of components it can supply. However, as long as Edwards provides sufficient advance orders, each supplier can devote its capacity to component 1, component 2, or any combination of the two components, if the total number of units ordered is within its capacity. Supplier capacities are as follows:

Supplier	1	2	3
Capacity	600	1000	800

If the Edwards production plan for the next period includes 1000 units of component 1 and 800 units of component 2, what purchases do you recommend? That is, how many units of each component should be ordered from each supplier? What is the total purchase cost for the components?

12. The Atlantic Seafood Company (ASC) is a buyer and distributor of seafood products that are sold to restaurants and specialty seafood outlets throughout the Northeast. ASC has a frozen storage facility in New York City that serves as the primary distribution point for all products. One of the ASC products is frozen large black tiger shrimp, which are sized at 16–20 pieces per pound. Each Saturday ASC can purchase more tiger shrimp or sell the tiger shrimp at the existing New York City warehouse market price. The ASC goal is to

buy tiger shrimp at a low weekly price and sell it later at a higher price. ASC currently has 20,000 pounds of tiger shrimp in storage. Space is available to store a maximum of 100,000 pounds of tiger shrimp each week. In addition, ASC developed the following estimates of tiger shrimp prices for the next four weeks:

Week	Price/lb
1	$6.00
2	$6.20
3	$6.65
4	$5.55

ASC would like to determine the optimal buying-storing-selling strategy for the next four weeks. The cost to store a pound of shrimp for one week is $0.15, and to account for unforeseen changes in supply or demand, management also indicated that 25,000 pounds of tiger shrimp must be in storage at the end of week 4. Determine the optimal buying-storing-selling strategy for ASC. What is the projected four-week profit?

13. Romans Food Market, located in Saratoga, New York, carries a variety of specialty foods from around the world. Two of the store's leading products use the Romans Food Market name: Romans Regular Coffee and Romans DeCaf Coffee. These coffees are blends of Brazilian Natural and Colombian Mild coffee beans, which are purchased from a distributor located in New York City. Because Romans purchases large quantities, the coffee beans may be purchased on an as-needed basis for a price 10% higher than the market price the distributor pays for the beans. The current market price is $0.47 per pound for Brazilian Natural and $0.62 per pound for Colombian Mild. The compositions of each coffee blend are as follows:

		Blend
Bean	Regular	DeCaf
Brazilian Natural	75%	40%
Colombian Mild	25%	60%

Romans sells the Regular blend for $3.60 per pound and the DeCaf blend for $4.40 per pound. Romans would like to place an order for the Brazilian and Colombian coffee beans that will enable the production of 1000 pounds of Romans Regular coffee and 500 pounds of Romans DeCaf coffee. The production cost is $0.80 per pound for the Regular blend. Because of the extra steps required to produce DeCaf, the production cost for the DeCaf blend is $1.05 per pound. Packaging costs for both products are $0.25 per pound. Formulate a linear programming model that can be used to determine the pounds of Brazilian Natural and Colombian Mild that will maximize the total contribution to profit. What is the optimal solution and what is the contribution to profit?

14. The production manager for the Classic Boat Corporation must determine how many units of the Classic 21 model to produce over the next four quarters. The company has a beginning inventory of 100 Classic 21 boats, and demand for the four quarters is 2000 units in quarter 1, 4000 units in quarter 2, 3000 units in quarter 3, and 1500 units in quarter 4. The firm has limited production capacity in each quarter. That is, up to 4000 units can be produced in quarter 1, 3000 units in quarter 2, 2000 units in quarter 3, and 4000 units in quarter 4. Each boat held in inventory in quarters 1 and 2 incurs an inventory holding cost of $250 per unit; the holding cost for quarters 3 and 4 is $300 per unit. The production costs for the first quarter are $10,000 per unit; these costs are expected to increase by 10% each quarter because of increases in labor and material costs. Management specified that the ending inventory for quarter 4 must be at least 500 boats.

a. Formulate a linear programming model that can be used to determine the production schedule that will minimize the total cost of meeting demand in each quarter subject to the production capacities in each quarter and also to the required ending inventory in quarter 4.

b. Solve the linear program formulated in part (a). Then develop a table that will show for each quarter the number of units to manufacture, the ending inventory, and the costs incurred.

c. Interpret each of the dual values corresponding to the constraints developed to meet demand in each quarter. Based on these dual values, what advice would you give the production manager?

d. Interpret each of the dual values corresponding to the production capacity in each quarter. Based on each of these dual values, what advice would you give the production manager?

 SELF*test*

15. Seastrand Oil Company produces two grades of gasoline: regular and high octane. Both gasolines are produced by blending two types of crude oil. Although both types of crude oil contain the two important ingredients required to produce both gasolines, the percentage of important ingredients in each type of crude oil differs, as does the cost per gallon. The percentage of ingredients A and B in each type of crude oil and the cost per gallon are shown.

Crude Oil	Cost	Ingredient A	Ingredient B
1	$0.10	20%	60%
2	$0.15	50%	30%

Crude oil 1 is 60% ingredient B

Each gallon of regular gasoline must contain at least 40% of ingredient A, whereas each gallon of high octane can contain at most 50% of ingredient B. Daily demand for regular and high-octane gasoline is 800,000 and 500,000 gallons, respectively. How many gallons of each type of crude oil should be used in the two gasolines to satisfy daily demand at a minimum cost?

16. The Ferguson Paper Company produces rolls of paper for use in adding machines, desk calculators, and cash registers. The rolls, which are 200 feet long, are produced in widths of 1½, 2½, and 3½ inches. The production process provides 200-foot rolls in 10-inch widths only. The firm must therefore cut the rolls to the desired final product sizes. The seven cutting alternatives and the amount of waste generated by each are as follows:

Cutting Alternative	Number of Rolls			Waste (inches)
	1½ in.	2½ in.	3½ in.	
1	6	0	0	1
2	0	4	0	0
3	2	0	2	0
4	0	1	2	½
5	1	3	0	1
6	1	2	1	0
7	4	0	1	½

The minimum requirements for the three products are

Roll Width (inches)	1½	2½	3½
Units	1000	2000	4000

a. If the company wants to minimize the number of 10-inch rolls that must be manufactured, how many 10-inch rolls will be processed on each cutting alternative? How many rolls are required, and what is the total waste (inches)?

b. If the company wants to minimize the waste generated, how many 10-inch rolls will be processed on each cutting alternative? How many rolls are required, and what is the total waste (inches)?

c. What are the differences in parts (a) and (b) to this problem? In this case, which objective do you prefer? Explain. What types of situations would make the other objective more desirable?

17. Frandec Company manufactures, assembles, and rebuilds material-handling equipment used in warehouses and distribution centers. One product, called a Liftmaster, is assembled from four components: a frame, a motor, two supports, and a metal strap. Frandec's production schedule calls for 5000 Liftmasters to be made next month. Frandec purchases the motors from an outside supplier, but the frames, supports, and straps may be either manufactured by the company or purchased from an outside supplier. Manufacturing and purchase costs per unit are shown.

Component	Manufacturing Cost	Purchase Cost
Frame	$38.00	$51.00
Support	$11.50	$15.00
Strap	$ 6.50	$ 7.50

Three departments are involved in the production of these components. The time (in minutes per unit) required to process each component in each department and the available capacity (in hours) for the three departments are as follows:

		Department	
Component	Cutting	Milling	Shaping
Frame	3.5	2.2	3.1
Support	1.3	1.7	2.6
Strap	0.8	—	1.7
Capacity (hours)	350	420	680

a. Formulate and solve a linear programming model for this make-or-buy application. How many of each component should be manufactured and how many should be purchased?

b. What is the total cost of the manufacturing and purchasing plan?

c. How many hours of production time are used in each department?

d. How much should Frandec be willing to pay for an additional hour of time in the shaping department?

e. Another manufacturer has offered to sell frames to Frandec for $45 each. Could Frandec improve its position by pursuing this opportunity? Why or why not?

18. The Two-Rivers Oil Company near Pittsburgh transports gasoline to its distributors by truck. The company recently contracted to supply gasoline distributors in southern Ohio, and it has $600,000 available to spend on the necessary expansion of its fleet of gasoline tank trucks. Three models of gasoline tank trucks are available.

Truck Model	Capacity (gallons)	Purchase Cost	Monthly Operating Cost, Including Depreciation
Super Tanker	5,000	$67,000	$550
Regular Line	2,500	$55,000	$425
Econo-Tanker	1,000	$46,000	$350

The company estimates that the monthly demand for the region will be 550,000 gallons of gasoline. Because of the size and speed differences of the trucks, the number of deliveries or round trips possible per month for each truck model will vary. Trip capacities are estimated at 15 trips per month for the Super Tanker, 20 trips per month for the Regular Line, and 25 trips per month for the Econo-Tanker. Based on maintenance and driver availability, the firm does not want to add more than 15 new vehicles to its fleet. In addition, the company has decided to purchase at least three of the new Econo-Tankers for use on short-run, low-demand routes. As a final constraint, the company does not want more than half the new models to be Super Tankers.

a. If the company wishes to satisfy the gasoline demand with a minimum monthly operating expense, how many models of each truck should be purchased?

b. If the company did not require at least three Econo-Tankers and did not limit the number of Super Tankers to at most half the new models, how many models of each truck should be purchased?

SELF*test*

19. The Silver Star Bicycle Company will be manufacturing both men's and women's models for its Easy-Pedal 10-speed bicycles during the next two months. Management wants to develop a production schedule indicating how many bicycles of each model should be produced in each month. Current demand forecasts call for 150 men's and 125 women's models to be shipped during the first month and 200 men's and 150 women's models to be shipped during the second month. Additional data are shown:

Model	Production Costs	Labor Requirements (hours)		Current Inventory
		Manufacturing	Assembly	
Men's	$120	2.0	1.5	20
Women's	$ 90	1.6	1.0	30

Last month the company used a total of 1000 hours of labor. The company's labor relations policy will not allow the combined total hours of labor (manufacturing plus assembly) to increase or decrease by more than 100 hours from month to month. In addition, the company charges monthly inventory at the rate of 2% of the production cost based on the inventory levels at the end of the month. The company would like to have at least 25 units of each model in inventory at the end of the two months.

a. Establish a production schedule that minimizes production and inventory costs and satisfies the labor-smoothing, demand, and inventory requirements. What inventories will be maintained and what are the monthly labor requirements?

b. If the company changed the constraints so that monthly labor increases and decreases could not exceed 50 hours, what would happen to the production schedule? How much will the cost increase? What would you recommend?

20. Filtron Corporation produces filtration containers used in water treatment systems. Although business has been growing, the demand each month varies considerably. As a result, the company utilizes a mix of part-time and full-time employees to meet production demands. Although this approach provides Filtron with great flexibility, it has resulted in increased costs and morale problems among employees. For instance, if Filtron needs to increase production from one month to the next, additional part-time employees have to be hired and trained, and costs go up. If Filtron has to decrease production, the workforce has to be reduced and Filtron incurs additional costs in terms of unemployment benefits and decreased morale. Best estimates are that increasing the number of units produced from one month to the next will increase production costs by $1.25 per unit, and that decreasing the number of units produced will increase production costs by $1.00 per unit. In February Filtron produced 10,000 filtration containers but only sold 7500 units; 2500 units are currently in inventory. The sales forecasts for March, April, and May are for 12,000 units, 8000 units, and 15,000 units, respectively. In addition, Filtron has the capacity to store up to 3000 filtration containers at the end of any month. Management would like to determine the number of units to be produced in March, April, and May that will minimize the total cost of the monthly production increases and decreases.

21. Greenville Cabinets received a contract to produce speaker cabinets for a major speaker manufacturer. The contract calls for the production of 3300 bookshelf speakers and 4100 floor speakers over the next two months, with the following delivery schedule:

Model	Month 1	Month 2
Bookshelf	2100	1200
Floor	1500	2600

Greenville estimates that the production time for each bookshelf model is 0.7 hour and the production time for each floor model is 1 hour. The raw material costs are $10 for each bookshelf model and $12 for each floor model. Labor costs are $22 per hour using regular production time and $33 using overtime. Greenville has up to 2400 hours of regular production time available each month and up to 1000 additional hours of overtime available each month. If production for either cabinet exceeds demand in month 1, the cabinets can be stored at a cost of $5 per cabinet. For each product, determine the number of units that should be manufactured each month on regular time and on overtime to minimize total production and storage costs.

22. TriCity Manufacturing (TCM) makes Styrofoam cups, plates, and sandwich and meal containers. Next week's schedule calls for the production of 80,000 small sandwich containers, 80,000 large sandwich containers, and 65,000 meal containers. To make these containers, Styrofoam sheets are melted and formed into final products using three machines: M1, M2, and M3. Machine M1 can process Styrofoam sheets with a maximum width of 12 inches. The width capacity of machine M2 is 16 inches, and the width capacity of machine M3 is 20 inches. The small sandwich containers require 10-inch-wide Styrofoam sheets; thus, these containers can be produced on each of the three machines. The large sandwich containers require 12-inch-wide sheets; thus, these containers can also be produced on each of the three machines. However, the meal containers require 16-inch-wide Styrofoam sheets, so the meal containers cannot be produced on machine M1. Waste is incurred in the production of all three containers because Styrofoam is lost in the heating and forming process as well as in the final trimming of the product. The amount of waste generated varies depending upon the container produced and the machine used. The following table shows the waste in square inches for each machine and product combination. The waste material is recycled for future use.

Machine	Small Sandwich	Large Sandwich	Meal
M1	20	15	—
M2	24	28	18
M3	32	35	36

Production rates also depend upon the container produced and the machine used. The following table shows the production rates in units per minute for each machine and product combination. Machine capacities are limited for the next week. Time available is 35 hours for machine M1, 35 hours for machine M2, and 40 hours for machine M3.

Machine	Small Sandwich	Large Sandwich	Meal
M1	30	25	—
M2	45	40	30
M3	60	52	44

a. Costs associated with reprocessing the waste material have been increasing. Thus, TCM would like to minimize the amount of waste generated in meeting next week's production schedule. Formulate a linear programming model that can be used to determine the best production schedule.

b. Solve the linear program formulated in part (a) to determine the production schedule. How much waste is generated? Which machines, if any, have idle capacity?

23. EZ-Windows, Inc., manufactures replacement windows for the home remodeling business. In January, the company produced 15,000 windows and ended the month with 9000 windows in inventory. EZ-Windows' management team would like to develop a production schedule for the next three months. A smooth production schedule is obviously desirable because it maintains the current workforce and provides a similar month-to-month operation. However, given the sales forecasts, the production capacities, and the storage capabilities as shown, the management team does not think a smooth production schedule with the same production quantity each month possible.

	February	March	April
Sales forecast	15,000	16,500	20,000
Production capacity	14,000	14,000	18,000
Storage capacity	6,000	6,000	6,000

The company's cost accounting department estimates that increasing production by one window from one month to the next will increase total costs by $1.00 for each unit increase in the production level. In addition, decreasing production by one unit from one month to the next will increase total costs by $0.65 for each unit decrease in the production level. Ignoring production and inventory carrying costs, formulate and solve a linear programming model that will minimize the cost of changing production levels while still satisfying the monthly sales forecasts.

24. Morton Financial must decide on the percentage of available funds to commit to each of two investments, referred to as A and B, over the next four periods. The following table shows the amount of new funds available for each of the four periods, as well as the cash expenditure required for each investment (negative values) or the cash income from the investment (positive values). The data shown (in thousands of dollars) reflect the amount of expenditure or income if 100% of the funds available in any period are invested in either A or B. For example, if Morton decides to invest 100% of the funds available in any period in investment A, it will incur cash expenditures of $1000 in period 1, $800 in period 2, $200 in period 3, and income of $200 in period 4. Note, however, if Morton made the decision to invest 80% in investment A, the cash expenditures or income would be 80% of the values shown.

Period	New Investment Funds Available	Investment A	Investment B
1	1500	−1000	−800
2	400	−800	−500
3	500	−200	−300
4	100	200	300

The amount of funds available in any period is the sum of the new investment funds for the period, the new loan funds, the savings from the previous period, the cash income from investment A, and the cash income from investment B. The funds available in any period can be used to pay the loan and interest from the previous period, placed in savings, used to pay the cash expenditures for investment A, or used to pay the cash expenditures for investment B.

Assume an interest rate of 10% per period for savings and an interest rate of 18% per period on borrowed funds. Let

$$S(t) = \text{the savings for period } t$$
$$L(t) = \text{the new loan funds for period } t$$

Then, in any period t, the savings income from the previous period is $1.1S(t-1)$, and the loan and interest expenditure from the previous period is $1.18L(t-1)$.

At the end of period 4, investment A is expected to have a cash value of \$3200 (assuming a 100% investment in A), and investment B is expected to have a cash value of \$2500 (assuming a 100% investment in B). Additional income and expenses at the end of period 4 will be income from savings in period 4 less the repayment of the period 4 loan plus interest.

Suppose that the decision variables are defined as

$$x_1 = \text{the proportion of investment A undertaken}$$
$$x_2 = \text{the proportion of investment B undertaken}$$

For example, if $x_1 = 0.5$, \$500 would be invested in investment A during the first period, and all remaining cash flows and ending investment A values would be multiplied by 0.5. The same holds for investment B. The model must include constraints $x_1 \le 1$ and $x_2 \le 1$ to make sure that no more than 100% of the investments can be undertaken.

If no more than \$200 can be borrowed in any period, determine the proportions of investments A and B and the amount of savings and borrowing in each period that will maximize the cash value for the firm at the end of the four periods.

25. Western Family Steakhouse offers a variety of low-cost meals and quick service. Other than management, the steakhouse operates with two full-time employees who work 8 hours per day. The rest of the employees are part-time employees who are scheduled for 4-hour shifts during peak meal times. On Saturdays the steakhouse is open from 11:00 A.M. to 10:00 P.M. Management wants to develop a schedule for part-time employees that will minimize labor costs and still provide excellent customer service. The average wage rate for the part-time employees is \$7.60 per hour. The total number of full-time and part-time employees needed varies with the time of day as shown.

Time	Total Number of Employees Needed
11:00 A.M.–Noon	9
Noon–1:00 P.M.	9
1:00 P.M.–2:00 P.M.	9
2:00 P.M.–3:00 P.M.	3
3:00 P.M.–4:00 P.M.	3
4:00 P.M.–5:00 P.M.	3
5:00 P.M.–6:00 P.M.	6
6:00 P.M.–7:00 P.M.	12
7:00 P.M.–8:00 P.M.	12
8:00 P.M.–9:00 P.M.	7
9:00 P.M.–10:00 P.M.	7

One full-time employee comes on duty at 11:00 A.M., works 4 hours, takes an hour off, and returns for another 4 hours. The other full-time employee comes to work at 1:00 P.M. and works the same 4-hours-on, 1-hour-off, 4-hours-on pattern.

a. Develop a minimum-cost schedule for part-time employees.
b. What is the total payroll for the part-time employees? How many part-time shifts are needed? Use the surplus variables to comment on the desirability of scheduling at least some of the part-time employees for 3-hour shifts.
c. Assume that part-time employees can be assigned either a 3-hour or a 4-hour shift. Develop a minimum-cost schedule for the part-time employees. How many part-time shifts are needed, and what is the cost savings compared to the previous schedule?

Case Problem 1   PLANNING AN ADVERTISING CAMPAIGN

The Flamingo Grill is an upscale restaurant located in St. Petersburg, Florida. To help plan an advertising campaign for the coming season, Flamingo's management team hired the advertising firm of Haskell & Johnson (HJ). The management team requested HJ's recommendation concerning how the advertising budget should be distributed across television, radio, and online advertisements. The budget has been set at $279,000.

In a meeting with Flamingo's management team, HJ consultants provided the following information about the industry exposure effectiveness rating per ad, their estimate of the number of potential new customers reached per ad, and the cost for each ad:

Advertising Media	Exposure Rating per Ad	New Customers per Ad	Cost per Ad
Television	90	4,000	$10,000
Radio	25	2,000	$ 3,000
Online	10	1,000	$ 1,000

The exposure rating is viewed as a measure of the value of the ad to both existing customers and potential new customers. It is a function of such things as image, message recall, visual and audio appeal, and so on. As expected, the more expensive television advertisement has the highest exposure effectiveness rating along with the greatest potential for reaching new customers.

At this point, the HJ consultants pointed out that the data concerning exposure and reach were only applicable to the first few ads in each medium. For television, HJ stated that the exposure rating of 90 and the 4000 new customers reached per ad were reliable for the first 10 television ads. After 10 ads, the benefit is expected to decline. For planning purposes, HJ recommended reducing the exposure rating to 55 and the estimate of the potential new customers reached to 1500 for any television ads beyond 10. For radio ads, the preceding data are reliable up to a maximum of 15 ads. Beyond 15 ads, the exposure rating declines to 20 and the number of new customers reached declines to 1200 per ad. Similarly, for online ads, the preceding data are reliable up to a maximum of 20; the exposure rating declines to 5 and the potential number of new customers reached declines to 800 for additional ads.

Flamingo's management team accepted maximizing the total exposure rating, across all media, as the objective of the advertising campaign. Because of management's concern with attracting new customers, management stated that the advertising campaign must reach at least 100,000 new customers. To balance the advertising campaign and make use of all advertising media, Flamingo's management team also adopted the following guidelines:

- Use at least twice as many radio advertisements as television advertisements.
- Use no more than 20 television advertisements.
- The television budget should be at least $140,000.
- The radio advertising budget is restricted to a maximum of $99,000.
- The online budget is to be at least $30,000.

HJ agreed to work with these guidelines and provide a recommendation as to how the $279,000 advertising budget should be allocated among television, radio, and online advertising.

Managerial Report

Develop a model that can be used to determine the advertising budget allocation for the Flamingo Grill. Include a discussion of the following in your report:

1. A schedule showing the recommended number of television, radio, and online advertisements and the budget allocation for each medium. Show the total exposure and indicate the total number of potential new customers reached.

2. How would the total exposure change if an additional $10,000 were added to the advertising budget?
3. A discussion of the ranges for the objective function coefficients. What do the ranges indicate about how sensitive the recommended solution is to HJ's exposure rating coefficients?
4. After reviewing HJ's recommendation, the Flamingo's management team asked how the recommendation would change if the objective of the advertising campaign was to maximize the number of potential new customers reached. Develop the media schedule under this objective.
5. Compare the recommendations from parts 1 and 4. What is your recommendation for the Flamingo Grill's advertising campaign?

Case Problem 2   SCHNEIDER'S SWEET SHOP

Schneider's Sweet Shop specializes in homemade candies and ice cream. Schneider produces its ice cream in-house, in batches of 50 pounds. The first stage in ice cream making is the blending of ingredients to obtain a mix which meets pre-specified requirements on the percentages of certain constituents of the mix. The desired composition is as follows:

1.	Fat	16.00%
2.	Serum solids	8.00%
3.	Sugar solids	16.00%
4.	Egg solids	.35%
5.	Stabilizer	.25%
6.	Emulsifier	.15%
7.	Water	59.25%

The mix can be composed of ingredients from the following list:

Ingredient	Cost ($/lb.)
1. 40% Cream	$1.19
2. 23% Cream	.70
3. Butter	2.32
4. Plastic cream	2.30
5. Butter oil	2.87
6. 4% Milk	.25
7. Skim condensed milk	.35
8. Skim milk powder	.65
9. Liquid sugar	.25
10. Sugared frozen fresh egg yolk	1.75
11. Powdered egg yolk	4.45
12. Stabilizer	2.45
13. Emulsifier	1.68
14. Water	.00

The number of pounds of a constituent found in a pound of an ingredient is shown in the next list. Note that a pound of stabilizer contributes only to the stabilizer requirement (one pound), one pound of emulsifier contributes only to the emulsifier requirement (one pound), and that water contributes only to the water requirement (one pound).

Constituent							Ingredient							
PRIVATE	1	2	3	4	5	6	7	8	9	10	11	12	13	14
1	.4	.2	.8	.8	.9	.1				.5	.6			
2	.1			.1		.1	.3	1						
3									.7	.1				
4										.4	.4			
5												1		
6													1	
7	.5	.8	.2	.1	.1	.8	.7		.3					1

Young Jack Schneider has recently acquired the shop from his father. Jack's father has in the past used the following mixture: 9.73 pounds of plastic cream, 3.03 pounds of skim milk powder, 11.37 pounds of liquid sugar, 0.44 pounds of sugared frozen fresh egg yolk, 0.12 pounds of stabilizer, 0.07 pounds of emulsifier, and 25.24 pounds of water. (The scale at Schneider's is only accurate to 100th of a pound.) Jack feels that perhaps it is possible to produce the ice cream in a more cost-effective manner. He would like to find the cheapest mix for producing a batch of ice cream, which meets the requirements specified above.

Jack is also curious about the cost effect of being a little more flexible in the requirements listed above. He wants to know the cheapest mix if the composition meets the following tolerances:

1. Fat   15.00–17.00%
2. Serum solids   7.00–9.00%
3. Sugar solids   15.50–16.50%
4. Egg solids   .30–.40%
5. Stabilizer   .20–.30%
6. Emulsifier   .10–.20%
7. Water   58.00–59.50%

Managerial Report

Write a managerial report which compares the cost of Papa Jack's approach to (a) the cost-minimized approach using the desired composition and (b) the cost-minimized approach with the more flexible requirements. Include the following in your report:

1. The cost of 50 pounds of ice cream under each of the three approaches
2. The amount of each ingredient used in the mix for each of the three approaches
3. A recommendation as to which approach should be used

Case Problem 3   TEXTILE MILL SCHEDULING

The Scottsville Textile Mill* produces five different fabrics. Each fabric can be woven on one or more of the mill's 38 looms. The sales department's forecast of demand for the next month is shown in Table 4.16, along with data on the selling price per yard, variable cost per yard, and purchase price per yard. The mill operates 24 hours a day and is scheduled for 30 days during the coming month.

The mill has two types of looms: dobby and regular. The dobbie looms are more versatile and can be used for all five fabrics. The regular looms can produce only three of the fabrics. The mill has a total of 38 looms: 8 are dobby and 30 are regular. The rate of production for each fabric on each type of loom is given in Table 4.17. The time required

---

*This case is based on the Calhoun Textile Mill Case by Jeffrey D. Camm, P. M. Dearing, and Suresh K. Tadisnia, 1987.

TABLE 4.16   MONTHLY DEMAND, SELLING PRICE, VARIABLE COST, AND PURCHASE PRICE DATA FOR SCOTTSVILLE TEXTILE MILL FABRICS

Fabric	Demand (yards)	Selling Price ($/yard)	Variable Cost ($/yard)	Purchase Price ($/yard)
1	16,500	0.99	0.66	0.80
2	22,000	0.86	0.55	0.70
3	62,000	1.10	0.49	0.60
4	7,500	1.24	0.51	0.70
5	62,000	0.70	0.50	0.70

TABLE 4.17   LOOM PRODUCTION RATES FOR THE SCOTTSVILLE TEXTILE MILL

	Loom Rate (yards/hour)	
Fabric	Dobby	Regular
1	4.63	—
2	4.63	—
3	5.23	5.23
4	5.23	5.23
5	4.17	4.17

Note: Fabrics 1 and 2 can be manufactured only on the dobbie loom.

to change over from producing one fabric to another is negligible and does not have to be considered.

The Scottsville Textile Mill satisfies all demand with either its own fabric or fabric purchased from another mill. Fabrics that cannot be woven at the Scottsville Mill because of limited loom capacity will be purchased from another mill. The purchase price of each fabric is also shown in Table 4.16.

Managerial Report

Develop a model that can be used to schedule production for the Scottsville Textile Mill, and at the same time, determine how many yards of each fabric must be purchased from another mill. Include a discussion and analysis of the following items in your report:

1. The final production schedule and loom assignments for each fabric.
2. The projected total contribution to profit.
3. A discussion of the value of additional loom time. (The mill is considering purchasing a ninth dobbie loom. What is your estimate of the monthly profit contribution of this additional loom?)
4. A discussion of the objective coefficients' ranges.
5. A discussion of how the objective of minimizing total costs would provide a different model than the objective of maximizing total profit contribution. (How would the interpretation of the objective coefficients' ranges differ for these two models?)

Case Problem 4   WORKFORCE SCHEDULING

Davis Instruments has two manufacturing plants located in Atlanta, Georgia. Product demand varies considerably from month to month, causing Davis extreme difficulty in workforce scheduling. Recently Davis started hiring temporary workers supplied by WorkForce Unlimited, a company that specializes in providing temporary employees for firms in the greater Atlanta area. WorkForce Unlimited offered to provide temporary employees under three contract options that differ in terms of the length of employment and the cost. The three options are summarized:

Option	Length of Employment	Cost
1	One month	$2000
2	Two months	$4800
3	Three months	$7500

The longer contract periods are more expensive because WorkForce Unlimited experiences greater difficulty finding temporary workers who are willing to commit to longer work assignments.

Over the next six months, Davis projects the following needs for additional employees:

Month	January	February	March	April	May	June
Employees Needed	10	23	19	26	20	14

Each month, Davis can hire as many temporary employees as needed under each of the three options. For instance, if Davis hires five employees in January under Option 2, WorkForce Unlimited will supply Davis with five temporary workers who will work for two months: January and February. For these workers, Davis will have to pay 5($4800) = $24,000. Because of some merger negotiations under way, Davis does not want to commit to any contractual obligations for temporary employees that extend beyond June.

Davis's quality control program requires each temporary employee to receive training at the time of hire. The training program is required even if the person worked for Davis Instruments in the past. Davis estimates that the cost of training is $875 each time a temporary employee is hired. Thus, if a temporary employee is hired for one month, Davis will incur a training cost of $875, but will incur no additional training cost if the employee is on a two- or three-month contract.

Managerial Report

Develop a model that can be used to determine the number of temporary employees Davis should hire each month under each contract plan in order to meet the projected needs at a minimum total cost. Include the following items in your report:

1. A schedule that shows the number of temporary employees that Davis should hire each month for each contract option.
2. A summary table that shows the number of temporary employees that Davis should hire under each contract option, the associated contract cost for each option, and the associated training cost for each option. Provide summary totals showing the total number of temporary employees hired, total contract costs, and total training costs.
3. If the cost to train each temporary employee could be reduced to $700 per month, what effect would this change have on the hiring plan? Explain. Discuss the implications that this effect on the hiring plan has for identifying methods for reducing training costs. How much of a reduction in training costs would be required to change the hiring plan based on a training cost of $875 per temporary employee?
4. Suppose that Davis hired 10 full-time employees at the beginning of January in order to satisfy part of the labor requirements over the next six months. If Davis can hire full-time employees for $16.50 per hour, including fringe benefits, what effect would it have on total labor and training costs over the six-month period as compared to hiring only temporary employees? Assume that full-time and temporary employees both work approximately 160 hours per month. Provide a recommendation regarding the decision to hire additional full-time employees.

Case Problem 5   DUKE ENERGY COAL ALLOCATION*

Duke Energy manufactures and distributes electricity to customers in the United States and Latin America. Duke purchased Cinergy Corporation, which has generating facilities and energy customers in Indiana, Kentucky, and Ohio. For these customers Cinergy has been spending $725 to $750 million each year for the fuel needed to operate its coal-fired and gas-fired power plants; 92% to 95% of the fuel used is coal. In this region, Duke Energy uses 10 coal-burning generating plants: five located inland and five located on the Ohio River. Some plants have more than one generating unit. Duke Energy uses 28–29 million tons of coal per year at a cost of approximately $2 million every day in this region.

The company purchases coal using fixed-tonnage or variable-tonnage contracts from mines in Indiana (49%), West Virginia (20%), Ohio (12%), Kentucky (11%), Illinois (5%), and Pennsylvania (3%). The company must purchase all of the coal contracted for on fixed-tonnage contracts, but on variable-tonnage contracts it can purchase varying amounts up to the limit specified in the contract. The coal is shipped from the mines to Duke Energy's generating facilities in Ohio, Kentucky, and Indiana. The cost of coal varies from $19 to $35 per ton and transportation/delivery charges range from $1.50 to $5.00 per ton.

A model is used to determine the megawatt-hours (mWh) of electricity that each generating unit is expected to produce and to provide a measure of each generating unit's efficiency, referred to as the heat rate. The heat rate is the total BTUs required to produce 1 kilowatt-hour (kWh) of electrical power.

Coal Allocation Model

Duke Energy uses a linear programming model, called the coal allocation model, to allocate coal to its generating facilities. The objective of the coal allocation model is to determine the lowest-cost method for purchasing and distributing coal to the generating units. The supply/availability of the coal is determined by the contracts with the various mines, and the demand for coal at the generating units is determined indirectly by the megawatt-hours of electricity each unit must produce.

The cost to process coal, called the add-on cost, depends upon the characteristics of the coal (moisture content, ash content, BTU content, sulfur content, and grindability) and the efficiency of the generating unit. The add-on cost plus the transportation cost are added to the purchase cost of the coal to determine the total cost to purchase and use the coal.

Current Problem

Duke Energy signed three fixed-tonnage contracts and four variable-tonnage contracts. The company would like to determine the least-cost way to allocate the coal available through these contracts to five generating units. The relevant data for the three fixed-tonnage contracts are as follows:

Supplier	Number of Tons Contracted For	Cost ($/ton)	BTUs/lb
RAG	350,000	22	13,000
Peabody Coal Sales	300,000	26	13,300
American Coal Sales	275,000	22	12,600

---

*The authors are indebted to Thomas Mason and David Bossee of Duke Energy Corporation, formerly Cinergy Corp., for their contribution to this case problem.

For example, the contract signed with RAG requires Duke Energy to purchase 350,000 tons of coal at a price of $22 per ton; each pound of this particular coal provides 13,000 BTUs.

The data for the four variable-tonnage contracts follow:

Supplier	Number of Tons Available	Cost ($/ton)	BTUs/lb
Consol, Inc.	200,000	32	12,250
Cyprus Amax	175,000	35	12,000
Addington Mining	200,000	31	12,000
Waterloo	180,000	33	11,300

For example, the contract with Consol, Inc., enables Duke Energy to purchase up to 200,000 tons of coal at a cost of $32 per ton; each pound of this coal provides 12,250 BTUs.

The number of megawatt-hours of electricity that each generating unit must produce and the heat rate provided are as follows:

Generating Unit	Electricity Produced (mWh)	Heat Rate (BTUs per kWh)
Miami Fort Unit 5	550,000	10,500
Miami Fort Unit 7	500,000	10,200
Beckjord Unit 1	650,000	10,100
East Bend Unit 2	750,000	10,000
Zimmer Unit 1	1,100,000	10,000

For example, Miami Fort Unit 5 must produce 550,000 megawatt-hours of electricity, and 10,500 BTUs are needed to produce each kilowatt-hour.

The transportation cost and the add-on cost in dollars per ton are shown here:

Supplier	Transportation Cost ($/ton)				
	Miami Fort Unit 5	Miami Fort Unit 7	Beckjord Unit 1	East Bend Unit 2	Zimmer Unit 1
RAG	5.00	5.00	4.75	5.00	4.75
Peabody	3.75	3.75	3.50	3.75	3.50
American	3.00	3.00	2.75	3.00	2.75
Consol	3.25	3.25	2.85	3.25	2.85
Cyprus	5.00	5.00	4.75	5.00	4.75
Addington	2.25	2.25	2.00	2.25	2.00
Waterloo	2.00	2.00	1.60	2.00	1.60

Supplier	Add-On Cost ($/ton)				
	Miami Fort Unit 5	Miami Fort Unit 7	Beckjord Unit 1	East Bend Unit 2	Zimmer Unit 1
RAG	10.00	10.00	10.00	5.00	6.00
Peabody	10.00	10.00	11.00	6.00	7.00
American	13.00	13.00	15.00	9.00	9.00
Consol	10.00	10.00	11.00	7.00	7.00
Cyprus	10.00	10.00	10.00	5.00	6.00
Addington	5.00	5.00	6.00	4.00	4.00
Waterloo	11.00	11.00	11.00	7.00	9.00

Managerial Report

Prepare a report that summarizes your recommendations regarding Duke Energy's coal allocation problem. Be sure to include information and analysis for the following issues:

1. Determine how much coal to purchase from each of the mining companies and how it should be allocated to the generating units. What is the cost to purchase, deliver, and process the coal?
2. Compute the average cost of coal in cents per million BTUs for each generating unit (a measure of the cost of fuel for the generating units).
3. Compute the average number of BTUs per pound of coal received at each generating unit (a measure of the energy efficiency of the coal received at each unit).
4. Suppose that Duke Energy can purchase an additional 80,000 tons of coal from American Coal Sales as an "all or nothing deal" for $30 per ton. Should Duke Energy purchase the additional 80,000 tons of coal?
5. Suppose that Duke Energy learns that the energy content of the coal from Cyprus Amax is actually 13,000 BTUs per pound. Should Duke Energy revise its procurement plan?
6. Duke Energy has learned from its trading group that Duke Energy can sell 50,000 megawatt-hours of electricity over the grid (to other electricity suppliers) at a price of $30 per megawatt-hour. Should Duke Energy sell the electricity? If so, which generating units should produce the additional electricity?

Appendix 4.1 EXCEL SOLUTION OF HEWLITT CORPORATION FINANCIAL PLANNING PROBLEM

In Appendix 2.1 we showed how Excel could be used to solve the Par, Inc.'s linear programming problem. To illustrate the use of Excel in solving a more complex linear programming problem, we show the solution to the Hewlitt Corporation financial planning problem presented in Section 4.2.

The spreadsheet formulation and solution of the Hewlitt Corporation problem are shown in Figure 4.10. As described in Appendix 2.1, our practice is to put the data required for the problem in the top part of the worksheet and build the model in the bottom part of the worksheet. The model consists of a set of cells for the decision variables, a cell for the objective function, a set of cells for the left-hand-side functions, and a set of cells for the right-hand sides of the constraints. The cells for each of these model components are screened; the cells for the decision variables are also enclosed by a boldface line. Descriptive labels are used to make the spreadsheet easy to read.

Formulation

The data and descriptive labels are contained in cells A1:G12. The screened cells in the bottom portion of the spreadsheet contain the key elements of the model required by the Excel Solver.

Decision Variables	Cells A17:L17 are reserved for the decision variables. The optimal values (rounded to three places) are shown to be $F = 1728.794$, $B_1 = 144.988$, $B_2 = 187.856$, $B_3 = 228.188$, $S_1 = 636.148$, $S_2 = 501.606$, $S_3 = 349.682$, $S_4 = 182.681$, and $S_5 = S_6 = S_7 = S_8 = 0$.
Objective Function	The formula $=A17$ has been placed into cell B20 to reflect the total funds required. It is simply the value of the decision variable, F. The total fund required by the optimal solution is shown to be $1,728,794$.
Left-Hand Sides	The left-hand sides for the eight constraints represent the annual net cash flow. They are placed into cells G21:G28. Cell G21 $=E21-F21$ (Copy to G22:G28)

FIGURE 4.10   EXCEL SOLUTION FOR THE HEWLITT CORPORATION PROBLEM

MODEL *file*

Hewlitt

	A	B	C	D	E	F	G	H	I	J	K	L
1	Hewlitt Corporation Cash Requirements											
2												
3		Cash										
4	Year	Rqmt.				Bond						
5	1	430			1	2	3					
6	2	210		Price ($1000)	1.15	1	1.35					
7	3	222		Rate	0.08875	0.055	0.1175					
8	4	231		Years to Maturity	5	6	7					
9	5	240										
10	6	195		Annual Savings Multiple	1.04							
11	7	225										
12	8	255										
13												
14	Model											
15												
16	F	B1	B2	B3	S1	S2	S3	S4	S5	S6	S7	S8
17	1728.794	144.988	187.856	228.188	636.148	501.606	349.682	182.681	0	0	0	0
18												
19					Cash Flow		Net Cash		Cash			
20	Min Funds	1728.7939		Constraints	In	Out	Flow		Rqmt.			
21				Year 1	1728.794	1298.794	430	=	430			
22				Year 2	711.6057	501.6057	210	=	210			
23				Year 3	571.6818	349.6818	222	=	222			
24				Year 4	413.6809	182.6809	231	=	231			
25				Year 5	240	0	240	=	240			
26				Year 6	195	0	195	=	195			
27				Year 7	225	0	225	=	225			
28				Year 8	255	0	255	=	255			

For this problem, some of the left-hand-side cells reference other cells that contain formulas. These referenced cells provide Hewlitt's cash flow in and cash flow out for each of the eight years.[*] The cells and their formulas are as follows:

Cell E21 $=A17$

Cell E22 $=SUMPRODUCT(\$E\$7:\$G\$7,\$B\$17:\$D\$17)+\$F\$10*E17$

Cell E23 $=SUMPRODUCT(\$E\$7:\$G\$7,\$B\$17:\$D\$17)+\$F\$10*F17$

Cell E24 $=SUMPRODUCT(\$E\$7:\$G\$7,\$B\$17:\$D\$17)+\$F\$10*G17$

Cell E25 $=SUMPRODUCT(\$E\$7:\$G\$7,\$B\$17:\$D\$17)+\$F\$10*H17$

Cell E26 $=(1+E7)*B17+F7*C17+G7*D17+F10*I17$

Cell E27 $=(1+F7)*C17+G7*D17+F10*J17$

Cell E28 $=(1+G7)*D17+F10*K17$

Cell F21 $=SUMPRODUCT(E6:G6,B17:D17)+E17$

Cell F22 $=F17$

Cell F23 $=G17$

Cell F24 $=H17$

Cell F25 $=I17$

Cell F26 $=J17$

Cell F27 $=K17$

Cell F28 $=L17$

---

[*]The cash flow in is the sum of the positive terms in each constraint equation in the mathematical model, and the cash flow out is the sum of the negative terms in each constraint equation.

Right-Hand Sides   The right-hand sides for the eight constraints represent the annual cash requirements. They are placed into cells I21:I28.

Cell I21 $=B5$ (Copy to I22:I28)

Excel Solution

We are now ready to use the information in the worksheet to determine the optimal solution to the Hewlitt Corporation problem. The following steps describe how to use Excel to obtain the optimal solution:

Step 1. Select the **Data** tab on the Ribbon

Step 2. Select **Solver** from the **Analyze** group

Step 3. When the **Solver Parameters** dialog box appears (see Figure 4.11):

Enter *B20* in the **Set Objective** box

Select the **To: Min** option

Enter *A17:L17* in the **By Changing Variable Cells** box

Step 4. Choose **Add**

When the **Add Constraint** dialog box appears:

Enter *G21:G28* in the left-hand box of the **Cell Reference** area

Select = from the middle drop-down button

FIGURE 4.11   SOLVER PARAMETERS DIALOG BOX FOR THE HEWLITT CORPORATION PROBLEM

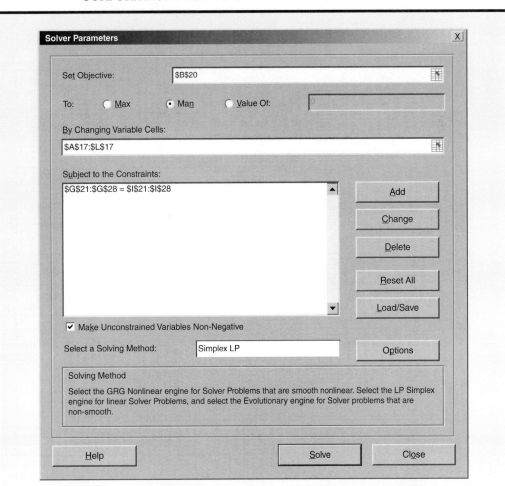

Enter *I21:I28* in the **Constraint** area
Click **OK**

Step 5. When the **Solver Parameters** dialog box reappears (see Figure 4.11):
Select **Make Unconstrained Variables Non-Negative**

Step 6. Select the **Select a Solving Method** drop-down button
Select **Simplex LP**

Step 7. Click **Solve**

Step 8. When the **Solver Results** dialog box appears:
Select **Keep Solver Solution**
Select **Sensitivity** in the **Reports** box
Click **OK**

The Solver Parameters dialog box is shown in Figure 4.11. The optimal solution is shown in Figure 4.10; the accompanying sensitivity report is shown in Figure 4.12.

Discussion

Figures 4.10 and 4.12 contain essentially the same information as that provided in Figure 4.4. Recall that the Excel sensitivity report uses the term *shadow price* to describe the *change* in value of the solution per unit increase in the right-hand side of a constraint. This is the same as the Dual Value in Figure 4.4.

FIGURE 4.12   EXCEL'S SENSITIVITY REPORT FOR THE HEWLITT
CORPORATION PROBLEM

Adjustable Cells

Cell	Name	Final Value	Reduced Cost	Objective Coefficient	Allowable Increase	Allowable Decrease
$A$17	F	1728.793855	0	1	1E + 30	1
$B$17	B1	144.9881496	0	0	0.067026339	0.013026775
$C$17	B2	187.8558478	0	0	0.012795531	0.020273774
$D$17	B3	228.1879195	0	0	0.022906851	0.749663022
$E$17	S1	636.1479438	0	0	0.109559907	0.05507386
$F$17	S2	501.605712	0	0	0.143307365	0.056948823
$G$17	S3	349.681791	0	0	0.210854199	0.059039182
$H$17	S4	182.680913	0	0	0.413598622	0.061382404
$I$17	S5	0	0.064025159	0	1E + 30	0.064025159
$J$17	S6	0	0.012613604	0	1E + 30	0.012613604
$K$17	S7	0	0.021318233	0	1E + 30	0.021318233
$L$17	S8	0	0.670839393	0	1E + 30	0.670839393

Constraints

Cell	Name	Final Value	Shadow Price	Constraint R.H. Side	Allowable Increase	Allowable Decrease
$G$21	Year 1 Flow	430	1	430	1E + 30	1728.793855
$G$22	Year 2 Flow	210	0.961538462	210	1E + 30	661.5938616
$G$23	Year 3 Flow	222	0.924556213	222	1E + 30	521.6699405
$G$24	Year 4 Flow	231	0.888996359	231	1E + 30	363.6690626
$G$25	Year 5 Flow	240	0.854804191	240	1E + 30	189.9881496
$G$26	Year 6 Flow	195	0.760364454	195	2149.927647	157.8558478
$G$27	Year 7 Flow	225	0.718991202	225	3027.962172	198.1879195
$G$28	Year 8 Flow	255	0.670839393	255	1583.881915	255

CHAPTER 5

Advanced Linear Programming Applications

CONTENTS

This chapter continues the study of linear programming applications. Four new applications of linear programming are introduced. We begin with data envelopment analysis (DEA), which is an application of linear programming used to measure the relative efficiency of operating units with the same goals and objectives. We illustrate how this technique is used to evaluate the performance of hospitals. In Section 5.2, we introduce the topic of revenue management. Revenue management involves managing the short-term demand for a fixed perishable inventory in order to maximize the revenue potential for an organization. Revenue management is critically important in the airline industry, and we illustrate the concept by determining the optimal full-fare and discount-fare seat allocations for flights among five cities.

Management science has a major impact in finance. Section 5.3 shows how linear programming is used to design portfolios that are consistent with a client's risk preferences. In Section 5.4, we introduce game theory, which is the study of how two or more decision makers (players) can compete against each other in an optimal fashion. We illustrate with a linear programming model for two firms competing against each other by trying to gain market share.

5.1   DATA ENVELOPMENT ANALYSIS

Data envelopment analysis (DEA) is an application of linear programming used to measure the relative efficiency of operating units with the same goals and objectives. For example, DEA has been used within individual fast-food outlets in the same chain. In this case, the goal of DEA was to identify the inefficient outlets that should be targeted for further study and, if necessary, corrective action. Other applications of DEA have measured the relative efficiencies of hospitals, banks, courts, schools, and so on. In these applications, the performance of each institution or organization was measured relative to the performance of all operating units in the same system. The Management Science in Action, American Red Cross Evaluates the Efficiency of Service, describes how one of the world's largest non profit social service organizations used DEA to determine which of its chapters were operating inefficiently.

MANAGEMENT SCIENCE IN ACTION

AMERICAN RED CROSS EVALUATES THE EFFICIENCY OF SERVICE*

The American Red Cross (ARC) is one of the largest non-profit service organizations in the world. ARC has approximately 1000 chapters in the United States. Each chapter covers a geographic territory, providing disaster relief, armed forces emergency communications, and health and safety training to the general public.

Historically, ARC chapters reported their performance data to the national headquarters in Washington, DC, but little feedback was provided and no analysis was given for chapters to compare their performance to the performance of other similar chapters. Like many other non-profit service agencies, ARC is under increased pressure to be more efficient and accountable for its budget. As a result, ARC sought a system that would provide relevant performance feedback to the chapters with the ultimate goal of improving performance.

ARC developed a system based on data envelopment analysis (DEA) to identify underperforming chapters. DEA is a data-driven approach for measuring the relative performance of an operating unit based on how it converts inputs to outputs. In the case of ARC, chapter inputs include revenues from contracts and donations, number of volunteers, and number of paid staff among others. Measures of chapter output include metrics such as number of clients receiving disaster relief, number of emergency communications provided, and number of people trained in safety and health courses. Using linear programming models, DEA assesses if a chapter is efficient or inefficient relative to other similar chapters.

The ARC chapter evaluation system was created using Visual Basic for Applications (VBA). VBA is used to clean and format the data, automate the solution of thousands of linear optimization models needed to score the chapters, and generate reports that will be useful to chapter management. By identifying inefficient chapters and peer groups from which they can learn, DEA provides a way for inefficient chapters to improve their performance.

In the previous approach, chapters had to collect and analyze their own data, generate a report and send it to headquarters, and then would receive little feedback. Based on past experience, this process consumed at least 160,000 person-hours each year. The new automated system saves at least $700,000 in analysis and report generating costs per year. More importantly, it has fostered a culture of continuous improvement at ARC, so that chapter managers can learn from one another and this has led to improved effectiveness in service.

*Based on K.S. Pasupathy and A. Medina-Borja, "Integrating Excel, Access and Visual Basic to Deploy Performance Measurement and Evaluation at American Red Cross," *Interfaces* 38, no. 4 (July–August 2008): 324–337.

The operating units of most organizations have multiple inputs such as staff size, salaries, hours of operation, and advertising budget, as well as multiple outputs such as profit, market share, and growth rate. In these situations, it is often difficult for a manager to determine which operating units are inefficient in converting their multiple inputs into multiple outputs. This particular area is where data envelopment analysis has proven to be a helpful managerial tool. We illustrate the application of data envelopment analysis by evaluating the performance of a group of four hospitals.

Evaluating the Performance of Hospitals

The hospital administrators at General Hospital, University Hospital, County Hospital, and State Hospital have been meeting to discuss ways in which they can help one another improve the performance at each of their hospitals. A consultant suggested that they consider using DEA to measure the performance of each hospital relative to the performance of all four hospitals. In discussing how this evaluation could be done, the following three input measures and four output measures were identified:

Input Measures
1. The number of full-time equivalent (FTE) nonphysician personnel
2. The amount spent on supplies
3. The number of bed-days available

Output Measures
1. Patient-days of service under Medicare
2. Patient-days of service not under Medicare
3. Number of nurses trained
4. Number of interns trained

Problem 1 asks you to formulate and solve a linear program to assess the relative efficiency of General Hospital.

Summaries of the input and output measures for a one-year period at each of the four hospitals are shown in Tables 5.1 and 5.2. Let us show how DEA can use these data to identify relatively inefficient hospitals.

Overview of the DEA Approach

In this application of DEA, a linear programming model is developed for each hospital whose efficiency is to be evaluated. To illustrate the modeling process, we formulate a linear program that can be used to determine the relative efficiency of County Hospital.

First, using a linear programming model, we construct a **hypothetical composite,** in this case a composite hospital, based on the outputs and inputs for all operating units with the same goals. For each of the four hospitals' output measures, the output for the composite hospital is determined by computing a weighted average of the corresponding outputs for all four hospitals. For each of the three input measures, the input for the composite hospital is determined by using the same weights to compute a weighted average of the corresponding inputs for all four hospitals. Constraints in the linear programming model require all outputs for the composite hospital to be *greater than or equal to* the outputs of County Hospital, the hospital being evaluated. If the inputs for the composite unit can be shown to be *less than* the inputs for County Hospital, the composite hospital is shown to have the same, or

TABLE 5.1   ANNUAL RESOURCES CONSUMED (INPUTS) BY THE FOUR HOSPITALS

	Hospital			
Input Measure	General	University	County	State
Full-time equivalent nonphysicians	285.20	162.30	275.70	210.40
Supply expense ($1000s)	123.80	128.70	348.50	154.10
Bed-days available (1000s)	106.72	64.21	104.10	104.04

TABLE 5.2   ANNUAL SERVICES PROVIDED (OUTPUTS) BY THE FOUR HOSPITALS

	Hospital			
Output Measure	General	University	County	State
Medicare patient-days (1000s)	48.14	34.62	36.72	33.16
Non-Medicare patient-days (1000s)	43.10	27.11	45.98	56.46
Nurses trained	253	148	175	160
Interns trained	41	27	23	84

more, output for *less input*. In this case, the model shows that the composite hospital is more efficient than County Hospital. In other words, the hospital being evaluated is *less efficient* than the composite hospital. Because the composite hospital is based on all four hospitals, the hospital being evaluated can be judged *relatively inefficient* when compared to the other hospitals in the group.

DEA Linear Programming Model

To determine the weight that each hospital will have in computing the outputs and inputs for the composite hospital, we use the following decision variables:

$$wg = \text{weight applied to inputs and outputs for General Hospital}$$
$$wu = \text{weight applied to inputs and outputs for University Hospital}$$
$$wc = \text{weight applied to inputs and outputs for County Hospital}$$
$$ws = \text{weight applied to inputs and outputs for State Hospital}$$

The DEA approach requires that the sum of these weights equal 1. Thus, the first constraint is

$$wg + wu + wc + ws = 1$$

In general, every DEA linear programming model will include a constraint that requires the weights for the operating units to sum to 1.

As we stated previously, for each output measure, the output for the composite hospital is determined by computing a weighted average of the corresponding outputs for all four hospitals. For instance, for output measure 1, the number of patient-days of service under Medicare, the output for the composite hospital is

$$\begin{pmatrix} \text{Medicare patient-days} \\ \text{for Composite Hospital} \end{pmatrix} = \begin{pmatrix} \text{Medicare patient-days} \\ \text{for General Hospital} \end{pmatrix} wg + \begin{pmatrix} \text{Medicare patient-days} \\ \text{for University Hospital} \end{pmatrix} wu$$
$$+ \begin{pmatrix} \text{Medicare patient-days} \\ \text{for County Hospital} \end{pmatrix} wc + \begin{pmatrix} \text{Medicare patient-days} \\ \text{for State Hospital} \end{pmatrix} ws$$

Substituting the number of Medicare patient-days for each hospital as shown in Table 5.2, we obtain the following expression:

$$\text{Medicare patient-days for Composite Hospital} = 48.14wg + 34.62wu + 36.72wc + 33.16ws$$

The other output measures for the composite hospital are computed in a similar fashion. Figure 5.1 provides a summary of the results.

For each of the four output measures, we need to write a constraint that requires the output for the composite hospital to be greater than or equal to the output for County Hospital. Thus, the general form of the output constraints is

$$\text{Output for the Composite Hospital} \geq \text{Output for County Hospital}$$

Because the number of Medicare patient-days for County Hospital is 36.72, the output constraint corresponding to the number of Medicare patient-days is

$$48.14wg + 34.62wu + 36.72wc + 33.16ws \geq 36.72$$

In a similar fashion, we formulated a constraint for each of the other three output measures, with the results as shown:

$$43.10wg + 27.11wu + 45.98wc + 56.46ws \geq 45.98 \quad \text{Non-Medicare}$$
$$253wg + 148wu + 175wc + 160ws \geq 175 \quad \text{Nurses}$$
$$41wg + 27wu + 23wc + 84ws \geq 23 \quad \text{Interns}$$

The four output constraints require the linear programming solution to provide weights that will make each output measure for the composite hospital greater than or equal to the corresponding output measure for County Hospital. Thus, if a solution satisfying the output constraints can be found, the composite hospital will have produced at least as much of each output as County Hospital.

FIGURE 5.1 RELATIONSHIP BETWEEN THE OUTPUT MEASURES FOR THE FOUR HOSPITALS AND THE OUTPUT MEASURES FOR THE COMPOSITE HOSPITAL

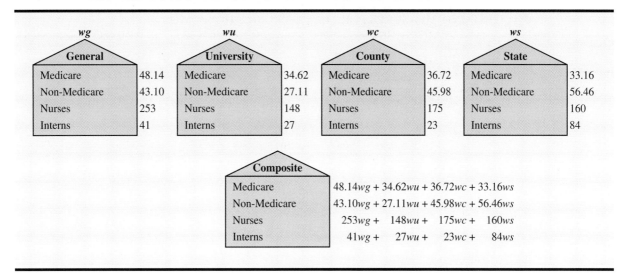

Next, we need to consider the constraints needed to model the relationship between the inputs for the composite hospital and the resources available to the composite hospital. A constraint is required for each of the three input measures. The general form for the input constraints is as follows:

$$\begin{array}{c}\text{Input for the}\\\text{Composite Hospital}\end{array} \leq \begin{array}{c}\text{Resources available to}\\\text{the Composite Hospital}\end{array}$$

For each input measure, the input for the composite hospital is a weighted average of the corresponding input for each of the four hospitals. Thus, for input measure 1, the number of full-time equivalent nonphysicians, the input for the composite hospital is

$$\begin{array}{c}\text{FTE nonphysicians}\\\text{for Composite Hospital}\end{array} = \left(\begin{array}{c}\text{FTE nonphysicians}\\\text{for General Hospital}\end{array}\right)wg + \left(\begin{array}{c}\text{FTE nonphysicians}\\\text{for University Hospital}\end{array}\right)wu$$

$$+ \left(\begin{array}{c}\text{FTE nonphysicians}\\\text{for County Hospital}\end{array}\right)wc + \left(\begin{array}{c}\text{FTE nonphysicians}\\\text{for State Hospital}\end{array}\right)ws$$

Substituting the values for the number of full-time equivalent nonphysicians for each hospital as shown in Table 5.1, we obtain the following expression for the number of full-time equivalent nonphysicians for the composite hospital:

$$285.20wg + 162.30wu + 275.70wc + 210.40ws$$

In a similar manner, we can write expressions for each of the other two input measures as shown in Figure 5.2.

To complete the formulation of the input constraints, we must write expressions for the right-hand-side values for each constraint. First, note that the right-hand-side values are the resources available to the composite hospital. In the DEA approach, these right-hand-side values are a percentage of the input values for County Hospital. Thus, we must introduce the following decision variable:

The logic of a DEA model is to determine whether a hypothetical composite facility can achieve the same or more output while requiring less input. If more output with less input can be achieved, the facility being evaluated is judged to be relatively inefficient.

E = the fraction of County Hospital's input available to the Composite Hospital

To illustrate the important role that E plays in the DEA approach, we show how to write the expression for the number of FTE nonphysicians available to the composite hospital.

FIGURE 5.2   RELATIONSHIP BETWEEN THE INPUT MEASURES FOR THE FOUR HOSPITALS
                  AND THE INPUT MEASURES FOR THE COMPOSITE HOSPITAL

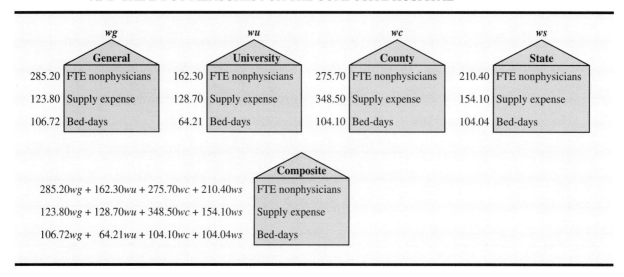

Table 5.1 shows that the number of FTE nonphysicians used by County Hospital was 275.70; thus, 275.70E is the number of FTE nonphysicians available to the composite hospital. If $E = 1$, the number of FTE nonphysicians available to the composite hospital is 275.70, the same as the number of FTE nonphysicians used by County Hospital. However, if E is greater than 1, the composite hospital would have available proportionally more nonphysicians, whereas if E is less than 1, the composite hospital would have available proportionally fewer FTE nonphysicians. Because of the effect that E has in determining the resources available to the composite hospital, E is referred to as the **efficiency index.**

We can now write the input constraint corresponding to the number of FTE nonphysicians available to the composite hospital:

$$285.50wg + 162.30wu + 275.70wc + 210.40ws \leq 275.70E$$

In a similar manner, we can write the input constraints for the supplies and bed-days available to the composite hospital. First, using the data in Table 5.1, we note that for each of these resources, the amount that is available to the composite hospital is 348.50E and 104.10E, respectively. Thus, the input constraints for the supplies and bed-days are written as follows:

$$123.80wg + 128.70wu + 348.50wc + 154.10ws \leq 348.50E \quad \text{Supplies}$$
$$106.72wg + 64.21wu + 104.10wc + 104.04ws \leq 104.10E \quad \text{Bed-days}$$

If a solution with $E < 1$ can be found, the composite hospital does not need as many resources as County Hospital needs to produce the same level of output.

The objective function for the DEA model is to minimize the value of E, which is equivalent to minimizing the input resources available to the composite hospital. Thus, the objective function is written as

$$\text{Min } E$$

The DEA efficiency conclusion is based on the optimal objective function value for E. The decision rule is as follows:

If $E = 1$, the composite hospital requires *as much input* as County Hospital does. There is no evidence that County Hospital is inefficient.

If $E < 1$, the composite hospital requires *less input* to obtain the output achieved by County Hospital. The composite hospital is more efficient; thus, County Hospital can be judged relatively inefficient.

The objective function in a DEA model is always Min E. The facility being evaluated (County Hospital in this example) can be judged relavtively inefficient if the optimal solution provides E less than 1, indicating that the composite facility requires less in input resources.

The DEA linear programming model for the efficiency evaluation of County Hospital has five decision variables and eight constraints. The complete model is rewritten as follows:

Min E

s.t.

$$wg + wu + wc + ws = 1$$
$$48.14wg + 34.62wu + 36.72wc + 33.16ws \geq 36.72$$
$$43.10wg + 27.11wu + 45.98wc + 56.46ws \geq 45.98$$
$$253wg + 148wu + 175wc + 160ws \geq 175$$
$$41wg + 27wu + 23wc + 84ws \geq 23$$
$$285.20wg + 162.30wu + 275.70wc + 210.40ws \leq 275.70E$$
$$123.80wg + 128.70wu + 348.50wc + 154.10ws \leq 348.50E$$
$$106.72wg + 64.21wu + 104.10wc + 104.04ws \leq 104.10E$$

$$E, wg, wu, wc, ws \geq 0$$

The optimal solution is shown in Figure 5.3. We first note that the value of the objective function shows that the efficiency score for County Hospital is 0.905. This score tells us

FIGURE 5.3   THE SOLUTION FOR THE COUNTY HOSPITAL DATA ENVELOPMENT
ANALYSIS PROBLEM

```
Optimal Objective Value =          0.90524

        Variable              Value              Reduced Cost
      -------------      ---------------        ---------------
           wg                 0.21227               0.00000
           wu                 0.26045               0.00000
           wc                 0.00000               0.09476
           ws                 0.52729               0.00000
           E                  0.90524               0.00000

        Constraint        Slack/Surplus             Dual Value
      -------------      ---------------        ---------------
            1                0.00000               -0.23889
            2                0.00000                0.01396
            3                0.00000                0.01373
            4                1.61539                0.00000
            5               37.02707                0.00000
            6               35.82408                0.00000
            7              174.42242                0.00000
            8                0.00000               -0.00961

                          Objective         Allowable          Allowable
        Variable         Coefficient         Increase           Decrease
      -----------      --------------      -----------        -----------
           wg             0.00000            0.44643            0.19991
           wu             0.00000            0.36384            Infinite
           wc             0.00000            Infinite           0.09476
           ws             0.00000            0.17972            0.42671
           E              1.00000            Infinite           1.00000

                             RHS            Allowable          Allowable
        Constraint          Value           Increase           Decrease
      -----------      --------------      -----------        -----------
            1              1.00000            0.01462            0.08491
            2             36.72000            8.19078            0.23486
            3             45.98000            7.30499            2.15097
            4            175.00000            1.61539            Infinite
            5             23.00000           37.02707            Infinite
            6              0.00000            Infinite          35.82408
            7              0.00000            Infinite         174.42242
            8              0.00000           13.52661            Infinite
```

County

that the composite hospital can obtain at least the level of each output that County Hospital obtains by having available no more than 90.5% of the input resources required by County Hospital. Thus, the composite hospital is more efficient, and the DEA analysis identified County Hospital as being relatively inefficient.

From the solution in Figure 5.3, we see that the composite hospital is formed from the weighted average of General Hospital ($wg = 0.212$), University Hospital ($wu = 0.260$), and State Hospital ($ws = 0.527$). Each input and output of the composite hospital is determined by the same weighted average of the inputs and outputs of these three hospitals.

The Slack/Surplus column provides some additional information about the efficiency of County Hospital compared to the composite hospital. Specifically, the composite hospital has at least as much of each output as County Hospital has (constraints 2–5) and provides

1.6 more nurses trained (surplus for constraint 4) and 37 more interns trained (surplus for constraint 5). The slack of zero from constraint 8 shows that the composite hospital uses approximately 90.5% of the bed-days used by County Hospital. The slack values for constraints 6 and 7 show that less than 90.5% of the FTE nonphysician and the supplies expense resources used at County Hospital are used by the composite hospital.

Clearly, the composite hospital is more efficient than County Hospital, and we are justified in concluding that County Hospital is relatively inefficient compared to the other hospitals in the group. Given the results of the DEA analysis, hospital administrators should examine operations to determine how County Hospital resources can be more effectively utilized.

Summary of the DEA Approach

To use data envelopment analysis to measure the relative efficiency of County Hospital, we used a linear programming model to construct a hypothetical composite hospital based on the outputs and inputs for the four hospitals in the problem. The approach to solving other types of problems using DEA is similar. For each operating unit that we want to measure the efficiency of, we must formulate and solve a linear programming model similar to the linear program we solved to measure the relative efficiency of County Hospital. The following step-by-step procedure should help you in formulating a linear programming model for other types of DEA applications. Note that the operating unit that we want to measure the relative efficiency of is referred to as the jth operating unit.

Step 1. Define decision variables or weights (one for each operating unit) that can be used to determine the inputs and outputs for the composite operating unit.
Step 2. Write a constraint that requires the weights to sum to 1.
Step 3. For each output measure, write a constraint that requires the output for the composite operating unit to be greater than or equal to the corresponding output for the jth operating unit.
Step 4. Define a decision variable, E, which determines the fraction of the jth operating unit's input available to the composite operating unit.
Step 5. For each input measure, write a constraint that requires the input for the composite operating unit to be less than or equal to the resources available to the composite operating unit.
Step 6. Write the objective function as Min E.

NOTES AND COMMENTS

1. Remember that the goal of data envelopment analysis is to identify operating units that are relatively inefficient. The method *does not* necessarily identify the operating units that are *relatively efficient*. Just because the efficiency index is $E = 1$, we cannot conclude that the unit being analyzed is relatively efficient. Indeed, any unit that has the largest output on any one of the output measures cannot be judged relatively inefficient.

2. It is possible for DEA to show all but one unit to be relatively inefficient. Such would be the case if a unit producing the most of every output also consumes the least of every input. Such cases are extremely rare in practice.

3. In applying data envelopment analysis to problems involving a large group of operating units, practitioners have found that roughly 50% of the operating units can be identified as inefficient. Comparing each relatively inefficient unit to the units contributing to the composite unit may be helpful in understanding how the operation of each relatively inefficient unit can be improved.

5.2   REVENUE MANAGEMENT

Revenue management involves managing the short-term demand for a fixed perishable inventory in order to maximize the revenue potential for an organization. The methodology, originally developed for American Airlines, was first used to determine how many airline flight seats to sell at an early

MANAGEMENT SCIENCE IN ACTION

REVENUE MANAGEMENT AT THE CARLSON REZIDOR HOTEL GROUP*

With over 1400 hotels in 115 countries, the Carlson Rezidor Hotel Group (CRHG) is one of the world's largest hotel companies. CRHG consists of a number of well-known hotel brands including Radisson, Park Plaza, and Country Inn & Suites. CRHG is recognized as an industry leader in the use of revenue management.

CRHG developed a revenue management system known as Stay Night Automated Pricing (SNAP). SNAP relies on demand forecasts and a pricing optimization model to manage its inventory of rooms and pricing. Demand forecasting is done by hotel, rate segment (type of rate purchased, for example, nonrefundable), requested length of stay, day of week, and the number of days before arrival at the time of booking. Based on these demand forecasts, the estimated price elasticity of demand, competitor rates, remaining room inventory, and other business rules, a large-scale optimization model is used to dynamically optimize the rate charged for each night of the stay.

The estimated annual impact of the SNAP system in CRHG's North American hotels was an increase in revenue of $16 million. Additional increases in revenue are anticipated as the recommended prices are more pervasively implemented by the hotels. The SNAP system is being implemented by CRHG globally, with an initial rollout in Europe, the Middle East, Africa, and Asia. The anticipated increase in annual revenue is expected to exceed $30 million once the model is implemented throughout the organization.

*Based on P. Pekgün. Menich et al., "Carlson Rezidor Hotel Group Maximizes Revenue Through Improved Demand Management and Price Optimization," *Interfaces* 43, no. 1 (January–February 2013): 21–36.

reservation discount fare and how many airline flight seats to sell at a full fare. By making the optimal decision for the number of discount-fare seats and the number of full-fare seats on each flight, the airline is able to increase its average number of passengers per flight and maximize the total revenue generated by the combined sale of discount-fare and full-fare seats. Today, all major airlines use some form of revenue management.

Given the success of revenue management in the airline industry, it was not long before other industries began using this approach. Revenue management systems often include pricing strategies, overbooking policies, short-term supply decisions, and the management of nonperishable assets. Application areas now include hotels, apartment rentals, car rentals, cruise lines, and golf courses. The Management Science in Action, Revenue Management at Carlson Rezidor Hotel Group (CRHG), discusses how CRHG implemented revenue management to improve its performance.

The development of a revenue management system can be expensive and time-consuming, but the potential payoffs may be substantial. For instance, the revenue management system used at American Airlines generates nearly $1 billion in annual incremental revenue. To illustrate the fundamentals of revenue management, we will use a linear programming model to develop a revenue management plan for Leisure Air, a regional airline that provides service for Pittsburgh, Newark, Charlotte, Myrtle Beach, and Orlando.

Leisure Air has two Boeing 737-400 airplanes, one based in Pittsburgh and the other in Newark. Both airplanes have a coach section with a 132-seat capacity. Each morning the Pittsburgh-based plane flies to Orlando with a stopover in Charlotte, and the Newark-based plane flies to Myrtle Beach, also with a stopover in Charlotte. At the end of the day, both planes return to their home bases. To keep the size of the problem reasonable, we restrict our attention to the Pittsburgh–Charlotte, Charlotte–Orlando, Newark–Charlotte, and Charlotte–Myrtle Beach flight legs for the morning flights. Figure 5.4 illustrates the logistics of the Leisure Air problem situation.

Leisure Air uses two fare classes: a discount-fare Q class and a full-fare Y class. Reservations using the discount-fare Q class must be made 14 days in advance and must include a Saturday night stay in the destination city. Reservations using the full-fare Y class may be made anytime, with no penalty for changing the reservation at a later date. To determine the itinerary and fare

FIGURE 5.4   LOGISTICS OF THE LEISURE AIR PROBLEM

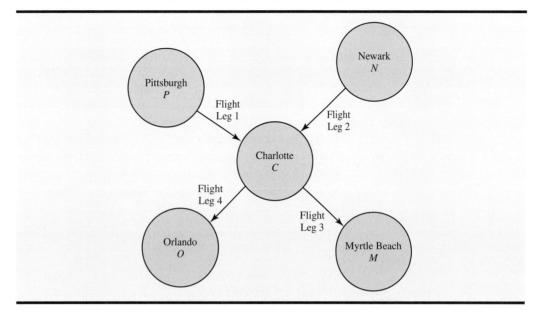

alternatives that Leisure Air can offer its customers, we must consider not only the origin and the destination of each flight, but also the fare class. For instance, possible products include Pittsburgh to Charlotte using Q class, Newark to Orlando using Q class, Charlotte to Myrtle Beach using Y class, and so on. Each product is referred to as an origin-destination-itinerary fare (ODIF). For May 5, Leisure Air established fares and developed forecasts of customer demand for each of 16 ODIFs. These data are shown in Table 5.3.

Suppose that on April 4 a customer calls the Leisure Air reservation office and requests a Q class seat on the May 5 flight from Pittsburgh to Myrtle Beach. Should Leisure Air accept the reservation? The difficulty in making this decision is that even though Leisure Air may

TABLE 5.3   FARE AND DEMAND DATA FOR 16 LEISURE AIR
ORIGIN-DESTINATION-ITINERARY FARES (ODIFs)

ODIF	Origin	Destination	Fare Class	ODIF Code	Fare	Forecasted Demand
1	Pittsburgh	Charlotte	Q	PCQ	$178	33
2	Pittsburgh	Myrtle Beach	Q	PMQ	268	44
3	Pittsburgh	Orlando	Q	POQ	228	45
4	Pittsburgh	Charlotte	Y	PCY	380	16
5	Pittsburgh	Myrtle Beach	Y	PMY	456	6
6	Pittsburgh	Orlando	Y	POY	560	11
7	Newark	Charlotte	Q	NCQ	199	26
8	Newark	Myrtle Beach	Q	NMQ	249	56
9	Newark	Orlando	Q	NOQ	349	39
10	Newark	Charlotte	Y	NCY	385	15
11	Newark	Myrtle Beach	Y	NMY	444	7
12	Newark	Orlando	Y	NOY	580	9
13	Charlotte	Myrtle Beach	Q	CMQ	179	64
14	Charlotte	Myrtle Beach	Y	CMY	380	8
15	Charlotte	Orlando	Q	COQ	224	46
16	Charlotte	Orlando	Y	COY	582	10

have seats available, the company may not want to accept this reservation at the Q class fare of \$268, especially if it is possible to sell the same reservation later at the Y class fare of \$456. Thus, determining how many Q and Y class seats to make available is an important decision that Leisure Air must make in order to operate its reservation system.

To develop a linear programming model that can be used to determine how many seats Leisure Air should allocate to each fare class, we need to define 16 decision variables, one for each ODIF alternative. Using P for Pittsburgh, N for Newark, C for Charlotte, M for Myrtle Beach, and O for Orlando, the decision variables take the following form:

PCQ = number of seats allocated to Pittsburgh–Charlotte Q class
PMQ = number of seats allocated to Pittsburgh–Myrtle Beach Q class
POQ = number of seats allocated to Pittsburgh–Orlando Q class
PCY = number of seats allocated to Pittsburgh–Charlotte Y class
$\vdots$
NCQ = number of seats allocated to Newark–Charlotte Q class
$\vdots$
COY = number of seats allocated to Charlotte–Orlando Y class

The objective is to maximize total revenue. Using the fares shown in Table 5.3, we can write the objective function for the linear programming model as follows:

$$\text{Max } 178PCQ + 268PMQ + 228POQ + 380PCY + 456PMY + 560POY$$
$$+ 199NCQ + 249NMQ + 349NOQ + 385NCY + 444NMY$$
$$+ 580NOY + 179CMQ + 380CMY + 224COQ + 582COY$$

Next, we must write the constraints. We need two types of constraints: capacity and demand. We begin with the capacity constraints.

Consider the Pittsburgh–Charlotte flight leg in Figure 5.4. The Boeing 737-400 airplane has a 132-seat capacity. Three possible final destinations for passengers on this flight (Charlotte, Myrtle Beach, or Orlando) and two fare classes (Q and Y) provide six ODIF alternatives: (1) Pittsburgh–Charlotte Q class, (2) Pittsburgh–Myrtle Beach Q class, (3) Pittsburgh–Orlando Q class, (4) Pittsburgh–Charlotte Y class, (5) Pittsburgh–Myrtle Beach Y class, and (6) Pittsburgh–Orlando Y class. Thus, the number of seats allocated to the Pittsburgh–Charlotte flight leg is $PCQ + PMQ + POQ + PCY + PMY + POY$. With the capacity of 132 seats, the capacity constraint is as follows:

$$PCQ + PMQ + POQ + PCY + PMY + POY \leq 132 \quad \text{Pittsburgh–Charlotte}$$

The capacity constraints for the Newark–Charlotte, Charlotte–Myrtle Beach, and Charlotte–Orlando flight legs are developed in a similar manner. These three constraints are as follows:

$$NCQ + NMQ + NOQ + NCY + NMY + NOY \leq 132 \quad \text{Newark–Charlotte}$$
$$PMQ + PMY + NMQ + NMY + CMQ + CMY \leq 132 \quad \text{Charlotte–Myrtle Beach}$$
$$POQ + POY + NOQ + NOY + COQ + COY \leq 132 \quad \text{Charlotte–Orlando}$$

The demand constraints limit the number of seats for each ODIF based on the forecasted demand. Using the demand forecasts in Table 5.3, 16 demand constraints must be added to the model. The first four demand constraints are as follows:

$$PCQ \leq 33 \quad \text{Pittsburgh–Charlotte Q class}$$
$$PMQ \leq 44 \quad \text{Pittsburgh–Myrtle Beach Q class}$$
$$POQ \leq 45 \quad \text{Pittsburgh–Orlando Q class}$$
$$PCY \leq 16 \quad \text{Pittsburgh–Charlotte Y class}$$

The complete linear programming model with 16 decision variables, 4 capacity constraints, and 16 demand constraints is as follows:

Max $178PCQ + 268PMQ + 228POQ + 380PCY + 456PMY + 560POY$
$+ 199NCQ + 249NMQ + 349NOQ + 385NCY + 444NMY$
$+ 580NOY + 179CMQ + 380CMY + 224COQ + 582COY$

s.t.

$$PCQ + PMQ + POQ + PCY + PMY + POY \le 132 \quad \text{Pittsburgh–Charlotte}$$
$$NCQ + NMQ + NOQ + NCY + NMY + NOY \le 132 \quad \text{Newark–Charlotte}$$
$$PMQ + PMY + NMQ + NMY + CMQ + CMY \le 132 \quad \text{Charlotte–Myrtle Beach}$$
$$POQ + POY + NOQ + NOY + COQ + COY \le 132 \quad \text{Charlotte–Orlando}$$

$$
\begin{aligned}
PCQ &\le 33 \\
PMQ &\le 44 \\
POQ &\le 45 \\
PCY &\le 16 \\
PMY &\le 6 \\
POY &\le 11 \\
NCQ &\le 26 \\
NMQ &\le 56 \\
NOQ &\le 39 \\
NCY &\le 15 \\
NMY &\le 7 \\
NOY &\le 9 \\
CMQ &\le 64 \\
CMY &\le 8 \\
COQ &\le 46 \\
COY &\le 10
\end{aligned}
\right\} \text{Demand Constraints}
$$

$$PCQ, PMQ, POQ, PCY, \ldots, COY \ge 0$$

The optimal solution to the Leisure Air revenue management problem is shown in Figure 5.5. The value of the optimal solution is \$103,103. The optimal solution shows that $PCQ = 33$, $PMQ = 44$, $POQ = 22$, $PCY = 16$, and so on. Thus, to maximize revenue, Leisure Air should allocate 33 Q class seats to Pittsburgh–Charlotte, 44 Q class seats to Pittsburgh–Myrtle Beach, 22 Q class seats to Pittsburgh–Orlando, 16 Y class seats to Pittsburgh–Charlotte, and so on.

Over time, reservations will come into the system and the number of remaining seats available for each ODIF will decrease. For example, the optimal solution allocated 44 Q class seats to Pittsburgh–Myrtle Beach. Suppose that two weeks prior to the departure date of May 5, all 44 seats have been sold. Now, suppose that a new customer calls the Leisure Air reservation office and requests a Q class seat for the Pittsburgh–Myrtle Beach flight. Should Leisure Air accept the new reservation even though it exceeds the original 44-seat allocation? The dual value for the Pittsburgh–Myrtle Beach Q class demand constraint will provide information that will help a Leisure Air reservation agent make this decision.

Dual values tell reservation agents the additional revenue associated with overbooking each ODIF.

Constraint 6, $PMQ \le 44$, restricts the number of Q class seats that can be allocated to Pittsburgh–Myrtle Beach to 44 seats. In Figure 5.5 we see that the dual value for constraint 6 is \$85. The dual value tells us that if one more Q class seat were available from Pittsburgh to Myrtle Beach, revenue would increase by \$85. This increase in revenue is referred to as the bid price for this ODIF. In general, the bid price for an ODIF tells a Leisure Air reservation agent the value of one additional reservation once a particular ODIF has been sold out.

FIGURE 5.5   THE SOLUTION FOR THE LEISURE AIR REVENUE
MANAGEMENT PROBLEM

MODEL *file*

Leisure

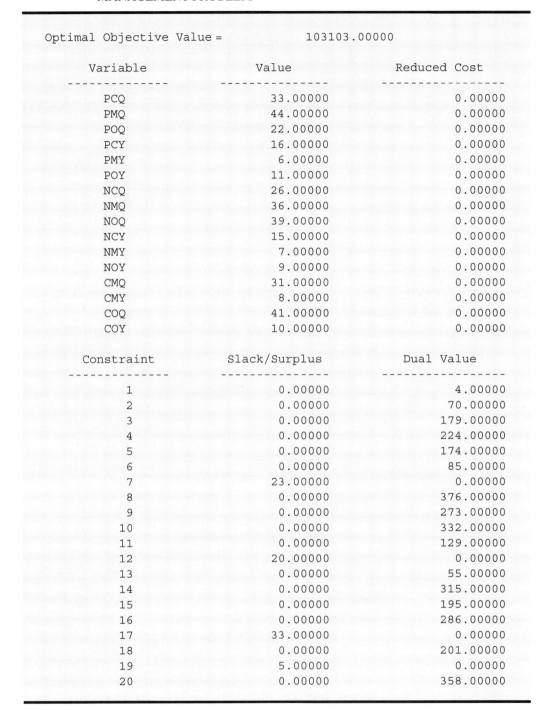

Optimal Objective Value =   103103.00000

Variable	Value	Reduced Cost
PCQ	33.00000	0.00000
PMQ	44.00000	0.00000
POQ	22.00000	0.00000
PCY	16.00000	0.00000
PMY	6.00000	0.00000
POY	11.00000	0.00000
NCQ	26.00000	0.00000
NMQ	36.00000	0.00000
NOQ	39.00000	0.00000
NCY	15.00000	0.00000
NMY	7.00000	0.00000
NOY	9.00000	0.00000
CMQ	31.00000	0.00000
CMY	8.00000	0.00000
COQ	41.00000	0.00000
COY	10.00000	0.00000

Constraint	Slack/Surplus	Dual Value
1	0.00000	4.00000
2	0.00000	70.00000
3	0.00000	179.00000
4	0.00000	224.00000
5	0.00000	174.00000
6	0.00000	85.00000
7	23.00000	0.00000
8	0.00000	376.00000
9	0.00000	273.00000
10	0.00000	332.00000
11	0.00000	129.00000
12	20.00000	0.00000
13	0.00000	55.00000
14	0.00000	315.00000
15	0.00000	195.00000
16	0.00000	286.00000
17	33.00000	0.00000
18	0.00000	201.00000
19	5.00000	0.00000
20	0.00000	358.00000

By looking at the dual values for the demand constraints in Figure 5.5, we see that the highest dual value (bid price) is $376 for constraint 8, $PCY \leq 16$. This constraint corresponds to the Pittsburgh–Charlotte Y class itinerary. Thus, if all 16 seats allocated to this itinerary have been sold, accepting another reservation will provide additional revenue of $376. Given this revenue contribution, a reservation agent would most likely accept the additional reservation even if it resulted in an overbooking of the flight. Other dual values for the demand constraints show a value of \$358 for constraint 20 (*COY*) and a value of \$332 for constraint 10 (*POY*). Thus, accepting additional reservations for the Charlotte–Orlando Y class and the Pittsburgh–Orlando Y class itineraries is a good choice for increasing revenue.

A revenue management system like the one at Leisure Air must be flexible and adjust to the ever-changing reservation status. Conceptually, each time a reservation is accepted for an ODIF that is at its capacity, the linear programming model should be updated and re-solved to obtain new seat allocations along with the revised bid price information. In practice, updating the allocations on a real-time basis is not practical because of the large number of itineraries involved. However, the bid prices from a current solution and some simple decision rules enable reservation agents to make decisions that improve the revenue for the firm. Then, on a periodic basis such as once a day or once a week, the entire linear programming model can be updated and re-solved to generate new seat allocations and revised bid price information.

5.3   PORTFOLIO MODELS AND ASSET ALLOCATION

In 1952 Harry Markowitz showed how to develop a portfolio that optimized the trade-off between risk and return. His work earned him a share of the 1990 Nobel Prize in Economics.

Asset allocation refers to the process of determining how to allocate investment funds across a variety of asset classes such as stocks, bonds, mutual funds, real estate, and cash. Portfolio models are used to determine the percentage of the investment funds that should be made in each asset class. The goal is to create a portfolio that provides the best balance between risk and return. In this section we show how linear programming models can be developed to determine an optimal portfolio involving a mix of mutual funds. The first model is designed for conservative investors who are strongly averse to risk. The second model is designed for investors with a variety of risk tolerances. The Management Science in Action, Meeting Personal Financial Goals Through Optimization, is a discussion of how linear programming is used by Optimized Financial Systems to help its clients with retirement planning.

MANAGEMENT SCIENCE IN ACTION

MEETING PERSONAL FINANCIAL GOALS THROUGH OPTIMIZATION*

Every individual faces the challenge of saving enough money for a comfortable retirement. Having well-defined financial goals and a strategy for achieving those goals will help ensure that a person's desired standard of living in retirement is achieved. Achieving one's goals takes discipline, focus, and an intentional strategy that has a high probability of success. There are numerous options to consider when investing for retirement, including the annual or monthly amount to save, the type of savings account, and how to allocate the money across the various investment alternatives to achieve return and risk goals.

In the United States, many individuals have an Individual Retirement Account (IRA). Introduced in 1974, an IRA is an account that allows the owner of the account to invest in a variety of investment alternatives with certain tax advantages. There are a number of different types of IRAs, including among others, traditional IRAs and Roth IRAs.

A traditional IRA is a tax-deferred savings account in which pre-tax money is invested and the investor pays taxes on the money invested and any accrued interest, dividends, and capital gains only upon withdrawal of funds. By deferring taxes, the traditional IRA allows the investment to grow faster and for many individuals, since the tax rate in retirement will be lower, pay less in taxes upon withdrawal. A Roth IRA is different than a traditional IRA in that after-tax dollars (rather than pre-tax dollars) are invested. The investor has already paid taxes on the money invested, but the growth of the investment is tax free, even at the time of withdrawal. Also, while the investor must start to take withdrawals from a traditional IRA after the age of 70.5 and can no longer contribute after that age, no withdrawals are required for a Roth IRA and contributions are not age-restricted. While Roth IRAs originally had income restrictions, those income restrictions were eliminated and the option of converting traditional IRAs to Roth IRAs is now available.

(continued)

What is the right mix of traditional and Roth IRAs? When should a traditional IRA be converted to a Roth IRA? How should funds be allocated to each type of IRA?

Optimized Financial Systems, located in Austin, Texas, uses a linear optimization model to assist its clients in answering these types of retirement financial-planning questions. Given the goal of the investor, the linear programming model determines the amounts to contribute to each type of IRA, the amount to convert from a traditional IRA to a Roth IRA each year and in retirement, and the amount to spend in each year given a spend constraint. The linear program solves two different objectives sequentially. The first objective is to minimize shortfall, defined as the difference between the after-tax budgeted spend and the amount spent in a given year. The second objective is to minimize the expected after-tax net present value of the client's estate. Constraints include cash flow balances over time including tax and shortfall calculations.

*Based on J. Woodruff et al., "Optimized Financial Systems Helps Customers Meet Their Personal Finance Goals with Optimization," *Interfaces* 46, no. 4 (July–August 2016), 345–359.

A Portfolio of Mutual Funds

Hauck Investment Services designs annuities, Individual Retirement Accounts (IRAs), 401(k) plans, and other investment vehicles for investors with a variety of risk tolerances. Hauck would like to develop a portfolio model that can be used to determine an optimal portfolio involving a mix of six mutual funds. A variety of measures can be used to indicate risk, but for portfolios of financial assets all are related to variability in return. Table 5.4 shows the annual return (%) for five 1-year periods for the six mutual funds. Year 1 represents a year in which the annual returns are good for all the mutual funds. Year 2 is also a good year for most of the mutual funds. But year 3 is a bad year for the small-cap value fund; year 4 is a bad year for the intermediate-term bond fund; and Year 5 is a bad year for four of the six mutual funds.

It is not possible to predict exactly the returns for any of the funds over the next 12 months, but the portfolio managers at Hauck Financial Services think that the returns for the five years shown in Table 5.4 are scenarios that can be used to represent the possibilities for the next year. For the purpose of building portfolios for their clients, Hauck's portfolio managers will choose a mix of these six mutual funds and assume that one of the five possible scenarios will describe the return over the next 12 months.

Conservative Portfolio

One of Hauck's portfolio managers has been asked to develop a portfolio for the firm's conservative clients who express a strong aversion to risk. The manager's task is to determine the proportion of the portfolio to invest in each of the six mutual funds so that the portfolio provides the best return possible with a minimum risk. Let us see how linear programming can be used to develop a portfolio for these clients.

In portfolio models, risk is minimized by diversification. To see the value of diversification, suppose we first consider investing the entire portfolio in just one of the six mutual funds. Assuming the data in Table 5.4 represent the possible outcomes over the next 12 months, the

TABLE 5.4 MUTUAL FUND PERFORMANCE IN FIVE SELECTED YEARS (USED AS PLANNING SCENARIOS FOR THE NEXT 12 MONTHS)

Mutual Fund	Annual Return (%)				
	Year 1	Year 2	Year 3	Year 4	Year 5
Foreign Stock	10.06	13.12	13.47	45.42	−21.93
Intermediate-Term Bond	17.64	3.25	7.51	−1.33	7.36
Large-Cap Growth	32.41	18.71	33.28	41.46	−23.26
Large-Cap Value	32.36	20.61	12.93	7.06	−5.37
Small-Cap Growth	33.44	19.40	3.85	58.68	−9.02
Small-Cap Value	24.56	25.32	−6.70	5.43	17.31

clients run the risk of losing 21.93% over the next 12 months if the entire portfolio is invested in the foreign stock mutual fund. Similarly, if the entire portfolio is invested in any one of the other five mutual funds, the clients will also run the risk of losing money; that is, the possible losses are 1.33% for the intermediate-term bond fund, 23.26% for the large-cap growth fund, 5.37% for the large-cap value fund, 9.02% for the small-cap growth fund, and 6.70% for the small-cap value fund. Let us now see how we can construct a diversified portfolio of these mutual funds that minimizes the risk of a loss.

To determine the proportion of the portfolio that will be invested in each of the mutual funds we use the following decision variables:

FS = proportion of portfolio invested in the foreign stock mutual fund

IB = proportion of portfolio invested in the intermediate-term bond fund

LG = proportion of portfolio invested in the large-cap growth fund

LV = proportion of portfolio invested in the large-cap value fund

SG = proportion of portfolio invested in the small-cap growth fund

SV = proportion of portfolio invested in the small-cap value fund

Because the sum of these proportions must equal 1, we need the following constraint:

$$FS + IB + LG + LV + SG + SV = 1$$

The other constraints are concerned with the return that the portfolio will earn under each of the planning scenarios in Table 5.4.

The portfolio return over the next 12 months depends on which of the possible scenarios (years 1 through 5) in Table 5.4 occurs. Let $R1$ denote the portfolio return if the scenario represented by year 1 occurs, $R2$ denote the portfolio return if the scenario represented by year 2 occurs, and so on. The portfolio returns for the five planning scenarios are as follows:

Scenario 1 return:

$$R1 = 10.06FS + 17.64IB + 32.41LG + 32.36LV + 33.44SG + 24.56SV$$

Scenario 2 return:

$$R2 = 13.12FS + 3.25IB + 18.71LG + 20.61LV + 19.40SG + 25.32SV$$

Scenario 3 return:

$$R3 = 13.47FS + 7.51IB + 33.28LG + 12.93LV + 3.85SG - 6.70SV$$

Scenario 4 return:

$$R4 = 45.42FS - 1.33IB + 41.46LG + 7.06LV + 58.68SG + 5.43SV$$

Scenario 5 return:

$$R5 = -21.93FS + 7.36IB - 23.26LG - 5.37LV - 9.02SG + 17.31SV$$

Let us now introduce a variable M to represent the minimum return for the portfolio. As we have already shown, one of the five possible scenarios in Table 5.4 will determine the portfolio return. Thus, the minimum possible return for the portfolio will be determined by the scenario which provides the worst case return. But we don't know which of the scenarios will turn out to represent what happens over the next 12 months. To ensure that the return under each scenario is at least as large as the minimum return M, we must add the following minimum-return constraints:

$$R1 \geq M \qquad \text{scenario 1 minimum return}$$
$$R2 \geq M \qquad \text{scenario 2 minimum return}$$

$$R3 \geq M \qquad \text{scenario 3 minimum return}$$
$$R4 \geq M \qquad \text{scenario 4 minimum return}$$
$$R5 \geq M \qquad \text{scenario 5 minimum return}$$

Substituting the values shown previously for $R1$, $R2$, and so on provides the following five minimum-return constraints:

$$10.06FS + 17.64IB + 32.41LG + 32.36LV + 33.44SG + 24.56SV \geq M \quad \text{scenario 1}$$
$$13.12FS + 3.25IB + 18.71LG + 20.61LV + 19.40SG + 25.32SV \geq M \quad \text{scenario 2}$$
$$13.47FS + 7.51IB + 33.28LG + 12.93LV + 3.85SG - 6.70SV \geq M \quad \text{scenario 3}$$
$$45.42FS + 1.33IB + 41.46LG + 7.06LV + 58.68SG + 5.43SV \geq M \quad \text{scenario 4}$$
$$-21.93FS + 7.36IB - 23.26LG - 5.37LV - 9.02SG + 17.31SV \geq M \quad \text{scenario 5}$$

To develop a portfolio that provides the best return possible with a minimum risk, we need to maximize the minimum return for the portfolio. Thus, the objective function is simple:

$$\text{Max } M$$

With the five minimum-return constraints present, the optimal value of M will equal the value of the minimum return scenario. The objective is to maximize the value of the minimum return scenario.

Because the linear programming model was designed to maximize the minimum return over all the scenarios considered, we refer to it as the *maximin* model. The complete maximin model for the problem of choosing a portfolio of mutual funds for a conservative, risk-averse investor involves seven variables and six constraints. The complete maximin model is written as follows:

Max M

s.t.

$$10.06FS + 17.64IB + 32.41LG + 32.36LV + 33.44SG + 24.56SV \geq M$$
$$13.12FS + 3.25IB + 18.71LG + 20.61LV + 19.40SG + 25.32SV \geq M$$
$$13.47FS + 7.51IB + 33.28LG + 12.93LV + 3.85SG - 6.70SV \geq M$$
$$45.42FS + 1.33IB + 41.46LG + 7.06LV + 58.68SG + 5.43SV \geq M$$
$$-21.93FS + 7.36IB - 23.26LG - 5.37LV - 9.02SG + 17.31SV \geq M$$
$$FS + IB + LG + LV + SG + SV = 1$$
$$M, FS, IB, LG, LV, SG, SV \geq 0$$

Note that we have written the constraint that requires the sum of the proportion of the portfolio invested in each mutual fund as the last constraint in the model. In this way, when we interpret the computer solution of the model, constraint 1 will correspond to planning scenario 1, constraint 2 will correspond to planning scenario 2, and so on.

The optimal solution to the Hauck maximin model is shown in Figure 5.6. The optimal value of the objective function is 6.445; thus, the optimal portfolio will earn 6.445% in the worst-case scenario. The optimal solution calls for 55.4% of the portfolio to be invested in the intermediate-term bond fund, 13.2% of the portfolio to be invested in the large-cap growth fund, and 31.4% of the portfolio to be invested in the small-cap value fund.

Because we do not know at the time of solving the model which of the five possible scenarios will occur, we cannot say for sure that the portfolio return will be 6.445%. However, using the surplus variables, we can learn what the portfolio return will be under each of the scenarios. Constraints 3, 4, and 5 correspond to scenarios 3, 4, and 5 (years 3, 4, and 5 in Table 5.4). The surplus variables for these constraints are zero to indicate that the portfolio return will be $M = 6.445\%$ if any of these three scenarios occur. The surplus variable for constraint 1 is 15.321, indicating that the portfolio return will exceed $M = 6.445$ by

FIGURE 5.6   THE SOLUTION FOR THE HAUCK MAXIMIN PORTFOLIO MODEL

MODEL *file*

Maximin

```
Optimal Objective Value =              6.44516

        Variable              Value         Reduced Cost
      --------------     --------------    ----------------
          FS                 0.00000            -6.76838
          IB                 0.55357             0.00000
          LG                 0.13204             0.00000
          LV                 0.00000            -3.15571
          SG                 0.00000            -2.76428
          SV                 0.31439             0.00000
          M                  6.44516             0.00000


       Constraint        Slack/Surplus        Dual Value
      --------------     --------------    ----------------
           1                15.32060            0.00000
           2                 5.78469            0.00000
           3                 0.00000           -0.39703
           4                 0.00000           -0.11213
           5                 0.00000           -0.49084
           6                 0.00000            6.44516
```

15.321 if scenario 1 occurs. So, if scenario 1 occurs, the portfolio return will be 6.445% + 15.321% = 21.766%. Referring to the surplus variable for constraint 2, we see that the portfolio return will be 6.445% + 5.785% = 12.230% if scenario 2 occurs.

We must also keep in mind that in order to develop the portfolio model, Hauck made the assumption that over the next 12 months one of the five possible scenarios in Table 5.4 will occur. But we also recognize that the actual scenario that occurs over the next 12 months may be different from the scenarios Hauck considered. Thus, Hauck's experience and judgment in selecting representative scenarios plays a key part in determining how valuable the model recommendations will be for the client.

Moderate Risk Portfolio

Hauck's portfolio manager would like to also construct a portfolio for clients who are willing to accept a moderate amount of risk in order to attempt to achieve better returns. Suppose that clients in this risk category are willing to accept some risk but do not want the annual return for the portfolio to drop below 2%. By setting $M = 2$ in the minimum-return constraints in the maximin model, we can constrain the model to provide a solution with an annual return of at least 2%. The minimum-return constraints needed to provide an annual return of at least 2% are as follows:

$$R1 \geq 2 \quad \text{Scenario 1 minimum return}$$
$$R2 \geq 2 \quad \text{Scenario 2 minimum return}$$
$$R3 \geq 2 \quad \text{Scenario 3 minimum return}$$
$$R4 \geq 2 \quad \text{Scenario 4 minimum return}$$
$$R5 \geq 2 \quad \text{Scenario 5 minimum return}$$

In addition to these five minimum-return constraints, we still need the constraint that requires that the sum of the proportions invested in the separate mutual funds is 1.

$$FS + IB + LG + LV + SG + SV = 1$$

A different objective is needed for this portfolio optimization problem. A common approach is to maximize the expected value of the return for the portfolio. For instance, if we assume that the planning scenarios are equally likely, we would assign a probability of 0.20 to each scenario. In this case, the objective function is to maximize

$$\text{Expected value of the return} = 0.2R1 + 0.2R2 + 0.2R3 + 0.2R4 + 0.2R5$$

Because the objective is to maximize the expected value of the return, we write Hauck's objective as follows:

$$\text{Max} \quad 0.2R1 + 0.2R2 + 0.2R3 + 0.2R4 + 0.2R5$$

The complete linear programming formulation for this version of the portfolio optimization problem involves 11 variables and 11 constraints.

Max $0.2R1 + 0.2R2 + 0.2R3 + 0.2R4 + 0.2R5$	(5.1)
s.t.	
$10.06FS + 17.64IB + 32.41LG + 32.36LV + 33.44SG + 24.56SV = R1$	(5.2)
$13.12FS + 3.25IB + 18.71LG + 20.61LV + 19.40SG + 25.32SV = R2$	(5.3)
$13.47FS + 7.51IB + 33.28LG + 12.93LV + 3.85SG + 6.70SV = R3$	(5.4)
$45.42FS - 1.33IB + 41.46LG + 7.06LV + 58.68SG - 5.43SV = R4$	(5.5)
$-21.93FS + 7.36IB + 23.26LG - 5.37LV + 9.02SG + 17.31SV = R5$	(5.6)
$R1 \geq 2$	(5.7)
$R2 \geq 2$	(5.8)
$R3 \geq 2$	(5.9)
$R4 \geq 2$	(5.10)
$R5 \geq 2$	(5.11)
$FS + IB + LG + LV + SG + SV = 1$	(5.12)
$FS, IB, LG, LV, SG, SV \geq 0$	(5.13)

NOTES AND COMMENTS

1. In this formulation, unlike in the previous maximin model, we keep the variables $R1$, $R2$, $R3$, $R4$, $R5$ in the model. The variables $R1$, $R2$, $R3$, $R4$, and $R5$ defined in constraints (5.2)–(5.6) are often called *definitional variables* (a variable that is defined in terms of other variables). These variables could be substituted out of the formulation, resulting in a smaller model. However, we believe that when formulating a model, clarity is of utmost importance and definitional variables often make the model easier to read and understand. Furthermore, stating the model as we have eliminates the need for the user to do the arithmetic calculations necessary to simplify the model. These calculations can lead to error and are best left to the software.

2. Most optimization codes have *preprocessing routines* that will eliminate and substitute out the definitional variables in constraints (5.2)–(5.6). Indeed, the optimization model actually solved by the solver may differ considerably from the actual model formulation. This is why we recommend the user focus on clarity when model building.

3. When building a model such as (5.1)–(5.13) in Excel, we recommend defining adjustable cells for only investment variables, that is, FS, IB, LG, LV, SG, and SV. There will be cells with formulas that calculate the returns given in (5.2)–(5.6), but they need not be adjustable. The Excel Solver model should have only six adjustable cells. See the Excel file *ModerateRisk* that illustrates this point.

FIGURE 5.7   THE SOLUTION FOR THE MODERATE RISK PORTFOLIO MODEL

Optimal Objective Value =   17.33172

Variable	Value	Reduced Cost
R1	29.09269	0.00000
R2	22.14934	0.00000
R3	2.00000	0.00000
R4	31.41658	0.00000
R5	2.00000	0.00000
FS	0.00000	12.24634
IB	0.00000	7.14602
LG	0.10814	0.00000
LV	0.00000	4.35448
SG	0.41484	0.00000
SV	0.47702	0.00000

Constraint	Slack/Surplus	Dual Value
1	0.00000	−0.20000
2	0.00000	−0.20000
3	0.00000	−0.41594
4	0.00000	−0.20000
5	0.00000	−0.59363
6	27.09269	0.00000
7	20.14934	0.00000
8	0.00000	−0.21594
9	29.41658	0.00000
10	0.00000	−0.39363
11	0.00000	18.55087

ModerateRisk

The optimal solution is shown in Figure 5.7. The optimal allocation is to invest 10.8% of the portfolio in a large-cap growth mutual fund, 41.5% in a small-cap growth mutual fund, and 47.7% in a small-cap value mutual fund. The objective function value shows that this allocation provides a maximum expected return of 17.33%. From the surplus variables, we see that the portfolio return will only be 2% if scenario 3 or 5 occurs (Constraints 8 and 10 are binding). The returns will be excellent if scenario 1, 2, or 4 occurs: The portfolio return will be 29.093% if scenario 1 occurs, 22.149% if scenario 2 occurs, and 31.417% if Scenario 4 occurs.

The moderate risk portfolio exposes Hauck's clients to more risk than the maximin portfolio developed for a conservative investor. With the maximin portfolio, the worst-case scenario provided a return of 6.44%. With this moderate risk portfolio, the worst-case scenarios (scenarios 3 and 5) only provide a return of 2%, but the portfolio also provides the possibility of higher returns.

The formulation we have developed for a moderate risk portfolio can be modified to account for other risk tolerances. If an investor can tolerate the risk of no return, the right-hand sides of the minimum-return constraints would be set to 0. If an investor can tolerate a *loss* of 3%, the right-hand side of the minimum-return constraints would be set equal to −3. In practice, we would expect Hauck to provide the client with a sensitivity analysis that gives the expected return as a function of minimum risk. Linear programming models can be solved quickly, so it is certainly practical to solve a series of linear programs where the minimum return is varied from, for example, −5% to 15% in increments of 1%, and the optimal expected return is calculated for each value of minimum return. Clients can then select an expected value and minimum return combination that they feel is most consistent with their risk preference.

MANAGEMENT SCIENCE IN ACTION

ASSET ALLOCATION AND VARIABLE ANNUITIES*

Insurance companies use portfolio models for asset allocation to structure a portfolio for their clients who purchase variable annuities. A variable annuity is an insurance contract that involves an accumulation phase and a distribution phase. In the accumulation phase the individual either makes a lump sum contribution or contributes to the annuity over a period of time. In the distribution phase the investor receives payments either in a lump sum or over a period of time. The distribution phase usually occurs at retirement, but because a variable annuity is an insurance product, a benefit is paid to a beneficiary should the annuitant die before or during the distribution period.

Most insurance companies selling variable annuities offer their clients the benefit of an asset allocation model to help them decide how to allocate their investment among a family of mutual funds. Usually the client fills out a questionnaire to assess his or her level of risk tolerance. Then, given that risk tolerance, the insurance company's asset allocation model recommends how the client's investment should be allocated over a family of mutual funds. American Skandia, a Prudential Financial Company, markets variable annuities that provide the types of services mentioned. A questionnaire is used to assess the client's risk tolerance, and the Morningstar Asset Allocator is used to develop portfolios for five levels of risk tolerance. Clients with low levels of risk tolerance are guided to portfolios consisting of bond funds and T-bills, and the most risk-tolerant investors are guided to portfolios consisting of a large proportion of growth stock mutual funds. Investors with intermediate, or moderate, risk tolerances are guided to portfolios that may consist of suitable mixtures of value and growth stock funds as well as some bond funds.

*Based on information provided by James R. Martin of the Martin Company, a financial services company.

5.4   GAME THEORY

In **game theory,** two or more decision makers, called players, compete against each other. Each player selects one of several strategies without knowing in advance the strategy selected by the other player or players. The combination of the competing strategies provides the value of the game to the players. Game theory applications have been developed for situations in which the competing players are teams, companies, political candidates, and contract bidders. The Management Science in Action, Game Theory Used in 700-MHZ Auction, describes how participants in an auction run by the Federal Communications Commission used game theory to develop bidding strategies.

In this section, we describe **two-person, zero-sum games.** *Two-person* means that two players participate in the game. *Zero-sum* means that the gain (or loss) for one player is equal to the loss (or gain) for the other player. As a result, the gain and loss balance out (resulting in a zero-sum) for the game. What one player wins, the other player loses. Let us demonstrate a two-person, zero-sum game and its solution by considering two companies competing for market share.

Competing for Market Share

Suppose that two companies are the only manufacturers of a particular product; they compete against each other for market share. In planning a marketing strategy for the coming year, each company will select one of three strategies designed to take market share from the other company. The three strategies, which are assumed to be the same for both companies, are as follows:

Strategy 1: Increase advertising.

Strategy 2: Provide quantity discounts.

Strategy 3: Extend warranty.

A payoff table showing the percentage gain in the market share for Company A for each combination of strategies is shown in Table 5.5. Because it is a zero-sum game, any gain in market share for Company A is a loss in market share for Company B.

GAME THEORY USED IN 700-MHZ AUCTION*

On January 24, 2008 the Federal Communications Commission (FCC) auctioned the rights to operate the 700-MHz frequency band in the United States. This bandwidth became available due to the switch of over-the-air television broadcasts from analog to digital transmission. The 700-MHz frequency bandwidth is highly desirable to companies because the high frequency can penetrate walls and other obstacles. Companies including Google, AT&T, Verizon Wireless, and many others placed bids on the rights to operate in this frequency band.

Game theory was central to this auction, as it was used by the FCC to establish the overall rules and procedures for the auction. To promote competition, the FCC used a "blind auction" format in which each bid was anonymous. A blind auction assures that each bidder does not know which competitor(s) they are bidding against. Thus, large firms could not use their market dominance and deep pockets to intimidate smaller firms from placing additional bids. Further, bidding was allowed to continue until no new bids were received in order to prevent last-second winning bids (a practice known as auction sniping).

Most participants hired game theorists to devise bid strategies. Economists, mathematicians, engineers, and many others assisted companies in developing optimal bid plans. The auction lasted 261 rounds over 38 days and resulted in 101 winning bidders. The auction generated over $19 billion in revenue for the FCC.

*Based on E. Woyke, "Peeking into the Spectrum Auction," Forbes, 2007.

TABLE 5.5 PAYOFF TABLE SHOWING THE PERCENTAGE GAIN IN MARKET SHARE FOR COMPANY A

		Company B		
		Increase Advertising b_1	Quantity Discounts b_2	Extend Warranty b_3
Company A	Increase Advertising a_1	4	3	2
	Quantity Discounts a_2	−1	4	1
	Extend Warranty a_3	5	−2	0

In interpreting the entries in the table, we see that if Company A increases advertising (a_1) and Company B increases advertising (b_1), Company A will come out ahead with an increase in market share of 4%, while Company B will have a decrease in market share of 4%. On the other hand, if Company A provides quantity discounts (a_2) and Company B increases advertising (b_1), Company A will lose 1% of market share, while Company B will gain 1% of market share. Therefore, Company A wants to maximize the payoff that is its increase in market share. Company B wants to minimize the payoff because the increase in market share for Company A is the decrease in market share for Company B.

This market-share game meets the requirements of a two-person, zero-sum game. The two companies are the two players, and the zero-sum occurs because the gain (or loss) in market share for Company A is the same as the loss (or gain) in market share for Company B. Each company will select one of its three alternative strategies. Because of the planning horizon, each company will have to select its strategy before knowing the other company's strategy. What is the optimal strategy for each company?

The logic of game theory assumes that each player has the same information and will select a strategy that provides the best possible payoff from its point of view. Suppose Company A selects strategy a_1. Market share increases of 4%, 3%, or 2% are possible depending upon Company B's strategy. At this point, Company A assumes that Company B

TABLE 5.6　PAYOFF TABLE WITH ROW MINIMUMS

| | | Company B | | | |
		Increase Advertising b_1	Quantity Discounts b_2	Extend Warranty b_3	Row Minimum
	Increase Advertising a_1	4	3	2	② ←Maximum
Company A	Quantity Discounts a_2	−1	4	1	−1
	Extend Warranty a_3	5	−2	0	−2

will select the strategy that is best for it. Thus, if Company A selects strategy a_1, Company A assumes Company B will select its best strategy (b_3), which will limit Company A's increase in market share to 2%. Continuing with this logic, Company A analyzes the game by protecting itself against the strategy that may be taken by Company B. Doing so, Company A identifies the minimum payoff for each of its strategies, which is the minimum value in each row of the payoff table. These row minimums are shown in Table 5.6.

The player seeking to maximize the value of the game selects a maximin strategy.

Considering the entries in the Row Minimum column, we see that Company A can be guaranteed an increase in market share of at least 2% by selecting strategy a_1. Strategy a_2 could result in a decrease in market share of 1% and strategy a_3 could result in a decrease in market share of 2%. After comparing the row minimum values, Company A selects the strategy that provides the *maximum* of the row *minimum* values. This is called a **maximin** strategy. Thus, Company A selects strategy a_1 as its optimal strategy; an increase in market share of at least 2% is guaranteed.

Let us now look at the payoff table from the point of view of the other player, Company B. The entries in the payoff table represent gains in market share for Company A, which correspond to losses in market share for Company B. Consider what happens if Company B selects strategy b_1. Company B market share decreases of 4%, –1%, and 5% are possible. Under the assumption that Company A will select the strategy that is best for it, Company B assumes Company A will select strategy a_3, resulting in a gain in market share of 5% for Company A and a loss in market share of 5% for Company B. At this point, Company B analyzes the game by protecting itself against the strategy taken by Company A. Doing so, Company B identifies the maximum payoff to Company A for each of its strategies b_1, b_2, and b_3. This payoff value is the maximum value in each column of the payoff table. These column maximums are shown in Table 5.7.

The player seeking to minimize the value of the game selects a minimax strategy.

Considering the entries in the Column Maximum row, Company B can be guaranteed a decrease in market share of no more than 2% by selecting strategy b_3. Strategy b_1 could result in a decrease in market share of 5% and strategy b_2 could result in a decrease in market

TABLE 5.7　PAYOFF TABLE WITH COLUMN MAXIMUMS

| | | Company B | | | |
		Increase Advertising b_1	Quantity Discounts b_2	Extend Warranty b_3	Row Minimum
	Increase Advertising a_1	4	3	2	② ←Maximum
Company A	Quantity Discounts a_2	−1	4	1	−1
	Extend Warranty a_3	5	−2	0	−2
	Column Maximum	5	4	② ←Minimum	

share of 4%. After comparing the column maximum values, Company B selects the strategy that provides the *minimum* of the column *maximum* values. This is called a **minimax** strategy. Thus, Company B selects b_3 as its optimal strategy. Company B has guaranteed that Company A cannot gain more than 2% in market share.

Identifying a Pure Strategy Solution

If it is optimal for both players to select one strategy and stay with that strategy regardless of what the other player does, the game has a **pure strategy** solution. Whenever the maximum of the row minimums *equals* the minimum of the column maximums, the players cannot improve their payoff by changing to a different strategy. The game is said to have a **saddle point,** or an equilibrium point. Thus, a pure strategy is the optimal strategy for the players. The requirement for a pure strategy solution is as follows:

A Game Has a Pure Strategy Solution If:

Maximum (Row minimums) = Minimum (Column maximums)

Because this equality is the case in our example, the solution to the game is for Company A to increase advertising (strategy a_1) and for Company B to extend the warranty (strategy b_3). Company A's market share will increase by 2% and Company B's market share will decrease by 2%.

With Company A selecting its pure strategy a_1, let us see what happens if Company B tries to change from its pure strategy b_3. Company A's market share will increase 4% if b_1 is selected or will increase 3% if b_2 is selected. Company B must stay with its pure Strategy b_3 to limit Company A to a 2% increase in market share. Similarly, with Company B selecting its pure Strategy b_3, let us see what happens if Company A tries to change from its pure strategy a_1. Company A's market share will increase only 1% if a_2 is selected or will not increase at all if a_3 is selected. Company A must stay with its pure strategy a_1 in order to keep its 2% increase in market share. Thus, even if one of the companies discovers its opponent's pure strategy in advance, neither company can gain any advantage by switching from its pure strategy.

If a pure strategy solution exists, it is the optimal solution to the game. The following steps can be used to determine when a game has a pure strategy solution and to identify the optimal pure strategy for each player:

Analyze a two-person, zero-sum game by first checking to see whether a pure strategy solution exists.

Step 1. Compute the minimum payoff for each row (Player A).

Step 2. For Player A, select the strategy that provides the maximum of the row minimums.

Step 3. Compute the maximum payoff for each column (Player B).

Step 4. For Player B, select the strategy that provides the minimum of the column maximums.

Step 5. If the maximum of the row minimums is equal to the minimum of the column maximums, this value is the value of the game and a pure strategy solution exists. The optimal pure strategy for Player A is identified in Step 2, and the optimal pure strategy for Player B is identified in Step 4.

If the maximum of the row minimums *does not equal* the minimum of the column maximums, a pure strategy solution does not exist. In this case, a mixed strategy solution becomes optimal. In the following discussion, we define a mixed strategy solution and show how linear programming can be used to identify the optimal mixed strategy for each player.

Identifying a Mixed Strategy Solution

Let us continue with the two-company market-share game and consider a slight modification in the payoff table as shown in Table 5.8. Only one payoff has changed. If both Company A

TABLE 5.8   MODIFIED PAYOFF TABLE SHOWING THE PERCENTAGE GAIN IN MARKET
SHARE FOR COMPANY A

		Company B			
		Increase Advertising b_1	Quantity Discounts b_2	Extend Warranty b_3	Row Minimum
	Increase Advertising a_1	4	3	2	② ←Maximum
Company A	Quantity Discounts a_2	−1	4	1	−1
	Extend Warranty a_3	5	−2	5	−2
	Column Maximum	5	④	5	

Minimum

and Company B choose the extended warranty strategy, the payoff to Company A is now a 5% increase in market share rather than the previous 0%. The row minimums do not change, but the column maximums do. Note that the column maximum for Strategy b_3 is 5% instead of the previous 2%.

In analyzing the game to determine whether a pure strategy solution exists, we find that the maximum of the row minimums is 2% while the minimum of the row maximums is 4%. Because these values are not equal, a pure strategy solution does not exist. In this case, it is not optimal for each company to be predictable and select a pure strategy regardless of what the other company does. The optimal solution is for both players to adopt a mixed strategy.

With a **mixed strategy,** each player selects its strategy according to a probability distribution. In the market share example, each company will first determine an optimal probability distribution for selecting whether to increase advertising, provide quantity discounts, or extend warranty. Then, when the game is played, each company will use its probability distribution to randomly select one of its three strategies.

First, consider the game from the point of view of Company A. Company A will select one of its three strategies based on the following probabilities:

$PA1$ = the probability that Company A selects Strategy a_1

$PA2$ = the probability that Company A selects Strategy a_2

$PA3$ = the probability that Company A selects Strategy a_3

The expected value, computed by multiplying each payoff by its probability and summing, can be interpreted as a long-run average payoff for a mixed strategy.

Using these probabilities for Company A's mixed strategy, what happens if Company B selects Strategy b_1? Using the payoffs in the b_1 column of Table 5.8, we see Company A will experience an increase in market share of 4% with probability $PA1$, a decrease in market share of 1% with probability $PA2$, and an increase in market share of 5% with probability $PA3$. Weighting each payoff by its probability and summing provides the **expected value** of the increase in market share for Company A. If Company B selects Strategy b_1, this expected value, referred to as the *expected gain* if Strategy b_1 is selected, can be written as follows:

$$EG(b_1) = 4PA1 - 1PA2 = 5PA3$$

The expression for the expected gain in market share for Company A for each Company B strategy is provided in Table 5.9.

TABLE 5.9 EXPECTED GAIN IN MARKET SHARE FOR COMPANY A FOR EACH
COMPANY B STRATEGY

Company B Strategy	Expected Gain for Company A
b_1	$EG(b_1) = 4PA1 - 1PA2 + 5PA3$
b_2	$EG(b_2) = 3PA1 + 4PA2 - 2PA3$
b_3	$EG(b_3) = 2PA1 + 1PA2 + 5PA3$

For example, if Company A uses a mixed strategy with equal probabilities ($PA1 = \frac{1}{3}$, $PA2 = \frac{1}{3}$, and $PA3 = \frac{1}{3}$), Company A's expected gain in market share for each Company B strategy is as follows:

$$EG(b_1) = 4PA1 - 1PA2 + 5PA3 = 4(\tfrac{1}{3}) - 1(\tfrac{1}{3}) + 5(\tfrac{1}{3}) = \tfrac{8}{3} = 2.67$$

$$EG(b_2) = 3PA1 + 4PA2 - 2PA3 = 3(\tfrac{1}{3}) + 4(\tfrac{1}{3}) - 2(\tfrac{1}{3}) = \tfrac{5}{3} = 1.67$$

$$EG(b_3) = 2PA1 + 1PA2 + 5PA3 = 2(\tfrac{1}{3}) + 1(\tfrac{1}{3}) + 5(\tfrac{1}{3}) = \tfrac{8}{3} = 2.67$$

The logic of game theory assumes that if Company A uses a mixed strategy, Company B will select the strategy that will minimize Company A's expected gain. Using these results, Company A assumes Company B will select Strategy b_2 and limit Company A's expected gain in market share to 1.67%. Because Company A's pure Strategy a_1 provides a 2% increase in market share, the mixed strategy with equal probabilities, $PA1 = \frac{1}{3}$, $PA2 = \frac{1}{3}$, and $PA3 = \frac{1}{3}$, is not the optimal strategy for Company A.

Let us show how Company A can use linear programming to find its optimal mixed strategy. Our goal is to find probabilities, $PA1$, $PA2$, and $PA3$, that maximize the expected gain in market share for Company A regardless of the strategy selected by Company B. In effect, Company A will protect itself against any strategy selected by Company B by being sure its expected gain in market share is as large as possible even if Company B selects its own optimal strategy.

Given the probabilities $PA1$, $PA2$, and $PA3$ and the expected gain expressions in Table 5.9, game theory assumes that Company B will select a strategy that provides the minimum expected gain for Company A. Thus, Company B will select b_1, b_2, or b_3 based on

$$\text{Min } \{EG(b_1), EG(b_2), EG(b_3)\}$$

When Company B selects its strategy, the value of the game will be the minimum expected gain. This strategy will minimize Company A's expected gain in market share.

The player seeking to maximize the value of the game selects a maximin strategy by maximizing the minimum expected gain.

Company A will select its optimal mixed strategy using a *maximin* strategy, which will maximize the minimum expected gain. This objective is written as follows:

$$\text{Max } [\text{Min } \{EG(b_1), EG(b_2), EG(b_3)\}]$$

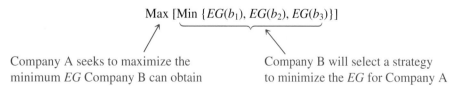

Company A seeks to maximize the
minimum *EG* Company B can obtain

Company B will select a strategy
to minimize the *EG* for Company A

Define *GAINA* to be the optimal expected gain in market share for Company A. Because Company B will select a strategy that minimizes this expected gain, we know *GAINA* is equal to Min $\{EG(b_1), EG(b_2), EG(b_3)\}$. Thus, the individual expected gains, $EG(b_1)$, $EG(b_2)$, and $EG(b_3)$, must all be *greater than or equal to GAINA*. If Company B selects Strategy b_1, we know

$$EG(b_1) \geq GAINA$$

Using the probabilities $PA1$, $PA2$, and $PA3$ and the expected gain expression in Table 5.9, this condition can be written as follows:

$$4PA1 - 1PA2 + 5PA3 \geq GAINA$$

Similarly, for Company B Strategies b_2 and b_3, the fact that both $EG(b_2) \geq GAINA$ and $EG(b_3) \geq GAINA$ provides the following two expressions:

$$3PA1 + 4PA2 - 2PA3 \geq GAINA$$
$$2PA1 + 1PA2 + 5PA3 \geq GAINA$$

In addition, we know that the sum of the Company A's mixed strategy probabilities must equal 1.

$$PA1 + PA2 + PA3 = 1$$

Finally, realizing that the objective of Company A is to maximize its expected gain, $GAINA$, we have the following linear programming model. Solving this linear program will provide Company A's optimal mixed strategy.

			Company B strategy
Max	$GAINA$		
s.t.			
	$4PA1 - 1PA2 + 5PA3 \geq GAINA$		(Strategy b_1)
	$3PA1 + 4PA2 - 2PA3 \geq GAINA$		(Strategy b_2)
	$2PA1 + 1PA2 + 5PA3 \geq GAINA$		(Strategy b_3)
	$PA1 + PA2 + PA3$	$= 1$	
	$PA1, PA2, PA3, GAINA \geq 0$		

The solution of Company A's linear program is shown in Figure 5.8.

From Figure 5.8, we see Company A's optimal mixed strategy is to increase advertising (a_1) with a probability of 0.875 and extend warranty (a_3) with a probability of 0.125. Company A should never provide quantity discounts (a_2) because $PA2 = 0$. The expected value of this mixed strategy is a 2.375% increase in market share for Company A.

FIGURE 5.8   THE SOLUTION FOR COMPANY A'S OPTIMAL MIXED STRATEGY

MODEL *file*

StrategyA

Optimal Objective Value =		2.37500
Variable	**Value**	**Reduced Costs**
PA1	0.87500	0.00000
PA2	0.00000	−0.25000
PA3	0.12500	0.00000
GAINA	2.37500	0.00000
Constraint	**Slack/Surplus**	**Dual Value**
1	1.75000	0.00000
2	0.00000	−0.37500
3	0.00000	−0.62500
4	0.00000	2.37500

Let us show what happens to the expected gain if Company A uses this optimal mixed strategy. Company A's expected gain for each Company B strategy follows:

$$EG(b_1) = 4PA1 - 1PA2 + 5PA3 = 4(0.875) - 1(0) + 5(0.125) = 4.125$$

$$EG(b_2) = 3PA1 + 4PA2 - 2PA3 = 3(0.875) + 4(0) - 2(0.125) = 2.375$$

$$EG(b_3) = 2PA1 + 1PA2 + 5PA3 = 2(0.875) + 1(0) + 5(0.125) = 2.375$$

Company B will minimize Company A's expected gain by selecting either Strategy b_2 or b_3. However, Company A has selected its optimal mixed strategy by maximizing this minimum expected gain. Thus, Company A obtains an expected gain in market share of 2.375% regardless of the strategy selected by Company B. The mixed strategy with $PA1 = 0.875$, $PA2 = 0.0$, and $PA3 = 0.125$ is the optimal strategy for Company A. The expected gain of 2.375% is better than Company A's best pure strategy (a_1), which provides a 2% increase in market share.

Now consider the game from the point of view of Company B. Company B will select one of its strategies based on the following probabilities:

$PB1$ = the probability that Company B selects strategy b_1

$PB2$ = the probability that Company B selects strategy b_2

$PB3$ = the probability that Company B selects strategy b_3

Based on these probabilities for Company B's mixed strategy, what happens if Company A selects strategy a_1? Using the payoffs in the a_1 row of Table 5.8, Company B will experience a decrease in market share of 4% with probability $PB1$, a decrease in market share of 3% with probability $PB2$, and a decrease in market share of 2% with probability $PB3$. If Company A selects strategy a_1, the expected value, referred to as Company B's *expected loss* if strategy a_1 is selected, can be written as follows:

$$EL(a_1) = 4PB1 + 3PB2 + 2PB3$$

The expression for the expected loss in market share for Company B for each Company A strategy is provided in Table 5.10.

Let us show how Company B can use linear programming to find its optimal mixed strategy. Our goal is to find the probabilities, $PB1$, $PB2$, and $PB3$, that minimize the expected loss in market share to Company B regardless of the strategy selected by Company A. In effect, Company B will protect itself from any strategy selected by Company A by being sure its expected loss in market share is as small as possible even if Company A selects its own optimal strategy.

Given the probabilities $PB1$, $PB2$, and $PB3$ and the expected loss expressions in Table 5.10, game theory assumes that Company A will select a strategy that provides the maximum expected loss for Company B. Thus, Company A will select a_1, a_2, or a_3 based on

$$\text{Max } \{EL(a_1), EL(a_2), EL(a_3)\}$$

TABLE 5.10 EXPECTED LOSS IN MARKET SHARE FOR COMPANY B FOR EACH COMPANY A STRATEGY

Company A Strategy	Expected Loss for Company B
a_1	$4PB1 + 3PB2 + 2PB3$
a_2	$-1PB1 + 4PB2 + 1PB3$
a_3	$5PB1 - 2PB2 + 5PB3$

When Company A selects its strategy, the value of the game will be the expected loss, which will maximize Company B's expected loss in market share.

Company B will select its optimal mixed strategy using a *minimax* strategy to minimize the maximum expected loss. This objective is written as follows:

The player seeking to minimize the value of the game selects a minimax strategy by minimizing the maximum expected loss.

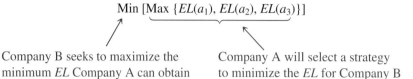

$$\text{Min } [\text{Max } \{EL(a_1), EL(a_2), EL(a_3)\}]$$

Company B seeks to maximize the minimum *EL* Company A can obtain

Company A will select a strategy to minimize the *EL* for Company B

Define *LOSSB* to be the optimal expected loss in market share for Company B. Because Company A will select a strategy that maximizes this expected loss, we know *LOSSB* is equal to Max $\{EL(a_1), EL(a_2), EL(a_3)\}$. Thus, the individual expected losses, $EL(a_1)$, $EL(a_2)$, and $EL(a_3)$, must all be *less than or equal to LOSSB*. If Company A selects Strategy a_1 we know

$$EL(a_1) \leq LOSSB$$

Using the probabilities *PB*1, *PB*2, and *PB*3 and the expected loss expression for $EL(a_1)$ in Table 5.10, this condition can be written as follows:

$$4PB1 + 3PB2 + 2PB3 \leq LOSSB$$

Similarly, for Company A Strategies a_2 and a_3, the fact that both $EL(a_2) \leq LOSSB$ and $EL(a_3) \leq LOSSB$ provides the following two expressions:

$$-1PB1 + 4PB2 + 1PB3 \leq LOSSB$$
$$5PB1 - 2PB2 + 5PB3 \leq LOSSB$$

In addition, we know that the sum of the Company B's mixed strategy probabilities must equal 1.

$$PB1 + PB2 + PB3 = 1$$

Finally, realizing that the objective of Company B is to minimize its expected loss, *LOSSB*, we have the following linear programming model. Solving this linear program will provide Company B's optimal mixed strategy.

$$
\begin{aligned}
\text{Min} \quad & LOSSB & & \text{Company A strategy} \\
\text{s.t.} \quad & 4PB1 + 3PB2 + 2PB3 \leq LOSSB & & (\text{Strategy } a_1) \\
& -1PB1 + 4PB2 + 1PB3 \leq LOSSB & & (\text{Strategy } a_2) \\
& 5PB1 - 2PB2 + 5PB3 \leq LOSSB & & (\text{Strategy } a_3) \\
& PB1 + PB2 + PB3 = 1 \\
& PB1, PB2, PB3, LOSSB \geq 0
\end{aligned}
$$

The solution of Company B's linear program is shown in Figure 5.9.

From Figure 5.9, we see Company B's optimal mixed strategy is to provide quantity discounts (b_2) with a probability of 0.375 and extend warranty (b_3) with a probability of 0.625. Company B should not increase advertising (b_1), because $PB1 = 0$. The expected value or expected loss of this mixed strategy is 2.375%. Note that the expected loss of 2.375% of the market share for Company B is the same as the expected gain in market share for Company A. The mixed strategy solution shows the zero-sum for the expected payoffs.

FIGURE 5.9 THE SOLUTION FOR COMPANY B'S OPTIMAL MIXED STRATEGY

MODEL *file*

StrategyB

```
Optimal Objective Value =            2.37500

        Variable            Value           Reduced Cost
      ------------      ------------      ----------------
          PB1             0.00000            1.75000
          PB2             0.37500            0.00000
          PB3             0.62500            0.00000
         LOSSB            2.37500            0.00000


       Constraint       Slack/Surplus        Dual Value
      ------------      ------------      ----------------
           1              0.00000            2.37500
           2              0.00000           -0.87500
           3              0.25000            0.00000
           4              0.00000           -0.12500
```

Let us show what happens to the expected loss if Company B uses this optimal mixed strategy. Company B's expected loss for each Company A strategy follows:

$$EL(a_1) = \quad 4PB1 + 3PB2 + 2PB3 = \quad 4(0) + 3(0.375) + 2(0.625) = 2.375$$
$$EL(a_2) = -1PB1 + 4PB2 + 1PB3 = -1(0) + 4(0.375) + 1(0.625) = 2.125$$
$$EL(a_3) = \quad 5PB1 - 2PB2 + 5PB3 = \quad 5(0) - 2(0.375) + 5(0.625) = 2.375$$

Company A will maximize Company B's expected loss by selecting either Strategy a_1 or a_3. However, Company B has selected its optimal mixed strategy by minimizing this maximum expected loss. Thus, Company B obtains an expected loss in market share of 2.375% regardless of the strategy selected by Company A. The mixed strategy with $PB1 = 0.0$, $PB2 = 0.375$, and $PB3 = 0.625$ is the optimal strategy for Company B. The expected loss of 2.375% is better than Company B's best pure strategy (b_2), which provides a 4% loss in market share.

The optimal mixed strategy solution with a value of 2.375% is an equilibrium solution. Given Company A's mixed strategy probabilities, Company B cannot improve the value of the game by changing $PB1$, $PB2$, or $PB3$. Likewise, given Company B's mixed strategy probabilities, Company A cannot improve the value of the game by changing $PA1$, $PA2$, or $PA3$. In general, the solution to the linear program will provide an equilibrium optimal mixed strategy solution for the game.

With a mixed strategy game, only solve the linear program for one of the players. Provided the value of the game is greater than zero, the absolute value of the dual values provides the optimal mixed strategy solution for the other player.

Let us conclude this linear programming application by making some observations and suggestions about using linear programming to solve mixed strategy two-person, zero-sum games. First of all, consider the dual value for constraint 2 in the solution of the Company A linear program in Figure 5.8. This dual value is –0.375. Recall that constraint 2 provides Company A's expected gain if Company B selects strategy b_2. The *absolute value* of the dual value is Company B's optimal probability for this strategy. Thus, we know $PB2 = 0.375$ without having to solve the Company B linear program. Using the absolute value of the dual values for the Company A linear program in Figure 5.8, we know that the optimal mixed strategy solution for Company B is $PB1 = 0.0$, $PB2 = 0.375$, and $PB3 = 0.625$. Therefore, when a two-person, zero-sum game has a mixed strategy, we only need to solve the linear program for one of the players. The optimal mixed strategy for the other player can be found by using the absolute value of the dual values.

Finally, note that a nonnegativity constraint in the linear program for Company A requires the value of the game, *GAINA*, to be greater than or equal to 0. A similar nonnegativity constraint in the linear program for Company B requires the value of the game, *LOSSB*, to be greater than or equal to 0. Because the value of the game in our example was 2.375%, we met these nonnegativity requirements. However, consider a two-person, zero-sum game where the payoff table contains several negative payoffs for player A. It may turn out that when player A selects an optimal mixed strategy, a negative value of the game is the best the player can do. In this case *GAINA* and *LOSSB* would be negative, which causes the linear program to have an infeasible solution.

If this condition exists or may exist, the following strategy can be used to modify the game and ensure that the linear program has a feasible solution. Define a constant c as follows:

$$c = \text{the absolute value of the largest negative payoff for player A}$$

If the value of a mixed strategy game may be negative, this procedure will guarantee that the linear program used to determine the optimal mixed strategy will have a feasible solution.

A revised payoff table can be created by adding c to each payoff, turning it into an equivalent two-person, zero-sum game. Because the revised payoff table contains no negative payoffs, the nonnegativity constraint for the value of the game will be satisfied and a feasible solution will exist for the linear program. More importantly, the optimal mixed strategy using the revised payoffs *will be the same* as the optimal mixed strategy for the original game. By subtracting c from the optimal objective function value for the game with the revised payoffs, you will obtain the objective function value for the original game.

NOTES AND COMMENTS

1. The analysis of a two-person, zero-sum game begins with checking to see whether a pure strategy solution exists. If the maximum of the row minimums for player A, V_A, is not equal to the minimum of the column maximums for player B, V_B, a pure strategy solution does not exist. At this point, we can also conclude that a mixed strategy solution is optimal and that the value of the game will be *between* V_A and V_B. For example, in our mixed strategy market-share game, the maximum of the row minimums was 2% and the minimum of the column maximums was 4%. Thus, we can conclude that a mixed strategy solution exists and that the value of the game is between 2% and 4%. We would know this result before solving the mixed strategy linear program.

    If the maximum of the row minimums, V_A, is positive and the minimum of the column maximums, V_B, is positive, we know that the value of the mixed strategy game will be positive. In this case, it is not necessary to revise the payoff

    table by the constant c to obtain a feasible linear programming solution. However, if one or both V_A and V_B are negative, the value of the mixed strategy game can be negative. In this case, it is desirable to revise the payoff table by adding the constant c to all payoffs prior to solving the linear program.

2. The linear programming formulation presented in this section used nonnegativity constraints $GAINA \geq 0$ and $LOSSB \geq 0$ so that the two-person, mixed strategy game could be solved with traditional linear programming software. If you are using software such as LINGO or Excel, these variables do not have to be nonnegative. In this case, eliminate the nonnegative requirements and make *GAINA* and *LOSSB* unrestricted in sign. This treatment guarantees that the linear program will have a feasible solution and eliminates the need to add a constant to the payoffs in situations where *GAINA* and *LOSSB* may be negative.

SUMMARY

In this chapter we presented selected advanced linear programming applications. In particular, we applied linear programming to evaluating the performance of hospitals, maximizing revenue for airlines, constructing mutual fund portfolios, and competing for market share. In practice, most of the modeling effort in these types of linear programming applications involves clearly understanding the problem, stating the problem mathematically, and then finding reliable data in the format required by the model.

GLOSSARY

Data envelopment analysis (DEA)   A linear programming application used to measure the relative efficiency of operating units with the same goals and objectives.

Efficiency index   Percentage of an individual operating unit's resources that are available to the composite operating unit.

Expected value In a mixed strategy game, a value computed by multiplying each payoff by its probability and summing. It can be interpreted as the long-run average payoff for the mixed strategy.

Game theory A decision-making situation in which two or more decision makers compete by each selecting one of several strategies. The combination of the competing strategies provides the value of the game to the players.

Hypothetical composite A weighted average of outputs and inputs of all operating units with similar goals.

Maximin strategy A strategy where the player seeking to maximize the value of the game selects the strategy that maximizes the minimum payoff obtainable by the other player.

Minimax strategy A strategy where the player seeking to minimize the value of the game selects the strategy that minimizes the maximum payoff obtainable by the other player.

Mixed strategy When a player randomly selects its strategy based on a probability distribution. The strategy selected can vary each time the game is played.

Pure strategy When one of the available strategies is optimal and the player always selects this strategy regardless of the strategy selected by the other player.

Saddle point A condition that exists when pure strategies are optimal for both players. Neither player can improve the value of the game by changing from the optimal pure strategy.

Two-person, zero-sum game A game with two players in which the gain to one player is equal to the loss to the other player.

PROBLEMS

Note: The following problems have been designed to give you an understanding and appreciation of the broad range of problems that can be formulated as linear programs. You should be able to formulate a linear programming model for each of the problems. However, you will need access to a linear programming computer package (e.g., Excel Solver or LINGO) to develop the solutions and make the requested interpretations.

1. In Section 5.1 data envelopment analysis was used to evaluate the relative efficiencies of four hospitals. Data for three input measures and four output measures were provided in Tables 5.1 and 5.2.

    a. Use these data to develop a linear programming model that could be used to evaluate the performance of General Hospital.

    b. The following solution is optimal. Does the solution indicate that General Hospital is relatively inefficient?

Objective Function Value = 1.000

Variable	Value	Reduced Costs
E	1.000	0.000
WG	1.000	0.000
WU	0.000	0.000
WC	0.000	0.331
WS	0.000	0.215

    c. Explain which hospital or hospitals make up the composite unit used to evaluate General Hospital and why.

2. Data envelopment analysis can measure the relative efficiency of a group of hospitals. The following data from a particular study involving seven teaching hospitals include three input measures and four output measures:

    a. Formulate a linear programming model so that data envelopment analysis can be used to evaluate the performance of hospital D.

b. Solve the model.

c. Is hospital D relatively inefficient? What is the interpretation of the value of the objective function?

Input Measures

Hospital	Full-Time Equivalent Nonphysicians	Supply Expense (1000s)	Bed-Days Available (1000s)
A	310.0	134.60	116.00
B	278.5	114.30	106.80
C	165.6	131.30	65.52
D	250.0	316.00	94.40
E	206.4	151.20	102.10
F	384.0	217.00	153.70
G	530.1	770.80	215.00

Output Measures

Hospital	Patient-Days (65 or older) (1000s)	Patient-Days (under 65) (1000s)	Nurses Trained	Interns Trained
A	55.31	49.52	291	47
B	37.64	55.63	156	3
C	32.91	25.77	141	26
D	33.53	41.99	160	21
E	32.48	55.30	157	82
F	48.78	81.92	285	92
G	58.41	119.70	111	89

d. How many patient-days of each type are produced by the composite hospital?

e. Which hospitals would you recommend hospital D consider emulating to improve the efficiency of its operation?

3. Refer again to the data presented in Problem 2.

a. Formulate a linear programming model that can be used to perform data envelopment analysis for hospital E.

b. Solve the model.

c. Is hospital E relatively inefficient? What is the interpretation of the value of the objective function?

d. Which hospitals are involved in making up the composite hospital? Can you make a general statement about which hospitals will make up the composite unit associated with a unit that is not inefficient?

4. The Ranch House, Inc., operates five fast-food restaurants. Input measures for the restaurants include weekly hours of operation, full-time equivalent staff, and weekly supply expenses. Output measures of performance include average weekly contribution to profit, market share, and annual growth rate. Data for the input and output measures are shown in the following tables:

Input Measures

Restaurant	Hours of Operation	FTE Staff	Supplies ($)
Bardstown	96	16	850
Clarksville	110	22	1400
Jeffersonville	100	18	1200
New Albany	125	25	1500
St. Matthews	120	24	1600

| | | Output Measures | |
Restaurant	Weekly Profit	Market Share (%)	Growth Rate (%)
Bardstown	$3800	25	8.0
Clarksville	$4600	32	8.5
Jeffersonville	$4400	35	8.0
New Albany	$6500	30	10.0
St. Matthews	$6000	28	9.0

    a. Develop a linear programming model that can be used to evaluate the performance of the Clarksville Ranch House restaurant.

    b. Solve the model.

    c. Is the Clarksville Ranch House restaurant relatively inefficient? Discuss.

    d. Where does the composite restaurant have more output than the Clarksville restaurant? How much less of each input resource does the composite restaurant require when compared to the Clarksville restaurant?

    e. What other restaurants should be studied to find suggested ways for the Clarksville restaurant to improve its efficiency?

5. Reconsider the Leisure Airlines problem from Section 5.2. The demand forecasts shown in Table 5.3 represent Leisure Air's best estimates of demand. But because demand cannot be forecasted perfectly, the number of seats actually sold for each origin-destination-itinerary fare (ODIF) may turn out to be smaller or larger than forecasted. Suppose that Leisure Air believes that economic conditions have improved and that their original forecast may be too low. To account for this possibility, Leisure Air is considering switching the Boeing 737-400 airplanes that are based in Pittsburgh and Newark with Boeing 757-200 airplanes that Leisure Air has available in other markets. The Boeing 757-200 airplane has a seating capacity of 158 in the coach section.

    a. Because of scheduling conflicts in other markets, suppose that Leisure Air is only able to obtain one Boeing 757-200. Should the larger plane be based in Pittsburgh or in Newark? Explain.

    b. Based upon your answer in part (a), determine a new allocation for the ODIFs. Briefly summarize the major differences between the new allocation using one Boeing 757-200 and the original allocation summarized in Figure 5.5.

    c. Suppose that two Boeing 757-200 airplanes are available. Determine a new allocation for the ODIFs using the two larger airplanes. Briefly summarize the major differences between the new allocation using two Boeing 757-200 airplanes and the original allocation shown in Figure 5.5.

    d. Consider the new solution obtained in part (b). Which ODIF has the highest bid price? What is the interpretation for this bid price?

6. Reconsider the Leisure Airlines problem from Section 5.2. Suppose that as of May 1 the following number of seats have been sold:

ODIF	1	2	3	4	5	6	7	8	9	10	11	12	13	14	15	16
Seats Sold	25	44	18	12	5	9	20	33	37	11	5	8	27	6	35	7

    a. Determine how many seats are still available for sale on each flight leg.

    b. Using the original demand forecasted for each ODIF, determine the remaining demand for each ODIF.

    c. Revise the linear programming model presented in Section 5.2 to account for the number of seats currently sold and a demand of one additional seat for the Pittsburgh–Myrtle Beach Q class ODIF. Resolve the linear programming model to determine a new allocation schedule for the ODIFs.

7. Hanson Inn is a 96-room hotel located near the airport and convention center in Louisville, Kentucky. When a convention or a special event is in town, Hanson increases its normal room rates and takes reservations based on a revenue management system. The Classic Corvette Owners Association scheduled its annual convention in Louisville for the

first weekend in June. Hanson Inn agreed to make at least 50% of its rooms available for convention attendees at a special convention rate in order to be listed as a recommended hotel for the convention. Although the majority of attendees at the annual meeting typically request a Friday and Saturday two-night package, some attendees may select a Friday night only or a Saturday night only reservation. Customers not attending the convention may also request a Friday and Saturday two-night package, or make a Friday night only or Saturday night only reservation. Thus, six types of reservations are possible: Convention customers/two-night package; convention customers/Friday night only; convention customers/Saturday night only; regular customers/two-night package; regular customers/Friday night only; and regular customers/Saturday night only. The cost for each type of reservation is shown here:

	Two-Night Package	Friday Night Only	Saturday Night Only
Convention	$225	$123	$130
Regular	$295	$146	$152

The anticipated demand for each type of reservation is as follows:

	Two-Night Package	Friday Night Only	Saturday Night Only
Convention	40	20	15
Regular	20	30	25

Hanson Inn would like to determine how many rooms to make available for each type of reservation in order to maximize total revenue.

a. Define the decision variables and state the objective function.

b. Formulate a linear programming model for this revenue management application.

c. What are the optimal allocation and the anticipated total revenue?

d. Suppose that one week before the convention the number of regular customers/Saturday night only rooms that were made available sell out. If another nonconvention customer calls and requests a Saturday night only room, what is the value of accepting this additional reservation?

8. In the latter part of Section 5.3 we developed a moderate risk portfolio model for Hauck Investment Services. Modify the model given so that it can be used to construct a portfolio for more aggressive investors. In particular, do the following:

a. Develop a portfolio model for investors who are willing to risk a portfolio with a return as low as 0%.

b. What is the recommended allocation for this type of investor?

c. How would you modify your recommendation in part (b) for an investor who also wants to have at least 10% of his or her portfolio invested in the foreign stock mutual fund? How does requiring at least 10% of the portfolio be invested in the foreign stock fund affect the expected return?

9. Table 5.11 shows data on the returns over five 1-year periods for six mutual funds. A firm's portfolio managers will assume that one of these scenarios will accurately reflect the investing climate over the next 12 months. The probabilities of each of the scenarios occurring are 0.1, 0.3, 0.1, 0.1, and 0.4 for years 1 to 5, respectively.

a. Develop a portfolio model for investors who are willing to risk a portfolio with a return no lower than 2%.

b. Solve the model in part (a) and recommend a portfolio allocation for the investor with this risk tolerance.

c. Modify the portfolio model in part (a) and solve it to develop a portfolio for an investor with a risk tolerance of 0%.

TABLE 5.11 RETURNS OVER FIVE 1-YEAR PERIODS FOR SIX MUTUAL FUNDS

	Planning Scenarios for Next 12 Months				
Mutual Funds	**Year 1**	**Year 2**	**Year 3**	**Year 4**	**Year 5**
Large-Cap Stock	35.3	20.0	28.3	10.4	−9.3
Mid-Cap Stock	32.3	23.2	−0.9	49.3	−22.8
Small-Cap Stock	20.8	22.5	6.0	33.3	6.1
Energy/Resources Sector	25.3	33.9	−20.5	20.9	−2.5
Health Sector	49.1	5.5	29.7	77.7	−24.9
Technology Sector	46.2	21.7	45.7	93.1	−20.1
Real Estate Sector	20.5	44.0	−21.1	2.6	5.1

    d. Is the expected return higher for investors following the portfolio recommendations in part (c) as compared to the returns for the portfolio in part (b)? If so, do you believe the returns are enough higher to justify investing in that portfolio?

SELF*test*

10. Consider the following two-person, zero-sum game. Payoffs are the winnings for Player A. Identify the pure strategy solution. What is the value of the game?

		Player B		
		b_1	b_2	b_3
Player A	a_1	8	5	7
	a_2	2	4	10

11. Assume that a two-person, zero-sum game has a pure strategy solution. If this game were solved using a linear programming formulation, how would you know from the linear programming solution that the game had a pure strategy solution?

12. Two opposing armies, Red and Blue, must each decide whether to attack or defend. These decisions are made without knowledge of the opposing army's decision. The payoff table, in terms of value of property gained or lost for the Red Army, appears below. Any gains for the Red Army are losses for the Blue Army.

		Blue Army	
		Attack	**Defend**
Red	**Attack**	30	50
Army	**Defend**	40	0

    a. What is the optimal mixed strategy for the Red Army?
    b. What is the optimal mixed strategy for the Blue Army?

13. Two television stations compete with each other for viewing audience. Local programming options for the 5:00 P.M. weekday time slot include a sitcom rerun, an early news program, or a home improvement show. Each station has the same programming options and must make its preseason program selection before knowing what the other television station will do. The viewing audience gains in thousands of viewers for Station A are shown in the payoff table.

| | | Station B | | |
		Sitcom Rerun b_1	News Program b_2	Home Improvement b_3
Station A	Sitcom Rerun a_1	10	−5	3
	News Program a_2	8	7	6
	Home Improvement a_3	4	8	7

Determine the optimal strategy for each station. What is the value of the game?

14. Two Indiana state senate candidates must decide which city to visit the day before the November election. The same four cities—Indianapolis, Evansville, Fort Wayne, and South Bend—are available for both candidates. Travel plans must be made in advance, so the candidates must decide which city to visit prior to knowing the city the other candidate will visit. Values in the payoff table show thousands of voters gained by the Republican candidate based on the strategies selected by the two candidates. Which city should each candidate visit and what is the value of the game?

| | | Democratic Candidate | | | |
		Indianapolis b_1	Evansville b_2	Fort Wayne b_3	South Bend b_4
Republican Candidate	Indianapolis a_1	0	−15	−8	20
	Evansville a_2	30	−5	5	−10
	Fort Wayne a_3	10	−25	0	20
	South Bend a_4	20	20	10	15

15. In a gambling game, Player A and Player B both have a \$1 and a \$5 bill. Each player selects one of the bills without the other player knowing the bill selected. Simultaneously they both reveal the bills selected. If the bills do not match, Player A wins Player B's bill. If the bills match, Player B wins Player A's bill.

  a. Develop the game theory table for this game. The values should be expressed as the gains (or losses) for Player A.

  b. Is there a pure strategy? Why or why not?

  c. Determine the optimal strategies and the value of this game. Does the game favor one player over the other?

  d. Suppose Player B decides to deviate from the optimal strategy and begins playing each bill 50% of the time. What should Player A do to improve Player A's winnings? Comment on why it is important to follow an optimal game theory strategy.

16. Two companies compete for a share of the soft drink market. Each has worked with an advertising agency to develop alternative advertising strategies for the coming year. A variety of television advertisements, newspaper advertisements, product promotions, and in-store displays have provided four different strategies for each company. The payoff table summarizes the gain in market share for Company A projected for the various combinations of Company A and Company B strategies. What is the optimal strategy for each company? What is the value of the game?

| | | Company B | | | |
		b_1	b_2	b_3	b_4
Company A	a_1	3	0	2	4
	a_2	2	−2	1	0
	a_3	4	2	5	6
	a_4	−2	6	−1	0

17. The offensive coordinator for the Chicago Bears professional football team is preparing a game plan for the upcoming game against the Green Bay Packers. A review of game tapes from previous Bears–Packers games provides data on the yardage gained for run plays and pass plays. Data show that when the Bears run against the Packers' run defense, the Bears gain an average of 2 yards. However, when the Bears run against the Packers' pass defense, the Bears gain an average of 6 yards. A similar analysis of pass plays reveals that if the Bears pass against the Packers' run defense, the Bears gain an average of 11 yards. However, if the Bears pass against the Packers' pass defense, the Bears average a loss of 1 yard. This loss, or negative gain of -1, includes the lost yardage due to quarterback sacks and interceptions. Develop a payoff table that shows the Bears' average yardage gain for each combination of the Bears' offensive strategy to run or pass and the Packers' strategy of using a run defense or a pass defense. What is the optimal strategy for the Chicago Bears during the upcoming game against the Green Bay Packers? What is the expected value of this strategy?

CHAPTER 6

Distribution and Network Models

CONTENTS

The models discussed in this chapter belong to a special class of linear programming problems called *network flow* problems. We begin by discussing models commonly encountered when dealing with problems related to supply chains, specifically transportation and transshipment problems. We then consider three other types of network problems: assignment problems, shortest-route problems, and maximal flow problems.

In each case, we present a graphical representation of the problem in the form of a *network*. We then show how the problem can be formulated and solved as a linear program. In the last section of the chapter we present a production and inventory problem that is an interesting application of the transshipment problem.

6.1 SUPPLY CHAIN MODELS

A **supply chain** describes the set of all interconnected resources involved in producing and distributing a product. For instance, a supply chain for automobiles could include raw material producers, automotive-parts suppliers, distribution centers for storing automotive parts, assembly plants, and car dealerships. All the materials needed to produce a finished automobile must flow through the supply chain. In general, supply chains are designed to satisfy customer demand for a product at minimum cost. Those that control the supply chain must make decisions such as where to produce the product, how much should be produced, and where it should be sent. We will look at two specific types of problems common in supply chain models that can be solved using linear programing: transportation problems and transshipment problems.

Transportation Problem

The **transportation problem** arises frequently in planning for the distribution of goods and services from several supply locations to several demand locations. Typically, the quantity of goods available at each supply location (origin) is limited, and the quantity of goods needed at each of several demand locations (destinations) is known. The usual objective in a transportation problem is to minimize the cost of shipping goods from the origins to the destinations.

Let us illustrate by considering a transportation problem faced by Foster Generators. This problem involves the transportation of a product from three plants to four distribution centers. Foster Generators operates plants in Cleveland, Ohio; Bedford, Indiana; and York, Pennsylvania. Production capacities over the next three-month planning period for one particular type of generator are as follows:

Origin	Plant	Three-Month Production Capacity (units)
1	Cleveland	5,000
2	Bedford	6,000
3	York	2,500
	Total	13,500

The firm distributes its generators through four regional distribution centers located in Boston, Chicago, St. Louis, and Lexington; the three-month forecast of demand for the distribution centers is as follows:

Destination	Distribution Center	Three-Month Demand Forecast (units)
1	Boston	6,000
2	Chicago	4,000
3	St. Louis	2,000
4	Lexington	1,500
	Total	13,500

Management would like to determine how much of its production should be shipped from each plant to each distribution center. Figure 6.1 shows graphically the 12 distribution routes Foster can use. Such a graph is called a **network**; the circles are referred to as **nodes** and the lines connecting the nodes as **arcs**. Each origin and destination is represented by a node, and each possible shipping route is represented by an arc. The amount of the supply is written next to each origin node, and the amount of the demand is written next to each destination node. The goods shipped from the origins to the destinations represent the flow in the network. Note that the direction of flow (from origin to destination) is indicated by the arrows.

FIGURE 6.1   THE NETWORK REPRESENTATION OF THE FOSTER GENERATORS TRANSPORTATION PROBLEM

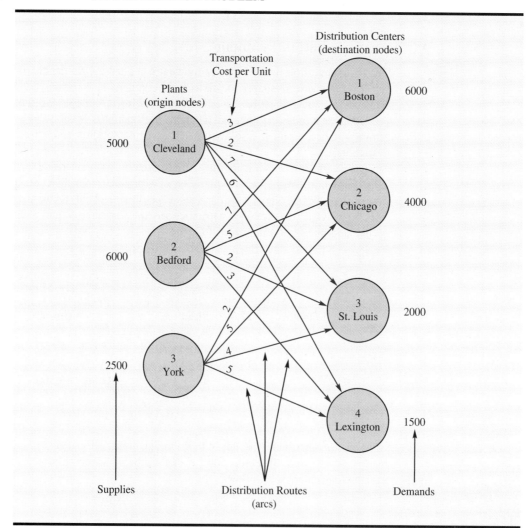

TABLE 6.1 TRANSPORTATION COST PER UNIT FOR THE FOSTER GENERATORS TRANSPORTATION PROBLEM

	Destination			
Origin	**Boston**	**Chicago**	**St. Louis**	**Lexington**
Cleveland	3	2	7	6
Bedford	7	5	2	3
York	2	5	4	5

Try Problem 1 for practice in developing a network model of a transportation problem.

For Foster's transportation problem, the objective is to determine the routes to be used and the quantity to be shipped via each route that will provide the minimum total transportation cost. The cost for each unit shipped on each route is given in Table 6.1 and is shown on each arc in Figure 6.1.

A linear programming model can be used to solve this transportation problem. We use double-subscripted decision variables, with x_{11} denoting the number of units shipped from origin 1 (Cleveland) to destination 1 (Boston), x_{12} denoting the number of units shipped from origin 1 (Cleveland) to destination 2 (Chicago), and so on. In general, the decision variables for a transportation problem having m origins and n destinations are written as follows:

The first subscript identifies the "from" node of the corresponding arc and the second subscript identifies the "to" node of the arc.

$$x_{ij} = \text{number of units shipped from origin } i \text{ to destination } j$$
$$\text{where } i = 1, 2, \ldots, m \text{ and } j = 1, 2, \ldots, n$$

Because the objective of the transportation problem is to minimize the total transportation cost, we can use the cost data in Table 6.1 or on the arcs in Figure 6.1 to develop the following cost expressions:

Transportation costs for
units shipped from Cleveland $= 3x_{11} + 2x_{12} + 7x_{13} + 6x_{14}$

Transportation costs for
units shipped from Bedford $= 7x_{21} + 5x_{22} + 2x_{23} + 3x_{24}$

Transportation costs for
units shipped from York $= 2x_{31} + 5x_{32} + 4x_{33} + 5x_{34}$

The sum of these expressions provides the objective function showing the total transportation cost for Foster Generators.

Transportation problems need constraints because each origin has a limited supply and each destination has a demand requirement. We consider the supply constraints first. The capacity at the Cleveland plant is 5000 units. With the total number of units shipped from the Cleveland plant expressed as $x_{11} + x_{12} + x_{13} + x_{14}$, the supply constraint for the Cleveland plant is

$$x_{11} + x_{12} + x_{13} + x_{14} \leq 5000 \quad \text{Cleveland supply}$$

With three origins (plants), the Foster transportation problem has three supply constraints. Given the capacity of 6000 units at the Bedford plant and 2500 units at the York plant, the two additional supply constraints are

$$x_{21} + x_{22} + x_{23} + x_{24} \leq 6000 \quad \text{Bedford supply}$$
$$x_{31} + x_{32} + x_{33} + x_{34} \leq 2500 \quad \text{York supply}$$

With the four distribution centers as the destinations, four demand constraints are needed to ensure that destination demands will be satisfied:

To obtain a feasible solution, the total supply must be greater than or equal to the total demand.

$$x_{11} + x_{21} + x_{31} = 6000 \quad \text{Boston demand}$$
$$x_{12} + x_{22} + x_{32} = 4000 \quad \text{Chicago demand}$$
$$x_{13} + x_{23} + x_{33} = 2000 \quad \text{St. Louis demand}$$
$$x_{14} + x_{24} + x_{34} = 1500 \quad \text{Lexington demand}$$

Combining the objective function and constraints into one model provides a 12-variable, 7-constraint linear programming formulation of the Foster Generators transportation problem:

$$\text{Min } 3x_{11} + 2x_{12} + 7x_{13} + 6x_{14} + 7x_{21} + 5x_{22} + 2x_{23} + 3x_{24} + 2x_{31} + 5x_{32} + 4x_{33} + 5x_{34}$$

s.t.

$$
\begin{array}{llll}
x_{11} + x_{12} + x_{13} + x_{14} & & & \le 5000 \\
x_{21} + x_{22} + x_{23} + x_{24} & & & \le 6000 \\
x_{31} + x_{32} + x_{33} + x_{34} & & & \le 2500 \\
x_{11} \quad\quad + x_{21} \quad\quad + x_{31} & & & = 6000 \\
x_{12} \quad\quad + x_{22} \quad\quad + x_{32} & & & = 4000 \\
x_{13} \quad\quad + x_{23} \quad\quad + x_{33} & & & = 2000 \\
x_{14} \quad\quad + x_{24} \quad\quad + x_{34} & & & = 1500 \\
\end{array}
$$

$$x_{ij} \ge 0 \quad \text{for } i = 1, 2, 3 \text{ and } j = 1, 2, 3, 4$$

Comparing the linear programming formulation to the network in Figure 6.1 leads to several observations: All the information needed for the linear programming formulation is on the network. Each node has one constraint and each arc has one variable. The sum of the variables corresponding to arcs from an origin node must be less than or equal to the origin's supply, and the sum of the variables corresponding to the arcs into a destination node must be equal to the destination's demand.

The optimal objective function values and optimal decision variable values for the Foster Generators problem are shown in Figure 6.2, which indicates that the minimum total transportation cost is $39,500. The values for the decision variables show the optimal amounts to ship over each route. For example, 3500 units should be shipped from Cleveland to Boston, and 1500 units should be shipped from Cleveland to Chicago. Other values of the decision variables indicate the remaining shipping quantities and routes. Table 6.2 shows the minimum cost transportation schedule, and Figure 6.3 summarizes the optimal solution on the network.

FIGURE 6.2   OPTIMAL SOLUTION FOR THE FOSTER GENERATORS TRANSPORTATION PROBLEM

MODEL file

Foster

Optimal Objective Value = 39500.00000

Variable	Value	Reduced Costs
X11	3500.00000	0.00000
X12	1500.00000	0.00000
X13	0.00000	8.00000
X14	0.00000	6.00000
X21	0.00000	1.00000
X22	2500.00000	0.00000
X23	2000.00000	0.00000
X24	1500.00000	0.00000
X31	2500.00000	0.00000
X32	0.00000	4.00000
X33	0.00000	6.00000
X34	0.00000	6.00000

TABLE 6.2 OPTIMAL SOLUTION TO THE FOSTER GENERATORS TRANSPORTATION PROBLEM

Route		Units	Cost	Total
From	**To**	**Shipped**	**per Unit**	**Cost**
Cleveland	Boston	3500	$3	$10,500
Cleveland	Chicago	1500	$2	$ 3,000
Bedford	Chicago	2500	$5	$12,500
Bedford	St. Louis	2000	$2	$ 4,000
Bedford	Lexington	1500	$3	$ 4,500
York	Boston	2500	$2	$ 5,000
				$39,500

FIGURE 6.3 NETWORK DIAGRAM FOR THE OPTIMAL SOLUTION TO THE FOSTER GENERATORS TRANSPORTATION PROBLEM

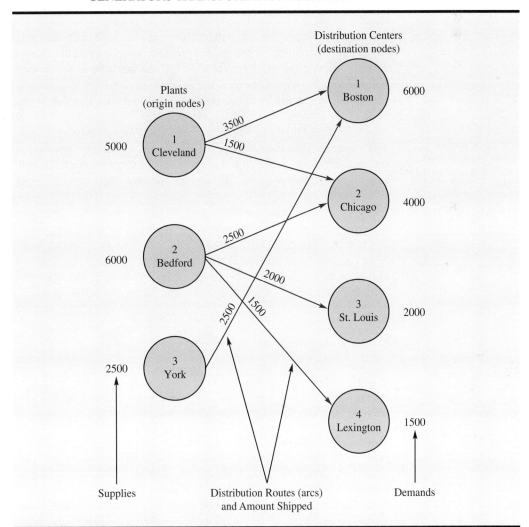

Problem Variations

The Foster Generators problem illustrates use of the basic transportation model. Variations of the basic transportation model may involve one or more of the following situations:

1. Total supply not equal to total demand
2. Maximization objective function
3. Route capacities or route minimums
4. Unacceptable routes

With slight modifications in the linear programming model, we can easily accommodate these situations.

Total Supply Not Equal to Total Demand   Often *the total supply is not equal to the total demand.* If total supply exceeds total demand, no modification in the linear programming formulation is necessary. Excess supply will appear as slack in the linear programming solution. Slack for any particular origin can be interpreted as the unused supply or amount not shipped from the origin.

Whenever total supply is less than total demand, the model does not determine how the unsatisfied demand is handled (e.g., backorders). The manager must handle this aspect of the problem.

If total supply is less than total demand, the linear programming model of a transportation problem will not have a feasible solution. In this case, we modify the network representation by adding a **dummy origin** with a supply equal to the difference between the total demand and the total supply. With the addition of the dummy origin and an arc from the dummy origin to each destination, the linear programming model will have a feasible solution. A zero cost per unit is assigned to each arc leaving the dummy origin so that the value of the optimal solution for the revised problem will represent the shipping cost for the units actually shipped (no shipments actually will be made from the dummy origin). When the optimal solution is implemented, the destinations showing shipments being received from the dummy origin will be the destinations experiencing a shortfall or unsatisfied demand.

Try Problem 6 for practice with a case in which demand is greater than supply with a maximization objective.

Maximization Objective Function   In some transportation problems, the objective is to find a solution that maximizes profit or revenue. Using the values for profit or revenue per unit as coefficients in the objective function, we simply solve a maximization rather than a minimization linear program. This change does not affect the constraints.

Route Capacities or Route Minimums   The linear programming formulation of the transportation problem also can accommodate capacities or minimum quantities for one or more of the routes. For example, suppose that in the Foster Generators problem the York–Boston route (origin 3 to destination 1) had a capacity of 1000 units because of limited space availability on its normal mode of transportation. With x_{31} denoting the amount shipped from York to Boston, the route capacity constraint for the York–Boston route would be

$$x_{31} \leq 1000$$

Similarly, route minimums can be specified. For example,

$$x_{22} \geq 2000$$

would guarantee that a previously committed order for a Bedford–Chicago delivery of at least 2000 units would be maintained in the optimal solution.

Unacceptable Routes   Finally, establishing a route from every origin to every destination may not be possible. To handle this situation, we simply drop the corresponding arc from the network and remove the corresponding variable from the linear programming formulation. For example, if the Cleveland–St. Louis route were unacceptable or unusable, the arc from Cleveland to St. Louis could be dropped in Figure 6.1, and x_{13} could be removed from the linear programming formulation. Solving the resulting 11-variable, 7-constraint model would provide the optimal solution while guaranteeing that the Cleveland–St. Louis route is not used.

A General Linear Programming Model

To show the general linear programming model for a transportation problem with m origins and n destinations, we use the following notation:

$$x_{ij} = \text{number of units shipped from origin } i \text{ to destination } j$$
$$c_{ij} = \text{cost per unit of shipping from origin } i \text{ to destination } j$$
$$s_i = \text{supply or capacity in units at origin } i$$
$$d_j = \text{demand in units at destination } j$$

The general linear programming model is as follows:

$$\text{Min} \quad \sum_{i=1}^{n} \sum_{j=1}^{n} c_{ij} x_{ij}$$

s.t.

$$\sum_{j=1}^{n} x_{ij} \leq s_i \qquad i = 1, 2, \ldots, m \quad \text{Supply}$$

$$\sum_{i=1}^{m} x_{ij} = d_j \qquad j = 1, 2, \ldots, n \quad \text{Demand}$$

$$x_{ij} \geq 0 \qquad \text{for all } i \text{ and } j$$

As mentioned previously, we can add constraints of the form $x_{ij} \leq L_{ij}$ if the route from origin i to destination j has capacity L_{ij}. A transportation problem that includes constraints of this type is called a **capacitated transportation problem**. Similarly, we can add route minimum constraints of the form $x_{ij} \geq M_{ij}$ if the route from origin i to destination j must handle at least M_{ij} units.

The Management Science in Action, Route Optimization at UPS Using ORION, describes how UPS uses optimization models to determine the best routes for its drivers resulting in huge savings for the company.

MANAGEMENT SCIENCE IN ACTION

ROUTE OPTIMIZATION AT UPS USING ORION*

UPS utilizes more than 100,000 delivery vehicles across the world to deliver nearly 5 billion packages per year. A delivery driver will deliver between 125 and 175 packages on a typical day, and UPS has approximately 55,000 different delivery routes in the United States alone. At the heart of UPS' system for determining the routes taken by delivery drivers is a system known as ORION: On-Road Integrated Optimization and Navigation. ORION represents one of the largest management science projects ever implemented by a company.

ORION's goal is to provide optimized routes to UPS drivers to minimize the time required for deliveries and to save on fuel costs. Each day, UPS examines data related to pickup and delivery requests as well as the availability of drivers and vehicles. ORION then applies advanced models, many of which are based on versions of the optimization models discussed in this chapter, to determine the best routes for its drivers.

ORION was an enormous project for UPS. It was developed over more than a decade and required UPS to invest significant resources in technology and better maps to use as input into the system. The full algorithm represents more than 1000 pages of code and utilizes high-powered computer equipment to determine the best routes for individual vehicles in seconds. ORION typically runs overnight to determine the optimal routes for its drivers for the next day.

UPS estimates that it saves more than 10 million gallons of fuel per year using ORION by reducing the annual miles driven by its vehicles by more than 100 million miles—he equivalent of more than 4000 trips around the world. This savings also translates into a reduction of about 100,000 metric tons of carbon dioxide emissions per year. UPS estimates that, in total, ORION will enable the company to save between $300 and $400 million dollars per year. In recognition for the exceptional contributions of the ORION system, UPS was awarded the 2016 Edelman Award by INFORMS, the leading organization for management scientists. The Edelman Award is the highest honor that an organization can receive to recognize achievements in the practice of management science.

*Based on information from www.ups.com and www.informs.org

Transshipment Problem

The **transshipment problem** is an extension of the transportation problem in which intermediate nodes, referred to as *transshipment nodes*, are added to account for locations such as warehouses. In this more general type of distribution problem, shipments may be made between any pair of the three general types of nodes: origin nodes, transshipment nodes, and destination nodes. For example, the transshipment problem permits shipments of goods from origins to intermediate nodes and on to destinations, from one origin to another origin, from one intermediate location to another, from one destination location to another, and directly from origins to destinations.

As was true for the transportation problem, the supply available at each origin is limited, and the demand at each destination is specified. The objective in the transshipment problem is to determine how many units should be shipped over each arc in the network so that all destination demands are satisfied with the minimum possible transportation cost.

Try Problem 11, part (a), for practice in developing a network representation of a transshipment problem.

Let us consider the transshipment problem faced by Ryan Electronics. Ryan is an electronics company with production facilities in Denver and Atlanta. Components produced at either facility may be shipped to either of the firm's regional warehouses, which are located in Kansas City and Louisville. From the regional warehouses, the firm supplies retail outlets in Detroit, Miami, Dallas, and New Orleans. The key features of the problem are shown in the network model depicted in Figure 6.4. Note that the supply at each origin and demand

FIGURE 6.4   NETWORK REPRESENTATION OF THE RYAN ELECTRONICS
TRANSSHIPMENT PROBLEM

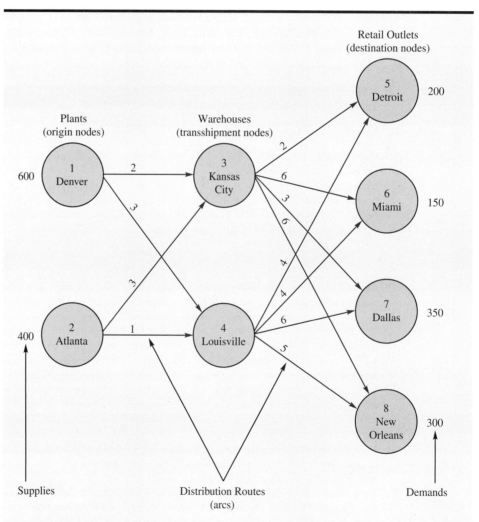

TABLE 6.3 TRANSPORTATION COST PER UNIT FOR THE RYAN ELECTRONICS TRANSSHIPMENT PROBLEM

	Warehouse	
Plant	**Kansas City**	**Louisville**
Denver	2	3
Atlanta	3	1

	Retail Outlet			
Warehouse	**Detroit**	**Miami**	**Dallas**	**New Orleans**
Kansas City	2	6	3	6
Louisville	4	4	6	5

at each destination are shown in the left and right margins, respectively. Nodes 1 and 2 are the origin nodes; nodes 3 and 4 are the transshipment nodes; and nodes 5, 6, 7, and 8 are the destination nodes. The transportation cost per unit for each distribution route is shown in Table 6.3 and on the arcs of the network model in Figure 6.4.

As with the transportation problem, we can formulate a linear programming model of the transshipment problem from a network representation. Again, we need a constraint for each node and a variable for each arc. Let x_{ij} denote the number of units shipped from node i to node j. For example, x_{13} denotes the number of units shipped from the Denver plant to the Kansas City warehouse, x_{14} denotes the number of units shipped from the Denver plant to the Louisville warehouse, and so on. Because the supply at the Denver plant is 600 units, the amount shipped from the Denver plant must be less than or equal to 600. Mathematically, we write this supply constraint as

$$x_{13} + x_{14} \leq 600$$

Similarly, for the Atlanta plant we have

$$x_{23} + x_{24} \leq 400$$

We now consider how to write the constraints corresponding to the two transshipment nodes. For node 3 (the Kansas City warehouse), we must guarantee that the number of units shipped out must equal the number of units shipped into the warehouse. If

Number of units
shipped out of node 3 $= x_{35} + x_{36} + x_{37} + x_{38}$

and

Number of units
shipped into node 3 $= x_{13} + x_{23}$

we obtain

$$x_{35} + x_{36} + x_{37} + x_{38} = x_{13} + x_{23}$$

Placing all the variables on the left-hand side provides the constraint corresponding to node 3 as

$$-x_{13} - x_{23} + x_{35} + x_{36} + x_{37} + x_{38} = 0$$

Similarly, the constraint corresponding to node 4 is

$$-x_{14} - x_{24} + x_{45} + x_{46} + x_{47} + x_{48} = 0$$

To develop the constraints associated with the destination nodes, we recognize that for each node the amount shipped to the destination must equal the demand. For example, to satisfy the demand for 200 units at node 5 (the Detroit retail outlet), we write

$$x_{35} + x_{45} = 200$$

Similarly, for nodes 6, 7, and 8, we have

$$x_{36} + x_{46} = 150$$
$$x_{37} + x_{47} = 350$$
$$x_{38} + x_{48} = 300$$

Try Problem 11, parts (b) and (c), for practice in developing the linear programming model and in solving a transshipment problem on the computer.

As usual, the objective function reflects the total shipping cost over the 12 shipping routes. Combining the objective function and constraints leads to a 12-variable, 8-constraint linear programming model of the Ryan Electronics transshipment problem (see Figure 6.5). Figure 6.6 shows the optimal solution and Table 6.4 summarizes the optimal solution.

FIGURE 6.5   LINEAR PROGRAMMING FORMULATION OF THE RYAN ELECTRONICS TRANSSHIPMENT PROBLEM

$$\text{Min } 2x_{13} + 3x_{14} + 3x_{23} + 1x_{24} + 2x_{35} + 6x_{36} + 3x_{37} + 6x_{38} + 4x_{45} + 4x_{46} + 6x_{47} + 5x_{48}$$

s.t.

$$
\begin{array}{llll}
x_{13} + x_{14} & & \leq 600 & \left.\begin{array}{l}\end{array}\right\} \text{Origin node} \\
\quad x_{23} + x_{24} & & \leq 400 & \text{constraints} \\
-x_{13} \quad - x_{23} \quad + x_{35} + x_{36} + x_{37} + x_{38} & & = 0 & \left.\begin{array}{l}\end{array}\right\} \text{Transshipment node} \\
\quad - x_{14} \quad - x_{24} \quad + x_{45} + x_{46} + x_{47} + x_{48} & = & 0 & \text{constraints} \\
\quad x_{35} \quad + x_{45} & & = 200 & \left.\begin{array}{l}\end{array}\right\} \\
\quad x_{36} \quad + x_{46} & & = 150 & \text{Destination node} \\
\quad x_{37} \quad + x_{47} & & = 350 & \text{constraints} \\
\quad x_{38} \quad + x_{48} & & = 300 &
\end{array}
$$

$$x_{ij} \geq 0 \text{ for all } i \text{ and } j$$

FIGURE 6.6   OPTIMAL SOLUTION FOR THE RYAN ELECTRONICS TRANSSHIPMENT PROBLEM

MODEL *file*

Ryan

```
Optimal Objective Value = 5200.00000

     Variable              Value            Reduced Costs
   --------------      ---------------     ----------------
        X13              550.00000             0.00000
        X14               50.00000             0.00000
        X23                0.00000             3.00000
        X24              400.00000             0.00000
        X35              200.00000             0.00000
        X36                0.00000             1.00000
        X37              350.00000             0.00000
        X38                0.00000             0.00000
        X45                0.00000             3.00000
        X46              150.00000             0.00000
        X47                0.00000             4.00000
        X48              300.00000             0.00000
```

TABLE 6.4 OPTIMAL SOLUTION TO THE RYAN ELECTRONICS TRANSSHIPMENT PROBLEM

| Route | | | Cost | |
From	To	Units Shipped	per Unit	Total Cost
Denver	Kansas City	550	$2	$1100
Denver	Louisville	50	$3	$ 150
Atlanta	Louisville	400	$1	$ 400
Kansas City	Detroit	200	$2	$ 400
Kansas City	Dallas	350	$3	$1050
Louisville	Miami	150	$4	$ 600
Louisville	New Orleans	300	$5	$1500
				$5200

As mentioned at the beginning of this section, in the transshipment problem, arcs may connect any pair of nodes. All such shipping patterns are possible in a transshipment problem. We still require only one constraint per node, but the constraint must include a variable for every arc entering or leaving the node. For origin nodes, the sum of the shipments out minus the sum of the shipments in must be less than or equal to the origin supply. For destination nodes, the sum of the shipments in minus the sum of the shipments out must equal demand. For transshipment nodes, the sum of the shipments out must equal the sum of the shipments in, as before.

For an illustration of this more general type of transshipment problem, let us modify the Ryan Electronics problem. Suppose that it is possible to ship directly from Atlanta to New Orleans at $4 per unit and from Dallas to New Orleans at $1 per unit. The network model corresponding to this modified Ryan Electronics problem is shown in Figure 6.7, the linear programming formulation is shown in Figure 6.8, and the optimal solution is shown in Figure 6.9.

Try Problem 12 for practice working with transshipment problems with this more general structure.

In Figure 6.7 we added two new arcs to the network model. Thus, two new variables are necessary in the linear programming formulation. Figure 6.8 shows that the new variables x_{28} and x_{78} appear in the objective function and in the constraints corresponding to the nodes to which the new arcs are connected. Figure 6.9 shows that the value of the optimal solution has been reduced $600 by allowing these additional shipping routes. The value of $x_{28} = 300$ indicates that 300 units are being shipped directly from Atlanta to New Orleans. The value of $x_{78} = 0$ indicates that no units are shipped from Dallas to New Orleans in this solution.[1]

Problem Variations

As with transportation problems, transshipment problems may be formulated with several variations, including

1. Total supply not equal to total demand
2. Maximization objective function
3. Route capacities or route minimums
4. Unacceptable routes

The linear programming model modifications required to accommodate these variations are identical to the modifications required for the transportation problem. When we add one or more constraints of the form $x_{ij} \leq L_{ij}$ to show that the route from node i to node j has capacity L_{ij}, we refer to the transshipment problem as a **capacitated transshipment problem**.

---

[1] This is an example of a linear programming with alternate optimal solutions. The solution $x_{13} = 600$, $x_{14} = 0$, $x_{23} = 0$, $x_{24} = 150$, $x_{28} = 250$, $x_{35} = 200$, $x_{36} = 0$, $x_{37} = 400$, $x_{38} = 0$, $x_{45} = 0$, $x_{46} = 150$, $x_{47} = 0$, $x_{48} = 0$, $x_{78} = 50$ is also optimal. Thus, in this solution both new routes are used: $x_{28} = 250$ units are shipped from Atlanta to New Orleans and $x_{78} = 50$ units are shipped from Dallas to New Orleans.

FIGURE 6.7   NETWORK REPRESENTATION OF THE MODIFIED RYAN ELECTRONICS
TRANSSHIPMENT PROBLEM

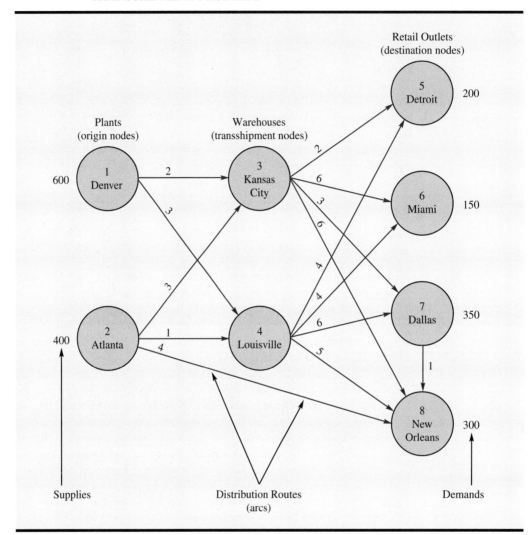

FIGURE 6.8   LINEAR PROGRAMMING FORMULATION OF THE MODIFIED RYAN ELECTRONICS
TRANSSHIPMENT PROBLEM

Min $2x_{13} + 3x_{14} + 3x_{23} + 1x_{24} + 2x_{35} + 6x_{36} + 3x_{37} + 6x_{38} + 4x_{45} + 4x_{46} + 6x_{47} + 5x_{48} + 4x_{28} + 1x_{78}$
s.t.

$$
\begin{array}{llllllll}
x_{13} + x_{14} & & & & & & \leq 600 & \left.\begin{array}{l}\\\\\end{array}\right\} \text{Origin node constraints} \\
& x_{23} + x_{24} & & & + x_{28} & & \leq 400 \\
-x_{13} & -x_{23} & + x_{35} + x_{36} + x_{37} + x_{38} & & & = 0 & \left.\begin{array}{l}\\\\\end{array}\right\} \begin{array}{l}\text{Transshipment node}\\ \text{constraints}\end{array} \\
-x_{14} & -x_{24} & & + x_{45} + x_{46} + x_{47} + x_{48} & & = 0 \\
& & x_{35} & + x_{45} & & = 200 & \left.\begin{array}{l}\\\\\\\end{array}\right\} \begin{array}{l}\text{Destination node}\\ \text{constraints}\end{array} \\
& & x_{36} & + x_{46} & & = 150 \\
& & x_{37} & + x_{47} & -x_{78} = 350 \\
& & x_{38} & + x_{48} + x_{28} + x_{78} & = 300 \\
\end{array}
$$

$x_{ij} \geq 0$ for all i and j

FIGURE 6.9 OPTIMAL SOLUTION FOR THE MODIFIED RYAN ELECTRONICS
TRANSSHIPMENT PROBLEM

MODEL *file*

ModifiedRyan

```
Optimal objective Value = 4600.00000
       Variable                  Value              Reduced Costs
    --------------           --------------         --------------
         X13                    550.000                0.00000
         X14                     50.000                0.00000
         X23                      0.000                3.00000
         X24                    100.000                0.00000
         X35                    200.000                0.00000
         X36                      0.000                1.00000
         X37                    350.000                0.00000
         X38                      0.000                2.00000
         X45                      0.000                3.00000
         X46                    150.000                0.00000
         X47                      0.000                4.00000
         X48                      0.000                2.00000
         X28                    300.000                0.00000
         X78                      0.000                0.00000
```

A General Linear Programming Model

To show the general linear programming model for the transshipment problem, we use the
following notation:

$$x_{ij} = \text{number of units shipped from node } i \text{ to node } j$$
$$c_{ij} = \text{cost per unit of shipping from node } i \text{ to node } j$$
$$s_i = \text{supply at origin node } i$$
$$d_j = \text{demand at destination node } j$$

The general linear programming model for the transshipment problem is as follows:

$$\text{Min} \sum_{\text{all arcs}} c_{ij}x_{ij}$$

s.t.

$$\sum_{\text{arcs out}} x_{ij} - \sum_{\text{arcs in}} x_{ij} \leq s_i \quad \text{Origin nodes } i$$

$$\sum_{\text{arcs out}} x_{ij} - \sum_{\text{arcs in}} x_{ij} = 0 \quad \text{Transshipment nodes}$$

$$\sum_{\text{arcs in}} x_{ij} - \sum_{\text{arcs out}} x_{ij} = d_j \quad \text{Destination nodes } j$$

$$x_{ij} \geq 0 \text{ for all } i \text{ and } j$$

The Management Science in Action, Product Sourcing Heuristic at Procter & Gamble,
describes a transshipment model used by Procter & Gamble to help make strategic decisions
related to sourcing and distribution.

NOTES AND COMMENTS

1. Supply chain models used in practice usually lead to large linear programs. Problems with 100 origins and 100 destinations are not unusual. Such a problem would involve (100)(100) = 10,000 variables.

2. To handle a situation in which some routes may be unacceptable, we stated that you could drop the corresponding arc from the network and remove the corresponding variable from the linear programming formulation. Another approach often used is to assign an extremely large objective function cost coefficient to any unacceptable arc. If the problem has already been formulated, another option is to add a constraint to the formulation that sets the variable you want to remove equal to zero.

3. The optimal solution to a transportation model will consist of integer values for the decision variables as long as all supply and demand values are integers. The reason is the special mathematical structure of the linear programming model. Each variable appears in exactly one supply and one demand constraint, and all coefficients in the constraint equations are 1 or 0.

4. In the general linear programming formulation of the transshipment problem, the constraints for the destination nodes are often written as

$$\sum_{\text{arcs out}} x_{ij} - \sum_{\text{arcs in}} x_{ij} = -d_j$$

The advantage of writing the constraints this way is that the left-hand side of each constraint then represents the flow out of the node minus the flow in.

MANAGEMENT SCIENCE IN ACTION

PRODUCT SOURCING HEURISTIC AT PROCTER & GAMBLE*

Another example of a successful implementation of management-science tools in supply-chain planning is provided by Procter & Gamble's (P&G) strategic-planning initiative known as the North American Product Sourcing Strategy. P&G wanted to consolidate its product sources and optimize its distribution system design throughout North America. A decision support system used to aid in this project was called the Product Sourcing Heuristic (PSH) and was based on a transshipment model much like the ones described in this chapter.

In a preprocessing phase, the many P&G products were aggregated into groups that shared the same technology and could be made at the same plant. The PSH employing the transshipment model was then used by product strategy teams responsible for developing product sourcing options for these product groups. The various plants that could produce the product group were the source nodes, the company's regional distribution centers were the transshipment nodes, and P&G's customer zones were the destinations. Direct shipments to customer zones as well as shipments through distribution centers were employed.

The product strategy teams used the heuristic interactively to explore a variety of questions concerning product sourcing and distribution. For instance, the team might be interested in the impact of closing two of five plants and consolidating production in the three remaining plants. The product sourcing heuristic would then delete the source nodes corresponding to the two closed plants, make any capacity modifications necessary to the sources corresponding to the remaining three plants, and re-solve the transshipment problem. The product strategy team could then examine the new solution, make some more modifications, solve again, and so on.

The Product Sourcing Heuristic was viewed as a valuable decision support system by all who used it. When P&G implemented the results of the study, it realized annual savings in the $200 million range. The PSH proved so successful in North America that P&G used it in other markets around the world.

*Based on information provided by Franz Dill and Tom Chorman of Procter & Gamble.

6.2   ASSIGNMENT PROBLEM

The **assignment problem** arises in a variety of decision-making situations; typical assignment problems involve assigning jobs to machines, agents to tasks, sales personnel to sales territories, contracts to bidders, and so on. A distinguishing feature of the assignment problem is that *one* agent is assigned to *one and only one* task. Specifically, we look for the set of assignments that will optimize a stated objective, such as minimize cost, minimize time, or maximize profits.

To illustrate the assignment problem, let us consider the case of Fowle Marketing Research, which has just received requests for market research studies from three new clients. The company faces the task of assigning a project leader (agent) to each client (task). Currently, three individuals have no other commitments and are available for the project leader assignments. Fowle's management realizes, however, that the time required to complete each study will depend on the experience and ability of the project leader assigned. The three projects have approximately the same priority, and management wants to assign project leaders to minimize the total number of days required to complete all three projects. If a project leader is to be assigned to one client only, which assignments should be made?

To answer the assignment question, Fowle's management must first consider all possible project leader–client assignments and then estimate the corresponding project completion times. With three project leaders and three clients, nine assignment alternatives are possible. The alternatives and the estimated project completion times in days are summarized in Table 6.5.

Try Problem 17, part (a), for practice in developing a network model for an assignment problem.

Figure 6.10 shows the network representation of Fowle's assignment problem. The nodes correspond to the project leaders and clients, and the arcs represent the possible assignments of project leaders to clients. The supply at each origin node and the demand at each destination node are 1; the cost of assigning a project leader to a client is the time it takes that project leader to complete the client's task. Note the similarity between the network models of the assignment problem (Figure 6.10) and the transportation problem (Figure 6.1). The assignment problem is a special case of the transportation problem in which all supply and demand values equal 1, and the amount shipped over each arc is either 0 or 1.

Because the assignment problem is a special case of the transportation problem, we can use the linear programming formulation for the transportation problem to solve the assignment problem. Again, we need a constraint for each node and a variable for each arc. Recall that in the transportation problem the double-subscripted decision variables x_{ij} denoted the number of units shipped from node i to node j. In the assignment problem, the value of each x_{ij} variable will either be 0 or 1 due to the structure of the problem. Therefore, if $x_{11} = 1$, we interpret this as "project leader 1 (Terry) is assigned to client 1," or if $x_{11} = 0$, we interpret this as "project leader 1 (Terry) is not assigned to client 1." In general, we interpret the decision variables for Fowle's assignment problem as

Due to the special structure of the assignment problem, the x_{ij} variables will either be 0 or 1 and not any value in between, e.g., 0.6. In Chapter 7, we discuss optimization problems which represent discrete choices with 0-1 (or binary) variables that must be explicitly constrained to avoid fractional values.

$$x_{ij} = \begin{cases} 1 & \text{if project leader } i \text{ is assigned to client } j \\ 0 & \text{otherwise} \end{cases}$$

where $i = 1, 2, 3$, and $j = 1, 2, 3$

Using this notation and the completion time data in Table 6.5, we develop completion time expressions:

Days required for Terry's assignment $= 10x_{11} + 15x_{12} + 9x_{13}$
Days required for Carle's assignment $= 9x_{21} + 18x_{22} + 5x_{23}$
Days required for McClymonds's assignment $= 6x_{31} + 14x_{32} + 3x_{33}$

TABLE 6.5 ESTIMATED PROJECT COMPLETION TIMES (DAYS) FOR THE FOWLE MARKETING RESEARCH ASSIGNMENT PROBLEM

		Client	
Project Leader	**1**	**2**	**3**
1. Terry	10	15	9
2. Carle	9	18	5
3. McClymonds	6	14	3

FIGURE 6.10   A NETWORK MODEL OF THE FOWLE MARKETING RESEARCH
ASSIGNMENT PROBLEM

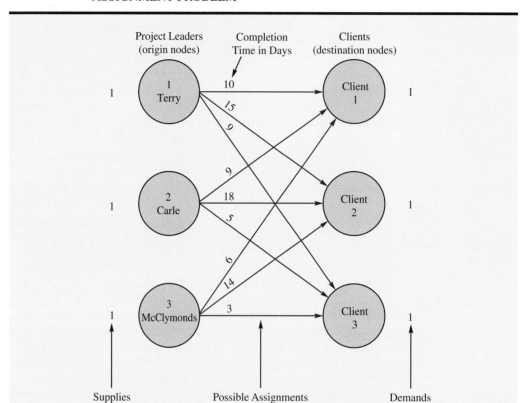

The sum of the completion times for the three project leaders will provide the total days required to complete the three assignments. Thus, the objective function is

$$\text{Min } 10x_{11} + 15x_{12} + 9x_{13} + 9x_{21} + 18x_{22} + 5x_{23} + 6x_{31} + 14x_{32} + 3x_{33}$$

Because the number of project leaders equals the number of clients, all the constraints could be written as equalities. But when the number of project leaders exceeds the number of clients, less-than-or-equal-to constraints must be used for the project leader constraints.

The constraints for the assignment problem reflect the conditions that each project leader can be assigned to at most one client and that each client must have one assigned project leader. These constraints are written as follows:

$$
\begin{array}{ll}
x_{11} + x_{12} + x_{13} \le 1 & \text{Terry's assignment} \\
x_{21} + x_{22} + x_{23} \le 1 & \text{Carle's assignment} \\
x_{31} + x_{32} + x_{33} \le 1 & \text{McClymonds's assignment} \\
x_{11} + x_{21} + x_{31} = 1 & \text{Client 1} \\
x_{12} + x_{22} + x_{32} = 1 & \text{Client 2} \\
x_{13} + x_{23} + x_{33} = 1 & \text{Client 3}
\end{array}
$$

Note that each node in Figure 6.10 has one constraint.

Try Problem 17, part (b), for practice in formulating and solving a linear programming model for an assignment problem on the computer.

Combining the objective function and constraints into one model provides the following nine-variable, six-constraint linear programming model of the Fowle Marketing Research assignment problem:

$$\text{Min} \quad 10x_{11} + 15x_{12} + 9x_{13} + 9x_{21} + 18x_{22} + 5x_{23} + 6x_{31} + 14x_{32} + 3x_{33}$$

s.t.

$$
\begin{array}{llllllll}
x_{11} + & x_{12} + & x_{13} & & & & & \leq 1 \\
& & & x_{21} + & x_{22} + & x_{23} & & \leq 1 \\
& & & & & & x_{31} + & x_{32} + & x_{33} \leq 1 \\
x_{11} & & & + x_{21} & & & + x_{31} & & = 1 \\
& x_{12} & & & + x_{22} & & & + x_{32} & = 1 \\
& & x_{13} & & & + x_{23} & & & + x_{33} = 1
\end{array}
$$

$$x_{ij} \geq 0 \quad \text{for } i = 1, 2, 3 \text{ and } j = 1, 2, 3$$

Figure 6.11 shows the optimal solution for this model. Terry is assigned to client 2 ($x_{12} = 1$), Carle is assigned to client 3 ($x_{23} = 1$), and McClymonds is assigned to client 1 ($x_{31} = 1$). The total completion time required is 26 days. This solution is summarized in Table 6.6.

Problem Variations

Because the assignment problem can be viewed as a special case of the transportation problem, the problem variations that may arise in an assignment problem parallel those for the transportation problem. Specifically, we can handle

1. Total number of agents (supply) not equal to the total number of tasks (demand)
2. A maximization objective function
3. Unacceptable assignments

FIGURE 6.11 OPTIMAL SOLUTION FOR THE FOWLE MARKETING RESEARCH ASSIGNMENT PROBLEM

MODEL *file*

Fowle

```
Optimal Objective Value = 26.00000

        Variable              Value            Reduced Costs
      -------------       ---------------     -----------------
          X11               0.00000               0.00000
          X12               1.00000               0.00000
          X13               0.00000               2.00000
          X21               0.00000               1.00000
          X22               0.00000               5.00000
          X23               1.00000               0.00000
          X31               1.00000               0.00000
          X32               0.00000               3.00000
          X33               0.00000               0.00000
```

TABLE 6.6 OPTIMAL PROJECT LEADER ASSIGNMENTS FOR THE FOWLE MARKETING RESEARCH ASSIGNMENT PROBLEM

Project Leader	Assigned Client	Days
Terry	2	15
Carle	3	5
McClymonds	1	6
	Total	26

The situation in which the number of agents does not equal the number of tasks is analogous to total supply not equaling total demand in a transportation problem. If the number of agents exceeds the number of tasks, the extra agents simply remain unassigned in the linear programming solution. If the number of tasks exceeds the number of agents, the linear programming model will not have a feasible solution. In this situation, a simple modification is to add enough dummy agents to equalize the number of agents and the number of tasks. For instance, in the Fowle problem we might have had five clients (tasks) and only three project leaders (agents). By adding two dummy project leaders, we can create a new assignment problem with the number of project leaders equal to the number of clients. The objective function coefficients for the assignment of dummy project leaders would be zero so that the value of the optimal solution would represent the total number of days required by the assignments actually made (no assignments will actually be made to the clients receiving dummy project leaders).

If the assignment alternatives are evaluated in terms of revenue or profit rather than time or cost, the linear programming formulation can be solved as a maximization rather than a minimization problem. In addition, if one or more assignments are unacceptable, the corresponding decision variable can be removed from the linear programming formulation. This situation could happen, for example, if an agent did not have the experience necessary for one or more of the tasks.

A General Linear Programming Model

In the general linear programming model for an assignment problem with m agents and n tasks, c_{ij} represents the cost of assigning agent i to task j and the value of x_{ij} represents whether (1) or not (0) agent i is assigned to task j. We express the formulation as:

$$\text{Min} \quad \sum_{i=1}^{m} \sum_{j=1}^{n} c_{ij} x_{ij}$$

s.t.

$$\sum_{j=1}^{n} x_{ij} \leq 1 \qquad i = 1, 2, \ldots, m \quad \text{Agents}$$

$$\sum_{i=1}^{m} x_{ij} = 1 \qquad j = 1, 2, \ldots, n \quad \text{Tasks}$$

$$x_{ij} \geq 0 \qquad \text{for all } i \text{ and } j$$

At the beginning of this section, we indicated that a distinguishing feature of the assignment problem is that *one* agent is assigned to *one and only one* task. In generalizations of the assignment problem where one agent can be assigned to two or more tasks, the linear programming formulation of the problem can be easily modified. For example, let us assume that in the Fowle Marketing Research problem Terry could be assigned up to two clients; in this case, the constraint representing Terry's assignment would be $x_{11} + x_{12} + x_{13} \leq 2$. In general, if a_i denotes the upper limit for the number of tasks to which agent i can be assigned, we write the agent constraints as

$$\sum_{j=1}^{n} x_{ij} \leq a_i \qquad i = 1, 2, \ldots, m$$

If some tasks require more than one agent, the linear programming formulation can also accommodate the situation. Use the number of agents required as the right-hand side of the appropriate task constraint.

NOTES AND COMMENTS

1. As noted, the assignment model is a special case of the transportation model. We stated in the Notes and Comments at the end of the preceding section that the optimal solution to the transportation problem will consist of integer values for the decision variables as long as the supplies and demands are integers. For the assignment problem, all supplies and demands equal 1; thus, the optimal solution must be integer valued and the integer values must be 0 or 1.

2. Combining the method for handling multiple assignments with the notion of a dummy agent provides another means of dealing with situations when the number of tasks exceeds the number of agents. That is, we add one dummy agent but provide the dummy agent with the capability to handle multiple tasks. The number of tasks the dummy agent can handle is equal to the difference between the number of tasks and the number of agents.

3. The Management Science in Action, Assigning Consultants to Clients at Energy Education, Inc. describes how a consulting company uses an assignment problem as part of an innovative model to minimize the travel costs for their clients.

MANAGEMENT SCIENCE IN ACTION

ASSIGNING CONSULTANTS TO CLIENTS AT ENERGY EDUCATION, INC.*

Energy Education, Inc. (EEI) is a consulting firm that provides experts to schools, universities, and other organizations to implement energy conservation programs. It is estimated that EEI has helped more than 1100 clients save in excess of $2.3 billion in energy costs over the course of the 25 years in which EEI has provided consulting services. EEI consultants spend almost all of their time working at the client location which results in frequent travel and high travel costs for the company. On average, a consultant for EEI spends about $1000 per week for air travel costs alone.

Because of the large expense associated with consultant travel, EEI seeks to minimize travel costs whenever possible. To help minimize consultant-travel cost, EEI created models that assign consultants to clients. The objective of these models is to minimize the total number of flights required each week while meeting all client needs. These models include an assignment-type problem similar to those described in this chapter as part of a more complicated framework that also considers the optimal routing of consultants among client locations.

The models developed by EEI are solved using dedicated optimization software, and the output of the models provides a weekly assignment and travel route for each consultant. The new models resulted in a 44% reduction in flight costs for EEI over a 12-week period in comparison to the consultant assignments and travel plans used previously. The number of consultants required to meet all client demands was also reduced using the new models, leading to a direct labor cost reduction of 15%. In total, EEI realized an annual cost savings of nearly $500,000 from implementing their models for assigning consultants to clients and optimizing consultant travel.

*Based on Junfang Yu and Randy Hoff, "Optimal Routing and Assignment of Consultants for Energy Education, Inc.," *Interfaces* 43, no. 2 (March–April 2013): 142–151.

6.3   SHORTEST-ROUTE PROBLEM

In this section we consider a problem in which the objective is to determine the **shortest route**, or *path*, between two nodes in a network. We will demonstrate the shortest-route problem by considering the situation facing the Gorman Construction Company. Gorman has several construction sites located throughout a three-county area. With multiple daily trips carrying personnel, equipment, and supplies from Gorman's office to the construction sites, the costs associated with transportation activities are substantial. The travel alternatives between Gorman's office and each construction site can be described by the road

FIGURE 6.12   ROAD NETWORK FOR THE GORMAN COMPANY
                  SHORTEST-ROUTE PROBLEM

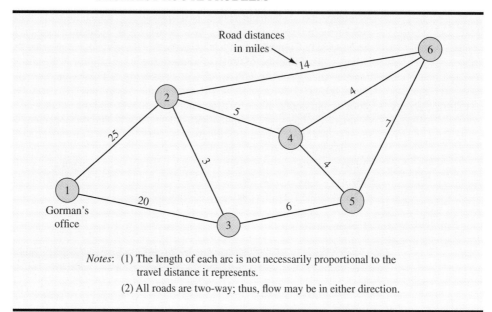

Notes: (1) The length of each arc is not necessarily proportional to the
              travel distance it represents.
          (2) All roads are two-way; thus, flow may be in either direction.

network shown in Figure 6.12. The road distances in miles between the nodes are shown above the corresponding arcs. In this application, Gorman would like to determine the route that will minimize the total travel distance between Gorman's office (located at node 1) and the construction site located at node 6.

A key to developing a model for the shortest-route problem is to understand that the problem is a special case of the transshipment problem. Specifically, the Gorman shortest-route problem can be viewed as a transshipment problem with one origin node (node 1), one destination node (node 6), and four transshipment nodes (nodes 2, 3, 4, and 5). The transshipment network for the Gorman shortest-route problem is shown in Figure 6.13. Arrows added to the arcs show the direction of flow, which is always *out* of the origin node and *into* the destination node. Note also that two directed arcs are shown between the pairs of transshipment nodes. For example, one arc going from node 2 to node 3 indicates that the shortest route may go from node 2 to node 3, and one arc going from node 3 to node 2 indicates that the shortest route may go from node 3 to node 2. The distance between two transshipment nodes is the same in either direction.

To find the shortest route between node 1 and node 6, think of node 1 as having a supply of 1 unit and node 6 as having a demand of 1 unit. Let x_{ij} denote the number of units that flow or are shipped from node i to node j. Because only 1 unit will be shipped from node 1 to node 6, the value of x_{ij} will be either 1 or 0. Thus, if $x_{ij} = 1$, the arc from node i to node j is on the shortest route from node 1 to node 6; if $x_{ij} = 0$, the arc from node i to node j is not on the shortest route. Because we are looking for the shortest route between node 1 and node 6, the objective function for the Gorman problem is

$$\text{Min}\quad 25x_{12} + 20x_{13} + 3x_{23} + 3x_{32} + 5x_{24} + 5x_{42} + 14x_{26} + 6x_{35} + 6x_{53}$$
$$+ 4x_{45} + 4x_{54} + 4x_{46} + 7x_{56}$$

To develop the constraints for the model, we begin with node 1. Because the supply at node 1 is 1 unit, the flow out of node 1 must equal 1. Thus, the constraint for node 1 is written as

$$x_{12} + x_{13} = 1$$

FIGURE 6.13 TRANSSHIPMENT NETWORK FOR THE GORMAN SHORTEST-ROUTE PROBLEM

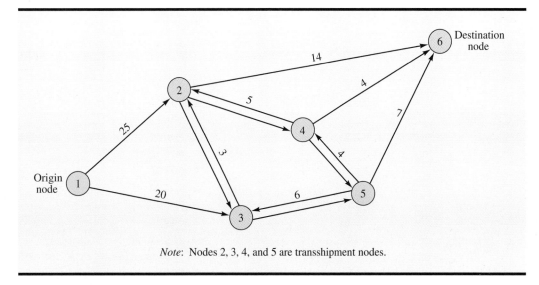

Note: Nodes 2, 3, 4, and 5 are transshipment nodes.

For transshipment nodes 2, 3, 4, and 5, the flow out of each node must equal the flow into each node; thus, the flow out minus the flow in must be 0. The constraints for the four transshipment nodes are as follows:

	Flow Out	**Flow In**
Node 2	$x_{23} + x_{24} + x_{26}$	$-x_{12} - x_{32} - x_{42} = 0$
Node 3	$x_{32} + x_{35}$	$-x_{13} - x_{23} - x_{53} = 0$
Node 4	$x_{42} + x_{45} + x_{46}$	$-x_{24} - x_{54} = 0$
Node 5	$x_{53} + x_{54} + x_{56}$	$-x_{35} - x_{45} = 0$

Because node 6 is the destination node with a demand of 1 unit, the flow into node 6 must equal 1. Thus, the constraint for node 6 is written as

$$x_{26} + x_{46} + x_{56} = 1$$

Including the negative constraints $x_{ij} \geq 0$ for all i and j, the linear programming model for the Gorman shortest-route problem is shown in Figure 6.14.

The optimal solution for the Gorman shortest-route problem is shown in Figure 6.15. The objective function value of 32 indicates that the shortest route between Gorman's

FIGURE 6.14 LINEAR PROGRAMMING FORMULATION OF THE GORMAN SHORTEST-ROUTE PROBLEM

Min $25x_{12} + 20x_{13} + 3x_{23} + 3x_{32} + 5x_{24} + 5x_{42} + 14x_{26} + 6x_{35} + 6x_{53} + 4x_{45} + 4x_{54} + 4x_{46} + 7x_{56}$
s.t.

$$
\begin{aligned}
x_{12} + \ x_{13} && = 1 \quad &\text{Origin node} \\
-x_{12} \quad\quad + x_{23} - x_{32} + x_{24} - x_{42} + \ x_{26} && = 0 \quad\;\, \\
- \ x_{13} - x_{23} + x_{32} \quad\quad\quad\quad\quad + x_{35} - x_{53} && = 0 \quad\;\,\, \\
- x_{24} + x_{42} \quad\quad\quad\quad + x_{45} - x_{54} + \ x_{46} && = 0 \quad\;\,\, \\
- x_{35} + x_{53} - x_{45} + x_{54} \quad\quad + x_{56} && = 0 \\
x_{26} \quad\quad\quad\quad\quad + x_{46} + \ x_{56} && = 1 \quad &\text{Destination node}
\end{aligned}
$$

$x_{ij} \geq 0$ for all i and j

FIGURE 6.15   OPTIMAL SOLUTION FOR THE GORMAN SHORTEST-ROUTE PROBLEM

```
Optimal Objective Value = 32.00000

          Variable              Value           Reduced Cost
        ------------        ---------------     ---------------
            X12                0.00000              2.00000
            X13                1.00000              0.00000
            X23                0.00000              6.00000
            X32                1.00000              0.00000
            X24                1.00000              0.00000
            X42                0.00000             10.00000
            X26                0.00000              5.00000
            X35                0.00000              0.00000
            X53                0.00000             12.00000
            X45                0.00000              7.00000
            X54                0.00000              1.00000
            X46                1.00000              0.00000
            X56                0.00000              0.00000
```

MODEL *file*

Gorman

Try Problem 23 to practice solving a shortest-route problem.

office located at node 1 to the construction site located at node 6 is 32 miles. With $x_{13} = 1$, $x_{32} = 1$, $x_{24} = 1$, and $x_{46} = 1$, the shortest route from node 1 to node 6 is 1–3–2–4–6; in other words, the shortest route takes us from node 1 to node 3; then from node 3 to node 2; then from node 2 to node 4; and finally from node 4 to node 6.

A General Linear Programming Model

Due to the special structure of the shortest-route problem, the x_{ij} variables will either be 0 or 1 and not any value in between, such as 0.6. In Chapter 7, we discuss optimization problems which represent discrete choices with 0-1 (or binary) variables that must be explicitly constrained to avoid fractional values.

The general linear programming model for the shortest-route problem is as follows:

$$\text{Min} \quad \sum_{\text{all arcs}} c_{ij} x_{ij}$$

s.t.

$$\sum_{\text{arcs out}} x_{ij} \qquad\qquad\qquad = 1 \qquad \text{Origin node } i$$

$$\sum_{\text{arcs out}} x_{ij} - \sum_{\text{arcs in}} x_{ij} = 0 \qquad \text{Transshipment nodes}$$

$$\sum_{\text{arcs in}} x_{ij} = 1 \qquad \text{Destination node } j$$

In this linear programming model, c_{ij} represents the distance, time, or cost associated with the arc from node i to node j, and the value of x_{ij} represents whether (1) or not (0) the arc from node i to node j is on the shortest route. If $x_{ij} = 1$, the arc from node i to node j is on the shortest route. If $x_{ij} = 0$, the arc from node i to node j is not on the shortest route.

NOTES AND COMMENTS

1. In the Gorman problem we assumed that all roads in the network are two-way. As a result, the road connecting nodes 2 and 3 in the road network resulted in the creation of two corresponding arcs in the transshipment network. Two decision variables, x_{23} and x_{32}, were required to show that the shortest route might go from node 2 to node 3 or from node 3 to node 2. If the road connecting nodes 2 and 3 had been a one-way road allowing flow only from node 2 to node 3, decision variable x_{32} would not have been included in the model.

6.4 MAXIMAL FLOW PROBLEM

The objective in a **maximal flow** problem is to determine the maximum amount of flow (vehicles, messages, fluid, etc.) that can enter and exit a network system in a given period of time. In this problem, we attempt to transmit flow through all arcs of the network as efficiently as possible. The amount of flow is limited due to capacity restrictions on the various arcs of the network. For example, highway types limit vehicle flow in a transportation system, while pipe sizes limit oil flow in an oil distribution system. The maximum or upper limit on the flow in an arc is referred to as the **flow capacity** of the arc. Even though we do not specify capacities for the nodes, we do assume that the flow out of a node is equal to the flow into the node.

As an example of the maximal flow problem, consider the north–south interstate highway system passing through Cincinnati, Ohio. The north–south vehicle flow reaches a level of 15,000 vehicles per hour at peak times. Due to a summer highway maintenance program, which calls for the temporary closing of lanes and lower speed limits, a network of alternate routes through Cincinnati has been proposed by a transportation planning committee. The alternate routes include other highways as well as city streets. Because of differences in speed limits and traffic patterns, flow capacities vary depending on the particular streets and roads used. The proposed network with arc flow capacities is shown in Figure 6.16.

The direction of flow for each arc is indicated, and the arc capacity is shown next to each arc. Note that most of the streets are one-way. However, a two-way street can be found between nodes 2 and 3 and between nodes 5 and 6. In both cases, the capacity is the same in each direction.

We will show how to develop a capacitated transshipment model for the maximal flow problem. First, we will add an arc from node 7 back to node 1 to represent the total flow through the highway system. Figure 6.17 shows the modified network. The newly added arc shows no capacity; indeed, we will want to maximize the flow over that arc. Maximizing the flow over the arc from node 7 to node 1 is equivalent to maximizing the number of cars that can get through the north–south highway system passing through Cincinnati.

The decision variables are as follows:

$$x_{ij} = \text{amount of traffic flow from node } i \text{ to node } j$$

The objective function that maximizes the flow over the highway system is

$$\text{Max } x_{71}$$

FIGURE 6.16 NETWORK OF HIGHWAY SYSTEM AND FLOW CAPACITIES (1000S/HOUR) FOR CINCINNATI

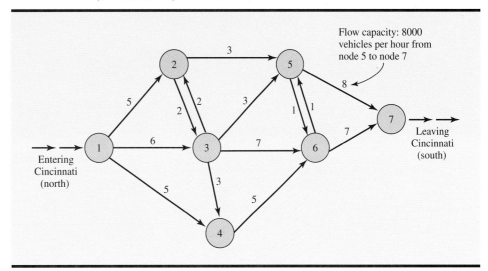

FIGURE 6.17   FLOW OVER ARC FROM NODE 7 TO NODE 1 TO REPRESENT
TOTAL FLOW THROUGH THE CINCINNATI HIGHWAY
SYSTEM

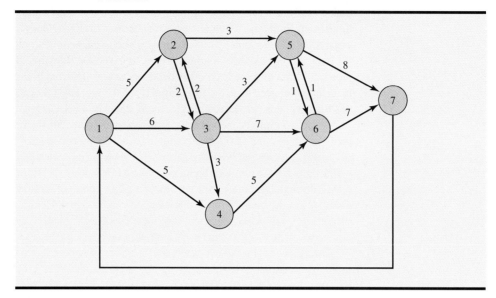

As with all transshipment problems, each arc generates a variable and each node generates a constraint. For each node, a conservation of flow constraint represents the requirement that the flow out must equal the flow in. Or, stated another way, the flow out minus the flow in must equal zero. For node 1, the flow out is $x_{12} + x_{13} + x_{14}$, and the flow in is x_{71}. Therefore, the constraint for node 1 is

$$x_{12} + x_{13} + x_{14} - x_{71} = 0$$

The conservation of flow constraints for the other six nodes are developed in a similar fashion.

	Flow Out	**Flow In**	
Node 2	$x_{23} + x_{25}$	$-x_{12} - x_{32}$	$= 0$
Node 3	$x_{32} + x_{34} + x_{35} + x_{36}$	$-x_{13} - x_{23}$	$= 0$
Node 4	x_{46}	$-x_{14} - x_{34}$	$= 0$
Node 5	$x_{56} + x_{57}$	$-x_{25} - x_{35} - x_{65}$	$= 0$
Node 6	$x_{65} + x_{67}$	$-x_{36} - x_{46} - x_{56}$	$= 0$
Node 7	x_{71}	$-x_{57} - x_{67}$	$= 0$

Additional constraints are needed to enforce the capacities on the arcs. These 14 simple upper-bound constraints are given.

$$x_{12} \le 5 \quad x_{13} \le 6 \quad x_{14} \le 5$$
$$x_{23} \le 2 \quad x_{25} \le 3$$
$$x_{32} \le 2 \quad x_{34} \le 3 \quad x_{35} \le 5 \quad x_{36} \le 7$$
$$x_{46} \le 5$$
$$x_{56} \le 1 \quad x_{57} \le 8$$
$$x_{65} \le 1 \quad x_{67} \le 7$$

FIGURE 6.18 OPTIMAL SOLUTION FOR THE CINCINNATI HIGHWAY SYSTEM MAXIMAL FLOW PROBLEM

MODEL *file*

Cincinnati

```
Optimal Objective Value = 14.00000

      Variable              Value            Reduced Cost
    ------------        ---------------     ---------------
        X12                3.00000              0.00000
        X13                6.00000              0.00000
        X14                5.00000              0.00000
        X23                0.00000              0.00000
        X25                3.00000              0.00000
        X34                0.00000              0.00000
        X35                3.00000              0.00000
        X36                3.00000              0.00000
        X32                0.00000              0.00000
        X46                5.00000              0.00000
        X56                0.00000              1.00000
        X57                7.00000              0.00000
        X65                1.00000              0.00000
        X67                7.00000              0.00000
        X71               14.00000              0.00000
```

Note that the only arc without a capacity is the one we added from node 7 to node 1.

The optimal solution for this 15-variable, 21-constraint linear programming problem is shown in Figure 6.18. We note that the value of the optimal solution is 14. This result implies that the maximal flow over the highway system is 14,000 vehicles. Figure 6.19 shows how the vehicle flow is routed through the original highway network. We note, for instance, that 3000 vehicles per hour are routed between nodes 1 and 2, 6000 vehicles per hour are routed between nodes 1 and 3, 0 vehicles are routed between nodes 2 and 3, and so on.

Try Problem 29 for practice in solving a maximal flow problem.

FIGURE 6.19 MAXIMAL FLOW PATTERN FOR THE CINCINNATI HIGHWAY SYSTEM NETWORK

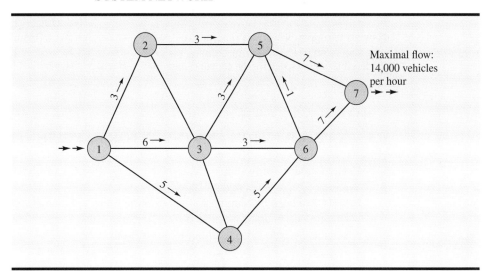

The results of the maximal flow analysis indicate that the planned highway network system will not handle the peak flow of 15,000 vehicles per hour. The transportation planners will have to expand the highway network, increase current arc flow capacities, or be prepared for serious traffic problems. If the network is extended or modified, another maximal flow analysis will determine the extent of any improved flow. The Management Science in Action, Finding the Shortest Paths for Containerships, describes how Danaos Corporation computes shortest path routes for their containerships to save millions of dollars in reduced fuel costs.

NOTES AND COMMENTS

1. The maximal flow problem of this section can also be solved with a slightly different formulation if the extra arc between nodes 7 and 1 is not used. The alternate approach is to maximize the flow into node 7 ($x_{57} + x_{67}$) and drop the conservation of flow constraints for nodes 1 and 7. However, the formulation used in this section is most common in practice.

2. Network models can be used to describe a variety of management science problems. Unfortunately, no one network solution algorithm can be used to solve every network problem. It is important to recognize the specific type of problem being modeled in order to select the correct specialized solution algorithm.

MANAGEMENT SCIENCE IN ACTION

FINDING THE SHORTEST PATHS FOR CONTAINERSHIPS*

Danaos Corporation is an international shipping company based in Greece that owns more than 60 containerships. Danaos' containerships travel millions of miles each year to transport millions of containers all around the world. Danaos has developed a powerful tool to improve shipping operations known as the Operations Research in Ship Management (ORISMA) tool. Part of this tool involves the solving of shortest-path problems to determine a containership's optimal route.

Optimizing the travel route for a containership generates substantial savings through the use of less fuel and because it allows the ship to generate more revenue in less time by visiting additional ports to pick up and deliver containers. A subcomponent of ORISMA determines the shortest-path route between two given waypoints (intermediate points of a ship's complete voyage) by defining nodes in the feasible sailing space for the containership.

Danaos determined that it generated $1.3 million in additional revenue in a single year by using ORISMA to reduce the amount of time containerships spent traveling between ports. Furthermore, it saved $3.2 million in reduced fuel costs during the same year. Danaos estimates that further use of ORISMA will increase profitability by 7–10% annually in the future. As a nice byproduct of Danaos' reduced travel times and decreased fuel usage, carbon emissions have been cut substantially and customers are happier to get their products with less lead time.

*Based on Takis Varelas, Sofia Archontaki, John Dimotikalis, Osman Turan, Iraklis Lazakis, and Orestis Varelas, "Optimizing Ship Routing to Maximize Fleet Revenue at Danaos," *Interfaces* 43, no. 1 (January–February 2013): 37–47.

6.5   A PRODUCTION AND INVENTORY APPLICATION

The introduction to supply chain models in Section 6.1 involved applications for the shipment of goods from several supply locations or origins to several demand sites or destinations. Although the shipment of goods is the subject of many supply chain problems, supply chain models can be developed for applications that have nothing to do with the physical shipment of goods from origins to destinations. In this section we show how to use a transshipment model to solve a production and inventory problem.

TABLE 6.7 PRODUCTION, DEMAND, AND COST ESTIMATES FOR CONTOIS CARPETS

Quarter	Production Capacity (square yards)	Demand (square yards)	Production Cost ($/square yard)	Inventory Cost ($/square yard)
1	600	400	2	0.25
2	300	500	5	0.25
3	500	400	3	0.25
4	400	400	3	0.25

Contois Carpets is a small manufacturer of carpeting for home and office installations. Production capacity, demand, production cost per square yard, and inventory holding cost per square yard for the next four quarters are shown in Table 6.7. Note that production capacity, demand, and production costs vary by quarter, whereas the cost of carrying inventory from one quarter to the next is constant at $0.25 per yard. Contois wants to determine how many yards of carpeting to manufacture each quarter to minimize the total production and inventory cost for the four-quarter period.

The network flows into and out of demand nodes are what make the model a transshipment model.

We begin by developing a network representation of the problem. First, we create four nodes corresponding to the production in each quarter and four nodes corresponding to the demand in each quarter. Each production node is connected by an outgoing arc to the demand node for the same period. The flow on the arc represents the number of square yards of carpet manufactured for the period. For each demand node, an outgoing arc represents the amount of inventory (square yards of carpet) carried over to the demand node for the next period. Figure 6.20 shows the network model. Note that nodes 1–4 represent the production for each quarter and that nodes 5–8 represent the demand for each quarter. The quarterly production capacities are shown in the left margin, and the quarterly demands are shown in the right margin.

The objective is to determine a production scheduling and inventory policy that will minimize the total production and inventory cost for the four quarters. Constraints involve production capacity and demand in each quarter. As usual, a linear programming model can be developed from the network by establishing a constraint for each node and a variable for each arc.

Let x_{15} denote the number of square yards of carpet manufactured in quarter 1. The capacity of the facility is 600 square yards in quarter 1, so the production capacity constraint is

$$x_{15} \leq 600$$

Using similar decision variables, we obtain the production capacities for quarters 2–4:

$$x_{26} \leq 300$$
$$x_{37} \leq 500$$
$$x_{48} \leq 400$$

We now consider the development of the constraints for each of the demand nodes. For node 5, one arc enters the node, which represents the number of square yards of carpet produced in quarter 1, and one arc leaves the node, which represents the number of square yards of carpet that will not be sold in quarter 1 and will be carried over for possible sale in quarter 2. In general, for each quarter the beginning inventory plus the production minus

FIGURE 6.20   NETWORK REPRESENTATION OF THE CONTOIS CARPETS PROBLEM

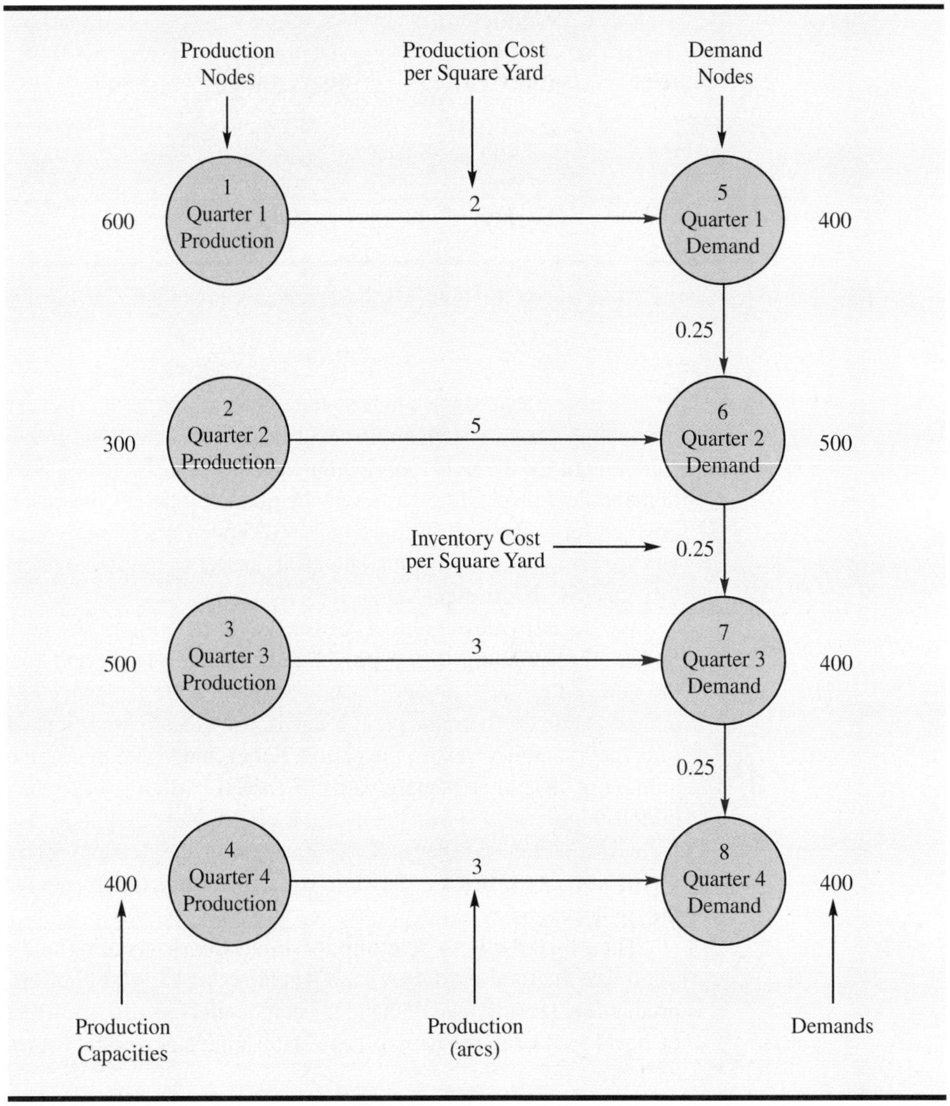

the ending inventory must equal demand. However, because quarter 1 has no beginning inventory, the constraint for node 5 is

$$x_{15} - x_{56} = 400$$

The constraints associated with the demand nodes in quarters 2, 3, and 4 are

$$x_{56} + x_{26} - x_{67} = 500$$
$$x_{67} + x_{37} - x_{78} = 400$$
$$x_{78} + x_{48} = 400$$

Note that the constraint for node 8 (fourth-quarter demand) involves only two variables because no provision is made for holding inventory for a fifth quarter.

The objective is to minimize total production and inventory cost, so we write the objective function as

$$\text{Min} \quad 2x_{15} + 5x_{26} + 3x_{37} + 3x_{48} + 0.25x_{56} + 0.25x_{67} + 0.25x_{78}$$

The complete linear programming formulation of the Contois Carpets problem is

FIGURE 6.21 OPTIMAL SOLUTION FOR THE CONTOIS CARPETS PROBLEM

Contois

```
Optimal Objective Value = 5150.00000

         Variable              Value           Reduced Cost
     ---------------       ---------------    ----------------
          X15               600.00000             0.00000
          X26               300.00000             0.00000
          X37               400.00000             0.00000
          X48               400.00000             0.00000
          X56               200.00000             0.00000
          X67                 0.00000             2.25000
          X78                 0.00000             0.00000
```

$$\text{Min} \quad 2x_{15} + 5x_{26} + 3x_{37} + 3x_{48} + 0.25x_{56} + 0.25x_{67} + 0.25x_{78}$$

s.t.

$$
\begin{aligned}
x_{15} & & & & & & & & \leq 600 \\
& x_{26} & & & & & & & \leq 300 \\
& & x_{37} & & & & & & \leq 500 \\
& & & x_{48} & & & & & \leq 400 \\
x_{15} & & & & - & x_{56} & & & = 400 \\
& x_{26} & & & + & x_{56} & - & x_{67} & = 500 \\
& & x_{37} & & & & + & x_{67} & - & x_{78} = 400 \\
& & & x_{48} & & & & & + & x_{78} = 400
\end{aligned}
$$

$$x_{ij} \geq 0 \quad \text{for all } i \text{ and } j$$

Figure 6.21 shows the optimal solution for this problem. Contois Carpets should manufacture 600 square yards of carpet in quarter 1, 300 square yards in quarter 2, 400 square yards in quarter 3, and 400 square yards in quarter 4. Note also that 200 square yards will be carried over from quarter 1 to quarter 2. The total production and inventory cost is $5150.

NOTES AND COMMENTS

1. For the network models presented in this chapter, the amount leaving the starting node for an arc is always equal to the amount entering the ending node for that arc. An extension of such a network model is the case where a gain or a loss occurs as an arc is traversed. The amount entering the destination node may be greater or smaller than the amount leaving the origin node. For instance, if cash is the commodity flowing across an arc, the cash earns interest from one period to the next. Thus, the amount of cash entering the next period is greater than the amount leaving the previous period by the amount of interest earned. Networks with gains or losses are treated in more advanced texts on network flow programming.

SUMMARY

In this chapter we introduced models related to supply chain problems—specifically, transportation and transshipment problems—as well as assignment, shortest-route, and maximal flow problems. All of these types of problems belong to the special category of linear programs called *network flow problems*. In general, the network model for these problems consists of nodes representing origins, destinations, and, if necessary, transshipment points in the network system. Arcs are used to represent the routes for shipment, travel, or flow between the various nodes.

Transportation problems and transshipment problems are commonly encountered when dealing with supply chains. The general transportation problem has m origins and n destinations. Given the supply at each origin, the demand at each destination, and unit shipping cost between each origin and each destination, the transportation model determines the optimal amounts to ship from each origin to each destination. The transshipment problem is an extension of the transportation problem involving transfer points referred to as transshipment nodes. In this more general model, we allow arcs between any pair of nodes in the network.

The assignment problem is a special case of the transportation problem in which all supply and all demand values are 1. We represent each agent as an origin node and each task as a destination node. The assignment model determines the minimum cost or maximum profit assignment of agents to tasks.

The shortest-route problem finds the shortest route or path between two nodes of a network. Distance, time, and cost are often the criteria used for this model. The shortest-route problem can be expressed as a transshipment problem with one origin and one destination. By shipping one unit from the origin to the destination, the solution will determine the shortest route through the network.

The maximal flow problem can be used to allocate flow to the arcs of the network so that flow through the network system is maximized. Arc capacities determine the maximum amount of flow for each arc. With these flow capacity constraints, the maximal flow problem is expressed as a capacitated transshipment problem.

In the last section of the chapter, we showed how a variation of the transshipment problem could be used to solve a production and inventory problem. In the chapter appendix we show how to use Excel to solve three of the distribution and network problems presented in the chapter.

GLOSSARY

Arcs The lines connecting the nodes in a network.

Assignment problem A network flow problem that often involves the assignment of agents to tasks; it can be formulated as a linear program and is a special case of the transportation problem.

Capacitated transportation problem A variation of the basic transportation problem in which some or all of the arcs are subject to capacity restrictions.

Capacitated transshipment problem A variation of the transshipment problem in which some or all of the arcs are subject to capacity restrictions.

Dummy origin An origin added to a transportation problem to make the total supply equal to the total demand. The supply assigned to the dummy origin is the difference between the total demand and the total supply.

Flow capacity The maximum flow for an arc of the network. The flow capacity in one direction may not equal the flow capacity in the reverse direction.

Maximal flow The maximum amount of flow that can enter and exit a network system during a given period of time.

Network A graphical representation of a problem consisting of numbered circles (nodes) interconnected by a series of lines (arcs); arrowheads on the arcs show the direction of flow. Transportation, assignment, and transshipment problems are network flow problems.

Nodes The intersection or junction points of a network.

Shortest route Shortest path between two nodes in a network.

Supply chain The set of all interconnected resources involved in producing and distributing a product.

Transportation problem A network flow problem that often involves minimizing the cost of shipping goods from a set of origins to a set of destinations; it can be formulated and solved as a linear program by including a variable for each arc and a constraint for each node.

Transshipment problem An extension of the transportation problem to distribution problems involving transfer points and possible shipments between any pair of nodes.

PROBLEMS

SELF*test*

1. A company imports goods at two ports: Philadelphia and New Orleans. Shipments of one product are made to customers in Atlanta, Dallas, Columbus, and Boston. For the next planning period, the supplies at each port, customer demands, and shipping costs per case from each port to each customer are as follows:

| | Customers | | | | Port |
Port	Atlanta	Dallas	Columbus	Boston	Supply
Philadelphia	2	6	6	2	5000
New Orleans	1	2	5	7	3000
Demand	1400	3200	2000	1400	

Develop a network representation of the distribution system (transportation problem).

SELF*test*

2. Consider the following network representation of a transportation problem:

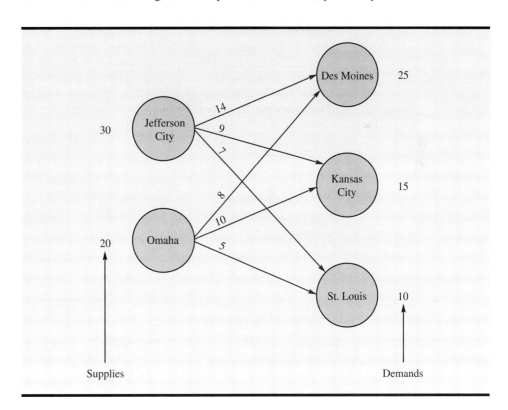

The supplies, demands, and transportation costs per unit are shown on the network.
   a. Develop a linear programming model for this problem; be sure to define the variables in your model.
   b. Solve the linear program to determine the optimal solution.

3. Tri-County Utilities, Inc., supplies natural gas to customers in a three-county area. The company purchases natural gas from two companies: Southern Gas and Northwest Gas.

Demand forecasts for the coming winter season are as follows: Hamilton County, 400 units; Butler County, 200 units; and Clermont County, 300 units. Contracts to provide the following quantities have been written: Southern Gas, 500 units; and Northwest Gas, 400 units. Distribution costs for the counties vary, depending upon the location of the suppliers. The distribution costs per unit (in thousands of dollars) are as follows:

| | | To | |
From	Hamilton	Butler	Clermont
Southern Gas	10	20	15
Northwest Gas	12	15	18

a. Develop a network representation of this problem.
b. Develop a linear programming model that can be used to determine the plan that will minimize total distribution costs.
c. Describe the distribution plan and show the total distribution cost.
d. Recent residential and industrial growth in Butler County has the potential for increasing demand by as much as 100 units. Which supplier should Tri-County contract with to supply the additional capacity?

4. GloFish, Inc., has genetically engineered a species of fish that glows in normal lighting conditions. The company believes the n ew fish will be a huge success as a new pet option for children and adults alike. GloFish, Inc., has developed two varieties of its glowing fish: one that glows red and one that glows blue. GloFish currently "grows" its fish at two different fish farms in the United States: one in Michigan and one in Texas. The Michigan farm can produce up to 1 million red and 1 million blue GloFish per year; the Texas farm can produce up to 600,000 GloFish, but only in the blue variety. GloFish ships its fish between the fish farms and its three retail stores using a third-party shipper. The shipment rates between origins and destinations are shown in the following table. These costs are per fish and do not depend on the color of the fish being shipped.

| | Cost of Shipping GloFish ($/fish) | | |
	Retailer 1	Retailer 2	Retailer 3
Michigan	1.00	2.50	0.50
Texas	2.00	1.50	2.80

Estimated demands by each retailer for each color of fish are shown in the following table:

| | Demand for GloFish | | |
	Retailer 1	Retailer 2	Retailer 3
Red	320,000	300,000	160,000
Blue	380,000	450,000	290,000

a. What is the optimal policy for the fish farms? How many red and blue fish should be produced in Michigan and shipped to each retailer? How many blue fish should be produced in Texas and shipped to each retailer?
b. What is the minimum shipping cost that can be incurred and still meet demand requirements at retailers 1, 2, and 3?
c. How much should GloFish be willing to invest to enable the Texas farm to produce both red and blue GloFish while maintaining the maximum of 600,000 total fish produced at the Texas farm?

5. Premier Consulting's two consultants, Avery and Baker, can be scheduled to work for clients up to a maximum of 160 hours each over the next four weeks. A third consultant, Campbell, has some administrative assignments already planned and is available for clients up to a maximum of 140 hours over the next four weeks. The company has four clients with projects in process. The estimated hourly requirements for each of the clients over the four-week period are as follows:

Client	Hours
A	180
B	75
C	100
D	85

Hourly rates vary for the consultant–client combination and are based on several factors, including project type and the consultant's experience. The rates (dollars per hour) for each consultant–client combination are as follows:

	Client			
Consultant	A	B	C	D
Avery	100	125	115	100
Baker	120	135	115	120
Campbell	155	150	140	130

a. Develop a network representation of the problem.
b. Formulate the problem as a linear program, with the optimal solution providing the hours each consultant should be scheduled for each client to maximize the consulting firm's billings. What is the schedule and what is the total billing?
c. New information shows that Avery doesn't have the experience to be scheduled for client B. If this consulting assignment is not permitted, what impact does it have on total billings? What is the revised schedule?

 SELF*test*

6. Klein Chemicals, Inc., produces a special oil-based material that is currently in short supply. Four of Klein's customers have already placed orders that together exceed the combined capacity of Klein's two plants. Klein's management faces the problem of deciding how many units it should supply to each customer. Because the four customers are in different industries, different prices can be charged because of the various industry pricing structures. However, slightly different production costs at the two plants and varying transportation costs between the plants and customers make a "sell to the highest bidder" strategy unacceptable. After considering price, production costs, and transportation costs, Klein established the following profit per unit for each plant–customer alternative:

	Customer			
Plant	D_1	D_2	D_3	D_4
Clifton Springs	$32	$34	$32	$40
Danville	$34	$30	$28	$38

The plant capacities and customer orders are as follows:

Plant	Capacity (units)	Distributor Orders (units)
Clifton Springs	5000	D_1 2000
		D_2 5000
Danville	3000	D_3 3000
		D_4 2000

How many units should each plant produce for each customer to maximize profits? Which customer demands will not be met? Show your network model and linear programming formulation.

7. Aggie Power Generation supplies electrical power to residential customers for many U.S. cities. Its main power generation plants are located in Los Angeles, Tulsa, and Seattle. The following table shows Aggie Power Generation's major residential markets, the annual demand in each market (in megawatts or MW), and the cost to supply electricity to each market from each power generation plant in $/MW):

| | Distribution Costs ($/MW) | | | |
City	Los Angeles	Tulsa	Seattle	Demand (MW)
Seattle	356.25	593.75	59.38	950.00
Portland	356.25	593.75	178.13	831.25
San Francisco	178.13	475.00	296.88	2375.00
Boise	356.25	475.00	296.88	593.75
Reno	237.50	475.00	356.25	950.00
Bozeman	415.63	415.63	296.88	593.75
Laramie	356.25	415.63	356.25	1187.50
Park City	356.25	356.25	475.00	712.50
Flagstaff	178.13	475.00	593.75	1187.50
Durango	356.25	296.88	593.75	1543.75

a. If there are no restrictions on the amount of power that can be supplied by any of the power plants, what is the optimal solution to this problem? Which cities should be supplied by which power plants? What is the total annual power distribution cost for this solution?

b. If at most 4000 MW of power can be supplied by any one of the power plants, what is the optimal solution? What is the annual increase in power distribution cost that results from adding these constraints to the original formulation?

8. Forbelt Corporation has a one-year contract to supply motors for all refrigerators produced by the Ice Age Corporation. Ice Age manufactures the refrigerators at four locations around the country: Boston, Dallas, Los Angeles, and St. Paul. Plans call for the following number (in thousands) of refrigerators to be produced at each location:

Boston	50
Dallas	70
Los Angeles	60
St. Paul	80

Forbelt's three plants are capable of producing the motors. The plants and production capacities (in thousands) are as follows:

Denver	100
Atlanta	100
Chicago	150

Because of varying production and transportation costs, the profit that Forbelt earns on each lot of 1000 units depends on which plant produced the lot and which destination it was shipped to. The following table gives the accounting department estimates of the profit per unit (shipments will be made in lots of 1000 units):

		Shipped To		
Produced At	**Boston**	**Dallas**	**Los Angeles**	**St. Paul**
Denver	7	11	8	13
Atlanta	20	17	12	10
Chicago	8	18	13	16

With profit maximization as a criterion, Forbelt's management wants to determine how many motors should be produced at each plant and how many motors should be shipped from each plant to each destination.

a. Develop a network representation of this problem.

b. Find the optimal solution.

9. The Ace Manufacturing Company has orders for three similar products:

Product	Orders (units)
A	2000
B	500
C	1200

Three machines are available for the manufacturing operations. All three machines can produce all the products at the same production rate. However, due to varying defect percentages of each product on each machine, the unit costs of the products vary depending on the machine used. Machine capacities for the next week and the unit costs are as follows:

Machine	Capacity (units)
1	1500
2	1500
3	1000

	Product		
Machine	A	B	C
1	$1.00	$1.20	$0.90
2	$1.30	$1.40	$1.20
3	$1.10	$1.00	$1.20

Use the transportation model to develop the minimum cost production schedule for the products and machines. Show the linear programming formulation.

10. Hatcher Enterprises uses a chemical called Rbase in production operations at five divisions. Only six suppliers of Rbase meet Hatcher's quality control standards. All six suppliers can produce Rbase in sufficient quantities to accommodate the needs of each division. The quantity of Rbase needed by each Hatcher division and the price per gallon charged by each supplier are as follows:

Division	Demand (1000s of gallons)	Supplier	Price per Gallon ($)
1	40	1	12.60
2	45	2	14.00
3	50	3	10.20
4	35	4	14.20
5	45	5	12.00
		6	13.00

The cost per gallon ($) for shipping from each supplier to each division is provided in the following table:

Division	Supplier					
	1	2	3	4	5	6
1	2.75	2.50	3.15	2.80	2.75	2.75
2	0.80	0.20	5.40	1.20	3.40	1.00
3	4.70	2.60	5.30	2.80	6.00	5.60
4	2.60	1.80	4.40	2.40	5.00	2.80
5	3.40	0.40	5.00	1.20	2.60	3.60

Hatcher believes in spreading its business among suppliers so that the company will be less affected by supplier problems (e.g., labor strikes or resource availability). Company policy requires that each division have a separate supplier.

a. For each supplier–division combination, compute the total cost of supplying the division's demand.

b. Determine the optimal assignment of suppliers to divisions.

11. The distribution system for the Herman Company consists of three plants, two warehouses, and four customers. Plant capacities and shipping costs per unit (in $) from each plant to each warehouse are as follows:

Plant	Warehouse		Capacity
	1	2	
1	4	7	450
2	8	5	600
3	5	6	380

Customer demand and shipping costs per unit (in $) from each warehouse to each customer are as follows:

Warehouse	Customer			
	1	2	3	4
1	6	4	8	4
2	3	6	7	7
Demand	300	300	300	400

a. Develop a network representation of this problem.

b. Formulate a linear programming model of the problem.

c. Solve the linear program to determine the optimal shipping plan.

12. Refer to Problem 11. Suppose that shipments between the two warehouses are permitted at $2 per unit and that direct shipments can be made from Plant 3 to Customer 4 at a cost of $7 per unit.

a. Develop a network representation of this problem.

b. Formulate a linear programming model of this problem.

c. Solve the linear program to determine the optimal shipping plan.

13. Sports of All Sorts produces, distributes, and sells high-quality skateboards. Its supply chain consists of three factories (located in Detroit, Los Angeles, and Austin) that produce skateboards. The Detroit and Los Angeles facilities can produce 350 skateboards per week, but the Austin plant is larger and can produce up to 700 skateboards per week. Skateboards must be shipped from the factories to one of four distribution centers, or DCs (located in

Iowa, Maryland, Idaho, and Arkansas). Each distribution center can process (repackage, mark for sale, and ship) at most 500 skateboards per week.

Skateboards are then shipped from the distribution centers to retailers. Sports of All Sorts supplies three major U.S. retailers: Just Sports, Sports 'N Stuff, and The Sports Dude. The weekly demands are 200 skateboards at Just Sports, 500 skateboards at Sports 'N Stuff, and 650 skateboards at The Sports Dude. The following tables display the per-unit costs for shipping skateboards between the factories and DCs and for shipping between the DCs and the retailers:

Shipping Costs ($ per skateboard)

Factory/DCs	Iowa	Maryland	Idaho	Arkansas
Detroit	25.00	25.00	35.00	40.00
Los Angeles	35.00	45.00	35.00	42.50
Austin	40.00	40.00	42.50	32.50

Retailers/DCs	Iowa	Maryland	Idaho	Arkansas
Just Sports	30.00	20.00	35.00	27.50
Sports 'N Stuff	27.50	32.50	40.00	25.00
The Sports Dude	30.00	40.00	32.50	42.50

   a. Draw the network representation for this problem.

   b. Build a model to minimize the transportation cost of a logistics system that will deliver skateboards from the factories to the distribution centers and from the distribution centers to the retailers. What is the optimal production strategy and shipping pattern for Sports of All Sorts? What is the minimum attainable transportation cost?

   c. Sports of All Sorts is considering expansion of the Iowa DC capacity to 800 units per week. The annual amortized cost of expansion is $40,000. Should the company expand the Iowa DC capacity so that it can process 800 skateboards per week? (Assume 50 operating weeks per year.)

14. The Moore & Harman Company is in the business of buying and selling grain. An important aspect of the company's business is arranging for the purchased grain to be shipped to customers. If the company can keep freight costs low, profitability will improve.

The company recently purchased three rail cars of grain at Muncie, Indiana; six rail cars at Brazil, Indiana; and five rail cars at Xenia, Ohio. Twelve carloads of grain have been sold. The locations and the amount sold at each location are as follows:

Location	Number of Rail Car Loads
Macon, GA	2
Greenwood, SC	4
Concord, SC	3
Chatham, NC	3

All shipments must be routed through either Louisville or Cincinnati. Shown are the shipping costs per bushel (in cents) from the origins to Louisville and Cincinnati and the costs per bushel to ship from Louisville and Cincinnati to the destinations.

	To	
From	Louisville	Cincinnati
Muncie	8	6
Brazil	3	8
Xenia	9	3

← Cost per bushel from Muncie to Cincinnati is 6¢

From	Macon	To Greenwood	Concord	Chatham
Louisville	44	34	34	32
Cincinnati	57	35	28	24

Cost per bushel from
Cincinnati to Greenwood is 35¢

Determine a shipping schedule that will minimize the freight costs necessary to satisfy demand. Which (if any) rail cars of grain must be held at the origin until buyers can be found?

15. The following linear programming formulation is for a transshipment problem:

$$\text{Min} \quad 11x_{13} + 12x_{14} + 10x_{21} + 8x_{34} + 10x_{35} + 11x_{42} + 9x_{45} + 12x_{52}$$

s.t.

$$x_{13} + x_{14} - x_{21} \leq 5$$
$$x_{21} \quad\quad - x_{42} \quad - x_{52} \leq 3$$
$$x_{13} \quad - x_{34} - x_{35} \leq 6$$
$$- x_{14} \quad - x_{34} \quad + x_{42} + x_{45} \leq 2$$
$$x_{35} \quad + x_{45} - x_{52} \leq 4$$

$$x_{ij} \geq 0 \quad \text{for all } i, j$$

Show the network representation of this problem.

16. A rental car company has an imbalance of cars at seven of its locations. The following network shows the locations of concern (the nodes) and the cost to move a car between locations. A positive number by a node indicates an excess supply at the node, and a negative number indicates an excess demand.

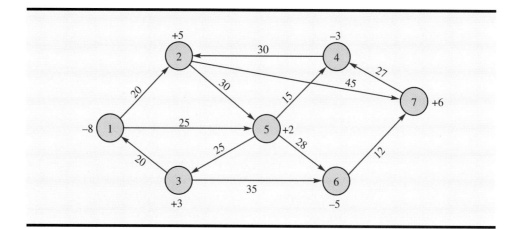

a. Develop a linear programming model of this problem.
b. Solve the model formulated in part (a) to determine how the cars should be redistributed among the locations.

SELF*test*

17. Scott and Associates, Inc., is an accounting firm that has three new clients. Project leaders will be assigned to the three clients. Based on the different backgrounds and experiences of the leaders, the various leader–client assignments differ in terms of projected completion times. The possible assignments and the estimated completion times in days are as follows:

	Client		
Project Leader	**1**	**2**	**3**
Jackson	10	16	32
Ellis	14	22	40
Smith	22	24	34

    a. Develop a network representation of this problem.
    b. Formulate the problem as a linear program, and solve. What is the total time required?

18. CarpetPlus sells and installs floor covering for commercial buildings. Brad Sweeney, a CarpetPlus account executive, was just awarded the contract for five jobs. Brad must now assign a CarpetPlus installation crew to each of the five jobs. Because the commission Brad will earn depends on the profit CarpetPlus makes, Brad would like to determine an assignment that will minimize total installation costs. Currently, five installation crews are available for assignment. Each crew is identified by a color code, which aids in tracking of job progress on a large white board. The following table shows the costs (in hundreds of dollars) for each crew to complete each of the five jobs:

	Job				
Crew	**1**	**2**	**3**	**4**	**5**
Red	30	44	38	47	31
White	25	32	45	44	25
Blue	23	40	37	39	29
Green	26	38	37	45	28
Brown	26	34	44	43	28

    a. Develop a network representation of the problem.
    b. Formulate and solve a linear programming model to determine the minimum cost assignment.

19. A local television station plans to drop four Friday evening programs at the end of the season. Steve Botuchis, the station manager, developed a list of six potential replacement programs. Estimates of the advertising revenue ($) that can be expected for each of the new programs in the four vacated time slots are as follows. Mr. Botuchis asked you to find the assignment of programs to time slots that will maximize total advertising revenue.

	5:00–5:30 P.M.	**5:30–6:00 P.M.**	**7:00–7:30 P.M.**	**8:00–8:30 P.M.**
Comedy Live	5000	3000	6000	4000
World News	7500	8000	7000	5500
NASCAR Live	8500	5000	6500	8000
Wall Street Today	7000	6000	6500	5000
Hollywood Briefings	7000	8000	3000	6000
This Week in Hockey	6000	4000	4500	7000

20. The U.S. Cable Company uses a distribution system with five distribution centers and eight customer zones. Each customer zone is assigned a sole source supplier; each customer zone receives all of its cable products from the same distribution center. In an effort to balance demand and workload at the distribution centers, the company's vice president of logistics specified that distribution centers may not be assigned more than three customer zones. The following table shows the five distribution centers and cost of supplying each customer zone (in thousands of dollars):

Distribution Centers	Customer Zones							
	Los Angeles	Chicago	Columbus	Atlanta	Newark	Kansas City	Denver	Dallas
Plano	70	47	22	53	98	21	27	13
Nashville	75	38	19	58	90	34	40	26
Flagstaff	15	78	37	82	111	40	29	32
Springfield	60	23	8	39	82	36	32	45
Boulder	45	40	29	75	86	25	11	37

  a. Determine the assignment of customer zones to distribution centers that will minimize cost.
  b. Which distribution centers, if any, are not used?
  c. Suppose that each distribution center is limited to a maximum of two customer zones. How does this constraint change the assignment and the cost of supplying customer zones?

21. United Express Service (UES) uses large quantities of packaging materials at its four distribution hubs. After screening potential suppliers, UES identified six vendors that can provide packaging materials that will satisfy its quality standards. UES asked each of the six vendors to submit bids to satisfy annual demand at each of its four distribution hubs over the next year. The following table lists the bids received (in thousands of dollars). UES wants to ensure that each of the distribution hubs is serviced by a different vendor. Which bids should UES accept, and which vendors should UES select to supply each distribution hub?

Bidder	Distribution Hub			
	1	2	3	4
Martin Products	190	175	125	230
Schmidt Materials	150	235	155	220
Miller Containers	210	225	135	260
D&J Burns	170	185	190	280
Larbes Furnishings	220	190	140	240
Lawler Depot	270	200	130	260

22. The quantitative methods department head at a major midwestern university will be scheduling faculty to teach courses during the coming autumn term. Four core courses need to be covered. The four courses are at the undergraduate (UG), master of business administration (MBA), master of science (MS), and doctor of philosophy (Ph.D.) levels. Four professors will be assigned to the courses, with each professor receiving one of the courses. Student evaluations of professors are available from previous terms. Based on a rating scale of 4 (excellent), 3 (very good), 2 (average), 1 (fair), and 0 (poor), the average student evaluations for each professor are shown. Professor D does not have a Ph.D. and cannot be assigned to teach the Ph.D. level course. If the department head makes teaching assign-ments based on maximizing the student evaluation ratings over all four courses, what staff-ing assignments should be made?

		Course		
Professor	UG	MBA	MS	Ph.D.
A	2.8	2.2	3.3	3.0
B	3.2	3.0	3.6	3.6
C	3.3	3.2	3.5	3.5
D	3.2	2.8	2.5	—

SELF*test*

23. Find the shortest route from node 1 to node 7 in the network shown.

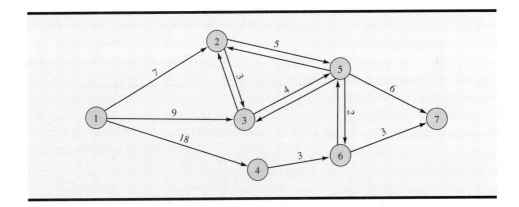

24. In the original Gorman Construction Company problem, we found the shortest distance from the office (node 1) to the construction site located at node 6. Because some of the roads are highways and others are city streets, the shortest-distance routes between the office and the construction site may not necessarily provide the quickest or shortest-time route. Shown here is the Gorman road network with travel time rather than distance. Find the shortest route from Gorman's office to the construction site at node 6 if the objective is to minimize travel time rather than distance.

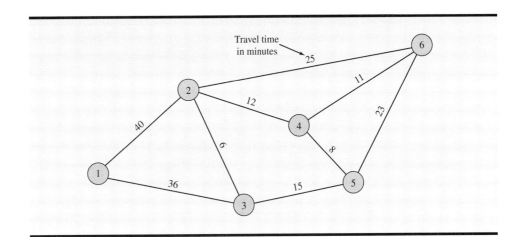

25. Cleveland Area Rapid Delivery (CARD) operates a delivery service in the Cleveland met-ropolitan area. Most of CARD's business involves rapid delivery of documents and parcels between offices during the business day. CARD promotes its ability to make fast and on-time deliveries anywhere in the metropolitan area. When a customer calls with a delivery request, CARD quotes a guaranteed delivery time. The following network shows the street routes available. The numbers above each arc indicate the travel time in minutes between the two locations.

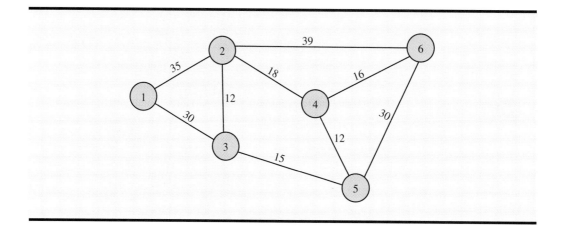

a. Develop a linear programming model that can be used to find the minimum time re-quired to make a delivery from location 1 to location 6.
b. How long does it take to make a delivery from location 1 to location 6?
c. Assume that it is now 1:00 P.M. and that CARD just received a request for a pickup at location 1. The closest CARD courier is 8 minutes away from location 1. If CARD provides a 20% safety margin in guaranteeing a delivery time, what is the guaranteed delivery time if the package picked up at location 1 is to be delivered to location 6?

26. Morgan Trucking Company operates a special pickup and delivery service between Chicago and six other cities located in a four-state area. When Morgan receives a request for service, it dispatches a truck from Chicago to the city requesting service as soon as possible. With both fast service and minimum travel costs as objectives for Morgan, it is important that the dispatched truck take the shortest route from Chicago to the specified city. Assume that the following network (not drawn to scale) with distances given in miles represents the highway network for this problem. Find the shortest-route distances from Chicago to node 6.

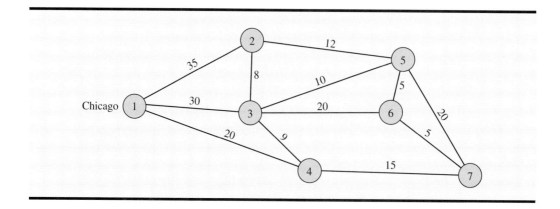

27. City Cab Company identified 10 primary pickup and drop locations for cab riders in New York City. In an effort to minimize travel time and improve customer service and the utilization of the company's fleet of cabs, management would like the cab drivers to take the shortest route between locations whenever possible. Using the following network of roads and streets, what is the route a driver beginning at location 1 should take to reach location 10? The travel times in minutes are shown on the arcs of the network. Note that there are two one-way streets and that the direction is shown by the arrows.

28. The five nodes in the following network represent points one year apart over a four-year period. Each node indicates a time when a decision is made to keep or replace a firm's computer equipment. If a decision is made to replace the equipment, a decision must also be made as to how long the new equipment will be used. The arc from node 0 to node 1 represents the decision to keep the current equipment one year and replace it at the end of the year. The arc from node 0 to node 2 represents the decision to keep the current equipment two years and replace it at the end of year 2. The numbers above the arcs indicate the total cost associated with the equipment replacement decisions. These costs include discounted purchase price, trade-in value, operating costs, and maintenance costs. Use a shortest-route model to determine the minimum cost equipment replacement policy for the four-year period.

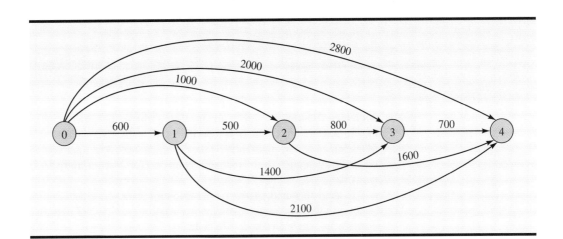

29. The north–south highway system passing through Albany, New York, can accommodate the capacities shown.

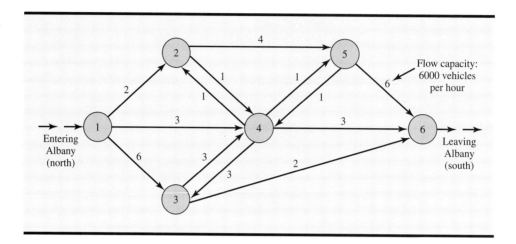

Can the highway system accommodate a north–south flow of 10,000 vehicles per hour?

30. If the Albany highway system described in Problem 29 has revised flow capacities as shown in the following network, what is the maximal flow in vehicles per hour through the system? How many vehicles per hour must travel over each road (arc) to obtain this maximal flow?

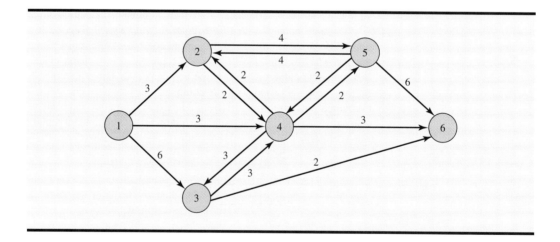

31. An Internet-service provider company uses a fiber-optic network to transmit data between locations. Data are carried through fiber-optic cables and switching nodes. A portion of the company's transmission network is shown here. The numbers above each arc show the capacity in gigabits of data per second that can be transmitted over that branch of the network.

To keep up with the volume of information transmitted between origin and destination points, use the network to determine the maximum amount of data, in gigabits per second, that may be sent from a node 1 to node 7.

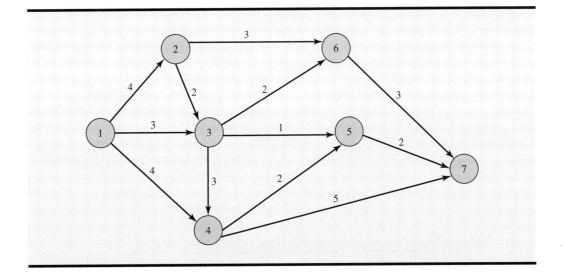

32. The High-Price Oil Company owns a pipeline network that is used to convey oil from its source to several storage locations. A portion of the network is as follows:

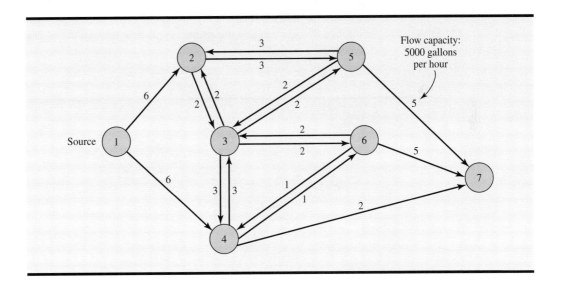

Due to the varying pipe sizes, the flow capacities vary. By selectively opening and closing sections of the pipeline network, the firm can supply any of the storage locations.

a. If the firm wants to fully utilize the system capacity to supply location 7, how long will it take to satisfy a location 7 demand of 100,000 gallons? What is the maximal flow for this pipeline system?

b. If a break occurs on line 2–3 and that line is closed down, what is the maximal flow for the system? How long will it take to transmit 100,000 gallons to location 7?

33. For the following highway network system, determine the maximal flow in vehicles per hour:

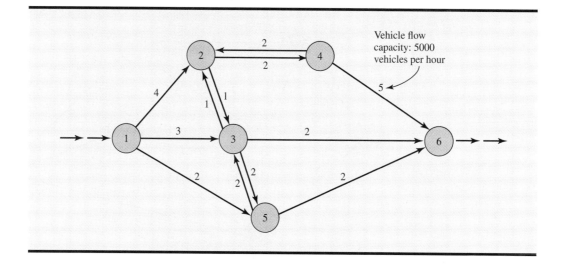

The highway commission is considering adding segment 3–4 to permit a flow of 2000 vehicles per hour or, at an additional cost, a flow of 3000 vehicles per hour. What is your recommendation for the proposed segment 3–4 of the highway network?

34. A chemical processing plant has a network of pipes that are used to transfer liquid chemical products from one part of the plant to another. The following pipe network has pipe flow capacities in gallons per minute as shown. What is the maximum flow capacity for the system if the company wishes to transfer as much liquid chemical as possible from location 1 to location 9? How much of the chemical will flow through the section of pipe from node 3 to node 5?

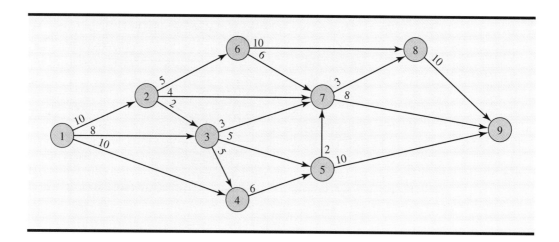

35. Refer to the Contois Carpets problem, for which the network representation is shown in Figure 6.20. Suppose that Contois has a beginning inventory of 50 yards of carpet and requires an inventory of 100 yards at the end of quarter 4.
   a. Develop a network representation of this modified problem.
   b. Develop a linear programming model and solve for the optimal solution.

36. Sanders Fishing Supply of Naples, Florida, manufactures a variety of fishing equipment that it sells throughout the United States. For the next three months, Sanders estimates demand for a particular product at 150, 250, and 300 units, respectively. Sanders can supply this demand by producing on regular time or overtime. Because of other commitments and

anticipated cost increases in month 3, the production capacities in units and the production costs per unit are as follows:

Production	Capacity (units)	Cost per Unit
Month 1—Regular	275	$ 50
Month 1—Overtime	100	$ 80
Month 2—Regular	200	$ 50
Month 2—Overtime	50	$ 80
Month 3—Regular	100	$ 60
Month 3—Overtime	50	$100

Inventory may be carried from one month to the next, but the cost is $20 per unit per month. For example, regular production from month 1 used to meet demand in month 2 would cost Sanders $50 + $20 = $70 per unit. This same month 1 production used to meet demand in month 3 would cost Sanders $50 + 2($20) = $90 per unit.

a. Develop a network representation of this production scheduling problem as a transportation problem. (*Hint*: Use six origin nodes; the supply for origin node 1 is the maximum that can be produced in month 1 on regular time, and so on.)

b. Develop a linear programming model that can be used to schedule regular and overtime production for each of the three months.

c. What is the production schedule, how many units are carried in inventory each month, and what is the total cost?

d. Is there any unused production capacity? If so, where?

Case Problem 1   SOLUTIONS PLUS

Solutions Plus is an industrial chemicals company that produces specialized cleaning fluids and solvents for a wide variety of applications. Solutions Plus just received an invitation to submit a bid to supply Great North American railroad with a cleaning fluid for locomotives. Great North American needs the cleaning fluid at 11 locations (railway stations); it provided the following information to Solutions Plus regarding the number of gallons of cleaning fluid required at each location (see Table 6.8).

Solutions Plus can produce the cleaning fluid at its Cincinnati plant for $1.20 per gallon. Even though the Cincinnati location is its only plant, Solutions Plus has negotiated with an industrial chemicals company located in Oakland, California, to produce and ship up to 500,000 gallons of the locomotive cleaning fluid to selected Solutions Plus customer locations. The Oakland company will charge Solutions Plus $1.65 per gallon to produce the cleaning fluid, but Solutions Plus thinks that the lower shipping costs from Oakland to some customer locations may offset the added cost to produce the product.

TABLE 6.8   GALLONS OF CLEANING FLUID REQUIRED AT EACH LOCATION

Location	Gallons Required	Location	Gallons Required
Santa Ana	22,418	Glendale	33,689
El Paso	6,800	Jacksonville	68,486
Pendleton	80,290	Little Rock	148,586
Houston	100,447	Bridgeport	111,475
Kansas City	24,570	Sacramento	112,000
Los Angeles	64,761		

TABLE 6.9   FREIGHT COST ($ PER GALLON)

	Cincinnati	Oakland
Santa Ana	—	0.22
El Paso	0.84	0.74
Pendleton	0.83	0.49
Houston	0.45	—
Kansas City	0.36	—
Los Angeles	—	0.22
Glendale	—	0.22
Jacksonville	0.34	—
Little Rock	0.34	—
Bridgeport	0.34	—
Sacramento	—	0.15

The president of Solutions Plus, Charlie Weaver, contacted several trucking companies to negotiate shipping rates between the two production facilities (Cincinnati and Oakland) and the locations where the railroad locomotives are cleaned. Table 6.9 shows the quotes received in terms of dollars per gallon. The "—" entries in Table 6.9 identify shipping routes that will not be considered because of the large distances involved. These quotes for shipping rates are guaranteed for one year.

To submit a bid to the railroad company, Solutions Plus must determine the price per gallon it will charge. Solutions Plus usually sells its cleaning fluids for 15% more than its cost to produce and deliver the product. For this big contract, however, Fred Roedel, the director of marketing, suggested that maybe the company should consider a smaller profit margin. In addition, to ensure that if Solutions Plus wins the bid, it will have adequate capacity to satisfy existing orders as well as accept orders for other new business, the management team decided to limit the number of gallons of the locomotive cleaning fluid produced in the Cincinnati plant to 500,000 gallons at most.

Managerial Report

You are asked to make recommendations that will help Solutions Plus prepare a bid. Your report should address, but not be limited to, the following issues:

1. If Solutions Plus wins the bid, which production facility (Cincinnati or Oakland) should supply the cleaning fluid to the locations where the railroad locomotives are cleaned? How much should be shipped from each facility to each location?
2. What is the breakeven point for Solutions Plus? That is, how low can the company go on its bid without losing money?
3. If Solutions Plus wants to use its standard 15% markup, how much should it bid?
4. Freight costs are significantly affected by the price of oil. The contract on which Solutions Plus is bidding is for two years. Discuss how fluctuation in freight costs might affect the bid Solutions Plus submits.

Case Problem 2   SUPPLY CHAIN DESIGN

The Darby Company manufactures and distributes meters used to measure electric power consumption. The company started with a small production plant in El Paso and gradually built a customer base throughout Texas. A distribution center was established in Fort Worth, Texas, and later, as business expanded, a second distribution center was established in Santa Fe, New Mexico.

The El Paso plant was expanded when the company began marketing its meters in Arizona, California, Nevada, and Utah. With the growth of the West Coast business, the Darby Company opened a third distribution center in Las Vegas and just two years ago opened a second production plant in San Bernardino, California.

Manufacturing costs differ between the company's production plants. The cost of each meter produced at the El Paso plant is $10.50. The San Bernardino plant utilizes newer and more efficient equipment; as a result, manufacturing cost is $0.50 per meter less than at the El Paso plant.

Due to the company's rapid growth, not much attention had been paid to the efficiency of its supply chain, but Darby's management decided that it is time to address this issue. The cost of shipping a meter from each of the two plants to each of the three distribution centers is shown in Table 6.10.

The quarterly production capacity is 30,000 meters at the older El Paso plant and 20,000 meters at the San Bernardino plant. Note that no shipments are allowed from the San Bernardino plant to the Fort Worth distribution center.

The company serves nine customer zones from the three distribution centers. The forecast of the number of meters needed in each customer zone for the next quarter is shown in Table 6.11.

The cost per unit of shipping from each distribution center to each customer zone is given in Table 6.12; note that some distribution centers cannot serve certain customer zones. These are indicated by a dash, "—".

In its current supply chain, demand at the Dallas, San Antonio, Wichita, and Kansas City customer zones is satisfied by shipments from the Fort Worth distribution center. In a similar manner, the Denver, Salt Lake City, and Phoenix customer zones are served by the Santa Fe distribution center, and the Los Angeles and San Diego customer zones are served by the Las Vegas distribution center. To determine how many units to ship from each plant,

TABLE 6.10 SHIPPING COST PER UNIT FROM PRODUCTION PLANTS TO DISTRIBUTION CENTERS (IN $)

	Distribution Center		
Plant	Fort Worth	Santa Fe	Las Vegas
El Paso	3.20	2.20	4.20
San Bernardino	—	3.90	1.20

TABLE 6.11 QUARTERLY DEMAND FORECAST

Customer Zone	Demand (meters)
Dallas	6300
San Antonio	4880
Wichita	2130
Kansas City	1210
Denver	6120
Salt Lake City	4830
Phoenix	2750
Los Angeles	8580
San Diego	4460

TABLE 6.12   SHIPPING COST FROM THE DISTRIBUTION CENTERS TO THE CUSTOMER ZONES

Distribution Center	Dallas	San Antonio	Wichita	Kansas City	Denver	Salt Lake City	Phoenix	Los Angeles	San Diego
					Customer Zone				
Fort Worth	0.3	2.1	3.1	4.4	6.0	—	—	—	—
Santa Fe	5.2	5.4	4.5	6.0	2.7	4.7	3.4	3.3	2.7
Las Vegas	—	—	—	—	5.4	3.3	2.4	2.1	2.5

the quarterly customer demand forecasts are aggregated at the distribution centers, and a transportation model is used to minimize the cost of shipping from the production plants to the distribution centers.

Managerial Report

You are asked to make recommendations for improving Darby Company's supply chain. Your report should address, but not be limited to, the following issues:

1. If the company does not change its current supply chain, what will its distribution costs be for the following quarter?
2. Suppose that the company is willing to consider dropping the distribution center limitations; that is, customers could be served by any of the distribution centers for which costs are available. Can costs be reduced? If so, by how much?
3. The company wants to explore the possibility of satisfying some of the customer demand directly from the production plants. In particular, the shipping cost is $0.30 per unit from San Bernardino to Los Angeles and $0.70 from San Bernardino to San Diego. The cost for direct shipments from El Paso to San Antonio is $3.50 per unit. Can distribution costs be further reduced by considering these direct plant-to-customer shipments?
4. Over the next five years, Darby is anticipating moderate growth (5000 meters) to the north and west. Would you recommend that Darby consider plant expansion at this time?

Appendix 6.1   EXCEL SOLUTION OF TRANSPORTATION, TRANSSHIPMENT, AND ASSIGNMENT PROBLEMS

In this appendix we will use an Excel worksheet to solve transportation, transshipment, and assignment problems. We start with the Foster Generators transportation problem (see Section 6.1).

Transportation Problem

The first step is to enter the data for the transportation costs, the origin supplies, and the destination demands in the top portion of the worksheet. Then the linear programming model is developed in the bottom portion of the worksheet. As with all linear programs, the worksheet model has four key elements: the decision variables, the objective function, the constraint left-hand sides, and the constraint right-hand sides. For a transportation problem, the decision variables are the amounts shipped from each origin to each destination; the objective function is the total transportation cost; the left-hand sides are the number of units shipped from each origin and the number of units shipped into each destination; and the right-hand sides are the origin supplies and the destination demands.

FIGURE 6.22   EXCEL SOLUTION OF THE FOSTER GENERATORS PROBLEM

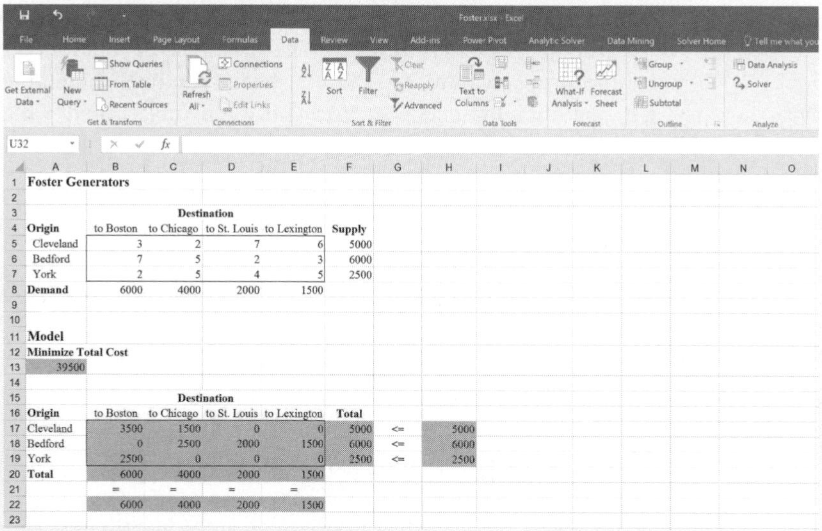

MODEL *file*

Foster

The formulation and solution of the Foster Generators problem are shown in Figure 6.22. The data are in the top portion of the worksheet. The model appears in the bottom portion of the worksheet.

Formulation

The data and descriptive labels are contained in cells A1:F8. The transportation costs are in cells B5:E7. The origin supplies are in cells F5:F7, and the destination demands are in cells B8:E8. The key elements of the model required by the Excel Solver are the decision variables, the objective function, the constraint left-hand sides, and the constraint right-hand sides.

Decision Variables   Cells B17:E19 are reserved for the decision variables. The optimal values are shown to be $x_{11} = 3500$, $x_{12} = 1500$, $x_{22} = 2500$, $x_{23} = 2000$, $x_{24} = 1500$, and $x_{41} = 2500$. All other decision variables equal zero, indicating that nothing will be shipped over the corresponding routes.

Objective Function   The formula $=SUMPRODUCT(B5:E7,B17:E19)$ has been placed into cell A13 to compute the cost of the solution. The minimum cost solution is shown to have a value of \$39,500.

Left-Hand Sides   Cells F17:F19 contain the left-hand sides for the supply constraints, and cells B20:E20 contain the left-hand sides for the demand constraints.

  Cell F17 $=SUM(B17:E17)$ (Copy to F18:F19)
  Cell B20 $=SUM(B17:B19)$ (Copy to C20:E20)

Right-Hand Sides   Cells H17:H19 contain the right-hand sides for the supply constraints, and cells B22:E22 contain the right-hand sides for the demand constraints.

  Cell H17 $=F5$ (Copy to H18:H19)
  Cell B22 $=B8$ (Copy to C22:E22)

Excel Solution

The solution shown in Figure 6.22 can be obtained by clicking **Data** on the Ribbon, and then selecting **Solver** from the **Analyze** group. The Data tab is displayed at the top of the worksheet in Figure 6.22. When the **Solver Parameters** dialog box appears, enter the proper values for the constraints and the objective function, select **Simplex LP,** and click the checkbox for **Make Unconstrained Variables Non-negative.** Then click **Solve.** The information entered into the Solver Parameters dialog box is shown in Figure 6.23.

Transshipment Problem

The worksheet model we present for the transshipment problem can be used for all the network flow problems (transportation, transshipment, and assignment) in this chapter. We organize the worksheet into two sections: an arc section and a node section. Let us illustrate by showing the worksheet formulation and solution of the Ryan Electronics transshipment problem. Refer to Figure 6.24 as we describe the steps involved.

Formulation

The arc section uses cells A4:C16. Each arc is identified in cells A5:A16. The arc costs are identified in cells B5:B16, and cells C5:C16 are reserved for the values of the decision variables (the amount shipped over the arcs).

    The node section uses cells F5:K14. Each of the nodes is identified in cells F7:F14. The following formulas are entered into cells G7:H14 to represent the flow out and the flow in for each node:

Units shipped in:	Cell G9 $\ =C5+C7$
	Cell G10 $=C6+C8$
	Cell G11 $=C9+C13$
	Cell G12 $=C10+C14$
	Cell G13 $=C11+C15$
	Cell G14 $=C12+C16$
Units shipped out:	Cell H7 $\ =SUM(C5:C6)$
	Cell H8 $\ =SUM(C7:C8)$
	Cell H9 $\ =SUM(C9:C12)$
	Cell H10 $=SUM(C13:C16)$

The net shipments in cells I7:I14 are the flows out minus the flows in for each node. For supply nodes, the flow out will exceed the flow in, resulting in positive net shipments. For demand nodes, the flow out will be less than the flow in, resulting in negative net shipments. The "net" supply appears in cells K7:K14. Note that the net supply is negative for demand nodes.

Decision Variables	Cells C5:C16 are reserved for the decision variables. The optimal number of units to ship over each arc is shown.
Objective Function	The formula $=SUMPRODUCT(B5:B16,C5:C16)$ is placed into cell G18 to show the total cost associated with the solution. As shown, the minimum total cost is $5200.
Left-Hand Sides	The left-hand sides of the constraints represent the net shipments for each node. Cells I7:I14 are reserved for these constraints. Cell I7 $=H7-G7$ (Copy to I8:I14)
Right-Hand Sides	The right-hand sides of the constraints represent the supply at each node. Cells K7:K14 are reserved for these values. (Note the negative supply at the four demand nodes.)

FIGURE 6.23   EXCEL SOLVER PARAMETERS DIALOG BOX FOR THE FOSTER
GENERATORS PROBLEM

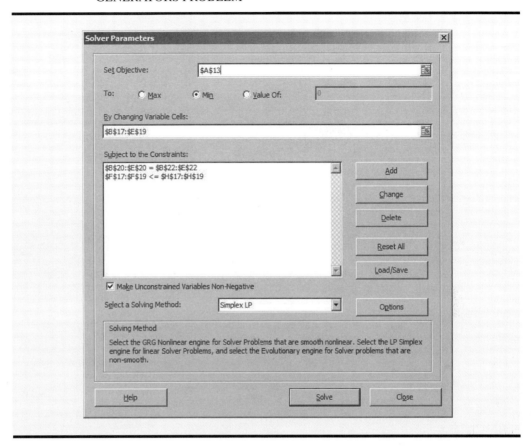

FIGURE 6.24   EXCEL SOLUTION FOR THE RYAN ELECTRONICS PROBLEM

MODEL *file*

Ryan

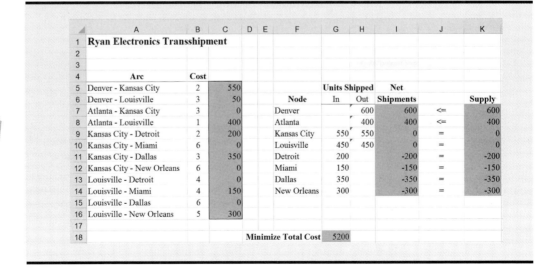

	A	B	C	D	E	F	G	H	I	J	K
1	**Ryan Electronics Transshipment**										
2											
3											
4	**Arc**	**Cost**									
5	Denver - Kansas City	2	550				**Units Shipped**		**Net**		
6	Denver - Louisville	3	50			**Node**	In	Out	**Shipments**		**Supply**
7	Atlanta - Kansas City	3	0			Denver		600	600	<=	600
8	Atlanta - Louisville	1	400			Atlanta		400	400	<=	400
9	Kansas City - Detroit	2	200			Kansas City	550	550	0	=	0
10	Kansas City - Miami	6	0			Louisville	450	450	0	=	0
11	Kansas City - Dallas	3	350			Detroit	200		-200	=	-200
12	Kansas City - New Orleans	6	0			Miami	150		-150	=	-150
13	Louisville - Detroit	4	0			Dallas	350		-350	=	-350
14	Louisville - Miami	4	150			New Orleans	300		-300	=	-300
15	Louisville - Dallas	6	0								
16	Louisville - New Orleans	5	300								
17											
18						**Minimize Total Cost**	5200				

Excel Solution

The solution can be obtained by clicking **Data** on the Ribbon, and then selecting **Solver** from the **Analyze** group. When the **Solver Parameters** dialog box appears, enter the proper values for the constraints and the objective function, select **Simplex LP**, and click the checkbox

FIGURE 6.25   EXCEL SOLVER PARAMETERS DIALOG BOX FOR THE RYAN
ELECTRONICS PROBLEM

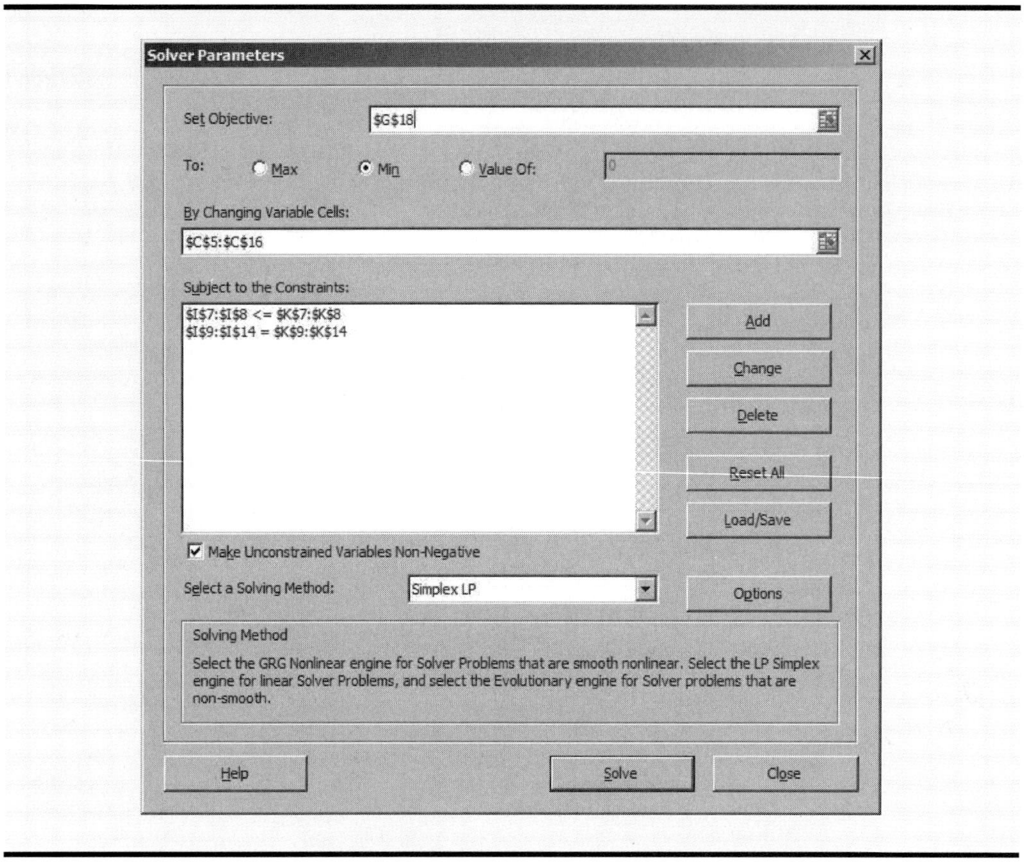

for **Make Unconstrained Variables Non-negative.** Then click **Solve.** The information
entered into the Solver Parameters dialog box is shown in Figure 6.25.

Assignment Problem

The first step is to enter the data for the assignment costs in the top portion of the worksheet. Even though the assignment model is a special case of the transportation model, it is
not necessary to enter values for origin supplies and destination demands because they are
always equal to 1.

The linear programming model is developed in the bottom portion of the worksheet. As
with all linear programs, the model has four key elements: the decision variables, the objective
function, the constraint left-hand sides, and the constraint right-hand sides. For an assignment
problem the decision variables indicate whether an agent is assigned to a task (with a 1 for yes
or 0 for no); the objective function is the total cost of all assignments; the constraint left-hand
sides are the number of tasks that are assigned to each agent and the number of agents that are
assigned to each task; and the right-hand sides are the number of tasks each agent can handle
(1) and the number of agents each task requires (1). The worksheet formulation and solution
for the Fowle marketing research problem are shown in Figure 6.26.

Formulation

The data and descriptive labels are contained in cells A3:D7. Note that we have not inserted
supply and demand values because they are always equal to 1 in an assignment problem. The
model appears in the bottom portion of the worksheet.

FIGURE 6.26   EXCEL SOLUTION OF THE FOWLE MARKETING RESEARCH
PROBLEM

	A	B	C	D	E	F	G
1	**Fowle Marketing Research**						
2							
3			**Client**				
4	**Project Leader**	1	2	3			
5	Terry	10	15	9			
6	Carle	9	18	5			
7	McClymonds	6	14	3			
8							
9							
10	**Model**						
11							
12	**Minimize Completion Time**		26				
13							
14							
15	**Project Leader**	to Client 1	to Client 2	to Client 3	**Total**		
16	Terry	0	1	0	1	<=	1
17	Carle	0	0	1	1	<=	1
18	McClymonds	1	0	0	1	<=	1
19	**Total**	1	1	1			
20		=	=	=			
21		1	1	1			

MODEL *file*

Fowle

Decision Variables	Cells B16:D18 are reserved for the decision variables. The optimal values are shown to be $x_{12} = 1$, $x_{23} = 1$, and $x_{31} = 1$, with all other variables $= 0$.
Objective Function	The formula $=SUMPRODUCT(B5:D7,B16:D18)$ has been placed into cell C12 to compute the number of days required to complete all the jobs. The minimum time solution has a value of 26 days.
Left-Hand Sides	Cells E16:E18 contain the left-hand sides of the constraints for the number of clients each project leader can handle. Cells B19:D19 contain the left-hand sides of the constraints requiring that each client must be assigned a project leader.
	Cell E16 $=SUM(B16:D16)$ (Copy to E17:E18)
	Cell B19 $=SUM(B16:B18)$ (Copy to C19:D19)
Right-Hand Sides	Cells G16:G18 contain the right-hand sides for the project leader constraints, and cells B21:D21 contain the right-hand sides for the client constraints. All right-hand-side cell values are 1.

Excel Solution

The solution shown in Figure 6.26 can be obtained by clicking **Data** on the Ribbon, and then selecting **Solver** from the **Analyze** group. When the Solver Parameters dialog box appears, enter the proper values for the constraints and the objective function, select **Simplex LP,** and click the checkbox for **Make Unconstrained Variables Nonnegative.** Then click Solve. The information entered into the Solver Parameters dialog box is shown in Figure 6.27.

FIGURE 6.27   EXCEL SOLVER PARAMETERS DIALOG BOX FOR THE FOWLE
MARKETING RESEARCH PROBLEM

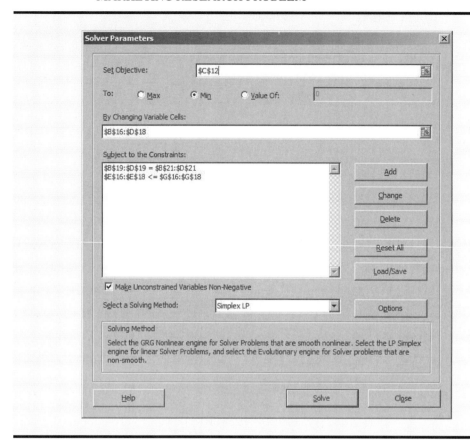

CHAPTER 7

Integer Linear Programming

CONTENTS

In this chapter we discuss a class of problems that are modeled as linear programs with the additional requirement that one or more variables must be integer. Such problems are called **integer linear programs.** If all variables must be integer, we have an all-integer linear program. If some, but not all, variables must be integer, we have a mixed-integer linear program. In many applications of integer linear programming, one or more integer variables are required to equal either 0 or 1. Such variables are called 0-1 or *binary variables.* If all variables are 0-1 variables, we have a 0-1 integer linear program.

Integer variables—especially 0-1 variables—provide substantial modeling flexibility. As a result, the number of applications that can be addressed with linear programming methodology is expanded. For instance, the Management Science in Action, Optimizing the Transport of Oil Rig Crews, describes how Petrobras uses a model with 0-1 variables for assigning helicopters to flights for transporting crews to and from its oil rigs. Later Management Science in Actions describe how the Virginia Court of Appeals uses a 0-1 integer program for scheduling panels of judges to preside over appeal hearings and how the modeling flexibility provided by 0-1 variables helped Ketron build a customer order allocation model for a sporting goods company. Many other applications of integer programming are described throughout the chapter.

The objective of this chapter is to provide an applications-oriented introduction to integer linear programming. First, we discuss the different types of integer linear programming models. Then we show the formulation, graphical solution, and computer solution of an all-integer linear program. In Section 7.3 we discuss five applications of integer linear programming that make use of 0-1 variables: capital budgeting, fixed cost, distribution system design, bank location, and market share optimization problems. In Section 7.4 we provide additional illustrations of the modeling flexibility provided by 0-1 variables. Chapter appendices illustrate the use of Excel and LINGO for solving integer programs.

The cost of the added modeling flexibility provided by integer programming is that problems involving integer variables are often much more difficult to solve. A linear programming problem with several thousand continuous variables can be solved with any of several commercial linear programming solvers. However, an all-integer linear programming problem with fewer than 100 variables can be extremely difficult to solve. Experienced management scientists can help identify the types of integer linear programs that are easy, or at least reasonable, to solve. Commercial computer software packages, such as LINGO, CPLEX, Gurobi, Xpress-MP, and the commercial version of Solver, have extensive integer programming capability, and very robust open-source software packages for integer programming are also available.

Information about open-source software can be found at the COIN-OR foundation website.

MANAGEMENT SCIENCE IN ACTION

OPTIMIZING THE TRANSPORT OF OIL RIG CREWS*

Petrobras, the largest corporation in Brazil, operates approximately 80 offshore oil production and exploration platforms in the oil-rich Campos Basin. One of Petrobras' biggest challenges is the planning of its logistics, including how to efficiently and safely transport nearly 1900 employees per day from its four mainland bases to the offshore platforms. Every day, planners must route and schedule the helicopters used to transport Petrobras employees from the mainland to the offshore locations and back to the mainland. This routing and scheduling problem is challenging because there are over a billion possible combinations of schedules and routes.

Petrobras uses mixed integer linear optimization to solve its helicopter transport scheduling and routing problem. The objective function of the optimization model is a weighted function designed to ensure safety, minimize unmet demand, and minimize the cost of the transport of its crews. Because offshore landings are the riskiest part of the transport, the safety objective is met by minimizing the number of offshore landings required in the schedule. Numerous constraints must be met in planning these routes and schedule. These include limiting the number of departures from a platform at certain times; ensuring no time conflicts for a given helicopter and pilot; ensuring proper breaks for pilots; limiting the number of flights per day for a given helicopter and routing restrictions. The decision variables include binary variables for assigning helicopters to flights and pilots to break times, as well as variables on the number of passengers per flight.

Compared to the previously used manual approach to this problem, the new approach using the integer optimization model transports the same number of passengers but with 18% fewer offshore landings, 8% less flight time, and a reduction in cost of 14%. The annual cost savings is estimated to be approximately $24 million.

*Based on F. Menezes et al., "Optimizing Helicopter Transport of Oil Rig Crews at Petrobras," *Interfaces* 40, no. 5 (September–October 2010): 408–416.

NOTES AND COMMENTS

1. Because integer linear programs are harder to solve than linear programs, one should not try to solve a problem as an integer program if simply rounding the linear programming solution is adequate. In many linear programming problems, such as those in previous chapters, rounding has little economic consequence on the objective function, and feasibility is not an issue. But, in problems such as determining how many jet engines to manufacture, the consequences of rounding can be substantial and integer programming methodology should be employed.

2. Some linear programming problems have a special structure, which guarantees that the variables will have integer values. The assignment, transportation, and transshipment problems of Chapter 6 have such structures. If the supply and the demand for transportation and transshipment problems are integer, the optimal linear programming solution will provide integer amounts shipped. For the assignment problem, the optimal linear programming solution will consist of 0s and 1s. So, for these specially structured problems, linear programming methodology can be used to find optimal integer solutions. Integer linear programming algorithms are not necessary.

7.1 TYPES OF INTEGER LINEAR PROGRAMMING MODELS

The only difference between the problems studied in this chapter and the ones studied in earlier chapters on linear programming is that one or more variables are required to be integer. If all variables are required to be integer, we have an **all-integer linear program.** The following is a two-variable, all-integer linear programming model:

$$\text{Max} \quad 2x_1 + 3x_2$$

s.t.

$$3x_1 + 3x_2 \leq 12$$
$$\tfrac{2}{3}x_1 + 1x_2 \leq 4$$
$$1x_1 + 2x_2 \leq 6$$
$$x_1, x_2 \geq 0 \text{ and integer}$$

If we drop the phrase "and integer" from the last line of this model, we have the familiar two-variable linear program. The linear program that results from dropping the integer requirements is called the **LP Relaxation** of the integer linear program.

If some, but not necessarily all, variables are required to be integer, we have a **mixed-integer linear program.** The following is a two-variable, mixed-integer linear program:

$$\text{Max} \quad 3x_1 + 4x_2$$

s.t.

$$-1x_1 + 2x_2 \leq 8$$
$$1x_1 + 2x_2 \leq 12$$
$$2x_1 + 1x_2 \leq 16$$
$$x_1, x_2 \geq 0 \text{ and } x_2 \text{ integer}$$

We obtain the LP Relaxation of this mixed-integer linear program by dropping the requirement that x_2 be integer.

In some applications, the integer variables may only take on the values 0 or 1. Then we have a **0-1 linear integer program.** As we see later in the chapter, 0-1 variables provide additional modeling capability. The Management Science in Action, Scheduling the Virginia Court of Appeals, describes how a 0-1 integer program is used to schedule hearings for its appeals and how it constructs the panels of judges to ensure that laws governing the process are followed.

MANAGEMENT SCIENCE IN ACTION

SCHEDULING THE VIRGINIA COURT OF APPEALS*

Every city and county in the state of Virginia has a circuit court that hears felony cases as well as claims of more than $25,000. In order to ensure fair outcomes, the Court of Appeals of the state of Virginia hears appeals of decisions handed down by the circuit courts. The Court of Appeals consists of 11 judges, who sit in panels of 3 judges for hearing sessions. A number of full-court sessions are also held, which by law must consist of at least 8 of the 11 judges. In order to ensure a fair and equitable judicial system for its citizens, Virginia law specifies a variety of constraints for how often, when, and where these sessions are scheduled and the makeup of each panel of judges.

The scheduling of the appeal hearings is based on forecasted case load. The construction of each panel of judges, when done by hand, is a complex and arduous task. The manual process was to use a wall-sized calendar with color-coded magnets to construct a full schedule based on extensive trial and error, often requiring 150 hours to complete. Court of Appeals staff members approached Virginia Commonwealth University about the possibility of automating the scheduling process. Working with the information technology department of the Court of Appeals, the Department of Statistics and Operations Research at Virginia Commonwealth developed a binary integer program to solve this complex problem.

Virginia law dictates that numerous restrictions must be satisfied with the schedule for the hearings. For example, no panel sessions may be scheduled during a week of a full-court session. Panels must be held in each of the State's four districts, and in a given district, hearings must be at least three weeks apart. Each of the four districts must have a session in the month of September, and dates on which there are judge's conferences or retreats as well as certain holidays must be avoided.

Likewise, restrictions exist on the makeup of the judge's panel for each session. Each judge must serve on a panel with every other judge at least once and any two judges can be on at most three of the same three-judge panels. Each judge must have a panel in each district, but can have at most two panels in any district that is not his/her home district. Other constraints similar to these must also be enforced.

In addition to the restrictions mentioned, each judge specifies times to be avoided if possible. The objective of the integer programming model is to minimize the number of assignments where a judge is assigned to a session that he/she requested to be avoided. The decision variables for the model are binary variables that indicate (1) if a judge is assigned to a session or not, (2) if a session is held or not, (3) if a judge serves in a given month or not, and (4) if a pair of judges works in a given session or not.

The resulting integer programming model is quite large, but with some preprocessing to eliminate obvious infeasible options, the model size was reduced from more than 80,000 variables and millions of constraints to 10,000 variables and approximately 100,000 constraints. Rather than buying software to solve the problem, the team used an optimization service available over the web to solve the problem. The solution time was about 10 hours. The team also constructed a back-end solution processor in Microsoft Access to allow easy visualization of the schedule, which is important for presenting the proposed solution for approval. Through the use of the optimization model, the deputy clerk is now free to use the 150 hours previously spent on scheduling for more productive activities.

*Based on J. Paul Brooks, "The Court of Appeals of Virginia Uses Integer Programming and Cloud Computing to Schedule Sessions, *Interfaces* Vol. 42, No. 6 (November/December 2012): 544–553.

7.2   GRAPHICAL AND COMPUTER SOLUTIONS FOR AN ALL-INTEGER LINEAR PROGRAM

Eastborne Realty has $2 million available for the purchase of new rental property. After an initial screening, Eastborne reduced the investment alternatives to townhouses and apartment buildings. Each townhouse can be purchased for $282,000, and five are available. Each apartment building can be purchased for $400,000, and the developer will construct as many buildings as Eastborne wants to purchase.

Eastborne's property manager can devote up to 140 hours per month to these new properties; each townhouse is expected to require 4 hours per month, and each apartment building is expected to require 40 hours per month. The annual cash flow, after deducting mortgage payments and operating expenses, is estimated to be $10,000 per townhouse and $15,000 per apartment building. Eastborne's owner would like to determine the number of townhouses and the number of apartment buildings to purchase to maximize annual cash flow.

We begin by defining the decision variables as follows:

$$T = \text{number of townhouses to purchase}$$
$$A = \text{number of apartment buildings to purchase}$$

The objective function for cash flow (in thousands of dollars) is

$$\text{Max } 10T + 15A$$

Three constraints must be satisfied:

$$282T + 400A \leq 2000 \quad \text{Funds available (\$1000s)}$$
$$4T + 40A \leq 140 \quad \text{Manager's time (hours)}$$
$$T \leq 5 \quad \text{Townhouses available}$$

The variables T and A must be nonnegative. In addition, the purchase of a fractional number of townhouses and/or a fractional number of apartment buildings is unacceptable. Thus, T and A must be integer. The model for the Eastborne Realty problem is the following all-integer linear program:

$$\text{Max } 10T + 15A$$
$$\text{s.t.}$$
$$282T + 400A \leq 2000$$
$$4T + 40A \leq 140$$
$$T \leq 5$$
$$T, A \geq 0 \text{ and integer}$$

Graphical Solution of the LP Relaxation

Suppose that we drop the integer requirements for T and A and solve the LP Relaxation of the Eastborne Realty problem. Using the graphical solution procedure, as presented in Chapter 2, the optimal linear programming solution is shown in Figure 7.1. It is $T = 2.479$ townhouses and $A = 3.252$ apartment buildings. The optimal value of the objective function is 73.574, which indicates an annual cash flow of $73,574. Unfortunately, Eastborne cannot purchase fractional numbers of townhouses and apartment buildings; further analysis is necessary.

Rounding to Obtain an Integer Solution

In many cases, a noninteger solution can be rounded to obtain an acceptable integer solution. For instance, a linear programming solution to a production scheduling problem might call for the production of 15,132.4 cases of breakfast cereal. The rounded integer solution of 15,132 cases would probably have minimal impact on the value of the objective function and the feasibility of the solution. Rounding would be a sensible approach. Indeed,

FIGURE 7.1   GRAPHICAL SOLUTION TO THE LP RELAXATION OF THE EASTBORNE
REALTY PROBLEM

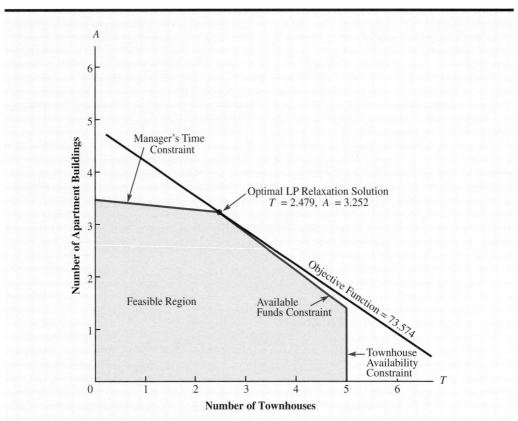

whenever rounding has a minimal impact on the objective function and constraints, most managers find it acceptable. A near-optimal solution is fine.

However, rounding may not always be a good strategy. When the decision variables take on small values that have a major impact on the value of the objective function or feasibility, an optimal integer solution is needed. Let us return to the Eastborne Realty problem and examine the impact of rounding. The optimal solution to the LP Relaxation for Eastborne Realty resulted in $T = 2.479$ townhouses and $A = 3.252$ apartment buildings. Because each townhouse costs $282,000 and each apartment building costs $400,000, rounding to an integer solution can be expected to have a significant economic impact on the problem.

Suppose that we round the solution to the LP Relaxation to obtain the integer solution $T = 2$ and $A = 3$, with an objective function value of $10(2) + 15(3) = 65$. The annual cash flow of $65,000 is substantially less than the annual cash flow of $73,574 provided by the solution to the LP Relaxation. Do other rounding possibilities exist? Exploring other rounding alternatives shows that the integer solution $T = 3$ and $A = 3$ is infeasible because it requires more funds than the $2,000,000 Eastborne has available. The rounded solution of $T = 2$ and $A = 4$ is also infeasible for the same reason. At this point, rounding has led to two townhouses and three apartment buildings with an annual cash flow of $65,000 as the best feasible integer solution to the problem. Unfortunately, we don't know whether this solution is the best integer solution to the problem.

Rounding to an integer solution is a trial-and-error approach. Each rounded solution must be evaluated for feasibility as well as for its impact on the value of the objective function. Even in cases where a rounded solution is feasible, we do not have a guarantee that we have found the optimal integer solution. We will see shortly that the rounded solution ($T = 2$ and $A = 3$) is not optimal for Eastborne Realty.

If a problem has only less-than-or-equal-to constraints with nonnegative coefficients for the variables, rounding down will always provide a feasible integer solution.

Graphical Solution of the All-Integer Problem

Try Problem 2 for practice with the graphical solution of an integer program.

Figure 7.2 shows the changes in the linear programming graphical solution procedure required to solve the Eastborne Realty integer linear programming problem. First, the graph of the feasible region is drawn exactly as in the LP Relaxation of the problem. Then, because the optimal solution must have integer values, we identify the feasible integer solutions with the dots shown in Figure 7.2. Finally, instead of moving the objective function line to the best extreme point in the feasible region, we move it in an improving direction as far as possible until reaching the dot (feasible integer point) providing the best value for the objective function. Viewing Figure 7.2, we see that the optimal integer solution occurs at $T = 4$ townhouses and $A = 2$ apartment buildings. The objective function value is $10(4) + 15(2) = 70$, providing an annual cash flow of $70,000. This solution is significantly better than the best solution found by rounding: $T = 2$, $A = 3$, with an annual cash flow of $65,000. Thus, we see that rounding would not have been the best strategy for Eastborne Realty.

Using the LP Relaxation to Establish Bounds

An important observation can be made from the analysis of the Eastborne Realty problem. It has to do with the relationship between the value of the optimal integer solution and the value of the optimal solution to the LP Relaxation.

> For integer linear programs involving maximization, the value of the optimal solution to the LP Relaxation provides an upper bound on the value of the optimal integer solution. For integer linear programs involving minimization, the value of the optimal solution to the LP Relaxation provides a lower bound on the value of the optimal integer solution.

FIGURE 7.2   GRAPHICAL SOLUTION OF THE EASTBORNE REALTY INTEGER PROBLEM

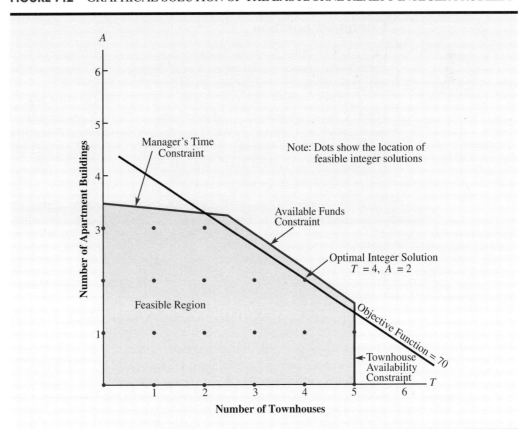

FIGURE 7.3   THE SOLUTION FOR THE EASTBORNE REALTY PROBLEM

MODEL *file*

Eastborne

```
         Optimal Objective Value = 70.00000

              Variable                    Value
          ---------------            ---------------

                 T                        4.00000
                 A                        2.00000


             Constraint                Slack/Surplus
          ---------------            ---------------

                 1                       72.00000
                 2                       44.00000
                 3                        1.00000
```

This observation is valid for the Eastborne Realty problem. The value of the optimal integer solution is $70,000, and the value of the optimal solution to the LP Relaxation is $73,574. Thus, we know from the LP Relaxation solution that the upper bound for the value of the objective function is $73,574.

Try Problem 5 for the graphical solution of a mixed-integer program.

The bounding property of the LP Relaxation allows us to conclude that if, by chance, the solution to an LP Relaxation turns out to be an integer solution, it is also optimal for the integer linear program. This bounding property can also be helpful in determining whether a rounded solution is "good enough." If a rounded LP Relaxation solution is feasible and provides a value of the objective function that is "almost as good as" the value of the objective function for the LP Relaxation, we know the rounded solution is a near-optimal integer solution. In this case, we can avoid having to solve the problem as an integer linear program.

Computer Solution

LINGO or Frontline Systems' Solver can be used to solve most of the integer linear programs in this chapter. In the appendices at the end of this chapter, we discuss how to solve integer linear programs using Solver and LINGO.

Specifying both T and A as integers provides the optimal integer solution shown in Figure 7.3. The solution of $T = 4$ townhouses and $A = 2$ apartment buildings has a maximum annual cash flow of $70,000. The values of the slack variables tell us that the optimal solution has $72,000 of available funds unused, 44 hours of the manager's time still available, and 1 of the available townhouses not purchased.

NOTES AND COMMENTS

The computer output we show in this chapter for integer programs does not include reduced costs, dual values, or sensitivity ranges because these are not meaningful for integer programs.

7.3   APPLICATIONS INVOLVING 0-1 VARIABLES

Much of the modeling flexibility provided by integer linear programming is due to the use of 0-1 variables. In many applications, 0-1 variables provide selections or choices with the value of the variable equal to 1 if a corresponding activity is undertaken and equal to 0 if the corresponding activity is not undertaken. The capital budgeting, fixed cost, distribution system design, bank location, and product design/market share applications presented in this section make use of 0-1 variables.

Capital Budgeting

The Ice-Cold Refrigerator Company is considering investing in several projects that have varying capital requirements over the next four years. Faced with limited capital each year, management would like to select the most profitable projects. The estimated net present value for each project,[1] the capital requirements, and the available capital over the four-year period are shown in Table 7.1.

The four 0-1 decision variables are as follows:

$P = 1$ if the plant expansion project is accepted; 0 if rejected
$W = 1$ if the warehouse expansion project is accepted; 0 if rejected
$M = 1$ if the new machinery project is accepted; 0 if rejected
$R = 1$ if the new product research project is accepted; 0 if rejected

In a **capital budgeting problem,** the company's objective function is to maximize the net present value of the capital budgeting projects. This problem has four constraints: one for the funds available in each of the next four years.

A 0-1 integer linear programming model with dollars in thousands is as follows:

$$\text{Max } 90P + 40W + 10M + 37R$$

s.t.

$$
\begin{aligned}
15P + 10W + 10M + 15R &\le 40 \quad \text{(Year 1 capital available)} \\
20P + 15W + 10R &\le 50 \quad \text{(Year 2 capital available)} \\
20P + 20W + 10R &\le 40 \quad \text{(Year 3 capital available)} \\
15P + 5W + 4M + 10R &\le 35 \quad \text{(Year 4 capital available)} \\
P, W, M, R &= 0, 1
\end{aligned}
$$

The integer programming solution is shown in Figure 7.4. The optimal solution is $P = 1$, $W = 1$, $M = 1$, $R = 0$, with a total estimated net present value of $140,000. Thus, the company should fund the plant expansion, the warehouse expansion, and the new machinery projects. The new product research project should be put on hold unless additional capital funds become available. The values of the slack variables (see Figure 7.4) show that the company will have $5,000 remaining in year 1, $15,000 remaining in year 2, and $11,000 remaining in year 4. Checking the capital requirements for the new product research project, we see that enough funds are available for this project in year 2 and year 4. However, the company would have to find additional capital funds of $10,000 in year 1 and $10,000 in year 3 to fund the new product research project.

TABLE 7.1 PROJECT NET PRESENT VALUE, CAPITAL REQUIREMENTS, AND AVAILABLE CAPITAL FOR THE ICE-COLD REFRIGERATOR COMPANY

	Project				
	Plant Expansion	Warehouse Expansion	New Machinery	New Product Research	Total Capital Available
Present Value	$90,000	$40,000	$10,000	$37,000	
Year 1 Cap Rqmt	$15,000	$10,000	$10,000	$15,000	$40,000
Year 2 Cap Rqmt	$20,000	$15,000		$10,000	$50,000
Year 3 Cap Rqmt	$20,000	$20,000		$10,000	$40,000
Year 4 Cap Rqmt	$15,000	$ 5,000	$ 4,000	$10,000	$35,000

[1] The estimated net present value is the net cash flow discounted back to the beginning of year 1.

FIGURE 7.4   THE SOLUTION FOR THE ICE-COLD REFRIGERATOR COMPANY PROBLEM

```
           Optimal Objective Value = 140.00000

                 Variable                   Value
              --------------            ---------------

                    P                       1.00000
                    W                       1.00000
                    M                       1.00000
                    R                       0.00000


               Constraint              Slack/Surplus
              --------------            ---------------

                    1                       5.00000
                    2                      15.00000
                    3                       0.00000
                    4                      11.00000
```

MODEL *file*

Ice-Cold

Fixed Cost

In many applications, the cost of production has two components: a setup cost, which is a fixed cost, and a variable cost, which is directly related to the production quantity. The use of 0-1 variables makes including the setup cost possible in a model for a production application.

As an example of a **fixed cost problem,** consider the RMC problem. Three raw materials are used to produce three products: a fuel additive, a solvent base, and a carpet cleaning fluid. The following decision variables are used:

$$F = \text{tons of fuel additive produced}$$
$$S = \text{tons of solvent base produced}$$
$$C = \text{tons of carpet cleaning fluid produced}$$

The profit contributions are $40 per ton for the fuel additive, $30 per ton for the solvent base, and $50 per ton for the carpet cleaning fluid. Each ton of fuel additive is a blend of 0.4 tons of material 1 and 0.6 tons of material 3. Each ton of solvent base requires 0.5 tons of material 1, 0.2 tons of material 2, and 0.3 tons of material 3. Each ton of carpet cleaning fluid is a blend of 0.6 tons of material 1, 0.1 tons of material 2, and 0.3 tons of material 3. RMC has 20 tons of material 1, 5 tons of material 2, and 21 tons of material 3 and is interested in determining the optimal production quantities for the upcoming planning period.

A linear programming model of the RMC problem is shown:

$$\text{Max} \quad 40F + 30S + 50C$$

s.t.

$$0.4F + 0.5S + 0.6C \leq 20 \quad \text{Material 1}$$
$$0.2S + 0.1C \leq 5 \quad \text{Material 2}$$
$$0.6F + 0.3S + 0.3C \leq 21 \quad \text{Material 3}$$
$$F, S, C \geq 0$$

The optimal solution consists of 27.5 tons of fuel additive, 0 tons of solvent base, and 15 tons of carpet cleaning fluid, with a value of $1850, as shown in Figure 7.5.

This linear programming formulation of the RMC problem does not include a fixed cost for production setup of the products. Suppose that the following data are available

FIGURE 7.5 THE SOLUTION TO THE RMC PROBLEM

```
Optimal Objective Value = 1850.00000

     Variable              Value          Reduced Costs
   --------------     ---------------     -----------------
        F                27.50000              0.00000
        S                 0.00000            -12.50000
        C                15.00000              0.00000
```

concerning the setup cost and the maximum production quantity for each of the three products:

Product	Setup Cost	Maximum Production
Fuel additive	$200	50 tons
Solvent base	$ 50	25 tons
Carpet cleaning fluid	$400	40 tons

The modeling flexibility provided by 0-1 variables can now be used to incorporate the fixed setup costs into the production model. The 0-1 variables are defined as follows:

$$SF = 1 \text{ if the fuel additive is produced; 0 if not}$$
$$SS = 1 \text{ if the solvent base is produced; 0 if not}$$
$$SC = 1 \text{ if the carpet cleaning fluid is produced; 0 if not}$$

Using these setup variables, the total setup cost is

$$200SF + 50SS + 400SC$$

We can now rewrite the objective function to include the setup cost. Thus, the net profit objective function becomes

$$\text{Max} \quad 40F + 30S + 50C - 200SF - 50SS - 400SC$$

Next, we must write production capacity constraints so that if a setup variable equals 0, production of the corresponding product is not permitted and, if a setup variable equals 1, production is permitted up to the maximum quantity. For the fuel additive, we do so by adding the following constraint:

$$F \leq 50SF$$

Note that, with this constraint present, production of the fuel additive is not permitted when $SF = 0$. When $SF = 1$, production of up to 50 tons of fuel additive is permitted. We can think of the setup variable as a switch. When it is off ($SF = 0$), production is not permitted; when it is on ($SF = 1$), production is permitted.

Similar production capacity constraints, using 0-1 variables, are added for the solvent base and carpet cleaning products:

$$S \leq 25SS$$
$$C \leq 40SC$$

FIGURE 7.6   THE SOLUTION TO THE RMC PROBLEM WITH SETUP COSTS

```
              Optimal Objective Value = 1350.00000

                  Variable              Value
                  --------            ---------
                     F                 25.00000
                     S                 20.00000
                     C                  0.00000
                     SF                 1.00000
                     SS                 1.00000
                     SC                 0.00000
```

We have then the following fixed cost model for the RMC problem:

$$\text{Max} \quad 40F + 30S + 50C - 200SF - 50SS - 400SC$$

s.t.

$0.4F + 0.5S + 0.6C$	$\leq \quad 20$	Material 1
$0.2S + 0.1C$	$\leq \quad 5$	Material 2
$0.6F + 0.3S + 0.3C$	$\leq \quad 21$	Material 3
F	$\leq 50SF$	Maximum F
S	$\leq 25SS$	Maximum S
C	$\leq 40SC$	Maximum C

$$F, S, C \geq 0; \ SF, SS, SC = 0, 1$$

The solution to the RMC problem with setup costs is shown in Figure 7.6. The optimal solution shows 25 tons of fuel additive and 20 tons of solvent base. The value of the objective function after deducting the setup cost is $1350. The setup cost for the fuel additive and the solvent base is $200 + $50 = $250. The optimal solution shows $SC = 0$, which indicates that the more expensive $400 setup cost for the carpet cleaning fluid should be avoided. Thus, the carpet cleaning fluid is not produced.

The key to developing a fixed-cost model is the introduction of a 0-1 variable for each fixed cost and the specification of an upper bound for the corresponding production variable. For a production quantity x, a constraint of the form $x \leq My$ can then be used to allow production when the setup variable $y = 1$ and not to allow production when the setup variable $y = 0$. The value of the maximum production quantity M should be large enough to allow for all reasonable levels of production. But research has shown that choosing values of M excessively large will slow the solution procedure.

Distribution System Design

The Martin-Beck Company operates a plant in St. Louis with an annual capacity of 30,000 units. Product is shipped to regional distribution centers located in Boston, Atlanta, and Houston. Because of an anticipated increase in demand, Martin-Beck plans to increase capacity by constructing a new plant in one or more of the following cities: Detroit, Toledo, Denver, or Kansas City. The estimated annual fixed cost and the annual capacity for the four proposed plants are as follows:

Proposed Plant	Annual Fixed Cost	Annual Capacity
Detroit	$175,000	10,000
Toledo	$300,000	20,000
Denver	$375,000	30,000
Kansas City	$500,000	40,000

The company's long-range planning group developed forecasts of the anticipated annual demand at the distribution centers as follows:

Distribution Center	Annual Demand
Boston	30,000
Atlanta	20,000
Houston	20,000

The shipping cost per unit from each plant to each distribution center is shown in Table 7.2. A network representation of the potential Martin-Beck distribution system is shown in Figure 7.7. Each potential plant location is shown; capacities and demands are shown in thousands of units. This network representation is for a transportation problem with a plant at St. Louis and at all four proposed sites. However, the decision has not yet been made as to which new plant or plants will be constructed.

Let us now show how 0-1 variables can be used in this **distribution system design problem** to develop a model for choosing the best plant locations and for determining how much to ship from each plant to each distribution center. We can use the following 0-1 variables to represent the plant construction decision:

$$y_1 = 1 \text{ if a plant is constructed in Detroit; 0 if not}$$
$$y_2 = 1 \text{ if a plant is constructed in Toledo; 0 if not}$$
$$y_3 = 1 \text{ if a plant is constructed in Denver; 0 if not}$$
$$y_4 = 1 \text{ if a plant is constructed in Kansas City; 0 if not}$$

The variables representing the amount shipped from each plant site to each distribution center are defined just as for a transportation problem.

$$x_{ij} = \text{the units shipped in thousands from plant } i \text{ to distribution center } j$$
$$i = 1, 2, 3, 4, 5 \quad \text{and} \quad j = 1, 2, 3$$

Using the shipping cost data in Table 7.2, the annual transportation cost in thousands of dollars is written as

$$5x_{11} + 2x_{12} + 3x_{13} + 4x_{21} + 3x_{22} + 4x_{23} + 9x_{31} + 7x_{32} + 5x_{33}$$
$$+ 10x_{41} + 4x_{42} + 2x_{43} + 8x_{51} + 4x_{52} + 3x_{53}$$

The annual fixed cost of operating the new plant or plants in thousands of dollars is written as

$$175y_1 + 300y_2 + 375y_3 + 500y_4$$

Note that the 0-1 variables are defined so that the annual fixed cost of operating the new plants is only calculated for the plant or plants that are actually constructed (i.e., $y_i = 1$). If a plant is not constructed, $y_i = 0$ and the corresponding annual fixed cost is $0.

TABLE 7.2   SHIPPING COST PER UNIT FOR THE MARTIN-BECK DISTRIBUTION SYSTEM

	Distribution Centers		
Plant Site	Boston	Atlanta	Houston
Detroit	5	2	3
Toledo	4	3	4
Denver	9	7	5
Kansas City	10	4	2
St. Louis	8	4	3

FIGURE 7.7   THE NETWORK REPRESENTATION OF THE MARTIN-BECK COMPANY
DISTRIBUTION SYSTEM PROBLEM

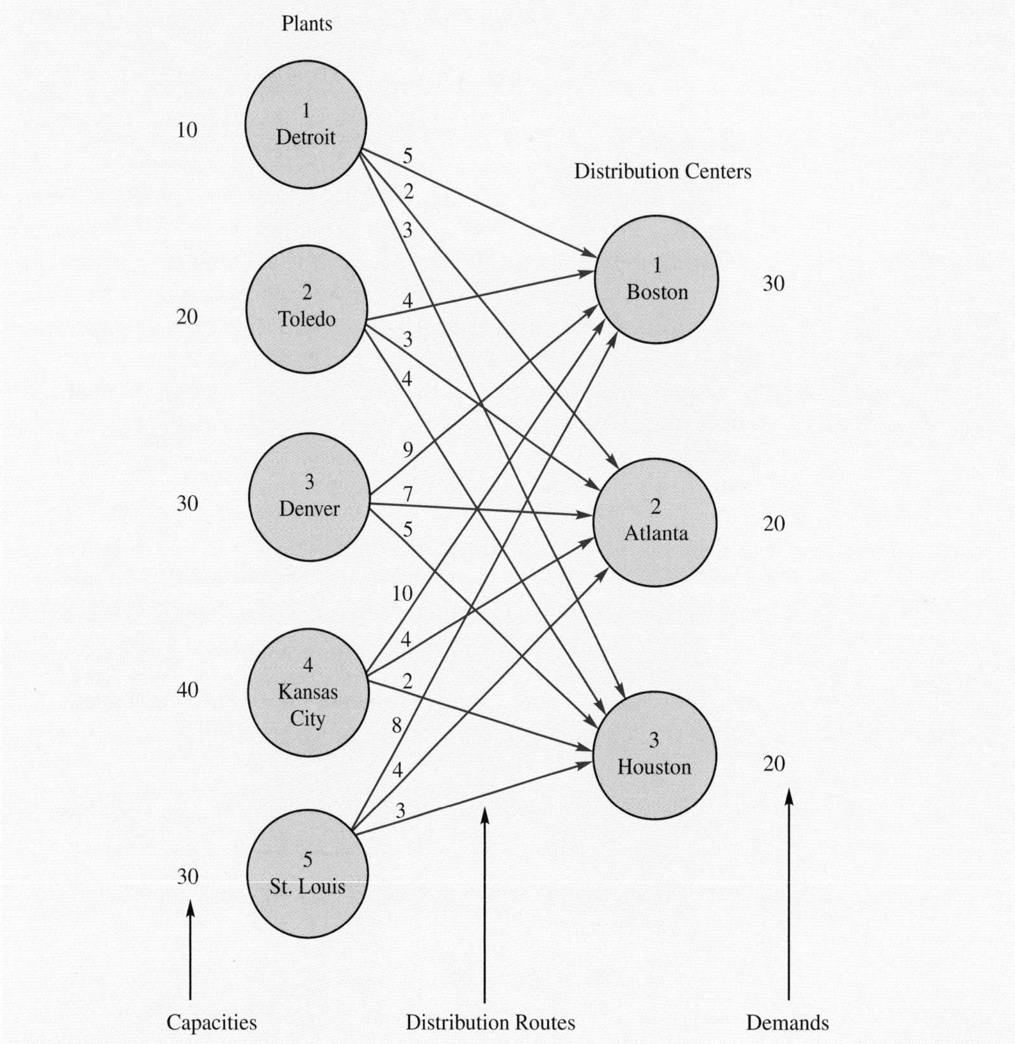

The Martin-Beck objective function is the sum of the annual transportation cost plus the annual fixed cost of operating the newly constructed plants.

Now let us consider the capacity constraints at the four proposed plants. Using Detroit as an example, we write the following constraint:

$$x_{11} + x_{12} + x_{13} \le 10y_1 \quad \text{Detroit capacity}$$

If the Detroit plant is constructed, $y_1 = 1$ and the total amount shipped from Detroit to the three distribution centers must be less than or equal to Detroit's 10,000-unit capacity. If the Detroit plant is not constructed, $y_1 = 0$ will result in a 0 capacity at Detroit. In this case, the variables corresponding to the shipments from Detroit must all equal zero: $x_{11} = 0$, $x_{12} = 0$, and $x_{13} = 0$.

In a similar fashion, the capacity constraint for the proposed plant in Toledo can be written as

$$x_{21} + x_{22} + x_{23} \le 20y_2 \quad \text{Toledo capacity}$$

Similar constraints can be written for the proposed plants in Denver and Kansas City. Note that because a plant already exists in St. Louis, we do not define a 0-1 variable for this plant. Its capacity constraint can be written as follows:

$$x_{51} + x_{52} + x_{53} \leq 30 \quad \text{St. Louis capacity}$$

Three demand constraints will be needed, one for each of the three distribution centers. The demand constraint for the Boston distribution center with units in thousands is written as

$$x_{11} + x_{21} + x_{31} + x_{51} = 30 \quad \text{Boston demand}$$

Similar constraints appear for the Atlanta and Houston distribution centers.

The complete model for the Martin-Beck distribution system design problem is as follows:

$$\text{Min } 5x_{11} + 2x_{12} + 3x_{13} + 4x_{21} + 3x_{22} + 4x_{23} + 9x_{31} + 7x_{32} + 5x_{33} + 10x_{41} + 4x_{42}$$
$$+ 2x_{43} + 8x_{51} + 4x_{52} + 3x_{53} + 175y_1 + 300y_2 + 375y_3 + 500y_4$$

s.t.

$x_{11} + x_{12} + x_{13}$	$\leq 10y_1$	Detroit capacity
$x_{21} + x_{22} + x_{23}$	$\leq 20y_2$	Toledo capacity
$x_{31} + x_{32} + x_{33}$	$\leq 30y_3$	Denver capacity
$x_{41} + x_{42} + x_{43}$	$\leq 40y_4$	Kansas City capacity
$x_{51} + x_{52} + x_{53}$	≤ 30	St. Louis capacity
$x_{11} + x_{21} + x_{31} + x_{41} + x_{51}$	$= 30$	Boston demand
$x_{12} + x_{22} + x_{32} + x_{42} + x_{52}$	$= 20$	Atlanta demand
$x_{13} + x_{23} + x_{33} + x_{43} + x_{53}$	$= 20$	Houston demand

$$x_{ij} \geq 0 \text{ for all } i \text{ and } j; \ y_1, y_2, y_3, y_4 = 0, 1$$

The solution for the Martin-Beck problem is shown in Figure 7.8. The optimal solution calls for the construction of a plant in Kansas City ($y_4 = 1$); 20,000 units will be shipped from Kansas City to Atlanta ($x_{42} = 20$), 20,000 units will be shipped from Kansas City to Houston ($x_{43} = 20$), and 30,000 units will be shipped from St. Louis to Boston ($x_{51} = 30$). Note that the total cost of this solution including the fixed cost of $500,000 for the plant in Kansas City is $860,000.

This basic model can be expanded to accommodate distribution systems involving direct shipments from plants to warehouses, from plants to retail outlets, and multiple products.[2] Using the special properties of 0-1 variables, the model can also be expanded to accommodate a variety of configuration constraints on the plant locations. For example, suppose in another problem, site 1 were in Dallas and site 2 were in Fort Worth. A company might not want to locate plants in both Dallas and Fort Worth because the cities are so close together. To *Problem 13, which is based* prevent this result from happening, the following constraint can be added to the model:

on the Martin-Beck dis-
tribution system problem,
provides additional practice
involving 0-1 variables.

$$y_1 + y_2 \leq 1$$

This constraint allows either y_1 or y_2 to equal 1, but not both. If we had written the constraints as an equality, it would require that a plant be located in either Dallas or Fort Worth.

Bank Location

The long-range planning department for the Ohio Trust Company is considering expanding its operation into a 20-county region in northeastern Ohio (see Figure 7.9). Currently,

---

[2] For computational reasons, it is usually preferable to replace the m plant capacity constraints with mn shipping route capacity constraints of the form $x_{ij} \leq \text{Min } \{s_i, d_j\} \ y_i$ for $i = 1, \ldots, m$, and $j = 1, \ldots, n$. The coefficient for y_i in each of these constraints is the smaller of the origin capacity (s_i) or the destination demand (d_j). These additional constraints often cause the solution of the LP Relaxation to be integer.

FIGURE 7.8 THE SOLUTION FOR THE MARTIN-BECK COMPANY DISTRIBUTION
SYSTEM PROBLEM

MODEL *file*

Martin-Beck

```
            Optimal Objective Value = 860.00000

              Variable                  Value
            --------------          ----------------
                X11                      0.00000
                X12                      0.00000
                X13                      0.00000
                X21                      0.00000
                X22                      0.00000
                X23                      0.00000
                X31                      0.00000
                X32                      0.00000
                X33                      0.00000
                X41                      0.00000
                X42                     20.00000
                X43                     20.00000
                X51                     30.00000
                X52                      0.00000
                X53                      0.00000
                Y1                       0.00000
                Y2                       0.00000
                Y3                       0.00000
                Y4                       1.00000

              Constraint             Slack/Surplus
            --------------          ----------------
                 1                       0.00000
                 2                       0.00000
                 3                       0.00000
                 4                       0.00000
                 5                       0.00000
                 6                       0.00000
                 7                       0.00000
                 8                       0.00000
```

Ohio Trust does not have a principal place of business (PPB) in any of the 20 counties. According to the banking laws in Ohio, if a bank establishes a PPB in any county, branch banks can be established in that county and in any adjacent county. However, to establish a new PPB, Ohio Trust must either obtain approval for a new bank from the state's superintendent of banks or purchase an existing bank.

Table 7.3 lists the 20 counties in the region and adjacent counties. For example, Ashtabula County is adjacent to Lake, Geauga, and Trumbull counties; Lake County is adjacent to Ashtabula, Cuyahoga, and Geauga counties; and so on.

As an initial step in its planning, Ohio Trust would like to determine the minimum number of PPBs necessary to do business throughout the 20-county region. A 0-1 integer programming model can be used to solve this **location problem** for Ohio Trust. We define the variables as

$$x_i = 1 \text{ if a PPB is established in county } i; 0 \text{ otherwise}$$

FIGURE 7.9   THE 20-COUNTY REGION IN NORTHEASTERN OHIO

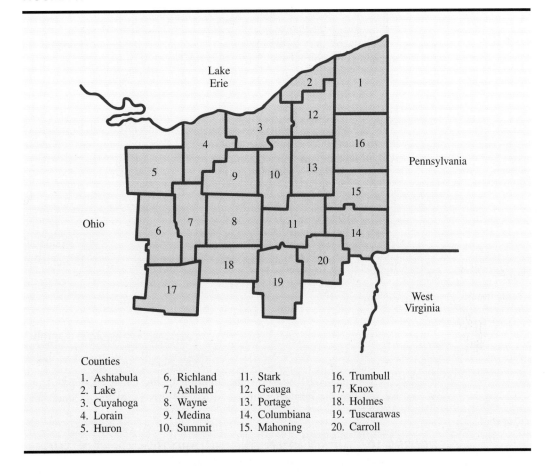

Counties

1. Ashtabula	6. Richland	11. Stark	16. Trumbull
2. Lake	7. Ashland	12. Geauga	17. Knox
3. Cuyahoga	8. Wayne	13. Portage	18. Holmes
4. Lorain	9. Medina	14. Columbiana	19. Tuscarawas
5. Huron	10. Summit	15. Mahoning	20. Carroll

TABLE 7.3   COUNTIES IN THE OHIO TRUST EXPANSION REGION

Counties Under Consideration	Adjacent Counties (by Number)
1. Ashtabula	2, 12, 16
2. Lake	1, 3, 12
3. Cuyahoga	2, 4, 9, 10, 12, 13
4. Lorain	3, 5, 7, 9
5. Huron	4, 6, 7
6. Richland	5, 7, 17
7. Ashland	4, 5, 6, 8, 9, 17, 18
8. Wayne	7, 9, 10, 11, 18
9. Medina	3, 4, 7, 8, 10
10. Summit	3, 8, 9, 11, 12, 13
11. Stark	8, 10, 13, 14, 15, 18, 19, 20
12. Geauga	1, 2, 3, 10, 13, 16
13. Portage	3, 10, 11, 12, 15, 16
14. Columbiana	11, 15, 20
15. Mahoning	11, 13, 14, 16
16. Trumbull	1, 12, 13, 15
17. Knox	6, 7, 18
18. Holmes	7, 8, 11, 17, 19
19. Tuscarawas	11, 18, 20
20. Carroll	11, 14, 19

To minimize the number of PPBs needed, we write the objective function as

$$\text{Min} \quad x_1 + x_2 + \cdots + x_{20}$$

The bank may locate branches in a county if the county contains a PPB or is adjacent to another county with a PPB. Thus, the linear program will need one constraint for each county. For example, the constraint for Ashtabula County is

$$x_1 + x_2 + x_{12} + x_{16} \geq 1 \quad \text{Ashtabula}$$

Note that satisfaction of this constraint ensures that a PPB will be placed in Ashtabula County *or* in one or more of the adjacent counties. This constraint thus guarantees that Ohio Trust will be able to place branch banks in Ashtabula County.

The complete statement of the bank location problem is

$$
\begin{aligned}
\text{Min} \quad & x_1 + x_2 + \quad \cdots \quad + x_{20} \\
\text{s.t.} \quad & \\
& x_1 + x_2 \quad + x_{12} + x_{16} \quad\quad \geq 1 \quad \text{Ashtabula} \\
& x_1 + x_2 + x_3 + x_{12} \quad\quad\quad \geq 1 \quad \text{Lake} \\
& \qquad\qquad \vdots \qquad\qquad\qquad\qquad \vdots \\
& x_{11} + x_{14} + x_{19} + x_{20} \geq 1 \quad \text{Carroll} \\
& x_i = 0, 1 \quad i = 1, 2, \ldots, 20
\end{aligned}
$$

In Figure 7.10 we show the solution to the Ohio Trust problem. Using the output, we see that the optimal solution calls for PPBs in Ashland, Stark, and Geauga counties.

FIGURE 7.10   THE SOLUTION FOR THE OHIO TRUST PPB LOCATION PROBLEM

MODEL *file*

OhioTrust

```
              Optimal Objective Value = 3.00000

                  Variable                  Value
              ---------------           ---------------
                     X1                     0.00000
                     X2                     0.00000
                     X3                     0.00000
                     X4                     0.00000
                     X5                     0.00000
                     X6                     0.00000
                     X7                     1.00000
                     X8                     0.00000
                     X9                     0.00000
                    X10                     0.00000
                    X11                     1.00000
                    X12                     1.00000
                    X13                     0.00000
                    X14                     0.00000
                    X15                     0.00000
                    X16                     0.00000
                    X17                     0.00000
                    X18                     0.00000
                    X19                     0.00000
                    X20                     0.00000
```

FIGURE 7.11   PRINCIPAL PLACE OF BUSINESS COUNTIES FOR OHIO TRUST

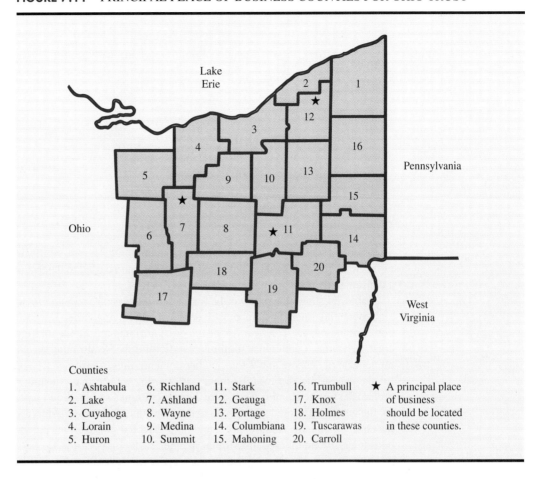

Counties

1. Ashtabula	6. Richland	11. Stark	16. Trumbull	★	A principal place
2. Lake	7. Ashland	12. Geauga	17. Knox		of business
3. Cuyahoga	8. Wayne	13. Portage	18. Holmes		should be located
4. Lorain	9. Medina	14. Columbiana	19. Tuscarawas		in these counties.
5. Huron	10. Summit	15. Mahoning	20. Carroll		

Problem 15 extends the Ohio Trust example to include all of the counties in Ohio.

With PPBs in these three counties, Ohio Trust can place branch banks in all 20 counties (see Figure 7.11). All other decision variables have an optimal value of zero, indicating that a PPB should not be placed in these counties. Clearly the integer programming model could be enlarged to allow for expansion into a larger area or throughout the entire state.

Product Design and Market Share Optimization

Conjoint analysis is a market research technique that can be used to learn how prospective buyers of a product value the product's attributes. In this section we will show how the results of conjoint analysis can be used in an integer programming model of a **product design and market share optimization problem.** We illustrate the approach by considering a problem facing Salem Foods, a major producer of frozen foods.

Salem Foods is planning to enter the frozen pizza market. Currently, two existing brands, Antonio's and King's, have the major share of the market. In trying to develop a sausage pizza that will capture a significant share of the market, Salem determined that the four most important attributes when consumers purchase a frozen sausage pizza are crust, cheese, sauce, and sausage flavor. The crust attribute has two levels (thin and thick); the cheese attribute has two levels (mozzarella and blend); the sauce attribute has two levels (smooth and chunky); and the sausage flavor attribute has three levels (mild, medium, and hot).

In a typical conjoint analysis, a sample of consumers are asked to express their preference for specially prepared pizzas with chosen levels for the attributes. Then regression analysis is used to determine the part-worth for each of the attribute levels. In essence, the part-worth is the utility value that a consumer attaches to each level of each attribute. A

TABLE 7.4   PART-WORTHS FOR THE SALEM FOODS PROBLEM

Consumer	Crust Thin	Crust Thick	Cheese Mozzarella	Cheese Blend	Sauce Smooth	Sauce Chunky	Sausage Flavor Mild	Sausage Flavor Medium	Sausage Flavor Hot
1	11	2	6	7	3	17	26	27	8
2	11	7	15	17	16	26	14	1	10
3	7	5	8	14	16	7	29	16	19
4	13	20	20	17	17	14	25	29	10
5	2	8	6	11	30	20	15	5	12
6	12	17	11	9	2	30	22	12	20
7	9	19	12	16	16	25	30	23	19
8	5	9	4	14	23	16	16	30	3

discussion of how to use regression analysis to compute the part-worths is beyond the scope of this text, but we will show how the part-worths can be used to determine the overall value a consumer attaches to a particular pizza.

Table 7.4 shows the part-worths for each level of each attribute provided by a sample of eight potential Salem customers who are currently buying either King's or Antonio's pizza. For consumer 1, the part-worths for the crust attribute are 11 for thin crust and 2 for thick crust, indicating a preference for thin crust. For the cheese attribute, the part-worths are 6 for the mozzarella cheese and 7 for the cheese blend; thus, consumer 1 has a slight preference for the cheese blend. From the other part-worths, we see that consumer 1 shows a strong preference for the chunky sauce over the smooth sauce (17 to 3) and has a slight preference for the medium-flavored sausage. Note that consumer 2 shows a preference for the thin crust, the cheese blend, the chunky sauce, and mild-flavored sausage. The part-worths for the other consumers are interpreted in a similar manner.

The part-worths can be used to determine the overall value (utility) each consumer attaches to a particular type of pizza. For instance, consumer 1's current favorite pizza is the Antonio's brand, which has a thick crust, mozzarella cheese, chunky sauce, and medium-flavored sausage. We can determine consumer 1's utility for this particular type of pizza using the part-worths in Table 7.4. For consumer 1, the part-worths are 2 for thick crust, 6 for mozzarella cheese, 17 for chunky sauce, and 27 for medium-flavored sausage. Thus, consumer 1's utility for the Antonio's brand pizza is 2 + 6 + 17 + 27 = 52. We can compute consumer 1's utility for a King's brand pizza in a similar manner. The King's brand pizza has a thin crust, a cheese blend, smooth sauce, and mild-flavored sausage. Because the part-worths for consumer 1 are 11 for thin crust, 7 for cheese blend, 3 for smooth sauce, and 26 for mild-flavored sausage, consumer 1's utility for the King's brand pizza is 11 + 7 + 3 + 26 = 47. In general, each consumer's utility for a particular type of pizza is just the sum of the appropriate part-worths.

In order to be successful with its brand, Salem Foods realizes that it must entice consumers in the marketplace to switch from their current favorite brand of pizza to the Salem product. That is, Salem must design a pizza (choose the type of crust, cheese, sauce, and sausage flavor) that will have the highest utility for enough people to ensure sufficient sales to justify making the product. Assuming the sample of eight consumers in the current study is representative of the marketplace for frozen sausage pizza, we can formulate and solve an integer programming model that can help Salem come up with such a design. In marketing literature, the problem being solved is called the *share of choices* problem.

The decision variables are defined as follows:

$$l_{ij} = 1 \text{ if Salem chooses level } i \text{ for attribute } j; 0 \text{ otherwise}$$
$$y_k = 1 \text{ if consumer } k \text{ chooses the Salem brand}; 0 \text{ otherwise}$$

The objective is to choose the levels of each attribute that will maximize the number of consumers preferring the Salem brand pizza. Because the number of customers preferring the Salem brand pizza is just the sum of the y_k variables, the objective function is

$$\text{Max } y_1 + y_2 + \cdots + y_8$$

One constraint is needed for each consumer in the sample. To illustrate how the constraints are formulated, let us consider the constraint corresponding to consumer 1. For consumer 1, the utility of a particular type of pizza can be expressed as the sum of the part-worths:

$$\text{Utility for Consumer } 1 = 11l_{11} + 2l_{21} + 6l_{12} + 7l_{22} + 3l_{13} + 17l_{23}$$
$$+ 26l_{14} + 27l_{24} + 8l_{34}$$

In order for consumer 1 to prefer the Salem pizza, the utility for the Salem pizza must be greater than the utility for consumer 1's current favorite. Recall that consumer 1's current favorite brand of pizza is Antonio's, with a utility of 52. Thus, consumer 1 will only purchase the Salem brand if the levels of the attributes for the Salem brand are chosen such that

$$11l_{11} + 2l_{21} + 6l_{12} + 7l_{22} + 3l_{13} + 17l_{23} + 26l_{14} + 27l_{24} + 8l_{34} > 52$$

Given the definitions of the y_k decision variables, we want $y_1 = 1$ when the consumer prefers the Salem brand and $y_1 = 0$ when the consumer does not prefer the Salem brand. Thus, we write the constraint for consumer 1 as follows:

$$11l_{11} + 2l_{21} + 6l_{12} + 7l_{22} + 3l_{13} + 17l_{23} + 26l_{14} + 27l_{24} + 8l_{34} \geq 1 + 52y_1$$

With this constraint, y_1 cannot equal 1 unless the utility for the Salem design (the left-hand side of the constraint) exceeds the utility for consumer 1's current favorite by at least 1. Because the objective function is to maximize the sum of the y_k variables, the optimization will seek a product design that will allow as many y_k as possible to equal 1.

A similar constraint is written for each consumer in the sample. The coefficients for the l_{ij} variables in the utility functions are taken from Table 7.4 and the coefficients for the y_k variables are obtained by computing the overall utility of the consumer's current favorite brand of pizza. The following constraints correspond to the eight consumers in the study:

Antonio's brand is the current favorite pizza for consumers 1, 4, 6, 7, and 8. King's brand is the current favorite pizza for consumers 2, 3, and 5.

$$11l_{11} + \ 2l_{21} + \ \ 6l_{12} + \ \ 7l_{22} + \ 3l_{13} + 17l_{23} + 26l_{14} + 27l_{24} + \ 8l_{34} \geq 1 + 52y_1$$
$$11l_{11} + \ 7l_{21} + \ 15l_{12} + \ 17l_{22} + 16l_{13} + 26l_{23} + 14l_{14} + \ \ 1l_{24} + 10l_{34} \geq 1 + 58y_2$$
$$\ 7l_{11} + \ 5l_{21} + \ \ 8l_{12} + \ 14l_{22} + 16l_{13} + \ 7l_{23} + 29l_{14} + 16l_{24} + 19l_{34} \geq 1 + 66y_3$$
$$13l_{11} + 20l_{21} + \ 20l_{12} + \ 17l_{22} + 17l_{13} + 14l_{23} + 25l_{14} + 29l_{24} + 10l_{34} \geq 1 + 83y_4$$
$$\ 2l_{11} + \ 8l_{21} + \ \ 6l_{12} + \ 11l_{22} + 30l_{13} + 20l_{23} + 15l_{14} + \ 5l_{24} + 12l_{34} \geq 1 + 58y_5$$
$$12l_{11} + 17l_{21} + \ 11l_{12} + \ \ 9l_{22} + \ 2l_{13} + 30l_{23} + 22l_{14} + 12l_{24} + 20l_{34} \geq 1 + 70y_6$$
$$\ 9l_{11} + 19l_{21} + \ 12l_{12} + \ 16l_{22} + 16l_{13} + 25l_{23} + 30l_{14} + 23l_{24} + 19l_{34} \geq 1 + 79y_7$$
$$\ 5l_{11} + \ 9l_{21} + \ \ 4l_{12} + \ 14l_{22} + 23l_{13} + 16l_{23} + 16l_{14} + 30l_{24} + \ 3l_{34} \geq 1 + 59y_8$$

Four more constraints must be added, one for each attribute. These constraints are necessary to ensure that one and only one level is selected for each attribute. For attribute 1 (crust), we must add the constraint

$$l_{11} + l_{21} = 1$$

Because l_{11} and l_{21} are both 0-1 variables, this constraint requires that one of the two variables equals 1 and the other equals 0. The following three constraints ensure that one and only one level is selected for each of the other three attributes:

$$l_{12} + l_{22} = 1$$
$$l_{13} + l_{23} = 1$$
$$l_{14} + l_{24} + l_{34} = 1$$

MODEL *file*

Salem

The optimal solution to this integer linear program is $l_{11} = l_{22} = l_{23} = l_{14} = 1$ and $y_1 = y_2 = y_6 = y_7 = 1$. The value of the optimal solution is 4, indicating that if Salem makes this type of pizza, it will be preferable to the current favorite for four of the eight consumers. With $l_{11} = l_{22} = l_{23} = l_{14} = 1$, the pizza design that obtains the largest market share for Salem has a thin crust, a cheese blend, a chunky sauce, and mild-flavored sausage. Note also that with $y_1 = y_2 = y_6 = y_7 = 1$, consumers 1, 2, 6, and 7 will prefer the Salem pizza. With this information Salem may choose to market this type of pizza.

NOTES AND COMMENTS

1. Most practical applications of integer linear programming involve only 0-1 integer variables. Indeed, some mixed-integer computer codes are designed to handle only integer variables with binary values. However, if a clever mathematical trick is employed, these codes can still be used for problems involving general integer variables. The trick is called *binary expansion* and requires that an upper bound be established for each integer variable. More advanced texts on integer programming show how it can be done.

2. The Management Science in Action, Optimizing the Scheduling of Automobile Crash Tests at Ford Motor Company, describes how Ford Motor company uses integer programming with 0-1 variables to schedule efficient and cost-effective crash tests to ensure vehicle safety.

3. General-purpose, mixed-integer linear programming codes and some spreadsheet packages can be used for linear programming problems, all-integer problems, and problems involving some continuous and some integer variables. General-purpose codes are seldom the fastest for solving problems with special structure (such as the transportation, assignment, and transshipment problems); however, unless the problems are very large, speed is usually not a critical issue. Thus, most practitioners prefer to use one general-purpose computer package that can be used on a variety of problems rather than to maintain a variety of computer programs designed for special problems.

MANAGEMENT SCIENCE IN ACTION

OPTIMIZING THE SCHEDULING OF AUTOMOBILE CRASH TESTS AT FORD MOTOR COMPANY*

Crash testing of automotive vehicles began in the 1930s and has without question dramatically improved the safety of automobile travel. Crash testing is destructive testing used to test the impact of automobile design and new features on vehicle safety. A variety of different crash tests are used to mimic what might happen to the vehicle on the road. These tests include frontal impact, rear and side impact as well as vehicle roll over. Every automobile manufacturer now uses crash testing to test the safety of proposed new vehicles.

Automaker Ford Motor Company, headquartered in Dearborn, Michigan, has conducted over 20,000 crash tests since 1954. To test new designs and features, Ford conducts these safety tests on prototype vehicles, which can cost over $200,000 per vehicle. Because of the cost of these prototypes and the fact that the crash testing is destructive, Ford takes a very scientific approach to prototype design and testing. This ensures that the testing process is comprehensive, effective, and cost efficient.

Due to the number of combinations of new features, designs, and the types of tests that need to be performed, the scheduling of crash tests can be quite complex. The same prototype vehicle can be used for some tests, so real efficiencies can be gained by intelligently scheduling which vehicles will be subjected to which tests and when.

Ford uses an integer programming model to solve the crash-testing scheduling problem. The models assign sequences of tests to prototype vehicles and the starting time for each test to minimize the cost of the testing. Constraints used in the model include restrictions on the timing of the tests and which tests are feasible for each vehicle. The timing constraints ensure all testing stays on schedule based on prototype availability and manufacturing schedules. The vehicle-test feasibility enforces that certain pairs of tests cannot both be performed on the same vehicle because for example, the first test renders the vehicle structurally unfit for the second test.

Pilot use of the integer programming model for scheduling the crash testing resulted in estimated annual savings of $1 million. Subsequently the approach has been used for testing a variety of vehicles including EcoSport, Mustang, Fusion, and Edge models.

*Based on D. Reich et al., "Scheduling Crash Tests at Ford Motor Company," *Interfaces* 46, no. 5, (September–October 2016): 409–423.

7.4   MODELING FLEXIBILITY PROVIDED BY 0-1 INTEGER VARIABLES

In Section 7.3 we presented four applications involving 0-1 integer variables. In this section we continue the discussion of the use of 0-1 integer variables in modeling. First, we show how 0-1 integer variables can be used to model multiple-choice and mutually exclusive constraints. Then, we show how 0-1 integer variables can be used to model situations in which k projects out of a set of n projects must be selected, as well as situations in which the acceptance of one project is conditional on the acceptance of another. We close the section with a cautionary note on the role of sensitivity analysis in integer linear programming.

Multiple-Choice and Mutually Exclusive Constraints

Recall the Ice-Cold Refrigerator capital budgeting problem introduced in Section 7.3. The decision variables were defined as

$P = 1$ if the plant expansion project is accepted; 0 if rejected
$W = 1$ if the warehouse expansion project is accepted; 0 if rejected
$M = 1$ if the new machinery project is accepted; 0 if rejected
$R = 1$ if the new product research project is accepted; 0 if rejected

Suppose that, instead of one warehouse expansion project, the Ice-Cold Refrigerator Company actually has three warehouse expansion projects under consideration. One of the warehouses *must* be expanded because of increasing product demand, but new demand is not sufficient to make expansion of more than one warehouse necessary. The following variable definitions and **multiple-choice constraint** could be incorporated into the previous 0-1 integer linear programming model to reflect this situation. Let

$W_1 = 1$ if the original warehouse expansion project is accepted; 0 if rejected
$W_2 = 1$ if the second warehouse expansion project is accepted; 0 if rejected
$W_3 = 1$ if the third warehouse expansion project is accepted; 0 if rejected

The following multiple-choice constraint reflects the requirement that exactly one of these projects must be selected:

$$W_1 + W_2 + W_3 = 1$$

If W_1, W_2, and W_3 are allowed to assume only the values 0 or 1, then one and only one of these projects will be selected from among the three choices.

If the requirement that one warehouse must be expanded did not exist, the multiple-choice constraint could be modified as follows:

$$W_1 + W_2 + W_3 \leq 1$$

This modification allows for the case of no warehouse expansion ($W_1 = W_2 = W_3 = 0$) but does not permit more than one warehouse to be expanded. This type of constraint is often called a **mutually exclusive constraint.**

k out of *n* Alternatives Constraint

An extension of the notion of a multiple-choice constraint can be used to model situations in which k *out of a set of* n projects must be selected—a *k* **out of** *n* **alternatives constraint.** Suppose that W_1, W_2, W_3, W_4, and W_5 represent five potential warehouse expansion projects and that two of the five projects must be accepted. The constraint that satisfies this new requirement is

$$W_1 + W_2 + W_3 + W_4 + W_5 = 2$$

If no more than two of the projects are to be selected, we would use the following less-than-or-equal-to constraint:

$$W_1 + W_2 + W_3 + W_4 + W_5 \leq 2$$

Again, each of these variables must be restricted to 0-1 values.

Conditional and Corequisite Constraints

Sometimes the acceptance of one project is conditional on the acceptance of another. For example, suppose for the Ice-Cold Refrigerator Company that the warehouse expansion project was conditional on the plant expansion project. That is, management will not consider expanding the warehouse unless the plant is expanded. With P representing plant expansion and W representing warehouse expansion, a **conditional constraint** could be introduced to enforce this requirement:

$$W \leq P$$

Both P and W must be 0 or 1; whenever P is 0, W will be forced to 0. When P is 1, W is also allowed to be 1; thus, both the plant and the warehouse can be expanded. However, we note that the preceding constraint does not force the warehouse expansion project (W) to be accepted if the plant expansion project (P) is accepted.

Try Problem 7 for practice with the modeling flexibility provided by 0-1 variables.

If the warehouse expansion project had to be accepted whenever the plant expansion project was, and vice versa, we would say that P and W represented **corequisite constraint** projects. To model such a situation, we simply write the preceding constraint as an equality:

$$W = P$$

The constraint forces P and W to take on the same value.

The Management Science in Action, Customer Order Allocation Model at Ketron, describes how the modeling flexibility provided by 0-1 variables helped Ketron build a customer order allocation model for a sporting goods company.

MANAGEMENT SCIENCE IN ACTION

CUSTOMER ORDER ALLOCATION MODEL AT KETRON*

Ketron Management Science provides consulting services for the design and implementation of mathematical programming applications. One such application involved the development of a mixed-integer programming model of the customer order allocation problem for a major sporting goods company. The sporting goods company markets approximately 300 products and has about 30 sources of supply (factory and warehouse locations). The problem is to determine how best to allocate customer orders to the various sources of supply such that the total manufacturing cost for the products ordered is minimized. Figure 7.12 provides a graphical representation of this problem. Note in the figure that each customer can receive shipments from only a few of the various sources of supply. For example, we see that customer 1 may be supplied by source A or B, customer 2 may be supplied only by source A, and so on.

The sporting equipment company classifies each customer order as either a "guaranteed" or "secondary" order. Guaranteed orders are single-source orders in that they must be filled by a single supplier to ensure that the complete order will be delivered to the customer at one time. This single-source requirement necessitates the use of 0-1 integer variables in the model. Approximately 80% of the company's orders are guaranteed orders. Secondary orders can be split among the various sources of supply. These orders are made by customers restocking inventory, and receiving partial shipments from different sources at different times is not a problem. The 0-1 variables are used to represent the assignment of a guaranteed order to a supplier and continuous variables are used to represent the secondary orders.

Constraints for the problem involve raw material capacities, manufacturing capacities, and individual product capacities. A fairly typical problem has about 800 constraints, 2000 0-1 assignment variables, and 500 continuous variables associated with the secondary orders. The customer order allocation problem is solved periodically as orders are received. In a typical period, between 20 and 40 customers are to be supplied. Because most customers require several products, usually between 600 and 800 orders must be assigned to the sources of supply.

*Based on information provided by J. A. Tomlin of Ketron Management Science.

A Cautionary Note About Sensitivity Analysis

Sensitivity analysis often is more crucial for integer linear programming problems than for linear programming problems. A small change in one of the coefficients in the constraints can cause a relatively large change in the value of the optimal solution. To understand why, consider the following integer programming model of a simple capital budgeting problem involving four projects and a budgetary constraint for a single time period:

$$\text{Max} \quad 40x_1 + 60x_2 + 70x_3 + 160x_4$$
$$\text{s.t.}$$
$$16x_1 + 35x_2 + 45x_3 + 85x_4 \leq 100$$
$$x_1, x_2, x_3, x_4 = 0, 1$$

We can obtain the optimal solution to this problem by enumerating the alternatives. It is $x_1 = 1$, $x_2 = 1$, $x_3 = 1$, and $x_4 = 0$, with an objective function value of $170. However, note that if the budget available is increased by $1 (from $100 to $101), the optimal solution changes to $x_1 = 1$, $x_2 = 0$, $x_3 = 0$, and $x_4 = 1$, with an objective function value of $200. That is, one additional dollar in the budget would lead to a $30 increase in the return. Surely management, when faced with such a situation, would increase the budget by $1. Because of the extreme sensitivity of the value of the optimal solution to the constraint coefficients, practitioners usually recommend re-solving the integer linear program several times with slight variations in the coefficients before attempting to choose the best solution for implementation.

FIGURE 7.12 GRAPHICAL REPRESENTATION OF THE CUSTOMER ORDER ALLOCATION PROBLEM

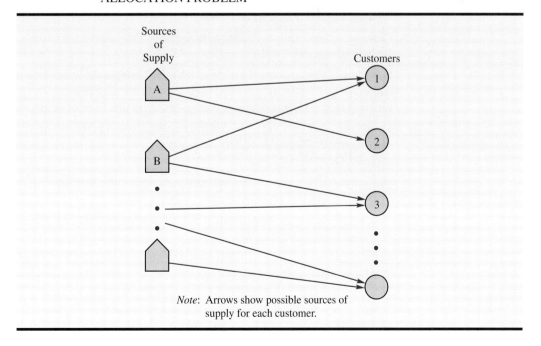

Note: Arrows show possible sources of supply for each customer.

SUMMARY

In this chapter we introduced the important extension of linear programming referred to as *integer linear programming.* The only difference between the integer linear programming problems discussed in this chapter and the linear programming problems studied in previous chapters is that one or more of the variables must be integer. If all variables must be integer, we have an all-integer linear program. If some, but not necessarily all, variables must be integer, we have a mixed-integer linear program. Most integer programming applications involve 0-1, or binary, variables.

Studying integer linear programming is important for two major reasons. First, integer linear programming may be helpful when fractional values for the variables are not permitted. Rounding a linear programming solution may not provide an optimal integer solution; methods for finding optimal integer solutions are needed when the economic consequences of rounding are significant. A second reason for studying integer linear programming is the increased modeling flexibility provided through the use of 0-1 variables. We showed how 0-1 variables could be used to model important managerial considerations in capital budgeting, fixed cost, distribution system design, bank location, and product design/market share applications.

The number of applications of integer linear programming continues to grow rapidly. This growth is due in part to the availability of good integer linear programming software packages. As researchers develop solution procedures capable of solving larger integer linear programs and as computer speed increases, a continuation of the growth of integer programming applications is expected.

GLOSSARY

0-1 integer linear program   An all-integer or mixed-integer linear program in which the integer variables are only permitted to assume the values 0 or 1. Also called *binary integer program.*

All-integer linear program   An integer linear program in which all variables are required to be integer.

Capital budgeting problem   A 0-1 integer programming problem that involves choosing which projects or activities provide the best investment return.

Conditional constraint   A constraint involving 0-1 variables that does not allow certain variables to equal 1 unless certain other variables are equal to 1.

Corequisite constraint   A constraint requiring that two 0-1 variables be equal. Thus, they are both in or out of solution together.

Distribution system design problem   A mixed-integer linear program in which the binary integer variables usually represent sites selected for warehouses or plants and continuous variables represent the amount shipped over arcs in the distribution network.

Fixed cost problem   A 0-1 mixed-integer programming problem in which the binary variables represent whether an activity, such as a production run, is undertaken (variable $= 1$) or not (variable $= 0$).

Integer linear program   A linear program with the additional requirement that one or more of the variables must be integer.

k out of n alternatives constraint   An extension of the multiple-choice constraint. This constraint requires that the sum of n 0-1 variables equal k.

Location problem   A 0-1 integer programming problem in which the objective is to select the best locations to meet a stated objective. Variations of this problem (see the bank location problem in Section 7.3) are known as covering problems.

LP Relaxation   The linear program that results from dropping the integer requirements for the variables in an integer linear program.

Mixed-integer linear program An integer linear program in which some, but not necessarily all, variables are required to be integer.

Multiple-choice constraint A constraint requiring that the sum of two or more 0-1 variables equal 1. Thus, any feasible solution makes a choice of which variable to set equal to 1.

Mutually exclusive constraint A constraint requiring that the sum of two or more 0-1 variables be less than or equal to 1. Thus, if one of the variables equals 1, the others must equal 0. However, all variables could equal 0.

Product design and market share optimization problem Sometimes called the share of choices problem, it involves choosing a product design that maximizes the number of consumers preferring it.

PROBLEMS

1. Indicate which of the following is an all-integer linear program and which is a mixed-integer linear program. Write the LP Relaxation for the problem but do not attempt to solve.

   a. Max $\quad 30x_1 + 25x_2$

      s.t.

$$3x_1 + 1.5x_2 \leq 400$$
$$1.5x_1 + 2x_2 \leq 250$$
$$1x_1 + 1x_2 \leq 150$$
$$x_1, x_2 \geq 0 \text{ and } x_2 \text{ integer}$$

   b. Min $\quad 3x_1 + 4x_2$

      s.t.

$$2x_1 + 4x_2 \geq 8$$
$$2x_1 + 6x_2 \geq 12$$
$$x_1, x_2 \geq 0 \text{ and integer}$$

 SELFtest

2. Consider the following all-integer linear program:

$$\text{Max } 5x_1 + 8x_2$$

   s.t.

$$6x_1 + 5x_2 \leq 30$$
$$9x_1 + 4x_2 \leq 36$$
$$1x_1 + 2x_2 \leq 10$$
$$x_1, x_2 \geq 0 \text{ and integer}$$

   a. Graph the constraints for this problem. Use dots to indicate all feasible integer solutions.
   b. Find the optimal solution to the LP Relaxation. Round down to find a feasible integer solution.
   c. Find the optimal integer solution. Is it the same as the solution obtained in part (b) by rounding down?

3. Consider the following all-integer linear program:

$$\text{Max } \quad 1x_1 + 1x_2$$

   s.t.

$$4x_1 + 6x_2 \leq 22$$
$$1x_1 + 5x_2 \leq 15$$
$$2x_1 + 1x_2 \leq 9$$
$$x_1, x_2 \geq 0 \text{ and integer}$$

   a. Graph the constraints for this problem. Use dots to indicate all feasible integer solutions.
   b. Solve the LP Relaxation of this problem.
   c. Find the optimal integer solution.

4. Consider the following all-integer linear program:

$$\text{Max} \quad 10x_1 + 3x_2$$
$$\text{s.t.}$$
$$6x_1 + 7x_2 \le 40$$
$$3x_1 + 1x_2 \le 11$$
$$x_1, x_2 \ge 0 \text{ and integer}$$

a. Formulate and solve the LP Relaxation of the problem. Solve it graphically, and round down to find a feasible solution. Specify an upper bound on the value of the optimal solution.

b. Solve the integer linear program graphically. Compare the value of this solution with the solution obtained in part (a).

c. Suppose the objective function changes to Max $3x_1 + 6x_2$. Repeat parts (a) and (b).

 5. Consider the following mixed-integer linear program:

$$\text{Max} \quad 2x_1 + 3x_2$$
$$\text{s.t.}$$
$$4x_1 + 9x_2 \le 36$$
$$7x_1 + 5x_2 \le 35$$
$$x_1, x_2 \ge 0 \text{ and } x_1 \text{ integer}$$

a. Graph the constraints for this problem. Indicate on your graph all feasible mixed-integer solutions.

b. Find the optimal solution to the LP Relaxation. Round the value of x_1 down to find a feasible mixed-integer solution. Is this solution optimal? Why or why not?

c. Find the optimal solution for the mixed-integer linear program.

6. Consider the following mixed-integer linear program:

$$\text{Max} \quad 1x_1 + 1x_2$$
$$\text{s.t.}$$
$$7x_1 + 9x_2 \le 63$$
$$9x_1 + 5x_2 \le 45$$
$$3x_1 + 1x_2 \le 12$$
$$x_1, x_2 \ge 0 \text{ and } x_2 \text{ integer}$$

a. Graph the constraints for this problem. Indicate on your graph all feasible mixed-integer solutions.

b. Find the optimal solution to the LP Relaxation. Round the value of x_2 down to find a feasible mixed-integer solution. Specify upper and lower bounds on the value of the optimal solution to the mixed-integer linear program.

c. Find the optimal solution to the mixed-integer linear program.

7. The following questions refer to a capital budgeting problem with six projects represented by 0-1 variables $x_1, x_2, x_3, x_4, x_5,$ and x_6:

a. Write a constraint modeling a situation in which two of the projects 1, 3, 5, and 6 must be undertaken.

b. Write a constraint modeling a situation in which, if projects 3 and 5 must be undertaken, they must be undertaken simultaneously.

c. Write a constraint modeling a situation in which project 1 or 4 must be undertaken, but not both.

d. Write constraints modeling a situation where project 4 cannot be undertaken unless projects 1 and 3 also are undertaken.

e. In addition to the requirement in part (d), assume that when projects 1 and 3 are undertaken, project 4 also must be undertaken.

8. Spencer Enterprises must choose among a series of new investment alternatives. The potential investment alternatives, the net present value of the future stream of returns, the capital requirements, and the available capital funds over the next three years are summarized as follows:

Alternative	Net Present Value ($)	Capital Requirements ($)		
		Year 1	Year 2	Year 3
Limited warehouse expansion	4,000	3,000	1,000	4,000
Extensive warehouse expansion	6,000	2,500	3,500	3,500
Test market new product	10,500	6,000	4,000	5,000
Advertising campaign	4,000	2,000	1,500	1,800
Basic research	8,000	5,000	1,000	4,000
Purchase new equipment	3,000	1,000	500	900
Capital funds available		10,500	7,000	8,750

a. Develop and solve an integer programming model for maximizing the net present value.

b. Assume that only one of the warehouse expansion projects can be implemented. Modify your model of part (a).

c. Suppose that, if test marketing of the new product is carried out, the advertising campaign also must be conducted. Modify your formulation of part (b) to reflect this new situation.

9. Hawkins Manufacturing Company produces connecting rods for 4- and 6-cylinder automobile engines using the same production line. The cost required to set up the production line to produce the 4-cylinder connecting rods is $2000, and the cost required to set up the production line for the 6-cylinder connecting rods is $3500. Manufacturing costs are $15 for each 4-cylinder connecting rod and $18 for each 6-cylinder connecting rod. Hawkins makes a decision at the end of each week as to which product will be manufactured the following week. If a production changeover is necessary from one week to the next, the weekend is used to reconfigure the production line. Once the line has been set up, the weekly production capacities are 6000 6-cylinder connecting rods and 8000 4-cylinder connecting rods. Let

x_4 = the number of 4-cylinder connecting rods produced next week

x_6 = the number of 6-cylinder connecting rods produced next week

s_4 = 1 if the production line is set up to produce the 4-cylinder connecting rods; 0 if otherwise

s_6 = 1 if the production line is set up to produce the 6-cylinder connecting rods; 0 if otherwise

a. Using the decision variables x_4 and s_4, write a constraint that limits next week's production of the 4-cylinder connecting rods to either 0 or 8000 units.

b. Using the decision variables x_6 and s_6, write a constraint that limits next week's production of the 6-cylinder connecting rods to either 0 or 6000 units.

c. Write three constraints that, taken together, limit the production of connecting rods for next week.

d. Write an objective function for minimizing the cost of production for next week.

10. Grave City is considering the relocation of several police substations to obtain better enforcement in high-crime areas. The locations under consideration together with the areas that can be covered from these locations are given in the following table:

Potential Locations for Substations	Areas Covered
A	1, 5, 7
B	1, 2, 5, 7
C	1, 3, 5
D	2, 4, 5
E	3, 4, 6
F	4, 5, 6
G	1, 5, 6, 7

a. Formulate an integer programming model that could be used to find the minimum number of locations necessary to provide coverage to all areas.
b. Solve the problem in part (a).

11. Hart Manufacturing makes three products. Each product requires manufacturing operations in three departments: A, B, and C. The labor-hour requirements, by department, are as follows:

Department	Product 1	Product 2	Product 3
A	1.50	3.00	2.00
B	2.00	1.00	2.50
C	0.25	0.25	0.25

During the next production period, the labor-hours available are 450 in department A, 350 in department B, and 50 in department C. The profit contributions per unit are $25 for product 1, $28 for product 2, and $30 for product 3.

a. Formulate a linear programming model for maximizing total profit contribution.
b. Solve the linear program formulated in part (a). How much of each product should be produced, and what is the projected total profit contribution?
c. After evaluating the solution obtained in part (b), one of the production supervisors noted that production setup costs had not been taken into account. She noted that setup costs are $400 for product 1, $550 for product 2, and $600 for product 3. If the solution developed in part (b) is to be used, what is the total profit contribution after taking into account the setup costs?
d. Management realized that the optimal product mix, taking setup costs into account, might be different from the one recommended in part (b). Formulate a mixed-integer linear program that takes setup costs into account. Management also stated that we should not consider making more than 175 units of product 1, 150 units of product 2, or 140 units of product 3.
e. Solve the mixed-integer linear program formulated in part (d). How much of each product should be produced, and what is the projected total profit contribution? Compare this profit contribution to that obtained in part (c).

12. Offhaus Manufacturing produces office supplies but outsources the delivery of its products to third-party carriers. Offhaus ships to 20 cities from its Dayton, Ohio, manufacturing facility and has asked a variety of carriers to bid on its business. Seven carriers have responded with bids. The resulting bids (in dollars per truckload) are shown in the table. For example, the table shows that carrier 1 bid on the business to cities 11–20. The right side of the table provides the number of truckloads scheduled for each destination in the next quarter.

Bid $/Truckload	Carrier 1	Carrier 2	Carrier 3	Carrier 4	Carrier 5	Carrier 6	Carrier 7	Destination	Demand (Truckloads)
City 1					$2188	$1666	$1790	City 1	30
City 2		$1453			$2602	$1767		City 2	10
City 3		$1534			$2283	$1857	$1870	City 3	20
City 4		$1687			$2617	$1738		City 4	40
City 5		$1523			$2239	$1771	$1855	City 5	10
City 6		$1521			$1571		$1545	City 6	10
City 7		$2100		$1922	$1938		$2050	City 7	12
City 8		$1800		$1432	$1416		$1739	City 8	25
City 9		$1134		$1233	$1181		$1150	City 9	25
City 10		$672		$610	$669		$678	City 10	33
City 11	$724		$723	$627	$657		$706	City 11	11
City 12	$766		$766	$721	$682		$733	City 12	29
City 13	$741		$745		$682		$733	City 13	12
City 14	$815	$800	$828		$745		$832	City 14	24
City 15	$904		$880		$891		$914	City 15	10
City 16	$958		$933		$891		$914	City 16	10
City 17	$925		$929		$937		$984	City 17	23
City 18	$892		$869	$822	$829		$864	City 18	25
City 19	$927		$969		$967		$1008	City 19	12
City 20	$963		$938		$955		$995	City 20	10
Number of Bids	10	10	10	7	20	5	18		

DATA file

Offhaus

Because dealing with too many carriers can be cumbersome, Offhaus would like to limit the number of carriers it uses to three. Also, for customer relationship reasons, Offhaus wants each city to be assigned to only one carrier (that is, there is no splitting of the demand to a given city across carriers).

a. Develop a model that will yield the three selected carriers and the city-carrier assignments that minimize the cost of shipping. Solve the model and report the solution.

b. Offhaus is not sure whether three is the correct number of carriers to select. Run the model you developed in part (a) for allowable carriers varying from 1 up to 7. Based on your results, how many carriers would you recommend and why?

 SELF*test*

13. Recall the Martin-Beck Company distribution system problem in Section 7.3.

a. Modify the formulation shown in Section 7.3 to account for the policy restriction that one plant, but not two, must be located either in Detroit or in Toledo.

b. Modify the formulation shown in Section 7.3 to account for the policy restriction that no more than two plants can be located in Denver, Kansas City, and St. Louis.

14. An automobile manufacturer has five outdated plants: one each in Michigan, Ohio, and California and two in New York. Management is considering modernizing these plants to manufacture engine blocks and transmissions for a new model car. The cost to modernize each plant and the manufacturing capacity after modernization are as follows:

Plant	Cost ($ millions)	Engine Blocks (1000s)	Transmissions (1000s)
Michigan	25	500	300
New York	35	800	400
New York	35	400	800
Ohio	40	900	600
California	20	200	300

The projected needs are for total capacities of 900,000 engine blocks and 900,000 transmissions. Management wants to determine which plants to modernize to meet projected manufacturing needs and, at the same time, minimize the total cost of modernization.

   a. Develop a table that lists every possible option available to management. As part of your table, indicate the total engine block capacity and transmission capacity for each possible option, whether the option is feasible based on the projected needs, and the total modernization cost for each option.

   b. Based on your analysis in part (a), what recommendation would you provide management?

   c. Formulate a 0-1 integer programming model that could be used to determine the optimal solution to the modernization question facing management.

   d. Solve the model formulated in part (c) to provide a recommendation for management.

DATA *file*

OhioTrustFull

15. Consider again the Ohio Trust bank location problem discussed in Section 7.3. The file *OhioTrustFull* contains data for all of Ohio's 88 counties. The file contains an 88 × 88 matrix with the rows and columns each being the 88 counties. The entries in the matrix are zeros and ones and indicate if the county of the row shares a border with the county of the column (1 = yes and 0 = no).

   a. Create a model to find the location of required principal places of business (PPBs) to minimize the number of PPBs needed to open all counties to branches.

   b. Solve the model constructed in part (a). What is the minimum number PPBs needed to open up the entire state to Ohio Trust branches?

16. The Northshore Bank is working to develop an efficient work schedule for full-time and part-time tellers. The schedule must provide for efficient operation of the bank including adequate customer service, employee breaks, and so on. On Fridays the bank is open from 9:00 A.M. to 7:00 P.M. The number of tellers necessary to provide adequate customer service during each hour of operation is summarized here.

Time	Number of Tellers	Time	Number of Tellers
9:00 A.M.–10:00 A.M.	6	2:00 P.M.–3:00 P.M.	6
10:00 A.M.–11:00 A.M.	4	3:00 P.M.–4:00 P.M.	4
11:00 A.M.–Noon	8	4:00 P.M.–5:00 P.M.	7
Noon–1:00 P.M.	10	5:00 P.M.–6:00 P.M.	6
1:00 P.M.–2:00 P.M.	9	6:00 P.M.–7:00 P.M.	6

Each full-time employee starts on the hour and works a 4-hour shift, followed by 1 hour for lunch and then a 3-hour shift. Part-time employees work one 4-hour shift beginning on the hour. Considering salary and fringe benefits, full-time employees cost the bank $15 per hour ($105 a day), and part-time employees cost the bank $8 per hour ($32 per day).

   a. Formulate an integer programming model that can be used to develop a schedule that will satisfy customer service needs at a minimum employee cost. (*Hint:* Let x_i = number of full-time employees coming on duty at the beginning of hour i and y_i = number of part-time employees coming on duty at the beginning of hour i.)

   b. Solve the LP Relaxation of your model in part (a).

   c. Solve for the optimal schedule of tellers. Comment on the solution.

   d. After reviewing the solution to part (c), the bank manager realized that some additional requirements must be specified. Specifically, she wants to ensure that one full-time employee is on duty at all times and that there is a staff of at least five full-time employees. Revise your model to incorporate these additional requirements and solve for the optimal solution.

DATA *file*

OhioTrustPop

17. Consider again the Ohio Trust problem described in Problem 15. Suppose only a limited number of PPBs can be placed. Ohio Trust would like to place this limited number of PPBs in counties so that the allowable branches can reach the maximum possible population. The

file *OhioTrustPop* contains the county adjacency matrix described in Problem 15 as well as the population of each county.

    a. Assume that only a fixed number of PPBs, denoted k, can be established. Formulate a linear binary integer program that will tell Ohio Trust where to locate the fixed number of PPBs in order to maximize the population reached. (*Hint:* Introduce variable $y_i = 1$ if it is possible to establish a branch in county i, and $y_i = 0$ otherwise; that is, if county i is covered by a PPB, then the population can be counted as covered.)

    b. Suppose that two PPBs can be established. Where should they be located to maximize the population served?

    c. Solve your model from part (a) for allowable number of PPBs ranging from 1 to 10. In other words, solve the model 10 times, with k set to 1, 2, ..., 10. Record the population reached for each value of k. Graph the results by plotting the population reached versus number of PPBs allowed. Based on their cost calculations, Ohio Trust considers an additional PPB to be a fiscally prudent only if it increases the population reached by at least 500,000 people. Based on this graph, what is the number of PPBs you recommend to be implemented?

18. Refer to the Salem Foods share of choices problem in Section 7.3 and address the following issues. It is rumored that King's is getting out of the frozen pizza business. If so, the major competitor for Salem Foods will be the Antonio's brand pizza.

    a. Compute the overall utility for the Antonio's brand pizza for each of the consumers in Table 7.4.

    b. Assume that Salem's only competitor is the Antonio's brand pizza. Formulate and solve the share of choices problem that will maximize market share. What is the best product design and what share of the market can be expected?

19. Burnside Marketing Research conducted a study for Barker Foods on some designs for a new dry cereal. Three attributes were found to be most influential in determining which cereal had the best taste: ratio of wheat to corn in the cereal flake, type of sweetener (sugar, honey, or artificial), and the presence or absence of flavor bits. Seven children participated in taste tests and provided the following part-worths for the attributes:

Child	Wheat/Corn		Sweetener			Flavor Bits	
	Low	High	Sugar	Honey	Artificial	Present	Absent
1	15	35	30	40	25	15	9
2	30	20	40	35	35	8	11
3	40	25	20	40	10	7	14
4	35	30	25	20	30	15	18
5	25	40	40	20	35	18	14
6	20	25	20	35	30	9	16
7	30	15	25	40	40	20	11

    a. Suppose the overall utility (sum of part-worths) of the current favorite cereal is 75 for each child. What is the product design that will maximize the share of choices for the seven children in the sample?

    b. Assume the overall utility of the current favorite cereal for the first four children in the group is 70, and the overall utility of the current favorite cereal for the last three children in the group is 80. What is the product design that will maximize the share of choices for the seven children in the sample?

20. Refer to Problem 14. Suppose that management determined that its cost estimates to modernize the New York plants were too low. Specifically, suppose that the actual cost is $40 million to modernize each plant.

    a. What changes in your previous 0-1 integer linear programming model are needed to incorporate these changes in costs?

    b. For these cost changes, what recommendations would you now provide management regarding the modernization plan?

c. Reconsider the solution obtained using the revised cost figures. Suppose that management decides that closing two plants in the same state is not acceptable. How could this policy restriction be added to your 0-1 integer programming model?

d. Based on the cost revision and the policy restriction presented in part (c), what recommendations would you now provide management regarding the modernization plan?

21. The Bayside Art Gallery is considering installing a video camera security system to reduce its insurance premiums. A diagram of the eight display rooms that Bayside uses for exhibitions is shown in Figure 7.13; the openings between the rooms are numbered 1 through 13. A security firm proposed that two-way cameras be installed at some room openings. Each camera has the ability to monitor the two rooms between which the camera is located. For example, if a camera were located at opening number 4, rooms 1 and 4 would be covered; if a camera were located at opening 11, rooms 7 and 8 would be covered; and so on. Management decided not to locate a camera system at the entrance to the display rooms. The

FIGURE 7.13 DIAGRAM OF DISPLAY ROOMS FOR BAYSIDE ART GALLERY

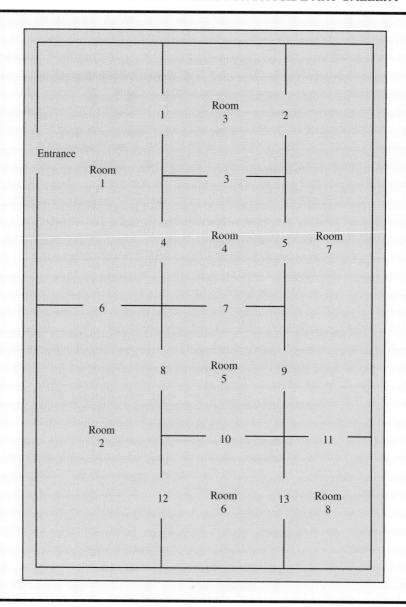

objective is to provide security coverage for all eight rooms using the minimum number of two-way cameras.

a. Formulate a 0-1 integer linear programming model that will enable Bayside's management to determine the locations for the camera systems.

b. Solve the model formulated in part (a) to determine how many two-way cameras to purchase and where they should be located.

c. Suppose that management wants to provide additional security coverage for room 7. Specifically, management wants room 7 to be covered by two cameras. How would your model formulated in part (a) have to change to accommodate this policy restriction?

d. With the policy restriction specified in part (c), determine how many two-way camera systems will need to be purchased and where they will be located.

22. The Delta Group is a management consulting firm specializing in the health care industry. A team is being formed to study possible new markets, and a linear programming model has been developed for selecting team members. However, one constraint the president imposed is a team size of three, five, or seven members. The staff cannot figure out how to incorporate this requirement in the model. The current model requires that team members be selected from three departments and uses the following variable definitions:

$$x_1 = \text{the number of employees selected from department 1}$$
$$x_2 = \text{the number of employees selected from department 2}$$
$$x_3 = \text{the number of employees selected from department 3}$$

Show the staff how to write constraints that will ensure that the team will consist of three, five, or seven employees. The following integer variables should be helpful:

$$y_1 = \begin{cases} 1 & \text{if team size is 3} \\ 0 & \text{otherwise} \end{cases}$$

$$y_2 = \begin{cases} 1 & \text{if team size is 5} \\ 0 & \text{otherwise} \end{cases}$$

$$y_3 = \begin{cases} 1 & \text{if team size is 7} \\ 0 & \text{otherwise} \end{cases}$$

23. Roedel Electronics produces a variety of electrical components, including a remote controller for televisions and a remote controller for DVRs. Each controller consists of three subassemblies that are manufactured by Roedel: a base, a cartridge, and a keypad. Both controllers use the same base subassembly, but different cartridge and keypad subassemblies.

Roedel's sales forecast indicates that 7000 TV controllers and 5000 DVR controllers will be needed to satisfy demand during the upcoming Christmas season. Because only 500 hours of in-house manufacturing time are available, Roedel is considering purchasing some, or all, of the subassemblies from outside suppliers. If Roedel manufactures a subassembly in-house, it incurs a fixed setup cost as well as a variable manufacturing cost. The following table shows the setup cost, the manufacturing time per subassembly, the manufacturing cost per subassembly, and the cost to purchase each of the subassemblies from an outside supplier:

Subassembly	Setup Cost ($)	Manufacturing Time per Unit (min.)	Manufacturing Cost per Unit ($)	Purchase Cost per Unit ($)
Base	1000	0.9	0.40	0.65
TV cartridge	1200	2.2	2.90	3.45
DVR cartridge	1900	3.0	3.15	3.70
TV keypad	1500	0.8	0.30	0.50
DVR keypad	1500	1.0	0.55	0.70

a. Determine how many units of each subassembly Roedel should manufacture and how many units Roedel should purchase. What is the total manufacturing and purchase cost associated with your recommendation?

b. Suppose Roedel is considering purchasing new machinery to produce DVR cartridges. For the new machinery, the setup cost is $3000; the manufacturing time is 2.5 minutes per cartridge, and the manufacturing cost is $2.60 per cartridge. Assuming that the new machinery is purchased, determine how many units of each subassembly Roedel should manufacture and how many units of each subassembly Roedel should purchase. What is the total manufacturing and purchase cost associated with your recommendation? Do you think the new machinery should be purchased? Explain.

24. Dave has $100,000 to invest in 10 mutual fund alternatives with the following restrictions. For diversification, no more than $25,000 can be invested in any one fund. If a fund is chosen for investment, then at least $10,000 will be invested in it. No more than two of the funds can be pure growth funds, and at least one pure bond fund must be selected. The total amount invested in pure bond funds must be at least as much as the amount invested in pure growth funds. Using the following expected annual returns, formulate and solve a model that will determine the investment strategy that will maximize expected annual return. What assumptions have you made in your model? How often would you expect to run your model?

DATA *file*

DaveMutualFunds

Fund	Type	Expected Annual Return (%)
1	Growth	6.70
2	Growth	7.65
3	Growth	7.55
4	Growth	7.45
5	Growth & Income	7.50
6	Growth & Income	6.45
7	Growth & Income	7.05
8	Stock & Bond	6.90
9	Bond	5.20
10	Bond	5.90

25. East Coast Trucking provides service from Boston to Miami using regional offices located in Boston, New York, Philadelphia, Baltimore, Washington, Richmond, Raleigh, Florence, Savannah, Jacksonville, and Tampa. The number of miles between each of the regional offices is provided in the following table:

	New York	Philadelphia	Baltimore	Washington	Richmond	Raleigh	Florence	Savannah	Jacksonville	Tampa	Miami
Boston	211	320	424	459	565	713	884	1056	1196	1399	1669
New York		109	213	248	354	502	673	845	985	1188	1458
Philadelphia			104	139	245	393	564	736	876	1079	1349
Baltimore				35	141	289	460	632	772	975	1245
Washington					106	254	425	597	737	940	1210
Richmond						148	319	491	631	834	1104
Raleigh							171	343	483	686	956
Florence								172	312	515	785
Savannah									140	343	613
Jacksonville										203	473
Tampa											270

The company's expansion plans involve constructing service facilities in some of the cities where a regional office is located. Each regional office must be within 400 miles of a service facility. For instance, if a service facility is constructed in Richmond, it can provide service to regional offices located in New York, Philadelphia, Baltimore, Washington, Richmond, Raleigh, and Florence. Management would like to determine the minimum number of service facilities needed and where they should be located.

a. Formulate an integer linear program that can be used to determine the minimum number of service facilities needed and their location.
b. Solve the linear program formulated in part (a). How many service facilities are required, and where should they be located?
c. Suppose that each service facility can only provide service to regional offices within 300 miles. How many service facilities are required, and where should they be located?

Case Problem 1 TEXTBOOK PUBLISHING

ASW Publishing, Inc., a small publisher of college textbooks, must make a decision regarding which books to publish next year. The books under consideration are listed in the following table, along with the projected three-year sales expected from each book:

Book Subject	Type of Book	Projected Sales ($1000s)
Business calculus	New	20
Finite mathematics	Revision	30
General statistics	New	15
Mathematical statistics	New	10
Business statistics	Revision	25
Finance	New	18
Financial accounting	New	25
Managerial accounting	Revision	50
English literature	New	20
German	New	30

The books listed as revisions are texts that ASW already has under contract; these texts are being considered for publication as new editions. The books that are listed as new have been reviewed by the company, but contracts have not yet been signed.

Three individuals in the company can be assigned to these projects, all of whom have varying amounts of time available; John has 60 days available, and Susan and Monica both have 40 days available. The days required by each person to complete each project are shown in the following table. For instance, if the business calculus book is published, it will require 30 days of John's time and 40 days of Susan's time. An "X" indicates that the person will not be used on the project. Note that at least two staff members will be assigned to each project except the finance book.

Book Subject	John	Susan	Monica
Business calculus	30	40	X
Finite mathematics	16	24	X
General statistics	24	X	30
Mathematical statistics	20	X	24
Business statistics	10	X	16
Finance	X	X	14
Financial accounting	X	24	26
Managerial accounting	X	28	30
English literature	40	34	30
German	X	50	36

ASW will not publish more than two statistics books or more than one accounting text in a single year. In addition, management decided that one of the mathematics books (business calculus or finite math) must be published, but not both.

Managerial Report

Prepare a report for the managing editor of ASW that describes your findings and recommendations regarding the best publication strategy for next year. In carrying out your analysis, assume that the fixed costs and the sales revenues per unit are approximately equal for all books; management is interested primarily in maximizing the total unit sales volume.

The managing editor also asked that you include recommendations regarding the following possible changes:

1. If it would be advantageous to do so, Susan can be moved off another project to allow her to work 12 more days.
2. If it would be advantageous to do so, Monica can also be made available for another 10 days.
3. If one or more of the revisions could be postponed for another year, should they be? Clearly the company will risk losing market share by postponing a revision.

Include details of your analysis in an appendix to your report.

Case Problem 2   YEAGER NATIONAL BANK

Using aggressive mail promotion with low introductory interest rates, Yeager National Bank (YNB) built a large base of credit card customers throughout the continental United States. Currently, customers who mail their payments to YNB send their regular payments to the bank's corporate office located in Charlotte, North Carolina. Daily collections from customers making their regular payments are substantial, with an average of approximately $600,000. YNB estimates that it makes about 15% on its funds and would like to ensure that customer payments are credited to the bank's account as soon as possible. For instance, if it takes five days for a customer's payment to be sent through the mail, processed, and credited to the bank's account, YNB has potentially lost five days' worth of interest income. Although the time needed for this collection process cannot be completely eliminated, reducing it can be beneficial given the large amounts of money involved.

Instead of having all its credit card customers send their payments to Charlotte, YNB is considering having customers send their payments to one or more regional collection centers, referred to in the banking industry as lockboxes. Four lockbox locations have been proposed: Phoenix, Salt Lake City, Atlanta, and Boston. To determine which lockboxes to open and where lockbox customers should send their payments, YNB divided its customer base into five geographical regions: Northwest, Southwest, Central, Northeast, and Southeast. Every customer in the same region will be instructed to send his or her payment to the same lockbox. The following table shows the average number of days it takes before a customer's payment is credited to the bank's account when the payment is sent from each of the regions to each of the potential lockboxes:

Customer Zone	Location of Lockbox				Daily Collection ($1000s)
	Phoenix	Salt Lake City	Atlanta	Boston	
Northwest	4	2	4	4	80
Southwest	2	3	4	6	90
Central	5	3	3	4	150
Northeast	5	4	3	2	180
Southeast	4	6	2	3	100

Managerial Report

Dave Wolff, the vice president for cash management, asked you to prepare a report containing your recommendations for the number of lockboxes and the best lockbox locations. Mr. Wolff is primarily concerned with minimizing lost interest income, but he wants you to also consider the effect of an annual fee charged for maintaining a lockbox at any location. Although the amount of the fee is unknown at this time, we can assume that the fees will be in the range of $20,000 to $30,000 per location. Once good potential locations have been selected, Mr. Wolff will inquire as to the annual fees.

Case Problem 3   PRODUCTION SCHEDULING WITH CHANGEOVER COSTS

Buckeye Manufacturing produces heads for engines used in the manufacture of trucks. The production line is highly complex, and it measures 900 feet in length. Two types of engine heads are produced on this line: the P-Head and the H-Head. The P-Head is used in heavy-duty trucks and the H-Head is used in smaller trucks. Because only one type of head can be produced at a time, the line is set up to manufacture either the P-Head or the H-Head, but not both. Changeovers are made over a weekend; costs are $500 in going from a setup for the P-Head to a setup for the H-Head, and vice versa. When set up for the P-Head, the maximum production rate is 100 units per week and when set up for the H-Head, the maximum production rate is 80 units per week.

Buckeye just shut down for the week after using the line to produce the P-Head. The manager wants to plan production and changeovers for the next eight weeks. Currently, Buckeye's inventory consists of 125 P-Heads and 143 H-Heads. Inventory carrying costs are charged at an annual rate of 19.5% of the value of inventory. The production cost for the P-Head is $225, and the production cost for the H-Head is $310. The objective in developing a production schedule is to minimize the sum of production cost, plus inventory carrying cost, plus changeover cost.

Buckeye received the following requirements schedule from its customer (an engine assembly plant) for the next nine weeks:

	Product Demand	
Week	**P-Head**	**H-Head**
1	55	38
2	55	38
3	44	30
4	0	0
5	45	48
6	45	48
7	36	58
8	35	57
9	35	58

Safety stock requirements are such that week-ending inventory must provide for at least 80% of the next week's demand.

Managerial Report

Prepare a report for Buckeye's management with a production and changeover schedule for the next eight weeks. Be sure to note how much of the total cost is due to production, how much is due to inventory, and how much is due to changeover.

Case Problem 4   APPLECORE CHILDREN'S CLOTHING

Applecore Children's Clothing is a retailer that sells high-end clothes for toddlers (ages 1–3) primarily in shopping malls. Applecore also has a successful Internet-based sales division. Recently Dave Walker, vice president of the e-commerce division, has been given the directive to expand the company's Internet sales. He commissioned a major study on the effectiveness of Internet ads placed on news websites. The results were favorable: Current patrons who purchased via the Internet and saw the ads on news websites spent more, on average, than did comparable Internet customers who did not see the ads.

With this new information on Internet ads, Walker continued to investigate how new Internet customers could most effectively be reached. One of these ideas involved strategically purchasing ads on news websites prior to and during the holiday season. To determine which news sites might be the most effective for ads, Walker conducted a follow-up study. An e-mail questionnaire was administered to a sample of 1200 current Internet customers to ascertain which of 30 news sites they regularly visit. The idea is that websites with high proportions of current customer visits would be viable sources of future customers of Applecore products.

Walker would like to ascertain which news sites should be selected for ads. The problem is complicated because Walker does not want to count multiple exposures. So, if a respondent visits mutiple sites with Applecore ads or visits a given site multiple times, that respondent should be counted as reached but not more than once. In other words, a customer is considered reached if he or she has visited at least one website with an Applecore ad.

Data from the customer e-mail survey have begun to trickle in. Walker wants to develop a prototype model based on the current survey results. So far, 53 surveys have been returned. To keep the prototype model manageable, Walker wants to proceed with model development using the data from the 53 returned surveys and using only the first ten news sites in the questionnaire. The costs of ads per week for the ten websites are given in the following table, and the budget is $10,000 per week. For each of the 53 responses received, which of the ten websites are regularly visited is given as shown below. For a given customer–website pair, a one indicates that the customer regularly visits that website, and a zero indicates that the customer does not regularly visit that site.

Data for Applecore Customer Visits to News Websites (respondents 5–33 hidden)

	Website									
	1	2	3	4	5	6	7	8	9	10
Cost/Wk ($000)	$5.0	$8.0	$3.5	$5.5	$7.0	$4.5	$6.0	$5.0	$3.0	$2.2
	Website									
Customer	1	2	3	4	5	6	7	8	9	10
1	0	0	0	0	0	0	0	0	0	1
2	1	0	0	1	0	0	0	0	0	0
3	1	0	0	0	0	0	0	0	0	0
4	0	0	0	0	1	1	0	0	0	0
34	0	0	0	1	1	0	0	0	0	0
35	1	0	0	0	1	1	0	0	0	0
36	1	0	1	0	0	0	0	0	0	0
37	0	0	1	0	1	0	0	1	0	0
38	0	0	1	0	0	0	0	0	0	0
39	0	1	0	0	0	0	1	0	0	0
40	0	1	0	0	0	0	1	0	0	0
41	0	0	0	0	0	0	1	0	0	0
42	0	0	0	1	1	1	0	0	0	0
43	0	0	0	0	0	0	0	0	0	0
44	0	0	0	0	1	0	0	0	0	1
45	1	1	0	0	0	0	0	0	0	0
46	0	0	0	0	0	0	1	0	0	0
47	1	0	0	0	1	0	0	0	0	1
48	0	0	1	0	0	0	0	0	0	0
49	1	0	1	1	0	0	0	0	0	0
50	0	0	0	0	0	0	0	0	0	0
51	0	1	0	0	0	1	0	0	0	0
52	0	0	0	0	0	0	0	0	0	0
53	0	1	0	0	1	0	0	1	1	1

DATA *file*

Applecore

Managerial Report:

1. Develop a model that will allow Applecore to maximize the number of customers reached for a budget of $10,000 for one week of promotion.
2. Solve the model. What is the maximum number of customers reached for the $10,000 budget?
3. Perform a sensitivity analysis on the budget for values from $5000 to $35,000 in increments of $5000. Construct a graph of percentage reach versus budget. Is the additional increase in percentage reach monotonically decreasing as the budget allocation increases? Why or why not? What is your recommended budget? Explain.

Appendix 7.1   EXCEL SOLUTION OF INTEGER LINEAR PROGRAMS

Worksheet formulation and solution for integer linear programs are similar to that for linear programming problems. Actually the worksheet formulation is exactly the same, but additional information must be provided when setting up the **Solver Parameters** dialog box. In the **Solver Parameters** dialog box it is necessary to identify the integer variables. The user should also be aware of settings related to integer linear programming in the **Solver Options** dialog box.

Let us demonstrate the Excel solution of an integer linear program by showing how Excel can be used to solve the Eastborne Realty problem. The worksheet with the optimal solution is shown in Figure 7.14. We will describe the key elements of the worksheet and how to obtain the solution, and then interpret the solution.

Formulation

The data and descriptive labels appear in cells A1:G7 of the worksheet in Figure 7.14. The screened cells in the lower portion of the worksheet contain the information required by the Excel Solver (decision variables, objective function, constraint left-hand sides, and constraint right-hand sides).

Decision Variables   Cells B17:C17 are reserved for the decision variables. The optimal solution is to purchase four townhouses and two apartment buildings.

FIGURE 7.14   EXCEL SOLUTION FOR THE EASTBORNE REALTY PROBLEM

MODEL _file_

Eastborne

	A	B	C	D	E	F	G	H
1	**Eastborne Realty Problem**							
2								
3		Townhouse	Apt. Bldg.					
4	Price($1000s)	282	400		**Funds Avl.($1000s)**		2000	
5	Mgr. Time	4	40		**Mgr. Time Avl.**		140	
6					**Townhouses Avl.**		5	
7	Ann. Cash Flow ($1000s)	10	15					
8								
9								
10	**Model**							
11								
12								
13	**Max Cash Flow**	70						
14					**Constraints**	**LHS**		**RHS**
15		**Number of**			Funds	1928	<=	2000
16		Townhouses	Apt. Bldgs.		Time	96	<=	140
17	**Purchase Plan**	4	2		Townhouses	4	<=	5
18								

Objective Function   The formula =SUMPRODUCT(B7:C7,B17:C17) has been placed into cell B13 to reflect the annual cash flow associated with the solution. The optimal solution provides an annual cash flow of $70,000.

Left-Hand Sides   The left-hand sides for the three constraints are placed into cells F15:F17.

    Cell F15 =SUMPRODUCT(B4:C4,$B$17:$C$17)

        (Copy to cell F16)

    Cell F17 =B17

Right-Hand Sides   The right-hand sides for the three constraints are placed into cells H15:H17.

      Cell H15 =G4 (Copy to cells H16:H17)

Excel Solution

Begin the solution procedure by selecting the **Data** tab and **Solver** from the **Analyze** group, and entering the proper values into the **Solver Parameters** dialog box as shown in Figure 7.15. The first constraint shown is $B$17:$C$17 = integer. This constraint tells Solver that the decision variables in cell B17 and cell C17 must be integer.

FIGURE 7.15   SOLVER PARAMETERS DIALOG BOX FOR THE EASTBORNE REALTY PROBLEM

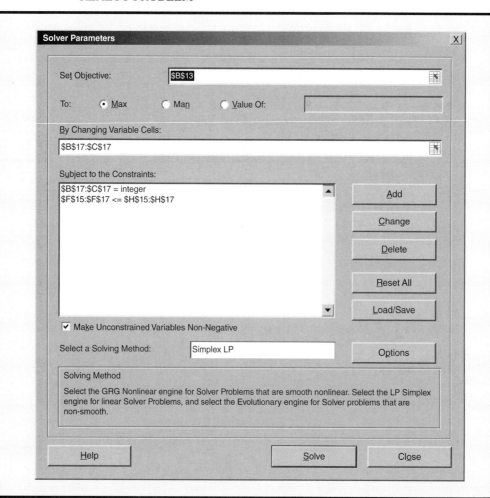

The integer requirement is created by using the **Add Constraint** procedure. $B$17:$C17 is entered in the left-hand box of the **Cell Reference** area and **int** rather than <=, =, or => is selected as the form of the constraint from the dropdown menu. When **int** is selected, the term "integer" automatically appears as the right-hand side of the constraint. Figure 7.15 shows the additional information required to complete the **Solver Parameters** dialog box. Note that the checkbox **Make Unconstrained Variables Non-Negative** is selected.

If binary variables are present in an integer linear programming problem, you must select the designation **bin** instead of **int** when setting up the constraints in the **Solver Parameters** dialog box.

*0-1 variables are identified with the **bin** designation in the **Solver Parameters** dialog box.*

Next select the **Options** button. The **Solver** options are shown in Figure 7.16. When solving an integer linear program make sure that the **Ignore Integer Constraints** checkbox is not selected. Also, the time required to obtain an optimal solution can be highly

FIGURE 7.16   SOLVER OPTIONS DIALOG BOX FOR THE EASTBORNE REALTY PROBLEM

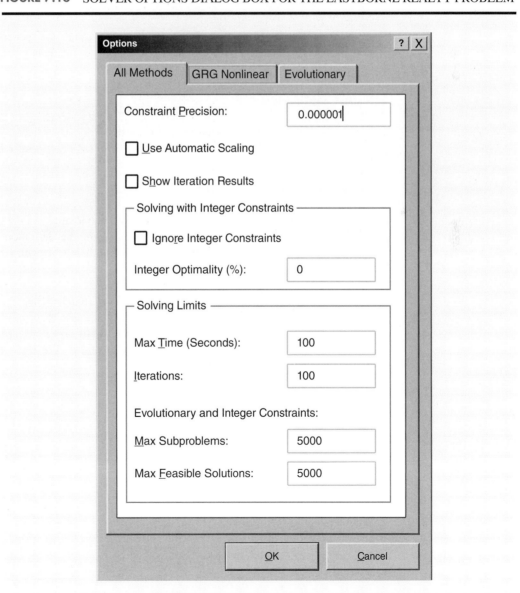

variable for integer linear programs. As shown in Figure 7.16, **Integer Optimality (%)** is set to 0 by default. This means that an optimal integer solution will be found. For larger problems it may be necessary to make this option positive. For example, if this option value were set to 5, then Solver will stop its search when it can guarantee that the best solution it has found so far is within 5% of the optimal solution in terms of objective function value.

Clicking **OK** in the Solver **Options** dialog box and selecting **Solve** in the **Solver Parameters** dialog box will instruct Solver to compute the optimal integer solution. The worksheet in Figure 7.14 shows that the optimal solution is to purchase four townhouses and two apartment buildings. The annual cash flow is $70,000.

Appendix 7.2   LINGO SOLUTION OF INTEGER LINEAR PROGRAMS

LINGO may be used to solve linear integer programs. An integer linear model is entered into LINGO exactly as described in Appendix 2.2, but with additional statements for declaring variables as either general integer or binary. For example, to declare a variable x integer, you need to include the following statement:

@GIN(x);

Note the use of the semicolon to end the statement. GIN stands for "general integer." Likewise to declare a variable y a binary variable, the following statement is required:

@BIN(y);

BIN stands for "binary."

To illustrate the use of integer variables, the following statements are used to model the Eastborne Reality problem discussed in this chapter:

First, we enter the following:

MODEL:
TITLE   EASTBORNE REALTY;

This statement gives the LINGO model the title Eastborne Realty.

Next, we enter the following two lines to document the definition of our decision variables (recall that ! denotes a comment, and each comment ends with a semicolon).

! T = NUMBER OF TOWNHOUSES PURCHASED;
! A = NUMBER OF APARTMENT BUILDINGS PURCHASED;

Next, we enter the objective function and constraints, each with a descriptive comment.

! MAXIMIZE THE CASH FLOW;
MAX = 10*T + 15*A;

! FUNDS AVAILABLE ($1000);
282*T + 400*A <= 2000;

! TIME AVAILABLILITY;
4*T + 40*A <= 140;

! TOWNHOUSES AVAILABLE;
T <= 5;

Finally, we must declare the variables T and A as general integer variables. Again, to document the model we begin with a descriptive comment and then declare each variable as a general integer variable:

    ! DECLARE THE VARIABLES TO BE GENERAL INTEGER VARIABLES;
    @GIN(T);
    @GIN(A);

Eastborne

The complete LINGO model is available in the LINGO file *Eastborne*.

CHAPTER 8

Nonlinear Optimization Models

CONTENTS

Many business processes behave in a nonlinear manner. For example, the price of a bond is a nonlinear function of interest rates, and the price of a stock option is a nonlinear function of the price of the underlying stock. The marginal cost of production often decreases with the quantity produced, and the quantity demanded for a product is usually a nonlinear function of the price. These and many other nonlinear relationships are present in many business applications.

A **nonlinear optimization problem** is any optimization problem in which at least one term in the objective function or a constraint is nonlinear. We begin our study of nonlinear applications by considering a production problem in which the objective function is a nonlinear function of the decision variables. In Section 8.2 we develop a nonlinear application that involves designing a portfolio of securities to track a stock market index. We extend our treatment of portfolio models in Section 8.3 by presenting the Nobel Prize–winning Markowitz model for managing the trade-off between risk and return. Section 8.4 provides a nonlinear application of the linear programming blending model introduced in Chapter 4. In Section 8.5, we present a well-known and successful model used in forecasting sales or adoptions of a new product. As a further illustration of the use of nonlinear optimization in practice, the Management Science in Action, Optimizing Retail Pricing at Intercontinental Hotels, discusses how the hotel chain is using a nonlinear optimization model to determine room prices at over 2000 different hotels. The Management Science in Action, Reducing the Risk from Pandemics using Nonlinear Optimization, discusses how experts at the Centers for Disease Control and Prevention have worked with researchers from Georgia Tech to develop mathematical models to contain the spread of disease pandemics.

Chapter appendices describe how to solve nonlinear programs using Excel Solver and LINGO.

MANAGEMENT SCIENCE IN ACTION

OPTIMIZING RETAIL PRICING AT INTERCONTINENTAL HOTELS*

InterContinental Hotel Group (IHG) owns, leases, or franchises over 4500 hotels in about 100 countries around the world. It offers in excess of 650,000 guest rooms, more than any other hotel. InterContinental Hotels, Crowne Plaza Hotels and Resorts, Holiday Inn Hotels and Resorts, and Holiday Inn Express are some of InterContinental's brands.

Like airlines and rental car companies, hotels offer a perishable good; that is, hotels have a limited time window in which to sell the product, after which the value perishes. For example, an empty seat on an airline flight is of no value, as is a hotel room that goes empty overnight. In dealing with perishable goods, how to price them in such a way as to maximize revenue is a challenge. Price the hotel room too high, and it will sit empty overnight and generate zero revenue. Price the hotel room too low, the hotel will be filled, but revenue likely will be lower than it could have been with higher pricing, even if fewer rooms were booked.

Revenue management (RM) is a term used to describe analytical approaches to this pricing problem.

IHG developed a novel approach to the hotel room pricing problem that uses a nonlinear optimization model to determine prices to charge for its rooms. Each day, IHG searches the Internet to acquire competitors' prices. The competitors' prices are factored into IHG's pricing optimization model, which is run daily. The model is nonlinear because the objective function is to maximize contribution (revenue – cost), but both demand and revenue are a function of the price variable. Over 2000 IHG hotels have started using this pricing model, and its use has led to increased revenue in excess of $145 million.

*Based on D. Kosuhik, J. A. Higbie, and C. Eister, "Retail Price Optimization at InterContinental Hotels Group," *Interfaces* 42, no. 1 (January–February 2012): 45–57.

8.1   A PRODUCTION APPLICATION—PAR, INC., REVISITED

We introduce constrained and unconstrained nonlinear optimization problems by considering an extension of the Par, Inc., linear program introduced in Chapter 2. We first consider the case in which the relationship between price and quantity sold causes the objective function to become nonlinear. The resulting unconstrained nonlinear program is then solved, and we observe that the unconstrained optimal solution does not satisfy the production constraints. Adding the production constraints back into the problem allows us to show the formulation and solution of a constrained nonlinear program. The section closes with a discussion of local and global optima.

An Unconstrained Problem

Let us consider a revision of the Par, Inc., problem from Chapter 2. Recall that Par, Inc., decided to manufacture standard and deluxe golf bags. In formulating the linear programming model for the Par Inc.'s problem, we assumed that it could sell all of the standard and deluxe bags it could produce. However, depending on the price of the golf bags, this assumption may not hold. An inverse relationship usually exists between price and demand. As price goes up, the quantity demanded goes down. Let P_S denote the price Par, Inc., charges for each standard bag and P_D denote the price for each deluxe bag. Assume that the demand for standard bags S and the demand for deluxe bags D are given by

$$S = 2250 - 15P_S \qquad (8.1)$$
$$D = 1500 - 5P_D \qquad (8.2)$$

The revenue generated from standard bags is the price of each standard bag P_S times the number of standard bags sold S. If the cost to produce a standard bag is $70, the cost to produce S standard bags is $70S$. Thus the profit contribution for producing and selling S standard bags (revenue − cost) is

$$P_S S - 70S \qquad (8.3)$$

We can solve equation (8.1) for P_S to show how the price of a standard bag is related to the number of standard bags sold. It is $P_S = 150 - \frac{1}{15}S$. Substituting $150 - \frac{1}{15}S$ for P_S in equation (8.3), the profit contribution for standard bags is

$$P_S S - 70S = (150 - \tfrac{1}{15}S)S - 70S = 80S - \tfrac{1}{15}S^2 \qquad (8.4)$$

Suppose that the cost to produce each deluxe golf bag is $150. Using the same logic we used to develop equation (8.4), the profit contribution for deluxe bags is

$$P_D D - 150D = (300 - \tfrac{1}{5}D)D - 150D = 150D - \tfrac{1}{5}D^2$$

Total profit contribution is the sum of the profit contribution for standard bags and the profit contribution for deluxe bags. Thus, total profit contribution is written as

$$\text{Total profit contribution} = 80S - \tfrac{1}{15}S^2 + 150D - \tfrac{1}{5}D^2 \qquad (8.5)$$

Note that the two linear demand functions, equations (8.1) and (8.2), give a nonlinear total profit contribution function, equation (8.5). This function is an example of a *quadratic function* because the nonlinear terms have a power of 2.

Using a computer solution method such as LINGO (see Appendix 8.2), we find that the values of S and D that maximize the profit contribution function are $S = 600$ and $D = 375$. The corresponding prices are \$110 for standard bags and \$225 for deluxe bags, and the profit contribution is \$52,125. These values provide the optimal solution for Par, Inc., if all production constraints are also satisfied.

A Constrained Problem

Unfortunately, Par, Inc., cannot make the profit contribution associated with the optimal solution to the unconstrained problem because the constraints defining the feasible region are violated. For instance, the cutting and dyeing constraint is

$$\tfrac{7}{10}S + D \le 630$$

A production quantity of 600 standard bags and 375 deluxe bags will require $\tfrac{7}{10}(600) + 1(375) = 795$ hours, which exceeds the limit of 630 hours by 165 hours. The feasible region for the original Par, Inc., problem along with the unconstrained optimal solution point (600, 375) is shown in Figure 8.1. The unconstrained optimum of (600, 375) is obviously outside the feasible region.

Clearly, the problem that Par, Inc., must solve is to maximize the total profit contribution

$$80S - \tfrac{1}{15}S^2 + 150D - \tfrac{1}{5}D^2$$

subject to all of the departmental labor hour constraints that were given in Chapter 2. The complete mathematical model for the Par, Inc., constrained nonlinear maximization problem follows:

$$\text{Max} \;\; 80S - \tfrac{1}{15}S^2 + 150D - \tfrac{1}{5}D^2$$

s.t.

MODEL *file*

ParNonlinear

$\tfrac{7}{10}S + \phantom{\tfrac{5}{6}}D \le 630$	Cutting and Dyeing
$\tfrac{1}{2}S + \tfrac{5}{6}D \le 600$	Sewing
$S + \tfrac{2}{3}D \le 708$	Finishing
$\tfrac{1}{10}S + \tfrac{1}{4}D \le 135$	Inspection and Packaging
$S, D \ge 0$	

This maximization problem is exactly the same as the Par, Inc., problem in Chapter 2 except for the nonlinear objective function. The solution to this constrained nonlinear maximization problem is shown in Figure 8.2.

The optimal value of the objective function is \$49,920.55. The Variable section shows that the optimal solution is to produce 459.7166 standard bags and 308.1984 deluxe bags. In the Slack/Surplus column of the Constraint section, the value of 0 in Constraint 1 means that the optimal solution uses all the labor hours in the cutting and dyeing department; but the nonzero values in rows 2–4 indicate that slack hours are available in the other departments.

A graphical view of the optimal solution of 459.7166 standard bags and 308.1984 deluxe bags is shown in Figure 8.3.

Note that the optimal solution is no longer at an extreme point of the feasible region. The optimal solution lies on the cutting and dyeing constraint line

$$\tfrac{7}{10}S + D = 630$$

but *not* at the extreme point formed by the intersection of the cutting and dyeing constraint and the finishing constraint, or the extreme point formed by the intersection of the cutting

FIGURE 8.1   THE PAR, INC., FEASIBLE REGION AND THE OPTIMAL SOLUTION FOR
THE UNCONSTRAINED OPTIMIZATION PROBLEM

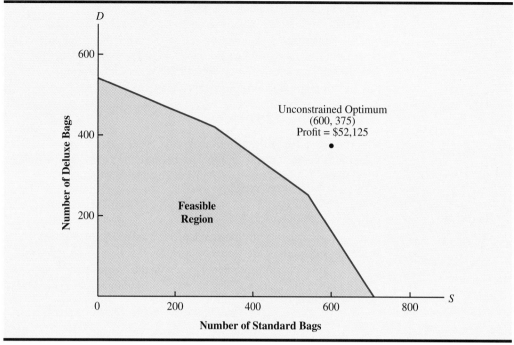

FIGURE 8.2   SOLUTION FOR THE NONLINEAR PAR, INC., PROBLEM

```
Optimal Objective Value = 49920.54655

        Variable              Value              Reduced Cost
      -------------        -------------        ---------------

           S                 459.71660              0.00000
           D                 308.19838              0.00000


       Constraint          Slack/Surplus           Dual Value
      -------------        -------------        ---------------

           1                   0.00000             26.72059
           2                 113.31074              0.00000
           3                  42.81679              0.00000
           4                  11.97875              0.00000
```

and dyeing constraint and the inspection and packaging constraint. To understand why, we look at Figure 8.3.

In Figure 8.3 we see three profit contribution *contour lines*. Each point on the same contour line is a point of equal profit. Here, the contour lines show profit contributions of $45,000, $49,920.55, and $51,500. In the original Par, Inc., problem described in Chapter 2 the objective function is linear and thus the profit contours are straight lines. However, for the Par, Inc., problem with a quadratic objective function, the profit contours are ellipses.

Because part of the $45,000 profit contour line cuts through the feasible region, we know an infinite number of combinations of standard and deluxe bags will yield a profit of $45,000. An infinite number of combinations of standard and deluxe bags also provide a profit of $51,500. However, none of the points on the $51,500 contour profit line are in the

Figure 8.3 shows that the profit contribution contour lines for the nonlinear Par, Inc., problem are ellipses.

FIGURE 8.3   THE PAR, INC., FEASIBLE REGION WITH OBJECTIVE FUNCTION CONTOUR LINES

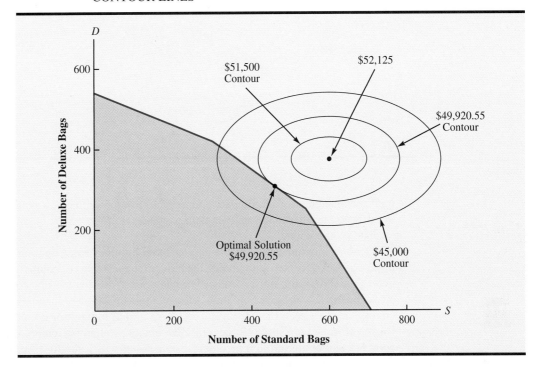

feasible region. As the contour lines move further out from the unconstrained optimum of (600, 375), the profit contribution associated with each contour line decreases. The contour line representing a profit of $49,920.55 intersects the feasible region at a single point. This solution provides the maximum possible profit. No contour line that has a profit contribution greater than $49,920.55 will intersect the feasible region. Because the contour lines are nonlinear, the contour line with the highest profit can touch the boundary of the feasible region at any point, not just an extreme point. In the Par, Inc., case the optimal solution is on the cutting and dyeing constraint line part way between two extreme points.

It is also possible for the optimal solution to a nonlinear optimization problem to lie in the interior of the feasible region. For instance, if the right-hand sides of the constraints in the Par, Inc., problem were all increased by a sufficient amount, the feasible region would expand so that the optimal unconstrained solution point of (600, 375) in Figure 8.3 would be in the interior of the feasible region. Many linear programming algorithms (e.g., the simplex method) optimize by examining only the extreme points and selecting the extreme point that gives the best solution value. As the solution to the constrained Par, Inc., nonlinear problem illustrates, such a method will not work in the nonlinear case because the optimal solution is generally not an extreme point solution. Hence, nonlinear programming algorithms are more complex than linear programming algorithms, and the details are beyond the scope of this text. Fortunately, we don't need to know how nonlinear algorithms work; we just need to know how to use them. Computer software packages such as Excel Solver and LINGO are available to solve nonlinear programming problems, and we describe how to use these software packages in the chapter appendices.

Local and Global Optima

A feasible solution is a **local optimum** if no other feasible solutions with a better objective function value are found in the immediate neighborhood. For example, for the constrained Par, Inc., problem, the local optimum corresponds to a **local maximum;** a point is a local maximum if no other feasible solutions with a larger objective function value are in the

FIGURE 8.4   A CONCAVE FUNCTION $f(X, Y) = -X^2 - Y^2$

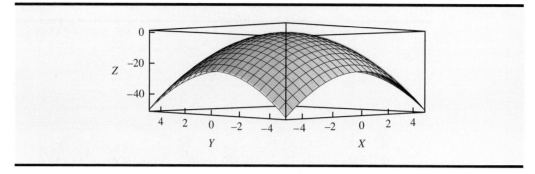

immediate neighborhood. Similarly, for a minimization problem, a point is a **local minimum** if no other feasible solutions with a smaller objective function value are in the immediate neighborhood.

Nonlinear optimization problems can have multiple local optimal solutions, which means we are concerned with finding the best of the local optimal solutions. A feasible solution is a **global optimum** if no other feasible points with a better objective function value are found in the feasible region. In the case of a maximization problem, the global optimum corresponds to a global maximum. A point is a **global maximum** if no other points in the feasible region give a strictly larger objective function value. For a minimization problem, a point is a **global minimum** if no other feasible points with a strictly smaller objective function value are in the feasible region. Obviously a global maximum is also a local maximum, and a global minimum is also a local minimum.

Nonlinear problems with multiple local optima are difficult to solve. But in many nonlinear applications, a single local optimal solution is also the global optimal solution. For such problems, we only need to find a local optimal solution. We will now present some of the more common classes of nonlinear problems of this type.

Consider the function $f(X, Y) = -X^2 - Y^2$. The shape of this function is illustrated in Figure 8.4. A function that is bowl-shaped down is called a **concave function.** The maximum value for this particular function is 0, and the point $(0, 0)$ gives the optimal value of 0. The point $(0, 0)$ is a local maximum, but it is also a *global maximum* because no point gives a larger function value. In other words, no values of X or Y result in an objective function value greater than 0. Functions that are concave, such as $f(X, Y) = -X^2 - Y^2$, have a single local maximum that is also a global maximum. This type of nonlinear problem is relatively easy to maximize.

The objective function for the nonlinear Par, Inc., problem is another example of a concave function.

$$80S - \tfrac{1}{15}S^2 + 150D - \tfrac{1}{5}D^2$$

In general, if all of the squared terms in a quadratic function have a negative coefficient and there are no cross-product terms, such as xy, then the function is a concave quadratic function. Thus, for the Par, Inc., problem, we are assured that the local maximum identified by LINGO in Figure 8.2 is the global maximum.

Let us now consider another type of function with a single local optimum that is also a global optimum. Consider the function $f(X, Y) = X^2 + Y^2$. The shape of this function is illustrated in Figure 8.5. It is bowl-shaped up and called a **convex function.** The minimum value for this particular function is 0, and the point $(0, 0)$ gives the minimum value of 0. The point $(0, 0)$ is a local minimum and a global minimum because no values of X or Y give an objective function value less than 0. Functions that are convex, such as $f(X, Y) = X^2 + Y^2$, have a single local minimum and are relatively easy to minimize.

For a concave function, we can be assured that if our computer software finds a local maximum, it is a global maximum. Similarly, for a convex function, we know that if our computer software finds a local minimum, it is a global minimum. Concave and convex

FIGURE 8.5   A CONVEX FUNCTION $f(X, Y) = X^2 + Y^2$

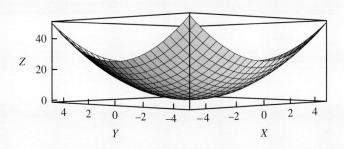

functions are well behaved. However, some nonlinear functions have multiple local optima. For example, Figure 8.6 shows the graph of the following function[1]:

$$f(X, Y) = 3(1 - X)^2 e^{-X^2 - (Y+1)^2} - 10(X/5 - X^3 - Y^5)e^{-X^2 - Y^2} - e^{-(X+1)^2 - Y^2}/3.$$

The hills and valleys in this graph show that this function has several local maximums and local minimums. These concepts are further illustrated in Figure 8.7, which is the same function as in Figure 8.6 but from a different viewpoint. It indicates two local minimums and three local maximums. One of the local minimums is also the global minimum, and one of the local maximums is also the global maximum.

Note that the output we use in this chapter for nonlinear optimization uses the label Optimal Objective Value. However, the solution may be either a local or a global optimum, depending on the problem characteristics.

From a technical standpoint, functions with multiple local optima pose a serious challenge for optimization software; most nonlinear optimization software methods can get "stuck" and terminate at a local optimum. Unfortunately, many applications can be nonlinear, and there is a severe penalty for finding a local optimum that is not a global optimum. Developing algorithms capable of finding the global optimum is currently an active research area. But the problem of minimizing a convex quadratic function over a linear constraint set is relatively easy, and for problems of this type there is no danger in getting stuck at a local minimum that is not a global

FIGURE 8.6   A FUNCTION WITH LOCAL MAXIMUMS AND MINIMUMS

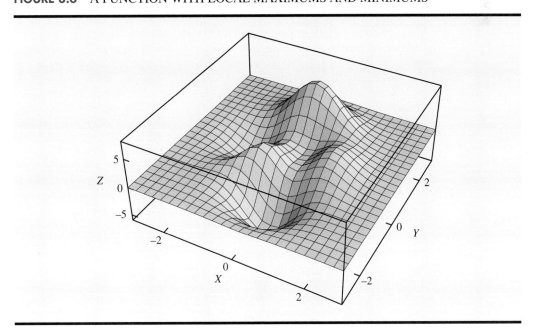

---

[1] This example is taken from the LINDO API manual available at www.lindo.com.

FIGURE 8.7   ANOTHER VIEWPOINT OF A FUNCTION WITH LOCAL MAXIMUMS
AND MINIMUMS

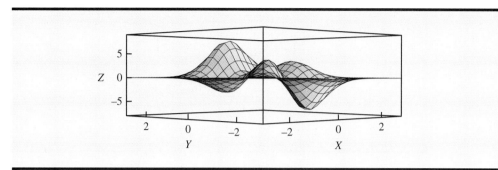

minimum. Similarly, the problem of maximizing a concave quadratic function over a linear constraint set is also relatively easy to solve without getting stuck at a local maximum that is not the global maximum.

Dual Values

We conclude this section with a brief discussion of dual values. The concept of a dual value was introduced in Chapter 3. Recall that the dual value is the change in the value of the optimal solution per unit increase in the right-hand side of the constraint. The interpretation of the dual value for nonlinear models is exactly the same as it is for linear programs. However, for nonlinear problems the allowable increase and decrease are not usually reported. This is because for typical nonlinear problems the allowable increase and decrease are zero. That is, if you change the right-hand side by even a small amount, the dual value changes.

MANAGEMENT SCIENCE IN ACTION

REDUCING THE RISK FROM PANDEMICS USING NONLINEAR OPTIMIZATION*

A pandemic is defined as the occurrence of an infectious disease affecting a large number of people across a very large geographic area (even worldwide). Pandemics are commonly associated with the influenza virus. One of the most recent examples of an influenza pandemic was the H1N1 pandemic in 2009. While the exact number of individuals infected by the H1N1 virus is unknown, the Centers for Disease Control and Prevention (CDC) estimates that there were approximately 60 million cases of H1N1 infection in the United States resulting in about 275,000 hospitalizations and more than 12,000 deaths.

Medical experts from the CDC and management science researchers from Georgia Institute of Technology have teamed up to develop models for vaccine distribution to contain the effects of a pandemic. One aspect of a vaccine distribution plan is the practice of prioritizing certain individuals for receiving vaccines first to best contain the spread of the disease. Traditionally, healthcare workers, children, and the elderly have often received priority for receiving vaccines. However, there are also

benefits to following a non-prioritization strategy to vaccinate as many people in the population as possible. Thus, key decisions are: (1) how to prioritize individuals for receiving the vaccine; and (2) when to switch from a prioritization strategy to a non-prioritization strategy.

The researchers from the CDC and Georgia Tech developed some of the first management science models that take into account disease propagation and vaccine-dispensing operations to develop optimal vaccine-distribution strategies. Part of this approach uses a nonlinear optimization model that minimizes the overall mortality rate from the spread of the disease. The model also contains constraints to make sure that the number of vaccines administered does not exceed the total vaccine supply based on available inventory.

The researchers compare their model-developed vaccine distribution strategies to what actually occurred in response to the 2009 H1N1 pandemic. Through computer simulation studies, the researchers find that their distribution strategies could have reduced the mortality rate from the H1N1 virus significantly. The researchers also confirmed the importance of switching from a prioritization strategy to a non-prioritization strategy depending on the transmission characteristics of the virus. As a result of the findings from examining the response to the 2009 H1N1 pandemic, the CDC established a system known as RealOpt-MCMOpt, which has been in use since 2011 to provide guidance on vaccine distribution and prioritization strategies. The goal of this work is to reduce both the number of infections overall and the patient mortality, from future pandemics.

*Based on Eva K. Lee, Fan Yuan, Ferdinand H. Pietz, Bernard A Benecke, Greg Burel, "Vaccine Prioritization for Effective Pandemic Response," *Interfaces* 45, no. 5 (September–October 2015) pp. 425–443.

8.2 CONSTRUCTING AN INDEX FUND

In Section 5.4 we studied portfolio and asset allocation models for Hauck Financial Services. Several linear programs were built to model different client attitudes toward risk. In this section we study an important related application.

Index funds are an extremely popular investment vehicle in the mutual fund industry. Indeed, the Vanguard 500 Index Fund is the single largest mutual fund in the United States, with more than $176 billion in net assets in 2014. An **index fund** is an example of passive asset management. The key idea behind an index fund is to construct a portfolio of stocks, mutual funds, or other securities that matches as closely as possible the performance of a broad market index such as the S&P 500.

Table 8.1 shows the one-year returns for four Vanguard Index Funds[2] and the returns for the corresponding market indexes. Several interesting issues are illustrated in this table. First, Vanguard has index funds for numerous types of investments. For example, the first two index funds are stock funds: the S&P 500 Index Fund and the MSCI Broad Market fund. The MSCI REIT fund is an investment in the real estate market, and the Short-Term Bond (Barclays US 1-5 Yr) fund is an investment in the corporate and United States government bond markets. Second, notice that even though the returns show considerable variation between the funds, the index funds do a good job of matching the return of the corresponding market index.

Why are index funds so popular? Behind the popularity of index funds is a substantial amount of research in finance that basically says, "You can't beat the market." In fact, the vast majority of mutual fund managers actually underperform leading market indexes such as the S&P 500. Therefore, many investors are satisfied with investments that provide a return that more closely matches the market return.

Now, let's revisit the Hauck Financial Services example from Chapter 5. Assume that Hauck has a substantial number of clients who wish to own a mutual fund portfolio with the characteristic that the portfolio, as a whole, closely matches the performance of the S&P 500 stock index. What percentage of the portfolio should be invested in each mutual fund in order to most closely mimic the performance of the entire S&P 500 index?

TABLE 8.1 ONE-YEAR RETURNS FOR FOUR VANGUARD INDEX FUNDS

Vanguard Fund	Vanguard Fund Return	Market Index	Market Index Return
500 Index Fund	25.81%	S&P 500	25.25%
Total Stock Index	24.71%	MSCI Broad Market	24.93%
REIT Index	24.18%	MSCI REIT	24.41%
Short-Term Bond	1.09%	Barclays US 1-5 Yr	1.10%

[2] These data were taken from www.vanguard.com and are for the one-year period ending August 31, 2014.

TABLE 8.2　MUTUAL FUND PERFORMANCE IN FIVE SELECTED YEARS USED AS PLANNING SCENARIOS FOR THE NEXT 12 MONTHS

Mutual Fund	Planning Scenarios				
	Year 1	Year 2	Year 3	Year 4	Year 5
Foreign Stock	10.06	13.12	13.47	45.42	−21.93
Intermediate-Term Bond	17.64	3.25	7.51	−1.33	7.36
Large-Cap Growth	32.41	18.71	33.28	41.46	−23.26
Large-Cap Value	32.36	20.61	12.93	7.06	−5.37
Small-Cap Growth	33.44	19.40	3.85	58.68	−9.02
Small-Cap Value	24.56	25.32	−6.70	5.43	17.31
S&P 500 Return	**25.00**	**20.00**	**8.00**	**30.00**	**−10.00**

In Table 8.2 we reproduce Table 5.4 (see Chapter 5), with an additional row that gives the S&P 500 return for each planning scenario. Recall that the columns show the actual percentage return that was earned by each mutual fund in that year. These five columns represent the most likely scenarios for the coming year.

The variables used in the model presented in Section 5.4 represented the proportion of the portfolio invested in each mutual fund.

FS = proportion of portfolio invested in a foreign stock mutual fund

IB = proportion of portfolio invested in an intermediate-term bond fund

LG = proportion of portfolio invested in a large-cap growth fund

LV = proportion of portfolio invested in a large-cap value fund

SG = proportion of portfolio invested in a small-cap growth fund

SV = proportion of portfolio invested in a small-cap value fund

The portfolio models presented in Section 5.4 chose the proportion of the portfolio to invest in each mutual fund in order to maximize return subject to constraints on the portfolio risk. Here we wish to choose the proportion of the portfolio to invest in each mutual fund in order to track as closely as possible the S&P 500 return.

For clarity of model exposition, we introduce variables $R1$, $R2$, $R3$, $R4$, and $R5$, which measure the portfolio return for each scenario. Consider, for example, variable $R1$. If the scenario represented by year 1 reflects what happens over the next 12 months, the portfolio return under scenario 1 is

$$R1 = 10.06FS + 17.64IB + 32.41LG + 32.36LV + 33.44SG + 24.56SV$$

Similarly, if scenarios 2–5 reflect the returns obtained over the next 12 months, the portfolio returns under scenarios 2–5 are as follows:

Scenario 2 return:

$$R2 = 13.12FS + 3.25IB + 18.71LG + 20.61LV + 19.40SG + 25.32SV$$

Scenario 3 return:

$$R3 = 13.47FS + 7.51IB + 33.28LG + 12.93LV + 3.85SG - 6.70SV$$

Scenario 4 return:

$$R4 = 45.42FS - 1.33IB + 41.46LG + 7.06LV + 58.68SG + 5.43SV$$

Scenario 5 return:

$$R5 = -21.93FS + 7.36IB - 23.26LG - 5.37LV - 9.02SG + 17.31SV$$

Next, for each scenario we compute the deviation between the return for the scenario and the S&P 500 return. Based on the last row of Table 8.2, the deviations are

$$R1 - 25, \quad R2 - 20, \quad R3 - 8, \quad R4 - 30, \quad R5 - (-10) \qquad (8.6)$$

The objective is for the portfolio returns to match as closely as possible the S&P 500 returns. To do so, we might try minimizing the sum of the deviations given in equation (8.6) as follows:

$$\text{Min} \quad (R1 - 25) + (R2 - 20) + (R3 - 8) + (R4 - 30) + (R5 - [-10]) \qquad (8.7)$$

Unfortunately, if we use expression (8.7), positive and negative deviations will cancel each other out, so a portfolio that has a small value for expression (8.7) might actually behave quite differently than the target index. Also, because we want to get as close to the target returns as possible, it makes sense to assign a higher marginal penalty cost for large deviations than for small deviations. A function that achieves this goal is

$$\text{Min} \ (R1 - 25)^2 + (R2 - 20)^2 + (R3 - 8)^2 + (R4 - 30)^2 + (R5 - [-10])^2$$

When we square each term, positive and negative deviations do not cancel each other out, and the marginal penalty cost for deviations increases as the deviation gets larger. The complete mathematical model we have developed involves 11 variables and 6 constraints (excluding the nonnegativity constraints).

MODEL *file*

HauckIndex

$$\begin{aligned}
\text{Min} \quad & (R1 - 25)^2 + (R2 - 20)^2 + (R3 - 8)^2 + (R4 - 30)^2 + (R5 - [-10])^2 \\
\text{s.t.} \quad & \\
R1 = \ & 10.06FS + 17.64IB + 32.41LG + 32.36LV + 33.44SG + 24.56SV \\
R2 = \ & 13.12FS + \ 3.25IB + 18.71LG + 20.61LV + 19.40SG + 25.32SV \\
R3 = \ & 13.47FS + \ 7.51IB + 33.28LG + 12.93LV + \ 3.85SG - \ 6.70SV \\
R4 = \ & 45.42FS - \ 1.33IB + 41.46LG + \ 7.06LV + 58.68SG + \ 5.43SV \\
R5 = \ & -21.93FS + \ 7.36IB - 23.26LG - \ 5.37LV - \ 9.02SG + 17.31SV \\
& FS + \ IB + \ LG + \ LV + \ SG + \ SV = 1 \\
& FS, IB, LG, LV, SG, SV \geq 0
\end{aligned}$$

This minimization problem is nonlinear because of the quadratic terms that appear in the objective function. For example, in the term $(R1 - 25)^2$ the variable $R1$ is raised to a power of 2 and is therefore nonlinear. However, because the coefficient of each squared term is positive, and there are no cross-product terms, the objective function is a convex function. Therefore, we are guaranteed that any local minimum is also a global minimum.

The solution for the Hauck Financial Services problem is given in Figure 8.8. The optimal value of the objective function is 4.42689, the sum of the squares of the return deviations. The portfolio calls for approximately 30% of the funds to be invested in the foreign stock fund ($FS = 0.30334$), 36% of the funds to be invested in the large-cap value fund ($LV = 0.36498$), 23% of the funds to be invested in the small-cap growth fund ($SG = 0.22655$), and 11% of the funds to be invested in the small-cap value fund ($SV = 0.10513$).

Table 8.3 shows a comparison of the portfolio return (see $R1$, $R2$, $R3$, $R4$, and $R5$ in Figure 8.8) to the S&P 500 return for each scenario. Notice how closely the portfolio returns match the S&P 500 returns. Based on historical data, a portfolio with this mix of Hauck mutual funds will indeed closely match the returns for the S&P 500 stock index.

We just illustrated an important application of nonlinear programming in finance. In the next section we show how the Markowitz model can be used to construct a portfolio that minimizes risk subject to a constraint requiring a minimum level of return.

FIGURE 8.8   SOLUTION FOR THE HAUCK FINANCIAL SERVICES PROBLEM

```
Optimal Objective Value = 4.42689

          Variable            Value          Reduced Cost
        -------------      -------------    ---------------
             FS              0.30334            0.00000
             IB              0.00000           64.84640
             LG              0.00000           18.51296
             LV              0.36498            0.00000
             SG              0.22655            0.00000
             SV              0.10513            0.00000
             R1             25.02024            0.00000
             R2             18.55903            0.00000
             R3              8.97303            0.00000
             R4             30.21926            0.00000
             R5             -8.83586            0.00000


        Constraint        Slack/Surplus        Dual Value
        -------------     -------------       ---------------
             1              0.00000              0.04047
             2              0.00000             -2.88192
             3              0.00000              1.94607
             4              0.00000              0.43855
             5              0.00000              2.32829
             6              0.00000            -42.33078
```

TABLE 8.3   PORTFOLIO RETURN VERSUS S&P 500 RETURN

Scenario	Portfolio Return	S&P 500 Return
1	25.02	25
2	18.56	20
3	8.97	8
4	30.22	30
5	−8.84	−10

NOTES AND COMMENTS

1. The returns for the planning scenarios in Table 8.2 are the actual returns for five years in the past. They were chosen as the past data most likely to represent what could happen over the next year. By using actual past data, the correlation among the mutual funds is automatically incorporated into the model.

2. Notice that the return variables ($R1, R2, \ldots, R5$) in the Hauck model are not restricted to be ≥ 0. This is because it might be that the best investment strategy results in a negative return in a given year. From Figure 8.8 you can see that the optimal value of $R5$ is -8.84, a return of -8.84%. A variable may be designated in LINGO as a free variable using the statement @FREE. For example, @FREE(R1); would designate R1 as a free variable. For an Excel model with some variables restricted to be nonnegative and others unrestricted, do not check **Make Unconstrained Variables Non-Negative** and add any required nonnegativity constraints in the constraint section of the **Solver Dialog** box.

3. While we used variables $R1, R2, \ldots, R5$ for model clarity in the Hauck model, they are not needed to solve the problem. They do, however, make the model simpler to read and interpret. Also, a model user is likely to be interested in the investment return in each year and these

variables provide this information. The use of extra variables for clarity exposes an interesting difference between LINGO models and Excel models. In a LINGO model these quantities must be designated decision variables. In an Excel model the returns can simply be calculated in a cell used in the model and do not have to be designated as variable cells (because they are functions of variable cells).

4. It would not be practical for an individual investor who desires to receive the same return as the S&P 500 to purchase all the S&P 500 stocks. The index fund we have constructed permits such an investor to approximate the S&P 500 return.
5. In this section we constructed an index fund from among mutual funds. The investment alternatives used to develop the index fund could also be individual stocks that are part of the S&P 500.

8.3   MARKOWITZ PORTFOLIO MODEL

Harry Markowitz received the 1990 Nobel Prize for his path-breaking work in portfolio optimization. The Markowitz mean-variance portfolio model is a classic application of non-linear programming. In this section we present the **Markowitz mean-variance portfolio model.** Numerous variations of this basic model are used by money management firms throughout the world.

A key trade-off in most portfolio optimization models must be made between risk and return. In order to get greater returns, the investor must also face greater risk. The index fund model of the previous section managed the trade-off passively. An investor in the index fund we constructed must be satisfied with the risk/return characteristics of the S&P 500. Other portfolio models explicitly quantify the trade-off between risk and return. In most portfolio optimization models, the return used is the expected return (or average) of the possible outcomes.

Consider the Hauck Financial Services example developed in the previous section. Five scenarios represented the possible outcomes over a one-year planning horizon. The return under each scenario was defined by the variables $R1$, $R2$, $R3$, $R4$, and $R5$, respectively. If p_s is the probability of scenario s among n possible scenarios, then the *expected return* for the portfolio $\bar{R}$ is

$$\bar{R} = \sum_{s=1}^{n} p_s R_s \tag{8.8}$$

If we assume that the five planning scenarios in the Hauck Financial Services model are equally likely, then

$$\bar{R} = \sum_{s=1}^{5} \tfrac{1}{5} R_s = \tfrac{1}{5} \sum_{s=1}^{5} R_s$$

Measuring risk is a bit more difficult. Entire books are devoted to the topic. The measure of risk most often associated with the Markowitz portfolio model is the variance of the portfolio. If the expected return is defined by equation (8.8), the portfolio *variance* is

$$Var = \sum_{s=1}^{n} p_s (R_s - \bar{R})^2 \tag{8.9}$$

For the Hauck Financial Services example, the five planning scenarios are equally likely. Thus,

$$Var = \sum_{s=1}^{5} \tfrac{1}{5}(R_s - \bar{R})^2 = \tfrac{1}{5} \sum_{s=1}^{5} (R_s - \bar{R})^2$$

The portfolio variance is the average of the sum of the squares of the deviations from the mean value under each scenario. The larger this number, the more widely dispersed the scenario returns are about their average value. If the portfolio variance were equal to zero, then every scenario return R_i would be equal.

Two basic ways to formulate the Markowitz model are (1) minimize the variance of the portfolio subject to a constraint on the expected return of the portfolio and (2) maximize the expected return of the portfolio subject to a constraint on variance. Consider the first case. Assume that Hauck clients would like to construct a portfolio from the six mutual funds listed in Table 8.2 that will minimize their risk as measured by the portfolio variance. However, the clients also require the expected portfolio return to be at least 10%. In our notation, the objective function is

$$\text{Min } \frac{1}{5}\sum_{s=1}^{5}(R_s - \overline{R})^2$$

The constraint on expected portfolio return is $\overline{R} \geq 10$. The complete Markowitz model involves 12 variables and 8 constraints (excluding the nonnegativity constraints).

MODEL *file*

HauckMarkowitz

$$\text{Min } \frac{1}{5}\sum_{s=1}^{5}(R_s - \overline{R})^2 \tag{8.10}$$

s.t.

$$R1 = 10.06FS + 17.64IB + 32.41LG + 32.36LV + 33.44SG + 24.56SV \tag{8.11}$$

$$R2 = 13.12FS + 3.25IB + 18.71LG + 20.61LV + 19.40SG + 25.32SV \tag{8.12}$$

$$R3 = 13.47FS + 7.51IB + 33.28LG + 12.93LV + 3.85SG - 6.70SV \tag{8.13}$$

$$R4 = 45.42FS - 1.33IB + 41.46LG + 7.06LV + 58.68SG + 5.43SV \tag{8.14}$$

$$R5 = -21.93FS + 7.36IB - 23.26LG - 5.37LV - 9.02SG + 17.31SV \tag{8.15}$$

$$FS + IB + LG + LV + SG + SV = 1 \tag{8.16}$$

$$\frac{1}{5}\sum_{s=1}^{5}R_s = \overline{R} \tag{8.17}$$

$$\overline{R} \geq 10 \tag{8.18}$$

$$FS, IB, LG, LV, SG, SV \geq 0 \tag{8.19}$$

The objective for the Markowitz model is to minimize portfolio variance. Note that equations (8.11) through (8.15) were present in the index fund model presented in Section 8.2. These equations define the return for each scenario. Equation (8.16), which was also present in the index fund model, requires all of the money to be invested in the mutual funds; this constraint is often called the *unity constraint*. Equation (8.17) defines $\overline{R}$, which is the expected return of the portfolio. Equation (8.18) requires the portfolio return to be at least 10%. Finally, expression (8.19) requires a nonnegative investment in each Hauck mutual fund.

A portion of the solution for this model using a required return of at least 10% appears in Figure 8.9. The minimum value for the portfolio variance is 27.13615. This solution implies that the clients will get an expected return of 10% (RBAR = 10.00000) and minimize their risk as measured by portfolio variance by investing approximately 16% of the portfolio in the foreign stock fund ($FS = 0.15841$), 53% in the intermediate bond fund ($IB = 0.52548$), 4% in the large-cap growth fund ($LG = 0.04207$), and 27% in the small-cap value fund ($SV = 0.27405$).

The Markowitz portfolio model provides a convenient way for an investor to trade off risk versus return. In practice, this model is typically solved iteratively for different values of return. Figure 8.10 graphs these minimum portfolio variances versus required expected returns as required expected return is varied from 8% to 12% in increments of 1%. In finance this graph is called the *efficient frontier*. Each point on the efficient frontier is the minimum possible risk (measured by portfolio variance) for the given return. By looking at the graph of the efficient frontier an investor can pick the mean-variance trade-off that he or she is most comfortable with.

FIGURE 8.9   SOLUTION FOR THE HAUCK MINIMUM VARIANCE PORTFOLIO WITH
A REQUIRED RETURN OF AT LEAST 10%

```
Optimal Objective Value = 27.13615
```

Variable	Value	Reduced Cost
FS	0.15841	0.00000
IB	0.52548	0.00000
LG	0.04207	0.00000
LV	0.00000	41.64139
SG	0.00000	15.60953
SV	0.27405	0.00000
R1	18.95698	0.00000
R2	11.51205	0.00000
R3	5.64390	0.00000
R4	9.72807	0.00000
R5	4.15899	0.00000
RBAR	10.00000	0.00000

FIGURE 8.10   AN EFFICIENT FRONTIER FOR THE MARKOWITZ PORTFOLIO MODEL

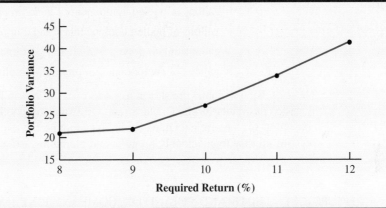

NOTES AND COMMENTS

1. Upper and lower bounds on the amount of an asset type in the portfolio can be easily modeled. Notice that the solution given in Figure 8.9 has more than 50% of the portfolio invested in the intermediate-term bond fund. It may be unwise to let one asset contribute so heavily to the portfolio. Hence upper bounds are often placed on the percentage of the portfolio invested in a single asset. Likewise, it might be undesirable to include an extremely small quantity of an asset in the portfolio. Thus, there may be constraints that require nonzero amounts of an asset to be at least a minimum percentage of the portfolio.

2. In the Hauck example, 100% of the available portfolio was invested in mutual funds. However, risk-averse investors often prefer to have some of their money in a "risk-free" asset such as U.S. Treasury bills. Thus, many portfolio optimization models allow funds to be invested in a risk-free asset.

3. In this section portfolio variance was used to measure risk. However, variance as it is defined counts deviations both above and below the mean. Most investors are happy with returns above the mean but wish to avoid returns below the mean. Hence, numerous portfolio models allow for flexible risk measures.

4. In practice, both brokers and mutual fund companies readjust portfolios as new information becomes available. However, constantly readjusting a portfolio may lead to large transaction costs. Case Problem 1 requires the student to develop a modification of the Markowitz portfolio selection problem in order to account for transaction costs.

8.4   BLENDING: THE POOLING PROBLEM

In Chapter 4 we showed how to use linear programming to solve the Grand Strand Oil Company blending problem. Recall that the Grand Strand refinery wanted to refine three petroleum components into regular and premium gasoline in order to maximize profit. In the Grand Strand model presented in Chapter 4 we assumed that all three petroleum components have separate storage tanks; as a result, components were not mixed together prior to producing gasoline. However, in practice it is often the case that at a blending site the number of storage facilities that hold the blending components is less than the number of components. In this case the components must share a storage tank or storage facility. Similarly, when transporting the components, the components often must share a pipeline or transportation container. Components that share a storage facility or pipeline are called *pooled* components. This pooling is illustrated in Figure 8.11.

Consider Figure 8.11. Components 1 and 2 are pooled in a single storage tank and component 3 has its own storage tank. Regular and premium gasoline are made from blending the pooled components and component 3. Two types of decisions must be made. First, what percentages of component 1 and component 2 should be used in the pooled mixture? Second, how much of the mixture of components 1 and 2 from the pooling tank are to be blended with component 3 to make regular and premium gasoline? These decisions require the following six decision variables:

y_1 = gallons of component 1 in the pooling tank

y_2 = gallons of component 2 in the pooling tank

x_{pr} = gallons of pooled components 1 and 2 in regular gasoline

x_{pp} = gallons of pooled components 1 and 2 in premium gasoline

x_{3r} = gallons of component 3 in regular gasoline

x_{3p} = gallons of component 3 in premium gasoline

These decision variables are shown as flows over the arcs in Figure 8.11.

The constraints for the Grand Strand Oil Company pooling problem are similar to the constraints for the original Grand Strand blending problem in Chapter 4. First, we need expressions for the total amount of regular and premium gasoline produced.

FIGURE 8.11   THE GRAND STRAND OIL COMPANY POOLING PROBLEM

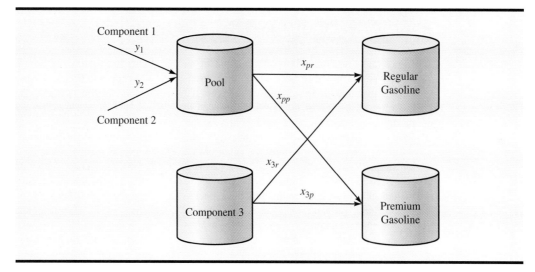

Total Gallons Produced Because the gasoline produced is a blend of the input components, the total number of gallons of each type of gasoline produced is the sum of the pooled components and component 3.

$$\text{Regular gasoline} = x_{pr} + x_{3r}$$
$$\text{Premium gasoline} = x_{pp} + x_{3p}$$

Total Petroleum Component Use The total gallons of components 1 and 2 consumed are the amount of the pooled mixture used in making regular and premium gasoline. The total gallons of component 3 consumed are the amount of component 3 used in regular gasoline plus the amount used in premium gasoline.

$$\text{Components 1 and 2 consumed:} \quad y_1 + y_2 = x_{pr} + x_{pp}$$
$$\text{Component 3 consumed:} \quad x_{3r} + x_{3p}$$

The equation involving components 1 and 2 is referred to as a *conservation equation;* this equation shows that the total amount of components 1 and 2 consumed must equal the amount of the pooled mixture used to make regular and premium gasoline.

Component Availability For the current production planning period, the maximum numbers of gallons available for the three components are 5000, 10,000, and 10,000, respectively. Thus, the three constraints that limit the availability of the three components are

$$\text{Component 1} \quad y_1 \leq 5000$$
$$\text{Component 2} \quad y_2 \leq 10,000$$
$$\text{Component 3} \quad x_{3r} + x_{3p} \leq 10,000$$

Product Specifications The product specifications for the regular and premium gasoline are the same as in Table 4.14 in Chapter 4. They are reproduced in Table 8.4 for ease of reference. Incorporating the blending specifications from Table 8.4 is a bit more difficult for the pooling problem because the amount of components 1 and 2 that go into the regular and premium gasoline depends on the proportion of these components in the pooled tank. For example, consider the constraint that component 1 can account for no more than 30% of the total gallons of regular gasoline produced. If x_{pr} gallons of the pooled components are blended with component 3 to make regular gasoline, it is necessary to know the percentage of component 1 in x_{pr}. The total gallons of components 1 and 2 in the pooled tank are $y_1 + y_2$; therefore, the fraction of component 1 in the pooled tank is

$$\left(\frac{y_1}{y_1 + y_2} \right)$$

TABLE 8.4 PRODUCT SPECIFICATIONS FOR THE GRAND STRAND BLENDING PROBLEM

Product	Specifications
Regular gasoline	At most 30% component 1
	At least 40% component 2
	At most 20% component 3
Premium gasoline	At least 25% component 1
	At most 45% component 2
	At least 30% component 3

As a result,

$$\left(\frac{y_1}{y_1 + y_2}\right)x_{pr}$$

is the number of gallons of component 1 used to blend regular gasoline. The total number of gallons of regular gasoline is $x_{pr} + x_{3r}$. So the constraint that the number of gallons of component 1 can account for no more than 30% of the total gallons of regular gasoline produced is

$$\left(\frac{y_1}{y_1 + y_2}\right)x_{pr} \leq 0.3(x_{pr} + x_{3r})$$

This expression is nonlinear because it involves the ratio of variables multiplied by another variable. The logic is similar for the other constraints required to implement the product specifications given in Table 8.4.

As in Section 4.3, the objective is to maximize the total profit contribution. Thus, we want to develop the objective function by maximizing the difference between the total revenue from both gasolines and the total cost of the three petroleum components. Recall that the price per gallon of the regular gasoline is $2.90 and the price per gallon of premium gasoline is $3.00. The cost of components 1, 2, and 3 is $2.50, $2.60, and $2.84, respectively. Finally, at least 10,000 gallons of regular gasoline must be produced.

The complete nonlinear model for the Grand Strand pooling problem, containing 6 decision variables and 11 constraints (excluding nonnegativity), follows:

Max $2.9\,(x_{pr} + x_{3r}) + 3.00(x_{pp} + x_{3p}) - 2.5y_1 - 2.6y_2 - 2.84(x_{3r} + x_{3p})$

s.t.

$$y_1 + y_2 = x_{pr} + x_{pp}$$

$$\left(\frac{y_1}{y_1 + y_2}\right)x_{pr} \leq 0.3(x_{pr} + x_{3r})$$

$$\left(\frac{y_2}{y_1 + y_2}\right)x_{pr} \geq 0.4(x_{pr} + x_{3r})$$

$$x_{3r} \leq 0.2(x_{pr} + x_{3r})$$

$$\left(\frac{y_1}{y_1 + y_2}\right)x_{pp} \geq 0.25(x_{pp} + x_{3p})$$

$$\left(\frac{y_2}{y_1 + y_2}\right)x_{pp} \leq 0.45(x_{pp} + x_{3p})$$

$$x_{3p} \geq 0.3(x_{pp} + x_{3p})$$

$$y_1 \leq 5000$$

$$y_2 \leq 10{,}000$$

$$x_{3r} + x_{3p} \leq 10{,}000$$

$$x_{pr} + x_{3r} \geq 10{,}000$$

$$x_{pr}, x_{pp}, x_{3r}, x_{3p}, y_1, y_2 \geq 0$$

MODEL *file*

GrandPooling

The optimal solution to the Grand Strand pooling problem is shown in Figure 8.12. The number of gallons of each component used and the percentage in regular and premium gasoline are shown in Table 8.5. For example, the 10,000 gallons of regular gasoline contain 2857.143 gallons of component 1. The number 2857.143 does not appear directly in the solution in Figure 8.12. It must be calculated. In the solution, $y_1 = 5000$, $y_2 = 9000$, and $x_{pr} = 8000$, which means that the number of gallons of component 1 in regular gasoline is

$$\left(\frac{y_1}{y_1 + y_2}\right)x_{pr} = \left(\frac{5000}{5000 + 9000}\right)8000 = 2857.143$$

FIGURE 8.12 SOLUTION TO THE GRAND STRAND POOLING PROBLEM

```
Optimal Objective Value = 5831.42857

         Variable            Value           Reduced Cost
       --------------     ---------------    ----------------
           XPR             8000.00000           0.00000
           X3R             2000.00000           0.00000
           XPP             6000.00000           0.00000
           X3P             2571.42857           0.00000
           Y1              5000.00000           0.00000
           Y2              9000.00000           0.00000


        Constraint        Slack/Surplus         Dual Value
       --------------     ---------------      ----------------
            1               0.00000               1.41200
            2            1000.00000               0.00000
            3            5428.57143               0.00000
            4               0.00000              -3.06134
            5             142.85714               0.00000
            6            1142.85714               0.00000
            7               0.00000               0.22857
            8               0.00000              -2.19657
            9               0.00000               0.86476
           10               0.00000               0.00000
           11               0.00000              -0.12286
```

TABLE 8.5 GRAND STRAND POOLING SOLUTION

	Gallons of Component (percentage)			
Gasoline	**Component 1**	**Component 2**	**Component 3**	**Total**
Regular	2857.143 (28.57%)	5142.857 (51.43%)	2000 (20%)	10,000
Premium	2142.857 (25%)	3857.143 (45%)	2571.429 (30%)	8571.429

In Figure 8.12 the objective value of 5831.429 corresponds to a total profit contribution of $5831.43. In Section 4.3 we found that the value of the optimal solution to the original Grand Strand blending problem is $7100. Why is the total profit contribution smaller for the model where components 1 and 2 are pooled? Note that any feasible solution to the problem with pooled components is feasible to the problem with no pooling. However, the converse is not true. For example, Figure 8.12 shows that the ratio of the number of gallons of component 1 to the number of gallons of component 2 in both regular and premium gasoline is constant. That is,

$$\frac{2857.143}{5142.857} = 0.556 = \frac{2142.857}{3857.143}$$

This must be the case because this ratio is y_1/y_2, the ratio of component 1 to component 2 in the pooled mixture. Table 8.6 shows the solution to the original Grand Strand problem without pooling (this table also appears in Section 4.3). The ratio of component 1 to component 2 in regular gasoline is $1250/6750 = 0.1852$, and the ratio of component 1 to component 2 in premium gasoline is $3750/3250 = 1.1538$, which is a large difference. By forcing us to use the same ratio of component 1 to component 2 in the pooling model, we lose flexibility and must spend more on the petroleum components used to make the gasoline.

TABLE 8.6 SOLUTION TO THE GRAND STRAND PROBLEM WITHOUT POOLING

Gasoline	Gallons of Component (percentage)			
	Component 1	**Component 2**	**Component 3**	**Total**
Regular	1250 (12.50%)	6750 (67.50%)	2000 (20%)	10,000
Premium	3750 (25%)	3250 (21.67%)	8000 (53.33%)	15,000

The lack of enough storage tanks for all the components reduces the number of blending feasible solutions, which in turn leads to a lower profit. Indeed, one use of this model is to provide management with a good estimate of the profit loss due to a shortage of storage tanks. Management would then be able to assess the profitability of purchasing additional storage tanks.

8.5 FORECASTING ADOPTION OF A NEW PRODUCT

Forecasting new adoptions after a product introduction is an important marketing problem. In this section we introduce a forecasting model developed by Frank Bass that has proven to be particularly effective in forecasting the adoption of innovative and new technologies in the marketplace.[3] Nonlinear programming is used to estimate the parameters of the Bass forecasting model. The model has three parameters that must be estimated.

m = the number of people estimated to eventually adopt the new product

A company introducing a new product is obviously interested in the value of this parameter.

q = the coefficient of imitation

This parameter measures the likelihood of adoption due to a potential adopter being influenced by someone who has already adopted the product. It measures the word-of-mouth and social media effects influencing purchases.

p = the coefficient of innovation

This parameter measures the likelihood of adoption, assuming no influence from someone who has already purchased (adopted) the product. It is the likelihood of someone adopting the product due to her or his own interest in the innovation.

Using these parameters, let us now develop the forecasting model. Let C_{t-1} denote the number of people who have adopted the product through time $t - 1$. Because m is the number of people estimated to eventually adopt the product, $m - C_{t-1}$ is the number of potential adopters remaining at time $t - 1$. We refer to the time interval between time $t - 1$ and time t as time period t. During period t, some percentage of the remaining number of potential adopters, $m - C_{t-1}$, will adopt the product. This value depends upon the likelihood of a new adoption.

Loosely speaking, the likelihood of a new adoption is the likelihood of adoption due to imitation plus the likelihood of adoption due to innovation. The likelihood of adoption due to imitation is a function of the number of people who have already adopted the product. The larger the current pool of adopters, the greater their influence through word-of-mouth and social media. Because C_{t-1}/m is the fraction of the number of people estimated to adopt the product by time $t-1$, the likelihood of adoption due to imitation is computed by multiplying this fraction by q, the coefficient of imitation. Thus, the likelihood of adoption due to imitation is

$$q(C_{t-1}/m)$$

---

[3] See Frank M. Bass, "A New Product Growth for Model Consumer Durables," *Management Science* 15 (1969).

The likelihood of adoption due to innovation is simply p, the coefficient of innovation. Thus, the likelihood of adoption is

$$p + q(C_{t-1}/m)$$

Using the likelihood of adoption, we can develop a forecast of the remaining number of potential customers who will adopt the product during time period t. Thus, F_t, the forecast of the number of new adopters during time period t, is

The Bass forecasting model given in equation (8.20) can be rigorously derived from statistical principles. Rather than providing such a derivation, we have emphasized the intuitive aspects of the model.

$$F_t = [p + q(C_{t-1}/m)](m - C_{t-1}) \qquad (8.20)$$

In developing a forecast of new adoptions in period t using the Bass model, the value of C_{t-1} will be known from past sales data. But we also need to know the values of the parameters to use in the model. Let us now see how nonlinear programming is used to estimate the parameter values m, p, and q.

Consider Figure 8.13. This figure shows the graph of box office revenues (in $ millions) for two different films, an independent studio film and a summer blockbuster action movie, over the first 12 weeks after release. Strictly speaking, box office revenues for time period t are not the same as the number of adopters during time period t. But the number of repeat customers is usually small and box office revenues are a multiple of the number of movie goers. The Bass forecasting model seems appropriate here.

These two films illustrate drastically different adoption patterns. Note that revenues for the independent studio film grow until they peak in week 4 and then they decline. For this film, much of the revenue is obviously due to word-of-mouth and social media influences. In terms of the Bass model, the imitation factor dominates the innovation factor, and we expect $q > p$. However, for the summer blockbuster, revenues peak in week 1 and drop sharply afterward. The innovation factor dominates the imitation factor, and we expect $q < p$.

The forecasting model given in equation (8.20) can be incorporated into a nonlinear optimization problem to find the values of p, q, and m that give the best forecasts for a set of data. Assume that N periods of data are available. Let S_t denote the actual number of adopters (or a multiple of that number, such as sales) in period t for $t = 1, \ldots, N$. Then the forecast in each period and the corresponding forecast error E_t are defined by

$$F_t = [p + q(C_{t-1}/m)](m - C_{t-1})$$
$$E_t = F_t - S_t$$

FIGURE 8.13   WEEKLY BOX OFFICE REVENUES FOR THE INDEPENDENT STUDIO FILM AND THE SUMMER BLOCKBUSTER

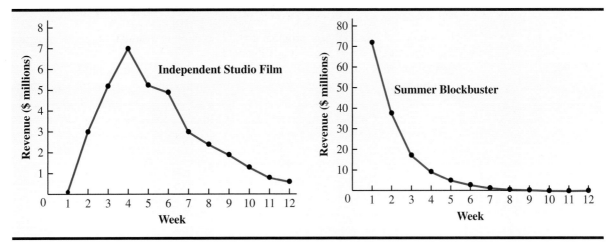

Notice that the forecast error is the difference between the forecast value F_t and the actual value S_t. It is common statistical practice to estimate parameters by minimizing the sum of errors squared.

Doing so for the Bass forecasting model leads to the following nonlinear optimization problem:

MODEL *file*

BassIndependent

$$\text{Min} \sum_{t=1}^{N} E_t^2 \tag{8.21}$$

s.t.

$$F_t = [p + q(C_{t-1}/m)](m - C_{t-1}), \quad t = 1, \ldots, N \tag{8.22}$$

$$E_t = F_t - S_t, \ t = 1, \ldots, N \tag{8.23}$$

Note that the parameters of the Bass forecasting model are the decision variables in this nonlinear optimization model.

Because equations (8.21) and (8.22) both contain nonlinear terms, this model is a nonlinear minimization problem.

The data in Table 8.7 provide the revenue and cumulative revenues for the independent studio film in weeks 1–12. Using these data, the nonlinear model to estimate the parameters of the Bass forecasting model for the independent studio film follows:

$$\text{Min} \quad E_1^2 + E_2^2 + \cdots + E_{12}^2$$

$$\text{s.t.} \quad F_1 = (p)m$$

$$F_2 = [p + q(0.10/m)] \, (m - 0.10)$$

$$F_3 = [p + q(3.10/m)] \, (m - 3.10)$$

$$\cdot$$
$$\cdot$$
$$\cdot$$

$$F_{12} = [p + q(34.85/m)] \, (m - 34.85)$$

$$E_1 = F_1 - 0.10$$

$$E_2 = F_2 - 3.00$$

$$\cdot$$
$$\cdot$$
$$\cdot$$

$$E_{12} = F_{12} - 0.60$$

Problem 23 asks you to formulate and solve a nonlinear model for the summer blockbuster.

The solution to this nonlinear program and the solution to a similar nonlinear program for the summer blockbuster are given in Table 8.8.

The optimal forecasting parameter values given in Table 8.8 are intuitively appealing and consistent with Figure 8.13. For the independent studio film, which has the largest revenues in week 4, the value of the imitation parameter q is 0.490; this value is substantially larger than the innovation parameter $p = 0.074$. The film picks up momentum over time due to favorable word of mouth. After week 4 revenues decline as more and more of the potential market for the film has already seen it. Contrast these data with those for the summer blockbuster, which has a negative value of -0.018 for the imitation parameter and an innovation parameter of 0.490. The greatest number of adoptions is in week 1, and new adoptions decline afterward. Obviously the word-of-mouth and social media influences were not favorable.

TABLE 8.7   BOX OFFICE REVENUES AND CUMULATIVE REVENUES IN $ MILLIONS FOR THE INDEPENDENT STUDIO FILM

Week	Revenues S_t	Cumulative Revenues C_t
1	0.10	0.10
2	3.00	3.10
3	5.20	8.30
4	7.00	15.30
5	5.25	20.55
6	4.90	25.45
7	3.00	28.45
8	2.40	30.85
9	1.90	32.75
10	1.30	34.05
11	0.80	34.85
12	0.60	35.45

TABLE 8.8   OPTIMAL FORECAST PARAMETERS FOR THE INDEPENDENT STUDIO FILM AND THE SUMMER BLOCKBUSTER

Parameter	Independent Studio Film	Summer Blockbuster
p	0.074	0.490
q	0.490	−0.018
m	34.850	149.540

FIGURE 8.14   FORECAST AND ACTUAL WEEKLY BOX OFFICE REVENUES FOR THE INDEPENDENT STUDIO FILM AND THE SUMMER BLOCKBUSTER

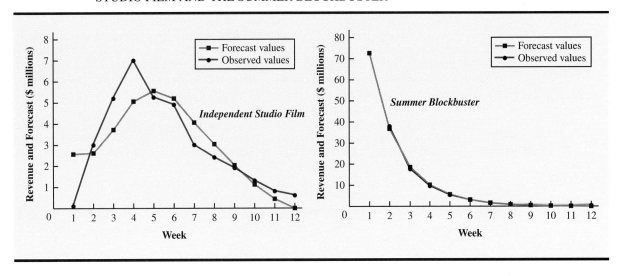

In Figure 8.14 we show the forecast values based on the parameters in Table 8.8 and the observed values in the same graph. The forecast values are denoted by a ■. The Bass forecasting model does a good job of tracking revenue for the independent studio film.

For the summer blockbuster, the Bass model does an outstanding job; it is virtually impossible to distinguish the forecast line from the actual adoption line.

You may wonder what good a forecasting model is if we must wait until after the adoption cycle is complete to estimate the parameters. One way to use the Bass forecasting model for a new product is to assume that sales of the new product will behave in a way that is similar to a previous product for which p and q have been calculated and to subjectively estimate m, the potential market for the new product. For example, one might assume that box office receipts for movies next summer will behave similarly to box office receipts for movies last summer. Then the p and q used for next summer's movies would be the p and q values calculated from the actual box office receipts last summer. The Management Science in Action, Forecasting Shale Oil Production with the Bass Model, describes how this approach was used to forecast shale oil production for an oil field in Texas.

A second approach is to wait until several periods of data for the new product are available. For example, if five periods of data are available, the sales data for these five periods could be used to forecast demand for period 6. Then, after six periods of sales are observed, a forecast for period 7 is made. This method is often called a rolling-horizon approach.

MANAGEMENT SCIENCE IN ACTION

FORECASTING SHALE OIL PRODUCTION WITH THE BASS MODEL*

The Bass model is considered one of the most influential formulas ever derived in the field of marketing. The model was originally developed by Frank Bass as a theoretical construct using the ideas that products are first adopted by customers who are more likely to take a risk on unproved or unknown products and services. These early-adopting customers, known as innovators, then influence other customers, known as imitators, through word-of-mouth to purchase the product or service.

Since its development in the 1960s, empirical evidence has shown that the Bass model is accurate for many different products and services. The Bass model has been used to model adoption of durable products such as stoves and refrigerators, as well as new electronics such as televisions and mobile phones, and even new services such as satellite-television adoption.

One of the more recent uses of the Bass model is to predict shale oil production. Shale oil is considered an unconventional type of oil because it is generally harder to extract usable oil from shale oil than from conventional oil wells. However, very large deposits of shale oil have been discovered in the United States and recent technological breakthroughs have made it cost effective to extract usable oil from shale oil. Therefore, the growth in the production of shale oil has been rapid.

The Bass model has been used very successfully to forecast the production of shale oil in an area in Texas known as the Eagle Ford Shale area that contained about 12,000 oil wells in 2015. To build the Bass model, data from 2006 to 2010 were used to estimate the value of m, the coefficient of imitation. Because there is limited history of shale oil product, the parameters p (coefficient of innovation) and q (coefficient of imitation) were estimated based on broader historical data from conventional oil well production.

The forecasts generated for shale oil production in the Eagle Ford Shale area have so far proven to be quite accurate. The Bass model forecasts predict that shale oil production will peak around the year 2020 at about 2.6 million barrels per day.

*Based on Thomas Tunstall, "Iterative Bass Model Forecasts for Unconventional Oil Production in the Eagle Ford Shale," *Energy* no. 93 (December 2015) pp. 580–588.

NOTES AND COMMENTS

The optimization model used to determine the parameter values for the Bass forecasting model is an example of a hard nonlinear optimization problem. It is neither convex nor concave. For such models, local optima may give values that are much worse than the global optimum. See the discussion in Appendix 8.1 and Appendix 8.2 on how to use Excel Solver and LINGO to find a global optimum.

SUMMARY

In this chapter we introduced nonlinear optimization models. A nonlinear optimization model is a model with at least one nonlinear term in either a constraint or the objective function. Because so many processes in business and nature behave in a nonlinear fashion, allowing nonlinear terms greatly increases the number of important applications that can be modeled as an optimization problem. Numerous problems in portfolio optimization, pricing, blending, economics, marketing, facility location, forecasting, and scheduling lend themselves to nonlinear models.

Unfortunately, nonlinear optimization models are not as easy to solve as linear optimization models, or even linear integer optimization models. As a rule of thumb, if a problem can be modeled realistically as a linear or linear integer problem, then it is probably best to do so. Many nonlinear formulations have local optima that are not globally optimal. Because most nonlinear optimization codes will terminate with a local optimum, the solution returned by the code may not be the best solution available. However, as pointed out in this chapter, numerous important classes of optimization problems, such as the Markowitz portfolio model, are convex optimization problems. For a convex optimization problem, a local optimum is also the global optimum. Additionally, the development of nonlinear optimization codes that do find global optimal solutions is proceeding at a rapid rate.

GLOSSARY

Concave function A function that is bowl-shaped down: For example, the functions $f(x) = -5x^2 - 5x$ and $f(x, y) = -x^2 - 11y^2$ are concave functions.

Convex function A function that is bowl-shaped up: For example, the functions $f(x) = x^2 - 5x$ and $f(x, y) = x^2 + 5y^2$ are convex functions.

Global maximum A feasible solution is a global maximum if there are no other feasible points with a larger objective function value in the entire feasible region. A global maximum is also a local maximum.

Global minimum A feasible solution is a global minimum if there are no other feasible points with a smaller objective function value in the entire feasible region. A global minimum is also a local minimum.

Global optimum A feasible solution is a global optimum if there are no other feasible points with a better objective function value in the entire feasible region. A global optimum may be either a global maximum or a global minimum.

Index fund A portfolio of stocks, mutual funds, or other securities that matches as closely as possible the performance of a broad market index such as the S&P 500.

Local maximum A feasible solution is a local maximum if there are no other feasible solutions with a larger objective function value in the immediate neighborhood.

Local minimum A feasible solution is a local minimum if there are no other feasible solutions with a smaller objective function value in the immediate neighborhood.

Local optimum A feasible solution is a local optimum if there are no other feasible solutions with a better objective function value in the immediate neighborhood. A local optimum may be either a local maximum or a local minimum.

Markowitz mean-variance portfolio model A portfolio optimization model used to construct a portfolio that minimizes risk subject to a constraint requiring a minimum level of return.

Nonlinear optimization problem An optimization problem that contains at least one nonlinear term in the objective function or a constraint.

PROBLEMS

1. The purpose of this exercise is to provide practice using Excel Solver or LINGO. Find the values of X and Y that minimize the function

$$\text{Min} \quad X^2 - 4X + Y^2 + 8Y + 20$$

Do not assume nonnegativity of the X and Y variables. Recall that by default LINGO assumes nonnegative variables. In order to allow the variables to take on negative values you can add

$$@FREE(X); \quad @FREE(Y);$$

Alternatively, if you want LINGO to allow for negative values by default, in the LINGO menu select **Options** and then click **General Solver,** and then uncheck the **Variables assumed nonnegative** tab. To allow for negative values in Excel Solver, make sure that the **Make Unconstrained Variables Non-Negative** box is not checked in the **Solver Parameters** dialog box.

SELF*test*

2. Consider the problem

$$\text{Min} \quad 2X^2 - 20X + 2XY + Y^2 - 14Y + 58$$
$$\text{s.t.} \quad X + 4Y \le 8$$

   a. Find the minimum solution to this problem.
   b. If the right-hand side of the constraint is increased from 8 to 9, how much do you expect the objective function to change?
   c. Resolve the problem with a new right-hand side of 9. How does the actual change compare with your estimate?

3. Jim's Camera shop sells two high-end cameras, the Sky Eagle and Horizon. The demands and selling prices for these two cameras are as follows: D_S = demand for the Sky Eagle, P_S is the selling price of the sky Eagle, D_H is the demand for the Horizon, and P_H is the selling price of the Horizon.

$$D_S = 222 - 0.60P_S + 0.35P_H$$
$$D_H = 270 + 0.10P_S - 0.64P_H$$

The store wishes to determine the selling price that maximizes revenue for these two products. Develop the revenue function for these two models, and find the revenue maximizing prices.

4. Lawn King manufactures two types of riding lawn mowers. One is a low-cost mower sold primarily to residential home owners; the other is an industrial model sold to landscaping and lawn service companies. The company is interested in establishing a pricing policy for the two mowers that will maximize the gross profit for the product line. A study of the relationships between sales prices and quantities sold of the two mowers has validated the following price–quantity relationships.

$$q_1 = 950 - 1.5p_1 + 0.7p_2$$
$$q_2 = 2500 + 0.3p_1 - 0.5p_2$$

where

$$q_1 = \text{number of residential mowers sold}$$
$$q_2 = \text{number of industrial mowers sold}$$
$$p_1 = \text{selling price of the residential mower in dollars}$$
$$p_2 = \text{selling price of the industrial mower in dollars}$$

The accounting department developed cost information on the fixed and variable cost of producing the two mowers. The fixed cost of production for the residential mower is $10,000 and the variable cost is $1500 per mower. The fixed cost of production for the industrial mower is $30,000 and the variable cost is $4000 per mower.

   a. Lawn King traditionally priced the lawn mowers at $2000 and $6000 for the residential and industrial mowers, respectively. Gross profit is computed as the sales revenue minus production cost. How many mowers will be sold, and what is the gross profit with this pricing policy?

b. Following the approach of Section 8.1, develop an expression for gross profit as a function of the selling prices for the two mowers.

c. What are the optimal prices for Lawn King to charge? How many units of each mower will be sold at these prices and what will the gross profit be?

d. Try a different formulation for this problem. Write the objective function as

$$\text{Max} \quad p_1 q_1 + p_2 q_2 - c_1 - c_2$$

where c_1 and c_2 represent the production costs for the two mowers. Then add four constraints to the problem, two based on the price–quantity relationships and two based on the cost functions. Solve this new constrained optimization problem to see whether you get the same answer. What are the advantages of this formulation, if any?

SELF*test*

5. GreenLawns provides a lawn fertilizer and weed control service. The company is adding a special aeration treatment as a low-cost extra service option, which it hopes will help attract new customers. Management is planning to promote this new service in two media: radio and direct-mail advertising. A media budget of $3000 is available for this promotional campaign. Based on past experience in promoting its other services, GreenLawns obtained the following estimate of the relationship between sales and the amount spent on promotion in these two media:

$$S = -2R^2 - 10M^2 - 8RM + 18R + 34M$$

where

S = total sales in thousands of dollars
R = thousands of dollars spent on radio advertising
M = thousands of dollars spent on direct-mail advertising

GreenLawns would like to develop a promotional strategy that will lead to maximum sales subject to the restriction provided by the media budget.

a. What is the value of sales if $2000 is spent on radio advertising and $1000 is spent on direct-mail advertising?

b. Formulate an optimization problem that can be solved to maximize sales subject to the media budget.

c. Determine the optimal amount to spend on radio and direct-mail advertising. How much money will be generated in sales?

6. The economic order quantity (EOQ) model is a classical model used for controlling inventory and satisfying demand. Costs included in the model are holding cost per unit, ordering cost, and the cost of goods ordered. The assumptions for that model are that only a single item is considered, that the entire quantity ordered arrives at one time, that the demand for the item is constant over time, and that no shortages are allowed.

Suppose we relax the first assumption and allow for multiple items that are independent except for a restriction on the amount of space available to store the products. The following model describes this situation:

Let

D_j = annual demand for item j
C_j = unit cost of item j
S_j = cost per order placed for item j
w_j = space required for item j
W = the maximum amount of space available for all goods
i = inventory carrying charge as a percentage of the cost per unit

The decision variables are Q_j, the amount of item j to order. The model is:

$$\text{Minimize} \quad \sum_{j=1}^{N} \left[C_j D_j + \frac{S_j D_j}{Q_j} + i C_j \frac{Q_j}{2} \right]$$

$$\text{s.t.} \quad \sum_{j=1}^{N} w_j Q_j \leq W$$

$$Q_j \geq 0$$

In the objective function, the first term is the annual cost of goods, the second is the annual ordering cost (D_j/Q_j is the number of orders), and the last term is the annual inventory holding cost ($Q_i/2$ is the average amount of inventory).

Set up and solve a nonlinear optimization model for the following data:

	Item 1	Item 2	Item 3
Annual Demand	2000	2000	1000
Item Cost ($)	100	50	80
Order Cost ($)	150	135	125
Space Required (sq. feet)	50	25	40
$W = 5000$			
$i = 0.20$			

7. The Cobb-Douglas production function is a classic model from economics used to model output as a function of capital and labor. It has the form

$$f(L, C) = c_0 L^{c_1} C^{c_2}$$

where c_0, c_1, and c_2 are constants. The variable L represents the units of input of labor and the variable C represents the units of input of capital.

a. In this example, assume $c_0 = 5$, $c_1 = 0.25$, and $c_2 = 0.75$. Assume each unit of labor costs $25 and each unit of capital costs $75. With $75,000 available in the budget, develop an optimization model for determining how the budgeted amount should be allocated between capital and labor in order to maximize output.

b. Find the optimal solution to the model you formulated in part (a). *Hint:* Put bound constraints on the variables based on the budget constraint. Use $L \leq 3000$ and $C \leq 1000$ and use the Multistart option as described in Appendix 8.1.

8. Let S represent the amount of steel produced (in tons). Steel production is related to the amount of labor used (L) and the amount of capital used (C) by the following function:

$$S = 20L^{0.30}C^{0.70}$$

In this formula L represents the units of labor input and C the units of capital input. Each unit of labor costs $50, and each unit of capital costs $100.

a. Formulate an optimization problem that will determine how much labor and capital are needed in order to produce 50,000 tons of steel at minimum cost.

b. Solve the optimization problem you formulated in part (a). *Hint:* Use the Multistart option as described in Appendix 8.1. Add lower and upper bound constraints of 0 and 5000 for both L and C before solving.

9. The profit function for two products is

$$Profit = -3x_1^2 + 42x_1 - 3x_2^2 + 48x_2 + 700$$

where x_1 represents units of production of product 1 and x_2 represents units of production of product 2. Producing one unit of product 1 requires 4 labor-hours and producing one unit of product 2 requires 6 labor-hours. Currently, 24 labor-hours are available. The cost of labor-hours is already factored into the profit function. However, it is possible to schedule overtime at a premium of $5 per hour.

a. Formulate an optimization problem that can be used to find the optimal production quantity of product 1 and the optimal number of overtime hours to schedule.

b. Solve the optimization model you formulated in part (a). How much should be produced and how many overtime hours should be scheduled?

 SELF*test*

10. Heller Manufacturing has two production facilities that manufacture baseball gloves. Production costs at the two facilities differ because of varying labor rates, local property taxes, type of equipment, capacity, and so on. The Dayton plant has weekly costs that can be expressed as a function of the number of gloves produced:

$$TCD(X) = X^2 - X + 5$$

where X is the weekly production volume in thousands of units and $TCD(X)$ is the cost in thousands of dollars. The Hamilton plant's weekly production costs are given by

$$TCH(Y) = Y^2 + 2Y + 3$$

where Y is the weekly production volume in thousands of units and $TCH(Y)$ is the cost in thousands of dollars. Heller Manufacturing would like to produce 8000 gloves per week at the lowest possible cost.

a. Formulate a mathematical model that can be used to determine the optimal number of gloves to produce each week at each facility.

b. Use Excel Solver or LINGO to find the solution to your mathematical model to determine the optimal number of gloves to produce at each facility.

 SELF*test*

11. In the Markowitz portfolio optimization model defined in equations (8.10) through (8.19), the decision variables represent the percentage of the portfolio invested in each of the mutual funds. For example, $FS = 0.25$ in the solution means that 25% of the money in the portfolio is invested in the foreign stock mutual fund. It is possible to define the decision variables to represent the actual dollar amount invested in each mutual fund or stock. Redefine the decision variables so that now each variable represents the dollar amount invested in the mutual fund. Assume an investor has $50,000 to invest and wants to minimize the variance of his or her portfolio subject to a constraint that the portfolio returns a minimum of 10%. Reformulate the model given by (8.10) through (8.19) based on the new definition of the decision variables. Solve the revised model with Excel Solver or LINGO.

12. Many forecasting models use parameters that are estimated using nonlinear optimization. A good example is the Bass model introduced in this chapter. Another example is the exponential smoothing forecasting model. The exponential smoothing model is common in practice and is described in further detail in Chapter 15. For instance, the basic exponential smoothing model for forecasting sales is

$$F_{t+1} = \alpha Y_t + (1 - \alpha)F_t$$

where

$$F_{t+1} = \text{forecast of sales for period } t + 1$$
$$Y_t = \text{actual value of sales for period } t$$
$$F_t = \text{forecast of sales for period } t$$
$$\alpha = \text{smoothing constant } 0 \leq \alpha \leq 1$$

This model is used recursively; the forecast for time period $t + 1$ is based on the forecast for period t, F_t, the observed value of sales in period t, Y_t, and the smoothing parameter α. The use of this model to forecast sales for 12 months is illustrated in Table 8.9 with the smoothing constant $\alpha = 0.3$. The forecast errors, $Y_t - F_t$, are calculated in the fourth column. The value of α is often chosen by minimizing the sum of squared forecast errors, commonly referred to as the mean squared error (MSE). The last column of Table 8.9 shows the square of the forecast error and the sum of squared forecast errors.

In using exponential smoothing models one tries to choose the value of α that provides the best forecasts. Build an Excel Solver or LINGO optimization model that will find the smoothing parameter, α, that minimizes the sum of forecast errors squared. You may find it easiest to put Table 8.9 into an Excel spreadsheet and then use Solver to find the optimal value of α.

Stock price data can be downloaded from many sites on the Internet including Yahoo! Finance, Google Finance, and others.

13. The purpose of this exercise is to learn how to calculate stock returns for portfolio models using actual stock price data. Ten years worth of stock price data are included in the file *StockReturns* for Apple Computer (AAPL), Advanced Micro Devices (AMD), and Oracle Corporation (ORCL). These data contain closing prices that are adjusted for stock dividends and splits.

Using these stock price data, we now want to calculate the annual returns for each stock for the Years 1 through 9. Returns are often calculated using continuous compounding. If the stock prices are adjusted for splits and stock dividends, then the price of stock i in period $t + 1$, $p_{i,t+1}$, is given by

$$p_{i,t+1} = p_{i,t}e^{r_{i,t}}$$

TABLE 8.9   EXPONENTIAL SMOOTHING MODEL FOR $\alpha = 0.3$

Week (t)	Observed Value (Y_t)	Forecast (F_t)	Forecast Error ($Y_t - F_t$)	Squared Forecast Error ($Y_t - F_t)^2$
1	17	17.00	0.00	0.00
2	21	17.00	4.00	16.00
3	19	18.20	0.80	0.64
4	23	18.44	4.56	20.79
5	18	19.81	−1.81	3.27
6	16	19.27	−3.27	10.66
7	20	18.29	1.71	2.94
8	18	18.80	−0.80	0.64
9	22	18.56	3.44	11.83
10	20	19.59	0.41	0.17
11	15	19.71	−4.71	22.23
12	22	18.30	3.70	13.69
				SUM = 102.86

where $p_{i,t}$ is the price of stock i in period t and $r_{i,t}$ is the return on stock i in period t. This calculation assumes no cash dividends were paid, which is true of Apple Computer, Advanced Micro Devices, and Oracle Corporation for the years included here. Solving the equation $p_{i,t+1} = p_{i,t}e^{r_{i,t}}$ for the return on stock i in period t gives

$$r_{i,t} = \ln\left(\frac{p_{i,t+1}}{p_{i,t}}\right)$$

For example, the Apple Computer adjusted closing price in Year 9 was \$38.45. The closing price in Year 10 was \$75.51. Thus, the continuously compounded return for Apple Computer from Year 9 to Year 10 is

$$\ln\,(75.51/38.45) = 0.6749$$

We use this calculation as our estimate of the annual return for Apple Computer for Year 9.

Take the closing stock prices shown in Figure 8.15 and calculate the annual returns for Years 1 through 9 for AAPL, AMD, and ORCL using $r_{i,t} = \ln(p_{i,t+1}/p_{i,t})$. If you calculate the returns properly, your results should appear as in the final three columns of Figure 8.15.

14. Formulate and solve the Markowitz portfolio optimization model to minimize portfolio variance subject to a required expected return of 10 percent that was defined in equations (8.10) through (8.19) using the data from Problem 13. In this case, nine scenarios

FIGURE 8.15   YEARLY RETURNS FOR AAPL, AMD, AND ORCL

DATA *file*

StockReturns

Year	AAPL Adj. Close (\$)	AMD Adj. Close (\$)	ORCL Adj. Close (\$)	AAPL Return	AMD Return	ORCL Return
1	4.16	17.57	4.32	0.0962	−0.5537	−0.1074
2	4.58	10.1	3.88	0.8104	0.1272	0.8666
3	10.3	11.47	9.23	0.9236	0.4506	0.9956
4	25.94	18	24.98	−0.8753	0.3124	0.1533
5	10.81	24.6	29.12	0.1340	−0.4270	−0.5230
6	12.36	16.05	17.26	−0.5432	−1.1194	−0.3610
7	7.18	5.24	12.03	0.4517	1.0424	0.1416
8	11.28	14.86	13.86	1.2263	0.0613	−0.0065
9	38.45	15.8	13.77	0.6749	0.9729	−0.0912
10	75.51	41.8	12.57			

Data Source: CSI
Web site: www.csidata.com

correspond to the yearly returns from Years 1 through 9. Treat each scenario as being equally likely and use the scenario returns that were calculated in Problem 13.

SELF*test*

15. Using the data obtained in Problem 13, construct a portfolio from AAPL, AMD, and ORCL that matches the Information Technology S&P index as closely as possible. Use the return data for the Information Technology S&P index given in the following table. The model for constructing the portfolio should be similar to the one developed for Hauck Financial Services in Section 8.2.

Year	Return
1	28.54%
2	78.14
3	78.74
4	−40.90
5	−25.87
6	−37.41
7	48.40
8	2.56
9	0.99

16. Most investors are happy when their returns are "above average," but not so happy when they are "below average." In the Markowitz portfolio optimization problem given by equations (8.10) through (8.19), the objective function is to minimize variance, which is given by

$$\text{Min } \tfrac{1}{5} \sum_{s=1}^{5} (R_s - \overline{R})^2$$

where R_s is the portfolio return under scenario s and $\overline{R}$ is the expected or average return of the portfolio.

With this objective function, we are choosing a portfolio that minimizes deviations both above and below the average, $\overline{R}$. However, most investors are happy when $R_s > \overline{R}$, but unhappy when $R_s < R$. With this preference in mind, an alternative to the variance measure in the objective function for the Markowitz model is the *semivariance*. The semivariance is calculated by only considering deviations below $\overline{R}$.

Let $D_{sp} - D_{sn} = R_s - \overline{R}$, and restrict D_{sp} and D_{sn} to be nonnegative. Then D_{sp} measures the positive deviation from the mean return in scenario s (i.e., $D_{sp} = R_s - \overline{R}$ when $R_s > \overline{R}$). In the case where the scenario return is below the average return, $R_s < \overline{R}$, we have $-D_{sn} = R_s - \overline{R}$. Using these new variables, we can reformulate the Markowitz model to minimize only the square of negative deviations below the average return. By doing so, we will use the semivariance rather than the variance in the objective function.

Reformulate the Markowitz portfolio optimization model given in equations (8.10) through (8.19) to use semivariance in the objective function. Solve the model using either Excel Solver or LINGO. *Hint:* When using Excel Solver, put an upper bound of 1 on each proportion variable and use the Multistart option as described in Appendix 8.1.

17. A second version of the Markowitz portfolio model maximizes return subject to a constraint that the variance of the portfolio must be less than or equal to some specified amount. Consider again the Hauck Financial Service data given in Table 8.2.

	Annual Return (%)				
Mutual Fund	**Year 1**	**Year 2**	**Year 3**	**Year 4**	**Year 5**
Foreign Stock	10.06	13.12	13.47	45.42	−21.93
Intermediate-Term Bond	17.64	3.25	7.51	−1.33	7.36
Large-Cap Growth	32.41	18.71	33.28	41.46	−23.26
Large-Cap Value	32.36	20.61	12.93	7.06	−5.37
Small-Cap Growth	33.44	19.40	3.85	58.68	−9.02
Small-Cap Value	24.56	25.32	−6.70	5.43	17.31

a. Construct this version of the Markowitz model for a maximum variance of 30.

b. Solve the model developed in part (a).

18. Refer to Problem 17. Use the model developed there to construct an efficient frontier by varying the maximum allowable variance from 20 to 60 in increments of 5 and solving for the maximum return for each. Plot the efficient frontier and compare it to Figure 8.10.

19. This problem requires a basic understanding of the normal probability distribution. Investors are often interested in knowing the probabilities of poor returns. For example, for what cutoff return will the probability of the actual return falling below this cutoff value be at most 1%?

Consider the solution to the Markowitz portfolio problem given in Figure 8.9. The mean return of the portfolio is 10% and the standard deviation (calculated by taking the square root of the variance, which is the objective function value) is

$$\sigma = \sqrt{27.13615} = 5.209237$$

Assume that the portfolio scenario returns are normally distributed about the mean return. From the normal probability table, we see that less than 1% of the returns fall more than 2.33 standard deviations below the mean. This result implies a probability of 1% or less that a portfolio return will fall below

$$10 - (2.33)(5.209237) = -2.1375$$

Stated another way, if the initial value of the portfolio is $1, then the investor faces a probability of 1% of incurring a loss of 2.1375 cents or more. The value at risk is 2.1375 cents at 1%. This measure of risk is called the *value at risk*, or VaR. It was popularized by JPMorgan Chase & Co. in the early 1990s (then, just JP Morgan).

A table of normal probabilities appears in Appendix B, but they are also easily calculated in LINGO and Excel. In LINGO the function @PSN(Z) and the equivalent function NORM.DIST in Excel provide the probability that a standard normal random variable is less than Z.

a. Consider the Markowitz portfolio problem given in equations (8.10) through (8.19). Delete the required return constraint (8.18), and reformulate this problem to minimize the VaR at 1%.

b. Is minimizing the VaR the same as minimizing the variances of the portfolio? Answer Yes or No, and justify.

c. For a fixed return, is minimizing the VaR the same as minimizing the variances of the portfolio? Answer Yes or No, and justify.

20. Options are popular instruments in the world of finance. A *call option* on a stock gives the owner the right to buy the stock at a predetermined price before the expiration date of the option. For example, suppose that call options are selling for Procter & Gamble stock that give the owner of the option the right to buy a share of stock for $60 within the next 21 days. The asking price on the option was $1.45 at the market close. How are options priced? A pricing formula for options was developed by Fischer Black and Myron Scholes and published in 1973. Scholes was later awarded the Nobel Prize for this work in 1997 (Black was deceased). The Black-Scholes pricing model is widely used today by hedge funds and traders. The Black-Scholes formula for the price of a call option is

$$C = S[PSN(Z)] - Xe^{-rT}[PSN(Z - \sigma\sqrt{T})]$$

where

$$C = \text{market price of the call option}$$
$$X = \text{strike or exercise price of the stock}$$
$$S = \text{current price of the stock}$$
$$r = \text{annual risk-free interest rate}$$
$$T = \text{time to maturity of the option}$$
$$\sigma = \text{yearly standard deviation}$$

In the Black-Scholes formula, $Z = [(r + \sigma^2/2)T + \ln(S/X)]/(\sigma\sqrt{T})$ and $PSN(Z)$ is the probability of an observation of Z or less for a normal distribution with mean 0 and variance 1.

The purpose of this exercise is to price a Procter & Gamble call option offered today that expires 21 days later. Use the yield on three-month Treasury bills as the risk-free interest rate, which you can assume is currently 0.0494. The strike price on the option is $60 today, the stock is currently trading at $60.87. In order to use the Black-Scholes formula, the yearly standard deviation, σ is required. One way to obtain this number is to estimate the weekly variance of Procter & Gamble stock, multiply the weekly variance by 52, and then take the square root to get the annual standard deviation. For this problem, use a weekly variance of 0.000479376. Use these data to calculate the option price using the Black-Scholes formula.

Problem 21 is an example of a quadratic assignment problem. The quadratic assignment problem is a powerful model. It is used in a number of facility location problems and components on circuit boards. It is also used to assign jets to gates at airports to minimize product of passengers and distance walked.

21. The port of Lajitas has three loading docks. The distance (in meters) between the loading docks is given in the following table:

	1	2	3
1	0	100	150
2	100	0	50
3	150	50	0

Three tankers currently at sea are coming into Lajitas. It is necessary to assign a dock for each tanker. Also, only one tanker can anchor in a given dock. Currently, ships 2 and 3 are empty and have no cargo. However, ship 1 has cargo that must be loaded onto the other two ships. The number of tons that must be transferred are as follows:

		To		
		1	2	3
From	1	0	60	80

Formulate and solve with Excel Solver or LINGO an optimization problem with binary decision variables (where 1 means an assignment and 0 means no assignment) that will assign ships to docks so that the product of tonnage moved times distance is minimized. There are 12 nonzero terms in the objective function. (*Hints:* This problem is an extension of the assignment problem introduced in Chapter 6. Also, be careful with the objective function. Only include the nonzero terms. Each of the 12 nonzero terms in the objective function is a quadratic term, or the product of two variables.)

22. Andalus Furniture Company has two manufacturing plants, one at Aynor and another at Spartanburg. The cost of producing Q_1 kitchen chairs at Aynor is

$$75Q_1 + 5Q_1^2 + 100$$

and the cost of producing Q_2 kitchen chairs at Spartanburg is

$$25Q_2 + 2.5Q_2^2 + 150$$

Andalus needs to manufacture a total of 40 kitchen chairs to meet an order just received. How many chairs should be made at Aynor and how many should be made at Spartanburg in order to minimize total production cost?

23. The weekly box office revenues (in $ millions) for the summer blockbuster movie are given here. Use these data in the Bass forecasting model given by equations (8.21) through (8.23) to estimate the parameters p, q, and m. Solve the model using Excel Solver and see whether you can duplicate the results in Table 8.8.

Week	Summer Blockbuster
1	72.39
2	37.93
3	17.58
4	9.57
5	5.39
6	3.13
7	1.62
8	0.87
9	0.61
10	0.26
11	0.19
12	0.35

The Bass forecasting model is a good example of a "hard" nonlinear program and the answer you get may be a local optimum that is not nearly as good as the result given in Table 8.8. If you find your results do not match those in Table 8.8, use the Multistart option as described in Appendix 8.1. Use a lower bound of -1 and an upper bound of 1 on both p and q. Use a lower bound of 100 and an upper bound of 1000 on m.

Case Problem 1   PORTFOLIO OPTIMIZATION WITH TRANSACTION COSTS[4]

Hauck Financial Services has a number of passive, buy-and-hold clients. For these clients, Hauck offers an investment account whereby clients agree to put their money into a portfolio of mutual funds that is rebalanced once a year. When the rebalancing occurs, Hauck determines the mix of mutual funds in each investor's portfolio by solving an extension of the Markowitz portfolio model that incorporates transaction costs. Investors are charged a small transaction cost for the annual rebalancing of their portfolio. For simplicity, assume the following:

- At the beginning of the time period (in this case one year), the portfolio is rebalanced by buying and selling Hauck mutual funds.
- The transaction costs associated with buying and selling mutual funds are paid at the beginning of the period when the portfolio is rebalanced, which, in effect, reduces the amount of money available to reinvest.
- No further transactions are made until the end of the time period, at which point the new value of the portfolio is observed.
- The transaction cost is a linear function of the dollar amount of mutual funds bought or sold.

Jean Delgado is one of Hauck's buy-and-hold clients. We briefly describe the model as it is used by Hauck for rebalancing her portfolio. The mix of mutual funds that are being considered for her portfolio are a foreign stock fund (FS), an intermediate-term bond fund (IB), a large-cap growth fund (LG), a large-cap value fund (LV), a small-cap growth fund (SG), and a small-cap value fund (SV). In the traditional Markowitz model, the variables are usually interpreted as the *proportion* of the portfolio invested in the asset represented by the variable. For example, FS is the proportion of the portfolio invested in the foreign stock fund. However, it is equally correct to interpret FS as the dollar amount invested in the foreign stock fund. Then $FS = 25,000$ implies $25,000 is invested in the foreign stock fund.

---

[4] The authors appreciate helpful input from Linus Schrage on this case.

Based on these assumptions, the initial portfolio value must equal the amount of money spent on transaction costs plus the amount invested in all the assets after rebalancing. That is,

Initial portfolio value = Amount invested in all assets after rebalancing
+ Transaction costs

The extension of the Markowitz model that Hauck uses for rebalancing portfolios requires a balance constraint for each mutual fund. This balance constraint is

Amount invested in fund i = Initial holding of fund i +
Amount of fund i purchased − Amount of fund i sold

Using this balance constraint requires three additional variables for each fund: one for the amount invested prior to rebalancing, one for the amount sold, and one for the amount purchased. For instance, the balance constraint for the foreign stock fund is

$$FS = FS\_START + FS\_BUY - FS\_SELL$$

Jean Delgado has \$100,000 in her account prior to the annual rebalancing, and she has specified a minimum acceptable return of 10%. Hauck plans to use the following model to rebalance Ms. Delgado's portfolio. The complete model with transaction costs is

$$\text{Min } \tfrac{1}{5} \sum_{s=1}^{5} (R_s - \overline{R})^2$$

s.t.

$$0.1006FS + 0.1764IB + 0.3241LG + 0.3236LV + 0.3344SG + 0.2456SV = R1$$
$$0.1312FS + 3.25IB \quad + 0.1871LG + 0.2061LV + 0.1940SG + 0.2532SV = R2$$
$$0.1347FS + 0.0751IB + 0.3328LG + 0.1293LV + 0.385SG - 0.0670SV = R3$$
$$0.4542FS - 0.0133IB + 0.4146LG + 0.0706LV + 0.5868SG + 0.0543SV = R4$$
$$-0.2193FS + 0.0736IB - 0.2326LG - 0.0537LV - 0.0902SG + 0.1731SV = R5$$

$$\tfrac{1}{5} \sum_{s=1}^{5} R_s = \overline{R}$$

$$\overline{R} \geq 10{,}000$$
$$FS + IB + LG + LV + SG + SV + TRANS\ COST = 100{,}000$$
$$FS\_START + FS\_BUY - FS\_SELL = FS$$
$$IB\_START + IB\_BUY - IB\_SELL \ = IB$$
$$LG\_START + LG\_BUY - LG\_SELL = LG$$
$$LV\_START + LV\_BUY - LV\_SELL \ = LV$$
$$SG\_START + SG\_BUY - SG\_SELL = SG$$
$$SV\_START + SV\_BUY - SV\_SELL = SV$$

$$TRANS\_FEE * (FS\_BUY + FS\_SELL + IB\_BUY + IB\_SELL +$$
$$LG\_BUY + LG\_SELL + LV\_BUY + LV\_SELL + SG\_BUY + SG\_SELL +$$
$$SV\_BUY + SV\_SELL) = TRANS\_COST$$
$$FS\_START = 10{,}000$$
$$IB\_START = 10{,}000$$
$$LG\_START = 10{,}000$$
$$LV\_START = 40{,}000$$
$$SG\_START = 10{,}000$$
$$SV\_START = 20{,}000$$
$$TRANS\_FEE = 0.01$$
$$FS, IB, LG, LV, SG, SV \geq 0$$

Notice that the transaction fee is set at 1% in the model (the last equality constraint) and that the transaction cost for buying and selling shares of the mutual funds is a linear function of the amount bought and sold. With this model, the transaction costs are deducted from the client's account at the time of rebalancing and thus reduce the amount of money invested. The LINGO solution for Ms. Delgado's rebalancing problem is shown in Figure 8.16.

Managerial Report

Assume you are a newly employed quantitative analyst hired by Hauck Financial Services. One of your first tasks is to review the portfolio rebalancing model in order to help resolve a dispute with Jean Delgado. Ms. Delgado has had one of the Hauck passively managed

FIGURE 8.16 SOLUTION TO HAUCK MINIMUM VARIANCE PORTFOLIO WITH TRANSACTION COSTS

MODEL *file*

HauckCase

```
Global optimal solution found.
    Objective value:                    0.2721946E+08
    Infeasibilities:                    0.000000
    Total solver iterations:            16
    Elapsed runtime seconds:            0.12
Model is convex quadratic

         Variable              Value            Reduced Cost
    --------------        ----------------      -----------------
              R1              18953.28             0.000000
            RBAR              10000.00             0.000000
              R2              11569.21             0.000000
              R3              5663.961             0.000000
              R4              9693.921             0.000000
              R5              4119.631             0.000000
              FS              15026.86             0.000000
              IB              51268.51             0.000000
              LG              4939.312             0.000000
              LV              0.000000             418.5587
              SG              0.000000             149.1254
              SV              27675.00             0.000000
      TRANS_COST             1090.311             0.000000
        FS_START             10000.00             0.000000
          FS_BUY             5026.863             0.000000
         FS_SELL             0.000000             1.516067
        IB_START             10000.00             0.000000
          IB_BUY             41268.51             0.000000
         IB_SELL             0.000000             1.516067
        LG_START             10000.00             0.000000
          LG_BUY             0.000000             1.516067
         LG_SELL             5060.688             0.000000
        LV_START             40000.00             0.000000
          LV_BUY             0.000000             1.516067
         LV_SELL             40000.00             0.000000
        SG_START             10000.00             0.000000
          SG_BUY             0.000000             1.516067
         SG_SELL             10000.00             0.000000
        SV_START             20000.00             0.000000
          SV_BUY             7675.004             0.000000
         SV_SELL             0.000000             1.516067
       TRANS_FEE             0.010000             0.000000
```

portfolios for the last five years and has complained that she is not getting the rate of return of 10% that she specified. After a review of her annual statements for the last five years, she feels that she is actually getting less than 10% on average.

1. According to the model solution in Figure 8.16, *IB_BUY* = $41,268.51. How much transaction cost did Ms. Delgado pay for purchasing additional shares of the intermediate-term bond fund?
2. Based on the model solution given in Figure 8.16, what is the total transaction cost associated with rebalancing Ms. Delgado's portfolio?
3. After paying transaction costs, how much did Ms. Delgado have invested in mutual funds after her portfolio was rebalanced?
4. According to the model solution in Figure 8.16, *IB* = $51,268.51. How much can Ms. Delgado expect to have in the intermediate-term bond fund at the end of the year?
5. According to the model solution in Figure 8.16, the expected return of the portfolio is $10,000. What is the expected dollar amount in Ms. Delgado's portfolio at the end of the year? Can she expect to earn 10% on the $100,000 she had at the beginning of the year?
6. It is now time to prepare a report to management to explain why Ms. Delgado did not earn 10% each year on her investment. Make a recommendation in terms of a revised portfolio model that can be used so that Jean Delgado can have an expected portfolio balance of $110,000 at the end of next year. Prepare a report that includes a modified optimization model that will give an expected return of 10% on the amount of money available at the beginning of the year before paying the transaction costs. Explain why the current model does not do this.
7. Solve the formulation in part (6) for Jean Delgado. How does the portfolio composition differ from that shown in Figure 8.16?

Case Problem 2 CAFE COMPLIANCE IN THE AUTO INDUSTRY

The Corporate Average Fuel Economy (CAFE) regulations were put into law by Congress in 1975 to promote the sale of fuel-efficient automobiles and light trucks. The law requires automakers to boost their fleet gas mileages to certain averages by specified dates. Encouraging consumers to purchase more fuel-efficient vehicles is one way for car manufacturers to meet CAFE standards. This can be done by lowering the price of more fuel-efficient cars. Of course, these pricing changes should be done in a way to keep profits as large as possible while meeting CAFE constraints.

In order to meet CAFE constraints while maximizing profits, General Motors (GM) has used mathematical models to coordinate their pricing and production decisions. The objective function in this model is nonlinear, similar to the Par, Inc., model that we developed in this chapter. In this case we build a model similar to the one built for General Motors. The CAFE requirement on fleet miles per gallon is based on an average. The harmonic average is used to calculate the CAFE requirement on average miles per gallon.

In order to understand the harmonic average, assume that there is a passenger car and a light truck. The passenger car gets 30 miles per gallon (MPG) and the light truck gets 20 MPG. Assume each vehicle is driven exactly one mile. Then the passenger car consumes $\frac{1}{30}$ gallon of gasoline in driving one mile and the light truck consumes $\frac{1}{20}$ gallon of gasoline in driving one mile. The amount of gasoline consumed in total is

$$\text{Gas consumption} = (\tfrac{1}{30}) + (\tfrac{1}{20}) = (\tfrac{5}{60}) = (\tfrac{1}{12}) \text{ gallon}$$

The average MPG of the two vehicles calculated the "normal way" is $(30 + 20)/2 = 25$ MPG. If both vehicles are "average," and each vehicle is driven exactly one mile, then the total gasoline consumption is

$$\text{Gas consumption} = (\tfrac{1}{25}) + (\tfrac{1}{25}) = (\tfrac{2}{25}) \text{ gallon}$$

Because $(\frac{2}{25})$ is not equal to $(\frac{5}{60})$, the total gas consumption of two "average vehicles" driving exactly one mile is not equal to the total gas consumption of each of the original vehicles driving exactly one mile. This is unfortunate. In order to make it easy for the government to impose and enforce MPG constraints on the auto companies, it would be nice to have a single target value MPG that every company in the auto industry must meet. As just illustrated, there is a problem with requiring an average MPG on the industry because it will incorrectly estimate the gas mileage consumption of the fleet. Fortunately, there is a statistic called the **harmonic average** so that total gas consumption by harmonic average vehicles is equal to gas consumption of the actual vehicles.

For simplicity, first assume that there are two types of vehicles in the fleet, passenger cars and light trucks. If there is one passenger car getting 30 MPG and there is one light truck getting 20 MPG, the harmonic average of these two vehicles is

$$\frac{2}{\dfrac{1}{30} + \dfrac{1}{20}} = \frac{2}{\dfrac{5}{60}} = \frac{120}{5} = 24$$

If each vehicle were to drive exactly one mile, each vehicle would consume $\frac{1}{24}$ gallon of gasoline for a total of $\frac{2}{24} = \frac{1}{12}$ gallon of gasoline. In this case each "average" vehicle driving exactly one mile results in total gas consumption equal to the total gas consumption of each vehicle with a different MPG rating driving exactly one mile.

If there are three passenger vehicles and two light trucks, the harmonic average is given by

$$\frac{5}{\dfrac{3}{30} + \dfrac{2}{20}} = \frac{5}{0.1 + 0.1} = \frac{5}{0.2} = 25$$

In general, when calculating the harmonic average, the numerator is the total number of vehicles. The denominator is the sum of two terms. Each term is the ratio of the number of vehicles in that class to the MPG of cars in that class. For example, the first ratio in the denominator is $\frac{3}{30}$ because there are 3 cars (the numerator) each getting 30 MPG (the denominator). These calculations are illustrated in Figure 8.17.

Based on Figure 8.17, if each of the 5 cars is average and drives exactly one mile, $(\frac{5}{25}) = (\frac{1}{5})$ gallon of gas is consumed. If three cars getting 30 MPG drive exactly one mile each and two cars getting 20 MPG drive exactly one mile, then $(\frac{3}{30}) + (\frac{2}{20}) = (\frac{2}{10}) = (\frac{1}{5})$ gallon is consumed. Thus, the average cars exactly duplicate the gas consumption of the fleet with varying MPG.

Now assume that the demand function for passenger cars is

$$\text{Demand} = 750 - P_C \tag{8.24}$$

FIGURE 8.17   AN EXCEL SPREADSHEET WITH A CAFE CALCULATION

	A	B	C	D
1			Number	
2		MPG	of Vehicles	Cafe Weight
3	Passenger Cars	30	3	0.1000
4	Light Trucks	20	3	0.1000
5			5	0.2000
6				
7	Cafe Average	25		

where P_C is the price of a passenger car. Similarly, the demand function for light trucks is

$$\text{Demand} = 830 - P_T \tag{8.25}$$

where P_T is the price of a light truck.

Managerial Report

1. Using the formulas given in equations (8.24) and (8.25), develop an expression for the total profit contribution as a function of the price of cars and the price of light trucks.
2. Using Excel Solver or LINGO, find the price for each car so that the total profit contribution is maximized.
3. Given the prices determined above, calculate the number of passenger cars sold and the number of light trucks sold.
4. Duplicate the spreadsheet in Figure 8.17. Your spreadsheet should have formulas in cells D3:D5 and B7 and be able to calculate the harmonic (CAFE) average for any MPG rating and any number of vehicles in each category.
5. Again, assume that passenger cars get 30 MPG and light trucks get 20 MPG; calculate the CAFE average for the fleet size from part (3).
6. If you do the calculation in part (5) correctly, the CAFE average of the fleet is 23.57. Add a constraint that the fleet average must be 25 MPG and re-solve the model to get the maximum total profit contribution subject to meeting the CAFE constraint.

Appendix 8.1   SOLVING NONLINEAR PROBLEMS WITH EXCEL SOLVER

Excel Solver can be used for nonlinear optimization. The Excel formulation of the nonlinear version of the Par, Inc., problem developed in Section 8.1 is shown in Figure 8.18. A worksheet model is constructed just as in the linear case. The formula in cell B18 is the objective function. The formulas in cells B21:B24 are the left-hand sides of constraint inequalities. And the formulas in cells D21:D24 provide the right-hand sides for the constraint inequalities.

Note how the nonlinearity comes into the model. The formula in cell B18, the objective function cell, is

=B27*B16 + B28*C16− B9*B16 − C9*C16

This formula takes the product of the variable cell B16 corresponding to the number of standard bags produced and multiplies it by cell B27 which is the price function for standard bags. But cell B27 also contains the standard bag variable cell B16 in the formula. This creates a nonlinear term and means Excel cannot solve using the standard LP Simplex Solver engine.

Refer to Figure 8.19, which is the **Solver Parameters** dialog box. To solve nonlinear models with Excel Solver, select **GRG Nonlinear** from the **Select a Solving Method** dropdown button. Solver uses a nonlinear algorithm known as the Generalized Reduced Gradient (GRG) technique. GRG uses a tool from calculus called the gradient. The gradient essentially calculates a direction of improvement for the objective function based on contour lines.

In Section 8.1, we discussed the difficulties associated with functions that have local optima. Excel Solver has an option that is helpful in overcoming local optimal solutions to find the global optimal solution. The **Multistart** option is found by selecting the **Options** button from the **Solver Parameters** dialog box, selecting the **GRG Nonlinear** tab and selecting the **Multistart** checkbox from the **Multistart** section. This option works best

FIGURE 8.18   THE MODIFIED PAR, INC., PROBLEM IN EXCEL SOLVER

	A	B	C	D
1	Par, Inc.			
2				
3			Production Time	
4	Operation	Standard	Deluxe	Time Available
5	Cutting and Dyeing	0.7	1	630
6	Sewing	0.5	0.83333	600
7	Finishing	1	0.66667	708
8	Inspection and Packaging	0.1	0.25	135
9	Marginal Cost	70	150	
10				
11				
12	Model			
13				
14		Decision Variables		
15		Standard	Deluxe	
16	Bags Produced	459.716599481299	308.198380121294	
17				
18	Maximize Total Profit	=B27*B16+B28*C16-B9*B16-C9*C16		
19				
20	Constraints	Hours Used (LHS)		Hours Available (RHS)
21	Cutting and Dyeing	=B5*B16+C5*C16	<=	=D5
22	Sewing	=B6*B16+C6*C16	<=	=D6
23	Finishing	=B7*B16+C7*C16	<=	=D7
24	Inspection and Packaging	=B8*B16+C8*C16	<=	=D8
25				
26				
27	Standard Bag Price Function	=150-(1/15)*SB$16		
28	Deluxe Bag Price Function	=300-(1/15)*SC$16		

MODEL *file*

ParNonlinear

	A	B	C	D
1	Par, Inc.			
2				
3			Production Time	
4	Operation	Standard	Deluxe	Time Available
5	Cutting and Dyeing	0.7	1	630
6	Sewing	0.5	0.833	600
7	Finishing	1	0.667	708
8	Inspection and Packaging	0.1	0.25	135
9	Marginal Cost	70	150	
10				
11				
12	Model			
13				
14		Decision Variables		
15		Standard	Deluxe	
16	Bags Produced	459.717	308.198	
17				
18	Maximize Total Profit	49921		
19				
20	Constraints	Hours Used (LHS)		Hours Available (RHS)
21	Cutting and Dyeing	630.000	<=	630
22	Sewing	486.689	<=	600
23	Finishing	665.183	<=	708
24	Inspection and Packaging	123.021	<=	135
25				
26				
27	Standard Bag Price Function	119.352		
28	Deluxe Bag Price Function	238.360		

FIGURE 8.19   THE MODIFIED PAR, INC., SOLVER PARAMETERS DIALOG BOX

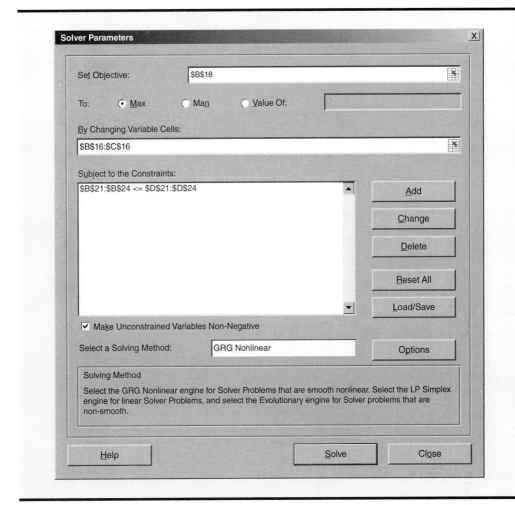

when you can specify reasonable lower and upper bounds on each variable. In this case you should also select the **Require Bounds on Variables** checkbox in the **Multistart** section (see Figure 8.20).

When using Excel, one must exercise care in how the minus sign is used. When used in a cell formula such as =A1 − B1^2, the minus sign is a binary operator because it connects two terms, A1 and B1^2. By convention, exponentiation has higher "precedence" than the minus, so if cell A1 contains 2 and cell B1 contains −1, the expression =A1 − B1^2 evaluates to

$$=A1 - B1\text{\textasciicircum}2 = 2 - (-1)^2 = 2 - 1 = 1$$

However, in the expression −B1^2 + A1, the minus sign is a unary operator because it does not combine terms. Excel, by default, assigns the unary minus sign higher precedence than exponentiation. Thus, if cell A1 contains 2 and cell B1 contains −1, the expression −B1^2 + A1 evaluates to

$$-B1\text{\textasciicircum}2 + A1 = (-B1)^2 + A1 + 1^2 + 2 = 3$$

This is a potential source of confusion. In this text we, like many authors, expect $-x^2$ to be interpreted as $-(x^2)$, not $(-x)^2$. LINGO (covered in Appendix 8.2) also treats the unary minus sign in this fashion.

FIGURE 8.20   THE MODIFIED PAR, INC., SOLVER OPTIONS DIALOG BOX

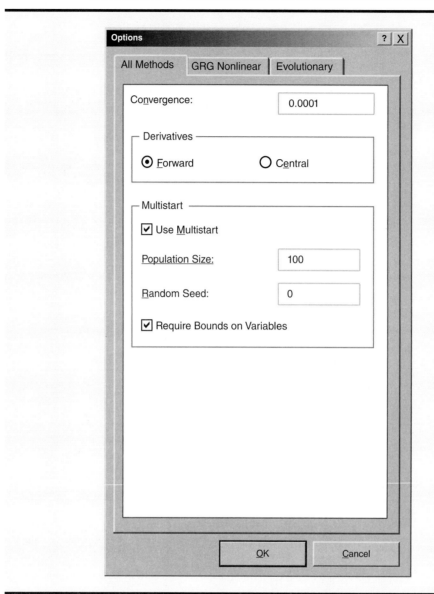

Appendix 8.2   SOLVING NONLINEAR PROBLEMS WITH LINGO

Appendix 2.2 shows how to use LINGO to solve linear programs.

Solving a nonlinear optimization problem in LINGO is no different from solving a linear optimization problem in LINGO. Simply type in the formulation, select the **LINGO** menu and choose the **Solve** option. Just remember that LINGO uses the ^ sign for exponentiation and the / sign for division. Also note that an asterisk (*) must be used to indicate multiplication.

We show how the unconstrained Par, Inc., problem from Section 8.1 is solved using LINGO. After starting LINGO, we type in the problem formulation in the model window as follows:

$$\text{MAX} = 80*S - (1/15)*S^2 + 150*D - (1/5)*D^2;$$

The solution obtained is shown in Figure 8.21. To solve the problem, select the **Solve** command from the **LINGO** menu or press the **Solve** button on the toolbar. Note that the value of the objective function is 52125.00, $S = 600$, and $D = 375$.

Now solve the constrained Par, Inc., problem from Section 8.1 using LINGO. The only difference from the constrained problem is that four lines must be added to the formulation

FIGURE 8.21   THE LINGO OPTIMAL SOLUTION FOR THE UNCONSTRAINED
PAR, INC., PROBLEM

```
Global optimal solution found.
    Objective value:                        52125.00
    Infeasibilities:                        0.000000
    Total solver iterations:                      10
    Elapsed runtime seconds:                    0.06
    Model is convex quadratic

Model Class:                                      QP

Total variables:                2
Nonlinear variables:            2
Integer variables:              0

Total constraints:              1
Nonlinear constraints:          1

Total nonzeros:                 2
Nonlinear nonzeros:             2

         Variable              Value          Reduced Cost
              S            600.0000         0.1107082E-07
              D            375.0000         0.1707244E-07

           Row    Slack or Surplus            Dual Price
             1            52125.00              1.000000
```

to account for the production constraints. After starting LINGO, we type in the problem formulation in the model window as follows:

$$\text{MAX} = 80*S - (1/15)*S^2 + 150*D - (1/5)*D^2;$$
$$(7/10)*S + D < 630;$$
$$(1/2)*S + (5/6)*D < 600;$$
$$S + (2/3)*D < 708;$$
$$(1/10)*S + (1/4)*D < 135;$$

Note that at the end of the objective function and each constraint a semicolon is used. After selecting the **Solve** command from the **Solver** menu, the solution shown in Figure 8.2 is obtained.

In the Par, Inc., problem, all the variables are constrained to be nonnegative. If some of the variables may assume negative values, extra lines must be added to the LINGO formulation and the @FREE command must be used. For instance, the Hauck index fund model shown in Section 8.2 did not contain nonnegativity constraints for variables $R1$, $R2$, $R3$, $R4$, and $R5$ because these variables are allowed to assume negative values. Thus, after entering the objective function and constraints, the following five lines must be added to the LINGO model to produce the solution shown in Figure 8.8.

$$@\text{FREE}(R1);$$
$$@\text{FREE}(R2);$$
$$@\text{FREE}(R3);$$
$$@\text{FREE}(R4);$$
$$@\text{FREE}(R5);$$

LINGO also provides the user with a wide variety of nonlinear functions that are useful in finance, inventory management, statistics, and other applications. To get a list of these functions, use the online LINGO User's Manual that is available under the Help menu. In the User's Manual you will find a chapter entitled "LINGO's Operators and Functions." This chapter contains a list of the available functions. When using a LINGO function you must precede the function name with the @ sign. For example, if you wanted to take the natural logarithm of X, you would write @LOG(X).

The demo version of LINGO provided for this text allows only five variables for problems that use the global solver.

We have discussed the concept of global versus local optimum. By default, LINGO finds a local optimum and the global solver is turned off. In order to turn on the global solver, select **Options...** from the **Solver** menu. When the **Lingo Options** dialog box appears, select the **Global Solver** tab and check the **Use Global Solver** box.

When using LINGO one must exercise care in how the minus sign is used. When used in an expression such as $y - x^2$, the minus sign is a binary operator because it connects two terms y and x^2. By convention, exponentiation has higher "precedence" than the minus; so if $y = 2$ and $x = -1$, the expression $y - x^2$ evaluates to

$$y - x^2 = 2 - (-1)^2 = 2 - 1 = 1$$

However, in the expression $-x^2 + y$, the minus sign is a unary operator because it does not combine terms. LINGO, by default, assigns the unary minus sign higher precedence than exponentiation. Thus, if $y = 2$ and $x = -1$ the expression $-x^2 + y$ evaluates to

$$-x^2 + y = (-x)^2 + y = 1^2 + 2 = 3$$

This is a potential source of confusion. In this text we, like many authors, expect $-x^2$ to be interpreted as $-(x^2)$, not $(-x)^2$. Excel also treats the unary minus sign in this fashion.

CHAPTER 9

Project Scheduling: PERT/CPM

CONTENTS

In many situations managers are responsible for planning, scheduling, and controlling projects that consist of numerous separate jobs or tasks performed by a variety of departments and individuals. Often these projects are so large or complex that the manager cannot possibly remember all the information pertaining to the plan, schedule, and progress of the project. In these situations the **program evaluation and review technique (PERT)** and the **critical path method (CPM)** have proven to be extremely valuable.

PERT and CPM can be used to plan, schedule, and control a wide variety of projects. Common applications include:

1. Research and development of new products and processes
2. Construction of plants, buildings, and highways
3. Maintenance of large and complex equipment
4. Design and installation of new systems

Henry L. Gantt developed the Gantt Chart as a graphical aid to scheduling jobs on machines. This application was the first of what has become known as project scheduling techniques.

In these types of projects, project managers must schedule and coordinate the various jobs or **activities** so that the entire project is completed on time. A complicating factor in carrying out this task is the interdependence of the activities; for example, some activities depend on the completion of other activities before they can be started. Because projects may comprise as many as several thousand activities, project managers look for procedures that will help them answer questions such as the following:

1. What is the total time to complete the project?
2. What are the scheduled start and finish dates for each specific activity?
3. Which activities are "critical" and must be completed *exactly* as scheduled to keep the project on schedule?
4. How long can "noncritical" activities be delayed before they cause an increase in the total project completion time?

PERT and CPM can help answer these questions.

Although PERT and CPM have the same general purpose and utilize much of the same terminology, the techniques were developed independently. PERT was developed in the late 1950s by the Navy specifically for the Polaris missile project. Many activities associated with this project had never been attempted previously, so PERT was developed to handle uncertain activity times. CPM was developed originally by DuPont and Remington Rand primarily for industrial projects for which activity times were certain and variability was not a concern. CPM offered the option of reducing activity times by adding more workers and/ or resources, usually at an increased cost. Thus, a distinguishing feature of CPM was that it identified trade-offs between time and cost for various project activities.

Today's computerized versions of PERT and CPM combine the best features of both approaches. Thus, the distinction between the two techniques is no longer necessary. As a result, we refer to the project scheduling procedures covered in this chapter as PERT/CPM. We begin the discussion of PERT/CPM by considering a project for the expansion of the Western Hills Shopping Center. At the end of the section, we describe how the investment securities firm of Seasongood & Mayer used PERT/CPM to schedule a $31 million hospital revenue bond project.

9.1   PROJECT SCHEDULING BASED ON EXPECTED ACTIVITY TIMES

The owner of the Western Hills Shopping Center plans to modernize and expand the current 32-business shopping center complex. The project is expected to provide room for 8 to 10 new businesses. Financing has been arranged through a private investor. All that remains is for the owner of the shopping center to plan, schedule, and complete the expansion project. Let us show how PERT/CPM can help.

The first step in the PERT/CPM scheduling process is to develop a list of the activities that make up the project. Table 9.1 shows the list of activities for the Western Hills

TABLE 9.1 LIST OF ACTIVITIES FOR THE WESTERN HILLS SHOPPING CENTER PROJECT

Activity	Activity Description	Immediate Predecessor	Expected Activity Time
A	Prepare architectural drawings	—	5
B	Identify potential new tenants	—	6
C	Develop prospectus for tenants	A	4
D	Select contractor	A	3
E	Prepare building permits	A	1
F	Obtain approval for building permits	E	4
G	Perform construction	D, F	14
H	Finalize contracts with tenants	B, C	12
I	Tenants move in	G, H	2
		Total	51

The effort that goes into identifying activities, determining interrelationships among activities, and estimating activity times is crucial to the success of PERT/ CPM. A substantial amount of time may be needed to complete this initial phase of the project scheduling process.

Immediate predecessor information determines whether activities can be completed in parallel (worked on simultaneously) or in series (one completed before another begins). Generally, a project with more series relationships will take longer to complete.

A project network is extremely helpful in visualizing the interrelationships among the activities. No rules guide the conversion of a list of activities and immediate predecessor information into a project network. The process of constructing a project network generally improves with practice and experience.

Problem 3 provides the immediate predecessor information for a project with seven activities and asks you to develop the project network.

Shopping Center expansion project. Nine activities are described and denoted A through I for later reference. Table 9.1 also shows the immediate predecessor(s) and the activity time (in weeks) for each activity. For a given activity, the **immediate predecessor** column identifies the activities that must be completed *immediately prior* to the start of that activity. Activities A and B do not have immediate predecessors and can be started as soon as the project begins; thus, a dash is written in the immediate predecessor column for these activities. The other entries in the immediate predecessor column show that activities C, D, and E cannot be started until activity A has been completed; activity F cannot be started until activity E has been completed; activity G cannot be started until both activities D and F have been completed; activity H cannot be started until both activities B and C have been completed; and, finally, activity I cannot be started until both activities G and H have been completed. The project is finished when activity I is completed.

The last column in Table 9.1 shows the expected number of weeks required to complete each activity. For example, activity A is expected to take 5 weeks, activity B is expected to take 6 weeks, and so on. The sum of expected activity times is 51. As a result, you may think that the total time required to complete the project is 51 weeks. However, as we show, two or more activities often may be scheduled concurrently (assuming sufficient availability of other required resources, such as labor and equipment), thus shortening the completion time for the project. Ultimately, PERT/CPM will provide a detailed activity schedule for completing the project in the shortest time possible.

Using the immediate predecessor information in Table 9.1, we can construct a graphical representation of the project, or the **project network**. Figure 9.1 depicts the project network for Western Hills Shopping Center. The activities correspond to the *nodes* of the network (drawn as rectangles), and the *arcs* (the lines with arrows) show the precedence relationships among the activities. In addition, nodes have been added to the network to denote the start and the finish of the project. A project network will help a manager visualize the activity relationships and provide a basis for carrying out the PERT/CPM computations.

The Concept of a Critical Path

To facilitate the PERT/CPM computations, we modified the project network as shown in Figure 9.2. Note that the upper left-hand corner of each node contains the corresponding activity letter. The activity time appears immediately below the letter.

To determine the project completion time, we have to analyze the network and identify what is called the **critical path** for the network. However, before doing so, we need to define the concept of a path through the network. A **path** is a sequence of connected nodes that leads from the Start node to the Finish node. For instance, one path for the network in Figure 9.2 is defined by the sequence of nodes A-E-F-G-I. By inspection, we see that other

FIGURE 9.1   PROJECT NETWORK FOR THE WESTERN HILLS SHOPPING CENTER

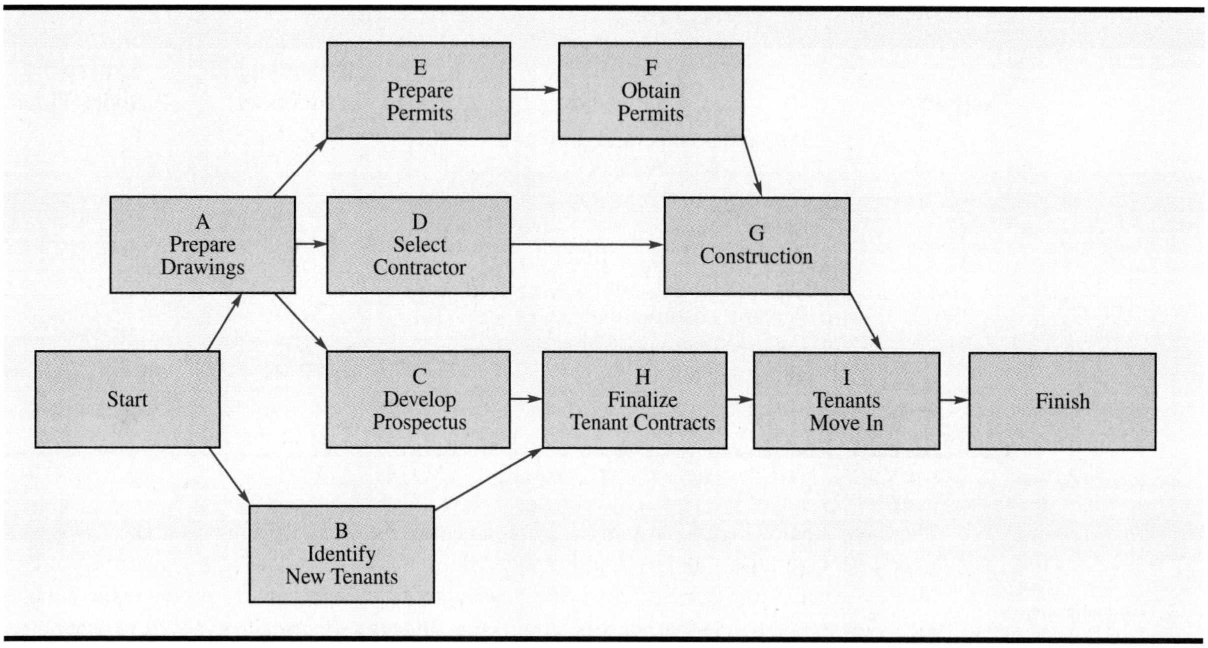

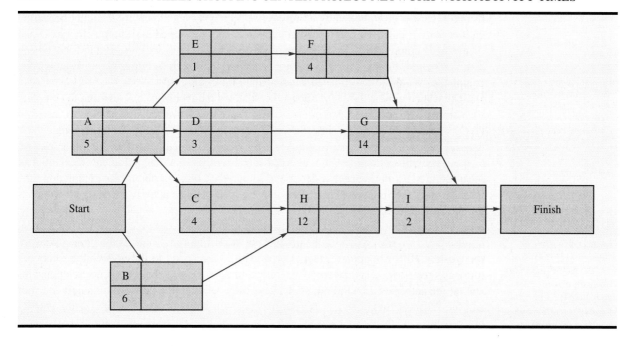

FIGURE 9.2   WESTERN HILLS SHOPPING CENTER PROJECT NETWORK WITH ACTIVITY TIMES

For convenience, we use the convention of referencing activities with letters. Generally, we assign the letters in approximate order as we move from left to right through the project network.

paths are possible, such as A-D-G-I, A-C-H-I, and B-H-I. All paths in the network must be traversed in order to complete the project, so we will look for the path that requires the greatest time. Because all other paths are shorter in duration, this *longest* path determines the total time required to complete the project. If activities on the longest path are delayed, the entire project will be delayed. Thus, the longest path is the *critical path*. Activities on the critical path are referred to as the **critical activities** for the project. The following discussion presents a step-by-step algorithm for finding the critical path in a project network.

Determining the Critical Path

We begin by finding the **earliest start time** and the **latest start time** for all activities in the network. Let

$$ES = \text{earliest start time for an activity}$$
$$EF = \text{earliest finish time for an activity}$$
$$t = \text{expected activity time}$$

The **earliest finish time** for any activity is

$$EF = ES + t \qquad\qquad (9.1)$$

Activity A can start as soon as the project starts, so we set the earliest start time for activity A equal to 0. With an expected activity time of 5 weeks, the earliest finish time for activity A is $EF = ES + t = 0 + 5 = 5$.

We will write the earliest start and earliest finish times in the node to the right of the activity letter. Using activity A as an example, we have

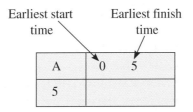

Because an activity cannot be started until *all* immediately preceding activities have been finished, the following rule can be used to determine the earliest start time for each activity:

The earliest start time for an activity is equal to the *largest* (i.e., *latest*) of the earliest finish times for all its immediate predecessors.

Determining the expected completion time of a project via critical path calculations implicitly assumes that sufficient resources (labor, equipment, supplies, etc.) are available to execute activities in parallel. If the resources available are insufficient to support the schedule generated by PERT/CPM, then more advanced techniques such as an integer linear programming model (Chapter 7) can be applied.

Let us apply the earliest start time rule to the portion of the network involving nodes A, B, C, and H, as shown in Figure 9.3. With an earliest start time of 0 and an activity time of 6 for activity B, we show $ES = 0$ and $EF = ES + t = 0 + 6 = 6$ in the node for activity B. Looking at node C, we note that activity A is the only immediate predecessor for activity C. The earliest finish time for activity A is 5, so the earliest start time for activity C must be $ES = 5$. Thus, with an activity time of 4, the earliest finish time for activity C is $EF = ES + t = 5 + 4 = 9$. Both the earliest start time and the earliest finish time can be shown in the node for activity C (see Figure 9.4).

Continuing with Figure 9.4, we move on to activity H and apply the earliest start time rule for this activity. With both activities B and C as immediate predecessors, the earliest start time for activity H must be equal to the largest of the earliest finish times for activities B and C. Thus, with $EF = 6$ for activity B and $EF = 9$ for activity C, we select the largest value, 9, as the earliest start time for activity H ($ES = 9$). With an activity time of 12 as shown in the node for activity H, the earliest finish time is $EF = ES + t = 9 + 12 = 21$. The $ES = 9$ and $EF = 21$ values can now be entered in the node for activity H in Figure 9.4.

FIGURE 9.3   A PORTION OF THE WESTERN HILLS SHOPPING CENTER PROJECT
NETWORK, SHOWING ACTIVITIES A, B, C, AND H

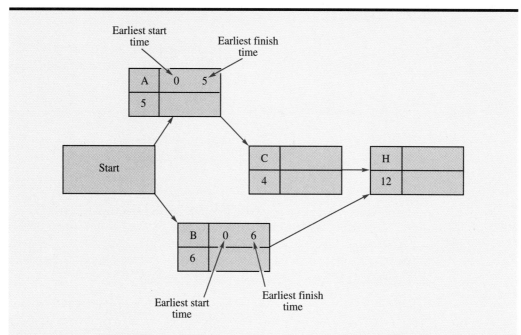

FIGURE 9.4   DETERMINING THE EARLIEST START TIME FOR ACTIVITY H

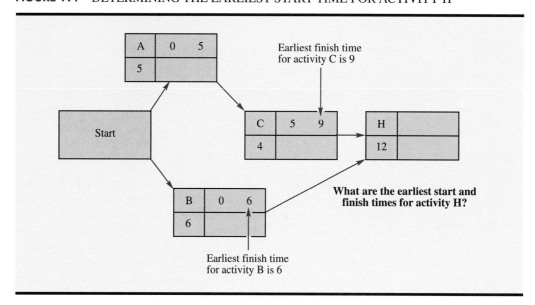

Continuing with this **forward pass** through the network, we can establish the earliest start time and the earliest finish time for each activity in the network. Figure 9.5 shows the Western Hills Shopping Center project network with the *ES* and *EF* values for each activity. Note that the earliest finish time for activity I, the last activity in the project, is 26 weeks. Therefore, we now know that the expected completion time for the entire project is 26 weeks.

We now continue the algorithm for finding the critical path by making a **backward pass** through the network. Because the expected completion time for the entire project is 26 weeks, we begin the backward pass with a **latest finish time** of 26 for activity I. Once the

FIGURE 9.5   WESTERN HILLS SHOPPING CENTER PROJECT NETWORK WITH EARLIEST START
AND EARLIEST FINISH TIMES SHOWN FOR ALL ACTIVITIES

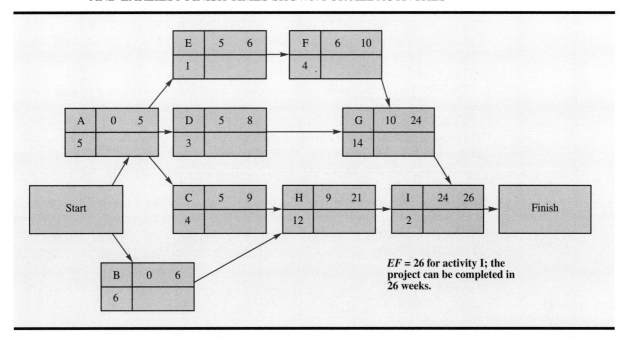

latest finish time for an activity is known, the *latest start time* for an activity can be computed
as follows. Let

$$LS = \text{latest start time for an activity}$$
$$LF = \text{latest finish time for an activity}$$

Then

$$LS = LF - t \qquad (9.2)$$

Beginning the backward pass with activity I, we know that the latest finish time is
$LF = 26$ and that the activity time is $t = 2$. Thus, the latest start time for activity I is
$LS = LF - t = 26 - 2 = 24$. We will write the LS and LF values in the node directly below
the earliest start (ES) and earliest finish (EF) times. Thus, for node I, we have

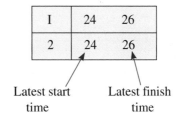

The following rule can be used to determine the latest finish time for each activity in the
network:

> The latest finish time for an activity is the *smallest (i.e., earliest)* of the latest start
> times for all activities that immediately follow the activity.

Logically, this rule states that the latest time an activity can be finished equals the earliest (smallest) value for the latest start time of following activities. Figure 9.6 shows the complete project network with the *LS* and *LF* backward pass results. We can use the latest finish time rule to verify the *LS* and *LF* values shown for activity H. The latest finish time for activity H must be the latest start time for activity I. Thus, we set $LF = 24$ for activity H. Using equation (9.2), we find that $LS = LF - t = 24 - 12 = 12$ as the latest start time for activity H. These values are shown in the node for activity H in Figure 9.6.

Activity A requires a more involved application of the latest start time rule. First, note that three activities (C, D, and E) immediately follow activity A. Figure 9.6 shows that the latest start times for activities C, D, and E are $LS = 8$, $LS = 7$, and $LS = 5$, respectively. The latest finish time rule for activity A states that the *LF* for activity A is the smallest of the latest start times for activities C, D, and E. With the smallest value being 5 for activity E, we set the latest finish time for activity A to $LF = 5$. Verify this result and the other latest start times and latest finish times shown in the nodes in Figure 9.6.

After we complete the forward and backward passes, we can determine the amount of slack associated with each activity. **Slack** is the length of time an activity can be delayed without increasing the project completion time. The amount of slack for an activity is computed as follows:

$$\text{Slack} = LS - ES = LF - EF \tag{9.3}$$

One of the primary contributions of PERT/CPM is the identification of the critical activities. The project manager will want to monitor critical activities closely because a delay in any one of these activities will lengthen the project completion time.

For example, the slack associated with activity C is $LS - ES = 8 - 5 = 3$ weeks. Hence, activity C can be delayed up to 3 weeks, and the entire project can still be completed in 26 weeks. In this sense, activity C is not critical to the completion of the entire project in 26 weeks. Next, we consider activity E. Using the information in Figure 9.6, we find that the slack is $LS - ES = 5 - 5 = 0$. Thus, activity E has zero, or no, slack. Consequently, this activity cannot be delayed without increasing the completion time for the entire project. In other words, completing activity E exactly as scheduled is critical in terms of keeping the project on schedule, and so activity E is a critical activity. In general, the *critical activities* are the activities with zero slack.

FIGURE 9.6   WESTERN HILLS SHOPPING CENTER PROJECT NETWORK WITH LATEST START AND LATEST FINISH TIMES SHOWN IN EACH NODE

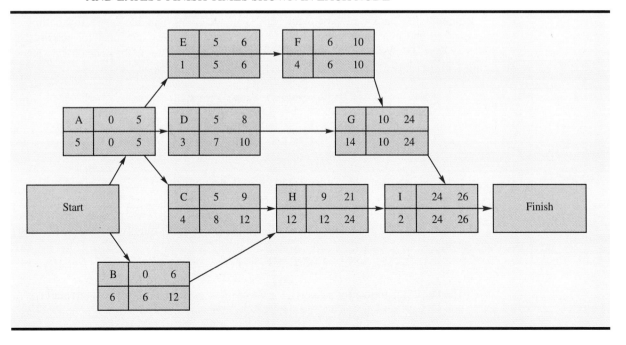

TABLE 9.2   ACTIVITY SCHEDULE FOR THE WESTERN HILLS SHOPPING
CENTER PROJECT

Activity	Earliest Start (ES)	Latest Start (LS)	Earliest Finish (EF)	Latest Finish (LF)	Slack (LS − ES)	Critical Path?
A	0	0	5	5	0	Yes
B	0	6	6	12	6	
C	5	8	9	12	3	
D	5	7	8	10	2	
E	5	5	6	6	0	Yes
F	6	6	10	10	0	Yes
G	10	10	24	24	0	Yes
H	9	12	21	24	3	
I	24	24	26	26	0	Yes

The critical path algorithm is a longest path algorithm. From the start node to the finish node, the critical path identifies the path that requires the most time.

The start and finish times shown in Figure 9.6 can be used to develop a detailed start time and finish time schedule for all activities. Putting this information in tabular form provides the activity schedule shown in Table 9.2. Note that the slack column shows that activities A, E, F, G, and I have zero slack. Hence, these activities are the critical activities for the project; the path formed by nodes A-E-F-G-I is the *critical path* in the Western Hills Shopping Center project network. The detailed schedule shown in Table 9.2 indicates the slack or delay that can be tolerated for the noncritical activities before these activities will increase project completion time.

Contributions of PERT/CPM

We previously stated that project managers look for procedures that will help answer important questions regarding the planning, scheduling, and controlling of projects. Let us reconsider these questions in light of the information that the critical path calculations have given us.

1. How long will the project take to complete?
    Answer: The project can be completed in 26 weeks if each activity is completed on schedule.
2. What are the scheduled start and completion times for each activity?
    Answer: The activity schedule (see Table 9.2) shows the earliest start, latest start, earliest finish, and latest finish times for each activity.
3. Which activities are critical and must be completed *exactly* as scheduled to keep the project on schedule?
    Answer: A, E, F, G, and I are the critical activities.
4. How long can noncritical activities be delayed before they cause an increase in the completion time for the project?
    Answer: The activity schedule (see Table 9.2) shows the slack associated with each activity.

Such information is valuable in managing any project. Although the effort required to develop the immediate predecessor relationships and the activity time estimates generally increases with the size of the project, the procedure and contribution of PERT/CPM to larger projects are identical to those shown for the shopping center expansion project. The Management Science in Action, Hospital Revenue Bond at Seasongood & Mayer, describes a 23-activity project that introduced a $31 million hospital revenue bond. PERT/CPM was used to identify the critical activities, the expected project completion time of 29 weeks, and the activity start times and finish times necessary to keep the entire project on schedule.

Summary of the PERT/CPM Critical Path Procedure

Before leaving this section, let us summarize the PERT/CPM critical path procedure.

Step 1. Develop a list of the activities that make up the project.

Step 2. Determine the immediate predecessor(s) for each activity in the project.

Step 3. Estimate the expected completion time for each activity.

Step 4. Draw a project network depicting the activities and immediate predecessors listed in steps 1 and 2.

Step 5. Use the project network and the activity time estimates to determine the earliest start and the earliest finish time for each activity by making a forward pass through the network. The earliest finish time for the last activity in the project identifies the expected time required to complete the entire project.

Step 6. Use the expected project completion time identified in step 5 as the latest finish time for the last activity and make a backward pass through the network to identify the latest start and latest finish time for each activity.

Step 7. Use the difference between the latest start time and the earliest start time for each activity to determine the slack for each activity.

Step 8. Find the activities with zero slack; these are the critical activities.

Step 9. Use the information from steps 5 and 6 to develop the activity schedule for the project.

MANAGEMENT SCIENCE IN ACTION

HOSPITAL REVENUE BOND AT SEASONGOOD & MAYER

Seasongood & Mayer is an investment securities firm located in Cincinnati, Ohio. The firm engages in municipal financing, including the underwriting of new issues of municipal bonds, acting as a market maker for previously issued bonds, and performing other investment banking services.

Seasongood & Mayer provided the underwriting for a $31 million issue of hospital facilities revenue bonds for Providence Hospital in Hamilton County, Ohio. The project of underwriting this municipal bond issue began with activities such as drafting the legal documents, drafting a description of the existing hospital facilities, and completing a feasibility study. A total of 23 activities defined the project that would be completed when the hospital

signed the construction contract and then made the bond proceeds available. The immediate predecessor relationships for the activities and the activity times were developed by a project management team.

PERT/CPM analysis of the project network identified the 10 critical path activities. The analysis also provided the expected completion time of 29 weeks, or approximately seven months. The activity schedule showed the start time and finish time for each activity and provided the information necessary to monitor the project and keep it on schedule. PERT/CPM was instrumental in helping Seasongood & Mayer obtain the financing for the project within the time specified in the construction bid.

NOTES AND COMMENTS

1. Software packages such as Microsoft Project perform the critical path calculations quickly and efficiently. Program inputs include the activities, their immediate predecessors, and expected activity times. The project manager can modify any aspect of the project and quickly determine how the modification affects the activity schedule and the expected time required to complete the project.

2. Suppose that, after analyzing a PERT/CPM network, the project manager finds that the project

completion time is unacceptable (i.e., the project is going to take too long). In this case, the manager must take one or both of the following steps. First, review the original PERT/CPM network to see whether any immediate predecessor relationships can be modified so that at least some of the critical path activities can be done simultaneously. Second, consider adding resources to critical path activities in an attempt to shorten the critical path; we discuss this alternative, referred to as *crashing*, in Section 9.3.

9.2 PROJECT SCHEDULING CONSIDERING UNCERTAIN ACTIVITY TIMES

In this section we consider the details of project scheduling for a problem involving new-product research and development. Because many of the activities in such a project have never been attempted by this organization, the project manager wants to account for uncertainties in the activity times. Let us show how project scheduling can be conducted with uncertain activity times.

The Daugherty Porta-Vac Project

The H. S. Daugherty Company has manufactured industrial vacuum cleaning systems for many years. Recently, a member of the company's new-product research team submitted a report suggesting that the company consider manufacturing a cordless vacuum cleaner. The new product, referred to as Porta-Vac, could contribute to Daugherty's expansion into the household market. Management hopes that the Porta-Vac can be manufactured at a reasonable cost and that its portability and no-cord convenience will make it extremely attractive to potential consumers.

Accurate activity time estimates are important in the development of an activity schedule. When activity times are uncertain, the three time estimates— optimistic, most probable, and pessimistic—allow the project manager to take uncertainty into consideration in determining the critical path and the activity schedule. This approach was developed by the designers of PERT.

Daugherty's management wants to study the feasibility of manufacturing the Porta-Vac product. The feasibility study will provide a recommendation on the action to be taken. To complete this study, information must be obtained from the firm's research and development (R&D), product testing, manufacturing, cost estimating, and market research groups. How long will it take to complete this feasibility study? In the following discussion, we show how to answer this question and provide an activity schedule for the project.

Again, the first step in the project scheduling process is to identify all activities that make up the project and determine the immediate predecessor(s) for each activity. Table 9.3 shows this information for the Porta-Vac project.

The Porta-Vac project network is shown in Figure 9.7. Verify that the network does in fact maintain the immediate predecessor relationships shown in Table 9.3.

Uncertain Activity Times

Once we develop the project network, we will need information on the time required to complete each activity. This information is used in calculating the total time required to complete the project and in scheduling of specific activities. For repeat projects, such as construction and maintenance projects, managers may have the experience and historical data necessary to provide accurate activity time estimates. However, for new or unique projects, estimating the time for each activity may be quite difficult. In fact, in many cases activity times are uncertain and are best described by a range of possible values rather than by one specific time estimate. In these instances, the uncertain activity times are treated as random variables

TABLE 9.3 ACTIVITY LIST FOR THE PORTA-VAC PROJECT

Activity	Description	Immediate Predecessor
A	Develop product design	—
B	Plan market research	—
C	Prepare routing (manufacturing engineering)	A
D	Build prototype model	A
E	Prepare marketing brochure	A
F	Prepare cost estimates (industrial engineering)	C
G	Do preliminary product testing	D
H	Complete market survey	B, E
I	Prepare pricing and forecast report	H
J	Prepare final report	F, G, I

FIGURE 9.7   PORTA-VAC CORDLESS VACUUM CLEANER PROJECT NETWORK

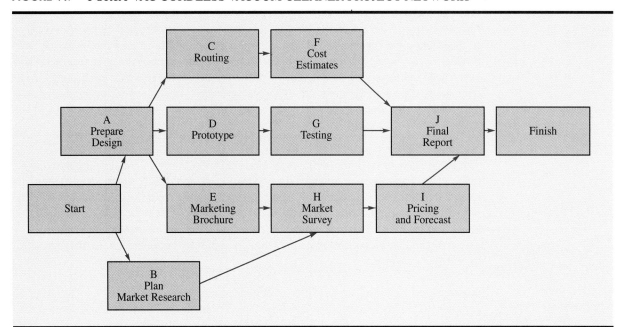

with associated probability distributions. As a result, probability statements will be provided about the ability to meet a specific project completion date.

To incorporate uncertain activity times into the analysis, we need to obtain three time estimates for each activity:

Optimistic time a = the minimum activity time if everything progresses ideally

Most probable time m = the most probable activity time under normal conditions

Pessimistic time b = the maximum activity time if substantial delays are encountered

To illustrate the PERT/CPM procedure with uncertain activity times, let us consider the optimistic, most probable, and pessimistic time estimates for the Porta-Vac activities as presented in Table 9.4. Using activity A as an example, we see that the most probable time is 5 weeks, with a range from 4 weeks (optimistic) to 12 weeks (pessimistic). If the activity could be repeated a large number of times, what is the average time for the activity? This average or **expected time** (t) is as follows:

$$t = \frac{a + 4m + b}{6} \tag{9.4}$$

For activity A we have an average or expected time of

$$t_A = \frac{4 + 4(5) + 12}{6} = \frac{36}{6} = 6 \text{ weeks}$$

With uncertain activity times, we can use the *variance* to describe the dispersion or variation in the activity time values. The variance of the activity time is given by the formula[1]

$$\sigma^2 = \left(\frac{b - a}{6}\right)^2 \tag{9.5}$$

---

[1] The variance equation is based on the notion that a standard deviation is approximately $\frac{1}{6}$ of the difference between the extreme values of the distribution: $(b - a)/6$. The variance is the square of the standard deviation.

TABLE 9.4 OPTIMISTIC, MOST PROBABLE, AND PESSIMISTIC ACTIVITY TIME
ESTIMATES (IN WEEKS) FOR THE PORTA-VAC PROJECT

Activity	Optimistic (a)	Most Probable (m)	Pessimistic (b)
A	4	5	12
B	1	1.5	5
C	2	3	4
D	3	4	11
E	2	3	4
F	1.5	2	2.5
G	1.5	3	4.5
H	2.5	3.5	7.5
I	1.5	2	2.5
J	1	2	3

The difference between the pessimistic (b) and optimistic (a) time estimates greatly affects
the value of the variance. Large differences in these two values reflect a high degree of uncertainty in the activity time. Using equation (9.5), we obtain the measure of uncertainty—
that is, the variance—of activity A, denoted σ_A^2:

$$\sigma_A^2 = \left(\frac{12 - 4}{6}\right)^2 = \left(\frac{8}{6}\right)^2 = 1.78$$

Equations (9.4) and (9.5) are based on the assumption that the activity time distribution
can be described by a **beta probability distribution**.[2] With this assumption, the probability
distribution for the time to complete activity A is as shown in Figure 9.8. Using equations
(9.4) and (9.5) and the data in Table 9.4, we calculated the expected time and variance
for each Porta-Vac activity; the results are summarized in Table 9.5. The Porta-Vac project
network with expected activity times is shown in Figure 9.9.

FIGURE 9.8 ACTIVITY TIME DISTRIBUTION FOR PRODUCT DESIGN (ACTIVITY A)
FOR THE PORTA-VAC PROJECT

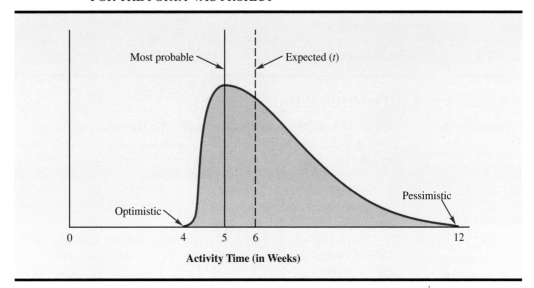

Activity Time (in Weeks)

---

[2] The equations for t and σ^2 require additional assumptions about the parameters of the beta probability distribution.
However, even when these additional assumptions are not made, the equations still provide good approximations of
t and σ^2.

TABLE 9.5 EXPECTED TIMES AND VARIANCES FOR THE PORTA-VAC PROJECT ACTIVITIES

Activity	Expected Time (weeks)	Variance
A	6	1.78
B	2	0.44
C	3	0.11
D	5	1.78
E	3	0.11
F	2	0.03
G	3	0.25
H	4	0.69
I	2	0.03
J	2	0.11
Total	32	

FIGURE 9.9 PORTA-VAC PROJECT NETWORK WITH EXPECTED ACTIVITY TIMES

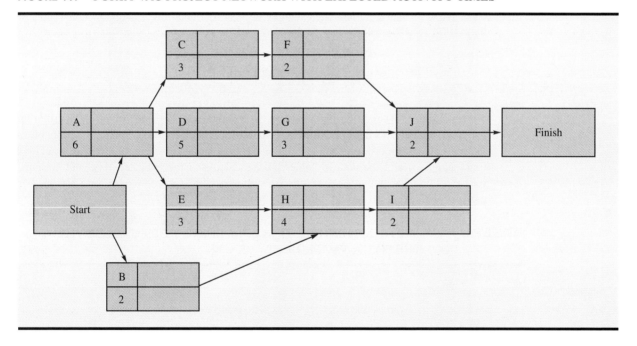

The Critical Path

When uncertain activity times are considered, the actual time required to complete the project may differ from the expected time to complete the project provided by the critical path calculations. However, for planning purposes, the expected time provides valuable information for the project manager.

When we have the project network and the expected activity times, we are ready to proceed with the critical path calculations necessary to determine the expected time required to complete the project and determine the activity schedule. In these calculations, we find the critical path for the Porta-Vac project by applying the critical path procedure introduced in Section 9.1 to the expected activity times (Table 9.5). After the critical activities and the expected time to complete the project have been determined, we analyze the effect of the activity time variability.

Proceeding with a forward pass through the network shown in Figure 9.9, we can establish the earliest start (*ES*) and earliest finish (*EF*) times for each activity. Figure 9.10 shows the project network with the *ES* and *EF* values. Note that the earliest finish time for activity J, the last activity, is 17 weeks. Thus, the expected completion time for the project is 17 weeks. Next, we make a backward pass through the network. The backward pass provides the latest start (*LS*) and latest finish (*LF*) times shown in Figure 9.11.

FIGURE 9.10 PORTA-VAC PROJECT NETWORK WITH EARLIEST START AND EARLIEST FINISH TIMES

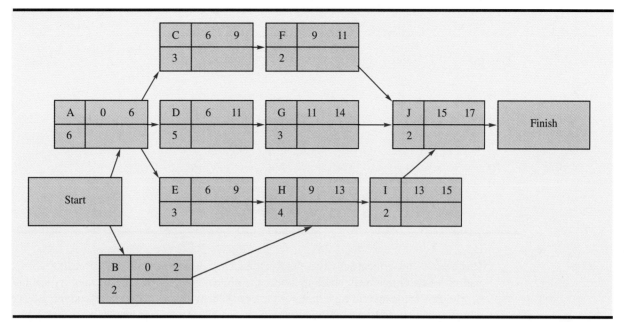

FIGURE 9.11 PORTA-VAC PROJECT NETWORK WITH LATEST START AND LATEST FINISH TIMES

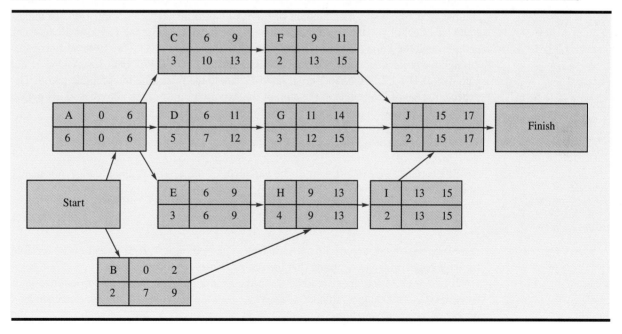

The activity schedule for the Porta-Vac project is shown in Table 9.6. Note that the slack time ($LS - ES$) is also shown for each activity. The activities with zero slack (A, E, H, I, and J) form the critical path for the Porta-Vac project network.

Variability in Project Completion Time

We know that for the Porta-Vac project the critical path of A-E-H-I-J resulted in an expected total project completion time of 17 weeks. However, variation in activities can cause variation in the project completion time. Variation in noncritical activities ordinarily has no effect on the project completion time because of the slack time associated with these activities.

TABLE 9.6   ACTIVITY SCHEDULE FOR THE PORTA-VAC PROJECT

Activity	Earliest Start (ES)	Latest Start (LS)	Earliest Finish (EF)	Latest Finish (LF)	Slack (LS − ES)	Critical Path?
A	0	0	6	6	0	Yes
B	0	7	2	9	7	
C	6	10	9	13	4	
D	6	7	11	12	1	
E	6	6	9	9	0	Yes
F	9	13	11	15	4	
G	11	12	14	15	1	
H	9	9	13	13	0	Yes
I	13	13	15	15	0	Yes
J	15	15	17	17	0	Yes

However, if a noncritical activity is delayed long enough to expend its slack time, it becomes part of a new critical path and may affect the project completion time. Variability leading to a longer-than-expected total time for the critical activities will always extend the project completion time, and, conversely, variability that results in a shorter-than-expected total time for the critical activities will reduce the project completion time, unless other activities become critical.

For a project involving uncertain activity times, the probability that the project can be completed within a specified amount of time is helpful managerial information. To understand the effect of variability on project management, we consider the variation along every path through the Porta-Vac project network. Examining Figure 9.11, we observe four paths through the project network: path 1 = A-E-H-I-J, path 2 = A-C-F-J, path 3 = A-D-G-J, and path 4 = B-H-I-J. Let the random variable T_i denote the total time to complete path i. The expected value of T_i is equal to the sum of the expected times of the activities along path i. For path 1 (the critical path), the expected time is

$$E(T_1) = t_A + t_E + t_H + t_I + t_J = 6 + 3 + 4 + 2 + 2 = 17 \text{ weeks}$$

The variance of T_i is the sum of the variances of the activities along path i. For path 1 (the critical path), the variance in completion time is

$$\sigma_1^2 = \sigma_A^2 + \sigma_E^2 + \sigma_H^2 + \sigma_I^2 + \sigma_J^2 = 1.78 + 0.11 + 0.69 + 0.03 + 0.11 = 2.72 \text{ weeks}^2$$

where σ_A^2, σ_E^2, σ_H^2, σ_I^2, and σ_J^2 are the variances of the activities A, E, H, I, and J. The formula for σ_1^2 is based on the assumption that the activity times are independent.

If two or more activities are dependent, the formula provides only an approximation of the variance of the path completion time. The closer the activities are to being independent, the better the approximation.

Knowing that the standard deviation is the square root of the variance, we compute the standard deviation σ_1 for the path 1 completion time as

$$\sigma_1 = \sqrt{\sigma_1^2} = \sqrt{2.72} = 1.65$$

Assuming that the distribution of the path completion time T_1 follows a normal or bell-shaped distribution[3] allows us to draw the distribution shown in Figure 9.12. With this distribution, we can compute the probability that a path of activities will meet be completed

---

[3] Use of the normal distribution as an approximation is based on the central limit theorem, which indicates that the sum of independent activity times follows a normal distribution as the number of activity times becomes large.

FIGURE 9.12 NORMAL DISTRIBUTION OF THE CRITICAL PATH COMPLETION TIME
FOR THE PORTA-VAC PROJECT

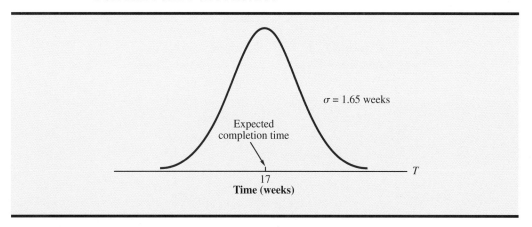

within a specified time. For example, suppose that management allotted 20 weeks for the
Porta-Vac project. What is the probability that path 1 will be completed within 20 weeks? We
are asking for the probability that $T_1 \leq 20$, which corresponds graphically to the shaded area
in Figure 9.13. The z-score for the normal probability distribution at $T_1 = 20$ is

$$z_1 = \frac{20 - 17}{1.65} = 1.82$$

*The normal distribution
tends to be a better
approximation of the
distribution of completion
time for larger projects.*

Using $z = 1.82$ and the table for the normal distribution (see Appendix B), we find that the
probability of path 1 meeting the 20-week deadline is 0.9656.

In Table 9.7, we repeat the calculation of the expected completion time and variance
in completion time for the other paths through the project network (including path 1 again
for completeness). As Table 9.7 shows, path 2 and path 4 are virtually guaranteed to be
completed by the 20-week deadline and path 3 has a probability of 0.9783 of meeting the
20-week deadline.

*Appendix 9.1 describes how
to compute cumulative
probabilities for normal
random variables in
Excel.*

One method for estimating the probability that the entire Porta-Vac project will be
completed by the 20-week deadline is to consider only the path with the smallest completion probability. As is often the case, the critical path (path 1) has the smallest completion
probability. So a simple estimate of the probability that the entire Porta-Vac project will be
complete within 20 weeks is 0.9656.

FIGURE 9.13 PROBABILITY THE CRITICAL PATH WILL BE COMPLETED BY THE
20-WEEK DEADLINE

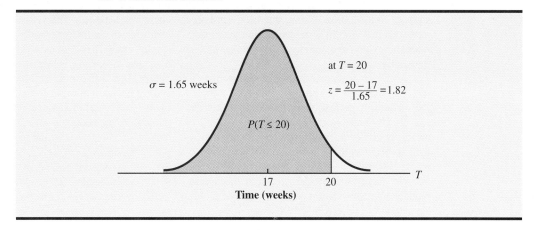

TABLE 9.7   COMPUTING THE PROBABILITY OF EACH PROJECT PATH MEETING
THE 20-WEEK DEADLINE

Expected Path Completion Time	Standard Deviation of Path Completion Time	z-Score	Probability of Meeting Deadline
$E(T_1) = 6 + 3 + 4 + 2$ $+ 2 = 17$	$\sigma_1^2 = 1.78 + 0.11 + 0.69$ $+ 0.03 + 0.11$ $= 2.72$	$z_1 = \dfrac{20 - 17}{\sqrt{2.72}}$ $= 1.82$	0.9656
$E(T_2) = 6 + 3 + 2 + 2$ $= 13$	$\sigma_2^2 = 1.78 + 0.11 + 0.03$ $+ 0.11 = 2.03$	$z_2 = \dfrac{20 - 13}{\sqrt{2.03}}$ $= 4.91$	> 0.9999
$E(T_3) = 6 + 5 + 3 + 2$ $= 16$	$\sigma_3^2 = 1.78 + 1.78 + 0.25$ $+ 0.11 = 3.92$	$z_3 = \dfrac{20 - 16}{\sqrt{3.92}}$ $= 2.02$	0.9783
$E(T_4) = 2 + 4 + 2 + 2$ $= 10$	$\sigma_4^2 = 0.44 + 0.69 + 0.03$ $+ 0.11 = 1.27$	$z_4 = \dfrac{20 - 10}{\sqrt{1.27}}$ $= 7.02$	> 0.9999

A common computational shortcut is to base the probability estimate of the entire project being complete by a deadline solely on the critical path. However, a probability estimate based only on the critical activities may be overly optimistic. When uncertain activity times exist, longer-than-expected completion times for one or more noncritical activities may cause an original noncritical activity to become critical and hence increase the time required to complete the project.

Because all paths must be completed in order for the entire project to be completed, an alternative method for computing the entire project's chance of completion by the deadline is

$P(path\ 1\ completed\ by\ deadline) \times P(path\ 2\ completed\ by\ deadline)$
$\times P(path\ 3\ completed\ by\ deadline) \times P(path\ 4\ completed\ by\ deadline)$
$0.9656 \times 1.0 \times 0.9783 \times 1.0 = 0.9446$

MANAGEMENT SCIENCE IN ACTION

PROJECT MANAGEMENT HELPS THE U.S. AIR FORCE REDUCE MAINTENANCE TIME*

Warner Robins Air Logistics Center (WR-ALC) provides maintenance and repair services for U.S. Air Force aircraft and ground equipment. To support combat zone efforts, the U.S. Air Force requested that WR-ALC reduce the amount of time it took to complete maintenance service on its C-5 transporter aircraft.

To identify ways to improve the management of its repair and overhaul process, WR-ALC adopted the method of critical chain project management (CCPM) by viewing each aircraft at its facility as a project with a series of tasks, precedence dependencies between these tasks, and resource requirements. Identifying tasks at a level of detail that allowed supervisors to clearly assign mechanics, maintenance tools, and facilities resulted in a project network of approximately 450 activities.

By explicitly accounting for each task's resource requirements (mechanics, aircraft parts, maintenance tools, etc.), CCPM identifies a "critical chain" of activities. Efforts to reduce the critical chain led to the insight that a task should not be started until all resources needed to complete the task are available. While this approach, called "pipelining," often results in an initial delay to the start of a task, it allows for the quicker completion of the task by eliminating delays after the task's launch and by reducing efficiency-robbing multitasking (across tasks) by the mechanics.

*Based on M. M. Srinivasan, W. D. Best, and S. Chandrasekaran, "Warner Robins Air Logistics Center Streamlines Aircraft Repair and Overhaul," *Interfaces* 37, no. 1 (2007), pp. 7–21.

Simulation is another technique used in project management and is particularly useful for estimating the probability of an extremely complex project being completed by a specified deadline.

This calculation assumes that each path is independent. As all of these paths share at least one common activity, this assumption is violated. Consequentially, this estimate will be a pessimistic estimate of the likelihood of meeting the project deadline.

Regardless of the method to estimate the completion probability, a project manager should frequently monitor the progress of the project. In particular, the project manager should monitor activities with large variances in their activity times. The Management Science in Action, Project Management Helps the U.S. Air Force Reduce Maintenance Time, describes how closely managing the progress of individual activities and the assignment of resources led to dramatic improvements in the maintenance of military aircraft.

9.3   CONSIDERING TIME–COST TRADE-OFFS

Using additional resources to reduce activity times was proposed by the developers of CPM. The shortening of activity times is referred to as crashing.

When determining the time estimates for activities in a project, the project manager bases these estimates on the amount of resources (workers, equipment, etc.) that will be assigned to an activity. The original developers of CPM provided the project manager with the option of adding resources to selected activities to reduce project completion time. Added resources (such as more workers, overtime, and so on) generally increase project costs, so the decision to reduce activity times must take into consideration the additional cost involved. In effect, the project manager must make a decision that involves trading additional project costs for reduced activity time.

Table 9.8 defines a two-machine maintenance project consisting of five activities. Management has substantial experience with similar projects and the times for maintenance activities have very little variability; hence, a single time estimate is given for each activity. The project network is shown in Figure 9.14.

TABLE 9.8   ACTIVITY LIST FOR THE TWO-MACHINE MAINTENANCE PROJECT

Activity	Description	Immediate Predecessor	Expected Time (days)
A	Overhaul machine I	—	7
B	Adjust machine I	A	3
C	Overhaul machine II	—	6
D	Adjust machine II	C	3
E	Test system	B, D	2

FIGURE 9.14   TWO-MACHINE MAINTENANCE PROJECT NETWORK

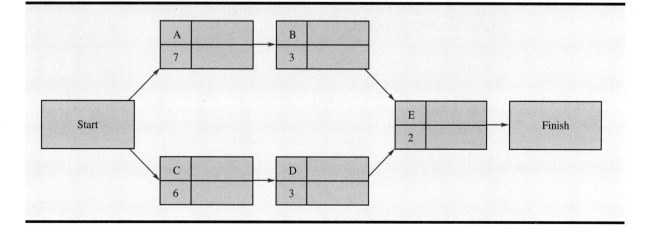

TABLE 9.9   ACTIVITY SCHEDULE FOR THE TWO-MACHINE MAINTENANCE PROJECT

Activity	Earliest Start (*ES*)	Latest Start (*LS*)	Earliest Finish (*EF*)	Latest Finish (*LF*)	Slack (*LS* − *ES*)	Critical Path?
A	0	0	7	7	0	Yes
B	7	7	10	10	0	Yes
C	0	1	6	7	1	
D	6	7	9	10	1	
E	10	10	12	12	0	Yes

The procedure for making critical path calculations for the maintenance project network is the same one that was used to find the critical path in the networks for both the Western Hills Shopping Center expansion project and the Porta-Vac project. Making the forward pass and backward pass calculations for the network in Figure 9.14, we obtained the activity schedule shown in Table 9.9. The zero slack times, and thus the critical path, are associated with activities A-B-E. The length of the critical path, and thus the total time required to complete the project, is 12 days.

Crashing Activity Times

Now suppose that current production levels make completing the maintenance project within 10 days imperative. By looking at the length of the critical path of the network (12 days), we realize that meeting the desired project completion time is impossible unless we can shorten selected activity times. This shortening of activity times, which usually can be achieved by adding resources, is referred to as **crashing**. Because the added resources associated with crashing activity times usually result in added project costs, we will want to identify the activities that cost the least to crash and then crash those activities by only the amount necessary to meet the desired project completion time.

To determine where and how much to crash activity times, we need information on how much each activity can be crashed and how much the crashing process costs. Hence, we must ask for the following information:

1. Activity cost under the normal or expected activity time
2. Time to complete the activity under maximum crashing (i.e., the shortest possible activity time)
3. Activity cost under maximum crashing

Let

$$\tau_i = \text{expected time for activity } i$$

$$\tau_i' = \text{time for activity } i \text{ under maximum crashing}$$

$$M_i = \text{maximum possible reduction in time for activity } i \text{ due to crashing}$$

Given τ_i and τ_i', we can compute M_i:

$$M_i = \tau_i - \tau_i' \tag{9.6}$$

Equation (9.7) assumes that each unit of time gained by crashing an activity has the same associated cost. It is possible that the first few units of time gained by crashing an activity cost less than ensuing units of time gained by crashing the activity.

Next, let C_i denote the cost for activity i under the normal or expected activity time and let C_i' denote the cost for activity i under maximum crashing. Thus, per unit of time (e.g., per day), the crashing cost K_i for each activity is given by

$$K_i = \frac{C_i' - C_i}{M_i} \tag{9.7}$$

For example, if the normal or expected time for activity A is 7 days at a cost of $C_A = \$500$ and the time under maximum crashing is 4 days at a cost of $C'_A = \$800$, equations (9.6) and (9.7) show that the maximum possible reduction in time for activity A is

$$M_A = 7 - 4 = 3 \text{ days}$$

with a crashing cost of

$$K_A = \frac{C'_A - C_A}{M_A} = \frac{800 - 500}{3} = \frac{300}{3} = \$100 \text{ per day}$$

We make the assumption that any portion or fraction of the activity crash time can be achieved for a corresponding portion of the activity crashing cost. For example, if we decided to crash activity A by only 1.5 days, the added cost would be 1.5 ($100) = $150, which results in a total activity cost of $500 + $150 = $650. Figure 9.15 shows the graph of the time–cost relationship for activity A. The complete normal and crash activity data for the two-machine maintenance project are given in Table 9.10.

FIGURE 9.15   TIME–COST RELATIONSHIP FOR ACTIVITY A

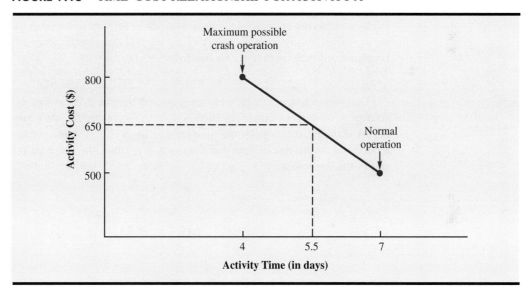

TABLE 9.10   NORMAL AND CRASH ACTIVITY DATA FOR THE TWO-MACHINE MAINTENANCE PROJECT

Activity	Time (days) Normal	Time (days) Crash	Total Cost Normal (C_i)	Total Cost Crash (C'_i)	Maximum Reduction in Time (M_i)	Crash Cost per Day $\left(K_i = \dfrac{C'_i - C_i}{M_i}\right)$
A	7	4	$ 500	$ 800	3	$100
B	3	2	200	350	1	150
C	6	4	500	900	2	200
D	3	1	200	500	2	150
E	2	1	300	550	1	250
			$1700	$3100		

Which activities should be crashed—and by how much—to meet the 10-day project completion deadline at minimum cost? Your first reaction to this question may be to consider crashing the critical activities—A, B, or E. Activity A has the lowest crashing cost per day of the three, and crashing this activity by 2 days will reduce the A-B-E path to the desired 10 days. Keep in mind, however, that as you crash the current critical activities, other paths may become critical. Thus, you will need to check the critical path in the revised network and perhaps either identify additional activities to crash or modify your initial crashing decision. For a small network, this trial-and-error approach can be used to make crashing decisions; in larger networks, however, a mathematical procedure is required to determine the optimal crashing decisions.

Linear Programming Model for Crashing

Let us describe how linear programming can be used to solve the network crashing problem. With PERT/CPM, we know that when an activity starts at its earliest start time, then

$$\text{Finish time} = \text{Earliest start time} + \text{Activity time}$$

However, if slack time is associated with an activity, then the activity need not start at its earliest start time. In this case, we may have

$$\text{Finish time} > \text{Earliest start time} + \text{Activity time}$$

Because we do not know ahead of time whether an activity will start at its earliest start time, we use the following inequality to show the general relationship among finish time, earliest start time, and activity time for each activity:

$$\text{Finish time} \geq \text{Earliest start time} + \text{Activity time}$$

Consider activity A, which has an expected time of 7 days. Let x_A = finish time for activity A, and y_A = amount of time activity A is crashed. If we assume that the project begins at time 0, the earliest start time for activity A is 0. Because the time for activity A is reduced by the amount of time that activity A is crashed, the finish time for activity A must satisfy the relationship

$$x_A \geq 0 + (7 - y_A)$$

Moving y_A to the left side

$$x_A + y_A \geq 7$$

In general, let

$$x_i = \text{the finish time for activity } i \qquad\qquad i = A, B, C, D, E$$

$$y_i = \text{the amount of time activity } i \text{ is crashed} \qquad i = A, B, C, D, E$$

If we follow the same approach that we used for activity A, the constraint corresponding to the finish time for activity C (expected time = 6 days) is

$$x_C \geq 0 + (6 - y_C) \quad \text{or} \quad x_C + y_C \geq 6$$

Continuing with the forward pass of the PERT/CPM procedure, we see that the earliest start time for activity B is x_A, the finish time for activity A. Thus, the constraint corresponding to the finish time for activity B is

$$x_B \geq x_A + (3 - y_B) \quad \text{or} \quad x_B + y_B - x_A \geq 3$$

Similarly, we obtain the constraint for the finish time for activity D:

$$x_D \geq x_C + (3 - y_D) \quad \text{or} \quad x_D + y_D - x_C \geq 3$$

Finally, we consider activity E. The earliest start time for activity E equals the *largest* of the finish times for activities B and D. Because the finish times for both activities B and D will be determined by the crashing procedure, we must write two constraints for activity E, one based on the finish time for activity B and one based on the finish time for activity D:

$$x_E + y_E - x_B \geq 2 \quad \text{and} \quad x_E + y_E - x_D \geq 2$$

Recall that current production levels made completing the maintenance project within 10 days imperative. Thus, the constraint for the finish time for activity E is

$$x_E \leq 10$$

In addition, we must add the following five constraints corresponding to the maximum allowable crashing time for each activity:

$$y_A \leq 3, \quad y_B \leq 1, \quad y_C \leq 2, \quad y_D \leq 2, \quad \text{and} \quad y_E \leq 1$$

As with all linear programs, we add the usual nonnegativity requirements for the decision variables.

All that remains is to develop an objective function for the model. Because the total project cost for a normal completion time is fixed at $1700 (see Table 9.10), we can minimize the total project cost (normal cost plus crashing cost) by minimizing the total crashing costs. Thus, the linear programming objective function becomes

$$\text{Min } 100y_A + 150y_B + 200y_C + 150y_D + 250y_E$$

Thus, to determine the optimal crashing for each of the activities, we must solve a 10-variable, 12-constraint linear programming model. Optimization software, such as Excel Solver, provides the optimal solution of crashing activity A by 1 day and activity E by 1 day, with a total crashing cost of $100 + $250 = $350. With the minimum cost crashing solution, the activity times are as follows:

Activity	Time in Days
A	6 (Crash 1 day)
B	3
C	6
D	3
E	1 (Crash 1 day)

The linear programming solution provided the revised activity times, but not the revised earliest start time, latest start time, and slack information. The revised activity times and the usual PERT/CPM procedure must be used to develop the activity schedule for the project.

NOTES AND COMMENTS

1. Note that the two-machine maintenance project network for the crashing illustration (see Figure 9.14) has only one activity, activity E, leading directly to the Finish node. As a result, the project completion time is equal to the completion time for activity E. Thus, the linear programming constraint requiring the project completion in 10 days or less could be written $x_E \leq 10$.

If two or more activities lead directly to the Finish node of a project network, a slight modification is required in the linear programming model for crashing. Consider the portion of the project network shown here. In this case, we suggest creating an additional variable, x_{FIN}, which indicates the finish or completion time for the entire project. The fact that the project cannot be finished until both activities E and G are completed can be modeled by the two constraints

$$x_{FIN} \geq x_E \quad \text{or} \quad x_{FIN} - x_E \geq 0$$

$$x_{FIN} \geq x_G \quad \text{or} \quad x_{FIN} - x_G \geq 0$$

The constraint that the project must be finished by time T can be added as $x_{FIN} \leq T$. Problem 22 gives you practice with this type of project network.

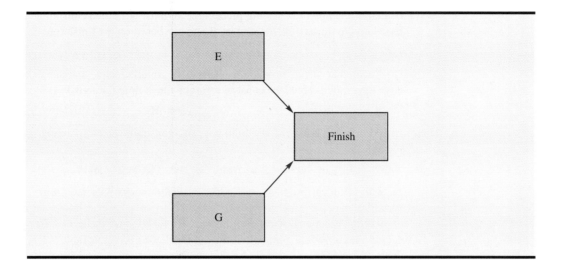

SUMMARY

In this chapter we showed how PERT/CPM can be used to plan, schedule, and control a wide variety of projects. The key to this approach to project scheduling is the development of a PERT/CPM project network that depicts the activities and their precedence relationships. From this project network and activity time estimates, the critical path for the network and the associated critical activities can be identified. In the process, an activity schedule showing the earliest start and earliest finish times, the latest start and latest finish times, and the slack for each activity can be identified.

We showed how we can include capabilities for handling variable or uncertain activity times and how to use this information to provide a probability statement about the chances the project can be completed in a specified period of time. We introduced crashing as a procedure for reducing activity times to meet project completion deadlines, and we showed how a linear programming model can be used to determine the crashing decisions that will minimize the cost of reducing the project completion time.

GLOSSARY

Activities   Specific jobs or tasks that are components of a project. Activities are represented by nodes in a project network.

Backward pass   Part of the PERT/CPM procedure that involves moving backward through the network to determine the latest start and latest finish times for each activity.

Beta probability distribution   A probability distribution used to describe activity times.

Crashing   The shortening of activity times by adding resources and hence usually increasing cost.

Critical activities   The activities on the critical path.

Critical path   The longest path in a project network.

Critical path method (CPM)   A network-based project scheduling procedure.

Earliest finish time   The earliest time an activity may be completed.

Earliest start time   The earliest time an activity may begin.

Expected time   The average activity time.

Forward pass   Part of the PERT/CPM procedure that involves moving forward through the project network to determine the earliest start and earliest finish times for each activity.

Immediate predecessors   The activities that must be completed immediately prior to the start of a given activity.

Latest finish time   The latest time an activity may be completed without increasing the project completion time.

Latest start time   The latest time an activity may begin without increasing the project completion time.

Most probable time   The most probable activity time under normal conditions.

Optimistic time   The minimum activity time if everything progresses ideally.

Path   A sequence of connected nodes that leads from the Start node to the Finish node.

Pessimistic time   The maximum activity time if substantial delays are encountered.

Program evaluation and review technique (PERT)   A network-based project scheduling procedure.

Project network   A graphical representation of a project that depicts the activities and shows the predecessor relationships among the activities.

Slack   The length of time an activity can be delayed without affecting the project completion time.

PROBLEMS

1. The Mohawk Discount Store is designing a management training program for individuals at its corporate headquarters. The company wants to design the program so that trainees can complete it as quickly as possible. Important precedence relationships must be maintained between assignments or activities in the program. For example, a trainee cannot serve as an assistant to the store manager until the trainee has obtained experience in the credit department and at least one sales department. The following activities are the assignments that must be completed by each trainee in the program. Construct a project network for this problem. Do not perform any further analysis.

Activity	A	B	C	D	E	F	G	H
Immediate Predecessor	—	—	A	A, B	A, B	C	D, F	E, G

2. Bridge City Developers is coordinating the construction of an office complex. As part of the planning process, the company generated the following activity list. Draw a project network that can be used to assist in the scheduling of the project activities.

Activity	A	B	C	D	E	F	G	H	I	J
Immediate Predecessor	—	—	—	A, B	A, B	D	E	C	C	F, G, H, I

 SELF*test*

3. Construct a project network for the following project. The project is completed when activities F and G are both complete.

Activity	A	B	C	D	E	F	G
Immediate Predecessor	—	—	A	A	C, B	C, B	D, E

4. Assume that the project in Problem 3 has the following activity times (in months):

Activity	A	B	C	D	E	F	G
Time	4	6	2	6	3	3	5

    a. Find the critical path.
    b. The project must be completed in 1.5 years. Do you anticipate difficulty in meeting the deadline? Explain.

5. Consider the Western Hills Shopping Center project summarized by Figure 9.6 and Table 9.2. Suppose the project has been underway for seven weeks. Activities A and E have been completed. Activity F has commenced but has three weeks remaining. Activities C and D have not started yet. Activity B has one week remaining (it was not started until week 2). Update the activity schedule for the project. In particular, how has the slack for each activity changed?

✓SELF*test*

6. Consider the following project network and activity times (in weeks):

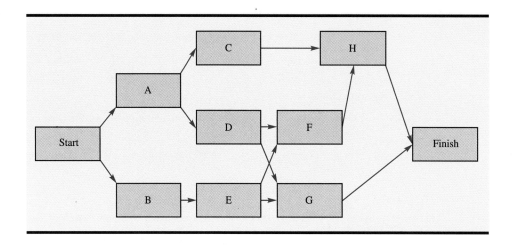

Activity	A	B	C	D	E	F	G	H
Time	5	3	7	6	7	3	10	8

a. Identify the critical path.
b. How much time will be needed to complete this project?
c. Can activity D be delayed without delaying the entire project? If so, by how many weeks?
d. Can activity C be delayed without delaying the entire project? If so, by how many weeks?
e. What is the schedule for activity E?

7. Embassy Club Condominium, located on the west coast of Florida, is undertaking a summer renovation of its main building. The project is scheduled to begin May 1, and a September 1 (17-week) completion date is desired. The condominium manager identified the following renovation activities and their estimated times:

Activity	Immediate Predecessor	Time
A	—	3
B	—	1
C	—	2
D	A, B, C	4
E	C, D	5
F	A	3
G	D, F	6
H	E	4

a. Draw a project network.
b. What are the critical activities?
c. What activity has the most slack time?
d. Will the project be completed by September 1?

8. Colonial State College is considering building a new multipurpose athletic complex on campus. The complex would provide a new gymnasium for intercollegiate basketball games, expanded office space, classrooms, and intramural facilities. The following activities would have to be undertaken before construction can begin:

Activity	Description	Immediate Predecessor	Time (weeks)
A	Survey building site	—	6
B	Develop initial design	—	8
C	Obtain board approval	A, B	12
D	Select architect	C	4
E	Establish budget	C	6
F	Finalize design	D, E	15
G	Obtain financing	E	12
H	Hire contractor	F, G	8

a. Draw a project network.
b. Identify the critical path.
c. Develop the activity schedule for the project.
d. Does it appear reasonable that construction of the athletic complex could begin one year after the decision to begin the project with the site survey and initial design plans? What is the expected completion time for the project?

9. At a local university, the Student Commission on Programming and Entertainment (SCOPE) is preparing to host its first rock concert of the school year. To successfully produce this rock concert, SCOPE has listed the requisite activities and related information in the following table (duration estimates measured in days).

Activity	Immediate Predecessor(s)	Optimistic	Most Probable	Pessimistic
A: Negotiate contract with selected musicians	—	8	10	15
B: Reserve site	—	7	8	9
C: Manage travel logistics for music group	A	5	6	10
D: Screen & hire security personnel	B	3	3	3
E: Arrange advertising & ticketing	B, C	1	5	9
F: Hire parking staff	D	4	7	10
G: Arrange concession sales	E	3	8	10

a. Draw the project network.
b. Compute the expected duration and variance of each activity.
c. Determine the critical path in the project network.
d. What is the expected duration and variance of the critical path?
e. Based only on the critical path, what is the likelihood that the project will be completed within 30 days?
f. If activity B is delayed by six days beyond its early start time, how does this affect the expected project duration?
g. Using all paths through the project network, estimate the probability that the project will be completed within 30 days. Compare your answer to the answer in part e and explain.

10. The following estimates of activity times (in days) are available for a small project:

Activity	Optimistic	Most Probable	Pessimistic
A	4	5.0	6
B	8	9.0	10
C	7	7.5	11
D	7	9.0	10
E	6	7.0	9
F	5	6.0	7

  a. Compute the expected activity completion times and the variance for each activity.
  b. An analyst determined that the critical path consists of activities B-D-F. Compute the expected project completion time and the variance of this path.

11. Building a backyard swimming pool consists of nine major activities. The activities and their immediate predecessors are shown. Develop the project network.

Activity	A	B	C	D	E	F	G	H	I
Immediate Predecessor	—	—	A, B	A, B	B	C	D	D, F	E, G, H

12. Assume that the activity time estimates (in days) for the swimming pool construction project in Problem 11 are as follows:

Activity	Optimistic	Most Probable	Pessimistic
A	3	5	6
B	2	4	6
C	5	6	7
D	7	9	10
E	2	4	6
F	1	2	3
G	5	8	10
H	6	8	10
I	3	4	5

  a. What are the critical activities?
  b. What is the expected time to complete the project?
  c. Based only on the critical path, what is the estimated probability that the project can be completed in 25 or fewer days?

13. Suppose that the following estimates of activity times (in weeks) were provided for the network shown in Problem 6:

Activity	Optimistic	Most Probable	Pessimistic
A	4.0	5.0	6.0
B	2.5	3.0	3.5
C	6.0	7.0	8.0
D	5.0	5.5	9.0
E	5.0	7.0	9.0
F	2.0	3.0	4.0
G	8.0	10.0	12.0
H	6.0	7.0	14.0

Based only on the critical path, what is the estimated probability that the project will be completed
  a. Within 21 weeks?
  b. Within 22 weeks?
  c. Within 25 weeks?

14. Davison Construction Company is building a luxury lakefront home in the Finger Lakes region of New York. Coordination of the architect and subcontractors will require a major effort to meet the 44-week (approximately 10-month) completion date requested by the owner. The Davison project manager prepared the following project network:

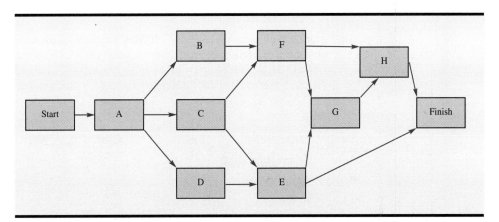

Estimates of the optimistic, most probable, and pessimistic times (in weeks) for the activities are as follows:

Activity	Optimistic	Most Probable	Pessimistic
A	4	8	12
B	6	7	8
C	6	12	18
D	3	5	7
E	6	9	18
F	5	8	17
G	10	15	20
H	5	6	13

a. Find the critical path.
b. What is the expected project completion time?
c. Based only on the critical path, what is the estimated probability the project can be completed in 44 weeks as requested by the owner?
d. Based only on the critical path, what is the estimated probability the building project could run more than 3 months late? Use 57 weeks for this calculation.
e. What should the construction company tell the owner?

15. Doug Casey is in charge of planning and coordinating next spring's sales management training program for his company. Doug listed the following activity information for this project:

Activity	Description	Immediate Predecessor	Time (weeks) Optimistic	Most Probable	Pessimistic
A	Plan topic	—	1.5	2.0	2.5
B	Obtain speakers	A	2.0	2.5	6.0
C	List meeting locations	—	1.0	2.0	3.0
D	Select location	C	1.5	2.0	2.5
E	Finalize speaker travel plans	B, D	0.5	1.0	1.5
F	Make final check with speakers	E	1.0	2.0	3.0
G	Prepare and mail brochure	B, D	3.0	3.5	7.0
H	Take reservations	G	3.0	4.0	5.0
I	Handle last-minute details	F, H	1.5	2.0	2.5

   a. Draw a project network.
   b. Prepare an activity schedule.
   c. What are the critical activities and what is the expected project completion time?
   d. If Doug wants a 0.99 probability of completing the project on time, how far ahead of the scheduled meeting date should he begin working on the project? Base your calculation solely on the critical path.

16. Management Decision Systems (MDS) is a consulting company that specializes in the development of decision support systems. MDS has a four-person team working on a current project with a small company to set up a system that scrapes data from a collection of websites and then automatically generates a report for management on a daily basis.

Activity	Description	Immediate Predecessor	Optimistic	Time (Weeks) Most Probable	Pessimistic
A	Report generation	—	1	7	11
B	Web scraping	—	3	8	10
C	Testing	A, B	1	1	1

   a. Construct the project network.
   b. Based solely on the critical path, estimate the probability that the project will be complete within 10 weeks.
   c. Using all paths through project network, estimate the probability that the project will be complete within 10 weeks.
   d. Should you use the estimate in (b) or (c)?

17. The Porsche Shop, founded in 1985 by Dale Jensen, specializes in the restoration of vintage Porsche automobiles. One of Jensen's regular customers asked him to prepare an estimate for the restoration of a 1964 model 356SC Porsche. To estimate the time and cost to perform such a restoration, Jensen broke the restoration process into four separate activities: disassembly and initial preparation work (A), body restoration (B), engine restoration (C), and final assembly (D). Once activity A has been completed, activities B and C can be performed independently of each other; however, activity D can be started only if both activities B and C have been completed. Based on his inspection of the car, Jensen believes that the following time estimates (in days) are applicable:

Activity	Optimistic	Most Probable	Pessimistic
A	3	4	8
B	5	8	11
C	2	4	6
D	4	5	12

   Jensen estimates that the parts needed to restore the body will cost $3000 and that the parts needed to restore the engine will cost $5000. His current labor costs are $400 a day.
   a. Develop a project network.
   b. What is the expected project completion time?
   c. Jensen's business philosophy is based on making decisions using a best- and worst-case scenario. Develop cost estimates for completing the restoration based on both a best- and worst-case analysis. Assume that the total restoration cost is the sum of the labor cost plus the material cost.
   d. If Jensen obtains the job with a bid that is based on the costs associated with an expected completion time, what is the probability that he will lose money on the job?
   e. If Jensen obtains the job based on a bid of $16,800, what is the probability that he will lose money on the job?

18. The manager of the Oak Hills Swimming Club is planning the club's swimming team program. The first team practice is scheduled for May 1. The activities, their immediate predecessors, and the activity time estimates (in weeks) are as follows:

Activity	Description	Immediate Predecessor	Time (weeks)		
			Optimistic	Most Probable	Pessimistic
A	Meet with board	—	1	1	2
B	Hire coaches	A	4	6	8
C	Reserve pool	A	2	4	6
D	Announce program	B, C	1	2	3
E	Meet with coaches	B	2	3	4
F	Order team suits	A	1	2	3
G	Register swimmers	D	1	2	3
H	Collect fees	G	1	2	3
I	Plan first practice	E, H, F	1	1	1

    a. Draw a project network.
    b. Develop an activity schedule.
    c. What are the critical activities, and what is the expected project completion time?
    d. If the club manager plans to start the project on February 1, calculate the probability the swimming program will be ready by the scheduled May 1 date (13 weeks) based solely on the critical path. Should the manager begin planning the swimming program before February 1?

19. The product development group at Landon Corporation has been working on a new computer software product that has the potential to capture a large market share. Through outside sources, Landon's management learned that a competitor is working to introduce a similar product. As a result, Landon's top management increased its pressure on the product development group. The group's leader turned to PERT/CPM as an aid to scheduling the activities remaining before the new product can be brought to the market. The project network is as follows:

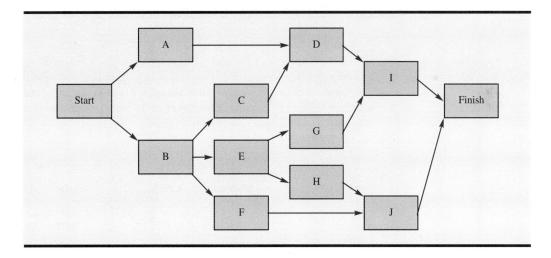

The activity time estimates (in weeks) are as follows:

Activity	Optimistic	Most Probable	Pessimistic
A	3.0	4.0	5.0
B	3.0	3.5	7.0
C	4.0	5.0	6.0
D	2.0	3.0	4.0
E	6.0	10.0	14.0
F	7.5	8.5	12.5
G	4.5	6.0	7.5
H	5.0	6.0	13.0
I	2.0	2.5	6.0
J	4.0	5.0	6.0

a. Develop an activity schedule for this project and identify the critical path activities.

b. Based solely on the critical path, what is the probability that the project will be completed so that Landon Corporation may introduce the new product within 25 weeks? Within 30 weeks?

20. Norton Industries is installing a new computer system. The activities, the activity times, and the project network are as follows:

Activity	Time	Activity	Time
A	3	E	4
B	6	F	3
C	2	G	9
D	5	H	3

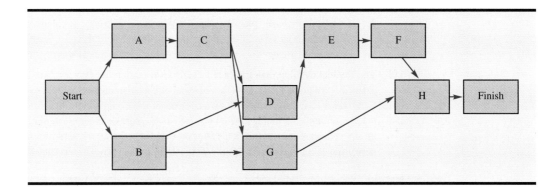

The critical path calculation shows B-D-E-F-H is the critical path, and the expected project completion time is 21 weeks. After viewing this information, management requested overtime be used to complete the project in 16 weeks. Thus, crashing of the project is necessary. The following information is relevant:

	Time (weeks)		Cost ($)	
Activity	Normal	Crash	Normal	Crash
A	3	1	900	1700
B	6	3	2000	4000
C	2	1	500	1000
D	5	3	1800	2400
E	4	3	1500	1850
F	3	1	3000	3900
G	9	4	8000	9800
H	3	2	1000	2000

a. Formulate a linear programming model that can be used to make the crashing decisions for this project.

b. Solve the linear programming model and make the minimum cost crashing decisions. What is the added cost of meeting the 16-week completion time?

c. Develop a complete activity schedule based on the crashed activity times.

21. Consider the following project network and activity times (in days):

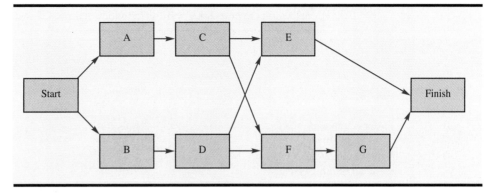

Activity	A	B	C	D	E	F	G
Time	3	2	5	5	6	2	2

The crashing data for this project are as follows:

	Time (days)		Cost ($)	
Activity	**Normal**	**Crash**	**Normal**	**Crash**
A	3	2	800	1400
B	2	1	1200	1900
C	5	3	2000	2800
D	5	3	1500	2300
E	6	4	1800	2800
F	2	1	600	1000
G	2	1	500	1000

   a. Find the critical path and the expected project completion time.
   b. What is the total project cost using the normal times?

22. Refer to Problem 21. Assume that management desires a 12-day project completion time.
   a. Formulate a linear programming model that can be used to assist with the crashing decisions.
   b. What activities should be crashed?
   c. What is the total project cost for the 12-day completion time?

23. Consider the following project network. Note that the normal or expected activity times are denoted τ_i, $i = $ A, B, . . . , I. Let $x_i = $ the earliest finish time for activity i. Formulate a linear programming model that can be used to determine the length of the critical path.

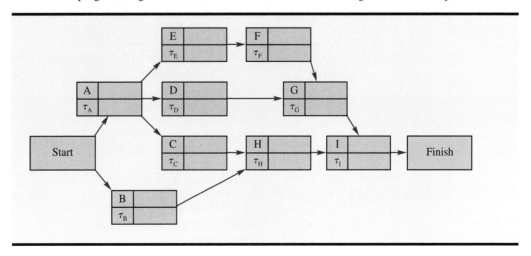

24. Office Automation, Inc., developed a proposal for introducing a new computerized office system that will standardize the electronic archiving of invoices for a particular company. Contained in the proposal is a list of activities that must be accomplished to complete the new office system project. Use the following relevant information about the activities:

Activity	Description	Immediate Predecessor	Time (weeks) Normal	Time (weeks) Crash	Cost ($1000s) Normal	Cost ($1000s) Crash
A	Plan needs	—	10	8	30	70
B	Order equipment	A	8	6	120	150
C	Install equipment	B	10	7	100	160
D	Set up training lab	A	7	6	40	50
E	Conduct training course	D	10	8	50	75
F	Test system	C, E	3	3	60	—

  a. Develop a project network.
  b. Develop an activity schedule.
  c. What are the critical activities, and what is the expected project completion time?
  d. Assume that the company wants to complete the project in six months or 26 weeks. What crashing decisions do you recommend to meet the desired completion time at the least possible cost? Work through the network and attempt to make the crashing decisions by inspection.
  e. Develop an activity schedule for the crashed project.
  f. What added project cost is required to meet the six-month completion time?

25. Because Landon Corporation (see Problem 19) is being pressured to complete the product development project at the earliest possible date, the project leader requested that the possibility of crashing the project be evaluated.
  a. Formulate a linear programming model that could be used in making the crashing decisions.
  b. What information would have to be provided before the linear programming model could be implemented?

Case Problem 1   R. C. COLEMAN

R. C. Coleman distributes a variety of food products that are sold through grocery store and supermarket outlets. The company receives orders directly from the individual outlets, with a typical order requesting the delivery of several cases of anywhere from 20 to 50 different products. Under the company's current warehouse operation, warehouse clerks dispatch order-picking personnel to fill each order and have the goods moved to the warehouse shipping area. Because of the high labor costs and relatively low productivity of hand order-picking, management has decided to automate the warehouse operation by installing a computer-controlled order-picking system, along with a conveyor system for moving goods from storage to the warehouse shipping area.

Activity	Description	Immediate Predecessor
A	Determine equipment needs	—
B	Obtain vendor proposals	—
C	Select vendor	A, B
D	Order system	C
E	Design new warehouse layout	C
F	Design warehouse	E
G	Design computer interface	C
H	Interface computer	D, F, G
I	Install system	D, F
J	Train system operators	H
K	Test system	I, J

| | | Time (weeks) | |
Activity	Optimistic	Most Probable	Pessimistic
A	4	6	8
B	6	8	16
C	2	4	6
D	8	10	24
E	7	10	13
F	4	6	8
G	4	6	20
H	4	6	8
I	4	6	14
J	3	4	5
K	2	4	6

R. C. Coleman's director of material management has been named the project manager in charge of the automated warehouse system. After consulting with members of the engineering staff and warehouse management personnel, the director compiled a list of activities associated with the project. The optimistic, most probable, and pessimistic times (in weeks) have also been provided for each activity.

Managerial Report

Develop a report that presents the activity schedule and expected project completion time for the warehouse expansion project. Include a project network in the report. In addition, take into consideration the following issues:

1. R. C. Coleman's top management established a required 40-week completion time for the project. Can this completion time be achieved? Include probability information in your discussion. What recommendations do you have if the 40-week completion time is required?

2. Suppose that management requests that activity times be shortened to provide an 80% chance of meeting the 40-week completion time. If the variance in the project completion time is the same as you found in part (1), how much should the expected project completion time be shortened to achieve the goal of an 80% chance of completion within 40 weeks?

3. Using the expected activity times as the normal times and the following crashing information, determine the activity crashing decisions and revised activity schedule for the warehouse expansion project:

| | Crashed Activity Time | Cost ($) | |
Activity	(weeks)	Normal	Crashed
A	4	1,000	1,900
B	7	1,000	1,800
C	2	1,500	2,700
D	8	2,000	3,200
E	7	5,000	8,000
F	4	3,000	4,100
G	5	8,000	10,250
H	4	5,000	6,400
I	4	10,000	12,400
J	3	4,000	4,400
K	3	5,000	5,500

Appendix 9.1   FINDING CUMULATIVE PROBABILITIES FOR NORMALLY DISTRIBUTED RANDOM VARIABLES

Excel can be used to find the probability a project with uncertain activity times will be completed in some given completion time (assuming the project completion time is normally distributed). We demonstrate this on the Porta-Vac project we considered in Section 9.2. Recall that management allotted 20 days to complete the project. We have found the z value that corresponds to $T = 20$:

$$z = \frac{20 - 17}{1.65} = 1.82$$

Now we will make use of the Excel function

$$=\text{NORM.S.DIST}(z, \text{TRUE})$$

by substituting the value of z we have found into the function (entering "TRUE" for the second argument signifies that we desire the cumulative probability associated with z). Enter the following function into any empty cell in an Excel worksheet:

$$=\text{NORM.S.DIST}(1.82, \text{TRUE})$$

The resulting value is 0.96562, which is the probability that the completion time for the Porta-Vac project will be no more than 20 days.

CHAPTER 10

Inventory Models

CONTENTS

Inventory refers to idle goods or materials held by an organization for use sometime in the future. Items carried in inventory include raw materials, purchased parts, components, subassemblies, work-in-process, finished goods, and supplies. Two primary reasons organizations stock inventory are: (1) to take advantage of economies-of-scale that exist due to the fixed cost of ordering items, and (2) to buffer against uncertainty in customer demand or disruptions in supply. Even though inventory serves an important and essential role, the expense associated with financing and maintaining inventories is a substantial part of the cost of doing business. In large organizations, the cost associated with inventory can run into the millions of dollars.

In applications involving inventory, managers must answer two important questions.

1. *How much* should be ordered when the inventory is replenished?
2. *When* should the inventory be replenished?

The inventory procedure described for the drugstore industry is discussed in detail in Section 10.7.

Virtually every business uses some sort of inventory management model or system to address the preceding questions. Hewlett-Packard works with its retailers to help determine the retailer's inventory replenishment strategies for the printers and other HP products. IBM developed inventory management policies for a range of microelectronic parts that are used in IBM plants as well as sold to a number of outside customers. The Management Science in Action, Inventory Management at CVS Corporation, describes an inventory system used to determine order quantities in the drugstore industry.

The purpose of this chapter is to show how quantitative models can assist in making the how-much-to-order and when-to-order inventory decisions. We will first consider *deterministic* inventory models, for which we assume that the rate of demand for the item is constant or nearly constant. Later we will consider *probabilistic* inventory models, for which the demand for the item fluctuates and can be described only in probabilistic terms.

MANAGEMENT SCIENCE IN ACTION

INVENTORY MANAGEMENT AT CVS CORPORATION*

CVS is one of the largest drugstore chains in the United States. The primary inventory management area in the drugstore involves the numerous basic products that are carried in inventory on an everyday basis. For these items, the most important issue is the replenishment quantity or order size each time an order is placed. In most drugstore chains, basic products are ordered under a periodic review inventory system, with the review period being one week.

The weekly review system uses electronic ordering equipment that scans an order label affixed to the shelf directly below each item. Among other information on the label is the item's replenishment level or order-to-quantity. The store employee placing the order determines the weekly order quantity by counting the number of units of the product on the shelf and subtracting this quantity from the replenishment level. A computer program determines the replenishment quantity for each item in each individual store, based on each store's movement rather than on the company movement. To minimize stock-outs the replenishment quantity is set equal to the store's three-week demand or movement for the product.

*Based on information provided by Bob Carver. (The inventory system described was originally implemented in the CVS stores formerly known as SupeRX.)

10.1 ECONOMIC ORDER QUANTITY (EOQ) MODEL

The **economic order quantity (EOQ)** model is applicable when the demand for an item shows a constant, or nearly constant, rate and when the entire quantity ordered arrives in inventory at one point in time. The **constant demand rate** assumption means that the same number of units is taken from inventory each period of time such as 5 units every day, 25 units every week, 100 units every four-week period, and so on.

The cost associated with developing and maintaining inventory is larger than many people think. Models such as the ones presented in this chapter can be used to develop cost-effective inventory management decisions.

To illustrate the EOQ model, let us consider the situation faced by the R&B Beverage Company. R&B Beverage is a distributor of beer, wine, and soft drink products. From a main warehouse located in Columbus, Ohio, R&B supplies nearly 1000 retail stores with beverage products. The beer inventory, which constitutes about 40% of the company's total inventory, averages approximately 50,000 cases. With an average cost per case of approximately $8, R&B estimates the value of its beer inventory to be $400,000.

The warehouse manager decided to conduct a detailed study of the inventory costs associated with Bub Beer, the number-one-selling R&B beer. The purpose of the study is to establish the how-much-to-order and the when-to-order decisions for Bub Beer that will result in the lowest possible total cost. As the first step in the study, the warehouse manager obtained the following demand data for the past 10 weeks:

One of the most criticized assumptions of the EOQ model is the constant demand rate. Obviously, the model would be inappropriate for items with widely fluctuating and variable demand rates. However, as this example shows, the EOQ model can provide a realistic approximation of the optimal order quantity when demand is relatively stable and occurs at a nearly constant rate.

Week	Demand (cases)
1	2000
2	2025
3	1950
4	2000
5	2100
6	2050
7	2000
8	1975
9	1900
10	2000
Total cases	20,000
Average cases per week	2000

Strictly speaking, these weekly demand figures do not show a constant demand rate. However, given the relatively low variability exhibited by the weekly demand, inventory planning with a constant demand rate of 2000 cases per week appears acceptable. In practice, you will find that the actual inventory situation seldom, if ever, satisfies the assumptions of the model exactly. Thus, in any particular application, the manager must determine whether the model assumptions are close enough to reality for the model to be useful. In this situation, because demand varies from a low of 1900 cases to a high of 2100 cases, the assumption of constant demand of 2000 cases per week appears to be a reasonable approximation.

The how-much-to-order decision involves selecting an order quantity that draws a compromise between (1) keeping small inventories and ordering frequently, and (2) keeping large inventories and ordering infrequently. The first alternative can result in undesirably high ordering costs, while the second alternative can result in undesirably high inventory holding costs. To find an optimal compromise between these conflicting alternatives, let us consider a mathematical model that shows the total cost as the sum of the holding cost and the ordering cost.[1]

Holding costs are the costs associated with maintaining or carrying a given level of inventory; these costs depend on the size of the inventory. The first holding cost to consider is the cost of financing the inventory investment. When a firm borrows money, it incurs an interest charge. If the firm uses its own money, it experiences an opportunity cost associated with not being able to use the money for other investments. In either case, an interest cost exists for the capital tied up in inventory. This **cost of capital** is usually expressed as a percentage of the amount invested. R&B estimates its cost of capital at an annual rate of 18%.

As with other quantitative models, accurate estimates of cost parameters are critical. In the EOQ model, estimates of both the inventory holding cost and the ordering cost are needed. Also see footnote 1, which refers to relevant costs.

---

[1]Even though analysts typically refer to "total cost" models for inventory systems, often these models describe only the total variable or total relevant costs for the decision being considered. Costs that are not affected by the how-much-to-order decision are considered fixed or constant and are not included in the model.

A number of other holding costs, such as insurance, taxes, breakage, pilferage, and warehouse overhead, also depend on the value of the inventory. R&B estimates these other costs at an annual rate of approximately 7% of the value of its inventory. Thus, the total holding cost for the R&B beer inventory is 18% + 7% = 25% of the value of the inventory. The cost of one case of Bub Beer is $8. With an annual holding cost rate of 25%, the cost of holding one case of Bub Beer in inventory for 1 year is 0.25($8) = $2.00.

The next step in the inventory analysis is to determine the **ordering cost**. This cost, which is considered fixed regardless of the order quantity, covers the preparation of the voucher; and the processing of the order, including payment, postage, telephone, transportation, invoice verification, receiving, and so on. For R&B Beverage, the largest portion of the ordering cost involves the salaries of the purchasers. An analysis of the purchasing process showed that a purchaser spends approximately 45 minutes preparing and processing an order for Bub Beer. With a wage rate and fringe benefit cost for purchasers of $20 per hour, the labor portion of the ordering cost is $15. Making allowances for paper, postage, telephone, transportation, and receiving costs at $17 per order, the manager estimates that the ordering cost is $32 per order. That is, R&B is paying $32 per order regardless of the quantity requested in the order.

The holding cost, ordering cost, and demand information are the three data items that must be known prior to the use of the EOQ model. After developing these data for the R&B problem, we can look at how they are used to develop a total cost model. We begin by defining Q as the order quantity. Thus, the how-much-to-order decision involves finding the value of Q that will minimize the sum of holding and ordering costs.

The inventory for Bub Beer will have a maximum value of Q units when an order of size Q is received from the supplier. R&B will then satisfy customer demand from inventory until the inventory is depleted, at which time another shipment of Q units will be received. Thus, assuming a constant demand, the graph of the inventory for Bub Beer is as shown in Figure 10.1. Note that the graph indicates an average inventory of $\frac{1}{2}Q$ for the period in question. This level should appear reasonable because the maximum inventory is Q, the minimum is zero, and the inventory declines at a constant rate over the period.

Most inventory cost models use an annual cost. Thus, demand should be expressed in units per year, and inventory holding cost should be based on an annual rate.

Figure 10.1 shows the inventory pattern during one order cycle of length T. As time goes on, this pattern will repeat. The complete inventory pattern is shown in Figure 10.2. If the average inventory during each cycle is $\frac{1}{2}Q$, the average inventory over any number of cycles is also $\frac{1}{2}Q$.

The holding cost can be calculated using the average inventory. That is, we can calculate the holding cost by multiplying the average inventory by the cost of carrying one unit in

FIGURE 10.1   INVENTORY FOR BUB BEER

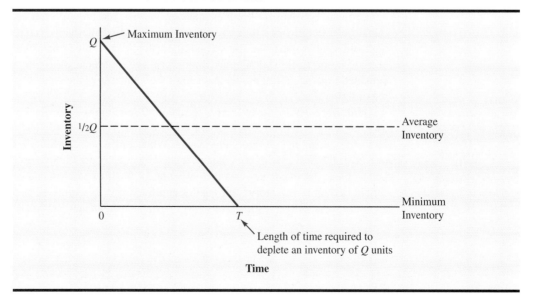

FIGURE 10.2 INVENTORY PATTERN FOR THE EOQ INVENTORY MODEL

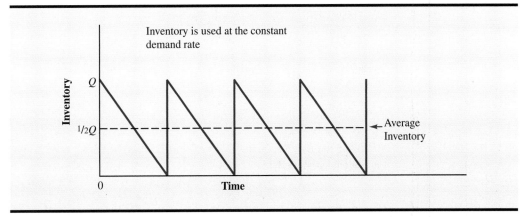

inventory for the stated period. The period selected for the model is up to you; it could be one week, one month, one year, or more. However, because the holding cost for many industries and businesses is expressed as an *annual* percentage, most inventory models are developed on an *annual* cost basis.

Let

$$I = \text{annual holding cost rate}$$
$$C = \text{unit cost of the inventory item}$$
$$C_h = \text{annual cost of holding one unit in inventory}$$

The annual cost of holding one unit in inventory is

$$C_h = IC \qquad (10.1)$$

C_h is the cost of holding one unit in inventory for one year. Because smaller order quantities Q will result in lower inventory, total annual holding cost can be reduced by using smaller order quantities.

The general equation for the annual holding cost for the average inventory of $\frac{1}{2}Q$ units is as follows:

$$\begin{pmatrix} \text{Annual} \\ \text{holding cost} \end{pmatrix} = \begin{pmatrix} \text{Average} \\ \text{inventory} \end{pmatrix} \begin{pmatrix} \text{Annual holding} \\ \text{cost} \\ \text{per unit} \end{pmatrix}$$

$$= \frac{1}{2} Q C_h \qquad (10.2)$$

To complete the total cost model, we must now include the annual ordering cost. The goal is to express the annual ordering cost in terms of the order quantity Q. The first question is, How many orders will be placed during the year? Let D denote the annual demand for the product. For R&B Beverage, $D = (52 \text{ weeks})(2000 \text{ cases per week}) = 104{,}000$ cases per year. We know that by ordering Q units every time we order, we will have to place D/Q orders per year. If C_o is the cost of placing one order, the general equation for the annual ordering cost is as follows:

C_o, the fixed cost per order, is independent of the amount ordered. For a given annual demand of D units, the total annual ordering cost can be reduced by using larger order quantities.

$$\begin{pmatrix} \text{Annual} \\ \text{ordering cost} \end{pmatrix} = \begin{pmatrix} \text{Number of} \\ \text{orders} \\ \text{per year} \end{pmatrix} \begin{pmatrix} \text{Cost} \\ \text{per} \\ \text{order} \end{pmatrix}$$

$$= \begin{pmatrix} \dfrac{D}{Q} \end{pmatrix} C_o \qquad (10.3)$$

Thus, the total annual cost, denoted *TC*, can be expressed as follows:

$$
\begin{array}{ccc}
\text{Total} & \text{Annual} & \text{Annual} \\
\text{annual} = & \text{holding} + & \text{ordering} \\
\text{cost} & \text{cost} & \text{cost}
\end{array}
$$

$$
TC = \frac{1}{2} Q C_h + \frac{D}{Q} C_o \qquad (10.4)
$$

Using the Bub Beer data $[C_h = IC = (0.25)(\$8) = \$2, C_o = \$32,$ and $D = 104{,}000]$, the total annual cost model is

$$
TC = \frac{1}{2} Q(\$2) + \frac{104{,}000}{Q}(\$32) = Q + \frac{3{,}328{,}000}{Q}
$$

The development of the total cost model goes a long way toward solving the inventory problem. We now are able to express the total annual cost as a function of *how much* should be ordered. The development of a realistic total cost model is perhaps the most important part of the application of quantitative methods to inventory decision making. Equation (10.4) is the general total cost equation for inventory situations for which the assumptions of the economic order quantity model are valid.

The How-Much-to-Order Decision

The next step is to find the order quantity Q that will minimize the total annual cost for Bub Beer. Using a trial-and-error approach, we can compute the total annual cost for several possible order quantities. As a starting point, let us consider $Q = 8000$. The total annual cost for Bub Beer is

$$
\begin{aligned}
TC &= Q + \frac{3{,}328{,}000}{Q} \\
&= 8000 + \frac{3{,}328{,}000}{8000} = \$8416
\end{aligned}
$$

A trial order quantity of 5000 gives

$$
TC = 5000 + \frac{3{,}328{,}000}{5000} = \$5666
$$

The results of several other trial order quantities are shown in Table 10.1. It shows the lowest cost solution to be about 2000 cases. Graphs of the annual holding and ordering costs and total annual costs are shown in Figure 10.3.

The advantage of the trial-and-error approach is that it is rather easy to do and provides the total annual cost for a number of possible order quantity decisions. In this case, the

TABLE 10.1   ANNUAL HOLDING, ORDERING, AND TOTAL COSTS FOR VARIOUS
ORDER QUANTITIES OF BUB BEER

Order Quantity	Annual Cost		
	Holding	**Ordering**	**Total**
5000	$5000	$ 666	$5666
4000	$4000	$ 832	$4832
3000	$3000	$1109	$4109
2000	$2000	$1664	$3664
1000	$1000	$3328	$4328

FIGURE 10.3 ANNUAL HOLDING, ORDERING, AND TOTAL COSTS FOR BUB BEER

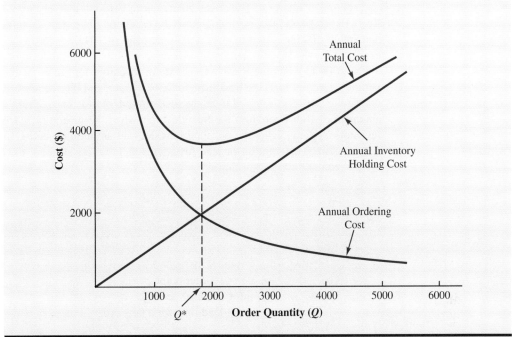

The EOQ formula determines the optimal order quantity by balancing the annual holding cost and the annual ordering cost.

minimum cost order quantity appears to be approximately 2000 cases. The disadvantage of this approach, however, is that it does not provide the exact minimum cost order quantity.

Refer to Figure 10.3. The minimum total cost order quantity is denoted by an order size of Q^*. By using differential calculus, it can be shown (see Appendix 10.1) that the value of Q^* that minimizes the total annual cost is given by the formula

$$Q^* = \sqrt{\frac{2DC_o}{C_h}} \qquad (10.5)$$

This formula is referred to as the *economic order quantity (EOQ) formula*.

Using equation (10.5), the minimum total annual cost order quantity for Bub Beer is

Problem 2 at the end of the chapter asks you to show that equal holding and ordering costs is a property of the EOQ model.

$$Q^* = \sqrt{\frac{2(104,000)32}{2}} = 1824 \text{ cases}$$

The use of an order quantity of 1824 in equation (10.4) shows that the minimum cost inventory policy for Bub Beer has a total annual cost of $3649. Note that $Q^* = 1824$ balances the holding and ordering costs. Check for yourself to see that these costs are equal.[2]

The When-to-Order Decision

The reorder point is expressed in terms of inventory position, the amount of inventory on hand plus the amount on order. With short lead times, inventory position is usually the same as the inventory on hand. However, with long lead times, inventory position may be larger than inventory on hand.

Now that we know how much to order, we want to address the question of *when* to order. To answer this question, we need to introduce the concept of inventory position. The **inventory position** is defined as the amount of inventory on hand plus the amount of inventory on

---

[2]Actually, Q^* from equation (10.5) is 1824.28, but because we cannot order fractional cases of beer, a Q^* of 1824 is shown. This value of Q^* may cause a few cents deviation between the two costs. If Q^* is used at its exact value, the holding and ordering costs will be exactly the same.

order. The when-to-order decision is expressed in terms of a **reorder point**—the inventory position at which a new order should be placed.

The manufacturer of Bub Beer guarantees a two-day delivery on any order placed by R&B Beverage. Hence, assuming R&B Beverage operates 250 days per year, the annual demand of 104,000 cases implies a daily demand of $104,000/250 = 416$ cases. Thus, we expect (2 days)(416 cases per day) = 832 cases of Bub to be sold during the two days it takes a new order to reach the R&B warehouse. In inventory terminology, the two-day delivery period is referred to as the **lead time** for a new order, and the 832-case demand anticipated during this period is referred to as the **lead-time demand**. Thus, R&B should order a new shipment of Bub Beer from the manufacturer when the inventory reaches 832 cases. For inventory systems using the constant demand rate assumption and a fixed lead time, the reorder point is the same as the lead-time demand. For these systems, the general expression for the reorder point is as follows:

$$r = dm \tag{10.6}$$

where

$$r = \text{reorder point}$$
$$d = \text{demand per day}$$
$$m = \text{lead time for a new order in days}$$

The question of how frequently the order will be placed can now be answered. The period between orders is referred to as the **cycle time**. Previously in equation (10.3), we defined D/Q as the number of orders that will be placed in a year. Thus, $D/Q^* = 104,000/1824 = 57$ is the number of orders R&B Beverage will place for Bub Beer each year. If R&B places 57 orders over 250 working days, it will order approximately every $250/57 = 4.39$ working days. Thus, the cycle time is 4.39 working days. The general expression for a cycle time[3] of T days is given by

$$T = \frac{250}{D/Q^*} = \frac{250Q^*}{D} \tag{10.7}$$

Sensitivity Analysis for the EOQ Model

Even though substantial time may have been spent in arriving at the cost per order ($32) and the holding cost rate (25%), we should realize that these figures are at best good estimates. Thus, we may want to consider how much the recommended order quantity would change with different estimated ordering and holding costs. To determine the effects of various cost scenarios, we can calculate the recommended order quantity under several different cost conditions. Table 10.2 shows the minimum total cost order quantity for several cost possibilities. As you can see from the table, the value of Q^* appears relatively stable, even with some variations in the cost estimates. Based on these results, the best order quantity for Bub Beer is in the range of 1700–2000 cases. If operated properly, the total cost for the Bub Beer inventory system should be close to $3400–$3800 per year. We also note that little risk is associated with implementing the calculated order quantity of 1824. For example, if R&B implements an order quantity of 1824 cases (using cost estimates based on $32 per order and 25% annual holding rate), but the actual cost per order turns out to be $34 and the

---

[3]This general expression for cycle time is based on 250 working days per year. If the firm operated 300 working days per year and wanted to express cycle time in terms of working days, the cycle time would be given by $T = 300Q^*/D$.

TABLE 10.2 OPTIMAL ORDER QUANTITIES FOR SEVERAL COST POSSIBILITIES

Possible Inventory Holding Cost (%)	Possible Cost per Order	Optimal Order Quantity (Q^*)	Projected Total Annual Cost	
			Using Q^*	Using $Q = 1824$
24	$30	1803	$3461	$3462
24	34	1919	3685	3690
26	30	1732	3603	3607
26	34	1844	3835	3836

actual annual holding rate turns out to be 24%, then R&B experiences only a $5 increase ($3690–$3685) in the total annual cost.

From the preceding analysis, we would say that this EOQ model is insensitive to small variations or errors in the cost estimates. This insensitivity is a property of EOQ models in general, which indicates that if we have at least reasonable estimates of ordering cost and holding cost, we can expect to obtain a good approximation of the true minimum cost order quantity.

Excel Solution of the EOQ Model

Inventory models such as the EOQ model are easily implemented with the aid of spread-sheets. The Excel EOQ worksheet for Bub Beer is shown in Figure 10.4. The worksheet view of the formulas is on the left and the worksheet view of the values is on the right. Data on annual demand, ordering cost, annual inventory holding cost rate, cost per unit, working days per year, and lead time in days are input in cells B3 to B8. The appropriate EOQ model

FIGURE 10.4 WORKSHEET FOR THE BUB BEER EOQ INVENTORY MODEL

MODEL *file*

EOQ

	A	B
1	**Economic Order Quantity**	
2		
3	Annual Demand	104000
4	Ordering Cost	32
5	Annual Inventory Holding Rate %	25
6	Cost per Unit	8
7	Working Days per Year	250
8	Lead Time (Days)	2
9		
10		
11	**Optimal Inventory Policy**	
12		
13	Economic Order Quantity	=SQRT(2*B3*B4/(B5/100*B6))
14	Annual Inventory Holding Cost	=(1/2)*B13*(B5/100*B6)
15	Annual Ordering Cost	=(B3/B13)*B4
16	Total Annual Cost	=B14+B15
17	Maximum Inventory Level	=B13
18	Average Inventory Level	=B17/2
19	Reorder Point	=(B3/B7)*B8
20	Number of Orders per Year	=B3/B13
21	Cycle Time (Days)	=B7/B20

	A	B
1	**Economic Order Quantity**	
2		
3	Annual Demand	104,000
4	Ordering Cost	$32.00
5	Annual Inventory Holding Rate %	25
6	Cost per Unit	$8.00
7	Working Days per Year	250
8	Lead Time (Days)	2
9		
10		
11	**Optimal Inventory Policy**	
12		
13	Economic Order Quantity	1824.28
14	Annual Inventory Holding Cost	$1,824.28
15	Annual Ordering Cost	$1,824.28
16	Total Annual Cost	$3,648.56
17	Maximum Inventory Level	1,824.28
18	Average Inventory Level	912.14
19	Reorder Point	832.00
20	Number of Orders per Year	57.01
21	Cycle Time (Days)	4.39

TABLE 10.3   THE EOQ MODEL ASSUMPTIONS

1. Demand D is deterministic and occurs at a constant rate.
2. The order quantity Q is the same for each order. The inventory level increases by Q units each time an order is received.
3. The cost per order, C_o, is constant and does not depend on the quantity ordered.
4. The purchase cost per unit, C, is constant and does not depend on the quantity ordered.
5. The inventory holding cost per unit per time period, C_h, is constant. The total inventory holding cost depends on both C_h and the size of the inventory.
6. Shortages such as stock-outs or backorders are not permitted.
7. The lead time for an order is constant.
8. The inventory position is reviewed continuously. As a result, an order is placed as soon as the inventory position reaches the reorder point.

formulas, which determine the optimal inventory policy, are placed in cells B13 to B21. For example, cell B13 computes the optimal economic order quantity 1824.28, and cell B16 computes the total annual cost $3648.56. If sensitivity analysis is desired, one or more of the input data values can be modified. The impact of any change or changes on the optimal inventory policy will then appear in the worksheet.

The Excel worksheet in Figure 10.4 is a template that can be used for the EOQ model. This worksheet and similar Excel worksheets for the other inventory models presented in this chapter are available at the MODELfiles link on the website that accompanies this text.

Summary of the EOQ Model Assumptions

You should carefully review the assumptions of the inventory model before applying it in an actual situation. Several inventory models discussed later in this chapter alter one or more of the assumptions of the EOQ model.

To use the optimal order quantity and reorder point model described in this section, an analyst must make assumptions about how the inventory system operates. The EOQ model with its economic order quantity formula is based on some specific assumptions about the R&B inventory system. A summary of the assumptions for this model is provided in Table 10.3. Before using the EOQ formula, carefully review these assumptions to ensure that they are applicable to the inventory system being analyzed. If the assumptions are not reasonable, seek a different inventory model.

Various types of inventory systems are used in practice, and the inventory models presented in the following sections alter one or more of the EOQ model assumptions shown in Table 10.3. When the assumptions change, a different inventory model with different optimal operating policies becomes necessary.

NOTES AND COMMENTS

1. With relatively long lead times, the lead-time demand and the resulting reorder point r, determined by equation (10.6), may exceed Q^*. If this condition occurs, at least one order will be outstanding when a new order is placed. For example, assume that Bub Beer has a lead time of $m = 6$ days. With a daily demand of $d = 432$ cases, equation (10.6) shows that the reorder point would be $r = dm = 6 \times 432 = 2592$ cases. Note that this reorder point exceeds $Q^* = 1824$ which also corresponds to the maximum inventory level (see Figure 10.1). At first glance, this seems impossible—how can we order when

inventory drops to 2592 cases when the maximum inventory level is 1824? The key is to remember that the reorder point is expressed in terms of inventory position which equals cases "on-hand" + cases "on the way." Thus, to interpret the $r = 2592$, realize that 2592 total cases will occur when there are 1824 cases on the way (from a previous order) and 768 on-hand. So, the model states that we should place another order when the on-hand inventory level is 768 cases. That is, because the lead time is so long (6 days), we have to place an order of Q units before the last order of Q units has even arrived!

10.2 ECONOMIC PRODUCTION LOT SIZE MODEL

The inventory model in this section alters assumption 2 of the EOQ model (see Table 10.3). The assumption concerning the arrival of Q units each time an order is received is changed to a constant production supply rate.

The inventory model presented in this section is similar to the EOQ model in that we are attempting to determine *how much* we should order and *when* the order should be placed. We again assume a constant demand rate. However, instead of assuming that the order arrives in a shipment of size Q^*, as in the EOQ model, we assume that units are supplied to inventory at a constant rate over several days or several weeks. The **constant supply rate** assumption implies that the same number of units is supplied to inventory each period of time (e.g., 10 units every day or 50 units every week). This model is designed for production situations for which, once an order is placed, production begins and a constant number of units is added to inventory each day until the production run has been completed.

If we have a production system that produces 50 units per day and we decide to schedule 10 days of production, we have a $50(10) = 500$-unit production lot size. The **lot size** is the number of units in an order. In general, if we let Q indicate the production lot size, the approach to the inventory decisions is similar to the EOQ model; that is, we build a holding and ordering cost model that expresses the total cost as a function of the production lot size. Then we attempt to find the production lot size that minimizes the total cost.

One other condition that should be mentioned at this time is that the model only applies to situations where the production rate is greater than the demand rate; the production system must be able to satisfy demand. For instance, if the constant demand rate is 400 units per day, the production rate must be at least 400 units per day to satisfy demand.

During the production run, demand reduces the inventory while production adds to inventory. Because we assume that the production rate exceeds the demand rate, each day during a production run we produce more units than are demanded. Thus, the excess production causes a gradual inventory buildup during the production period. When the production run is completed, the continuing demand causes the inventory to gradually decline until a new production run is started. The inventory pattern for this system is shown in Figure 10.5.

This model differs from the EOQ model in that a setup cost replaces the ordering cost, and the saw-tooth inventory pattern shown in Figure 10.5 differs from the inventory pattern shown in Figure 10.2.

As in the EOQ model, we are now dealing with two costs, the holding cost and the ordering cost. Here the holding cost is identical to the definition in the EOQ model, but the interpretation of the ordering cost is slightly different. In fact, in a production situation the ordering cost is more correctly referred to as the production **setup cost**. This cost, which includes labor, material, and lost production costs incurred while preparing the production system for operation, is a fixed cost that occurs for every production run regardless of the production lot size.

Total Cost Model

Let us begin building the production lot size model by writing the holding cost in terms of the production lot size Q. Again, the approach is to develop an expression for average

FIGURE 10.5 INVENTORY PATTERN FOR THE PRODUCTION LOT SIZE INVENTORY MODEL

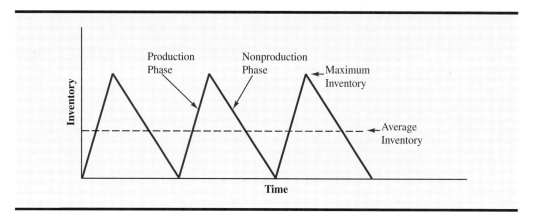

inventory and then establish the holding costs associated with the average inventory. We use a one-year time period and an annual cost for the model.

In the EOQ model the average inventory is one-half the maximum inventory, or $\frac{1}{2}Q$. Figure 10.5 shows that for a production lot size model, a constant inventory buildup rate occurs during the production run, and a constant inventory depletion rate occurs during the nonproduction period; thus, the average inventory will be one-half the maximum inventory. However, in this inventory system the production lot size Q does not go into inventory at one point in time, and thus the inventory never reaches a level of Q units.

To show how we can compute the maximum inventory, let

$$d = \text{daily demand rate}$$
$$p = \text{daily production rate}$$
$$t = \text{number of days for a production run}$$

At this point, the logic of the production lot size model is easier to follow using a daily demand rate d and a daily production rate p. However, when the total annual cost model is eventually developed, we recommend that inputs to the model be expressed in terms of the annual demand rate D and the annual production rate P.

Because we are assuming that p will be larger than d, the daily inventory buildup rate during the production phase is $p - d$. If we run production for t days and place $p - d$ units in inventory each day, the inventory at the end of the production run will be $(p - d)t$. From Figure 10.5 we can see that the inventory at the end of the production run is also the maximum inventory. Thus,

$$\text{Maximum inventory} = (p - d)t \tag{10.8}$$

If we know we are producing a production lot size of Q units at a daily production rate of p units, then $Q = pt$, and the length of the production run t must be

$$t = \frac{Q}{p} \text{ days} \tag{10.9}$$

Thus,

$$\text{Maximum inventory} = (p - d)t = (p - d)\left(\frac{Q}{p}\right)$$
$$= \left(1 - \frac{d}{p}\right)Q \tag{10.10}$$

The average inventory, which is one-half the maximum inventory, is given by

$$\text{Average inventory} = \frac{1}{2}\left(1 - \frac{d}{p}\right)Q \tag{10.11}$$

With an annual per-unit holding cost of C_h, the general equation for annual holding cost is as follows:

$$\begin{array}{c} \text{Annual} \\ \text{holding cost} \end{array} = \left(\begin{array}{c} \text{Average} \\ \text{inventory} \end{array}\right)\left(\begin{array}{c} \text{Annual} \\ \text{cost} \\ \text{per unit} \end{array}\right)$$
$$= \frac{1}{2}\left(1 - \frac{d}{p}\right)QC_h \tag{10.12}$$

If D is the annual demand for the product and C_o is the setup cost for a production run, then the annual setup cost, which takes the place of the annual ordering cost in the EOQ model, is as follows:

$$\text{Annual setup cost} = \left(\begin{array}{c}\text{Number of production} \\ \text{runs per year}\end{array}\right)\left(\begin{array}{c}\text{Setup cost} \\ \text{per run}\end{array}\right)$$

$$= \frac{D}{Q}C_o \qquad\qquad (10.13)$$

Thus, the total annual cost (TC) model is

$$TC = \frac{1}{2}\left(1 - \frac{d}{p}\right)QC_h + \frac{D}{Q}C_o \qquad\qquad (10.14)$$

Suppose that a production facility operates 250 days per year. Then we can write daily demand d in terms of annual demand D as follows:

$$d = \frac{D}{250}$$

Now let P denote the annual production for the product if the product were produced every day. Then

$$P = 250p \quad\text{and}\quad p = \frac{P}{250}$$

Thus,[4]

$$\frac{d}{p} = \frac{D/250}{P/250} = \frac{D}{P}$$

Therefore, we can write the total annual cost model as follows:

$$TC = \frac{1}{2}\left(1 - \frac{D}{P}\right)QC_h + \frac{D}{Q}C_o \qquad\qquad (10.15)$$

Equations (10.14) and (10.15) are equivalent. However, equation (10.15) may be used more frequently because an *annual* cost model tends to make the analyst think in terms of collecting *annual* demand data (D) and *annual* production data (P) rather than daily data.

Economic Production Lot Size

As the production rate P approaches infinity, D/P approaches zero. In this case, equation (10.16) is equivalent to the EOQ model in equation (10.5).

Given estimates of the holding cost (C_h), setup cost (C_o), annual demand rate (D), and annual production rate (P), we could use a trial-and-error approach to compute the total annual cost for various production lot sizes (Q). However, trial and error is not necessary; we can use the minimum cost formula for Q^* that has been developed using differential calculus (see Appendix 10.2). The equation is as follows:

$$Q^* = \sqrt{\frac{2DC_o}{(1 - D/P)C_h}} \qquad\qquad (10.16)$$

[4]The ratio $d/p = D/P$ holds regardless of the number of days of operation; 250 days is used here merely as an illustration.

LotSize

Work Problem 13 as an example of an economic production lot size model.

An Example   Beauty Bar Soap is produced on a production line that has an annual capacity of 60,000 cases. The annual demand is estimated at 26,000 cases, with the demand rate essentially constant throughout the year. The cleaning, preparation, and setup of the production line cost approximately $135. The manufacturing cost per case is $4.50, and the annual holding cost is figured at a 24% rate. Thus, $C_h = IC = 0.24(\$4.50) = \$1.08$. What is the recommended production lot size?

Using equation (10.16), we have

$$Q^* = \sqrt{\frac{2(26,000)(135)}{(1 - 26,000/60,000)(1.08)}} = 3387$$

The total annual cost using equation (10.15) and $Q^* = 3387$ is $2073.

Other relevant data include a five-day lead time to schedule and set up a production run and 250 working days per year. Thus, the lead-time demand of $(26,000/250)(5) = 520$ cases is the reorder point. The cycle time is the time between production runs. Using equation (10.7), the cycle time is $T = 250Q^*/D = [(250)(3387)]/26,000$, or 33 working days. Thus, we should plan a production run of 3387 units every 33 working days.

10.3   INVENTORY MODEL WITH PLANNED SHORTAGES

The assumptions of the EOQ model in Table 10.3 apply to this inventory model with the exception that shortages, referred to as backorders, are now permitted.

A **shortage** or **stock-out** occurs when demand exceeds the amount of inventory on hand. In many situations, shortages are undesirable and should be avoided if at all possible. However, in other cases it may be desirable—from an economic point of view—to plan for and allow shortages. In practice, these types of situations are most commonly found where the value of the inventory per unit is high and hence the holding cost is high. An example of this type of situation is a new car dealer's inventory. Often a specific car that a customer wants is not in stock. However, if the customer is willing to wait a few weeks, the dealer is usually able to order the car.

The model developed in this section takes into account a type of shortage known as a **backorder**. In a backorder situation, we assume that when a customer places an order and discovers that the supplier is out of stock, the customer waits until the new shipment arrives, and then the order is filled. Frequently, the waiting period in backorder situations is relatively short. Thus, by promising the customer top priority and immediate delivery when the goods become available, companies may be able to convince the customer to wait until the order arrives. In these cases, the backorder assumption is valid.

The backorder model that we develop is an extension of the EOQ model presented in Section 10.1. We use the EOQ model for which all goods arrive in inventory at one time and are subject to a constant demand rate. If we let S indicate the number of backorders that have accumulated by the time a new shipment of size Q is received, then the inventory system for the backorder case has the following characteristics:

- If S backorders exist when a new shipment of size Q arrives, then S backorders are shipped to the appropriate customers, and the remaining $Q - S$ units are placed in inventory. Therefore, $Q - S$ is the maximum inventory.
- The inventory cycle of T days is divided into two distinct phases: t_1 days when inventory is on hand and orders are filled as they occur, and t_2 days when stock-outs occur and all new orders are placed on backorder.

The inventory pattern for the inventory model with backorders, where negative inventory represents the number of backorders, is shown in Figure 10.6.

With the inventory pattern now defined, we can proceed with the basic step of all inventory models—namely, the development of a total cost model. For the inventory model with backorders, we encounter the usual holding costs and ordering costs. We also incur a backorder cost in terms of the labor and special delivery costs directly associated with the handling of the backorders. Another portion of the backorder cost accounts for the loss of goodwill because some customers will have to wait for their orders. Because the **goodwill cost** depends

FIGURE 10.6   INVENTORY PATTERN FOR AN INVENTORY MODEL WITH BACKORDERS

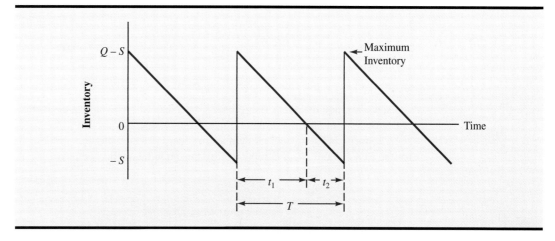

on how long a customer has to wait, it is customary to adopt the convention of expressing backorder cost in terms of the cost of having a unit on backorder for a stated period of time. This method of costing backorders on a time basis is similar to the method used to compute the inventory holding cost, and we can use it to compute a total annual cost of backorders once the average backorder level and the backorder cost per unit per period are known.

Let us begin the development of a total cost model by calculating the average inventory for a hypothetical problem. If we have an average inventory of two units for three days and no inventory on the fourth day, what is the average inventory over the four-day period? It is

$$\frac{2 \text{ units (3 days)} + 0 \text{ units (1 day)}}{4 \text{ days}} = \frac{6}{4} = 1.5 \text{ units}$$

Refer to Figure 10.6. You can see that this situation is what happens in the backorder model. With a maximum inventory of $Q - S$ units, the t_1 days we have inventory on hand will have an average inventory of $(Q - S)/2$. No inventory is carried for the t_2 days in which we experience backorders. Thus, over the total cycle time of $T = t_1 + t_2$ days, we can compute the average inventory as follows:

$$\text{Average inventory} = \frac{\frac{1}{2}(Q - S)t_1 + 0t_2}{t_1 + t_2} = \frac{\frac{1}{2}(Q - S)t_1}{T} \qquad (10.17)$$

Can we find other ways of expressing t_1 and T? Because we know that the maximum inventory is $Q - S$ and that d represents the constant daily demand, we have

$$t_1 = \frac{Q - S}{d} \text{ days} \qquad (10.18)$$

That is, the maximum inventory of $Q - S$ units will be used up in $(Q - S)/d$ days. Because Q units are ordered for each cycle, we know the length of a cycle must be

$$T = \frac{Q}{d} \text{ days} \qquad (10.19)$$

Combining equations (10.18) and (10.19) with equation (10.17), we can compute the average inventory as follows:

$$\text{Average inventory} = \frac{\frac{1}{2}(Q - S)[(Q - S)/d]}{Q/d} = \frac{(Q - S)^2}{2Q} \tag{10.20}$$

Thus, the average inventory is expressed in terms of two inventory decisions: how much we will order (Q) and the maximum number of backorders (S).

The formula for the annual number of orders placed using this model is identical to that for the EOQ model. With D representing the annual demand, we have

$$\text{Annual number of orders} = \frac{D}{Q} \tag{10.21}$$

The next step is to develop an expression for the average backorder level. Because we know the maximum for backorders is S, we can use the same logic we used to establish average inventory in finding the average number of backorders. We have an average number of backorders during the period t_2 of $\frac{1}{2}$ the maximum number of backorders or $\frac{1}{2}S$. We do not have any backorders during the t_1 days we have inventory; therefore, we can calculate the average backorders in a manner similar to equation (10.17). Using this approach, we have

$$\text{Average backorders} = \frac{0t_1 + (S/2)t_2}{T} = \frac{(S/2)t_2}{T} \tag{10.22}$$

When we let the maximum number of backorders reach an amount S at a daily rate of d, the length of the backorder portion of the inventory cycle is

$$t_2 = \frac{S}{d} \tag{10.23}$$

Using equations (10.23) and (10.19) in equation (10.22), we have

$$\text{Average backorders} = \frac{(S/2)(S/d)}{Q/d} = \frac{S^2}{2Q} \tag{10.24}$$

Let

C_h = cost to hold one unit in inventory for one year
C_o = cost per order
C_b = cost to maintain one unit on backorder for one year

The backorder cost C_b is one of the most difficult costs to estimate in inventory models. The reason is that it attempts to measure the cost associated with the loss of goodwill when a customer must wait for an order. Expressing this cost on an annual basis adds to the difficulty.

The total annual cost (TC) for the inventory model with backorders becomes

$$TC = \frac{(Q - S)^2}{2Q}C_h + \frac{D}{Q}C_o + \frac{S^2}{2Q}C_b \tag{10.25}$$

Given C_h, C_o, and C_b and the annual demand D, differential calculus can be used to show that the minimum cost values for the order quantity Q^* and the planned backorders S^* are as follows:

$$Q^* = \sqrt{\frac{2DC_o}{C_h}\left(\frac{C_h + C_b}{C_b}\right)} \qquad (10.26)$$

$$S^* = Q^*\left(\frac{C_h}{C_h + C_b}\right) \qquad (10.27)$$

MODEL *file*

Shortage

An inventory situation that incorporates backorder costs is considered in Problem 15.

An Example   Suppose that the Higley Radio Components Company has a product for which the assumptions of the inventory model with backorders are valid. Information obtained by the company is as follows:

$$D = 2000 \text{ units per year}$$
$$I = 20\%$$
$$C = \$50 \text{ per unit}$$
$$C_h = IC = (0.20)(\$50) = \$10 \text{ per unit per year}$$
$$C_o = \$25 = \text{per order}$$

The company is considering the possibility of allowing some backorders to occur for the product. The annual backorder cost is estimated to be $30 per unit per year. Using equations (10.26) and (10.27), we have

$$Q^* = \sqrt{\frac{2(2000)(25)}{10}\left(\frac{10 + 30}{30}\right)} = 115$$

and

$$S^* = 115\left(\frac{10}{10 + 30}\right) = 29$$

If this solution is implemented, the system will operate with the following properties:

$$\text{Maximum inventory} = Q - S = 115 - 29 = 86$$
$$\text{Cycle time} = T = \frac{Q}{D}(250) = \frac{115}{2000}(250) = 14 \text{ working days}$$

If backorders can be tolerated, the total cost including the backorder cost will be less than the total cost of the EOQ model. Some people think the model with backorders will have a greater cost because it includes a backorder cost in addition to the usual inventory holding and ordering costs. You can point out the fallacy in this thinking by noting that the backorder model leads to lower inventory and hence lower inventory holding costs.

The total annual cost is

$$\text{Holding cost} = \frac{(86)^2}{2(115)}(10) = \$322$$
$$\text{Ordering cost} = \frac{2000}{115}(25) = \$435$$
$$\text{Backorder cost} = \frac{(29)^2}{2(115)}(30) = \$110$$
$$\text{Total cost} = \$867$$

If the company chooses to prohibit backorders and adopts the regular EOQ model, the recommended inventory decision would be

$$Q^* = \sqrt{\frac{2(2000)(25)}{10}} = \sqrt{10,000} = 100$$

This order quantity would result in a holding cost and an ordering cost of $500 each or a total annual cost of $1000. Thus, in this problem, allowing backorders is projecting a $1000 − $867 = $133, or 13.3%, savings in cost from the no-stock-out EOQ model. The preceding comparison and conclusion are based on the assumption that the backorder model with an annual cost per backordered unit of $30 is a valid model for the actual inventory situation. If the company is concerned that stock-outs might lead to lost sales, then the savings might not be enough to warrant switching to an inventory policy that allows for planned shortages.

NOTES AND COMMENTS

1. Equation (10.27) shows that the optimal number of planned backorders S^* is proportional to the ratio $C_h/(C_h + C_b)$, where C_h is the annual holding cost per unit and C_b is the annual backorder cost per unit. Whenever C_h increases, this ratio becomes larger, and the number of planned backorders increases. This relationship explains why items that have a high per-unit cost and a correspondingly high annual holding cost are more economically handled on a backorder basis. On the other hand, whenever the backorder cost C_b increases, the ratio becomes smaller, and the number of planned backorders decreases. Thus, the model provides the intuitive result that items with high backorder costs will be handled with few backorders. In fact, with high backorder costs, the backorder model and the EOQ model with no backordering allowed provide similar inventory policies.

10.4 QUANTITY DISCOUNTS FOR THE EOQ MODEL

In the quantity discount model, assumption 4 of the EOQ model in Table 10.3 is altered. The cost per unit varies depending on the quantity ordered.

Quantity discounts occur in numerous situations for which suppliers provide an incentive for large order quantities by offering a lower purchase cost when items are ordered in larger quantities. In this section we show how the EOQ model can be used when quantity discounts are available.

Assume that we have a product for which the basic EOQ model (see Table 10.3) is applicable. Instead of a fixed unit cost, the supplier quotes the following discount schedule:

Discount Category	Order Size	Discount (%)	Unit Cost
1	0 to 999	0	$5.00
2	1000 to 2499	3	4.85
3	2500 and over	5	4.75

The 5% discount for the 2500-unit minimum order quantity looks tempting. However, realizing that higher order quantities result in higher inventory holding costs, we should prepare a thorough cost analysis before making a final ordering and inventory policy recommendation.

Suppose that the data and cost analyses show an annual holding cost rate of 20%, an ordering cost of $49 per order, and an annual demand of 5000 units; what order quantity should we select? The following three-step procedure shows the calculations necessary to make this decision. In the preliminary calculations, we use Q_1 to indicate the order quantity for discount category 1, Q_2 for discount category 2, and Q_3 for discount category 3.

Step 1. For each discount category, compute a Q^* using the EOQ formula based on the unit cost associated with the discount category.

Recall that the EOQ model provides $Q^* = \sqrt{2DC_o/C_h}$, where $C_h = IC = (0.20)C$. With three discount categories providing three different unit costs C, we obtain

MODEL *file*

Discount

$$Q_1^* = \sqrt{\frac{2(5000)49}{(0.20)(5.00)}} = 700$$

$$Q_2^* = \sqrt{\frac{2(5000)49}{(0.20)(4.85)}} = 711$$

$$Q_3^* = \sqrt{\frac{2(5000)49}{(0.20)(4.75)}} = 718$$

Because the only differences in the EOQ formulas come from slight differences in the holding cost, the economic order quantities resulting from this step will be approximately the same. However, these order quantities will usually not all be of the size necessary to qualify for the discount price assumed. In the preceding case, both Q_2^* and Q_3^* are insufficient order quantities to obtain their assumed discounted costs of \$4.85 and \$4.75, respectively. For those order quantities for which the assumed price cannot be obtained, the following procedure must be used:

Step 2. For the Q^* that is too small to qualify for the assumed discount price, adjust the order quantity upward to the nearest order quantity that will allow the product to be purchased at the assumed price.

In our example, this adjustment causes us to set

$$Q_2^* = 1000$$

and

$$Q_3^* = 2500$$

If a calculated Q^* for a given discount price is large enough to qualify for a bigger discount, that value of Q^* cannot lead to an optimal solution. Although the reason may not be obvious, it does turn out to be a property of the EOQ quantity discount model.

In the previous inventory models considered, the annual purchase cost of the item was not included because it was constant and never affected by the inventory order policy decision. However, in the quantity discount model, the annual purchase cost depends on the order quantity and the associated unit cost. Thus, annual purchase cost (annual demand $D \times$ unit cost C) is included in the equation for total cost as shown here.

In the EOQ model with quantity discounts, the annual purchase cost must be included because purchase cost depends on the order quantity. Thus, it is a relevant cost.

$$TC = \frac{Q}{2} C_h + \frac{D}{Q} C_o + DC \tag{10.28}$$

Using this total cost equation, we can determine the optimal order quantity for the EOQ discount model in step 3.

Problem 21 will give you practice in applying the EOQ model to situations with quantity discounts.

Step 3. For each order quantity resulting from steps 1 and 2, compute the total annual cost using the unit price from the appropriate discount category and equation (10.28). The order quantity yielding the minimum total annual cost is the optimal order quantity.

The step 3 calculations for the example problem are summarized in Table 10.4. As you can see, a decision to order 1000 units at the 3% discount rate yields the minimum cost solution. Even though the 2500-unit order quantity would result in a 5% discount, its excessive holding cost makes it the second-best solution. Figure 10.7 shows the total cost curve for each of the three discount categories. Note that $Q^* = 1000$ provides the minimum cost order quantity.

TABLE 10.4 TOTAL ANNUAL COST CALCULATIONS FOR THE EOQ MODEL WITH QUANTITY DISCOUNTS

Discount Category	Unit Cost	Order Quantity	Annual Cost			
			Holding	**Ordering**	**Purchase**	**Total**
1	\$5.00	700	\$ 350	\$350	\$25,000	\$25,700
2	4.85	1000	\$ 485	\$245	\$24,250	\$24,980
3	4.75	2500	\$1188	\$ 98	\$23,750	\$25,036

FIGURE 10.7   TOTAL COST CURVES FOR THE THREE DISCOUNT CATEGORIES

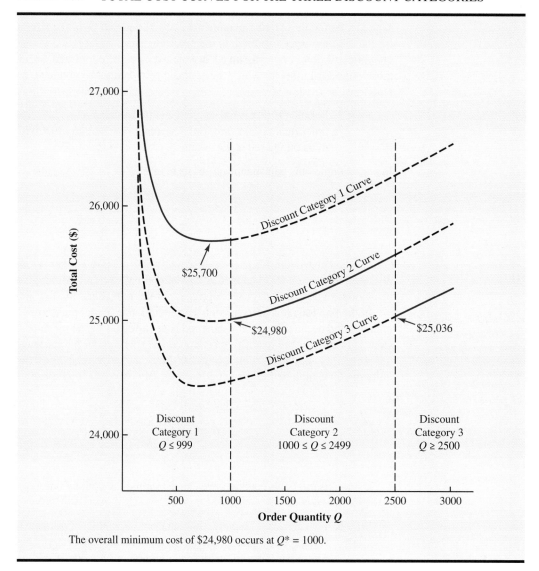

The overall minimum cost of $24,980 occurs at $Q^* = 1000$.

10.5   SINGLE-PERIOD INVENTORY MODEL WITH PROBABILISTIC DEMAND

The inventory models discussed thus far were based on the assumption that the demand rate is constant and **deterministic** throughout the year. We developed minimum cost order quantity and reorder point policies based on this assumption. In situations for which the demand rate is not deterministic, other models treat demand as **probabilistic** and best described by a probability distribution. In this section we consider a single-period inventory model with probabilistic demand.

The single-period inventory model refers to inventory situations for which *one* order is placed for the product; at the end of the period, the product has either sold out, or a surplus of unsold items will be sold for a salvage value. The single-period inventory model is applicable in situations involving seasonal or perishable items that cannot be carried in inventory and sold in future periods. Seasonal clothing (such as bathing suits and winter coats) are typically handled in a single-period manner. In these situations, a buyer places one preseason order for each item and then experiences a stock-out or holds a clearance sale on the surplus stock at the end of the season. No items are carried in inventory and sold the following year. Newspapers are another example of a product that is ordered one time and is either sold or not sold during the single period. Although newspapers are ordered daily, they cannot be carried in inventory and sold in later periods. Thus, newspaper orders may be treated as a sequence of single-period models; that is, each day or period is separate, and a single-period inventory decision must be made each period (day). Because we order only once for the period, the only inventory decision we must make is *how much* of the product to order at the start of the period.

Obviously, if the demand were known for a single-period inventory situation, the solution would be easy; we would simply order the amount we knew would be demanded. However, in most single-period models, the exact demand is not known. In fact, forecasts may show that demand can have a wide variety of values. If we are going to analyze this type of inventory problem in a quantitative manner, we need information about the probabilities associated with the various demand values. Thus, the single-period model presented in this section is based on probabilistic demand.

This inventory model is the first in the chapter that explicitly treats probabilistic demand. Unlike the EOQ model, it is for a single period, and unused inventory is not carried over to future periods.

Neiman Marcus

Let us consider a single-period inventory model that could be used to make a how-much-to-order decision for Neiman Marcus, a high-end fashion store. The buyer for Neiman Marcus decided to order Manolo Blahnik heels shown at a buyers' meeting in New York City. The shoe will be part of the company's spring–summer promotion and will be sold through nine retail stores in the Chicago area. Because the shoe is designed for spring and summer months, it cannot be expected to sell in the fall. Neiman Marcus plans to hold a special August clearance sale in an attempt to sell all shoes not sold by July 31. The shoes cost $700 a pair and retail for $900 a pair. At the sale price of $600 a pair, all surplus shoes can be expected to sell during the August sale. If you were the buyer for Neiman Marcus, how many pairs of the shoes would you order?

To answer the question of how much to order, we need information on the demand for the shoe. Specifically, we would need to construct a probability distribution for the possible values of demand. Let us suppose that the uniform probability distribution shown in Figure 10.8 can be used to describe the demand for the Manolo Blahnik heels. In particular, note that the range of demand is from 350 to 650 pairs of shoes, with an average, or expected, demand of 500 pairs of shoes.

Incremental analysis is a method that can be used to determine the optimal order quantity for a single-period inventory model. Incremental analysis addresses the how-much-to-order question by comparing the cost or loss of *ordering one additional unit* with the cost or loss of *not ordering one additional unit*. The costs involved are defined as follows:

c_o = cost per unit of *overestimating* demand. This cost represents the loss of ordering one additional unit and finding that it cannot be sold.

c_u = cost per unit of *underestimating* demand. This cost represents the opportunity loss of not ordering one additional unit and finding that it could have been sold.

FIGURE 10.8   UNIFORM PROBABILITY DISTRIBUTION OF DEMAND FOR NEIMAN MARCUS PROBLEM

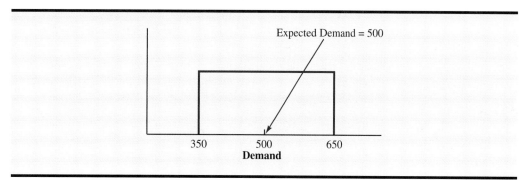

In the Neiman Marcus problem, the company will incur the cost of overestimating demand whenever it orders too many pairs and has to sell the extra shoes during the August clearance sale. Thus, the cost per unit of overestimating demand is equal to the purchase cost per unit minus the August sales price per unit; that is, $c_o = \$700 - \$600 = \$100$. Therefore, Neiman Marcus will lose \$100 for each pair of shoes that it orders over the quantity demanded. The cost of underestimating demand is the lost profit (often referred to as an opportunity cost) because a pair of shoes that could have been sold was not available in inventory. Thus, the per-unit cost of underestimating demand is the difference between the regular selling price per unit and the purchase cost per unit; that is, $c_u = \$900 - \$700 = \$200$.

Because the exact level of demand for the Manolo Blahnik heels is unknown, we have to consider the probability of demand and thus the probability of obtaining the associated costs or losses. For example, let us assume that Neiman Marcus management wishes to consider an order quantity equal to the average or expected demand for 500 pairs of shoes. In incremental analysis, we consider the possible losses associated with an order quantity of 501 (ordering one additional unit) and an order quantity of 500 (not ordering one additional unit). The order quantity alternatives and the possible losses are summarized here.

The key to incremental analysis is to focus on the costs that are different when comparing an order quantity $Q + 1$ to an order quantity Q.

Order Quantity Alternatives	Loss Occurs If	Possible Loss	Probability Loss Occurs
$Q = 501$	Demand overestimated; the additional unit *cannot* be sold	$c_o = \$100$	$P(\text{demand} \leq 500)$
$Q = 500$	Demand underestimated; an additional unit *could have* been sold	$c_u = \$200$	$P(\text{demand} > 500)$

Using the demand probability distribution in Figure 10.8, we see that $P(\text{demand} \leq 500) = 0.50$ and that $P(\text{demand} > 500) = 0.50$. By multiplying the possible losses, $c_o = \$100$ and $c_u = \$200$, by the probability of obtaining the loss, we can compute the expected value of the loss, or simply the *expected loss* (EL), associated with the order quantity alternatives. Thus,

$$\text{EL}(Q = 501) = c_o P(\text{demand} \leq 500) = \$100(0.50) = \$50$$
$$\text{EL}(Q = 500) = c_u P(\text{demand} > 500) = \$200(0.50) = \$100$$

Based on these expected losses, do you prefer an order quantity of 501 or 500 pairs of shoes? Because the expected loss is greater for $Q = 500$, and because we want to avoid this higher cost or loss, we should make $Q = 501$ the preferred decision. We could now consider incrementing the order quantity one additional unit to $Q = 502$ and repeating the expected loss calculations.

Although we could continue this unit-by-unit analysis, it would be time-consuming and cumbersome. We would have to evaluate $Q = 502$, $Q = 503$, $Q = 504$, and so on until we found the value of Q where the expected loss of ordering one incremental unit is equal to the expected loss of not ordering one incremental unit; that is, the optimal order quantity Q^* occurs when the incremental analysis shows that

$$\text{EL}(Q^* + 1) = \text{EL}(Q^*) \tag{10.29}$$

When this relationship holds, increasing the order quantity by one additional unit has no economic advantage. Using the logic with which we computed the expected losses for the order quantities of 501 and 500, the general expressions for $\text{EL}(Q^* + 1)$ and $\text{EL}(Q^*)$ can be written as

$$\text{EL}(Q^* + 1) = c_o P(\text{demand} \leq Q^*) \tag{10.30}$$
$$\text{EL}(Q^*) = c_u P(\text{demand} > Q^*) \tag{10.31}$$

Because demand $\leq Q^*$ and demand $> Q^*$ are complementary events, we know from basic probability that

$$P(\text{demand} \leq Q^*) + P(\text{demand} > Q^*) = 1 \qquad (10.32)$$

and we can write

$$P(\text{demand} > Q^*) = 1 - P(\text{demand} \leq Q^*) \qquad (10.33)$$

Using this expression, equation (10.31) can be rewritten as

$$EL(Q^*) = c_u[1 - P(\text{demand} \leq Q^*)] \qquad (10.34)$$

Equations (10.30) and (10.34) can be used to show that $EL(Q^* + 1) = EL(Q^*)$ whenever

$$c_o P(\text{demand} \leq Q^*) = c_u[1 - P(\text{demand} \leq Q^*)] \qquad (10.35)$$

Solving for $P(\text{demand} \leq Q^*)$, we have

$$P(\text{demand} \leq Q^*) = \frac{c_u}{c_u + c_o} \qquad (10.36)$$

This expression provides the general condition for the optimal order quantity Q^* in the single-period inventory model.

In the Neiman Marcus problem, $c_o = \$100$ and $c_u = \$200$. Thus, equation (10.36) shows that the optimal order size for the Manolo Blahnik heels must satisfy the following condition:

$$P(\text{demand} \leq Q^*) = \frac{c_u}{c_u + c_o} = \frac{200}{200 + 100} = \frac{200}{300} = \frac{2}{3}$$

We can find the optimal order quantity Q^* by referring to the probability distribution shown in Figure 10.8 and finding the value of Q that will provide $P(\text{demand} \leq Q^*) = \frac{2}{3}$. To find this solution, we note that in the uniform distribution the probability is evenly distributed over the entire range of 350–650 pairs of shoes. Thus, we can satisfy the expression for Q^* by moving two-thirds of the way from 350 to 650. Because this range is $650 - 350 = 300$, we move 200 units from 350 toward 650.

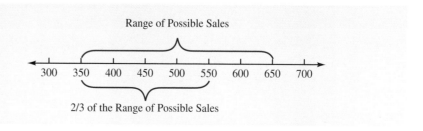

Doing so provides the optimal order quantity of 550 pairs of shoes.

In summary, the key to establishing an optimal order quantity for single-period inventory models is to identify the probability distribution that describes the demand for the item and to calculate the per-unit costs of overestimation and underestimation. Then, using the information for the per-unit costs of overestimation and underestimation, equation (10.36) can be used to find the location of Q^* in the probability distribution.

Nationwide Car Rental

As another example of a single-period inventory model with probabilistic demand, consider the situation faced by Nationwide Car Rental. Nationwide must decide how many automobiles to have available at each car rental location at specific points in time throughout the year. Using the Myrtle Beach, South Carolina, location as an example, management would like to know the number of full-sized automobiles to have available for the Labor Day weekend. Based on previous experience, customer demand for full-sized automobiles for the Labor Day weekend has a normal distribution with a mean of 150 automobiles and a standard deviation of 14 automobiles.

The Nationwide Car Rental situation can benefit from use of a single-period inventory model. The company must establish the number of full-sized automobiles to have available prior to the weekend. Customer demand over the weekend will then result in either a stock-out or a surplus. Let us denote the number of full-sized automobiles available by Q. If Q is greater than customer demand, Nationwide will have a surplus of cars. The cost of a surplus is the cost of overestimating demand. This cost is set at $80 per car, which reflects, in part, the opportunity cost of not having the car available for rent elsewhere.

If Q is less than customer demand, Nationwide will rent all available cars and experience a stock-out or shortage. A shortage results in an underestimation cost of $200 per car. This figure reflects the cost due to lost profit and the lost goodwill of not having a car available for a customer. Given this information, how many full-sized automobiles should Nationwide make available for the Labor Day weekend?

Using the cost of underestimation, $c_u = \$200$, and the cost of overestimation, $c_o = \$80$, equation (10.36) indicates that the optimal order quantity must satisfy the following condition:

$$P(\text{demand} \leq Q^*) = \frac{c_u}{(c_u + c_o)} = \frac{200}{200 + 80} = 0.7143$$

We can use the normal probability distribution for demand as shown in Figure 10.9 to find the order quantity that satisfies the condition that $P(\text{demand} \leq Q^*) = 0.7143$. From Appendix B, we see that 0.7143 of the area in the left tail of the normal probability

FIGURE 10.9   PROBABILITY DISTRIBUTION OF DEMAND FOR THE NATIONWIDE CAR RENTAL PROBLEM SHOWING THE LOCATION OF Q^*

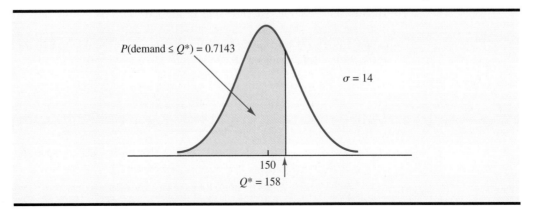

MODEL *file*

SinglePeriod

An example of a single-period inventory model with probabilistic demand described by a normal probability distribution is considered in Problem 25.

distribution occurs at $z = 0.57$ standard deviations *above* the mean. With a mean demand of $\mu = 150$ automobiles and a standard deviation of $\sigma = 14$ automobiles, we have

$$Q^* = \mu + 0.57\sigma$$
$$= 150 + 0.57(14) = 158$$

Thus, Nationwide Car Rental should plan to have 158 full-sized automobiles available in Myrtle Beach for the Labor Day weekend. Note that in this case the cost of overestimation is less than the cost of underestimation. Thus, Nationwide is willing to risk a higher probability of overestimating demand and hence a higher probability of a surplus. In fact, Nationwide's optimal order quantity has a 0.7143 probability of a surplus and a $1 - 0.7143 = 0.2857$ probability of a stock-out. As a result, the probability is 0.2857 that all 158 full-sized automobiles will be rented during the Labor Day weekend.

NOTES AND COMMENTS

1. In any probabilistic inventory model, the assumption about the probability distribution for demand is critical and can affect the recommended inventory decision. In the problems presented in this section, we used the uniform and the normal probability distributions to describe demand. In some situations, other probability distributions may be more appropriate. In using probabilistic inventory models, we must exercise care in selecting the probability distribution that most realistically describes demand.

2. In the single-period inventory model, the value of $c_u/(c_u + c_o)$ plays a critical role in selecting the order quantity [see equation (10.36)]. Whenever $c_u = c_o$, $c_u/(c_u + c_o)$ equals 0.50; in this case, we should select an order quantity corresponding to the median demand. With this choice, a stock-out is just as likely as a surplus because the two costs are equal. However, whenever $c_u < c_o$, a smaller order quantity will be recommended. In this case, the smaller order quantity will provide a higher probability of a stock-out; however, the more expensive cost of overestimating demand and having a surplus will tend to be avoided. Finally, whenever $c_u > c_o$, a larger order quantity will be recommended. In this case, the larger order quantity provides a lower probability of a stock-out in an attempt to avoid the more expensive cost of underestimating demand and experiencing a stock-out.

10.6 ORDER-QUANTITY, REORDER POINT MODEL WITH PROBABILISTIC DEMAND

In the previous section we considered a single-period inventory model with probabilistic demand. In this section we extend our discussion to a multiperiod order-quantity, reorder point inventory model with probabilistic demand. In the multiperiod model, the inventory system operates continuously with many repeating periods or cycles; inventory can be carried from one period to the next. Whenever the inventory position reaches the reorder point, an order for Q units is placed. Because demand is probabilistic, the time the reorder point will be reached, the time between orders, and the time the order of Q units will arrive in inventory cannot be determined in advance.

The inventory model in this section is based on the assumptions of the EOQ model shown in Table 10.3, with the exception that demand is probabilistic rather than deterministic. With probabilistic demand, occasional shortages may occur.

The inventory pattern for the order-quantity, reorder point model with probabilistic demand will have the general appearance shown in Figure 10.10. Note that the increases, or jumps, in the inventory occur whenever an order of Q units arrives. The inventory decreases at a nonconstant rate based on the probabilistic demand. A new order is placed whenever the reorder point is reached. At times, the order quantity of Q units will arrive before inventory reaches zero. However, at other times, higher demand will cause a stock-out before a new order is received. As with other order-quantity, reorder point models, the manager must determine the order quantity Q and the reorder point r for the inventory system.

The exact mathematical formulation of an order-quantity, reorder point inventory model with probabilistic demand is beyond the scope of this text. However, we present

FIGURE 10.10   INVENTORY PATTERN FOR AN ORDER-QUANTITY, REORDER POINT
MODEL WITH PROBABILISTIC DEMAND

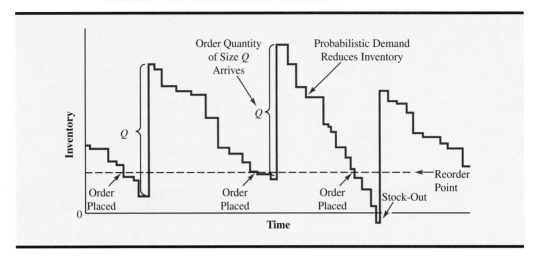

a procedure that can be used to obtain good, workable order-quantity and reorder point inventory policies. The solution procedure can be expected to provide only an approximation of the optimal solution, but it can yield good solutions in many practical situations.

Let us consider the inventory problem of Dabco Industrial Lighting Distributors. Dabco purchases a special high-intensity lightbulb for industrial lighting systems from a well-known lightbulb manufacturer. Dabco would like a recommendation on how much to order and when to order so that a low-cost inventory policy can be maintained. Pertinent facts are that the ordering cost is $12 per order, one bulb costs $6, and Dabco uses a 20% annual holding cost rate for its inventory ($C_h = IC = 0.20 \times \$6 = \$1.20$). Dabco, which has more than 1000 customers, experiences a probabilistic demand; in fact, the number of units demanded varies considerably from day to day and from week to week. The lead time for a new order of lightbulbs is one week. Historical sales data indicate that demand during a one-week lead time can be described by a normal probability distribution with a mean of 154 lightbulbs and a standard deviation of 25 lightbulbs. The normal distribution of demand during the lead time is shown in Figure 10.11. Because the mean demand during one week is 154 units, Dabco can anticipate a mean or expected annual demand of 154 units per week $\times$ 52 weeks per year = 8008 units per year.

FIGURE 10.11   LEAD-TIME DEMAND PROBABILITY DISTRIBUTION
FOR DABCO LIGHTBULBS

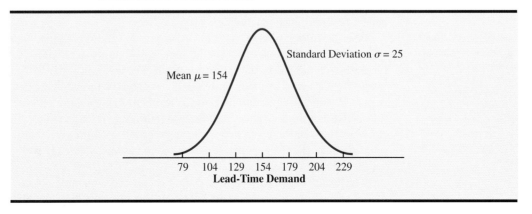

The How-Much-to-Order Decision

Although we are in a probabilistic demand situation, we have an estimate of the expected annual demand of 8008 units. We can apply the EOQ model from Section 10.1 as an approximation of the best order quantity, with the expected annual demand used for D. In Dabco's case

$$Q^* = \sqrt{\frac{2DC_o}{C_h}} = \sqrt{\frac{2(8008)(12)}{(1.20)}} = 400 \text{ units}$$

When we studied the sensitivity of the EOQ model, we learned that the total cost of operating an inventory system was relatively insensitive to order quantities that were in the neighborhood of Q^*. Using this knowledge, we expect 400 units per order to be a good approximation of the optimal order quantity. Even if annual demand were as low as 7000 units or as high as 9000 units, an order quantity of 400 units should be a relatively good low-cost order size. Thus, given our best estimate of annual demand at 8008 units, we will use $Q^* = 400$.

We have established the 400-unit order quantity by ignoring the fact that demand is probabilistic. Using $Q^* = 400$, Dabco can anticipate placing approximately $D/Q^* = 8008/400 = 20$ orders per year with an average of approximately $250/20 = 12.5$ working days between orders.

The When-to-Order Decision

The probability of a stock-out during any one inventory cycle is easiest to estimate by first determining the number of orders that are expected during the year. The inventory manager can usually state a willingness to allow perhaps one, two, or three stock-outs during the year. The allowable stock-outs per year divided by the number of orders per year will provide the desired probability of a stock-out.

We now want to establish a when-to-order decision rule or reorder point that will trigger the ordering process. With a mean lead-time demand of 154 units, you might first suggest a 154-unit reorder point. However, considering the probability of demand now becomes extremely important. If 154 is the mean lead-time demand, and if demand is symmetrically distributed about 154, then the lead-time demand will be more than 154 units roughly 50% of the time. When the demand during the one-week lead time exceeds 154 units, Dabco will experience a shortage or stock-out. Thus, using a reorder point of 154 units, approximately 50% of the time (10 of the 20 orders a year, on average) Dabco will be short of bulbs before the new supply arrives. This shortage rate would most likely be viewed as unacceptable.

Refer to the **lead-time demand distribution** shown in Figure 10.11. Given this distribution, we can now determine how the reorder point r affects the probability of a stock-out. Because stock-outs occur whenever the demand during the lead time exceeds the reorder point, we can find the probability of a stock-out by using the lead-time demand distribution to compute the probability that demand will exceed r.

We could now approach the when-to-order problem by defining a cost per stock-out and then attempting to include this cost in a total cost equation. Alternatively, we can ask management to specify the average number of stock-outs that can be tolerated per year. If demand for a product is probabilistic, a manager who will never tolerate a stock-out is being somewhat unrealistic because attempting to avoid stock-outs completely will require high reorder points, high inventory, and an associated high holding cost.

Suppose in this case that Dabco management is willing to tolerate an average of one stock-out per year. Because Dabco places 20 orders per year, this decision implies that management is willing to allow demand during lead time to exceed the reorder point one time in 20, or 5% of the time. The reorder point r can be found by using the lead-time demand distribution to find the value of r with a 5% chance of having a lead-time demand that will exceed it. This situation is shown graphically in Figure 10.12.

From the standard normal probability distribution table in Appendix B, we see that $1 - 0.05 = 0.95$ of the area in the left tail of the normal probability distribution occurs at $z = 1.645$ standard deviations above the mean. Therefore, for the assumed normal distribution for lead-time demand with $\mu = 154$ and $\sigma = 25$, the reorder point r is

$$r = 154 + 1.645(25) = 195$$

FIGURE 10.12   REORDER POINT *R* THAT ALLOWS A 5% CHANCE OF A STOCK-OUT FOR DABCO LIGHTBULBS

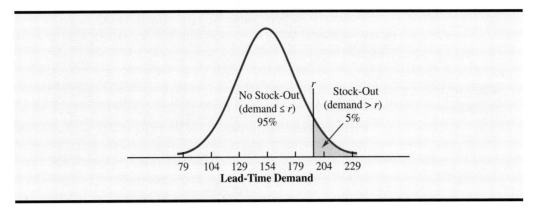

If a normal distribution is used for lead-time demand, the general equation for *r* is

$$r = \mu + z\sigma \qquad\qquad (10.37)$$

where z is the number of standard deviations necessary to obtain the acceptable stock-out probability.

Try Problem 29 as an example of an order-quantity, reorder point model with probabilistic demand.

Thus, the recommended inventory decision is to order 400 units whenever the inventory reaches the reorder point of 195. Because the mean or expected demand during the lead time is 154 units, the $195 - 154 = 41$ units serve as a **safety stock**, which absorbs higher-than-usual demand during the lead time. Roughly 95% of the time, the 195 units will be able to satisfy demand during the lead time. The anticipated annual cost for this system is as follows:

Holding cost, normal inventory $(Q/2)C_h = (400/2)(1.20) = \$240$

Holding cost, safety stock $(41)C_h = 41(1.20) = \$\ 49$

Ordering cost $(D/Q)C_o = (8008/400)12 = \underline{\$240}$

Total $\$529$

If Dabco could assume that a known, constant demand rate of 8008 units per year existed for the lightbulbs, then $Q^* = 400$, $r = 154$, and a total annual cost of $\$240 + \$240 = \$480$ would be optimal. When demand is uncertain and can only be expressed in probabilistic terms, a larger total cost can be expected. The larger cost occurs in the form of larger holding costs because more inventory must be maintained to limit the number of stock-outs. For Dabco, this additional inventory or safety stock was 41 units, with an additional annual holding cost of $49. The Management Science in Action, Inventory Models at Microsoft, describes how Microsoft has employed inventory models to increase customer service levels as well as reduce inventory costs.

NOTES AND COMMENTS

1. The safety stock required at Microsoft in the Management Science in Action, Inventory Models at Microsoft, was based on a service level defined by the probability of being able to satisfy all customer demand during an order cycle. If Microsoft wanted to guarantee that it would be able to meet all demand in 95% of all order cycles, then we would say that Microsoft has a 95% service level. This is sometimes referred to as a *Type-I* service level or a *cycle service level*. However, other definitions of *service level* may include the percentage of all customer demand that can be satisfied from inventory. Thus, when an inventory manager expresses a desired service level, it is a good idea to clarify exactly what the manager means by the term *service level*.

MANAGEMENT SCIENCE IN ACTION

INVENTORY MODELS AT MICROSOFT*

While known more for its operating system software, Microsoft has steadily increased its presence in consumer electronics. Microsoft produces Xbox video game consoles and a variety of personal-computer accessories such as mice and keyboards. In 2008 the consumer-electronics division of Microsoft generated over $8 billion in revenue compared to $52 billion in revenue from software. While products such as the Xbox are sold year-round, approximately 40% of annual sales occur in October, November, and December. Therefore, it is critical that Microsoft has sufficient inventory available to meet demand for the holiday season.

In conjunction with the supply-chain-services company Optiant, Microsoft began an ambitious effort in 2005 to improve its inventory management systems. Microsoft developed new forecasting techniques to better estimate future demand for its products. It then set service-level requirements for each product based on profit margins and demand forecasts. These service levels were used in safety-stock model calculations to determine target inventory levels that drove production plans. The new safety-stock models were used for more than 10,000 different consumer-electronics products sold by Microsoft.

Microsoft has experienced substantial inventory level reductions since implementing its new models and policies. Corporate-wide, Microsoft has reduced its inventories by $1.5 billion (60%). The consumer-electronics division of Microsoft posted its first ever profitable year in 2008. Microsoft largely credits these cost savings and profitability to superior forecasting and inventory models.

*Based on J.J. Neale and S.P. Willems, "Managing Inventory in Supply Chains with Nonstationary Demand," *Interfaces* 39, no. 5 (September 2009): 388–399.

10.7   PERIODIC REVIEW MODEL WITH PROBABILISTIC DEMAND

Up to this point, we have assumed that the inventory position is reviewed continuously so that an order can be placed as soon as the inventory position reaches the reorder point. The inventory model in this section assumes probabilistic demand and a periodic review of the inventory position.

The order-quantity, reorder point inventory models previously discussed require a **continuous review inventory system**. In a continuous review inventory system, the inventory position is monitored continuously so that an order can be placed whenever the reorder point is reached. Computerized inventory systems can easily provide the continuous review required by the order-quantity, reorder point models.

An alternative to the continuous review system is the **periodic review inventory system**. With a periodic review system, the inventory is checked and reordering is done only at specified points in time. For example, inventory may be checked and orders placed on a weekly, biweekly, monthly, or some other periodic basis. When a firm or business handles multiple products, the periodic review system offers the advantage of requiring that orders for several items be placed at the same preset periodic review time. With this type of inventory system, the shipping and receiving of orders for multiple products are easily coordinated. Under the previously discussed order-quantity, reorder point systems, the reorder points for various products can be encountered at substantially different points in time, making the coordination of orders for multiple products more difficult.

To illustrate this system, let us consider Dollar Discounts, a firm with several retail stores that carry a wide variety of products for household use. The company operates its inventory system with a two-week periodic review. Under this system, a retail store manager may order any number of units of any product from the Dollar Discounts central warehouse every two weeks. Orders for all products going to a particular store are combined into one shipment. When making the order quantity decision for each product at a given review period, the store manager knows that a reorder for the product cannot be made until the next review period.

Assuming that the lead time is less than the length of the review period, an order placed at a review period will be received prior to the next review period. In this case, the how-much-to-order decision at any review period is determined using the following:

$$Q = M - H \qquad\qquad (10.38)$$

where

Q = the order quantity

M = the replenishment level

H = the inventory on hand at the review period

Because the demand is probabilistic, the inventory on hand at the review period, H, will vary. Thus, the order quantity that must be sufficient to bring the inventory position back to its maximum or replenishment level M can be expected to vary each period. For example, if the replenishment level for a particular product is 50 units and the inventory on hand at the review period is $H = 12$ units, an order of $Q = M - H = 50 - 12 = 38$ units should be made. Thus, under the periodic review model, enough units are ordered each review period to bring the inventory position back up to the replenishment level.

A typical inventory pattern for a periodic review system with probabilistic demand is shown in Figure 10.13. Note that the time between periodic reviews is predetermined and fixed. The order quantity Q at each review period can vary and is shown to be the difference between the replenishment level and the inventory on hand. Finally, as with other probabilistic models, an unusually high demand can result in an occasional stock-out.

The decision variable in the periodic review model is the replenishment level M. To determine M, we could begin by developing a total cost model, including holding, ordering, and stock-out costs. Instead, we describe an approach that is often used in practice. In this approach, the objective is to determine a replenishment level that will meet a desired performance level, such as a reasonably low probability of stock-out or a reasonably low number of stock-outs per year.

FIGURE 10.13   INVENTORY PATTERN FOR PERIODIC REVIEW MODEL
WITH PROBABILISTIC DEMAND

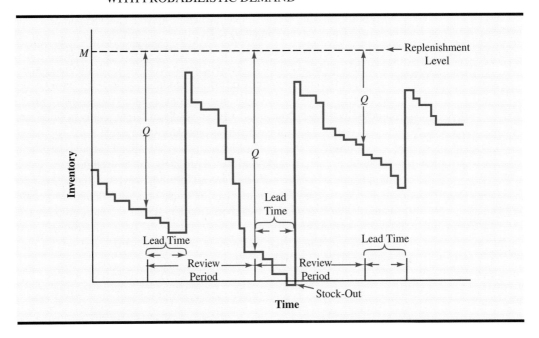

In the Dollar Discounts problem, we assume that management's objective is to determine the replenishment level with only a 1% chance of a stock-out. In the periodic review model, the order quantity at each review period must be sufficient to cover *demand for the review period plus the demand for the following lead time.* Suppose that an order is to be placed at time *t*. To determine this order quantity, we must realize that the quantity ordered at time *t* must last until the next time inventory is replenished, which will be time (*t* + review period + lead time). Thus, the total length of time that the order quantity at time *t* must last is equal to the review period plus the lead time. Figure 10.14 shows the normal probability distribution of demand during the review period plus the lead-time period for one of the Dollar Discounts products. The mean demand is 250 units, and the standard deviation of demand is 45 units. Given this situation, the logic used to establish *M* is similar to the logic used to establish the reorder point in Section 10.6. Figure 10.15 shows the replenishment level *M* with a 1% chance that demand will exceed that replenishment level. In other words, Figure 10.15 shows the replenishment level that allows a 1% chance of a stock-out associated with the replenishment decision. Using the normal probability distribution table in Appendix B, we see that $1 - 0.01 = 0.99$ of the area in the left tail of the normal probability distribution occurs at $z = 2.33$ standard deviations above the mean. Therefore, for the assumed normal probability distribution with $\mu = 250$ and $\sigma = 45$, the replenishment level is determined by

Periodic

$$M = 250 + 2.33(45) = 355$$

FIGURE 10.14   PROBABILITY DISTRIBUTION OF DEMAND DURING THE REVIEW
PERIOD AND LEAD TIME FOR THE DOLLAR DISCOUNTS PROBLEM

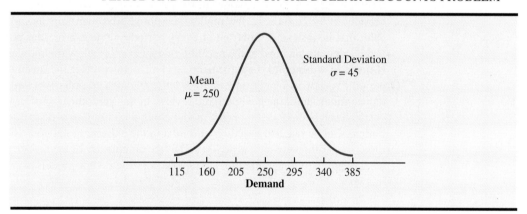

FIGURE 10.15   REPLENISHMENT LEVEL *M* THAT ALLOWS A 1% CHANCE
OF A STOCK-OUT FOR THE DOLLAR DISCOUNTS PROBLEM

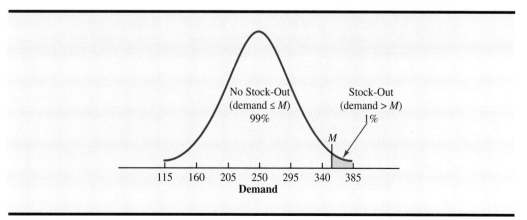

Problem 33 gives you practice in computing the replenishment level for a periodic review model with probabilistic demand.

Although other probability distributions can be used to express the demand during the review period plus the lead-time period, if the normal probability distribution is used, the general expression for M is

$$M = \mu + z\sigma \qquad (10.39)$$

Periodic review systems provide advantages of coordinated orders for multiple items. However, periodic review systems require larger safety-stock levels than corresponding continuous review systems.

where z is the number of standard deviations necessary to obtain the acceptable stock-out probability.

If demand had been deterministic rather than probabilistic, the replenishment level would have been the demand during the review period plus the demand during the lead-time period. In this case, the replenishment level would have been 250 units, and no stock-out would have occurred. However, with the probabilistic demand, we have seen that higher inventory is necessary to allow for uncertain demand and to control the probability of a stock-out. In the Dollar Discounts problem, $355 - 250 = 105$ is the safety stock that is necessary to absorb any higher-than-usual demand during the review period plus the demand during the lead-time period. This safety stock limits the probability of a stock-out to 1%.

More Complex Periodic Review Models

The periodic review model just discussed is one approach to determining a replenishment level for the periodic review inventory system with probabilistic demand. More complex versions of the periodic review model incorporate a reorder point as another decision variable; that is, instead of ordering at every periodic review, a reorder point is established. If the inventory on hand at the periodic review is at or below the reorder point, a decision is made to order up to the replenishment level. However, if the inventory on hand at the periodic review is greater than the reorder level, such an order is not placed, and the system continues until the next periodic review. In this case, the cost of ordering is a relevant cost and can be included in a cost model along with holding and stock-out costs. Optimal policies can be reached based on minimizing the expected total cost. Situations with lead times longer than the review period add to the complexity of the model. The mathematical level required to treat these more extensive periodic review models is beyond the scope of this text.

NOTES AND COMMENTS

1. The periodic review model presented in this section is based on the assumption that the lead time for an order is less than the periodic review period. Most periodic review systems operate under this condition. However, the case for which the lead time is longer than the review period can be handled by defining H in equation (10.38) as the inventory position, where H includes the inventory on hand plus the inventory on order. In this case, the order quantity at any review period is the amount needed for the inventory on hand plus all outstanding orders needed to reach the replenishment level.

2. In the order-quantity, reorder point model discussed in Section 10.6, a continuous review was used to initiate an order whenever the reorder point was reached. The safety stock for this model was based on the probabilistic demand during the lead time. The periodic review model presented in this section also determined a recommended safety stock. However, because the inventory review was only periodic, the safety stock was based on the probabilistic demand during the review period plus the lead-time period. This longer period for the safety stock computation means that periodic review systems tend to require a larger safety stock than do continuous review systems.

SUMMARY

In this chapter we presented some of the approaches used to assist managers in establishing low-cost inventory policies. We first considered cases for which the demand rate for the product is constant. In analyzing these inventory systems, total cost models were developed; these models included ordering costs, holding costs, and, in some cases, backorder costs. Then minimum cost formulas for the order quantity Q were presented. A reorder point r can be established by considering the lead-time demand.

In addition, we discussed inventory models for which a deterministic and constant rate could not be assumed, and thus demand was described by a probability distribution. A critical issue with these probabilistic inventory models is obtaining a probability distribution that most realistically approximates the demand distribution. We first described a single-period model where only one order is placed for the product and, at the end of the period, either the product has sold out or a surplus remains of unsold products that will be sold for a salvage value. Solution procedures were then presented for multiperiod models based on either an order-quantity, reorder point, continuous review system or a replenishment-level, periodic review system.

In closing this chapter, we reemphasize that inventory and inventory systems can be an expensive phase of a firm's operation. It is important for managers to be aware of the cost of inventory systems and to make the best possible operating policy decisions for the inventory system. Inventory models, as presented in this chapter, can help managers to develop good inventory policies.

GLOSSARY

Backorder The receipt of an order for a product when no units are in inventory. These backorders are eventually satisfied when a new supply of the product becomes available.

Constant demand rate An assumption of many inventory models that states that the same number of units are taken from inventory each period of time.

Constant supply rate A situation in which the inventory is built up at a constant rate over a period of time.

Continuous review inventory system A system in which the inventory position is monitored or reviewed on a continuous basis so that a new order can be placed as soon as the reorder point is reached.

Cost of capital The cost a firm incurs to obtain capital for investment. It may be stated as an annual percentage rate, and it is part of the holding cost associated with maintaining inventory.

Cycle time The length of time between the placing of two consecutive orders.

Deterministic inventory model A model where demand is considered known and not subject to uncertainty.

Economic order quantity (EOQ) The order quantity that minimizes the annual holding cost plus the annual ordering cost.

Goodwill cost A cost associated with a backorder, a lost sale, or any form of stock-out or unsatisfied demand. This cost may be used to reflect the loss of future profits because a customer experienced an unsatisfied demand.

Holding cost The cost associated with maintaining an inventory investment, including the cost of the capital investment in the inventory, insurance, taxes, warehouse overhead, and so on. This cost may be stated as a percentage of the inventory investment or as a cost per unit.

Incremental analysis A method used to determine an optimal order quantity by comparing the cost of ordering an additional unit with the cost of not ordering an additional unit.

Inventory position The inventory on hand plus the inventory on order.

Lead time   The time between the placing of an order and its receipt in the inventory system.

Lead-time demand   The number of units demanded during the lead-time period.

Lead-time demand distribution   The distribution of demand that occurs during the lead-time period.

Lot size   The order quantity in the production inventory model.

Ordering cost   The fixed cost (salaries, paper, transportation, etc.) associated with placing an order for an item.

Periodic review inventory system   A system in which the inventory position is checked or reviewed at predetermined periodic points in time. Reorders are placed only at periodic review points.

Probabilistic inventory model   A model where demand is not known exactly; probabilities must be associated with the possible values for demand.

Quantity discounts   Discounts or lower unit costs offered by the manufacturer when a customer purchases larger quantities of the product.

Reorder point   The inventory position at which a new order should be placed.

Safety stock   Inventory maintained in order to reduce the number of stock-outs resulting from higher-than-expected demand.

Setup cost   The fixed cost (labor, materials, lost production) associated with preparing for a new production run.

Shortage or stock-out   Occurrence when demand cannot be supplied from inventory.

Single-period inventory model   An inventory model in which only one order is placed for the product, and at the end of the period either the item has sold out or a surplus of unsold items will be sold for a salvage value.

PROBLEMS

 SELF*test*

1.   Suppose that the R&B Beverage Company has a soft drink product that shows a constant annual demand rate of 3600 cases. A case of the soft drink costs R&B $3. Ordering costs are $20 per order and holding costs are 25% of the value of the inventory. R&B has 250 working days per year, and the lead time is 5 days. Identify the following aspects of the inventory policy:
     a.   Economic order quantity
     b.   Reorder point
     c.   Cycle time
     d.   Total annual cost

2.   A general property of the EOQ inventory model is that total inventory holding and total ordering costs are equal at the optimal solution. Use the data in Problem 1 to show that this result is true. Use equations (10.1), (10.2), and (10.3) to show that, in general, total holding costs and total ordering costs are equal whenever Q^* is used.

3.   The reorder point [see equation (10.6)] is defined as the lead-time demand for an item. In cases of long lead times, the lead-time demand and thus the reorder point may exceed the economic order quantity Q^*. In such cases, the inventory position will not equal the inventory on hand when an order is placed, and the reorder point may be expressed in terms of either the inventory position or the inventory on hand. Consider the economic order quantity model with $D = 5000$, $C_o = \$32$, $C_h = \$2$, and 250 working days per year. Identify the reorder point in terms of the inventory position and in terms of the inventory on hand for each of the following lead times:
     a.   5 days
     b.   15 days
     c.   25 days
     d.   45 days

4. Westside Auto purchases a component used in the manufacture of automobile generators directly from the supplier. Westside's generator production operation, which is operated at a constant rate, will require 1000 components per month throughout the year (12,000 units annually). Assume that the ordering costs are $25 per order, the unit cost is $2.50 per component, and annual holding costs are 20% of the value of the inventory. Westside has 250 working days per year and a lead time of 5 days. Answer the following inventory policy questions:
   a. What is the EOQ for this component?
   b. What is the reorder point?
   c. What is the cycle time?
   d. What are the total annual holding and ordering costs associated with your recommended EOQ?

5. The Metropolitan Bus Company (MBC) purchases diesel fuel from American Petroleum Supply. In addition to the fuel cost, American Petroleum Supply charges MBC $250 per order to cover the expenses of delivering and transferring the fuel to MBC's storage tanks. The lead time for a new shipment from American Petroleum is 10 days; the cost of holding a gallon of fuel in the storage tanks is $0.04 per month, or $0.48 per year; and annual fuel usage is 150,000 gallons. MBC buses operate 300 days a year.
   a. What is the optimal order quantity for MBC?
   b. How frequently should MBC order to replenish the gasoline supply?
   c. The MBC storage tanks have a capacity of 15,000 gallons. Should MBC consider expanding the capacity of its storage tanks?
   d. What is the reorder point?

6. The manager at a local university bookstore wishes to apply the EOQ model to determine the respective order quantities for two products: ballpoint pens and mechanical pencils. The annual demand for pens and pencils is 1500 and 400, respectively. The ordering cost for each product is $20 per order and the wholesale price of a pen and pencil is $1.50 and $4, respectively. Assume the bookstore's annual holding rate is 10% and that the bookstore operates 240 days per year.
   a. Determine the optimal order quantity and the order cycle time for each product. What is the total cost (summed over both products)?
   b. The bookstore orders the pens and pencils from the same supplier. If these two products had the same cycle time, the corresponding shipment consolidation would reduce the ordering cost to $15. How much money does the bookstore save by consolidating the orders for these two products? (*Hint:* By setting the cycle times equal, we have $Q_{pens}/(1500/240) = Q_{pencils}/(400/240)$ or $Q_{pens} = 3.75Q_{pencils}$. Make this substitution into the combined cost equation so that it is a function only of $Q_{pencils}$ and apply equation (10.5) with the appropriate values to determine $Q_{pencils}$ (and subsequently Q_{pens}).

7. A large distributor of oil-well drilling equipment operated over the past two years with EOQ policies based on an annual holding cost rate of 22%. Under the EOQ policy, a particular product has been ordered with a $Q^* = 80$. A recent evaluation of holding costs shows that because of an increase in the interest rate associated with bank loans, the annual holding cost rate should be 27%. Observe that we cannot directly use the EOQ equation to compute the order quantity considering the new holding cost rate of 27% because we are not given the annual demand, fixed ordering cost, and ordering price. However, we can use the original value of Q and knowledge of how we computed it to determine the revised economic order quantity corresponding to the updated holding cost rate.
   a. Develop a general expression showing how the economic order quantity changes when the annual holding cost rate is changed from I to I'.
   b. Using the formula you derived in part a, compute the new economic order quantity for the product.

8. Nation-Wide Bus Lines is proud of its six-week bus driver–training program that it conducts for all new Nation-Wide drivers. As long as the class size remains less than or equal to 35, a six-week training program costs Nation-Wide $22,000 for instructors, equipment, and so on. The Nation-Wide training program must provide the company with approximately five new drivers per month. After completing the training program, new drivers are paid $1600 per month but do not work until a full-time driver position is open. Nation-Wide views the $1600 per month

paid to each idle new driver as a holding cost necessary to maintain a supply of newly trained drivers available for immediate service. Viewing new drivers as inventory-type units, how large should the training classes be to minimize Nation-Wide's total annual training and new driver idle-time costs? How many training classes should the company hold each year? What is the total annual cost associated with your recommendation?

9. Cress Electronic Products manufactures components used in the automotive industry. Cress purchases parts for use in its manufacturing operation from a variety of different suppliers. One particular supplier provides a part where the assumptions of the EOQ model are realistic. The annual demand is 5000 units, the ordering cost is $80 per order, and the annual holding cost rate is 25%.

   a. If the cost of the part is $20 per unit, what is the economic order quantity?

   b. Assume 250 days of operation per year. If the lead time for an order is 12 days, what is the reorder point?

   c. If the lead time for the part is seven weeks (35 days), what is the reorder point? Compare this with the economic order quantity from part (a). Explain the relative size of these two quantities. *Hint:* Remember that the reorder point is expressed in terms of inventory position.

   d. What is the reorder point for part (c) if the reorder point is expressed in terms of the inventory on hand rather than the inventory position?

10. All-Star Bat Manufacturing, Inc., supplies baseball bats to major and minor league baseball teams. After an initial order in January, demand over the six-month baseball season is approximately constant at 1000 bats per month. Assuming that the bat production process can handle up to 4000 bats per month, the bat production setup costs are $150 per setup, the production cost is $10 per bat, and the holding costs have a monthly rate of 2%, what production lot size would you recommend to meet the demand during the baseball season? If All-Star operates 20 days per month, how often will the production process operate, and what is the length of a production run?

11. Assume that a production line operates such that the production lot size model of Section 10.2 is applicable. Assume that $D = 6400$ units per year, $C_o = \$100$, and $C_h = \$2$ per unit per year.

   a. Compute the minimum cost production lot size for each of the following production rates: (i) 8000 units per year, (ii) 10,000 units per year, (iii) 32,000 units per year, and (iv) 100,000 units per year.

   b. Compute the EOQ recommended lot size using equation (10.5). Comparing the EOQ lot size to the various production lot sizes in part a, what two observations can you make about the relationship between the EOQ model and the production lot size model?

12. EL Computer produces its multimedia notebook computer on a production line that has an annual capacity of 16,000 units. EL Computer estimates the annual demand for this model at 6000 units. The cost to set up the production line is $2345, and the annual holding cost is $20 per unit. Current practice calls for production runs of 500 notebook computers each month.

   a. What is the optimal production lot size?

   b. How many production runs should be made each year? What is the recommended cycle time?

   c. Would you recommend changing the current production lot size policy from the monthly 500-unit production runs? Why or why not? What is the projected savings of your recommendation?

 SELF*test*

13. Wilson Publishing Company produces books for the retail market. Demand for a current book is expected to occur at a constant annual rate of 7200 copies. The cost of one copy of the book is $14.50. The holding cost is based on an 18% annual rate, and production setup costs are $150 per setup. The equipment with which the book is produced has an annual production volume of 25,000 copies. Wilson has 250 working days per year, and the lead time for a production run is 15 days. Use the production lot size model to compute the following values:

   a. Minimum cost production lot size

   b. Number of production runs per year

   c. Cycle time

   d. Length of a production run

   e. Maximum inventory

   f. Total annual cost

   g. Reorder point

14. A well-known manufacturer of several brands of toothpaste uses the production lot size model to determine production quantities for its various products. The product known as Extra White is currently being produced in production lot sizes of 5000 units. The length of the production run for this quantity is 10 days. Because of a recent shortage of a particular raw material, the supplier of the material announced that a cost increase will be passed along to the manufacturer of Extra White. Current estimates are that the new raw material cost will increase the manufacturing cost of the toothpaste products by 23% per unit. What will be the effect of this price increase on the production lot sizes for Extra White?

15. Suppose that Westside Auto of Problem 4, with $D = 12,000$ units per year, $C_h = (2.50)$ $(0.20) = \$0.50$, and $C_o = \$25$, decided to operate with a backorder inventory policy. Backorder costs are estimated to be \$5 per unit per year. Identify the following:
    a. Minimum cost order quantity
    b. Maximum number of backorders
    c. Maximum inventory
    d. Cycle time
    e. Total annual cost

16. Assuming 250 days of operation per year and a lead time of five days, what is the reorder point for Westside Auto in Problem 15? Show the general formula for the reorder point for the EOQ model with backorders. In general, is the reorder point when backorders are allowed greater than or less than the reorder point when backorders are not allowed? Explain.

17. A manager of an inventory system believes that inventory models are important decision-making aids. The manager has experience with the EOQ policy, but has never considered a backorder model because of the assumption that backorders were "bad" and should be avoided. However, with upper management's continued pressure for cost reduction, you have been asked to analyze the economics of a backorder policy for some products that can possibly be backordered. For a specific product with $D = 800$ units per year, $C_o = \$150$, $C_h = \$3$, and $C_b = \$20$, what is the difference in total annual cost between the EOQ model and the planned shortage or backorder model? If the manager adds constraints that no more than 25% of the units can be backordered and that no customer will have to wait more than 15 days for an order, should the backorder inventory policy be adopted? Assume 250 working days per year.

18. If the lead time for new orders is 20 days for the inventory system discussed in Problem 17, find the reorder point for both the EOQ and the backorder models.

19. The A&M Hobby Shop carries a line of radio-controlled model racing cars. Demand for the cars is assumed to be constant at a rate of 40 cars per month. The cars cost \$60 each, and ordering costs are approximately \$15 per order, regardless of the order size. The annual holding cost rate is 20%.
    a. Determine the economic order quantity and total annual cost under the assumption that no backorders are permitted.
    b. Using a \$45 per-unit per-year backorder cost, determine the minimum cost inventory policy and total annual cost for the model racing cars.
    c. What is the maximum number of days a customer would have to wait for a backorder under the policy in part (b)? Assume that the Hobby Shop is open for business 300 days per year.
    d. Would you recommend a no-backorder or a backorder inventory policy for this product? Explain.
    e. If the lead time is six days, what is the reorder point for both the no-backorder and backorder inventory policies?

20. Assume that the following quantity discount schedule is appropriate. If annual demand is 120 units, ordering costs are \$20 per order, and the annual holding cost rate is 25%, what order quantity would you recommend?

Order Size	Discount (%)	Unit Cost
0 to 49	0	\$30.00
50 to 99	5	\$28.50
100 or more	10	\$27.00

SELF*test*

21. Apply the EOQ model to the following quantity discount situation for which $D = 500$ units per year, $C_o = \$40$, and the annual holding cost rate is 20%. What order quantity do you recommend?

Discount Category	Order Size	Discount (%)	Unit Cost
1	0 to 99	0	$10.00
2	100 or more	3	$ 9.70

22. Keith Shoe Stores carries a basic black dress shoe for men that sells at an approximately constant rate of 500 pairs of shoes every three months. Keith's current buying policy is to order 500 pairs each time an order is placed. It costs Keith $30 to place an order. The annual holding cost rate is 20%. With the order quantity of 500, Keith obtains the shoes at the lowest possible unit cost of $28 per pair. Other quantity discounts offered by the manufacturer are as follows. What is the minimum cost order quantity for the shoes? What are the annual savings of your inventory policy over the policy currently being used by Keith?

Order Quantity	Price per Pair
0–99	$36
100–199	$32
200–299	$30
300 or more	$28

23. In the EOQ model with quantity discounts, we stated that if the Q^* for a price category is larger than necessary to qualify for the category price, the category cannot be optimal. Use the two discount categories in Problem 21 to show that this statement is true. That is, plot total cost curves for the two categories and show that if the category 2 minimum cost Q is an acceptable solution, we do not have to consider category 1.

24. University of Iowa Sports Information (UISI) procures its game-day football magazines from a publishing company at a price of $9.00 per magazine. UISI sells the magazines on the day of the corresponding football game at a retail price of $10.00. To sell these magazines, UISI hires vendors and pays them $0.50 for each program that they sell. For the first game of the season, UISI has determined that demand for the game-day football magazines is normally distributed with a mean of 9000 magazines and a standard deviation of 400 magazines. Any magazines that are not sold on the day of the game are worthless and UISI recycles them.
  a. What is UISI's optimal order quantity of game-day football magazines for the first game of the season?
  b. Instead of recycling the unsold programs, suppose the publisher offers to buy back any unsold programs for $8.00. Under this scenario, what is UISI's optimal order quantity?

SELF*test*

25. The Gilbert Air-Conditioning Company is considering the purchase of a special shipment of portable air conditioners manufactured in Japan. Each unit will cost Gilbert $80, and it will be sold for $125. Gilbert does not want to carry surplus air conditioners over until the following year. Thus, all surplus air conditioners will be sold to a wholesaler for $50 per unit. Assume that the air conditioner demand follows a normal probability distribution with $\mu = 20$ and $\sigma = 8$.
  a. What is the recommended order quantity?
  b. What is the probability that Gilbert will sell all units it orders?

26. The Bridgeport city manager and the chief of police agreed on the size of the police force necessary for normal daily operations. However, they need assistance in determining the number of additional police officers needed to cover daily absences due to injuries, sickness, vacations, and personal leave. Records over the past three years show that the daily demand for additional police officers is normally distributed with a mean of 50 officers and a standard deviation of 10 officers. The cost of an additional police officer is based on the average pay rate of $150 per day. If the daily demand for additional police officers exceeds the number of additional officers available, the excess demand will be covered by overtime at the pay rate of $240 per day for each overtime officer.

a. If the number of additional police officers available is greater than demand, the city will have to pay for more additional police officers than needed. What is the cost of overestimating demand?

b. If the number of additional police officers available is less than demand, the city will have to use overtime to meet the demand. What is the cost of underestimating demand?

c. What is the optimal number of additional police officers that should be included in the police force?

d. On a typical day, what is the probability that overtime will be necessary?

27. A perishable dairy product is ordered daily at a particular supermarket. The product costs $1.19 per unit and sells for $1.65 per unit. If units are unsold at the end of the day, the supplier takes them back at a rebate of $1 per unit. Assume that daily demand is approximately normally distributed with $\mu = 150$ and $\sigma = 30$.

a. What is your recommended daily order quantity for the supermarket?

b. What is the probability that the supermarket will sell all the units it orders?

c. In problems such as these, why would the supplier offer a rebate as high as $1? For example, why not offer a nominal rebate of, say, 25¢ per unit? What happens to the supermarket order quantity as the rebate is reduced?

28. A retail outlet sells holiday candy for $10 per bag. The cost of the product is $8 per bag. All units not sold during the selling season prior to the holiday are sold for half the retail price in a postholiday clearance sale. Assume that demand for bags of holiday candy during the selling season is uniformly distributed between 200 and 800.

a. What is the recommended order quantity?

b. What is the probability that at least some customers will ask to purchase the product after the outlet is sold out? That is, what is the probability of a stock-out using your order quantity in part (a)?

c. To keep customers happy and returning to the store later, the owner feels that stock-outs should be avoided if at all possible. What is your recommended order quantity if the owner is willing to tolerate a 0.15 probability of a stock-out?

d. Using your answer to part (c), what is the goodwill cost you are assigning to a stock-out?

 SELF*test*

29. Floyd Distributors, Inc., provides a variety of auto parts to small local garages. Floyd purchases parts from manufacturers according to the EOQ model and then ships the parts from a regional warehouse direct to its customers. For a particular type of muffler, Floyd's EOQ analysis recommends orders with $Q^* = 25$ to satisfy an annual demand of 200 mufflers. Floyd's has 250 working days per year, and the lead time averages 15 days.

a. What is the reorder point if Floyd assumes a constant demand rate?

b. Suppose that an analysis of Floyd's muffler demand shows that the lead-time demand follows a normal probability distribution with $\mu = 12$ and $\sigma = 2.5$. If Floyd's management can tolerate one stock-out per year, what is the revised reorder point?

c. What is the safety stock for part (b)? If $C_h = \$5$/unit/year, what is the extra cost due to the uncertainty of demand?

30. To serve "to-go" orders, Terrapin Coffeehouse faces normally distributed weekly demand with an average of 300 paper cups and a standard deviation of 75 cups per week. Terrapin orders cups by the box. Each box costs $10 and contains 100 cups. For each order placed, Terrapin pays a fixed $15 shipping fee (regardless of the number of boxes ordered) and the order arrives one week after Terrapin places it with the cup supplier. Terrapin estimates that holding costs are 15% per dollar per year. Due to the importance of cups to business, Terrapin wants no more than a 1% chance of a stock-out during the one-week lead time for cup replenishment. Assume that there are 52 weeks in a year.

a. What is the optimal order quantity (in terms of number of boxes)?

b. What is the optimal reorder point (in terms of number of cups)?

31. A product with an annual demand of 1000 units has $C_o = \$25.50$ and $C_h = \$8$. The demand exhibits some variability such that the lead-time demand follows a normal probability distribution with $\mu = 25$ and $\sigma = 5$.

   a. What is the recommended order quantity?

   b. What are the reorder point and safety stock if the firm desires at most a 2% probability of stock-out on any given order cycle?

   c. If a manager sets the reorder point at 30, what is the probability of a stock-out on any given order cycle? How many times would you expect a stock-out during the year if this reorder point were used?

32. The B&S Novelty and Craft Shop in Bennington, Vermont, sells a variety of quality handmade items to tourists. B&S will sell 300 hand-carved miniature replicas of a Colonial soldier each year, but the demand pattern during the year is uncertain. The replicas sell for $20 each, and B&S uses a 15% annual inventory holding cost rate. Ordering costs are $5 per order, and demand during the lead time follows a normal probability distribution with $\mu = 15$ and $\sigma = 6$.

   a. What is the recommended order quantity?

   b. If B&S is willing to accept a stock-out roughly twice a year, what reorder point would you recommend? What is the probability that B&S will have a stock-out in any one order cycle?

   c. What are the safety stock and annual safety stock costs for this product?

 SELFtest

33. A firm uses a one-week periodic review inventory system. A two-day lead time is needed for any order, and the firm is willing to tolerate an average of one stock-out per year.

   a. Using the firm's service guideline, what is the probability of a stock-out associated with each replenishment decision?

   b. What is the replenishment level if demand during the review period plus lead-time period is normally distributed with a mean of 60 units and a standard deviation of 12 units?

   c. What is the replenishment level if demand during the review period plus lead-time period is uniformly distributed between 35 and 85 units?

34. Foster Drugs, Inc., handles a variety of health and beauty aid products. A particular hair conditioner product costs Foster Drugs $2.95 per unit. The annual holding cost rate is 20%. An order-quantity, reorder point inventory model recommends an order quantity of 300 units per order.

   a. Lead time is one week, and the lead-time demand is normally distributed with a mean of 150 units and a standard deviation of 40 units. What is the reorder point if the firm is willing to tolerate a 1% chance of stock-out on any one cycle?

   b. What safety stock and annual safety stock costs are associated with your recommendation in part (a)?

   c. The order-quantity, reorder point model requires a continuous review system. Management is considering making a transition to a periodic review system in an attempt to coordinate ordering for many of its products. The demand during the proposed two-week review period and the one-week lead-time period is normally distributed with a mean of 450 units and a standard deviation of 70 units. What is the recommended replenishment level for this periodic review system if the firm is willing to tolerate the same 1% chance of stock-out associated with any replenishment decision?

   d. What safety stock and annual safety stock costs are associated with your recommendation in part (c)?

   e. Compare your answers to parts (b) and (d). The company is seriously considering the periodic review system. Would you support this decision? Explain.

   f. Would you tend to favor the continuous review system for more expensive items? For example, assume that the product in the preceding example sold for $295 per unit. Explain.

35. Statewide Auto Parts uses a four-week periodic review system to reorder parts for its inventory stock. A one-week lead time is required to fill the order. Demand for one particular part during the five-week replenishment period is normally distributed with a mean of 18 units and a standard deviation of 6 units.

   a. At a particular periodic review, 8 units are in inventory. The parts manager places an order for 16 units. What is the probability that this part will have a stock-out before an order that is placed at the next four-week review period arrives?

    b. Assume that the company is willing to tolerate a 2.5% chance of a stock-out associated with a replenishment decision. How many parts should the manager have ordered in part (a)? What is the replenishment level for the four-week periodic review system?

36. Rose Office Supplies, Inc., which is open six days a week, uses a two-week periodic review for its store inventory. On alternating Monday mornings, the store manager fills out an order sheet requiring a shipment of various items from the company's warehouse. A particular three-ring notebook sells at an average rate of 16 notebooks per week. The standard deviation in sales is 5 notebooks per week. The lead time for a new shipment is three days. The mean lead-time demand is 8 notebooks with a standard deviation of 3.5.

    a. What is the mean or expected demand during the review period plus the lead-time period?

    b. Under the assumption of independent demand from week to week, the variances in demands are additive. Thus, the variance of the demand during the review period plus the lead-time period is equal to the variance of demand during the first week plus the variance of demand during the second week plus the variance of demand during the lead-time period. What is the variance of demand during the review period plus the lead-time period? What is the standard deviation of demand during the review period plus the lead-time period?

    c. Assuming that demand has a normal probability distribution, what is the replenishment level that will provide an expected stock-out rate of one per year?

    d. On Monday, March 22, 18 notebooks remain in inventory at the store. How many notebooks should the store manager order?

Case Problem 1   WAGNER FABRICATING COMPANY

Managers at Wagner Fabricating Company are reviewing the economic feasibility of manufacturing a part that the company currently purchases from a supplier. Forecasted annual demand for the part is 3200 units. Wagner operates 250 days per year.

    Wagner's financial analysts established a cost of capital of 14% for the use of funds for investments within the company. In addition, over the past year $600,000 was the average investment in the company's inventory. Accounting information shows that a total of $24,000 was spent on taxes and insurance related to the company's inventory. In addition, an estimated $9000 was lost due to inventory shrinkage, which included damaged goods as well as pilferage. A remaining $15,000 was spent on warehouse overhead, including utility expenses for heating and lighting.

    An analysis of the purchasing operation shows that approximately two hours are required to process and coordinate an order for the part regardless of the quantity ordered. Purchasing salaries average $28 per hour, including employee benefits. In addition, a detailed analysis of 125 orders showed that $2375 was spent on telephone, paper, and postage directly related to the ordering process.

    A one-week lead time is required to obtain the part from the supplier. An analysis of demand during the lead time shows it is approximately normally distributed with a mean of 64 units and a standard deviation of 10 units. Service-level guidelines indicate that one stock-out per year is acceptable.

    Currently, the company has a contract to purchase the part from a supplier at a cost of $18 per unit. However, over the past few months, the company's production capacity has been expanded. As a result, excess capacity is now available in certain production departments, and the company is considering the alternative of producing the parts itself.

    Forecasted utilization of equipment shows that production capacity will be available for the part being considered. The production capacity is available at the rate of 1000 units per month, with up to five months of production time available. Management believes that with a two-week lead time, schedules can be arranged so that the part can be produced whenever needed. The demand during the two-week lead time is approximately normally distributed, with a mean of 128 units and a standard deviation of 20 units. Production costs are expected to be $17 per part.

A concern of management is that setup costs will be substantial. The total cost of labor and lost production time is estimated to be $50 per hour, and a full eight-hour shift will be needed to set up the equipment for producing the part.

Managerial Report

Develop a report for management of Wagner Fabricating that will address the question of whether the company should continue to purchase the part from the supplier or begin to produce the part itself. Include the following factors in your report:

1. An analysis of the holding costs, including the appropriate annual holding cost rate
2. An analysis of ordering costs, including the appropriate cost per order from the supplier
3. An analysis of setup costs for the production operation
4. A development of the inventory policy for the following two alternatives:
    a. Ordering a fixed quantity Q from the supplier
    b. Ordering a fixed quantity Q from in-plant production
5. Include the following in the policies of parts 4(a) and 4(b):
    a. Optimal quantity Q^*
    b. Number of order or production runs per year
    c. Cycle time
    d. Reorder point
    e. Amount of safety stock
    f. Expected maximum inventory
    g. Average inventory
    h. Annual holding cost
    i. Annual ordering cost
    j. Annual cost of the units purchased or manufactured
    k. Total annual cost of the purchase policy and the total annual cost of the production policy
6. Make a recommendation as to whether the company should purchase or manufacture the part. What savings are associated with your recommendation as compared with the other alternative?

Case Problem 2   RIVER CITY FIRE DEPARTMENT

The River City Fire Department (RCFD) fights fires and provides a variety of rescue operations in the River City metropolitan area. The RCFD staffs 13 ladder companies, 26 pumper companies, and several rescue units and ambulances. Normal staffing requires 186 firefighters to be on duty every day.

RCFD is organized with three firefighting units. Each unit works a full 24-hour day and then has two days (48 hours) off. For example, Unit 1 covers Monday, Unit 2 covers Tuesday, and Unit 3 covers Wednesday. Then Unit 1 returns on Thursday, and so on. Over a three-week (21-day) scheduling period, each unit will be scheduled for seven days. On a rotational basis, firefighters within each unit are given one of the seven regularly scheduled days off. This day off is referred to as a Kelley day. Thus, over a three-week scheduling period, each firefighter in a unit works six of the seven scheduled unit days and gets one Kelley day off.

Determining the number of firefighters to be assigned to each unit includes the 186 firefighters who must be on duty plus the number of firefighters in the unit who are off for a Kelley day. Furthermore, each unit needs additional staffing to cover firefighter absences due to injury, sick leave, vacations, or personal time. This additional staffing involves finding the best mix of adding full-time firefighters to each unit and the selective use of overtime. If the number of absences on a particular day brings the number of available firefighters below the required 186, firefighters who are currently off (e.g., on a Kelley day) must be scheduled to work overtime. Overtime is compensated at 1.55 times the regular pay rate.

Analysis of the records maintained over the last several years concerning the number of daily absences shows a normal probability distribution with a mean of 20 and a standard deviation of 5 provides a good approximation of the probability distribution for the number of daily absences.

Managerial Report

Develop a report that will enable Fire Chief O. E. Smith to determine the necessary numbers for the Fire Department. Include, at a minimum, the following items in your report:

1. Assuming no daily absences and taking into account the need to staff Kelley days, determine the base number of firefighters needed by each unit.
2. Using a minimum cost criterion, how many additional firefighters should be added to each unit in order to cover the daily absences? These extra daily needs will be filled by the additional firefighters and, when necessary, the more expensive use of overtime by off-duty firefighters.
3. On a given day, what is the probability that Kelley-day firefighters will be called in to work overtime?
4. Based on the three-unit organization, how many firefighters should be assigned to each unit? What is the total number of full-time firefighters required for the River City Fire Department?

Appendix 10.1   DEVELOPMENT OF THE OPTIMAL ORDER QUANTITY (Q) FORMULA FOR THE EOQ MODEL

Given equation (10.4) as the total annual cost for the EOQ model,

$$TC = \frac{1}{2}QC_h + \frac{D}{Q}C_o \tag{10.4}$$

we can find the order quantity Q that minimizes the total cost by setting the derivative, dTC/dQ, equal to zero and solving for Q^*.

$$\frac{dTC}{dQ} = \frac{1}{2}C_h - \frac{D}{Q^2}C_o = 0$$

$$\frac{1}{2}C_h = \frac{D}{Q^2}C_o$$

$$C_hQ^2 = 2DC_o$$

$$Q^2 = \frac{2DC_o}{C_h}$$

Hence,

$$Q^* = \sqrt{\frac{2DC_o}{C_h}} \tag{10.5}$$

The second derivative is

$$\frac{d^2TC}{dQ^2} = \frac{2D}{Q^3}C_o$$

Because the value of the second derivative is greater than zero, Q^* from equation (10.5) is the minimum-cost solution.

Appendix 10.2   DEVELOPMENT OF THE OPTIMAL LOT SIZE ($Q*$) FORMULA FOR THE PRODUCTION LOT SIZE MODEL

Given equation (10.15) as the total annual cost for the production lot size model,

$$TC = \frac{1}{2}\left(1 - \frac{D}{P}\right)QC_h + \frac{D}{Q}C_o \tag{10.15}$$

we can find the order quantity Q that minimizes the total cost by setting the derivative, dTC/dQ, equal to zero and solving for $Q*$.

$$\frac{dTC}{dQ} = \frac{1}{2}\left(1 - \frac{D}{P}\right)C_h - \frac{D}{Q^2}C_o = 0$$

Solving for $Q*$, we have

$$\frac{1}{2}\left(1 - \frac{D}{P}\right)C_h = \frac{D}{Q^2}C_o$$

$$\left(1 - \frac{D}{P}\right)C_hQ^2 = 2DC_o$$

$$Q^2 = \frac{2DC_o}{(1 - D/P)C_h}$$

Hence,

$$Q* = \sqrt{\frac{2DC_o}{(1 - D/P)C_h}} \tag{10.16}$$

The second derivative is

$$\frac{d^2TC}{dQ^2} = \frac{2DC_o}{Q^3}$$

Because the value of the second derivative is greater than zero, $Q*$ from equation (10.16) is a minimum-cost solution.

CHAPTER 11

Waiting Line Models

CONTENTS

Recall the last time that you had to wait at a supermarket checkout counter, for a teller at your local bank, or to be served at a fast-food restaurant. In these and many other waiting line situations, the time spent waiting is undesirable. Adding more checkout clerks, bank tellers, or servers is not always the most economical strategy for improving service, so businesses need to determine ways to keep waiting times within tolerable limits.

Models have been developed to help managers understand and make better decisions concerning the operation of waiting lines. In management science terminology, a waiting line is also known as a **queue**, and the body of knowledge dealing with waiting lines is known as **queueing theory**. In the early 1900s, A. K. Erlang, a Danish telephone engineer, began a study of the congestion and waiting times occurring in the completion of telephone calls. Since then, queueing theory has grown far more sophisticated, with applications in a wide variety of waiting line situations.

Waiting line models consist of mathematical formulas and relationships that can be used to determine the **operating characteristics** (performance measures) for a waiting line. Operating characteristics of interest include these:

1. The probability that no units are in the system (i.e., the system is idle)
2. The average number of units in the waiting line
3. The average number of units in the system (the number of units in the waiting line plus the number of units being served)
4. The average time a unit spends in the waiting line
5. The average time a unit spends in the system (the waiting time plus the service time)
6. The probability that an arriving unit has to wait for service

Managers who have such information are better able to make decisions that balance desirable service levels against the cost of providing the service.

The Management Science in Action, ATM Waiting Times at Citibank, describes how a waiting line model was used to help determine the number of automatic teller machines to place at New York City banking centers. A waiting line model prompted the creation of a new kind of line and a chief line director to implement first-come, first-served queue discipline at Whole Foods Market in the Chelsea neighborhood of New York City. In addition, a waiting line model helped the New Haven, Connecticut, fire department develop policies to improve response time for both fire and medical emergencies.

MANAGEMENT SCIENCE IN ACTION

ATM WAITING TIMES AT CITIBANK*

The waiting line model used at Citibank is discussed in Section 11.3.

The New York City franchise of U.S. Citibank operates more than 250 banking centers. Each center provides one or more automatic teller machines (ATMs) capable of performing a variety of banking transactions. At each center, a waiting line is formed by randomly arriving customers who seek service at one of the ATMs.

In order to make decisions on the number of ATMs to have at selected banking center locations, management needed information about potential waiting times and general customer service. Waiting line operating characteristics such as average number of customers in the waiting line, average time a customer spends waiting, and the probability that an arriving customer has to wait would help management determine the number of ATMs to recommend at each banking center.

For example, one busy Midtown Manhattan center had a peak arrival rate of 172 customers per hour. A multiple-server waiting line model with six ATMs showed that 88% of the customers would have to wait, with an average wait time between six and seven minutes. This level of service was judged unacceptable. Expansion to seven ATMs was recommended for this location based on the waiting line model's projection of acceptable waiting times. Use of the waiting line model provided guidelines for making incremental ATM decisions at each banking center location.

*Based on information provided by Stacey Karter of Citibank.

11.1   STRUCTURE OF A WAITING LINE SYSTEM

To illustrate the basic features of a waiting line model, we consider the waiting line at the Burger Dome fast-food restaurant. Burger Dome sells hamburgers, cheeseburgers, french fries, soft drinks, and milk shakes, as well as a limited number of specialty items and dessert selections. Although Burger Dome would like to serve each customer immediately, at times more customers arrive than can be handled by the Burger Dome food service staff. Thus, customers wait in line to place and receive their orders.

Burger Dome is concerned that the methods currently used to serve customers are resulting in excessive waiting times and a possible loss of sales. Management wants to conduct a waiting line study to help determine the best approach to reduce waiting times and improve service.

Single-Server Waiting Line

In the current Burger Dome operation, an employee takes a customer's order, determines the total cost of the order, receives payment from the customer, and then fills the order. Once the first customer's order is filled, the employee takes the order of the next customer waiting for service. This operation is an example of a **single-server waiting line**. Each customer entering the Burger Dome restaurant is served by a single order-filling station that handles order placement, bill payment, and food delivery. When more customers arrive than can be served immediately, they form a waiting line and wait for the order-filling station to become available. A diagram of the Burger Dome single-server waiting line is shown in Figure 11.1.

Distribution of Arrivals

Defining the arrival process for a waiting line involves determining the probability distribution for the number of arrivals in a given period of time. For many waiting line situations, the arrivals occur *randomly and independently* of other arrivals, and we cannot predict when an arrival will occur. In such cases, analysts have found that the **Poisson probability distribution** provides a good description of the arrival pattern.

The Poisson probability function provides the probability of x arrivals in a specific time period. The probability function is as follows[1]:

$$P(x) = \frac{\lambda^x e^{-\lambda}}{x!} \quad \text{for } x = 0, 1, 2, \ldots \tag{11.1}$$

FIGURE 11.1   THE BURGER DOME SINGLE-SERVER WAITING LINE

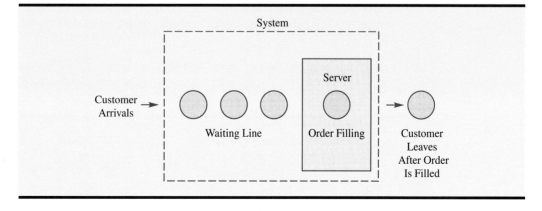

---

[1]The term $x!$, *x factorial*, is defined as $x! = x(x-1)(x-2) \ldots (2)(1)$. For example, $4! = (4)(3)(2)(1) = 24$. For the special case of $x = 0$, $0! = 1$ by definition.

where

$$x = \text{the number of arrivals in the time period}$$
$$\lambda = \text{the } \textit{mean} \text{ number of arrivals per time period}$$
$$e = 2.71828$$

The mean number of arrivals per time period, λ, is called the **arrival rate**. Values of $e^{-\lambda}$ can be found using a calculator or by using Appendix C.

Suppose that Burger Dome analyzed data on customer arrivals and concluded that the arrival rate is 45 customers per hour. For a one-minute period, the arrival rate would be $\lambda = 45$ customers $\div$ 60 minutes $= 0.75$ customers per minute. Thus, we can use the following Poisson probability function to compute the probability of x customer arrivals during a one-minute period:

$$P(x) = \frac{\lambda^x e^{-\lambda}}{x!} = \frac{0.75^x e^{-0.75}}{x!} \tag{11.2}$$

Thus, the probabilities of 0, 1, and 2 customer arrivals during a one-minute period are

$$P(0) = \frac{(0.75)^0 e^{-0.75}}{0!} = e^{-0.75} = 0.4724$$

$$P(1) = \frac{(0.75)^1 e^{-0.75}}{1!} = 0.75 e^{-0.75} = 0.75(0.4724) = 0.3543$$

$$P(2) = \frac{(0.75)^2 e^{-0.75}}{2!} = \frac{(0.5625)(0.4724)}{2} = 0.1329$$

The probability of no customers in a one-minute period is 0.4724, the probability of one customer in a one-minute period is 0.3543, and the probability of two customers in a one-minute period is 0.1329. Table 11.1 shows the Poisson probabilities for customer arrivals during a one-minute period.

The waiting line models that will be presented in Sections 11.2 and 11.3 use the Poisson probability distribution to describe the customer arrivals at Burger Dome. In practice, you should record the actual number of arrivals per time period for several days or weeks and compare the frequency distribution of the observed number of arrivals to the Poisson probability distribution to determine whether the Poisson probability distribution provides a reasonable approximation of the arrival distribution.

Distribution of Service Times

The service time is the time a customer spends at the service facility once the service has started. At Burger Dome, the service time starts when a customer begins to place the order

TABLE 11.1　POISSON PROBABILITIES FOR THE NUMBER OF CUSTOMER ARRIVALS AT A BURGER DOME RESTAURANT DURING A ONE-MINUTE PERIOD ($\lambda = 0.75$)

Number of Arrivals	Probability
0	0.4724
1	0.3543
2	0.1329
3	0.0332
4	0.0062
5 or more	0.0010

with the employee and continues until the customer receives the order. Service times are rarely constant. At Burger Dome, the number of items ordered and the mix of items ordered vary considerably from one customer to the next. Small orders can be handled in a matter of seconds, but large orders may require more than two minutes.

If the probability distribution for the service time can be assumed to follow an **exponential probability distribution**, formulas are available for providing useful information about the operation of the waiting line. Using an exponential probability distribution, the probability that the service time will be less than or equal to a time of length t is

$$P(\text{service time} \leq t) = 1 - e^{-\mu t} \tag{11.3}$$

where

$\mu = $ the *mean* number of units that can be served per time period
$e = 2.71828$

The mean number of units that can be served per time period, μ, is called the **service rate**.

Suppose that Burger Dome studied the order-filling process and found that a single employee can process an average of 60 customer orders per hour. On a one-minute basis, the service rate would be $\mu = 60$ customers $\div$ 60 minutes $= 1$ customer per minute. For example, with $\mu = 1$, we can use equation (11.3) to compute probabilities such as the probability that an order can be processed in $^1/_2$ minute or less, 1 minute or less, and 2 minutes or less. These computations are

A property of the exponential probability distribution is that there is a 0.6321 probability that the random variable takes on a value less than its mean. In waiting line applications, the exponential probability distribution indicates that approximately 63% of the service times are less than the mean service time and approximately 37% of the service times are greater than the mean service time.

$$P(\text{service time} \leq 0.5 \text{ min.}) = 1 - e^{-1(0.5)} = 1 - 0.6065 = 0.3935$$
$$P(\text{service time} \leq 1.0 \text{ min.}) = 1 - e^{-1(1.0)} = 1 - 0.3679 = 0.6321$$
$$P(\text{service time} \leq 2.0 \text{ min.}) = 1 - e^{-1(2.0)} = 1 - 0.1353 = 0.8647$$

Thus, we would conclude that there is a 0.3935 probability that an order can be processed in $^1/_2$ minute or less, a 0.6321 probability that it can be processed in 1 minute or less, and a 0.8647 probability that it can be processed in 2 minutes or less.

In several waiting line models presented in this chapter, we assume that the probability distribution for the service time follows an exponential probability distribution. In practice, you should collect data on actual service times to determine whether the exponential probability distribution is a reasonable approximation of the service times for your application.

Queue Discipline

In describing a waiting line system, we must define the manner in which the waiting units are arranged for service. For the Burger Dome waiting line, and in general for most customer-oriented waiting lines, the units waiting for service are arranged on a **first-come, first-served** basis; this approach is referred to as an **FCFS** queue discipline. However, some situations call for different queue disciplines. For example, when people board an airplane, the last passengers to board are typically the first to deplane since many airlines have the passengers with seat assignments in the back of the plane board first. On the other hand, it does not seem prudent for hospital emergency rooms to operate under either of these queue disciplines, and so we have other types of queue disciplines that assign priorities to the waiting units and then serve the unit with the highest priority first. In this chapter we consider only waiting lines based on a first-come, first-served queue discipline.

Steady-State Operation

When the Burger Dome restaurant opens in the morning, no customers are in the restaurant, and the characteristics of the waiting line system fluctuate depending on realized arrival and service times. Gradually, activity builds up to a normal or steady state. The beginning or startup period is referred to as the **transient period**. The transient period ends when the system reaches the normal or **steady-state operation**. Waiting line models describe the steady-state operating characteristics of a waiting line.

11.2 SINGLE-SERVER WAITING LINE MODEL WITH POISSON ARRIVALS AND EXPONENTIAL SERVICE TIMES

Waiting line models are often based on assumptions such as Poisson arrivals and exponential service times. When applying any waiting line model, data should be collected on the actual system to ensure that the assumptions of the model are reasonable.

In this section we present formulas that can be used to determine the steady-state operating characteristics for a single-server waiting line. The formulas are applicable if the arrivals follow a Poisson probability distribution and the service times follow an exponential probability distribution. As these assumptions apply to the Burger Dome waiting line problem introduced in Section 11.1, we show how formulas can be used to determine Burger Dome's operating characteristics and thus provide management with helpful decision-making information.

The mathematical methodology used to derive the formulas for the operating characteristics of waiting lines is rather complex. However, our purpose in this chapter is not to provide the theoretical development of waiting line models, but rather to show how the formulas that have been developed can provide information about operating characteristics of the waiting line. Readers interested in the mathematical development of the formulas can consult the specialized texts listed in Appendix D at the end of the text.

Operating Characteristics

The following formulas can be used to compute the steady-state operating characteristics for a single-server waiting line with Poisson arrivals and exponential service times, where

$$\lambda = \text{the mean number of arrivals per time period (the arrival rate)}$$

$$\mu = \text{the mean number of services per time period (the service rate)}$$

Equations (11.4) through (11.10) do not provide formulas for optimal conditions. Rather, these equations provide information about the steady-state operating characteristics of a waiting line.

1. The probability that no units are in the system:

$$P_0 = 1 - \frac{\lambda}{\mu} \tag{11.4}$$

2. The average number of units in the waiting line:

$$L_q = \frac{\lambda^2}{\mu(\mu - \lambda)} \tag{11.5}$$

3. The average number of units in the system:

$$L = L_q + \frac{\lambda}{\mu} \tag{11.6}$$

4. The average time a unit spends in the waiting line:

$$W_q = \frac{L_q}{\lambda} \tag{11.7}$$

5.   The average time a unit spends in the system:

$$W = W_q + \frac{1}{\mu} \qquad (11.8)$$

6.   The probability that an arriving unit has to wait for service:

$$P_w = \frac{\lambda}{\mu} \qquad (11.9)$$

7.   The probability of n units in the system:

$$P_n = \left(\frac{\lambda}{\mu}\right)^n P_0 \qquad (11.10)$$

The values of the arrival rate λ and the service rate μ are clearly important components in determining the operating characteristics. Equation (11.9) shows that the ratio of the arrival rate to the service rate, λ/μ, provides the probability that an arriving unit has to wait because the service facility is in use. Hence, λ/μ is referred to as the *utilization factor* for the service facility.

The operating characteristics presented in equations (11.4) through (11.10) are applicable only when the service rate μ is *greater than* the arrival rate λ—in other words, when $\lambda/\mu < 1$. If this condition does not exist, the waiting line will continue to grow without limit because the service facility does not have sufficient capacity to handle the arriving units. Thus, in using equations (11.4) through (11.10), we must have $\mu > \lambda$.

Operating Characteristics for the Burger Dome Problem

Recall that for the Burger Dome problem we had an arrival rate of $\lambda = 0.75$ customers per minute and a service rate of $\mu = 1$ customer per minute. Thus, with $\mu > \lambda$, equations (11.4) through (11.10) can be used to provide operating characteristics for the Burger Dome single-server waiting line:

Problem 5 asks you to compute the operating characteristics for a single-server waiting line application.

$$P_0 = 1 - \frac{\lambda}{\mu} = 1 - \frac{0.75}{1} = 0.25$$

$$L_q = \frac{\lambda^2}{\mu(\mu - \lambda)} = \frac{0.75^2}{1(1 - 0.75)} = 2.25 \text{ customers}$$

$$L = L_q + \frac{\lambda}{\mu} = 2.25 + \frac{0.75}{1} = 3 \text{ customers}$$

$$W_q = \frac{L_q}{\lambda} = \frac{2.25}{0.75} = 3 \text{ minutes}$$

$$W = W_q + \frac{1}{\mu} = 3 + \frac{1}{1} = 4 \text{ minutes}$$

$$P_w = \frac{\lambda}{\mu} = \frac{0.75}{1} = 0.75$$

Equation (11.10) can be used to determine the probability of any number of customers in the system. Applying this equation provides the probability information in Table 11.2.

TABLE 11.2   THE PROBABILITY OF *n* CUSTOMERS IN THE SYSTEM FOR THE BURGER
DOME WAITING LINE PROBLEM

Number of Customers	Probability
0	0.2500
1	0.1875
2	0.1406
3	0.1055
4	0.0791
5	0.0593
6	0.0445
7 or more	0.1335

Managers' Use of Waiting Line Models

The results of the single-server waiting line for Burger Dome show several important things about the operation of the waiting line. In particular, customers wait an average of three minutes before beginning to place an order, which appears somewhat long for a business based on fast service. In addition, the facts that the average number of customers waiting in line is 2.25 and that 75% of the arriving customers have to wait for service are indicators that something should be done to improve the waiting line operation. Table 11.2 shows a 0.1335 probability that seven or more customers are in the Burger Dome system at one time. This condition indicates a fairly high probability that Burger Dome will experience some long waiting lines if it continues to use the single-server operation.

If the operating characteristics are unsatisfactory in terms of meeting company standards for service, Burger Dome's management should consider alternative designs or plans for improving the waiting line operation.

Improving the Waiting Line Operation

Waiting line models often indicate when improvements in operating characteristics are desirable. However, the decision of how to modify the waiting line configuration to improve the operating characteristics must be based on the insights and creativity of the analyst.

After reviewing the operating characteristics provided by the waiting line model, Burger Dome's management concluded that improvements designed to reduce waiting times were desirable. To make improvements in the waiting line operation, analysts often focus on ways to improve the service rate. Generally, service rate improvements are obtained by making either or both of the following changes:

1. Increase the service rate by making a creative design change or by using new technology.
2. Add one or more servers so that more customers can be served simultaneously.

Assume that in considering Alternative 1, Burger Dome's management decides to employ a design change that allows the customer to fill out and submit a paper order form directly to the kitchen while they are waiting in line. This allows the customer's food to be ready by the time the employee collects payment from the customer. With this design, Burger Dome's management estimates that the service rate can be increased from the current 60 customers per hour to 75 customers per hour. Thus, the service rate for the revised system is $\mu = 75$ customers $\div$ 60 minutes $= 1.25$ customers per minute. For $\lambda = 0.75$ customers per minute and $\mu = 1.25$ customers per minute, equations (11.4) through (11.10) can be used to provide the new operating characteristics for the Burger Dome waiting line. These operating characteristics are summarized in Table 11.3.

The information in Table 11.3 indicates that all operating characteristics have improved because of the increased service rate. In particular, the average time a customer spends in the

TABLE 11.3   OPERATING CHARACTERISTICS FOR THE BURGER DOME SYSTEM WITH
THE SERVICE RATE INCREASED TO $\mu = 1.25$ CUSTOMERS PER MINUTE

Probability of no customers in the system	0.400
Average number of customers in the waiting line	0.900
Average number of customers in the system	1.500
Average time in the waiting line	1.200 minutes
Average time in the system	2.000 minutes
Probability that an arriving customer has to wait	0.600
Probability that seven or more customers are in the system	0.028

Problem 11 asks you to determine whether a change in the service rate will meet the company's service guideline for its customers.

waiting line has been reduced from 3 to 1.2 minutes, and the average time a customer spends in the system has been reduced from 4 to 2 minutes. Are any other alternatives available that Burger Dome can use to increase the service rate? If so, and if the mean service rate μ can be identified for each alternative, equations (11.4) through (11.10) can be used to determine the revised operating characteristics and any improvements in the waiting line system. The added cost of any proposed change can be compared to the corresponding service improvements to help the manager determine whether the proposed service improvements are worthwhile.

As mentioned previously in Alternative 2, another option often available is to add one or more servers so that orders for multiple customers can be filled simultaneously. The extension of the single-server waiting line model to the multiple-server waiting line model is the topic of the next section.

Excel Solution of Waiting Line Model

Waiting line models are easily implemented with the aid of spreadsheets. The Excel worksheet for the Burger Dome single-server waiting line is shown in Figure 11.2. The worksheet view showing the formulas is on the left and the worksheet view showing the values is on the right. The arrival rate and the service rate are entered in cells B7 and B8. The formulas for the waiting line's operating characteristics are placed in cells C13 to C18. The worksheet computes the same values for the operating characteristics that we obtained earlier. Modifications in the waiting line design can be evaluated by entering different arrival rates and/or service rates into cells B7 and B8. The new operating characteristics of the waiting line will be shown immediately. The Excel worksheet in Figure 11.2 is a template that can be used with any single-server waiting line model with Poisson arrivals and exponential service times.

NOTES AND COMMENTS

1. The assumption that arrivals follow a Poisson probability distribution is equivalent to the assumption that the time between arrivals has an exponential probability distribution. For example, if the arrivals for a waiting line follow a Poisson probability distribution with a mean of 20 arrivals per hour, the time between arrivals will follow an exponential probability distribution, with a mean time between arrivals of $1/20$ or 0.05 hour.

2. Many individuals believe that whenever the service rate μ is greater than the arrival rate λ, the system should be able to handle or serve all arrivals without any customer waiting for service. This would be true if the time between customer arrivals was constant and the service time was constant. However, as the Burger Dome example shows, the variability of arrival times and service times may result in long waiting times even when the service rate exceeds the arrival rate. A contribution of waiting line models is that they can point out undesirable waiting line operating characteristics even when the $\mu > \lambda$ condition appears satisfactory.

FIGURE 11.2   WORKSHEET FOR THE BURGER DOME SINGLE-SERVER WAITING LINE

	A	B	C
1	**Single-Server Waiting Line Model**		
2			
3	**Assumptions**		
4	**Poisson Arrivals**		
5	**Exponential Service Times**		
6			
7	Arrival Rate	0.75	
8	Service Rate	1	
9			
10			
11	**Operating Characteristics**		
12			
13	Probability that no customers are in the system, P_0		=1-B7/B8
14	Average number of customers in the waiting line, L_q		=B7^2/(B8*(B8-B7))
15	Average number of customers in the system, L		=C14+B7/B8
16	Average time a customer spends in the waiting line, W_q		=C14/B7
17	Average time a customer spends in the system, W		=C16+1/B8
18	Probability an arriving customer has to wait, P_w		=B7/B8

MODEL *file*

Single

	A	B	C
1	**Single-Server Waiting Line Model**		
2			
3	**Assumptions**		
4	**Poisson Arrivals**		
5	**Exponential Service Times**		
6			
7	Arrival Rate	0.75	
8	Service Rate	1	
9			
10			
11	**Operating Characteristics**		
12			
13	Probability that no customers are in the system, P_0		0.2500
14	Average number of customers in the waiting line, L_q		2.2500
15	Average number of customers in the system, L		3.0000
16	Average time a customer spends in the waiting line, W_q		3.0000
17	Average time a customer spends in the system, W		4.0000
18	Probability an arriving customer has to wait, P_w		0.7500

11.3   MULTIPLE-SERVER WAITING LINE MODEL WITH POISSON ARRIVALS AND EXPONENTIAL SERVICE TIMES

A **multiple-server waiting line** consists of two or more servers that are assumed to be identical in terms of service capability. For multiple-server systems, there are two typical queueing possibilities: (1) arriving customers wait in a single waiting line (called a "pooled" or "shared" queue) and then move to the first available server for processing, or (2) each server has a "dedicated" queue and an arriving customer selects one of these lines to join (and typically is not allowed to switch lines). In this chapter, we focus on the system design with a single shared waiting line for all servers. Operating characteristics for a multiple-server system are typically better when a single shared queue, rather than multiple dedicated waiting lines, is used. The single-server Burger Dome operation can be expanded to a two-server system by opening a second server. Figure 11.3 shows a diagram of the Burger Dome two-server waiting line.

In this section we present formulas that can be used to determine the steady-state operating characteristics for a multiple-server waiting line. These formulas are applicable if the following conditions exist:

1. The arrivals follow a Poisson probability distribution.
2. The service time for each server follows an exponential probability distribution.
3. The service rate μ is the same for each server.
4. The arrivals wait in a single waiting line and then move to the first open server for service.

FIGURE 11.3   THE BURGER DOME TWO-SERVER WAITING LINE

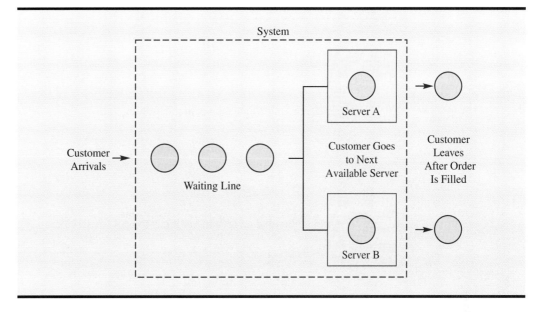

Operating Characteristics

The following formulas can be used to compute the steady-state operating characteristics for multiple-server waiting lines, where

$$\lambda = \text{the arrival rate for the system}$$
$$\mu = \text{the service rate for \textit{each} server}$$
$$k = \text{the number of servers}$$

1. The probability that no units are in the system:

$$P_0 = \cfrac{1}{\displaystyle\sum_{n=0}^{k-1} \frac{(\lambda/\mu)^n}{n!} + \frac{(\lambda/\mu)^k}{k!}\left(\frac{k\mu}{k\mu - \lambda}\right)} \tag{11.11}$$

2. The average number of units in the waiting line:

$$L_q = \frac{(\lambda/\mu)^k \lambda\mu}{(k-1)!(k\mu - \lambda)^2} P_0 \tag{11.12}$$

3. The average number of units in the system:

$$L = L_q + \frac{\lambda}{\mu} \tag{11.13}$$

4. The average time a unit spends in the waiting line:

$$W_q = \frac{L_q}{\lambda} \qquad (11.14)$$

5. The average time a unit spends in the system:

$$W = W_q + \frac{1}{\mu} \qquad (11.15)$$

6. The probability that an arriving unit has to wait for service:

$$P_w = \frac{1}{k!}\left(\frac{\lambda}{\mu}\right)^k \left(\frac{k\mu}{k\mu - \lambda}\right) P_0 \qquad (11.16)$$

7. The probability of n units in the system:

$$P_n = \frac{(\lambda/\mu)^n}{n!} P_0 \qquad \text{for } n \leq k \qquad (11.17)$$

$$P_n = \frac{(\lambda/\mu)^n}{k!k^{(n-k)}} P_0 \qquad \text{for } n > k \qquad (11.18)$$

Because μ is the service rate for each server, $k\mu$ is the service rate for the multiple-server system. As was true for the single-server waiting line model, the formulas for the operating characteristics of multiple-server waiting lines can be applied only in situations where the service rate for the system exceeds the arrival rate for the system; in other words, the formulas are applicable only if $k\mu$ is greater than λ.

Some expressions for the operating characteristics of multiple-server waiting lines are more complex than their single-server counterparts. However, equations (11.11) through (11.18) provide the same information as provided by the single-server model. To help simplify the use of the multiple-server equations, Table 11.4 contains values of P_0 for selected values of λ/μ and k. The values provided in the table correspond to cases where $k\mu > \lambda$, and hence the service rate is sufficient to process all arrivals.

Operating Characteristics for the Burger Dome Problem

To illustrate the multiple-server waiting line model, we return to the Burger Dome fast-food restaurant waiting line problem. Suppose that management wants to evaluate the desirability of opening a second order-processing station so that two customers can be served simultaneously. Assume a single waiting line with the first customer in line moving to the first available server. Let us evaluate the operating characteristics for this two-server system.

We use equations (11.11) through (11.18) for the $k = 2$-server system. For an arrival rate of $\lambda = 0.75$ customers per minute and a service rate of $\mu = 1$ customer per minute for each server, we obtain the operating characteristics:

$$P_0 = 0.4545 \qquad \text{(from Table 11.4 with } \lambda/\mu = 0.75)$$

TABLE 11.4   VALUES OF P_0 FOR MULTIPLE-SERVER WAITING LINES WITH POISSON ARRIVALS AND EXPONENTIAL SERVICE TIMES

Ratio λ/μ	Number of Servers (k)			
	2	3	4	5
0.15	0.8605	0.8607	0.8607	0.8607
0.20	0.8182	0.8187	0.8187	0.8187
0.25	0.7778	0.7788	0.7788	0.7788
0.30	0.7391	0.7407	0.7408	0.7408
0.35	0.7021	0.7046	0.7047	0.7047
0.40	0.6667	0.6701	0.6703	0.6703
0.45	0.6327	0.6373	0.6376	0.6376
0.50	0.6000	0.6061	0.6065	0.6065
0.55	0.5686	0.5763	0.5769	0.5769
0.60	0.5385	0.5479	0.5487	0.5488
0.65	0.5094	0.5209	0.5219	0.5220
0.70	0.4815	0.4952	0.4965	0.4966
0.75	0.4545	0.4706	0.4722	0.4724
0.80	0.4286	0.4472	0.4491	0.4493
0.85	0.4035	0.4248	0.4271	0.4274
0.90	0.3793	0.4035	0.4062	0.4065
0.95	0.3559	0.3831	0.3863	0.3867
1.00	0.3333	0.3636	0.3673	0.3678
1.20	0.2500	0.2941	0.3002	0.3011
1.40	0.1765	0.2360	0.2449	0.2463
1.60	0.1111	0.1872	0.1993	0.2014
1.80	0.0526	0.1460	0.1616	0.1646
2.00		0.1111	0.1304	0.1343
2.20		0.0815	0.1046	0.1094
2.40		0.0562	0.0831	0.0889
2.60		0.0345	0.0651	0.0721
2.80		0.0160	0.0521	0.0581
3.00			0.0377	0.0466
3.20			0.0273	0.0372
3.40			0.0186	0.0293
3.60			0.0113	0.0228
3.80			0.0051	0.0174
4.00				0.0130
4.20				0.0093
4.40				0.0063
4.60				0.0038
4.80				0.0017

MODEL *file*

Multiple

$$L_q = \frac{(0.75/1)^2(0.75)(1)}{(2-1)![2(1)-0.75]^2}(0.4545) = 0.1227 \text{ customer}$$

$$L = L_q + \frac{\lambda}{\mu} = 0.1227 + \frac{0.75}{1} = 0.8727 \text{ customer}$$

$$W_q = \frac{L_q}{\lambda} = \frac{0.1227}{0.75} = 0.1636 \text{ minute}$$

$$W = W_q + \frac{1}{\mu} = 0.1636 + \frac{1}{1} = 1.1636 \text{ minutes}$$

$$P_w = \frac{1}{2!}\left(\frac{0.75}{1}\right)^2\left[\frac{2(1)}{2(1)-0.75}\right](0.4545) = 0.2045$$

Try Problem 18 for practice in determining the operating characteristics for a two-server waiting line.
Using equations (11.17) and (11.18), we can compute the probabilities of n customers in the system. The results from these computations are summarized in Table 11.5.

We can now compare the steady-state operating characteristics of the two-server system to the operating characteristics of the original single-server system discussed in Section 11.2.

1. The average time a customer spends in the system (waiting time plus service time) is reduced from $W = 4$ minutes to $W = 1.1636$ minutes.
2. The average number of customers in the waiting line is reduced from $L_q = 2.25$ customers to $L_q = 0.1227$ customers.
3. The average time a customer spends in the waiting line is reduced from $W_q = 3$ minutes to $W_q = 0.1636$ minutes.
4. The probability that a customer has to wait for service is reduced from $P_w = 0.75$ to $P_w = 0.2045$.

Clearly the two-server system will substantially improve the operating characteristics of the waiting line. The waiting line study provides the operating characteristics that can be anticipated under three configurations: the original single-server system, a single-server system with the design change involving direct submission of paper order form to kitchen, and a two-server system composed of two order-filling employees. After considering these results, what action would you recommend? In this case, Burger Dome adopted the following policy statement: For periods when customer arrivals are expected to average 45 customers per hour, Burger Dome will open two order-processing servers with one employee assigned to each.

By changing the arrival rate λ to reflect arrival rates at different times of the day and then computing the operating characteristics, Burger Dome's management can establish guidelines and policies that tell the store managers when to schedule service operations with a single server, two servers, or perhaps even three or more servers.

TABLE 11.5   THE PROBABILITY OF n CUSTOMERS IN THE SYSTEM FOR THE BURGER DOME TWO-SERVER WAITING LINE

Number of Customers	Probability
0	0.4545
1	0.3409
2	0.1278
3	0.0479
4	0.0180
5 or more	0.0109

NOTES AND COMMENTS

1. The multiple-server waiting line model is based on a single waiting line. You may have also encountered situations where each of the k servers has its own waiting line. Analysts have shown that the operating characteristics of multiple-server systems are better if a single waiting line is used. Also, people tend to like them better; no one who comes in after you can be served ahead of you, and so they appeal to one's sense of fairness. Thus, when possible, banks, airline reservation counters, airport security systems, food-service establishments, and other businesses frequently use a single waiting line for a multiple-server system.

11.4 SOME GENERAL RELATIONSHIPS FOR WAITING LINE MODELS

In Sections 11.2 and 11.3 we presented formulas for computing the operating characteristics for single-server and multiple-server waiting lines with Poisson arrivals and exponential service times. The operating characteristics of interest included

L_q = the average number of units in the waiting line

L = the average number of units in the system

W_q = the average time a unit spends in the waiting line

W = the average time a unit spends in the system

John D. C. Little showed that several relationships exist among these four characteristics and that these relationships apply to a variety of different waiting line systems. Two of the relationships, referred to as *Little's flow equations*, are

$$L = \lambda W \tag{11.19}$$

$$L_q = \lambda W_q \tag{11.20}$$

Equation (11.19) shows that the average number of units in the system, L, can be found by multiplying the arrival rate, λ, by the average time a unit spends in the system, W. Equation (11.20) shows that the same relationship holds between the average number of units in the waiting line, L_q, and the average time a unit spends in the waiting line, W_q.

Using equation (11.20) and solving for W_q, we obtain

$$W_q = \frac{L_q}{\lambda} \tag{11.21}$$

Equation (11.21) follows directly from Little's second flow equation. We used it for the single-server waiting line model in Section 11.2 and the multiple-server waiting line model in Section 11.3 [see equations (11.7) and (11.14)]. Once L_q is computed for either of these models, equation (11.21) can then be used to compute W_q.

Another general expression that applies to waiting line models is that the average time in the system, W, is equal to the average time in the waiting line, W_q, plus the average service time. For a system with a service rate μ, the mean service time is $1/\mu$. Thus, we have the general relationship

$$W = W_q + \frac{1}{\mu} \tag{11.22}$$

Recall that we used equation (11.22) to provide the average time in the system for both the single- and multiple-server waiting line models [see equations (11.8) and (11.15)].

The importance of Little's flow equations is that they apply to *any waiting line model* regardless of whether arrivals follow the Poisson probability distribution and regardless of whether service times follow the exponential probability distribution. For example, in a study of the grocery checkout counters at Murphy's Foodliner, an analyst concluded that arrivals follow the Poisson probability distribution with an arrival rate of 24 customers per hour, or $\lambda = 24/60 = 0.40$ customers per minute. However, the analyst found that

The advantage of Little's flow equations is that they show how operating characteristics L, L_q, W, and W_q are related in any waiting line system. Arrivals and service times do not have to follow specific probability distributions for the flow equations to be applicable.

service times follow a normal probability distribution rather than an exponential probability distribution. The service rate was found to be 30 customers per hour, or $\mu = 30/60 = 0.50$ customers per minute. A time study of actual customer waiting times showed that, on average, a customer spends 4.5 minutes in the system (waiting time plus checkout time); that is, $W = 4.5$. Using the waiting line relationships discussed in this section, we can now compute other operating characteristics for this waiting line.

First, using equation (11.22) and solving for W_q, we have

$$W_q = W - \frac{1}{\mu} = 4.5 - \frac{1}{0.50} = 2.5 \text{ minutes.}$$

With both W and W_q known, we can use Little's flow equations, (11.19) and (11.20), to compute

$$L = \lambda W = 0.40(4.5) = 1.8 \text{ customers}$$
$$L_q = \lambda W_q = 0.40(2.5) = 1 \text{ customer}$$

The application of Little's flow equations is demonstrated in Problem 24.

The manager of Murphy's Foodliner can now review these operating characteristics to see whether action should be taken to improve the service and to reduce the waiting time and the length of the waiting line.

NOTES AND COMMENTS

1. In waiting line systems where the length of the waiting line is limited (e.g., a small waiting area), some arriving units will be blocked from joining the waiting line and will be lost. In this case, the blocked or lost arrivals will make the mean number of units entering the system something less than the arrival rate. In other instances, arrivals will decide the line is too long and will leave. By defining λ as the mean number of units *joining the system*, rather than the arrival rate, the relationships discussed in this section can be used to determine W, L, W_q, and L_q.

11.5 ECONOMIC ANALYSIS OF WAITING LINES

Frequently, decisions involving the design of waiting lines will be based on a subjective evaluation of the operating characteristics of the waiting line. For example, a manager may decide that an average waiting time of one minute or less and an average of two customers or fewer in the system are reasonable goals. The waiting line models presented in the preceding sections can be used to determine the number of servers that will meet the manager's waiting line performance goals.

On the other hand, a manager may want to identify the cost of operating the waiting line system and then base the decision regarding system design on a minimum hourly or daily operating cost. Before an economic analysis of a waiting line can be conducted, a total cost model, which includes the cost of waiting and the cost of service, must be developed.

Waiting cost is based on average number of units in the system. It includes the time spent waiting in line plus the time spent being served.

To develop a total cost model for a waiting line, we begin by defining the notation to be used:

c_w = the waiting cost per time period for each unit

L = the average number of units in the system

c_s = the service cost per time period for each server

k = the number of servers

TC = the total cost per time period

The total cost is the sum of the waiting cost and the service cost; that is,

$$TC = c_w L + c_s k \tag{11.23}$$

Adding more servers always improves the operating characteristics of the waiting line and reduces the waiting cost. However, additional servers increase the service cost. An economic analysis of waiting lines attempts to find the number of servers that will minimize total cost by balancing the waiting cost and the service cost.

To conduct an economic analysis of a waiting line, we must obtain reasonable estimates of the waiting cost and the service cost. Of these two costs, the waiting cost is usually the more difficult to evaluate. In the Burger Dome restaurant problem, the waiting cost would be the cost per minute for a customer waiting for service. This cost is not a direct cost to Burger Dome. However, if Burger Dome ignores this cost and allows long waiting lines, customers ultimately will take their business elsewhere. Thus, Burger Dome will experience lost sales and, in effect, incur a cost.

The service cost is generally easier to determine as it relates to any cost associated with establishing each server operation. In the Burger Dome problem, this cost would include the server's wages, benefits, and any other direct costs associated with establishing a server. At Burger Dome, this cost is estimated to be $10 per hour.

To demonstrate the use of equation (11.23), we assume that Burger Dome is willing to assign a cost of $15 per hour for customer waiting time. We use the average number of units in the system, L, as computed in Sections 11.2 and 11.3 to obtain the total hourly cost for the single-server and two-server systems:

Single-server system ($L = 3$ customers):

$$TC = c_w L + c_s k$$
$$= 15(3) + 10(1) = \$55.00 \text{ per hour}$$

Two-server system ($L = 0.8727$ customer):

$$TC = c_w L + c_s k$$
$$= 15(0.8727) + 10(2) = \$33.09 \text{ per hour}$$

Thus, based on the cost data provided by Burger Dome, the two-server system provides the more economical operation. Note that when the cost of serving a customer c_s exceeds the cost of customer waiting time c_w by a sufficient amount, the single-server system will be more economical for Burger Dome.

Problem 21 tests your ability to conduct an economic analysis of proposed single-server and two-server waiting line systems.

Figure 11.4 shows the general shape of the cost curves in the economic analysis of waiting lines. The service cost increases as the number of servers is increased. However, with more servers, the service is better. As a result, waiting time and cost decrease as the number of servers is increased. The number of servers that will provide a good approximation of

FIGURE 11.4 THE GENERAL SHAPE OF WAITING COST, SERVICE COST, AND TOTAL COST CURVES IN WAITING LINE MODELS

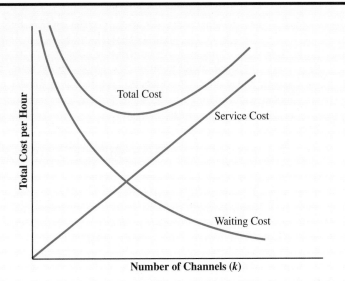

the minimum total cost design can be found by evaluating the total cost for several design alternatives.

1. In dealing with government agencies and utility companies, customers may not be able to take their business elsewhere. In these situations, no lost business occurs when long waiting times are encountered. This condition is one reason that service in such organizations may be poor and that customers in such situations may experience long waiting times.
2. In some instances, the organization providing the service also employs the units waiting for the service. For example, consider the case of a company that owns and operates the trucks used to deliver goods to and from its manufacturing plant. In addition to the costs associated with the trucks waiting to be loaded or unloaded, the firm also pays the wages of the truck loaders and unloaders who are effectively operating as servers. In this case, the cost of having the trucks wait and the cost of operating the servers are direct expenses to the firm. An economic analysis of the waiting line system is highly recommended for these types of situations.

11.6   OTHER WAITING LINE MODELS

D. G. Kendall suggested a notation that is helpful in classifying the wide variety of different waiting line models that have been developed. The three-symbol Kendall notation is as follows:

$$A/B/k$$

where

A denotes the probability distribution for the arrivals

B denotes the probability distribution for the service time

k denotes the number of servers

Depending on the letter appearing in the A or B position, a variety of waiting line systems can be described. The letters that are commonly used are as follows:

M designates a Poisson probability distribution for the arrivals or an exponential probability distribution for service time

D designates that the arrivals or the service times are deterministic or constant

G designates that the arrivals or the service times have a general probability distribution with a known mean and variance

Using the Kendall notation, the single-server waiting line model with Poisson arrivals and exponential service times is classified as an $M/M/1$ model. The two-server waiting line model with Poisson arrivals and exponential service times presented in Section 11.3 would be classified as an $M/M/2$ model.

1. In some cases, the Kendall notation is extended to five symbols. The fourth symbol indicates the largest number of units that can be in the system, and the fifth symbol indicates the size of the population. The fourth symbol is used in situations where the waiting line can hold a finite or maximum number of units, and the fifth symbol is necessary when the population of arriving units or customers is finite. When the fourth and fifth symbols of the Kendall notation are omitted, the waiting line system is assumed to have infinite capacity, and the population is assumed to be infinite.

11.7 SINGLE-SERVER WAITING LINE MODEL WITH POISSON ARRIVALS AND ARBITRARY SERVICE TIMES

Let us return to the single-server waiting line model where arrivals are described by a Poisson probability distribution. However, we now assume that the probability distribution for the service times is not an exponential probability distribution. Thus, using the Kendall notation, the waiting line model that is appropriate is an *M/G/1* model, where *G* denotes a general or unspecified probability distribution.

When providing input to the M/G/1 model, be consistent in terms of the time period. For example, if λ and μ are expressed in terms of the number of units per hour, the standard deviation of the service time should be expressed in hours. The example that follows uses minutes as the time period for the arrival and service data.

Operating Characteristics for the *M/G/1* Model

The notation used to describe the operating characteristics for the *M/G/1* model is

λ = the arrival rate
μ = the service rate
σ = the standard deviation of the service time

Some of the steady-state operating characteristics of the *M/G/1* waiting line model are as follows:

1. The probability that no units are in the system:

$$P_0 = 1 - \frac{\lambda}{\mu} \tag{11.24}$$

2. The average number of units in the waiting line:

$$L_q = \frac{\lambda^2\sigma^2 + (\lambda/\mu)^2}{2(1 - \lambda/\mu)} \tag{11.25}$$

3. The average number of units in the system:

$$L = L_q + \frac{\lambda}{\mu} \tag{11.26}$$

4. The average time a unit spends in the waiting line:

$$W_q = \frac{L_q}{\lambda} \tag{11.27}$$

5. The average time a unit spends in the system:

$$W = W_q + \frac{1}{\mu} \tag{11.28}$$

6. The probability that an arriving unit has to wait for service:

$$P_w = \frac{\lambda}{\mu} \tag{11.29}$$

Note that the relationships for L, W_q, and W are the same as the relationships used for the waiting line models in Sections 11.2 and 11.3. They are given by Little's flow equations.

Problem 27 provides another application of a single-server waiting line with Poisson arrivals and arbitrary service times.

An Example   Retail sales at Hartlage's Seafood Supply are handled by one clerk. Customer arrivals follow a Poisson distribution, and the arrival rate is 21 customers per hour or $\lambda = 21/60 = 0.35$ customers per minute. A study of the service process shows that the service time is a random variable with an average of 2 minutes per customer and a standard deviation of $\sigma = 1.2$ minutes. The mean time of 2 minutes per customer shows that the clerk has a service rate of $\mu = \frac{1}{2} = 0.50$ customers per minute. The operating characteristics of this $M/G/1$ waiting line system are as follows:

MODEL *file*

SingleArbitrary

$$P_0 = 1 - \frac{\lambda}{\mu} = 1 - \frac{0.35}{0.50} = 0.30$$

$$L_q = \frac{(0.35)^2(1.2)^2 + (0.35/0.50)^2}{2(1 - 0.35/0.50)} = 1.1107 \text{ customers}$$

$$L = L_q + \frac{\lambda}{\mu} = 1.1107 + \frac{0.35}{0.50} = 1.8107 \text{ customers}$$

$$W_q = \frac{L_q}{\lambda} = \frac{1.1107}{0.35} = 3.1733 \text{ minutes}$$

$$W = W_q + \frac{1}{\mu} = 3.1733 + \frac{1}{0.50} = 5.1733 \text{ minutes}$$

$$P_w = \frac{\lambda}{\mu} = \frac{0.35}{0.50} = 0.70$$

Hartlage's manager can review these operating characteristics to determine whether scheduling a second clerk appears to be worthwhile.

Constant Service Times

We want to comment briefly on the single-server waiting line model that assumes random arrivals but constant service times. Such a waiting line can occur in production and manufacturing environments where machine-controlled service times are generally constant. This waiting line is described by the $M/D/1$ model, with the D referring to the deterministic service times. With the $M/D/1$ model, the average number of units in the waiting line, L_q, can be found by using equation (11.25) with the condition that the standard deviation of the constant service time is $\sigma = 0$. Thus, the expression for the average number of units in the waiting line for the $M/D/1$ waiting line becomes

$$L_q = \frac{(\lambda/\mu)^2}{2(1 - \lambda/\mu)} \tag{11.30}$$

The other expressions presented earlier in this section can be used to determine additional operating characteristics of the $M/D/1$ system.

NOTES AND COMMENTS

1. Whenever the operating characteristics of a waiting line are unacceptable, managers often try to improve service by increasing the service rate μ. This approach is good, but equation (11.25) shows that the variation in the service times also affects the operating characteristics of the waiting line. Because the standard deviation of service times, σ, appears in the numerator of equation (11.25), a larger variation in service times results in a larger average number of units in the waiting line. Hence, another alternative for improving the service capabilities of a waiting line is to reduce the variation in the service times. Thus, even when the service rate of the service facility cannot be increased, a reduction in σ will reduce the average number of units in the waiting line and improve the operating characteristics of the system.

11.8 MULTIPLE-SERVER MODEL WITH POISSON ARRIVALS, ARBITRARY SERVICE TIMES, AND NO WAITING LINE

An interesting variation of the waiting line models discussed so far involves a system in which no waiting is allowed. Arriving units or customers seek service from one of several servers. If all servers are busy, arriving units are denied access to the system. In waiting line terminology, arrivals occurring when the system is full are **blocked** and are cleared from the system. Such customers may be lost or may attempt a return to the system later.

The specific model considered in this section is based on the following assumptions:

1. The system has k servers.
2. The arrivals follow a Poisson probability distribution, with arrival rate λ.
3. The service times for each server may have any probability distribution.
4. The service rate μ is the same for each server.
5. An arrival enters the system only if at least one server is available. An arrival occurring when all servers are busy is blocked—that is, denied service and not allowed to enter the system.

With G denoting a general or unspecified probability distribution for service times, the appropriate model for this situation is referred to as an $M/G/k$ model with "blocked customers cleared." The question addressed in this type of situation is, How many servers should be used?

A primary application of this model involves the design of telephone and other communication systems where the arrivals are the calls and the servers are the number of telephone or communication lines available. In such a system, the calls are made to one telephone number, with each call automatically switched to an open server if possible. When all servers are busy, additional calls receive a busy signal and are denied access to the system.

Operating Characteristics for the $M/G/k$ Model with Blocked Customers Cleared

With no waiting allowed, operating characteristics L_q and W_q considered in previous waiting line models are automatically zero regardless of the number of servers. In this situation, the more important design consideration involves determining how the percentage of blocked customers is affected by the number of servers.

We approach the problem of selecting the best number of servers by computing the steady-state probabilities that j of the k servers will be busy. These probabilities are

$$P_j = \frac{(\lambda/\mu)^j/j!}{\displaystyle\sum_{i=0}^{k} (\lambda/\mu)^i/i!} \tag{11.31}$$

where

$\quad \lambda$ = the arrival rate

$\quad \mu$ = the service rate for each server

$\quad k$ = the number of servers

$\quad P_j$ = the probability that j of the k servers are busy
$\qquad$ for $j = 0, 1, 2, \ldots, k$

The most important probability value is P_k, which is the probability that all k servers are busy. Thus, P_k also indicates the percentage of arrivals that are blocked and denied access to the system.

Another operating characteristic of interest is the average number of units in the system; note that this number is equivalent to the average number of servers in use. Letting L denote the average number of units in the system, we have

$$L = \frac{\lambda}{\mu}(1 - P_k) \tag{11.32}$$

where L will certainly be less than k.

An Example   Microdata Software, Inc., uses a telephone ordering system for its computer software products. Callers place orders with Microdata by using the company's 800 telephone number. Assume that calls to this telephone number arrive at a rate of $\lambda = 12$ calls per hour. The time required to process a telephone order varies considerably from order to order. However, each Microdata sales representative can be expected to handle $\mu = 6$ calls per hour. Currently, the Microdata 800 telephone number has three internal lines or servers, each operated by a separate sales representative. Calls received on the 800 number are automatically transferred to an open line or server if available.

Whenever all three lines are busy, callers receive a busy signal. In the past, Microdata's management assumed that callers receiving a busy signal would call back later. However, recent research on telephone ordering showed that a substantial number of callers who are denied access do not call back later. These lost calls represent lost revenues for the firm, so Microdata's management requested an analysis of the telephone ordering system. Specifically, management wanted to know the percentage of callers who get busy signals and are blocked from the system. If management's goal is to provide sufficient capacity to handle 90% of the callers, how many telephone lines and sales representatives should Microdata use?

We can demonstrate the use of equation (11.31) by computing P_3, the probability that all three of the currently available telephone lines will be in use and additional callers will be blocked:

MODEL *file*

NoWaiting

$$P_3 = \frac{(^{12}/_6)^3/3!}{(^{12}/_6)^0/0! + (^{12}/_6)^1/1! + (^{12}/_6)^2/2! + (^{12}/_6)^3/3!} = \frac{1.3333}{6.3333} = 0.2105$$

Problem 30 provides practice in calculating probabilities for multiple-server systems with no waiting line.

With $P_3 = 0.2105$, approximately 21% of the calls, or slightly more than one in five calls, are being blocked. Only 79% of the calls are being handled immediately by the three-line system.

Let us assume that Microdata expands to a four-line system. Then, the probability that all four servers will be in use and that callers will be blocked is

$$P_4 = \frac{(^{12}/_6)^4/4!}{(^{12}/_6)^0/0! + (^{12}/_6)^1/1! + (^{12}/_6)^2/2! + (^{12}/_6)^3/3! + (^{12}/_6)^4/4!} = \frac{0.667}{7} = 0.0952$$

With only 9.52% of the callers blocked, 90.48% of the callers will reach the Microdata sales representatives. Thus, Microdata should expand its order-processing operation to four lines to meet management's goal of providing sufficient capacity to handle at least 90% of the callers. The average number of calls in the four-line system and thus the average number of lines and sales representatives that will be busy is

$$L = \frac{\lambda}{\mu}(1 - P_4) = \frac{12}{6}(1 - 0.0952) = 1.8095$$

Although an average of fewer than two lines will be busy, the four-line system is necessary to provide the capacity to handle at least 90% of the callers. We used equation (11.31) to calculate the probability that 0, 1, 2, 3, or 4 lines will be busy. These probabilities are summarized in Table 11.6.

TABLE 11.6   PROBABILITIES OF BUSY LINES FOR THE MICRODATA FOUR-LINE SYSTEM

Number of Busy Lines	Probability
0	0.1429
1	0.2857
2	0.2857
3	0.1905
4	0.0952

As discussed in Section 11.5, an economic analysis of waiting lines can be used to guide system design decisions. In the Microdata system, the cost of the additional line and additional sales representative should be relatively easy to establish. This cost can be balanced against the cost of the blocked calls. With 9.52% of the calls blocked and $\lambda = 12$ calls per hour, an eight-hour day will have an average of $8(12)(0.0952) = 9.1$ blocked calls. If Microdata can estimate the cost of possible lost sales, the cost of these blocked calls can be established. The economic analysis based on the service cost and the blocked-call cost can assist in determining the optimal number of lines for the system.

11.9   WAITING LINE MODELS WITH FINITE CALLING POPULATIONS

In previous waiting line models, the arrival rate was constant and independent of the number of units in the system. With a finite calling population, the arrival rate decreases as the number of units in the system increases because, with more units in the system, fewer units are available for arrivals.

For the waiting line models introduced so far, the population of units or customers arriving for service has been considered to be unlimited. In technical terms, when no limit is placed on how many units may seek service, the model is said to have an **infinite calling population**. Under this assumption, the arrival rate λ remains constant regardless of how many units are in the waiting line system. This assumption of an infinite calling population is made in most waiting line models.

In other cases, the maximum number of units or customers that may seek service is assumed to be finite. In this situation the arrival rate for the system changes, depending on the number of units in the waiting line, and the waiting line model is said to have a **finite calling population**. The formulas for the operating characteristics of the previous waiting line models must be modified to account for the effect of the finite calling population.

The finite calling population model discussed in this section is based on the following assumptions:

1. The arrivals for *each unit* follow a Poisson probability distribution, with arrival rate λ.
2. The service times follow an exponential probability distribution, with service rate μ.
3. The population of units that may seek service is finite.

With a single server, the waiting line model is referred to as an $M/M/1$ model with a finite calling population.

The arrival rate for the $M/M/1$ model with a finite calling population is defined in terms of how often each unit arrives or seeks service. This situation differs from that for previous waiting line models, in which λ denoted the arrival rate for the system. With a finite calling population, the arrival rate for the system varies depending on the number of units in the system. Instead of adjusting for the changing system arrival rate, in the finite calling population model λ indicates the arrival rate for each unit.

Operating Characteristics for the $M/M/1$ Model with a Finite Calling Population

The following formulas are used to determine the steady-state operating characteristics for an $M/M/1$ model with a finite calling population, where

$$\lambda = \text{the arrival rate for each unit}$$

$$\mu = \text{the service rate}$$

$$N = \text{the size of the population}$$

1. The probability that no units are in the system:

$$P_0 = \frac{1}{\displaystyle\sum_{n=0}^{N} \frac{N!}{(N-n)!} \left(\frac{\lambda}{\mu}\right)^n} \tag{11.33}$$

The arrival rate λ is defined differently for the finite calling population model. Specifically, λ is defined in terms of the arrival rate for each unit.

2. The average number of units in the waiting line:

$$L_q = N - \frac{\lambda + \mu}{\lambda}(1 - P_0) \qquad (11.34)$$

3. The average number of units in the system:

$$L = L_q + (1 - P_0) \qquad (11.35)$$

4. The average time a unit spends in the waiting line:

$$W_q = \frac{L_q}{(N - L)\lambda} \qquad (11.36)$$

5. The average time a unit spends in the system:

$$W = W_q + \frac{1}{\mu} \qquad (11.37)$$

6. The probability an arriving unit has to wait for service:

$$P_w = 1 - P_0 \qquad (11.38)$$

7. The probability of n units in the system:

$$P_n = \frac{N!}{(N - n)!}\left(\frac{\lambda}{\mu}\right)^n P_0 \qquad \text{for } n = 0, 1, \ldots, N \qquad (11.39)$$

One of the primary applications of the $M/M/1$ model with a finite calling population is referred to as the *machine repair problem*. In this problem, a group of machines is considered to be the finite population of "customers" that may request repair service. Whenever a machine breaks down, an arrival occurs in the sense that a new repair request is initiated. If another machine breaks down before the repair work has been completed on the first machine, the second machine begins to form a "waiting line" for repair service. Additional breakdowns by other machines will add to the length of the waiting line. The assumption of first-come, first-served indicates that machines are repaired in the order they break down. The $M/M/1$ model shows that one person or one server is available to perform the repair service. To return the machine to operation, each machine with a breakdown must be repaired by the single-server operation. This model is often applied by computer maintenance departments of various organizations.

An Example   The Kolkmeyer Manufacturing Company uses a group of six identical machines, each of which operates an average of 20 hours between breakdowns. Thus, the arrival rate or request for repair service for each machine is $\lambda = \frac{1}{20} = 0.05$ per hour. With randomly occurring breakdowns, the Poisson probability distribution is used to describe the machine breakdown arrival process. One person from the maintenance department provides the single-server repair service for the six machines. The exponentially distributed service times have a mean of two hours per machine, or a service rate of $\mu = \frac{1}{2} = 0.50$ machines per hour.

With $\lambda = 0.05$ and $\mu = 0.50$, we use equations (11.33) through (11.38) to compute the operating characteristics for this system. Note that the use of equation (11.33) makes the computations involved somewhat cumbersome. Confirm for yourself that equation (11.33) provides the value of $P_0 = 0.4845$. The computations for the other operating characteristics are

$$L_q = 6 - \left(\frac{0.05 + 0.50}{0.05} \right)(1 - 0.4845) = 0.3297 \text{ machines}$$

$$L = 0.3295 + (1 - 0.4845) = 0.8451 \text{ machines}$$

$$W_q = \frac{0.3295}{(6 - 0.845)0.50} = 1.279 \text{ hours}$$

$$W = 1.279 + \frac{1}{0.50} = 3.279 \text{ hours}$$

$$P_w = 1 - P_0 = 1 - 0.4845 = 0.5155$$

Operating characteristics of an M/M/1 waiting line with a finite calling population are considered in Problem 34.

Finally, equation (11.39) can be used to compute the probabilities of any number of machines being in the repair system.

As with other waiting line models, the operating characteristics provide the manager with useful information about the operation of the waiting line. In this case, the fact that a machine breakdown waits an average of $W_q = 1.279$ hours before maintenance begins and the fact that more than 50% of the machine breakdowns must wait for service, $P_w = 0.5155$, indicate that a two-server system may be needed to improve the machine repair service.

An Excel worksheet template at the MODELfiles link on the website that accompanies this text may be used to analyze the multiple-server finite calling population model.

Computations of the operating characteristics of a multiple-server finite calling population waiting line are more complex than those for the single-server model. A computer solution is virtually mandatory in this case. The Excel worksheet for the Kolkmeyer two-server machine repair system is shown in Figure 11.5. With two repair personnel, the average

FIGURE 11.5   WORKSHEET FOR THE KOLKMEYER TWO-SERVER MACHINE REPAIR
PROBLEM

MODEL *file*

Finite

	A	B	C
1	**Waiting Line Model with a Finite Calling Population**		
2			
3	**Assumptions**		
4	Poisson Arrivals		
5	Exponential Service Times		
6	Finite Calling Population		
7			
8	Number of Servers	2	
9	Arrival Rate For Each Unit	0.05	
10	Service Rate For Each Server	0.5	
11	Population Size	6	
12			
13			
14	**Operating Characteristics**		
15			
16	Probability that no customers are in the system, P_0		0.5602
17	Average number of customers in the waiting line, L_q		0.0227
18	Average number of customers in the system, L		0.5661
19	Average time a customer spends in the waiting line, W_q		0.0834
20	Average time a customer spends in the system, W		2.0834
21	Probability an arriving customer has to wait, P_w		0.1036

machine breakdown waiting time is reduced to $W_q = 0.0834$ hours, or 5 minutes, and only 10%, $P_w = 0.1036$, of the machine breakdowns wait for service. Thus, the two-server system significantly improves the machine repair service operation. Ultimately, by considering the cost of machine downtime and the cost of the repair personnel, management can determine whether the improved service of the two-server system is cost effective.

SUMMARY

In this chapter we presented a variety of waiting line models that have been developed to help managers make better decisions concerning the operation of waiting lines. For each model we presented formulas that could be used to develop operating characteristics or performance measures for the system being studied. The operating characteristics presented include the following:

1. Probability that no units are in the system
2. Average number of units in the waiting line
3. Average number of units in the system
4. Average time a unit spends in the waiting line
5. Average time a unit spends in the system
6. Probability that arriving units will have to wait for service

We also showed how an economic analysis of the waiting line could be conducted by developing a total cost model that includes the cost associated with units waiting for service and the cost required to operate the service facility.

As many of the examples in this chapter show, the most obvious applications of waiting line models are situations in which customers arrive for service such as at a grocery checkout counter, bank, or restaurant. However, with a little creativity, waiting line models can be applied to many different situations, such as telephone calls waiting for connections, mail orders waiting for processing, machines waiting for repairs, manufacturing jobs waiting to be processed, and money waiting to be spent or invested. The Management Science in

MANAGEMENT SCIENCE IN ACTION

ALLOCATING VOTING MACHINES TO POLLING LOCATIONS*

In the 2004 U.S. presidential election, many voters waited more than ten hours to cast their ballots. Similar problems with long lines at the voting booth were reported in the United States in the 2006 and 2008 elections as well as in the 2010 elections in the United Kingdom. Long lines at a voting booth can result in a voter leaving without casting her/his ballot. Queueing models can be used to diagnose why these long lines are occurring and offer improvements.

Many of the problems occurring in the U.S. elections can be linked to the implementation of direct-recording electronic (DRE) voting machines (better known as touch-screen systems). Because these systems are quite expensive, many election boards had only a relatively few DRE voting machines to allocate to polling locations. Voters' unfamiliarity with the systems also resulted in increased voting times when using DRE machines. Most election boards initially allocated voting machines to polling locations without considering queueing effects.

Starting in 2008, the Board of Elections in Franklin County, Ohio (the location of the state capital, Columbus) has used queueing models to help determine the optimal allocation of voting machines to polling locations. Voting machines can be considered as servers in this context and the voters can be thought of as customers. Queueing models were used to predict voter waiting times based on expected voter turnout, number of registered voters, and ballot lengths. The use of queueing models was credited with greatly reducing the waiting times for Franklin County voters in the 2010 presidential election, even though voter turnout was at a record high.

*Based on work done by Ted Allen (The Ohio State University), Mike Fry and David Kelton (University of Cincinnati), and Muer Yang (University of St. Thomas).

Action, Allocating Voting Machines to Polling Locations, describes an application in which a waiting line model helped decrease the waiting times voters experience on Election Day.

The complexity and diversity of waiting line systems found in practice often prevent an analyst from finding an existing waiting line model that fits the specific application being studied. Simulation, the topic discussed in Chapter 16, provides an approach to determining the operating characteristics of such waiting line systems.

GLOSSARY

Arrival rate   The mean number of customers or units arriving in a given period of time.

Blocked   When arriving units cannot enter the waiting line because the system is full. Blocked units can occur when waiting lines are not allowed or when waiting lines have a finite capacity.

Exponential probability distribution   A probability distribution used to describe the service time for some waiting line models.

Finite calling population   The population of customers or units that may seek service has a fixed and finite value.

First-come, first-served (FCFS)   The queue discipline that serves waiting units on a first-come, first-served basis.

Infinite calling population   The population of customers or units that may seek service has no specified upper limit.

Multiple-server waiting line   A waiting line with two or more parallel service facilities.

Operating characteristics   The performance measures for a waiting line, including the probability that no units are in the system, the average number of units in the waiting line, the average waiting time, and so on.

Poisson probability distribution   A probability distribution used to describe the arrival pattern for some waiting line models.

Queue   A waiting line.

Queueing theory   The body of knowledge dealing with waiting lines.

Service rate   The mean number of customers or units that can be served by one service facility in a given period of time.

Single-server waiting line   A waiting line with only one service facility.

Steady-state operation   The normal operation of the waiting line after it has gone through a startup or transient period. The operating characteristics of waiting lines are computed for steady-state conditions.

Transient period   The startup period for a waiting line, occurring before the waiting line reaches a normal or steady-state operation.

PROBLEMS

1.   Willow Brook National Bank operates a drive-up teller window that allows customers to complete bank transactions without getting out of their cars. On weekday mornings, arrivals to the drive-up teller window occur at random, with an arrival rate of 24 customers per hour or 0.4 customers per minute.

    a.   What is the mean or expected number of customers that will arrive in a five-minute period?

    b.   Assume that the Poisson probability distribution can be used to describe the arrival process. Use the arrival rate in part (a) and compute the probabilities that exactly 0, 1, 2, and 3 customers will arrive during a five-minute period.

    c.   Delays are expected if more than three customers arrive during any five-minute period. What is the probability that delays will occur?

2. In the Willow Brook National Bank waiting line system (see Problem 1), assume that the service times for the drive-up teller follow an exponential probability distribution with a service rate of 36 customers per hour, or 0.6 customers per minute. Use the exponential probability distribution to answer the following questions:
    a. What is the probability that the service time is one minute or less?
    b. What is the probability that the service time is two minutes or less?
    c. What is the probability that the service time is more than two minutes?

3. Use the single-server drive-up bank teller operation referred to in Problems 1 and 2 to determine the following operating characteristics for the system:
    a. The probability that no customers are in the system
    b. The average number of customers waiting
    c. The average number of customers in the system
    d. The average time a customer spends waiting
    e. The average time a customer spends in the system
    f. The probability that arriving customers will have to wait for service

 SELF*test*

4. Use the single-server drive-up bank teller operation referred to in Problems 1–3 to determine the probabilities of 0, 1, 2, and 3 customers in the system. What is the probability that more than three customers will be in the drive-up teller system at the same time?

5. The reference desk of a university library receives requests for assistance. Assume that a Poisson probability distribution with an arrival rate of 10 requests per hour can be used to describe the arrival pattern and that service times follow an exponential probability distribution with a service rate of 12 requests per hour.
    a. What is the probability that no requests for assistance are in the system?
    b. What is the average number of requests that will be waiting for service?
    c. What is the average waiting time in minutes before service begins?
    d. What is the average time at the reference desk in minutes (waiting time plus service time)?
    e. What is the probability that a new arrival has to wait for service?

6. Movies Tonight is a typical video and DVD movie rental outlet for home-viewing customers. During the weeknight evenings, customers arrive at Movies Tonight with an arrival rate of 1.25 customers per minute. The checkout clerk has a service rate of 2 customers per minute. Assume Poisson arrivals and exponential service times.
    a. What is the probability that no customers are in the system?
    b. What is the average number of customers waiting for service?
    c. What is the average time a customer waits for service to begin?
    d. What is the probability that an arriving customer will have to wait for service?
    e. Do the operating characteristics indicate that the one-clerk checkout system provides an acceptable level of service?

7. Speedy Oil provides a single-server automobile oil change and lubrication service. Customers provide an arrival rate of 2.5 cars per hour. The service rate is 5 cars per hour. Assume that arrivals follow a Poisson probability distribution and that service times follow an exponential probability distribution.
    a. What is the average number of cars in the system?
    b. What is the average time that a car waits for the oil and lubrication service to begin?
    c. What is the average time a car spends in the system?
    d. What is the probability that an arrival has to wait for service?

8. For the Burger Dome single-server waiting line in Section 11.2, assume that the arrival rate is increased to 1 customer per minute and that the service rate is increased to 1.25 customers per minute. Compute the following operating characteristics for the new system: P_0, L_q, L, W_q, W, and P_w. Does this system provide better or poorer service compared to the original system? Discuss any differences and the reason for these differences.

9. Marty's Barber Shop has one barber. Customers have an arrival rate of 2.2 customers per hour, and haircuts are given with a service rate of 5 per hour. Use the Poisson arrivals and exponential service times model to answer the following questions:
    a. What is the probability that no units are in the system?
    b. What is the probability that one customer is receiving a haircut and no one is waiting?

    c. What is the probability that one customer is receiving a haircut and one customer is waiting?

    d. What is the probability that one customer is receiving a haircut and two customers are waiting?

    e. What is the probability that more than two customers are waiting?

    f. What is the average time a customer waits for service?

10. Trosper Tire Company decided to hire a new mechanic to handle all tire changes for customers ordering a new set of tires. Two mechanics applied for the job. One mechanic has limited experience, can be hired for $14 per hour, and can service an average of three customers per hour. The other mechanic has several years of experience, can service an average of four customers per hour, but must be paid $20 per hour. Assume that customers arrive at the Trosper garage at the rate of two customers per hour.

    a. What are the waiting line operating characteristics using each mechanic, assuming Poisson arrivals and exponential service times?

    b. If the company assigns a customer waiting cost of $30 per hour, which mechanic provides the lower operating cost?

SELFtest

11. Agan Interior Design provides home and office decorating assistance to its customers. In normal operation, an average of 2.5 customers arrive each hour. One design consultant is available to answer customer questions and make product recommendations. The consultant averages 10 minutes with each customer.

    a. Compute the operating characteristics of the customer waiting line, assuming Poisson arrivals and exponential service times.

    b. Service goals dictate that an arriving customer should not wait for service more than an average of 5 minutes. Is this goal being met? If not, what action do you recommend?

    c. If the consultant can reduce the average time spent per customer to 8 minutes, what is the mean service rate? Will the service goal be met?

12. Pete's Market is a small local grocery store with only one checkout counter. Assume that shoppers arrive at the checkout lane according to a Poisson probability distribution, with an arrival rate of 15 customers per hour. The checkout service times follow an exponential probability distribution, with a service rate of 20 customers per hour.

    a. Compute the operating characteristics for this waiting line.

    b. If the manager's service goal is to limit the waiting time prior to beginning the checkout process to no more than five minutes, what recommendations would you provide regarding the current checkout system?

13. After reviewing the waiting line analysis of Problem 12, the manager of Pete's Market wants to consider one of the following alternatives for improving service. What alternative would you recommend? Justify your recommendation.

    a. Hire a second person to bag the groceries while the cash register operator is entering the cost data and collecting money from the customer. With this improved single-server operation, the service rate could be increased to 30 customers per hour.

    b. Hire a second person to operate a second checkout counter. The two-server operation would have a service rate of 20 customers per hour for each server.

14. Ocala Software Systems operates a technical support center for its software customers. If customers have installation or use problems with Ocala software products, they may telephone the technical support center and obtain free consultation. Currently, Ocala operates its support center with one consultant. If the consultant is busy when a new customer call arrives, the customer hears a recorded message stating that all consultants are currently busy with other customers. The customer is then asked to hold and is told that a consultant will provide assistance as soon as possible. The customer calls follow a Poisson probability distribution, with an arrival rate of five calls per hour. On average, it takes 7.5 minutes for a consultant to answer a customer's questions. The service time follows an exponential probability distribution.

    a. What is the service rate in terms of customers per hour?

    b. What is the probability that no customers are in the system and the consultant is idle?

    c. What is the average number of customers waiting for a consultant?

    d. What is the average time a customer waits for a consultant?

    e. What is the probability that a customer will have to wait for a consultant?

f. Ocala's customer service department recently received several letters from customers complaining about the difficulty in obtaining technical support. If Ocala's customer service guidelines state that no more than 35% of all customers should have to wait for technical support and that the average waiting time should be two minutes or less, does your waiting line analysis indicate that Ocala is or is not meeting its customer service guidelines? What action, if any, would you recommend?

15. To improve customer service, Ocala Software Systems (see Problem 14) wants to investigate the effect of using a second consultant at its technical support center. What effect would the additional consultant have on customer service? Would two technical consultants enable Ocala to meet its service guidelines (no more than 35% of all customers having to wait for technical support and an average customer waiting time of two minutes or less)? Discuss.

16. The new Fore and Aft Marina is to be located on the Ohio River near Madison, Indiana. Assume that Fore and Aft decides to build a docking facility where one boat at a time can stop for gas and servicing. Assume that arrivals follow a Poisson probability distribution, with an arrival rate of 5 boats per hour, and that service times follow an exponential probability distribution, with a service rate of 10 boats per hour. Answer the following questions:
a. What is the probability that no boats are in the system?
b. What is the average number of boats that will be waiting for service?
c. What is the average time a boat will spend waiting for service?
d. What is the average time a boat will spend at the dock?
e. If you were the manager of Fore and Aft Marina, would you be satisfied with the service level your system will be providing? Why or why not?

17. The manager of the Fore and Aft Marina in Problem 16 wants to investigate the possibility of enlarging the docking facility so that two boats can stop for gas and servicing simultaneously. Assume that the arrival rate is 5 boats per hour and that the service rate for each server is 10 boats per hour.
a. What is the probability that the boat dock will be idle?
b. What is the average number of boats that will be waiting for service?
c. What is the average time a boat will spend waiting for service?
d. What is the average time a boat will spend at the dock?
e. If you were the manager of Fore and Aft Marina, would you be satisfied with the service level your system will be providing? Why or why not?

✓SELF*test* **18.** All airplane passengers at the Lake City Regional Airport must pass through a security screening area before proceeding to the boarding area. The airport has three screening stations available, and the facility manager must decide how many to have open at any particular time. The service rate for processing passengers at each screening station is 3 passengers per minute. On Monday morning the arrival rate is 5.4 passengers per minute. Assume that processing times at each screening station follow an exponential distribution and that arrivals follow a Poisson distribution.
a. Suppose two of the three screening stations are open on Monday morning. Compute the operating characteristics for the screening facility.
b. Because of space considerations, the facility manager's goal is to limit the average number of passengers waiting in line to 10 or fewer. Will the two-screening-station system be able to meet the manager's goal?
c. What is the average time required for a passenger to pass through security screening?

19. Refer again to the Lake City Regional Airport described in Problem 18. When the security level is raised to high, the service rate for processing passengers is reduced to 2 passengers per minute at each screening station. Suppose the security level is raised to high on Monday morning. The arrival rate is 5.4 passengers per minute.
a. The facility manager's goal is to limit the average number of passengers waiting in line to 10 or fewer. How many screening stations must be open in order to satisfy the manager's goal?
b. What is the average time required for a passenger to pass through security screening?

20. A Florida coastal community experiences a population increase during the winter months, with seasonal residents arriving from northern states and Canada. Staffing at a local post office is often in a state of change due to the relatively low volume of customers in the summer months and the relatively high volume of customers in the winter months. The service rate of a postal clerk is 0.75 customers per minute. The post office counter has a maximum of three workstations. The target maximum time a customer waits in the system is five minutes.

a. For a particular Monday morning in November, the anticipated arrival rate is 1.2 customers per minute. What is the recommended staffing for this Monday morning? Show the operating characteristics of the waiting line.

b. A new population growth study suggests that over the next two years the arrival rate at the postal office during the busy winter months can be expected to be 2.1 customers per minute. Use a waiting line analysis to make a recommendation to the post office manager.

21. Refer to the Agan Interior Design situation in Problem 11. Agan's management would like to evaluate two alternatives:
   - Use one consultant with an average service time of 8 minutes per customer.
   - Expand to two consultants, each of whom has an average service time of 10 minutes per customer.

   If the consultants are paid $16 per hour and the customer waiting time is valued at $25 per hour for waiting time prior to service, should Agan expand to the two-consultant system? Explain.

22. A fast-food franchise is considering operating a drive-up window food-service operation. Assume that customer arrivals follow a Poisson probability distribution, with an arrival rate of 24 cars per hour, and that service times follow an exponential probability distribution. Arriving customers place orders at an intercom station at the back of the parking lot and then drive to the service window to pay for and receive their orders. The following three service alternatives are being considered:
   - A single-server operation in which one employee fills the order and takes the money from the customer. The average service time for this alternative is 2 minutes.
   - A single-server operation in which one employee fills the order while a second employee takes the money from the customer. The average service time for this alternative is 1.25 minutes.
   - A two-server operation with two service windows and two employees. The employee stationed at each window fills the order and takes the money for customers arriving at the window. The average service time for this alternative is 2 minutes for each server.

   For each of the three design alternatives, answer the following questions. Then, recommend one of the design options.
   a. What is the probability that no cars are in the system?
   b. What is the average number of cars waiting for service?
   c. What is the average number of cars in the system?
   d. What is the average time a car waits for service?
   e. What is the average time in the system?
   f. What is the probability that an arriving car will have to wait for service?

23. The following cost information is available for the fast-food franchise in Problem 22:
   - Customer waiting time is valued at $25 per hour to reflect the fact that waiting time is costly to the fast-food business.
   - The cost of each employee is $6.50 per hour.
   - To account for equipment and space, an additional cost of $20 per hour is attributable to each server.

   What is the lowest-cost design for the fast-food business?

24. A study of the multiple-server food-service operation at the Red Birds baseball park shows that the average time between the arrival of a customer at the food-service counter and his or her departure with a filled order is 10 minutes. During the game, customers arrive at the rate of four per minute. The food-service operation requires an average of 2 minutes per customer order.
   a. What is the service rate per server in terms of customers per minute?
   b. What is the average waiting time in the line prior to placing an order?
   c. On average, how many customers are in the food-service system?

25. To understand how a multiple-server waiting line system with a shared queue compares to a multiple-server waiting line system with a dedicated queue for each server, reconsider the Burger Dome example. Suppose Burger Dome establishes two servers but arranges the restaurant layout so that an arriving customer must decide which server's queue to join. Assume that this system equally splits the customer arrivals so that each server sees half of the customers. How does this system compare with the two-server waiting line system with a shared queue from Section 11.3? Compare the average number of customers waiting, average number of customers in the system, average waiting time, and average time in the system.

26. Manning Autos operates an automotive service. To complete their repair work, Manning mechanics often need to retrieve parts from the company's parts department counter. Mechanics arrive at the parts counter at a rate of four per hour. The parts coordinator spends an average of six minutes with each mechanic, discussing the parts the mechanic needs and retrieving the parts from inventory.

    a. Currently, Manning has one parts coordinator. On average, each mechanic waits four minutes before the parts coordinator is available to answer questions or retrieve parts from inventory. Find L_q, W, and L for this single-server parts operation.

    b. A trial period with a second parts coordinator showed that, on average, each mechanic waited only one minute before a parts coordinator was available. Find L_q, W, and L for this two-server parts operation.

    c. If the cost of each mechanic is $20 per hour and the cost of each parts coordinator is $12 per hour, is the one-server or the two-server system more economical?

27. Gubser Welding, Inc., operates a welding service for construction and automotive repair jobs. Assume that the arrival of jobs at the company's office can be described by a Poisson probability distribution with an arrival rate of two jobs per 8-hour day. The time required to complete the jobs follows a normal probability distribution, with a mean time of 3.2 hours and a standard deviation of 2 hours. Answer the following questions, assuming that Gubser uses one welder to complete all jobs:

    a. What is the mean arrival rate in jobs per hour?
    b. What is the mean service rate in jobs per hour?
    c. What is the average number of jobs waiting for service?
    d. What is the average time a job waits before the welder can begin working on it?
    e. What is the average number of hours between when a job is received and when it is completed?
    f. What percentage of the time is Gubser's welder busy?

28. Jobs arrive randomly at a particular assembly plant; assume that the arrival rate is five jobs per hour. Service times (in minutes per job) do not follow the exponential probability distribution. Two proposed designs for the plant's assembly operation are shown.

| | Service Time | |
Design	Mean	Standard Deviation
A	6.0	3.0
B	6.25	0.6

    a. What is the service rate in jobs per hour for each design?
    b. For the service rates in part (a), what design appears to provide the best or fastest service rate?
    c. What are the standard deviations of the service times in hours?
    d. Use the $M/G/1$ model to compute the operating characteristics for each design.
    e. Which design provides the best operating characteristics? Why?

29. The Robotics Manufacturing Company operates an equipment repair business where emergency jobs arrive randomly at the rate of three jobs per 8-hour day. The company's repair facility is a single-server system operated by a repair technician. The service time varies, with a mean repair time of 2 hours and a standard deviation of 1.5 hours. The company's

cost of the repair operation is $28 per hour. In the economic analysis of the waiting line system, Robotics uses $35 per hour cost for customers waiting during the repair process.

a.   What are the arrival rate and service rate in jobs per hour?

b.   Show the operating characteristics, including the total cost per hour.

c.   The company is considering purchasing a computer-based equipment repair system that would enable a constant repair time of 2 hours. For practical purposes, the standard deviation is 0. Because of the computer-based system, the company's cost of the new operation would be $32 per hour. The firm's director of operations rejected the request for the new system because the hourly cost is $4 higher and the mean repair time is the same. Do you agree? What effect will the new system have on the waiting line characteristics of the repair service?

d.   Does paying for the computer-based system to reduce the variation in service time make economic sense? How much will the new system save the company during a 40-hour workweek?

SELF*test*

30.   A large insurance company maintains a central computing system that contains a variety of information about customer accounts. Insurance agents in a six-state area use telephone lines to access the customer information database. Currently, the company's central computer system allows three users to access the central computer simultaneously. Agents who attempt to use the system when it is full are denied access; no waiting is allowed. Management realizes that with its expanding business, more requests will be made to the central information system. Being denied access to the system is inefficient as well as annoying for agents. Access requests follow a Poisson probability distribution, with a mean of 42 calls per hour. The service rate per line is 20 calls per hour.

a.   What is the probability that 0, 1, 2, and 3 access lines will be in use?

b.   What is the probability that an agent will be denied access to the system?

c.   What is the average number of access lines in use?

d.   In planning for the future, management wants to be able to handle $\lambda = 50$ calls per hour; in addition, the probability that an agent will be denied access to the system should be no greater than the value computed in part (b). How many access lines should this system have?

31.   Mid-West Publishing Company publishes college textbooks. The company operates an 800 telephone number whereby potential adopters can ask questions about forthcoming texts, request examination copies of texts, and place orders. Currently, two extension lines are used, with two representatives handling the telephone inquiries. Calls occurring when both extension lines are being used receive a busy signal; no waiting is allowed. Each representative can accommodate an average of 12 calls per hour. The arrival rate is 20 calls per hour.

a.   How many extension lines should be used if the company wants to handle 90% of the calls immediately?

b.   What is the average number of extension lines that will be busy if your recommendation in part (a) is used?

c.   What percentage of calls receive a busy signal for the current telephone system with two extension lines?

32.   City Cab, Inc., uses two dispatchers to handle requests for service and to dispatch the cabs. The telephone calls that are made to City Cab use a common telephone number. When both dispatchers are busy, the caller hears a busy signal; no waiting is allowed. Callers who receive a busy signal can call back later or call another cab service. Assume that the arrival of calls follows a Poisson probability distribution, with a mean of 40 calls per hour, and that each dispatcher can handle a mean of 30 calls per hour.

a.   What percentage of time are both dispatchers idle?

b.   What percentage of time are both dispatchers busy?

c.   What is the probability that callers will receive a busy signal if two, three, or four dispatchers are used?

d.   If management wants no more than 12% of the callers to receive a busy signal, how many dispatchers should be used?

33. Kolkmeyer Manufacturing Company (see Section 11.9) is considering adding two machines to its manufacturing operation. This addition will bring the number of machines to eight. The president of Kolkmeyer asked for a study of the need to add a second employee to the repair operation. The arrival rate is 0.05 machines per hour for each machine, and the service rate for each individual assigned to the repair operation is 0.50 machines per hour.
   a. Compute the operating characteristics if the company retains the single-employee repair operation.
   b. Compute the operating characteristics if a second employee is added to the machine repair operation.
   c. Each employee is paid $20 per hour. Machine downtime is valued at $80 per hour. From an economic point of view, should one or two employees handle the machine repair operation? Explain.

SELF*test*

34. Five administrative assistants use an office copier. The average time between arrivals for each assistant is 40 minutes, which is equivalent to an arrival rate of $1/40 = 0.025$ arrivals per minute. The mean time each assistant spends at the copier is 5 minutes, which is equivalent to a service rate of $1/5 = 0.20$ per minute. Use the $M/M/1$ model with a finite calling population to determine the following:
   a. The probability that the copier is idle
   b. The average number of administrative assistants in the waiting line
   c. The average number of administrative assistants at the copier
   d. The average time an assistant spends waiting for the copier
   e. The average time an assistant spends at the copier
   f. During an 8-hour day, how many minutes does an assistant spend at the copier? How much of this time is waiting time?
   g. Should management consider purchasing a second copier? Explain.

35. Schips Department Store operates a fleet of 10 trucks. The trucks arrive at random times throughout the day at the store's truck dock to be loaded with new deliveries or to have incoming shipments from the regional warehouse unloaded. Each truck returns to the truck dock for service two times per 8-hour day. Thus, the arrival rate per truck is 0.25 trucks per hour. The service rate is 4 trucks per hour. Using the Poisson arrivals and exponential service times model with a finite calling population of 10 trucks, determine the following operating characteristics:
   a. The probability that no trucks are at the truck dock
   b. The average number of trucks waiting for loading/unloading
   c. The average number of trucks in the truck dock area
   d. The average waiting time before loading/unloading begins
   e. The average waiting time in the system
   f. What is the hourly cost of operation if the cost is $50 per hour for each truck and $30 per hour for the truck dock?
   g. Consider a two-server truck dock operation where the second server could be operated for an additional $30 per hour. How much would the average number of trucks waiting for loading/unloading have to be reduced to make the two-server truck dock economically feasible?
   h. Should the company consider expanding to the two-server truck dock? Explain.

Case Problem 1   REGIONAL AIRLINES

Regional Airlines is establishing a new telephone system for handling flight reservations. During the 10:00 A.M. to 11:00 A.M. time period, calls to the reservation agent occur randomly at an average of one call every 3.75 minutes. Historical service time data show that a reservation agent spends an average of 3 minutes with each customer. The waiting line model assumptions of Poisson arrivals and exponential service times appear reasonable for the telephone reservation system.

Regional Airlines' management believes that offering an efficient telephone reservation system is an important part of establishing an image as a service-oriented airline. If the system is properly implemented, Regional Airlines will establish good customer relations, which in the long run will increase business. However, if the telephone reservation system is frequently overloaded and customers have difficulty contacting an agent, a negative customer reaction may lead to an eventual loss of business. The cost of a ticket reservation agent is $20 per hour. Thus, management wants to provide good service, but it does not want to incur the cost of overstaffing the telephone reservation operation by using more agents than necessary.

At a planning meeting, Regional's management team agreed that an acceptable customer service goal is to answer at least 85% of the incoming calls immediately. During the planning meeting, Regional's vice president of administration pointed out that the data show that the average service rate for an agent is faster than the average arrival rate of the telephone calls. The vice president's conclusion was that personnel costs could be minimized by using one agent and that the single agent should be able to handle the telephone reservations and still have some idle time. The vice president of marketing restated the importance of customer service and expressed support for at least two reservation agents.

The current telephone reservation system design does not allow callers to wait. Callers who attempt to reach a reservation agent when all agents are occupied receive a busy signal and are blocked from the system. A representative from the telephone company suggested that Regional Airlines consider an expanded system that accommodates waiting. In the expanded system, when a customer calls and all agents are busy, a recorded message tells the customer that the call is being held in the order received and that an agent will be available shortly. The customer can stay on the line and listen to background music while waiting for an agent. Regional's management will need more information before switching to the expanded system.

Managerial Report

Prepare a managerial report for Regional Airlines analyzing the telephone reservation system. Evaluate both the system that does not allow waiting and the expanded system that allows waiting. Include the following information in your report:

1. A detailed analysis of the operating characteristics of the reservation system with one agent as proposed by the vice president of administration. What is your recommendation concerning a single-agent system?
2. A detailed analysis of the operating characteristics of the reservation system based on your recommendation regarding the number of agents Regional should use.
3. A detailed analysis of the advantages or disadvantages of the expanded system. Discuss the number of waiting callers the expanded system would need to accommodate.
4. This report represents a pilot study of the reservation system for the 10:00 A.M. to 11:00 A.M. time period during which an average of one call arrives every 3.75 minutes; however, the arrival rate of incoming calls is expected to change from hour to hour. Describe how your waiting line analysis could be used to develop a ticket agent staffing plan that would enable the company to provide different levels of staffing for the ticket reservation system at different times during the day. Indicate the information that you would need to develop this staffing plan.

Case Problem 2   OFFICE EQUIPMENT, INC.

Office Equipment, Inc. (OEI), leases automatic mailing machines to business customers in Fort Wayne, Indiana. The company built its success on a reputation of providing timely maintenance and repair service. Each OEI service contract states that a service technician will arrive at a customer's business site within an average of three hours from the time that the customer notifies OEI of an equipment problem.

Currently, OEI has 10 customers with service contracts. One service technician is responsible for handling all service calls. A statistical analysis of historical service records indicates that a customer requests a service call at an average rate of one call per 50 hours of operation. If the service technician is available when a customer calls for service, it takes the technician an average of 1 hour of travel time to reach the customer's office and an average of 1.5 hours to complete the repair service. However, if the service technician is busy with another customer when a new customer calls for service, the technician completes the current service call and any other waiting service calls before responding to the new service call. In such cases, once the technician is free from all existing service commitments, the technician takes an average of 1 hour of travel time to reach the new customer's office and an average of 1.5 hours to complete the repair service. The cost of the service technician is $80 per hour. The downtime cost (wait time and service time) for customers is $100 per hour.

OEI is planning to expand its business. Within one year, OEI projects that it will have 20 customers, and within two years, OEI projects that it will have 30 customers. Although OEI is satisfied that one service technician can handle the 10 existing customers, management is concerned about the ability of one technician to meet the average three-hour service call guarantee when the OEI customer base expands. In a recent planning meeting, the marketing manager made a proposal to add a second service technician when OEI reaches 20 customers and to add a third service technician when OEI reaches 30 customers. Before making a final decision, management would like an analysis of OEI service capabilities. OEI is particularly interested in meeting the average three-hour waiting time guarantee at the lowest possible total cost.

Managerial Report

Develop a managerial report summarizing your analysis of the OEI service capabilities. Make recommendations regarding the number of technicians to be used when OEI reaches 20 customers and when OEI reaches 30 customers. Include a discussion of the following issues in your report:

1. What is the arrival rate for each customer per hour?
2. What is the service rate in terms of the number of customers per hour? Note that the average travel time of 1 hour becomes part of the service time because the time that the service technician is busy handling a service call includes the travel time plus the time required to complete the repair.
3. Waiting line models generally assume that the arriving customers are in the same location as the service facility. Discuss the OEI situation in light of the fact that a service technician travels an average of 1 hour to reach each customer. How should the travel time and the waiting time predicted by the waiting line model be combined to determine the total customer waiting time?
4. OEI is satisfied that one service technician can handle the 10 existing customers. Use a waiting line model to determine the following information:
   - Probability that no customers are in the system
   - Average number of customers in the waiting line
   - Average number of customers in the system
   - Average time a customer waits until the service technician arrives
   - Average time a customer waits until the machine is back in operation
   - Probability that a customer will have to wait more than one hour for the service technician to arrive
   - The total cost per hour for the service operation

   Do you agree with OEI management that one technician can meet the average three-hour service call guarantee? Explain.
5. What is your recommendation for the number of service technicians to hire when OEI expands to 20 customers? Use the information that you developed in part (4) to justify your answer.
6. What is your recommendation for the number of service technicians to hire when OEI expands to 30 customers? Use the information that you developed in part (4) to justify your answer.
7. What are the annual savings of your recommendation in part (6) compared to the planning committee's proposal that 30 customers will require three service technicians? Assume 250 days of operation per year.

CHAPTER 12

Simulation

CONTENTS

MANAGEMENT SCIENCE IN ACTION

REDUCING PATIENT INFECTIONS IN THE ICU*

Approximately 2 million patients acquire an infection after being admitted to the hospital in the United States each year. More than 100,000 of these patients die as a result of their hospital-acquired infections. This problem is expected to worsen as pathogens continue to develop greater resistance to antibiotics.

Two methods of decreasing the rate of hospital-acquired infections are (1) patient isolation and (2) greater adherence to hand-washing hygiene. If infected patients can be identified quickly, they can be quarantined to prevent greater outbreaks. Furthermore, proper hand washing can greatly reduce the number of pathogens present on the skin and thereby also lead to fewer infections. Yet previous studies have found that less than half of all health workers completely and correctly follow hand-hygiene protocols.

A group of researchers used data from the intensive-care unit (ICU) at Cook County Hospital in Chicago to create a simulation model of the movements of patients, health care workers,

hospital visitors, and actual pathogens that lead to infections. The researchers were able to simulate both the creation of a new isolation ward in the ICU and model better hand-hygiene habits. The simulation estimated rates of infection and impacts on hospital costs in each scenario.

The simulation showed that both patient isolation and better hand-hygiene can greatly reduce infection rates. Improving hand-hygiene is considerably cheaper than building and maintaining additional quarantine facilities, but the researchers point out that even the best simulations do not consider psychological responses of health care workers. The simulation cannot detect why hand-hygiene compliance is currently low, so improving adherence in practice could be challenging.

*From R. Hagtvedt, P. Griffin, P. Keskinocak, and R. Roberts, "A Simulation Model to Compare Strategies for the Reduction of Health-Care-Associated Infections," *Interfaces* 39, no. 3 (May–June 2009): 256–270.

Uncertainty pervades decision making in business, government, and our personal lives. This chapter introduces the use of **simulation** to evaluate the impact of uncertainty on a decision. Simulation models have been successfully used in a variety of disciplines. Financial applications include investment planning, project selection, and option pricing. Marketing applications include new product development and the timing of market entry for a product. Operations applications include project management, inventory management, capacity planning, and revenue management (prominent in the airline, hotel, and car rental industries). Simulation can also be used to evaluate the implications of a management policy, as described by the Management Science in Action, Reducing Patient Infections in the ICU. In each of these applications, there are uncertain quantities that complicate the decision process.

As we will demonstrate, a spreadsheet simulation analysis requires a model foundation of logical formulas that correctly express the relationships between **parameters** and decisions to generate outputs of interest. A simulation model replaces the use of single values for parameters with a range of possible values. For example, a simple spreadsheet model may compute a clothing retailer's profit, given values for the number of ski jackets ordered from the manufacturer and the number of ski jackets demanded by customers. A simulation analysis extends this model by replacing the single value used for ski jacket demand with a **probability distribution** of possible values of ski jacket demand. A probability distribution of ski jacket demand represents not only the range of possible values but also the relative likelihood of various levels of demand.

To evaluate a decision with a simulation model, an analyst identifies parameters that are not known with a high degree of certainty and treats these parameters as random, or uncertain, variables. The values for the **random variables** or **uncertain variables** are randomly generated from the specified probability distributions. The simulation model uses the randomly generated values of the random variables and the relationships between parameters and decisions to compute the corresponding values of an output. Specifically, a simulation experiment produces a *distribution* of output values that correspond to the randomly generated values of the uncertain input variables. This probability distribution of the output values describes the range of possible outcomes as well as the relative likelihood of each outcome. After reviewing the simulation results, the analyst is often able to make decision recommendations for the **controllable inputs** that address the *average* output and the *variability* of the output. When making a decision in the presence of uncertainty, decision makers should not only be interested in the average, or expected, outcome, but they should also be interested in information regarding the variability of possible outcomes. Specifically, decision makers are interested **risk analysis**, i.e., quantifying the likelihood and magnitude of an undesirable outcome.

12.1   WHAT-IF ANALYSIS

In this section, we show how to perform a basic assessment of a business venture by varying input parameters to generate a small set of what-if scenarios. This approach provides the basis for the more sophisticated simulation modeling we discuss later in the chapter.

Sanotronics

Sanotronics is a startup company that manufactures medical devices for use in hospital clinics. Inspired by experiences with family members who have battled cancer, Sanotronics's founders have developed a prototype for a new device that limits health care workers' exposure to chemotherapy treatments while they are preparing, administering, and disposing of these hazardous medications. This new device features an innovative design and has the potential to capture a substantial share of the market.

Santronics would like an analysis of the first-year profit potential of the device. Because of Sanotronics's tight cash flow situation, management is particularly concerned about the potential for a loss. Sanotronics has identified the key parameters in determining first-year profit: selling price per unit (p), first-year administrative and advertising costs (c_a), direct labor cost per unit (c_l), parts cost per unit (c_p), and first-year demand (d). After conducting market research and a financial analysis, Sanotronics estimates with a high level of certainty that the device's selling price will be $249 per unit, and the first-year administrative and advertising costs will total $1,000,000.

Sanotronics is not certain about the values for the cost of direct labor, the cost of parts, and the first-year demand. At this stage of the planning process, Sanotronics's base estimates of these inputs are $45 per unit for the direct labor cost, $90 per unit for the parts cost, and 15,000 units for the first-year demand.

Base-Case Scenario

Sanotronics's first-year profit is computed by

$$\text{Profit} = (p - c_l - c_p) \times d - c_a \tag{12.1}$$

Recall that Sanotronics is certain of a selling price of $249 per unit, and administrative and advertising costs total $1,000,000. Substituting these values into equation (12.1) yields

$$\text{Profit} = (249 - c_l - c_p) \times d - 1,000,000 \tag{12.2}$$

Sanotronics's base-case estimates of the direct labor cost per unit, the parts cost per unit, and first-year demand are $45, $90, and 15,000 units, respectively. These values constitute the **base-case scenario** for Sanotronics. Substituting these values into equation (12.2) yields the following profit projection:

$$\text{Profit} = (249 - 45 - 90)(15,000) - 1,000,000 = 710,000$$

Thus, the base-case scenario leads to an anticipated profit of $710,000.

While the base-case scenario looks appealing, Sanotronics is aware that the values of direct labor cost per unit, parts cost per unit, and first-year demand are uncertain, so the base-case scenario may not occur. To help Sanotronics gauge the impact of the uncertainty, a **what-if analysis** involves considering alternative values for the random variables (direct labor cost, parts cost, and first-year demand) and computing the resulting value for the output (profit).

Sanotronics is interested in what happens if the estimates of the direct labor cost per unit, parts cost per unit, and first-year demand do not turn out to be as expected under the base-case scenario. For instance, suppose that Sanotronics believes that direct labor costs could range from $43 to $47 per unit, the parts cost could range from $80 to $100 per unit, and the first-year demand could range from 0 to 30,000 units. Using these ranges, what-if analysis can be used to evaluate a **worst-case scenario** and a **best-case scenario**.

Worst-Case Scenario

The worst-case value for the direct labor cost is $47 (the highest value), the worst-case value for the parts cost is $100 (the highest value), and the worst-case value for demand is 0 units (the lowest value). Substituting these values into equation (12.2) leads to the following profit projection:

$$\text{Profit} = (249 - 47 - 100)(0) - 1,000,000 = -1,000,000$$

So, the worst-case scenario leads to a projected *loss* of $1,000,000.

Best-Case Scenario

The best-case value for the direct labor cost is $43 (the lowest value), the best-case value for the parts cost is $80 (the lowest value), and the best-case value for demand is 30,000 units (the highest value). Substituting these values into equation (12.2) leads to the following profit projection:

$$\text{Profit} = (249 - 43 - 80)(30,000) - 1,000,000 = 2,780,000$$

So the best-case scenario leads to a projected profit of $2,780,000.

At this point, the what-if analysis provides the conclusion that profits may range from a loss of $1,000,000 to a profit of $2,780,000 with a base-case profit of $710,000. Although the base-case profit of $710,000 is possible, the what-if analysis indicates that either a substantial loss or a substantial profit is also possible. Sanotronics can repeat this what-if analysis for other scenarios. However, simple what-if analyses do not indicate the likelihood of the various profit or loss values. In particular, we do not know anything about the probability of a loss. To conduct a more thorough evaluation of risk by obtaining insight on the potential magnitude and probability of undesirable outcomes, we now turn to developing a spreadsheet simulation model.

12.2 SIMULATION OF SANOTRONICS PROBLEM

In the chapter appendix we demonstrate how the Excel add-in Analytic Solver facilitates the construction of simulation models.

In this section, we show how to construct a simulation model and conduct a risk analysis using native Excel functionality. The first step in constructing a spreadsheet simulation model is to express the relationship between the inputs and the outputs with appropriate formula logic. Figure 12.1 provides the formula and value view for the Sanotronics spreadsheet. Data on selling price per unit, administrative and advertising cost, direct labor cost per unit, parts cost per unit, and demand are in cells B4 to B8. The profit calculation, corresponding to equation (12.1), is expressed in cell B11 using appropriate cell references and formula logic. For the values shown in Figure 12.1, the spreadsheet model computes profit for the base-case scenario. By changing one or more values for the input parameters, the spreadsheet model can be used to conduct a manual what-if analysis (e.g., the best-case and worst-case scenarios).

FIGURE 12.1   EXCEL WORKSHEET FOR SANOTRONICS

◢	A	B
1	Sanotronics	
2		
3	Parameters	
4	Selling Price per Unit	249
5	Administrative & Advertising Cost	1000000
6	Direct Labor Cost per Unit	45
7	Parts Cost per Unit	90
8	Demand	15000
9		
10	Model	
11	Profit	=((B4-B6-B7)*B8)-B5
12		

◢	A	B
1	Sanotronics	
2		
3	Parameters	
4	Selling Price per Unit	$249.00
5	Administrative & Advertising Cost	$1,000,000
6	Direct Labor Cost per Unit	$45.00
7	Parts Cost per Unit	$90.00
8	Demand	15,000
9		
10	Model	
11	Profit	$710,000.00

Use of Probability Distributions to Represent Random Variables

MODEL *file*

Sanotronics

Using the what-if approach to risk analysis, we manually select values for the random variables (direct labor cost per unit, parts cost per unit, and first-year demand) and then compute the resulting profit. Instead of manually selecting the values for the random variables, a simulation model randomly generates values for the random variables so that the values used reflect what we might observe in practice. A probability distribution describes the possible values of a random variable and the relative likelihood of the random variable realizing these values. The analyst can use historical data and knowledge of the random variable (such as the range, mean, mode, standard deviation) to specify the probability distribution for a random variable. As described below, Sanotronics examined the random variables to identify probability distributions for the direct labor cost per unit, the parts cost per unit, and first-year demand.

Direct Labor Cost   Based on recent wage rates and estimated processing requirements of the device, Sanotronics believes that the direct labor cost will range from $43 to $47 per unit and is described by the discrete probability distribution shown in Figure 12.2. Thus, we see that there is 0.1 probability that the direct labor cost will be $43 per unit, a 0.2 probability that the direct labor cost will be $44 per unit, and so on. The highest probability of 0.4 is associated with a direct labor cost of $45 per unit. Because Sanotronics models the direct labor cost per unit with a **discrete probability distribution**, the direct labor cost per unit can *only* take on a value of $43, $44, $45, $46, or $47 (no other values are possible).

FIGURE 12.2   PROBABILITY DISTRIBUTION FOR DIRECT LABOR COST PER UNIT

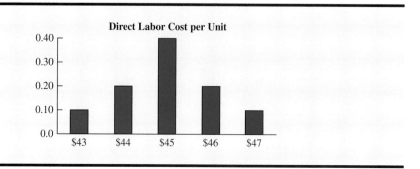

FIGURE 12.3   UNIFORM PROBABILITY DISTRIBUTION FOR PARTS COST PER UNIT

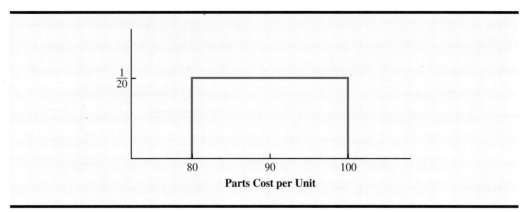

Parts Cost   Sanotronics is relatively unsure of the value of the parts cost because it depends on many factors, including the general economy, the overall demand for parts, and the pricing policy of Sanotronics's parts suppliers. Sanotronics is confident that the parts cost will be between $80 and $100 per unit but is unsure if any particular values between $80 and $100 are more likely than others. Therefore, Sanotronics decides to describe the uncertainty in parts cost with a uniform probability distribution, as shown in Figure 12.3. Costs per unit between $80 and $100 are equally likely. A uniform probability distribution is an example of a **continuous probability distribution**; this means that the parts cost can take on *any* value between $80 and $100 with equal likelihood.

One advantage of simulation is that the analyst can adjust the probability distributions of the random variables to determine the impact of the assumptions about the "shape" of the uncertainty on the results (and ultimately the sensitivity of the decision to the distribution assumptions about the random variables).

First-Year Demand   Based on sales of comparable medical devices, Sanotronics believes that first-year demand is described by the normal probability distribution shown in Figure 12.4. The mean or expected value of first-year demand is 15,000 units. The standard deviation of 4500 units describes the variability in the first-year demand. The normal probability distribution is a continuous probability distribution in which any value is possible, but values far larger or smaller than the mean are increasingly unlikely.

Generating Values for Random Variables with Excel

To simulate the Sanotronics problem, we must generate values for the three random variables and compute the resulting profit. A set of values for the random variables is called a trial. We then generate another trial, compute a second value for profit, and

FIGURE 12.4   NORMAL PROBABILITY DISTRIBUTION FOR FIRST-YEAR DEMAND

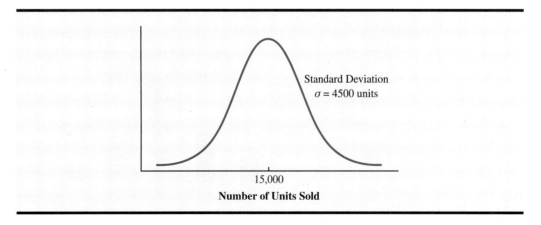

so on. We continue this process until we are satisfied that sufficient trials have been conducted to describe the probability distribution for profit. Put simply, simulation is the process of generating values of random variables and computing the corresponding output measures.

In the Sanotronics model, representative values must be generated for the random variables corresponding to the direct labor cost per unit, the parts cost per unit, and the first-year demand. To illustrate how to generate these values, we need to introduce the concept of computer-generated random numbers.

Computer-generated random numbers[1] are randomly selected numbers from 0 up to, but not including, 1; this interval is denoted as [0, 1). All values of the computer-generated random numbers are equally likely and so are uniformly distributed over the interval from 0 to 1. Computer-generated random numbers can be obtained using built-in functions available in computer simulation packages and spreadsheets. For example, placing the formula =RAND() in a cell of an Excel worksheet will result in a random number between 0 and 1 being placed into that cell.

Let us show how random numbers can be used to generate values corresponding to the probability distributions for the random variables in the Sanotronics example. We begin by showing how to generate a value for the direct labor cost per unit. The approach described is applicable for generating values from any discrete probability distribution.

Table 12.1 illustrates the process of partitioning the interval from 0 to 1 into subintervals so that the probability of generating a random number in a subinterval is equal to the probability of the corresponding direct labor cost. The interval of random numbers from 0 up to but not including 0.1, [0, 0.1), is associated with a direct labor cost of $43, the interval of random numbers from 0.1 up to but not including 0.3, [0.1, 0.3), is associated with a direct labor cost of $44, and so on. With this assignment of random number intervals to the possible values of the direct labor cost, the probability of generating a random number in any interval is equal to the probability of obtaining the corresponding value for the direct labor cost. Thus, to select a value for the direct labor cost, we generate a random number between 0 and 1 using the RAND function in Excel. If the random number is at least 0.0 but less than 0.1, we set the direct labor cost equal to $43. If the random number is at least 0.1 but less than 0.3, we set the direct labor cost equal to $44, and so on.

Each trial of the simulation requires a value for the direct labor cost. Suppose that on the first trial the random number is 0.9109. From Table 12.1, because 0.9109 is in the interval [0.9, 1.0), the corresponding simulated value for the direct labor cost is $47 per unit. Suppose that on the second trial the random number is 0.2841. From Table 12.1, the simulated value for the direct labor cost is $44 per unit.

Each trial in the simulation also requires a value of the parts cost and first-year demand. Let us now turn to the issue of generating values for the parts cost. The probability distribution

TABLE 12.1 RANDOM NUMBER INTERVALS FOR GENERATING VALUE OF DIRECT LABOR COST PER UNIT

Direct Labor Cost per Unit	Probability	Interval of Random Numbers
$43	0.1	[0.0, 0.1)
$44	0.2	[0.1, 0.3)
$45	0.4	[0.3, 0.7)
$46	0.2	[0.7, 0.9)
$47	0.1	[0.9, 1.0)

---

[1]Computer-generated random numbers are formally called pseudorandom numbers because they are generated through the use of mathematical formulas and are therefore not technically random. The difference between random numbers and pseudorandom numbers is primarily philosophical, and we use the term random numbers regardless of whether they are generated by a computer.

for the parts cost per unit is the uniform distribution shown in Figure 12.3. Because this random variable has a different probability distribution than direct labor cost, we use random numbers in a slightly different way to generate simulated values for parts cost. To generate a value for a random variable characterized by a continuous uniform distribution, the following Excel formula is used:

$$\text{Value of uniform random variable} = \text{lower bound} + \\ (\text{upper bound} - \text{lower bound}) \times \text{RAND()} \tag{12.3}$$

For Sanotronics, parts cost per unit is a uniformly distributed random variable with a lower bound of \$80 and an upper bound of \$100. Applying equation (12.3) leads to the following formula for generating the parts cost:

$$\text{Parts cost} = 80 + 20 \times \text{RAND()} \tag{12.4}$$

By closely examining equation (12.4), we can understand how it uses random numbers to generate uniformly distributed values for parts cost. The first term of equation (12.4) is 80, since Sanotronics is assuming that the parts cost will never drop below \$80 per unit. Since RAND is between 0 and 1, the second term, $20 \times \text{RAND()}$, corresponds to how much more than the lower bound the simulated value of parts cost is. Since RAND is equally likely to be any value between 0 and 1, the simulated value for the parts cost is equally likely to be between the lower bound $(80 + 0 = 80)$ and the upper bound $(80 + 20 = 100)$. For example, suppose that a random number of 0.4576 is obtained. As illustrated by Figure 12.5, the value for the parts cost is

$$\text{Parts cost} = 80 + 20 \times 0.4576 = 80 + 9.15 = 89.15 \text{ per unit}$$

Suppose that a random number of 0.5842 is generated on the next trial. The value for the parts cost is

$$\text{Parts cost} = 80 + 20 \times 0.5842 = 80 + 11.68 = 91.68 \text{ per unit}$$

With appropriate choices of the lower bound and the upper bound, equation (12.3) can be used to generate values for any uniform probability distribution.

Lastly, we need a procedure for generating the first-year demand from computer-generated random numbers. Because first-year demand is normally distributed with a mean of 15,000 units and a standard deviation of 4500 units (see Figure 12.4), we need a procedure for generating random values from this normal probability distribution.

FIGURE 12.5   GENERATION OF VALUE FOR PARTS COST PER UNIT CORRESPONDING TO RANDOM NUMBER 0.4576

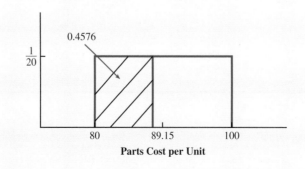

Once again we will use random numbers between 0 and 1 to simulate values for first-year demand. To generate a value for a random variable characterized by a normal distribution with a specified mean and standard deviation, the following Excel formula is used:

With appropriate specification of the mean and standard deviation, equation (12.5) can be used to generate values for any normal probability distribution.

$$\text{Value of normal random variable} = \text{NORM.INV(RAND(),} \atop \text{mean, standard deviation)} \qquad (12.5)$$

For Sanotronics, first-year demand is a normally distributed random variable with a mean of 15,000 and a standard deviation of 4500. Applying equation (12.5) leads to the following formula for generating the first-year demand:

$$\text{Demand} = \text{NORM.INV(RAND(), 15000, 4500)} \qquad (12.6)$$

Suppose that the random number of 0.6026 is produced by the RAND function; applying equation (12.6) then results in Demand =NORM.INV(0.6026, 15000, 4500) = 16,170 units. To understand how equation (12.6) uses random numbers to generate normally distributed values for first-year demand, we note that the Excel expression =NORM.INV(0.6026, 15000, 4500) provides the value for a normal distribution with a mean of 15,000 and a standard deviation of 4500, such that 60.26% of the area under the normal curve is to the left of this value (see Figure 12.6). Now suppose that the random number produced by the RAND function is 0.3551; applying equation (12.6) then results in Demand =NORM.INV(0.3551, 15000, 4500) = 13,328 units. Because half of this normal distribution lies below the mean of 15,000 and half lies above, RAND values less than 0.5 result in values of first-year demand below the average of 15,000 units and RAND value above 0.5 correspond to values of first-year demand above the average of 15,000 units.

Now that we know how to randomly generate values for the random variables (direct labor cost, parts cost, first-year demand) from their respective probability distributions, we modify the spreadsheet by adding this information. The static values in Figure 12.1 for these parameters in cells B6, B7, and B8 are replaced with cell formulas that will randomly generate values whenever the spreadsheet is recalculated (as shown in Figure 12.7). Corresponding to Table 12.1, cell B6 uses a random number generated by the RAND function and looks up the corresponding cost per unit by applying the VLOOKUP function to the table of intervals contained in cells A15:C19 (which corresponds to Table 12.1). Cell B7 executes equation (12.4) using references to the lower bound and upper bound of the uniform distribution

For further description of the VLOOKUP function, refer to Appendix A.

FIGURE 12.6   GENERATION OF VALUE FOR FIRST-YEAR DEMAND CORRESPONDING TO RANDOM NUMBER 0.6026

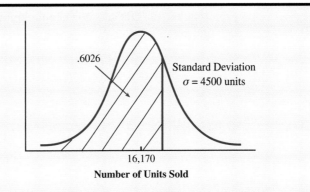

FIGURE 12.7 FORMULA WORKSHEET FOR SANOTRONICS

	A	B	C	D	E	F
1	Sanotronics					
2						
3	Parameters					
4	Selling Price per Unit	249				
5	Administrative & Advertising Cost	1000000				
6	Direct Labor Cost per Unit	=VLOOKUP(RAND(),A15:C19,3,TRUE)				
7	Parts Cost per Unit	=F14+(F15-F14)*RAND()				
8	Demand	=NORM.INV(RAND(),F18,F19)				
9						
10	Model					
11	Profit	=((B4-B6-B7)*B8)-B5				
12						
13	Direct Labor Cost				Parts Cost (Uniform Distribution)	
14	Lower End of Interval	Upper End of Interval	Cost per Unit	Probability	Lower Bound	80
15	0	=D15+A15	43	0.1	Upper Bound	100
16	=B15	=D16+A16	44	0.2		
17	=B16	=D17+A17	45	0.4	Demand (Normal Distribution)	
18	=B17	=D18+A18	46	0.2	Mean	15000
19	=B18	1	47	0.1	Standard Deviation	4500
20						

of the parts cost in cells F14 and F15, respectively.[2] Cell B8 executes equation (12.6) using references to the mean and standard deviation of the normal distribution of the first-year demand in cells F18 and F19, respectively.[3]

Executing Simulation Trials with Excel

For a detailed description of Excel's Data Table functionality, see Appendix A.

Each trial in the simulation involves randomly generating values for the random variables (direct labor cost, parts cost, and first-year demand) and computing profit. To facilitate the execution of multiple simulation trials, we use Excel's Data Table functionality in an unorthodox, but effective, manner. To set up the spreadsheet for the execution of 1000 simulation trials, we structure a table as shown in cells A21 through E1021 in Figure 12.8. As Figure 12.8 shows, A22:A1021 numbers the 1000 simulation trials (rows 25 through 1019 are hidden). To populate cells A23 through E1021 of the data table, we execute the following steps:

MODEL *file*

Sanotronics

These steps iteratively select the simulation trial number from the range A22 through A1021 and substitute it into the blank cell selected in Step 4 (D1). This substitution has no bearing on the spreadsheet, but it forces Excel to recalculate the spreadsheet each time, thereby generating new random numbers with the RAND functions in cells B6, B7, and B8.

Step 1. Select cell range A22:E1021
Step 2. Click the **Data** tab in the Ribbon
Step 3. Click **What-If Analysis** in the **Forecast** group and select **Data Table**
Step 4. When the **Data Table** dialog box appears, enter any blank cell in the spreadsheet (e.g., D1) into the **Column input cell:** box
Step 5. Click **OK**

---

[2]Technically, random variables modeled with continuous probability distributions should be appropriately rounded to avoid modeling error (e.g., the simulated values of parts cost per unit should be rounded to the nearest penny). To simplify exposition, we do not worry about the small amount of modeling error that results. To model these random variables more accurately, the formula in cell B7 should be =ROUND(F12+(F13-F12)*RAND(),2).

[3]In addition to being a continuous distribution that technically requires rounding when applied to discrete phenomena (like units of medical device demand), the normal distribution also allows negative values. The probability of a negative value is quite small in the case of first-year demand, and we simply ignore the small amount of modeling error for the sake of simplicity. To model first-year demand more accurately, the formula in cell B8 should be =MAX(ROUND(NORM. INV(RAND(),F16,F17),0),0).

FIGURE 12.8 SETTING UP SANOTRONICS SPREADSHEET FOR MULTIPLE SIMULATION TRIALS

	A	B	C	D	E	F
1	Sanotronics					
2						
3	**Parameters**					
4	Selling Price per Unit	249				
5	Administrative & Advertising Cost	1000000				
6	Direct Labor Cost per Unit	=VLOOKUP(RAND(), A15:C19,3,TRUE)				
7	Parts Cost per Unit	=F14+(F15-F14)*RAND()				
8	Demand	=NORM.INV(RAND(),F18,F19)				
9						
10	**Model**					
11	Profit	=((B4-B6-B7)*B8)-B5				
12						
13	Direct Labor Cost				Parts Cost (Uniform Distribution)	
14	Lower End of Interval	Upper End of Interval	Cost per Unit	Probability	Lower Bound	80
15	0	=D15+A15	43	0.1	Upper Bound	100
16	-B15	=D16+A16	44	0.2		
17	-B16	=D17+A17	45	0.4	Demand (Normal Distribution)	
18	-B17	=D18+A18	46	0.2	Mean	15000
19	-B18	1	47	0.1	Standard Deviation	4500
20						
21	Simulation Trial	Direct Labor Cost per Unit	Parts Cost per Unit	Demand	Profit	
22	1	=B6	=B7	=B8	=B11	
23	2					
24	3					
1019	998					
1020	999					
1021	1000					

Data Table dialog box (shown overlaying the spreadsheet):

Data Table

Row input cell:

Column input cell: D1

OK   Cancel

Pressing the F9 key recalculates the spreadsheet, thereby generating a new set of simulation trials.

Figure 12.8 shows the results of our simulation. After executing the simulation with the data table, each row in this table corresponds to a distinct simulation trial consisting of different values of the random variables. In trial 1 (row 22 in the spreadsheet), we see that the direct labor cost is $45 per unit, the parts cost is $86.29 per unit, and first-year demand is 19,976 units, resulting in profit of $1,351,439. In trial 2 (row 23 in the spreadsheet), we observe random variables of $45 for the direct labor cost, $81.02 for the parts cost, and 14,910 for first-year demand. These values provide a simulated profit of $833,700 on the second simulation trial.

Measuring and Analyzing Simulation Output

The analysis of the output observed over the set of simulation trials is a critical part of the simulation process. For the collection of simulation trials, it is helpful to compute descriptive statistics such as sample average, sample standard deviation, minimum, maximum, and sample proportion. To compute these statistics for the Sanotronics example, we use the following Excel functions:

Cell H22   =AVERAGE(E22:E1021)

Cell H23   =STDEV.S(E22:E1021)

Cell H24   =MIN(E22:E1021

Cell H25   =MAX(E22:E1021)

Cell H26   =COUNTIF(E22:E1021,"<0") / COUNT(E22:E1021)

Simulation studies enable an objective estimate of the probability of a loss, which is an important aspect of risk analysis.

Cell H26 computes the ratio of the number of trials whose profit is less than zero over the total number of trials. By changing the value of the second argument in the COUNTIF function, the probability that the profit is less than any specified value can be computed in cell H26.

As shown in Figure 12.9, we observe a mean profit of $717,663, standard deviation of $521,536, extremes ranging between −$996,547 and $2,253,674, and a 0.078 estimated probability of a loss.

To visualize the distribution of profit on which these descriptive statistics are based, we use Excel's FREQUENCY function and a column chart. In Figure 12.9, cells J23:J41

FIGURE 12.9   OUTPUT FROM SANOTRONICS SIMULATION

	A	B	C	D	E	F	G	H	I	J	K
1	Sanotronics										
2											
3	Parameters										
4	Selling Price per Unit	$249									
5	Administrative & Advertising Cost	$1,000,000									
6	Direct Labor Cost per Unit	$45									
7	Parts Cost per Unit	$86.29									
8	Demand	19,976									
9											
10	Model										
11	Profit	$1,351,439									
12											
13	Direct Labor Cost				Parts Cost (Uniform Distribution)						
14	Lower End of Interval	Upper End of Interval	Cost per Unit	Probability	Lower Bound	$80					
15	0.0	0.1	$43	0.1	Upper Bound	$100					
16	0.1	0.3	$44	0.2							
17	0.3	0.7	$45	0.4	Demand (Normal Distribution)						
18	0.7	0.9	$46	0.2	Mean	15,000					
19	0.9	1.0	$47	0.1	Standard Deviation	4,500					
20											
21	Simulation Trial	Direct Labor Cost per Unit	Parts Cost per Unit	Demand	Profit		Profit Summary Statistics				
22	1	$45	$86.29	19,976	$1,351,439		Mean	$717,663		Bin	Frequency
23	2	$45	$81.02	14,910	$833,700		Standard Deviation	$521,536		−$1,500,000	0
24	3	$46	$98.15	18,570	$947,064		Minimum Profit	−$996,547		−$1,250,000	0
25	4	$45	$92.29	12,561	$403,085		Maximum Profit	$2,253,674		−$1,000,000	0
26	5	$47	$88.82	6,844	−$225,345		P(Profit < $0)	0.078		−$750,000	3
27	6	$45	$95.98	15,337	$656,778					−$500,000	4
28	7	$44	$88.23	18,723	$1,186,276					−$250,000	22
29	8	$47	$96.20	17,589	$861,005					$0	49
30	9	$44	$85.97	19,967	$1,376,760					$250,000	113
31	10	$45	$89.62	14,056	$607,650					$500,000	151
32	11	$45	$85.96	11,204	$322,448					$750,000	188
33	12	$45	$92.06	11,150	$248,172					$1,000,000	193
34	13	$47	$85.34	11,880	$385,901					$1,250,000	122
35	14	$44	$80.05	24,733	$2,090,469					$1,500,000	79
36	15	$46	$92.47	10,933	$208,447					$1,750,000	47
37	16	$45	$81.61	17,453	$1,136,087					$2,000,000	20
38	17	$45	$84.16	13,205	$582,483					$2,250,000	7
39	18	$45	$93.07	15,809	$753,735					$2,500,000	2
40	19	$47	$85.33	9,422	$99,247					$2,750,000	0
41	20	$43	$83.58	13,599	$664,800					$3,000,000	0
42	21	$47	$92.23	17,168	$884,578					>$3,000,000	0
1021	1,000	$45	$92.87	22,467	$1,496,677						
1022											

contain the upper limits of the bins into which we wish to group the 1000 simulated observations of profit listed in cells E22:E1021.

Step 1. Select cells K23:K42
Step 2. In the Formula Bar, type the formula =FREQUENCY(E22:E1021, J23:J41).
Step 3. Press **CTRL+SHIFT+ENTER** after typing the formula in Step 2.

Pressing CTRL+SHIFT+ENTER in Excel indicates that the function should return an array of values to fill the cell range K23:K42. For example, cell K23 contains the number of profit observations less than −$1,500,000, cell K24 contains the number of profit observations greater than or equal to −$1,500,000 and less than −$1,250,000, cell K25 contains the number of profit observations greater than or equal to −$1,250,000 and less than −$1,000,000, etc.

To construct the column chart based on this frequency data:

Step 1. Select cells J23:K42
Step 2. Click the **Insert** tab on the Ribbon
Step 3. Click the **Insert Column Chart** button in the **Charts** group
Step 4. When the list of bar chart subtypes appears, click the **Clustered Column** button in the **2-D Column** section.

Figure 12.9 shows that the distribution of profit values is fairly symmetric, with a large number of values in the range of $250,000 to $1,250,000. The probability of a large loss or a large gain is small. Only 7 trials out of 1000 resulted in a loss of more than $500,000, and only 9 trials resulted in a profit greater than $2,000,000. The bin with the largest number of values has profit ranging between $750,000 and $1,000,000.

In comparing the simulation approach to the manual what-if approach, we observe that much more information is obtained by using simulation. Recall from the what-if analysis in Section 12.1, we learned that the base-case scenario projected a profit of $710,000, the worst-case scenario projected a loss of $1,000,000, and the best-case scenario projected a profit of $2,591,000. From the 1000 trials of the simulation run, we see that the worst- and best-case scenarios, although possible, are unlikely. Indeed, the advantage of simulation for risk analysis is the information it provides on the likely values of the output. We now know the probability of a loss, how the profit values are distributed over their range, and what profit values are most likely.

The simulation results help Sanotronics's management better understand the profit/loss potential of the new medical device. The 0.078 probability of a loss may be acceptable to management. On the other hand, Sanotronics might want to conduct further market research before deciding whether to introduce the product. In any case, the simulation results should be helpful in reaching an appropriate decision.

NOTES AND COMMENTS

1. In the preceding section, we showed how to generate values for random variables from a custom discrete distribution, a uniform distribution, and a normal distribution. Generating values for a normally distributed random variable required the use of NORM.INV and the RAND functions. When using the Excel formula =NORM.INV(RAND(), m, s), the RAND function generates a random number r between 0 and 1 and then the NORM.INV function identifies the smallest value k such that $P(X \leq k) \geq r$, where X is a normal random variable with mean m and standard deviation s. Similarly, the RAND function can be used with the Excel functions BETA.INV, BINOM.INV, GAMMA.INV, and LOGNORM.INV to generate values for a random variable with a beta distribution, binomial distribution, gamma distribution, or lognormal distribution, respectively. In Appendix 12.1, we describe several additional types of random variables and how to generate them with Excel functions. Using a different probablity distribution for a random variable simply changes the relative likelihood of the random variable realizing certain values. The choice of probability distribution to use for a random variable should be based on historical data and knowledge of the analyst.

12.3   INVENTORY SIMULATION

In this section, we describe how simulation can be used to establish an inventory policy for a product that has an uncertain demand. In our example, we consider the Butler Internet Company, which distributes a wireless router. Each router costs Butler $75 and sells for $125. Thus Butler realizes a gross profit of $125 − $75 = $50 for each router sold. Monthly demand for the router is described by a normal probability distribution with a mean of 100 units and a standard deviation of 20 units.

Butler receives monthly deliveries from its supplier and replenishes its inventory to a level of Q at the beginning of each month. This beginning inventory level is referred to as the replenishment level. If monthly demand is less than the replenishment level, an inventory holding cost of $15 is charged for each unit that is not sold. However, if monthly demand is greater than the replenishment level, a stock-out occurs and a shortage cost is incurred. Because Butler assigns a loss-of-goodwill cost of $30 for each customer turned away, a shortage cost of $30 is charged for each unit of demand that cannot be satisfied. Management would like to use a simulation model to determine the average monthly net profit resulting from using particular replenishment levels. Management would also like information on the percentage of total demand that will be satisfied. This percentage is referred to as the *service level*.

The controllable input to the Butler simulation model is the replenishment level, Q. The monthly demand, D, is a random variable. The two output measures are the average monthly net profit and the service level. Computation of the service level requires that we keep track of the number of routers sold each month and the total demand for routers for each month. The service level will be computed at the end of the simulation run as the ratio of total units sold to total demand.

When demand is less than or equal to the replenishment level ($D \le Q$), D units are sold, and an inventory holding cost of $15 is incurred for each of the $Q - D$ units that remain in inventory. Net profit for this case is computed as follows:

Case 1: $D \le Q$

$$\text{Gross profit} = \$50D$$
$$\text{Holding cost} = \$15(Q - D)$$
$$\text{Net profit} = \text{Gross profit} - \text{Holding cost} = \$50D - \$15(Q - D)$$

When demand is greater than the replenishment level ($D > Q$), Q routers are sold, and a shortage cost of $30 is imposed for each of the $D - Q$ units of demand not satisfied. Net profit for this case is computed as follows:

Case 2: $D > Q$

$$\text{Gross profit} = \$50Q$$
$$\text{Shortage cost} = \$30(D - Q)$$
$$\text{Net profit} = \text{Gross profit} - \text{Shortage cost} = \$50Q - \$30(D - Q)$$

Figure 12.10 shows a flowchart that defines the sequence of logical and mathematical operations required to simulate the Butler inventory system. Each trial in the simulation represents one month of operation. The simulation is run for 1000 months using a given replenishment level, Q. Then, the average profit and service level output measures are computed. Let us describe the steps involved in the simulation by illustrating the results for the first two months of a simulation run using a replenishment level of $Q = 100$.

The first block of the flowchart in Figure 12.10 sets the values of the model parameters: gross profit = $50 per unit, holding cost = $15 per unit, and shortage cost = $30 per unit. The next block shows that a replenishment level of Q is selected; in our illustration, $Q = 100$. A value for monthly demand is then generated from a normal distribution with a mean of 100 units and a standard deviation of 20 units; this can be done in Excel with the command =NORM.INV(RAND(), 100, 20). Suppose that a value of $D = 79$ is generated on

FIGURE 12.10   FLOWCHART FOR THE BUTLER INVENTORY SIMULATION

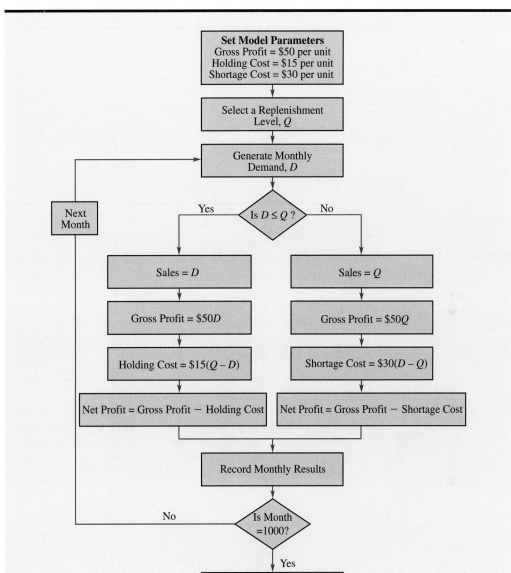

the first trial. This value of demand is then compared with the replenishment level, Q. With the replenishment level set at $Q = 100$, demand is less than the replenishment level, and the left branch of the flowchart is followed. Sales are set equal to demand (79), and gross profit, holding cost, and net profit are computed as follows:

$$\text{Gross profit} = 50D = 50(79) = 3950$$
$$\text{Holding cost} = 15(Q - D) = 15(100 - 79) = 315$$
$$\text{Net profit} = \text{Gross profit} - \text{Holding cost} = 3950 - 315 = 3635$$

The values of demand, sales, gross profit, holding cost, and net profit are recorded for the first month. The first row of Table 12.2 summarizes the information for this first trial.

For the second month, suppose that a value of 111 is generated for monthly demand. Because demand is greater than the replenishment level, the right branch of the flowchart is

TABLE 12.2   BUTLER INVENTORY SIMULATION RESULTS FOR FIVE TRIALS
WITH $Q = 100$

Month	Demand	Sales	Gross Profit ($)	Holding Cost ($)	Shortage Cost ($)	Net Profit ($)
1	79	79	3,950	315	0	3,635
2	111	100	5,000	0	330	4,670
3	93	93	4,650	105	0	4,545
4	100	100	5,000	0	0	5,000
5	118	100	5,000	0	540	4,460
Totals	501	472	23,600	420	870	22,310
Average	100	94	$4,720	$84	$174	$4,462

followed. Sales are set equal to the replenishment level (100), and gross profit, shortage cost, and net profit are computed as follows:

$$\text{Gross profit} = 50Q = 50(100) = 5000$$

$$\text{Shortage cost} = 30(D - Q) = 30(111 - 100) = 330$$

$$\text{Net profit} = \text{Gross profit} - \text{Shortage cost} = 5000 - 330 = 4670$$

The values of demand, sales, gross profit, holding cost, shortage cost, and net profit are recorded for the second month. The second row of Table 12.2 summarizes the information generated in the second trial.

Table 12.2 shows results for five trials (months) of the simulation. The totals show an accumulated total net profit of $22,310, which is an average monthly net profit of $22,310/5 = $4462. Total unit sales are 472, and total demand is 501. Thus, the service level is 472/501 = 0.942, indicating Butler has been able to satisfy 94.2% of demand during the five-month period.

Simulation of the Butler Inventory Problem

MODEL *file*

Butler

Using Excel, we simulate the Butler inventory operation for 1000 months. The worksheet used to carry out the simulation is shown in Figure 12.11. Note that the simulation results for months 22 through 999 have been hidden so that the results can be displayed in a reasonably sized figure. If desired, the rows for these months can be shown and the simulation results displayed for all 1000 months. Let us describe the details of the Excel worksheet that provided the Butler inventory simulation.

The gross profit per unit, holding cost per unit, and shortage cost per unit data are entered directly into cells B4, B5, and B6. The mean and standard deviation of the normal probability distribution for demand are entered into cells E6 and E7. The replenishment level (a controllable input) is entered into cell B10. At this point, we are ready to insert Excel formulas that will be executed for each simulation month or trial.

To generate values for demand, the cell formula in cell B7 is =NORM.INV(RAND(), E6, E7). Next, compute the sales, which is equal to demand (cell B7) if demand is less than or equal to the replenishment level, or is equal to the replenishment level (cell B10) if demand is greater than the replenishment level.

Cell B11   Compute sales =MIN(B7, B10)

Cell B12   Calculate gross profit =B11*B4

Cell B13   Calculate the holding cost if demand is less than or equal to the replenishment
             level
             =IF(B10>B7, (B10-B7)*B5, 0)

FIGURE 12.11 OUTPUT FROM BUTLER INVENTORY SIMULATION

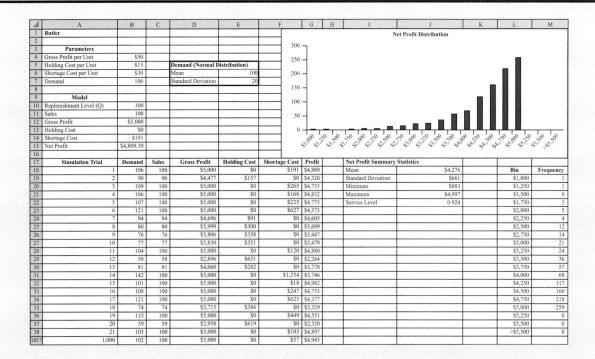

Cell B14   Calculate the shortage cost if demand is greater than the replenishment level
$$=IF(B7>B10, (B7-B10)*B6, 0)$$
Cell B15   Calculate net profit $=B12-B13-B14$

     The table of simulation trials in cells A18:G1017 and the summary statistics are generated using the steps described in Section 12.2. The summary statistics in Figure 12.11 show what can be anticipated over 1000 months if Butler operates its inventory system using a replenishment level of 100. The average net profit is $4276 per month and the service level is 92.4%. A closer look at the distribution of net profit shows that the maximum net profit never exceeds $5000 (indeed the maximum monthly net profit of $5000 occurs when monthly demand is 100 routers and matches the replenishment level). The most likely monthly net profit levels are between $4750 and $5000, but net profits below $1000 are also possible.

     By varying the values of controllable inputs, simulation models can be used to identify good operating policies and decisions. For Butler, the simulation model can be used to test the impact of different replenishment levels on the monthly net profit. Table 12.3 summarizes the results of varying the replenishment levels of 110, 120, 130, and 140 units

TABLE 12.3 BUTLER INVENTORY SIMULATION RESULTS FOR 1000 TRIALS

Replenishment Level	Average Net Profit ($)	Standard Deviation Profit ($)	Service Level (%)
100	4276	661	92.4
110	4498	853	96.2
120	4573	1078	98.1
130	4462	1201	99.4
140	4327	1247	99.9

by showing the average monthly net profit, standard deviation of monthly net profit, and the service level for the respective replenishment levels. From Table 12.3, we observe that average monthly net profit increases as the replenishment level increases from 100 to 120, but then decreases as the replenishment level is further increased to 130 and beyond. The standard deviation of monthly net profit increases as the replenishment level increases, suggesting that the monthly profit is more variable as Butler stocks more inventory. This occurs because as Butler increases its replenishment level, it can achieve more sales during months with high demand, but also is exposed to increased holding costs during months with low demand. The service level increases as the replenishment level increases because with more inventory on-hand, Butler is more likely to be able to satisfy demand.

Simulation allows the user to consider different operating policies and changes to model parameters and then observe the impact of the changes on output measures such as profit or service level.

On the basis of these results, Butler selected a replenishment level of $Q = 120$, which achieves the highest monthly net profit of \$4573 with an acceptable service level of 98.1%. Experimental simulation studies, such as this one for Butler's inventory policy, can help identify good operating policies and decisions. Butler's management used simulation to choose a replenishment level of 120 for the wireless router. With the simulation model in place, management can also explore the sensitivity of this decision to some of the model parameters. For instance, we assigned a shortage cost of \$30 for any customer demand not met. With this shortage cost, the replenishment level was $Q = 120$ and the service level was 98.1%. If management felt a more appropriate shortage cost was \$10 per unit, running the simulation again using \$10 as the shortage cost would be a simple matter.

Earlier we mentioned that simulation is not an optimization technique. Even though we used simulation to choose a replenishment level, it does not guarantee that this choice is optimal. All possible replenishment levels were not tested. Perhaps a manager would like to consider additional simulation runs with replenishment levels of $Q = 115$ and $Q = 125$ to search for a superior inventory policy. We also have no guarantee that the replenishment level with the highest profit would be the same for another set of 1000 randomly generated demand values. However, with a large number of simulation trials, we should find a near-optimal solution.

12.4   WAITING LINE SIMULATION

The simulation models discussed thus far have been based on independent trials (i.e., simulation experiments in which the results for one trial do not affect what happens in subsequent trials). In this sense, the system being modeled does not change or evolve over time. Simulation models such as the ones for the Sanotronics problem and the Butler inventory problem are referred to as **static simulation models**. In this section, we develop a simulation model of a waiting line system where the state of the system, including the number of customers in the waiting line and whether the service facility is busy or idle, changes or evolves over time. To incorporate time into the simulation model, we use a simulation clock to record the time that each customer arrives for service as well as the time that each customer completes service. Simulation models that must take into account how the system changes or evolves over time are referred to as **dynamic simulation models**. In a situation in which the simulation experiment is managed as a discrete sequence of events (e.g., arrivals and departures of customers) over time, a dynamic simulation model is also referred to as a **discrete-event simulation**.

One common application of discrete-event simulation is the analysis of waiting lines. In a waiting line simulation, the random variables are the interarrival times of the customers and the service times of the servers, which together determine the waiting time and completion time of the customers. In Chapter 11 we presented formulas that could be used to compute the steady-state operating characteristics of a waiting line, including the average waiting time, the average number of units in the waiting line, the probability of a customer experiencing a wait, and so on. In most cases, the waiting line formulas were based on specific assumptions about the probability distribution for arrivals, the probability distribution for service times, the queue discipline, and so on. Simulation, as an alternative for studying waiting lines, is more flexible. In applications where the assumptions required by the waiting line formulas are not reasonable, simulation may be the only feasible approach to studying the waiting line system. In this section, we discuss the simulation of the waiting line at the quality inspection department for Black Sheep Scarves.

Black Sheep Scarves

Black Sheep Scarves will open several new production facilities during the coming year. Each new production facility is designed to have one quality inspector who checks the knitting of the wool scarves before they are shipped to retailers. The arrival of hand-knit wool scarves to the quality inspection department is variable over the 24-hour work day. A concern is that during busy periods, the shipment of scarves to retailers may be delayed as they wait to be inspected. This concern prompted Black Sheep Scarves to undertake a study of the flow of scarves into the quality inspection department as a waiting line. Black Sheep Scarves's vice president wants to determine whether one quality inspector per facility will be sufficient. Black Sheep Scarves established service guidelines stating that the average delay waiting for quality inspection should be no more than one minute. Let us show how a simulation model can be used to study the quality inspection for a particular production facility. Note that each scarf can be viewed as a customer in this example, since scarves are the flow unit passing through the system.

Customer (Scarf) Arrival Times

A uniform probability distribution of interarrival times is used here to illustrate the simulation computations. Actually, any interarrival time probability distribution can be assumed, and the fundamental logic of the waiting line simulation model will not change.

One random variable in the Black Sheep Scarves simulation model is the arrival times of scarves to the quality inspection department. In waiting line simulations, arrival times are determined by randomly generating the time between successive arrivals, referred to as the *interarrival time*. For the quality inspection department being studied, the scarf interarrival times are assumed to be uniformly distributed between 0 and 5 minutes, as shown in Figure 12.12. As shown by equation (12.3) in Section 12.2, values from a uniform probability distribution with a lower bound of 0 and upper bound of 5 can be generated using the Excel function =RAND()*5.

Assume that the simulation run begins at time = 0. A random number of 0.2804 generates an interarrival time of 5(0.2804) = 1.4 minutes for scarf 1. Thus, scarf 1 arrives 1.4 minutes after the simulation run begins. A second random number of 0.2598 generates an interarrival time of 5(0.2598) = 1.3 minutes, indicating that scarf 2 arrives 1.3 minutes after scarf 1. Thus, scarf 2 arrives 1.4 + 1.3 = 2.7 minutes after the simulation begins. Continuing, a third random number of 0.9802 indicates that scarf 3 arrives 4.9 minutes after scarf 2, which is 7.6 minutes after the simulation begins.

Customer (Scarf) Service (Inspection) Times

Another random variable in the Black Sheep Scarves simulation model is service time, which is the time it takes a quality inspector to check a scarf. Past data from similar quality

FIGURE 12.12   UNIFORM PROBABILITY DISTRIBUTION OF INTERARRIVAL TIMES
                              FOR THE BLACK SHEEP SCARVES PROBLEM

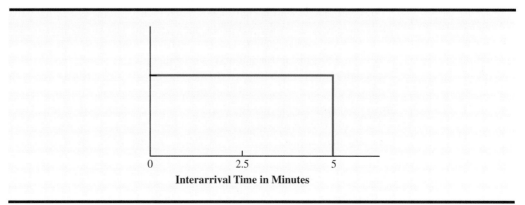

Interarrival Time in Minutes

FIGURE 12.13   NORMAL PROBABILITY DISTRIBUTION OF SERVICE TIMES
FOR THE BLACK SHEEP SCARVES PROBLEM

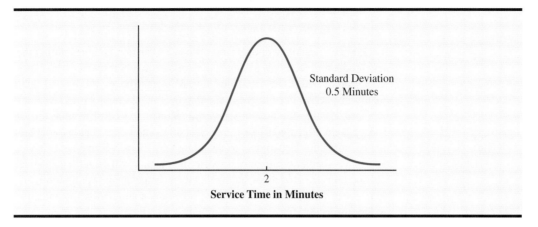

inspection departments indicate that a normal probability distribution with a mean of 2 minutes and a standard deviation of 0.5 minutes, as shown in Figure 12.13, can be used to describe service (inspection) times. As shown by equation (12.5) in Section 12.2, values from a normal probability distribution with mean 2 and standard deviation 0.5 can be generated using the Excel function =NORMINV(RAND(), 2, 0.5). For example, the random number of 0.7257 generates a scarf service time of 2.3 minutes.

Simulation Model

The random variables for the Black Sheep Scarves simulation model are the interarrival time and the service time. The controllable input is the number of quality inspectors. The output will consist of various operating characteristics such as the probability of waiting, the average waiting time, the maximum waiting time, and so on. Figure 12.14 shows a flowchart that defines the sequence of logical and mathematical operations required to simulate the Black Sheep Scarves system. The flowchart uses the following notation:

$$IAT = \text{Interarrival time generated}$$
$$\text{Arrival time } (i) = \text{Time at which scarf } i \text{ arrives}$$
$$\text{Start time } (i) = \text{Time at which scarf } i \text{ starts service}$$
$$\text{Wait time } (i) = \text{Waiting time for scarf } i$$
$$ST = \text{Service time generated}$$
$$\text{Completion time } (i) = \text{Time at which scarf } i \text{ completes service}$$
$$\text{System time } (i) = \text{System time for scarf } i \text{ (completion time } - \text{ arrival time)}$$

The logic for determining whether the server (the quality inspector in the Black Sheep Scarves example) is idle or busy is the most difficult aspect of the logic in a waiting line simulation model.

Referring to Figure 12.14, we see that the simulation is initialized in the first block of the flowchart. A new scarf is then created. An interarrival time is generated to determine the time that has passed since the preceding scarf arrived.[4] The arrival time for the new scarf is then computed by adding the interarrival time to the arrival time of the preceding scarf.

The arrival time for the new scarf must be compared to the completion time of the preceding scarf to determine whether the quality inspector is idle or busy. If the arrival time of the new scarf is greater than the completion time of the preceding scarf, the preceding scarf will have finished service (been inspected) prior to the arrival of the new scarf. In this case, the quality inspector will be idle, and the new scarf can begin service immediately. In such cases the service start time for the new scarf is equal to the arrival

---

[4]For the first scarf, the interarrival time determines how much time since the beginning of the simulation ($t = 0$) that the first scarf arrives.

FIGURE 12.14   FLOWCHART OF THE BLACK SHEEP SCARVES SIMULATION

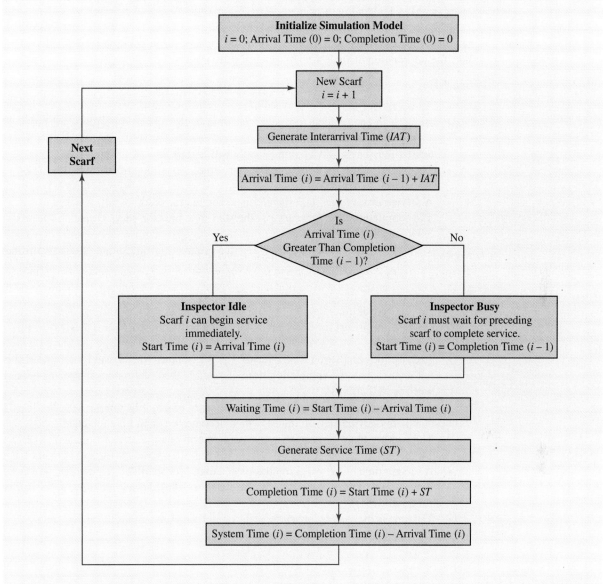

time of the new scarf. However, if the arrival time for the new scarf is not greater than the completion time of the preceding scarf, the new scarf arrived before the preceding scarf finished service. In this case, the quality inspector is busy, and inspection of the new scarf cannot begin until the quality inspector completes the inspection of the preceding scarf. The service start time for the new scarf is equal to the completion time of the preceding scarf.

Note that the time the new scarf has to wait to use the quality inspector is the difference between the scarf's service start time and the scarf's arrival time. At this point, the scarf is ready to use the quality inspector, and the simulation run continues with the generation of the scarf's service time. The time at which the scarf begins service plus the service time generated determine the scarf's completion time, which then becomes the earliest start time for inspection of the next scarf that arrives. Finally, the total time the scarf spends in the system is the difference between the scarf's service completion time and the scarf's arrival time. At this point, the computations are complete for the current scarf, and the simulation continues with the next scarf. The simulation is continued until a specified number of scarves have been served by the quality inspector.

Simulation results for a set of 10 scarves are shown in Table 12.4. We discuss the computations for the first three scarves to illustrate the logic of the simulation model and to show how the information in Table 12.4 was developed.

Scarf 1

- An interarrival time of $IAT = 1.4$ minutes is generated.
- Because the simulation run begins at time 0, the arrival time for scarf 1 is $0 + 1.4 = 1.4$ minutes.
- Scarf 1 may begin service immediately with a start time of 1.4 minutes.
- The waiting time for scarf 1 is the start time minus the arrival time: $1.4 - 1.4 = 0$ minutes.
- A service time of $ST = 2.3$ minutes is generated for scarf 1.
- The completion time for scarf 1 is the start time plus the service time: $1.4 + 2.3 = 3.7$ minutes.
- The time in the system for scarf 1 is the completion time minus the arrival time: $3.7 - 1.4 = 2.3$ minutes.

Scarf 2

- An interarrival time of $IAT = 1.3$ minutes is generated.
- Because the arrival time of scarf 1 is 1.4, the arrival time for scarf 2 is $1.4 + 1.3 = 2.7$ minutes.
- Because the completion time of scarf 1 is 3.7 minutes, the arrival time of scarf 2 is not greater than the completion time of scarf 1; thus, the quality inspector is busy when scarf 2 arrives.
- Scarf 2 must wait for scarf 1 to complete service before beginning service. Scarf 1 completes service at 3.7 minutes, which becomes the start time for scarf 2.
- The waiting time for scarf 2 is the start time minus the arrival time: $3.7 - 2.7 = 1$ minute.
- A service time of $ST = 1.5$ minutes is generated for scarf 2.
- The completion time for scarf 2 is the start time plus the service time: $3.7 + 1.5 = 5.2$ minutes.
- The time in the system for scarf 2 is the completion time minus the arrival time: $5.2 - 2.7 = 2.5$ minutes.

TABLE 12.4   SIMULATION RESULTS FOR 10 SCARVES

Scarf	Interarrival Time	Arrival Time	Service Start Time	Waiting Time	Service Time	Completion Time	Time in System
1	1.4	1.4	1.4	0.0	2.3	3.7	2.3
2	1.3	2.7	3.7	1.0	1.5	5.2	2.5
3	4.9	7.6	7.6	0.0	2.2	9.8	2.2
4	3.5	11.1	11.1	0.0	2.5	13.6	2.5
5	0.7	11.8	13.6	1.8	1.8	15.4	3.6
6	2.8	14.6	15.4	0.8	2.4	17.8	3.2
7	2.1	16.7	17.8	1.1	2.1	19.9	3.2
8	0.6	17.3	19.9	2.6	1.8	21.7	4.4
9	2.5	19.8	21.7	1.9	2.0	23.7	3.9
10	1.9	21.7	23.7	2.0	2.3	26.0	4.3
Totals	21.7			11.2	20.9		32.1
Averages	2.17			1.12	2.09		3.21

Scarf 3

- An interarrival time of $IAT = 4.9$ minutes is generated.
- Because the arrival time of scarf 2 was 2.7 minutes, the arrival time for scarf 3 is 2.7 + 4.9 = 7.6 minutes.
- The completion time of scarf 2 is 5.2 minutes, so the arrival time for scarf 3 is greater than the completion time of scarf 2. Thus, the quality inspector is idle when scarf 3 arrives.
- Scarf 3 begins service immediately with a start time of 7.6 minutes.
- The waiting time for scarf 3 is the start time minus the arrival time: 7.6 − 7.6 = 0 minutes.
- A service time of $ST = 2.2$ minutes is generated for scarf 3.
- The completion time for scarf 3 is the start time plus the service time: 7.6 + 2.2 = 9.8 minutes.
- The time in the system for scarf 3 is the completion time minus the arrival time: 9.8 − 7.6 = 2.2 minutes.

Using the totals in Table 12.4, we can compute an average waiting time for the 10 scarves of 11.2/10 = 1.12 minutes, and an average time in the system of 32.1/10 = 3.21 minutes. Table 12.4 shows that 7 of the 10 scarves had to wait. The total time for the 10-scarf simulation is given by the completion time of the 10th scarf: 26.0 minutes. However, at this point, we realize that a simulation for 10 scarves is much too short a period to draw any firm conclusions about the operation of the waiting line.

Simulation of Black Sheep Scarves

Using an Excel worksheet, we simulated the operation of the waiting line for the Black Sheep Scarves's quality inspection of 1000 scarves. The worksheet used to carry out the simulation is shown in Figure 12.15. Note that the simulation results for scarves 3 through

FIGURE 12.15 OUTPUT FOR BLACK SHEEP SCARVES WITH ONE QUALITY INSPECTOR

	A	B	C	D	E	F	G	H
1	**Black sheep Scarves with One Quality Inspector**							
2								
3	**Parameters**							
4	**Interarrival Times (Uniform Distribution)**							
5	Smallest Value	0.0						
6	Largest Value	5.0						
7								
8	**Service Times (Normal Distribution)**							
9	Mean	2.0						
10	Standard Dev	0.5						
11								
12	**Model**							
13	Customer	Interarrival Time	Arrival Time	Service Start Time	Waiting Time	Service Time	Completion Time	Time in System
14	1	2.6	2.6	2.6	0.0	1.8	4.4	1.8
15	2	0.6	3.1	4.4	1.3	1.7	6.1	3.0
16	3	4.1	7.3	7.3	0.0	0.9	8.2	0.9
1012	999	2.9	2565.7	2565.9	0.3	1.9	2567.8	2.1
1013	1000	4.5	2570.1	2570.1	0.0	1.9	2572.0	1.9
1014								
1015	**Summary Statistic**			**Wait Time Range**	**Bin**	**Frequency**		
1016	Number Waiting	531		0–1	1	521.0		
1017	Number of Customers	900		1–2	2	164.0		
1018	Probability of Waiting	0.5900		2–3	3	89.0		
1019	Average Waiting Time	1.21		3–4	4	65.0		
1020	Maximum Waiting Time	8.6		4–5	5	29.0		
1021	Utilization of Quality Inspector	0.7829		5–6	6	15.0		
1022	Number Waiting > 1 Min	379		6–7	7	12.0		
1023	Probability Waiting > 1 Min	0.4211		7–8	8	3.0		
1024				8–9	9	2.0		
1025				9–10	10	0.0		

998 have been hidden so that the results can be shown in a reasonably sized figure. If desired, the rows for these scarves can be shown and the simulation results displayed for all 1000 scarves.

Before discussing the summary statistics, let us point out that many simulation studies of dynamic systems focus on the operation of the system during its long-run or steady-state operation. To ensure that the effects of start-up conditions are not included in the steady-state calculations, a dynamic simulation model is usually run for a specified period without collecting any data about the operation of the system. The length of the startup period can vary depending on the application but can be determined by experimenting with the simulation model. Because the Black Sheep Scarves production facility operates 24 hours per day, we will avoid the transient effects by treating the results for the first 100 scarves as the startup period. Thus, the summary statistics shown in Figure 12.15 are for the 900 scarves arriving during the steady-state period.

The summary statistics show that 531 of the 900 scarves had to wait. This result provides a 531/900 = 0.59 probability that a scarf will have to wait for service. In other words, approximately 59% of the scarves will have to wait some amount of time because the quality inspector is in use when they arrive. The average waiting time is 1.21 minutes per scarf, with at least one scarf waiting the maximum time of 8.6 minutes. The utilization rate of 0.7829 indicates that the quality inspector is in use approximately 78% of the time. Finally, 379 of the 900 scarves had to wait more than 1 minute (approximately 42% of all scarves). From the wait time distribution, we observe 17 scarves (about 2% of all scarves) had a wait time greater than 6 minutes. Note that if we had used all 1000 simulated arrivals, these estimates could have been substantially different because the scarves that arrived early in the simulation had to wait less often and for less time.

The simulation supports the conclusion that the production facility will have a busy quality inspection department. With an average scarf wait time of 1.21 minutes, the system does not satisfy Black Sheep's service guideline of an average scarf wait time of less than one minute. This production facility is a good candidate for a second quality inspector or a more efficient inspection process.

Simulation with Two Quality Inspectors

In this section, we extend the logic of the Black Sheep simulation model to account for two quality inspectors. For the second quality inspector we also assume that the service time is normally distributed with a mean of 2 minutes and a standard deviation of 0.5 minutes. Table 12.5 shows the simulation results for the first 10 scarves. In comparing

TABLE 12.5   SIMULATION RESULTS FOR 10 SCARVES FOR A TWO-QUALITY INSPECTOR SYSTEM

Scarf	Interarrival Time	Arrival Time	Service Start Time	Waiting Time	Service Time	Completion Time	Time in System	Time QI 1	Available QI 2
1	1.7	1.7	1.7	0.0	2.1	3.8	2.1	3.8	0.0
2	0.7	2.4	2.4	0.0	2.0	4.4	2.0	3.8	4.4
3	2.0	4.4	4.4	0.0	1.4	5.8	1.4	5.8	4.4
4	0.1	4.5	4.5	0.0	0.9	5.4	0.9	5.8	5.4
5	4.6	9.1	9.1	0.0	2.2	11.3	2.2	5.8	11.3
6	1.3	10.4	10.4	0.0	1.6	12.0	1.6	12.0	11.3
7	0.6	11.0	11.3	0.3	1.7	13.0	2.0	12.0	13.0
8	0.3	11.3	12.0	0.7	2.2	14.2	2.9	14.2	13.0
9	3.4	14.7	14.7	0.0	2.9	17.6	2.9	14.2	17.6
10	0.1	14.8	14.8	0.0	2.8	17.6	2.8	17.6	17.6
Totals	14.8			1.0	19.8		20.8		
Averages	1.48			0.1	1.98		2.08		

the two quality inspector system results in Table 12.5 with the single quality inspector simulation results shown in Table 12.4, we see that two additional columns are needed. These two columns show when each quality inspector becomes available for scarf service. We assume that, when a new scarf arrives, the scarf will be served by the quality inspector who is available first. When the simulation begins, the first scarf is arbitrarily assigned to quality inspector 1.

Table 12.5 shows that scarf 7 is the first scarf that has to wait to use a quality inspector. We describe how scarves 6, 7, and 8 are processed to show how the logic of the simulation run for two quality inspectors differs from that with a single quality inspector.

Scarf 6

- An interarrival time of 1.3 minutes is generated, and scarf 6 arrives 9.1 + 1.3 = 10.4 minutes into the simulation.
- From the scarf 5 row, we see that quality inspector 1 frees up at 5.8 minutes, and quality inspector 2 will free up at 11.3 minutes into the simulation. Because quality inspector 1 is free, scarf 6 does not wait and begins service on quality inspector 1 at the arrival time of 10.4 minutes.
- A service time of 1.6 minutes is generated for scarf 6. So scarf 6 has a completion time of 10.4 + 1.6 = 12.0 minutes.
- The time quality inspector 1 will next become available is set at 12.0 minutes; the time available for quality inspector 2 remains 11.3 minutes.

Scarf 7

- An interarrival time of 0.6 minute is generated, and scarf 7 arrives 10.4 + 0.6 = 11.0 minutes into the simulation.
- From the previous row, we see that quality inspector 1 will not be available until 12.0 minutes, and quality inspector 2 will not be available until 11.3 minutes. So scarf 7 must wait to use a quality inspector. Because quality inspector 2 will free up first, scarf 7 begins service on that machine at a start time of 11.3 minutes. With an arrival time of 11.0 and a service start time of 11.3, scarf 7 experiences a waiting time of 11.3 − 11.0 = 0.3 minute.
- A service time of 1.7 minutes is generated, leading to a completion time of 11.3 + 1.7 = 13.0 minutes.
- The time available for quality inspector 2 is updated to 13.0 minutes, and the time available for quality inspector 1 remains at 12.0 minutes.

Scarf 8

- An interarrival time of 0.3 minute is generated, and scarf 8 arrives 11.0 + 0.3 = 11.3 minutes into the simulation.
- From the previous row, we see that quality inspector 1 will be the first available. Thus, scarf 8 starts service on quality inspector 1 at 12.0 minutes, resulting in a waiting time of 12.0 − 11.3 = 0.7 minute.
- A service time of 2.2 minutes is generated, resulting in a completion time of 12.0 + 2.2 = 14.2 minutes and a system time of 0.7 + 2.2 = 2.9 minutes.
- The time available for quality inspector 1 is updated to 14.2 minutes, and the time available for quality inspector 2 remains at 13.0 minutes.

From the totals in Table 12.5, we see that the average waiting time for these 10 scarves is only 1.0/10 = 0.1 minute. Of course, a much longer simulation will be necessary before any reliable conclusions can be drawn.

Simulation Results with Two Quality Inspectors

The Excel worksheet that we used to conduct a simulation for 1000 scarves using two quality inspectors is shown in Figure 12.16. Results for the first 100 scarves were discarded

FIGURE 12.16   OUTPUT FOR BLACK SHEEP SCARVES WITH TWO QUALITY INSPECTORS

	A	B	C	D	E	F	G	H	I	J
1	Black Sheep Scarves with Two Quality Inspectors									
2										
3	**Parameters**									
4	**Interarrival Times (Uniform Distribution**									
5	Smallest value	0.0								
6	Largest Value	5.0								
7										
8	**Service Times (Normal Diributiion)**									
9	Mean	2.0								
10	Standerd Dev	0.5								
11										
12	**Model**									
13	Customer	Interarrival Time	Arrival Time	Service Start Time	Waiting Time	Service Time	Completion Time	Time in System	Inspector 1 Available	Inspector 2 Available
14	1	4.4	4.4	4.4	0.0	1.6	6.0	1.6	6.0	0.0
15	2	0.8	5.2	5.2	0.0	2.0	7.2	2.0	6.0	7.2
16	3	2.1	7.3	7.3	0.0	1.8	9.1	1.8	9.1	7.2
1012	999	2.6	2507.0	2507.0	0.0	2.3	2509.3	2.3	2507.3	2509.3
1013	1000	3.0	2510.0	2510.0	0.0	3.0	2513.0	3.0	2513.0	2509.3
1014										
1015	**Summary Statistics**			Wait Time Range	Bin	Frequency				
1016	Number Waiting	87		0–1	1	876.0				
1017	Number of Customers	900		1–2	2	18.0				
1018	Probability of Waiting	0.0967		2–3	3	6.0				
1019	Average Waiting Time	0.07		3–4	4	0.0				
1020	Maximum Waiting Time	2.8		4–5	5	0.0				
1021	Utilization of Quality Inspectors	0.3961		5–6	6	0.0				
1022	Number Waiting > 1 Min	24		6–7	7	0.0				
1023	Probability of Waiting > 1 Min	0.0267		7–8	8	0.0				
1024				8–9	9	0.0				
1025				9–10	10	0.0				
1026				10–11	11	0.0				
1027				11–12	12	0.0				

to account for the startup period. With two quality inspectors, the number of scarves that had to wait was reduced from 531 to 87. This reduction results in a 87/900 = 0.0967 probability that a scarf will have to wait for service when two quality inspectors are used. The two-quality inspector system also reduced the average waiting time to 0.07 minute (4.2 seconds) per scarf. The maximum waiting time was reduced from 8.6 to 2.8 minutes, and the quality inspectors were in use 39.61% of the time. Finally, only 24 of the 900 scarves had to wait more than 1 minute for a quality inspector to become available. Thus, only 2.67% of scarves had to wait more than 1 minute. The simulation results demonstrate the performance benefits of adding a second quality inspector, and in combination with cost information of this second quality inspector, Black Sheep Scarves can evaluate the decision to expand to two quality inspectors.

The simulation models that we developed can now be used to study the quality inspection at other production facilities. In each case, assumptions must be made about the appropriate interarrival time and service time probability distributions. However, once appropriate assumptions have been made, the same simulation models can be used to determine the operating characteristics of the quality inspector waiting line system.

MODEL *file*

BlackSheepTwo

NOTES AND COMMENTS

1. The Black Sheep Scarves waiting line model was based on uniformly distributed interarrival times and normally distributed service times. One advantage of simulation is its flexibility in accommodating a variety of different probability distributions. For instance, if we believe an exponential distribution is more appropriate for interarrival times, this waiting line simulation could easily be repeated by simply changing the way the interarrival times are generated.

2. At the beginning of this section, we defined discrete-event simulation as involving a dynamic system that evolves over time. The simulation computations focus on the sequence of events as they occur at discrete points in time. In the Black Sheep Scarves waiting line example, scarf arrivals and the scarf service

completions were the discrete events. Refer-ring to the arrival times and completion times in the following table, we see that the first five discrete events for this waiting line simulation were as follows:

Event	Time
Scarf 1 arrives	1.4
Scarf 2 arrives	2.7
Scarf 1 finished	3.7
Scarf 2 finished	5.2
Scarf 3 arrives	7.6

3. We did not keep track of the number of scarves in the quality inspection waiting line as we carried out the quality inspection simulation computations on a scarf-by-scarf basis. How-ever, we can determine the average number of scarves in the waiting line from other infor-mation in the simulation output. The follow-ing relationship is valid for any waiting line system:

$$\text{Average number in waiting line} = \frac{\text{Total waiting time}}{\text{Total time of simulation}}$$

For the system with one quality inspector, sup-pose the 100th scarf completed service at 247.8 minutes into the simulation. Thus, the total time of the simulation for the next 900 scarves was $2572.0 - 247.8 = 2324.2$ minutes. The average waiting time was 1.21 minutes. During the sim-ulation, the 900 scarves had a total waiting time of $900(1.21) = 1089$ minutes. Therefore, the average number of scarves in the waiting line is

$$\begin{aligned}\text{Average number in waiting line} &= 1089/2324.2 \\ &= 0.47 \text{ scarf}\end{aligned}$$

4. While it is possible to conduct small discrete-event simulations with native Excel functional-ity or with a Monte Carlo simulation package such as Analytic Solver®, discrete-event simu-lation modeling is best conducted with special-purpose software such as Arena®, ProModel®, AnyLogic®, and ExtendSim®. These packages have built-in simulation clocks, simplified methods for generating random variables, and procedures for collecting and summarizing the simulation output.

12.5 SIMULATION CONSIDERATIONS

Verification and Validation

An important step in any simulation study is confirmation that the simulation model accu-rately describes the real system. Inaccurate simulation models cannot be expected to provide worthwhile information. Thus, before using simulation results to draw conclusions about a real system, one must take steps to verify and validate the simulation model.

Verification is the process of determining that the computer procedure performing the simulation calculations is logically correct. Verification is largely a debugging task to ensure that there are no errors in the computer procedure that implements the simulation. In some cases, an analyst may compare computer results for a limited number of events with inde-pendent hand calculations. In other cases, tests may be performed to verify that the random variables are being generated correctly and that the output from the simulation model appears to be reasonable. The verification step is not complete until the user develops a high degree of confidence that the computer procedure is error free.

Validation is the process of ensuring that the simulation model provides an accurate repre-sentation of a real system. Validation requires an agreement among analysts and managers that the logic and the assumptions used in the design of the simulation model accurately reflect how the real system operates. The first phase of the validation process is done prior to, or in conjunction with, the development of the computer procedure for the simulation process. Vali-dation continues after the computer program has been developed, with the analyst reviewing the simulation output to see whether the simulation results closely approximate the performance of the real system. If possible, the output of the simulation model is compared to the output of the existing real system to make sure that the simulation output closely approximates the perfor-mance of the real system. If this form of validation is not possible, an analyst can experiment with the simulation model, and one or more individuals experienced with the operation of the real system can review the simulation output to determine whether it is a reasonable approxima-tion of what would be obtained with the real system under similar conditions.

Verification and validation are not tasks to be taken lightly. They are key steps in any simulation study and are necessary to ensure that decisions and conclusions based on the simulation results are appropriate for the real system.

Advantages and Disadvantages of Using Simulation

The primary advantages of simulation are that it is easy to understand and that the methodology can be used to model and learn about the behavior of complex systems that would be difficult, if not impossible, to deal with analytically. Simulation models are flexible; they can be used to describe systems without requiring the assumptions that are often required by mathematical models. In general, the larger the number of random variables a system has, the more likely that a simulation model will provide the most suitable approach for studying the system. Another advantage of simulation is that a simulation model provides a convenient experimental laboratory for the real system. Changing assumptions or operating policies in the simulation model and rerunning it can provide results that help us understand how such changes will affect the operation of the real system. Experimenting directly with a real system is often expensive or not feasible. Simulation models often warn against poor decision strategies by projecting disastrous outcomes such as system failures, large financial losses, and so on.

Simulation is not without disadvantages. For complex systems, the process of developing, verifying, and validating a simulation model can be time-consuming and expensive (however, the process of developing the model generally leads to a better understanding of the system, which is an important benefit). As with all mathematical models, the analyst must be mindful of the assumptions of the model in order to understand its limitations. In addition, each simulation run provides only a sample of how the real system will operate. As such, the summary of the simulation data provides only estimates or approximations about the real system. Nonetheless, the danger of obtaining poor solutions is greatly mitigated if the analyst exercises good judgment in developing the simulation model, follows proper verification and validation steps, and if the simulation process is run long enough under a wide variety of conditions so that the analyst has sufficient data to predict how the real system will operate.

SUMMARY

Simulation is a method for learning about a real system by experimenting with a model that represents the system. Some of the reasons simulation is frequently used are

1. It can be used for a wide variety of practical problems.
2. The simulation approach is relatively easy to explain and understand. As a result, management confidence is increased, and acceptance of the results is more easily obtained.
3. Spreadsheet packages now provide another alternative for model implementation, and third-party vendors have developed add-ins that expand the capabilities of the spreadsheet packages.
4. Computer software developers have produced simulation packages that make it easier to develop and implement simulation models for more complex problems.

In this chapter, we first analyzed uncertainty by considering the base-case, best-case, and worst-case scenarios. Then, we showed how native Excel functions can be used to execute a simulation to evaluate risk involving the development of a new product, the Sanotronics device. Next we used the Butler Inventory problem to demonstrate another example of simulation modeling. Finally, we illustrated how to use Excel to create a discrete-event simulation for the Black Sheep problem. These examples represent a wide range of problems that can be addressed with simulation modeling.

Our approach throughout this chapter was to develop simulation models that contained both controllable inputs and random variables. Procedures were developed for randomly generating values for the random variables, the sequence of logical and mathematical operations that describe the steps of the simulation process were modeled, and simulation results were obtained by running the simulation for a suitable number of trials. Simulation results were obtained and conclusions were drawn about the operation of the real system.

Summary of Steps for Conducting a Simulation Analysis

1. **Construct a spreadsheet model that computes output measures for given values of inputs.** The foundation of a good simulation model is logic that correctly relates input values to outputs. Audit the spreadsheet to assure that the cell formulas correctly evaluate the outputs over the entire range of possible input values.
2. **Identify inputs that are uncertain and specify probability distributions for these cells** (rather than just static numbers). Note that not all inputs may have a large enough degree of uncertainty to require modeling with a probability distribution. Other inputs may actually be decision variables, which are values that the decision maker can control and so are not random quantities to model with probability distributions.

Recall that for dynamic simulation models (discussed in Section 12.4), outputs are recorded for simulation trials occurring after an initial startup period.

3. **Select one or more outputs to record over the simulation trials.** Typical information recorded for an output includes a histogram of output values and summary statistics such as the mean, standard deviation, maximum, minimum, percentile values, etc.
4. **Execute the simulation for a specified number of trials.** For most simulation models, we recommend using at least 1000 trials. The amount of sampling error can be monitored by observing the degree by which simulation output measures fluctuate across multiple simulation runs.
5. **Analyze the outputs and interpret the implications on the decision-making process.** In addition to estimates of the mean output, simulation allows us to construct a distribution of possible output values.

GLOSSARY

Base-case scenario Determining the output assuming the most likely values for the random variables of a model.

Best-case scenario Determining the output assuming the best values that can be expected for the random variables of a model.

Continuous probability distribution A probability distribution where the possible values for a random variable can take any value between two specified values. The specified values can include negative and positive infinity.

Controllable input Input to a simulation model that is selected by the decision maker.

Discrete-event simulation model A simulation model that describes how a system evolves over time by managing a discrete sequence of events (i.e., customer arrival or departure, over time).

Discrete probability distribution A probability distribution where the possible values for a random variable can take on only specified discrete values.

Dynamic simulation model A simulation model used in situations where the state of the system affects how the system changes or evolves over time.

Parameters Numerical values that appear in the mathematical relationships of a model.

Probability distribution A description of the range and relative likelihood of possible values of an uncertain variable.

Random variable or uncertain variable Input to a simulation model whose value is uncertain and described by a probability distribution.

Risk analysis The process of evaluating a decision in the face of uncertainty by quantifying the likelihood and magnitude of an undesirable outcome.

Simulation A method that uses repeated random sampling of values to represent uncertainty in a model representing a real system and computes the values of model outputs.

Static simulation model   A simulation model in which each trial used in situations where the state of the system at one point in time does not affect the state of the system at future points in time. Each trial of the simulation is independent.

Validation   The process of determining that a simulation model provides an accurate representation of a real system.

Verification   The process of determining that a computer program implements a simulation model as it is intended.

What-if analysis   A trial-and-error approach to learning about the range of possible outputs for a model. Trial values are chosen for the model inputs (these are the what-ifs) and the value of the output(s) is computed.

Worst-case scenario   Determining the output assuming the worst values that can be expected for the random variables of a model.

PROBLEMS

1.   The management of Brinkley Corporation is interested in using simulation to estimate the profit per unit for a new product. The selling price for the product will be $45 per unit. Probability distributions for the purchase cost, the labor cost, and the transportation cost are estimated as follows:

Procurement Cost ($)	Probability	Labor Cost ($)	Probability	Transportation Cost ($)	Probability
10	0.25	20	0.10	3	0.75
11	0.45	22	0.25	5	0.25
12	0.30	24	0.35		
		25	0.30		

   a. Compute profit per unit for the base-case, worst-case, and best-case scenarios.
   b. Construct a simulation model to estimate the mean profit per unit.
   c. Why is the simulation approach to risk analysis preferable to generating a variety of what-if scenarios?
   d. Management believes the project may not be sustainable if the profit per unit is less than $5. Use simulation to estimate the probability the profit per unit will be less than $5.

2.   The management of Madeira Computing is considering the introduction of a wearable electronic device with the functionality of a laptop computer and phone. The fixed cost to launch this new product is $300,000. The variable cost for the product is expected to be between $160 and $240, with a most likely value of $200 per unit. The product will sell for $300 per unit. Demand estimates for the product vary widely, ranging from 0 to 20,000 units, with 4000 units the most likely.
   a. Compute profit for the base-case, worst-case, and best-case scenarios.
   b. Model the variable cost as a uniform random variable with a minimum of $160 and a maximum of $240. Model product demand as 1,000 times the value of a gamma random variable with the shape parameter (alpha) of 3 and a scale parameter (beta) of 2. Construct a simulation model to estimate the mean profit and the probability that that the project will result in a loss.
   c. What is your recommendation with regard to the introduction of the product?

3.   Grear Tire Company has produced a new tire with an estimated mean lifetime mileage of 36,500 miles. Management also believes that the standard deviation is 5000 miles and that tire mileage is normally distributed. To promote the new tire, Grear has offered to refund a portion of the purchase price if the tire fails to reach 30,000 miles before the tire needs to be replaced. Specifically, for tires with a lifetime below 30,000 miles, Grear will refund a customer $1 per 100 miles short of 30,000.
   a. For each tire sold, what is the expected cost of the promotion?
   b. What is the probability that Grear will refund more than $50 for a tire?
   c. What mileage should Grear set the promotion claim if it wants the expected cost to be $2?

4. Construct a spreadsheet simulation in which each trial consists of rolling of four dice. That is, there are four random variables each with an outcome of 1, 2, 3, 4, 5, or 6. For each trial, record the value of the first dice, the sum of the first two dice, the sum of the first three dice, and the sum of the first four dice. Using the FREQUENCY command, create a frequency distribution for each of these four computations on a separate plot. What phenonemon do you observe?

5. To generate leads for new business, Gustin Investment Services offers free financial planning seminars at major hotels in Southwest Florida. Gustin conducts seminars for groups of 25 individuals. Each seminar costs Gustin $3500, and the average first-year commission for each new account opened is $5000. Gustin estimates that for each individual attending the seminar, there is a 0.01 probability that he/she will open a new account.

   a. Determine the equation for computing Gustin's profit per seminar, given values of the relevant parameters.
   b. What type of random variable is the number of new accounts opened? *Hint:* Review Appendix 12.1 for descriptions of various types of probability distributions.
   c. Construct a spreadsheet simulation model to analyze the profitability of Gustin's seminars. Would you recommend that Gustin continue running the seminars?
   d. How large of an audience does Gustin need before a seminar's expected profit is greater than zero?

6. The Statewide Auto Insurance Company developed the following probability distribution for automobile collision claims paid during the past year:

Payment ($)	Probability
0	0.83
500	0.06
1,000	0.05
2,000	0.02
5,000	0.02
8,000	0.01
10,000	0.01

   a. Set up a table of intervals of random numbers that can be used with a VLOOKUP to generate automobile collision claim payments.
   b. Construct a simulation model to estimate the mean and standard deviation of claims payments. How accurate are these estimates? Compare them to the analytical calculation of the mean, $\mu = x_1 \times P(x = x_1) + x_2 \times P(x = x_2) + \cdots x_n \times P(x = x_n)$, and standard deviation, $\sqrt{\sigma} = (x_1 - \mu)^2 \times P(x = x_1) + (x_2 - \mu)^2 \times P(x = x_2) + \cdots (x_n - \mu)^2 \times P(x = x_n)(x_n - \mu)^2 \times P(x = x_n)$. How can we improve the accuracy of the simulation estimates?

7. Baseball's World Series is a maximum of seven games, with the winner being the first team to win four games. Assume that the Atlanta Braves and the Minnesota Twins are playing in the World Series and that the first two games are to be played in Atlanta, the next three games at the Twins' ballpark, and the last two games, if necessary, back in Atlanta. Taking into account the projected starting pitchers for each game and the home field advantage, the probabilities of Atlanta winning each game are as follows:

Game	1	2	3	4	5	6	7
Probability of Win	0.60	0.55	0.48	0.45	0.48	0.55	0.50

   a. Set up a spreadsheet simulation model for which whether Atlanta wins or loses each game is a random variable.
   b. What is the probability that the Atlanta Braves win the World Series?
   c. What is the average number of games played regardless of winner?

SELF*test*

8. The current price of a share of a particular stock listed on the New York Stock Exchange is $39. The following probability distribution shows how the price per share is expected to change over a three-month period:

Stock Price Change ($)	Probability
−2	0.05
−1	0.10
0	0.25
+1	0.20
+2	0.20
+3	0.10
+4	0.10

a. Construct a spreadsheet simulation model that computes the value of the stock price in 3 months, 6 months, 9 months, and 12 months under the assumption that the change in stock price over any 3-month period is independent of the change in stock price over any other 3-month period.
b. With the current price of $39 per share, simulate the price per share for the next four 3-month periods. What is the average stock price per share in 12 months? What is the standard deviation of the stock price in 12 months?
c. Based on the model assumptions, what are the lowest and highest possible prices for this stock in 12 months? Based on your knowledge of the stock market, how valid do you think these prices are? Propose an alternative to modeling how stock prices evolve over 3-month periods.

9. The Iowa Energy of the National Basketball Association Developmental League (NBA-DL) are scheduled to play against the Maine Red Claws in an upcoming game. Because a player in the NBA-DL is still developing his skills, the number of points he scores in a game can vary dramatically. Assume that each player's point production can be represented as an integer uniform variable with the ranges provided in the table below.
a. Develop a spreadsheet model that simulates the points scored by each team.
b. What is the average and standard deviation of points scored by the Iowa Energy? What is the shape of the distribution of points scored by the Iowa Energy?
c. What are the average and standard deviation of points scored by the Maine Red Claws? What is the shape of the distribution of points scored by the Maine Red Claws?
d. Let Point Differential = Iowa Energy points − Maine Red Claw points. What is the average point differential between the Iowa Energy and Maine Red Claws? What is the standard deviation in the point differential? What is the shape of the point differential distribution?
e. What is the probability of that the Iowa Energy scores more points than the Maine Red Claws?
f. The coach of the Iowa Energy feels that they are the underdog and is considering a "riskier" game strategy. The effect of the riskier game strategy is that the range of each Energy player's point production increases symmetrically so that the new range is [0, original upper bound + original lower bound]. For example, Energy player 1's range with the risky strategy is [0, 25]. How does the new strategy affect the average and standard deviation of the Energy point total? How is the probability of the Iowa Energy scoring more points that the Maine Red Claws affected?

Player	Iowa Energy	Maine Red Claws
1	[5, 20]	[7, 12]
2	[7, 20]	[15, 20]
3	[5, 10]	[10, 20]
4	[10, 40]	[15, 30]
5	[6, 20]	[5, 10]
6	[3, 10]	[1, 20]
7	[2, 5]	[1, 4]
8	[2, 4]	[2, 4]

10. A project has four activities (A, B, C, and D) that must be performed sequentially. The probability distributions for the time required to complete each of the activities are as follows:

Activity	Activity Time (weeks)	Probability
A	5	0.25
	6	0.35
	7	0.25
	8	0.15
B	3	0.20
	5	0.55
	7	0.25
C	10	0.10
	12	0.25
	14	0.40
	16	0.20
	18	0.05
D	8	0.60
	10	0.40

a. Construct a spreadsheet simulation model to estimate the average length of the project and the standard deviation of the project length.

b. What is the estimated probability that the project will be completed in 35 weeks or less?

11. In preparing for the upcoming holiday season, Fresh Toy Company (FTC) designed a new doll called The Dougie that teaches children how to dance. The fixed cost to produce the doll is $100,000. The variable cost, which includes material, labor, and shipping costs, is $34 per doll. During the holiday selling season, FTC will sell the dolls for $42 each. If FTC overproduces the dolls, the excess dolls will be sold in January through a distributor who has agreed to pay FTC $10 per doll. Demand for new toys during the holiday selling season is extremely uncertain. Forecasts are for expected sales of 60,000 dolls with a standard deviation of 15,000. The normal probability distribution is assumed to be a good description of the demand. FTC has tentatively decided to produce 60,000 units (the same as average demand), but it wants to conduct an analysis regarding this production quantity before finalizing the decision.

a. Create a what-if spreadsheet model using a formula that relate the values of production quantity, demand, sales, revenue from sales, amount of surplus, revenue from sales of surplus, total cost, and net profit. What is the profit corresponding to average demand (60,000 units)?

b. Modeling demand as a normal random variable with a mean of 60,000 and a standard deviation of 15,000, simulate the sales of the Dougie doll using a production quantity of 60,000 units. What is the estimate of the average profit associated with the production quantity of 60,000 dolls? How does this compare to the profit corresponding to the average demand (as computed in part (a))?

c. Before making a final decision on the production quantity, management wants an analysis of a more aggressive 70,000-unit production quantity and a more conservative 50,000-unit production quantity. Run your simulation with these two production quantities. What is the mean profit associated with each?

d. In addition to mean profit, what other factors should FTC consider in determining a production quantity? Compare the three production quantities (50,000, 60,000, and 70,000) using all these factors. What trade-offs occur? What is your recommendation?

12. South Central Airlines (SCA) operates a commuter flight between Atlanta and Charlotte. The regional jet holds 50 passengers, and currently SCA only books up to 50 reservations. Past data show that SCA always sells all 50 reservations, but on average, two passengers do not show up for the flight. As a result, with 50 reservations the flight is often being flown with empty seats. To capture additional profit, SCA is considering an overbooking strategy in which they would accept 52 reservations even though the airplane holds only

50 passengers. SCA believes that it will be able to always book all 52 reservations. The probability distribution for the number of passengers showing up when 52 reservations are accepted is estimated as follows:

Passengers Showing Up	Probability
48	0.05
49	0.25
50	0.50
51	0.15
52	0.05

SCA receives a marginal profit of $100 for each passenger who books a reservation (regardless whether they show up or not). The airline will also incur a cost for any passenger denied seating on the flight. This cost covers added expenses of rescheduling the passenger as well as loss of goodwill, estimated to be $150 per passenger. Develop a spreadsheet simulation model for this overbooking system and simulate the number of passengers that show up for a flight.

a. What is the average net profit for each flight with the overbooking strategy?
b. What is the probability that the net profit with the overbooking strategy will be less than the net profit without overbooking (50*$100 = $5000)?
c. Explain how your simulation model could be used to evaluate other overbooking levels such as 51, 53, and 54 and for recommending a best overbooking strategy.

13. The wedding date for a couple is quickly approaching, and the wedding planner must provide the caterer an estimate of how many people will attend the reception so that the appropriate quantity of food is prepared for the buffet. The following table contains information on the number of RSVP guests for the 145 invitations. Unfortunately, the number of guests does not always correspond to the number of RSVPed guests.

Based on her experience, the wedding planner knows it is extremely rare for guests to attend a wedding if they notified that they will not be attending. Therefore, the wedding planner will assume that no one from these 50 invitations will attend. The wedding planner estimates that the each of the 25 guests planning to come solo has a 75% chance of attending alone, a 20% chance of not attending, and a 5% chance of bringing a companion. For each of the 60 RSVPs who plan to bring a companion, there is a 90% chance that she or he will attend with a companion, a 5% chance of attending solo, and a 5% chance of not attending at all. For the 10 people who have not responded, the wedding planner assumes that there is an 80% chance that each will not attend, a 15% chance each will attend alone, and a 5% chance each will attend with a companion.

RSVPed Guests	Number of Invitations
0	50
1	25
2	60
No response	10

a. Assist the wedding planner by constructing a spreadsheet simulation model to determine the expected number of guests who will attend the reception.
b. To be accommodating hosts, the couple has instructed the wedding planner to use the Monte Carlo simulation model to determine X, the minimum number of guests for which the caterer should prepare the meal, so that there is at least a 90% chance that the actual attendance is less than or equal to X. What is the best estimate for the value of X?

14. A building contractor is preparing a bid on a new construction project. Two other contractors will be submitting bids for the same project. Based on past bidding practices and the requirements of the project, the bid from Contractor A can be described with a uniform distribution between $600,000 and $800,000, while the bid from Contractor B can be described with a normal distribution with a mean of $700,000 and standard deviation of $50,000.

a. If the building contractor submits a bid of $750,000, what is the probability that the building contractor will obtain the bid?

b. The building contractor is also considering bids of $765,000 and $775,000. If the building contract would like to bid such that the probability of winning the bid is about 0.80, what bid would you recommend? Repeat the simulation with bids of $765,000 and $775,000 to justify your recommendation.

15. Strassel Investors buys real estate, develops it, and resells it for a profit. A new property is available, and Bud Strassel, the president and owner of Strassel Investors, believes if he purchases and develops this property, it can then be sold for $160,000. The current property owner has asked for bids and stated that the property will be sold for the highest bid in excess of $100,000. Two competitors will be submitting bids for the property. Strassel does not know what the competitors will bid, but he assumes for planning purposes that the amount bid by each competitor will be uniformly distributed between $100,000 and $150,000.

Due to its limit on the number of random variables, the version of Analytic Solver accessible to students may not be able to solve Problems 16, 17, 18, and 19. We recommend using native Excel functionality rather than Analytic Solver for these problems.

a. Develop a worksheet that can be used to simulate the bids made by the two competitors. Strassel is considering a bid of $130,000 for the property. Using a simulation of 1000 trials, what is the estimate of the probability Strassel will be able to obtain the property using a bid of $130,000?

b. How much does Strassel need to bid to be assured of obtaining the property? What is the profit associated with this bid?

c. Use the simulation model to compute the profit for each trial of the simulation run. With maximization of profit as Strassel's objective, use simulation to evaluate Strassel's bid alternatives of $130,000, $140,000, or $150,000. What is the recommended bid, and what is the expected profit?

BurgerDome

16. The Burger Dome is a fast-food restaurant that is currently appraising its customer service. In its current operation, an employee takes a customer's order, tabulates the cost, receives payment from the customer, and then fills the order. Once the customer's order is filled, the employee takes the order of the next customer waiting for service. Assume that time between each customer's arrival is an exponential random variable with a mean of 1.35 minutes. Assume also that the time for the employee to complete the customer's service is an exponential random variable with mean of 1 minute. Use the BurgerDome.xlsx template to complete a simulation model for the waiting line at Burger Dome for a 14-hour work day. Using the summary statistics gathered at the bottom of the spreadsheet model, answer the following questions:

a. What is the average wait time experienced by a customer?

b. What is the longest wait time experienced by a customer?

c. What is the probability that a customer waits more than 2 minutes?

d. Create a histogram depicting the wait time distribution with bins corresponding to 0-1 minutes, 1-2 minutes, 2-3 minutes, etc. What is the most common wait time bin?

e. By pressing the F9 key to generate a new set of simulation trials, one can observe the variability in the summary statistics from simulation to simulation. Typically, this variability can be reduced by increasing the number of trials. Why is this approach not appropriate for this problem?

17. One advantage of simulation is that a simulation model can be altered easily to reflect a change in the assumptions. Refer back to the Burger Dome analysis in Problem 12. Assume that the service time is more accurately described by a normal distribution with a mean of 1 minute and a standard deviation of 0.2 minutes. This distribution has less variability than the exponential distribution originally used. What is the impact of this change on the output measures?

BurgerDomeTwo

18. Refer back to the Burger Dome analysis in Problem 12. Burger Dome wants to consider the effect of hiring a second employee to serve customers (in parallel with the first employee). Use the BurgerDomeTwoServers.xlsx template to complete a simulation model that accounts for the second employee. *Hint:* The time that a customer begins service will depend on the availability of employees. What is the impact of this change on the output measures?

19. Telephone calls come into a 24-hour airline call center (handling calls worldwide) randomly at the mean rate of 15 calls per hour. The time between calls follows an exponential distribution with a mean of 4 minutes. When the two reservation agents are busy, a telephone message tells the caller that the call is important and to please wait on the line until the next reservation agent becomes available. The service time for each reservation agent is normally distributed with a mean of 4 minutes and a standard deviation of 1 minute. Use a two-server waiting line simulation model to evaluate this waiting line system. Simulate the operation of the call center for 800 customers. Discard the first 100 customers, and collect data over the next 700 customers.

a. Compute the mean interarrival time and the mean service time. If your simulation model is operating correctly, both of these should have means of approximately 4 minutes.

b. What is the mean customer waiting time for this system?

c. Use the =COUNTIF function to determine the number of customers who have to wait for a reservation agent. What percentage of the customers have to wait?

20. Blackjack, or 21, is a popular casino game that begins with each player and the dealer being dealt two cards. The value of each hand is determined by the point total of the cards in the hand. Face cards and 10s count 10 points, aces can be counted as either 1 or 11 points, and all other cards count at their face value. For instance, the value of a hand consisting of a jack and an 8 is 18; the value of a hand consisting of an ace and a two is either 3 or 13, depending on whether player counts the ace as 1 or 11 points. The goal is to obtain a hand with a value as close as possible to 21 without exceeding 21. After the initial deal, each player and the dealer may draw additional cards (called "taking a hit") in order to improve her or his hand. If a player or the dealer takes a hit and the value of the hand exceeds 21, that person "goes broke" and loses. The dealer's advantage is that each player must decide whether to take a hit before the dealer decides whether to take a hit. If a player takes a hit and goes over 21, the player loses even if the dealer later takes a hit and goes over 21. For this reason, players will often decide not to take a hit when the value of their hand is 12 or greater.

The dealer's hand is dealt with one card up (face showing) and one card down (face hidden). The player then decides whether to take a hit based on knowledge of the dealer's up card.

a. A gambling professional determined that when the dealer's up card is a 6, the following probabilities describe the ending value of the dealer's hand:

Value of Hand	17	18	19	20	21	Broke
Probability	0.1654	0.1063	0.1063	0.1017	0.0972	0.4231

Set up intervals of random numbers that can be used to simulate the ending value of the dealer's hand when the dealer has a 6 as the up card.

b. Suppose you are playing blackjack and your hand has a value of 16 for the two cards initially dealt. If you decide to take a hit, the following cards will improve your hand: ace, 2, 3, 4, and 5. Any card with a point count greater than 5 will result in you going broke. Assume that if you have a hand with a value of 16 and decide to take a hit, the following probabilities describe the ending value of your hand:

Value of Hand	17	18	19	20	21	Broke
Probability	0.0769	0.0769	0.0769	0.0769	0.0769	0.6155

Set up intervals of random numbers that can be used to simulate the ending value of your hand after taking a hit with a value of 16.

c. Use the results of parts (a) and (b) to simulate the result of 20 blackjack hands when the dealer has a 6 up and the player chooses to take a hit with a hand that has a value of 16. What is the probability of the dealer winning, a push (a tie), and the player winning, respectively?

d. If the player has a hand with a value of 16 and doesn't take a hit, the only way the player can win is if the dealer goes broke. What is the probability of the dealer winning, a push (tie), and the player winning, respectively? On the basis of this result and the results in part (d), would you recommend the player take a hit if the player has a hand with a value of 16 and the dealer has a 6 up?

Case Problem 1   FOUR CORNERS

What will your portfolio be worth in 10 years? In 20 years? When can you stop working? The Human Resources Department at Four Corners Corporation was asked to develop a financial planning model that would help employees address these questions. Tom Gifford was asked to lead this effort and decided to begin by developing a financial plan for himself. Tom is 40 years old, has a degree in business, and earns an annual salary of $85,000. Through contributions to his company's retirement program and the receipt of a small inheritance, Tom has accumulated a portfolio valued at $50,000. Tom plans to work 20 more years and hopes to accumulate a portfolio valued at $1,000,000. Can he do it?

Tom began with a few assumptions about his future salary, his new investment contributions, and his portfolio growth rate. He assumed a 5% annual salary growth rate and plans to make new investment contributions at 6% of his salary. After some research on historical stock market performance, Tom decided that a 10% annual portfolio growth rate was reasonable. Using these assumptions, Tom developed the Excel worksheet shown in the figure below. The worksheet provides a financial projection for the next five years. In computing the portfolio earnings for a given year, Tom assumed that his new investment contribution would occur evenly throughout the year, and thus half of the new investment could be included in the computation of the portfolio earnings for the year. From the figure below, we see that at age 45, Tom is projected to have a portfolio valued at $116,321.

Tom's plan was to use this worksheet as a template to develop financial plans for the company's employees. The data in the spreadsheet would be tailored for each employee, and rows would be added to the worksheet to reflect the employee's planning horizon. After adding another 15 rows to the worksheet, Tom found that he could expect to have a portfolio of $772,722 after 20 years. Tom then took his results to show his boss, Kate Krystkowiak.

Although Kate was pleased with Tom's progress, she voiced several criticisms. One of the criticisms was the assumption of a constant annual salary growth rate. She noted that most employees experience some variation in the annual salary growth rate from year to year. In addition, she pointed out that the constant annual portfolio growth rate was unrealistic and that the actual growth rate would vary considerably from year to year. She further suggested that a simulation model for the portfolio projection might allow Tom to account for the random variability in the salary growth rate and the portfolio growth rate.

After some research, Tom and Kate decided to assume that the annual salary growth rate would vary from 0% to 5% and that a uniform probability distribution would provide a realistic approximation. Four Corners's accountants suggested that the annual portfolio growth rate could be approximated by a normal probability distribution with a mean of 10% and a standard deviation of 5%. With this information, Tom set off to redesign his spreadsheet so that it could be used by the company's employees for financial planning.

Play the role of Tom Gifford and develop a simulation model for financial planning. Write a report for Tom's boss and, at a minimum, include the following:

MODEL *file*

FourCorners

◢	A	B	C	D	E	F	G
1	Four Corners						
2							
3	Age	40					
4	Current Salary	$85,000					
5	Current Portfolio	$50,000					
6	Annual Investment Rate	6%					
7	Salary Growth Rate	5%					
8	Portfolio Growth Rate	10%					
9							
10	Year	Beginning Balance	Salary	New Investment	Earnings	Ending Balance	Age
11	1	$50,000	$85,000	$5,100	$5,255	$60,355	41
12	2	$60,355	$89,250	$5,355	$6,303	$72,013	42
13	3	$72,013	$93,713	$5,623	$7,482	$85,118	43
14	4	$85,118	$98,398	$5,904	$8,807	$99,829	44
15	5	$99,829	$103,318	$6,199	$10,293	$116,321	45
16							

1. Without considering the random variability, extend the current worksheet to 20 years. Confirm that by using the constant annual salary growth rate and the constant annual portfolio growth rate, Tom can expect to have a 20-year portfolio of $772,722. What would Tom's annual investment rate have to increase to in order for his portfolio to reach a 20-year, $1,000,000 goal? *Hint:* Use Goal Seek.

For a review of Goal Seek, refer to Appendix A.

2. Redesign the spreadsheet model to incorporate the random variability of the annual salary growth rate and the annual portfolio growth rate into a simulation model. Assume that Tom is willing to use the annual investment rate that predicted a 20-year, $1,000,000 portfolio in part 1. Show how to simulate Tom's 20-year financial plan. Use results from the simulation model to comment on the uncertainty associated with Tom reaching the 20-year, $1,000,000 goal.

3. What recommendations do you have for employees with a current profile similar to Tom's after seeing the impact of the uncertainty in the annual salary growth rate and the annual portfolio growth rate?

4. Assume that Tom is willing to consider working 25 more years instead of 20 years. What is your assessment of this strategy if Tom's goal is to have a portfolio worth $1,000,000?

5. Discuss how the financial planning model developed for Tom Gifford can be used as a template to develop a financial plan for any of the company's employees.

Case Problem 2   HARBOR DUNES GOLF COURSE

Harbor Dunes Golf Course was recently honored as one of the top public golf courses in South Carolina. The course, situated on land that was once a rice plantation, offers some of the best views of saltwater marshes available in the Carolinas. Harbor Dunes targets the upper end of the golf market, and in the peak spring golfing season it charges green fees of $160 per person and golf cart fees of $20 per person.

MODEL *file*

BurgerDome

Harbor Dunes accepts reservations for tee times for groups of four players (foursomes) every nine minutes between 7:30 A.M. and 1:21 P.M. Two foursomes start at the same time: one on the front nine and one on the back nine of the course, with a new pair of foursomes teeing off every nine minutes. With the last tee time of the day set at 1:21 P.M. to ensure all players can complete 18 holes before dusk, Harbor Dunes can sell a maximum of 20 afternoon tee times.

Last year, Harbor Dunes was able to sell every morning tee time available for every day of the spring golf season. The same result is anticipated for the coming year. Afternoon tee times, however, are generally more difficult to sell. An analysis of the sales data for last year enabled Harbor Dunes to develop the probability distribution of sales for the afternoon tee times as shown in Table 12.6. For the season, Harbor Dunes averaged selling approximately 14 of the

TABLE 12.6   PROBABILITY DISTRIBUTION OF SALES FOR THE AFTERNOON TEE TIMES

Number of Tee Times Sold	Probability
8	0.01
9	0.04
10	0.06
11	0.08
12	0.10
13	0.11
14	0.12
15	0.15
16	0.10
17	0.09
18	0.07
19	0.05
20	0.02

TABLE 12.7 PROBABILITY DISTRIBUTIONS FOR THE NUMBER OF GROUPS
REQUESTING A REPLAY

Option 1: $25 per Person + Cart Fee		Option 2: $50 per Person + Cart Fee	
Number of Foursomes Requesting a Replay	**Probability**	**Number of Foursomes Requesting a Replay**	**Probability**
0	0.01	0	0.06
1	0.03	1	0.09
2	0.05	2	0.12
3	0.05	3	0.17
4	0.11	4	0.20
5	0.15	5	0.13
6	0.17	6	0.11
7	0.15	7	0.07
8	0.13	8	0.05
9	0.09		
10	0.06		

20 available afternoon tee times. The average income from afternoon green fees and cart fees has been $10,240. However, the average of six unused tee times per day resulted in lost revenue.

In an effort to increase the sale of afternoon tee times, Harbor Dunes is considering an idea popular at other golf courses. These courses offer foursomes that play in the morning the option to play another round of golf in the afternoon by paying a reduced fee for the afternoon round. Harbor Dunes is considering two replay options: (1) a green fee of $25 per player plus a cart fee of $20 per player; (2) a green fee of $50 per player plus a cart fee of $20 per player. For option 1, each foursome will generate additional revenues of $180; for option 2, each foursome will generate additional revenues of $280. The decision as to which option is best depends upon the number of groups that are induced to play a second round by each replay offer. Working with a consultant who has expertise in statistics and the golf industry, Harbor Dunes developed probability distributions for the number of foursomes requesting a replay for each of the two options. These probability distributions are shown in Table 12.7.

In offering these replay options, Harbor Dunes's first priority will be to sell full-price afternoon advance reservations. If the demand for replay tee times exceeds the number of afternoon tee times available, Harbor Dunes will post a notice that the course is full. In this case, any excess replay requests will not be accepted.

Managerial Report

Develop simulation models for both replay options. Prepare a report that will help management of Harbor Dunes Golf Course decide which replay option to implement for the upcoming spring golf season. In preparing your report, be sure to include the following:

1. Statistical summaries of the revenue expected under each replay option
2. Your recommendation as to the best replay option
3. Assuming a 90-day spring golf season, an estimate of the added revenue using your recommendation
4. Any other recommendations you have that might improve the income for Harbor Dunes

Case Problem 3   COUNTY BEVERAGE DRIVE-THRU

County Beverage Drive-Thru, Inc., operates a chain of beverage supply stores in northern Illinois. Each store has a single service lane; cars enter at one end of the store and exit at the other end. Customers pick up soft drinks, beer, snacks, and party supplies without getting out of their cars. When a new customer arrives at the store, the customer waits until the preceding customer's order is complete and then drives into the store for service.

Typically, three employees operate each store during peak periods; two clerks take and fill orders, and a third clerk serves as cashier and store supervisor. County Beverage is considering a revised store design in which computerized order-taking and payment are integrated with specialized warehousing equipment. Management hopes that the new design will permit operating each store with one clerk. To determine whether the new design is beneficial, management decided to build a new store using the revised design.

County Beverage's new store will be located near a major shopping center. Based on experience at other locations, management believes that during the peak late afternoon and evening hours, the time between arrivals will follow an exponential probability distribution with a mean of six minutes. These peak hours are the most critical time period for the company; most of their profit is generated during these peak hours.

An extensive study of times required to fill orders with a single clerk led to the following probability distribution of service times:

Service Time (minutes)	Probability
2	0.24
3	0.20
4	0.15
5	0.14
6	0.12
7	0.08
8	0.05
9	0.02
Total	1.00

In case customer waiting times prove to be too long with just a single clerk, County Beverage's management is considering two design alternatives: (1) adding a second clerk to assist the first clerk with bagging, taking orders, and related tasks (still serving one car at a time as a single-server system), or (2) enlarging the drive-through area so that two cars can be served at once (operating as a two-server system). With the two-server option, service times are expected to be the same for each server. With the second clerk teaming with the first clerk in the single server design, service times will be reduced and would be given by the probability distribution in the following table:

Service Time (minutes)	Probability
1	0.20
2	0.35
3	0.30
4	0.10
5	0.05
Total	1.00

County Beverage's management would like you to develop a spreadsheet simulation model of the new system and use it to compare the operation of the system using the following three designs:

Design

A   Single-server system operated by one clerk
B   Single-server system operated by two clerks
C   Two-server system operated by two clerks

Management is especially concerned with how long customers have to wait for service. As a guideline, management requires the average waiting time to be less than 1.5 minutes.

Managerial Report

Prepare a report that discusses the general development of the spreadsheet simulation model, and make any recommendations that you have regarding the best store design and staffing plan for County Beverage. One additional consideration is that the design allowing for a two-server system will cost an additional $10,000 to build.

1. Construct a separate simulation model to evaluate the performance of each design alternative.
2. Execute the simulation for 360 minutes (representing the peak hours of 4 P.M. to 10 P.M.). You may assume that the system begins empty at 4 P.M. You may want to make more than one run with each alternative. Record relevant summary statistics over the simulation runs and use this information to support your final recommendation.

Appendix 12.1   PROBABILITY DISTRIBUTIONS FOR RANDOM VARIABLES

Selecting the appropriate probability distribution to characterize a random variable in a simulation model can be a critical modeling decision. In this appendix, we review several of the distributions from which one can easily generate values with native Excel functionality. For each distribution, the parameters are the values required to completely specify the distribution. The range provides the minimum and maximum values that can be taken by a random variable that follows the given distribution. We also provide a short description of the overall shape and/or common uses of the distribution.

Continuous Probability Distributions

Random variables which can be many possible values (even if these values are discrete) are often modeled with a continuous probability distribution.

Normal Distribution

> **Parameters:** mean (μ), stdev (σ)
> **Range:** $-\infty$ to $+\infty$
> **Excel command:** NORM.INV(RAND(), μ, σ)
> **Description:** The normal distribution is a bell-shaped, symmetric distribution centered at its mean μ. The normal distribution is often a good way to characterize a quantity that is the sum of many independent random variables.
> **Example:** In human resource management, employee performance is often well-represented by a normal distribution. Typically the performance of 68% of employees is within one standard deviation of the average performance and the performance of 95% of the employees is within two standard deviations. Employees with exceptionally low or high performance are rare.

Log-normal Distribution

> **Parameters:** log_mean (m), log_stdev (s)
> **Range:** 0 to +infinity
> **Excel command:** LOGNORM.INV(RAND(), log_mean, log_stdev), where log_mean and log_stdev are the mean and standard deviation of the normally distributed random variable obtained when taking the logarithm of the log-normally distributed random variable.
> **Description:** The log-normal distribution is a unimodal distribution (like the normal distribution) that has a minimum value of 0 and a long right tail (unlike the normal distribution). The logarithm of a log-normally distributed random variable is normally distributed.
> **Example:** The income distribution of a population is often well-described using a log-normal distribution.

Uniform Distribution

Parameters: min (a), max (b)

Range: a to b

Excel command: RAND()*($b - a$) + a

Description: The uniform distribution is appropriate when a random variable is equally likely to be any value between a and b. In the case where little is known about a phenomenon besides its minimum and maximum possible values, the uniform distribution may be a conservative choice to model an uncertain quantity.

Example: A service technician making a house call may quote a four-hour time window in which he will arrive. If the technician is equally likely to arrive any time during this time window, then the arrival time of the technician in this time window may be described with a uniform distribution.

Exponential Distribution

As the exponential distribution with mean μ is equivalent to the gamma distribution with parameters alpha = 1 and beta = ($1/\mu$), an exponential random variable can also be generated by GAMMA. INV(RAND(), 1, $1/\mu$).

Parameters: mean (μ)

Range: 0 to $+\infty$

Excel command: LN(RAND())*($-\mu$)

Description: The exponential distribution is characterized by a mean value that is equal to its standard deviation and a long right tail stretching from a mode value of 0.

Example: The time between events, such as customer arrivals or customer defaults on bill payment, is commonly modeled with an exponential distribution. An exponential random variable possesses the "memoryless" property: the probability that there will be 25 or more minutes between customer arrivals if 10 minutes have passed since the last customer arrival is the same as the probability that there will be more than 15 minutes until the next arrival if a customer just arrived. That is, the probability of a customer arrival occurring in the next X minutes does not depend on how long it's been since the last arrival.

Gamma Distribution

Parameters: alpha (α), beta (β)

Range: 0 to +infinity

Excel command: GAMMA.INV(RAND(), alpha, beta)

Description: The gamma distribution has a very flexible shape controlled by the values of alpha and beta. The gamma distribution is useful in modeling an uncertain quantity that can be as small as zero but can also realize large values.

Example: The time it takes for α events to occur when the mean time between events is $1/\beta$ can be described by a gamma distribution.

Beta Distribution

Parameters: shape1 (α), shape2 (β), min (A), max (B)

Range: A to B

Excel command: BETA.INV(RAND(), α, β, A, B)

Description: The beta distribution has a very flexible shape that can be manipulated by adjusting α and β. The beta distribution is useful in modeling an uncertain quantity that has a known minimum value A and maximum value B.

Example: Setting $A = 0$ and $B = 1$, the beta distribution can be used to describe the likelihood of values for the true proportion of drivers in an age group who would favor one model of car over another.

Triangular Distribution

Parameters: min (a), likely (m), max (b)

Range: a to b

Excel command: IF(random < ($m - a$)/($b-a$), a + SQRT(($b-a$)*($m-a$)*random), b − SQRT(($b-a$)*($b-m$)*(1-random))) where *random* refers to a single cell containing =RAND()

Description: The triangular distribution is often used to subjectively assess uncertainty when little is known about a random variable besides its range, but it is thought to have a single mode. The distri bution is shaped like a triangle with vertices at a, m, and b.

Example: In corporate finance, a triangular distribution may be used to model a project's revenue growth in a net present value analysis if the analyst can reliably provide the minimum, most likely, and maximum estimates of growth.

Discrete Probability Distributions

Random variables which can be only a relatively small number of discrete values are often best modeled with a discrete distribution. The appropriate choice of discrete distribution relies on the specific situation. For discrete distributions, we provide the parameters required to specify the distribution, the possible values taken by a random variable that follows the distribution, and a short description of the distribution and an example of a possible application.

Bernoulli Distribution

As the Bernoulli distribution with probability of success p is equivalent to the binomial distribution with a single trial and probability of success p, a Bernoulli random variable can also be generated by BINOM. INV(1, p, RAND()).

Parameters: prob (p)
Possible values: 0 (event doesn't occur) or 1 (event occurs)
Excel command: IF(RAND() $< p$, 1, 0)
Description: A Bernoulli random variable corresponds to whether or not an event successfully occurs given a probability p of successfully occurring.
Example: Whether or not a particular stock increases in value over a defined length of time is a Bernoulli random variable.

Binomial Distribution

Parameters: trials (n), prob (p)
Possible values: 0, 1, 2, . . . , n
Excel command: BINOM.INV(n, p, RAND())
Description: A binomial random variable corresponds to the number of times an event successfully occurs in n trials, and the probability of a success at each trial is p and independent of whether a success occurs on other trials. Note that for $n = 1$, the binomial is equivalent to the Bernoulli distribution.
Example: In a portfolio of 20 similar stocks, each of which has the same probability of increasing in value of $p = 0.6$, the total number of stocks that increase in value can be described by a binomial distribution with parameters $n = 20$ and $p = 0.6$.

Integer Uniform Distribution

Parameters: lower (l), upper (u)
Possible values: l, $l + 1$, $l + 2$, . . . , $u - 2$, $u - 1$, u
Excel command: RANDBETWEEN(l, u)
Description: An integer uniform random variable assumes that the integer values between l and u are equally likely.
Example: The number of philanthropy volunteers from a class of 10 students may be an integer uniform variable with values 0, 1, 2, . . . , 10.

Discrete Uniform Distribution

Parameters: set of values $\{v_1, v_2, v_3, . . . , v_k\}$
Possible values: $v_1, v_2, v_3, . . . , v_k$
Excel command: CHOOSE(RANDBETWEEN(1, k), $v_1, v_2, . . . , v_k$)
Description: A discrete uniform random variable is equally likely to be any of the specified set of values $\{v_1, v_2, v_3, . . . , v_k\}$.
Example: Consider six envelopes containing \$1, \$5, \$10, \$20, \$50, \$100. If the game show reward that a contestant receives is randomly selected from one of these six, then the reward is a discrete uniform random variable with values $\{1, 5, 10, 20, 50, 100\}$.

Custom Discrete Distribution

Parameters: set of values $\{v_1, v_2, v_3, \ldots, v_k\}$ and corresponding weights $\{w_1, w_2, w_3, \ldots, w_k\}$ where $\sum_{j=1}^{k} w_j = 1$

Possible values: $v_1, v_2, v_3, \ldots, v_k$

Excel command: Use the RAND() function in conjunction with the VLOOKUP function referencing a table in which each row lists a possible value and a segment of the interval [0,1) representing the likelihood of the corresponding value. Figure 12.7 illustrates the implementation of a custom discrete distribution for direct labor cost in the Sanotronics LLC problem.

Description: A custom discrete distribution can be used to create a tailored distribution to model a discrete, uncertain quantity. The value of a custom discrete random variable is equal to the value v_i with probability w_i.

Example: Analysis of daily sales for the past 50 days at a car dealership shows that on 2 days no cars were sold, on 5 days one car was sold, on 9 days two cars were sold, on 24 days three cars were sold, on 7 days four cars were sold, and on 3 days five cars were sold. We can estimate the probability distribution of daily sales using the relative frequencies. An estimate of the probability that no cars are sold on a given day is 2/50 = 0.04, an estimate of the probability the one car is sold is 5/50 = 0.10, and so on. Daily sales may then be described by a custom discrete distribution with values of $\{0, 1, 2, 3, 4, 5\}$ with respective weights of $\{0.04, 0.10, 0.18, 0.48, 0.14, 0.06\}$.

Appendix 12.2   SIMULATION WITH ANALYTIC SOLVER

MODEL *file*

ButlerAS

In Section 12.3 we constructed a spreadsheet simulation model to analyze the inventory policy for the Butler Internet Company. This simulation model was constructed using only native Excel functionality. The use of specialized simulation packages facilitates the construction and analysis of simulation models. In this appendix, we demonstrate how Analytic Solver V2017 can be used to execute the Butler simulation model.

Formulating a Model in Analytic Solver

The first steps for building an Excel simulation model are very similar whether using native Excel functionality or Analytic Solver. As in Section 12.3, we begin by entering the problem data and cell formulas into the top portion of the worksheet. For the Butler model, we must enter the following parameters: gross profit per unit, holding cost per unit, shortage cost per unit, as well as the mean and standard deviation of the normally distributed demand. The controllable input (replenishment level) is entered and cell formulas are entered to compute sales, gross profit, holding cost, shortage cost, and net profit.

Instead of constructing a table of simulation trials and manually collecting summary statistics, Analytic Solver provides functionality to ease the process of executing simulation trials and analyzing the output. Recall that monthly demand is a random variable in the Butler problem. Analytic Solver refers to random variables as uncertain variables. Analytic Solver allows you to characterize each cell containing an uncertain variable with a distribution that describes its possible values and the corresponding likelihood of these values.

Generating Values for Butler's Uncertain Demand

We are now ready to define the probability distribution for the demand for Butler's routers.

Step 1. Select cell B7
Step 2. Click the **Analytic Solver** tab in the Ribbon
Step 3. Click **Distributions** in the **Simulation Model** group
　　　　　Select **Common** and click **Normal**
Step 4. When the $B$7 dialog box appears, in the **Parameters** area enter *E6* in the box to the right of **mean** and *E7* in the box to the right of **stdev** (see Figure 12.17)
Step 5. Click **Save**

FIGURE 12.17   NORMAL DISTRIBUTION FOR ROUTER DEMAND

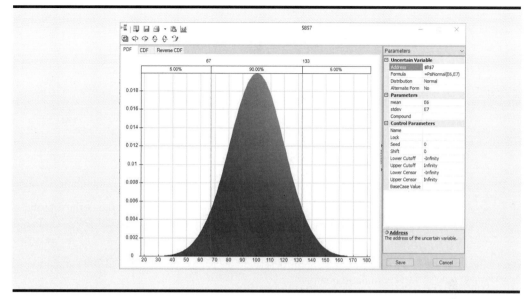

FIGURE 12.18   FORMULA VIEW OF BUTLER SIMULATION MODEL

	A	B	C	D	E
1	**Butler**				
2					
3	**Parameters**				
4	Gross Profit per Unit	50			
5	Holding Cost per Unit	15		**Demand (Normal Distribution)**	
6	Shortage Cost per Unit	30		Mean	100
7	Demand	=PsiNormal(E6, E7)		Standard Deviation	20
8					
9	**Model**				
10	Replenishment Level (Q)	140			
11	Sales	=MIN(B7,B10)			
12	Gross Profit	=B11*B4			
13	Holding Cost	=IF(B10>B7,(B10-B7)*B5,0)			
14	Shortage Cost	=IF(B7>B10,(B7-B10)*B6,0)			
15	Net Profit	=B12-B13-B14			

Figure 12.18 summarizes the construction of the model at this stage. Observe that Analytic Solver has placed the formula =PsiNormal(E6, E7) in cell B7, and pressing the F9 key causes the spreadsheet to generate a new value for demand from a normal distribution with mean of 100 units and standard deviation of 20 units.

Tracking Output for Butler

After defining the distribution for demand, we are ready to track the simulation output. The following steps show this process for cell B15, which is the cell calculating Butler's monthly net profit:

Step 1. Select cell B15
Step 2. Click the **Analytic Solver** tab in the Ribbon
Step 3. Click **Results** in the **Simulation Model** group
Select **Output**, and click **In Cell**

This procedure appends the formula in cell B15 with "+PsiOutput()" which triggers Analytic Solver to record the cell's value for each of the simulation trials. By collecting the value of net profit resulting from each simulation trial, Analytic Solver can then create a distribution of net profit.

Setting Simulation Options

Increasing the number of trials per simulation reduces the error in estimating the output.

For the Butler simulation, we only need to specify the number of trials.

Step 1. Click the **Analytic Solver** tab in the Ribbon
Step 2. In the **Tools** group, enter *1000* in the **Trials**: box

Running the Simulation

For each of the 1000 simulation trials, Analytic Solver automatically repeats three tasks:

1. A value is generated for demand according to the defined probability distributions.
2. A new simulated net profit is computed based on the new value of demand.
3. The new simulated net profit is recorded.

When the interactive simulation in Analytic Solver is activated, the spreadsheet will automatically rerun the simulation whenever the spreadsheet is changed or the F9 key is pressed.

The following steps describe how to execute the set of 1000 simulation trials and to analyze simulation output:

Step 1. Click the **Analytic Solver** tab in the Ribbon
Step 2. Click the arrow under **Simulate** from the **Solve Action** group
From the drop-down menu that appears, select **Interactive**

Note that the minimum and maximum values of net profit will tend to be more extreme as the number of simulation trials increases.

When the run of 1000 trials is complete, Analytic Solver displays the $B$15 dialog box in Figure 12.19, which shows a frequency distribution of Butler's monthly net profit values obtained over the 1000 simulation trials (months). We see that the mean monthly net profit in this simulation is $4,383.58 and the standard deviation of monthly net profit is $1,265.25. From Figure 12.19, we also observe that 5% the simulations resulted in a net profit less than $2,263.58 and 5% of the simulations resulted in a net profit larger than $6,502.87. The simulation results will vary slightly each time you perform another set of 1000 trials (by pressing the F9 key) because different random numbers will be used to generate the inputs.

FIGURE 12.19   BUTLER SIMULATION OUTPUT

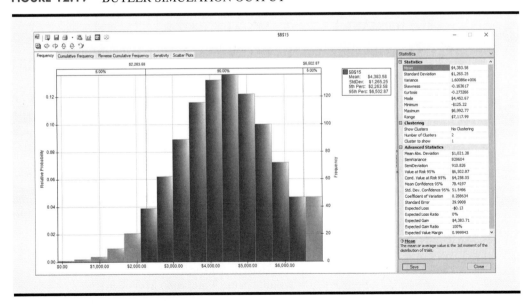

CHAPTER 13

Decision Analysis

CONTENTS

Decision analysis can be used to develop an optimal strategy when a decision maker is faced with several decision alternatives and an uncertain or risk-filled pattern of future events. For example, Ohio Edison used decision analysis to choose the best type of particulate control equipment for coal-fired generating units when it faced future uncertainties concerning sulfur content restrictions, construction costs, and so on. The State of North Carolina used decision analysis in evaluating whether to implement a medical screening test to detect metabolic disorders in newborns. The Management Science in Action, Natural Resource Management, discusses the use of decision analysis to evaluate alternative actions to protect endangered species.

Even when a careful decision analysis has been conducted, the uncertain future events make the final consequence uncertain. In some cases, the selected decision alternative may provide good or excellent results. In other cases, a relatively unlikely future event may occur, causing the selected decision alternative to provide only fair or even poor results. The risk associated with any decision alternative is a direct result of the uncertainty associated with the final consequence. A good decision analysis includes careful consideration of risk. Through risk analysis the decision maker is provided with probability information about the favorable as well as the unfavorable consequences that may occur.

We begin the study of decision analysis by considering problems that involve reasonably few decision alternatives and reasonably few possible future events. Influence diagrams and payoff tables are introduced to provide a structure for the decision problem and to illustrate the fundamentals of decision analysis. We then introduce decision trees to show the sequential nature of decision problems. Decision trees are used to analyze more complex problems and to identify an optimal sequence of decisions, referred to as an optimal decision strategy. Sensitivity analysis shows how changes in various aspects of the problem affect the recommended decision alternative.

MANAGEMENT SCIENCE IN ACTION

NATURAL RESOURCE MANAGEMENT*

Caution must be exercised when making decisions on what measures are taken to protect an endangered or threatened species. A conservative action may not be sufficient to save the species, while an aggressive action may have serious economic consequences, and decision analysis has long been used to strike a balance of these two concerns. However, in recent years policy analysts have been giving increasing consideration to another issue—the potential deleterious long-run effects—the decision ultimately may have on the endangered or threatened species' ecosystem. Conservationists and policy analysts are now recognizing that the resilience of an ecological system (the degree of disturbance that an ecological system can absorb without changing substantially) must be an important consideration when making these decisions.

In research funded by the U.S. Geological Survey and the U.S. Fish and Wildlife Service, B. Ken Williams of the Wildlife Society and Fred A. Johnson and James D. Nichols of the U.S. Geological Survey have developed a means for using decision analysis that considers resilience of an ecological system when assessing alternative strategies for protecting an endangered or threatened species. Although the resilience of the ecological system and the intended ecological and social benefits of various strategies for protecting a species are difficult to measure, this approach strives to consider them when selecting from various alternative strategies. Incorporating the resilience of the ecological system into decision analysis of alternative strategies for protecting endangered and threatened species promises to lead to actions that simultaneously enhance the probability of the species' survival and reduce the risk to the ecological system.

*Based on Fred A. Johnson, B. Ken Williams, and James D. Nichols, "Resilience Thinking and a Decision-Analytic Approach to Conservation: Strange Bedfellows or Essential Partners?" *Ecology and Society* 17, no. 4 (2013): 28.

FIGURE 13.2 DECISION TREE FOR THE PDC CONDOMINIUM PROJECT
(PAYOFFS IN $ MILLIONS)

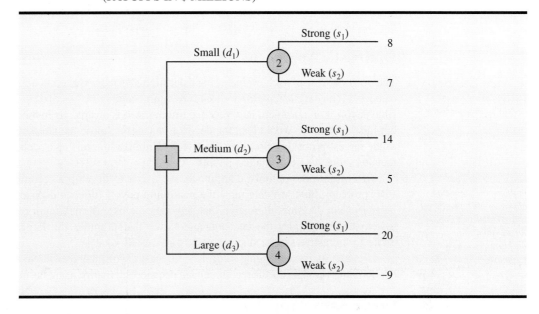

implemented, either state of nature s_1 or s_2 will occur. The number at each endpoint of the tree indicates the payoff associated with a particular sequence. For example, the topmost payoff of 8 indicates that an $8 million profit is anticipated if PDC constructs a small condominium complex (d_1) and demand turns out to be strong (s_1). The next payoff of 7 indicates an anticipated profit of $7 million if PDC constructs a small condominium complex (d_1) and demand turns out to be weak (s_2). Thus, the decision tree provides a graphical depiction of the sequences of decision alternatives and states of nature that provide the six possible payoffs for PDC.

If you have a payoff table, you can develop a decision tree. Try Problem 1, part (a).

The decision tree in Figure 13.2 shows four nodes, numbered 1–4. Squares are used to depict decision nodes and circles are used to depict chance nodes. Thus, node 1 is a decision node, and nodes 2, 3, and 4 are chance nodes. The **branches** connect the nodes; those leaving the decision node correspond to the decision alternatives. The branches leaving each chance node correspond to the states of nature. The payoffs are shown at the end of the states-of-nature branches. We now turn to the question: How can the decision maker use the information in the payoff table or the decision tree to select the best decision alternative? Several approaches may be used.

NOTES AND COMMENTS

1. The first step in solving a complex problem is to decompose the problem into a series of smaller subproblems. Decision trees provide a useful way to decompose a problem and illustrate the sequential nature of the decision process.

2. People often view the same problem from different perspectives. Thus, the discussion regarding the development of a decision tree may provide additional insight about the problem.

13.2 DECISION MAKING WITHOUT PROBABILITIES

In this section we consider approaches to decision making that do not require knowledge of the probabilities of the states of nature. These approaches are appropriate in situations in which the decision maker has little confidence in his or her ability to assess the probabilities,

Many people think of a good decision as one in which the consequence is good. However, in some instances, a good, well-thought-out decision may still lead to a bad or undesirable consequence, while a poor, ill-conceived decision may still lead to a good or desirable consequence.

or in which a simple best-case and worst-case analysis is desirable. Because different approaches sometimes lead to different decision recommendations, the decision maker must understand the approaches available and then select the specific approach that, according to the judgment of the decision maker, is the most appropriate.

Optimistic Approach

The **optimistic approach** evaluates each decision alternative in terms of the *best* payoff that can occur. The decision alternative that is recommended is the one that provides the best possible payoff. For a problem in which maximum profit is desired, as in the PDC problem, the optimistic approach would lead the decision maker to choose the alternative corresponding to the largest profit. For problems involving minimization, this approach leads to choosing the alternative with the smallest payoff.

For a maximization problem, the optimistic approach often is referred to as the maximax approach; for a minimization problem, the corresponding terminology is minimin.

To illustrate the optimistic approach, we use it to develop a recommendation for the PDC problem. First, we determine the maximum payoff for each decision alternative; then we select the decision alternative that provides the overall maximum payoff. These steps systematically identify the decision alternative that provides the largest possible profit. Table 13.2 illustrates these steps.

Because 20, corresponding to d_3, is the largest payoff, the decision to construct the large condominium complex is the recommended decision alternative using the optimistic approach.

Conservative Approach

For a maximization problem, the conservative approach is often referred to as the maximin approach; for a minimization problem, the corresponding terminology is minimax.

The **conservative approach** evaluates each decision alternative in terms of the *worst* payoff that can occur. The decision alternative recommended is the one that provides the best of the worst possible payoffs. For a problem in which the output measure is profit, as in the PDC problem, the conservative approach would lead the decision maker to choose the alternative that maximizes the minimum possible profit that could be obtained. For problems involving minimization, this approach identifies the alternative that will minimize the maximum payoff.

To illustrate the conservative approach, we use it to develop a recommendation for the PDC problem. First, we identify the minimum payoff for each of the decision alternatives; then we select the decision alternative that maximizes the minimum payoff. Table 13.3 illustrates these steps for the PDC problem.

Because 7, corresponding to d_1, yields the maximum of the minimum payoffs, the decision alternative of a small condominium complex is recommended. This decision approach is considered conservative because it identifies the worst possible payoffs and then recommends the decision alternative that avoids the possibility of extremely "bad" payoffs. In the

TABLE 13.2   MAXIMUM PAYOFF FOR EACH PDC DECISION ALTERNATIVE

Decision Alternative	Maximum Payoff	
Small complex, d_1	8	
Medium complex, d_2	14	
Large complex, d_3	20 ←	Maximum of the maximum payoff values

TABLE 13.3   MINIMUM PAYOFF FOR EACH PDC DECISION ALTERNATIVE

Decision Alternative	Minimum Payoff	
Small complex, d_1	7 ←	Maximum of the minimum payoff values
Medium complex, d_2	5	
Large complex, d_3	−9	

conservative approach, PDC is guaranteed a profit of at least $7 million. Although PDC may make more, it *cannot* make less than $7 million.

Minimax Regret Approach

In decision analysis, **regret** is the difference between the payoff associated with a particular decision alternative and the payoff associated with the decision that would yield the most desirable payoff for a given state of nature. Thus, regret represents how much potential payoff one would forgo by selecting a particular decision alternative given that a specific state of nature will occur. This is why regret is often referred to as **opportunity loss**.

As its name implies, under the **minimax regret approach** to decision making one would choose the decision alternative that minimizes the maximum state of regret that could occur over all possible states of nature. This approach is neither purely optimistic nor purely conservative. Let us illustrate the minimax regret approach by showing how it can be used to select a decision alternative for the PDC problem.

Suppose that PDC constructs a small condominium complex (d_1) and demand turns out to be strong (s_1). Table 13.1 showed that the resulting profit for PDC would be $8 million. However, given that the strong demand state of nature (s_1) has occurred, we realize that the decision to construct a large condominium complex (d_3), yielding a profit of $20 million, would have been the best decision. The difference between the payoff for the best decision alternative ($20 million) and the payoff for the decision to construct a small condominium complex ($8 million) is the regret or opportunity loss associated with decision alternative d_1 when state of nature s_1 occurs; thus, for this case, the opportunity loss or regret is $20 million − $8 million = $12 million. Similarly, if PDC makes the decision to construct a medium condominium complex (d_2) and the strong demand state of nature (s_1) occurs, the opportunity loss, or regret, associated with d_2 would be $20 million − $14 million = $6 million.

In general, the following expression represents the opportunity loss, or regret:

$$R_{ij} = |V_j^* - V_{ij}| \qquad (13.1)$$

where

> R_{ij} = the regret associated with decision alternative d_i and state of nature s_j
>
> V_j^* = the payoff value[1] corresponding to the best decision for the state of nature s_j
>
> V_{ij} = the payoff corresponding to decision alternative d_i and state of nature s_j

Note the role of the absolute value in equation (13.1). For minimization problems, the best payoff, V_j^*, is the smallest entry in column j. Because this value always is less than or equal to V_{ij}, the absolute value of the difference between V_j^* and V_{ij} ensures that the regret is always the magnitude of the difference.

Using equation (13.1) and the payoffs in Table 13.1, we can compute the regret associated with each combination of decision alternative d_i and state of nature s_j. Because the PDC problem is a maximization problem, V_j^* will be the largest entry in column j of the payoff table. Thus, to compute the regret, we simply subtract each entry in a column from the largest entry in the column. Table 13.4 shows the opportunity loss, or regret, table for the PDC problem.

The next step in applying the minimax regret approach is to list the maximum regret for each decision alternative; Table 13.5 shows the results for the PDC problem. Selecting the decision alternative with the *minimum* of the *maximum* regret values—hence, the name *minimax regret*—yields the minimax regret decision. For the PDC problem, the alternative

---

[1] In maximization problems, V_j^* will be the largest entry in column j of the payoff table. In minimization problems, V_j^* will be the smallest entry in column j of the payoff table.

TABLE 13.4   OPPORTUNITY LOSS, OR REGRET, TABLE FOR THE PDC CONDOMINIUM PROJECT ($ MILLIONS)

	State of Nature	
Decision Alternative	**Strong Demand s_1**	**Weak Demand s_2**
Small complex, d_1	12	0
Medium complex, d_2	6	2
Large complex, d_3	0	16

TABLE 13.5   MAXIMUM REGRET FOR EACH PDC DECISION ALTERNATIVE

Decision Alternative	**Maximum Regret**	
Small complex, d_1	12	
Medium complex, d_2	6	← Minimum of the maximum regret
Large complex, d_3	16	

For practice in developing a decision recommendation using the optimistic, conservative, and minimax regret approaches, try Problem 1, part (b).

to construct the medium condominium complex, with a corresponding maximum regret of $6 million, is the recommended minimax regret decision.

Note that the three approaches discussed in this section provide different recommendations, which in itself isn't bad. It simply reflects the difference in decision-making philosophies that underlie the various approaches. Ultimately, the decision maker will have to choose the most appropriate approach and then make the final decision accordingly. The main criticism of the approaches discussed in this section is that they do not consider any information about the probabilities of the various states of nature. In the next section we discuss an approach that utilizes probability information in selecting a decision alternative.

13.3   DECISION MAKING WITH PROBABILITIES

In many decision-making situations, we can obtain probability assessments for the states of nature. When such probabilities are available, we can use the **expected value approach** to identify the best decision alternative. Let us first define the expected value of a decision alternative and then apply it to the PDC problem.

Let

$$N = \text{the number of states of nature}$$

$$P(s_j) = \text{the probability of state of nature } s_j$$

Because one and only one of the N states of nature can occur, the probabilities must satisfy two conditions:

$$P(s_j) \geq 0 \qquad \text{for all states of nature} \qquad (13.2)$$

$$\sum_{j=1}^{N} P(s_j) = P(s_1) + P(s_2) + \cdots + P(s_N) = 1 \qquad (13.3)$$

The **expected value (EV)** of decision alternative d_i is defined as follows:

$$EV(d_i) = \sum_{j=1}^{N} P(s_j)V_{ij} \qquad (13.4)$$

In words, the expected value of a decision alternative is the sum of weighted payoffs for the decision alternative. The weight for a payoff is the probability of the associated state of nature and therefore the probability that the payoff will occur. Let us return to the PDC problem to see how the expected value approach can be applied.

PDC is optimistic about the potential for the luxury high-rise condominium complex. Suppose that this optimism leads to an initial subjective probability assessment of 0.8 that demand will be strong (s_1) and a corresponding probability of 0.2 that demand will be weak (s_2). Thus, $P(s_1) = 0.8$ and $P(s_2) = 0.2$. Using the payoff values in Table 13.1 and equation (13.4), we compute the expected value for each of the three decision alternatives as follows:

Can you now use the expected value approach to develop a decision recommendation? Try Problem 5.

$$EV(d_1) = 0.8(8) + 0.2(7) \quad = 7.8$$
$$EV(d_2) = 0.8(14) + 0.2(5) \quad = 12.2$$
$$EV(d_3) = 0.8(20) + 0.2(-9) = 14.2$$

Thus, using the expected value approach, we find that the large condominium complex, with an expected value of $14.2 million, is the recommended decision.

The calculations required to identify the decision alternative with the best expected value can be conveniently carried out on a decision tree. Figure 13.3 shows the decision tree for the PDC problem with state-of-nature branch probabilities. Working backward through the decision tree, we first compute the expected value at each chance node. That is, at each chance node, we weight each possible payoff by its probability of occurrence. By doing so, we obtain the expected values for nodes 2, 3, and 4, as shown in Figure 13.4.

Computer packages are available to help in constructing more complex decision trees. See Appendices 13.1 and 13.2.

Because the decision maker controls the branch leaving decision node 1 and because we are trying to maximize the expected profit, the best decision alternative at node 1 is d_3. Thus, the decision tree analysis leads to a recommendation of d_3, with an expected value of $14.2 million. Note that this recommendation is also obtained with the expected value approach in conjunction with the payoff table.

Other decision problems may be substantially more complex than the PDC problem, but if a reasonable number of decision alternatives and states of nature are present, you can use the decision tree approach outlined here. First, draw a decision tree consisting of decision nodes, chance nodes, and branches that describe the sequential nature of the problem. If you use the expected value approach, the next step is to determine the probabilities for each of the states of nature and compute the expected value at each chance node. Then select the

FIGURE 13.3   PDC DECISION TREE WITH STATE-OF-NATURE BRANCH PROBABILITIES

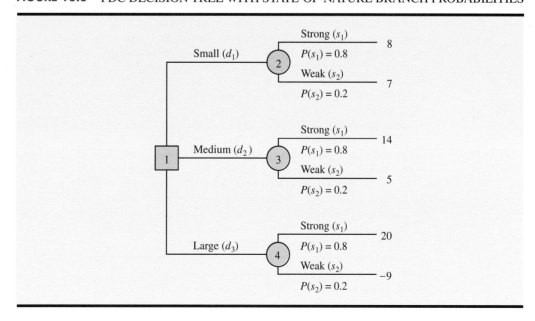

FIGURE 13.4   APPLYING THE EXPECTED VALUE APPROACH USING A DECISION TREE

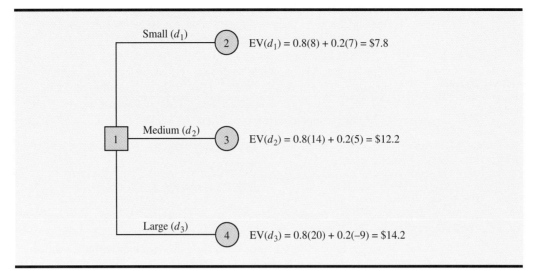

decision branch leading to the chance node with the best expected value. The decision alternative associated with this branch is the recommended decision.

The Management Science in Action, Gushers, Dry Wells, and Decision Analysis, describes the importance of using data in the oil and natural gas industry to accurately estimate the likelihoods and the profit associated with possible outcomes in order to make wise development decisions.

MANAGEMENT SCIENCE IN ACTION

GUSHERS, DRY WELLS, AND DECISION ANALYSIS*

Oil and natural gas are big businesses; nine of the top ten organizations in Fortune's Global 500 are oil and gas companies. The rewards in these industries can be high, but the associated risks are also great. Oil prices at or above $100 per barrel make an oil reservoir with potentially one million barrels of supply appear an enticing development venture. But as Adam Farris, Senior Vice President of Business Development for Drillinginfo, explains, realizing this potential $100 million stream of revenue is not simple. He points out that the acquisition, processing, and interpretation of the seismic data necessary to evaluate the potential well before drilling could cost $30 million. Typical deals involve the procurement of access to thousands of acres of land (a single well may require 120 acres) and land can cost $30,000 per acre. Drilling can cost from $5 million to $10 million for U.S. onshore wells and up to $100 million for offshore drilling. The costs of producing the oil and getting it to market are also substantial. And if the well is drilled and does not produce oil, the company has to incur the costs associated with the acquisition, processing, and interpretation of the seismic data, obtaining access to the land, and drilling with no resulting revenue.

"If you are a major integrated oil and gas company, your profit on $100 million will be $1 million to $12 million (a bit higher for independent operators)," states Farris. "Many will lose money overall. Analytical approaches that impact the success rate of finding or reducing the cost to develop and produce oil and gas can make energy more affordable, safer and environmentally conscious."

Decision analysis provides a means for oil exploration companies to assess the complex data in a systematic manner and extract information from the data that ultimately are used to decide whether to drill in a potential well site. Identifying well sites for which the potential gains exceed the costs and therefore justify the risk of drilling is critical to the economic success of these firms.

*Based on Adam Farris, "How Big Data Is Changing the Oil & Gas Industry," *Analytics* (November/December 2012).

Expected Value of Perfect Information

Suppose that PDC has the opportunity to conduct a market research study that would help evaluate buyer interest in the condominium project and provide information that management could use to improve the probability assessments for the states of nature. To determine the potential value of this information, we begin by supposing that the study could provide *perfect information* regarding the states of nature; that is, we assume for the moment that PDC could determine with certainty, prior to making a decision, which state of nature is going to occur. To make use of this perfect information, we will develop a decision strategy that PDC should follow once it knows which state of nature will occur. A decision strategy is simply a decision rule that specifies the decision alternative to be selected after new information becomes available.

To help determine the decision strategy for PDC, we reproduced PDC's payoff table as Table 13.6. Note that, if PDC knew for sure that state of nature s_1 would occur, the best decision alternative would be d_3, with a payoff of $20 million. Similarly, if PDC knew for sure that state of nature s_2 would occur, the best decision alternative would be d_1, with a payoff of $7 million. Thus, we can state PDC's optimal decision strategy when the perfect information becomes available as follows:

> If s_1, select d_3 and receive a payoff of $20 million.
>
> If s_2, select d_1 and receive a payoff of $7 million.

What is the expected value for this decision strategy? To compute the expected value with perfect information, we return to the original probabilities for the states of nature: $P(s_1) = 0.8$ and $P(s_2) = 0.2$. Thus, there is a 0.8 probability that the perfect information will indicate state of nature s_1, and the resulting decision alternative d_3 will provide a $20 million profit. Similarly, with a 0.2 probability for state of nature s_2, the optimal decision alternative d_1 will provide a $7 million profit. Thus, from equation (13.4) the expected value of the decision strategy that uses perfect information is $0.8(20) + 0.2(7) = 17.4$.

We refer to the expected value of $17.4 million as the *expected value with perfect information* (EVwPI).

Earlier in this section we showed that the recommended decision using the expected value approach is decision alternative d_3, with an expected value of $14.2 million. Because this decision recommendation and expected value computation were made without the benefit of perfect information, $14.2 million is referred to as the *expected value without perfect information* (EVwoPI).

The expected value with perfect information is $17.4 million, and the expected value without perfect information is $14.2; therefore, the expected value of the perfect information (EVPI) is $17.4 − $14.2 = $3.2 million. In other words, $3.2 million represents the additional expected value that can be obtained if perfect information were available about the states of nature.

It would be worth $3.2 million for PDC to learn the level of market acceptance before selecting a decision alternative.

Generally speaking, a market research study will not provide "perfect" information; however, if the market research study is a good one, the information gathered might be worth a sizable portion of the $3.2 million. Given the EVPI of $3.2 million, PDC might seriously consider a market survey as a way to obtain more information about the states of nature.

TABLE 13.6 PAYOFF TABLE FOR THE PDC CONDOMINIUM PROJECT ($ MILLIONS)

	State of Nature	
Decision Alternative	**Strong Demand s_1**	**Weak Demand s_2**
Small complex, d_1	8	7
Medium complex, d_2	14	5
Large complex, d_3	20	−9

In general, the **expected value of perfect information (EVPI)** is computed as follows:

$$EVPI = |EVwPI - EVwoPI| \qquad (13.5)$$

where

EVPI = expected value of perfect information

EVwPI = expected value *with* perfect information about the states of nature

EVwoPI = expected value *without* perfect information about the states of nature

For practice in determining the expected value of perfect information, try Problem 14.

Note the role of the absolute value in equation (13.5). For minimization problems, the expected value with perfect information is always less than or equal to the expected value without perfect information. In this case, EVPI is the magnitude of the difference between EVwPI and EVwoPI, or the absolute value of the difference as shown in equation (13.5).

NOTES AND COMMENTS

1. We restate the *opportunity loss,* or *regret,* table for the PDC problem (see Table 13.4) as follows:

	State of Nature	
	Strong Demand	**Weak Demand**
Decision	s_1	s_2
Small complex, d_1	12	0
Medium complex, d_2	6	2
Large complex, d_3	0	16

Using $P(s_1)$, $P(s_2)$, and the opportunity loss values, we can compute the *expected opportunity loss* (EOL) for each decision alternative. With $P(s_1) = 0.8$ and $P(s_2) = 0.2$, the expected

opportunity loss for each of the three decision alternatives is

$$EOL(d_1) = 0.8(12) + 0.2(0) = 9.6$$
$$EOL(d_2) = 0.8(6) + 0.2(2) = 5.2$$
$$EOL(d_3) = 0.8(0) + 0.2(16) = 3.2$$

Regardless of whether the decision analysis involves maximization or minimization, the *minimum* expected opportunity loss always provides the best decision alternative. Thus, with $EOL(d_3) = 3.2$, d_3 is the recommended decision. In addition, the minimum expected opportunity loss always is *equal to the expected value of perfect information.* That is, EOL(best decision) = EVPI; for the PDC problem, this value is $3.2 million.

13.4 RISK ANALYSIS AND SENSITIVITY ANALYSIS

Risk analysis helps the decision maker recognize the difference between the expected value of a decision alternative and the payoff that may actually occur. **Sensitivity analysis** also helps the decision maker by describing how changes in the state-of-nature probabilities and/or changes in the payoffs affect the recommended decision alternative.

Risk Analysis

A decision alternative and a state of nature combine to generate the payoff associated with a decision. The **risk profile** for a decision alternative shows the possible payoffs along with their associated probabilities.

Let us demonstrate risk analysis and the construction of a risk profile by returning to the PDC condominium construction project. Using the expected value approach, we identified the large condominium complex (d_3) as the best decision alternative. The expected value of $14.2 million for d_3 is based on a 0.8 probability of obtaining a $20 million profit and a 0.2 probability of obtaining a $9 million loss. The 0.8 probability for the $20 million payoff and the 0.2 probability for the $-$9 million payoff provide the risk profile for the large complex decision alternative. This risk profile is shown graphically in Figure 13.5.

FIGURE 13.5 RISK PROFILE FOR THE LARGE COMPLEX DECISION ALTERNATIVE FOR THE PDC CONDOMINIUM PROJECT

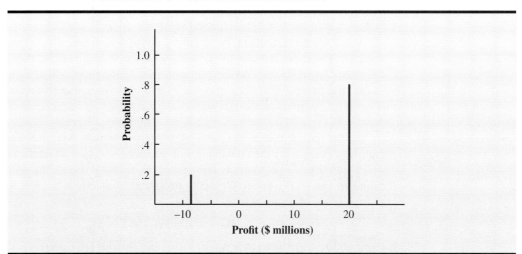

Sometimes a review of the risk profile associated with an optimal decision alternative may cause the decision maker to choose another decision alternative even though the expected value of the other decision alternative is not as good. For example, the risk profile for the medium complex decision alternative (d_2) shows a 0.8 probability for a $14 million payoff and a 0.2 probability for a $5 million payoff. Because no probability of a loss is associated with decision alternative d_2, the medium complex decision alternative would be judged less risky than the large complex decision alternative. As a result, a decision maker might prefer the less risky medium complex decision alternative even though it has an expected value of $2 million less than the large complex decision alternative.

Sensitivity Analysis

Sensitivity analysis can be used to determine how changes in the probabilities for the states of nature or changes in the payoffs affect the recommended decision alternative. In many cases, the probabilities for the states of nature and the payoffs are based on subjective assessments. Sensitivity analysis helps the decision maker understand which of these inputs are critical to the choice of the best decision alternative. If a small change in the value of one of the inputs causes a change in the recommended decision alternative, the solution to the decision analysis problem is sensitive to that particular input. Extra effort and care should be taken to make sure the input value is as accurate as possible. On the other hand, if a modest-to-large change in the value of one of the inputs does not cause a change in the recommended decision alternative, the solution to the decision analysis problem is not sensitive to that particular input. No extra time or effort would be needed to refine the estimated input value.

One approach to sensitivity analysis is to select different values for the probabilities of the states of nature and the payoffs and then resolve the decision analysis problem. If the recommended decision alternative changes, we know that the solution is sensitive to the changes made. For example, suppose that in the PDC problem the probability for a strong demand is revised to 0.2 and the probability for a weak demand is revised to 0.8. Would the recommended decision alternative change? Using $P(s_1) = 0.2$, $P(s_2) = 0.8$, and equation (13.4), the revised expected values for the three decision alternatives are

$$EV(d_1) = 0.2(8) + 0.8(7) = 7.2$$
$$EV(d_2) = 0.2(14) + 0.8(5) = 6.8$$
$$EV(d_3) = 0.2(20) + 0.8(-9) = -3.2$$

With these probability assessments, the recommended decision alternative is to construct a small condominium complex (d_1), with an expected value of \$7.2 million. The probability of strong demand is only 0.2, so constructing the large condominium complex (d_3) is the least preferred alternative, with an expected value of $-\$3.2$ million (a loss).

Thus, when the probability of strong demand is large, PDC should build the large complex; when the probability of strong demand is small, PDC should build the small complex. Obviously, we could continue to modify the probabilities of the states of nature and learn even more about how changes in the probabilities affect the recommended decision alternative. The drawback to this approach is the numerous calculations required to evaluate the effect of several possible changes in the state-of-nature probabilities.

Computer software packages for decision analysis make it easy to calculate these revised scenarios.

For the special case of two states of nature, a graphical procedure can be used to determine how changes for the probabilities of the states of nature affect the recommended decision alternative. To demonstrate this procedure, we let p denote the probability of state of nature s_1; that is, $P(s_1) = p$. With only two states of nature in the PDC problem, the probability of state of nature s_2 is

$$P(s_2) = 1 - P(s_1) = 1 - p$$

Using equation (13.4) and the payoff values in Table 13.1, we determine the expected value for decision alternative d_1 as follows:

$$
\begin{aligned}
EV(d_1) &= P(s_1)(8) + P(s_2)(7) \\
&= p(8) + (1-p)(7) \\
&= 8p + 7 - 7p = p + 7
\end{aligned}
\tag{13.6}
$$

Repeating the expected value computations for decision alternatives d_2 and d_3, we obtain expressions for the expected value of each decision alternative as a function of p:

$$EV(d_2) = 9p + 5 \tag{13.7}$$

$$EV(d_3) = 29p - 9 \tag{13.8}$$

Thus, we have developed three equations that show the expected value of the three decision alternatives as a function of the probability of state of nature s_1.

We continue by developing a graph with values of p on the horizontal axis and the associated EVs on the vertical axis. Because equations (13.6), (13.7), and (13.8) are linear equations, the graph of each equation is a straight line. For each equation, we can obtain the line by identifying two points that satisfy the equation and drawing a line through the points. For instance, if we let $p = 0$ in equation (13.6), $EV(d_1) = 7$. Then, letting $p = 1$, $EV(d_1) = 8$. Connecting these two points, (0,7) and (1,8), provides the line labeled $EV(d_1)$ in Figure 13.6. Similarly, we obtain the lines labeled $EV(d_2)$ and $EV(d_3)$; these lines are the graphs of equations (13.7) and (13.8), respectively.

Figure 13.6 shows how the recommended decision changes as p, the probability of the strong demand state of nature (s_1), changes. Note that for small values of p, decision alternative d_1 (small complex) provides the largest expected value and is thus the recommended decision. When the value of p increases to a certain point, decision alternative d_2 (medium complex) provides the largest expected value and is the recommended decision. Finally, for large values of p, decision alternative d_3 (large complex) becomes the recommended decision.

The value of p for which the expected values of d_1 and d_2 are equal is the value of p corresponding to the intersection of the $EV(d_1)$ and the $EV(d_2)$ lines. To determine this value, we set $EV(d_1) = EV(d_2)$ and solve for the value of p:

$$
\begin{aligned}
p + 7 &= 9p + 5 \\
8p &= 2 \\
p &= \frac{2}{8} = 0.25
\end{aligned}
$$

FIGURE 13.6 EXPECTED VALUE FOR THE PDC DECISION ALTERNATIVES AS A FUNCTION OF p

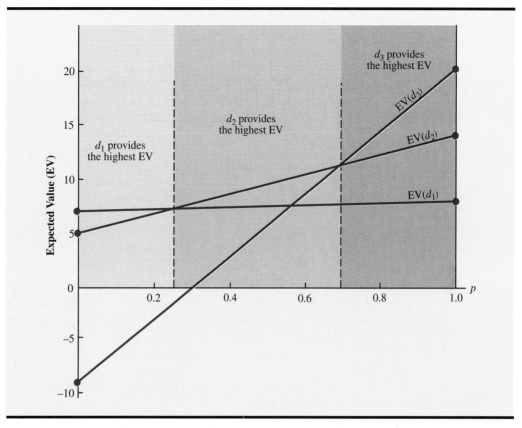

Graphical sensitivity analysis shows how changes in the probabilities for the states of nature affect the recommended decision alternative. Try Problem 8.

Hence, when $p = 0.25$, decision alternatives d_1 and d_2 provide the same expected value. Repeating this calculation for the value of p corresponding to the intersection of the $EV(d_2)$ and $EV(d_3)$ lines, we obtain $p = 0.70$.

Using Figure 13.6, we can conclude that decision alternative d_1 provides the largest expected value for $p \leq 0.25$, decision alternative d_2 provides the largest expected value for $0.25 \leq p \leq 0.70$, and decision alternative d_3 provides the largest expected value for $p \geq 0.70$. Because p is the probability of state of nature s_1 and $(1 - p)$ is the probability of state of nature s_2, we now have the sensitivity analysis information that tells us how changes in the state-of-nature probabilities affect the recommended decision alternative.

Sensitivity analysis calculations can also be made for the values of the payoffs. In the original PDC problem, the expected values for the three decision alternatives were as follows: $EV(d_1) = 7.8$, $EV(d_2) = 12.2$, and $EV(d_3) = 14.2$. Decision alternative d_3 (large complex) was recommended. Note that decision alternative d_2 with $EV(d_2) = 12.2$ was the second best decision alternative. Decision alternative d_3 will remain the optimal decision alternative as long as $EV(d_3)$ is greater than or equal to the expected value of the second best decision alternative. Thus, decision alternative d_3 will remain the optimal decision alternative as long as

$$EV(d_3) \geq 12.2 \qquad (13.9)$$

Let

S = the payoff of decision alternative d_3 when demand is strong
W = the payoff of decision alternative d_3 when demand is weak

Using $P(s_1) = 0.8$ and $P(s_2) = 0.2$, the general expression for EV(d_3) is

$$EV(d_3) = 0.8S + 0.2W \tag{13.10}$$

Assuming that the payoff for d_3 stays at its original value of $-\$9$ million when demand is weak, the large complex decision alternative will remain optimal as long as

$$EV(d_3) = 0.8S + 0.2(-9) \geq 12.2 \tag{13.11}$$

Solving for S, we have

$$0.8S - 1.8 \geq 12.2$$
$$0.8S \geq 14$$
$$S \geq 17.5$$

Recall that when demand is strong, decision alternative d_3 has an estimated payoff of $\$20$ million. The preceding calculation shows that decision alternative d_3 will remain optimal as long as the payoff for d_3 when demand is strong is at least $\$17.5$ million.

Assuming that the payoff for d_3 when demand is strong stays at its original value of $\$20$ million, we can make a similar calculation to learn how sensitive the optimal solution is with regard to the payoff for d_3 when demand is weak. Returning to the expected value calculation of equation (13.10), we know that the large complex decision alternative will remain optimal as long as

$$EV(d_3) = 0.8(20) + 0.2W \geq 12.2 \tag{13.12}$$

Solving for W, we have

$$16 + 0.2 \geq 12.2$$
$$0.2W \geq -3.8$$
$$W \geq -19$$

Recall that when demand is weak, decision alternative d_3 has an estimated payoff of $-\$9$ million. The preceding calculation shows that decision alternative d_3 will remain optimal as long as the payoff for d_3 when demand is weak is at least $-\$19$ million.

Based on this sensitivity analysis, we conclude that the payoffs for the large complex decision alternative (d_3) could vary considerably, and d_3 would remain the recommended decision alternative. Thus, we conclude that the optimal solution for the PDC decision problem is not particularly sensitive to the payoffs for the large complex decision alternative. We note, however, that this sensitivity analysis has been conducted based on only one change at a time. That is, only one payoff was changed and the probabilities for the states of nature remained $P(s_1) = 0.8$ and $P(s_2) = 0.2$. Note that similar sensitivity analysis calculations can be made for the payoffs associated with the small complex decision alternative d_1 and the medium complex decision alternative d_2. However, in these cases, decision alternative d_3 remains optimal only if the changes in the payoffs for decision alternatives d_1 and d_2 meet the requirements that EV(d_1) ≤ 14.2 and EV(d_2) ≤ 14.2.

Sensitivity analysis can assist management in deciding whether more time and effort should be spent obtaining better estimates of payoffs and probabilities.

NOTES AND COMMENTS

1. Some decision analysis software automatically provides the risk profiles for the optimal decision alternative. These packages also allow the user to obtain the risk profiles for other decision alternatives. After comparing the risk profiles, a decision maker may decide to select a decision alternative with a good risk profile even though the expected value of the decision alternative is not as good as the optimal decision alternative.

2. A *tornado diagram*, a graphical display, is particularly helpful when several inputs combine to determine the value of the optimal solution. By varying each input over its range of values, we obtain information about how each input affects the value of the optimal solution. To display this information, a bar is constructed for the input, with the width of the bar showing how the input affects the value of the optimal solution. The widest bar corresponds to the input that is most sensitive. The bars are arranged in a graph with the widest bar at the top, resulting in a graph that has the appearance of a tornado.

13.5 DECISION ANALYSIS WITH SAMPLE INFORMATION

In applying the expected value approach, we showed how probability information about the states of nature affects the expected value calculations and thus the decision recommendation. Frequently, decision makers have preliminary or **prior probability** assessments for the states of nature that are the best probability values available at that time. However, to make the best possible decision, the decision maker may want to seek additional information about the states of nature. This new information can be used to revise or update the prior probabilities so that the final decision is based on more accurate probabilities for the states of nature. Most often, additional information is obtained through experiments designed to provide **sample information** about the states of nature. Raw material sampling, product testing, and market research studies are examples of experiments (or studies) that may enable management to revise or update the state-of-nature probabilities. These revised probabilities are called **posterior probabilities**.

Let us return to the PDC problem and assume that management is considering a 6-month market research study designed to learn more about potential market acceptance of the PDC condominium project. Management anticipates that the market research study will provide one of the following two results:

1. Favorable report: A substantial number of the individuals contacted express interest in purchasing a PDC condominium.
2. Unfavorable report: Very few of the individuals contacted express interest in purchasing a PDC condominium.

Influence Diagram

By introducing the possibility of conducting a market research study, the PDC problem becomes more complex. The influence diagram for the expanded PDC problem is shown in Figure 13.7. Note that the two decision nodes correspond to the research study and the complex-size decisions. The two chance nodes correspond to the research study results and demand for the condominiums. Finally, the consequence node is the profit. From the arcs of the influence diagram, we see that demand influences both the research study results and profit. Although demand is currently unknown to PDC, some level of demand for the condominiums already exists in the Pittsburgh area. If existing demand is strong, the research study is likely to find a substantial number of individuals who express an interest in purchasing a condominium. However, if the existing demand is weak, the research study is more likely to find a substantial number of individuals who express little interest in purchasing a condominium. In this sense, existing demand for the condominiums will influence the research study results, and clearly, demand will have an influence upon PDC's profit.

The arc from the research study decision node to the complex-size decision node indicates that the research study decision precedes the complex-size decision. No arc spans from

FIGURE 13.7   INFLUENCE DIAGRAM FOR THE PDC PROBLEM WITH SAMPLE
INFORMATION

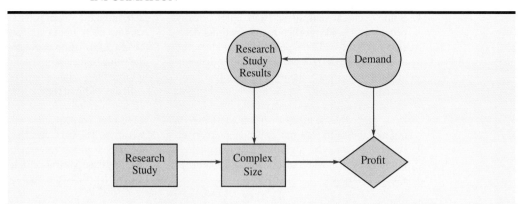

the research study decision node to the research study results node because the decision to conduct the research study does not actually influence the research study results. The decision to conduct the research study makes the research study results available, but it does not influence the results of the research study. Finally, the complex-size node and the demand node both influence profit. Note that if a stated cost to conduct the research study were given, the decision to conduct the research study would also influence profit. In such a case, we would need to add an arc from the research study decision node to the profit node to show the influence that the research study cost would have on profit.

Decision Tree

The decision tree for the PDC problem with sample information shows the logical sequence for the decisions and the chance events in Figure 13.8.

First, PDC's management must decide whether the market research should be conducted. If it is conducted, PDC's management must be prepared to make a decision about the size of the condominium project if the market research report is favorable and, possibly, a different decision about the size of the condominium project if the market research report is unfavorable. In Figure 13.8, the squares are decision nodes and the circles are chance nodes. At each decision node, the branch of the tree that is taken is based on the decision made. At each chance node, the branch of the tree that is taken is based on probability or chance. For example, decision node 1 shows that PDC must first make the decision of whether to conduct the market research study. If the market research study is undertaken, chance node 2 indicates that both the favorable report branch and the unfavorable report branch are not under PDC's control and will be determined by chance. Node 3 is a decision node, indicating that PDC must make the decision to construct the small, medium, or large complex if the market research report is favorable. Node 4 is a decision node showing that PDC must make the decision to construct the small, medium, or large complex if the market research report is unfavorable. Node 5 is a decision node indicating that PDC must make the decision to construct the small, medium, or large complex if the market research is not undertaken. Nodes 6 to 14 are chance nodes indicating that the strong demand or weak demand state-of-nature branches will be determined by chance.

Analysis of the decision tree and the choice of an optimal strategy require that we know the branch probabilities corresponding to all chance nodes. PDC has developed the following branch probabilities:

In Section 13.6 we explain how the branch probabilities for P(Favorable report) and P(Unfavorable report) can be developed.

If the market research study is undertaken

$$P(\text{Favorable report}) = 0.77$$
$$P(\text{Unfavorable report}) = 0.23$$

If the market research report is favorable

$$P(\text{Strong demand given a favorable report}) = 0.94$$
$$P(\text{Weak demand given a favorable report}) = 0.06$$

If the market research report is unfavorable

$$P(\text{Strong demand given an unfavorable report}) = 0.35$$
$$P(\text{Weak demand given an unfavorable report}) = 0.65$$

FIGURE 13.8 THE PDC DECISION TREE INCLUDING THE MARKET RESEARCH STUDY

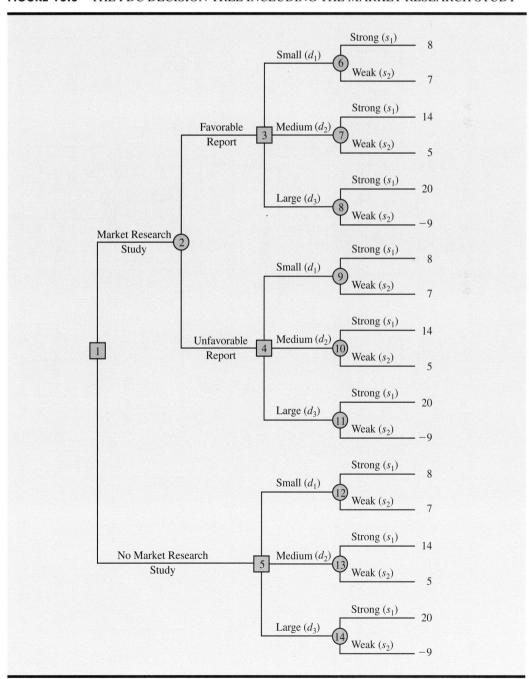

If the market research report is not undertaken, the prior probabilities are applicable.

$$P(\text{Strong demand}) = 0.80$$

$$P(\text{Weak demand}) = 0.20$$

The branch probabilities are shown on the decision tree in Figure 13.9.

Decision Strategy

A **decision strategy** is a sequence of decisions and chance outcomes where the decisions chosen depend on the yet-to-be-determined outcomes of chance events.

FIGURE 13.9   THE PDC DECISION TREE WITH BRANCH PROBABILITIES

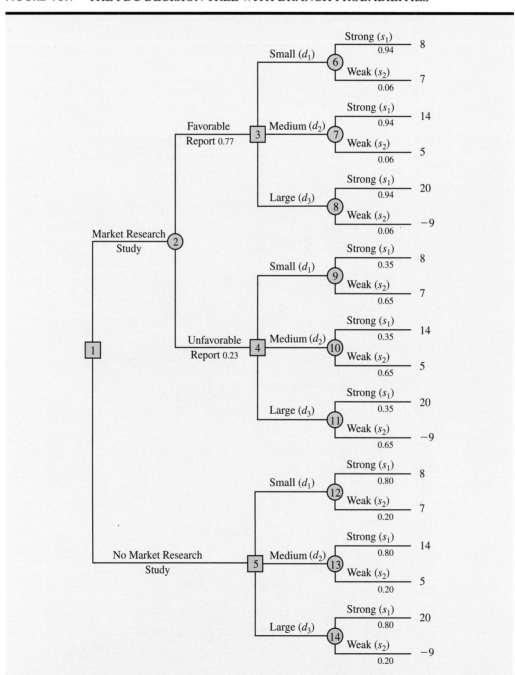

The approach used to determine the optimal decision strategy is based on a backward pass through the decision tree using the following steps:

1. At chance nodes, compute the expected value by multiplying the payoff at the end of each branch by the corresponding branch probabilities.
2. At decision nodes, select the decision branch that leads to the best expected value. This expected value becomes the expected value at the decision node.

Starting the backward pass calculations by computing the expected values at chance nodes 6 to 14 provides the following results:

$$
\begin{aligned}
EV(\text{Node } 6) &= 0.94(8) + 0.06(7) &&= 7.94 \\
EV(\text{Node } 7) &= 0.94(14) + 0.06(5) &&= 13.46 \\
EV(\text{Node } 8) &= 0.94(20) + 0.06(-9) &&= 18.26 \\
EV(\text{Node } 9) &= 0.35(8) + 0.65(7) &&= 7.35 \\
EV(\text{Node } 10) &= 0.35(14) + 0.65(5) &&= 8.15 \\
EV(\text{Node } 11) &= 0.35(20) + 0.65(-9) &&= 1.15 \\
EV(\text{Node } 12) &= 0.80(8) + 0.20(7) &&= 7.80 \\
EV(\text{Node } 13) &= 0.80(14) + 0.20(5) &&= 12.20 \\
EV(\text{Node } 14) &= 0.80(20) + 0.20(-9) &&= 14.20
\end{aligned}
$$

Figure 13.10 shows the reduced decision tree after computing expected values at these chance nodes.

Next, move to decision nodes 3, 4, and 5. For each of these nodes, we select the decision alternative branch that leads to the best expected value. For example, at node 3 we have the choice of the small complex branch with EV(Node 6) = 7.94, the medium complex branch with EV(Node 7) = 13.46, and the large complex branch with EV(Node 8) = 18.26. Thus, we select the large complex decision alternative branch and the expected value at node 3 becomes EV(Node 3) = 18.26.

For node 4, we select the best expected value from nodes 9, 10, and 11. The best decision alternative is the medium complex branch that provides EV(Node 4) = 8.15. For node 5, we select the best expected value from nodes 12, 13, and 14. The best decision alternative is the large complex branch that provides EV(Node 5) = 14.20. Figure 13.11 shows the reduced decision tree after choosing the best decisions at nodes 3, 4, and 5.

The expected value at chance node 2 can now be computed as follows:

$$
\begin{aligned}
EV(\text{Node } 2) &= 0.77EV(\text{Node } 3) + 0.23EV(\text{Node } 4) \\
&= 0.77(18.26) + 0.23(8.15) = 15.93
\end{aligned}
$$

This calculation reduces the decision tree to one involving only the two decision branches from node 1 (see Figure 13.12).

Finally, the decision can be made at decision node 1 by selecting the best expected values from nodes 2 and 5. This action leads to the decision alternative to conduct the market research study, which provides an overall expected value of 15.93.

Problem 16 will test your ability to develop an optimal decision strategy.

The optimal decision for PDC is to conduct the market research study and then carry out the following decision strategy:

If the market research is favorable, construct the large condominium complex.

If the market research is unfavorable, construct the medium condominium complex.

The analysis of the PDC decision tree describes the methods that can be used to analyze more complex sequential decision problems. First, draw a decision tree consisting of decision and chance nodes and branches that describe the sequential nature of the problem. Determine the probabilities for all chance outcomes. Then, by working backward through

FIGURE 13.10   PDC DECISION TREE AFTER COMPUTING EXPECTED VALUES
AT CHANCE NODES 6 TO 14

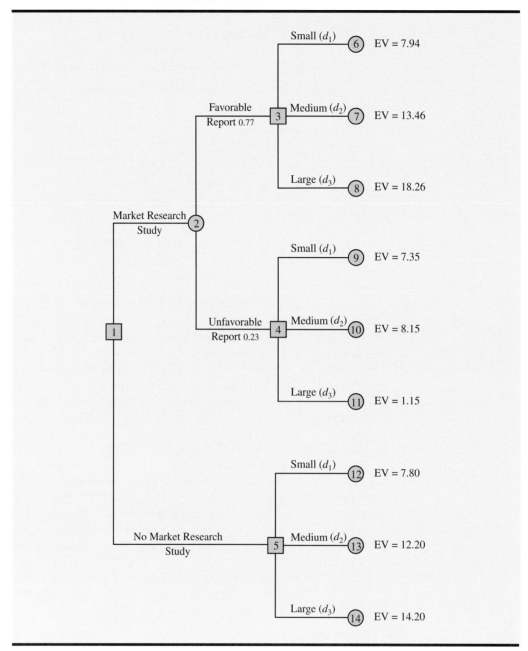

the tree, compute expected values at all chance nodes and select the best decision branch at all decision nodes. The sequence of optimal decision branches determines the optimal decision strategy for the problem.

The Management Science in Action, Decision Analysis At Bat, describes the application of decision analysis to guide a batter's strategy during an at-bat in a baseball game.

Risk Profile

Figure 13.13 provides a reduced decision tree showing only the sequence of decision alternatives and chance events for the PDC optimal decision strategy. By implementing the optimal decision strategy, PDC will obtain one of the four payoffs shown at the terminal branches of

FIGURE 13.11   PDC DECISION TREE AFTER CHOOSING BEST DECISIONS AT NODES 3, 4, AND 5

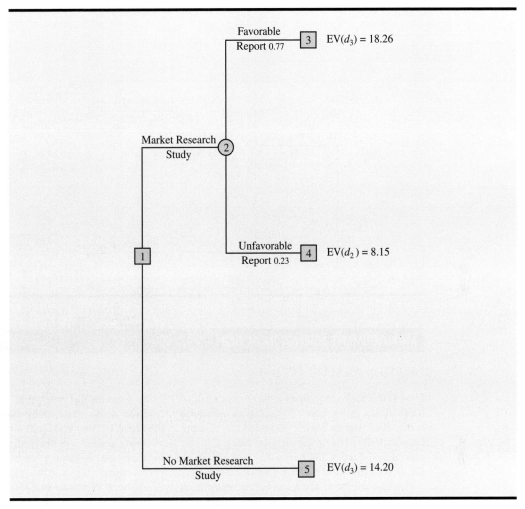

FIGURE 13.12   PDC DECISION TREE REDUCED TO TWO DECISION BRANCHES

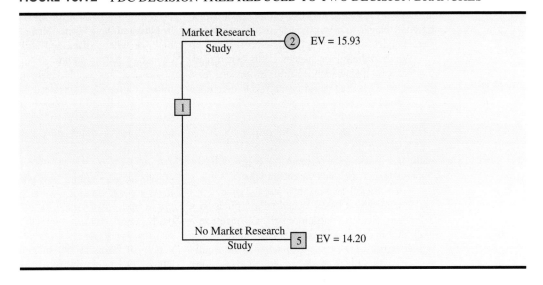

FIGURE 13.13   PDC DECISION TREE SHOWING ONLY BRANCHES ASSOCIATED WITH
OPTIMAL DECISION STRATEGY

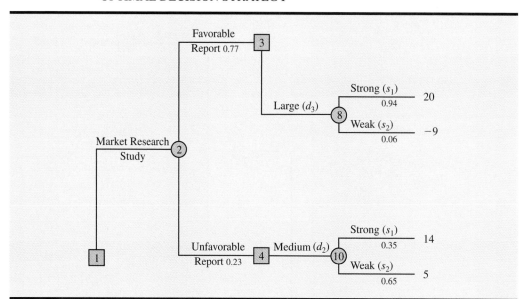

MANAGEMENT SCIENCE IN ACTION

DECISION ANALYSIS AT BAT*

Evan Gattis took a circuitous route to major league baseball. His path to becoming a 26-year-old rookie on the 2013 Atlanta Braves' roster has earned comparisons to Roy Hobbs, the mythical baseball player central to the novel and movie *The Natural*. As in the story of Roy Hobbs, Gattis dropped completely out of baseball for several years before returning in a big way. In his first month in the major leagues, he hit six home runs and was named the National League's Rookie of the Month. He duplicated both feats in his second month—he hit six more home runs and was again named the National League's Rookie of the Month. But what is most unusual about Gattis is that he may be the first major league baseball player to give credit to management science and decision analysis for his success.

While in the minor leagues Gattis began reading the work of University of Texas Professor J. Eric Bickel, who has used decision analysis to determine the optimal decisions for a hitter to make in each count. "One paper I wrote was how to act on different pitch counts," Bickel said. "Sometimes the batter will just let a pitch go by on purpose. If it's three balls, no strikes, a lot of times the coach will say, 'Don't swing at the pitch, no matter what.'"

What Bickel said is that most people don't understand why a batter would take a pitch on a 3-0 count. Because one more ball will result in a walk and put the batter on first base, under these circumstances the opposing pitcher will usually put a very hittable fastball through the heart of the

strike zone on the next pitch. However, Bickel's research demonstrates why taking a pitch when the count is three balls and no strikes rather than swinging at what will likely be a very hittable pitch increases the probability the batter will ultimately get on base.

"About 38 percent of all batters eventually get on base," Bickel said. "At 3-0, 77 percent of batters eventually get on base. Suppose you're sitting there with a 3-0 count. If you let the pitch go by, and the pitcher throws a strike, you're down to a 63 percent chance of getting on. If you instead put that ball in play, you only have a one-third chance of getting on base. Your choice is to put the ball in play and have a one-third chance of getting on base, or take a strike and still have a 63 percent chance of getting on base. That's why you take it."

Bickel has used decision analysis to determine a batter's optimal strategies for all ball-strike counts. His decision analysis and his lucid explanation of the resulting optimal strategies for various ball/strike counts have helped shape the way Gattis approaches each pitch when he is at bat.

*Based on Joe Lemire, "This Photo Is Just One Good Reason You Need to Know the Story of Evan Gattis," *Sports Illustrated* (June 10, 2013) and "Mastering the Numbers Game—Sports Illustrated Coverage," *Petroleum and Geosystems Engineering News*, University of Texas at Austin, http://www.pge.utexas.edu/news/136-eric-bickel.

the decision tree. Recall that a risk profile shows the possible payoffs with their associated probabilities. Thus, in order to construct a risk profile for the optimal decision strategy, we will need to compute the probability for each of the four payoffs.

Note that each payoff results from a sequence of branches leading from node 1 to the payoff. For instance, the payoff of $20 million is obtained by following the upper branch from node 1, the upper branch from node 2, the lower branch from node 3, and the upper branch from node 8. The probability of following that sequence of branches can be found by multiplying the probabilities for the branches from the chance nodes in the sequence. Thus, the probability of the $20 million payoff is $(0.77)(0.94) = 0.72$. Similarly, the probabilities for each of the other payoffs are obtained by multiplying the probabilities for the branches from the chance nodes leading to the payoffs. By doing so, we find the probability of the $-$9$ million payoff is $(0.77)(0.06) = 0.05$; the probability of the $14 million payoff is $(0.23)(0.35) = 0.08$; and the probability of the $5 million payoff is $(0.23)(0.65) = 0.15$. The following table showing the probability distribution for the payoffs for the PDC optimal decision strategy is the tabular representation of the risk profile for the optimal decision strategy:

Payoff ($ millions)	Probability
−9	0.05
5	0.15
14	0.08
20	0.72
	1.00

Figure 13.14 provides a graphical representation of the risk profile. Comparing Figures 13.5 and 13.14, we see that the PDC risk profile is changed by the strategy to conduct the market research study. In fact, the use of the market research study lowered the probability of the $9 million loss from 0.20 to 0.05. PDC's management would most likely view that change as a considerable reduction in the risk associated with the condominium project.

FIGURE 13.14 RISK PROFILE FOR PDC CONDOMINIUM PROJECT WITH SAMPLE INFORMATION SHOWING PAYOFFS ASSOCIATED WITH OPTIMAL DECISION STRATEGY

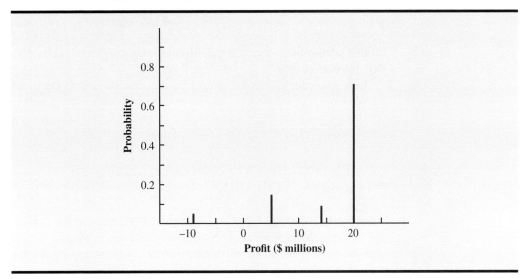

Expected Value of Sample Information

In the PDC problem, the market research study is the sample information used to determine the optimal decision strategy. The expected value associated with the market research study is $15.93. In Section 13.3 we showed that the best expected value if the market research study is *not* undertaken is $14.20. Thus, we can conclude that the difference, $15.93 − $14.20 = $1.73, is the **expected value of sample information (EVSI)**. In other words, conducting the market research study adds $1.73 million to the PDC expected value. In general, the expected value of sample information is as follows:

$$EVSI = \left| EVwSI - EVwoSI \right| \tag{13.13}$$

where

$$EVSI = \text{expected value of sample information}$$
$$EVwSI = \text{expected value } \textit{with} \text{ sample information about the states of nature}$$
$$EVwoSI = \text{expected value } \textit{without} \text{ sample information about the states of nature}$$

The EVSI = $1.73 million suggests PDC should be willing to pay up to $1.73 million to conduct the market research study.

Note the role of the absolute value in equation (13.13). For minimization problems, the expected value with sample information is always less than or equal to the expected value without sample information. In this case, EVSI is the magnitude of the difference between EVwSI and EVwoSI; thus, by taking the absolute value of the difference as shown in equation (13.13), we can handle both the maximization and minimization cases with one equation.

Efficiency of Sample Information

In Section 13.3 we showed that the expected value of perfect information (EVPI) for the PDC problem is $3.2 million. We never anticipated that the market research report would obtain perfect information, but we can use an **efficiency** measure to express the value of the market research information. With perfect information having an efficiency rating of 100%, the efficiency rating E for sample information is computed as follows:

$$E = \frac{EVSI}{EVPI} \times 100 \tag{13.14}$$

For the PDC problem,

$$E = \frac{1.73}{3.2} \times 100 = 54.1\%$$

In other words, the information from the market research study is 54.1% as efficient as perfect information.

Low efficiency ratings for sample information might lead the decision maker to look for other types of information. However, high efficiency ratings indicate that the sample information is almost as good as perfect information and that additional sources of information would not yield substantially better results.

13.6   COMPUTING BRANCH PROBABILITIES WITH BAYES' THEOREM

In Section 13.5 the branch probabilities for the PDC decision tree chance nodes were specified in the problem description. No computations were required to determine these probabilities. In this section we show how **Bayes' theorem** can be used to compute branch probabilities for decision trees.

The PDC decision tree is shown again in Figure 13.15:

$$F = \text{Favorable market research report}$$
$$U = \text{Unfavorable market research report}$$
$$s_1 = \text{Strong demand (state of nature 1)}$$
$$s_2 = \text{Weak demand (state of nature 2)}$$

At chance node 2, we need to know the branch probabilities $P(F)$ and $P(U)$. At chance nodes 6, 7, and 8, we need to know the branch probabilities $P(s_1 \mid F)$, the probability of state of nature 1 given a favorable market research report, and $P(s_2 \mid F)$, the probability of state of

FIGURE 13.15   THE PDC DECISION TREE

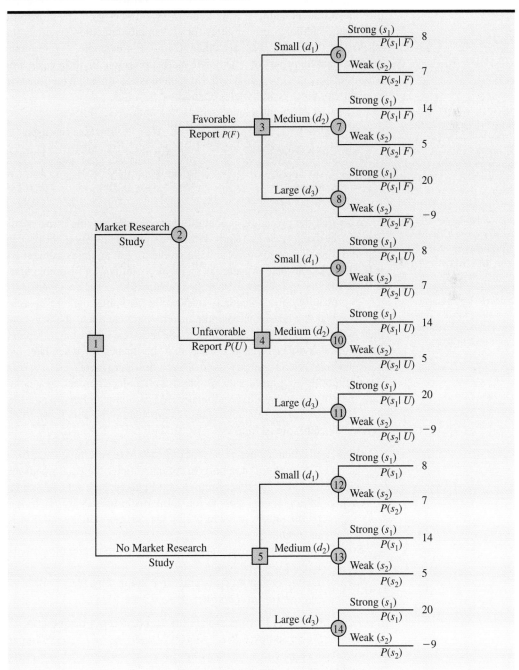

nature 2 given a favorable market research report. $P(s_1 \mid F)$ and $P(s_2 \mid F)$ are referred to as *posterior probabilities* because they are conditional probabilities based on the outcome of the sample information. At chance nodes 9, 10, and 11, we need to know the branch probabilities $P(s_1 \mid U)$ and $P(s_2 \mid U)$; note that these are also posterior probabilities, denoting the probabilities of the two states of nature *given* that the market research report is unfavorable. Finally, at chance nodes 12, 13, and 14, we need the probabilities for the states of nature, $P(s_1)$ and $P(s_2)$, if the market research study is not undertaken.

In performing the probability computations, we need to know PDC's assessment of the probabilities for the two states of nature, $P(s_1)$ and $P(s_2)$, which are the prior probabilities as discussed earlier. In addition, we must know the **conditional probability** of the market research outcomes (the sample information) *given* each state of nature. For example, we need to know the conditional probability of a favorable market research report given that the state of nature is strong demand for the PDC project; note that this conditional probability of F given state of nature s_1 is written $P(F \mid s_1)$. To carry out the probability calculations, we will need conditional probabilities for all sample outcomes given all states of nature, that is, $P(F \mid s_1)$, $P(F \mid s_2)$, $P(U \mid s_1)$, and $P(U \mid s_2)$. For example, $P(F \mid s_1)$ may be estimated via the historical frequency of a favorable market research report in cases where strong demand was ultimately observed. In the PDC problem we assume that the following assessments are available for these conditional probabilities:

	Market Research	
State of Nature	**Favorable, F**	**Unfavorable, U**
Strong demand, s_1	$P(F \mid s_1) = 0.90$	$P(U \mid s_1) = 0.10$
Weak demand, s_2	$P(F \mid s_2) = 0.25$	$P(U \mid s_2) = 0.75$

A favorable market research report given that the state of nature is weak demand is often referred to as a "false positive," while the converse (an unfavorable market research report given that the state of nature is strong demand) is referred to as a "false negative."

Note that the preceding probability assessments provide a reasonable degree of confidence in the market research study. If the true state of nature is s_1, the probability of a favorable market research report is 0.90, and the probability of an unfavorable market research report is 0.10. If the true state of nature is s_2, the probability of a favorable market research report is 0.25, and the probability of an unfavorable market research report is 0.75. The reason for a 0.25 probability of a potentially misleading favorable market research report for state of nature s_2 is that when some potential buyers first hear about the new condominium project, their enthusiasm may lead them to overstate their real interest in it. A potential buyer's initial favorable response can change quickly to a "no thank you" when later faced with the reality of signing a purchase contract and making a down payment.

In the following discussion we present a tabular approach as a convenient method for carrying out the probability computations. The computations for the PDC problem based on a favorable market research report (F) are summarized in Table 13.7. The steps used to develop this table are as follows:

Step 1. In column 1 enter the states of nature. In column 2 enter the *prior probabilities* for the states of nature. In column 3 enter the *conditional probabilities* of a favorable market research report (F) given each state of nature.

Step 2. In column 4 compute the **joint probabilities** by multiplying the prior probability values in column 2 by the corresponding conditional probability values in column 3.

Step 3. Sum the joint probabilities in column 4 to obtain the probability of a favorable market research report, $P(F)$.

Step 4. Divide each joint probability in column 4 by $P(F) = 0.77$ to obtain the revised or *posterior probabilities*, $P(s_1 \mid F)$ and $P(s_2 \mid F)$.

Table 13.7 shows that the probability of obtaining a favorable market research report is $P(F) = 0.77$. In addition, $P(s_1 \mid F) = 0.94$ and $P(s_2 \mid F) = 0.06$. In particular, note that a favorable market research report will prompt a revised or posterior probability of 0.94 that the market demand of the condominium will be strong, s_1.

TABLE 13.7 BRANCH PROBABILITIES FOR THE PDC CONDOMINIUM PROJECT BASED ON A FAVORABLE MARKET RESEARCH REPORT

States of Nature	Prior Probabilities	Conditional Probabilities	Joint Probabilities	Posterior Probabilities
s_j	$P(s_j)$	$P(F \mid s_j)$	$P(F \cap s_j)$	$P(s_j \mid F)$
s_1	0.8	0.90	0.72	0.94
s_2	0.2	0.25	0.05	0.06
	1.0		$P(F) = 0.77$	1.00

TABLE 13.8 BRANCH PROBABILITIES FOR THE PDC CONDOMINIUM PROJECT BASED ON AN UNFAVORABLE MARKET RESEARCH REPORT

States of Nature	Prior Probabilities	Conditional Probabilities	Joint Probabilities	Posterior Probabilities
s_j	$P(s_j)$	$P(U \mid s_j)$	$P(U \cap s_j)$	$P(s_j \mid U)$
s_1	0.8	0.10	0.08	0.35
s_2	0.2	0.75	0.15	0.65
	1.0		$P(U) = 0.23$	1.00

The tabular probability computation procedure must be repeated for each possible sample information outcome. Table 13.8 shows the computations of the branch probabilities of the PDC problem based on an unfavorable market research report. Note that the probability of obtaining an unfavorable market research report is $P(U) = 0.23$. If an unfavorable report is obtained, the posterior probability of a strong market demand, s_1, is 0.35 and of a weak market demand, s_2, is 0.65. The branch probabilities from Tables 13.7 and 13.8 were shown on the PDC decision tree in Figure 13.9.

Problem 23 asks you to compute the posterior probabilities.

The tabular method can be used directly to compute the branch probabilities in the decision tree. Alternatively, equation (13.15) provides a general formula for Bayes' theorem for computing posterior probabilities.

BAYES' THEOREM

$$P(A_i \mid B) = \frac{P(B \mid A_i)P(A_i)}{\Sigma_j P(B \mid A_j) P(A_j)} \tag{13.15}$$

To perform the Bayes' theorem calculations for $P(s_1 \mid U)$ with equation (13.15), we replace B with U (unfavorable report) and A_i with s_1 in (13.15) so that we have,

$$P(s_1 \mid U) = \frac{P(U \mid s_1)P(s_1)}{\Sigma_j P(U \mid s_j) P(s_j)}$$

$$= \frac{0.10 \times 0.80}{(0.10 \times 0.80) + (0.20 \times 0.75)} = 0.35$$

which provides the same value as the tabular approach used to generate the values in Table 13.7.

The discussion in this section shows an underlying relationship between the probabilities on the various branches in a decision tree. It would be inappropriate to assume different prior probabilities, $P(s_1)$ and $P(s_2)$, without determining how these changes would alter $P(F)$ and $P(U)$, as well as the posterior probabilities $P(s_1 \mid F)$, $P(s_2 \mid F)$, $P(s_1 \mid U)$, and $P(s_2 \mid U)$.

MANAGEMENT SCIENCE IN ACTION

DECISION ANALYSIS HELPS TREAT AND PREVENT HEPATITIS B*

Hepatitis B is a viral disease that left untreated can lead to fatal liver conditions such as cirrhosis and cancer. The hepatitis B virus can be treated, and there exists a vaccine to prevent it. However, in order to make economically prudent allocations of their limited health care budgets, public health officials require analysis on the cost effectiveness (health benefit per dollar investment) of any potential health program. Unfortunately, since hepatitis B is a slow-progressing condition whose victims are often un-aware of their potentially fatal infection, gathering data on the benefits of any public health policy ad-dressing hepatitis B would take decades.

A multidisciplinary team consisting of manage-ment science researchers and a liver transplant surgeon from Stanford University applied decision analysis techniques to determine which combina-tion of hepatitis B screening, treatment, and vacci-nation would be appropriate in the United States. Their decision tree contained the sequential deci-sions of (1) whether or not to perform a blood test to screen an individual for a hepatitis B infection, (2) whether or not to treat infected individuals, and (3) whether or not to vaccinate a noninfected (or nonscreened) individual.

For each policy, composed of a sequence of screening, treatment, and vaccination decisions, the researchers utilized existing infection and treatment knowledge to model future disease progression. Implementing their decision model in an Excel spreadsheet, the researchers concluded that it is cost effective to screen adult Asian and Pacific Islanders so that infected individuals can be treated (these individuals are genetically at a high risk for hepatitis B infection). Although it is not cost effective to universally vaccinate all U.S. adult Asian and Pacific Islanders, it proves to be cost effective to vaccinate people in close contact with infected individuals. Influenced by these findings, the Centers for Disease Control and Prevention updated its official policy in 2008 to recommend screening all adult Asian and Pacific Islanders and all adults in areas of intermediate (2% to 7%) hepatitis B prevalence.

*Based on David W. Hutton, Margaret L. Brandeau, and Samuel K. So, "Doing Good with Good OR: Supporting Cost-Effective Hepatitis B Interventions," *Interfaces* 41(May/June 2011): 289–300.

The Management Science in Action, Decision Analysis Helps Treat and Prevent Hepati-tis B, discusses how medical researchers use posterior probability information and decision analysis to understand the risks and costs associated with treatment and screening procedures.

13.7   UTILITY THEORY

The decision analysis situations presented so far in this chapter expressed outcomes (payoffs) in terms of monetary values. With probability information available about the outcomes of the chance events, we defined the optimal decision alternative as the one that provided the best expected value. However, in some situations the decision alternative with the best expected value may not be the preferred alternative. A decision maker may also wish to consider intan-gible factors such as risk, image, or other nonmonetary criteria in order to evaluate the decision alternatives. When monetary value does not necessarily lead to the most preferred decision, expressing the value (or worth) of a consequence in terms of its utility will permit the use of expected utility to identify the most desirable decision alternative. The discussion of utility and its application in decision analysis is presented in this section.

Utility is a measure of the total worth or relative desirability of a particular outcome; it reflects the decision maker's attitude toward a collection of factors such as profit, loss, and risk. Researchers have found that as long as the monetary value of payoffs stays within a range that the decision maker considers reasonable, selecting the decision alternative with the best expected value usually leads to selection of the most preferred decision. However, when the payoffs are extreme, decision makers are often unsatisfied or uneasy with the deci-sion that simply provides the best expected value.

As an example of a situation in which utility can help in selecting the best decision alternative, let us consider the problem faced by Swofford, Inc., a relatively small real estate investment firm located in Atlanta, Georgia. Swofford currently has two investment opportunities that require approximately the same cash outlay. The cash requirements necessary prohibit Swofford from making more than one investment at this time. Consequently, three possible decision alternatives may be considered.

The three decision alternatives, denoted d_1, d_2, and d_3, are

$$d_1 = \text{make investment A}$$
$$d_2 = \text{make investment B}$$
$$d_3 = \text{do not invest}$$

The monetary payoffs associated with the investment opportunities depend on the investment decision and on the direction of the real estate market during the next six months (the chance event). Real estate prices will go up, remain stable, or go down. Thus the states of nature, denoted s_1, s_2, and s_3, are

$$s_1 = \text{real estate prices go up}$$
$$s_2 = \text{real estate prices remain stable}$$
$$s_3 = \text{real estate prices go down}$$

Using the best information available, Swofford has estimated the profits, or payoffs, associated with each decision alternative and state-of-nature combination. The resulting payoff table is shown in Table 13.9.

The best estimate of the probability that real estate prices will go up is 0.3; the best estimate of the probability that prices will remain stable is 0.5; and the best estimate of the probability that prices will go down is 0.2. Thus the expected values for the three decision alternatives are

$$EV(d_1) = 0.3(30,000) + 0.5(20,000) + 0.2(-50,000) = 9,000$$
$$EV(d_2) = 0.3(50,000) + 0.5(-20,000) + 0.2(-30,000) = -11,000$$
$$EV(d_3) = 0.3(0) + 0.5(0) + 0.2(0) = 0$$

Using the expected value approach, the optimal decision is to select investment A with an expected value of $9000. Is it really the best decision alternative? Let us consider some other relevant factors that relate to Swofford's capability for absorbing the loss of $50,000 if investment A is made and prices actually go down.

Actually, Swofford's current financial position is weak. This condition is partly reflected in Swofford's ability to make only one investment. More important, however, the firm's president believes that, if the next investment results in a substantial loss, Swofford's future will be in jeopardy. Although the expected value approach leads to a recommendation for d_1, do you think the firm's president would prefer this decision? We suspect that the president would select d_2 or d_3 to avoid the possibility of incurring a $50,000 loss. In fact, a reasonable conclusion is that, if a loss of even $30,000 could drive Swofford out of business, the president would select d_3, believing that both investments A and B are too risky for Swofford's current financial position.

TABLE 13.9 PAYOFF TABLE FOR SWOFFORD, INC.

Decision Alternative	State of Nature		
	Prices Go Up s_1	Prices Stable s_2	Prices Go Down s_3
Investment A, d_1	$30,000	$20,000	-$50,000
Investment B, d_2	$50,000	-$20,000	-$30,000
Do Not Invest, d_3	0	0	0

The way we resolve Swofford's dilemma is first to determine Swofford's utility for the various outcomes. Recall that the utility of any outcome is the total worth of that outcome, taking into account all risks and consequences involved. If the utilities for the various consequences are assessed correctly, the decision alternative with the highest expected utility is the most preferred, or best, alternative. We next show how to determine the utility of the outcomes so that the alternative with the highest expected utility can be identified.

Utility and Decision Analysis

The procedure we use to establish a utility for each of the payoffs in Swofford's situation requires that we first assign a utility to the best and worst possible payoffs. Any values will work as long as the utility assigned to the best payoff is greater than the utility assigned to the worst payoff. In this case, $50,000 is the best payoff and −$50,000 is the worst. Suppose, then, that we arbitrarily make assignments to these two payoffs as follows:

Utility values of 0 and 1 could have been selected here; we selected 0 and 10 to avoid any possible confusion between the utility value for a payoff and the probability p.

p *is often referred to as the* indifference probability.

$$\text{Utility of } -\$50,000 = U(-50,000) = 0$$
$$\text{Utility of } \$50,000 = U(50,000) = 10$$

Let us now determine the utility associated with every other payoff.

Consider the process of establishing the utility of a payoff of $30,000. First we ask Swofford's president to state a preference between a guaranteed $30,000 payoff and an opportunity to engage in the following lottery, or bet, for some probability of p that we select:

Lottery: Swofford obtains a payoff of $50,000 with probability p and a payoff of −$50,000 with probability $(1 - p)$.

Obviously, if p is very close to 1, Swofford's president would prefer the lottery to the guaranteed payoff of $30,000 because the firm would virtually ensure itself a payoff of $50,000. If p is very close to 0, Swofford's president would clearly prefer the guarantee of $30,000. In any event, as p increases continuously from 0 to 1, the preference for the guaranteed payoff of $30,000 decreases and at some point is equal to the preference for the lottery. At this value of p, Swofford's president would have equal preference for the guaranteed payoff of $30,000 and the lottery; at greater values of p, Swofford's president would prefer the lottery to the guaranteed $30,000 payoff. For example, let us assume that when $p = 0.95$, Swofford's president is indifferent between the guaranteed payoff of $30,000 and the lottery. For this value of p, we can compute the utility of a $30,000 payoff as follows:

$$
\begin{aligned}
U(30,000) &= pU(50,000) + (1 - p)U(-50,000) \\
&= 0.95(10) + (0.05)(0) \\
&= 9.5
\end{aligned}
$$

Obviously, if we had started with a different assignment of utilities for a payoff of $50,000 and −$50,000, the result would have been a different utility for $30,000. For example, if we had started with an assignment of 100 for $50,000 and 10 for −$50,000, the utility of a $30,000 payoff would be

$$
\begin{aligned}
U(30,000) &= 0.95(100) + 0.05(10) \\
&= 95.0 + 0.5 \\
&= 95.5
\end{aligned}
$$

Hence, we must conclude that the utility assigned to each payoff is not unique but merely depends on the initial choice of utilities for the best and worst payoffs.

Before computing the utility for the other payoffs, let us consider the implication of Swofford's president assigning a utility of 9.5 to a payoff of $30,000. Clearly, when $p = 0.95$, the expected value of the lottery is

$$
\begin{aligned}
EV(\text{lottery}) &= 0.95(\$50,000) + 0.05(-\$50,000) \\
&= \$47,500 - \$2,500 \\
&= \$45,000
\end{aligned}
$$

The difference between the expected value of the lottery and the guaranteed payoff can be viewed as the risk premium the decision maker is willing to pay.

Although the expected value of the lottery when $p = 0.95$ is \$45,000, Swofford's president is indifferent between the lottery (and its associated risk) and a guaranteed payoff of \$30,000. Thus, Swofford's president is taking a conservative, or risk-avoiding, viewpoint. A decision maker who would choose a guaranteed payoff over a lottery with a superior expected payoff is a **risk avoider** (or is said to be risk averse). The president would rather have \$30,000 for certain than risk anything greater than a 5 percent chance of incurring a loss of \$50,000. In other words, the difference between the EV of \$45,000 and the guaranteed payoff of \$30,000 is the risk premium that Swofford's president would be willing to pay to avoid the 5 percent chance of losing \$50,000.

To compute the utility associated with a payoff of −\$20,000, we must ask Swofford's president to state a preference between a guaranteed −\$20,000 payoff and an opportunity to engage again in the following lottery:

Lottery: Swofford obtains a payoff of \$50,000 with probability p and a payoff of −\$50,000 with probability $(1 − p)$.

Note that this lottery is exactly the same as the one we used to establish the utility of a payoff of \$30,000 (in fact, we can use this lottery to establish the utility for any value in the Swofford payoff table). We need to determine the value of p that would make the president indifferent between a guaranteed payoff of −\$20,000 and the lottery. For example, we might begin by asking the president to choose between a certain loss of \$20,000 and the lottery with a payoff of \$50,000 with probability $p = 0.90$ and a payoff of −\$50,000 with probability $(1 − p) = 0.10$. What answer do you think we would get? Surely, with this high probability of obtaining a payoff of \$50,000, the president would elect the lottery. Next, we might ask whether $p = 0.85$ would result in indifference between the loss of \$20,000 for certain and the lottery. Again the president might prefer the lottery. Suppose that we continue until we get to $p = 0.55$, at which point the president is indifferent between the payoff of −\$20,000 and the lottery. In other words, for any value of p less than 0.55, the president would take a loss of \$20,000 for certain rather than risk the potential loss of \$50,000 with the lottery; and for any value of p above 0.55, the president would choose the lottery. Thus, the utility assigned to a payoff of −\$20,000 is

$$U(-\$20,000) = pU(50,000) + (1 − p)U(-\$50,000)$$
$$= 0.55(10) + 0.45(0)$$
$$= 5.5$$

Again let us assess the implication of this assignment by comparing it to the expected value approach. When $p = 0.55$, the expected value of the lottery is

$$EV(\text{lottery}) = 0.55(\$50,000) + 0.45(-\$50,000)$$
$$= \$27,500 − \$22,500$$
$$= \$5,000$$

Thus, Swofford's president would just as soon absorb a certain loss of \$20,000 as take the lottery and its associated risk, even though the expected value of the lottery is \$5,000. Once again this preference demonstrates the conservative, or risk-avoiding, point of view of Swofford's president.

In these two examples, we computed the utility for the payoffs of \$30,000 and −\$20,000. We can determine the utility for any payoff M in a similar fashion. First, we must find the probability p for which the decision maker is indifferent between a guaranteed payoff of M and a lottery with a payoff of \$50,000 with probability p and −\$50,000 with probability $(1 − p)$. The utility of M is then computed as follows:

$$U(M) = pU(\$50,000) + (1 − p)U(-\$50,000)$$
$$= p(10) + (1 − p)0$$
$$= 10p$$

Using this procedure we developed a utility for each of the remaining payoffs in Swofford's problem. The results are presented in Table 13.10.

TABLE 13.10   UTILITY OF MONETARY PAYOFFS FOR SWOFFORD, INC.

Monetary Value	Indifference Value of p	Utility
$50,000	Does not apply	10.0
30,000	0.95	9.5
20,000	0.90	9.0
0	0.75	7.5
−20,000	0.55	5.5
−30,000	0.40	4.0
−50,000	Does not apply	0

TABLE 13.11   UTILITY TABLE FOR SWOFFORD, INC.

	State of Nature		
Decision Alternative	Prices Up s_1	Prices Stable s_2	Prices Down s_3
Investment A, d_1	9.5	9.0	0
Investment B, d_2	10.0	5.5	4.0
Do Not Invest, d_3	7.5	7.5	7.5

Now that we have determined the utility of each of the possible monetary values, we can write the original payoff table in terms of utility. Table 13.11 shows the utility for the various outcomes in the Swofford problem. The notation we use for the entries in the utility table is U_{ij}, which denotes the utility associated with decision alternative d_i and state of nature s_j. Using this notation, we see that $U_{23} = 4.0$.

We can now compute the **expected utility (EU)** of the utilities in Table 13.11 in a similar fashion as we computed expected value in Section 13.3. In other words, to identify an optimal decision alternative for Swofford, Inc., the expected utility approach requires the analyst to compute the expected utility for each decision alternative and then select the alternative yielding the highest expected utility. With N possible states of nature, the expected utility of a decision alternative d_i is given by

EXPECTED UTILITY (EU)

$$EU(d_i) = \sum_{j=1}^{N} P(s_j)U_{ij} \tag{13.16}$$

The expected utility for each of the decision alternatives in the Swofford problem is

$$EU(d_1) = 0.3(9.5) + 0.5(9.0) + 0.2(0) = 7.35$$
$$EU(d_2) = 0.3(10) + 0.5(5.5) + 0.2(4.0) = 6.55$$
$$EU(d_3) = 0.3(7.5) + 0.5(7.5) + 0.2(7.5) = 7.50$$

Note that the optimal decision using the expected utility approach is d_3, do not invest. The ranking of alternatives according to the president's utility assignments and the associated monetary values are as follows:

Ranking of Decision Alternatives	Expected Utility	Expected Value
Do Not Invest	7.50	0
Investment A	7.35	9000
Investment B	6.55	−1000

Note that, although investment A had the highest expected value of $9000, the analysis indicates that Swofford should decline this investment. The rationale behind not selecting investment A is that the 0.20 probability of a $50,000 loss was considered to involve a serious risk by Swofford's president. The seriousness of this risk and its associated impact on the company were not adequately reflected by the expected value of investment A. We assessed the utility for each payoff to assess this risk adequately.

The following steps state in general terms the procedure used to solve the Swofford, Inc., investment problem:

Step 1. Develop a payoff table using monetary values
Step 2. Identify the best and worst payoff values in the table and assign each a utility, with U(best payoff) $>$ U(worst payoff)
Step 3. For every other monetary value M in the original payoff table, do the following to determine its utility:
    a. Define the lottery such that there is a probability p of the best payoff and a probability $(1 - p)$ of the worst payoff
    b. Determine the value of p such that the decision maker is indifferent between a guaranteed payoff of M and the lottery defined in step 3(a)
    c. Calculate the utility of M as follows:

$$U(M) = pU(\text{best payoff}) + (1 - p)U(\text{worst payoff})$$

Step 4. Convert each monetary value in the payoff table to a utility
Step 5. Apply the expected utility approach to the utility table developed in step 4 and select the decision alternative with the highest expected utility

The procedure we described for determining the utility of monetary consequences can also be used to develop a utility measure for nonmonetary consequences. Assign the best consequence a utility of 10 and the worst a utility of 0. Then create a lottery with a probability of p for the best consequence and $(1 - p)$ for the worst consequence. For each of the other consequences, find the value of p that makes the decision maker indifferent between the lottery and the consequence. Then calculate the utility of the consequence in question as follows:

$$U(\text{consequence}) = pU(\text{best consequence}) + (1 - p)U(\text{worst consequence})$$

Utility Functions

Next we describe how different decision makers may approach risk in terms of their assessment of utility. The financial position of Swofford, Inc., was such that the firm's president evaluated investment opportunities from a conservative, or risk-avoiding, point of view. However, if the firm had a surplus of cash and a stable future, Swofford's president might have been looking for investment alternatives that, although perhaps risky, contained a potential for substantial profit. That type of behavior would demonstrate that the president is a risk taker with respect to this decision.

A **risk taker** is a decision maker who would choose a lottery over a guaranteed payoff when the expected value of the lottery is inferior to the guaranteed payoff. In this section, we analyze the decision problem faced by Swofford from the point of view of a decision maker who would be classified as a risk taker. We then compare the conservative point of view of Swofford's president (a risk avoider) with the behavior of a decision maker who is a risk taker.

For the decision problem facing Swofford, Inc., using the general procedure for developing utilities as discussed previously, a risk taker might express the utility for the various payoffs shown in Table 13.12. As before, $U(50,000) = 10$ and $U(-50,000) = 0$. Note the difference in behavior reflected in Table 13.12 and Table 13.10. In other words, in determining the value of p at which the decision maker is indifferent between a guaranteed payoff of M and a lottery in which $50,000 is obtained with probability p and $-$50,000 with

TABLE 13.12   REVISED UTILITIES FOR SWOFFORD, INC., ASSUMING A
                  RISK TAKER

Monetary Value	Indifference Value of p	Utility
$50,000	Does not apply	10.0
30,000	0.50	5.0
20,000	0.40	4.0
0	0.25	2.5
−20,000	0.15	1.5
−30,000	0.10	1.0
−50,000	Does not apply	0

probability $(1 - p)$, the risk taker is willing to accept a greater risk of incurring a loss of $50,000 in order to gain the opportunity to realize a profit of $50,000.

To help develop the utility table for the risk taker, we have reproduced the Swofford, Inc, payoff table in Table 13.13. Using these payoffs and the risk taker's utilities given in Table 13.12, we can write the risk taker's utility table as shown in Table 13.14. Using the state-of-nature probabilities $P(s_1) = 0.3$, $P(s_2) = 0.5$, and $P(s_3) = 0.2$, the expected utility for each decision alternative is

$$EU(d_1) = 0.3(5.0) + 0.5(4.0) + 0.2(0) = 3.50$$
$$EU(d_2) = 0.3(10) + 0.5(1.5) + 0.2(1.0) = 3.95$$
$$EU(d_3) = 0.3(2.5) + 0.5(2.5) + 0.2(2.5) = 2.50$$

What is the recommended decision? Perhaps somewhat to your surprise, the analysis recommends investment B, with the highest expected utility of 3.95. Recall that this investment has a −$1,000 expected value. Why is it now the recommended decision? Remember that the decision maker in this revised problem is a risk taker. Thus, although the expected value of investment B is negative, utility analysis has shown that this decision maker is enough of a risk taker to prefer investment B and its potential for the $50,000 profit.

TABLE 13.13   PAYOFF TABLE FOR SWOFFORD, INC.

| Decision Alternative | State of Nature | | |
	Prices Up s_1	Prices Stable s_2	Prices Down s_3
Investment A, d_1	$30,000	$20,000	−$50,000
Investment B, d_2	$50,000	−$20,000	−$30,000
Do Not Invest, d_3	0	0	0

TABLE 13.14   UTILITY TABLE OF A RISK TAKER FOR SWOFFORD, INC.

| Decision Alternative | State of Nature | | |
	Prices Up s_1	Prices Stable s_2	Prices Down s_3
Investment A, d_1	5.0	4.0	0
Investment B, d_2	10.0	1.5	1.0
Do Not Invest, d_3	2.5	2.5	2.5

Ranking by the expected utilities generates the following order of preference of the decision alternatives for the risk taker and the associated expected values:

Ranking of Decision Alternatives	Expected Utility	Expected Value
Investment B	3.95	−$1000
Investment A	3.50	$9000
Do Not Invest	2.50	0

Comparing the utility analysis for a risk taker with the more conservative preferences of the president of Swofford, Inc., who is a risk avoider, we see that, even with the same decision problem, different attitudes toward risk can lead to different recommended decisions. The utilities established by Swofford's president indicated that the firm should not invest at this time, whereas the utilities established by the risk taker showed a preference for investment B. Note that both of these decisions differ from the best expected value decision, which was investment A.

We can obtain another perspective of the difference between behaviors of a risk avoider and a risk taker by developing a graph that depicts the relationship between monetary value and utility. We use the horizontal axis of the graph to represent monetary values and the vertical axis to represent the utility associated with each monetary value. Now, consider the data in Table 13.10, with a utility corresponding to each monetary value for the original Swofford, Inc., problem. These values can be plotted on a graph to produce the top curve in Figure 13.16. The resulting curve is the **utility function for money** for Swofford's president. Recall that these points reflected the conservative, or risk-avoiding, nature of Swofford's president. Hence, we refer to the top curve in Figure 13.16 as a utility function for a risk avoider. Using the data in Table 13.12 developed for a risk taker, we can plot these points to produce the bottom curve in Figure 13.16. The resulting curve depicts the utility function for a risk taker.

By looking at the utility functions in Figure 13.16, we can begin to generalize about the utility functions for risk avoiders and risk takers. Although the exact shape of the utility

FIGURE 13.16 UTILITY FUNCTION FOR MONEY FOR RISK-AVOIDER, RISK-TAKER, AND RISK-NEUTRAL DECISION MAKERS

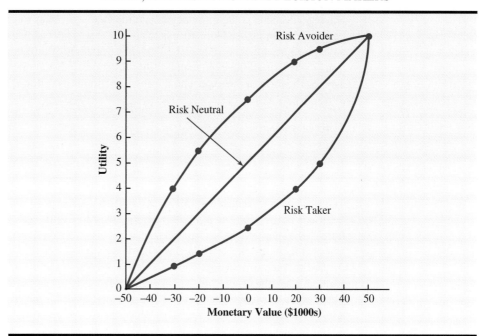

function will vary from one decision maker to another, we can see the general shape of these two types of utility functions. The utility function for a risk avoider shows a diminishing marginal return for money. For example, the increase in utility going from a monetary value of −$30,000 to $0 is 7.5 − 4.0 = 3.5, whereas the increase in utility in going from $0 to $30,000 is only 9.5 − 7.5 = 2.0.

However, the utility function for a risk taker shows an increasing marginal return for money. For example, in Figure 13.16, the increase in utility for the risk taker in going from −$30,000 to $0 is 2.5 − 1.0 = 1.5, whereas the increase in utility in going from $0 to $30,000 for the risk taker is 5.0 − 2.5 = 2.5. Note also that in either case the utility function is always increasing; that is, more money leads to more utility. All utility functions possess this property.

We concluded that the utility function for a risk avoider shows a diminishing marginal return for money and that the utility function for a risk taker shows an increasing marginal return. When the marginal return for money is neither decreasing nor increasing but remains constant, the corresponding utility function describes the behavior of a decision maker who is neutral to risk. The following characteristics are associated with a **risk-neutral** decision maker:

1. The utility function can be drawn as a straight line connecting the "best" and the "worst" points.
2. The expected utility approach and the expected value approach applied to monetary payoffs result in the same action.

The straight, diagonal line in Figure 13.16 depicts the utility function of a risk-neutral decision maker using the Swofford, Inc., problem data.

Generally, when the payoffs for a particular decision-making problem fall into a reasonable range—the best is not too good and the worst is not too bad—decision makers tend to express preferences in agreement with the expected value approach. Thus, we suggest asking the decision maker to consider the best and worst possible payoffs for a problem and assess their reasonableness. If the decision maker believes that they are in the reasonable range, the decision alternative with the best expected value can be used. However, if the payoffs appear unreasonably large or unreasonably small (for example, a huge loss) and if the decision maker believes that monetary values do not adequately reflect her or his true preferences for the payoffs, a utility analysis of the problem should be considered.

Exponential Utility Function

Having a decision maker provide enough indifference values to create a utility function can be time consuming. An alternative is to assume that the decision maker's utility is defined by an exponential function. Figure 13.17 shows examples of different exponential utility functions. Note that all the exponential utility functions indicate that the decision maker is risk averse. The form of the exponential utility function is as follows:

In equation (13.17), the number $e \approx 2.718282\ldots$ *is a mathematical constant corresponding to the base of the natural logarithm. In Excel,* e^x *can be evaluated for any power* x *using the function EXP(x).*

EXPONENTIAL UTILITY FUNCTION

$$U(x) = 1 - e^{-x/R} \qquad (13.17)$$

The R parameter in equation (13.17) represents the decision maker's risk tolerance; it controls the shape of the exponential utility function. Larger R values create flatter exponential functions, indicating that the decision maker is less risk averse (closer to risk neutral). Smaller R values indicate that the decision maker has less risk tolerance (is more risk averse). A common method to determine an approximate risk tolerance is to ask the decision maker to consider a scenario where he or she could win R with probability 0.5 and lose $R/2$ with probability 0.5. The R value to use in equation (13.17) is the largest R for which the decision maker would accept this gamble. For instance, if the decision maker is comfortable accepting a gamble with a 50 percent chance of winning $2000 and a 50 percent chance of losing $1000, but not with

FIGURE 13.17   EXPONENTIAL UTILITY FUNCTIONS WITH DIFFERENT RISK
TOLERANCE (R) VALUES

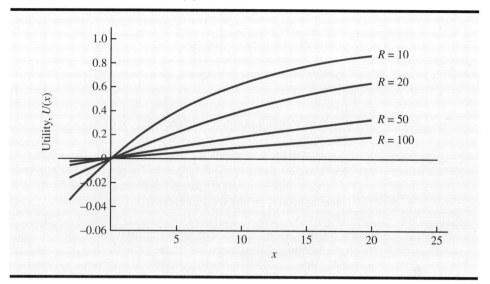

a gamble with a 50 percent chance of winning $3000 and a 50 percent chance of losing $1500
then we would use $R = \$2000$ in equation (13.17). Determining the maximum gamble that a
decision maker is willing to take and then using this value in the exponential utility function
can be much less time consuming than generating a complete table of indifference probabilities. One should remember that using an exponential utility function assumes that the decision
maker is risk averse; however, this is often true in practice for business decisions.

NOTES AND COMMENTS

1. In the Swofford problem, we have been using
a utility of 10 for the best payoff and 0 for the
worst. We could have chosen any values as long
as the utility associated with the best payoff exceeds the utility associated with the worst payoff. Alternatively, a utility of 1 can be associated
with the best payoff and a utility of 0 associated
with the worst payoff. Had we made this choice,
the utility for any monetary value M would have
been the value of p at which the decision maker
was indifferent between a guaranteed payoff
of M and a lottery in which the best payoff is
obtained with probability p and the worst payoff
is obtained with probability $(1 - p)$. Thus, the
utility for any monetary value would have been
equal to the probability of earning the best payoff. Often this choice is made because of the ease
in computation. We chose not to do so to emphasize the distinction between the utilities and the
indifference probabilities for the lottery.

2. Circumstances often dictate whether one acts as
a risk avoider or a risk taker when making a decision. For example, you may think of yourself
as a risk avoider when faced with financial decisions, but if you have ever purchased a lottery

ticket, you have actually acted as a risk taker.
For example, suppose you purchase a $1 lottery
ticket for a simple lottery in which the object is
to pick the six numbers that will be drawn from
50 potential numbers. Also suppose that the
winner (who correctly chooses all six numbers
that are drawn) will receive $1,000,000. There
are 15,890,700 possible winning combinations,
so your probability of winning is 1/15,890,700
= 0.00000006292989809763 (i.e., *very low*)
and the expected value of your ticket is

$$\frac{1}{15,890,700}(\$1,000,000 - \$1) + \left(1 - \frac{1}{15,890,700}\right)(-\$1)$$

$$= -\$0.93707$$

or about $-\$0.94$.

   If a lottery ticket has a negative expected
value, why does anyone play? The answer is in
utility; most people who play lotteries associate
great utility with the possibility of winning the
$1,000,000 prize and relatively little utility with
the $1 cost for a ticket, and so the expected value
of the utility of the lottery ticket is positive even
though the expected value of the ticket is negative.

SUMMARY

Decision analysis can be used to determine a recommended decision alternative or an optimal decision strategy when a decision maker is faced with an uncertain and risk-filled pattern of future events. The goal of decision analysis is to identify the best decision alternative or the optimal decision strategy given information about the uncertain events and the possible consequences or payoffs. The uncertain future events are called chance events, and the outcomes of the chance events are called states of nature. The "best" decision should consider the risk preference of the decision maker in evaluating outcomes.

We showed how influence diagrams, payoff tables, and decision trees could be used to structure a decision problem and describe the relationships among the decisions, the chance events, and the consequences. We presented three approaches to decision making without probabilities: the optimistic approach, the conservative approach, and the minimax regret approach. When probability assessments are provided for the states of nature, the expected value approach can be used to identify the recommended decision alternative or decision strategy.

Even though the expected value approach can be used to obtain a recommended decision alternative or optimal decision strategy, the payoff that actually occurs will usually have a value different from the expected value. A risk profile provides a probability distribution for the possible payoffs and can assist the decision maker in assessing the risks associated with different decision alternatives. Finally, sensitivity analysis can be conducted to determine the effect changes in the probabilities for the states of nature and changes in the values of the payoffs have on the recommended decision alternative.

In cases where sample information about the chance events is available, a sequence of decisions has to be made. First we must decide whether to obtain the sample information. If the answer to this decision is yes, an optimal decision strategy based on the specific sample information must be developed. In this situation, decision trees and the expected value approach can be used to determine the optimal decision strategy.

Bayes' theorem can be used to compute branch probabilities for decision trees. Bayes' theorem updates a decision maker's prior probabilities regarding the states of nature using sample information to compute revised posterior probabilities.

We showed how utility could be used in decision-making situations in which monetary value did not provide an adequate measure of the payoffs. Utility is a measure of the total worth of an outcome. As such, utility takes into account the decision maker's assessment of all aspects of a consequence, including profit, loss, risk, and perhaps additional nonmonetary factors. The examples showed how the use of expected utility can lead to decision recommendations that differ from those based on expected value.

A decision maker's judgment must be used to establish the utility for each consequence. We presented a step-by-step procedure to determine a decision maker's utility for monetary payoffs. We also discussed how conservative, risk-avoiding decision makers assess utility differently from more aggressive, risk-taking decision makers.

GLOSSARY

Bayes' theorem   A theorem that enables the use of sample information to revise prior probabilities.

Branch   Lines showing the alternatives from decision nodes and the outcomes from chance nodes.

Chance event   An uncertain future event affecting the consequence, or payoff, associated with a decision.

Chance nodes   Nodes indicating points where an uncertain event will occur.

Conditional probabilities   The probability of one event given the known outcome of a (possibly) related event.

Consequence The result obtained when a decision alternative is chosen and a chance event occurs. A measure of the consequence is often called a payoff.

Consequence nodes Nodes of an influence diagram indicating points where a payoff will occur.

Conservative approach An approach to choosing a decision alternative without using probabilities. For a maximization problem, it leads to choosing the decision alternative that maximizes the minimum payoff; for a minimization problem, it leads to choosing the decision alternative that minimizes the maximum payoff.

Decision alternatives Options available to the decision maker.

Decision nodes Nodes indicating points where a decision is made.

Decision strategy A strategy involving a sequence of decisions and chance outcomes to provide the optimal solution to a decision problem.

Decision tree A graphical representation of the decision problem that shows the sequential nature of the decision-making process.

Efficiency The ratio of EVSI to EVPI as a percentage; perfect information is 100% efficient.

Expected utility (EU) The weighted average of the utilities associated with a decision alternative. The weights are the state-of-nature probabilities.

Expected value (EV) For a chance node, it is the weighted average of the payoffs. The weights are the state-of-nature probabilities.

Expected value approach An approach to choosing a decision alternative based on the expected value of each decision alternative. The recommended decision alternative is the one that provides the best expected value.

Expected value of perfect information (EVPI) The expected value of information that would tell the decision maker exactly which state of nature is going to occur (i.e., perfect information).

Expected value of sample information (EVSI) The difference between the expected value of an optimal strategy based on sample information and the "best" expected value without any sample information.

Influence diagram A graphical device that shows the relationship among decisions, chance events, and consequences for a decision problem.

Joint probabilities The probabilities of both sample information and a particular state of nature occurring simultaneously.

Minimax regret approach An approach to choosing a decision alternative without using probabilities. For each alternative, the maximum regret is computed, which leads to choosing the decision alternative that minimizes the maximum regret.

Node An intersection or junction point of an influence diagram or a decision tree.

Opportunity loss, or regret The amount of loss (lower profit or higher cost) from not making the best decision for each state of nature.

Optimistic approach An approach to choosing a decision alternative without using probabilities. For a maximization problem, it leads to choosing the decision alternative corresponding to the largest payoff; for a minimization problem, it leads to choosing the decision alternative corresponding to the smallest payoff.

Payoff A measure of the consequence of a decision such as profit, cost, or time. Each combination of a decision alternative and a state of nature has an associated payoff (consequence).

Payoff table A tabular representation of the payoffs for a decision problem.

Posterior (revised) probabilities The probabilities of the states of nature after revising the prior probabilities based on sample information.

Prior probabilities   The probabilities of the states of nature prior to obtaining sample information.

Risk neutral   A decision maker who is neutral to risk. For this decision maker the decision alternative with the best expected value is identical to the alternative with the highest expected utility.

Risk analysis   The study of the possible payoffs and probabilities associated with a decision alternative or a decision strategy.

Risk avoider   A decision maker who would choose a guaranteed payoff over a lottery with a better expected payoff.

Risk profile   The probability distribution of the possible payoffs associated with a decision alternative or decision strategy.

Risk taker   A decision maker who would choose a lottery over a better guaranteed payoff.

Sample information   New information obtained through research or experimentation that enables an updating or revision of the state-of-nature probabilities.

Sensitivity analysis   The study of how changes in the probability assessments for the states of nature or changes in the payoffs affect the recommended decision alternative.

States of nature   The possible outcomes for chance events that affect the payoff associated with a decision alternative.

Utility   A measure of the total worth of a consequence reflecting a decision maker's attitude toward considerations such as profit, loss, and risk.

Utility function for money   A curve that depicts the relationship between monetary value and utility.

PROBLEMS

 SELF*test*

1. The following payoff table shows profit for a decision analysis problem with two decision alternatives and three states of nature:

	State of Nature		
Decision Alternative	s_1	s_2	s_3
d_1	250	100	25
d_2	100	100	75

   a. Construct a decision tree for this problem.
   b. If the decision maker knows nothing about the probabilities of the three states of nature, what is the recommended decision using the optimistic, conservative, and minimax regret approaches?

2. Suppose that a decision maker faced with four decision alternatives and four states of nature develops the following profit payoff table:

	State of Nature			
Decision Alternative	s_1	s_2	s_3	s_4
d_1	14	9	10	5
d_2	11	10	8	7
d_3	9	10	10	11
d_4	8	10	11	13

a. If the decision maker knows nothing about the probabilities of the four states of nature, what is the recommended decision using the optimistic, conservative, and minimax regret approaches?

b. Which approach do you prefer? Explain. Is establishing the most appropriate approach before analyzing the problem important for the decision maker? Explain.

c. Assume that the payoff table provides *cost* rather than profit payoffs. What is the recommended decision using the optimistic, conservative, and minimax regret approaches?

 SELF*test*

3. Southland Corporation's decision to produce a new line of recreational products resulted in the need to construct either a small plant or a large plant. The best selection of plant size depends on how the marketplace reacts to the new product line. To conduct an analysis, marketing management has decided to view the possible long-run demand as low, medium, or high. The following payoff table shows the projected profit in millions of dollars:

Plant Size	Long-Run Demand		
	Low	Medium	High
Small	150	200	200
Large	50	200	500

a. What is the decision to be made, and what is the chance event for Southland's problem?
b. Construct an influence diagram.
c. Construct a decision tree.
d. Recommend a decision based on the use of the optimistic, conservative, and minimax regret approaches.

4. Amy Lloyd is interested in leasing a new Honda and has contacted three automobile dealers for pricing information. Each dealer offered Amy a closed-end 36-month lease with no down payment due at the time of signing. Each lease includes a monthly charge and a mileage allowance. Additional miles receive a surcharge on a per-mile basis. The monthly lease cost, the mileage allowance, and the cost for additional miles follow:

Dealer	Monthly Cost	Mileage Allowance	Cost per Additional Mile
Hepburn Honda	$299	36,000	$0.15
Midtown Motors	$310	45,000	$0.20
Hopkins Automotive	$325	54,000	$0.15

Amy decided to choose the lease option that will minimize her total 36-month cost. The difficulty is that Amy is not sure how many miles she will drive over the next three years. For purposes of this decision, she believes it is reasonable to assume that she will drive 12,000 miles per year, 15,000 miles per year, or 18,000 miles per year. With this assumption Amy estimated her total costs for the three lease options. For example, she figures that the Hepburn Honda lease will cost her $10,764 if she drives 12,000 miles per year, $12,114 if she drives 15,000 miles per year, or $13,464 if she drives 18,000 miles per year.

a. What is the decision, and what is the chance event?
b. Construct a payoff table for Amy's problem.
c. If Amy has no idea which of the three mileage assumptions is most appropriate, what is the recommended decision (leasing option) using the optimistic, conservative, and minimax regret approaches?
d. Suppose that the probabilities that Amy drives 12,000, 15,000, and 18,000 miles per year are 0.5, 0.4, and 0.1, respectively. What option should Amy choose using the expected value approach?
e. Develop a risk profile for the decision selected in part (d). What is the most likely cost, and what is its probability?
f. Suppose that after further consideration Amy concludes that the probabilities that she will drive 12,000, 15,000, and 18,000 miles per year are 0.3, 0.4, and 0.3, respectively. What decision should Amy make using the expected value approach?

5. The following profit payoff table was presented in Problem 1. Suppose that the decision maker obtained the probability assessments $P(s_1) = 0.65$, $P(s_2) = 0.15$, and $P(s_3) = 0.20$. Use the expected value approach to determine the optimal decision.

	State of Nature		
Decision Alternative	s_1	s_2	s_3
d_1	250	100	25
d_2	100	100	75

6. Investment advisors estimated the stock market returns for four market segments: computers, financial, manufacturing, and pharmaceuticals. Annual return projections vary depending on whether the general economic conditions are improving, stable, or declining. The anticipated annual return percentages for each market segment under each economic condition are as follows:

	Economic Condition		
Market Segment	Improving	Stable	Declining
Computers	10	2	-4
Financial	8	5	-3
Manufacturing	6	4	-2
Pharmaceuticals	6	5	-1

a. Assume that an individual investor wants to select one market segment for a new investment. A forecast shows stable to declining economic conditions with the following probabilities: improving (0.2), stable (0.5), and declining (0.3). What is the preferred market segment for the investor, and what is the expected return percentage?

b. At a later date, a revised forecast shows a potential for an improvement in economic conditions. New probabilities are as follows: improving (0.4), stable (0.4), and declining (0.2). What is the preferred market segment for the investor based on these new probabilities? What is the expected return percentage?

7. Hudson Corporation is considering three options for managing its data processing operation: continuing with its own staff, hiring an outside vendor to do the managing (referred to as *outsourcing*), or using a combination of its own staff and an outside vendor. The cost of the operation depends on future demand. The annual cost of each option (in thousands of dollars) depends on demand as follows:

	Demand		
Staffing Options	High	Medium	Low
Own staff	650	650	600
Outside vendor	900	600	300
Combination	800	650	500

a. If the demand probabilities are 0.2, 0.5, and 0.3, which decision alternative will minimize the expected cost of the data processing operation? What is the expected annual cost associated with that recommendation?

b. Construct a risk profile for the optimal decision in part (a). What is the probability of the cost exceeding $700,000?

8. The following payoff table shows the profit for a decision problem with two states of nature and two decision alternatives:

	State of Nature	
Decision Alternative	s_1	s_2
d_1	10	1
d_2	4	3

a. Use graphical sensitivity analysis to determine the range of probabilities of state of nature s_1 for which each of the decision alternatives has the largest expected value.

b. Suppose $P(s_1) = 0.2$ and $P(s_2) = 0.8$. What is the best decision using the expected value approach?

c. Perform sensitivity analysis on the payoffs for decision alternative d_1. Assume the probabilities are as given in part (b), and find the range of payoffs under states of nature s_1 and s_2 that will keep the solution found in part (b) optimal. Is the solution more sensitive to the payoff under state of nature s_1 or s_2?

9. Myrtle Air Express decided to offer direct service from Cleveland to Myrtle Beach. Management must decide between a full-price service using the company's new fleet of jet aircraft and a discount service using smaller capacity commuter planes. It is clear that the best choice depends on the market reaction to the service Myrtle Air offers. Management developed estimates of the contribution to profit for each type of service based upon two possible levels of demand for service to Myrtle Beach: strong and weak. The following table shows the estimated quarterly profits (in thousands of dollars):

	Demand for Service	
Service	Strong	Weak
Full price	$960	−$490
Discount	$670	$320

a. What is the decision to be made, what is the chance event, and what is the consequence for this problem? How many decision alternatives are there? How many outcomes are there for the chance event?

b. If nothing is known about the probabilities of the chance outcomes, what is the recommended decision using the optimistic, conservative, and minimax regret approaches?

c. Suppose that management of Myrtle Air Express believes that the probability of strong demand is 0.7 and the probability of weak demand is 0.3. Use the expected value approach to determine an optimal decision.

d. Suppose that the probability of strong demand is 0.8 and the probability of weak demand is 0.2. What is the optimal decision using the expected value approach?

e. Use graphical sensitivity analysis to determine the range of demand probabilities for which each of the decision alternatives has the largest expected value.

10. Video Tech is considering marketing one of two new video games for the coming holiday season: Battle Pacific or Space Pirates. Battle Pacific is a unique game and appears to have no competition. Estimated profits (in thousands of dollars) under high, medium, and low demand are as follows:

	Demand		
Battle Pacific	High	Medium	Low
Profit	$1000	$700	$300
Probability	0.2	0.5	0.3

Video Tech is optimistic about its Space Pirates game. However, the concern is that profitability will be affected by a competitor's introduction of a video game viewed as similar to Space Pirates. Estimated profits (in thousands of dollars) with and without competition are as follows:

Space Pirates with Competition	Demand		
	High	Medium	Low
Profit	$800	$400	$200
Probability	0.3	0.4	0.3

Space Pirates without Competition	Demand		
	High	**Medium**	**Low**
Profit	$1600	$800	$400
Probability	0.5	0.3	0.2

    a. Develop a decision tree for the Video Tech problem.

    b. For planning purposes, Video Tech believes there is a 0.6 probability that its competitor will produce a new game similar to Space Pirates. Given this probability of competition, the director of planning recommends marketing the Battle Pacific video game. Using expected value, what is your recommended decision?

    c. Show a risk profile for your recommended decision.

    d. Use sensitivity analysis to determine what the probability of competition for Space Pirates would have to be for you to change your recommended decision alternative.

11. For the Pittsburgh Development Corporation problem in Section 13.3, the decision alternative to build the large condominium complex was found to be optimal using the expected value approach. In Section 13.4 we conducted a sensitivity analysis for the payoffs associated with this decision alternative. We found that the large complex remained optimal as long as the payoff for the strong demand was greater than or equal to $17.5 million and as long as the payoff for the weak demand was greater than or equal to $-$19 million.

    a. Consider the medium complex decision. How much could the payoff under strong demand increase and still keep decision alternative d_3 the optimal solution?

    b. Consider the small complex decision. How much could the payoff under strong demand increase and still keep decision alternative d_3 the optimal solution?

12. The distance from Potsdam to larger markets and limited air service have hindered the town in attracting new industry. Air Express, a major overnight delivery service, is considering establishing a regional distribution center in Potsdam. However, Air Express will not establish the center unless the length of the runway at the local airport is increased. Another candidate for new development is Diagnostic Research, Inc. (DRI), a leading producer of medical testing equipment. DRI is considering building a new manufacturing plant. Increasing the length of the runway is not a requirement for DRI, but the planning commission feels that doing so will help convince DRI to locate its new plant in Potsdam. Assuming that the town lengthens the runway, the Potsdam planning commission believes that the probabilities shown in the following table are applicable:

	DRI Plant	**No DRI Plant**
Air Express Center	0.30	0.10
No Air Express Center	0.40	0.20

For instance, the probability that Air Express will establish a distribution center and DRI will build a plant is 0.30.

    The estimated annual revenue to the town, after deducting the cost of lengthening the runway, is as follows:

	DRI Plant	**No DRI Plant**
Air Express Center	$600,000	$150,000
No Air Express Center	$250,000	$-$200,000

If the runway expansion project is not conducted, the planning commission assesses the probability that DRI will locate its new plant in Potsdam at 0.6; in this case, the estimated annual revenue to the town will be $450,000. If the runway expansion project is not conducted and DRI does not locate in Potsdam, the annual revenue will be $0 because no cost will have been incurred and no revenues will be forthcoming.

a. What is the decision to be made, what is the chance event, and what is the consequence?

b. Compute the expected annual revenue associated with the decision alternative to lengthen the runway.

c. Compute the expected annual revenue associated with the decision alternative not to lengthen the runway.

d. Should the town elect to lengthen the runway? Explain.

e. Suppose that the probabilities associated with lengthening the runway were as follows:

	DRI Plant	No DRI Plant
Air Express Center	0.40	0.10
No Air Express Center	0.30	0.20

What effect, if any, would this change in the probabilities have on the recommended decision?

13. Seneca Hill Winery recently purchased land for the purpose of establishing a new vineyard. Management is considering two varieties of white grapes for the new vineyard: Chardonnay and Riesling. The Chardonnay grapes would be used to produce a dry Chardonnay wine, and the Riesling grapes would be used to produce a semidry Riesling wine. It takes approximately four years from the time of planting before new grapes can be harvested. This length of time creates a great deal of uncertainty concerning future demand and makes the decision about the type of grapes to plant difficult. Three possibilities are being considered: Chardonnay grapes only; Riesling grapes only; and both Chardonnay and Riesling grapes. Seneca management decided that for planning purposes it would be adequate to consider only two demand possibilities for each type of wine: strong or weak. With two possibilities for each type of wine, it was necessary to assess four probabilities. With the help of some forecasts in industry publications, management made the following probability assessments:

	Riesling Demand	
Chardonnay Demand	Weak	Strong
Weak	0.05	0.50
Strong	0.25	0.20

Revenue projections show an annual contribution to profit of $20,000 if Seneca Hill only plants Chardonnay grapes and demand is weak for Chardonnay wine, and $70,000 if Seneca only plants Chardonnay grapes and demand is strong for Chardonnay wine. If Seneca only plants Riesling grapes, the annual profit projection is $25,000 if demand is weak for Riesling grapes and $45,000 if demand is strong for Riesling grapes. If Seneca plants both types of grapes, the annual profit projections are shown in the following table:

	Riesling Demand	
Chardonnay Demand	Weak	Strong
Weak	$22,000	$40,000
Strong	$26,000	$60,000

a. What is the decision to be made, what is the chance event, and what is the consequence? Identify the alternatives for the decisions and the possible outcomes for the chance events.

b. Develop a decision tree.

c. Use the expected value approach to recommend which alternative Seneca Hill Winery should follow in order to maximize expected annual profit.

d. Suppose management is concerned about the probability assessments when demand for Chardonnay wine is strong. Some believe it is likely for Riesling demand to also be strong in this case. Suppose the probability of strong demand for Chardonnay and weak demand for Riesling is 0.05 and that the probability of strong demand for Chardonnay and strong demand for Riesling is 0.40. How does this change the recommended decision? Assume that the probabilities when Chardonnay demand is weak are still 0.05 and 0.50.

e. Other members of the management team expect the Chardonnay market to become saturated at some point in the future, causing a fall in prices. Suppose that the annual profit projections fall to $50,000 when demand for Chardonnay is strong and Chardonnay grapes only are planted. Using the original probability assessments, determine how this change would affect the optimal decision.

 SELF*test*

14. The following profit payoff table was presented in Problem 1:

	State of Nature		
Decision Alternative	s_1	s_2	s_3
d_1	250	100	25
d_2	100	100	75

The probabilities for the states of nature are $P(s_1) = 0.65$, $P(s_2) = 0.15$, and $P(s_3) = 0.20$.

a. What is the optimal decision strategy if perfect information were available?
b. What is the expected value for the decision strategy developed in part (a)?
c. Using the expected value approach, what is the recommended decision without perfect information? What is its expected value?
d. What is the expected value of perfect information?

15. The Lake Placid Town Council decided to build a new community center to be used for conventions, concerts, and other public events, but considerable controversy surrounds the appropriate size. Many influential citizens want a large center that would be a showcase for the area. But the mayor feels that if demand does not support such a center, the community will lose a large amount of money. To provide structure for the decision process, the council narrowed the building alternatives to three sizes: small, medium, and large. Everybody agreed that the critical factor in choosing the best size is the number of people who will want to use the new facility. A regional planning consultant provided demand estimates under three scenarios: worst case, base case, and best case. The worst-case scenario corresponds to a situation in which tourism drops substantially; the base-case scenario corresponds to a situation in which Lake Placid continues to attract visitors at current levels; and the best-case scenario corresponds to a substantial increase in tourism. The consultant has provided probability assessments of 0.10, 0.60, and 0.30 for the worst-case, base-case, and best-case scenarios, respectively.

The town council suggested using net cash flow over a 5-year planning horizon as the criterion for deciding on the best size. The following projections of net cash flow (in thousands of dollars) for a 5-year planning horizon have been developed. All costs, including the consultant's fee, have been included.

	Demand Scenario		
Center Size	Worst Case	Base Case	Best Case
Small	400	500	660
Medium	−250	650	800
Large	−400	580	990

a. What decision should Lake Placid make using the expected value approach?
b. Construct risk profiles for the medium and large alternatives. Given the mayor's concern over the possibility of losing money and the result of part (a), which alternative would you recommend?

c. Compute the expected value of perfect information. Do you think it would be worth trying to obtain additional information concerning which scenario is likely to occur?

d. Suppose the probability of the worst-case scenario increases to 0.2, the probability of the base-case scenario decreases to 0.5, and the probability of the best-case scenario remains at 0.3. What effect, if any, would these changes have on the decision recommendation?

e. The consultant has suggested that an expenditure of $150,000 on a promotional campaign over the planning horizon will effectively reduce the probability of the worst-case scenario to zero. If the campaign can be expected to also increase the probability of the best-case scenario to 0.4, is it a good investment?

SELF*test*

16. Consider a variation of the PDC decision tree shown in Figure 13.9. The company must first decide whether to undertake the market research study. If the market research study is conducted, the outcome will either be favorable (F) or unfavorable (U). Assume there are only two decision alternatives, d_1 and d_2, and two states of nature, s_1 and s_2. The payoff table showing profit is as follows:

| | State of Nature | |
Decision Alternative	s_1	s_2
d_1	100	300
d_2	400	200

a. Show the decision tree.

b. Using the following probabilities, what is the optimal decision strategy?

$P(F) = 0.56$ $P(s_1 \mid F) = 0.57$ $P(s_1 \mid U) = 0.18$ $P(s_1) = 0.40$

$P(U) = 0.44$ $P(s_2 \mid F) = 0.43$ $P(s_2 \mid U) = 0.82$ $P(s_2) = 0.60$

17. Hemmingway, Inc., is considering a $5 million research and development (R&D) project. Profit projections appear promising, but Hemmingway's president is concerned because the probability that the R&D project will be successful is only 0.50. Furthermore, the president knows that even if the project is successful, it will require that the company build a new production facility at a cost of $20 million in order to manufacture the product. If the facility is built, uncertainty remains about the demand and thus uncertainty about the profit that will be realized. Another option is that if the R&D project is successful, the company could sell the rights to the product for an estimated $25 million. Under this option, the company would not build the $20 million production facility.

The decision tree is shown in Figure 13.18. The profit projection for each outcome is shown at the end of the branches. For example, the revenue projection for the high demand outcome is $59 million. However, the cost of the R&D project ($5 million) and the cost of the production facility ($20 million) show the profit of this outcome to be $59 − $5 − $20 = $34 million. Branch probabilities are also shown for the chance events.

a. Analyze the decision tree to determine whether the company should undertake the R&D project. If it does, and if the R&D project is successful, what should the company do? What is the expected value of your strategy?

b. What must the selling price be for the company to consider selling the rights to the product?

c. Develop a risk profile for the optimal strategy.

18. Dante Development Corporation is considering bidding on a contract for a new office building complex. Figure 13.19 shows the decision tree prepared by one of Dante's analysts. At node 1, the company must decide whether to bid on the contract. The cost of preparing the bid is $200,000. The upper branch from node 2 shows that the company has a 0.8 probability of winning the contract if it submits a bid. If the company wins the bid, it will have to pay $2,000,000 to become a partner in the project. Node 3 shows that the company will then consider doing a market research study to forecast demand for the office units prior to beginning construction. The cost of this study is $150,000. Node 4 is a chance node showing the possible outcomes of the market research study.

FIGURE 13.18   DECISION TREE FOR HEMMINGWAY, INC.

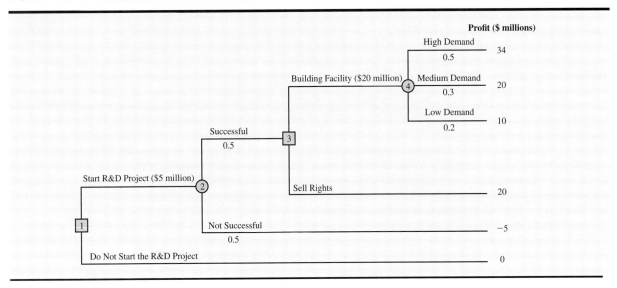

FIGURE 13.19   DECISION TREE FOR THE DANTE DEVELOPMENT CORPORATION

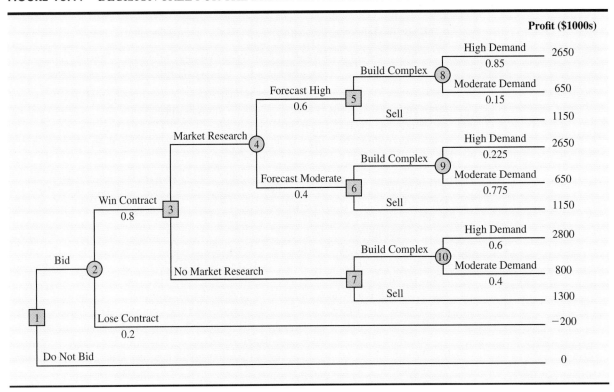

Nodes 5, 6, and 7 are similar in that they are the decision nodes for Dante to either build the office complex or sell the rights in the project to another developer. The decision to build the complex will result in an income of $5,000,000 if demand is high and $3,000,000 if demand is moderate. If Dante chooses to sell its rights in the project to another developer, income from the sale is estimated to be $3,500,000. The probabilities shown at nodes 4, 8, and 9 are based on the projected outcomes of the market research study.

a. Verify Dante's profit projections shown at the ending branches of the decision tree by calculating the payoffs of $2,650,000 and $650,000 for first two outcomes.

    b. What is the optimal decision strategy for Dante, and what is the expected profit for this project?

    c. What would the cost of the market research study have to be before Dante would change its decision about the market research study?

    d. Develop a risk profile for Dante.

19. Hale's TV Productions is considering producing a pilot for a comedy series in the hope of selling it to a major television network. The network may decide to reject the series, but it may also decide to purchase the rights to the series for either one or two years. At this point in time, Hale may either produce the pilot and wait for the network's decision or transfer the rights for the pilot and series to a competitor for $100,000. Hale's decision alternatives and profits (in thousands of dollars) are as follows:

		State of Nature	
Decision Alternative	**Reject, s_1**	**1 Year, s_2**	**2 Years, s_3**
Produce pilot, d_1	-100	50	150
Sell to competitor, d_2	100	100	100

The probabilities for the states of nature are $P(s_1) = 0.20$, $P(s_2) = 0.30$, and $P(s_3) = 0.50$. For a consulting fee of $5000, an agency will review the plans for the comedy series and indicate the overall chances of a favorable network reaction to the series. Assume that the agency review will result in a favorable (F) or an unfavorable (U) review and that the following probabilities are relevant:

$$P(F) = 0.69 \qquad P(s_1 \mid F) = 0.09 \qquad P(s_1 \mid U) = 0.45$$
$$P(U) = 0.31 \qquad P(s_2 \mid F) = 0.26 \qquad P(s_2 \mid U) = 0.39$$
$$P(s_3 \mid F) = 0.65 \qquad P(s_3 \mid U) = 0.16$$

    a. Construct a decision tree for this problem.

    b. What is the recommended decision if the agency opinion is not used? What is the expected value?

    c. What is the expected value of perfect information?

    d. What is Hale's optimal decision strategy assuming the agency's information is used?

    e. What is the expected value of the agency's information?

    f. Is the agency's information worth the $5000 fee? What is the maximum that Hale should be willing to pay for the information?

    g. What is the recommended decision?

20. Embassy Publishing Company received a six-chapter manuscript for a new college textbook. The editor of the college division is familiar with the manuscript and estimated a 0.65 probability that the textbook will be successful. If successful, a profit of $750,000 will be realized. If the company decides to publish the textbook and it is unsuccessful, a loss of $250,000 will occur.

    Before making the decision to accept or reject the manuscript, the editor is considering sending the manuscript out for review. A review process provides either a favorable (F) or unfavorable (U) evaluation of the manuscript. Past experience with the review process suggests that probabilities $P(F) = 0.7$ and $P(U) = 0.3$ apply. Let s_1 = the textbook is successful, and s_2 = the textbook is unsuccessful. The editor's initial probabilities of s_1 and s_2 will be revised based on whether the review is favorable or unfavorable. The revised probabilities are as follows:

$$P(s_1 \mid F) = 0.75 \qquad P(s_1 \mid U) = 0.417$$
$$P(s_2 \mid F) = 0.25 \qquad P(s_2 \mid U) = 0.583$$

    a. Construct a decision tree assuming that the company will first make the decision of whether to send the manuscript out for review and then make the decision to accept or reject the manuscript.

b. Analyze the decision tree to determine the optimal decision strategy for the publishing company.

c. If the manuscript review costs $5000, what is your recommendation?

d. What is the expected value of perfect information? What does this EVPI suggest for the company?

21. A real estate investor has the opportunity to purchase land currently zoned residential. If the county board approves a request to rezone the property as commercial within the next year, the investor will be able to lease the land to a large discount firm that wants to open a new store on the property. However, if the zoning change is not approved, the investor will have to sell the property at a loss. Profits (in thousands of dollars) are shown in the following payoff table:

	State of Nature	
	Rezoning Approved	Rezoning Not Approved
Decision Alternative	s_1	s_2
Purchase, d_1	600	-200
Do not purchase, d_2	0	0

a. If the probability that the rezoning will be approved is 0.5, what decision is recommended? What is the expected profit?

b. The investor can purchase an option to buy the land. Under the option, the investor maintains the rights to purchase the land anytime during the next three months while learning more about possible resistance to the rezoning proposal from area residents. Probabilities are as follows:

Let H = High resistance to rezoning

L = Low resistance to rezoning

$P(H) = 0.55$	$P(s_1 \mid H) = 0.18$	$P(s_2 \mid H) = 0.82$
$P(L) = 0.45$	$P(s_1 \mid L) = 0.89$	$P(s_2 \mid L) = 0.11$

What is the optimal decision strategy if the investor uses the option period to learn more about the resistance from area residents before making the purchase decision?

c. If the option will cost the investor an additional $10,000, should the investor purchase the option? Why or why not? What is the maximum that the investor should be willing to pay for the option?

22. Lawson's Department Store faces a buying decision for a seasonal product for which demand can be high, medium, or low. The purchaser for Lawson's can order one, two, or three lots of the product before the season begins but cannot reorder later. Profit projections (in thousands of dollars) are shown as follows:

	State of Nature		
	High Demand	Medium Demand	Low Demand
Decision Alternative	s_1	s_2	s_3
Order 1 lot, d_1	60	60	50
Order 2 lots, d_2	80	80	30
Order 3 lots, d_3	100	70	10

a. If the prior probabilities for the three states of nature are 0.3, 0.3, and 0.4, respectively, what is the recommended order quantity?

b. At each preseason sales meeting, the vice president of sales provides a personal opinion regarding potential demand for this product. Because of the vice president's enthusiasm and optimistic nature, the predictions of market conditions have always been either "excellent" (E) or "very good" (V). Probabilities are as follows:

$$P(E) = 0.70 \qquad P(s_1 \mid E) = 0.34 \qquad P(s_1 \mid V) = 0.20$$
$$P(V) = 0.30 \qquad P(s_2 \mid E) = 0.32 \qquad P(s_2 \mid V) = 0.26$$
$$P(s_3 \mid E) = 0.34 \qquad P(s_3 \mid V) = 0.54$$

What is the optimal decision strategy?

c. Use the efficiency of sample information and discuss whether the firm should consider a consulting expert who could provide independent forecasts of market conditions for the product.

23. Suppose that you are given a decision situation with three possible states of nature: s_1, s_2, and s_3. The prior probabilities are $P(s_1) = 0.2$, $P(s_2) = 0.5$, and $P(s_3) = 0.3$. With sample information I, $P(I \mid s_1) = 0.1$, $P(I \mid s_2) = 0.05$, and $P(I \mid s_3) = 0.2$. Compute the revised or posterior probabilities: $P(s_1 \mid I)$, $P(s_2 \mid I)$, and $P(s_3 \mid I)$.

24. To save on expenses, Rona and Jerry agreed to form a carpool for traveling to and from work. Rona preferred to use the somewhat longer but more consistent Queen City Avenue. Although Jerry preferred the quicker expressway, he agreed with Rona that they should take Queen City Avenue if the expressway had a traffic jam. The following payoff table provides the one-way time estimate in minutes for traveling to or from work:

	State of Nature	
	Expressway Open	Expressway Jammed
Decision Alternative	s_1	s_2
Queen City Avenue, d_1	30	30
Expressway, d_2	25	45

Based on their experience with traffic problems, Rona and Jerry agreed on a 0.15 probability that the expressway would be jammed.

In addition, they agreed that weather seemed to affect the traffic conditions on the expressway. Let

$$C = \text{clear}$$
$$O = \text{overcast}$$
$$R = \text{rain}$$

The following conditional probabilities apply:

$$P(C \mid s_1) = 0.8 \qquad P(O \mid s_1) = 0.2 \qquad P(R \mid s_1) = 0.0$$
$$P(C \mid s_2) = 0.1 \qquad P(O \mid s_2) = 0.3 \qquad P(R \mid s_2) = 0.6$$

a. Use Bayes' theorem for probability revision to compute the probability of each weather condition and the conditional probability of the expressway open, s_1, or jammed, s_2, given each weather condition.

b. Show the decision tree for this problem.

c. What is the optimal decision strategy, and what is the expected travel time?

25. The Gorman Manufacturing Company must decide whether to manufacture a component part at its Milan, Michigan, plant or purchase the component part from a supplier. The resulting profit is dependent upon the demand for the product. The following payoff table shows the projected profit (in thousands of dollars):

	State of Nature		
	Low Demand	Medium Demand	High Demand
Decision Alternative	s_1	s_2	s_3
Manufacture, d_1	−20	40	100
Purchase, d_2	10	45	70

The state-of-nature probabilities are $P(s_1) = 0.35$, $P(s_2) = 0.35$, and $P(s_3) = 0.30$.

a. Use a decision tree to recommend a decision.

b. Use EVPI to determine whether Gorman should attempt to obtain a better estimate of demand.

c. A test market study of the potential demand for the product is expected to report either a favorable (F) or unfavorable (U) condition. The relevant conditional probabilities are as follows:

$$P(F \mid s_1) = 0.10 \qquad P(U \mid s_1) = 0.90$$
$$P(F \mid s_2) = 0.40 \qquad P(U \mid s_2) = 0.60$$
$$P(F \mid s_3) = 0.60 \qquad P(U \mid s_3) = 0.40$$

What is the probability that the market research report will be favorable?

d. What is Gorman's optimal decision strategy?

e. What is the expected value of the market research information?

f. What is the efficiency of the information?

26. Alexander Industries is considering purchasing an insurance policy for its new office building in St. Louis, Missouri. The policy has an annual cost of $10,000. If Alexander Industries doesn't purchase the insurance and minor fire damage occurs, a cost of $100,000 is anticipated; the cost if major or total destruction occurs is $200,000. The costs, including the state-of-nature probabilities, are as follows:

	Damage		
	None	Minor	Major
Decision Alternative	s_1	s_2	s_3
Purchase Insurance, d_1	10,000	10,000	10,000
Do Not Purchase Insurance, d_2	0	100,000	200,000
Probabilities	0.96	0.03	0.01

a. Using the expected value approach, what decision do you recommend?

b. What lottery would you use to assess utilities? (*Note:* Because the data are costs, the best payoff is $0.)

c. Assume that you found the following indifference probabilities for the lottery defined in part (b). What decision would you recommend?

Cost	Indifference Probability
10,000	$p = 0.99$
100,000	$p = 0.60$

d. Do you favor using expected value or expected utility for this decision problem? Why?

27. In a certain state lottery, a lottery ticket costs $2. In terms of the decision to purchase or not to purchase a lottery ticket, suppose that the following payoff table applies:

	State of Nature	
	Win	Lose
Decision Alternatives	s_1	s_2
Purchase Lottery Ticket, d_1	300,000	−2
Do Not Purchase Lottery Ticket, d_2	0	0

a. A realistic estimate of the chances of winning is 1 in 250,000. Use the expected value approach to recommend a decision.

b. If a particular decision maker assigns an indifference probability of 0.000001 to the $0 payoff, would this individual purchase a lottery ticket? Use expected utility to justify your answer.

28. Three decision makers have assessed utilities for the following decision problem (payoff in dollars):

	State of Nature		
Decision Alternative	s_1	s_2	s_3
d_1	20	50	-20
d_2	80	100	-100

The indifference probabilities are as follows:

	Indifference Probability (p)		
Payoff	Decision Maker A	Decision Maker B	Decision Maker C
100	1.00	1.00	1.00
80	0.95	0.70	0.90
50	0.90	0.60	0.75
20	0.70	0.45	0.60
-20	0.50	0.25	0.40
-100	0.00	0.00	0.00

a. Plot the utility function for money for each decision maker.
b. Classify each decision maker as a risk avoider, a risk taker, or risk neutral.
c. For the payoff of 20, what is the premium that the risk avoider will pay to avoid risk? What is the premium that the risk taker will pay to have the opportunity of the high payoff?

29. In Problem 28, if $P(s_1) = 0.25$, $P(s_2) = 0.50$, and $P(s_3) = 0.25$, find a recommended decision for each of the three decision makers. (*Note:* For the same decision problem, different utilities can lead to different decisions.)

30. Translate the following monetary payoffs into utilities for a decision maker whose utility function is described by an exponential function with $R = 250$: $-\$200$, $-\$100$, $\$0$, $\$100$, $\$200$, $\$300$, $\$400$, $\$500$.

31. Consider a decision maker who is comfortable with an investment decision that has a 50 percent chance of earning $25,000 and a 50 percent chance of losing $12,500, but not with any larger investments that have the same relative payoffs.
a. Write the equation for the exponential function that approximates this decision maker's utility function.
b. Plot the exponential utility function for this decision maker for x values between $-20,000$ and 35,000. Is this decision maker risk seeking, risk neutral, or risk averse?
c. Suppose the decision maker decides that she would actually be willing to make an investment that has a 50 percent chance of earning $30,000 and a 50 percent chance of losing $15,000. Plot the exponential function that approximates this utility function and compare it to the utility function from part (b). Is the decision maker becoming more risk seeking or more risk averse?

Case Problem 1   PROPERTY PURCHASE STRATEGY

Glenn Foreman, president of Oceanview Development Corporation, is considering submitting a bid to purchase property that will be sold by sealed bid at a county tax foreclosure. Glenn's initial judgment is to submit a bid of $5 million. Based on his experience, Glenn estimates that a bid of $5 million will have a 0.2 probability of being the highest bid and securing the property for Oceanview. The current date is June 1. Sealed bids for the property must be submitted by August 15. The winning bid will be announced on September 1.

If Oceanview submits the highest bid and obtains the property, the firm plans to build and sell a complex of luxury condominiums. However, a complicating factor is that the property is currently zoned for single-family residences only. Glenn believes that a referendum could be placed on the voting ballot in time for the November election. Passage of the referendum would change the zoning of the property and permit construction of the condominiums.

The sealed-bid procedure requires the bid to be submitted with a certified check for 10% of the amount bid. If the bid is rejected, the deposit is refunded. If the bid is accepted, the deposit is the down payment for the property. However, if the bid is accepted and the bidder does not follow through with the purchase and meet the remainder of the financial obligation within six months, the deposit will be forfeited. In this case, the county will offer the property to the next highest bidder.

To determine whether Oceanview should submit the $5 million bid, Glenn conducted some preliminary analysis. This preliminary work provided an assessment of 0.3 for the probability that the referendum for a zoning change will be approved and resulted in the following estimates of the costs and revenues that will be incurred if the condominiums are built:

Cost and Revenue Estimates

Revenue from condominium sales	$15,000,000
Cost	
Property	$5,000,000
Construction expenses	$8,000,000

If Oceanview obtains the property and the zoning change is rejected in November, Glenn believes that the best option would be for the firm not to complete the purchase of the property. In this case, Oceanview would forfeit the 10% deposit that accompanied the bid.

Because the likelihood that the zoning referendum will be approved is such an important factor in the decision process, Glenn suggested that the firm hire a market research service to conduct a survey of voters. The survey would provide a better estimate of the likelihood that the referendum for a zoning change would be approved. The market research firm that Oceanview Development has worked with in the past has agreed to do the study for $15,000. The results of the study will be available on August 1, so that Oceanview will have this information before the August 15 bid deadline. The results of the survey will be either a prediction that the zoning change will be approved or a prediction that the zoning change will be rejected. After considering the record of the market research service in previous studies conducted for Oceanview, Glenn developed the following probability estimates concerning the accuracy of the market research information:

$$P(A \mid s_1) = 0.9 \qquad P(N \mid s_1) = 0.1$$
$$P(A \mid s_2) = 0.2 \qquad P(N \mid s_2) = 0.8$$

where

A = prediction of zoning change approval

N = prediction that zoning change will not be approved

s_1 = the zoning change is approved by the voters

s_2 = the zoning change is rejected by the voters

Managerial Report

Perform an analysis of the problem facing the Oceanview Development Corporation, and prepare a report that summarizes your findings and recommendations. Include the following items in your report:

1. A decision tree that shows the logical sequence of the decision problem
2. A recommendation regarding what Oceanview should do if the market research information is not available

3. A decision strategy that Oceanview should follow if the market research is conducted
4. A recommendation as to whether Oceanview should employ the market research firm, along with the value of the information provided by the market research firm

Include the details of your analysis as an appendix to your report.

Case Problem 2   LAWSUIT DEFENSE STRATEGY

John Campbell, an employee of Manhattan Construction Company, claims to have injured his back as a result of a fall while repairing the roof at one of the Eastview apartment buildings. He filed a lawsuit against Doug Reynolds, the owner of Eastview Apartments, asking for damages of $1,500,000. John claims that the roof had rotten sections and that his fall could have been prevented if Mr. Reynolds had told Manhattan Construction about the problem. Mr. Reynolds notified his insurance company, Allied Insurance, of the lawsuit. Allied must defend Mr. Reynolds and decide what action to take regarding the lawsuit.

Some depositions and a series of discussions took place between both sides. As a result, John Campbell offered to accept a settlement of $750,000. Thus, one option is for Allied to pay John $750,000 to settle the claim. Allied is also considering making John a counteroffer of $400,000 in the hope that he will accept a lesser amount to avoid the time and cost of going to trial. Allied's preliminary investigation shows that John's case is strong; Allied is concerned that John may reject its counteroffer and request a jury trial. Allied's lawyers spent some time exploring John's likely reaction if they make a counteroffer of $400,000.

The lawyers concluded that it is adequate to consider three possible outcomes to represent John's possible reaction to a counteroffer of $400,000: (1) John will accept the counteroffer and the case will be closed; (2) John will reject the counteroffer and elect to have a jury decide the settlement amount; or (3) John will make a counteroffer to Allied of $600,000. If John does make a counteroffer, Allied decided that it will not make additional counteroffers. It will either accept John's counteroffer of $600,000 or go to trial.

If the case goes to a jury trial, Allied considers three outcomes possible: (1) the jury may reject John's claim and Allied will not be required to pay any damages; (2) the jury will find in favor of John and award him $750,000 in damages; or (3) the jury will conclude that John has a strong case and award him the full amount of $1,500,000.

Key considerations as Allied develops its strategy for disposing of the case are the probabilities associated with John's response to an Allied counteroffer of $400,000 and the probabilities associated with the three possible trial outcomes. Allied's lawyers believe that the probability that John will accept a counteroffer of $400,000 is 0.10, the probability that John will reject a counteroffer of $400,000 is 0.40, and the probability that John will, himself, make a counteroffer to Allied of $600,000 is 0.50. If the case goes to court, they believe that the probability that the jury will award John damages of $1,500,000 is 0.30, the probability that the jury will award John damages of $750,000 is 0.50, and the probability that the jury will award John nothing is 0.20.

Managerial Report

Perform an analysis of the problem facing Allied Insurance and prepare a report that summarizes your findings and recommendations. Be sure to include the following items:

1. A decision tree
2. A recommendation regarding whether Allied should accept John's initial offer to settle the claim for $750,000
3. A decision strategy that Allied should follow if they decide to make John a counteroffer of $400,000
4. A risk profile for your recommended strategy

Case Problem 3   ROB'S MARKET

Rob's Market (RM) is a regional food store chain in the southwest United States. David White, director of Business Intelligence for RM, would like to initiate a study of the purchase behavior of customers who use the RM loyalty card (a card that customers scan at checkout to qualify for discounted prices). The use of the loyalty card allows RM to capture what is known as "point-of-sale" data, that is, a list of products purchased by a given customer as he/she checks out of the market. David feels that better understanding of which products tend to be purchased together could lead to insights for better pricing and display strategies as well as a better understanding of sales and the potential impact of different levels of coupon discounts. This type of analysis is known as market basket analysis, as it is a study of what different customers have in their "shopping baskets" as they check out of the store.

As a prototype study, David wants to investigate customer buying behavior with regard to bread, jelly, and peanut butter. RM's Information Technology (IT) group, at David's request, has provided a data set of purchases made by 1000 customers over a one-week period. The data set contains the following variables for each customer:

- Bread—wheat, white, or none
- Jelly—grape, strawberry, or none
- Peanut Butter—creamy, natural, or none

The variables appear in the above order from left to right in the data set, where each row is a customer. For example, the first record of the data set is:

white   grape   none

which means that customer #1 purchased white bread, grape jelly, and no peanut butter. The second record is:

white   strawberry   none

which means that customer #2 purchased white bread, strawberry jelly, and no peanut butter. The sixth record in the data set is:

none   none   none

which means that the sixth customer did not purchase bread, jelly, or peanut butter.
Other records are interpreted in a similar fashion.

David would like you to do an initial study of the data to get a better understanding of RM customer behavior with regard to these three products.

DATA *file*

MarketBasket

Managerial Report

Prepare a report that gives insight into the purchase behavior of customers who use the RM loyalty card. At a minimum your report should include estimates of the following:

1. The probability that a random customer does not purchase any of the three products (bread, jelly, or peanut butter).
2. The probability that a random customer purchases white bread.
3. The probability that a random customer purchases wheat bread.
4. The probability that a random customer purchases grape jelly given that he/she purchases white bread.
5. The probability that a random customer purchases strawberry jelly given that he/she purchases white bread.
6. The probability that a random customer purchases creamy peanut butter given that he/she purchases white bread.

One way to answer these questions is to use pivot tables (discussed in Chapter 2) to obtain absolute frequencies and use the pivot table results to calculate the relevant probabilities.

7. The probability that a random customer purchases natural peanut butter given that he/she purchases white bread.
8. The probability that a random customer purchases creamy peanut butter given that he/she purchases wheat bread.
9. The probability that a random customer purchases natural peanut butter given that he/she purchases wheat bread.
10. The probability that a random customer purchases white bread, grape jelly, and creamy peanut butter.

Case Problem 4   COLLEGE SOFTBALL RECRUITING

College softball programs have a limited number of scholarships to offer promising high school seniors, so the programs invest a great deal of effort in evaluating these players. One measure of performance the programs commonly use to evaluate recruits is the *batting average*—the proportion of at-bats (excluding times when the player is walked or hit by a pitch) in which the player gets a hit. For example, a player who gets 50 hits in 150 at-bats has a batting average of

$$\frac{50}{150} = 0.333$$

A college softball program is considering two players, Fran Hayes and Millie Marshall, who have recently completed their senior years of high school. Their respective statistics for their junior and senior years are as shown in Table 13.15.

Managerial Report

The Athletic Director and Coach of the women's softball team at a large public university are trying to decide to which of these two players they will offer an athletic scholarship (i.e., an opportunity to attend the university for free in exchange for playing on the university's softball team). Take the following steps to determine which player had the better batting average over the two-year period provided in the table, and use your results to advise the Athletic Director and Coach on their decision.

1. Calculate the batting average of each player for her junior year; then also calculate the batting average of each player for her senior year. Which player would this analysis lead you to choose?
2. Calculate the batting average of each player for her combined junior and senior years. Which player would this analysis lead you to choose?
3. After considering both of your analyses, which player would you choose? Why?
4. Prepare a report on your findings for the athletic director and coach of the college program. Focus on clearly explaining the discrepancy in your two analyses.

TABLE 13.15   SUMMARY OF BATTING PERFORMANCES IN JUNIOR AND SENIOR YEARS BY HAYES AND MARSHALL

	Junior Year		**Senior Year**	
	At-Bats	**Hits**	**At-Bats**	**Hits**
Fran Hayes	200	70	40	15
Millie Marshall	196	67	205	76

Appendix 13.1   DECISION TREES WITH ANALYTIC SOLVER

In this appendix, we describe how Analytic Solver V2017 can be used to develop a decision tree for the PDC problem presented in Section 13.3. The decision tree for the PDC problem is shown in Figure 13.20.

Getting Started: An Initial Decision Tree

To build a decision tree for the PDC problem using Analytic Solver, follow these steps in a blank workbook in Excel:

Step 2 will open the Solver Options and Model Specifications task pane.

Step 1. Select cell A1
Step 2. Click the **Analytic Solver** tab on the Ribbon
Step 3. In the **Solver Options and Model Specifications** task pane, right-click on **Decision Tree** (see Figure 13.21)
　　　　　　Select **Add Node**
Step 4. When the **Decision Tree** dialog box appears, verify that **Decision** is selected for **Node Type**, and click **OK**

A decision tree with one decision node and two branches (initially labeled as "Decision 1" and "Decision 2") appears, as shown in Figure 13.22.

Adding a Branch

When selecting a cell (such as B5 in Step 1 of Adding a Branch), be sure that the cell is selected rather than the tree node laying on top of the spreadsheet. One way to do ensure this is to type the cell location in Excel's Name Box (left of the Formula Bar).

The PDC problem has three decision alternatives (small, medium, and large condominium complexes), so we must add another decision branch to the tree.

Step 1. Select cell B5
Step 2. Right click **New Node** under **Decision Tree** in **Solver Options and Model Specifications** Task Pane
　　　　　　Select **Add Branch**

FIGURE 13.20   DECISION TREE FOR THE PDC CONDOMINIUM PROJECT (PAYOFFS IN MILLIONS OF $)

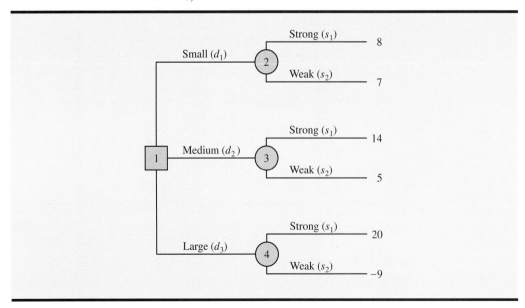

FIGURE 13.21   DECISION TREES IN SOLVER OPTIONS AND MODEL SPECIFICATIONS
TASK PANE

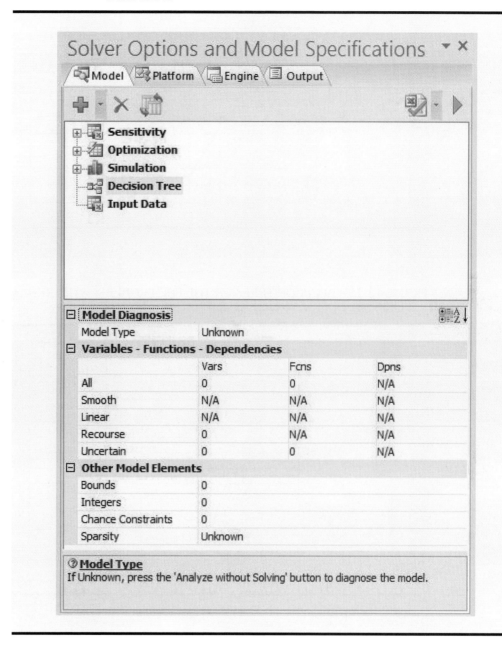

Step 3.   When the **Decision Tree** dialog box appears:
          Verify that **Decision** is selected for **Node Type**
          In the **Branches:** area, double click **Decision 1** and change the name to *Small*
          In the **Branches:** area, double click **Decision 2** and change the name to *Medium*
          In the **Branches:** area, double click **New Branch** and change the name to *Large*
Step 4. Click **OK**

A revised tree with three decision branches now appears in the Excel worksheet as shown
in Figure 13.23.

FIGURE 13.22   DECISION TREE WITH ONE DECISION NODE AND TWO BRANCHES
CREATED WITH ANALYTIC SOLVER

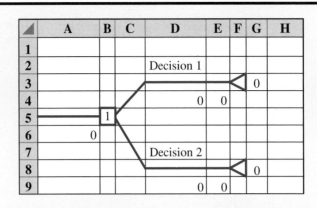

FIGURE 13.23   DECISION TREE FOR THE PDC PROBLEM WITH RENAMED BRANCHES
CREATED WITH ANALYTIC SOLVER

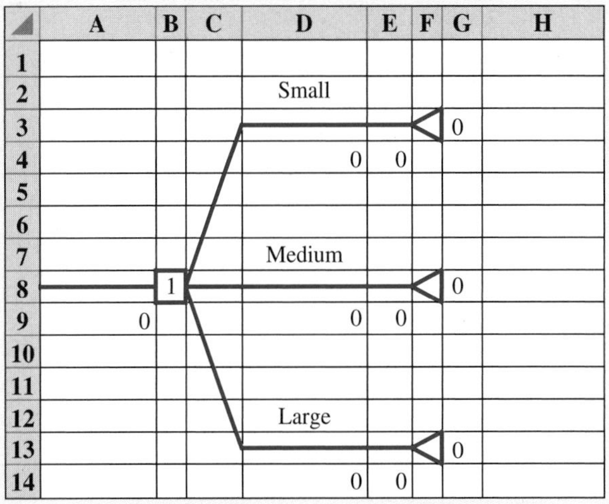

Adding Chance Nodes

When selecting a cell (such as F3 in Step 1 of Adding Chance Nodes), be sure that the cell is selected rather than the tree node laying on top of the spreadsheet. One way to do ensure this is to type the cell location in Excel's Name Box (left of the Formula Bar).

The chance event for the PDC problem is the demand for the condominiums, which may be either strong or weak. Thus, a chance node with two branches must be added at the end of each decision alternative branch. To add a chance node with two branches to the top decision alternative branch:

Step 1. Select cell F3
Step 2. Click the **Analytic Solver** tab in the Ribbon to reveal the **Solver Options and Model Specifications** task pane
Step 3. Under **Decision Tree** in the **Solver Options and Model Specification** task pane
Right click **Terminal** below **Small**
Select **Add Node**

Step 4. When the **Decision Tree** dialog box appears, select **Event/Chance** in the
Node Type area
Click **OK**

The tree now appears as shown in Figure 13.24. We then repeat this process for the
Medium and Large nodes.

Next we would like to rename "Event 1" and "Event 2" as *Strong* and *Weak*, respectively,
to provide the proper names for the PDC states of nature. To rename these events, we follow
the steps below.

Step 1. Right click **Event 1** in the **Solver Options and Model Specifications** task pane
Select **Edit**
Step 2. When the **Decision Tree** dialog box opens
Double click **Event 1** in the **Branches:** area
Change the name to *Strong*
Double click **Event 2** in the **Branches:** area
Change the name to *Weak*
Click **OK**

This copy-and-paste procedure places a chance node at the end of the Small decision
branch. Repeating the same copy-and-paste procedure for the Medium and Large decision
branches completes the structure of the PDC decision tree, as shown in Figure 13.25.

Inserting Probabilities and Payoffs

We can now insert probabilities and payoffs into the decision tree. In Figure 13.25, we see
that an equal probability of 0.5 is assigned automatically to each of the chance outcomes and
all payoffs are set to 0. For PDC, the probability of strong demand is 0.8 and the probability
of weak demand is 1 minus the probability of strong demand, $1 - 0.8 = 0.2$. The payoffs for
each outcome, dependent on the decision alternative selected and the state of nature, were
given in Table 13.1.

We can enter these values for our decision tree by following the steps below.

Step 1. Right click on **New Node** under the **Small** decision branch in the **Solver
Options and Model Specifications** task pane
Select **Edit**

FIGURE 13.24   DECISION TREE FOR THE PDC PROBLEM WITH AN ADDED
CHANCE NODE CREATED WITH ANALYTIC SOLVER

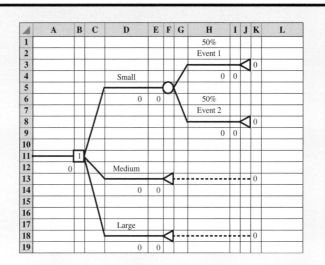

FIGURE 13.25   PDC DECISION TREE CREATED WITH ANALYTIC SOLVER

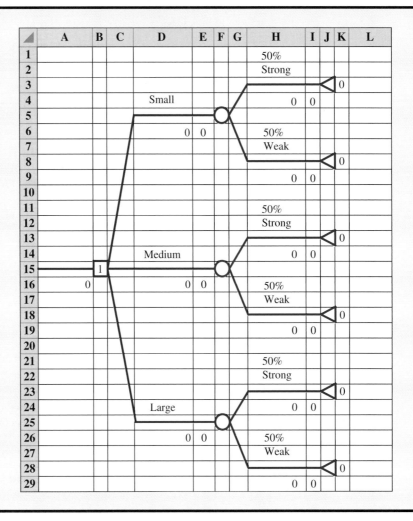

Step 2. When the **Decision Tree** dialog box opens

In the **Branches:** area, double click on **0.5** in the **Chance** column for **Strong**

Change this value to *0.8*

Double click on **0.5** in the **Chance** column for **Weak**

Change this value to *0.2*

Double click on **0** in the **Value** column for **Strong**

Change this value to *8*

Double click on **0** in the **Value** column for **Weak**

Change this value to *7*

Click **OK**

We can then enter chance probabilities for the Medium and Large decision branches as follows:

Step 3. Right click on **New Node** under the **Medium** decision branch in the **Solver Options and Model Specifications** task

Select **Edit**

Step 4. When the **Decision Tree** dialog box opens
In the **Branches:** area, double click on **0.5** in the **Chance** column for **Strong**
Change this value to *0.8*
Double click on **0.5** in the **Chance** column for **Weak**
Change this value to *0.2*
Double click on **0** in the **Value** column for **Strong**
Change this value to *14*
Double click on **0** in the **Value** column for **Weak**
Change this value to *5*
Click **OK**

Step 5. Right click on **New Node** under the **Large** decision branch in the **Solver Options and Model Specifications** task pane
Select **Edit**

Step 6. When the **Decision Tree** dialog box opens
In the **Branches:** area, double click on **0.5** in the **Chance** column for **Strong**
Change this value to *0.8*
Double click on **0.5** in the **Chance** column for **Weak**
Change this value to *0.2*
Double click on **0** in the **Value** column for **Strong**
Change this value to *20*
Double click on **0** in the **Value** column for **Weak**
Change this value to *-9*
Click **OK**

In Figure 13.26, we see that Analytic Solver places the probabilities and payoffs in column H in Excel. The probabilities appear above the branches and the payoffs appear below the branches. Note that the payoffs also appear in the right-hand margin of the decision tree (column K in Figure 13.26). The payoffs in the right margin are computed by a formula that adds the payoffs on all the branches leading to the associated terminal node. For the PDC problem, no payoffs are associated with the decision alternative branches, so we see that the payoff values below the Small, Medium, and Large decision branches are set to 0 in cells D6, D16, and D26. The PDC decision tree is now complete as shown in Figure 13.26.

Interpreting the Result

When probabilities and payoffs are inserted, Analytic Solver automatically makes the rollback computations necessary to determine the optimal solution. Optimal decisions are identified by the number in the corresponding decision node. In the PDC decision tree in Figure 13.26, cell B15 contains the decision node. Note that a 3 appears in this node, which tells us that decision alternative branch 3 provides the optimal decision. We can also easily identify the best decision using the Highlight function in Analytic Solver. To highlight the best decision follow these steps:

Step 1. Click the **Analytic Solver** tab in the Ribbon
Step 2. Click **Tools** and then click **Decision Tree**
Select **Highlight**, and click **Highlight Best**

Analytic Solver highlights the best decision for the PDC problem. From Figure 13.27, we see that decision analysis recommends that PDC construct the large condominium complex. The expected value of this decision appears at the beginning of the tree in cell A16. Thus, we see that the optimal expected value is $14.2 million. The expected values of the other decision alternatives are displayed at the end of the corresponding decision branch. Thus, referring to cells E6 and E16, we see that the expected value of the small complex is $7.8 million and the expected value of the medium complex is $12.2 million.

FIGURE 13.26   PDC DECISION TREE WITH BRANCH PROBABILITIES AND PAYOFFS CREATED WITH ANALYTIC SOLVER

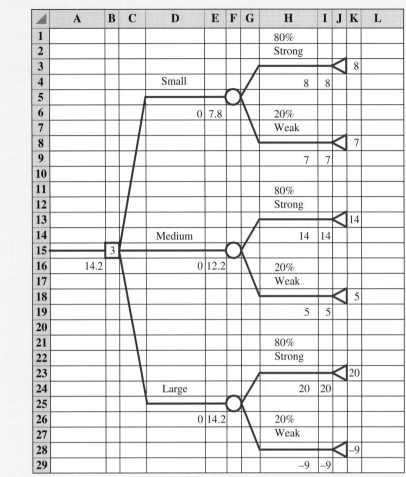

Using software such as Analytic Solver to develop decision trees allows for easy sensitivity analysis. We can analyze the impact of changing branch probabilities and payoffs by simply changing these values in Analytic Solver and observing the impact on the optimal decision. For instance, if we want to examine the impact of different probabilities of Strong and Weak demand on our decision, we can follow the steps below.

Step 1. Right click on **New Node** under the **Small** decision branch in the **Solver Options and Model Specifications** task pane
     Select **Edit**

Step 2. When the **Decision Tree** dialog box opens
     In the **Branches:** area, double click on **0.8** in the **Chance** column for **Strong**
          Change this value to *0.6*
     Double click on **0.2** in the **Chance** column for **Weak**
          Change this value to *0.4*
     Click **OK**

We then repeat Steps 1 and 2 above for the Medium and Large decision branches.

FIGURE 13.27   DECISION TREE FOR THE PDC PROBLEM WITH BEST DECISION HIGHLIGHTED CREATED WITH ANALYTIC SOLVER

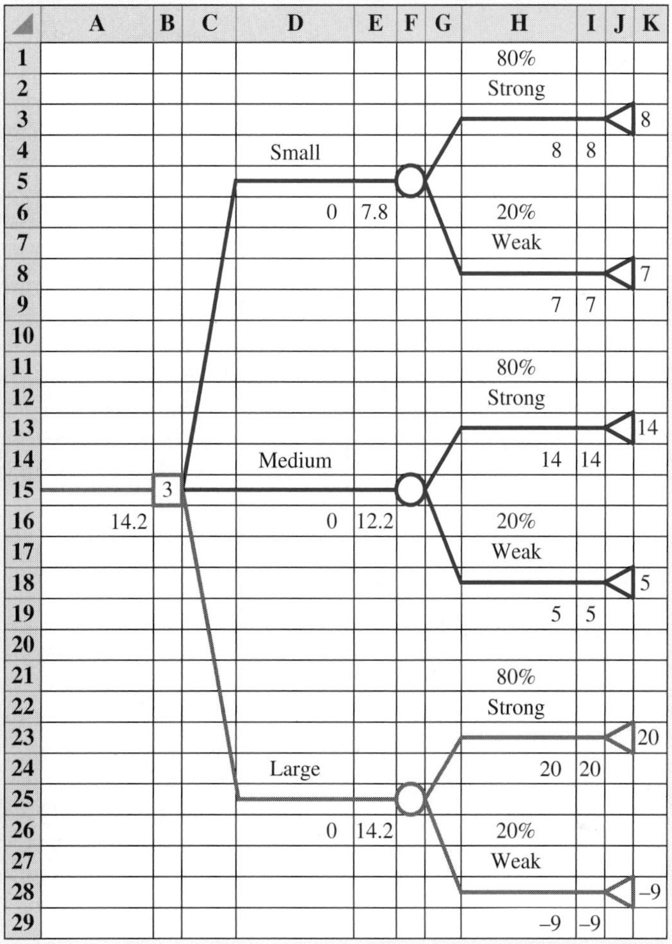

	A	B	C	D	E	F	G	H	I	J	K
1								80%			
2								Strong			
3											8
4				Small				8	8		
5							○				
6					0	7.8		20%			
7								Weak			
8											7
9								7	7		
10											
11								80%			
12								Strong			
13											14
14				Medium				14	14		
15			3				○				
16	14.2				0	12.2		20%			
17								Weak			
18											5
19								5	5		
20											
21								80%			
22								Strong			
23											20
24				Large				20	20		
25							○				
26					0	14.2		20%			
27								Weak			
28											−9
29								−9	−9		

Figure 13.28 indicates that with 0.6 probability of Strong demand and 0.4 probability of Weak demand, the optimal decision alternative is 2, building a Medium complex. The expected value of building a Medium complex in this scenario is $10.4 million.

Using the Exponential Utility Function in Analytic Solver

By default, the decision trees created in Analytic Solver use the expected value (risk-neutral) approach for calculating the best decisions. However, we can easily change this setting so that Analytic Solver will use an exponential utility function to calculate utilities and determine the best decisions with a risk-averse approach. To do this, we will modify the settings using the Solver Options and Model Specifications task pane of Analytic Solver. To change the settings in a decision tree to use the exponential utility function, we use the following steps:

If the Solver Options and Model Specifications task pane is not visible, it can be activated by clicking the Model button in the Model group under the Analytic Solver tab in the Ribbon.

Step 1. Click the **Analytic Solver** tab in the Ribbon to reveal the **Solver Options and Model Specifications** task pane

FIGURE 13.28   DECISION TREE FOR THE PDC PROBLEM WITH MODIFIED
PROBABILITIES

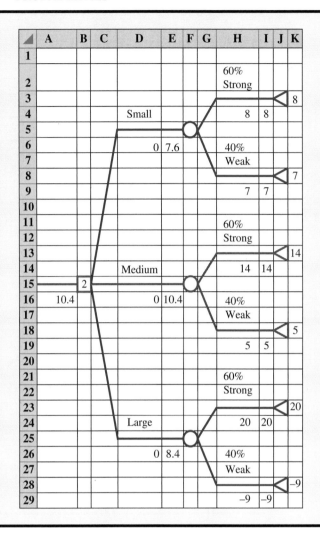

Step 2. In the **Solver Options and Model Specifications** task pane, click the **Model** tab
Select **Decision Tree** in the **Solver Options and Model Specifications**
task pane
Step 3. In the **Decision Tree** area at the bottom of the **Solver Options and Model Specifications** task pane, click **Expected Values** next to **Certainty Equivalents**
Change this value to **Exponential Utility Function**
Step 4. We also must provide the risk tolerance value (*R* in equation 13.17) to be used
in the exponential utility function. In the **Decision Tree** area at the bottom of
the **Solver Options and Model Specifications** task pane, change the value next
to **Risk Tolerance** to *N1*.

This allows us to enter the Risk Tolerance value in cell N1 in Excel. For instance, if we
enter *1.0* in cell N1, the output appears as shown in Figure 13.29.

Figure 13.29 shows the completed decision tree using the exponential utility function
for the PDC problem with modified probability values of 0.6 for Strong demand and 0.4
for Weak demand. Step 4 indicates that we are using a value of $1 million as the *R* value in
equation (13.17). We know that the units here are in millions of dollars because those are

MODEL *file*

PDCModel

FIGURE 13.29   DECISION TREE IN ANALYTIC SOLVER USING MODIFIED PROBABILITIES AND AN EXPONENTIAL UTILITY FUNCTION WITH $R = \$1$ MILLION

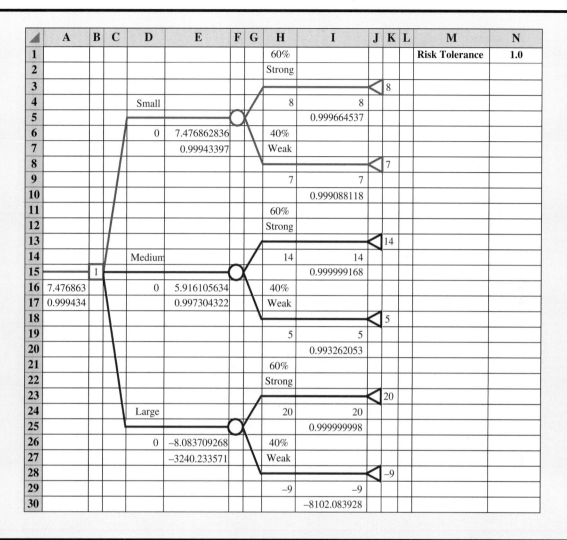

the units used by the values in our decision tree. Recall that a small risk tolerance (R value), relative to the payoff values in the decision tree, indicates that the decision maker is very risk averse.

Once we make this change in Analytic Solver, the decision tree calculations are done using utilities based on the exponential function rather than using the expected value method.

In Figure 13.29, we see that the decision maker prefers to build the Small complex to limit downside risk due to the decision maker being very risk averse. However, if we change the risk tolerance (R) to be $9 million by entering *9.0* in cell N1. This means that the decision maker is less risk averse. Figure 13.30 shows the decision tree with an exponential utility function and $R = \$9$ million; here we see that the decision maker chooses the Medium complex. Figure 13.30 reflects a decision maker who is less risk averse and more willing to accept decisions that could have higher payoffs but that also have higher likelihoods of worse payoffs.

The complete decision tree and data table for the PDC problem are contained in the file *PDCModel*.

FIGURE 13.30 DECISION TREE IN ANALYTIC SOLVER USING MODIFIED PROBABILITIES AND AN EXPONENTIAL UTILITY FUNCTION WITH $R = \$9$ MILLION

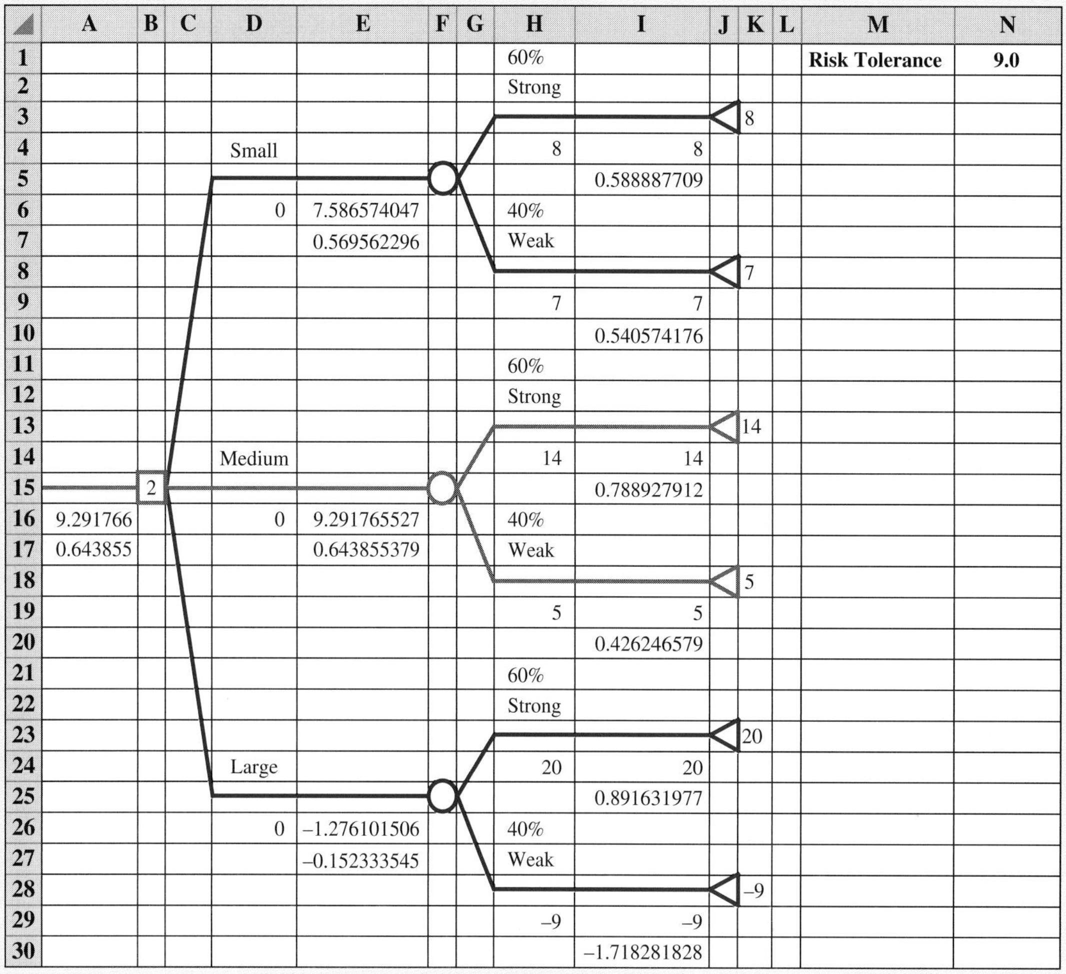

	A	B	C	D	E	F	G	H	I	J	K	L	M	N
1								60%					**Risk Tolerance**	**9.0**
2								Strong						
3											8			
4				Small				8	8					
5						○			0.588887709					
6				0	7.586574047			40%						
7					0.569562296			Weak						
8											7			
9								7	7					
10									0.540574176					
11								60%						
12								Strong						
13											14			
14				Medium				14	14					
15		2				○			0.788927912					
16	9.291766			0	9.291765527			40%						
17	0.643855				0.643855379			Weak						
18											5			
19								5	5					
20									0.426246579					
21								60%						
22								Strong						
23											20			
24				Large				20	20					
25						○			0.891631977					
26				0	−1.276101506			40%						
27					−0.152333545			Weak						
28											−9			
29								−9	−9					
30									−1.718281828					

CHAPTER 14

Multicriteria Decisions

CONTENTS

In previous chapters we showed how a variety of quantitative methods can help managers make better decisions. Whenever we desired an optimal solution, we utilized a single criterion (e.g., maximize profit, minimize cost, minimize time). In this chapter we discuss techniques that are appropriate for situations in which the decision maker needs to consider multiple criteria in arriving at the overall best decision. For example, consider a company involved in selecting a location for a new manufacturing plant. The cost of land and construction may vary from location to location, so one criterion in selecting the best site could be the cost involved in building the plant; if cost were the sole criterion of interest, management would simply select the location that minimizes land cost plus construction cost. Before making any decision, however, management might also want to consider additional criteria such as the availability of transportation from the plant to the firm's distribution centers, the attractiveness of the proposed location in terms of hiring and retaining employees, energy costs at the proposed site, and state and local taxes. In such situations the complexity of the problem increases because one location may be more desirable in terms of one criterion and less desirable in terms of one or more of the other criteria.

To introduce the topic of multicriteria decision making, we consider a technique referred to as **goal programming.** This technique has been developed to handle multiple-criteria situations within the general framework of linear programming. We next consider a *scoring model* as a relatively easy way to identify the best decision alternative for a multicriteria problem. Finally, we introduce a method known as the *analytical hierarchy process (AHP)*, which allows the user to make pairwise comparisons among the criteria and a series of pairwise comparisons among the decision alternatives in order to arrive at a prioritized ranking of the decision alternatives.

14.1   GOAL PROGRAMMING: FORMULATION AND GRAPHICAL SOLUTION

To illustrate the goal programming approach to multicriteria decision problems, let us consider a problem facing Nicolo Investment Advisors. A client has $80,000 to invest and, as an initial strategy, would like the investment portfolio restricted to two stocks:

Stock	Price/Share	Estimated Annual Return/Share	Risk Index/Share
U.S. Oil	$25	$3	0.50
Hub Properties	$50	$5	0.25

U.S. Oil, which has a return of $3 on a $25 share price, provides an annual rate of return of 12%, whereas Hub Properties provides an annual rate of return of 10%. The risk index per share, 0.50 for U.S. Oil and 0.25 for Hub Properties, is a rating Nicolo assigned to measure the relative risk of the two investments. Higher risk index values imply greater risk; hence, Nicolo judged U.S. Oil to be the riskier investment. By specifying a maximum portfolio risk index, Nicolo will avoid placing too much of the portfolio in high-risk investments.

To illustrate how to use the risk index per share to measure the total portfolio risk, suppose that Nicolo chooses a portfolio that invests all $80,000 in U.S. Oil, the higher risk, but higher return, investment. Nicolo could purchase $80,000/$25 = 3200 shares of U.S. Oil, and the portfolio would have a risk index of 3200(0.50) = 1600. Conversely, if Nicolo purchases no shares of either stock, the portfolio will have no risk, but also no return. Thus, the portfolio risk index will vary from 0 (least risk) to 1600 (most risk).

Nicolo's client would like to avoid a high-risk portfolio; thus, investing all funds in U.S. Oil would not be desirable. However, the client agreed that an acceptable level of risk would correspond to portfolios with a maximum total risk index of 700. Thus, considering only risk, one *goal* is to find a portfolio with a risk index of 700 or less.

Another goal of the client is to obtain an annual return of at least $9000. This goal can be achieved with a portfolio consisting of 2000 shares of U.S. Oil [at a cost of 2000($25) = $50,000] and 600 shares of Hub Properties [at a cost of 600($50) = $30,000]; the annual return in this case would be 2000($3) + 600($5) = $9000. Note, however, that the portfolio risk index for this investment strategy would be 2000(0.50) + 600(0.25) = 1150; thus, this portfolio achieves the annual return goal but does not satisfy the portfolio risk index goal.

Thus, the portfolio selection problem is a multicriteria decision problem involving two conflicting goals: one dealing with risk and one dealing with annual return. The goal programming approach was developed precisely for this kind of problem. Goal programming can be used to identify a portfolio that comes closest to achieving both goals. Before applying the methodology, the client must determine which, if either, goal is more important.

Suppose that the client's top-priority goal is to restrict the risk; that is, keeping the portfolio risk index at 700 or less is so important that the client is not willing to trade the achievement of this goal for any amount of an increase in annual return. As long as the portfolio risk index does not exceed 700, the client seeks the best possible return. Based on this statement of priorities, the goals for the problem are as follows:

Primary Goal (Priority Level 1)

Goal 1: Find a portfolio that has a risk index of 700 or less.

Secondary Goal (Priority Level 2)

Goal 2: Find a portfolio that will provide an annual return of at least $9000.

In goal programming with preemptive priorities, we never permit trade-offs between higher and lower level goals.

The primary goal is called a *priority level 1 goal*, and the secondary goal is called a *priority level 2 goal*. In goal programming terminology, they are called **preemptive priorities** because the decision maker is not willing to sacrifice any amount of achievement of the priority level 1 goal for the lower priority goal. The portfolio risk index of 700 is the **target value** for the priority level 1 (primary) goal, and the annual return of $9000 is the target value for the priority level 2 (secondary) goal. The difficulty in finding a solution that will achieve these goals is that only $80,000 is available for investment.

Developing the Constraints and the Goal Equations

We begin by defining the decision variables:

$$U = \text{number of shares of U.S. Oil purchased}$$
$$H = \text{number of shares of Hub Properties purchased}$$

Constraints for goal programming problems are handled in the same way as in an ordinary linear programming problem. In the Nicolo Investment Advisors problem, one constraint corresponds to the funds available. Because each share of U.S. Oil costs $25 and each share of Hub Properties costs $50, the constraint representing the funds available is

$$25U + 50H \leq 80,000$$

To complete the formulation of the model, we must develop a **goal equation** for each goal. Let us begin by writing the goal equation for the primary goal. Each share of U.S. Oil has a risk index of 0.50 and each share of Hub Properties has a risk index of 0.25; therefore, the portfolio risk index is $0.50U + 0.25H$. Depending on the values of U and H, the portfolio risk index may be less than, equal to, or greater than the target value of 700. To represent these possibilities mathematically, we create the goal equation

$$0.50U + 0.25H = 700 + d_1^+ - d_1^-$$

where

$$d_1^+ = \text{the amount by which the portfolio risk index exceeds the target value of 700}$$

$$d_1^- = \text{the amount by which the portfolio risk index is less than the target value of 700}$$

To achieve a goal exactly, the two deviation variables must both equal zero.

In goal programming, d_1^+ and d_1^- are called **deviation variables.** The purpose of deviation variables is to allow for the possibility of not meeting the target value exactly. Consider, for example, a portfolio that consists of $U = 2000$ shares of U.S. Oil and $H = 0$ shares of Hub Properties. The portfolio risk index is $0.50(2000) = 0.25(0) = 1000$. In this case, $d_1^+ = 300$ reflects the fact that the portfolio risk index exceeds the target value by 300 units; note also that because d_1^+ is greater than zero, the value of d_1^- must be zero. For a portfolio consisting of $U = 0$ shares of U.S. Oil and $H = 1000$ shares of Hub Properties, the portfolio risk index would be $0.50(0) + 0.25(1000) = 250$. In this case, $d_1^- = 450$ and $d_1^+ = 0$, indicating that the solution provides a portfolio risk index of 450 less than the target value of 700.

In general, the letter d is used for deviation variables in a goal programming model. A superscript of plus $(+)$ or minus $(-)$ is used to indicate whether the variable corresponds to a positive or negative deviation from the target value. If we bring the deviation variables to the left-hand side, we can rewrite the goal equation for the primary goal as

$$0.50U + 0.25H - d_1^+ + d_1^- = 700$$

Note that the value on the right-hand side of the goal equation is the target value for the goal. The left-hand side of the goal equation consists of two parts:

1. A function that defines the amount of goal achievement in terms of the decision variables (e.g., $0.50U + 0.25H$)
2. Deviation variables representing the difference between the target value for the goal and the level achieved

To develop a goal equation for the secondary goal, we begin by writing a function representing the annual return for the investment:

$$\text{Annual return} = 3U + 5H$$

Then we define two deviation variables that represent the amount of over- or underachievement of the goal. Doing so, we obtain

$d_2^+ = $ the amount by which the annual return for the portfolio is greater
than the target value of \$9000

$d_2^- = $ the amount by which the annual return for the portfolio is less
than the target value of \$9000

Using these two deviation variables, we write the goal equation for goal 2 as

$$3U + 5H = 9000 + d_2^+ - d_2^-$$

or

$$3U + 5H - d_2^+ + d_2^- = 9000$$

This step completes the development of the goal equations and the constraints for the Nicolo portfolio problem. We are now ready to develop an appropriate objective function for the problem.

Developing an Objective Function with Preemptive Priorities

The objective function in a goal programming model calls for minimizing a function of the deviation variables. In the portfolio selection problem, the most important goal, denoted P_1, is to find a portfolio with a risk index of 700 or less. This problem has only two goals, and the client is unwilling to accept a portfolio risk index greater than 700 to achieve the secondary annual return goal. Therefore, the secondary goal is denoted P_2. As we stated previously, these goal priorities are referred to as preemptive priorities because the satisfaction of a higher level goal cannot be traded for the satisfaction of a lower level goal.

Goal programming problems with preemptive priorities are solved by treating priority level 1 goals (P_1) first in an objective function. The idea is to start by finding a solution that comes closest to satisfying the priority level 1 goals. This solution is then modified by solving a problem with an objective function involving only priority level 2 goals (P_2); however, revisions in the solution are permitted only if they do not hinder achievement of the P_1 goals. In general, solving a goal programming problem with preemptive priorities involves solving a sequence of linear programs with different objective functions; P_1 goals are considered first, P_2 goals second, P_3 goals third, and so on. At each stage of the procedure, a revision in the solution is permitted only if it causes no reduction in the achievement of a higher priority goal.

We must solve one linear program for each priority level.

The number of linear programs that we must solve in sequence to develop the solution to a goal programming problem is determined by the number of priority levels. One linear program must be solved for each priority level. We will call the first linear program solved the priority level 1 problem, the second linear program solved the priority level 2 problem, and so on. Each linear program is obtained from the one at the next higher level by changing the objective function and adding a constraint.

We first formulate the objective function for the priority level 1 problem. The client stated that the portfolio risk index should not exceed 700. Is underachieving the target value of 700 a concern? Clearly, the answer is no because portfolio risk index values of less than 700 correspond to less risk. Is overachieving the target value of 700 a concern? The answer is yes because portfolios with a risk index greater than 700 correspond to unacceptable levels of risk. Thus, the objective function corresponding to the priority level 1 linear program should minimize the value of d_1^+.

The goal equations and the funds available constraint have already been developed. Thus, the priority level 1 linear program can now be stated.

P_1 Problem

Min d_1^+

s.t.

$$
\begin{array}{rclcl}
25U + 50H & & & \leq & 80,000 \quad \text{Funds available} \\
0.50U + 0.25H - d_1^+ + d_1^- & & & = & 700 \quad P_1 \text{ goal} \\
3U + 5H & - d_2^+ + d_2^- & & = & 9000 \quad P_2 \text{ goal} \\
\end{array}
$$

$$U, H, d_1^+, d_1^-, d_2^+, d_2^- \geq 0$$

Graphical Solution Procedure

One approach that can often be used to solve a difficult problem is to break the problem into two or more smaller or easier problems. The linear programming procedure we use to solve the goal programming problem is based on this approach.

The graphical solution procedure for goal programming is similar to that for linear programming presented in Chapter 2. The only difference is that the procedure for goal programming involves a separate solution for each priority level. Recall that the linear programming graphical solution procedure uses a graph to display the values for the decision variables. Because the decision variables are nonnegative, we consider only that portion of the graph where $U \geq 0$ and $H \geq 0$. Recall also that every point on the graph is called a *solution point*.

We begin the graphical solution procedure for the Nicolo Investment problem by identifying all solution points that satisfy the available funds constraint:

$$25U + 50H \leq 80,000$$

The shaded region in Figure 14.1, feasible portfolios, consists of all points that satisfy this constraint—that is, values of U and H for which $25U + 50H \leq 80,000$.

The objective for the priority level 1 linear program is to minimize d_1^+, the amount by which the portfolio index exceeds the target value of 700. Recall that the P_1 goal equation is

$$0.50U + 0.25H - d_1^+ + d_1^- = 700$$

When the P_1 goal is met exactly, $d_1^+ = 0$ and $d_1^- = 0$; the goal equation then reduces to $0.50U + 0.25H = 700$. Figure 14.2 shows the graph of this equation; the shaded region identifies all solution points that satisfy the available funds constraint and also result in the value of $d_1^+ = 0$. Thus, the shaded region contains all the feasible solution points that achieve the priority level 1 goal.

FIGURE 14.1   PORTFOLIOS THAT SATISFY THE AVAILABLE FUNDS CONSTRAINT

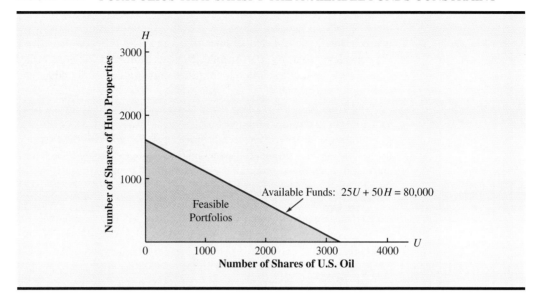

FIGURE 14.2   PORTFOLIOS THAT SATISFY THE P_1 GOAL

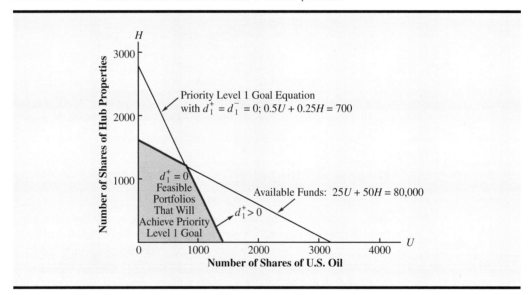

At this point, we have solved the priority level 1 problem. Note that alternative optimal solutions are possible; in fact, all solution points in the shaded region in Figure 14.2 maintain a portfolio risk index of 700 or less, and hence $d_1^+ = 0$.

The priority level 2 goal for the Nicolo Investment problem is to find a portfolio that will provide an annual return of at least $9000. Is overachieving the target value of $9000 a concern? Clearly, the answer is no because portfolios with an annual return of more than $9000 correspond to higher returns. Is underachieving the target value of $9000 a concern? The answer is yes because portfolios with an annual return of less than $9000 are not acceptable to the client. Thus, the objective function corresponding to the priority level 2 linear program should minimize the value of d_2^-. However, because goal 2 is a secondary goal, the solution to the priority level 2 linear program must not degrade the optimal solution to the priority level 1 problem. Thus, the priority level 2 linear program can now be stated.

P_2 Problem

Min d_2^-

s.t.

$$
\begin{array}{rrcll}
25U + & 50H & \leq & 80{,}000 & \text{Funds available} \\
0.50U + 0.25H - d_1^+ + d_1^- & = & 700 & P_1 \text{ goal} \\
3U + & 5H & - d_2^+ + d_2^- = & 9000 & P_2 \text{ goal} \\
& d_1^+ & = & 0 & \text{Maintain achievement} \\
& & & & \text{of } P_1 \text{ goal}
\end{array}
$$

$$U, H, d_1^+, d_1^-, d_2^+, d_2^- \geq 0$$

Note that the priority level 2 linear program differs from the priority level 1 linear program in two ways. The objective function involves minimizing the amount by which the portfolio annual return underachieves the level 2 goal, and another constraint has been added to ensure that no amount of achievement of the priority level 1 goal is sacrificed.

Let us now continue the graphical solution procedure. The goal equation for the priority level 2 goal is

$$3U + 5H - d_2^+ + d_2^- = 9000$$

When both d_2^+ and d_2^- equal zero, this equation reduces to $3U + 5H = 9000$; we show the graph with this equation in Figure 14.3.

At this stage, we cannot consider any solution point that will degrade the achievement of the priority level 1 goal. Figure 14.3 shows that no solution points will achieve the priority level 2 goal and maintain the values we were able to achieve for the priority level 1 goal. In fact, the best solution that can be obtained when considering the priority level 2 goal is given by the point ($U = 800$, $H = 1200$); in other words, this point comes the closest to satisfying the priority level 2 goal from among those solutions satisfying the priority level 1 goal. Because the annual return corresponding to this solution point is $3(800) + $5(1200) = 8400, identifying a portfolio that will satisfy both the priority level 1 and the priority level 2 goals is impossible. In fact, the best solution underachieves goal 2 by $d_2^- = $9000 - $8400 = 600.

Thus, the goal programming solution for the Nicolo Investment problem recommends that the $80,000 available for investment be used to purchase 800 shares of U.S. Oil and

FIGURE 14.3   BEST SOLUTION WITH RESPECT TO BOTH GOALS
                 (SOLUTION TO P_2 PROBLEM)

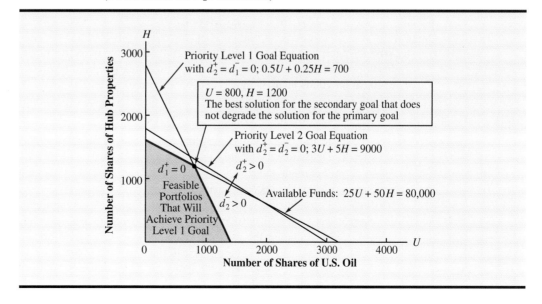

1200 shares of Hub Properties. Note that the priority level 1 goal of a portfolio risk index of 700 or less has been achieved. However, the priority level 2 goal of at least a $9000 annual return is not achievable. The annual return for the recommended portfolio is $8400.

In summary, the graphical solution procedure for goal programming involves the following steps:

Step 1. Identify the feasible solution points that satisfy the problem constraints.
Step 2. Identify all feasible solutions that achieve the highest priority goal; if no feasible solutions will achieve the highest priority goal, identify the solution(s) that comes closest to achieving it.
Step 3. Move down one priority level, and determine the "best" solution possible without sacrificing any achievement of higher priority goals.
Step 4. Repeat step 3 until all priority levels have been considered.

Problem 2 will test your ability to formulate a goal programming model and use the graphical solution procedure to obtain a solution.

Although the graphical solution procedure is a convenient method for solving goal programming problems involving two decision variables, the solution of larger problems requires a computer-aided approach. In Section 14.2 we illustrate how to use a computer software package to solve more complex goal programming problems.

Goal Programming Model

As we stated, preemptive goal programming problems are solved as a sequence of linear programs: one linear program for each priority level. However, notation that permits writing a goal programming problem in one concise statement is helpful.

In writing the overall objective for the portfolio selection problem, we must write the objective function in a way that reminds us of the preemptive priorities. We can do so by writing the objective function as

$$\text{Min } P_1(d_1^+) + P_2(d_2^-)$$

The priority levels P_1 and P_2 are not numerical weights on the deviation variables, but simply labels that remind us of the priority levels for the goals.

We now write the complete goal programming model as

$$\text{Min } P_1(d_1^+) + P_2(d_2^-)$$

s.t.

$25U + 50H$	$\leq$	$80,000$	Funds available
$0.50U + 0.25H - d_1^+ + d_1^-$	$=$	700	P_1 goal
$3U + 5H \qquad - d_2^+ + d_2^-$	$=$	9000	P_2 goal

$$U, H, d_1^+, d_1^-, d_2^+, d_2^- \geq 0$$

With the exception of the P_1 and P_2 priority levels in the objective function, this model is a linear programming model. The solution of this linear program involves solving a sequence of linear programs involving goals at decreasing priority levels.

We now summarize the procedure used to develop a goal programming model.

Step 1. Identify the goals and any constraints that reflect resource capacities or other restrictions that may prevent achievement of the goals.
Step 2. Determine the priority level of each goal; goals with priority level P_1 are most important, those with priority level P_2 are next most important, and so on.
Step 3. Define the decision variables.
Step 4. Formulate the constraints in the usual linear programming fashion.
Step 5. For each goal, develop a goal equation, with the right-hand side specifying the target value for the goal. Deviation variables d_i^+ and d_i^- are included in each goal equation to reflect the possible deviations above or below the target value.
Step 6. Write the objective function in terms of minimizing a prioritized function of the deviation variables.

NOTES AND COMMENTS

1. The constraints in the general goal programming model are of two types: goal equations and ordinary linear programming constraints. Some analysts call the goal equations *goal constraints* and the ordinary linear programming constraints *system constraints*.

2. You might think of the general goal programming model as having "hard" and "soft" constraints. The hard constraints are the ordinary linear programming constraints that cannot be violated. The soft constraints are the ones resulting from the goal equations. Soft constraints can be violated but with a penalty for doing so. The penalty is reflected by the coefficient of the deviation variable in the objective function. In Section 14.2 we illustrate this point with a problem that has a coefficient of 2 for one of the deviation variables.

3. Note that the constraint added in moving from the linear programming problem at one priority level to the linear programming problem at the next lower priority level is a hard constraint that ensures that no amount of achievement of the higher priority goal is sacrificed to achieve the lower priority goal.

14.2   GOAL PROGRAMMING: SOLVING MORE COMPLEX PROBLEMS

In Section 14.1 we formulated and solved a goal programming model that involved one priority level 1 goal and one priority level 2 goal. In this section we show how to formulate and solve goal programming models that involve multiple goals within the same priority level. Although specially developed computer programs can solve goal programming models, these programs are not as readily available as general purpose linear programming software packages. Thus, the computer solution procedure outlined in this section develops a solution to a goal programming model by solving a sequence of linear programming models with a general purpose linear programming software package.

Suncoast Office Supplies Problem

The management of Suncoast Office Supplies establishes monthly goals, or quotas, for the types of customers contacted. For the next four weeks, Suncoast's customer contact strategy calls for the salesforce, which consists of four salespeople, to make 200 contacts with established customers who have previously purchased supplies from the firm. In addition, the strategy calls for 120 contacts of new customers. The purpose of this latter goal is to ensure that the salesforce is continuing to investigate new sources of sales.

After making allowances for travel and waiting time, as well as for demonstration and direct sales time, Suncoast allocated two hours of salesforce effort to each contact of an established customer. New customer contacts tend to take longer and require three hours per contact. Normally, each salesperson works 40 hours per week, or 160 hours over the four-week planning horizon; under a normal work schedule, the four salespeople will have $4(160) = 640$ hours of salesforce time available for customer contacts.

Management is willing to use some overtime, if needed, but is also willing to accept a solution that uses less than the scheduled 640 hours available. However, management wants both overtime and underutilization of the workforce limited to no more than 40 hours over the four-week period. Thus, in terms of overtime, management's goal is to use no more than $640 + 40 = 680$ hours of salesforce time; and in terms of labor utilization, management's goal is to use at least $640 - 40 = 600$ hours of salesforce time.

In addition to the customer contact goals, Suncoast established a goal regarding sales volume. Based on its experience, Suncoast estimates that each established customer contacted will generate $250 of sales and that each new customer contacted will generate $125 of sales. Management wants to generate sales revenue of at least $70,000 for the next month.

Given Suncoast's small salesforce and the short time frame involved, management decided that the overtime goal and the labor utilization goal are both priority level 1 goals. Management also concluded that the $70,000 sales revenue goal should be a priority level 2 goal and that the two customer contact goals should be priority level 3 goals. Based on these priorities, we can now summarize the goals.

Priority Level 1 Goals

Goal 1: Do not use any more than 680 hours of salesforce time.

Goal 2: Do not use any less than 600 hours of salesforce time.

Priority Level 2 Goal

Goal 3: Generate sales revenue of at least $70,000.

Priority Level 3 Goals

Goal 4: Call on at least 200 established customers.

Goal 5: Call on at least 120 new customers.

Formulating the Goal Equations

Next, we must define the decision variables whose values will be used to determine whether we are able to achieve the goals. Let

$$E = \text{the number of established customers contacted}$$
$$N = \text{the number of new customers contacted}$$

Using these decision variables and appropriate deviation variables, we can develop a goal equation for each goal. The procedure used parallels the approach introduced in the preceding section. A summary of the results obtained is shown for each goal.

Goal 1

$$2E + 3N - d_1^+ + d_1^- = 680$$

where

$d_1^+ =$ the amount by which the number of hours used by the salesforce is greater than the target value of 680 hours

$d_1^- =$ the amount by which the number of hours used by the salesforce is less than the target value of 680 hours

Goal 2

$$2E + 3N - d_2^+ + d_2^- = 600$$

where

$d_2^+ =$ the amount by which the number of hours used by the salesforce is greater than the target value of 600 hours

$d_2^- =$ the amount by which the number of hours used by the salesforce is less than the target value of 600 hours

Goal 3

$$250E + 125N = d_3^+ + d_3^- = 70,000$$

where

$d_3^+ =$ the amount by which the sales revenue is greater than the target value of $70,000

$d_3^- =$ the amount by which the sales revenue is less than the target value of $70,000

Goal 4

$$E - d_4^+ + d_4^- = 200$$

where

> d_4^+ = the amount by which the number of established customer contacts is greater than the target value of 200 established customer contacts
>
> d_4^- = the amount by which the number of established customer contacts is less than the target value of 200 established customer contacts

Goal 5

$$N - d_5^+ + d_5^- = 120$$

where

> d_5^+ = the amount by which the number of new customer contacts is greater than the target value of 120 new customer contacts
>
> d_5^- = the amount by which the number of new customer contacts is less than the target value of 120 new customer contacts

Formulating the Objective Function

To develop the objective function for the Suncoast Office Supplies problem, we begin by considering the priority level 1 goals. When considering goal 1, if $d_1^+ = 0$, we will have found a solution that uses no more than 680 hours of salesforce time. Because solutions for which d_1^+ is greater than zero represent overtime beyond the desired level, the objective function should minimize the value of d_1^+. When considering goal 2, if $d_2^- = 0$, we will have found a solution that uses *at least* 600 hours of sales force time. If d_2^- is greater than zero, however, labor utilization will not have reached the acceptable level. Thus, the objective function for the priority level 1 goals should minimize the value of d_2^-. Because both priority level 1 goals are equally important, the objective function for the priority level 1 problem is

$$\text{Min} \quad d_1^+ + d_2^-$$

In considering the priority level 2 goal, we note that management wants to achieve sales revenues of at least $70,000. If $d_3^- = 0$, Suncoast will achieve revenues of *at least* $70,000, and if $d_3^- > 0$, revenues of less than $70,000 will be obtained. Thus, the objective function for the priority level 2 problem is

$$\text{Min} \quad d_3^-$$

Next, we consider what the objective function must be for the priority level 3 problem. When considering goal 4, if $d_4^- = 0$, we will have found a solution with *at least* 200 established customer contacts; however, if $d_4^- > 0$, we will have underachieved the goal of contacting at least 200 established customers. Thus, for goal 4 the objective is to minimize d_4^-. When considering goal 5, if $d_5^- = 0$, we will have found a solution with *at least* 120 new customer contacts; however, if $d_5^- > 0$, we will have underachieved the goal of contacting at least 120 new customers. Thus, for goal 5 the objective is to minimize d_5^-. If goals 4 and 5 are equal in importance, the objective function for the priority level 3 problem would be

$$\text{Min} \quad d_4^- + d_5^-$$

However, suppose that management believes that generating new customers is vital to the long-run success of the firm and that goal 5 should be weighted more than goal 4. If management believes that goal 5 is twice as important as goal 4, the objective function for the priority level 3 problem would be

$$\text{Min} \quad d_4^- + 2d_5^-$$

Combining the objective functions for all three priority levels, we obtain the overall objective function for the Suncoast Office Supplies problem:

$$\text{Min} \quad P_1(d_1^+) + P_1(d_2^-) + P_2(d_3^-) + P_3(d_4^-) + P_3(2d_5^-)$$

As we indicated previously, P_1, P_2, and P_3 are simply labels that remind us that goals 1 and 2 are the priority level 1 goals, goal 3 is the priority level 2 goal, and goals 4 and 5 are the priority level 3 goals. We can now write the complete goal programming model for the Suncoast Office Supplies problem as follows:

$$\text{Min} \quad P_1(d_1^+) + P_1(d_2^-) + P_2(d_3^-) + P_3(d_4^-) + P_3(2d_5^-)$$

s.t.

$2E +$	$3N - d_1^+ + d_1^-$				$=$	680 Goal 1
$2E +$	$3N$	$- d_2^+ + d_2^-$			$=$	600 Goal 2
$250E + 125N$		$- d_3^+ + d_3^-$			$=$	70,000 Goal 3
E			$- d_4^+ + d_4^-$		$=$	200 Goal 4
	N			$- d_5^+ + d_5^- =$		120 Goal 5

$$E, N, d_1^+, \ d_1^-, \ d_2^+, \ d_2^-, \ d_3^+, \ d_3^-, \ d_4^+, \ d_4^-, \ d_5^+, \ d_5^- \geq 0$$

Computer Solution

The following computer procedure develops a solution to a goal programming model by solving a sequence of linear programming problems. The first problem comprises all the constraints and all the goal equations for the complete goal programming model; however, the objective function for this problem involves only the P_1 priority level goals. Again, we refer to this problem as the P_1 problem.

Whatever the solution to the P_1 problem, a P_2 problem is formed by adding a constraint to the P_1 model that ensures that subsequent problems will not degrade the solution obtained for the P_1 problem. The objective function for the priority level 2 problem takes into consideration only the P_2 goals. We continue the process until we have considered all priority levels.

To solve the Suncoast Office Supplies problem, we begin by solving the P_1 problem:

$$\text{Min} \quad d_1^+ + d_2^-$$

s.t.

$2E +$	$3N - d_1^+ + d_1^-$				$=$	680 Goal 1
$2E +$	$3N$	$- d_2^+ + d_2^-$			$=$	600 Goal 2
$250E + 125N$		$- d_3^+ + d_3^-$			$=$	70,000 Goal 3
E			$- d_4^+ + d_4^-$		$=$	200 Goal 4
	N			$- d_5^+ + d_5^- =$		120 Goal 5

$$E, N, d_1^+, \ d_1^-, \ d_2^+, \ d_2^-, \ d_3^+, \ d_3^-, \ d_4^+, \ d_4^-, \ d_5^+, \ d_5^- \geq 0$$

In Figure 14.4 we show the solution for this linear program. Note that D1PLUS refers to d_1^+, D2MINUS refers to d_2^-, D1MINUS refers to d_1^-, and so on. The solution shows $E = 250$ established customer contacts and $N = 60$ new customer contacts. Because D1PLUS $= 0$ and

D2MINUS = 0, we see that the solution achieves both goals 1 and 2. Alternatively, the value of the objective function is 0, confirming that both priority level 1 goals have been achieved. Next, we consider goal 3, the priority level 2 goal, which is to minimize D3MINUS. The solution in Figure 14.4 shows that D3MINUS = 0. Thus, the solution of $E = 250$ established customer contacts and $N = 60$ new customer contacts also achieves goal 3, the priority level 2 goal, which is to generate a sales revenue of at least \$70,000. The fact that D3PLUS = 0 indicates that the current solution satisfies goal 3 exactly at \$70,000. Finally, the solution in Figure 14.4 shows D4PLUS = 50 and D5MINUS = 60. These values tell us that goal 4 of the priority level 3 goals is overachieved by 50 established customers, but goal 5 is underachieved by 60 new customers. At this point, both the priority level 1 and 2 goals have been achieved, but we need to solve another linear program to determine whether a solution can be identified that will satisfy both of the priority level 3 goals. Therefore, we go directly to the P_3 problem.

The linear programming model for the P_3 problem is a modification of the linear programming model for the P_1 problem. Specifically, the objective function for the P_3 problem is expressed in terms of the priority level 3 goals. Thus, the P_3 problem objective function becomes to minimize D4MINUS + 2D5MINUS. The original five constraints of the P_1 problem appear in the P_3 problem. However, two additional constraints must be added to ensure that the solution to the P_3 problem continues to satisfy the priority level 1 and priority level 2 goals. Thus, we add the priority level 1 constraint D1PLUS + D2MINUS = 0 and the priority level 2 constraint D3MINUS = 0. Making these modifications to the P_1 problem, we obtain the solution to the P_3 problem shown in Figure 14.5.

Referring to Figure 14.5, we see the objective function value of 120 indicates that the priority level 3 goals cannot be achieved. Because D5MINUS = 60, the optimal solution of $E = 250$ and $N = 60$ results in 60 fewer new customer contacts than desired. However, the fact that we solved the P_3 problem tells us the goal programming solution comes as close as possible to satisfying priority level 3 goals given the achievement of both the priority level 1 and 2 goals. Because all priority levels have been considered, the solution procedure is finished. The optimal solution for Suncoast is to contact 250 established customers and 60 new customers. Although this solution will not achieve management's goal of contacting at least 120 new customers, it does achieve each of the other goals specified. If management isn't happy with this solution, a different set of priorities could be considered. Management must keep in mind, however, that in any situation involving multiple goals at different priority levels, rarely will all the goals be achieved with existing resources.

FIGURE 14.4   THE SOLUTION OF THE P_1 PROBLEM

```
Optimal Objective Value = 0.00000

        Variable              Value              Reduced Cost
     --------------      ---------------      ------------------
        D1PLUS               0.00000                1.00000
        D2MINUS              0.00000                1.00000
        E                  250.00000                0.00000
        N                   60.00000                0.00000
        D1MINUS              0.00000                0.00000
        D2PLUS              80.00000                0.00000
        D3PLUS               0.00000                0.00000
        D3MINUS              0.00000                0.00000
        D4PLUS              50.00000                0.00000
        D4MINUS              0.00000                0.00000
        D5PLUS               0.00000                0.00000
        D5MINUS             60.00000                0.00000
```

FIGURE 14.5   THE SOLUTION OF THE P_3 PROBLEM

```
Optimal Objective Value = 120.00000

        Variable              Value          Reduced Cost
      --------------      ---------------     ----------------
        D1PLUS               0.00000             0.00000
        D2MINUS              0.00000             1.00000
        E                  250.00000             0.00000
        N                   60.00000             0.00000
        D1MINUS              0.00000             1.00000
        D2PLUS              80.00000             0.00000
        D3PLUS               0.00000             0.08000
        D3MINUS              0.00000             0.00000
        D4PLUS              50.00000             0.00000
        D4MINUS              0.00000             1.00000
        D5PLUS               0.00000             2.00000
        D5MINUS             60.00000             0.00000
```

NOTES AND COMMENTS

1. Not all goal programming problems involve multiple priority levels. For problems with one priority level, only one linear program needs to be solved to obtain the goal programming solution. The analyst simply minimizes the weighted deviations from the goals. Trade-offs are permitted among the goals because they are all at the same priority level.

2. The goal programming approach can be used when the analyst is confronted with an infeasible solution to an ordinary linear program. Reformulating some constraints as goal equations with deviation variables allows a solution that minimizes the weighted sum of the deviation variables. Often, this approach will suggest a reasonable solution.

3. The approach that we used to solve goal programming problems with multiple priority levels is to solve a sequence of linear programs. These linear programs are closely related so that complete reformulation and solution are not necessary. By changing the objective function and adding a constraint, we can go from one linear program to the next.

14.3   SCORING MODELS

A scoring model is a relatively quick and easy way to identify the best decision alternative for a multicriteria decision problem. We will demonstrate the use of a scoring model for a job selection application.

Assume that a graduating college student with a double major in finance and accounting received job offers for the following three positions:

- A financial analyst for an investment firm located in Chicago
- An accountant for a manufacturing firm located in Denver
- An auditor for a CPA firm located in Houston

When asked about which job is preferred, the student made the following comments: "The financial analyst position in Chicago provides the best opportunity for my long-run career advancement. However, I would prefer living in Denver rather than in Chicago or Houston. On the other hand, I liked the management style and philosophy at the Houston CPA firm the best." The student's statement points out that this example is clearly a multicriteria decision problem. Considering only the *long-run career advancement* criterion, the financial analyst position in Chicago is the preferred decision alternative. Considering only the *location* criterion, the best decision alternative is the accountant position in Denver. Finally, considering only the *management style* criterion, the best alternative is the auditor position with the CPA firm in Houston. For most individuals, a multicriteria decision problem that requires a trade-off among the several criteria is difficult to solve. In this section, we describe how a **scoring model** can assist in analyzing a multicriteria decision problem and help identify the preferred decision alternative.

The steps required to develop a scoring model are as follows:

A scoring model enables a decision maker to identify the criteria and indicate the weight or importance of each criterion.

Step 1. Develop a list of the criteria to be considered. The criteria are the factors that the decision maker considers relevant for evaluating each decision alternative.

Step 2. Assign a weight to each criterion that describes the criterion's relative importance. Let

$$w_i = \text{the weight for criterion } i$$

Step 3. Assign a rating for each criterion that shows how well each decision alternative satisfies the criterion. Let

$$r_{ij} = \text{the rating for criterion } i \text{ and decision alternative } j$$

Step 4. Compute the score for each decision alternative. Let

$$S_j = \text{score for decision alternative } j$$

The equation used to compute S_j is as follows:

$$S_j = \sum_i w_i r_{ij} \tag{14.1}$$

Step 5. Order the decision alternatives from the highest score to the lowest score to provide the scoring model's ranking of the decision alternatives. The decision alternative with the highest score is the recommended decision alternative.

Let us return to the multicriteria job selection problem the graduating student was facing and illustrate the use of a scoring model to assist in the decision-making process. In carrying out step 1 of the scoring model procedure, the student listed seven criteria as important factors in the decision-making process. These criteria are as follows:

- Career advancement
- Location
- Management style
- Salary
- Prestige
- Job security
- Enjoyment of the work

In step 2, a weight is assigned to each criterion to indicate the criterion's relative importance in the decision-making process. For example, using a five-point scale, the question used to assign a weight to the career advancement criterion would be as follows:

Relative to the other criteria you are considering, how important is career advancement?

Importance	Weight
Very important	5
Somewhat important	4
Average importance	3
Somewhat unimportant	2
Very unimportant	1

TABLE 14.1   WEIGHTS FOR THE SEVEN JOB SELECTION CRITERIA

Criterion	Importance	Weight (w_i)
Career advancement	Very important	5
Location	Average importance	3
Management style	Somewhat important	4
Salary	Average importance	3
Prestige	Somewhat unimportant	2
Job security	Somewhat important	4
Enjoyment of the work	Very important	5

By repeating this question for each of the seven criteria, the student provided the criterion weights shown in Table 14.1. Using this table, we see that career advancement and enjoyment of the work are the two most important criteria, each receiving a weight of 5. The management style and job security criteria are both considered somewhat important, and thus each received a weight of 4. Location and salary are considered average in importance, each receiving a weight of 3. Finally, because prestige is considered to be somewhat unimportant, it received a weight of 2.

The weights shown in Table 14.1 are subjective values provided by the student. A different student would most likely choose to weight the criteria differently. One of the key advantages of a scoring model is that it uses the subjective weights that most closely reflect the preferences of the individual decision maker.

In step 3, each decision alternative is rated in terms of how well it satisfies each criterion. For example, using a nine-point scale, the question used to assign a rating for the "financial analyst in Chicago" alternative and the career advancement criterion would be as follows:

> To what extent does the financial analyst position in Chicago satisfy your career advancement criterion?
>
> | Level of Satisfaction | Rating |
> |---|---|
> | Extremely high | 9 |
> | Very high | 8 |
> | High | 7 |
> | Slightly high | 6 |
> | Average | 5 |
> | Slightly low | 4 |
> | Low | 3 |
> | Very low | 2 |
> | Extremely low | 1 |

A score of 8 on this question would indicate that the student believes the financial analyst position would be rated "very high" in terms of satisfying the career advancement criterion.

This scoring process must be completed for each combination of decision alternative and decision criterion. Because seven decision criteria and three decision alternatives need to be considered, $7 \times 3 = 21$ ratings must be provided. Table 14.2 summarizes the student's responses. Scanning this table provides some insights about how the student rates each decision criterion and decision alternative combination. For example, a rating of 9, corresponding to an extremely high level of satisfaction, only appears for the management style criterion and the auditor position in Houston. Thus, considering all combinations, the student rates the auditor position in Houston as the very best in terms of satisfying the management criterion. The lowest rating in the table is a 3 that appears for the location criterion of the

TABLE 14.2   RATINGS FOR EACH DECISION CRITERION AND EACH DECISION
ALTERNATIVE COMBINATION

	Decision Alternative		
Criterion	Financial Analyst Chicago	Accountant Denver	Auditor Houston
Career advancement	8	6	4
Location	3	8	7
Management style	5	6	9
Salary	6	7	5
Prestige	7	5	4
Job security	4	7	6
Enjoyment of the work	8	6	5

financial analyst position in Chicago. This rating indicates that Chicago is rated "low" in terms of satisfying the student's location criterion. Other insights and interpretations are possible, but the question at this point is how a scoring model uses the data in Tables 14.1 and 14.2 to identify the best overall decision alternative.

Step 4 of the procedure shows that equation (14.1) is used to compute the score for each decision alternative. The data in Table 14.1 provide the weight for each criterion (w_i) and the data in Table 14.2 provide the ratings of each decision alternative for each criterion (r_{ij}). Thus, for decision alternative 1, the score for the financial analyst position in Chicago is

By comparing the scores for each criterion, a decision maker can learn why a particular decision alternative has the highest score.

$$S_1 = \sum_i w_i r_{i1} = 5(8) + 3(3) + 4(5) + 3(6) + 2(7) + 4(4) + 5(8) = 157$$

The scores for the other decision alternatives are computed in the same manner. The computations are summarized in Table 14.3.

From Table 14.3, we see that the highest score of 167 corresponds to the accountant position in Denver. Thus, the accountant position in Denver is the recommended decision alternative. The financial analyst position in Chicago, with a score of 157, is ranked second, and the auditor position in Houston, with a score of 149, is ranked third.

The job selection example that illustrates the use of a scoring model involved seven criteria, each of which was assigned a weight from 1 to 5. In other applications the weights assigned to the criteria may be percentages that reflect the importance of each of the criteria.

TABLE 14.3   COMPUTATION OF SCORES FOR THE THREE DECISION ALTERNATIVES

		Decision Alternative					
		Financial Analyst Chicago		Accountant Denver		Auditor Houston	
Criterion	Weight w_i	Rating r_{i1}	Score $w_i r_{i1}$	Rating r_{i2}	Score $w_i r_{i2}$	Rating r_{i3}	Score $w_i r_{i3}$
Career advancement	5	8	40	6	30	4	20
Location	3	3	9	8	24	7	21
Management style	4	5	20	6	24	9	36
Salary	3	6	18	7	21	5	15
Prestige	2	7	14	5	10	4	8
Job security	4	4	16	7	28	6	24
Enjoyment of the work	5	8	40	6	30	5	25
Score			157		167		149

In addition, multicriteria problems often involve additional subcriteria that enable the decision maker to incorporate additional detail into the decision process. For instance, consider the location criterion in the job selection example. This criterion might be further subdivided into the following three subcriteria:

- Affordability of housing
- Recreational opportunities
- Climate

In this case, the three subcriteria would have to be assigned weights, and a score for each decision alternative would have to be computed for each subcriterion.

14.4 ANALYTIC HIERARCHY PROCESS

The **analytic hierarchy process (AHP),** developed by Thomas L. Saaty,[1] is designed to solve complex multicriteria decision problems. AHP requires the decision maker to provide judgments about the relative importance of each criterion and then specify a preference for each decision alternative using each criterion. The output of AHP is a prioritized ranking of the decision alternatives based on the overall preferences expressed by the decision maker.

To introduce AHP, we consider a car purchasing decision problem faced by Diane Payne. After a preliminary analysis of the makes and models of several used cars, Diane narrowed her list of decision alternatives to three cars: a Honda Accord, a Ford Taurus, and a Chevrolet Cruze. Table 14.4 summarizes the information Diane collected about these cars.

Diane decided that the following criteria were relevant for her car selection decision process:

- Price
- Miles per gallon (MPG)
- Comfort
- Style

Data regarding the Price and MPG are provided in Table 14.4. However, measures of Comfort and Style cannot be specified so directly. Diane will need to consider factors such as the car's interior, type of entertainment system, ease of entry, seat adjustments, and driver visibility in order to determine the comfort level of each car. The style criterion will have to be based on Diane's subjective evaluation of the color and the general appearance of each car.

TABLE 14.4   INFORMATION FOR THE CAR SELECTION PROBLEM

	Decision Alternative		
Characteristics	**Accord**	**Taurus**	**Cruze**
Price	$21,600	$24,200	$22,500
Color	Black	Red	Blue
Miles per gallon	19	23	28
Interior	Deluxe	Above Average	Standard
Body type	4-door midsize	2-door sport	2-door compact
Entertainment system	Deluxe	Basic	Basic

[1]T. Saaty, *Decision Making for Leaders: The Analytic Hierarchy Process for Decisions in a Complex World,* 3rd rev. ed. RWS, 2012.

FIGURE 14.6 HIERARCHY FOR THE CAR SELECTION PROBLEM

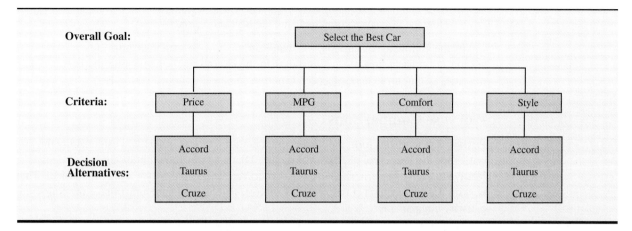

AHP allows a decision maker to express personal preferences and subjective judgments about the various aspects of a multicriteria problem.

Even when a criterion such as price can be easily measured, subjectivity becomes an issue whenever a decision maker indicates his or her personal preference for the decision alternatives based on price. For instance, the price of the Accord ($21,600) is $3600 more than the price of the Cruze ($22,500). The $3600 difference might represent a great deal of money to one person, but not much of a difference to another person. Thus, whether the Accord is considered "extremely more expensive" than the Cruze or perhaps only "moderately more expensive" than the Cruze depends upon the financial status and the subjective opinion of the person making the comparison. An advantage of AHP is that it can handle situations in which the unique subjective judgments of the individual decision maker constitute an important part of the decision-making process.

Developing the Hierarchy

The first step in AHP is to develop a graphical representation of the problem in terms of the overall goal, the criteria to be used, and the decision alternatives. Such a graph depicts the **hierarchy** for the problem. Figure 14.6 shows the hierarchy for the car selection problem. Note that the first level of the hierarchy shows that the overall goal is to select the best car. At the second level, the four criteria (Price, MPG, Comfort, and Style) each contribute to the achievement of the overall goal. Finally, at the third level, each decision alternative— Accord, Taurus, and Cruze—contributes to each criterion in a unique way.

Using AHP, the decision maker specifies judgments about the relative importance of each of the four criteria in terms of its contribution to the achievement of the overall goal. At the next level, the decision maker indicates a preference for each decision alternative based on each criterion. A mathematical process is used to synthesize the information on the relative importance of the criteria and the preferences for the decision alternatives to provide an overall priority ranking of the decision alternatives. In the car selection problem, AHP will use Diane's personal preferences to provide a priority ranking of the three cars in terms of how well each car meets the overall goal of being the *best* car.

14.5 ESTABLISHING PRIORITIES USING AHP

In this section we show how AHP uses pairwise comparisons expressed by the decision maker to establish priorities for the criteria and priorities for the decision alternatives based on each criterion. Using the car selection example, we show how AHP determines priorities for each of the following:

1. How the four criteria contribute to the overall goal of selecting the best car
2. How the three cars compare using the Price criterion

3. How the three cars compare using the MPG criterion
4. How the three cars compare using the Comfort criterion
5. How the three cars compare using the Style criterion

In the following discussion we demonstrate how to establish priorities for the four criteria in terms of how each contributes to the overall goal of selecting the best car. The priorities of the three cars using each criterion can be determined similarly.

Pairwise Comparisons

Pairwise comparisons form the fundamental building blocks of AHP. In establishing the priorities for the four criteria, AHP will require Diane to state how important each criterion is relative to each other criterion when the criteria are compared two at a time (pairwise). That is, with the four criteria (Price, MPG, Comfort, and Style) Diane must make the following pairwise comparisons:

Price compared to MPG

Price compared to Comfort

Price compared to Style

MPG compared to Comfort

MPG compared to Style

Comfort compared to Style

In each comparison, Diane must select the more important criterion and then express a judgment of how much more important the selected criterion is.

For example, in the Price-MPG pairwise comparison, assume that Diane indicates that Price is more important than MPG. To measure how much more important Price is compared to MPG, AHP uses a scale with values from 1 to 9. Table 14.5 shows how the decision maker's verbal description of the relative importance between the two criteria is converted into a numerical rating. In the car selection example, suppose that Diane states that Price is "moderately more important" than MPG. In this case, a numerical rating of 3 is assigned to the Price-MPG pairwise comparison. From Table 14.5, we see "strongly more important" receives a numerical rating of 5, whereas "very strongly more important" receives a numerical rating of 7. Intermediate judgments such as "strongly to very strongly more important" are possible and would receive a numerical rating of 6.

Table 14.6 provides a summary of the six pairwise comparisons Diane provided for the car selection problem. Using the information in this table, Diane has specified that

Price is moderately more important than MPG.

Price is equally to moderately more important than Comfort.

TABLE 14.5   COMPARISON SCALE FOR THE IMPORTANCE OF CRITERIA USING AHP

Verbal Judgment	Numerical Rating
Extremely more important	9
	8
Very strongly more important	7
	6
Strongly more important	5
	4
Moderately more important	3
	2
Equally important	1

Price is equally to moderately more important than Style.

Comfort is moderately to strongly more important than MPG.

Style is moderately to strongly more important than MPG.

Style is equally to moderately more important than Comfort.

AHP uses the numerical ratings from the pairwise comparisons to establish a priority or importance measure for each criterion.

As shown, the flexibility of AHP can accommodate the unique preferences of each individual decision maker. First, the choice of the criteria that are considered can vary depending upon the decision maker. Not everyone would agree that Price, MPG, Comfort, and Style are the only criteria to be considered in a car selection problem. Perhaps you would want to add safety, resale value, and/or other criteria if you were making the car selection decision. AHP can accommodate any set of criteria specified by the decision maker. Of course, if additional criteria are added, more pairwise comparisons will be necessary. In addition, if you agree with Diane that Price, MPG, Comfort, and Style are the four criteria to use, you would probably disagree with her as to the relative importance of the criteria. Using the format of Table 14.6, you could provide your own assessment of the importance of each pairwise comparison, and AHP would adjust the numerical ratings to reflect your personal preferences.

Pairwise Comparison Matrix

To determine the priorities for the four criteria, we need to construct a matrix of the pairwise comparison ratings provided in Table 14.6. Using the four criteria, the **pairwise comparison matrix** will consist of four rows and four columns as shown here:

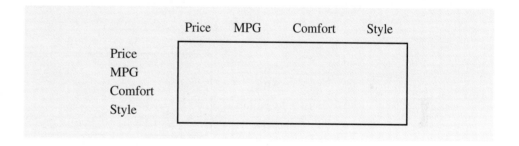

Each of the numerical ratings in Table 14.6 must be entered into the pairwise comparison matrix. As an illustration of this process consider the numerical rating of 3 for the Price–MPG pairwise comparison. Table 14.6 shows that for this pairwise comparison that Price is the most important criterion. Thus, we must enter a 3 into the row labeled Price and the column labeled MPG in the pairwise comparison matrix. In general, the entries

TABLE 14.6 SUMMARY OF DIANE PAYNE'S PAIRWISE COMPARISONS OF THE FOUR CRITERIA FOR THE CAR SELECTION PROBLEM

Pairwise Comparison	More Important Criterion	How Much More Important	Numerical Rating
Price–MPG	Price	Moderately	3
Price–Comfort	Price	Equally to moderately	2
Price–Style	Price	Equally to moderately	2
MPG–Comfort	Comfort	Moderately to strongly	4
MPG–Style	Style	Moderately to strongly	4
Comfort–Style	Style	Equally to moderately	2

in the column labeled Most Important Criterion in Table 14.6 indicate which row of the pairwise comparison matrix the numerical rating must be placed in. As another illustration, consider the MPG-Comfort pairwise comparison. Table 14.6 shows that Comfort is the most important criterion for this pairwise comparison and that the numerical rating is 4. Thus, we enter a 4 into the row labeled Comfort and into the column labeled MPG. Following this procedure for the other pairwise comparisons shown in Table 14.6, we obtain the following pairwise comparison matrix:

	Price	MPG	Comfort	Style
Price		3	2	2
MPG				
Comfort		4		
Style		4	2	

Because the diagonal elements are comparing each criterion to itself, the diagonal elements of the pairwise comparison matrix are always equal to 1. For example, if Price is compared to Price, the verbal judgment would be "equally important" with a rating of 1; thus, a 1 would be placed into the row labeled Price and into the column labeled Price in the pairwise comparison matrix. At this point, the pairwise comparison matrix appears as follows:

	Price	MPG	Comfort	Style
Price	1	3	2	2
MPG		1		
Comfort		4	1	
Style		4	2	1

All that remains is to complete the entries for the remaining cells of the matrix. To illustrate how these values are obtained, consider the numerical rating of 3 for the Price-MPG pairwise comparison. This rating implies that the MPG-Price pairwise comparison should have a rating of $\frac{1}{3}$. That is, because Diane already indicated Price is moderately more important than MPG (a rating of 3), we can infer that a pairwise comparison of MPG relative to Price should be $\frac{1}{3}$. Similarly, because the Comfort-MPG pairwise comparison has a rating of 4, the MPG-Comfort pairwise comparison would be $\frac{1}{4}$. Thus, the complete pairwise comparison matrix for the car selection criteria is as follows:

	Price	MPG	Comfort	Style
Price	1	3	2	2
MPG	$\frac{1}{3}$	1	$\frac{1}{4}$	$\frac{1}{4}$
Comfort	$\frac{1}{2}$	4	1	$\frac{1}{2}$
Style	$\frac{1}{2}$	4	2	1

Synthesization

Using the pairwise comparison matrix, we can now calculate the priority of each criterion in terms of its contribution to the overall goal of selecting the best car. This aspect of AHP is referred to as **synthesization.** The exact mathematical procedure required to perform synthesization is beyond the scope of this text. However, the following three-step procedure provides a good approximation of the synthesization results:

1. Sum the values in each column of the pairwise comparison matrix.
2. Divide each element in the pairwise comparison matrix by its column total; the resulting matrix is referred to as the **normalized pairwise comparison matrix.**
3. Compute the average of the elements in each row of the normalized pairwise comparison matrix; these averages provide the priorities for the criteria.

To show how the synthesization process works, we carry out this three-step procedure for the criteria pairwise comparison matrix.

Step 1. Sum the values in each column.

	Price	MPG	Comfort	Style
Price	1	3	2	2
MPG	⅓	1	¼	¼
Comfort	½	4	1	½
Style	½	4	2	1
Sum	2.333	12.000	5.250	3.750

Step 2. Divide each element of the matrix by its column total.

	Price	MPG	Comfort	Style
Price	0.429	0.250	0.381	0.533
MPG	0.143	0.083	0.048	0.067
Comfort	0.214	0.333	0.190	0.133
Style	0.214	0.333	0.381	0.267

Step 3. Average the elements in each row to determine the priority of each criterion.

	Price	MPG	Comfort	Style	Priority
Price	0.429	0.250	0.381	0.533	0.398
MPG	0.143	0.083	0.048	0.067	0.085
Comfort	0.214	0.333	0.190	0.133	0.218
Style	0.214	0.333	0.381	0.267	0.299

The AHP synthesization procedure provides the priority of each criterion in terms of its contribution to the overall goal of selecting the best car. Thus, using Diane's pairwise comparisons provided in Table 14.6, AHP determines that Price, with a priority of 0.398, is the most important criterion in the car selection process. Style, with a priority of 0.299, ranks second in importance and is closely followed by Comfort, with a priority of 0.218. MPG is the least important criterion, with a priority of 0.085.

Consistency

A key step in AHP is the making of several pairwise comparisons, as previously described. An important consideration in this process is the **consistency** of the pairwise judgments provided by the decision maker. For example, if criterion A compared to criterion B has a numerical rating of 3 and if criterion B compared to criterion C has a numerical rating of 2, perfect consistency of criterion A compared to criterion C would have a numerical rating of 3 × 2 = 6. If the A to C numerical rating assigned by the decision maker was 4 or 5, some inconsistency would exist among the pairwise comparison.

With numerous pairwise comparisons, perfect consistency is difficult to achieve. In fact, some degree of inconsistency can be expected to exist in almost any set of pairwise comparisons. To handle the consistency issue, AHP provides a method for measuring the degree of consistency among the pairwise comparisons provided by the decision maker. If the degree of consistency is unacceptable, the decision maker should review and revise the pairwise comparisons before proceeding with the AHP analysis.

A consistency ratio greater than 0.10 indicates inconsistency in the pairwise comparisons. In such cases, the decision maker should review the pairwise comparisons before proceeding.

AHP provides a measure of the consistency for the pairwise comparisons by computing a **consistency ratio.** This ratio is designed in such a way that a value *greater than* 0.10 indicates an inconsistency in the pairwise judgments. Thus, if the consistency ratio is 0.10 or less, the consistency of the pairwise comparisons is considered reasonable, and the AHP process can continue with the synthesization computations.

Although the exact mathematical computation of the consistency ratio is beyond the scope of this text, an approximation of the ratio can be obtained with little difficulty. The step-by-step procedure for estimating the consistency ratio for the criteria of the car selection problem follows:

Step 1. Multiply each value in the first column of the pairwise comparison matrix by the priority of the first item; multiply each value in the second column of the pairwise comparison matrix by the priority of the second item; continue this process for all columns of the pairwise comparison matrix. Sum the values across the rows to obtain a vector of values labeled "weighted sum." This computation for the car selection problem is as follows:

$$0.398\begin{bmatrix}1\\ 1/3\\ 1/2\\ 1/2\end{bmatrix} + 0.085\begin{bmatrix}3\\ 1\\ 4\\ 4\end{bmatrix} + 0.218\begin{bmatrix}2\\ 1/2\\ 1\\ 2\end{bmatrix} + 0.299\begin{bmatrix}2\\ 1/4\\ 1/2\\ 1\end{bmatrix} =$$

$$\begin{bmatrix}0.398\\ 0.133\\ 0.199\\ 0.199\end{bmatrix} + \begin{bmatrix}0.255\\ 0.085\\ 0.340\\ 0.340\end{bmatrix} + \begin{bmatrix}0.436\\ 0.054\\ 0.218\\ 0.436\end{bmatrix} + \begin{bmatrix}0.598\\ 0.075\\ 0.149\\ 0.299\end{bmatrix} = \begin{bmatrix}1.687\\ 0.347\\ 0.907\\ 1.274\end{bmatrix}$$

Step 2. Divide the elements of the weighted sum vector obtained in step 1 by the corresponding priority for each criterion.

$$\text{Price} \quad \frac{1.687}{0.398} = 4.236$$

$$\text{MPG} \quad \frac{0.347}{0.085} = 4.077$$

$$\text{Comfort} \quad \frac{0.907}{0.218} = 4.163$$

$$\text{Style} \quad \frac{1.274}{0.299} = 4.264$$

Step 3. Compute the average of the values found in step 2; this average is denoted λ_{max}.

$$\lambda_{max} = \frac{(4.236 + 4.077 + 4.163 + 4.264)}{4} = 4.185$$

Step 4. Compute the consistency index (CI) as follows:

$$CI = \frac{\lambda_{max} - n}{n - 1}$$

where n is the number of items being compared. Thus, we have

$$CI = \frac{4.185 - 4}{4 - 1} = 0.0616$$

Step 5. Compute the consistency ratio, which is defined as

$$CR = \frac{CI}{RI}$$

where RI is the consistency index of a *randomly* generated pairwise comparison matrix. The value of RI depends on the number of items being compared and is given as follows:

n	3	4	5	6	7	8
RI	0.58	0.90	1.12	1.24	1.32	1.41

Thus, for the car selection problem with $n = 4$ criteria, we have RI = 0.90 and a consistency ratio

$$CR = \frac{0.0616}{0.90} = 0.068$$

As mentioned previously, a consistency ratio of 0.10 or less is considered acceptable. Because the pairwise comparisons for the car selection criteria show CR = 0.068, we can conclude that the degree of consistency in the pairwise comparisons is acceptable.

Other Pairwise Comparisons for the Car Selection Problem

Practice setting up a pairwise comparison matrix and determine whether judgments are consistent by working Problem 20.

Continuing with the AHP analysis of the car selection problem, we need to use the pairwise comparison procedure to determine the priorities for the three cars using each of the criteria: Price, MPG, Comfort, and Style. Determining these priorities requires Diane to express pairwise comparison preferences for the cars using each criterion one at a time. For example, using the Price criterion, Diane must make the following pairwise comparisons:

the Accord compared to the Taurus

the Accord compared to the Cruze

the Taurus compared to the Cruze

In each comparison, Diane must select the more preferred car and then express a judgment of how much more preferred the selected car is.

For example, using Price as the basis for comparison, assume that Diane considers the Accord-Taurus pairwise comparison and indicates that the less expensive Taurus is preferred. Table 14.7 shows how AHP uses Diane's verbal description of the preference between the Accord and Taurus to determine a numerical rating of the preference. For example, suppose that Diane states that based on Price, the Taurus is "moderately more preferred" to the Accord. Thus, using the Price criterion, a numerical rating of 3 is assigned to the Taurus row and Accord column of the pairwise comparison matrix.

Table 14.8 shows the summary of the car pairwise comparisons that Diane provided for each criterion of the car selection problem. Using this table and referring to selected pairwise comparison entries, we see that Diane stated the following preferences:

In terms of Price, the Cruze is moderately to strongly more preferred than the Accord.

In terms of MPG, the Cruze is moderately more preferred than the Taurus.

In terms of Comfort, the Accord is very strongly to extremely more preferred than the Cruze.

In terms of Style, the Taurus is moderately more preferred than the Accord.

Problem 16 will give you practice with the synthesization calculations and determining the consistency ratio.

Using the pairwise comparison matrixes in Table 14.8, many other insights may be gained about the preferences Diane expressed for the cars. However, at this point AHP continues by synthesizing each of the four pairwise comparison matrixes in Table 14.8 in order to determine the priority of each car using each criterion. A synthesization is conducted for each pairwise comparison matrix, using the three-step procedure described previously for the criteria pairwise comparison matrix. Four synthesization computations provide the four sets of priorities shown in Table 14.9. Using this table, we see that the Cruze is the preferred alternative based on Price (0.557), the Cruze is the preferred alternative based on MPG (0.639), the Accord is the preferred alternative based on Comfort (0.593), and the Taurus is the preferred alternative based on Style (0.656). At this point, no car is the clear, overall best. The next section shows how to combine the priorities for the criteria and the priorities in Table 14.9 to develop an overall priority ranking for the three cars.

TABLE 14.7   PAIRWISE COMPARISON SCALE FOR THE PREFERENCE OF DECISION ALTERNATIVES USING AHP

Verbal Judgment	Numerical Rating
Extremely preferred	9
	8
Very strongly preferred	7
	6
Strongly preferred	5
	4
Moderately preferred	3
	2
Equally preferred	1

TABLE 14.8   PAIRWISE COMPARISON MATRIXES SHOWING PREFERENCES
FOR THE CARS USING EACH CRITERION

Price	Accord	Taurus	Cruze		MPG	Accord	Taurus	Cruze
Accord	1	⅓	¼		Accord	1	¼	⅙
Taurus	3	1	½		Taurus	4	1	⅓
Cruze	4	2	1		Cruze	6	3	1

Comfort	Accord	Taurus	Cruze		Style	Accord	Taurus	Cruze
Accord	1	2	8		Accord	1	⅓	4
Taurus	½	1	6		Taurus	3	1	7
Cruze	⅛	⅙	1		Cruze	¼	⅐	1

TABLE 14.9   PRIORITIES FOR EACH CAR USING EACH CRITERION

	Criterion			
	Price	MPG	Comfort	Style
Accord	0.123	0.087	0.593	0.265
Taurus	0.320	0.274	0.341	0.656
Cruze	0.557	0.639	0.065	0.080

14.6   USING AHP TO DEVELOP AN OVERALL PRIORITY RANKING

In Section 14.5 we used Diane's pairwise comparisons of the four criteria to develop the priorities of 0.398 for Price, 0.085 for MPG, 0.218 for Comfort, and 0.299 for Style. We now want to use these priorities and the priorities shown in Table 14.9 to develop an overall priority ranking for the three cars.

The procedure used to compute the overall priority is to weight each car's priority shown in Table 14.9 by the corresponding criterion priority. For example, the Price criterion has a priority of 0.398, and the Accord has a priority of 0.123 in terms of the Price criterion. Thus, $0.398 \times 0.123 = 0.049$ is the priority value of the Accord based on the Price criterion. To obtain the overall priority of the Accord, we need to make similar computations for the MPG, Comfort, and Style criteria and then add the values to obtain the overall priority. This calculation is as follows:

Overall Priority of the Accord:

$$0.398(0.123) + 0.085(0.087) + 0.218(0.593) + 0.299(0.265) = 0.265$$

Repeating this calculation for the Taurus and the Cruze, we obtain the following results:

Overall Priority of the Taurus:

$$0.398(0.320) + 0.085(0.274) + 0.218(0.341) + 0.299(0.656) = 0.421$$

Overall Priority of the Cruze:

$$0.398(0.557) + 0.085(0.639) + 0.218(0.065) + 0.299(0.080) = 0.314$$

Ranking these priorities, we have the AHP ranking of the decision alternatives:

Car	Priority
1. Taurus	0.421
2. Cruze	0.314
3. Accord	0.265

Work Problem 24 and determine the AHP priorities for the two decision alternatives.

These results provide a basis for Diane to make a decision regarding the purchase of a car. As long as Diane believes that her judgments regarding the importance of the criteria and her preferences for the cars using each criterion are valid, the AHP priorities show that the Taurus is preferred. In addition to the recommendation of the Taurus as the best car, the AHP analysis helped Diane gain a better understanding of the trade-offs in the decision-making process and a clearer understanding of why the Taurus is the AHP recommended alternative. The Management Science in Action, Distribution Companies Use Analytic Hierarchy Process to Develop Environmentally Sustainable Transportation Routes, describes the use of AHP by two distribution companies and a team of researchers in Spain to determine the most environmentally friendly transportation route across the Pyrenees Mountains from Spain into France. This example combines data on pollution levels with expert opinions on multiple decision criteria to determine the best transportation route for minimizing environmental damage.

MANAGEMENT SCIENCE IN ACTION

DISTRIBUTION COMPANIES USE ANALYTIC HIERARCHY PROCESS TO DEVELOP ENVIRONMENTALLY SUSTAINABLE TRANSPORTATION ROUTES*

Many organizations are striving to incorporate environmental sustainability into their business operations. Organizations are taking action to minimize their harmful environmental impact by reducing the pollution caused by their manufacturing activities, using less fuel in their distribution systems, and reducing the packaging used by their products. Several distribution companies in Europe have used AHP to help them choose the most environmentally sustainable routes to reduce the amount of pollution caused by their distribution activities.

Two Spanish distributors, Hydro Inasa and GamesaEólica, used the analytic hierarchy process to help them identify the transportation route from Pamplona, Spain, through the Pyrenees Mountains and into France that resulted in the least environmental impact. To determine this transportation route, data was collected on the pollution in different areas on five potential routes and a multicriteria decision model was developed to help the decision makers evaluate these alternative transportation routes.

Three main criteria of Economic, Social, and Natural Areas were defined that could be associated with a particular area affected by the transportation route. Each main criterion included subcriteria to further define the issues associated with a particular area of a transportation route. For

instance, the Social main criterion included subcriteria related to whether the transportation route passed near an urban center, heritage site, or recreational zone.

Pairwise comparisons of the main criteria and subcriteria were then made based on interviews with transportation and environmental experts. From these pairwise comparisons, priorities were established to provide a ranking of the five possible routes through the Pyrenees Mountains. The results of AHP showed that two of the routes were considered superior, but that the priority scores for these two routes were quite close. Therefore, a sensitivity analysis was conducted by randomly perturbing the priorities of the criteria and subcriteria. The results of the sensitivity analysis indicated that one of the two routes was considered superior in 91% of the scenarios; thus, this route was selected as the best candidate that was then used by both Hydro Inasa and GamesaEólica.

*Based on Javier Faulin, Esteban de Paz, Fernando Lera-López, Ángel Juan, and Israel Gil-Ramírez, "Distribution Companies Use Analytical Hierarchy Process for Environmental Assessment Transportation Routes Crossing Pyrenees in Navarre, Spain," *Interfaces* 43, no. 13 (May–June 2013): 285–287.

NOTES AND COMMENTS

1. The scoring model in Section 14.3 used the following equation to compute the overall score of a decision alternative:

$$S_j = \sum_i w_i \, r_{ij}$$

where

w_i = the weight for criterion i

r_{ij} = the rating for criterion i and decision alternative j

In Section 14.5 AHP used the same calculation to determine the overall priority of each decision alternative. The difference between the two approaches is that the scoring model required the decision maker to estimate the values of w_i and r_{ij} directly. AHP used synthesization to compute the criterion priorities w_i and the decision alternative priorities r_{ij} based on the pairwise comparison information provided by the decision maker.

2. The software package Expert Choice® provides a user-friendly procedure for implementing AHP on a personal computer. Expert Choice takes the decision maker through the pairwise comparison process in a step-by-step manner. Once the decision maker responds to the pairwise comparison prompts, Expert Choice automatically constructs the pairwise comparison matrix, conducts the synthesization calculations, and presents the overall priorities. Expert Choice is a software package that should warrant consideration by a decision maker who anticipates solving a variety of multicriteria decision problems.

SUMMARY

In this chapter we used goal programming to solve problems with multiple goals within the linear programming framework. We showed that the goal programming model contains one or more goal equations and an objective function designed to minimize deviations from the goals. In situations where resource capacities or other restrictions affect the achievement of the goals, the model will contain constraints that are formulated and treated in the same manner as constraints in an ordinary linear programming model.

In goal programming problems with preemptive priorities, priority level 1 goals are treated first in an objective function to identify a solution that will best satisfy these goals. This solution is then revised by considering an objective function involving only the priority level 2 goals; solution modifications are considered only if they do not degrade the solution obtained for the priority level 1 goals. This process continues until all priority levels have been considered.

We showed how a variation of the linear programming graphical solution procedure can be used to solve goal programming problems with two decision variables. Specialized goal programming computer packages are available for solving the general goal programming problem, but such computer codes are not as readily available as are general purpose linear programming computer packages. As a result, we showed how linear programming can be used to solve a goal programming problem.

We then presented a scoring model as a quick and relatively easy way to identify the most desired decision alternative in a multicriteria problem. The decision maker provides a subjective weight indicating the importance of each criterion. Then the decision maker rates each decision alternative in terms of how well it satisfies each criterion. The end result is a score for each decision alternative that indicates the preference for the decision alternative considering all criteria.

We also presented an approach to multicriteria decision making called the analytic hierarchy process (AHP). We showed that a key part of AHP is the development of judgments concerning the relative importance of, or preference for, the elements being compared. A consistency ratio is computed to determine the degree of consistency exhibited by the decision maker in making the pairwise comparisons. Values of the consistency ratio less than or equal to 0.10 are considered acceptable.

Once the set of all pairwise comparisons has been developed, a process referred to as synthesization is used to determine the priorities for the elements being compared. The final step of the analytic hierarchy process involves multiplying the priority levels established for the decision alternatives relative to each criterion by the priority levels reflecting the importance of the criteria themselves; the sum of these products over all the criteria provides the overall priority level for each decision alternative.

GLOSSARY

Analytic hierarchy process (AHP)   An approach to multicriteria decision making based on pairwise comparisons for elements in a hierarchy.

Consistency   A concept developed to assess the quality of the judgments made during a series of pairwise comparisons. It is a measure of the internal consistency of these comparisons.

Consistency ratio   A numerical measure of the degree of consistency in a series of pairwise comparisons. Values less than or equal to 0.10 are considered reasonable.

Deviation variables   Variables that are added to the goal equation to allow the solution to deviate from the goal's target value.

Goal equation   An equation whose right-hand side is the target value for the goal; the left-hand side of the goal equation consists of (1) a function representing the level of achievement and (2) deviation variables representing the difference between the target value for the goal and the level achieved.

Goal programming   A linear programming approach to multicriteria decision problems whereby the objective function is designed to minimize the deviations from goals.

Hierarchy   A diagram that shows the levels of a problem in terms of the overall goal, the criteria, and the decision alternatives.

Normalized pairwise comparison matrix   The matrix obtained by dividing each element of the pairwise comparison matrix by its column total. This matrix is computed as an intermediate step in the synthesization of priorities.

Pairwise comparison matrix   A matrix that consists of the preference, or relative importance, ratings provided during a series of pairwise comparisons.

Preemptive priorities   Priorities assigned to goals that ensure that the satisfaction of a higher level goal cannot be traded for the satisfaction of a lower level goal.

Scoring model   An approach to multicriteria decision making that requires the user to assign weights to each criterion that describe the criterion's relative importance and to assign a rating that shows how well each decision alternative satisfies each criterion. The output is a score for each decision alternative.

Synthesization   A mathematical process that uses the preference or relative importance values in the pairwise comparison matrix to develop priorities.

Target value   A value specified in the statement of the goal. Based on the context of the problem, management will want the solution to the goal programming problem to result in a value for the goal that is less than, equal to, or greater than the target value.

PROBLEMS

1.   The RMC Corporation blends three raw materials to produce two products: a fuel additive and a solvent base. Each ton of fuel additive is a mixture of $\frac{2}{5}$ ton of material 1 and $\frac{3}{5}$ ton of material 3. A ton of solvent base is a mixture of $\frac{1}{2}$ ton of material 1, $\frac{1}{5}$ ton of material 2, and $\frac{3}{10}$ ton of material 3. RMC's production is constrained by a limited availability of the three raw materials. For the current production period, RMC has the following quantities of each raw material: material 1, 20 tons; material 2, 5 tons; material 3, 21 tons. Management wants to achieve the following P_1 priority level goals:

Goal 1: Produce at least 30 tons of fuel additive.

Goal 2: Produce at least 15 tons of solvent base.

Assume there are no other goals.

a. Is it possible for management to achieve both P_1 level goals given the constraints on the amounts of each material available? Explain.

b. Treating the amounts of each material available as constraints, formulate a goal programming model to determine the optimal product mix. Assume that both P_1 priority level goals are equally important to management.

c. Use the graphical goal programming procedure to solve the model formulated in part (b).

d. If goal 1 is twice as important as goal 2, what is the optimal product mix?

 SELF*test*

2. DJS Investment Services must develop an investment portfolio for a new client. As an initial investment strategy, the new client would like to restrict the portfolio to a mix of two stocks:

Stock	Price/Share	Estimated Annual Return (%)
AGA Products	$ 50	6
Key Oil	100	10

The client wants to invest $50,000 and established the following two investment goals:

Priority Level 1 Goal

Goal 1: Obtain an annual return of at least 9%.

Priority Level 2 Goal

Goal 2: Limit the investment in Key Oil, the riskier investment, to no more than 60% of the total investment.

a. Formulate a goal programming model for the DJS Investment problem.

b. Use the graphical goal programming procedure to obtain a solution.

3. The L. Young & Sons Manufacturing Company produces two products, which have the following profit and resource requirement characteristics:

Characteristic	Product 1	Product 2
Profit/unit	$4	$2
Dept. A hours/unit	1	1
Dept. B hours/unit	2	5

Last month's production schedule used 350 hours of labor in department A and 1000 hours of labor in department B.

Young's management has been experiencing workforce morale and labor union problems during the past six months because of monthly departmental workload fluctuations. New hiring, layoffs, and interdepartmental transfers have been common because the firm has not attempted to stabilize workload requirements.

Management would like to develop a production schedule for the coming month that will achieve the following goals:

Goal 1: Use 350 hours of labor in department A.

Goal 2: Use 1000 hours of labor in department B.

Goal 3: Earn a profit of at least $1300.

a. Formulate a goal programming model for this problem, assuming that goals 1 and 2 are P_1 level goals and goal 3 is a P_2 level goal; assume that goals 1 and 2 are equally important.

b. Solve the model formulated in part (a) using the graphical goal programming procedure.

c. Suppose that the firm ignores the workload fluctuations and considers the 350 hours in department A and the 1000 hours in department B as the maximum available. Formulate and solve a linear programming problem to maximize profit subject to these constraints.

    d. Compare the solutions obtained in parts (b) and (c). Discuss which approach you favor, and why.

    e. Reconsider part (a) assuming that the priority level 1 goal is goal 3 and the priority level 2 goals are goals 1 and 2; as before, assume that goals 1 and 2 are equally important. Solve this revised problem using the graphical goal programming procedure, and compare your solution to the one obtained for the original problem.

4. Industrial Chemicals produces two adhesives used in the manufacturing process for airplanes. The two adhesives, which have different bonding strengths, require different amounts of production time: the IC-100 adhesive requires 20 minutes of production time per gallon of finished product, and the IC-200 adhesive uses 30 minutes of production time per gallon. Both products use 1 pound of a highly perishable resin for each gallon of finished product. Inventory currently holds 300 pounds of the resin, and more can be obtained if necessary. However, because of the limited shelf life of the material, any amount not used in the next two weeks will be discarded.

    The firm has existing orders for 100 gallons of IC-100 and 120 gallons of IC-200. Under normal conditions, the production process operates eight hours per day, five days per week. Management wants to schedule production for the next two weeks to achieve the following goals:

Priority Level 1 Goals

Goal 1: Avoid underutilization of the production process.

Goal 2: Avoid overtime in excess of 20 hours for the two weeks.

Priority Level 2 Goals

Goal 3: Satisfy existing orders for the IC-100 adhesive; that is, produce at least 100 gallons of IC-100.

Goal 4: Satisfy existing orders for the IC-200 adhesive; that is, produce at least 120 gallons of IC-200.

Priority Level 3 Goal

Goal 5: Use all the available resin.

    a. Formulate a goal programming model for the Industrial Chemicals problem. Assume that both priority level 1 goals and both priority level 2 goals are equally important.

    b. Use the graphical goal programming procedure to develop a solution for the model formulated in part (a).

5. Standard Pump recently won a $14 million contract with the U.S. Navy to supply 2000 custom-designed submersible pumps over the next four months. The contract calls for the delivery of 200 pumps at the end of May, 600 pumps at the end of June, 600 pumps at the end of July, and 600 pumps at the end of August. Standard's production capacity is 500 pumps in May, 400 pumps in June, 800 pumps in July, and 500 pumps in August. Management would like to develop a production schedule that will keep monthly ending inventories low while at the same time minimizing the fluctuations in inventory levels from month to month. In attempting to develop a goal programming model of the problem, the company's production scheduler let x_m denote the number of pumps produced in month m and s_m denote the number of pumps in inventory at the end of month m. Here, $m = 1$ refers to May, $m = 2$ refers to June, $m = 3$ refers to July, and $m = 4$ refers to August. Management asks you to assist the production scheduler in model development.

    a. Using these variables, develop a constraint for each month that will satisfy the following demand requirement:

$$\begin{pmatrix} \text{Beginning} \\ \text{Inventory} \end{pmatrix} + \begin{pmatrix} \text{Current} \\ \text{Production} \end{pmatrix} - \begin{pmatrix} \text{Ending} \\ \text{Inventory} \end{pmatrix} = \begin{pmatrix} \text{This Month's} \\ \text{Demand} \end{pmatrix}$$

    b. Write goal equations that represent the fluctuations in the production level from May to June, June to July, and July to August.

    c. Inventory carrying costs are high. Is it possible for Standard to avoid carrying any monthly ending inventories over the scheduling period of May to August? If not, develop goal equations with a target of zero for the ending inventory in May, June, and July.

d. Besides the goal equations developed in parts (b) and (c), what other constraints are needed in the model?

e. Assuming the production fluctuation and inventory goals are of equal importance, develop and solve a goal programming model to determine the best production schedule.

f. Can you find a way to reduce the variables and constraints needed in your model by eliminating the goal equations and deviation variables for ending inventory levels? Explain.

6. Michigan Motors Corporation (MMC) just introduced a new luxury touring sedan. As part of its promotional campaign, the marketing department decided to send personalized invitations to test-drive the new sedan to two target groups: (1) current owners of an MMC luxury automobile and (2) owners of luxury cars manufactured by one of MMC's competitors. The cost of sending a personalized invitation to each customer is estimated to be $1 per letter. Based on previous experience with this type of advertising, MMC estimates that 25% of the customers contacted from group 1 and 10% of the customers contacted from group 2 will test-drive the new sedan. As part of this campaign, MMC set the following goals:

Goal 1: Get at least 10,000 customers from group 1 to test-drive the new sedan.

Goal 2: Get at least 5000 customers from group 2 to test-drive the new sedan.

Goal 3: Limit the expense of sending out the invitations to $70,000.

Assume that goals 1 and 2 are P_1 priority level goals and that goal 3 is a P_2 priority level goal.

a. Suppose that goals 1 and 2 are equally important; formulate a goal programming model of the MMC problem.

b. Use the goal programming computer procedure illustrated in Section 14.2 to solve the model formulated in part (a).

c. If management believes that contacting customers from group 2 is twice as important as contacting customers from group 1, what should MMC do?

7. A committee in charge of promoting a Ladies Professional Golf Association tournament is trying to determine how best to advertise the event during the two weeks prior to the tournament. The committee obtained the following information about the three advertising media they are considering using:

Category	Audience Reached per Advertisement	Cost per Advertisement	Maximum Number of Advertisements
TV	200,000	$2,500	10
Radio	50,000	$ 400	15
Internet	100,000	$ 500	20

The last column in this table shows the maximum number of advertisements that can be run during the next two weeks; these values should be treated as constraints. The committee established the following goals for the campaign:

Priority Level 1 Goal

Goal 1: Reach at least 4 million people.

Priority Level 2 Goal

Goal 2: The number of television advertisements should be at least 30% of the total number of advertisements.

Priority Level 3 Goal

Goal 3: The number of radio advertisements should not exceed 20% of the total number of advertisements.

Priority Level 4 Goal

Goal 4: Limit the total amount spent for advertising to $20,000.

a. Formulate a goal programming model for this problem.

b. Use the goal programming computer procedure illustrated in Section 14.2 to solve the model formulated in part (a).

8. Morley Company is attempting to determine the best location for a new machine in an existing layout of three machines. The existing machines are located at the following x_1, x_2 coordinates on the shop floor:

$$\text{Machine 1:}\quad x_1 = 1, x_2 = 7$$
$$\text{Machine 2:}\quad x_1 = 5, x_2 = 9$$
$$\text{Machine 3:}\quad x_1 = 6, x_2 = 2$$

a. Develop a goal programming model that can be solved to minimize the total distance of the new machine from the three existing machines. The distance is to be measured rectangularly. For example, if the location of the new machine is ($x_1 = 3$, $x_2 = 5$), it is considered to be a distance of $|3 - 1| + |5 - 7| = 2 + 2 = 4$ from machine 1. *Hint:* In the goal programming formulation, let

$x_1 =$ first coordinate of the new machine location

$x_2 =$ second coordinate of the new machine location

$d_i^+ =$ amount by which the x_1 coordinate of the new machine exceeds the x_1 coordinate of machine i ($i = 1, 2, 3$)

$d_i^- =$ amount by which the x_1 coordinate of machine i exceeds the x_1 coordinate of the new machine ($i = 1, 2, 3$)

$e_i^+ =$ amount by which the x_2 coordinate of the new machine exceeds the x_2 coordinate of machine i ($i = 1, 2, 3$)

$e_i^- =$ amount by which the x_2 coordinate of machine i exceeds the x_2 coordinate of the new machine ($i = 1, 2, 3$)

b. What is the optimal location for the new machine?

SELF*test*

9. One advantage of using the multicriteria decision-making methods presented in this chapter is that the criteria weights and the decision alternative ratings may be modified to reflect the unique interests and preferences of each individual decision maker. For example, assume that another graduating college student had the same three job offers described in Section 14.3. This student provided the following scoring model information. Rank the overall preference for the three positions. Which position is recommended?

		Ratings		
Criteria	Weight	Analyst Chicago	Accountant Denver	Auditor Houston
Career advancement	5	7	4	4
Location	2	5	6	4
Management style	5	6	5	7
Salary	4	7	8	4
Prestige	4	8	5	6
Job security	2	4	5	8
Enjoyment of the work	4	7	5	5

10. The Kenyon Manufacturing Company is interested in selecting the best location for a new plant. After a detailed study of 10 sites, the three location finalists are Georgetown, Kentucky; Marysville, Ohio; and Clarksville, Tennessee. The Kenyon management team

provided the following data on location criteria, criteria importance, and location ratings. Use a scoring model to determine the best location for the new plant.

		Ratings		
Criteria	Weight	Georgetown, Kentucky	Marysville, Ohio	Clarksville, Tennessee
Land cost	4	7	4	5
Labor cost	3	6	5	8
Labor availability	5	7	8	6
Construction cost	4	6	7	5
Transportation	3	5	7	4
Access to customers	5	6	8	5
Long-range goals	4	7	6	5

11. The Davis family of Atlanta, Georgia, is planning its annual summer vacation. Three vacation locations along with criteria weights and location ratings follow. What is the recommended vacation location?

		Ratings		
Criteria	Weight	Myrtle Beach, South Carolina	Smoky Mountains	Branson, Missouri
Travel distance	2	5	7	3
Vacation cost	5	5	6	4
Entertainment available	3	7	4	8
Outdoor activities	2	9	6	5
Unique experience	4	6	7	8
Family fun	5	8	7	7

12. A high school senior is considering attending one of the following four colleges or universities. Eight criteria, criteria weights, and school ratings are also shown. What is the recommended choice?

		Ratings			
Criteria	Weight	Midwestern University	State College at Newport	Handover College	Tecumseh State
School prestige	3	8	6	7	5
Number of students	4	3	5	8	7
Average class size	5	4	5	8	7
Cost	5	5	8	3	6
Distance from home	2	7	8	7	6
Sports program	4	9	5	4	6
Housing desirability	4	6	5	7	6
Beauty of campus	3	5	3	8	5

13. A real estate investor is interested in purchasing condominium property in Naples, Florida. The three most preferred condominiums are listed along with criteria weights and rating information. Which condominium is preferred?

			Ratings	
Criteria	Weight	Park Shore	The Terrace	Gulf View
Cost	5	5	6	5
Location	4	7	4	9
Appearance	5	7	4	7
Parking	2	5	8	5
Floor plan	4	8	7	5
Swimming pool	1	7	2	3
View	3	5	4	9
Kitchen	4	8	7	6
Closet space	3	6	8	4

14. Clark and Julie Anderson are interested in purchasing a new boat and have limited their choice to one of three boats manufactured by Sea Ray, Inc.: the 220 Bowrider, the 230 Overnighter, and the 240 Sundancer. The Bowrider weighs 3100 pounds, has no overnight capability, and has a price of $28,500. The 230 Overnighter weighs 4300 pounds, has a reasonable overnight capability, and has a price of $37,500. The 240 Sundancer weighs 4500 pounds, has an excellent overnight capability (kitchen, bath, and bed), and has a price of $48,200. The Andersons provided the scoring model information separately, as shown here:

Clark Anderson

		Ratings		
Criteria	Weight	220 Bowrider	230 Overnighter	240 Sundancer
Cost	5	8	5	3
Overnight capability	3	2	6	9
Kitchen/bath facilities	2	1	4	7
Appearance	5	7	7	6
Engine/speed	5	6	8	4
Towing/handling	4	8	5	2
Maintenance	4	7	5	3
Resale value	3	7	5	6

Julie Anderson

		Ratings		
Criteria	Weight	220 Bowrider	230 Overnighter	240 Sundancer
Cost	3	7	6	5
Overnight capability	5	1	6	8
Kitchen/bath facilities	5	1	3	7
Appearance	4	5	7	7
Engine/speed	2	4	5	3
Towing/handling	2	8	6	2
Maintenance	1	6	5	4
Resale value	2	5	6	6

a. Which boat does Clark Anderson prefer?

b. Which boat does Julie Anderson prefer?

15. Use the pairwise comparison matrix for the price criterion shown in Table 14.8 to verify that the priorities after synthesization are 0.123, 0.320, and 0.557. Compute the consistency ratio and comment on its acceptability.

16. Use the pairwise comparison matrix for the style criterion, as shown in Table 14.8, to verify that the priorities after synthesization are 0.265, 0.656, and 0.080. Compute the consistency ratio and comment on its acceptability.

17. Dan Joseph was considering entering one of two graduate schools of business to pursue studies for an MBA degree. When asked how he compared the two schools with respect to reputation, he responded that he preferred school A strongly to very strongly to school B.

a. Set up the pairwise comparison matrix for this problem.

b. Determine the priorities for the two schools relative to this criterion.

18. An organization was investigating relocating its corporate headquarters to one of three possible cities. The following pairwise comparison matrix shows the president's judgments regarding the desirability for the three cities:

	City 1	City 2	City 3
City 1	1	5	7
City 2	⅕	1	3
City 3	⅐	⅓	1

a. Determine the priorities for the three cities.

b. Is the president consistent in terms of the judgments provided? Explain.

19. The following pairwise comparison matrix contains the judgments of an individual regarding the fairness of two proposed tax programs, A and B:

	A	B
A	1	3
B	⅓	1

a. Determine the priorities for the two programs.

b. Are the individual's judgments consistent? Explain.

20. Asked to compare three soft drinks with respect to flavor, an individual stated that

A is moderately more preferable than B.

A is equally to moderately more preferable than C.

B is strongly more preferable than C.

a. Set up the pairwise comparison matrix for this problem.

b. Determine the priorities for the soft drinks with respect to the flavor criterion.

c. Compute the consistency ratio. Are the individual's judgments consistent? Explain.

21. Refer to Problem 20. Suppose that the individual had stated the following judgments instead of those given in Problem 20:

A is strongly more preferable than C.

B is equally to moderately more preferable than A.

B is strongly more preferable than C.

Answer parts (a), (b), and (c) as stated in Problem 20.

 SELF*test*

22. The national sales director for Jones Office Supplies needs to determine the best location for the next national sales meeting. Three locations have been proposed: Dallas, San Francisco, and New York. One criterion considered important in the decision is the desirability of the location in terms of restaurants, entertainment, and so on. The national sales manager made the following judgments with regard to this criterion:

> New York is very strongly more preferred than Dallas.
>
> New York is moderately more preferred than San Francisco.
>
> San Francisco is moderately to strongly more preferred than Dallas.

  a. Set up the pairwise comparison matrix for this problem.
  b. Determine the priorities for the desirability criterion.
  c. Compute the consistency ratio. Are the sales manager's judgments consistent? Explain.

23. A study comparing four personal computers resulted in the following pairwise comparison matrix for the performance criterion:

	1	2	3	4
1	1	3	7	1/3
2	1/3	1	4	1/4
3	1/7	1/4	1	1/6
4	3	4	6	1

  a. Determine the priorities for the four computers relative to the performance criterion.
  b. Compute the consistency ratio. Are the judgments regarding performance consistent? Explain.

 SELF*test*

24. An individual was interested in determining which of two stocks to invest in, Central Computing Company (CCC) or Software Research, Inc. (SRI). The criteria thought to be most relevant in making the decision are the potential yield of the stock and the risk associated with the investment. The pairwise comparison matrixes for this problem are

Criterion	Yield	Risk
Yield	1	2
Risk	1/2	1

Yield	CCC	SRI
CCC	1	3
SRI	1/3	1

Risk	CCC	SRI
CCC	1	1/2
SRI	2	1

  a. Compute the priorities for each pairwise comparison matrix.
  b. Determine the overall priority for the two investments, CCC and SRI. Which investment is preferred based on yield and risk?

25. The vice president of Harling Equipment needs to select a new director of marketing. The two possible candidates are Bill Jacobs and Sue Martin, and the criteria thought to be most relevant in the selection are leadership ability (L), personal skills (P), and administrative skills (A). The following pairwise comparison matrixes were obtained:

Criterion	L	P	A
L	1	1/3	1/4
P	3	1	2
A	4	1/2	1

Leadership	Jacobs	Martin
Jacobs	1	4
Martin	1/4	1

Personal	Jacobs	Martin
Jacobs	1	⅓
Martin	3	1

Administrative	Jacobs	Martin
Jacobs	1	2
Martin	½	1

    a. Compute the priorities for each pairwise comparison matrix.

    b. Determine an overall priority for each candidate. Which candidate is preferred?

26. A woman considering the purchase of a custom sound stereo system for her car looked at three different systems (A, B, and C), which varied in terms of price, sound quality, and FM reception. The following pairwise comparison matrixes were developed:

Criterion	Price	Sound	Reception
Price	1	3	4
Sound	⅓	1	3
Reception	¼	⅓	1

Price	A	B	C
A	1	4	2
B	¼	1	⅓
C	½	3	1

Sound	A	B	C
A	1	½	¼
B	2	1	⅓
C	4	3	1

Reception	A	B	C
A	1	4	2
B	¼	1	1
C	½	1	1

    a. Compute the priorities for each pairwise comparison matrix.

    b. Determine an overall priority for each system. Which stereo system is preferred?

Case Problem 1   EZ TRAILERS, INC.

EZ Trailers, Inc., manufactures a variety of general purpose trailers, including a complete line of boat trailers. Two of their best-selling boat trailers are the EZ-190 and the EZ-250. The EZ-190 is designed for boats up to 19 feet in length, and the EZ-250 can be used for boats up to 25 feet in length.

    EZ Trailers would like to schedule production for the next two months for these two models. Each unit of the EZ-190 requires four hours of production time, and each unit of the EZ-250 uses six hours of production time. The following orders have been received for March and April:

Model	March	April
EZ-190	800	600
EZ-250	1100	1200

The ending inventory from February was 200 units of the EZ-190 and 300 units of the EZ-250. The total number of hours of production time used in February was 6300 hours.

    The management of EZ Trailers is concerned about being able to satisfy existing orders for the EZ-250 for both March and April. In fact, it believes that this goal is the most important one that a production schedule should meet. Next in importance is satisfying existing orders for the EZ-190. In addition, management doesn't want to implement any production schedule that would involve significant labor fluctuations from month to month. In this regard, its goal is to develop a production schedule that would limit fluctuations in labor hours used to a maximum of 1000 hours from one month to the next.

Managerial Report

Perform an analysis of EZ Trailers' production scheduling problem, and prepare a report for EZ's president that summarizes your findings. Include a discussion and analysis of the following items in your report:

1. The production schedule that best achieves the goals as specified by management.
2. Suppose that EZ Trailers' storage facilities would accommodate only a maximum of 300 trailers in any one month. What effect would this have on the production schedule?
3. Suppose that EZ Trailers can store only a maximum of 300 trailers in any one month. In addition, suppose management would like to have an ending inventory in April of at least 100 units of each model. What effect would both changes have on the production schedule?
4. What changes would occur in the production schedule if the labor fluctuation goal were the highest priority goal?

Appendix 14.1   SCORING MODELS WITH EXCEL

Excel provides an efficient way to analyze a multicriteria decision problem that can be described by a scoring model. We will use the job selection application from Section 14.3 to demonstrate this procedure.

A worksheet for the job selection scoring model is shown in Figure 14.7. The criteria weights are placed into cells B6 to B12. The ratings for each criterion and decision alternative are entered into cells C6 to E12.

The calculations used to compute the score for each decision alternative are shown in the bottom portion of the worksheet. The calculation for cell C18 is provided by the cell formula

$$=\$B6*C6$$

This cell formula can be copied from cell C18 to cells C18:E24 to provide the results shown in rows 18 to 24. The score for the financial analyst position in Chicago is found by placing the following formula in cell C26:

$$=SUM(C18:C24)$$

Copying cell C26 to cells D26:E26 provides the scores for the accountant in Denver and the auditor in Houston positions.

FIGURE 14.7   WORKSHEET FOR THE JOB SELECTION SCORING MODEL

DATA *file*

Scoring

	A	B	C	D	E	F
1	**Job Selection Scoring Model**					
2						
3				**Ratings**		
4			**Analyst**	**Accountant**	**Auditor**	
5	**Criteria**	**Weight**	**Chicago**	**Denver**	**Houston**	
6	Career Advancement	5	8	6	4	
7	Location	3	3	8	7	
8	Management	4	5	6	9	
9	Salary	3	6	7	5	
10	Prestige	2	7	5	4	
11	Job Security	4	4	7	6	
12	Enjoy the Work	5	8	6	5	
13						
14						
15	**Scoring Calculations**					
16			**Analyst**	**Accountant**	**Auditor**	
17	**Criteria**		**Chicago**	**Denver**	**Houston**	
18	Career Advancement		40	30	20	
19	Location		9	24	21	
20	Management		20	24	36	
21	Salary		18	21	15	
22	Prestige		14	10	8	
23	Job Security		16	28	24	
24	Enjoy the Work		40	30	25	
25						
26	**Score**		157	167	149	

CHAPTER 15

Time Series Analysis and Forecasting

CONTENTS

The purpose of this chapter is to provide an introduction to time series analysis and forecasting. Suppose we are asked to provide quarterly forecasts of sales for one of our company's products over the coming one-year period. Production schedules, raw materials purchasing, inventory policies, and sales quotas will all be affected by the quarterly forecasts we provide. Consequently, poor forecasts may result in poor planning and increased costs for the company. How should we go about providing the quarterly sales forecasts? Good judgment, intuition, and an awareness of the state of the economy may give us a rough idea or "feeling" of what is likely to happen in the future, but converting that feeling into a number that can be used as next year's sales forecast is challenging. The Management Science in Action, Forecasting Energy Needs in the Utility Industry, describes the role that forecasting plays in the utility industry.

A forecast is simply a prediction of what will happen in the future. Managers must accept that regardless of the technique used, they will not be able to develop perfect forecasts.

Forecasting methods can be classified as qualitative or quantitative. Qualitative methods generally involve the use of expert judgment to develop forecasts. Such methods are appropriate when historical data on the variable being forecast are either unavailable or not applicable. Quantitative forecasting methods can be used when (1) past information about the variable being forecast is available, (2) the information can be quantified, and (3) it is reasonable to assume that past is prologue (i.e., the pattern of the past will continue into the future). We will focus exclusively on quantitative forecasting methods in this chapter.

If the historical data are restricted to past values of the variable to be forecast, the forecasting procedure is called a *time series method* and the historical data are referred to as a time series. The objective of time series analysis is to uncover a pattern in the historical data or time series and then extrapolate the pattern into the future; the forecast is based solely on past values of the variable and/or on past forecast errors.

In Section 15.1 we discuss the various kinds of time series that a forecaster might be faced with in practice. These include a constant or horizontal pattern, a trend, a seasonal pattern, both a trend and a seasonal pattern, and a cyclical pattern. In order to build a quantitative

MANAGEMENT SCIENCE IN ACTION

FORECASTING ENERGY NEEDS IN THE UTILITY INDUSTRY*

Duke Energy is a diversified energy company with a portfolio of natural gas and electric businesses and an affiliated real estate company. In 2006, Duke Energy merged with Cinergy of Cincinnati, Ohio, to create one of North America's largest energy companies, with assets totaling more than $70 billion. As a result of this merger the Cincinnati Gas & Electric Company became part of Duke Energy. Today, Duke Energy services over 5.5 million retail electric and gas customers in North Carolina, South Carolina, Ohio, Kentucky, Indiana, and Ontario, Canada.

Forecasting in the utility industry offers some unique perspectives. Because energy is difficult to store, this product must be generated to meet the instantaneous requirements of the customers. Electrical shortages are not just lost sales, but "brownouts" or "blackouts." This situation places an unusual burden on the utility forecaster. On the positive side, the demand for energy and the sale of energy are more predictable than for many other products. Also, unlike the situation in a multiproduct firm, a great amount of forecasting effort and expertise can be concentrated on the two products: gas and electricity.

The largest observed electric demand for any given period, such as an hour, a day, a month, or a year, is defined as the peak load. The forecast of the annual electric peak load guides the timing decision for constructing future generating units, and the financial impact of this decision is great. Obviously, a timing decision that leads to having the unit available no sooner than necessary is crucial.

The energy forecasts are important in other ways also. For example, purchases of coal as fuel for the generating units are based on the forecast levels of energy needed. The revenue from the electric operations of the company is determined from forecasted sales, which in turn enters into the planning of rate changes and external financing. These planning and decision-making processes are among the most important managerial activities in the company. It is imperative that the decision makers have the best forecast information available to assist them in arriving at these decisions.

*Based on information provided by Dr. Richard Evans of Duke Energy.

forecasting model it is also necessary to have a measurement of forecast accuracy. Different measurements of forecast accuracy, and their respective advantages and disadvantages, are discussed in Section 15.2. In Section 15.3 we consider the simplest case, which is a horizontal or constant pattern. For this pattern, we develop the classical moving average, weighted moving average, and exponential smoothing models. Many time series have a trend, and taking this trend into account is important; in Section 15.4 we provide regression models for finding the best model parameters when a linear trend is present. Finally, in Section 15.5 we show how to incorporate both a trend and seasonality into a forecasting model.

15.1 TIME SERIES PATTERNS

A **time series** is a sequence of observations on a variable measured at successive points in time or over successive periods of time. The measurements may be taken every hour, day, week, month, or year, or at any other regular interval.[1] The pattern of the data is an important factor in understanding how the time series has behaved in the past. If such behavior can be expected to continue in the future, we can use it to guide us in selecting an appropriate forecasting method.

To identify the underlying pattern in the data, a useful first step is to construct a time series plot. A **time series plot** is a graphical presentation of the relationship between time and the time series variable; time is represented on the horizontal axis and values of the time series variable are shown on the vertical axis. Let us first review some of the common types of data patterns that can be identified when examining a time series plot.

Horizontal Pattern

A horizontal pattern exists when the data fluctuate randomly around a constant mean over time. To illustrate a time series with a horizontal pattern, consider the 12 weeks of data in Table 15.1. These data show the number of gallons of gasoline (in 1000s) sold by a gasoline distributor in Bennington, Vermont, over the past 12 weeks. The average value or mean for this time series is 19.25 or 19,250 gallons per week. Figure 15.1 shows a time series plot for these data. Note how the data fluctuate around the sample mean of 19,250 gallons. Although random variability is present, we would say that these data follow a horizontal pattern.

TABLE 15.1   GASOLINE SALES TIME SERIES

DATA *file*

Gasoline

Week	Sales (1000s of gallons)
1	17
2	21
3	19
4	23
5	18
6	16
7	20
8	18
9	22
10	20
11	15
12	22

---

[1]We limit our discussion to time series for which the values of the series are recorded at equal intervals. Cases in which the observations are made at unequal intervals are beyond the scope of this text.

FIGURE 15.1   GASOLINE SALES TIME SERIES PLOT

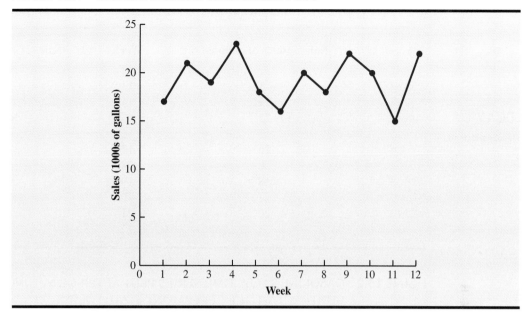

The term **stationary time series**[2] is used to denote a time series whose statistical properties are independent of time. In particular this means that

1. The process generating the data has a constant mean.
2. The variability of the time series is constant over time.

A time series plot for a stationary time series will always exhibit a horizontal pattern with random fluctuations. However, simply observing a horizontal pattern is not sufficient evidence to conclude that the time series is stationary. More advanced texts on forecasting discuss procedures for determining if a time series is stationary and provide methods for transforming a time series that is nonstationary into a stationary series.

Changes in business conditions often result in a time series with a horizontal pattern that shifts to a new level at some point in time. For instance, suppose the gasoline distributor signs a contract with the Vermont Sate Police to provide gasoline for state police cars located in southern Vermont beginning in Week 13. With this new contract, the distributor naturally expects to see a substantial increase in weekly sales starting in Week 13. Table 15.2 shows the number of gallons of gasoline sold for the original time series and the 10 weeks after signing the new contract. Figure 15.2 shows the corresponding time series plot. Note the increased level of the time series beginning in Week 13. This change in the level of the time series makes it more difficult to choose an appropriate forecasting method. Selecting a forecasting method that adapts well to changes in the level of a time series is an important consideration in many practical applications.

Trend Pattern

Although time series data generally exhibit random fluctuations, a time series may also show gradual shifts or movements to relatively higher or lower values over a longer period of time. If a time series plot exhibits this type of behavior, we say that a **trend pattern** exists. A trend is usually the result of long-term factors such as population increases or decreases, shifting demographic characteristics of the population, improving technology, and/or changes in consumer preferences.

---

[2]For a formal definition of stationarity, see K. Ord and R. Fildes (2012), *Principles of Business Forecasting*. Mason, OH: Cengage Learning, p. 155.

TABLE 15.2   GASOLINE SALES TIME SERIES AFTER OBTAINING THE CONTRACT
WITH THE VERMONT STATE POLICE

DATA *file*

GasolineRevised

Week	Sales (1000s of gallons)	Week	Sales (1000s of gallons)
1	17	12	22
2	21	13	31
3	19	14	34
4	23	15	31
5	18	16	33
6	16	17	28
7	20	18	32
8	18	19	30
9	22	20	29
10	20	21	34
11	15	22	33

FIGURE 15.2   GASOLINE SALES TIME SERIES PLOT AFTER OBTAINING THE
CONTRACT WITH THE VERMONT STATE POLICE

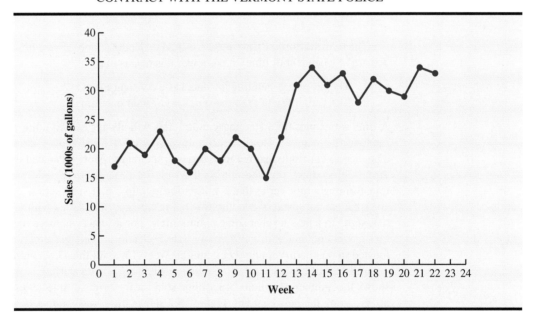

To illustrate a time series with a linear trend pattern, consider the time series of bicycle sales for a particular manufacturer over the past 10 years, as shown in Table 15.3 and Figure 15.3. Note that 21,600 bicycles were sold in Year 1, 22,900 were sold in Year 2, and so on. In Year 10, the most recent year, 31,400 bicycles were sold. Visual inspection of the time series plot shows some up and down movement over the past 10 years, but the time series seems also to have a systematically increasing or upward trend.

The trend for the bicycle sales time series appears to be linear and increasing over time, but sometimes a trend can be described better by other types of patterns. For instance, the data in Table 15.4 and the corresponding time series plot in Figure 15.4 show the sales revenue for a cholesterol drug since the company won FDA approval for the drug 10 years ago. The time series increases in a nonlinear fashion; that is, the rate of change of revenue does not increase by a constant amount from one year to the next. In fact, the revenue appears to be growing in an exponential fashion. Exponential relationships such as this are appropriate when the percentage change from one period to the next is relatively constant.

TABLE 15.3 BICYCLE SALES TIME SERIES

DATA *file*

Bicycle

Year	Sales (1000s)
1	21.6
2	22.9
3	25.5
4	21.9
5	23.9
6	27.5
7	31.5
8	29.7
9	28.6
10	31.4

FIGURE 15.3 BICYCLE SALES TIME SERIES PLOT

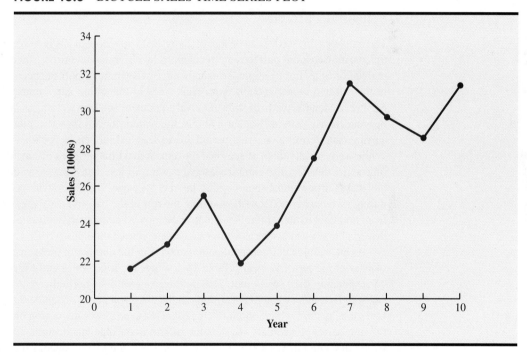

TABLE 15.4 CHOLESTEROL DRUG REVENUE TIME SERIES ($ MILLIONS)

DATA *file*

Cholesterol

Year	Revenue
1	23.1
2	21.3
3	27.4
4	34.6
5	33.8
6	43.2
7	59.5
8	64.4
9	74.2
10	99.3

FIGURE 15.4   CHOLESTEROL DRUG REVENUE TIME SERIES PLOT ($ MILLIONS)

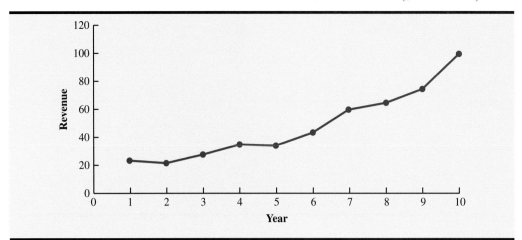

Seasonal Pattern

The trend of a time series can be identified by analyzing movements in historical data over multiple years. **Seasonal patterns** are recognized by observing recurring patterns over successive periods of time. For example, a manufacturer of swimming pools expects low sales activity in the fall and winter months, with peak sales in the spring and summer months to occur each year. Manufacturers of snow removal equipment and heavy clothing, however, expect the opposite yearly pattern. Not surprisingly, the pattern for a time series plot that exhibits a recurring pattern over a one-year period due to seasonal influences is called a seasonal pattern. While we generally think of seasonal movement in a time series as occurring within one year, time series data can also exhibit seasonal patterns of less than one year in duration. For example, daily traffic volume shows within-the-day "seasonal" behavior, with peak levels occurring during rush hours, moderate flow during the rest of the day and early evening, and light flow from midnight to early morning. Another example of an industry with sales that exhibit easily discernable seasonal patterns within a day is the restaurant industry.

As an example of a seasonal pattern, consider the number of umbrellas sold at a clothing store over the past five years. Table 15.5 shows the time series and Figure 15.5 shows the corresponding time series plot. The time series plot does not indicate a long-term trend in sales. In fact, unless you look carefully at the data, you might conclude that the data follow a horizontal pattern with random fluctuation. However, closer inspection of the fluctuations in the time series plot reveals a systematic pattern in the data that occurs within each year. That is, the first and third quarters have moderate sales, the second quarter has the highest sales, and the fourth quarter tends to have the lowest sales volume. Thus, we would conclude that a quarterly seasonal pattern is present.

Trend and Seasonal Pattern

Some time series include both a trend and a seasonal pattern. For instance, the data in Table 15.6 and the corresponding time series plot in Figure 15.6 show quarterly smartphone sales for a particular manufacturer over the past four years. Clearly an increasing trend is present. However, Figure 15.6 also indicates that sales are lowest in the second quarter of each year and highest in quarters 3 and 4. Thus, we conclude that a seasonal pattern also exists for smartphones sales. In such cases we need to use a forecasting method that is capable of dealing with both trend and seasonality.

Cyclical Pattern

A **cyclical pattern** exists if the time series plot shows an alternating sequence of points below and above the trend line that lasts for more than one year. Many economic time series exhibit

TABLE 15.5   UMBRELLA SALES TIME SERIES

Year	Quarter	Sales
1	1	125
	2	153
	3	106
	4	88
2	1	118
	2	161
	3	133
	4	102
3	1	138
	2	144
	3	113
	4	80
4	1	109
	2	137
	3	125
	4	109
5	1	130
	2	165
	3	128
	4	96

DATA *file*

Umbrella

FIGURE 15.5   UMBRELLA SALES TIME SERIES PLOT

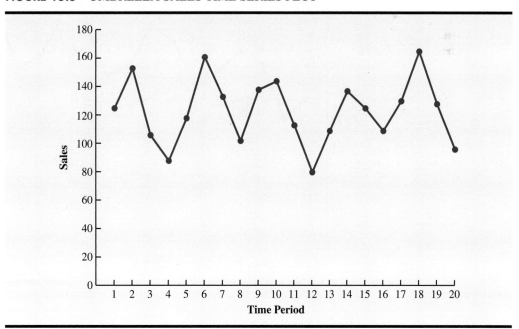

cyclical behavior with regular runs of observations below and above the trend line. Often the cyclical component of a time series is due to multiyear business cycles. For example, periods of moderate inflation followed by periods of rapid inflation can lead to a time series that alternates below and above a generally increasing trend line (e.g., a time series for housing costs). Business cycles are extremely difficult, if not impossible, to forecast. As a result, cyclical effects

TABLE 15.6   QUARTERLY SMARTPHONE SALES TIME SERIES

DATA *file*

SmartPhoneSales

Year	Quarter	Sales (1000s)
1	1	4.8
	2	4.1
	3	6.0
	4	6.5
2	1	5.8
	2	5.2
	3	6.8
	4	7.4
3	1	6.0
	2	5.6
	3	7.5
	4	7.8
4	1	6.3
	2	5.9
	3	8.0
	4	8.4

FIGURE 15.6   QUARTERLY SMARTPHONE SALES TIME SERIES PLOT

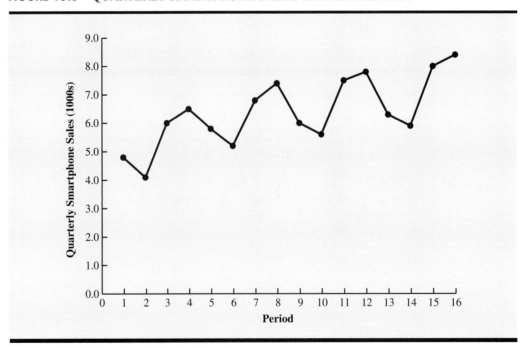

are often combined with long-term trend effects and referred to as trend-cycle effects. In this chapter we do not deal with cyclical effects that may be present in the time series.

Selecting a Forecasting Method

The underlying pattern in the time series is an important factor in selecting a forecasting method. Thus, a time series plot should be one of the first analytic tools employed when trying to determine which forecasting method to use. If we see a horizontal pattern, then we need to select a method appropriate for this type of pattern. Similarly, if we observe a trend in the data, then we need to use a forecasting method that is capable of handling a trend effectively. In the next two sections we illustrate methods for assessing forecast accuracy and consider forecasting models that can be used in situations for which the underlying pattern is horizontal; in other words, no trend or seasonal effects are present. We then consider methods appropriate when trend and/or seasonality are present in the data. The Management Science in Action, Forecasting Demand for a Broad Product Line of Office Products, describes the considerations made by ACCO Brands when forecasting demand for its consumer and office products.

MANAGEMENT SCIENCE IN ACTION

FORECASTING DEMAND FOR A BROAD PRODUCT LINE OF OFFICE PRODUCTS*

ACCO Brands Corporation is one of the world's largest suppliers of branded office and consumer products and print finishing solutions. The company's widely recognized brands include AT-A-GLANCE*, Day-Timer*, Five Star*, GBC*, Hilroy*, Kensington*, Marbig*, Mead*, NOBO, Quartet*, Rexel, Swingline*, Tilibra*, Wilson Jones*, and many others.

Because it produces and markets a wide array of products with a myriad of demand characteristics, ACCO Brands relies heavily on sales forecasts in planning its manufacturing, distribution, and marketing activities. By viewing its relationship in terms of a supply chain, ACCO Brands and its customers (which are generally retail chains) establish close collaborative relationships and consider each other to be valued partners. As a result, ACCO Brands' customers share valuable information and data that serve as inputs into ACCO Brands' forecasting process.

In her role as a forecasting manager for ACCO Brands, Vanessa Baker appreciates the importance of this additional Information. "We do separate forecasts of demand for each major customer," said Baker, "and we generally use twenty-four to thirty-six months of history to generate monthly forecasts twelve to eighteen months into the future. While trends are important, several of our major product lines, including school, planning and organizing, and decorative calendars, are heavily seasonal, and seasonal sales make up the bulk of our annual volume."

Daniel Marks, one of several account-level strategic forecast managers for ACCO Brands, adds:

The supply chain process includes the total lead time from identifying opportunities to making or procuring the product to getting the product on the shelves to align with the forecasted demand; this can potentially take several months, so the accuracy of our

forecasts is critical throughout each step of the supply chain. Adding to this challenge is the risk of obsolescence. We sell many dated items, such as planners and calendars, which have a natural, built-in obsolescence. In addition, many of our products feature designs that are fashion-conscious or contain pop culture images, and these products can also become obsolete very quickly as tastes and popularity change. An overly optimistic forecast for these products can be very costly, but an overly pessimistic forecast can result in lost sales potential and give our competitors an opportunity to take market share from us.

In addition to looking at trends, seasonal components, and cyclical patterns, Baker and Marks must contend with several other factors. Baker notes, "We have to adjust our forecasts for upcoming promotions by our customers." Marks agrees and adds:

We also have to go beyond just forecasting consumer demand; we must consider the retailer's specific needs in our order forecasts, such as what type of display will be used and how many units of a product must be on display to satisfy their presentation requirements. Current inventory is another factor—if a customer is carrying either too much or too little inventory, that will affect their future orders, and we need lo reflect that in our forecasts. Will the product have a short life because it is tied lo a cultural fad? What are the retailer's marketing and markdown strategics? Our knowledge of the environments in which our supply chain partners are competing helps us to forecast demand more accurately, and that reduces waste and makes our customers, as well as ACCO Brands, far more profitable.

*The authors are indebted to Vanessa Baker and Daniel Marks of ACCO Brands for providing input for this Management Science in Action.

15.2 FORECAST ACCURACY

In this section we begin by developing forecasts for the gasoline time series shown in Table 15.1 using the simplest of all the forecasting methods, an approach that uses the most recent week's sales volume as the forecast for the next week. For instance, the distributor sold 17,000 gallons of gasoline in Week 1; this value is used as the forecast for Week 2. Next, we use 21, the actual value of sales in Week 2, as the forecast for Week 3, and so on. The forecasts obtained for the historical data using this method are shown in Table 15.7 in the column labeled Forecast. Because of its simplicity, this method is often referred to as a naïve forecasting method.

How accurate are the forecasts obtained using this naïve forecasting method? To answer this question we will introduce several measures of forecast accuracy. These measures are used to determine how well a particular forecasting method is able to reproduce the time series data that are already available. By selecting the method that is most accurate for the data already known, we hope to increase the likelihood that we will obtain more accurate forecasts for future time periods.

The key concept associated with measuring forecast accuracy is **forecast error**. If we denote Y_t and F_t as the actual and forcasted values of the time series for period t, respectively, the forecasting error for period t is

$$e_t = Y_t - \hat{Y}_t \qquad (15.1)$$

That is, the forecast error for time period t is the difference between the actual and the forecasted values for period t.

For instance, because the distributor actually sold 21,000 gallons of gasoline in Week 2 and the forecast, using the sales volume in Week 1, was 17,000 gallons, the forecast error in Week 2 is

$$\text{Forecast Error in Week 2} = e_2 = Y_2 - \hat{Y}_2 = 21 - 17 = 4$$

The fact that the forecast error is positive indicates that in Week 2 the forecasting method underestimated the actual value of sales. Next we use 21, the actual value of sales in Week 2, as the forecast for Week 3. Since the actual value of sales in Week 3 is 19, the forecast error for Week 3 is $e_3 = 19 - 21 = -2$. In this case, the negative forecast error indicates the forecast overestimated the actual value for Week 3. Thus, the forecast error may be positive or negative, depending on whether the forecast is too low or too high. A complete summary of the forecast errors for this naïve forecasting method is shown in Table 15.7 in the column labeled Forecast Error. It is important to note that because we are using a past value of the time series to produce a forecast for period t, we do not have sufficient data to produce a naïve forecast for the first week of this time series.

A simple measure of forecast accuracy is the mean or average of the forecast errors. If we have n periods in our time series and k is the number of periods at the beginning of the time series for which we cannot produce a naïve forecast, the mean forecast error (MFE) is

$$\text{MFE} = \frac{\sum_{t=k+1}^{n} e_t}{n - k} \qquad (15.2)$$

Table 15.7 shows that the sum of the forecast errors for the gasoline sales time series is 5; thus, the mean or average error is 5/11 = 0.45. Because we do not have sufficient data to produce a naïve forecast for the first week of this time series, we must adjust our calculations in both the numerator and denominator accordingly. This is common in forecasting; we often use k past periods from the time series to produce forecasts, and so we frequently cannot produce forecasts for the first k periods. In those instances the summation in the numerator starts at the first value of t for which we have produced a forecast (so we begin the summation at $t = k + 1$), and the denominator (which is the number of periods in our time series for which we are able to produce a forecast) will also reflect these circumstances. In the gasoline example, although the time series consists of 12 values, to compute the mean error we divided the sum

TABLE 15.7 COMPUTING FORECASTS AND MEASURES OF FORECAST ACCURACY USING THE MOST RECENT VALUE AS THE FORECAST FOR THE NEXT PERIOD

Week	Time Series Value	Forecast	Forecast Error	Absolute Value of Forecast Error	Squared Forecast Error	Percentage Error	Absolute Value of Percentage Error
1	17						
2	21	17	4	4	16	19.05	19.05
3	19	21	−2	2	4	−10.53	10.53
4	23	19	4	4	16	17.39	17.39
5	18	23	−5	5	25	−27.78	27.78
6	16	18	−2	2	4	−12.50	12.50
7	20	16	4	4	16	20.00	20.00
8	18	20	−2	2	4	−11.11	11.11
9	22	18	4	4	16	18.18	18.18
10	20	22	−2	2	4	−10.00	10.00
11	15	20	−5	5	25	−33.33	33.33
12	22	15	7	7	49	31.82	31.82
		Total	5	41	179	1.19	211.69

of the forecast errors by 11 because there are only 11 forecast errors (we cannot generate forecast sales for the first week using this naïve forecasting method).

Also note that in the gasoline time series, the mean forecast error is positive, which implies that the method is generally underforecasting; in other words, the observed values tend to be greater than the forecasted values. Because positive and negative forecast errors tend to offset one another, the mean error is likely to be small; thus, the mean error is not a very useful measure of forecast accuracy.

The **mean absolute error**, denoted MAE, is a measure of forecast accuracy that avoids the problem of positive and negative forecast errors offsetting one another. As you might expect given its name, MAE is the average of the absolute values of the forecast errors:

$$\text{MAE} = \frac{\sum\limits_{t=k+1}^{n} |e_t|}{n - k} \tag{15.3}$$

This is also referred to as the mean absolute deviation or MAD. Table 15.7 shows that the sum of the absolute values of the forecast errors is 41; thus

$$\text{MAE} = \text{average of the absolute value of forecast errors} = \frac{41}{11} = 3.73$$

Another measure that avoids the problem of positive and negative errors offsetting each other is obtained by computing the average of the squared forecast errors. This measure of forecast accuracy, referred to as the **mean squared error**, is denoted as MSE:

$$\text{MSE} = \frac{\sum\limits_{t=k+1}^{n} e_t^2}{n - k} \tag{15.4}$$

From Table 15.7, the sum of the squared errors is 179; hence,

$$\text{MSE} = \text{average of the sum of squared forecast errors} = \frac{179}{11} = 16.27$$

The size of MAE and MSE depends upon the scale of the data. As a result, it is difficult to make comparisons for different time intervals (such as comparing a method of forecasting monthly gasoline sales to a method of forecasting weekly sales) or to make comparisons across different time series (such as monthly sales of gasoline and monthly sales of oil filters). To make comparisons such as these we need to work with relative or percentage error measures. The **mean absolute percentage error**, denoted as MAPE, is such a measure. To compute MAPE we must first compute the percentage error for each forecast:

$$\left(\frac{e_t}{Y_t}\right)100$$

For example, the percentage error corresponding to the forecast of 17 in Week 2 is computed by dividing the forecast error in Week 2 by the actual value in Week 2 and multiplying the result by 100. For Week 2 the percentage error is computed as follows:

$$\text{Percentage error for Week 2} = \left(\frac{e_2}{Y_2}\right)100 = \left(\frac{4}{21}\right)100 = 19.05\%$$

Thus, the forecast error for Week 2 is 19.05% of the observed value in Week 2. A complete summary of the percentage errors is shown in Table 15.7 in the column labeled Percentage Error. In the next column, we show the absolute value of the percentage error. Finally, we find the MAPE, which is calculated as

$$\text{MAPE} = \frac{\sum\limits_{t=k+1}^{n}\left|\left(\frac{e_t}{Y_t}\right)100\right|}{n-k} \qquad (15.5)$$

Table 15.7 shows that the sum of the absolute values of the percentage errors is 211.69; thus

$$\text{MAPE} = \text{average of the absolute value of percentage forecast errors}$$

$$= \frac{211.69}{11} = 19.24\%$$

In summary, using the naïve (most recent observation) forecasting method, we obtained the following measures of forecast accuracy:

$$\text{MAE} = 3.73$$
$$\text{MSE} = 16.27$$
$$\text{MAPE} = 19.24\%$$

Try Problem 1 for practice in computing measures of forecast accuracy.

These measures of forecast accuracy simply measure how well the forecasting method is able to forecast historical values of the time series. Now, suppose we want to forecast sales for a future time period, such as Week 13. In this case the forecast for Week 13 is 22, the actual value of the time series in Week 12. Is this an accurate estimate of sales for Week 13? Unfortunately there is no way to address the issue of accuracy associated with forecasts for future time periods. However, if we select a forecasting method that works well for the historical data, and we have reason to believe the historical pattern will continue into the future, we should obtain forecasts that will ultimately be shown to be accurate.

Before closing this section, let us consider another method for forecasting the gasoline sales time series in Table 15.1. Suppose we use the average of all the historical data available as the forecast for the next period. We begin by developing a forecast for Week 2. Since there is only one historical value available prior to Week 2, the forecast for Week 2 is

TABLE 15.8   COMPUTING FORECASTS AND MEASURES OF FORECAST ACCURACY
USING THE AVERAGE OF ALL THE HISTORICAL DATA AS THE
FORECAST FOR THE NEXT PERIOD

Week	Time Series Value	Forecast	Forecast Error	Absolute Value of Forecast Error	Squared Forecast Error	Percentage Error	Absolute Value of Percentage Error
1	17						
2	21	17.00	4.00	4.00	16.00	19.05	19.05
3	19	19.00	0.00	0.00	0.00	0.00	0.00
4	23	19.00	4.00	4.00	16.00	17.39	17.39
5	18	20.00	−2.00	2.00	4.00	−11.11	11.11
6	16	19.60	−3.60	3.60	12.96	−22.50	22.50
7	20	19.00	1.00	1.00	1.00	5.00	5.00
8	18	19.14	−1.14	1.14	1.31	−6.35	6.35
9	22	19.00	3.00	3.00	9.00	13.64	13.64
10	20	19.33	0.67	0.67	0.44	3.33	3.33
11	15	19.40	−4.40	4.40	19.36	−29.33	29.33
12	22	19.00	3.00	3.00	9.00	13.64	13.64
		Total	4.52	26.81	89.07	2.75	141.34

just the time series value in Week 1; thus, the forecast for Week 2 is 17,000 gallons of gasoline. To compute the forecast for Week 3, we take the average of the sales values in Weeks 1 and 2. Thus,

$$\hat{Y}_3 = \frac{17 + 21}{2} = 19$$

Similarly, the forecast for Week 4 is

$$\hat{Y}_4 = \frac{17 + 21 + 19}{3} = 19$$

The forecasts obtained using this method for the gasoline time series are shown in Table 15.8 in the column labeled Forecast. Using the results shown in Table 15.8, we obtained the following values of MAE, MSE, and MAPE:

$$MAE = \frac{26.81}{11} = 2.44$$

$$MSE = \frac{89.07}{11} = 8.10$$

$$MAPE = \frac{141.34}{11} = 12.85\%$$

We can now compare the accuracy of the two forecasting methods we have considered in this section by comparing the values of MAE, MSE, and MAPE for each method.

	Naïve Method	Average of Past Values
MAE	3.73	2.44
MSE	16.27	8.10
MAPE	19.24%	12.85%

For each of these measures, the average of past values provides more accurate forecasts than using the most recent observation as the forecast for the next period. In general, if the underlying time series is stationary, the average of all the historical data will provide the most accurate forecasts.

Evaluating different forecasts based on historical accuracy is only helpful if historical patterns continue in to the future. As we note in Section 15.1, the 12 observations of Table 15.1 comprise a stationary time series. In Section 15.1 we mentioned that changes in business conditions often result in a time series that is not stationary. We discussed a situation in which the gasoline distributor signed a contract with the Vermont State Police to provide gasoline for state police cars located in southern Vermont. Table 15.2 shows the number of gallons of gasoline sold for the original time series and the 10 weeks after signing the new contract, and Figure 15.2 shows the corresponding time series plot. Note the change in level in Week 13 for the resulting time series. When a shift to a new level such as this occurs, it takes several periods for the forecasting method that uses the average of all the historical data to adjust to the new level of the time series. However, in this case the simple naïve method adjusts very rapidly to the change in level because it uses only the most recent observation available as the forecast.

Measures of forecast accuracy are important factors in comparing different forecasting methods, but we have to be careful to not rely too heavily upon them. Good judgment and knowledge about business conditions that might affect the value of the variable to be forecast also have to be considered carefully when selecting a method. Historical forecast accuracy is not the sole consideration, especially if the pattern exhibited by the time series is likely to change in the future.

In the next section we will introduce more sophisticated methods for developing forecasts for a time series that exhibits a horizontal pattern. Using the measures of forecast accuracy developed here, we will be able to assess whether such methods provide more accurate forecasts than we obtained using the simple approaches illustrated in this section. The methods that we will introduce also have the advantage that they adapt well to situations in which the time series changes to a new level. The ability of a forecasting method to adapt quickly to changes in level is an important consideration, especially in short-term forecasting situations.

15.3   MOVING AVERAGES AND EXPONENTIAL SMOOTHING

In this section we discuss three forecasting methods that are appropriate for a time series with a horizontal pattern: moving averages, weighted moving averages, and exponential smoothing. These methods are also capable of adapting well to changes in the level of a horizontal pattern such as what we saw with the extended gasoline sales time series (Table 15.2 and Figure 15.2). However, without modification they are not appropriate when considerable trend, cyclical, or seasonal effects are present. Because the objective of each of these methods is to "smooth out" random fluctuations in the time series, they are referred to as smoothing methods. These methods are easy to use and generally provide a high level of accuracy for short-range forecasts, such as a forecast for the next time period.

Moving Averages

The moving averages method uses the average of the most recent k data values in the time series as the forecast for the next period. Mathematically, a **moving average** forecast of order k is as follows:

$$\hat{Y}_{t+1} = \frac{\sum(\text{most recent } k \text{ data values})}{k} = \frac{\sum_{i=t-k+1}^{t} Y_i}{k}$$

$$= \frac{Y_{t-k+1} + \cdots + Y_{t-1} + Y_t}{k} \tag{15.6}$$

where

$$\hat{Y}_{t+1} = \text{forecast of the time series for period } t + 1$$
$$Y_i = \text{actual value of the time series in period } i$$
$$k = \text{number of periods of time series data used to generate the forecast}$$

The term *moving* is used because every time a new observation becomes available for the time series, it replaces the oldest observation in the equation and a new average is computed. Thus, the periods over which the average is calculated change, or move, with each ensuing period.

To illustrate the moving averages method, let us return to the original 12 weeks of gasoline sales data in Table 15.1 and Figure 15.1. The time series plot in Figure 15.1 indicates that the gasoline sales time series has a horizontal pattern. Thus, the smoothing methods of this section are applicable.

To use moving averages to forecast a time series, we must first select the order k, or number of time series values to be included in the moving average. If only the most recent values of the time series are considered relevant, a small value of k is preferred. If a greater number of past values are considered relevant, then we generally opt for a larger value of k. As mentioned earlier, a time series with a horizontal pattern can shift to a new level over time. A moving average will adapt to the new level of the series and resume providing good forecasts in k periods. Thus a smaller value of k will track shifts in a time series more quickly (the naïve approach discussed earlier is actually a moving average for $k = 1$). On the other hand, larger values of k will be more effective in smoothing out random fluctuations. Thus, managerial judgment based on an understanding of the behavior of a time series is helpful in choosing an appropriate value of k.

To illustrate how moving averages can be used to forecast gasoline sales, we will use a three-week moving average ($k = 3$). We begin by computing the forecast of sales in Week 4 using the average of the time series values in Weeks 1 to 3.

$$\hat{Y}_4 = \text{average of Weeks 1 to 3} = \frac{17 + 21 + 19}{3} = 19$$

Thus, the moving average forecast of sales in Week 4 is 19 or 19,000 gallons of gasoline. Because the actual value observed in Week 4 is 23, the forecast error in Week 4 is $e_4 = 23 - 19 = 4$.

We next compute the forecast of sales in Week 5 by averaging the time series values in Weeks 2–4.

$$\hat{Y}_5 = \text{average of Weeks 2 to 4} = \frac{21 + 19 + 23}{3} = 21$$

Hence, the forecast of sales in Week 5 is 21 and the error associated with this forecast is $e_5 = 18 - 21 = -3$. A complete summary of the three-week moving average forecasts for the gasoline sales time series is provided in Table 15.9. Figure 15.7 shows the original time series plot and the three-week moving average forecasts. Note how the graph of the moving average forecasts has tended to smooth out the random fluctuations in the time series.

Can you now use moving averages to develop forecasts? Try Problem 7.

To forecast sales in Week 13, the next time period in the future, we simply compute the average of the time series values in Weeks 10, 11, and 12.

$$\hat{Y}_{13} = \text{average of Weeks 10 to 12} = \frac{20 + 15 + 22}{3} = 19$$

Thus, the forecast for Week 13 is 19 or 19,000 gallons of gasoline.

Forecast Accuracy   In Section 15.2 we discussed three measures of forecast accuracy: mean absolute error (MAE); mean squared error (MSE); and mean absolute percentage error

TABLE 15.9   SUMMARY OF THREE-WEEK MOVING AVERAGE CALCULATIONS

Week	Time Series Value	Forecast	Forecast Error	Absolute Value of Forecast Error	Squared Forecast Error	Percentage Error	Absolute Value of Percentage Error
1	17						
2	21						
3	19						
4	23	19	4	4	16	17.39	17.39
5	18	21	−3	3	9	−16.67	16.67
6	16	20	−4	4	16	−25.00	25.00
7	20	19	1	1	1	5.00	5.00
8	18	18	0	0	0	0.00	0.00
9	22	18	4	4	16	18.18	18.18
10	20	20	0	0	0	0.00	0.00
11	15	20	−5	5	25	−33.33	33.33
12	22	19	3	3	9	13.64	13.64
		Total	0	24	92	−20.79	129.21

FIGURE 15.7   GASOLINE SALES TIME SERIES PLOT AND THREE-WEEK MOVING AERAGE FORECASTS

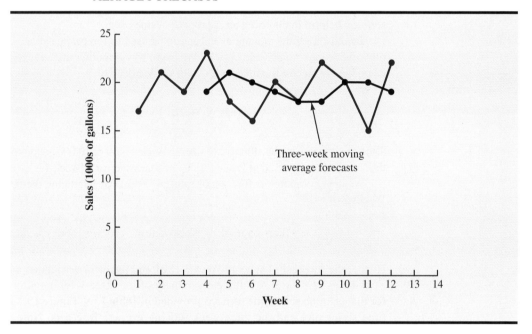

(MAPE). Using the three-week moving average calculations in Table 15.9, the values for these three measures of forecast accuracy are

$$\text{MAE} = \frac{\sum_{t=4}^{12} |e_t|}{12 - 3} = \frac{24}{9} = 2.67$$

$$\text{MSE} = \frac{\sum_{t=4}^{12} e_t^2}{12 - 3} = \frac{92}{9} = 10.22$$

$$\text{MAPE} = \frac{\sum_{t=4}^{12} \left| \left(\frac{e_t}{Y_t}\right) 100 \right|}{12 - 3} = \frac{129.21}{9} = 14.36\%$$

In situations where you need to compare forecasting methods for different time periods, such as comparing a forecast of weekly sales to a forecast of monthly sales, relative measures such as MAPE are preferred.

In Section 15.2 we showed that using the most recent observation as the forecast for the next week (a moving average of order $k = 1$) resulted in values of MAE = 3.73, MSE = 16.27, and MAPE = 19.24%. Thus, in each case the three-week moving average approach has provided more accurate forecasts than simply using the most recent observation as the forecast. Also note how the formulas for the MAE, MSE, and MAPE reflect that our use of a three-week moving average leaves us with insufficient data to generate forecasts for the first three weeks of our time series.

To determine if a moving average with a different order k can provide more accurate forecasts, we recommend using trial and error to determine the value of k that minimizes the MSE. For the gasoline sales time series, it can be shown that the minimum value of MSE corresponds to a moving average of order $k = 6$ with MSE = 6.79. If we are willing to assume that the order of the moving average that is best for the historical data will also be best for future values of the time series, the most accurate moving average forecasts of gasoline sales can be obtained using a moving average of order $k = 6$.

Weighted Moving Averages

A moving average forecast of order k is just a special case of the weighted moving averages method in which each weight is equal to 1/k; for example, a moving average forecast of order k = 3 is just a special case of the weighted moving averages method in which each weight is equal to $\frac{1}{3}$.

In the moving averages method, each observation in the moving average calculation receives equal weight. One variation, known as **weighted moving averages**, involves selecting a different weight for each data value in the moving average and then computing a weighted average of the most recent k values as the forecast.

$$\hat{Y}_{t+1} = w_t Y_t + w_{t-1} Y_{t-1} + \cdots + w_{t-k+1} Y_{t-k+1} \qquad (15.7)$$

where

$\hat{Y}_{t+1} =$ forecast of the time series for period $t + 1$

$Y_t =$ actual value of the time series in period t

$w_t =$ weight applied to the actual time series value for period t

$k =$ number of periods of time series data used to generate the forecast

Generally the most recent observation receives the largest weight, and the weight decreases with the relative age of the data values. Let us use the gasoline sales time series in Table 15.1 to illustrate the computation of a weighted three-week moving average. We will assign a weight of $w_t = \frac{3}{6}$ to the most recent observation, a weight of $w_{t-1} = \frac{2}{6}$ to the second most recent observation, and a weight of $w_{t-2} = \frac{1}{6}$ to the third most recent observation. Using this weighted average, our forecast for Week 4 is computed as follows:

$$\text{Forecast for Week 4} = \frac{1}{6}(17) + \frac{2}{6}(21) = \frac{3}{6}(19) = 19.33$$

Use Problem 8 to practice using weighted moving averages to produce forecasts.

Note that the sum of the weights is equal to 1 for the weighted moving average method.

Forecast Accuracy To use the weighted moving averages method, we must first select the number of data values to be included in the weighted moving average and then choose weights for each of these data values. In general, if we believe that the recent past is a better predictor of the future than the distant past, larger weights should be given to the more recent observations. However, when the time series is highly variable, selecting approximately equal weights for the data values may be preferable. The only requirements in selecting the weights are that they be nonnegative and that their sum must equal 1. To determine whether one particular combination of number of data values and weights provides a more accurate forecast than another combination, we recommend using MSE as the measure of forecast accuracy. That is, if we assume that the combination that is best for the past will also be best for the future, we would use the combination of number of data values and weights that minimized MSE for the historical time series to forecast the next value in the time series.

Exponential Smoothing

Exponential smoothing also uses a weighted average of past time series values as a forecast; it is a special case of the weighted moving averages method in which we select only one weight—the weight for the most recent observation. The weights for the other data values are computed automatically and become smaller as the observations move farther into the past. The exponential smoothing model follows.

$$\hat{Y}_{t+1} = \alpha Y_t + (1 - \alpha)\hat{Y}_t \qquad (15.8)$$

where

$$\hat{Y}_{t+1} = \text{forecast of the time series for period } t + 1$$
$$Y_t = \text{actual value of the time series in period } t$$
$$\hat{Y}_t = \text{forecast of the time series for period } t$$
$$\alpha = \text{smoothing constant } (0 \leq \alpha \leq 1)$$

There are several exponential smoothing procedures. Because it has a single smoothing constant α, the method presented here is often referred to as single exponential smoothing.

Equation (15.8) shows that the forecast for period $t + 1$ is a weighted average of the actual value in period t and the forecast for period t. The weight given to the actual value in period t is the **smoothing constant** α and the weight given to the forecast in period t is $1 - \alpha$. It turns out that the exponential smoothing forecast for any period is actually a weighted average of *all the previous actual values* of the time series. Let us illustrate by working with a time series involving only three periods of data: Y_1, Y_2, and Y_3.

To initiate the calculations, we let $\hat{Y}_1$ equal the actual value of the time series in period 1; that is, $\hat{Y}_1 = Y_1$. Hence, the forecast for period 2 is

$$\hat{Y}_2 = \alpha Y_1 + (1 - \alpha)\hat{Y}_1$$
$$= \alpha Y_1 + (1 - \alpha)Y_1$$
$$= Y_1$$

We see that the exponential smoothing forecast for period 2 is equal to the actual value of the time series in period 1.

The forecast for period 3 is

$$\hat{Y}_3 = \alpha Y_2 + (1 - \alpha)\hat{Y}_2 = \alpha Y_2 + (1 - \alpha)Y_1$$

Finally, substituting this expression for $\hat{Y}_3$ into the expression for $\hat{Y}_4$, we obtain

$$\hat{Y}_4 = \alpha Y_3 + (1 - \alpha)\hat{Y}_3$$
$$= \alpha Y_3 + (1 - \alpha)[\alpha Y_2 + (1 - \alpha)Y_1]$$
$$= \alpha Y_3 + \alpha(1 - \alpha)Y_2 + (1 - \alpha)^2 Y_1$$

The term exponential smoothing comes from the exponential nature of the weighting scheme for the historical values.

We now see that $\hat{Y}_4$ is a weighted average of the first three time series values. The sum of the coefficients, or weights, for Y_1, Y_2, and Y_3 equals 1. A similar argument can be made to show that, in general, any forecast $\hat{Y}_{t+1}$ is a weighted average of all the t previous time series values.

Despite the fact that exponential smoothing provides a forecast that is a weighted average of all past observations, all past data do not need to be retained to compute the forecast for the next period. In fact, equation (15.8) shows that once the value for the smoothing constant α is selected, only two pieces of information are needed to compute the forecast for period $t + 1$: Y_t, the actual value of the time series in period t; and $\hat{Y}_t$, the forecast for period t.

To illustrate the exponential smoothing approach to forecasting, let us again consider the gasoline sales time series in Table 15.1 and Figure 15.1. As indicated previously, to initialize the calculations we set the exponential smoothing forecast for period 2 equal to the actual value of the time series in period 1. Thus, with $Y_1 = 17$, we set $\hat{Y}_2 = 17$ to initiate the computations. Referring to the time series data in Table 15.1, we find an actual time series value in period 2 of $Y_2 = 21$. Thus, in period 2 we have a forecast error of $e_2 = 21 - 17 = 4$.

Continuing with the exponential smoothing computations using a smoothing constant of $\alpha = 0.2$, we obtain the following forecast for period 3:

$$\hat{Y}_3 = 0.2Y_2 + 0.8\hat{Y}_2 = 0.2(21) + 0.8(17) = 17.8$$

Once the actual time series value in period 3, $Y_3 = 19$, is known, we can generate a forecast for period 4 as follows:

$$\hat{Y}_4 = 0.2Y_3 + 0.8\hat{Y}_3 = 0.2(19) + 0.8(17.8) = 18.04$$

Continuing the exponential smoothing calculations, we obtain the weekly forecast values shown in Table 15.10. Note that we have not shown an exponential smoothing forecast or a forecast error for Week 1 because no forecast was made (we used actual sales for Week 1 as the forecasted sales for Week 2 to initialize the exponential smoothing process). For Week 12, we have $Y_{12} = 22$ and $\hat{Y}_{12} = 18.48$. We can we use this information to generate a forecast for Week 13.

$$\hat{Y}_{13} = 0.2Y_{12} + 0.8\hat{Y}_{12} = 0.2(22) + 0.8(18.48) = 19.18$$

Try Problem 9 for practice using exponential smoothing to produce forecasts.

Thus, the exponential smoothing forecast of the amount sold in Week 13 is 19.18, or 19,180 gallons of gasoline. With this forecast, the firm can make plans and decisions accordingly.

Figure 15.8 shows the time series plot of the actual and forecast time series values. Note in particular how the forecasts "smooth out" the irregular or random fluctuations in the time series.

TABLE 15.10 SUMMARY OF THE EXPONENTIAL SMOOTHING FORECASTS AND FORECAST ERRORS FOR THE GASOLINE SALES TIME SERIES WITH SMOOTHING CONSTANT $\alpha = 0.2$

Week	Time Series Value	Forecast	Forecast Error	Squared Forecast Error
1	17			
2	21	17.00	4.00	16.00
3	19	17.80	1.20	1.44
4	23	18.04	4.96	24.60
5	18	19.03	−1.03	1.06
6	16	18.83	−2.83	8.01
7	20	18.26	1.74	3.03
8	18	18.61	−0.61	0.37
9	22	18.49	3.51	12.32
10	20	19.19	0.81	0.66
11	15	19.35	−4.35	18.92
12	22	18.48	3.52	12.39
		Total	10.92	98.80

FIGURE 15.8   ACTUAL AND FORECAST GASOLINE TIME SERIES WITH SMOOTHING
CONSTANT $\alpha = 0.2$

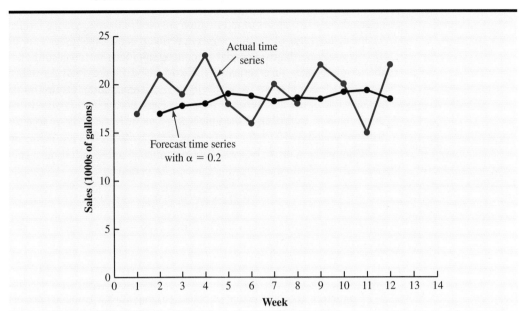

Forecast Accuracy   In the preceding exponential smoothing calculations, we used a smoothing constant of $\alpha = 0.2$. Although any value of α between 0 and 1 is acceptable, some values will yield more accurate forecasts than others. Insight into choosing a good value for α can be obtained by rewriting the basic exponential smoothing model as follows:

$$
\hat{Y}_{t+1} = \alpha Y_t + (1 - \alpha)\hat{Y}_t
$$
$$
\hat{Y}_{t+1} = \alpha Y_t + \hat{Y}_t - \alpha \hat{Y}_t \qquad (15.9)
$$
$$
\hat{Y}_{t+1} = \hat{Y}_t + \alpha(Y_t - \hat{Y}_t) = \hat{Y}_t + \alpha e_t
$$

Thus, the new forecast $\hat{Y}_{t+1}$ is equal to the previous forecast $\hat{Y}_t$ plus an adjustment, which is the smoothing constant α times the most recent forecast error, $e_t = Y_t - \hat{Y}_t$. That is, the forecast in period $t + 1$ is obtained by adjusting the forecast in period t by a fraction of the forecast error from period t. If the time series contains substantial random variability, a small value of the smoothing constant is preferred. The reason for this choice is that if much of the forecast error is due to random variability, we do not want to overreact and adjust the forecasts too quickly. For a time series with relatively little random variability, a forecast error is more likely to represent a real change in the level of the series. Thus, larger values of the smoothing constant provide the advantage of quickly adjusting the forecasts to changes in the time series; this allows the forecasts to react more quickly to changing conditions.

The criterion we will use to determine a desirable value for the smoothing constant α is the same as the criterion we proposed for determining the order or number of periods of data to include in the moving averages calculation. That is, we choose the value of α that minimizes the MSE. A summary of the MSE calculations for the exponential smoothing forecast of gasoline sales with $\alpha = 0.2$ is shown in Table 15.10. Note that there is one less squared error term than the number of time periods; this is because we had no past values with which to make a forecast for period 1. The value of the sum of squared forecast errors is 98.80; hence MSE = 98.80/11 = 8.98. Would a different value of α provide better results in terms of a lower MSE value? Trial and error is often used to determine if a different smoothing constant α can provide more accurate forecasts, but we can avoid trial and error and determine the value of α that minimizes MSE through the use of nonlinear optimization as discussed in Chapter 8 (see Problem 8.12).

NOTES AND COMMENTS

1. Spreadsheet packages are effective tools for implementing exponential smoothing. With the time series data and the forecasting formulas in a spreadsheet as shown in Table 15.10, you can use the MAE, MSE, and MAPE to evaluate different values of the smoothing constant α.

2. We presented the moving average, weighted moving average, and exponential smoothing methods in the context of a stationary time series. These methods can also be used to forecast a nonstationary time series that shifts in

level but exhibits no trend or seasonality. Moving averages with small values of k adapt more quickly than moving averages with larger values of k. Weighted moving averages that place relatively large weights on the most recent values adapt more quickly than weighted moving averages that place relatively equal weights on the k time series values used in calculating the forecast. Exponential smoothing models with smoothing constants closer to 1 adapt more quickly than models with smaller values of the smoothing constant.

15.4 LINEAR TREND PROJECTION

In this section we present forecasting methods that are appropriate for time series exhibiting trend patterns. Here we show how **regression analysis** may be used to forecast a time series with a linear trend. In Section 15.1 we used the bicycle sales time series in Table 15.3 and Figure 15.3 to illustrate a time series with a trend pattern. Let us now use this time series to illustrate how regression analysis can be used to forecast a time series with a linear trend. The data for the bicycle time series are repeated in Table 15.11 and Figure 15.9.

Although the time series plot in Figure 15.9 shows some up and down movement over the past 10 years, we might agree that the linear trend line shown in Figure 15.10 provides a reasonable approximation of the long-run movement in the series. We can use regression analysis to develop such a linear trend line for the bicycle sales time series.

In regression analysis we use known values of variables to estimate the relationship between one variable (called the **dependent variable**) and one or more other related variables (called **independent variables**). This relationship is usually found in a manner that minimizes the sum of squared errors (and so also minimizes the MSE). With this relationship we can then use values of the independent variables to estimate the associated value of the dependent variable. When we estimate a linear relationship between the dependent variable (which is usually denoted as y) and a single independent variable (which is usually denoted as x), this is referred to as **simple linear regression**. Estimating the relationship between the dependent variable and a single independent

TABLE 15.11   BICYCLE SALES TIME SERIES

DATA *file*

Bicycle

Year	Sales (1000s)
1	21.6
2	22.9
3	25.5
4	21.9
5	23.9
6	27.5
7	31.5
8	29.7
9	28.6
10	31.4

FIGURE 15.9   BICYCLE SALES TIME SERIES PLOT

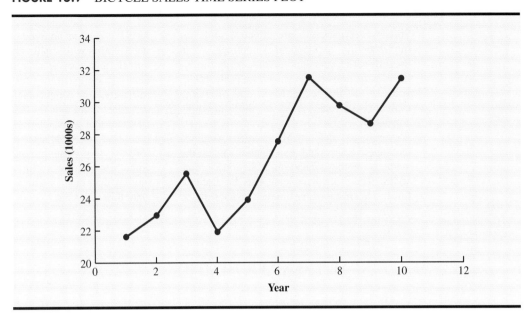

FIGURE 15.10   TREND REPRESENTED BY A LINEAR FUNCTION FOR THE BICYCLE
SALES TIME SERIES

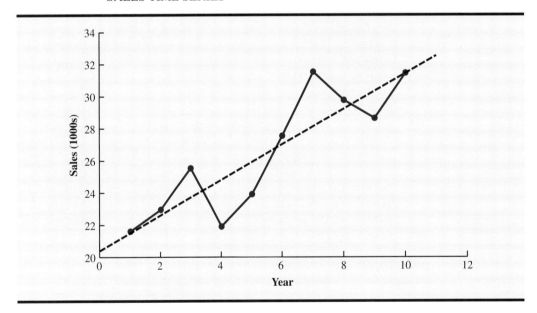

variable requires that we find the values of parameters b_0 and b_1 for the straight line $y = b_0 + b_1x$.

Because our use of simple linear regression analysis yields the linear relationship between the independent variable and the dependent variable that minimizes the MSE, we can use this approach to find a best-fitting line to a set of data that exhibits a linear trend. In finding a linear trend, the variable to be forecasted (Y_t, the actual value of the time series in period t) is the dependent variable and the trend variable (time period t) is the independent variable. We will use the following notation for our linear trendline:

$$\hat{Y}_t = b_0 + b_1 t \tag{15.10}$$

where

t = the time period
$\hat{Y}_t$ = linear trend forecast in period t (i.e., the estimated value of Y_t in period t)
b_0 = the Y-intercept of the linear trendline
b_1 = the slope of the linear trendline

In equation (15.10) the time variable begins at $t = 1$ corresponding to the first time series observation (Year 1 for the bicycle sales time series) and continues until $t = n$ corresponding to the most recent time series observation (Year 10 for the bicycle sales time series). Thus, for the bicycle sales time series $t = 1$ corresponds to the oldest time series value and $t = 10$ corresponds to the most recent year. Calculus may be used to show that the equations given below for b_0 and b_1 yield the line that minimizes the MSE. The equations for computing the values of b_0 and b_1 are

$$b_1 = \frac{\sum_{t=1}^{n} t Y_t - \sum_{t=1}^{n} t \sum_{t=1}^{n} Y_t \Big/ n}{\sum_{t=1}^{n} t^2 - \left(\sum_{t=1}^{n} t\right)^2 \Big/ n} \tag{15.11}$$

$$b_0 = \overline{Y} - b_1 \bar{t} \tag{15.12}$$

where

t = the time period
Y_t = actual value of the time series in period t
n = number of periods in the time series

$\overline{Y}$ = average value of the time series; that is, $\overline{Y} = \sum_{t=1}^{n} Y_t \Big/ n$

$\bar{t}$ = mean value of t; that is, $\bar{t} = \sum_{t=1}^{n} t \Big/ n$

Let us calculate b_0 and b_1 for the bicycle data in Table 15.11; the intermediate summary calculations necessary for computing the values of b_0 and b_1 are

t	Y_t	tY_t	t^2
1	21.6	21.6	1
2	22.9	45.8	4
3	25.5	76.5	9
4	21.9	87.6	16
5	23.9	119.5	25
6	27.5	165.0	36
7	31.5	220.5	49
8	29.7	237.6	64
9	28.6	257.4	81
10	31.4	314.0	100
Total 55	264.5	1545.5	385

And the final calculations of the values of b_0 and b_1 are

$$\bar{t} = \frac{55}{10} = 5.5$$

$$\bar{Y} = \frac{264.5}{10} = 26.45$$

$$b_1 = \frac{1545.5 - (55)(264.5)/10}{385 - 55^2/10} = 1.10$$

$$b_0 = 26.45 - 1.10(5.5) = 20.40$$

Problem 20 provides additional practice in using regression analysis to estimate the linear trend in a time series data set.

Therefore,

$$\hat{Y}_t = 20.4 + 1.1t \tag{15.13}$$

is the regression equation for the linear trend component for the bicycle sales time series.

The slope of 1.1 in this trend equation indicates that over the past 10 years, the firm has experienced an average growth in sales of about 1100 units per year. If we assume that the past 10-year trend in sales is a good indicator for the future, we can use equation (15.13) to project the trend component of the time series. For example, substituting $t = 11$ into equation (15.13) yields next year's trend projection, $\hat{Y}_{11}$:

$$\hat{Y}_{11} = 20.4 + 1.1(11) = 32.5$$

Thus, the linear trend model yields a sales forecast of 32,500 bicycles for the next year.

Table 15.12 shows the computation of the minimized sum of squared errors for the bicycle sales time series. As previously noted, minimizing sum of squared errors also minimizes the commonly used measure of accuracy, MSE. For the bicycle sales time series,

$$\text{MSE} = \frac{\sum_{t=1}^{n} e_t^2}{n} = \frac{30.7}{10} = 3.07$$

Note that in this example we are not using past values of the time series to produce forecasts, and so $k = 0$; that is, we can produce a forecast for each period of the time series and so do not have to adjust our calculations of the MAE, MSE, or MAPE for k.

TABLE 15.12   SUMMARY OF THE LINEAR TREND FORECASTS AND FORECAST ERRORS FOR THE BICYCLE SALES TIME SERIES

Week	Sales (1000s) Y_t	Forecast $\hat{Y}_t$	Forecast Error	Squared Forecast Error
1	21.6	21.5	0.1	0.01
2	22.9	22.6	0.3	0.09
3	25.5	23.7	1.8	3.24
4	21.9	24.8	−2.9	8.41
5	23.9	25.9	−2.0	4.00
6	27.5	27.0	0.5	0.25
7	31.5	28.1	3.4	11.56
8	29.7	29.2	0.5	0.25
9	28.6	30.3	−1.7	2.89
10	31.4	31.4	0.0	0.00
			Total	30.70

We can also use the trendline to forecast sales farther into the future. For instance, using equation (15.13), we develop annual forecasts for two and three years into the future as follows:

$$\hat{Y}_{12} = 20.4 + 1.1(12) = 33.6$$
$$\hat{Y}_{13} = 20.4 + 1.1(13) = 34.7$$

Note that the forecasted value increases by 1100 bicycles in each year.

NOTES AND COMMENTS

1. Statistical packages such as Minitab and SAS, as well as Excel, have routines to perform regression analysis. Regression analysis minimizes the sum of squared error and under certain assumptions it also allows the analyst to make statistical statements about the parameters and the forecasts.

2. While the use of a linear function to model the trend is common, some time series exhibit a curvilinear (nonlinear) trend. More advanced texts discuss how to develop nonlinear models such as quadratic models and exponential models for these more complex relationships.

In this section we used simple linear regression to estimate the relationship between the dependent variable (Y_t, the actual value of the time series in period t) and a single independent variable (the trend variable t). However, some regression models include several independent variables. When we estimate a linear relationship between the dependent variable and more than one independent variable, this is referred to as multiple linear regression. In the next section we will apply multiple linear regression to time series that include seasonal effects and to time series that include both seasonal effects and a linear trend.

15.5 SEASONALITY

In this section we show how to develop forecasts for a time series that has a seasonal pattern. To the extent that seasonality exists, we need to incorporate it into our forecasting models to ensure accurate forecasts. We begin the section by considering a seasonal time series with no trend and then discuss how to model seasonality with a linear trend.

Seasonality Without Trend

Let us consider again the data from Table 15.5, the number of umbrellas sold at a clothing store over the past five years. We repeat the data here in Table 15.13, and Figure 15.11 again shows the corresponding time series plot. The time series plot does not indicate any long-term trend in sales. In fact, unless you look carefully at the data, you might conclude that the data follow a horizontal pattern with random fluctuation and that single exponential smoothing could be used to forecast sales. However, closer inspection of the time series plot reveals a pattern in the fluctuations. That is, the first and third quarters have moderate sales, the second quarter the highest sales, and the fourth quarter tends to be the lowest quarter in terms of sales volume. Thus, we conclude that a quarterly seasonal pattern is present.

We can model a time series with a seasonal pattern by treating the season as a categorical variable. **Categorical variables** are data used to categorize observations of data. When a categorical variable has k levels, $k - 1$ dummy variables (sometimes called 0-1 variables) are required. So if there are four seasons, we need three dummy variables. For instance, in the umbrella sales time series, the quarter to which each observation corresponds is treated as a season; it is a categorical variable with four levels: Quarter 1, Quarter 2, Quarter 3, and

TABLE 15.13   UMBRELLA SALES TIME SERIES

DATA *file*

Umbrella

Year	Quarter	Sales
1	1	125
	2	153
	3	106
	4	88
2	1	118
	2	161
	3	133
	4	102
3	1	138
	2	144
	3	113
	4	80
4	1	109
	2	137
	3	125
	4	109
5	1	130
	2	165
	3	128
	4	96

FIGURE 15.11   UMBRELLA SALES TIME SERIES PLOT

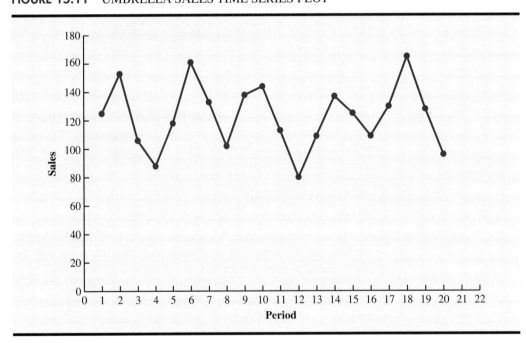

Quarter 4. Thus, to model the seasonal effects in the umbrella time series we need $4 - 1 = 3$ dummy variables. The three dummy variables can be coded as follows:

$$\text{Qtr1}_t = \begin{cases} 1 & \text{if period } t \text{ is a Quarter 1} \\ 0 & \text{otherwise} \end{cases}$$

$$\text{Qtr2}_t = \begin{cases} 1 & \text{if period } t \text{ is a Quarter 2} \\ 0 & \text{otherwise} \end{cases}$$

$$Qtr3_t = \begin{cases} 1 & \text{if period } t \text{ is a Quarter 3} \\ 0 & \text{otherwise} \end{cases}$$

Using $\hat{Y}_t$ to denote the forecasted value of sales for period t, the general form of the equation relating the number of umbrellas sold to the quarter the sales take place is as follows.

$$\hat{Y}_t = b_0 + b_1\,Qtr1_t + b_2\,Qtr2_t + b_3\,Qtr3_t \qquad (15.14)$$

Note that we have numbered the observations in Table 15.14 as periods 1 to 20. For example, Year 3, quarter 3 is observation 11.

Note that the fourth quarter will be denoted by a setting of all three dummy variables to 0. Table 15.14 shows the umbrella sales time series with the coded values of the dummy variables shown. We can use a multiple linear regression model to find the values of b_0, b_1, b_2, and b_3 that minimize the sum of squared errors. For this regression model Y_t is the dependent variable and the quarterly dummy variables $Qtr1_t$, $Qtr2_t$, and $Qtr3_t$ are the independent variables.

Using the data in Table 15.14 and regression analysis, we obtain the following equation:

$$\hat{Y}_t = 95.0 + 29.0\,Qtr1_t + 57.0\,Qtr2_t + 26.0\,Qtr3_t \qquad (15.15)$$

we can use Equation (15.15) to forecast quarterly sales for next year.

For practice using categorical variables to estimate seasonal effects, try Problem 24.

Quarter 1: Sales = 95.0 + 29.0(1) + 57.0(0) + 26.0(0) = 124
Quarter 2: Sales = 95.0 + 29.0(0) + 57.0(1) + 26.0(0) = 152
Quarter 3: Sales = 95.0 + 29.0(0) + 57.0(0) + 26.0(1) = 121
Quarter 4: Sales = 95.0 + 29.0(0) + 57.0(0) + 26.0(0) = 95

TABLE 15.14 UMBRELLA SALES TIME SERIES WITH DUMMY VARIABLES

Period	Year	Quarter	Qtr1	Qtr2	Qtr3	Sales
1	1	1	1	0	0	125
2		2	0	1	0	153
3		3	0	0	1	106
4		4	0	0	0	88
5	2	1	1	0	0	118
6		2	0	1	0	161
7		3	0	0	1	133
8		4	0	0	0	102
9	3	1	1	0	0	138
10		2	0	1	0	144
11		3	0	0	1	113
12		4	0	0	0	80
13	4	1	1	0	0	109
14		2	0	1	0	137
15		3	0	0	1	125
16		4	0	0	0	109
17	5	1	1	0	0	130
18		2	0	1	0	165
19		3	0	0	1	128
20		4	0	0	0	96

It is interesting to note that we could have obtained the quarterly forecasts for next year by simply computing the average number of umbrellas sold in each quarter, as shown in the following table:

Year	Quarter 1	Quarter 2	Quarter 3	Quarter 4
1	125	153	106	88
2	118	161	133	102
3	138	144	113	80
4	109	137	125	109
5	130	165	128	96
Average	124	152	121	95

Nonetheless, for more complex problem situations, such as dealing with a time series that has both trend and seasonal effects, this simple averaging approach will not work.

Seasonality with Trend

We now consider situations for which the time series contains both a seasonal effect and a linear trend by showing how to forecast the quarterly smartphone sales time series introduced in Section 15.1. The data for the smartphone time series are shown in Table 15.15. The time series plot in Figure 15.12 indicates that sales are lowest in the second quarter of each year and increase in quarters 3 and 4. Thus, we conclude that a seasonal pattern exists for smartphone sales. However, the time series also has an upward linear trend that will need to be accounted for in order to develop accurate forecasts of quarterly sales. This is easily done by combining the dummy variable approach for handling seasonality with the approach we discussed in Section 15.4 for handling a linear trend.

The general form of the regression equation for modeling both the quarterly seasonal effects and the linear trend in the smartphone time series is:

$$\hat{Y}_t = b_0 + b_1\text{Qtr1}_t + b_2\text{Qtr2}_t + b_3\text{Qtr3}_t + b_4t \qquad (15.16)$$

TABLE 15.15   SMARTPHONE SALES TIME SERIES

DATA *file*

SmartPhoneSales

Year	Quarter	Sales (1000s)
1	1	4.8
	2	4.1
	3	6.0
	4	6.5
2	1	5.8
	2	5.2
	3	6.8
	4	7.4
3	1	6.0
	2	5.6
	3	7.5
	4	7.8
4	1	6.3
	2	5.9
	3	8.0
	4	8.4

FIGURE 15.12   SMARTPHONE SALES TIME SERIES PLOT

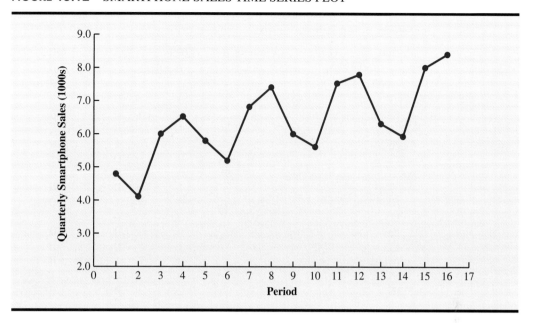

where

$$\hat{Y}_t = \text{forecast of sales in period } t$$

$\text{Qtr1}_t = 1$ if time period t corresponds to the first quarter of the year; 0, otherwise

$\text{Qtr2}_t = 1$ if time period t corresponds to the second quarter of the year; 0, otherwise

$\text{Qtr3}_t = 1$ if time period t corresponds to the third quarter of the year; 0, otherwise

$$t = \text{time period}$$

For this regression model Y_t is the dependent variable and the quarterly dummy variables Qtr1_t, Qtr2_t, and Qtr3_t and the time period t are the independent variables.

Table 15.16 shows the revised smartphone sales time series that includes the coded values of the dummy variables and the time period t. Using the data in Table 15.16 with the regression model that includes both the seasonal and trend components, we obtain the following equation that minimizes our sum of squared errors:

$$\hat{Y}_t = 6.07 - 1.36\,\text{Qtr1}_t - 2.03\,\text{Qtr2}_t - 0.304\,\text{Qtr3}_t + 0.146t \qquad (15.17)$$

We can now use equation (15.17) to forecast quarterly sales for next year. Next year is Year 5 for the smartphone sales time series; that is, time periods 17, 18, 19, and 20.

Forecast for Time Period 17 (Quarter 1 in Year 5)

$$\hat{Y}_{17} = 6.07 - 1.36(1) - 2.03(0) - 0.304(0) + 0.146(17) = 7.19$$

Forecast for Time Period 18 (Quarter 2 in Year 5)

$$\hat{Y}_{18} = 6.07 - 1.36(0) - 2.03(1) - 0.304(0) + 0.146(18) = 6.67$$

Forecast for Time Period 19 (Quarter 3 in Year 5)

$$\hat{Y}_{19} = 6.07 - 1.36(0) - 2.03(0) - 0.304(1) + 0.146(19) = 8.54$$

Forecast for Time Period 20 (Quarter 4 in Year 5)

$$\hat{Y}_{20} = 6.07 - 1.36(0) - 2.03(0) - 0.304(0) + 0.146(20) = 8.99$$

Thus, accounting for the seasonal effects and the linear trend in smartphone sales, the estimates of quarterly sales in Year 5 are 7190, 6670, 8540, and 8990.

TABLE 15.16   SMARTPHONE SALES TIME SERIES WITH DUMMY VARIABLES AND TIME PERIOD

Period	Year	Quarter	Qtr1	Qtr2	Qtr3	Sales (1000s)
1	1	1	1	0	0	4.8
2		2	0	1	0	4.1
3		3	0	0	1	6.0
4		4	0	0	0	6.5
5	2	1	1	0	0	5.8
6		2	0	1	0	5.2
7		3	0	0	1	6.8
8		4	0	0	0	7.4
9	3	1	1	0	0	6.0
10		2	0	1	0	5.6
11		3	0	0	1	7.5
12		4	0	0	0	7.8
13	4	1	1	0	0	6.3
14		2	0	1	0	5.9
15		3	0	0	1	8.0
16		4	0	0	0	8.4

The dummy variables in the equation actually provide four equations, one for each quarter. For instance, if time period t corresponds to quarter 1, the estimate of quarterly sales is

Quarter 1: Sales $= 6.07 - 1.36(1) - 2.03(0) - 0.304(0) + 0.146t = 4.71 + 0.146t$

Similarly, if time period t corresponds to quarters 2, 3, and 4, the estimates of quarterly sales are

Quarter 2: Sales $= 6.07 - 1.36(0) - 2.03(1) - 0.304(0) + 0.146t = 4.04 + 0.146t$

Quarter 3: Sales $= 6.07 - 1.36(0) - 2.03(0) - 0.304(1) + 0.146t = 5.77 + 0.146t$

Problem 28 provides another example of using regression analysis to forecast time series data with both trend and seasonal effects.

Quarter 4: Sales $= 6.07 - 1.36(0) - 2.03(0) - 0.304(0) + 0.146t = 6.07 + 0.146t$

The slope of the trend line for each quarterly forecast equation is 0.146, indicating a consistent growth in sales of about 146 sets per quarter. The only difference in the four equations is that they have different intercepts.

Models Based on Monthly Data

Whenever a categorical variable such as season has k levels, k − 1 dummy variables are required.

In the preceding smartphone sales example, we showed how dummy variables can be used to account for the quarterly seasonal effects in the time series. Because there were four levels for the categorical variable season, three dummy variables were required. However, many businesses use monthly rather than quarterly forecasts. For monthly data, season is a categorical variable with 12 levels, and thus $12 - 1 = 11$ dummy variables are required. For example, the 11 dummy variables could be coded as follows:

$$Month1 = \begin{cases} 1 & \text{if January} \\ 0 & \text{otherwise} \end{cases}$$

$$Month2 = \begin{cases} 1 & \text{if February} \\ 0 & \text{otherwise} \end{cases}$$

$$\vdots$$

$$Month11 = \begin{cases} 1 & \text{if November} \\ 0 & \text{otherwise} \end{cases}$$

Other than this change, the approach for handling seasonality remains the same.

SUMMARY

This chapter provided an introduction to basic methods of time series analysis and forecasting. We first showed that the underlying pattern in the time series can often be identified by constructing a time series plot. Several types of data patterns can be distinguished, including a horizontal pattern, a trend pattern, and a seasonal pattern. The forecasting methods we have discussed are based on which of these patterns are present in the time series.

We also discussed that the accuracy of the method is an important factor in determining which forecasting method to use. We considered three measures of forecast accuracy: mean absolute error (MAE), mean squared error (MSE), and mean absolute percentage error (MAPE). Each of these measures is designed to determine how well a particular forecasting method is able to reproduce the time series data that are already available. By selecting the method that is most accurate for the data already known, we hope to increase the likelihood that we will obtain more accurate forecasts for future time periods.

For a time series with a horizontal pattern, we showed how moving averages, weighted moving averages, and exponential smoothing can be used to develop a forecast. The moving averages method consists of computing an average of past data values and then using that average as the forecast for the next period. In the weighted moving average and exponential smoothing methods, weighted averages of past time series values are used to compute forecasts. These methods also adapt well to a horizontal pattern that shifts to a different level and then resumes a horizontal pattern.

For time series that have only a long-term linear trend, we showed how regression analysis can be used to make trend projections. For a time series with a seasonal pattern, we showed how dummy variables and regression analysis can be used to develop an equation with seasonal effects. We then extended the approach to include situations where the time series contains both a seasonal and a linear trend effect by showing how to combine the dummy variable approach for handling seasonality with the approach for handling a linear trend.

GLOSSARY

Categorical (dummy) variable A variable used to categorize observations of data. Used when modeling a time series with a seasonal pattern.

Cyclical pattern A cyclical pattern exists if the time series plot shows an alternating sequence of points below and above the trend line lasting more than one year.

Dependent variable The variable that is being predicted or explained in a regression analysis.

Exponential smoothing A forecasting method that uses a weighted average of past time series values as the forecast; it is a special case of the weighted moving averages method in which we select only one weight—the weight for the most recent observation.

Forecast error The difference between the actual time series value and the forecast.

Independent variable A variable used to predict or explain values of the dependent variable in regression analysis.

Mean absolute error (MAE) The average of the absolute values of the forecast errors.

Mean absolute percentage error (MAPE) The average of the absolute values of the percentage forecast errors.

Mean squared error (MSE) The average of the sum of squared forecast errors.

Moving averages A forecasting method that uses the average of the k most recent data values in the time series as the forecast for the next period.

Regression analysis A procedure for estimating values of a dependent variable given the values of one or more independent variables in a manner that minimizes the sum of the squared errors.

Seasonal pattern A seasonal pattern exists if the time series plot exhibits a repeating pattern over successive periods.

Smoothing constant   A parameter of the exponential smoothing model that provides the weight given to the most recent time series value in the calculation of the forecast value.

Stationary time series   A time series whose statistical properties are indepepndent of time. For a stationary time series, the process generating the data has a constant mean and the variability of the time series is constant over time.

Time series   A sequence of observations on a variable measured at successive points in time or over successive periods of time.

Time series plot   A graphical presentation of the relationship between time and the time series variable. Time is shown on the horizontal axis and the time series values are shown on the verical axis.

Trend pattern   A trend pattern exists if the time series plot shows gradual shifts or movements to relatively higher or lower values over a longer period of time.

Weighted moving averages   A forecasting method that involves selecting a different weight for the k most recent data values in the time series and then computing a weighted average of the of the values. The sum of the weights must equal one.

PROBLEMS

1.   Consider the following time series data:

Week	1	2	3	4	5	6
Value	18	13	16	11	17	14

Using the naïve method (most recent value) as the forecast for the next week, compute the following measures of forecast accuracy:
a.   Mean absolute error
b.   Mean squared error
c.   Mean absolute percentage error
d.   What is the forecast for Week 7?

2.   Refer to the time series data in Exercise 1. Using the average of all the historical data as a forecast for the next period, compute the following measures of forecast accuracy:
a.   Mean absolute error
b.   Mean squared error
c.   Mean absolute percentage error
d.   What is the forecast for Week 7?

3.   Exercises 1 and 2 used different forecasting methods. Which method appears to provide the more accurate forecasts for the historical data? Explain.

4.   Consider the following time series data:

Month	1	2	3	4	5	6	7
Value	24	13	20	12	19	23	15

a.   Compute MSE using the most recent value as the forecast for the next period. What is the forecast for Month 8?
b.   Compute MSE using the average of all the data available as the forecast for the next period. What is the forecast for Month 8?
c.   Which method appears to provide the better forecast?

5.   Consider the following time series data:

Week	1	2	3	4	5	6
Value	18	13	16	11	17	14

a. Construct a time series plot. What type of pattern exists in the data?
b. Develop a three-week moving average for this time series. Compute MSE and a forecast for Week 7.
c. Use $\alpha = 0.2$ to compute the exponential smoothing values for the time series. Compute MSE and a forecast for Week 7.
d. Compare the three-week moving average forecast with the exponential smoothing forecast using $\alpha = 0.2$. Which appears to provide the better forecast based on MSE? Explain.
e. Use trial and error to find a value of the exponential smoothing coefficient α that results in a smaller MSE than what you calculated for $\alpha = 0.2$.

6. Consider the following time series data:

Month	1	2	3	4	5	6	7
Value	24	13	20	12	19	23	15

a. Construct a time series plot. What type of pattern exists in the data?
b. Develop a three-week moving average for this time series. Compute MSE and a forecast for Month 8.
c. Use $\alpha = 0.2$ to compute the exponential smoothing values for the time series. Compute MSE and a forecast for Month 8.
d. Compare the three-week moving average forecast with the exponential smoothing forecast using $\alpha = 0.2$. Which appears to provide the better forecast based on MSE?
e. Use trial and error to find a value of the exponential smoothing coefficient α that results in a smaller MSE than what you calculated for $\alpha = 0.2$.

DATA *file*

Gasoline

7. Refer to the gasoline sales time series data in Table 15.1.
a. Compute four-week and five-week moving averages for the time series.
b. Compute the MSE for the four-week and five-week moving average forecasts.
c. What appears to be the best number of weeks of past data (three, four, or five) to use in the moving average computation? Recall that MSE for the three-week moving average is 10.22.

SELF_test_

8. Refer again to the gasoline sales time series data in Table 15.1.
a. Using a weight of 1/2 for the most recent observation, 1/3 for the second most recent, and 1/6 for third most recent, compute a three-week weighted moving average for the time series.
b. Compute the MSE for the weighted moving average in part (a). Do you prefer this weighted moving average to the unweighted moving average? Remember that the MSE for the unweighted moving average is 10.22.
c. Suppose you are allowed to choose any weights as long as they sum to 1. Could you always find a set of weights that would make the MSE smaller for a weighted moving average than for an unweighted moving average? Why or why not?

SELF_test_

9. With the gasoline time series data from Table 15.1, show the exponential smoothing forecasts using $\alpha = 0.1$.
a. Applying the MSE measure of forecast accuracy, would you prefer a smoothing constant of $\alpha = 0.1$ or $\alpha = 0.2$ for the gasoline sales time series?
b. Are the results the same if you apply MAE as the measure of accuracy?
c. What are the results if MAPE is used?

10. With a smoothing constant of $\alpha = 0.2$, equation (15.8) shows that the forecast for Week 13 of the gasoline sales data from Table 15.1 is given by $\hat{Y}_{13} = 0.2Y_{12} + 0.8\hat{Y}_{12}$. However, the forecast for Week 12 is given by $\hat{Y}_{12} = 0.2Y_{11} + 0.8\hat{Y}_{11}$. Thus, we could combine these two results to show that the forecast for Week 13 can be written as

$$\hat{Y}_{13} = 0.2Y_{12} + 0.8(0.2Y_{11} + 0.8\hat{Y}_{11}) = 0.2Y_{12} + 0.16Y_{11} + 0.64\hat{Y}_{11}$$

a. Making use of the fact that $\hat{Y}_{11} = 0.2Y_{10} + 0.8\hat{Y}_{10}$ (and similarly for $\hat{Y}_{10}$ and $\hat{Y}_9$), continue to expand the expression for $\hat{Y}_{13}$ until it is written in terms of the past data values $Y_{12}, Y_{11}, Y_{10}, Y_9, Y_8$, and the forecast for Week 8.

b. Refer to the coefficients or weights for the past values Y_{12}, Y_{11}, Y_{10}, Y_9, and Y_8. What observation can you make about how exponential smoothing weights past data values in arriving at new forecasts? Compare this weighting pattern with the weighting pattern of the moving averages method.

11. For the Hawkins Company, the monthly percentages of all shipments received on time over the past 12 months are 80, 82, 84, 83, 83, 84, 85, 84, 82, 83, 84, and 83.

  a. Construct a time series plot. What type of pattern exists in the data?

  b. Compare a three-month moving average forecast with an exponential smoothing forecast for $\alpha = 0.2$. Which provides the better forecasts using MSE as the measure of model accuracy?

  c. What is the forecast for next month?

12. Corporate triple A bond interest rates for 12 consecutive months follow.

9.5   9.3   9.4   9.6   9.8   9.7   9.8   10.5   9.9   9.7   9.6   9.6

  a. Construct a time series plot. What type of pattern exists in the data?

  b. Develop three-month and four-month moving averages for this time series. Does the three-month or four-month moving average provide the better forecasts based on MSE? Explain.

  c. What is the moving average forecast for the next month?

13. The values of Alabama building contracts (in millions of dollars) for a 12-month period follow.

240   350   230   260   280   320   220   310   240   310   240   230

  a. Construct a time series plot. What type of pattern exists in the data?

  b. Compare a three-month moving average forecast with an exponential smoothing forecast. Use $\alpha = 0.2$. Which provides the better forecasts based on MSE?

  c. What is the forecast for the next month?

14. The following time series shows the sales of a particular product over the past 12 months:

Month	Sales	Month	Sales
1	105	7	145
2	135	8	140
3	120	9	100
4	105	10	80
5	90	11	100
6	120	12	110

  a. Construct a time series plot. What type of pattern exists in the data?

  b. Use $\alpha = 0.3$ to compute the exponential smoothing values for the time series.

  c. Use trial and error to find a value of the exponential smoothing coefficient α that results in a relatively small MSE.

15. Ten weeks of data on the Commodity Futures Index are 7.35, 7.40, 7.55, 7.56, 7.60, 7.52, 7.52, 7.70, 7.62, and 7.55.

  a. Construct a time series plot. What type of pattern exists in the data?

  b. Use trial and error to find a value of the exponential smoothing coefficient α that results in a relatively small MSE.

16. Since its inception in 1967, the Super Bowl is one of the most watched events on television in the United States every year. The number of U.S. households that tuned in for each Super Bowl, reported by Nielson.com, is provided in the data set SuperBowlRatings.

  a. Construct a time series plot for the data. What type of pattern exists in the data? Discuss some of the patterns that may have resulted in the pattern exhibited in the time series plot of the data.

  b. Given the pattern of the time series plot developed in part (a), do you think the forecasting methods discussed in this chapter are appropriate to develop forecasts for this time series? Explain.

  c. Use simple linear regression analysis to find the parameters for the line that minimizes MSE for this time series.

SELF*test*

DATA *file*

SuperBowlRatings

17. Consider the following time series:

t	1	2	3	4	5
Y_t	6	11	9	14	15

  a. Construct a time series plot. What type of pattern exists in the data?
  b. Use simple linear regression analysis to find the parameters for the line that minimizes MSE for this time series.
  c. What is the forecast for $t = 6$?

18. The following table reports the percentage of stocks in a portfolio for nine quarters from 2012 to 2014:

Quarter	Stock%
1st—2012	29.8
2nd—2012	31.0
3rd—2012	29.9
4th—2012	30.1
1st—2013	32.2
2nd—2013	31.5
3rd—2013	32.0
4th—2013	31.9
1st—2014	30.0

  a. Construct a time series plot. What type of pattern exists in the data?
  b. Use trial and error to find a value of the exponential smoothing coefficient α that results in a relatively small MSE.
  c. Using the exponential smoothing model you developed in part (b), what is the forecast of the percentage of stocks in a typical portfolio for the second quarter of 2014?

19. Consider the following time series:

t	1	2	3	4	5	6	7
Y_t	120	110	100	96	94	92	88

  a. Construct a time series plot. What type of pattern exists in the data?
  b. Use simple linear regression analysis to find the parameters for the line that minimizes MSE for this time series.
  c. What is the forecast for $t = 8$?

20. Because of high tuition costs at state and private universities, enrollments at community colleges have increased dramatically in recent years. The following data show the enrollment (in thousands) for Jefferson Community College for the nine most recent years:

Year	Enrollment (1000s)
1	6.5
2	8.1
3	8.4
4	10.2
5	12.5
6	13.3
7	13.7
8	17.2
9	18.1

  a. Construct a time series plot. What type of pattern exists in the data?
  b. Use simple linear regression analysis to find the parameters for the line that minimizes MSE for this time series.
  c. What is the forecast for Year 10?

DATA *file*

AdultSmokers

21. The Centers for Disease Control and Prevention Office on Smoking and Health (OSH) is the lead federal agency responsible for comprehensive tobacco prevention and control. OSH was established in 1965 to reduce the death and disease caused by tobacco use and exposure to second-hand smoke. One of the many responsibilities of the OSH is to collect data on tobacco use. The following data show the percentage of adults in the United States who were users of tobacco from 2001 through 2011 (http://www.cdc.gov /tobacco/data_statistics/tables/trends/cig_smoking/index.htm):

Year	Percentage of Adults Who Smoke
2001	22.8
2002	22.5
2003	21.6
2004	20.9
2005	20.9
2006	20.8
2007	19.8
2008	20.6
2009	20.6
2010	19.3
2011	18.9

a. Construct a time series plot. What type of pattern exists in the data?
b. Use simple linear regression to find the parameters for the line that minimizes MSE for this time series.
c. One of OSH's *Healthy People 2020 Goals* is to cut the percentage of adults in the United States who were users of tobacco to 12% or less by the year 2020. Does your regression model from part (b) suggest that the OSH is on target to meet this goal? If not, use your model from part (b) to estimate the year in which the OSH will achieve this goal.

22. The president of a small manufacturing firm is concerned about the continual increase in manufacturing costs over the past several years. The following figures provide a time series of the cost per unit for the firm's leading product over the past eight years:

Year	Cost/Unit ($)	Year	Cost/Unit ($)
1	20.00	5	26.60
2	24.50	6	30.00
3	28.20	7	31.00
4	27.50	8	36.00

a. Construct a time series plot. What type of pattern exists in the data?
b. Use simple linear regression analysis to find the parameters for the line that minimizes MSE for this time series.
c. What is the average cost increase that the firm has been realizing per year?
d. Compute an estimate of the cost/unit for next year.

DATA *file*

Exercise

23. The medical community unanimously agrees on the health benefits of regular exercise, but are adults listening? During each of the past 15 years, a polling organization has surveyed Americans about their exercise habits. In the most recent of these polls, slightly over half of all American adults reported that they exercise for 30 or more minutes at least three times per week. The following data show the percentages of adults who reported that they exercise for 30 or more minutes at least three times per week during each of the 15 years of this study:

Year	Percentage of Adults Who Reported That They Exercise for 30 or More Minutes At Least Three Times per Week
1	41.0
2	44.9
3	47.1
4	45.7
5	46.6
6	44.5
7	47.6
8	49.8
9	48.1
10	48.9
11	49.9
12	52.1
13	50.6
14	54.6
15	52.4

a. Construct a time series plot. Does a linear trend appear to be present?

b. Use simple linear regression to find the parameters for the line that minimizes MSE for this time series.

c. Use the trend equation from part (b) to forecast the percentage of adults next year (Year 16 of the study) who will report that they exercise for 30 or more minutes at least three times per week.

d. Would you feel comfortable using the trend equation from part (b) to forecast the percentage of adults three years from now (Year 18 of the study) who will report that they exercise for 30 or more minutes at least three times per week?

SELF*test*

24. Consider the following time series:

Quarter	Year 1	Year 2	Year 3
1	71	68	62
2	49	41	51
3	58	60	53
4	78	81	72

a. Construct a time series plot. What type of pattern exists in the data?

b. Use a multiple linear regression model with dummy variables as follows to develop an equation to account for seasonal effects in the data. Qtr1 = 1 if Quarter 1, 0 otherwise; Qtr2 = 1 if Quarter 2, 0 otherwise; Qtr3 = 1 if Quarter 3, 0 otherwise.

c. Compute the quarterly forecasts for next year.

25. Consider the following time series data:

Quarter	Year 1	Year 2	Year 3
1	4	6	7
2	2	3	6
3	3	5	6
4	5	7	8

a. Construct a time series plot. What type of pattern exists in the data?

b. Use a multiple regression model with dummy variables as follows to develop an equation to account for seasonal effects in the data. Qtr1 = 1 if Quarter 1, 0 otherwise; Qtr2 = 1 if Quarter 2, 0 otherwise; Qtr3 = 1 if Quarter 3, 0 otherwise.

c. Compute the quarterly forecasts for next year.

26. The quarterly sales data (number of copies sold) for a college textbook over the past three years follow.

Quarter	Year 1	Year 2	Year 3
1	1690	1800	1850
2	940	900	1100
3	2625	2900	2930
4	2500	2360	2615

    a. Construct a time series plot. What type of pattern exists in the data?

    b. Use a regression model with dummy variables as follows to develop an equation to account for seasonal effects in the data. Qtr1 = 1 if Quarter 1, 0 otherwise; Qtr2 = 1 if Quarter 2, 0 otherwise; Qtr3 = 1 if Quarter 3, 0 otherwise.

    c. Compute the quarterly forecasts for next year.

    d. Let $t = 1$ to refer to the observation in Quarter 1 of Year 1; $t = 2$ to refer to the observation in Quarter 2 of Year 1; . . . ; and $t = 12$ to refer to the observation in Quarter 4 of Year 3. Using the dummy variables defined in part (b) and also using t, develop an equation to account for seasonal effects and any linear trend in the time series. Based upon the seasonal effects in the data and linear trend, compute the quarterly forecasts for next year.

Pollution

27. Air pollution control specialists in southern California monitor the amount of ozone, carbon dioxide, and nitrogen dioxide in the air on an hourly basis. The hourly time series data exhibit seasonality, with the levels of pollutants showing patterns that vary over the hours in the day. On July 15, 16, and 17, the following levels of nitrogen dioxide were observed for the 12 hours from 6:00 A.M. to 6:00 P.M.:

July 15: 25 28 35 50 60 60 40 35 30 25 25 20
July 16: 28 30 35 48 60 65 50 40 35 25 20 20
July 17: 35 42 45 70 72 75 60 45 40 25 25 25

    a. Construct a time series plot. What type of pattern exists in the data?

    b. Use a multiple linear regression model with dummy variables as follows to develop an equation to account for seasonal effects in the data:

        Hour1 = 1 if the reading was made between 6:00 A.M. and 7:00 A.M.; 0 otherwise

        Hour2 = 1 if the reading was made between 7:00 A.M. and 8:00 A.M.; 0 otherwise

$$\vdots$$

        Hour11 = 1 if the reading was made between 4:00 P.M. and 5:00 P.M.; 0 otherwise

    Note that when the values of the 11 dummy variables are equal to 0, the observation corresponds to the 5:00 P.M. to 6:00 P.M. hour.

    c. Using the equation developed in part (b), compute estimates of the levels of nitrogen dioxide for July 18.

    d. Let $t = 1$ to refer to the observation in Hour 1 on July 15; $t = 2$ to refer to the observation in Hour 2 of July 15; . . . ; and $t = 36$ to refer to the observation in Hour 12 of July 17. Using the dummy variables defined in part (b) and t, develop an equation to account for seasonal effects and any linear trend in the time series. Based upon the seasonal effects in the data and linear trend, compute estimates of the levels of nitrogen dioxide for July 18.

SouthShore

28. South Shore Construction builds permanent docks and seawalls along the southern shore of Long Island, New York. Although the firm has been in business for only five years, revenue has increased from $308,000 in the first year of operation to $1,084,000 in the most recent year. The following data show the quarterly sales revenue in thousands of dollars:

Quarter	Year 1	Year 2	Year 3	Year 4	Year 5
1	20	37	75	92	176
2	100	136	155	202	282
3	175	245	326	384	445
4	13	26	48	82	181

a. Construct a time series plot. What type of pattern exists in the data?
b. Use a multiple regression model with dummy variables as follows to develop an equation to account for seasonal effects in the data. Qtr1 = 1 if Quarter 1, 0 otherwise; Qtr2 = 1 if Quarter 2, 0 otherwise; Qtr3 = 1 if Quarter 3, 0 otherwise.
c. Let Period = 1 to refer to the observation in Quarter 1 of Year 1; Period = 2 to refer to the observation in Quarter 2 of Year 1; . . . and Period = 20 to refer to the observation in Quarter 4 of Year 5. Using the dummy variables defined in part (b) and Period, develop an equation to account for seasonal effects and any linear trend in the time series. Based upon the seasonal effects in the data and linear trend, compute estimates of quarterly sales for Year 6.

Case Problem 1   FORECASTING FOOD AND BEVERAGE SALES

The Vintage Restaurant, on Captiva Island near Fort Myers, Florida, is owned and operated by Karen Payne. The restaurant just completed its third year of operation. During that time, Karen sought to establish a reputation for the restaurant as a high-quality dining establishment that specializes in fresh seafood. Through the efforts of Karen and her staff, her restaurant has become one of the best and fastest-growing restaurants on the island.

To better plan for future growth of the restaurant, Karen needs to develop a system that will enable her to forecast food and beverage sales by month for up to one year in advance. Table 15.17 shows the value of food and beverage sales ($1000s) for the first three years of operation.

Managerial Report

Perform an analysis of the sales data for the Vintage Restaurant. Prepare a report for Karen that summarizes your findings, forecasts, and recommendations. Include the following:

1. A time series plot. Comment on the underlying pattern in the time series.
2. Using the dummy variable approach, forecast sales for January through December of the fourth year.

TABLE 15.17   FOOD AND BEVERAGE SALES FOR THE VINTAGE RESTAURANT ($1000s)

DATA file
Vintage

Month	First Year	Second Year	Third Year
January	242	263	282
February	235	238	255
March	232	247	265
April	178	193	205
May	184	193	210
June	140	149	160
July	145	157	166
August	152	161	174
September	110	122	126
October	130	130	148
November	152	167	173
December	206	230	235

Assume that January sales for the fourth year turn out to be $295,000. What was your forecast error? If this error is large, Karen may be puzzled about the difference between your forecast and the actual sales value. What can you do to resolve her uncertainty in the forecasting procedure?

Case Problem 2   FORECASTING LOST SALES

The Carlson Department Store suffered heavy damage when a hurricane struck on August 31. The store was closed for four months (September through December), and Carlson is now involved in a dispute with its insurance company about the amount of lost sales during the time the store was closed. Two key issues must be resolved: (1) the amount of sales Carlson would have made if the hurricane had not struck and (2) whether Carlson is entitled to any compensation for excess sales due to increased business activity after the storm. More than $8 billion in federal disaster relief and insurance money came into the county, resulting in increased sales at department stores and numerous other businesses.

Table 15.18 gives Carlson's sales data for the 48 months preceding the storm. Table 15.19 reports total sales for the 48 months preceding the storm for all department stores in the county, as well as the total sales in the county for the four months the Carlson Department Store was closed. Carlson's managers asked you to analyze these data and develop estimates of the lost sales at the Carlson Department Store for the months of September through December. They also asked you to determine whether a case can be made for excess storm-related sales during the same period. If such a case can be made, Carlson is entitled to compensation for excess sales it would have earned in addition to ordinary sales.

Managerial Report

Prepare a report for the managers of the Carlson Department Store that summarizes your findings, forecasts, and recommendations. Include the following:

1. An estimate of sales for Carlson Department Store had there been no hurricane
2. An estimate of countywide department store sales had there been no hurricane
3. An estimate of lost sales for the Carlson Department Store for September through December

In addition, use the countywide actual department stores sales for September through December and the estimate in part (2) to make a case for or against excess storm-related sales.

TABLE 15.18   SALES FOR CARLSON DEPARTMENT STORE ($ MILLIONS)

DATA *file*

CarlsonSales

Month	Year 1	Year 2	Year 3	Year 4	Year 5
January		1.45	2.31	2.31	2.56
February		1.80	1.89	1.99	2.28
March		2.03	2.02	2.42	2.69
April		1.99	2.23	2.45	2.48
May		2.32	2.39	2.57	2.73
June		2.20	2.14	2.42	2.37
July		2.13	2.27	2.40	2.31
August		2.43	2.21	2.50	2.23
September	1.71	1.90	1.89	2.09	
October	1.90	2.13	2.29	2.54	
November	2.74	2.56	2.83	2.97	
December	4.20	4.16	4.04	4.35	

TABLE 15.19   DEPARTMENT STORE SALES FOR THE COUNTY ($ MILLIONS)

Month	Year 1	Year 2	Year 3	Year 4	Year 5
January		46.80	46.80	43.80	48.00
February		48.00	48.60	45.60	51.60
March		60.00	59.40	57.60	57.60
April		57.60	58.20	53.40	58.20
May		61.80	60.60	56.40	60.00
June		58.20	55.20	52.80	57.00
July		56.40	51.00	54.00	57.60
August		63.00	58.80	60.60	61.80
September	55.80	57.60	49.80	47.40	69.00
October	56.40	53.40	54.60	54.60	75.00
November	71.40	71.40	65.40	67.80	85.20
December	117.60	114.00	102.00	100.20	121.80

DATA *file*

CountySales

Appendix 15.1   FORECASTING WITH EXCEL DATA ANALYSIS TOOLS

In this appendix we show how Excel can be used to develop forecasts using three forecasting methods: moving averages, exponential smoothing, and trend projection. We also show how to use Excel Solver for least-squares fitting of models to data.

Moving Averages

*If the **Data Analysis** option does not appear in the **Analyze** group, you will have to include the Add-In in Excel. To do so, click on the **File** tab, then click **Options**, and then **Add-Ins**. Click **Go** next to the **Excel Add-Ins** drop-down box. Click the box next to **Analysis ToolPak** and click **OK**.*

To show how Excel can be used to develop forecasts using the moving averages method, we develop a forecast for the gasoline sales time series in Table 15.1 and Figure 15.1. We assume that the user has entered the week in rows 2 through 13 of column A and the sales data for the 12 weeks into worksheet rows 2 through 13 of column B (as in Figure 15.13).

The following steps can be used to produce a three-week moving average:

Step 1. Select the **Data** tab
Step 2. From the **Analyze** group select the **Data Analysis** option
Step 3. When the **Data Analysis** dialog box appears, choose **Moving Average** and click **OK**
Step 4. When the **Moving Average** dialog box appears:
    Enter B2:B13 in the **Input Range** box
    Enter 3 in the **Interval** box
    Enter C2 in the **Output Range** box
    Click **OK**

Once you have completed this step (as shown in Figure 15.14), the three-week moving average forecasts will appear in column C of the worksheet as in Figure 15.15. Note that forecasts for periods of other lengths can be computed easily by entering a different value in the **Interval** box.

Exponential Smoothing

To show how Excel can be used for exponential smoothing, we again develop a forecast for the gasoline sales time series in Table 15.1 and Figure 15.1. We assume that the user has entered the week in rows 2 through 13 of column A and the sales data for the 12 weeks into worksheet rows 2 through 13 of column B (as in Figure 15.13), and that the smoothing constant is $\alpha = 0.2$. The following steps can be used to produce a forecast:

Step 1. Select the **Data** tab
Step 2. From the **Analyze** group select the **Data Analysis** option

FIGURE 15.13   GASOLINE SALES DATA IN EXCEL ARRANGED TO USE THE MOVING
AVERAGES FUNCTION TO DEVELOP FORECASTS

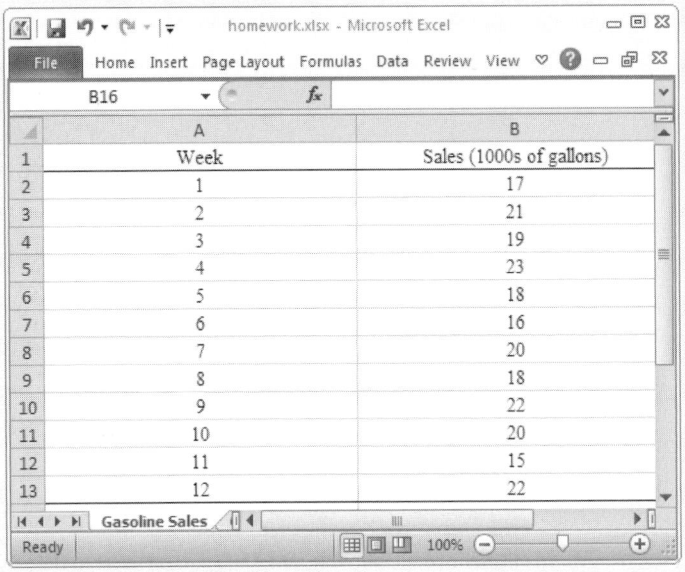

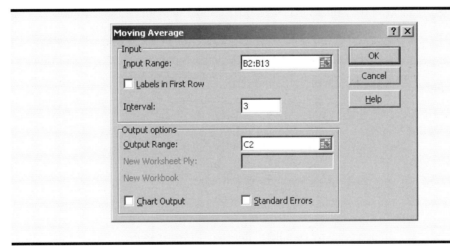

Week	Sales (1000s of gallons)
1	17
2	21
3	19
4	23
5	18
6	16
7	20
8	18
9	22
10	20
11	15
12	22

FIGURE 15.14   EXCEL MOVING AVERAGE DIALOGUE BOX FOR A 3-PERIOD MOVING
AVERAGE

Step 3. When the **Data Analysis** dialog box appears, choose **Exponential Smoothing**
and click **OK**

Step 4. When the **Exponential Smoothing** dialog box appears:
Enter B2:B13 in the **Input Range** box
Enter 0.8 in the **Damping factor** box
Enter C2 in the **Output Range** box
Click **OK**

Once you have completed this step (as shown in Figure 15.16), the exponential smoothing
forecasts will appear in column C of the worksheet (as in Figure 15.17). Note that the value
we entered in the **Damping factor** box is $1 - \alpha$; forecasts for other smoothing constants
can be computed easily by entering a different value for $1 - \alpha$ in the **Damping factor** box.

FIGURE 15.15   GASOLINE SALES DATA AND OUTPUT OF MOVING AVERAGES
FUNCTION IN EXCEL

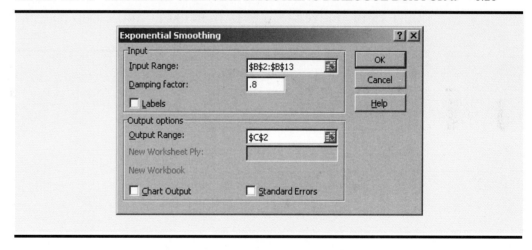

	A	B	C
1	Week	Sales (1000s of gallons)	F_t
2	1	17	#N/A
3	2	21	#N/A
4	3	19	19
5	4	23	21
6	5	18	20
7	6	16	19
8	7	20	18
9	8	18	18
10	9	22	20
11	10	20	20
12	11	15	19
13	12	22	19

FIGURE 15.16   EXCEL EXPONENTIAL SMOOTHING DIALOGUE BOX FOR $\alpha = 0.20$

Trend Projection

To show how Excel can be used for trend projection, we develop a forecast for the bicycle sales time series in Table 15.3 and Figure 15.3. We assume that the user has entered the year (1–10) for each observation into worksheet rows 2 through 11 of column A and the sales values into worksheet rows 2 through 11 of column B as shown in Figure 15.18. The following steps can be used to produce a forecast for Year 11 by trend projection:

Step 1. Select the **Formulas** tab
Step 2. Select two cells in the row where you want the regression coefficients b_1 and b_0 to appear (for this example, choose D1 and E1)
Step 3. Click on the **Insert Function** key
Step 4. When the **Insert Function** dialog box appears:
      Choose **Statistical** in the **Or select a category** box
      Choose **Linest** in the **Select a function** box
      Click **OK**

FIGURE 15.17   GASOLINE SALES DATA AND OUTPUT OF EXPONENTIAL
                   SMOOTHING FUNCTION IN EXCEL

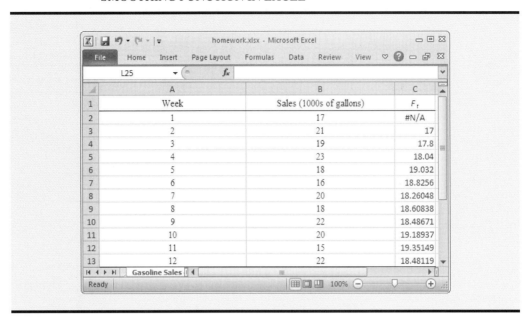

FIGURE 15.18   BICYCLE SALES DATA IN EXCEL ARRANGED TO USE THE LINEST
                   FUNCTION TO FIND THE LINEAR TREND

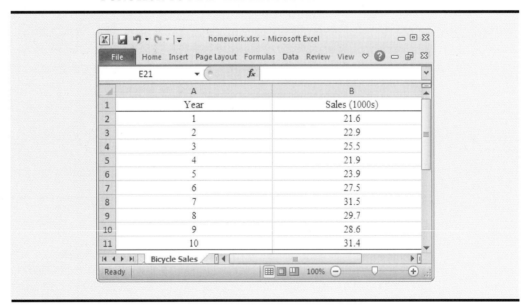

See Figure 15.19 for an example of this step.

Step 5. When the **Function Arguments** dialog box appears:
       Enter B2:B11 in the **Known_y's** box
       Enter A2:A11 in the **Known_x's** box
       Click **OK**

FIGURE 15.19   EXCEL INSERT FUNCTION DIALOGUE BOX FOR FINDING THE TREND LINE USING THE LINEST FUNCTION IN EXCEL

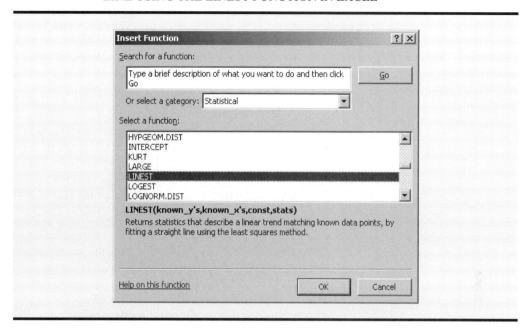

FIGURE 15.20   EXCEL FUNCTION ARGUMENTS DIALOGUE BOX FOR FINDING THE TREND LINE USING THE LINEST FUNCTION IN EXCEL

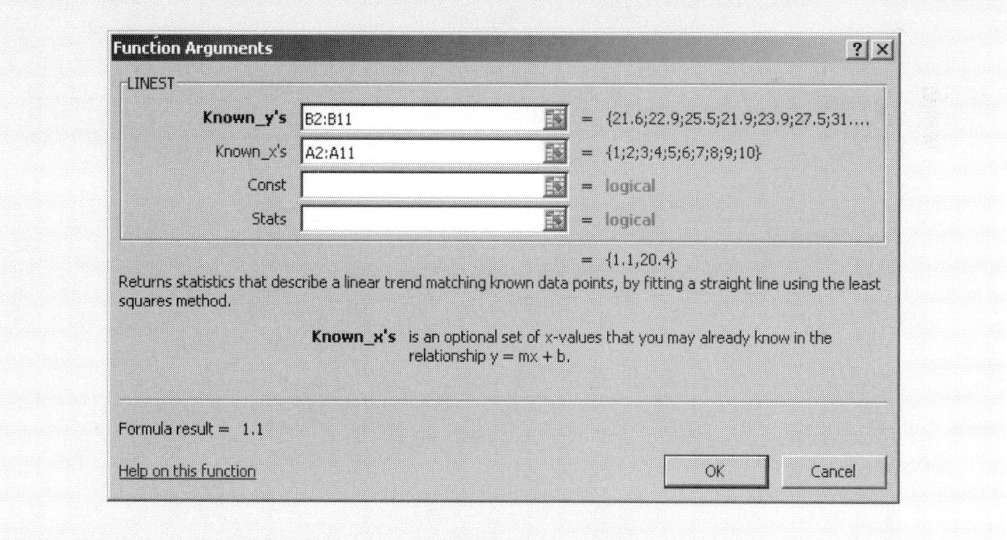

See Figure 15.20 for an example of this step.

Step 6. Hit the F2 key and then simultaneously hit the Shift, Control, and Enter keys (Shift + Control + Enter) to create an array that contains the values of the regression coefficients b_1 and b_0

At this point you have generated the regression coefficients b_1 and b_0 in the two cells you originally selected in step 1. It is important to note that cell D1 contains b_1 and cell E1 contains b_0.

To generate a forecast, in a blank cell, multiply the value of the independent variable t by b_1 and add the value of b_0 to this product. For example, if you wish to use this linear trend model to generate a forecast for Year 11 and the value of b_1 is in cell D1 and the value of b_0 is in cell E1, then enter $=11*D1+E1$ in a blank cell. The forecast for Year 11, in this case 32.5, will appear in the blank cell in which you enter this formula.

Models with Seasonality and No Trend

To show how Excel can be used to fit models with seasonality, we develop a forecast for the umbrella sales time series in Table 15.13 and Figure 15.11. We assume that the user has entered the year (1–5) for each observation into worksheet rows 3 through 22 of column A; the values for the quarter in worksheet rows 3 through 22 of column B; the values for the quarterly dummy variables Qtr1$_t$, Qtr2$_t$, and Qtr3$_t$ in worksheet rows 3 through 22 of columns C, D, and E, respectively; and the sales values into worksheet rows 3 through 22 of column F. The following steps can be used to produce a forecast for Year 11 by trend projection as shown in Figure 15.21.

Step 1. Select the **Formulas** tab
Step 2. Select four cells in the row where you want the regression coefficients b_3, b_2, b_1, and b_0 to appear (for this example, choose G1:J1)
Step 3. Click on the **Insert Function** key
Step 4. When the **Insert Function** dialog box appears:
　　　　Choose **Statistical** in the **Or select a category** box

FIGURE 15.21　UMBRELLA SALES DATA IN EXCEL ARRANGED TO USE THE LINEST
　　　　　　　　　FUNCTION TO FIND THE SEASONAL COMPONENTS

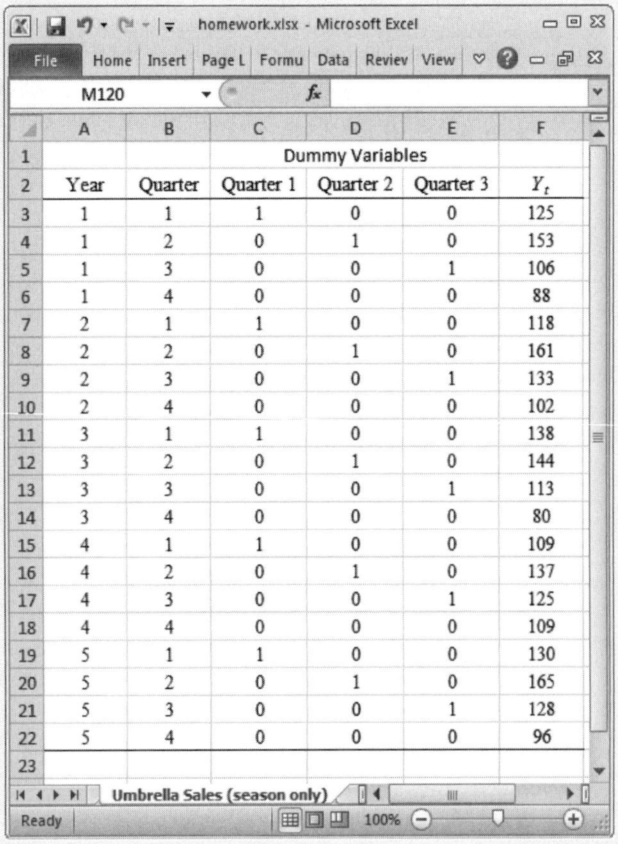

	A	B	C	D	E	F
1				Dummy Variables		
2	Year	Quarter	Quarter 1	Quarter 2	Quarter 3	Y_t
3	1	1	1	0	0	125
4	1	2	0	1	0	153
5	1	3	0	0	1	106
6	1	4	0	0	0	88
7	2	1	1	0	0	118
8	2	2	0	1	0	161
9	2	3	0	0	1	133
10	2	4	0	0	0	102
11	3	1	1	0	0	138
12	3	2	0	1	0	144
13	3	3	0	0	1	113
14	3	4	0	0	0	80
15	4	1	1	0	0	109
16	4	2	0	1	0	137
17	4	3	0	0	1	125
18	4	4	0	0	0	109
19	5	1	1	0	0	130
20	5	2	0	1	0	165
21	5	3	0	0	1	128
22	5	4	0	0	0	96
23						

Umbrella Sales (season only)

> Choose **LINEST** in the **Select a function** box
> Click **OK**

Step 5. When the **Function Arguments** dialog box appears:
> Enter F3:F22 in the **Known_y's** box
> Enter C3:E22 in the **Known_x's** box
> Click **OK**
> See Figure 15.22 for an example of this step.

Step 6. Hit the F2 key and then simultaneously hit the Shift, Control, and Enter keys (Shift + Control + Enter) to create an array that contains the values of the regression coefficients b_3, b_2, b_1, and b_0

At this point you have generated the regression coefficients b_3, b_2, b_1, and b_0 in cells G1:J1 selected in step 1. It is important to note that the first cell you selected contains b_3, the second cell you selected contains b_2, the third cell you selected contains b_1, and the fourth cell you selected contains b_0 (i.e., if you selected cells G1:J1 in step 1, the value of b_1 will be in cell G1, the value of b_2 will be in H1, the value of b_1 will be in I1, and the value of b_0 will be in cell J1).

To generate a forecast, in a blank cell, add together b_0 and the product of b_1 and Qtr1_t, the product of b_2 and Qtr2_t, and the product of b_3 and Qtr3_t. For example, if you wish to use this linear trend model to generate a forecast for the first quarter of next year and the value of b_3 is in cell G1, the value of b_2 is in cell H1, the value of b_1 is in cell I1, and the value of b_0 is in cell J1, then enter $=1*G1+0*H1+0*I1+J1$ in a blank cell. The forecast for the first quarter of next year, in this case 124.0, will appear in the blank cell in which you enter this formula.

Models with Seasonality and Linear Trend

To show how Excel can be used to fit models with seasonality and a linear trend, we develop a forecast for the umbrella set time series in Table 15.13 and Figure 15.11. We assume that the user has entered the year (1–5) for each observation into worksheet rows 3 through 22 of column A; the values for the quarter in worksheet rows 3 through 22 of column B; the values for the quarterly dummy variables Qtr1_t, Qtr2_t, and Qtr3_t into worksheet rows 3 through 22 of columns C, D, and E, respectively; the values of period t into worksheet rows 3 through 22 of column F; and the sales values into worksheet rows 3 through 22 of column G. The following steps can be used to produce a forecast for Year 11 by trend projection as shown in Figure 15.23.

FIGURE 15.22   EXCEL FUNCTION ARGUMENTS DIALOGUE BOX FOR FINDING THE SEASONAL COMPONENTS USING THE LINEST FUNCTION IN EXCEL

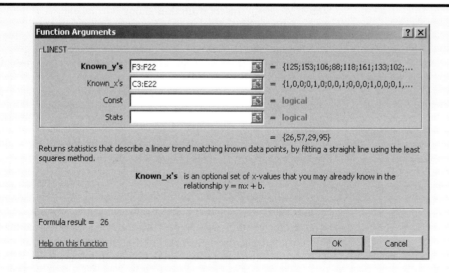

FIGURE 15.23   UMBRELLA TIME SERIES DATA IN EXCEL ARRANGED TO USE THE LINEST FUNCTION TO FIND BOTH THE SEASONAL COMPONENTS AND TREND COMPONENT

	A	B	C	D	E	F	G
1				Dummy Variables			
2	Year	Quarter	Quarter 1	Quarter 2	Quarter 3	t	Y_t
3	1	1	1	0	0	1	125
4	1	2	0	1	0	2	153
5	1	3	0	0	1	3	106
6	1	4	0	0	0	4	88
7	2	1	1	0	0	5	118
8	2	2	0	1	0	6	161
9	2	3	0	0	1	7	133
10	2	4	0	0	0	8	102
11	3	1	1	0	0	9	138
12	3	2	0	1	0	10	144
13	3	3	0	0	1	11	113
14	3	4	0	0	0	12	80
15	4	1	1	0	0	13	109
16	4	2	0	1	0	14	137
17	4	3	0	0	1	15	125
18	4	4	0	0	0	16	109
19	5	1	1	0	0	17	130
20	5	2	0	1	0	18	165
21	5	3	0	0	1	19	128
22	5	4	0	0	0	20	96
23							

Umbrella Sales (season & trend)

Step 1. Select the **Formulas** tab

Step 2. Select five cells in the row where you want the regression coefficients b_4, b_3, b_2, b_1, and b_0 to appear for this example; choose H1:L1

Step 3. Click on the **Insert Function** key

Step 4. When the **Insert Function** dialog box appears:
Choose **Statistical** in the **Or select a category** box
Choose **LINEST** in the **Select a function** box
Click **OK**

Step 5. When the **Function Arguments** dialog box appears:
Enter G3:G22 in the **Known_y's** box
Enter C3:F22 in the **Known_x's** box
Click **OK**

Step 6. Hit the F2 key and then simultaneously hit the Shift, Control, and Enter keys (Shift + Control + Enter) to create an array that contains the values of the regression coefficients b_4, b_3, b_2, b_1, and b_0

At this point you have generated the regression coefficients b_4, b_3, b_2, b_1, and b_0 in cells H1:L1 selected in step 1. It is important to note that the first cell you selected contains b_4, the second cell you selected contains b_3, the third cell you selected contains b_2, the fourth cell you selected contains b_1, and the fifth cell you selected contains b_0 (i.e., if you selected cells H1:L1 in step 1, the value of b_4 will be in cell H1, the value of b_1 will be in cell I1, the value of b_2 will be in J1, the value of b_1 will be in K1, and the value of b_0 will be in cell L1).

To generate a forecast, in a blank cell, add together b_0 and the product of b_1 and $Qtr1_t$, the product of b_2 and $Qtr2_t$, the product of b_3 and $Qtr3_t$, and the product of b_4 and t. For example, if you wish to use this linear trend model to generate a forecast for the first quarter of Year 5 and the value of b_4 is in cell H1, the value of b_3 is in cell I1, the value of b_2 is in cell J1, the value of b_1 is in cell K1, and the value of b_0 is in cell L1, then enter = 17*H1+1*I1+0*J1+0*K1+L1 in a blank cell. The forecast for the first quarter of next year, in this case 7.19, will appear in the blank cell in which you enter this formula.

Appendix 15.2   USING THE EXCEL FORECAST SHEET

Excel 2016 features a new tool called Forecast Sheet. This interface automatically produces forecasts using the Holt–Winters additive seasonal smoothing model, which is an exponential smoothing approach to estimating additive linear trend and seasonal effects. It also generates a variety of other outputs that are useful in assessing the accuracy of the forecast model it produces.

Excel refers to the forecasting approach used by Forecast: Sheet as the AAA exponential smoothing (ETS) algorithm, where AAA stands for additive error, additive trend, and additive seasonality.

We will demonstrate Forecast Sheet on the four years of quarterly smartphone sales that are provided in Table 15.6. A review of the time series plot of these data in Figure 15.6 provides clear evidence of an increasing linear trend and a seasonal pattern (sales are consistently lowest in the second quarter of each year and highest in quarters 3 and 4). We concluded in Section 15.1 that we need to use a forecasting method that is capable of dealing with both trend and seasonality when developing a forecasting model for this time series, and so it is appropriate to use Forecast Sheet to produce forecasts for these data.

We begin by putting the data into the format required by Forecast Sheet. The time series data must be collected on a consistent interval (i.e., annually, quarterly, monthly, etc.), and the spreadsheet must include two data series in contiguous columns or rows that include:

- a series with the dates or periods in the time series
- a series with corresponding time series values

DATA *file*

SmartPhoneSales

First, open the file *SmartPhoneSales*, then insert a column between column B (Quarter) and Column C (Sales (1000s)). Enter *Period* into cell C1; this will be the heading for the column of values that will represent the periods in our data. Next enter *1* in cell C2, *2* in cell C3, *3* in cell C4, and so on, ending with *16* in Cell C17 as shown in Figure 15.24.

Now that the data are properly formatted for Forecast Sheet, the following steps can be used to produce forecasts for the next four quarters (periods 17 through 20) with Forecast Sheet:

Step 1. Highlight cells C1:D17 (the data in column C of this highlighted section is what Forecast Sheet refers to as the **Timeline Range** and the data in column D is the **Values Range**).

Step 2. Click the **Data** tab in the Ribbon

Step 3. Click Forecast Sheet in the Forecast group

Step 4. When the **Create Forecast Worksheet** dialog box appears (Figure 15.25):

      Select **20** for **Forecast End**

      Click **Options** to expand the **Create Forecast Worksheet** dialog box and show the options (Figure 15.25)

          Select **16** for **Forecast Start**

          Select **95%** for **Confidence Interval**

          Under **Seasonality**, click on **Set Manually** and select **4**

          Select the checkbox for **Include forecast statistics**

          Click **Create**

Forecast Sheet requires that the period selected for Forecast Start is one of the periods of the original time series.

The results of Forecast Sheet will be output to a new worksheet as shown in Figure 15.26. The output of Forecast Sheet includes the following.

- The period for each of the 16 time series observations and the forecasted time periods in column A
- The actual time series data for periods 1 to 16 in column B

FIGURE 15.24   SMARTPHONE DATA REFORMATTED FOR FORECAST SHEET

	A	B	C	D
1	**Year**	**Quarter**	**Period**	**Sales (1000s)**
2	1	1	1	4.8
3	1	2	2	4.1
4	1	3	3	6.0
5	1	4	4	6.5
6	2	1	5	5.8
7	2	2	6	5.2
8	2	3	7	6.8
9	2	4	8	7.4
10	3	1	9	6.0
11	3	2	10	5.6
12	3	3	11	7.5
13	3	4	12	7.8
14	4	1	13	6.3
15	4	2	14	5.9
16	4	3	15	8.0
17	4	4	16	8.4

- The forecasts for periods 16 to 20 in column C
- The lower confidence bounds for the forecasts for periods 16 to 20 in column D
- The upper confidence bounds for the forecasts for periods 16 to 20 in column E
- A line graph of the time series, forecast values, and forecast interval
- The values of the three parameters (alpha, beta, and gamma) used in the Holt–Winters additive seasonal smoothing model in cells H2:H4 (these values are determined by an algorithm in Forecast Sheet)
- Measures of forecast accuracy in cells H5:H8, including:
  - the MASE, or mean absolute scaled error, in cell H5; MASE, which was not discussed in this chapter, is defined as:

$$\text{MASE} = \frac{1}{n}\sum_{t=1}^{n} \frac{|e_t|}{\frac{1}{n-1}\sum_{t=1}^{n}|y_t - y_{t-1}|}$$

  MASE compares the forecast error, e_t to a naïve forecast error given by $|y_t - y_{t-1}|$. If MASE > 1, then the forecast is considered inferior to a naïve forecast; if MASE < 1 the forecast is considered superior to a naïve forecast.

  - the SMAPE, or symmetric mean absolute percentage error, in cell H6; SMAPE, which was not discussed in this chapter, is defined as:

$$\text{SMAPE} = \frac{1}{n}\sum_{t=1}^{n} \frac{|e_t|}{(|y_t| + |\hat{y}_t|)/2}$$

  SMAPE is similar to mean absolute percentage error (MAPE), discussed in Section 8.2; both SMAPE and MAPE measure forecast error relative to actual values.

FIGURE 15.25   CREATE FORECAST WORKSHEET DIALOG BOX WITH OPTIONS OPEN
FOR QUARTERLY SMARTPHONE SALES DATA

- the MAE, or mean absolute error, (as defined in equation 8.3) in cell H7
- the RMSE, or root mean squared error, (which is the square root of the MSE, defined in equation 8.4) in cell H8

Forecast Sheet also features an algorithm for finding the number of time periods over which the seasonal pattern recurs. To use this algorithm, select the option for **Detect Automatically** under Seasonality in the **Create Forecast Worksheet** dialog box before clicking Create. We suggest using this feature only to confirm a suspected seasonal pattern (Forecast Sheet actually does successfully detect a four-period seasonal pattern in the quarterly smartphone sales data). Using this feature to find a seasonal effect may lead to identification of a spurious pattern that does not actually reflect seasonality and cannot be expected to persist in future periods. This would result in a model that is overfit on the observed time series data and would likely produce very inaccurate forecasts. A forecast model with seasonality should only be fit when the modeler has reason to suspect a specific seasonal pattern.

Forecast Sheet is actually an interface that implements several functions that are new to Excel 2016. We can recreate the output from Forecast Sheet using these Excel functions. For example, after reformatting the data in the same manner as we did in preparation

FIGURE 15.26 FORECAST SHEET RESULTS FOR QUARTERLY SMARTPHONE SALES DATA

	Period	Sales (1000s)	Forecast(Sales (1000s))	Lower Confidence Bound(Sales (1000s))	Upper Confidence Bound(Sales (1000s))		Statistic	Value
2	1	4.8					Alpha	0.50
3	2	4.1					Beta	0.00
4	3	6.0					Gamma	0.00
5	4	6.5					MASE	0.22
6	5	5.8					SMAPE	0.03
7	6	5.2					MAE	0.20
8	7	6.8					RMSE	0.27
9	8	7.4						
10	9	6.0						
11	10	5.6						
12	11	7.5						
13	12	7.8						
14	13	6.3						
15	14	5.9						
16	15	8.0						
17	16	8.4	8.4	8.4	8.4			
18	17		7.3	6.9	7.8			
19	18		6.6	6.2	7.1			
20	19		8.4	7.9	9.0			
21	20		9.0	8.4	9.6			

for using Forecast Sheet, we enter the values 17, 18, 19, and 20 into cells C18 through C21, respectively, to denote the periods for which we will be generating forecasts. We then enter the column titles *Forecast, Lower Confidence Interval, Upper Confidence Interval, Statistic,* and *Value* in cells E1 through I1, respectively. Next we enter the statistic labels *Alpha, Beta, Gamma, MASE, SMAPE, MAE,* and *RMSE* in cells H2 through H8, respectively. Finally, we enter the label Seasonality in cell H12. This updated worksheet is shown in Figure 15.27.

We can now recreate the Forecast Sheet results in the updated worksheet shown in Figure 15.27 as follows:

- The forecast generated by Forecast Sheet for period 17 for the smartphone quarterly sales data can be found by using the formula:

  =FORECAST.ETS(C18,D2:D17,C2:C17,TRUE).

  The arguments for this function are the forecast period, the time series values, the timeline associated with the time series values, and a seasonality indicator that is TRUE if Excel is to automatically detect a seasonal pattern for the forecast and FALSE otherwise.

- The margin of error for the confidence bounds generated by Forecast Sheet for period 17 for the smartphone quarterly sales data can be found by using the formula:

  =FORECAST.ETS.CONFINT(C18,D2:D17,C2:C17,0.95,TRUE)

  The confidence bounds generated by Forecast Sheet for period 17 for the smartphone quarterly sales data can be found by using the formulas:

  =E18-FORECAST.ETS.CONFINT(C18,D2:D17,C2:C17,0.95,TRUE)

FIGURE 15.27   SMARTPHONE DATA REFORMATTED FOR USE WITH EXCEL FORECAST FUNCTIONS

	A	B	C	D	E	F	G	H	I
1	Year	Quarter	Period	Sales (1000s)	Forecast	Lower Confidence Bound	Upper Confidence Bound	Statistic	Value
2	1	1	1	4.8				Alpha	
3	1	2	2	4.1				Beta	
4	1	3	3	6.0				Gamma	
5	1	4	4	6.5				MASE	
6	2	1	5	5.8				SMAPE	
7	2	2	6	5.2				MAE	
8	2	3	7	6.8				RMSE	
9	2	4	8	7.4					
10	3	1	9	6.0					
11	3	2	10	5.6					
12	3	3	11	7.5				Seasonality	
13	3	4	12	7.8					
14	4	1	13	6.3					
15	4	2	14	5.9					
16	4	3	15	8.0					
17	4	4	16	8.4					
18			17						
19			18						
20			19						
21			20						

and

$$=E18+FORECAST.ETS.CONFINT(C18,D2:D17,C2:C17,0.95,TRUE).$$

The arguments for this function are identical to the arguments for the FORECAST. ETS function.

The statistics generated by Forecast Sheet for the smartphone quarterly sales data can be found by using the formulas:

- Alpha

$$=FORECAST.ETS.STAT(D2:D17,C2:C17,1,TRUE)$$

- Beta

$$=FORECAST.ETS.STAT(D2:D17,C2:C17,2,TRUE)$$

- Gamma

$$=FORECAST.ETS.STAT(D2:D17,C2:C17,3,TRUE)$$

- MASE

$$=FORECAST.ETS.STAT(D2:D17,C2:C17,4,TRUE)$$

- SMAPE

$$=FORECAST.ETS.STAT(D2:D17,C2:C17,5,TRUE)$$

- MAE

$$=FORECAST.ETS.STAT(D2:D17,C2:C17,6,TRUE)$$

- RMSE

$$= FORECAST.ETS.STAT(D2:D17,C2:C17,7,TRUE)$$

The arguments for this function are the time series values, the timeline associated with the time series values, the statistic type, and a seasonality indicator that is TRUE if Excel is to automatically detect a seasonal pattern for the forecast and FALSE otherwise. The statistic-type argument indicates which statistic will be produced by this function. Values for the statistic-type argument include the following:

- Statistic type = 1: requests the alpha parameter used in the Holt–Winters additive seasonal smoothing model
- Statistic type = 2: requests the beta parameter used in the Holt–Winters additive seasonal smoothing model
- Statistic type = 3: requests the gamma parameter used in the Holt–Winters additive seasonal smoothing model
- Statistic type = 4: requests the MASE that results when the Holt–Winters additive seasonal smoothing model is applied to the original time series data
- Statistic type = 5: requests the SMAPE that results when the Holt–Winters additive seasonal smoothing model is applied to the original time series data
- Statistic type = 6: requests the MAE that results when the Holt–Winters additive seasonal smoothing model is applied to the original time series data
- Statistic type = 7: requests the RMSE that results when the Holt–Winters additive seasonal smoothing model is applied to the original time series data

We can also use the formula FORECAST.ETS.SEASONALITY to determine the number of periods in the seasonal pattern detected by the FORECAST.ETS formula in the smartphone quarterly sales data by entering the following formula:

=FORECAST.ETS.SEASONALITY(D2:D17,C2:C17)

We now illustrate the use of these Excel functions on the smartphone quarterly sales data. We use the:

- FORECAST.ETS function to generate forecasts for periods 17 to 20 in cells E18:E21
- FORECAST.ETS.CONFINT function to generate confidence bounds for these four forecasts in cells F18:G21 (we subtract these values from the corresponding forecast values in cells E18:E21 to create lower confidence bounds, and we add these values to the corresponding forecast values in cells E18:E21 to create upper confidence bounds)
- FORECAST.ETS.STAT function with the appropriate values for the statistics type argument to generate the parameters of our Holt–Winters additive seasonal smoothing model and measures of forecast accuracy in cells I2:I8
- FORECAST.ETS.SEASONALITY function in cell I12 to determine the number of periods in the seasonal pattern detected by the = FORECAST.ETS function.

FIGURE 15.28　FORECAST RESULTS FOR QUARTERLY SMARTPHONE SALES DATA USING EXCEL FUNCTIONS

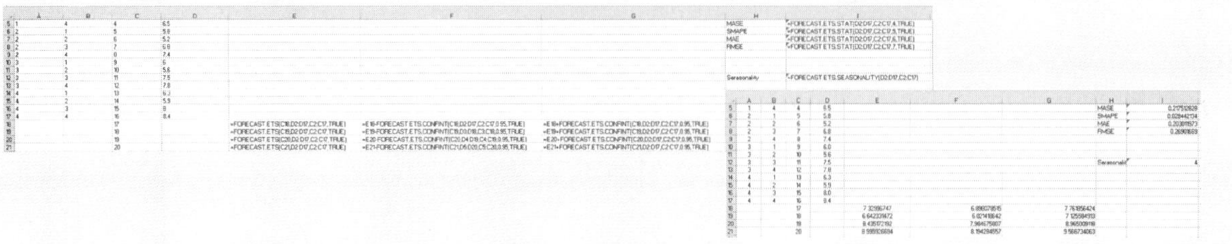

These results are provided in Figure 15.28.

Finally, note that:

- **Forecast Start** in the **Create Forecast Worksheet** dialog box controls both the first period to be forecasted and the last period to be used to generate the forecast model. If we had selected 15 for Forecast Start, we would have generated a forecast model for the smartphone monthly sales data based on only the first 15 periods of data in the original time series.
- Forecast Sheet can accommodate multiple observations for a single period of the time series. The **Aggregate Duplicates Using** option in the **Create Forecast Worksheet** dialog box allows the user to select from several ways to deal with this issue.
- Forecast Sheet allows for up to 30% of the values for the time series variable to be missing. In the smartphone quarterly sales data, the value of sales for up to 30% of the 16 periods (or 4 periods) could be missing and Forecast Sheet will still produce forecasts. The **Fill Missing Points Using** option in the **Create Forecast Worksheet** dialog box allows the user to select whether the missing values will be replaced with zero or with the result of linearly interpolating existing values in the time series.

APPENDICES

Appendix A Building Spreadsheet Models

The purpose of this appendix is twofold. First, we provide an overview of Excel and discuss the basic operations needed to work with Excel workbooks and worksheets. Second, we provide an introduction to building mathematical models using Excel, including a discussion of how to find and use particular Excel functions, how to design and build good spreadsheet models, and how to ensure that these models are free of errors.

OVERVIEW OF MICROSOFT EXCEL

A workbook is a file containing one or more worksheets.

When using Excel for modeling, the data and the model are displayed in workbooks, each of which contains a series of worksheets. Figure A.1 shows the layout of a blank workbook created each time Excel is opened. The workbook is named Book1 and contains a worksheet named Sheet1. Note that cell A1 is initially selected.

The wide bar located across the top of the workbook is referred to as the Ribbon. Tabs, located at the top of the Ribbon, provide quick access to groups of related commands. By default, eight tabs are included on the Ribbon in Excel: Home, Insert, Page Layout, Formulas, Data, Review, and View. Loading additional packages (such as Analytic Solver Platform or Acrobat) may create additional tabs. Each tab contains several groups of related commands. Note that the Home tab is selected when Excel is opened. The seven groups associated with the Home tab are displayed in Figure A.2. Under the Home tab there are seven groups of related commands: Clipboard, Font, Alignment, Number, Styles, Cells, and Editing. Commands are arranged within each group. For example, to change selected text to boldface, click the **Home** tab and click the **Bold** button B in the **Font** group.

FIGURE A.1 BLANK WORKBOOK CREATED WHEN EXCEL IS STARTED

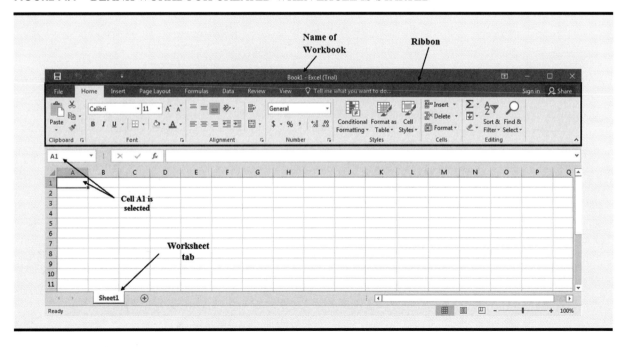

FIGURE A.2   PORTION OF THE HOME TAB

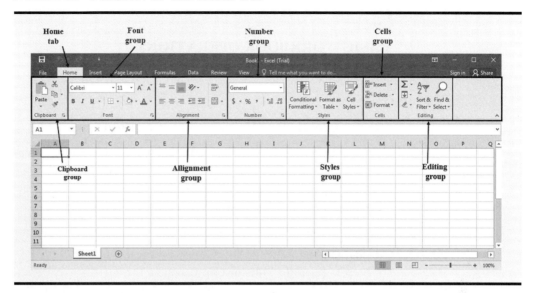

FIGURE A.3   EXCEL FILE TAB, QUICK ACCESS TOOLBAR, AND FORMULA BAR

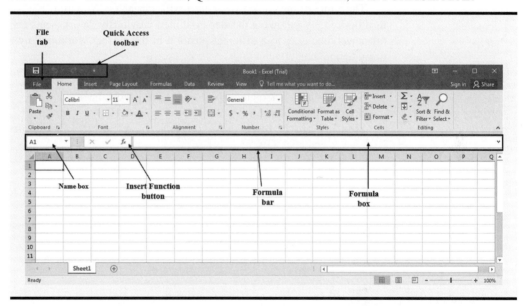

Figure A.3 illustrates the location of the File tab, the Quick Access Toolbar, and the Formula Bar. When you click the **File** tab, Excel provides a list of workbook options such as opening, saving, and printing (worksheets). The Quick Access Toolbar allows you to quickly access these workbook options. For instance, the **Quick Access Toolbar** shown in Figure A.3 includes a **Save** button 🔲 that can be used to save files without having to first click the **File** tab. To add or remove features on the **Quick Access Toolbar** click the **Customize Quick Access Toolbar** button ▼ on the **Quick Access Toolbar**.

The Formula Bar contains a Name box, the Insert Function button fx, and a Formula box. In Figure A.3, "A1" appears in the Name box because cell A1 is selected. You can select any other cell in the worksheet by using the mouse to move the cursor to another cell and clicking or by typing the new cell location in the name box and pressing the Enter key. The Formula box is used to display the formula in the currently selected cell. For instance, if you had entered $=A1+A2$ into cell A3, whenever you select cell A3, the formula $=A1+A2$ will be shown in the Formula box. This feature makes it very easy to see and edit a formula in a particular cell. The Insert Function button allows you to quickly access all of the functions available in Excel. Later, we show how to find and use a particular function.

BASIC WORKBOOK OPERATIONS

Figure A.4 illustrates the worksheet options that can be performed after right clicking on a worksheet tab.

Basic Spreadsheet Workbook Operations

To change the name of the current worksheet, we take the following steps:

Step 1. Right-click on the worksheet tab named **Sheet1**
Step 2. Select the **Rename** option
Step 3. Enter *Nowlin* to rename the worksheet and press **Enter**

You can create a copy of the newly renamed Nowlin worksheet by following these steps:

Step 1. Right-click the worksheet tab named **Nowlin**
Step 2. Select the **Move or Copy...** option
Step 3. When the **Move or Copy** dialog box appears, select the checkbox for **Create a Copy**, and click **OK**

The name of the copied worksheet will appear as "Nowlin (2)." You can then rename it, if desired, by following the steps outlined previously. Worksheets can also be moved to other workbooks or to a different position in the current workbook by using the Move or Copy option.

New worksheet can also be created using the insert worksheet button ⊕ at the bottom of the screen.

To create additional worksheets follow these steps:

Step 1. Right-click on the tab of any existing worksheet
Step 2. Select **Insert...**
Step 3. When the **Insert** dialog box appears, select **Worksheet** from the **General** area, and click **OK**

FIGURE A.4   WORKSHEET OPTIONS OBTAINED AFTER RIGHT CLICKING ON A WORKSHEET TAB

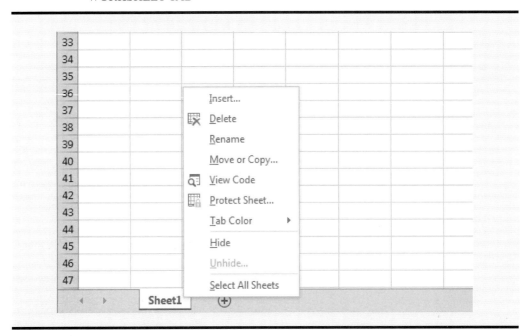

Worksheets can be deleted by right-clicking the worksheet tab and choosing **Delete**. After clicking Delete, a window may appear, warning you that any data appearing in the worksheet will be lost. Click **Delete** to confirm that you do want to delete the worksheet.

Creating, Saving, and Opening Files

As an illustration of manually entering, saving, and opening a file, we will use the Nowlin Plastics production example from Chapter 1. The objective is to compute the breakeven point for a product (the Viper cell phone cover) that has a fixed cost of $3000, a variable cost per unit of $2, and a selling price per unit of $5. We begin by creating a worksheet containing the problem data.

If you have just opened Excel, a blank workbook containing Sheet1 will be displayed. The Nowlin data can now be entered manually by simply typing the fixed cost of $3000, the variable cost of $2, and the selling price of $5 into one of the worksheets. If Excel is currently running and no blank workbook is displayed, you can create a new blank workbook using the following steps:

Step 1. Click the **File** tab on the Ribbon
Step 2. Click **New** in the list of options
Step 3. Click **Blank workbook**

A new workbook will appear.

We will place the data for the Nowlin example in the top portion of Sheet1 of the new workbook. First, we enter the label *Nowlin Plastics* into cell A1. To identify each of the three data values we enter the label *Fixed Cost* into cell A3, the label *Variable Cost per Unit* into cell A5, and the label *Selling Price per Unit* into cell A7. Next, we enter the actual cost and price data into the corresponding cells in column B: the value of *$3000* in cell B3; the value of *$2* in cell B5; and the value of *$5* into cell B7. Finally, we will change the name of the worksheet from "Sheet1" to *NowlinModel* using the procedure described previously. Figure A.5 shows a portion of the worksheet we have just developed.

Before we begin the development of the model portion of the worksheet, we recommend that you first save the current file; this will prevent you from having to reenter the data in

FIGURE A.5   NOWLIN PLASTICS DATA

	A	B
1	**Nowlin Plastics**	
2		
3	**Fixed Cost**	$3,000
4		
5	**Variable Cost Per Unit**	$2
6		
7	**Selling Price Per Unit**	$5
8		
9		
10		
11		
12		
13		
14		
15		
16		
17		
18		

case something happens that causes Excel to close. To save the workbook using the filename *Nowlin* we perform the following steps:

*In some versions of Windows, **This PC** in Step 3 may appear as **My Computer** or **Computer**.*

Step 1. Click the **File** tab on the Ribbon
Step 2. Click **Save** in the list of options
Step 3. Select **This PC** under **Save As** and click **Browse**
Step 4. When the **Save As** dialog box appears
Select the location where you want to save the file
Enter the file name *Nowlin* in the **File name:** box
Click **Save**

Excel's Save command is designed to save the file as an Excel workbook. As you work with and build models in Excel, you should follow the practice of periodically saving the file so that you will not lose any work. Simply follow the procedure described above, using the Save command.

*Keyboard shortcut: To save the file, press **CTRL S.***

Sometimes you may want to create a copy of an existing file. For instance, suppose you change one or more of the data values and would like to save the modified file using the filename *Nowlin*. The following steps show how to save the modified workbook using filename *NowlinMod*.

Step 1. Click the **File** tab in the Ribbon
Step 2. Click **Save As** in the list of options
Step 3. Select **This PC** under **Save As** and click **Browse**
Step 4. When the **Save As** dialog box appears
Select the location where you want to save the file
Type the file name *NowlinMod* in the **File name:** box
Click **Save**

Once the *NowlinMod* workbook has been saved, you can continue to work with the file to perform whatever type of analysis is appropriate. When you are finished working with the file, simply click the close window button **×** located at the top right-hand corner of the Ribbon.

You can easily access a saved file at another point in time. For example, the following steps show how to open the previously saved Nowlin workbook.

The filename Nowlin *may also appear under the **Recent Workbooks** list in Excel to allow you to open it directly without navigating to where you saved the file.*

Step 1. Click the **File** tab in the Ribbon
Step 2. Click **Open** in the list of options
Step 3. Select **This PC** under **Open** and click **Browse**
Step 4. When the **Open** dialog box appears:
Find the location where you previously saved the *Nowlin* file
Click on the filename **Nowlin** so that it appears in the **File name:** box
Click **Open**

CELLS, REFERENCES, AND FORMULAS IN EXCEL

Assume that the Nowlin workbook is open again and that we would like to develop a model that can be used to compute the profit or loss associated with a given production volume. We will use the bottom portion of the worksheet shown in Figure A.5 to develop the model. The model will contain formulas that *refer to the location of the data cells* in the upper section of the worksheet. By putting the location of the data cells in the formula, we will build a model that can be easily updated with new data. This will be discussed in more detail later in this appendix in the section Principles for Building Good Spreadsheet Models.

We enter the label *Model* into cell A10 to provide a visual reminder that the bottom portion of this worksheet will contain the model. Next, we enter the labels *Production Volume* into cell A12, *Total Cost* into cell A14, *Total Revenue* into cell A16, and *Total Profit (Loss)* into cell A18. Cell B12 is used to contain a value for the production volume. We will now enter formulas into cells B14, B16, and B18 that use the production volume in cell B12 to compute the values for total cost, total revenue, and total profit or loss.

*To display all formulas in the cells of a worksheet, hold down the **CTRL** key and then press the ~ key (usually located above the Tab key).*

Total cost is the sum of the fixed cost (cell B3) and the total variable cost. The total variable cost is the product of the variable cost per unit (cell B5) and production volume (cell B12). Thus, the formula for total variable cost is B5*B12 and to compute the value of total cost, we enter the formula $=B3+B5*B12$ into cell B14. Next, total revenue is the product of the selling price per unit (cell B7) and the number of units produced (cell B12), which we enter in cell B16 as the formula $=B7*B12$. Finally, the total profit or loss is the difference between the total revenue (cell B16) and the total cost (cell B14). Thus, in cell B18 we enter the formula $=B16-B14$. Figure A.6 shows a portion of the formula worksheet just described.

We can now compute the total profit or loss for a particular production volume by entering a value for the production volume into cell B12. Figure A.7 shows the results after

FIGURE A.6   NOWLIN PLASTICS DATA AND MODEL

	A	B
1	Nowlin Plastics	
2		
3	Fixed Cost	3000
4		
5	Variable Cost Per Unit	2
6		
7	Selling Price Per Unit	5
8		
9		
10	Models	
11		
12	Production Volume	
13		
14	Total Cost	=B3+B5*B12
15		
16	Total Revenue	=B7*B12
17		
18	Total Profit (Loss)	=B16-B14

FIGURE A.7   NOWLIN PLASTICS RESULTS

	A	B
1	Nowlin Plastics	
2		
3	Fixed Cost	$3,000
4		
5	Variable Cost Per Unit	$2
6		
7	Selling Price Per Unit	$5
8		
9		
10	Models	
11		
12	Production Volume	800
13		
14	Total Cost	$4,600
15		
16	Total Revenue	$4,000
17		
18	Total Profit (Loss)	−$600

entering a value of 800 into cell B12. We see that a production volume of 800 units results in a total cost of $4600, a total revenue of $4000, and a loss of $600.

WHAT-IF ANALYSIS

Excel offers a number of tools to facilitate what-if analysis. In this section we introduce two such tools, Data Tables and Goal Seek. Both of these tools are designed to rid the user of the tedious manual trial-and-error approach to analysis. Let us see how these two tools can help us analyze Nowlin's breakeven decision as discussed in Section 1.4.

Data Tables

An Excel Data Table quantifies the impact of changing the value of a specific input on an output of interest. Excel can generate either a one-way data table, which summarizes a single input's impact on the output, or a two-way data table, which summarizes two inputs' impact on the output.

Let us consider how profit for Nowlins Plastics changes as the quantity of Vipers produced changes. A one-way data table changing the production volume and reporting total profit (or loss) would be very useful. We will use the previously developed Nowlin spreadsheet for this analysis.

The first step in creating a one-way data table is to construct a sorted list of the values you would like to consider for the input. Let us investigate the production volume over a range from 0 to 1600 in increments of 100 units. Figure A.8 shows we have entered these data in cells D5 through D21, with a column label in D4. This column of data is the set of values that Excel will use as inputs for production volume. Since the output of interest is profit (or loss) (located in cell B18), we have entered the formula =B18 in cell E4. In general, set the cell to the right of the label to the cell location of the output variable of interest. Once the basic structure is in place, we invoke the **Data Table** tool using the following steps:

Step 1. Select cells D4:E21
Step 2. Click the **DATA** tab in the Ribbon

FIGURE A.8   THE INPUT FOR CONSTRUCTING A ONE-WAY DATA TABLE FOR NOWLIN PLASTICS

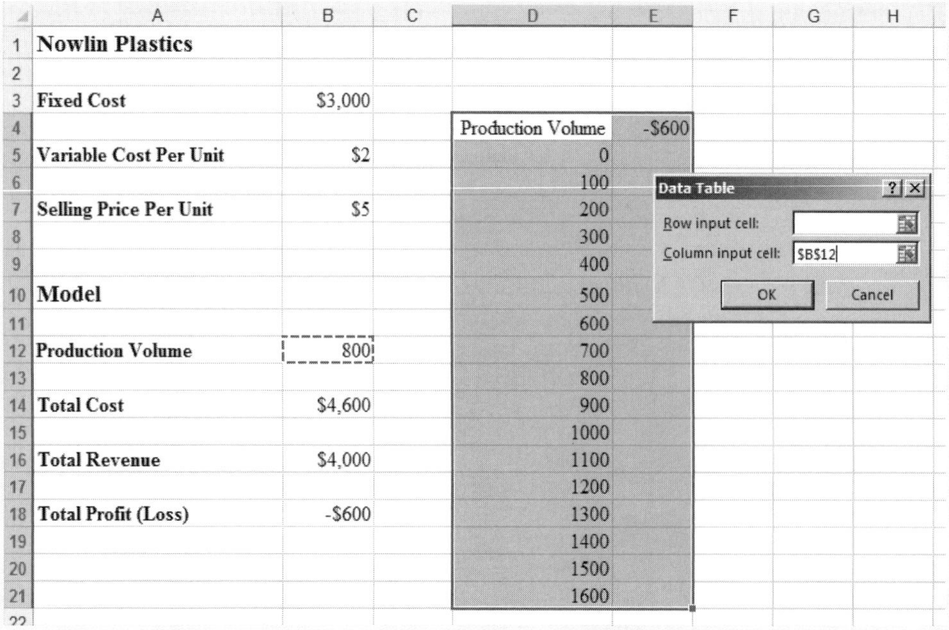

Entering B12 in the
Column input cell: *box*
indicates that the column
of data corresponds to
different values of the input
located in cell B12.

Step 3. Click **What-If Analysis** in the **Data Tools** group, and select **Data Table**

Step 4. When the **Data Table** dialog box appears, enter *B12* in the **Column input cell:** box

Click **OK**

As shown in Figure A.9, the table will be populated with profit (or loss) for each production volume in the table. For example, when production volume = 1200, profit = $600 and when production = 500, profit = 2$1,500. We see that for a production volume of 1000 units, profit = 0. Hence, 1000 units is the breakeven volume. If Nowlin produces more than 1000 units, it will earn a profit; if Nowlin produces fewer than 1000 units, it will suffer a loss.

Suppose Nowlin would like to better understand how the breakeven production volume changes as selling price changes. A two-way data table with rows corresponding to production quantity and columns corresponding to various selling prices would be helpful.

In Figure A.10, we have entered various quantities in cells D5 through D21, as in the one-way table. These correspond to cell B12 in our model. In cells E4 through L4, we have entered selling prices from $3 to $10 in increments of $1. These correspond to B7, the selling price per unit. In cell D4, above the column input values and to the left of the row input values, we have entered the formula =B18, the location of the output of interest, in this case, profit (or loss). Once the table inputs have been entered into the spreadsheet, we perform the following steps to construct the two-way Data Table.

Step 1. Select cells D4:L21

Step 2. Click the **DATA** tab in the Ribbon

Step 3. Click **What-If Analysis** in the **Data Tools** group, and select **Data Table**

Step 4. When the **Data Table** dialog box appears:

Enter *B7* in the **Row input cell:** box

Enter *B12* in the **Column input cell:** box

Click **OK**

FIGURE A.9   RESULTS OF ONE-WAY DATA TABLE FOR NOWLIN PLASTICS

	A	B	C	D	E	F
1	**Nowlin Plastics**					
2						
3	**Fixed Cost**	$3,000				
4				Production Volume	-$600	
5	**Variable Cost Per Unit**	$2		0	-$3,000	
6				100	-$2,700	
7	**Selling Price Per Unit**	$5		200	-$2,400	
8				300	-$2,100	
9				400	-$1,800	
10	**Model**			500	-$1,500	
11				600	-$1,200	
12	**Production Volume**	800		700	-$900	
13				800	-$600	
14	**Total Cost**	$4,600		900	-$300	
15				1000	$0	
16	**Total Revenue**	$4,000		1100	$300	
17				1200	$600	
18	**Total Profit (Loss)**	-$600		1300	$900	
19				1400	$1,200	
20				1500	$1,500	
21				1600	$1,800	

FIGURE A.10   THE INPUT FOR CONSTRUCTING A TWO-WAY DATA TABLE FOR NOWLIN PLASTICS

	A	B	C	D	E	F	G	H	I	J	K	L	M
1	Nowlin Plastics												
2													
3	Fixed Cost	$3,000											
4				-$600	$3	$4	$5	$6	$7	$8	$9	$10	
5	Variable Cost Per Unit	$2		0									
6				100									
7	Selling Price Per Unit	$5		200									
8				300									
9				400									
10	Model			500									
11				600									
12	Production Volume	800		700									
13				800									
14	Total Cost	$4,600		900									
15				1000									
16	Total Revenue	$4,000		1100									
17				1200									
18	Total Profit (Loss)	-$600		1300									
19				1400									
20				1500									
21				1600									
22													

Data Table
Row input cell: $B$7
Column input cell: $B$12
OK   Cancel

FIGURE A.11   RESULTS OF TWO-WAY DATA TABLE FOR NOWLIN PLASTICS

	A	B	C	D	E	F	G	H	I	J	K	L	M
1	Nowlin Plastics												
2													
3	Fixed Cost	$3,000											
4				-$600	$3	$4	$5	$6	$7	$8	$9	$10	
5	Variable Cost Per Unit	$2		0	-$3,000	-$3,000	-$3,000	-$3,000	-$3,000	-$3,000	-$3,000	-$3,000	
6				100	-$2,900	-$2,800	-$2,700	-$2,600	-$2,500	-$2,400	-$2,300	-$2,200	
7	Selling Price Per Unit	$5		200	-$2,800	-$2,600	-$2,400	-$2,200	-$2,000	-$1,800	-$1,600	-$1,400	
8				300	-$2,700	-$2,400	-$2,100	-$1,800	-$1,500	-$1,200	-$900	-$600	
9				400	-$2,600	-$2,200	-$1,800	-$1,400	-$1,000	-$600	-$200	$200	
10	Model			500	-$2,500	-$2,000	-$1,500	-$1,000	-$500	$0	$500	$1,000	
11				600	-$2,400	-$1,800	-$1,200	-$600	$0	$600	$1,200	$1,800	
12	Production Volume	800		700	-$2,300	-$1,600	-$900	-$200	$500	$1,200	$1,900	$2,600	
13				800	-$2,200	-$1,400	-$600	$200	$1,000	$1,800	$2,600	$3,400	
14	Total Cost	$4,600		900	-$2,100	-$1,200	-$300	$600	$1,500	$2,400	$3,300	$4,200	
15				1000	-$2,000	-$1,000	$0	$1,000	$2,000	$3,000	$4,000	$5,000	
16	Total Revenue	$4,000		1100	-$1,900	-$800	$300	$1,400	$2,500	$3,600	$4,700	$5,800	
17				1200	-$1,800	-$600	$600	$1,800	$3,000	$4,200	$5,400	$6,600	
18	Total Profit (Loss)	-$600		1300	-$1,700	-$400	$900	$2,200	$3,500	$4,800	$6,100	$7,400	
19				1400	-$1,600	-$200	$1,200	$2,600	$4,000	$5,400	$6,800	$8,200	
20				1500	-$1,500	$0	$1,500	$3,000	$4,500	$6,000	$7,500	$9,000	
21				1600	-$1,400	$200	$1,800	$3,400	$5,000	$6,600	$8,200	$9,800	
22													

Figure A.10 shows the selected cells and the Data Table dialog box. The results are shown in Figure A.11.

From this two-way data table, we can make a number of observations about the break-even production volume for various selling prices. For example, consider a selling price of $3; since losses are smaller at higher production volumes and there is a loss at 1600 units, we know that the breakeven production volume exceeds 1600 units. Likewise, we know the breakeven point for a selling price of $4 is 1500 units ($0 profit there). Similarly, we know the exact breakeven points for selling prices of $5, $7, and $8 are 1000, 600, and 500, respectively. Because of the change in sign from negative to positive (indicating a change from loss to profit), we see that the breakeven production volume for a selling price of $6 is between 700 and 800 units. For a selling price of $9, the breakeven is between 400 and 500 units, and for a selling price of $10 it is between 300 and 400 units. Next we show how to use Excel's Goal Seek tool to find the exact breakeven production volume for these selling prices.

Goal Seek

Excel's Goal Seek tool allows the user to determine the value of an input cell that will cause the value of a related output cell to equal some specified value (the *goal*). In the case of Nowlin Plastics, suppose we want to know the exact breakeven production volume for a selling price of $6. We know from the two-way data table in Figure A.11 that the breakeven volume for a selling price of $6 is between 700 and 800 units (that is where the profit goes from negative to positive). Somewhere in this range of 700 to 800 units, the profit equals zero, and the production quantity where this occurs is the breakeven point. After setting cell B7 to $6, the following steps show how to use Goal Seek to find the breakeven point for this selling price.

Step 1. Click the **DATA** tab in the Ribbon
Step 2. Click **What-If Analysis** in the **Data Tools** group, and select **Goal Seek**
Step 3. When the **Goal Seek** dialog box appears (Figure A.12):
  Enter *B18* in the **Set cell:** box
  Enter *0* in the **To value:** box
  Enter *B12* in the **By changing cell:** box
  Click **OK**
Step 4. When the **Goal Seek Status** dialog box appears, click **OK**

The completed Goal Seek dialog box is shown in Figure A.12.
  The results from Goal Seek are shown in Figure A.13. We see that the breakeven point for a selling price of $6 is 750 units.

FIGURE A.12 GOAL SEEK DIALOG BOX FOR NOWLIN PLASTICS

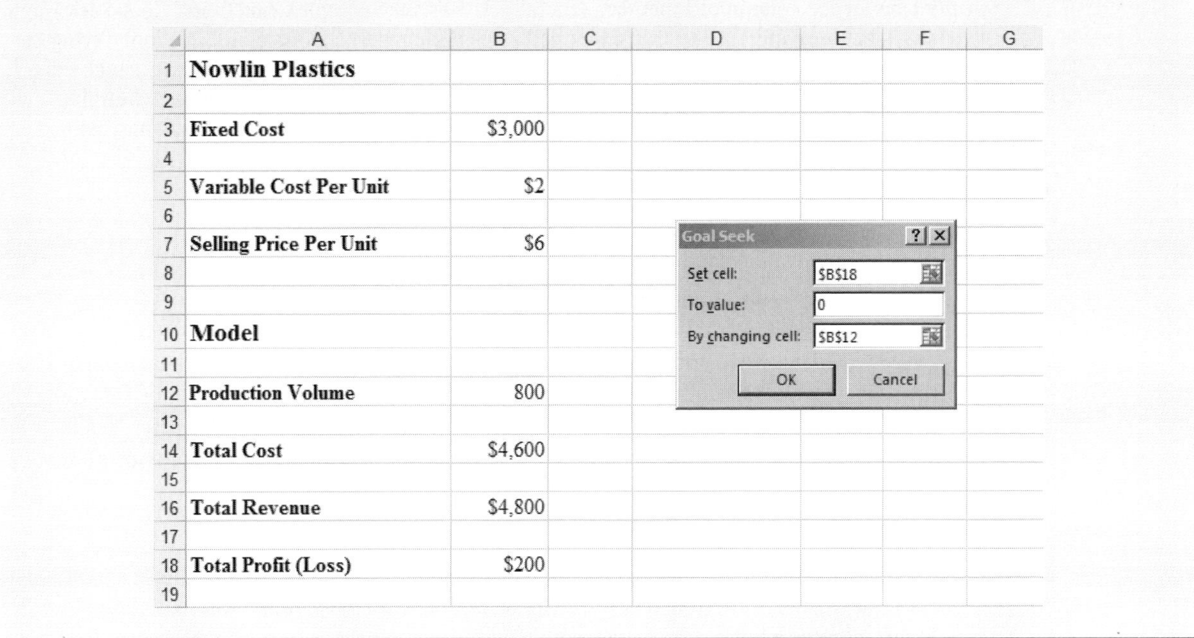

	A	B	C	D	E	F	G
1	**Nowlin Plastics**						
2							
3	**Fixed Cost**	$3,000					
4							
5	**Variable Cost Per Unit**	$2					
6							
7	**Selling Price Per Unit**	$6		Goal Seek		? X	
8				Set cell:	$B$18		
9				To value:	0		
10	**Model**			By changing cell:	$B$12		
11							
12	**Production Volume**	800		OK	Cancel		
13							
14	**Total Cost**	$4,600					
15							
16	**Total Revenue**	$4,800					
17							
18	**Total Profit (Loss)**	$200					
19							

FIGURE A.13   RESULTS FROM GOAL SEEK FOR NOWLIN PLASTICS

	A	B	C	D	E	F	G
1	**Nowlin Plastics**						
2							
3	**Fixed Cost**	$3,000					
4							
5	**Variable Cost Per Unit**	$2					
6							
7	**Selling Price Per Unit**	$6					
8							
9							
10	**Model**						
11							
12	**Production Volume**	750					
13							
14	**Total Cost**	$4,500					
15							
16	**Total Revenue**	$4,500					
17							
18	**Total Profit (Loss)**	$0					
19							

Goal Seek Status dialog box:
Goal Seeking with Cell B18 found a solution.
Target value: 0
Current value: $0
[Step] [Pause] [OK] [Cancel]

NOTES AND COMMENTS

1. We emphasize the location of the reference to the desired output in a one-way versus a two-way Data Table. For a one-way table, the reference to the output cell location is placed in the cell above and to the right of the column of input data so that it is in the cell just to the right of the label of the column of input data. For a two-way table, the reference to the output cell location is placed above the column of input data and to the left of the row input data.

2. Notice that in Figures A.9 and A.11, the tables are formatted as currency. This must be done manually after the table is constructed using the options in the **Number** group under the **HOME** tab in the Ribbon. It also a good idea to label the rows and the columns of the table.

3. For very complex functions, Goal Seek might not converge to a stable solution. Trying several different initial values (the actual value in the cell referenced in the **By changing cell:** box) when invoking Goal Seek may help..

USING EXCEL FUNCTIONS

Excel provides a wealth of built-in formulas or functions for developing mathematical models. If we know which function is needed and how to use it, we can simply enter the function into the appropriate worksheet cell. However, if we are not sure which functions are available to accomplish a task or are not sure how to use a particular function, Excel can provide assistance.

Finding the Right Excel Function

To identify the functions available in Excel, click the **Formulas** tab on the Ribbon and then click the **Insert Function** button in the **Function Library** group. Alternatively, click the **Insert Function** button *fx* on the formula bar. Either approach provides the **Insert Function dialog box** shown in Figure A.14.

FIGURE A.14   INSERT FUNCTION DIALOG BOX

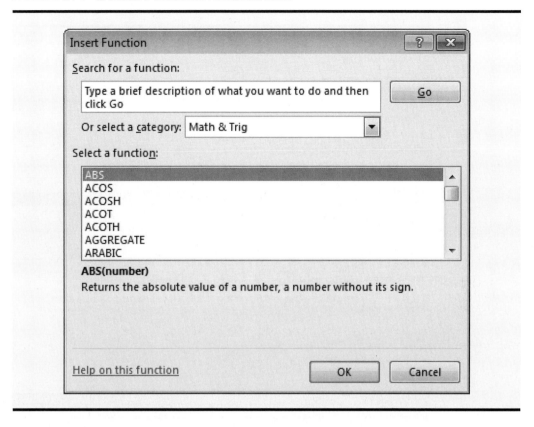

The **Search for a function** box at the top of the **Insert Function dialog box** enables us to type a brief description for what we want to do. After doing so and clicking **Go**, Excel will search for and display, in the **Select a function box**, the functions that may accomplish our task. In many situations, however, we may want to browse through an entire category of functions to see what is available. For this task, the **Or select a category box** is helpful.

It contains a dropdown list of several categories of functions provided by Excel. Figure A.14 shows that we selected the Math & Trig category. As a result, Excel's Math & Trig functions appear in alphabetical order in the Select a function box. We see the ABS function listed first, followed by the ACOS function, and so on.

Colon Notation

Although many functions, such as the ABS function, have a single argument, some Excel functions depend on arrays. Colon notation provides an efficient way to convey arrays and matrices of cells to functions. The colon notation may be described as follows: B3:B5 means cell B1 "through" cell B5, namely the array of values stored in the locations (B1,B2,B3,B4,B5). Consider for example the following function =SUM(B1:B5). The sum function adds up the elements contained in the function's argument. Hence, =SUM(B1:B5) evaluates the following formula:

$$=B1+B2+B3+B4+B5$$

Inserting a Function into a Worksheet Cell

Through the use of an example, we will now show how to use the Insert Function and Function Arguments dialog boxes to select a function, develop its arguments, and insert the function into a worksheet cell. We also illustrate the use of a very useful function, the SUM-PRODUCT function, and how to use colon notation in the argument of a function.

FIGURE A.15   DESCRIPTION OF THE SUMPRODUCT FUNCTION IN THE INSERT
FUNCTION DIALOG BOX

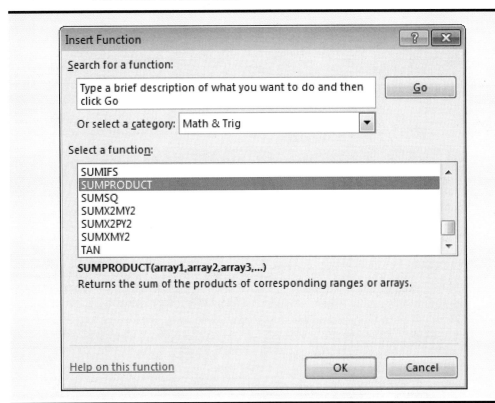

The SUMPRODUCT function, as shown in Figure A.15, is used in many of the Solver examples in the textbook. Note that SUMPRODUCT is now highlighted, and that immediately below the **Select a function** box we see SUMPRODUCT(array1,array2,array3, . . .), which indicates that the SUMPRODUCT function contains the array arguments array1, array2, array3, ... In addition, we see that the description of the SUMPRODUCT function is "Returns the sum of the products of corresponding ranges or arrays." For example, the function =SUMPRODUCT(A1:A3, B1:B3) evaluates the formula A1*B1 + A2*B2 + A3*B3. As shown in the following example, this function can be very useful in calculations of cost, profit, and other such functions involving multiple arrays of numbers.

Figure A.16 displays an Excel worksheet for the Foster Generators Problem that appears in Chapter 6. This problem involves the transportation of a product from three plants (Cleveland, Bedford, and York) to four distribution centers (Boston, Chicago, St. Louis, and Lexington). The costs for each unit shipped from each plant to each distribution center are shown in cells B5:E7, and the values in cells B17:E19 are the number of units shipped from each plant to each distribution center. Cell B13 will contain the total transportation cost corresponding to the transportation cost values in cells B5:E7 and the values of the number of units shipped in cells B17:E19.

The following steps show how to use the SUMPRODUCT function to compute the total transportation cost for Foster Generators.

Step 1. Select cell C13
Step 2. Click *fx* on the formula bar
Step 3. When the **Insert Function** dialog box appears:
  Select **Math & Trig** in the **Or select a category** box
  Select **SUMPRODUCT** in the **Select a function** box (as shown in Figure A.15)
  Click **OK**

FIGURE A.16   EXCEL WORKSHEET USED TO CALCULATE TOTAL SHIPPING COSTS
FOR THE FOSTER GENERATORS TRANSPORTATION PROBLEM

MODEL *file*

FosterGenerators

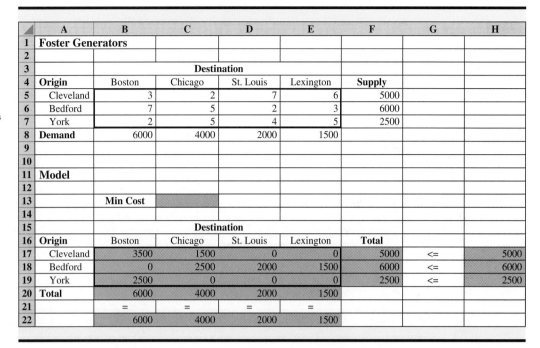

	A	B	C	D	E	F	G	H
1	**Foster Generators**							
2								
3				**Destination**				
4	**Origin**	Boston	Chicago	St. Louis	Lexington	**Supply**		
5	Cleveland	3	2	7	6	5000		
6	Bedford	7	5	2	3	6000		
7	York	2	5	4	5	2500		
8	**Demand**	6000	4000	2000	1500			
9								
10								
11	**Model**							
12								
13		**Min Cost**						
14								
15				**Destination**				
16	**Origin**	Boston	Chicago	St. Louis	Lexington	**Total**		
17	Cleveland	3500	1500	0	0	5000	<=	5000
18	Bedford	0	2500	2000	1500	6000	<=	6000
19	York	2500	0	0	0	2500	<=	2500
20	**Total**	6000	4000	2000	1500			
21		=	=	=	=			
22		6000	4000	2000	1500			

FIGURE A.17   COMPLETED FUNCTION ARGUMENTS DIALOG BOX FOR THE
SUMPRODUCT FUNCTION

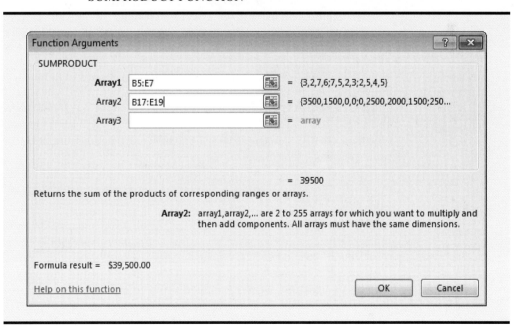

Step 4. When the **Function Arguments** box appears (see Figure A.17):
Enter *B5:E7* in the **Array1** box
Enter *B17:E19* in the **Array2** box
Click **OK**

FIGURE A.18   EXCEL WORKSHEET SHOWING THE USE OF EXCEL'S SUMPRODUCT
FUNCTION TO CALCULATE TOTAL SHIPPING COSTS

	A	B	C	D	E	F	G	H
1	Foster Generators							
2								
3			Destination					
4	Origin	Boston	Chicago	St. Louis	Lexington	Supply		
5	Cleveland	3	2	7	6	5000		
6	Bedford	7	5	2	3	6000		
7	York	2	5	4	5	2500		
8	Demand	6000	4000	2000	1500			
9								
10								
11	Model							
12								
13		Min Cost	39500					
14								
15			Destination					
16	Origin	Boston	Chicago	St. Louis	Lexington	Total		
17	Cleveland	3500	1500	0	0	5000	<=	5000
18	Bedford	0	2500	2000	1500	6000	<=	6000
19	York	2500	0	0	0	2500	<=	2500
20	Total	6000	4000	2000	1500			
21		=	=	=	=			
22		6000	4000	2000	1500			

The worksheet then appears as shown in Figure A.18. The value of the total transportation cost in cell C13 is 39500, or \$39,500.

We illustrated the use of Excel's capability to provide assistance in using the SUMPRODUCT function. The procedure is similar for all Excel functions. This capability is especially helpful if you do not know which function to use or forget the proper name and/ or syntax for a function.

ADDITIONAL EXCEL FUNCTIONS FOR MODELING

In this section we introduce some additional Excel functions that have proven useful in modeling decision problems.

IF and COUNTIF Functions

Let us consider the case of Gambrell Manufacturing. Gambrell Manufacturing produces car stereos. Stereos are composed of a variety of components that the company must carry in inventory to keep production running smoothly. However, because inventory can be a costly investment, Gambrell generally likes to keep the amount of inventory of the components it uses in manufacturing to a minimum. To help monitor and control its inventory of components, Gambrell uses an inventory policy known as an "order up to" policy. This type of inventory policy and others are discussed in detail in Chapter 10.

The "order up to" policy is as follows. Whenever the inventory on hand drops below a certain level, enough units are ordered to return the inventory to that predetermined level. If the current number of units in inventory, denoted by H, drops below M units, we order enough to get the inventory level back up to M units. M is called the Order Up to Point. Stated mathematically, if Q is the amount we order, then

$$Q = M - H$$

FIGURE A.19   THE GAMBRELL MANUFACTURING COMPONENT ORDERING MODEL

MODEL *file*

Gambrell

	A	B	C	D	E	F
4	Component ID	570	578	741	755	
5	Inventory On-Hand	5	30	70	17	
6	Up to Order Point	100	55	70	45	
7	Cost per unit	$4.50	$12.50	$3.26	$4.15	
8						
9	Fixed Cost per Order	$120				
10						
11	**Model**					
12						
13	Component ID	570	578	741	755	
14	Order Quantity	95	25	0	28	
15	Cost of Goods	$384.75	$312.50	$0.00	$116.20	
16						
17	Total Number of Orders	3				
18						
19	Total Fixed costs	$360.00				
20	Total Cost of Goods	$813.45				
21	Total Cost	$1,173.45				
22						

An inventory model for Gambrell Manufacturing appears in Figure A.19. In this worksheet, labeled *Order Quantity* in the upper half of the worksheet, the component ID number, inventory on hand (H), order up to point (M), and cost per unit are given for each of four components. Also given in this sheet is the fixed cost per order. The fixed cost is interpreted as follows: Each time a component is ordered, it costs Gambrell $120 to process the order. The fixed cost of $120 is incurred regardless of how many units are ordered.

The model portion of the worksheet calculates the order quantity for each component. For example, for component 570, $M = 100$ and $H = 5$, so $Q = M - H = 100 - 5 = 95$. For component 741, $M = 70$ and $H = 70$ and no units are ordered because the on-hand inventory of 70 units is equal to the order point of 70. The calculations are similar for the other two components.

Depending on the number of units ordered, Gambrell receives a discount on the cost per unit. If 50 or more units are ordered, there is a quantity discount of 10% on every unit purchased. For example, for component 741, the cost per unit is $4.50 and 95 units are ordered. Because 95 exceeds the 50-unit requirement, there is a 10% discount and the cost per unit is reduced to $4.50 - 0.1($4.50) = $4.50 - $0.45 = $4.05. Not including the fixed cost, the cost of goods purchased is then $4.05(95) = $384.75.

The Excel functions used to perform these calculations are shown in Figure A.20. The IF function is used to calculate the purchase cost of goods for each component in row 15. The general form of the IF function is

=IF(*condition, result if condition is true, result if condition is false*)

For example, in cell B15 we have =IF(B14>=50,0.9*B7,B7)*B14. This statement says if the order quantity (cell B14) is greater than or equal to 50, then the cost per unit is 0.9*B7 (there is a 10% discount); otherwise, there is no discount and the cost per unit is the amount given in cell B7. The purchase cost of goods for the other components is computed in a like manner.

The total cost in cell B21 is the sum of the purchase cost of goods ordered in row 15 and the fixed ordering costs. Because we place three orders (one each for components 570, 578, and 755), the fixed cost of the orders is 3*120 = $360.

The COUNTIF function in cell B17 is used to count how many times we order. In particular, it counts the number of components having a positive order quantity. The general form of the COUNTIF function is

=COUNTIF(*range, condition*)

FIGURE A.20   FORMULAS AND FUNCTIONS FOR GAMBRELL MANUFACTURING

	A	B	C	D	E
1					
2	**Gambrell Manufacturing**				
3					
4	Component ID	570	578	741	755
5	Inventory On-Hand	5	30	70	17
6	Up to Order Point	100	55	70	45
7	Cost per unit	4.5	12.5	3.26	4.15
8					
9	Fixed Cost per Order	120			
10					
11	**Model**				
12					
13	Component ID	=B4	=C4	=D4	=E4
14	Order Quantity	=B6-B5	=C6-C5	=D6-D5	=E6-E5
15	Cost of Goods	=IF(B14>=50,0.9*B7,B7)*B14	=IF(C14>=50, 0.9*C7,C7)*C14	=IF(D14>=50, 0.9*D7,D7)*D14	=IF(E14>=50, 0.9*E7,E7)*E14
16					
17	Total Number of Orders	=COUNTIF(B14:E14,">0")			
18					
19	Total Fixed Costs	=B17*B9			
20	Total Cost of Goods	=SUM(B15:E15)			
21	Total Cost	=SUM(B19:B20)			
22					

The *range* is the range to search for the *condition*. The condition is the test to be counted when satisfied. *Note that quotes are required for the condition with the COUNTIF function.* In the Gambrell model in Figure A.20, cell B17 counts the number of cells that are greater than zero in the range of cells B14:E14. In the model, because only cells B14, C14, and E14 are greater than zero, the COUNTIF function in cell B17 returns 3.

As we have seen, IF and COUNTIF are powerful functions that allow us to make calculations based on a condition holding (or not). There are other such conditional functions available in Excel. In the problems at the end of this appendix, we ask you to investigate one such function, the SUMIF function. Another conditional function that is extremely useful in modeling is the VLOOKUP function. We discuss the VLOOKUP function with an example in the next section.

VLOOKUP Function

Next, consider the workbook named *OM455* shown in Figure A.21. The worksheet named Grades is shown. This worksheet calculates the course grades for the course OM 455. There are 11 students in the course. Each student has a midterm exam score and a final exam score, and these are averaged in column D to get the course average. The scale given in the upper portion of the worksheet is used to determine the course grade for each student. Consider, for example, the performance of student Choi in row 16. This student earned an 82 on the midterm, an 80 on the final, and a course average of 81. From the grading scale, this equates to a course grade of B.

The course average is simply the average of the midterm and final scores, but how do we get Excel to look in the grading scale table and automatically assign the correct course letter grade to each student? The VLOOKUP function allows us to do just that. The formulas and functions used in *OM455* are shown in Figure A.22.

The VLOOKUP function allows the user to pull a subset of data from a larger table of data based on some criterion. The general form of the VLOOKUP function is

$$=VLOOKUP(arg1, arg2, arg3, arg4)$$

where *arg1* is the value to search for in the first column of the table, *arg2* is the table location, *arg3* is the column location in the table to be returned, and *arg4* is TRUE if looking for

FIGURE A.21   OM455 GRADE SPREADSHEET

MODEL *file*

OM455

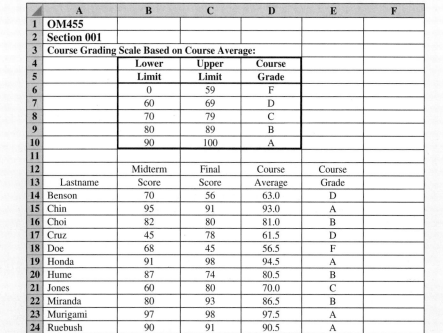

	A	B	C	D	E	F
1	OM455					
2	Section 001					
3	Course Grading Scale Based on Course Average:					
4		Lower	Upper	Course		
5		Limit	Limit	Grade		
6		0	59	F		
7		60	69	D		
8		70	79	C		
9		80	89	B		
10		90	100	A		
11						
12		Midterm	Final	Course	Course	
13	Lastname	Score	Score	Average	Grade	
14	Benson	70	56	63.0	D	
15	Chin	95	91	93.0	A	
16	Choi	82	80	81.0	B	
17	Cruz	45	78	61.5	D	
18	Doe	68	45	56.5	F	
19	Honda	91	98	94.5	A	
20	Hume	87	74	80.5	B	
21	Jones	60	80	70.0	C	
22	Miranda	80	93	86.5	B	
23	Murigami	97	98	97.5	A	
24	Ruebush	90	91	90.5	A	
25						

FIGURE A.22   THE FORMULAS AND FUNCTIONS USED IN OM455

	A	B	C	D	E
1	OM 455				
2	Section 001				
3	Course Grading Scale Based on Course Average:				
4		Lower	Upper	Course	
5		Limit	Limit	Grade	
6		0	59	F	
7		60	69	D	
8		70	79	C	
9		80	89	B	
10		90	100	A	
11					
12		Midterm	Final	Course	Course
13	Lastname	Score	Score	Average	Grade
14	Benson	70	56	=AVERAGE(B14:C14)	=VLOOKUP(D14,B6:D10,3,TRUE)
15	Chin	95	91	=AVERAGE(B15:C15)	=VLOOKUP(D15,B6:D10,3,TRUE)
16	Choi	82	80	=AVERAGE(B16:C16)	=VLOOKUP(D16,B6:D10,3,TRUE)
17	Cruz	45	78	=AVERAGE(B17:C17)	=VLOOKUP(D17,B6:D10,3,TRUE)
18	Doe	68	45	=AVERAGE(B18:C18)	=VLOOKUP(D18,B6:D10,3,TRUE)
19	Honda	91	98	=AVERAGE(B19:C19)	=VLOOKUP(D19,B6:D10,3,TRUE)
20	Hume	87	74	=AVERAGE(B20:C20)	=VLOOKUP(D20,B6:D10,3,TRUE)
21	Jones	60	80	=AVERAGE(B21:C21)	=VLOOKUP(D21,B6:D10,3,TRUE)
22	Miranda	80	93	=AVERAGE(B22:C22)	=VLOOKUP(D22,B6:D10,3,TRUE)
23	Murigami	97	98	=AVERAGE(B23:C23)	=VLOOKUP(D23,B6:D10,3,TRUE)
24	Ruebush	90	91	=AVERAGE(B24:C24)	=VLOOKUP(D24,B6:D10,3,TRUE)
25					

the first partial match of *arg1* and FALSE for looking for an exact match of *arg1*. We will explain the difference between a partial and exact match in a moment. VLOOKUP assumes that the first column of the table is sorted in ascending order.

The VLOOKUP function for student Choi in cell E16 is as follows:

$$=VLOOKUP(D16,B6:D10,3,TRUE)$$

This function uses the course average from cell D16 and searches the first column of the table defined by B6:D10. In the first column of the table (column B), Excel searches from the top until it finds a number strictly greater than the value of D16 (81). It then backs up one row (to row 9). That is, it finds the last value in the first column less than or equal to 81. Because there is a 3 in the third argument of the VLOOKUP function, it takes the element in row 9 in the third column of the table, which is the letter "B." In summary, the VLOOKUP takes the first argument and searches the first column of the table for the last row that is less than or equal to the first argument. It then selects from that row the element in the column number of the third argument.

Note: If the last element of the VLOOKUP function is "False," the only change is that Excel searches for an exact match of the first argument in the first column of the data. VLOOKUP is very useful when you seek subsets of a table based on a condition.

PRINCIPLES FOR BUILDING GOOD SPREADSHEET MODELS

We have covered some of the fundamentals of building spreadsheet models. There are some generally accepted guiding principles for how to build a spreadsheet so that it is more easily used by others and so that the risk of error is mitigated. In this section we discuss some of those principles.

Separate the Data from the Model

One of the first principles of good modeling is to separate the data from the model. This enables the user to update the model parameters without fear of mistakenly typing over a formula or function. For this reason, it is good practice to have a data section at the top of the spreadsheet. A separate model section should contain all calculations and in general should not be updated by a user. For a what-if model or an optimization model, there might also be a separate section for decision cells (values that are not data or calculations, but are the outputs we seek from the model).

The Nowlin model in Figure A.6 is a good example. The data section is in the upper part of the spreadsheet followed by the model section that contains the calculations. The Gambrell model in Figure A.19 does not totally employ the principle of data/model separation. A better model would have the 50-unit hurdle and the 90% cost (10% discount) as data in the upper section. Then the formulas in row 15 would simply refer to the cells in the upper section. This would allow the user to easily change the discount, for example, without having to change all four formulas in row 15.

Document the Model

A good spreadsheet model is well documented. Clear labels and proper formatting and alignment make the spreadsheet easier to navigate and understand. For example, if the values in a worksheet are cost, currency formatting should be used. No cells should be unlabeled. A new user should be able to easily understand the model and its calculations. Figure A.23 shows a better-documented version of the Foster Generators model previously discussed (Figure A.16). The tables are more explicitly labeled, and shading focuses the user on the objective and the decision cells (amount to ship). The per-unit shipping cost data and total (Min) cost have been properly formatted as currency.

Use Simple Formulas and Cell Names

Clear formulas can eliminate unnecessary calculations, reduce errors, and make it easier to maintain your spreadsheet. Long and complex calculations should be divided into several

FIGURE A.23   A BETTER-DOCUMENTED FOSTER GENERATORS MODEL

MODEL *file*

FosterRev

	A	B	C	D	E	F	G	H
1	**Foster Generators**							
2								
3	Origin to Destination—Cost per unit to ship							
4			**Destination**					
5	**Origin**	Boston	Chicago	St. Louis	Lexington	**Units Available**		
6	Cleveland	$3.00	$2.00	$7.00	$6.00	5000		
7	Bedford	$7.00	$5.00	$2.00	$3.00	6000		
8	York	$2.00	$5.00	$4.00	$5.00	2500		
9	**Units Demanded**	6000	4000	2000	1500			
10								
11								
12	**Model**							
13								
14		**Min Cost**	$39,500.00					
15								
16	Origin to Destination—Units Shipped							
17			**Destination**					
18	**Origin**	Boston	Chicago	St. Louis	Lexington	**Units Shipped**		
19	Cleveland	3500	1500	0	0	5000	<=	5000
20	Bedford	0	2500	2000	1500	6000	<=	6000
21	York	2500	0	0	0	2500	<=	2500
22	**Units Received**	6000	4000	2000	1500			
23		=	=	=	=			
24		6000	4000	2000	1500			

cells. This makes the formula easier to understand and easier to edit. Avoid using numbers in a formula. Instead, put the number in a cell in the data section of your worksheet and refer to the cell location of the data in the formula. Building the formula in this manner avoids having to edit the formula for a simple data change.

Using cell names can make a formula much easier to understand. To assign a name to a cell, use the following steps:

Step 1. Select the cell or range of cells you would like to name
Step 2. Select the **Formulas** tab on the Ribbon
Step 3. Choose **Define Name** from the **Defined Names** section
Step 4. The **New Name** dialog box will appear, as shown in Figure A.24
Enter the name you would like to use in the top portion of the dialog box and Click **OK**

Following this procedure and naming all cells in the *NowlinPlastics* spreadsheet model leads to the model shown in Figure A.25. Compare this to Figure A.6 to easily understand the formulas in the model.

A name is also easily applied to range as follows. First, highlight the range of interest. Then click on the **Name Box** in the **Formula Bar** (refer back to Figure A.3) and type in the desired range name.

Use of Relative and Absolute Cell References

There are a number of ways to copy a formula from one cell to another in an Excel worksheet. One way to copy a formula from one cell to another is presented here:

Step 1. Select the cell you would like to copy
Step 2. Right click on the mouse
Step 3. Click **Copy**

FIGURE A.24   THE NEW NAME DIALOG BOX

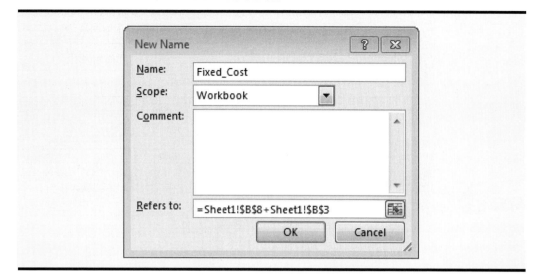

FIGURE A.25   THE NOWLIN PLASTICS MODEL FORMULAS WITH NAMED CELLS

	A	B
1	**Nowlin Plastics**	
2		
3	**Fixed Cost**	3000
4		
5	**Variable Cost Per Unit**	2
6		
7	**Selling Price Per Unit**	5
8		
9		
10	**Models**	
11		
12	**Production Volume**	800
13		
14	**Total Cost**	=Fixed_Cost+Variable_Cost*Production_Volume
15		
16	**Total Revenue**	=Selling_Price*Production_Volume
17		
18	**Total Profit (Loss)**	=Total_Revenue-Total_Cost

Step 4. Select the cell where you would like to put the copy
Step 5. Right click on the mouse
Step 6. Click **Paste**

When copying in Excel, one can use a relative or an absolute address. When copied, a relative address adjusts with the move of the copy, whereas an absolute address stays in its original form. Relative addresses are of the form C7. Absolute addresses have $ in front of the column and row, for example, $C$7. How you use relative and absolute addresses can have an impact on the amount of effort it takes to build a model and the opportunity for error in constructing the model.

Let us reconsider the OM455 grading spreadsheet previously discussed in this appendix and shown in Figure A.22. Recall that we used the VLOOKUP function to retrieve the appropriate letter grade for each student. The following formula is in cell E14:

$$=VLOOKUP(D14,B6:D10,3,TRUE)$$

Note that this formula contains only relative addresses. If we copy this to cell E15, we get the following result:

$$=VLOOKUP(D15,B7:D11,3,TRUE)$$

Although the first argument has correctly changed to D15 (we want to calculate the letter grade for the student in row 15), the table in the function has also shifted to B7:D11. What we desired was for this table location to remain the same. A better approach would have been to use the following formula in cell E14:

$$=VLOOKUP(D14,\$B\$6:\$D\$10,3,TRUE)$$

Copying this formula to cell E15 results in the following formula:

$$=VLOOKUP(D15,\$B\$6:\$D\$10,3,TRUE)$$

This correctly changes the first argument to D15 and keeps the data table intact. Using absolute referencing is extremely useful if you have a function that has a reference that should not change when applied to another cell and you are copying the formula to other locations. In the case of the OM455 workbook, instead of typing the VLOOKUP for each student, we can use absolute referencing on the table and then copy from row 14 to rows 15 through 24.

In this section we have discussed guidelines for good spreadsheet model building. In the next section we discuss EXCEL tools available for checking and debugging spreadsheet models.

AUDITING EXCEL MODELS

EXCEL contains a variety of tools to assist you in the development and debugging of spreadsheet models. These tools are found in the **Formula Auditing** group of the **Formulas** tab as shown in Figure A.26. Let us review each of the tools available in this group.

Trace Precedents and Dependents

The **Trace Precedents** button ⊞ Trace Precedents creates arrows pointing to the selected cell from cells that are part of the formula in that cell. The **Trace Dependents** button ⊞ Trace Dependents , on the other hand, shows arrows pointing from the selected cell, to cells that depend on the selected cell. Both of the tools are excellent for quickly ascertaining how parts of a model are linked.

An example of Trace Precedents is shown in Figure A.27. Here we have opened the *Foster Rev* worksheet, selected cell C14, and clicked the **Trace Precedents** button in

FIGURE A.26   THE FORMULA AUDITING GROUP OF THE FORMULAS TAB

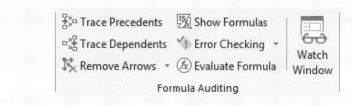

FIGURE A.27   TRACE PRECEDENTS FOR CELL C14 (COST) IN THE FOSTER GENERATORS REV MODEL

C14			f_x	=SUMPRODUCT(B6:E8,B19:E21)			
	A	**B**	**C**	**D**	**E**	**F**	**G**	**H**
1	**Foster Generators**							
2								
3	Origin to Destination—Cost per unit to ship							
4			**Destination**					
5	Origin	Boston	Chicago	St. Louis	Lexington	**Units Available**		
6	Cleveland	$3.00	$2.00	$7.00	$6.00	5000		
7	Bedford	$7.00	$5.00	$2.00	$3.00	6000		
8	York	$2.00	$5.00	$4.00	$5.00	2500		
9	**Units Demanded**	6000	4000	2000	1500			
10								
11								
12	**Model**							
13								
14		**Min Cost**	$39,500.00					
15								
16	Origin to Destination—Units Shipped							
17			**Destination**					
18	Origin	Boston	Chicago	St. Louis	Lexington	**Units Shipped**		
19	Cleveland	3500	1500	0	0	5000	<=	5000
20	Bedford	0	2500	2000	1500	6000	<=	6000
21	York	2500	0	0	0	2500	<=	2500
22	**Units Received**	6000	4000	2000	1500			
23		=	=	=	=			
24		6000	4000	2000	1500			

FIGURE A.28   TRACE DEPENDENTS FOR CELL C14 (COST) IN THE FOSTER GENERATORS REV MODEL

E20			f_x	1500			
	A	**B**	**C**	**D**	**E**	**F**	**G**	**H**
12	**Model**							
13								
14		**Min Cost**	$39,500.00					
15								
16	Origin to Destination—Units Shipped							
17			**Destination**					
18	Origin	Boston	Chicago	St. Louis	Lexington	**Units Shipped**		
19	Cleveland	3500	1500	0	0	5000	<=	5000
20	Bedford	0	2500	2000	1500	6000	<=	6000
21	York	2500	0	0	0	2500	<=	2500
22	**Units Received**	6000	4000	2000	1500			
23		=	=	=	=			
24		6000	4000	2000	1500			

the **Formula Auditing** group. Recall that the cost in cell C14 is calculated as the SUM-PRODUCT of the per-unit shipping cost and units shipped. In Figure A.27, to show this relationship, arrows are drawn to these respective areas of the spreadsheet to cell C14. These arrows may be removed by clicking on the **Remove Arrows** button in the **Auditing Tools** group.

An example of Trace Dependents is shown in Figure A.28. We have selected cell E20, the units shipped from Bedford to Lexington, and clicked on the **Trace Dependents** button in the **Formula Auditing** group. As shown in Figure A.28, units shipped from Bedford to Lexington impacts the cost function in cell C14, the total units shipped from Bedford given in cell F20, and the total units shipped to Lexington in cell E22. These arrows may be removed by clicking on the **Remove Arrows** button in the **Auditing Tools** group.

Trace Precedents and Trace Dependents can highlight errors in copying and formula construction by showing that incorrect sections of the worksheet are referenced.

Show Formulas

The **Show Formulas** button, 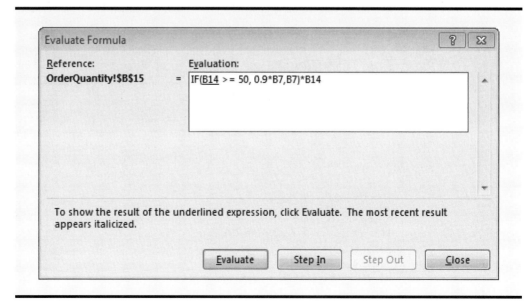 Show Formulas , does exactly that. To see the formulas in a worksheet, simply click on any cell in the worksheet and then click on **Show Formulas**. You will see the formulas that exist in that worksheet. To go back to hiding the formulas, click again on the **Show Formulas** button. Figure A.6 gives an example of the show formulas view. This allows you to inspect each formula in detail in its cell location.

Evaluate Formulas

The **Evaluate Formula** button, Evaluate Formula , allows you to investigate the calculations of particular cell in great detail. To invoke this tool, we simply select a cell containing a formula and click on the **Evaluate Formula** button in the **Formula Auditing** group. As an example, we select cell B15 of the Gambrell Manufacturing model (see Figures A.19 and A.20). Recall that we are calculating cost of goods based upon whether or not there is a quantity discount. Clicking on the Evaluate button allows you to evaluate this formula explicitly. The **Evaluate Formula** dialog box appears in Figure A.29. Figure A.30 shows the result of one click of the Evaluate button. The B14 has changed to its value of 95. Further clicks would evaluate in order, from left to right, the remaining components of the formula. We ask the reader to further explore this tool in an exercise at the end of this appendix.

The Evaluate Formula tool provides an excellent means of identifying the exact location of an error in a formula.

Error Checking

The **Error Checking** button, Error Checking ▾ , provides an automatic means of checking for mathematical errors within formulas of a worksheet. Clicking on the **Error Checking**

FIGURE A.29   THE EVALUATE FORMULA DIALOG BOX FOR CELL B15 OF THE
GAMBRELL MANUFACTURING MODEL

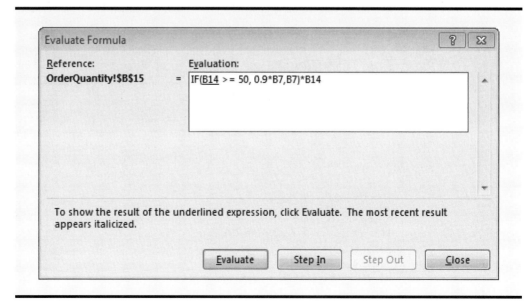

FIGURE A.30   THE EVALUATE FORMULA FOR CELL B15 OF THE GAMBRELL
MANUFACTURING MODEL AFTER ONE CLICK OF THE EVALUATE
BUTTON

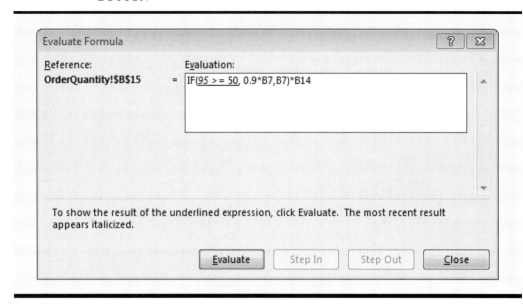

button causes Excel to check every formula in the sheet for calculation errors. If an error is
found, the **Error Checking** dialog box appears. An example for a hypothetical division by
zero error is shown in Figure A.31. From this box, the formula can be edited or the calculation steps can be observed (as in the previous section on **Evaluate Formulas**).

Watch Window

The **Watch Window**, located in the **Formula Auditing** group, allows the user to observe the
values of cells included in the **Watch Window** box list. This is useful for large models when
not all the model is observable on the screen or when multiple worksheets are used. The
user can monitor how the listed cells change with a change in the model without searching
through the worksheet or changing from one worksheet to another.

FIGURE A.31   THE ERROR CHECKING DIALOG BOX FOR A DIVISION
BY ZERO ERROR

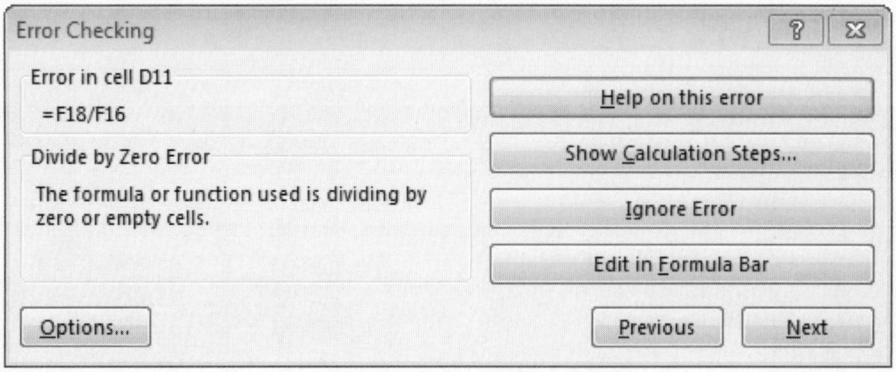

Error Checking

Error in cell D11

=F18/F16

Divide by Zero Error

The formula or function used is dividing by
zero or empty cells.

Help on this error

Show Calculation Steps...

Ignore Error

Edit in Formula Bar

Options...   Previous   Next

FIGURE A.32   THE WATCH WINDOW FOR THE GAMBRELL MANUFACTURING MODEL

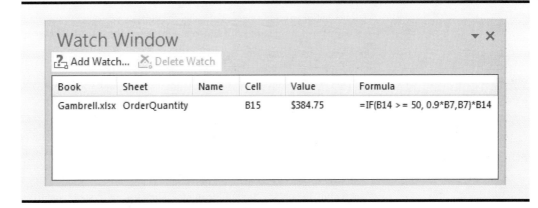

A Watch Window for the Gambrell Manufacturing model is shown in Figure A.32. The following steps were used from the OrderQuantity worksheet to add cell B15 of the OrderQuantity worksheet to the watch list:

Step 1. Select the **Formulas** tab
Step 2. Select **Watch Window** from the **Formula Auditing** group
The **Watch Window** will appear
Step 3. Select **Add Watch...**
Step 4. Click on the cell you would like to add to the watch list (in this case B15)

As shown in Figure A.32, the list gives the workbook name, worksheet name, cell name (if used), cell location, cell value, and cell formula. To delete a cell from the watch list, select the entry from the list and then click on the **Delete Watch** button in the upper part of the **Watch Window**.

The **Watch Window**, as shown in Figure A.32, allows us to monitor the value of B15 as we make changes elsewhere in the worksheet. Furthermore, if we had other worksheets in this workbook, we could monitor changes to B15 of the OrderQuantity worksheet even from these other worksheets. The **Watch Window** is observable regardless of where we are in any worksheet of a workbook.

SUMMARY

In this appendix we have discussed how to build effective spreadsheet models using Excel. We provided an overview on workbooks and worksheets and details on useful Excel functions. We also discussed a set of principles for good modeling and tools for auditing spreadsheet models.

PROBLEMS

MODEL *file*

NowlinPlastics

1. Open the file *NowlinPlastics*. Recall that we have modeled total profit for the product CD-50 in this spreadsheet. Suppose we have a second product called a CD-100, with the following characteristics:

$$\text{Fixed Cost} = \$2500$$

$$\text{Variable Cost per Unit} = \$1.67$$

$$\text{Selling Price per Unit} = \$4.40$$

Extend the model so that the profit is calculated for each product and then totaled to give an overall profit generated for the two products. Use a CD-100 production volume of 1200.

Save this file as *NowlinPlastics2*. *Hint:* Place the data for CD-100 in column C and copy the formulas in rows 14, 16, and 18 to column C.

2. Assume that in an empty Excel worksheet in cell A1 you enter the formula =B1*$F$3. You now copy this formula into cell E6. What is the modified formula that appears in E6?

MODEL *file*

FosterRev

3. Open the file *FosterRev*. Select cells B6:E8 and name these cells Shipping_Cost. Select cells B19:E21 and name these cells Units_Shipped. Use these names in the SUM-PRODUCT function in cell C14 to compute cost and verify that you obtain the same cost ($39,500).

4. Open the file *NowlinPlastics*. Recall that we have modeled total profit for the product CD-50 in this spreadsheet. Modify the spreadsheet to take into account production capacity and forecasted demand. If forecasted demand is less than or equal to capacity, Nowlin will produce only the forecasted demand; otherwise, they will produce the full capacity. For this example, use forecasted demand of 1200 and capacity of 1500. *Hint:* Enter demand and capacity into the data section of the model. Then use an IF statement to calculate production volume.

MODEL *file*

CoxElectric

5. Cox Electric makes electronic components and has estimated the following for a new design of one of its products:

Fixed Cost = $10,000

Revenue per Unit = $0.65

Material Cost per Unit = $0.15

Labor Cost per Unit = $0.10

These data are given in the spreadsheet *CoxElectric*. Also in the spreadsheet in row 14 is a profit model that gives the profit (or loss) for a specified volume (cell C14).

a. Use the Show Formula button in the Formula Auditing Group of the Formulas tab to see the formulas and cell references used in row 14.

b. Use the Trace Precedents tool to see how the formulas are dependent on the elements of the data section.

c. Use trial and error, by trying various values of volume in cell C14, to arrive at a break-even volume.

6. Return to the CoxElectric spreadsheet. Build a table of profits based on different volume levels by doing the following: In cell C15, enter a volume of 20,000. Look at each formula in row 14 and decide which references should be absolute or relative for purposes of copying the formulas to row 15. Make the necessary changes to row 14 (change any references that should be absolute by putting in $). Copy cells D14:I14 to row 15. Continue this with new rows until a positive profit is found. Save your file as *CoxBreakeven*.

MODEL *file*

OM455

7. Open the workbook *OM455*. Save the file under a new name, *OM455COUNTIF*. Suppose we wish to automatically count the number of each letter grade.

a. Begin by putting the letters A, B, C, D, and F in cells C29:C33. Use the COUNTIF function in cells D29:D33 to count the number of each letter grade. *Hint:* Create the necessary COUNTIF function in cell D29. Use absolute referencing on the range ($E14:$E$24) and then copy the function to cells D30:D33 to count the number of each of the other letter grades.

b. We are considering a different grading scale as follows:

Lower	Upper	Grade
0	69	F
70	76	D
77	84	C
85	92	B
93	100	A

For the current list of students, use the COUNTIF function to determine the number of A, B, C, D, and F letter grades earned under this new system.

MODEL *file*

OM455

8. Open the workbook *OM455*. Save the file under a new name, *OM4555Revised*. Suppose we wish to use a more refined grading system, as shown below:

Lower	Upper	Grade
0	59	F
60	69	D
70	72	C−
73	76	C−
77	79	C+
80	82	B−
83	86	B
87	89	B+
90	92	A−
93	100	A

Update the file to use this more refined grading system. How many of each letter grades are awarded under the new system? *Hint:* Build a new grading table and use VLOOKUP and an absolute reference to the table. Then use COUNTIF to count the number of each letter grade.

9. Richardson Ski Racing (RSR) sells equipment needed for downhill ski racing. One of RSR's products is fencing used on downhill courses. The fence product comes in 150-foot rolls and sells for $215 per roll. However, RSR offers quantity discounts. The following table shows the price per roll depending on order size:

DATA *file*

RSR

	Quantity Ordered	
From	To	Price per Roll
1	50	$215
51	100	$195
101	200	$175
201	and up	$155

The file *RSR* contains 172 orders that have arrived for the coming six weeks.
a. Use the VLOOKUP function with the preceding pricing table to determine the total revenue from these orders.
b. Use the COUNTIF function to determine the number of orders in each price bin.

DATA *file*

Williamson

10. Newton Manufacturing produces scientific calculators. The models are N350, N450, and the N900. Newton has planned its distribution of these products around eight customer zones: Brazil, China, France, Malaysia, U.S. Northeast, U.S. Southeast, U.S. Midwest, and U.S. West. Data for the current quarter (volume to be shipped in thousands of units) for each product and each customer zone are given in the file *NewtonData*.

Newton would like to know the total number of units going to each customer zone and also the total units of each product shipped. There are several ways to get this information from the data set. One way is to use the SUMIF function.

The SUMIF function extends the SUM function by allowing the user to add the values of cells meeting a logical condition. This general form of the function is

=SUMIF(*test range, condition, range to be summed*)

The *test range* is an area to search to test the *condition,* and the *range to be summed* is the position of the data to be summed. So, for example, using the *NewtonData* file, we would use the following function to get the total units sent to Malaysia:

$$=\text{SUMIF(A3:A26,A3,C3:C26)}$$

Here, A3 is Malaysia, A3:A26 is the range of customer zones, and C3:C26 are the volumes for each product for these customer zones. The SUMIF looks for matches of Malaysia in column A and, if a match is found, adds the volume to the total. Use the SUMIF function to get each total volume by zone and each total volume by product.

Williamson

11. Consider the transportation model given in the Excel file *Williamson*. It is a model that is very similar to the Foster Generators model. Williamson produces a single product and has plants in Atlanta, Lexington, Chicago, and Salt Lake City and warehouses in Portland, St. Paul, Las Vegas, Tuscon, and Cleveland. Each plant has a capacity and each warehouse has a demand. Williamson would like to find a low-cost shipping plan. Mr. Williamson has reviewed the results and notices right away that the total cost is way out of line. Use the Formula Auditing Tools under the Formulas tab in Excel to find any errors in this model. Correct the errors. *Hint:* There are two errors in this model. Be sure to check every formula.

Appendix B   Areas for the Standard Normal Distribution

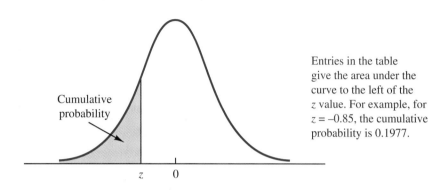

Cumulative probability

Entries in the table give the area under the curve to the left of the z value. For example, for $z = -0.85$, the cumulative probability is 0.1977.

z	0.00	0.01	0.02	0.03	0.04	0.05	0.06	0.07	0.08	0.09
−3.0	0.0013	0.0013	0.0013	0.0012	0.0012	0.0011	0.0011	0.0011	0.0010	0.0010
−2.9	0.0019	0.0018	0.0018	0.0017	0.0016	0.0016	0.0015	0.0015	0.0014	0.0014
−2.8	0.0026	0.0025	0.0024	0.0023	0.0023	0.0022	0.0021	0.0021	0.0020	0.0019
−2.7	0.0035	0.0034	0.0033	0.0032	0.0031	0.0030	0.0029	0.0028	0.0027	0.0026
−2.6	0.0047	0.0045	0.0044	0.0043	0.0041	0.0040	0.0039	0.0038	0.0037	0.0036
−2.5	0.0062	0.0060	0.0059	0.0057	0.0055	0.0054	0.0052	0.0051	0.0049	0.0048
−2.4	0.0082	0.0080	0.0078	0.0075	0.0073	0.0071	0.0069	0.0068	0.0066	0.0064
−2.3	0.0107	0.0104	0.0102	0.0099	0.0096	0.0094	0.0091	0.0089	0.0087	0.0084
−2.2	0.0139	0.0136	0.0132	0.0129	0.0125	0.0122	0.0119	0.0116	0.0113	0.0110
−2.1	0.0179	0.0174	0.0170	0.0166	0.0162	0.0158	0.0154	0.0150	0.0146	0.0143
−2.0	0.0228	0.0222	0.0217	0.0212	0.0207	0.0202	0.0197	0.0192	0.0188	0.0183
−1.9	0.0287	0.0281	0.0274	0.0268	0.0262	0.0256	0.0250	0.0244	0.0239	0.0233
−1.8	0.0359	0.0351	0.0344	0.0336	0.0329	0.0322	0.0314	0.0307	0.0301	0.0294
−1.7	0.0446	0.0436	0.0427	0.0418	0.0409	0.0401	0.0392	0.0384	0.0375	0.0367
−1.6	0.0548	0.0537	0.0526	0.0516	0.0505	0.0495	0.0485	0.0475	0.0465	0.0455
−1.5	0.0668	0.0655	0.0643	0.0630	0.0618	0.0606	0.0594	0.0582	0.0571	0.0559
−1.4	0.0808	0.0793	0.0778	0.0764	0.0749	0.0735	0.0721	0.0708	0.0694	0.0681
−1.3	0.0968	0.0951	0.0934	0.0918	0.0901	0.0885	0.0869	0.0853	0.0838	0.0823
−1.2	0.1151	0.1131	0.1112	0.1093	0.1075	0.1056	0.1038	0.1020	0.1003	0.0985
−1.1	0.1357	0.1335	0.1314	0.1292	0.1271	0.1251	0.1230	0.1210	0.1190	0.1170
−1.0	0.1587	0.1562	0.1539	0.1515	0.1492	0.1469	0.1446	0.1423	0.1401	0.1379
−0.9	0.1841	0.1814	0.1788	0.1762	0.1736	0.1711	0.1685	0.1660	0.1635	0.1611
−0.8	0.2119	0.2090	0.2061	0.2033	0.2005	0.1977	0.1949	0.1922	0.1894	0.1867
−0.7	0.2420	0.2389	0.2358	0.2327	0.2296	0.2266	0.2236	0.2206	0.2177	0.2148
−0.6	0.2743	0.2709	0.2676	0.2643	0.2611	0.2578	0.2546	0.2514	0.2483	0.2451
−0.5	0.3085	0.3050	0.3015	0.2981	0.2946	0.2912	0.2877	0.2843	0.2810	0.2776
−0.4	0.3446	0.3409	0.3372	0.3336	0.3300	0.3264	0.3228	0.3192	0.3156	0.3121
−0.3	0.3821	0.3783	0.3745	0.3707	0.3669	0.3632	0.3594	0.3557	0.3520	0.3483
−0.2	0.4207	0.4168	0.4129	0.4090	0.4052	0.4013	0.3974	0.3936	0.3897	0.3859
−0.1	0.4602	0.4562	0.4522	0.4483	0.4443	0.4404	0.4364	0.4325	0.4286	0.4247
−0.0	0.5000	0.4960	0.4920	0.4880	0.4840	0.4801	0.4761	0.4721	0.4681	0.4641

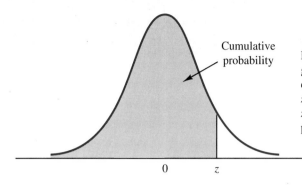

Cumulative probability

Entries in the table give the area under the curve to the left of the z value. For example, for $z = 1.25$, the cumulative probability is 0.8944.

z	0.00	0.01	0.02	0.03	0.04	0.05	0.06	0.07	0.08	0.09
0.0	0.5000	0.5040	0.5080	0.5120	0.5160	0.5199	0.5239	0.5279	0.5319	0.5359
0.1	0.5398	0.5438	0.5478	0.5517	0.5557	0.5596	0.5636	0.5675	0.5714	0.5753
0.2	0.5793	0.5832	0.5871	0.5910	0.5948	0.5987	0.6026	0.6064	0.6103	0.6141
0.3	0.6179	0.6217	0.6255	0.6293	0.6331	0.6368	0.6406	0.6443	0.6480	0.6517
0.4	0.6554	0.6591	0.6628	0.6664	0.6700	0.6736	0.6772	0.6808	0.6844	0.6879
0.5	0.6915	0.6950	0.6985	0.7019	0.7054	0.7088	0.7123	0.7157	0.7190	0.7224
0.6	0.7257	0.7291	0.7324	0.7357	0.7389	0.7422	0.7454	0.7486	0.7517	0.7549
0.7	0.7580	0.7611	0.7642	0.7673	0.7704	0.7734	0.7764	0.7794	0.7823	0.7852
0.8	0.7881	0.7910	0.7939	0.7967	0.7995	0.8023	0.8051	0.8078	0.8106	0.8133
0.9	0.8159	0.8186	0.8212	0.8238	0.8264	0.8289	0.8315	0.8340	0.8365	0.8389
1.0	0.8413	0.8438	0.8461	0.8485	0.8508	0.8531	0.8554	0.8577	0.8599	0.8621
1.1	0.8643	0.8665	0.8686	0.8708	0.8729	0.8749	0.8770	0.8790	0.8810	0.8830
1.2	0.8849	0.8869	0.8888	0.8907	0.8925	0.8944	0.8962	0.8980	0.8997	0.9015
1.3	0.9032	0.9049	0.9066	0.9082	0.9099	0.9115	0.9131	0.9147	0.9162	0.9177
1.4	0.9192	0.9207	0.9222	0.9236	0.9251	0.9265	0.9279	0.9292	0.9306	0.9319
1.5	0.9332	0.9345	0.9357	0.9370	0.9382	0.9394	0.9406	0.9418	0.9429	0.9441
1.6	0.9452	0.9463	0.9474	0.9484	0.9495	0.9505	0.9515	0.9525	0.9535	0.9545
1.7	0.9554	0.9564	0.9573	0.9582	0.9591	0.9599	0.9608	0.9616	0.9625	0.9633
1.8	0.9641	0.9649	0.9656	0.9664	0.9671	0.9678	0.9686	0.9693	0.9699	0.9706
1.9	0.9713	0.9719	0.9726	0.9732	0.9738	0.9744	0.9750	0.9756	0.9761	0.9767
2.0	0.9772	0.9778	0.9783	0.9788	0.9793	0.9798	0.9803	0.9808	0.9812	0.9817
2.1	0.9821	0.9826	0.9830	0.9834	0.9838	0.9842	0.9846	0.9850	0.9854	0.9857
2.2	0.9861	0.9864	0.9868	0.9871	0.9875	0.9878	0.9881	0.9884	0.9887	0.9890
2.3	0.9893	0.9896	0.9898	0.9901	0.9904	0.9906	0.9909	0.9911	0.9913	0.9913
2.4	0.9916	0.9920	0.9922	0.9925	0.9927	0.9929	0.9931	0.9932	0.9934	0.9936
2.5	0.9938	0.9940	0.9941	0.9943	0.9945	0.9946	0.9948	0.9949	0.9951	0.9952
2.6	0.9953	0.9955	0.9956	0.9957	0.9959	0.9960	0.9961	0.9962	0.9963	0.9964
2.7	0.9965	0.9966	0.9967	0.9968	0.9969	0.9970	0.9971	0.9972	0.9973	0.9974
2.8	0.9974	0.9975	0.9976	0.9977	0.9977	0.9978	0.9979	0.9979	0.9980	0.9981
2.9	0.9981	0.9982	0.9982	0.9983	0.9984	0.9984	0.9985	0.9985	0.9986	0.9986
3.0	0.9987	0.9987	0.9987	0.9988	0.9988	0.9989	0.9989	0.9989	0.9990	0.9990

Appendix C Values of $e^{-\lambda}$

λ	$e^{-\lambda}$	λ	$e^{-\lambda}$	λ	$e^{-\lambda}$
0.05	0.9512	2.05	0.1287	4.05	0.0174
0.10	0.9048	2.10	0.1225	4.10	0.0166
0.15	0.8607	2.15	0.1165	4.15	0.0158
0.20	0.8187	2.20	0.1108	4.20	0.0150
0.25	0.7788	2.25	0.1054	4.25	0.0143
0.30	0.7408	2.30	0.1003	4.30	0.0136
0.35	0.7047	2.35	0.0954	4.35	0.0129
0.40	0.6703	2.40	0.0907	4.40	0.0123
0.45	0.6376	2.45	0.0863	4.45	0.0117
0.50	0.6065	2.50	0.0821	4.50	0.0111
0.55	0.5769	2.55	0.0781	4.55	0.0106
0.60	0.5488	2.60	0.0743	4.60	0.0101
0.65	0.5220	2.65	0.0707	4.65	0.0096
0.70	0.4966	2.70	0.0672	4.70	0.0091
0.75	0.4724	2.75	0.0639	4.75	0.0087
0.80	0.4493	2.80	0.0608	4.80	0.0082
0.85	0.4274	2.85	0.0578	4.85	0.0078
0.90	0.4066	2.90	0.0550	4.90	0.0074
0.95	0.3867	2.95	0.0523	4.95	0.0071
1.00	0.3679	3.00	0.0498	5.00	0.0067
1.05	0.3499	3.05	0.0474	5.05	0.0064
1.10	0.3329	3.10	0.0450	5.10	0.0061
1.15	0.3166	3.15	0.0429	5.15	0.0058
1.20	0.3012	3.20	0.0408	5.20	0.0055
1.25	0.2865	3.25	0.0388	5.25	0.0052
1.30	0.2725	3.30	0.0369	5.30	0.0050
1.35	0.2592	3.35	0.0351	5.35	0.0047
1.40	0.2466	3.40	0.0334	5.40	0.0045
1.45	0.2346	3.45	0.0317	5.45	0.0043
1.50	0.2231	3.50	0.0302	5.50	0.0041
1.55	0.2122	3.55	0.0287	5.55	0.0039
1.60	0.2019	3.60	0.0273	5.60	0.0037
1.65	0.1920	3.65	0.0260	5.65	0.0035
1.70	0.1827	3.70	0.0247	5.70	0.0033
1.75	0.1738	3.75	0.0235	5.75	0.0032
1.80	0.1653	3.80	0.0224	5.80	0.0030
1.85	0.1572	3.85	0.0213	5.85	0.0029
1.90	0.1496	3.90	0.0202	5.90	0.0027
1.95	0.1423	3.95	0.0193	5.95	0.0026
2.00	0.1353	4.00	0.0183	6.00	0.0025
				7.00	0.0009
				8.00	0.000335
				9.00	0.000123
				10.00	0.000045

Appendix D References and Bibliography

Chapter 1 Introduction

Churchman, C. W., R. L. Ackoff, and E. L. Arnoff. *Introduction to Operations Research.* Wiley, 1957.

Horner, Peter. "The Sabre Story," *OR/MS Today* (June 2000).

Leon, Linda, Z. Przasnyski, and K. C. Seal. "Spreadsheets and OR/MS Models: An End-User Perspective," *Interfaces* (March/April 1996).

Powell, S. G. "Innovative Approaches to Management Science," *OR/MS Today* (October 1996).

Savage, S. "Weighing the Pros and Cons of Decision Technology and Spreadsheets," *OR/MS Today* (February 1997).

Winston, W. L. "The Teachers' Forum: Management Science with Spreadsheets for MBAs at Indiana University," *Interfaces* (March/April 1996).

Chapters 2 to 7 Linear, Integer Programming

Ahuja, R. K., T. L. Magnanti, and J. B. Orlin. *Network Flows, Theory, Algorithms, and Applications.* Prentice Hall, 1993.

Bazarra, M. S., J. J. Jarvis, and H. D. Sherali. *Linear Programming and Network Flows,* 2d ed. Wiley, 1990.

Carino, H. F., and C. H. Le Noir, Jr. "Optimizing Wood Procurement in Cabinet Manufacturing," *Interfaces* (March/April 1988): 10–19.

Dantzig, G. B. *Linear Programming and Extensions.* Princeton University Press, 1963.

Davis, Morton D. *Game Theory: A Nontechnical Introduction.* Dover, 1997.

Evans, J. R., and E. Minieka. *Optimization Algorithms for Networks and Graphs,* 2d ed. Marcel Dekker, 1992.

Ford, L. R., and D. R. Fulkerson. *Flows and Networks.* Princeton University Press, 1962.

Geoffrion, A., and G. Graves. "Better Distribution Planning with Computer Models," *Harvard Business Review* (July/August 1976).

Greenberg, H. J. "How to Analyze the Results of Linear Programs—Part 1: Preliminaries," *Interfaces* 23, no. 4 (July/August 1993): 56–67.

Greenberg, H. J. "How to Analyze the Results of Linear Programs—Part 2: Price Interpretation," *Interfaces* 23, no. 5 (September/October 1993): 97–114.

Greenberg, H. J. "How to Analyze the Results of Linear Programs—Part 3: Infeasibility Diagnosis," *Interfaces* 23, no. 6 (November/December 1993): 120–139.

Lillien, G., and A. Rangaswamy. *Marketing Engineering: Computer-Assisted Marketing Analysis and Planning.* Addison-Wesley, 1998.

Martin, R. K. *Large Scale Linear and Integer Optimization: A Unified Approach.* Kluwer Academic Publishers, 1999.

McMillian, John. *Games, Strategies, and Managers.* Oxford University Press, 1992.

Myerson, Roger B. *Game Theory: Analysis of Conflict.* Harvard University Press, 1997.

Nemhauser, G. L., and L. A. Wolsey. *Integer and Combinatorial Optimization.* Wiley, 1999.

Osborne, Martin J. *An Introduction to Game Theory.* Oxford University Press, 2004.

Schrage, Linus. *Optimization Modeling with LINDO,* 4th ed. LINDO Systems Inc., 2000.

Sherman, H. D. "Hospital Efficiency Measurement and Evaluation," *Medical Care* 22, no. 10 (October 1984): 922–938.

Winston, W. L., and S. C. Albright. *Practical Management Science,* 2d ed. Duxbury Press, 2001.

Chapter 8 Nonlinear Optimization Models

Bazarra, M. S., H. D. Sherali, and C. M. Shetty. *Nonlinear Programming Theory and Applications.* Wiley, 1993.

Benninga, Simon. *Financial Modeling.* MIT Press, 2000.

Luenberger, D. *Linear and Nonlinear Programming,* 2d ed. Addison-Wesley, 1984.

Rardin, R. L. *Optimization in Operations Research.* Prentice Hall, 1998.

Chapter 9 Project Scheduling: PERT/CPM

Moder, J. J., C. R. Phillips, and E. W. Davis. *Project Management with CPM, PERT and Precedence Diagramming,* 3d ed. Blitz, 1995.

Wasil, E. A., and A. A. Assad. "Project Management on the PC: Software, Applications, and Trends," *Interfaces* 18, no. 2 (March/April 1988): 75–84.

Wiest, J., and F. Levy. *Management Guide to PERT-CPM,* 2d ed. Prentice Hall, 1977.

Chapter 10 Inventory Models

Fogarty, D. W., J. H. Blackstone, and T. R. Hoffman. *Production and Inventory Management,* 2d ed. South-Western, 1990.

Hillier, F., and G. J. Lieberman. *Introduction to Operations Research,* 7th ed. McGraw-Hill, 2000.

Narasimhan, S. L., D. W. McLeavey, and P. B. Lington. *Production Planning and Inventory Control,* 2d ed. Prentice Hall, 1995.

Orlicky, J., and G. W. Plossi. *Orlicky's Material Requirements Planning.* McGraw-Hill, 1994.

Vollmann, T. E., W. L. Berry, and D. C. Whybark. *Manufacturing Planning and Control Systems,* 4th ed. McGraw-Hill, 1997.

Zipkin, P. H. *Foundations of Inventory Management.* McGraw-Hill/Irwin, 2000.

Chapter 11 Waiting Line Models

Bunday, B. D. *An Introduction to Queueing Theory.* Wiley, 1996.

Gross, D., and C. M. Harris. *Fundamentals of Queueing Theory,* 3d ed. Wiley, 1997.

Hall, R. W. *Queueing Methods: For Services and Manufacturing.* Prentice Hall, 1997.

Hillier, F., and G. J. Lieberman. *Introduction to Operations Research,* 7th ed. McGraw-Hill, 2000.

Kao, E. P. C. *An Introduction to Stochastic Processes.* Duxbury, 1996.

Chapter 12 Simulation

Banks, J., J. S. Carson, B. L. Nelson, and D. M. Nicol. *Discrete-Event System Simulation,* 5th ed. Pearson, 2009.

Bell, P. *Brent-Harbridge Developments, Inc.* Richard Ivey School of Business, University of Western Ontario, 1998.

Law, A. M. *Simulation Modeling and Analysis,* 5th ed. McGraw-Hill, 2014.

Ross, S. *Simulation.* Academic Press, 2013.

Savage, S. L., *Flaw of Averages.* Wiley, 2012.

Talib, N.N. *Fooled by Randomness.* Random House, 2004.

Wainer, H. *Picturing the Uncertain World.* Princeton University Press, 2009.

Winston, W. *Decision Making Under Uncertainty.* Palisade Corporation, 2007.

Chapter 13 Decision Analysis

Berger, J. O. *Statistical Decision Theory and Bayesian Analysis,* 2d ed. Springer-Verlag, 1985.

Chernoff, H., and L. E. Moses. *Elementary Decision Theory.* Dover, 1987.

Clemen, R. T., and T. Reilly. *Making Hard Decisions with Decision Tools.* Duxbury, 2001.

Goodwin, P., and G. Wright. *Decision Analysis for Management Judgment,* 2d ed. Wiley, 1999.

Gregory, G. *Decision Analysis.* Plenum, 1988.

Pratt, J. W., H. Raiffa, and R. Schlaifer. *Introduction to Statistical Decision Theory.* MIT Press, 1995.

Raiffa, H. *Decision Analysis.* McGraw-Hill, 1997.

Schlaifer, R. *Analysis of Decisions Under Uncertainty.* Krieger, 1978.

Chapter 14 Multicriteria Decisions

Dyer, J. S. "A Clarification of Remarks on the Analytic Hierarchy Process," *Management Science* 36, no. 3 (March 1990): 274–275.

Dyer, J. S. "Remarks on the Analytic Hierarchy Process," *Management Science* 36, no. 3 (March 1990): 249–258.

Harker, P. T., and L. G. Vargas. "Reply to Remarks on the Analytic Hierarchy Process by J. S. Dyer," *Management Science* 36, no. 3 (March 1990): 269–273.

Harker, P. T., and L. G. Vargas. "The Theory of Ratio Scale Estimation: Saaty's Analytic Hierarchy Process," *Management Science* 33, no. 11 (November 1987): 1383–1403.

Ignizio, J. *Introduction to Linear Goal Programming.* Sage, 1986.

Keeney, R. L., and H. Raiffa. *Decisions with Multiple Objectives: Preferences and Value Tradeoffs.* Cambridge, 1993.

Saaty, T. *Decision Making for Leaders: The Analytic Hierarchy Process for Decisions in a Complex World,* 3d ed. RWS, 1999.

Saaty, T. *Multicriteria Decision Making,* 2d ed. RWS, 1996.

Saaty, T. L. "An Exposition of the AHP in Reply to the Paper Remarks on the Analytic Hierarchy Process," *Management Science* 36, no. 3 (March 1990): 259–268.

Saaty, T. L. "Rank Generation, Preservation, and Reversal in the Analytic Hierarchy Decision Process," *Decision Sciences* 18 (1987): 157–177.

Winkler, R. L. "Decision Modeling and Rational Choice: AHP and Utility Theory," *Management Science* 36, no. 3 (March 1990): 247–248.

Chapter 15 Forecasting

Bowerman, B. L., and R. T. O'Connell. *Forecasting and Time Series: An Applied Approach,* 3d ed. Duxbury, 2000.

Box, G. E. P., G. M. Jenkins, and G. C. Reinsel. *Time Series Analysis: Forecasting and Control,* 3d ed. Prentice Hall, 1994.

Hanke, J. E., and A. G. Reitsch. *Business Forecasting,* 6th ed. Prentice Hall, 1998.

Makridakis, S. G., S. C. Wheelwright, and R. J. Hyndman. *Forecasting: Methods and Applications,* 3d ed. Wiley, 1997.

Wilson, J. H., and B. Keating. *Business Forecasting,* 3d ed. Irwin, 1998.

Chapter 16 Markov Processes

Bharucha-Reid, A. T. *Elements of the Theory of Markov Processes and Their Applications.* Dover, 1997.

Bhat, U. N. *Elements of Applied Stochastic Processes,* 2d ed. Wiley, 1984.

Filar, J. A., and K. Vrieze. *Competitive Markov Decision Processes.* Springer-Verlag, 1996.

Norris, J. *Markov Chains.* Cambridge, 1997.

Appendix E   Self-Test Solutions and Answers to Even-Numbered Exercises (online)

Completely worked-out solutions can be accessed by students and instructors online two ways:

1. Those with Mindtap access, Appendix E can be found within the Course Materials folder, linking to the free companion site
2. Appendix E can also be accessed at **www.cengagebrain.com** by creating an account to access the free materials that accompany your purchased product

Index